ANNOTATED
GUIDE TO THE INSOLVENCY LEGISLAT

D1587012

FIFTEENTH EDITION

VOLUME 2

ANNOTATED GUIDE TO THE INSOLVENCY LEGISLATION

Company Directors Disqualification Act 1986
EC Regulation on Insolvency Proceedings 2000
UNCITRAL Model Law on Cross-Border Insolvency
Cross-Border Insolvency Regulations 2006
Selected Statutes and Statutory Instruments

Fifteenth Edition

Volume 2

Len Sealy MA LLM PhD, Barrister and Solicitor (NZ)
SJ Berwin Professor Emeritus of Corporate Law,
University of Cambridge

David Milman LLB PhD
Professor of Law
Law School
Lancaster University
Professorial Associate at Exchange Chambers

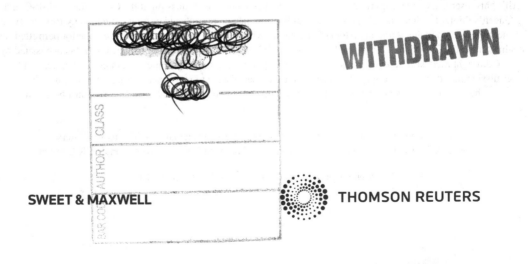

Disclaimer

This publication is sold on the understanding that the publisher is not engaged in rendering legal or accounting advice or other professional services. The publisher, its editors and any authors, consultants or general editors expressly disclaim all and any liability and responsibility to any person, whether a purchaser or reader of this publication or not, in respect of anything and of the consequences of anything, done or omitted to be done by any such person in reliance, whether wholly or partially, upon the whole or any part of the contents of this publication. While this publication is intended to provide accurate information in regard to the subject matter covered, readers entering into transactions on the basis of such information should seek the services of a competent professional adviser.

The publisher advises that any statutory or other materials issued by the Crown or other relevant bodies and reproduced or quoted in this publication are not the authorised official versions of those statutory or other materials. In their preparation, however, the greatest care has been taken to ensure exact conformity with the law as enacted or other material as issued.

While copyright in all statutory and other materials resides in the Crown or other relevant body, copyright in the remaining material in this publication is vested in the publisher.

Published in 2012 by Sweet & Maxwell, 100 Avenue Road, London NW3 3PF
part of Thomson Reuters (Professional) UK Limited (Registered in England & Wales,
Company No 1679046. Registered Office and address for service:
Aldgate House, 33 Aldgate High Street, London EC3N 1DL)

For further information on our products and services, visit
www.sweetandmaxwell.co.uk

Typeset by Interactive Sciences Ltd, Gloucester
Printed and bound in Great Britain by Ashford Colour Press Ltd, Gosport, Hants

No natural forests were destroyed to make this product; only farmed timber was used and replanted.

A CIP catalogue record for this book is available from the British Library

ISBN 978-0-414-02409-0

PREFACE TO THE FIFTEENTH EDITION

The Government's recently published insolvency statistics make interesting reading. The number of corporate insolvencies over the last few years has remained fairly steady, hovering around 21,000 in total (with a slight rise in 2011), while individual insolvencies (at just under 120,000) have begun a decline from their peak in 2009–2010. But a comparison between the present position and the average over the past 25 years tells a rather different story. The liquidation rate today (0.7 per cent of all registered companies) remains low compared with the peak of 2.6 per cent in 1993 and an average of 1.2 per cent reckoned over that 25-year period. (This is partly accounted for by the fact that the number of registered companies has risen considerably in that time.) In contrast for individual insolvencies the rate, after remaining steady for many years, has followed a steeply upward path since 2004 and is still elevated (about 1 insolvency per 360 individuals today compared with the 25-year average of 1 in 1600).

There is no doubt that the latter trend is primarily to be explained by the fact that since the enactment of the Insolvency Act 1986 (as amended by the Enterprise Act 2002) and more recently the Tribunals, Courts and Enforcement Act 2007, alternatives to bankruptcy have been made available for individuals in the form of individual voluntary arrangements and debt relief orders. These regimes are now recorded in the statistics, whereas the informal arrangements (such as they were) that they have in part replaced were not. On analysis, we see that over the last couple of years bankruptcy orders have decreased by almost half and that this substantial drop is broadly balanced by the growth in DROs. Relief has thus been provided for individual debtors, mainly at the lower end of the scale, in keeping with changes in government policy.

Some of the recently reported cases which are discussed in this new edition are concerned with developments in this area. In particular, we note the Supreme Court ruling on the DRO moratorium in *Secretary of State for Work and Pensions v Payne* [2011] UKSC 60; [2012] 2 W.L.R. 1, which has been partly counteracted by the Insolvency (Amendment) Rules 2012 (SI 2012/469). The Court of Appeal ruling in *Sharples v Places for People Homes*; *Godfrey v A2 Dominion Homes* [2011] EWCA Civ 813; [2011] B.P.I.R. 1488 on the rights of landlords during the DRO and bankruptcy moratoria is also covered. Reference is made to judicial attempts to curb "bankruptcy tourism". In the IVA context, the important Court of Appeal procedural precedent in *Kapoor v Nat West Bank* [2011] EWCA Civ 1083; [2011] B.P.I.R. 1180 is noted. Other rulings in cases of individual insolvency include *Brook v Reed* [2011] EWCA Civ 331; [2011] B.C.C. 423 (remuneration of office-holders), an authority generally applicable to all office holders.

In the corporate sphere, the ruling of the Supreme Court in *BNY Corporate Trustee Services Ltd v Belmont Park Investments Pty Ltd* [2011] UKSC 38; [2011] B.C.C. 734 explores the limits of the "anti-deprivation" rule. The same company was involved in *BNY Corporate Trustee Services Ltd v Eurosail-UK 2007-3BL plc* [2011] EWCA Civ 227; [2011] B.C.C. 399, in which the concept of "balance-sheet" insolvency is examined in detail. Another Supreme Court decision, *Re Kaupthing Singer & Friedlander Ltd* [2011] UKSC 48; [2012] B.C.C. 1 confirms the paramountcy of the "rule against double proof" in corporate liquidations. Prominent among several cases heard by the Court of Appeal are *Re Nortel GmbH, Bloom v Pensions Regulator* [2011] EWCA Civ 1124; [2012] B.C.C. 83 (super-priority of financial support direction), *Re Kaupthing Singer & Friedlander Ltd* [2010] EWCA Civ 518; [2011] B.C.C. 555 (set-off of loans repayable in the future) and *Re New Cap Reinsurance Corp Ltd* [2011] EWCA Civ 971; [2011] B.C.C. 937 (assistance for foreign court). We understand that some of these rulings are likely to go to appeal. Particularly topical is the flurry of cases (including *Minmar (929) Ltd v Khalastchi* [2011] EWHC 1159 (Ch); [2011] B.C.C. 486, *Re Frontsouth (Witham) Ltd* [2011] EWHC 1668 (Ch); [2011] B.C.C. 635 and *Re Care Matters Partnership Ltd* [2011] EWHC 2543 (Ch); [2011] B.C.C. 957 that have generated much controversy on points which have yet to be resolved by a higher court (defective administrator appointments, retrospective administration orders and majority-directors' decisions). Also in the news is the much debated "football creditors rule", on which we await a ruling as this work goes to press.

Developments in the law governing cross-border insolvencies and director disqualification are also fully covered. In the former context we have seen the blossoming of the common-law principle of international comity, though we await the views of the Supreme Court on the full legitimate extent of this development.

Although there has not been any new legislation of major importance in the area of insolvency law, we have included in Volume 2 the relevant parts of the Charities Act 2011 and brought up to date the text of the Financial Services and Markets Act 2000, the Companies Act 2006 and the Insolvency Rules. Substantial amendments have also been made to the Insolvency Regulations 1994 (SI 1994/2507), the Financial Markets and Insolvency (Settlement Finality) Regulations 1999 (SI 1999/2979) and the Insurers (Reorganisation and Winding Up) Regulations 2004 (SI 2004/353). These and many minor changes to the legislation included in Volume 2 have been noted, bringing the text fully up to date.

Of particular importance to practitioners is the new *Practice Direction: Insolvency Proceedings* (February 23, 2012), reported in [2012] B.C.C. 265, which supersedes all previous Practice Directions. The text is reproduced in full in this edition.

It is a pleasure once again to express our thanks to our friend and colleague Peter Bailey for his expert help and support, and to thank our publishers and their staff for help at all stages of production. Our debt to Claire Patient, Senior Editor, who masterminds the preparation of our copy, is immeasurable. We would also like to thank those of our readers who have sent us comments and queries, brought some unreported judgments to our notice and drawn our attention to errors. These contributions are always most welcome. We are grateful also to the officials of the Policy Unit of the Insolvency Service for their continuing assistance and support.

We have endeavoured to state the law as at February 29, 2012, although we have been able to add some later developments at proof stage where space permits. We would also assure those of our readers who subscribe to this *Guide* in its online form on Westlaw UK that the regular weekly updating of the 14th edition has continued throughout the time that this edition has been in production, and that the material in those updates will be brought forward into the electronic version of this new edition as soon as practicable after publication.

Len Sealy
David Milman

March 2012

ABOUT THE AUTHORS

Len Sealy MA, LLM, PhD, Barrister and Solicitor (NZ) is SJ Berwin Professor Emeritus of Corporate Law at the University of Cambridge. He is an eminent commentator on company and commercial law, having written and lectured extensively in these areas and is General Editor of British Company Law and Practice.

David Milman LLB, PhD is Professor of Law at Lancaster University. He is also Co-Author of Corporate Insolvency: Law and Practice and Co-General Editor of Insolvency Intelligence and a Professorial Associate at Exchange Chambers.

ABBREVIATIONS

The following abbreviations are used in this work:

BA 1914	Bankruptcy Act 1914
B(A)A 1926	Bankruptcy (Amendment) Act 1926
BIS	Department of Business, Innovation and Skills
BR 1952	Bankruptcy Rules 1952
BRO	Bankruptcy restrictions order
BRU	Bankruptcy restrictions undertaking
CA	Companies Act (e.g. CA 2006 = Companies Act 2006)
CBIR	Cross-Border Insolvency Regulations 2006
CDDA 1986	Company Directors Disqualification Act 1986
CFCSA 1972	Companies (Floating Charges and Receivers) (Scotland) Act 1972
CDO	Competition Disqualification Order
CDU	Competition Disqualification Undertaking
CJA	Criminal Justice Act (e.g. CJA 1988 = Criminal Justice Act 1988)
COMI	Centre of main interests
Cork Report	*Report of the Review Committee on Insolvency Law and Practice* (Cmnd.8558, 1982)
CPR	Civil Procedure Rules
CVA	Company voluntary arrangement
DBERR	Department for Business, Enterprise and Regulatory Reform
DBIS	Department for Business, Innovation and Skills
DRO	Debt relief order
DRRO	Debt relief restrictions order
DRRU	Debt relief restrictions undertaking
DTI	Department of Trade and Industry
EA 2002	Enterprise Act 2002
EC Regulation	EC Regulation on Insolvency Proceedings 2000
FA	Finance Act (e.g. FA 1985 = Finance Act 1985)
Finality Regulations	Financial Markets and Insolvency (Settlement Finality) Regulations 1999 (SI 1999/2979)
FSA 1986	Financial Services Act 1986
FSMA 2000	Financial Services and Markets Act 2000
G to E	Model Law on Cross-Border Insolvency Guide to Enactment
IA	Insolvency Act (e.g. IA 1985 = Insolvency Act 1985)
IPA	Income payments agreement
IPO	Income payments order
IR 1986	Insolvency Rules 1986
I(A)R	Insolvency (Amendment) Rules (e.g. I(A)R 1993 = Insolvency Amendment Rules 1993)
IVA	Individual voluntary arrangement

Judgments Regulation	Council Regulation (EC) 44/2001 of December 22, 2000 on jurisdiction and the recognition and enforcement of judgments in civil and commercial matters
LLP	Limited liability partnership
LLPA 2000	Limited Liability Partnerships Act 2000
LLPR 2001	Limited Liability Partnerships Regulations 2001 (SI 2001/1090)
LPA 1925	Law of Property Act 1925
LRO 2010	Legislative Reform (Insolvency) (Miscellaneous Amendments) Order 2010
OR	Official receiver
POCA 2002	Proceeds of Crime Act 2002
RSC	Rules of the Supreme Court
TCEA 2007	Tribunals, Courts and Enforcement Act 2007
TLATA 1996	Trusts of Land and Appointment of Trustees Act 1996
TUPE Regulations	Transfer of Undertakings (Protection of Employment) Regulations 2006
White Paper	*A Revised Framework for Insolvency Law* (Cmnd.9175, 1984)

Appendix I and Appendix II list the words and phrases which are given a special statutory definition or used in a particular sense in the legislation or the Rules, and give references to the provisions in which they and the accompanying commentary can be found.

CONTENTS

Case Table

References within square brackets are located in Volume 2.

The following abbreviations are used in the tables to denote the location of entries in all tables:

[CBIR]	Cross-Border Insolvency Regulations 2006
[CDDA]	Company Directors Disqualification Act 1986
EA	Enterprise Act 2002
[ER]	EC Regulation on Insolvency Proceedings 2000
IA	Insolvency Act 1986
IA 2000	Insolvency Act 2000
IR	Insolvency Rules 1986
[UML]	UNCITRAL Model Law on Cross-Border Insolvency

Provision

A

1st Credit (Finance) Ltd v Bartram [2010] EWHC 2910 (Ch); [2011] B.P.I.R. 1 . . . . IA 269, IR 6.5

4Eng Ltd v Harper [2009] EWHC 2633 (Ch); [2010] B.P.I.R. 1 . . . . IA 423(1)–(3), 425(1), 425(2), (3)

A Straume (UK) Ltd v Bradlor Developments Ltd [2000] B.C.C. 333, Ch D . . . . [IA 11(3)]

A&BC Chewing Gum, Re [1975] 1 W.L.R. 579; [1975] 1 All E.R. 1017 . IA 123

A&C Group Services Ltd, Re [1993] B.C.L.C. 1297, Ch D . . . . [CDDA 9(1)]

A&C Supplies Ltd, Re; sub nom. Sutton, Re [1998] B.C.C. 708, Ch D . IA 29(2), 45(1), (2), 172(1), (2)

A&J Fabrications (Batley) Ltd v Grant Thornton (a Firm) (No.1) [1999] B.C.C. 807, Ch D . . . . IA 212(1)

ABC Ltd (in liq.), Re. *See* XYZ v Revenue and Customs Commissioners . . . . IA 236

ACLI Metals (London) Ltd, Re (1989) 5 B.C.C. 749, Ch D . . . . IA 168(5)

AA Mutual International Insurance Co Ltd, Re [2004] EWHC 2430 (Ch) . . . IA Pt II, Sch.B1, paras 9, 11

AE Farr Ltd, Re [1992] B.C.C. 150, Ch D (Companies Ct) . . . . IA 236

AES Barry Ltd v TXU Europe Energy Trading (in admin.) [2004] EWHC 1757 (Ch) . . . . [IA 11(3)]

Provision

AET v Kermanshahchi. *See* Anglo Eastern Trust Ltd v Kermanshahchi

AG (Manchester) Ltd (formerly The Accident Group Ltd) (in liq.), Re; sub nom. Official Receiver v Langford; Official Receiver v Watson [2008] EWHC 64 (Ch); [2008] B.C.C. 497 . [CDDA 9(1)]

AE Realisations (1985) Ltd, Re [1988] 1 W.L.R. 200; (1987) 3 B.C.C. 136, Ch D . . . . IA 179, 181(1)–(3)

AI Levy (Holdings) Ltd, Re [1964] Ch. 19, Ch D . . . . IA 127

AIB Finance Ltd v Alsop; sub nom. AIB Finance Ltd v Debtors [1998] 2 All E.R. 929; [1998] B.C.C. 780, CA (Civ Div) . . . . IR 6.5

AJ Adams (Builders) Ltd, Re [1991] B.C.C. 62, Ch D (Companies Ct) . . . IA 108, 171(4)

AMEC Properties Ltd v Planning Research & Systems Plc [1992] 1 E.G.L.R. 70, CA (Civ Div) . . . . IA 37(1), (2), 44(1), (2)

AMF International Ltd, Re [1995] B.C.C. 439, Ch D . . . . IR 4.139– 4.148E

AMF International Ltd (No.2), Re; sub nom. Cohen v Ellis [1996] 1 W.L.R. 77; [1996] B.C.C. 335, Ch D . . . . IA 212(3)

AMP Enterprises Ltd v Hoffman; sub nom. AMP Music Box Enterprises Ltd v Hoffman [2002] EWHC 1899 (Ch); [2002] B.C.C. 996 . . . . IA 108

Case Table

	Provision		Provision

Daisytek-ISA Ltd, Re [2003] B.C.C. 562; [2004] B.P.I.R. 30, Ch D . . . . . . — [ER, art.3(1)]

Dallhold Estates (UK) Pty Ltd, Re [1992] B.C.C. 394, Ch D (Companies Ct) . . . . — IA 426(4), (5), (11), EA 254(1), [IA 8(1), (2)]

Daltel Europe Ltd (in liq.) v Makki (No.1) [2004] EWHC 726 (Ch) . . . . . — IA 236

Dana (UK) Ltd, Re [1999] 2 B.C.L.C. 239, Ch D . . . . — IA Sch.B1 paras 53, 54, 68(2), (3), [IA 24(1), (2), 25(1)]

Darrell v Miller [2003] EWHC 2811 (Ch); [2004] B.P.I.R. 470, Ch D . . . . — IA 172(1), (2)

Data Online Transactions (UK) Ltd, Re. *See* Apcar v Aftab

Davenham Trust Ltd v White [2010] EWHC 2748 (Ch); [2011] B.C.C. 77 — IA 244(3), IR 6.5

Davenham Trust Plc v CV Distribution (UK) Ltd; sub nom. Taylor (a Bankrupt), Re [2006] EWHC 3029 (Ch); [2007] Ch. 150 . . . . — IA 285(3), (4), 323

David Meek Plant Ltd, Re; David Meek Access Ltd, Re [1993] B.C.C. 175, Ch D . . . . — [IA 11(3)]

Davidson v Stanley [2004] EWHC 2595 (Ch); [2005] B.P.I.R. 279 . . . . . — IA 255(1), (2)

Davies (a Bankrupt), Re; sub nom. Davies v Patel [1997] B.P.I.R. 619, Ch D . . . . — IA 285(2)

Davies v Barnes Webster & Sons Ltd [2011] EWHC 2560 (Ch) . . . . — IR 6.5

Davis v Martin-Sklan. *See* Hussein (Essengin), Re

Dawes & Henderson (Agencies) Ltd (in liq.) (No.2), Re; sub nom. Shuttleworth v Secretary of State for Trade and Industry [2000] B.C.C. 204, Ch D . . . . — [CDDA 1(1)]

Dawodu v American Express Bank [2001] B.P.I.R. 983, Ch D . . . . — IR 6.25

Dawson Print Group Ltd, Re (1987) 3 B.C.C. 322; [1987] B.C.L.C. 601 . . . — [CDDA 9(1)]

Day v Haine; sub nom. Haine v Day (liquidator of Compound Sections Ltd) [2008] EWCA Civ 626; [2008] B.C.C. 845 . . . . — IA Sch.B1 para.99(5)–(6), IR 4.218(1)–(3), 12.3, 13.12

Dean v Stout [2004] EWHC 3315 (Ch); [2006] 1 F.L.R. 725; [2005] B.P.I.R. 1113 . . . . — IA 335A

Dean & Dean (a Firm) v Angel Airlines SA [2009] EWHC 447 (Ch); [2009] B.P.I.R. 409 . . . . — IA 267(1), (2), 271(1), (2), (4)

Dear v Reeves [2001] EWCA Civ 277; [2001] B.P.I.R. 577 . . . . — IA 436

Debtor (No.400 of 1940), Re; sub nom. Debtor v Dodwell [1949] Ch. 236; [1949] 1 All E.R. 510, Ch D . . . . — IA 168(5), 303(1)

Debtor (No.26A of 1975), Re [1985] 1 W.L.R. 6, Ch D . . . . — IA 303(2), 314(1), (2), (6)

Debtor (No.2A of 1980, Colchester), Re [1981] Ch. 148, Ch D . . . . — IA 373(2)

Debtor (No.707 of 1985), Re, The Times, January 21, 1988, CA (Civ Div) . . . . — IA 282(1), (3)

Debtor (No.1 of 1987), Re [1989] 1 W.L.R. 271, CA (Civ Div) . . . . — IA Pt IX, 268, IR 6.5, 7.55

Debtor (No.11 of 1987), Re, Independent, March 28, 1988 . . . . . . — IR 6.5

Debtor (No.190 of 1987), Re, The Times, May 21, 1988 . . . . — IA 268, IR 6.5, 7.55

Debtor (No.10 of 1988), Re [1989] 1 W.L.R. 405, Ch D . . . . — IA 268, IR 6.5

Debtor (No.83 of 1988), Re [1990] 1 W.L.R. 708, Ch D . . . . — IA 252(2), 256(5), 257(1), 262(4)–(7)

Debtor (No.310 of 1988), Re [1989] 1 W.L.R. 452 . . . . — IA 383(2)–(4), IR 6.1

Debtor (No.222 of 1990) Ex p. Bank of Ireland, Re (No.2) [1993] B.C.L.C. 233, Ch D . . . . — IA 262, IR 4.50–4.71

Debtor (No.259 of 1990), Re [1992] 1 W.L.R. 226, Ch D . . . . — IA 262

Debtor (No.26 of 1991), Re; sub nom. Holmes v Official Receiver [1996] B.C.C. 246; [1996] B.P.I.R. 279, Ch D . . . . — IA 279(3)–(5), IR 6.215, 6.216

Debtor (No.32/SD/1991) (No.2), Re [1994] B.C.C. 524, Ch D . . . . — IA 375(2), IR 6.5

Debtor (No.51/SD/1991), Re [1992] 1 W.L.R. 1294, Ch D . . . . — IA 267(1), (2), IR 6.111

Provision   **Provision**

Hellas Telecommunications (Luxembourg) II SCA (in admin.), Re [2011] EWHC 3176 (Ch) . . . . IA Sch.B1 para.84(1), (2), para.98(2)

Hemming (Deceased), Re [2008] EWHC 8565 (Ch); [2009] B.P.I.R. 50 — IA 436

Henderson v 3052775 Nova Scotia Ltd [2006] UKHL 21 . . . . IA 242

Henwood v Barlow Clowes International Ltd (in liq.) [2008] EWCA Civ 577 . . . . IA 265

Henwood v Customs and Excise [1998] B.P.I.R. 339, CA (Civ Div) . . . . IA 282(1), (3)

Heritage Joinery v Krasner [1999] B.P.I.R. 683, Ch D . . . . IA 263(1), (2)

Hewitt Brannan (Tools) Co Ltd, Re [1990] B.C.C. 354, Ch D (Companies Ct) . . . . IA 124(5)

Hibernian Merchants Ltd, Re [1958] Ch. 76, Ch D . . . . IA 221

Hickling v Baker [2007] EWCA Civ 287; (2007) 104(16) L.S.G. 26 . . . . . IA 364(1), 366(1)

High Street Services Ltd v Bank of Credit & Commerce International SA. *See* MS Fashions Ltd v Bank of Credit and Commerce International SA (in liq.)

Higham (a Bankrupt), Re; sub nom. Beer v Higham [1997] B.P.I.R. 349, Ch D . . . . IA 284(1)–(3), (6)

Highberry Ltd v Colt Telecom Group Plc (No.1); sub nom. Colt Telecom Group Plc, Re (No.1) [2002] EWHC 2503 (Ch) . . . . IA Sch.B1 para.11, IR 7.60, [IA 9(1)]

Highberry Ltd v Colt Telecom Group Plc (No.2); sub nom. Colt Telecom Group Plc (No.2), Re [2002] EWHC 2815 (Ch); [2003] B.P.I.R. 324 . . . . . [IA 8(1), (2), IR 2.1–2.3]

Hill Samuel & Co Ltd v Laing [1991] B.C.C. 665; 1989 S.C. 301, CS (IH 2 Div) . . . . IA 57(2), (4), (5)

Hill v Alex Lawrie Factors Ltd; sub nom. Burfoot (a Bankrupt), Re [2000] B.P.I.R. 1038, Ch D . . . . IA 344(1), (2)

Hill v East and West India Dock Co; sub nom. East and West India Dock

Co v Hill (1883–84) L.R. 9 App. Cas. 448 . . . . IA 181(1)–(3)

Hill v Haines; sub nom. Haines v Hill [2007] EWCA Civ 1284; [2008] Ch. 412; overruling [2007] EWHC 1012 (Ch); [2007] N.P.C. 58 . . . . IA 339(1)–(3), 340(4), (5), 382(3), (4)

Hill v Secretary of State [2005] EWHC 696 (Ch) . . . . IA 283(2), (3), 307(1), [CDDA 11]

Hill v Spread Trustee Co Ltd; sub nom. Nurkowski, Re [2006] EWCA Civ 542; [2006] B.C.C. 646; [2006] B.P.I.R. 789 . . . . IA 238(4), 423, 423(1)–(3)

Hill v Stokes plc [2010] EWHC 3726 (Ch); [2011] B.C.C. 473 . . . . IA Sch.B1 paras 26(2), (3), 28

Hill v Department for Business, Innovation and Skills, unreported, December 7, 2011 . . . . [CDDA 13]

Hill v Van Der Merwe [2007] EWHC 1613 (Ch); [2007] B.P.I.R. 1562 . . . . IR 9.2

Hillingdon LBC v Cutler; sub nom. Hillingdon Corp v Cutler [1968] 1 Q.B. 124, CA (Civ Div) . . . . [IA 9(2)]

Hindcastle Ltd v Barbara Attenborough Associates Ltd [1997] A.C. 70; [1996] B.C.C. 636, HL . . . . IA 181(1)–(3), 315, 315(3), (5)

Hirani v Rendle [2003] EWHC 2538 (Ch); [2004] B.P.I.R. 274 . . . . IA 282(1), (3)

Hoare, Re [1997] B.P.I.R. 683, Ch D . . IA 260(1), (2), (2A)

Hoare v Inland Revenue Commissioners [2002] EWHC 775 (Ch); [2002] B.P.I.R. 986 . . . . IA 282(1), (3)

Hobbs v Gibson [2010] EWHC 3676 (Ch) . . . . IA 108, Sch.B1 para.83(7)

Hocking v Canyon Holdings Ltd [2004] EWHC 1966 (Ch); [2005] B.P.I.R. 160. . . . . IA 339(1)–(3)

Hofer v Strawson [1999] 2 B.C.L.C. 336; [1999] B.P.I.R. 501, Ch D . . . . . IR 6.5

Holdenhurst Securities Plc v Cohen [2001] 1 B.C.L.C. 460, Ch D . . . . . . IA 7(3)

Holland v HM Revenue and Customs. *See* Revenue and Customs Commissioners v Holland

Hollicourt (Contracts) Ltd (in liq.) v Bank of Ireland; sub nom. Bank of Ireland v Hollicourt (Contracts) Ltd;

Provision | Provision

Case Table

	Provision		Provision

Mourant & Co Trustees Ltd v Sixty UK Ltd (in admin.) [2010] EWHC 1890 (Ch); [2010] B.C.C. 882; [2010] B.P.I.R. 1264 .... **IA 6**

Movitex Ltd, Re [1992] 1 W.L.R. 303; [1992] B.C.C. 101, CA (Civ Div) ... **IA 112(2), IR 4.218(1)–(3)**

Mulkerrins v PricewaterhouseCoopers; sub nom. Mulkerrins (formerly Woodward) v Pricewaterhouse Coopers (formerly t/a Coopers & Lybrand) [2003] UKHL 41; [2003] 1 W.L.R. 1937 .... **IA 306**

Mullarkey v Broad [2007] EWHC 3400 (Ch); [2008] 1 B.C.L.C. 638 .... **IA 212(3)**

Mulvey v Secretary of State for Social Security, 1997 S.C. (H.L.) 105; 1997 S.L.T. 753; [1997] B.P.I.R. 696, HL . **IA 306**

Mundy v Brown [2011] EWHC 377 (Ch) .... **IA 107**

Munns v Perkins [2002] B.P.I.R. 120, Ch D .... **IA 35(1), 36(1)**

Mumtaz Properties Ltd v Saeed Ahmed [2011] EWCA Civ 160 .... **IA 212(1)**

Munro and Rowe, Re; sub nom. Singer v Trustee of the Property of Munro [1981] 1 W.L.R. 1358, Ch D .... **IA 299(1), (2), IR 13.4**

Murjani (a Bankrupt), Re [1996] 1 W.L.R. 1498; [1996] B.C.C. 278, Ch D .... **IA 366(1)**

Murphy v Gooch [2007] EWCA Civ 603; [2007] 2 F.L.R. 934, CA (Civ Div) .... **IA 335A**

Muscovitch, Re [1939] Ch. 69, CA .... **[IA 9(2)]**

Myles J Callaghan Ltd (in rec.) v Glasgow DC, 1987 S.C. 171; (1987) 3 B.C.C. 337, CS (OH) .... **IA 53(6), (7), 55(1), (2), IR 4.90**

N

N (a Debtor), Re [2002] B.P.I.R. 1024, Ch D (Bankruptcy Ct) .... **IA 257(1), 262**

NP Engineering & Security Products Ltd, Re; sub nom. Official Receiver v Pafundo [2000] B.C.C. 164, CA (Civ Div) .... **[CDDA 6(3)–(3C), 7(1)]**

NS Distribution Ltd, Re [1990] B.C.L.C. 169, Ch D .... **[IA 17(2)]**

NT Gallagher & Son Ltd, Re; sub nom. NT Gallagher & Sons Ltd v Howard; Shierson v Tomlinson [2002] EWCA

Civ 404; [2002] B.C.C. 867; [2002] B.P.I.R. 565 .... **IA 7(4), 7A, 263(5), (6), IR 4.16–4.21B**

Naeem (a Bankrupt) (No.18 of 1988), Re [1990] 1 W.L.R. 48; (1989) 86(46) L.S.G. 37, Ch D .... **IA 4(3), 260(1), (2), (2A), 262**

Namco UK Ltd, Re [2003] EWHC 989 (Ch) .... **IA 135**

Namulas Pension Trustees Ltd v Mouzakis [2011] B.P.I.R. 1724 ..... **IA 257(2), (3), 260(1), (2), (2A), 262(1)–(3), (8), IR 12A.1, 12A.5**

Narinen v Finland (App. No.45027/98) [2004] B.P.I.R. 914, ECHR .... **IA 371(1)**

National Employers Mutual General Insurance Association Ltd (in liq.), Re [1995] B.C.C. 774, Ch D .... **IA 130(2)**

National Provincial Bank Ltd v Ainsworth [1965] A.C. 1175, HL ... **IA 335A**

National Union of Flint Glassworkers, Re [2006] B.C.C. 828, Ch D .... **IA 220(1)**

National Westminster Bank Ltd v Halesowen Presswork and Assemblies Ltd; sub nom. Halesowen Presswork & Assemblies v Westminster Bank Ltd [1972] A.C. 785, HL .... **IA 323, IR 4.90**

National Westminster Bank Ltd v Jones; sub nom. Jones v National Westminster Bank Plc [2001] EWCA Civ 1541; [2002] B.P.I.R. 361 ...... **IA 423(1)–(3)**

National Westminster Bank Plc v Kapoor [2011] EWCA Civ 1083; [2012] 1 All E.R. 1201; [2011] B.P.I.R. 1680 .... **IA Pt VIII, 262(1)–(3), (8), IR 5.21, 5.23**

National Westminster Bank Plc v Msaada Group [2011] EWHC 3423 (Ch); [2012] B.C.C. 226 .... **IA Sch.B1 para.26(2), (3)**

National Westminster Bank Plc v Scher. *See* Debtor (No.574 of 1995), Re

National Westminster Bank plc v Yadgaroff [2011] EWHC 3711 (Ch) . **IA 262(1)–(3), (8), 5.21, 5.22**

Nationwide Building Society v Wright [2009] B.P.I.R. 1047 .... **IA 346(1), (5)**

Neath Rugby Ltd, Re. *See* Cuddy v Hawkes

	Provision		Provision
Neath Rugby Ltd, Re (2009). *See* Hawkes v Cuddy		Ng (a Bankrupt), Re; sub nom. Trustee of the Estate of Ng v Ng [1997] B.C.C. 507; [1998] 2 F.L.R. 386, Ch D	IA 305(2), 336(3)–(5)
Neely v Inland Revenue Commissioners. *See* Debtor (No.383-SD-92), Re			
Nelson v Nelson [1997] 1 W.L.R. 233; [1997] B.P.I.R. 702, CA (Civ Div)	IA 306	Niagara Mechanical Services International Ltd (in admin.), Re; sub nom. Canary Wharf Contractors (DS6) Ltd v Niagara Mechanical Services International Ltd (in admin.) [2001] B.C.C. 393, Ch D (Companies Ct)	IA 107
Neuschild v British Equitorial Oil Co Ltd [1925] Ch. 346, Ch D	IA 194		
New Bullas Trading Ltd, Re [1994] B.C.C. 36, CA (Civ Div)	IA 40(1), (2)		
New Cap Reinsurance Corp Ltd v HIH Casualty & General Insurance Ltd. *See* HIH Casualty & General Insurance Ltd, Re		Nicholls v Lan [2006] EWHC 1255 (Ch); [2007] 1 F.L.R. 744; [2006] B.P.I.R. 1243	IA 335A
New Cap Reinsurance Corp Ltd (in liq.) v Grant [2011] EWCA Civ 971; [2012] 1 All E.R. 755; [2011] C.P. Rep. 48; [2011] B.C.C. 937; [2011] B.P.I.R. 1428	IA 426(4), (5)	Nicoll v Cutts [1985] P.C.C. 311; (1985) 1 B.C.C. 99,427, CA (Civ Div)	IA 37(1), (2), 44(1), (2)
New China Hong Kong Capital Ltd, Re [2003] EWHC 1573 (Ch); [2003] B.P.I.R. 1176	IA 236(2)	Nicoll v Steelpress (Supplies) Ltd; sub nom. Nicoll v Steel Press (Supplies) Ltd, 1992 S.C. 119; 1993 S.L.T. 533, CS (IH Ex Div)	IA 243(1), (2)
New Generation Engineers Ltd, Re [1993] B.C.L.C. 435, Ch D (Companies Ct)	[CDDA 9(1)]	Nine Miles Down UK Ltd, Re. *See* Singla v Hedman	
New Hampshire Insurance Co v Rush & Tompkins Group Plc [1998] 2 B.C.L.C. 471, CA (Civ Div)	IA 221	Noble Trees Ltd, Re [1993] B.C.C. 318; [1993] B.C.L.C. 1185, Ch D (Companies Ct)	[CDDA 7(2)]
New Millennium Experience Co Ltd, Re. *See* Greenwich Millennium Exhibition Ltd v New Millennium Experience Co Ltd		Nolton Business Centres Ltd, Re; sub nom. Eliades v City of London Common Council [1996] B.C.C. 500; [1996] R.A. 116, Ch D	IR 12.2
New Technology Systems Ltd, Re; sub nom. Official Receiver v Prior [1997] B.C.C. 810, CA (Civ Div)	[CDDA 1(1)]	Norditrack (UK) Ltd, Re [2000] 1 W.L.R. 343; [2000] B.C.C. 441, Ch D (Companies Ct)	IA 84(2A), (2B), 240(1), (3), [IA 18(1), (2)]
Newham LBC (08019113) [2010] B.P.I.R. 464	IA Pt IX Ch1		
Newhart Developments Ltd v Cooperative Commercial Bank Ltd [1978] Q.B. 814, CA (Civ Div)	IA Pt III	Norfolk House Plc (in rec.) v Repsol Petroleum Ltd, 1992 S.L.T. 235, CS (OH)	IA 72
Newlands (Seaford) Educational Trust (in admin.), Re. *See* Chittenden v Pepper		Norglen Ltd (in liq.) v Reeds Rains Prudential Ltd; Mayhew-Lewis v Westminster Scaffolding Group Plc; Levy v ABN AMRO Bank NV; Circuit Systems Ltd (in liq.) v Zuken-Redac (UK) Ltd [1999] 2 A.C. 1; [1998] B.C.C. 44, HL	IA Sch.4 para.6
Newman Shopfitters (Cleveland) Ltd, Re [1991] B.C.L.C. 407, Ch D	[IA 15(2), (5), (6)]		
Newport County Association Football Club Ltd, Re (1987) 3 B.C.C. 635, Ch D (Companies Ct)	[IA 8(1), (2), IR 2.1–2.3]	Norman Holding Co Ltd (in liq.), Re [1991] 1 W.L.R. 10; [1991] B.C.C. 11, Ch D	IR 4.90
Newscreen Media Group Plc (in liq.), Re; sub nom. Hardy v McLoughlin [2009] EWHC 944	[IA 20(2), (3)]	Normandy Marketing Ltd, Re [1993] B.C.C. 879, Ch D (Companies Ct)	IA 220, 225, 441

	Provision		Provision

Official Receiver v Zwirn; sub nom. Windows West Ltd, Re [2002] B.C.C. 760, Ch D (Companies Ct) .. **[CDDA 22(5)]**

Official Receiver for Northern Ireland v Rooney and Paulson [2008] NICh 22; [2009] B.P.I.R. 536, Ch D (NI) ..... **IA 336(3)–(5)**

Official Receiver for Northern Ireland v Stranaghan [2010] NICh 8; [2010] B.P.I.R. 928 .... **IA 339(1)–(3)**

Oldham v Kyrris. *See* Kyrris v Oldham

Olympia & York Canary Wharf Ltd (No.1), Re; sub nom. American Express Europe Ltd v Adamson [1993] B.C.C. 154, Ch D .... **[IA 11(3)]**

Omokwe v HFC Bank Ltd [2007] B.P.I.R. 1157, HC .... **IA 267(1), (2), 282(1), (3), IR 6.3**

Oracle (North West) Ltd v Pinnacle Financial Services (UK) Ltd [2008] EWHC 1920 (Ch); [2009] B.C.C. 159......................... **IA Sch.B1 para.13(1), (3)**

Ord v Upton [2000] Ch. 352, CA (Civ Div)........................... **IA 306**

Orient Power Holdings Ltd, Re [2009] B.C.C. 452, HK HC .... **IA 139**

Oriental Commercial Bank, Re; sub nom. European Bank Ex p. (1871–72) L.R. 7 Ch. App. 99, CA in Chancery .... **IR 4.73–4.85**

Oriental Inland Steam Co Ex p. Scinde Railway Co, Re (1873–74) L.R. 9 Ch. App. 557, CA in Chancery ..... **IA 183**

Orion Media Marketing Ltd v Media Brook Ltd [2003] B.P.I.R. 474, Ch D (Companies Ct) .... **IA 123**

Orleans Motor Co Ltd, Re [1911] 2 Ch. 41, Ch D .... **IA 245(2)**

Orrick, Herrington & Sutcliffe (Europe) Ltd v Frohlich [2012] B.P.I.R. 169 .. **IA 267(1), (2), 268**

Ortega Associates Ltd (in liq.), Re. *See* Green v Walkling

Osborn v Cole [1999] B.P.I.R. 251, Ch D .... **IA 303(1)**

Ouvaroff (a Bankrupt), Re [1997] B.P.I.R. 712, Ch D .... **IA 366(1)**

Oval 1742 Ltd (in CVL), Re; sub nom. Customs and Excise Commissioners v Royal Bank of Scotland Plc [2007] EWCA Civ 1262; [2008] B.C.C. 135 **IA 40(1), (2), 175**

Overnight Ltd, Re [2009] EWHC 601 (Ch); [2009] B.C.C. 787 .... **IA 213**

Overnight Ltd (No.2) (in liq.), Re; sub nom. Goldfarb v Higgins [2010] EWHC 613 (Ch); [2010] B.C.C. 796 **IA 213(2)**

Overnight Ltd (No.3) (in liq.), Re; sub nom. Goldfarb v Higgins [2010] EWHC 1587 (Ch); [2010] B.C.C. 808........................... **IA 213(2)**

Owo-Samson v Barclays Bank Plc (No.1); sub nom. Owo-Sampson v Barclays Bank Plc [2003] EWCA Civ 714; [2003] B.P.I.R. 1373 ...... **IA 282(1), (3)**

Owusu v Jackson (t/a Villa Holidays Bal Inn Villas) (C-281/02) [2005] Q.B. 801, ECJ .... **IA 125(1)**

Oxted Financial Services Ltd v Gordon [1998] B.P.I.R. 231, Ch D .... **IA 266(3), (4)**

Oxford Pharmaceuticals Ltd, Re; sub nom. Wilson v Masters International Ltd [2009] EWHC 1753 (Ch); [2010] B.C.C. 834.................... **IA 239(6), 241(2)**

P

P&C and R&T (Stockport) Ltd, Re; sub nom. Griffiths v Provincial & City Property Co [1991] B.C.C. 98, Ch D **[IA 14(1)]**

PFTZM Ltd, Re; sub nom. Jourdain v Paul [1995] B.C.C. 280, Ch D ...... **IA 214(1), 236, 240**

PNC Telecom Plc (in admin.), Re [2003] EWHC 2220 (Ch); [2004] B.P.I.R. 314 .... **IA 236**

PNC Telecom Plc v Thomas [2007] EWHC 2157 (Ch) .... **IA 212(3)**

Pacific & General Insurance Co Ltd v Hazell; Pacific & General Insurance Co Ltd v Home & Overseas Insurance Co Ltd [1997] L.R.L.R. 65; [1997] B.C.C. 400, QBD (Comm)...................... **IA 135**

Pacific & General Insurance Ltd (in liq.) v Home & Overseas Insurance Co Ltd. *See* Pacific & General Insurance Co Ltd v Hazell

Packaging Direct Ltd, Re; sub nom. Jones v Secretary of State for Trade and Industry [1994] B.C.C. 213, Ch D (Companies Ct) .... **[CDDA 7(2)]**

Paget Ex p. Official Receiver, Re [1927] 2 Ch. 85, CA .... **IA 290(3), (5)**

Painter v Hutchison [2007] EWHC 758 (Ch); [2008] B.P.I.R. 170, Ch D .... **IR 11.2, 11.3**

PAL SC Realisations 2007 Ltd (in liq.), Re. See Kelly v Inflexion Fund 2 Ltd

Provision   **Provision**

Secretary of State for Trade and Industry v Queen, 1998 S.L.T. 735; [1998] B.C.C. 678, CS (IH Ex Div) . **[CDDA 6(1)]**

Secretary of State for Trade and Industry v Reynard; sub nom. Reynard v Secretary of State for Trade and Industry [2002] EWCA Civ 497; [2002] B.C.C. 813 . . . . **[CDDA 6(1), 9(1)]**

Secretary of State for Trade and Industry v Rogers [1996] 1 W.L.R. 1569; [1997] B.C.C. 155, CA (Civ Div) . . . . **[CDDA 7(1)]**

Secretary of State for Trade and Industry v Rosenfield [1999] B.C.C. 413, Ch D . . . . **[CDDA 1(1)]**

Secretary of State for Trade and Industry v Sananes [1994] B.C.C. 375, CC (Nottingham) . . . . **[CDDA 7(3)]**

Secretary of State for Trade and Industry v Shakespeare [2005] B.C.C. 891, Ch D . . . . **[CDDA 6(3)–(3C)]**

Secretary of State for Trade and Industry v Slater [2008] B.C.C. 70; [2008] I.C.R. 54, EAT . . . . **IA 86**

Secretary of State for Trade and Industry v Swan; sub nom. Finelist Ltd, Re [2003] EWHC 1780 (Ch); [2004] B.C.C. 877 . . . . **[CDDA 7(1), 16]**

Secretary of State for Trade and Industry v Swan (No.2) [2005] EWHC 603 (Ch); [2005] B.C.C. 596 **[CDDA 9(1)]**

Secretary of State for Trade and Industry v Taylor; sub nom. CS Holidays Ltd, Re; Company (No.004803 of 1996), Re; Secretary of State for Trade and Industry v Gash [1997] 1 W.L.R. 407; [1997] B.C.C. 172, Ch D . . . . **[CDDA 9(1)]**

Secretary of State for Trade and Industry v Thornbury [2007] EWHC 3202 (Ch); [2008] B.C.C. 768 . . . . . . **[CDDA 9(1)]**

Secretary of State For Trade and Industry v Tillman. *See* Launchexcept Ltd, Re

Secretary of State for Trade and Industry v Tjolle [1998] B.C.C. 282; [1998] 1 B.C.L.C. 333, Ch D . . . . . . **[CDDA 1, 7(2), 22(5)]**

Secretary of State for Trade and Industry v Travel Time (UK) Ltd; sub nom. Company (No.5669 of 1998), Re; Secretary of State for Trade and Industry v Embassy Enterprises UK Ltd (No.5670 of 1998); Secretary of State for Trade and Industry v Harmony Holidays Ltd (No.5671 of 1998); Secretary of State for Trade and Industry v Marlborou; sub nom. Promotions Ltd (No.5672 of 1998) [2000] B.C.C. 792, Ch D (Companies Ct) . . . . **IA 124A**

Secretary of State for Trade and Industry v Van Hengel; sub nom. CSTC Ltd, Re [1995] B.C.C. 173, Ch D . . . . **[CDDA 9(1)]**

Secretary of State for Trade and Industry v Vohora [2007] EWHC 2656 (Ch); [2009] B.C.C. 369 . . . . . . **[CDDA 7(2)]**

Secretary of State for Trade and Industry v Walker. *See* Walker v Secretary of State for Trade and Industry

Secretary of State for Trade and Industry v Worth; sub nom. Dicetrade Ltd, Re [1994] B.C.C. 371, CA (Civ Div) . . . . **[CDDA 1(1), 17]**

Secretary of State for Work and Pensions v Payne. *See* R. (on the application of Payne) v Secretary of State for Work and Pensions

Secure & Provide Plc, Re [1992] B.C.C. 405, Ch D (Companies Ct) . . . . **IA 124A, IR 4.25–4.31**

Securum Finance Ltd v Camswell Ltd [1994] B.C.C. 434, Ch D . . . . **IA 123**

Segal v Pasram [2008] EWHC 3448 (Ch); [2008] 1 F.L.R. 271 . . . . **IA 339(1)–(3)**

Senator Hanseatische Verwaltungsgesellschaft mbH, Re; sub nom. Titan Marketing Gesellschaft, Re; Company (No.002613 of 1996), Re; Secretary of State for Trade and Industry v Glas [1997] 1 W.L.R. 515; [1997] B.C.C. 112, CA (Civ Div) . . . . **IA 124A**

Sendo Ltd, Re [2005] EWHC 1604 (Ch); [2006] 1 B.C.L.C. 395 . . . . **IA Sch.B1 para.111(1), 111(1A), 111(1B), [ER art.3(1)]**

Servaccomm Redhall Ltd, Re. *See* Cunningham v Secretary of State for Trade and Industry

	Provision		Provision

U

Statutes Table

Statutory Instruments Table

European and Other Legislation Table

Company Directors Disqualification Act 1986

Introductory note to the Act

This Act brings together in consolidated form the whole of the law relating to the disqualification of company directors (and, in some circumstances, other persons), either by order of the court or by an undertaking accepted in lieu of a court order.

The title of the Act is somewhat misleading, in that it may be read as applying only to company directors. While it is true that some of its provisions (e.g. ss.6–8 and 9A) are restricted to persons who are or have been directors, most of the rest of the Act is not so limited; and its scope has been extended by supplementary legislation so as to include other categories of persons such as the members of insolvent partnerships.

There has been a power to make disqualification orders in the Companies Acts since 1947, and this power was extended in later Companies Acts, notably in CA 1976 and CA 1981; but little use was made of the sanction prior to 1985, mainly because the necessary resources were not committed to investigation and enforcement. With the enactment of the insolvency reforms of 1985, there was manifested a new resolve on the part of Government to make much greater use of the power to disqualify directors. Difficulties which had been experienced in the operation of the earlier law (e.g. as regards the heavy burden of proof required in some circumstances) were overcome by amending legislation and new grounds for disqualification introduced. These reforms were brought into force on April 28, 1986, several months ahead of the general implementation of IA 1985. The Department of Trade and Industry (now the Department for Business, Innovation and Skills) established a special Disqualification Unit authorised to investigate cases of suspected breaches of the law and to institute proceedings for disqualification orders; and liquidators, administrators, receivers and other insolvency practitioners are required by law to make reports to the Department on the conduct of all the directors in every case of corporate insolvency.

Under the legislation as originally enacted, a person could be disqualified only by order of the court, but the Insolvency Act 2000 introduced the alternative of a disqualification *undertaking*, which applies only to cases under CDDA 1986 ss.6–8, i.e. cases where the basis of the charge is that the director has shown by his conduct that he is unfit to be concerned in the management of a company. A person who is prepared to accept liability may give an undertaking to the Secretary of State that he will not be a director or otherwise concerned in the management of a company for an agreed period, with the same consequences as would follow if a court order had been made in the same terms. Since the change came into force, undertakings have displaced disqualification orders in the great majority of cases.

The Act applies to "companies", an expression which (by s.22(2)) "includes any company which may be wound up under the Insolvency Act 1986". This means that it applies to "unregistered companies": see the note to IA 1986 s.220. As originally drafted, it did not apply to building societies or incorporated friendly societies, but it has since been extended so as to apply to the directors (or the members of the committee of management) and officers of both: see ss.22A and 22B, below. In 2004, the Act was extended to include the directors and officers (but not "shadow directors"—see below) of NHS Foundation Trusts: see s.22C, and in 2009 to open-ended investment companies (s.22D). It applies also to EEIGs: see the European Economic Interest Grouping Regulations 1989 (SI 1989/638) reg.20. The Co-operative and Community Benefit Societies and Credit Unions Act 2010, when it is brought into force, will extend the Act to industrial and provident societies (other than credit unions). Its application to other bodies remains uncertain: see the note to s.22(2).

Where an insolvent partnership is wound up as an unregistered company under Pt V of IA 1986 (see the note to IA 1986 s.420), any member or former member of the partnership or any other person who has or has had control or management of the partnership business is treated in the same way as the director of a company, and ss.1, 1A, 6 to 10, 13 to 15, 17, 19(c) and 20 and Sch.1 of CDDA 1986 apply: see the Insolvent Partnerships Order 1994 (SI 1994/2421) art.16 (as amended).

The provisions of CDDA 1986 are made to apply to limited liability partnerships by the Limited Liability Partnerships Regulations 2001 (SI 2001/1090 reg.4(2)), subject to certain modifications set out in Sch.2 Pt II of the Regulations. More particularly, references in the Act to a director or officer of a company are to be taken as including references to a member or officer of an LLP, and there is a new concept of "shadow member" corresponding to "shadow director".

For the purposes of the Act, "director" includes any person occupying the position of director, by whatever name called (s.22(3)), so that it is immaterial that, in the company in question, the members of the board may be called (e.g.) "trustees" or "governors". For the purposes of ss.6–9E, the term "director" includes a "shadow director", as defined in s.22(5). A de facto director has also been held to be within s.6: see the note to s.6(1) and, on the meaning of this term, the note to s.22(5).

All sections of CDDA 1986 apply to England and Wales and to Scotland, but not to Northern Ireland. However, equivalent legislation has been in force in that jurisdiction since 1986. Initially, this was brought about by the Companies (Northern Ireland) Order 1986 (SI 1986/1032 (NI 6)); but this has now been replaced by the Companies (Northern Ireland) Order 2002 (SI 2002/3150 (NI 4)). (See further the note to s.24(2).)

Generally speaking, the courts of England and Wales have no jurisdiction in matters of insolvency over companies registered in Scotland, and vice versa. Most sections of the CDDA 1986 also make it plain that this separation between the two jurisdictions applies also in relation to that Act (frequently by reference to the "court having jurisdiction to wind up the company" in question). One notable exception is s.8 (below), where the language is ambiguous and arguably would allow the Secretary of State to choose to start proceedings concerning a Scottish company in either jurisdiction; but in *Re Helene plc* [2000] 2 B.C.L.C. 249 Blackburne J. held that the distinction should be observed and it was competent only to make application to the court in Scotland. However, a disqualification order made (or an undertaking given) in either England and Wales or Scotland is operative in all parts of Britain (and, indeed, has unrestricted extraterritorial effect). And an amendment introduced by IA 2000 gives force throughout these jurisdictions to a Northern Ireland disqualification order or undertaking: see the note to s.12A, below.

In a number of cases relating to director disqualification an issue has arisen based on an allegation that there has been a violation of the European Convention for the Protection of Human Rights and Fundamental Freedoms (now largely embodied in UK domestic law following the enactment of the Human Rights Act 1998), and opinions have been expressed both by the courts in England and by the European Commission on Human Rights on the applicability of the Convention to disqualification proceedings.

In *EDC v United Kingdom (Application No.24433/94)* [1998] B.C.C. 370 the director concerned had been a respondent to an application for disqualification which had begun in August 1991 and was not finally disposed of until January 1996—nearly four and a half years from the start of the proceedings and seven years after the events had occurred on which the case was based. He alleged that there had been a violation of art.6(1) of the Convention, which states that "In the determination of his civil rights and obligations or of any criminal charge against him, everyone is entitled to a fair and public hearing within a reasonable time …". The Commission upheld his complaint, holding that the delay was in breach of the Convention (and accepting the view, incidentally, that the proceedings constituted a dispute over "civil rights and obligations").

In the later case of *DC, HS and AD v United Kingdom (Application No.39031/97)* [2000] B.C.C. 710 the European Court of Human Rights rejected an argument that disqualification proceedings constituted "criminal charges" within art.6(1): "the disqualification of directors is a matter which is regulatory rather than criminal". The applicants' main complaint was that it was unfair to base the disqualification proceedings on statements which had been obtained compulsorily under IA 1986 s.235, citing *Saunders v United Kingdom (Case 43/1994/490/572)* [1997] E.H.R.R. 313; [1997] B.C.C. 872. But this contention was rejected, one ground being that, unlike *Saunders*, this was not a criminal case. The court also ruled that the exclusion of evidence of the directors' good character was not incompatible with a fair hearing.

This ruling has been confirmed by the courts in this country. In *R. v Secretary of State for Trade and Industry Ex p. McCormick* [1998] B.C.C. 379, the Court of Appeal held that it was not unreasonable for the Secretary of State to continue to make use of compelled evidence in disqualification proceedings even though, in the light of the *Saunders* ruling, she had adopted a policy of not using compelled evidence in criminal cases. Again, in *Re Westminster Property Management Ltd, Official Receiver v Stern* [2000] 1 W.L.R. 2230; [2001] B.C.C. 121 the Court of Appeal, affirming Scott V.C. ruled that there had been no violation of the Convention on this ground, nor on the ground that an order would interfere with the freedom of establishment and freedom to provide services (arts 43, 49 of the Convention).

In *WGS and MSLS v United Kingdom (Application No.38172/97)* [2000] B.C.C. 719 the European Court of Human Rights held that director disqualification proceedings do not infringe art.8 of the Convention (respect for private life): in so far as the applicants' complaint was about press reporting of their case it was open to them to invoke the law of defamation. It was also ruled that no appeal could be made to the European Court until after the matter had been determined at a trial in the United Kingdom court and an order made.

It is normal practice for the Secretary of State to require that there should be attached to a disqualification undertaking a statement of the grounds on which the finding of unfitness against the director had been made: see the note to s.7. In *Re Blackspur Group plc (No.3), Secretary of State for Trade and Industry v Davies (No.2)* [2002] 2 B.C.L.C. 263 the court rejected a contention by the director that to impose such a requirement was a breach of his human rights. In another case concerning a different director of the same company, *Re Blackspur Group plc (No.3), Secretary of State for Trade and Industry v Eastaway* [2003] B.C.C. 520 a delay of over eight years was held not to have prevented the director from having a fair and public hearing of his case: the greater part of this delay was due to various unsuccessful actions taken by the applicant himself, trying to prevent the case from coming to trial. However, this issue was taken to the European Court of Human Rights (*Davies v UK* [2005] B.C.C. 401), where it was held that the Government was responsible for the greater part of the delay and was in breach of the Convention. On the strength of this ruling, the director applied to the domestic court to have the disqualification proceedings against him dismissed and his disqualification retrospectively set aside, but he was unsuccessful, both at first instance and on appeal: *Re Blackspur Group plc (No.4)* [2006] EWHC 299 (Ch); [2006] 2 B.C.L.C. 489; *Eastaway v Secretary of State for Trade and Industry* [2007] EWCA Civ 425; [2007] B.C.C. 550. See also, on the ECHR costs, *Eastaway v UK* [2006] 2 B.C.L.C. 361.

Although the Secretary of State may be compelled under IA 1986 to make disclosure of materials, this obligation is restricted to materials in his possession and does not extend to materials that could be in his possession: requirements of fairness under the Convention do not require him to interview or obtain documents from third parties (*Re Stakefield (Midlands) Ltd* [2010] EWHC 2518 (Ch)). Similarly, in *Secretary of State for Business, Innovation and Skills v Doffman* [2010] EWHC 2518 (Ch); [2011] 1 B.C.L.C. 597 it was held that neither the Convention nor his general duty to act fairly would normally extend to requiring the Secretary of State to obtain evidence or undertake investigations requested by the respondent.

Independently of the Human Rights legislation, a plea has been raised on occasion that it would be an infringement of the principle of "double jeopardy" to pursue disqualification proceedings against a defendant when he has been, or is concurrently being, faced with disciplinary proceedings by a professional body (e.g. the Financial Services Authority) in respect of the same charges. In *Re Barings plc (No.4)* [1999] B.C.C. 639; and *Re Migration Services International Ltd* [2000] B.C.C. 1,095 such an objection was not upheld, the court ruling that the issues in the two proceedings were materially different. An objection on the ground of "double jeopardy" was also not upheld in *Re Cedarwood Productions Ltd* [2001] EWCA Civ 1083; [2004] B.C.C. 65, where a disqualification order under CDDA 1986 s.2 had been made against the defendants as part of a criminal sentence and the Secretary of State wished to pursue civil proceedings for an order under s.6 which relied partly on the same facts. Although there was some overlap, the court in the latter proceedings would be looking at a wider picture. (See also *Re Denis Hilton Ltd* [2002] 1 B.C.L.C. 302.)

The present Act has its own definition section (s.22), but there is some cross-referencing between it and IA 1986, and also to the Companies Acts; and s.22(9) provides that any expression not specifically defined in this Act is to be interpreted by reference to the Companies Acts. The terms used in all of these Acts may therefore for the most part be taken to have the same meanings.

The Enterprise Act 2002 s.204, inserting new ss.9A–9E into CDDA 1986, introduced the regime of competition disqualification orders (CDOs) and competition disqualification undertakings (CDUs). This reform took effect from June 20, 2003: see the Enterprise Act 2002 (Commencement No.3, Transitional and Transitory Provisions and Savings) Order 2003 (SI 2003/1397 (C. 60)) arts 1, 2(1) and Sch.1. Under s.9A the court is empowered to make a disqualification order against a person who is or has been a director or shadow director of a company which has committed a breach of competition law where the court considers that his conduct as a director, taken together with his conduct in relation to one or more other undertakings, makes him unfit to be concerned in the management of a company. Responsibility under ss.9A–9E lies with the Office of Fair Trading and a number of named regulators, and not with the Secretary of State. See further the notes to ss.9A–9E.

The Enterprise Act 2002 s.257 also introduced the system of bankruptcy restrictions orders and undertakings (see the comment to IA 1986 s.281A and Sch.4A). The law governing these orders and undertakings closely parallels that already established by the present Act for director disqualification, and the CDDA cases are likely to be relevant. This will be the case also with debt relief restrictions orders and undertakings, a regime introduced (as IA 1986 Pt 7A) by the Tribunals, Courts and Enforcement Act 2007.

The Companies Act 2006 Pt 40 introduced (from October 1, 2009) new provisions relating to persons who are subject to restrictions similar to those imposed by a director disqualification order (or equivalent undertaking) under the law of a country or territory outside the United Kingdom. The Secretary of State is empowered to make regulations which either (a) automatically disqualify such persons from acting as director, etc. of a UK company or (b) may be disqualified by order of the court on the application of the Secretary of State; and there may be provision also in the regulations for the Secretary of State to accept a disqualification undertaking in lieu of an order. No regulations have yet been made.

Regulations relating to director disqualification were made under CA 1985 and replaced by new regulations in similar terms after the 1986 legislation became operative. Those currently in force are:

- the Insolvent Companies (Disqualification of Unfit Directors) Proceedings Rules 1987 (SI 1987/2023, as amended by SI 1999/1023, 2001/765, 2003/1367 and 2007/1906);

- the Insolvent Companies (Reports on Conduct of Directors) Rules 1996 (SI 1996/1909, as amended by SI 2001/764 and 2003/2096);

- the Insolvent Companies (Reports on Conduct of Directors) (Scotland) Rules 1996 (SI 1996/1910 (S 154), as amended by SI 2001/768.

Also of relevance are the Companies (Disqualification Orders) Regulations 2009 (SI 2009/2471, replacing SI 2001/967).

Attention should also be drawn to the *Practice Direction: Directors Disqualification Proceedings* [2007] B.C.C. 862 (reproduced as App.VI to this *Guide*).

Comparable secondary legislation has been introduced in Northern Ireland. See the note to s.24(2).

The Insolvent Companies (Disqualification of Unfit Directors) Proceedings Rules 2007 (SI 2007/1906), effective August 6, 2007 clarify the rules of procedure to be used in various applications made in the course of disqualification proceedings, e.g. applications for leave to act as a director notwithstanding a disqualification order.

Reference will be made at appropriate places in this section to Totty and Moss, *Insolvency* (Sweet & Maxwell, looseleaf), Pt B; and to Walters and Davis-White, *Directors' Disqualification & Insolvency Restrictions* (Sweet & Maxwell, 2009).

Company Directors Disqualification Act 1986

(1986 Chapter 46)

Arrangement of Sections

Company Directors Disqualification Act 1986

(1986 Chapter 46)

An Act to consolidate certain enactments relating to the disqualification of persons from being directors of companies, and from being otherwise concerned with a company's affairs.

[25th July 1986]

Preliminary

1 Disqualification orders: general

1(1) [Disqualification order] In the circumstances specified below in this Act a court may, and under sections 6 and 9A shall, make against a person a disqualification order, that is to say an order that for a period specified in the order–

   (a) he shall not be a director of a company, act as receiver of a company's property or in any way, whether directly or indirectly, be concerned or take part in the promotion, formation or management of a company unless (in each case) he has the leave of the court, and

   (b) he shall not act as an insolvency practitioner.

1(2) [Maximum, minimum periods] In each section of this Act which gives to a court power or, as the case may be, imposes on it the duty to make a disqualification order there is specified the maximum (and, in section 6, the minimum) period of disqualification which may or (as the case may be) must be imposed by means of the order and, unless the court otherwise orders, the period of disqualification so imposed shall begin at the end of the period of 21 days beginning with the date of the order.

1(3) [Where two orders] Where a disqualification order is made against a person who is already subject to such an order or to a disqualification undertaking, the periods specified in those orders or, as the case may be, in the order and the undertaking shall run concurrently.

1(4) [Criminal grounds] A disqualification order may be made on grounds which are or include matters other than criminal convictions, notwithstanding that the person in respect of whom it is to be made may be criminally liable in respect of those matters.

GENERAL NOTE

This section brings forward from CA 1985 s.295 the provisions defining a disqualification order and describing its effect. The wording has been altered in a number of respects by IA 2000, as noted in the comments to subss.(1) to (3) below.

Differing views have been expressed regarding the nature and purpose of a disqualification order. On the one hand, it may be seen as a form of punishment for misconduct—a view that is reinforced by the fact that the courts have, on occasion, revised or lifted a disqualification order when a person has appealed against a criminal sentence: see, e.g. *R. v Young* [1990] B.C.C. 549, where the court said that a disqualification order was "unquestionably a punishment", and ruled that it was quite inappropriate to link such an order with a conditional discharge, and *R. v Millard* (1993) 15 Cr. App. R. (S) 445.

On the other hand, it has been stressed in a far greater number of cases (and particularly those brought under ss.6–9 and 11) that the court's primary concern is to ensure the protection of the public: see, e.g. *Re Lo-Line Electric Motors Ltd* [1988] Ch. 477 at 486; (1988) 4 B.C.C. 415 at 419; *Re Sevenoaks Stationers (Retail) Ltd* [1991] Ch. 164 at 176, [1990] B.C.C. 765 at 773; *Secretary of State for Trade & Industry v Langridge, Re Cedac Ltd* [1991] Ch. 402 at 413–414; [1991] B.C.C. 148 at 153–155; *R. v Secretary of State for Trade & Industry Ex p. Lonrho plc* [1992] B.C.C. 325 at 333, 335. However, even so, an order is clearly restrictive of the liberty of the person against whom it is made, and its contravention can have penal consequences under s.13 (above). It has also been observed that a disqualification order involves the termination of a civil right and obligation (*R. v Secretary of State for Trade & Industry Ex p. McCormick* [1998] B.C.C. 379), that the objective of the legislation is to raise standards of responsibility (*Secretary of State for Trade & Industry v McTighe* [1997] B.C.C. 224) and that it is intended to have a real deterrent effect on others (*Re Blackspur Group plc* [1998] 1 W.L.R. 422; [1998] B.C.C. 11; *Secretary of State for Trade & Industry v Tjolle* [1998] B.C.C. 282). Of course, such remarks are often nothing more than observations made by a judge *en passant*; but in some cases the distinction has been squarely in issue before the court, and in these cases it has been emphasised that the jurisdiction is civil and not criminal in nature. For example the standard of proof is that of a balance of probabilities (*Re Living Images Ltd* [1996] B.C.C. 12)—although it is recognised that the more serious the allegations are, the more the court will require cogent evidence as proof (ibid., and see *Re Verby Print for Advertising Ltd* [1998] B.C.C. 652). Again, where dishonesty is alleged, evidence of good character has been ruled to be inadmissible, even though it would be relevant in criminal proceedings (*Secretary of State for Trade & Industry v Dawes* [1997] B.C.C. 121). However this is not always the approach: in *Secretary of State for Trade & Industry v Baker* [1998] Ch. 356 at 376, Scott V.C. said that disqualification proceedings "have, in many respects, much more in common with criminal proceedings than with civil litigation about private rights", and that it was appropriate for the Secretary of State to disclose to a respondent a report which in criminal proceedings would have to be disclosed. The Court of Appeal in *Re Westmid Packing Services Ltd Secretary of State for Trade & Industry v Griffiths* [1986] B.C.C. 836, while stating that protection of the public is the primary purpose of disqualification, admitted that in truth the exercise engaged in is little different from any sentencing exercise. Lord Woolf said (at 843) "The period of disqualification must reflect the gravity of the offence. It must contain deterrent elements. That is what sentencing is all about".

The view that disqualification proceedings are civil rather than criminal in nature has been endorsed in a number of cases where it has been claimed that the proceedings have involved, or would involve, a contravention of the European Convention for the Protection of Human Rights and Fundamental Freedoms (now incorporated into domestic legislation by the Human Rights Act 1998). See the Introductory note to CDDA 1986 at p.2 above.

In *R. v Holmes* [1991] B.C.C. 394 the Court of Appeal held that it was wrong in principle to make a compensation order and at the same time to disqualify the person concerned from acting as a company director, since his ability to earn the means with which to pay the compensation would be significantly diminished. The compensation order which had been imposed by the trial court following his conviction for fraudulent trading was accordingly quashed.

On this topic, see further Walters and Davis-White, *Directors' Disqualification & Insolvency Restrictions*, Ch.2; and Totty and Moss, *Insolvency*, B1–03.

The legislation as enacted in 1986 made no provision for a disqualification order to be made by consent, or for a respondent to admit the case against him and plead guilty. Every application for a disqualification order had to be brought before a court and proved by evidence. The delay and expense (and, for respondents, the uncertainty and stress) involved was costly in every sense, and a large backlog of cases soon built up. It was not until the case of *Re Carecraft Construction Co Ltd* [1994] 1 W.L.R. 172; [1993] B.C.C. 336 that a first step was taken, by judicial ingenuity, to deal with the problem. The *Carecraft* procedure allowed the court to deal with uncontested cases in a summary way. In the ensuing years this summary procedure was regularly followed where the facts were agreed or, at least, not disputed and both the Secretary of State and the director were willing for the case to proceed on the basis of those facts. The *Practice Direction: Directors Disqualification Proceedings* [2007] B.C.C. 862 contains guidance as to the procedure to be followed where a *Carecraft* application for summary trial is made: see App.VI, para.13.

The introduction of the *Carecraft* procedure enabled the parties in many cases to avoid the delay, stress and expense involved in a full-scale hearing, but it still involved the participation of the court and a considerable amount of documentation had to be prepared in order that the court could be fully apprised of the facts of the case. The procedure has now been rendered obsolete by the Insolvency Act 2000, which introduced the disqualification undertaking as an alternative to a disqualification order and has made the involvement of the court no longer necessary in the great majority of cases: see the notes to s.1A, below.

The offence of acting as a director while disqualified under this section is probably an absolute offence, on analogy with the position of an undischarged bankrupt: there is no requirement of mens rea. See *R. v Brockley* [1994] B.C.C. 131, and the note to s.11 below; and compare *R. v Cole, Lees & Birch* [1998] B.C.C. 87 (a decision on IA 1986 s.216).

A person who is subject to a disqualification order or undertaking under this Act (or under the corresponding legislation for Northern Ireland) is disqualified from being a trustee of a charity: Charities Act 2011 s.178(1), or the Scottish equivalent (Law Reform (Miscellaneous Provisions) (Scotland) Act 1990 s.8(1)(d)). Other legislation imposes an equivalent ban from holding office (or provides that disqualification order or undertaking shall be a ground for the person's removal) as the trustee of a pension trust scheme (Pensions Act 1995 s.29(1)(f)), a member of a police authority (Police Act 1996; Sch.2 para.11(1)(c); Sch.2A para.7(1)(c)), a Police Commissioner or member of a Police Service Authority (Police Act 1997 s.91(7)(b)) and Sch.2 para.3(1)(c)), a registered social landlord (Housing Act 1996 Sch.1 para.4(2)(b)), or a school governor (Schools Standards and Framework Act 1998 Sch.11 and Education (Company Directors Disqualification Act 1986: Amendments to Disqualification Provisions) (England) Regulations 2004 (SI 2004/3264)). In some of these cases there is provision for the court or the relevant authority to give leave to act or to grant a waiver, but in others there appears to be no dispensing power at all; compare *Re Westminster Property Management Ltd, Official Receiver v Stern (No.2)* [2001] EWCA Civ 111; [2002] B.C.C. 937.

In the last-mentioned case the question arose whether a disqualification order would prevent the person concerned from acting as a director of an overseas company. This would appear to turn on whether a UK court would have jurisdiction to wind up the particular company under Pt V of the Act, which in turn would require it to be shown by proper evidence that it had a "sufficient connection" with the jurisdiction.

The Insolvent Partnerships Order 1994 (SI 1994/2421, as amended by SI 2001/767) applies the greater part of CDDA 1986 to the members or former members of insolvent partnerships: see the note to IA 1986 s.420. Sections 22A, 22B, s.22C and 22D similarly extend this Act to building societies, incorporated friendly societies, NHS foundation trusts and open-ended investment companies: see the notes to those sections. Note prospective insertion of s.22E by the Co-operative and Community Benefit Societies and Credit Unions Act 2010 s.3, which (when brought into force) will extend the Act to Industrial and Provident Societies (other than Credit Unions). The Act applies also to EEIGs: see the European Economic Interest Grouping Regulations 1989 (SI 1989/638) reg.20.

In the application of CDDA 1986 to LLPs, references in the former to a director or shadow director are to be construed as references to a member or shadow member of an LLP (LLPR 2001 reg.4(2)(f), (g)); and accordingly a person who is subject to a director disqualification order is prohibited from being a member or shadow member of an LLP, except with the leave of the court.

S.1(1)

The wording of this subsection was changed by IA 2000 s.5(1), with effect from April 2, 2001, but the only change of substance is that the ban on acting as an insolvency practitioner has been separated off so that the prohibition is in that respect absolute, and not subject to the power of the court to grant leave to act. The former wording "for a specified period *beginning with the date of the order*" was also changed (by dropping the italicised words) for the reasons described in the note to s.1(2), below.

A disqualification order may be made against a company or other corporate body, since the section uses the word "person" rather than "individual". This is confirmed by s.14, below.

The word "shall" reflects the fact that the court has no discretion; and ss.6 and 9A are expressed in similar imperative terms.

Section 1(1) states clearly that a disqualification order is an order that the person shall not, without the leave of the court, engage in the activities listed in paras (a) and (b). On occasion, orders have been made in which some only of these activities have been specified. It has been ruled that it is not competent for a court to make an order limited in this way. However, such an order is not a nullity but an error capable of being corrected under CPR r.40.12 (formerly RSC Ord.20 r.11) (the "slip rule"). (See *Re Gower Enterprises Ltd (No.2)* [1995] B.C.C. 1,081; *Re Seagull Manufacturing Co Ltd (No.3)* [1995] B.C.C. 1,088; *Re Brian Sheridan Cars Ltd* [1995] B.C.C. 1,035; and *Re Cannonquest Ltd* [1997] B.C.C. 644). On the same reasoning, it is not competent for a court to make an order limiting the disqualification to acting in relation to public companies: *R. v Ward* [2001] EWCA Crim 1648; [2002] B.C.C. 953.

"Management" for the purposes of para.(a) includes both the internal and external affairs of a company: *R. v Austen* (1985) 1 B.C.C. 99,528 (a case concerning the fraudulent raising of finance). In *R. v Campbell* [1984] B.C.L.C. 83, a management consultant who acted as adviser to the board of a company was held to have "been concerned in" and "taken part in" its management. It is not necessary that there should be any actual misconduct of the company's affairs: in *R. v Georgiou* (1988) 4 B.C.C. 322, a disqualification order was made against a person who had carried on an unauthorised insurance business through the medium of a limited company. In *R. v Creggy* [2008] EWCA Crim 364; [2008] 1 B.C.L.C. 625 the appellant, a solicitor, had allowed his client account to be used for money-laundering and had set up a company for the purpose: this was held to be an offence "in connection with the management" of the company. In the Australian case *Re Magna Alloys & Research Pty Ltd* (1975) C.L.C. paras 40–227: (see: *British Company Law and Practice*, paras 37–150), a former director who acted as marketing adviser, and in that capacity attended directors' meetings, was held not to have taken part in the management of the company. In another part of the same judgment the court expressed the view that a majority shareholder might so use his position on questions of management as to infringe a prohibition on "taking part in management"; but it was thought that he would be free to vote as a shareholder, "even on a management matter".

In another Australian case, *CCA v Brecht* (1989) 7 A.C.L.C. 40, the court considered that the concept of "management" required an involvement of some kind in the decision-making process of the company, and a degree of responsibility. It may not exonerate the person concerned simply to show that some other person has the final say in decision-making or signs all the cheques. Negotiating terms of credit facilities, for instance, may be a management activity, even though those terms have to be confirmed. Advice given to management, participation in the decision-making process, and execution of management's decisions which goes beyond the mere carrying out of directions is sufficient (ibid.). In contrast, in *Re Clasper Group Services Ltd* (1988) 4 B.C.C. 673 the respondent, who was the son of the controlling shareholder and director, was employed as a "management trainee"; he did not appear "to have risen much above the status of an office boy and messenger", but he did have authority to sign company cheques. Warner J. held that his functions were too lowly to bring him within the phrase "is or has been concerned, or has taken part, in the … management of the company" for the purposes of IA 1986 s.212(1)(c). In *Drew v Lord Advocate*, 1996 S.L.T. 1062 a person who purported to act only as an employee of a small company which he had himself set up was held to have taken part in its management. Further discussion of this topic can be found in *Re a Company* [1980] Ch. 138 at 144; and *Re Market Wizard Systems (UK) Ltd* [1998] 2 B.C.L.C. 282 at 298–301, where Carnwath J. said (at 301): "Essentially it is a jury question. I would, however, agree with Ormiston J. [in *CCA v Brecht*] in emphasising that 'ultimate control' in not a necessary element, and further in the emphasis that he gives to those functions which are relevant to 'the solvency or probity of the corporation's administration'."

A disqualification order need not impose a total prohibition on the activities of the person concerned, since the court has power under this subsection to give leave. The Act gives no guidance as to the exercise of the court's discretion in considering whether to grant leave: the discretion is wholly unfettered (*Shuttleworth v Secretary of State for Trade and Industry* [2000] B.C.C. 204). A balance has to be struck between the applicant's need to be able to act in the manner requested and the importance of protecting the public. In *Re Cargo Agency Ltd* [1992] B.C.C. 388 (where leave to act as a director was refused, but the respondent was allowed to act as a general manager of the subsidiary of a large public company) Harman J. said, at 393: "It seems to me that … applications for leave pursuant to s.1 should only be granted where there is a need for them to be granted, and should only be granted upon evidence of adequate protection from danger." The question of "need" has occasioned some debate. It has been described as a "practical" need (*Re Tech Textiles Ltd* [1998] 1 B.C.L.C. 260). The need is that of the companies concerned (and its employees and other stakeholders) rather than that of the individual applicant (*Re Verby Print for Advertising Ltd* [1998] B.C.C. 652; *Secretary of State for Trade and Industry v Rosenfield* [1999] B.C.C. 413). An argument based on the need of the company carries little weight when the company is wholly or substantially owned by the applicant: *Secretary of State for Trade and Industry v Barnett* [1998] 2 B.C.L.C. 64; *Re Britannia Homes Centres Ltd* [2001] 2 B.C.L.C. 63. On the other hand, it has been said to be in the public interest that the applicant should be able to earn a living: *Shuttleworth v Secretary of State for Trade and Industry* [2000] B.C.C. 204. Somewhat exceptionally, in *Re Barings plc (No.5)* [1999] B.C.C. 960, where there had been no dishonesty and no abuse of the privilege of limited liability and the court was satisfied that the public would be adequately protected, leave was given despite the fact that "need" had not been demonstrated. In contrast, where there has been dishonesty or illegal conduct, considerations of public interest and the concern to protect the public will outweigh any argument based on "need": see, for instance *Re Amaron Ltd* [1998] B.C.C. 264; *Re Westminster Property Management Ltd, Official Receiver v Stern (No.2)* [2001] B.C.C 305 (on appeal [2001] EWCA Civ 111; [2002] B.C.C. 937).

As regards protection of the public, "the public for this purpose includes all relevant interest groups, such as shareholders, employees, lenders, customers and other creditors" (*Re Tech Textiles Ltd* (above), at 268). "The public" is not confined to people within the jurisdiction: the effect of a disqualification order extends to foreign jurisdictions and the question whether disqualification could be imposed on the same facts by a foreign court is irrelevant (*Re Westminster Property Management (No.2)* (above), at 358–359). In the *Tech Textiles* case Arden J. identified a number of key factors to be taken into account, including the grounds on which "unfitness" under s.6 was found (and in particular whether the applicant has misappropriated any assets or acted knowingly in breach of duty), the character of the applicant (and in particular his honesty, reliability and willingness to accept advice), the previous career of the applicant, and whether he had been disqualified previously. The court has also to consider the company or companies in relation to which he wishes to have leave to act: the nature of its business, its size and financial position, the number of directors, the risks involved in its business, and whether there is potential for the matters which were held to constitute unfitness to recur. See also *Re Hennelly's Utilities Ltd* [2004] EWHC 34 (Ch); [2005] B.C.C. 542; *Re Servaccomm Redhall Ltd* [2004] EWHC 760 (Ch); [2006] 1 B.C.L.C. 1.

The court may take into account for the purposes of an application for leave various factors which are treated as irrelevant when ruling on the question of a defendant's "unfitness". These factors include: the person's general good character; the fact that his management of other companies has been satisfactory; the likelihood that he will not offend again; and any period of de facto disqualification to which the applicant has been subject pending the hearing of his case.

The grant of leave is commonly made subject to conditions. Reported cases include: *Re Lo-Line Electric Motors Ltd* [1988] Ch. 477; (1988) 4 B.C.C. 415 (if another named person remained a director with voting control); *Re Majestic Recording Studios Ltd* (1988) 4 B.C.C. 519 (if a chartered accountant was willing to act as a co-director and audited accounts for the previous five years were produced and filed); *Re Chartmore Ltd* [1990] B.C.C. 673 (if monthly board meetings were held, attended by a representative of the auditors); *Re Godwin Warren Control Systems plc* [1992] B.C.C. 557 (if, in the case of two companies, the disqualification order and the reasons for making it were brought to the attention of the companies' boards of directors and, in regard to another, if similar disclosure was made to two outside shareholders); *Re Gibson Davies Ltd* [1995] B.C.C. 11 (a total of ten safeguards, including a ban on signing cheques without a countersignature and conditions that loans owed by the company to the applicant were not to be repaid and that the applicant should not take security over the company's assets); *Secretary of State for Trade and Industry v Arif* [1996] B.C.C. 960 (no loan to be made to associated company); *Secretary of State for Trade and Industry v Rosenfield* [1999] B.C.C. 413 (prompt settlement of inter-company debts; regular management accounts); *Re Barings plc* (above) (not undertaking executive duties or accepting fees); *Re TLL Realisations Ltd* [2000] B.C.C. 988 (that the person should perform only specified duties in a subordinate capacity). See also *Re Hennelly's Utilities Ltd* (above), where leave was granted (in a relatively serious case) subject to stringent conditions.

In *Re Brian Sheridan Cars Ltd* [1995] B.C.C. 1035 the applicant, who was already subject to a disqualification order, applied to the court to vary the order by removing the conditions on which he had been given leave to act, and to do so with retrospective effect. The court declined this request, which would have had the effect of decriminalising any past acts of his which were in breach of the conditions, and which would also have meant that third parties who might have had personal claims against him would have lost the right to sue him.

In *R. v Goodman* [1992] B.C.C. 625, it was held that there is no power under the Act to make an exception of a general kind, e.g. that the defendant be disqualified from being a director of a public company but given leave to be a director of any private company; compare *R. v Ward* [2001] EWCA Crim 1648; [2002] B.C.C. 953.

In *Re D J Matthews (Joinery Design) Ltd* (1988) 4 B.C.C. 513, there was a suggestion that the court might be more willing to consider granting a disqualified person leave to act as a director of a company if it was an unlimited company and he was prepared to assume unlimited personal liability. In *Shuttleworth v Secretary of State for Trade and Industry* [2000] B.C.C. 204 a director was allowed to act in relation to an unlimited company, so long as it did not convert to a limited company or have any limited subsidiaries. On similar reasoning, the courts have thought it appropriate that an applicant should act as a consultant (*Re Barings plc (No.5)* [1999] B.C.C. 960), or trade in partnership (*Re Amaron Ltd* [1998] B.C.C. 264), rather than be given leave to act as director of a limited company.

Leave to act under a disqualification order may be granted either at the time when the original order is made, or subsequently. The former course is desirable as "in everyone's interests" (*Re Dicetrade Ltd* [1994] B.C.C. 371 at 373). In the latter case application need not be made to the same court. See further s.17 below.

The Court of Appeal in *Re Westmid Packing Services Ltd Secretary of State for Trade and Industry v Griffiths* [1998] B.C.C. 836 gave guidance on what is relevant and admissible evidence in an application for leave under s.17.

Where the Secretary of State accepts a disqualification undertaking in lieu of applying to the court for a disqualification order; the person who has given the undertaking may apply to a court for leave to act notwithstanding the undertaking (s.1A(1)(a)). Section 17(3) and (4) gives guidance as to the appropriate court. The Secretary of State has no power to grant leave himself, or to accept an undertaking subject to conditions. This would be true also in the case of competition undertakings.

Neither the present Act nor any of the immediately relevant rules contain provisions dealing with appeals from a disqualification order. The current *Practice Direction: Insolvency Proceedings* [2012] B.C.C. 265 (see App.IV) provides that an appeal from a decision of a county court (whether made by a district judge or a circuit judge) or of a registrar of the High Court in insolvency proceedings (a "first appeal") lies to a judge of the High Court pursuant to IA 1986 s.375(2) and IR 1986 r.7.48(2) (as amended by s.55 of the Access to Justice Act 1999). A first appeal does not require the permission of any court (*Secretary of State for Trade and Industry v Paulin* [2005] EWHC 888 (Ch); [2005] B.C.C. 927). A first appeal (as defined above) does not, however, include an appeal from a decision of a judge of the High Court.

An appeal from a decision of a judge of the High Court made on a first appeal lies to the Court of Appeal, but only with the permission of the Court of Appeal. Such permission will not be granted unless the Court of Appeal considers that (a) the appeal will raise an important point of principle or practice; or (b) there is some other compelling reason for the Court of Appeal to hear it (Access to Justice Act 1999 s.55). An appeal from a judge of the High Court which is not a decision on a first appeal lies to the Court of Appeal with the permission of either the judge or the Court of Appeal. The procedure and practice for an appeal from such a decision or from a first appeal are governed by IR 1986 r.7.49A, which imports the procedure and practice of the Court of Appeal (CPR Pt 52).

Further guidance on these new provisions governing appeals may be found in *Tanfern Ltd v Cameron-MacDonald* [2000] 2 All E.R. 801; and *Clark (Inspector of Taxes) v Perks* [2000] 4 All E.R. 1.

It was stated in *Re New Technology Systems Ltd* [1997] B.C.C. 810 that an application for leave to appeal should normally be made to the appeal court rather than the trial court, unless some point of law or principle is in issue which the lower court considers appropriate to be reviewed on appeal.

An appeal in disqualification proceedings is, at least in the normal case, a "true" appeal rather than a rehearing: the appellant has the burden of proving that the ruling below was wrong: *Secretary of State for Trade and Industry v Jones* [1999] B.C.C. 336. However, very exceptionally, the court will sometimes in its discretion proceed by way of rehearing (relying on CPR r.52.11): *Lewis v Secretary of State for Trade and Industry* [2001] 2 B.C.L.C. 597. However, where there is little or no dispute as to the primary facts, the appellate court is in as good a position as the trial judge to form a judgment as to the respondent's unfitness, so that it is free to draw its own conclusion and, where appropriate, reverse the judge's finding on the question: *Re Grayan Building Services Ltd* [1995] B.C.C. 554; *Re Structural Concrete Ltd* [2001] B.C.C. 588. Fresh evidence will not be admitted on an appeal unless it is shown (a) that it could not with reasonable diligence have been obtained for use at the trial; (b) the evidence, if given, would probably have an important influence on the result of the case; and (c) the evidence is apparently credible: *Re Barings plc (No.5)* [2000] 1 B.C.L.C. 534.

The court on appeal may extend or reduce the period of disqualification or discharge the order altogether: *Secretary of State for Trade & Industry v Bannister* [1996] 1 W.L.R. 118 at 122; [1995] B.C.C. 1,027 at 1,030. But it will interfere with the period fixed by the trial judge only if the latter has erred in principle (e.g. by not having regard to the threefold "bracketing" of periods recommended in the *Sevenoaks Stationers* case (see the note to s.1(2) below), or has taken wrong factors into account: *Secretary of State for Trade and Industry v McTighe* [1997] B.C.C. 224; *Secretary of State for Trade and Industry v Griffiths, Re Westmid Packing Services Ltd (No.3)* [1998] 2 All E.R. 124; [1998] B.C.C. 836; *Re Saver Ltd* [1999] B.C.C. 221; *Re TLL Realisations Ltd* [2000] B.C.C. 998. Where the appeal is from the refusal of the lower court to make a disqualification order and the appeal is successful, the appeal court may either determine the appropriate length of disqualification itself or remit the question to the court below (*Secretary of State for Trade and Industry v Deverell* [2001] Ch. 340; [2000] B.C.C. 1057). If a disqualification order has been made and the director has been granted leave to take part in the management of a company, and the Secretary of State considers that the court erred by giving leave, it is open to him to appeal against the decision to grant leave: *Secretary of State for Trade and Industry v Collins* [2000] B.C.C. 998. But an appeal court will interfere with the decision of the trial judge to grant or refuse leave only if he has misdirected himself about material considerations or come to a plainly erroneous conclusion (ibid.).

There is no express provision in the Act or the rules giving a court power to suspend the operation of a disqualification order pending the hearing of an appeal, but in *Bannister's* case (above) it was held that both the High Court and the Court of Appeal may do so in their inherent jurisdiction. The question whether the county court has such a power was left open. However, the question is probably academic because the court in *Bannister's* case also made it clear that normally the better procedure would be for the director to be given leave to act under s.17 in relation to specified companies pending the hearing of the appeal, and that the power to grant a stay should be invoked only in extreme cases "in which the court below went badly wrong and the very existence of the disqualification order causes irreparable harm to the person apparently disqualified". In such an extreme case, it is more appropriate that the question of a stay should be determined by the appeal court rather than the court below: *Re Continental Assurance Co of London plc* [1996] B.C.C. 888 at 899.

No specific provision is made in the Act for the variation of a disqualification order; but that there is power to do so is perhaps confirmed by the Companies (Disqualification Orders) Regulations 2009 (SI 2009/2471) reg.4(b) and the Insolvent Companies (Disqualification of Unfit Directors) Rules 1987 (SI 1987/2023) r.8(2). This is in any case something which the High Court, at least, could do in its inherent jurisdiction. The court in *Re Brian Sheridan Cars Ltd* [1995] B.C.C. 1035 made an order varying the terms of an original order, but this was pursuant to a power reserved in the earlier order. The Act makes special provision for the court to order the variation of a disqualification undertaking in s.8A.

The normal rule that costs are in the discretion of the court applies to proceedings in relation to disqualification orders. For a period it had come to be accepted that certain practices favourable to the Crown should displace this rule: (1) that costs should not be awarded against the Secretary of State in situations where a prima facie case of unfitness had been made out against a director which was subsequently rebutted by evidence (see, e.g. *Re Douglas Construction Services Ltd* (1988) 4 B.C.C. 553; *Re Cladrose Ltd* [1990] B.C.C. 11); and (2) that where costs were awarded against an unsuccessful respondent in favour of the Secretary of State or official receiver, it should be on an indemnity and not on the standard basis (see, e.g. *Re Brooks Transport (Purfleet) Ltd* [1993] B.C.C. 766 and the cases there cited). However the former practice was disapproved of in *Re Southbourne Sheet Metal Co Ltd* [1993] 1 W.L.R. 244; [1992] B.C.C. 797, where Nourse L.J. made it clear that the ruling applied also where the applicant has discontinued the proceedings, and the latter practice was rejected by Chadwick J. in *Re Godwin Warren Control Systems plc* [1992] B.C.C. 557 (a decision subsequently approved by the Court of Appeal in *Re Dicetrade Ltd, Secretary of State for Trade & Industry v Worth* [1994] B.C.C. 371). In the latter case it was said that it would not usually be appropriate to make a separate costs order in favour of the Secretary of State in regard to an application for leave to act when the application was made contemporaneously with the main hearing; but that the position would be otherwise if the application for leave was made at a later date. This distinction was endorsed by the Court of Appeal in *Re TLL Realisations Ltd* [2000] B.C.C. 998. In *Re Smart-Tel (UK) plc* [2007] B.C.C. 896 the claimant discontinued the proceedings after the defendant had filed and served his evidence in answer, following three hearings and more than a year after the commencement of the case. The court ordered that the defendant's costs should be discounted by 20 per cent because his conduct in failing to provide the claimant with full access to the company's books and records had contributed to the prolongation of the case.

Where the application is made by the official receiver, he is entitled to an award of costs on the basis that he is a litigant in person: *Official Receiver v Brunt* [1998] 4 All E.R. 500; [1999] B.C.C. 571.

In *Re Sykes (Butchers) Ltd* [1998] B.C.C. 484 one respondent was ordered to pay part of the costs of a second respondent against whom the Secretary of State's application had been dismissed.

Costs on an indemnity basis were awarded against the Secretary of State, when proceedings against a director (in which fraud had been alleged without justification) had been discontinued, in *Re City Truck Group Ltd* [2006] B.C.C. 384.

S.1(2)
Only s.6(4) contains provision for a minimum period of disqualification (two years). (Although s.9A(1) makes it mandatory for the court to make an order if unfitness is found, no minimum period is fixed.) In *Re Bath Glass Ltd* (1988) 4 B.C.C. 130 at 133, Peter Gibson J. expressed the view that the fact that the legislature had imposed this minimum disqualification period for "unfitness" was relevant to deciding whether a person should be classed as "unfit": only conduct which was sufficiently serious to warrant such a period of disqualification would justify a conclusion that a person was unfit. There is no power to make an order of indefinite duration.

In *Re Sevenoaks Stationers (Retail) Ltd* [1991] Ch. 164; [1990] B.C.C. 765 (the first reported director disqualification case decided by the Court of Appeal), Dillon L.J. thought that it would be a helpful guide to the courts to divide the possible periods of disqualification under s.6 into three brackets. The top period of disqualification for periods of 10–15 years should be reserved for particularly serious cases. This might include cases where a director who had already been disqualified fell to be disqualified again. The minimum bracket of two to five years' disqualification should be applied where, although disqualification was mandatory, the case was relatively not very serious. The middle bracket of disqualification for from six to ten years should apply in serious cases which did not merit the top bracket. In *R. v Goodman* [1992] B.C.C. 625 at 628 the guidelines were not applied in criminal proceedings under s.2; but they were referred to in *R. v Millard* (1993) 15 Cr. App. R. (S) 445. In *Randhawa v Official Receiver* [2006] B.P.I.R. 1435 it was considered "helpful and appropriate" to adopt the same three brackets in the context of bankruptcy restriction orders. (See also *Official Receiver v Pyman* [2007] EWHC 2002 (Ch); [2007] B.P.I.R. 1150.)

The Court of Appeal has since given further guidance in *Re Westmid Packing Services Ltd, Secretary of State for Trade and Industry v Griffiths* [1998] B.C.C. 836. In determining the appropriate period of disqualification the court should start with an assessment of the correct period to fit the gravity of the offence, bearing in mind that the period has to contain deterrent elements, and then allow for mitigating factors (such factors not being restricted to the facts of the offence). The power to grant leave under s.17 (and the fact that the court is minded to grant leave) is, however, not relevant at this stage. Relevant matters include the director's general reputation and conduct in discharge of the office of director, his age and state of health, the length of time he has been in jeopardy, whether he had admitted the offence, his general conduct before and after the offence and the periods of disqualification meted out to any of his co-directors.

In the same case Lord Woolf M.R. stated that in the great majority of cases it is unnecessary and inappropriate for the court to be taken through the facts of previous cases in order to guide it on the period of disqualification: this, he said, was a jurisdiction which the court should exercise in a summary manner, using a "broad brush" approach.

In *Re Mea Corp Ltd* [2006] EWHC 1846 (Ch); [2007] B.C.C. 288 the disqualification period was increased from 7 to 11 years because the respondent was already subject to a disqualification order.

Chadwick J. in *Secretary of State for Trade and Industry v Arif* [1996] B.C.C. 586 considered that the court cannot take into account in fixing the period of disqualification the fact that the person has been suspended from acting as a director or has voluntarily refrained from doing so pending the hearing, but he added that de facto disqualification could be a relevant consideration on an application for leave to act under s.17. However, the Court of Appeal in *Re Westmid Packing Services Ltd, Secretary of State for Trade and Industry v Griffiths* [1998] B.C.C. 836 disagreed with that comment regarding the length of the disqualification period.

Section 1(1), prior to its amendment by IA 2000, stipulated that the period of disqualification should run "for a specified period beginning with the date of the order". This ran counter to the provision in the Insolvent Companies (Disqualification of Directors) Proceedings Rules 1987 r.9, which stated that unless the court ordered otherwise, an order should take effect at the beginning of the 21st day after the day on which the order was made. In practice, the judiciary turned a blind eye to the inconsistency and a 21-day period of grace became the norm. The IA 2000 amendment has removed the anomaly by writing the 21-day period into the Act and revoking r.9. The defendant is thus given a breathing space to sort out his affairs before the order takes effect. The discretion given to the court to order otherwise will allow this period to be extended or curtailed in special circumstances—even, conceivably, to make the disqualification run from the end of a custodial sentence.

S.1(3)

This statutory prohibition on making cumulative disqualification orders has been amended to deal with the case where an order is sought against a respondent who is already subject to a disqualification undertaking. The counterpart situation, where an undertaking is given by a person who is already disqualified, is dealt with in ss.1A(3) and 9B(6).

The rule applies where one order is made as part of a criminal sentence and another in civil proceedings (*Re Living Images Ltd* [1996] B.C.C. 112 at 136).

S.1(4)

This makes it clear that disqualification proceedings may go ahead independently and without regard to the possibility that a criminal prosecution may be brought in respect of the same matter. In *Re TransTec plc* [2005] EWHC 1723 (Ch); [2006] B.C.C. 295 respondents to disqualification proceedings sought a stay, and more particularly a direction that they should not be required to prepare and serve their written evidence, before the commencement of criminal proceedings arising out of their conduct as directors. The application was refused, but some conditions were imposed relating to the disclosure of the evidence prior to the end of the criminal trial to persons other than the Secretary of State.

In *Re Cedarwood Productions Ltd, Secretary of State for Trade and Industry v Rayna* [2001] EWCA Civ 1083; [2004] B.C.C. 65 disqualification proceedings had been stayed pending the outcome of criminal proceedings against the respondents. On conviction, the trial judge disqualified them for two years under CDDA 1986 s.2. The Secretary of State then successfully applied for the disqualification proceedings to be restored, on the ground that factors which might justify a longer period of disqualification could be taken into account for that purpose which would not have been available to the criminal court. See also *Re Denis Hilton Ltd* [2002] B.C.L.C. 302, and the note to s.2(1).

In *Re Rex Williams Leisure plc* [1994] Ch. 350; [1994] B.C.C. 551 the respondent director sought a stay of disqualification proceedings which had been brought against him by the Secretary of State until civil litigation in which he was a defendant had been disposed of. The same matters were material to both sets of proceedings. The court refused to grant a stay. The Court of Appeal, affirming Nicholls V.C. [1994] Ch. 1; [1993] B.C.C. 79, stated that the public interest in having disqualification orders made against unfit directors of insolvent companies should not be subordinated to private litigation.

1A   Disqualification undertakings: general

1A(1)   [Power of Secretary of State] In the circumstances specified in sections 7 and 8 the Secretary of State may accept a disqualification undertaking, that is to say an undertaking by any person that, for a period specified in the undertaking, the person–

(a)   will not be a director of a company, act as receiver of a company's property or in any way, whether directly or indirectly, be concerned or take part in the promotion, formation or management of a company unless (in each case) he has the leave of a court, and

(b)   will not act as an insolvency practitioner.

1A(2)   [Maximum period] The maximum period which may be specified in a disqualification undertaking is 15 years; and the minimum period which may be specified in a disqualification undertaking under section 7 is two years.

1A(3)   [Undertakings, etc. to run concurrently] Where a disqualification undertaking by a person who is already subject to such an undertaking or to a disqualification order is accepted, the periods specified in those undertakings or (as the case may be) the undertaking and the order shall run concurrently.

1A(4)   [Matters other than criminal convictions] In determining whether to accept a disqualification undertaking by any person, the Secretary of State may take account of matters other than criminal convictions, notwithstanding that the person may be criminally liable in respect of those matters.

GENERAL NOTE

Section 1A contains one of the major reforms made by IA 2000: the introduction of disqualification undertakings as an alternative to disqualification orders made by a court. This regime applies only to disqualification cases under ss.7 and 8, i.e. to situations based on "unfitness", but there is also parallel provision for competition undertakings in s.9B. The Secretary of State is empowered to dispose of a case administratively, without any involvement by the court, if the person concerned is prepared to give an undertaking and the Secretary of State to accept it and they are agreed on the period for which the undertaking is to run. The *Carecraft* procedure (see the note to s.7(1), below) has, in consequence, now fallen into disuse, with a considerable saving of court time and expense. An undertaking has for all practical purposes the same effect as a disqualification order, and the consequences of a breach are also the same. This may be contrasted with the handful of cases decided prior to 2000 in which, exceptionally, the court had been prepared to accept an undertaking from a respondent not to act as a director in lieu of making a disqualification order where, for example, he was not fit enough to face a full hearing (see, e.g. *Re Homes Assured Corp plc* [1993] B.C.C. 573). The undertaking in such a case was given to the court, and in the event of a breach would have been sanctioned by proceedings for contempt (which would have to be instituted by some interested party). Under s.1A, the civil consequences of a breach follow automatically under s.15 and criminal liability under ss.13–14 is strict, and the register of disqualification orders (s.18) now includes those who have given undertakings.

The Secretary of State is not obliged to accept an undertaking, even where the facts are admitted: he may (for instance) take a test case to the court, or consider that it is in the public interest that a full trial be held in a particular case. In *Re Blackspur Group plc (No.3), Secretary of State for Trade and Industry v Davies (No.2)* [2001] EWCA Civ 1595; [2002] 2 B.C.L.C. 363 the Court of Appeal, affirming Patten J., held that the Secretary of State was entitled to refuse to accept an undertaking unless the person giving the undertaking was prepared to sign a statement of agreed facts (which could be relied on, and would not be disputed, in any future proceedings).

If an undertaking is offered before proceedings have been issued, the Secretary of State will not usually seek to recover his costs, but if offered later, he normally will: see *Dear IP*, Ch.10(4).

If a person who has given an undertaking wishes to have leave to act, this must be sought from a court under s.17. The Secretary of State cannot give leave himself or accept an undertaking qualified by any concessions: *Re Morija plc* [2007] EWHC 3055 (Ch); [2008] 2 B.C.L.C. 313 at [7]. On an application to the court, the director cannot dispute the correctness of facts which he accepted when signing the disqualification undertaking (ibid.). The court also has power to vary an undertaking under s.8A, but only in limited respects: see the note to that section.

Rule 7.47 of IR 1986 (appeals in insolvency proceedings) applies only to appeals from orders of the court, and has no application to disqualification undertakings: *Eastaway v Secretary of State for Trade and Industry* [2007] EWCA Civ 425; [2007] B.C.C. 550.

S.1A(1), (2)
The detailed terms of an undertaking are identical with those of a disqualification order. The maximum period is 15 years under ss.7, 8 and 9B; there is a minimum of two years if the undertaking is given under s.7, but no minimum if it is under s.8 or 9B.

S.1A(3), (4)
These provisions correspond with s.1(3), (4). See the notes to those subsections.

Disqualification for general misconduct in connection with companies

2 Disqualification on conviction of indictable offence

2(1)　[Court's power] The court may make a disqualification order against a person where he is convicted of an indictable offence (whether on indictment or summarily) in connection with the promotion, formation, management, liquidation or striking off of a company, with the receivership of a company's property or with his being an administrative receiver of a company.

2(2)　["The court"] "The court" for this purpose means–

　(a)　any court having jurisdiction to wind up the company in relation to which the offence was committed, or

　(b)　the court by or before which the person is convicted of the offence, or

　(c)　in the case of a summary conviction in England and Wales, any other magistrates' court acting in the same local justice area;

and for the purposes of this section the definition of **"indictable offence"** in Schedule 1 to the Interpretation Act 1978 applies for Scotland as it does for England and Wales.

2(3) **[Maximum period]** The maximum period of disqualification under this section is–

(a) where the disqualification order is made by a court of summary jurisdiction, 5 years, and

(b) in any other case, 15 years.

S.2(1)

A conviction for an indictable offence is a precondition for the operation of this section (although the proceedings need not have been on indictment). The disqualification order may be made by the court by which the offender is convicted or by the same or another court on an application made subsequently.

The scope of s.2 is not confined to offences which arise out of the management of the internal affairs of the company: it may extend to offences in relation to third parties, e.g. defrauding finance companies (*R. v Corbin* (1984) 6 Cr. App. R. (S) 17) or an insurance company (*R. v Appleyard* (1985) 81 Cr. App. R. 319). In *R. v Georgiou* (1988) 4 B.C.C. 322 there was no actual misconduct of the company's affairs, internal or external: the offence of which the respondent was convicted was the carrying on of an unauthorised insurance business through the medium of a limited liability company. In *R. v Goodman* [1992] B.C.C. 625 the defendant had been convicted of insider dealing under the Company Securities (Insider Dealing) Act 1985, and sentenced to a term of imprisonment. The Court of Appeal held that it was competent also to impose a disqualification order: it was sufficient that the accused had been convicted of an indictable offence which had some relevant factual connection with the management of a company.

See also *R. v Millard* (1993) 15 Cr. App. R. (S) 445.

The fact that the court when imposing a criminal penalty has been invited to disqualify the defendant but has declined to do so is no bar to proceedings for disqualification on the ground of unfitness being taken by the Secretary of State: *Re Denis Hilton Ltd* [2002] 1 B.C.L.C. 302.

S.2(2)

The court having jurisdiction to wind up a company is defined by IA 1986 ss.117 et seq. (for England and Wales) and 120 et seq. (for Scotland). Where the application is made to such a court, the procedure is governed by s.16, below.

See also the note to s.6(3).

3 Disqualification for persistent breaches of companies legislation

3(1) **[Court's power]** The court may make a disqualification order against a person where it appears to it that he has been persistently in default in relation to provisions of the companies legislation requiring any return, account or other document to be filed with, delivered or sent, or notice of any matter to be given, to the registrar of companies.

3(2) **[Conclusive proof of default]** On an application to the court for an order to be made under this section, the fact that a person has been persistently in default in relation to such provisions as are mentioned above may (without prejudice to its proof in any other manner) be conclusively proved by showing that in the 5 years ending with the date of the application he has been adjudged guilty (whether or not on the same occasion) of three or more defaults in relation to those provisions.

3(3) **[Guilty of default under s.3(2)]** A person is to be treated under subsection (2) as being adjudged guilty of a default in relation to any provision of that legislation if–

(a) he is convicted (whether on indictment or summarily) of an offence consisting in a contravention of or failure to comply with that provision (whether on his own part or on the part of any company), or

(b) a default order is made against him, that is to say an order under any of the following provisions–

(i) section 452 of the Companies Act 2006 (order requiring delivery of company accounts), (ia) section 456 of that Act (order requiring preparation of revised accounts),

    (ii) section 1113 of that Act (enforcement of company's filing obligations),

    (iii) section 41 of the Insolvency Act 1986 (enforcement of receiver's or manager's duty to make returns), or

    (iv) section 170 of that Act (corresponding provision for liquidator in winding up),

in respect of any such contravention of or failure to comply with that provision (whether on his own part or on the part of any company).

3(4) **["The court"]** In this section **"the court"** means any court having jurisdiction to wind up any of the companies in relation to which the offence or other default has been or is alleged to have been committed.

3(4A) **["The companies legislation" in s.3]** In this section "the companies legislation" means the Companies Acts and Parts 1 to 7 of the Insolvency Act 1986 (company insolvency and winding up).

3(5) **[Maximum period]** The maximum period of disqualification under this section is 5 years.

GENERAL NOTE

This section runs closely parallel with s.5, which empowers the court entering a summary conviction against a person for a company law offence to make a disqualification order if he has had two or more similar convictions in the preceding five years. Minor textual amendments were made and s.3(4A) inserted by the Companies Act 2006 (Consequential Amendments, Transitional Provisions and Savings) Order 2009 (SI 2009/1941) art.2(1) and Sch.1 para.85(2) as from October 1, 2009.

S.3(1)

"Persistent default" in complying with the filing instructions of the companies legislation is made a ground for disqualification by this section. "Persistent default" may be established by invoking the presumptions contained in the following subsections.

    In *Re Arctic Engineering Ltd* [1986] 1 W.L.R. 686; (1985) 1 B.C.C. 99, 563 it was held that the term "persistently" requires some degree of continuance or repetition. A person may persist in the same default, or persistently commit a series of defaults. However, it is not necessary to show that he or she has been culpable, in the sense of evincing a *deliberate* disregard of the statutory requirements, although such culpability can be taken into account in considering whether to make a disqualification order and, if so, for how long.

S.3(2)

The meaning of "adjudged guilty" is explained in s.3(3).

S.3(3)

Section 3(3)(b) was amended by the Companies Act 2006 (Consequential Amendments etc.) Order 2008 (SI 2008/948) art.3(1) and Sch.1 para.106(2), as from April 6, 2008.

    The obligation to file documents with the registrar of companies is most often placed on the company itself rather than on any particular officer, but some duties (e.g. to deliver annual accounts) are specifically imposed on the directors, and others on the liquidator or some other office-holder. However, even where the duty lies with the company, it is ordinarily provided that the company and any "officer in default" shall be guilty of an offence—i.e. "any officer of the company who knowingly and wilfully authorises or permits the default ... or contravention" (CA 2006 s.1121(3)). A director can thus be guilty of an offence when his company is in breach of the Act, but for para(a) of the present subsection to apply, it is the director who must have been convicted, and not merely the company.

    The five statutory provisions mentioned in para.(b) empower the court to make an order directing a company and any officer of it to make good the default in question. This may be done on the application of the registrar of companies or any member (under IA 1986 s.170, any contributory) or creditor. Again, for para.(b) to apply, the default order must have been made against the person concerned and not merely his company.

S.3(4)

See the notes to ss.2(2) and 6(3) and, for the procedure, s.16.

4   Disqualification for fraud, etc., in winding up

4(1)   **[Court's power]** The court may make a disqualification order against a person if, in the course of the winding up of a company, it appears that he–

(a)   has been guilty of an offence for which he is liable (whether he has been convicted or not) under section 993 of the Companies Act 2006 (fraudulent trading), or

(b)   has otherwise been guilty, while an officer or liquidator of the company, receiver of the company's property or administrative receiver of the company, of any fraud in relation to the company or of any breach of his duty as such officer, liquidator, receiver or administrative receiver.

4(2)   **[Definitions]** In this section **"the court"** means any court having jurisdiction to wind up any of the companies in relation to which the offence or other default has been or is alleged to have been committed; and **"officer"** includes a shadow director.

4(3)   **[Maximum period]** The maximum period of disqualification under this section is 15 years.

S.4(1)

There is some overlap between this provision and s.2: the main points of distinction are that a conviction is a prerequisite for the operation of s.2, but not s.4, while a winding up is necessary for s.4, but not s.2.

The offence of fraudulent trading could formerly be committed only if the company ended up in liquidation, but this limitation was removed, so far as criminal proceedings are concerned, by CA 1981 s.96. However, the same limitation continues to apply in the present section, and so if a director is convicted under CA 2006 s.993 while his company is a going concern, any disqualification order must be sought under s.2 and not s.4.

There is also the possibility of an overlap between the present section and s.10, which allows a disqualification order to be made in the case where a person has had a declaration of liability made against him for fraudulent or wrongful trading.

Paragraph (b) does not appear to apply to an administrator or to the supervisor of a CVA.

For s.4(1)(b) to warrant the disqualification of an officer or office-holder, the "breach of duty" must be, if not fraudulent, at least very serious. The provision does not cover breaches of duty which are trivial or the result of a mistake: *Re Adbury Park Estates Ltd* [2003] B.C.C. 696. In this case the court also held that only a person with a tangible interest in the order sought had standing to bring an application.

Section 4(1)(a) was amended by the Companies Act 2006 (Commencement No.3, Consequential Amendments, Transitional Provisions and Savings) Order 2007 (SI 2007/2194 (C. 84)) art.9 and Sch.3 para.46 as from October 1, 2007.

S.4(2)

On the meaning of "the court", see the notes to ss.2(2) and 6(3).

The Companies Act definition of the term "officer" (CA 2006 s.1173) is incorporated into the present Act by s.22(9). For a discussion of this definition, see the note to IA 1986 s.206(3).

For the meaning of "shadow director", see s.22(5).

5   Disqualification on summary conviction

5(1)   **[Relevant offences]** An offence counting for the purposes of this section is one of which a person is convicted (either on indictment or summarily) in consequence of a contravention of, or failure to comply with, any provision of the companies legislation requiring a return, account or other document to be filed with, delivered or sent, or notice of any matter to be given, to the registrar of companies (whether the contravention or failure is on the person's own part or on the part of any company).

5(2)   **[Court's power]** Where a person is convicted of a summary offence counting for those purposes, the court by which he is convicted (or, in England and Wales, any other magistrates' court acting in the same local justice area) may make a disqualification order against him if the circumstances specified in the next subsection are present.

5(3)   **[Circumstances in s.5(2)]** Those circumstances are that, during the 5 years ending with the date of the conviction, the person has had made against him, or has been convicted of, in total not less than

3 default orders and offences counting for the purposes of this section; and those offences may include that of which he is convicted as mentioned in subsection (2) and any other offence of which he is convicted on the same occasion.

5(4) **[Definitions]** For the purposes of this section–

(a) the definition of **"summary offence"** in Schedule 1 to the Interpretation Act 1978 applies for Scotland as for England and Wales, and

(b) **"default order"** means the same as in section 3(3)(b).

5(4A) **["The companies legislation" in s.5]** In this section "the companies legislation" means the Companies Acts and Parts 1 to 7 of the Insolvency Act 1986 (company insolvency and winding up).

5(5) **[Maximum period]** The maximum period of disqualification under this section is 5 years.

GENERAL NOTE

Section 5(4A) was inserted by the Companies Act 2006 (Consequential Amendments, Transitional Provisions and Savings) Order 2009 (SI 2009/1941) art.2(1) and Sch.1 para.85(3) as from October 1, 2009.

This section and s.3 deal with very much the same situation, except that an order under s.3 may be made only by the court having jurisdiction to wind up one of the companies concerned, i.e. the High Court or in some cases the county court, and their Scottish counterparts. Prosecutions for failure to make company law returns will, however, invariably be brought summarily, and this section enables the court exercising summary jurisdiction in such a case itself to make a disqualification order for "persistent default".

For further discussion, see the note to s.3.

Disqualification for unfitness

6 Duty of court to disqualify unfit directors of insolvent companies

6(1) **[Court's duty]** The court shall make a disqualification order against a person in any case where, on an application under this section, it is satisfied–

(a) that he is or has been a director of a company which has at any time become insolvent (whether while he was a director or subsequently), and

(b) that his conduct as a director of that company (either taken alone or taken together with his conduct as a director of any other company or companies) makes him unfit to be concerned in the management of a company.

6(2) **[Interpretation]** For the purposes of this section and the next, a company becomes insolvent if–

(a) the company goes into liquidation at a time when its assets are insufficient for the payment of its debts and other liabilities and the expenses of the winding up,

(b) the company enters administration,

(c) an administrative receiver of the company is appointed;

and references to a person's conduct as a director of any company or companies include, where that company or any of those companies has become insolvent, that person's conduct in relation to any matter connected with or arising out of the insolvency of that company.

6(3) **["The court"]** In this section and section 7(2), **"the court"** means–

(a) where the company in question is being or has been wound up by the court, that court,

(b) where the company in question is being or has been wound up voluntarily, any court which has or (as the case may be) had jurisdiction to wind it up,

(c)   where neither paragraph (a) nor (b) applies but an administrator or administrative receiver has at any time been appointed in respect of the company in question, any court which has jurisdiction to wind it up.

6(3A)   [Application of Insolvency Act 1986 ss.117 and 120] Sections 117 and 120 of the Insolvency Act 1986 (jurisdiction) shall apply for the purposes of subsection (3) as if the references in the definitions of **"registered office"** to the presentation of the petition for winding up were references–

(a)   in a case within paragraph (b) of that subsection, to the passing of the resolution for voluntary winding up.

(b)   in a case within paragraph (c) of that subsection, to the appointment of the administrator or (as the case may be) administrative receiver,

6(3B)   [Wrong court] Nothing in subsection (3) invalidates any proceedings by reason of their being taken in the wrong court; and proceedings–

(a)   for or in connection with a disqualification order under this section, or

(b)   in connection with a disqualification undertaking accepted under section 7,

may be retained in the court in which the proceedings were commenced, although it may not be the court in which they ought to have been commenced.

6(3C)   ["Director"] In this section and section 7, **"director"** includes a shadow director.

6(4)   [Minimum, maximum periods] Under this section the minimum period of disqualification is 2 years, and the maximum period is 15 years.

GENERAL NOTE

This section is, without doubt, the "flagship" provision in the disqualification regime introduced by the 1985–86 reforms. Far more disqualification orders have been made under s.6 than under all the other sections put together; and it is only in relation to s.6 and the other "unfitness" section, s.8, that the alternative of a disqualification undertaking is available (although there are parallel provisions in ss.9A–9E as regards competition undertakings).

Only the Secretary of State (or the official receiver acting under directions from the Secretary of State) may institute proceedings under this section.

S.6(1)

Both the word "shall" and the use of the expression "duty" in the marginal note indicate that where unfitness is found the court is obliged to make a disqualification order. However, the court's discretion is not altogether excluded, since it is required to be "satisfied" that the director's conduct makes him "unfit to be concerned in the management of a company"; and a court which took the view that a director's conduct did not warrant the making of a disqualification order would be free to stop short of making such a finding. In *Re Bath Glass Ltd* (1988) 4 B.C.C. 133, Peter Gibson J. reached such a conclusion: though the director's conduct had been imprudent and, in part, improper, it was not so serious as to justify a finding of unfitness warranting a two-year disqualification. See also *Secretary of State for Trade and Industry v Lewis* [2003] B.C.C. 611; and *Secretary of State for Trade and Industry v Walker* [2003] EWHC 175 (Ch); [2003] 1 B.C.L.C. 363, where no order was made because although incompetence was found it was not of a sufficiently high degree. In *Re Polly Peck International plc, Secretary of State for Trade & Industry v Ellis (No.2)* [1993] B.C.C. 890, Lindsay J. took this factor into account in declining to grant the Secretary of State leave to issue proceedings out of time.

In *Re Polly Peck International plc, Secretary of State for Trade & Industry v Ellis (No.2)* (above) the court declined to qualify the wording of s.6(1)(b) by adding at the end the words "without the leave of the court": to do this would be to make the threshold which a claimant had to cross other than what parliament had by its language intended. In the same case it was held that "a company" in s.6(1)(b) meant "companies generally".

"Director" includes a shadow director: see ss.6(3C) and 22(4) and, for the meaning of the latter term, s.22(5). Former directors are also within the scope of the section. An order may also be made against a de facto director—i.e. a person who acts as a director without having been properly appointed, or whose appointment has expired: *Re Lo-Line Electric Motors Ltd* [1988] Ch. 477; (1988) 4 B.C.C. 415; *Re Cargo Agency Ltd* [1992] B.C.C. 388; *Re Hydrodan (Corby) Ltd* [1994] B.C.C. 161; *Re Moorgate Metals Ltd* [1995] B.C.C. 143; *Re Richborough Furniture*

Ltd [1996] B.C.C. 155. For further discussion of this term and the distinction between it and "shadow director", see the note to s.22(5). In *Re Eurostem Maritime Ltd* [1987] B.C.C. 190 the court expressed the view, obiter, that it had power to disqualify a director in respect of a foreign company that was being wound up in England, and it held that in proceedings against the director of an English company his conduct in relation to foreign companies of which he was also a director could be taken into consideration. (See also *Re Dominion International Group plc (No.2)* [1996] 1 B.C.L.C. 572.)

Section 6 contains no territorial restriction. It may be applied to persons, whether British subjects or foreigners, who are out of the jurisdiction at the relevant time and in respect of conduct which occurred outside the jurisdiction. However, the court has a discretion not to order that the proceedings be served out of the jurisdiction, which it will exercise where it is not satisfied that there is a good arguable case on the requirements of s.6(1): *Re Seagull Manufacturing Co Ltd (No.2)* [1994] 1 W.L.R. 453; [1993] B.C.C. 833.

The one exception to the extraterritorial scope of the court's jurisdiction (above) is that the courts in England and Wales and those in Scotland have mutually exclusive jurisdictions and will not make disqualification orders based on a person's conduct in relation to a company incorporated in the other part of Great Britain: *Re Helene plc* [2000] 2 B.C.L.C. 249. But once jurisdiction is established, the person's conduct as a director of such companies may be taken into account in determining his "unfitness".

The phrase "has become insolvent" is explained in s.6(2).

There is no anterior time limit fixed by s.6(1)(a): the court may inquire right back into the defendant's history as a director of the company and any other companies, and also into his conduct after he has ceased to be a director, if it relates to a matter "connected with or arising out of the insolvency of that company" (s.6(2)). It should be noted that an application has to be made no later than two years after the company "became insolvent": s.7(2).

The matters to be taken into account in determining the question of "unfitness" are dealt with by s.9 and Sch.1: see the note to s.9.

For a discussion of the term "management", see the note to s.1(1).

The court may take into account a person's conduct in relation to other companies: it is not necessary that those companies should also have "become insolvent", but it is only his conduct as a director of those companies that is relevant. In the cases it has become customary to refer to the company with reference to which the disqualification proceedings are brought as the "lead company" and the other companies as "collateral companies". It is permissible to specify more than one lead company in an application (*Re Surrey Leisure Ltd* [1999] B.C.C. 847); and the court may, in its discretion, allow an amendment to add a further lead company, but this is not appropriate where to do so would alter the fundamental focus and nature of the complaint against the defendant (*Re Diamond Computer Systems Ltd* [1997] 1 B.C.L.C. 174). If there is no finding of unfitness in relation to the lead company, the court cannot proceed to consider the defendant's conduct as director of the other companies (*Secretary of State for Trade and Industry v Tillman* [1999] B.C.C. 703).

In *Re Country Farm Inns Ltd* [1997] B.C.C. 801 it was emphasised that although Pt II of Sch.1 was relevant only if the collateral company (or companies) was insolvent, as well as the lead company, it was not necessary that the director's conduct in relation to the latter should be the same as, similar to or explanatory or confirmatory of the conduct relied on in relation to the lead company, and that there was no need for a nexus of any kind between the two, over and above the fact that the respondent had been a director of both companies and that his conduct in each case tended to show unfitness. It was held, however, in *Re Bath Glass Ltd* (above), that the director's conduct in relation to other companies is to be looked at only "for the purpose of finding additional matters of complaint": in other words, it is not open to the director to adduce evidence that his conduct in relation to other companies has been impeccable in an endeavour to show that a disqualification order would be inappropriate. In determining the question of unfitness, the court will also disregard a plea that the respondent has mended his ways: the question for the court is whether disqualification is merited on the evidence relied on in the application, and not whether the future protection of the public might or might not merit a disqualification: *Re Grayan Building Services Ltd* [1995] B.C.C. 554. On similar reasoning, it was held in *Secretary of State for Trade & Industry v Dawes* [1997] B.C.C. 121 that evidence of the respondent's general good character was inadmissible (compare *Re Oakframe Construction Ltd* [1996] B.C.C. 67; and *Re Pinemoor Ltd* [1997] B.C.C. 708, where the court struck out as irrelevant evidence by accountants which purported to express expert opinions on the issue before the court). However, once unfitness has been established, evidence of a person's general conduct which relates specifically to discharging the office of director may be admitted in determining the appropriate length of the disqualification period; and it may also be relevant to the question whether the court should give leave to act under s.17: *Re Barings plc, Secretary of State for Trade & Industry v Baker* [1998] B.C.C. 583 at 590 (a point not raised on appeal, [2001] B.C.C. 273); *Secretary of State for Trade and Industry v Griffiths* [1998] B.C.C. 836.

Note also that, although matters subsequent to the initiation of disqualification proceedings are not normally relevant to the case, the conduct of the respondent in the proceedings themselves may be taken into account, as in

Secretary of State for Trade and Industry v Blunt [2006] B.C.C. 112, where the defendant was given credit for admitting the allegations of misconduct; and in *Secretary of State for Trade and Industry v Reynard* [2002] B.C.C. 813, where the deceitful conduct of the director concerned in the witness box was held to justify a longer period of disqualification.

In *Secretary of State for Trade and Industry v Queen* [1998] B.C.C. 678 the court had regard to the fact that the respondent had been convicted of criminal offences as a director some years previously, even though these were now "spent" convictions under the Rehabilitation of Offenders Act 1974.

Procedural unfairness, such as not giving a respondent adequate notice of the charges that he has to face, may be a ground for refusing to make a disqualification order: *Re Cubelock Ltd* [2001] B.C.C. 523. In *Official Receiver v Key* [2009] B.C.C. 11 the applicant had chosen to issue disqualification proceedings against only one of two directors, who in the opinion of the court could have been considered equally culpable, and had accepted without making proper inquiries the evidence of the other director: the court declined to make an order.

S.6(2)

Before the jurisdiction of s.6 can be invoked, the company must have "become insolvent"; but this expression has an artificial meaning which will not necessarily mean that the company is insolvent in a business sense. Section 22(3) imports into the present Act the definition of "insolvency" in IA 1986 s.247(1)—a definition which is plainly concerned with various situations in which a company may find itself (e.g. liquidation, receivership) and not with its financial viability. (See further the discussion preceding IA 1986 s.230, and the note to s.247(1)).

Section 6 of the present Act uses the phrase "becomes insolvent" in the same sense, and so "insolvency" at the end of the present subsection should be understood accordingly. The financial situation of the company (i.e. its solvency in an everyday sense) will be relevant only in a liquidation (para.(a)); in the case of an administration or an administrative receivership (paras (b) and (c)) a company may be said to have "become insolvent" even when it might be reckoned financially solvent by at least some, and perhaps all, of the accepted tests of solvency.

Conversely, when a company has become insolvent in a business sense, the section will not necessarily apply—there must also have been one of the events listed in paras (a)–(c). It is no defence to disqualification proceedings under s.6 that the company's creditors have been, or could or might have been, paid in full (although this may be a factor in deciding whether unfitness is established): *Re Normanton Wells Properties Ltd* [2011] 1 B.C.L.C. 191.

It is not open to a respondent in disqualification proceedings to challenge the validity of the insolvency proceedings (liquidation, receivership, etc.) on the basis of which the company in question has "become insolvent": that issue must be resolved in other, appropriate, proceedings pending the determination of which the disqualification application may be adjourned or stayed (*Secretary of State for Trade & Industry v Jabble* [1998] B.C.C. 39).

In determining whether a company "becomes insolvent" within s.6(2)(a), "the expenses of the winding up" are to be brought into account. In *Official Receiver v Moore, Re Gower Enterprises Ltd* [1995] B.C.C. 293 Evans-Lombe J. held that (1) the assets and liabilities are to be valued by reference to the date of the liquidation, and not what they subsequently realised; (2) interest accruing on the debts after liquidation, and statutory interest under IA 1986 s.189, should be disregarded; and (3) that "the expenses of the winding up" should read as meaning "the reasonable expenses of the winding up". He went on to suggest, as a "rule of thumb", that in ascertaining the "reasonable expenses" the liquidator's remuneration should prima facie be determined by applying the official receiver's scale fees under the Insolvency Fees Order 1986 [see now the Insolvency Proceedings (Fees) Order 2004] to the realisable assets of the winding up but added the qualification that, if the expenses actually incurred proved to be less than the sum so calculated, the figure for the actual expenses should be substituted. However in further proceedings (reported at 297 et seq.) Blackburne J. held that where the expenses actually incurred included remuneration which has been properly fixed in accordance with the Rules (and, where applicable, the Insolvency Regulations) and had not been challenged, they should be regarded as reasonable whether the sum was higher or lower than the figure which would have been arrived at by these other methods.

The phrase "goes into liquidation" is also defined in IA 1986 s.247(2) and extended to this Act by s.22(3). A company "goes into liquidation" when it passes a resolution for voluntary winding up or when an order for its winding up is made by the court (unless it is then already in voluntary liquidation, when the time of the winding-up resolution will be the relevant time): see *Re Walter L Jacob & Co Ltd, Official Receiver v Jacob* [1993] B.C.C. 512.

S.6(3)–(3C)

On "the court having jurisdiction to wind up the company", see the note to s.2(2). Section 6(3) was recast, and s.6(3A)–(3C) added by IA 2000 (with effect from April 2, 2001) in order to resolve jurisdictional difficulties experienced under the former wording of the subsection, e.g. where the company in question had been dissolved (*Re*

Working Project Ltd [1995] B.C.C. 197; *Official Receiver v Pafundo* [2000] B.C.C. 164) or had changed its registered office from the district of one county court to another (*Re Lichfield Freight Terminal Ltd* [1997] B.C.C. 11). The phrase "has jurisdiction" in s.6(3)(c) means "has at the time of that appointment": *Secretary of State for Trade and Industry v Arnold* [2007] EWCA 1933 (Ch); [2008] B.C.C. 119. Even if a proceeding is instituted in the wrong court, s.6(3B) should deter the defendant from making objection to its jurisdiction. In *Secretary of State for Trade and Industry v Arnold* (above), H.H.J. Pelling Q.C. said that if proceedings against a dissolved company were held to be a nullity, so that an application to have the company reinstated was necessary, permission could be granted under s.7(2) to start disqualification proceedings out of time.

There can only ever be one county court that has jurisdiction to entertain a disqualification application under s.6(3), and there is no power to transfer an application from one county court to another, if the former is the correct court. If there is difficulty (e.g. if the proper court has no specialist knowledge) it may be appropriate to transfer the proceedings to the High Court. But this will not be possible where s.6(3)(a) applies. (*Secretary of State for Trade and Industry v Shakespeare* [2005] B.C.C. 891.)

S.6(4)
This is the only provision in the Act which fixes a minimum period of disqualification.

7   Disqualification order or undertaking; and reporting provisions

7(1)   [Application by Secretary of State, official receiver] If it appears to the Secretary of State that it is expedient in the public interest that a disqualification order under section 6 should be made against any person, an application for the making of such an order against that person may be made–

(a)   by the Secretary of State, or

(b)   if the Secretary of State so directs in the case of a person who is or has been a director of a company which is being or has been wound up by the court in England and Wales, by the official receiver.

7(2)   [Time for application] Except with the leave of the court, an application for the making under that section of a disqualification order against any person shall not be made after the end of the period of 2 years beginning with the day on which the company of which that person is or has been a director became insolvent.

7(2A)   [Acceptance of undertaking where s.6(1) satisfied] If it appears to the Secretary of State that the conditions mentioned in section 6(1) are satisfied as respects any person who has offered to give him a disqualification undertaking, he may accept the undertaking if it appears to him that it is expedient in the public interest that he should do so (instead of applying, or proceeding with an application, for a disqualification order).

7(3)   [Report to Secretary of State] If it appears to the office-holder responsible under this section, that is to say–

(a)   in the case of a company which is being wound up by the court in England and Wales, the official receiver,

(b)   in the case of a company which is being wound up otherwise, the liquidator,

(c)   in the case of a company which is in administration, the administrator, or

(d)   in the case of a company of which there is an administrative receiver, that receiver,

that the conditions mentioned in section 6(1) are satisfied as respects a person who is or has been a director of that company, the office-holder shall forthwith report the matter to the Secretary of State.

7(4)   [Extra information etc.] The Secretary of State or the official receiver may require the liquidator, administrator or administrative receiver of a company, or the former liquidator, administrator or administrative receiver of a company–

(a)   to furnish him with such information with respect to any person's conduct as a director of the company, and

(b)   to produce and permit inspection of such books, papers and other records relevant to that person's conduct as such a director,

as the Secretary of State or the official receiver may reasonably require for the purpose of determining whether to exercise, or of exercising, any function of his under this section.

S.7(1)

The Secretary of State, or the official receiver acting at his direction, alone has standing to make an application. The procedure is prescribed in detail by the Insolvent Companies (Disqualification of Unfit Directors) Proceedings Rules 1987 (SI 1987/2023) and by the *Practice Direction: Directors Disqualification Proceedings* issued by the Vice-Chancellor following the introduction of the Civil Procedure Rules 1998 (SI 1998/3132: the "CPR") and now reported (as amended) [2007] B.C.C. 842. The *Practice Direction* incorporates, where relevant, provisions from the 1987 Rules, and is reproduced in App.VI to this *Guide*. This procedure governs disqualification applications under ss.2(2)(a), 3, 4 and 8 as well as under the present section. An application is commenced by a claim form issued in the High Court, out of the office of the companies court registrar or a chancery district registry (or, in the county court, out of a county court office), in the form annexed to the *Practice Direction*. All disqualification proceedings are multi-track. The first hearing is before a registrar. Where the application is made under ss.7 or 8, the first hearing is on a summary basis and on that hearing a disqualification order of up to five years may be imposed; but if it appears that a longer period is justified on the evidence then before the court, the matter is adjourned to a later hearing. An adjournment may also be ordered if the registrar is of opinion that questions of law or fact arise which are not suitable for summary determination. The adjourned hearing may be before a registrar or a judge, as the registrar (or, at a later stage, the court) directs. Directions may also be given as to the subsequent management of the case, e.g. as to the filing and service of further evidence, a timetable for the steps to be taken prior to the hearing, etc. A pre-trial review may also be ordered. Special rules apply if the defendant does not intend to contest his liability and it is proposed to invite the court to adopt the *Carecraft* procedure (see below). The procedure set out in CPR Pt 8 applies, subject to any modification of that procedure under the *Practice Direction* or the Rules.

Evidence in disqualification applications is by affidavit (or, where the applicant is the official receiver, a written report, with or without affidavits by other persons, made by him (or his deputy: *Re Homes Assured Corp Ltd* [1993] B.C.C. 573); this, under the 1987 Rules, is prima facie evidence of any matter contained in it). (Note that the Legislative Reform (Insolvency) (Miscellaneous Provisions) Order 2010 (SI 2010/18) and the Insolvency (Amendment) Rules 2010 (SI 2010/686), which abolish the use of affidavits for many purposes in insolvency proceedings, do not extend to the CDDA 1986.) The same evidential status is accorded to any documents that are annexed to the report (*Re City Investments Ltd* [1992] B.C.L.C. 956). In practice, an affidavit from the insolvency practitioner concerned is invariably filed. (For a description of a typical affidavit and its contents, see D. S. Henry, (1992) 5 Insolv. Int. 1.) Guidance on the drawing up of affidavits and the official receiver's report is to be found also in *Re Pamstock Ltd* [1994] B.C.C. 264 (avoidance of excessive detail); *Secretary of State for Trade and Industry v Hickling* [1996] B.C.C. 678 (significant available evidence in favour of a respondent should not be omitted); *Re Pinemoor Ltd* [1997] B.C.C. 708 (evidence of opinion as to respondent's fitness (unless expert opinion) must be excluded); *Re Park House Properties Ltd* [1998] B.C.C. 847 (distinction to be made between matters of fact, inferences which the court is invited to draw and matters said to amount to unfitness on the part of a defendant). The office-holder's report is a public document and, subject to any question of privilege, should be made available to the defendant (*Re Barings plc (No.2)* [1998] B.C.C. 888).

The defendant has 28 days after service of the proceedings to file his own affidavit evidence in reply. Again, evidence of opinion must be excluded, unless that of an expert, as must evidence of good character (*Secretary of State for Trade and Industry v Dawes* [1997] B.C.C. 121). The *Practice Direction* states that, so far as possible, all evidence should be filed before the first hearing of the application.

Deponents may be cross-examined on their affidavit evidence (*Re Dominion International Group plc* [1995] B.C.C. 303). Disclosure (formerly discovery) may be ordered in the usual way, but an order for disclosure made against the Secretary of State will not extend to documents which are not held by him personally but by the insolvency practitioner on whose report the disqualification proceedings have been based: *Re Lombard Shipping and Forwarding Ltd* [1992] B.C.C. 700. (In practice, however, disclosure is always made available: *Re Thomas Christy Ltd* [1994] 2 B.C.L.C. 527 at 529.) Nor will it extend to internal departmental memoranda: *Re Astra Holdings plc* [1999] B.C.C. 121. Witness summonses (e.g. in a case prior to the introduction of the CPR, a *subpoena duces tecum*) may be issued, on general principles (*Re Global Information Ltd* [1999] 1 B.C.L.C. 74); but an order requiring the

Secretary of State to file replies to interrogatories (under the CPR, further information) was refused (and doubts expressed whether such an order would ever be appropriate) in *Re Sutton Glassworks Ltd* [1996] B.C.C. 174.

In *Official Receiver v Stojevic* [2007] EWHC 1186 (Ch); [2008] Bus.L.R. 641 findings of fraud had been made against the defendant director in a claim based on deceit. It was held that the judgment could be adduced as prima facie evidence in disqualification proceedings subsequently brought against him.

Where a report of inspectors appointed by the Secretary of State under Pt XIV of the Companies Act 1985 is to be put in evidence, s.441 of that Act provides that a certified copy of the inspectors' report shall be admissible in all legal proceedings. [These provisions are not consolidated within CA 2006.]

Rule 3(3) of the 1987 Rules requires that in the affidavit evidence (or, where appropriate, the official receiver's report) there shall be stated the matters by reference to which the defendant is alleged to be unfit to be concerned in the management of a company. In *Re Sevenoaks Stationers (Retail) Ltd* [1991] Ch. 164 at 177; [1990] B.C.C. 765 at 774 the Court of Appeal ruled that it was improper for matters not so stated to be taken into account by the court, either in determining the question of "unfitness" or in fixing the appropriate period of disqualification, unless the court had, in a proper exercise of its discretion, allowed the altered or new allegation to be relied on. This should be done only if there was no injustice to the accused director, and might call for the giving of prior notice or the granting of an adjournment, so that he would have an opportunity to put in new evidence if he wished, and generally a fair opportunity to answer the new allegations (*Re Jazzgold Ltd* [1992] B.C.C. 587 at 594). An amendment may be refused if its effect is to shift the fundamental focus of the complaint to the defendant's conduct in relation to a different company: *Re Diamond Computer Systems Ltd* [1997] 1 B.C.L.C. 174; *Secretary of State for Trade and Industry v Gill* [2004] EWHC 175 (Ch); [2005] B.C.C. 24. The cases of *Re Finelist Ltd* [2003] EWHC 170 (Ch); [2004] B.C.C. 877; and *Secretary of State for Trade and Industry v Gill* [2004] EWHC 175 (Ch); [2005] B.C.C. 24 emphasise the need for a respondent to disqualification proceedings to have a clear statement of the charges and the evidence in support which are brought against him, and the desirability of offering the director an opportunity before the proceedings are begun to proffer explanations for his conduct. In *Kappler v Secretary of State for Trade and Industry* [2006] B.C.C. 845 the allegation against the director was that he had "caused" the use by the company of fraudulent invoices, whereas the case was conducted on the basis that he knew of the fraud and had not put a stop to it. On appeal, he argued that there should have been a formal amendment of the allegation from "caused" to "allowed", but it was ruled that the lack of an amendment had not prevented the trial from being conducted fairly.

The report of the official receiver and other evidence on the court file is confidential: it is punishable as a contempt of court to publish this information in a newspaper before the hearing of the application: *Dobson v Hastings* [1992] Ch. 394; [1992] 2 All E.R. 94.

In *Re Rex Williams Leisure plc* [1994] Ch. 350; [1994] B.C.C. 551 the respondent directors wished (a) to object to much of the evidence put forward on behalf of the Secretary of State on the ground that is was hearsay and inadmissible; (b) to file no affidavit evidence of their own before the hearing and give no evidence at all until they had had an opportunity of submitting that there was no case to answer; and (c) to have the disqualification proceedings stayed until a civil action brought against one of the respondents had been disposed of. They failed on all three counts. The court ruled (a) that evidence put forward by an examiner of the investigations division of the Department of Trade and Industry had to be treated analogously with the reports of inspectors appointed under the Companies Act 1985 s.431, and was accordingly admissible as evidence of the facts it contained, even though the examiner was reporting on matters of which he had little or no first-hand knowledge; (b) that the procedure as regards evidence on affidavit laid down in the 1987 Rules (above) should be followed as the norm; and (c) that disqualification proceedings, being a matter of public interest, should not be held up pending the outcome of parallel private litigation. Similarly, objection may not be taken to evidence in an affidavit or report by the official receiver or an officeholder (or a professional person, such as an accountant, employed to report on his behalf) on the ground that it is or contains hearsay: this may go to the weight to be attached to the evidence, but not to its admissibility (*Re Moonbeam Cards Ltd* [1993] B.C.L.C. 1,099; *Re Circle Holidays International plc* [1994] B.C.C. 226; *Secretary of State for Trade and Industry v Moffatt* [1997] 2 B.C.L.C. 16; *Secretary of State for Trade and Industry v Ashcroft* [1998] Ch. 71; [1997] B.C.C. 634; *Re Barings plc (No.3)* [1999] B.C.C. 146). The Court of Appeal considered the position more generally in *Aaron v Secretary of State for Business, etc.* [2008] EWCA Civ 1146; [2009] B.C.C. 375, where the defendant challenged the admissibility of a report by the Financial Services Authority into complaints that had been made against the defendant's company, and also the decisions of the Financial Ombudsman Service in the same matter. It was held that in disqualification proceedings it was a well-established exception to the hearsay rule that material obtained under a statutory scheme for investigation was admissible as prima facie evidence and that it was a matter for the judge what weight should be given to it. Further, where the documents contained some inadmissible material (such as the recital of evidence given by complainants) this did not justify the exclusion of the documents as a whole and it would be for the judge to decide what weight should be attached to them.

Factual findings in an earlier civil case for breach of contract and wrongful dismissal are not admissible in later disqualification proceedings and the Secretary of State must make good his allegations afresh by legally admissible evidence (*Secretary of State for Trade and Industry v Bairstow* [2003] EWCA Civ 321; [2004] Ch. 1; [2003] B.C.C. 682; *Secretary of State for Trade and Industry v Arnold* [2007] EWCA 1933 (Ch); [2008] B.C.C. 119).

An order may be made in the absence of the defendant if he fails to appear. Where he has failed to file an acknowledgment of service and the time for doing so has expired, he may attend the hearing of the application but may not take part in the hearing unless the court gives permission (*Practical Direction: Directors Disqualification Proceedings* [2007] B.C.C. 862 (reproduced as App.VI to this *Guide*) para.8.4).

Disqualification proceedings are adversarial in nature. The court has no investigative function. It is up to the Secretary of State (or other claimant) to select the matters to be put to the court and if he decides, in the interest of saving time and costs, to weed our parts of the case which could possibly be advanced, he is justified in doing so (*Secretary of State for Trade and Industry v Tillman* [1999] B.C.C. 703). The judge has no power to open the case more widely than the applicant has chosen to present it (*Re SIG Security Services Ltd* [1998] B.C.C. 978). The burden of proof is on the applicant (*Re Verby Print for Advertising Ltd* [1998] B.C.C. 652).

As noted above (see the note to s.1), disqualification proceedings are essentially civil, but they differ from ordinary private law proceedings in many respects: "Significantly, the 1986 Act does not expressly equip the court with a discretion to deploy the armoury of common law and equitable remedies to restrain future misconduct (injunction or undertaking in lieu of injunction), to punish for disregard of restraints imposed by court order (contempt powers of imprisonment or fine), to compensate for past loss unlawfully inflicted (damages) or to restore benefits unjustly acquired (restitution)" (Lord Woolf M.R. in *Re Blackspur Group plc (No.2)* [1998] 1 W.L.R. 422 at 427D–E; [1998] B.C.C. 11 at 16B–C). However, there is no doubt that the court may, either under the Rules or in its inherent jurisdiction, exercise many powers which are not expressly conferred by the Act, e.g. to grant a stay or suspend an order pending an appeal (*Secretary of State for Trade and Industry v Bannister* [1996] 1 W.L.R. 118; [1995] B.C.C. 1,027; *Re Barings plc (No.4)* [1999] B.C.C. 639).

The legislation does not include any provision which expressly allows the court to make a disqualification order on the basis of a "plea of guilty" or an agreement reached between the Secretary of State or official receiver, on the one hand, and the respondent director, on the other. However, in practice this became possible as a result of the decision of Ferris J. in *Re Carecraft Construction Co Ltd* [1994] 1 W.L.R. 172; [1993] B.C.C. 336 and its subsequent endorsement (subject to some important qualifications) by the Court of Appeal in *Secretary of State for Trade & Industry v Rogers* [1996] 1 W.L.R. 1569; [1997] B.C.C. 155. This "summary procedure" (commonly referred to as the "*Carecraft* procedure") enabled a case to be dealt with expeditiously and without the expense of a full hearing. As a result, a very significant proportion of disqualification orders were made by this method in the years that followed.

However, the power given to the Secretary of State by IA 2000 to accept an undertaking in lieu of making, or continuing with, an application to court provides an even more convenient way of dealing with an uncontested case (see the notes to s.1A, above), and there will be little reason to follow the *Carecraft* procedure in most instances. One exceptional situation might be where there is no dispute as to the facts, but disagreement on the appropriate length of disqualification.

The Secretary of State has a general power to delegate his functions to an official receiver under IA 1986 s.400, and accordingly he may direct an official receiver to make an application under s.7(1)(a) even where (because the company in question is not being wound up by the court) the case does not come within s.7(1)(b). In such a situation the proceedings should be brought in the name of the Secretary of State and not that of the official receiver; but if an error is made in this respect it can be cured by amendment: *Official Receiver v Pafundo* [2000] B.C.C. 164; not following *Re Probe Data Systems Ltd* (1989) 5 B.C.C. 384.

S.7(2)

Section 6 is the only provision in CDDA 1986 which imposes a time limit. (Note that this is not a limitation provision conferring on the director immunity from suit, but merely a period after which proceedings can only be brought with permission: *Re Instant Access Properties Ltd* [2011] EWHC 3022 (Ch).) If the two-year limit expires on a day when the court office is closed, the time is extended until the next day when it is open (*Re Philipp & Lion Ltd* [1994] B.C.C. 261). An application for "making" an order is made when the application is brought, i.e. lodged in the court office: *Secretary of State for Trade and Industry v Vohora* [2007] EWHC 2656 (Ch); [2009] B.C.C. 369.

A company "becomes insolvent" for the purposes of s.7(2) on the happening of any of the events mentioned in s.6(2) (insolvent liquidation, administration, administrative receivership): see the note to that section. In the case of a compulsory winding up, the relevant date is the date of the order and not that of the petition (*Re Walter L Jacob & Co Ltd, Official Receiver v Jacob* [1993] B.C.C. 512).

Where, on an application for the appointment of an administrator under the original regime, the court first makes an interim order under IA 1986 s.9(4) and later makes an administration order under s.8 of that Act, it is the date of the latter order from which time should be reckoned for the purposes of the present provision: *Secretary of State for Trade & Industry v Palmer* [1993] B.C.C. 650.

Where more than one of the events mentioned in s.7(2) happen in succession to the same company (e.g. the company is first put into administrative receivership and then into compulsory liquidation), the period of two years runs from the first of those events: *Re Tasbian Ltd* [1990] B.C.C. 318. However, if the company were to return to a state of solvency between the happening of the two events, it is arguable that a fresh two-year period would start when it "became insolvent" for the second time (ibid.).

The procedure to be followed by the Secretary of State or the official receiver in making application for an extension of time under s.7(2) is set out in Pt 3 of the *Practice Direction: Directors Disqualification Proceedings* [2007] B.C.C. 842. (See App.VI to this Guide.) Application is made by Application Notice under CPR Pt 23.

The section does not indicate the grounds upon which the court might see fit to extend the two-year time limit. It is for the Secretary of State or official receiver to show a good reason for the extension of time (*Re Crestjoy Products Ltd* [1990] B.C.C. 23 at 29; *Re Copecrest Ltd* [1993] B.C.C. 844 at 847, 852). The matters to be taken into account are: (1) the length of delay; (2) the reasons for the delay; (3) the strength of the case against the director; and (4) the degree of prejudice caused to the director by the delay (*Re Probe Data Systems Ltd (No.3), Secretary of State for Trade & Industry v Desai* [1992] B.C.C. 110 at 118). This list is not expressed to be exclusive but in most cases is likely to be so (*Re Polly Peck International plc, Secretary of State for Trade & Industry v Ellis (No.2)* [1993] B.C.C. 890 at 894). When each of these four matters has been looked at separately, there then needs to take place a balancing exercise; but even before this, the application for leave should be rejected if the applicant's case is so weak that it could not lead to a disqualification (ibid., and see also *Re Manlon Trading Ltd* [1996] Ch. 136; [1995] B.C.C. 579).

Other cases have elaborated upon the matters listed above. In *Re Copecrest Ltd* (above) Hoffmann L.J. said that the two-year period under s.7(2) had to be treated as having built into it a contingency allowance for unexpected delays for which the applicant was not responsible, such as delays on the part of the liquidator or other office-holder; but on the other hand delays for which the respondent himself was to blame were a factor which it was proper to take into account. In *Re Crestjoy Products Ltd* (above) pressure of work and a shortage of staff in the Secretary of State's department was not considered a sufficient reason to grant leave out of time retrospectively, although the court indicated that an application made prior to the expiry of the statutory deadline would have been more favourably considered.

Notwithstanding the view expressed in the *Polly Peck* case (above) that the four factors mentioned will usually be sufficient, later cases have added to the list. These include: the director's own share of responsibility for the delay (*Secretary of State for Trade & Industry v McTighe* [1997] B.C.C. 224); the fact that the charges are particularly serious and that there is a public interest in having them determined (*Secretary of State for Trade & Industry v Davies* [1996] 4 All E.R. 289; [1997] B.C.C. 235); whether it is still possible to have a fair trial (*Secretary of State for Trade & Industry v Martin* [1998] B.C.C. 184). In *Re Instant Access Properties Ltd* [2011] EWHC 3022 (Ch) it was said that the gravity of the charge and the prospects of success could together measure the public interest in allowing the proceedings to continue. The mere fact that the delay after the two-year period is very short is not relevant (*Re Cedar Developments Ltd* [1995] B.C.C. 220); nor that the Secretary of State has a good reason for the delay: what must be shown is a good reason for being granted the extension of time (*Secretary of State for Trade & Industry v Davies* (above)).

Even though disqualification proceedings have been formally commenced in time, delay in bringing the case to a hearing may lead to the striking out or dismissal of the claim: *Secretary of State for Trade & Industry v Tjolle* [1998] B.C.C. 282. But where there has been no real prejudice to the defendant caused by the delay, or where his own acts have contributed to it, the courts will not readily take such a course: see, e.g. *Re Abermeadow Ltd* [2001] B.C.C. 724; *Re Rocksteady Service Ltd* [2001] B.C.C. 467; *Re Blackspur Group plc (No.3), Secretary of State for Trade and Industry v Eastaway* [2003] B.C.C. 520.

The European Commission of Human Rights has also ruled on the effects of delay, declaring in *EDC v United Kingdom (Application No.24433/94)* [1998] B.C.C. 370 that a stay of proceedings for seven years (pending the disposal of criminal proceedings against other parties) was excessive and breached the right of a respondent to have a hearing of the case within a reasonable time, as required by art.6(1) of the European Convention for the Protection of Human Rights and Fundamental Freedoms. In contrast, in the *Abermeadow* and *Blackspur* cases (above) a plea based on the ground that the Human Rights legislation had been infringed was unsuccessful.

Rule 3(1) of the Insolvent Companies (Disqualification of Directors) Proceedings Rules 1987 (SI 1987/2023) states that the evidence in support of an application for a disqualification order should be filed at the time when the summons is issued—although this provision is directory and not mandatory and failing to comply with it is an irregularity which the court may waive (*Re Jazzgold Ltd* [1992] B.C.C. 587; *Re Copecrest Ltd* [1993] B.C.C. 844 at 851). The evidence may take the form of, or include, a report by the official receiver (r.3(2)). The court may take into account evidence contained in a supplementary report filed after the expiry of the two-year limitation period (*Re Jazzgold Ltd* (above)). On the application for an extension of time, it is sufficient for the evidence to show that there is an arguable case (*Re Tasbian Ltd (No.3)* [1991] B.C.C. 435): the court will not, even where there is a conflict of evidence, virtually try the case (*Re Packaging Direct Ltd, Jones v Secretary of State for Trade & Industry* [1994] B.C.C. 213). It is not necessarily an obstacle to allowing the trial to proceed that the applicant's evidence has not been wholly accurate (*Re Tasbian Ltd (No.3)* (above)).

An application under s.7 may also be struck out for want of prosecution: *Re Noble Trees Ltd* [1993] B.C.C. 318; *Official Receiver v B Ltd* [1994] 2 B.C.L.C. 1.

S.7(2A)

On disqualification undertakings, see the note to s.1A. In *Gardiner v Secretary of State for Business, Enterprise and Regulatory Reform* [2009] B.C.C. 742 the applicant, who had given an undertaking after proceedings had been commenced against him, sought to have it rescinded or declared invalid on the grounds that the proceedings had been issued out of time. The court found that this was not so on the facts, but held that in any case an undertaking could be accepted by the Secretary of State even if the associated proceedings had not been commenced in time.

S.7(3)

This provision makes it the duty of the liquidator or other office-holder to report any case of suspected unfitness to the Secretary of State.

Rules were made under IA 1985 to reinforce these requirements, which imposed an obligation on the insolvency practitioner concerned to complete and return prescribed forms in a number of stipulated cases. These have been reissued and are now the Insolvent Companies (Reports on Conduct of Directors) Rules 1996 (SI 1996/1909 (as amended by SI 2001/764, as from April 2, 2001 and by SI 2003/2096 from September 15, 2003)) and the Insolvent Companies (Reports on Conduct of Directors) (Scotland) Rules 1996 (SI 1996/1910 (S 154) (as amended by SI 2001/768, as from April 2, 2001)). The former rules apply to (1) a voluntary winding up where the company is "insolvent" (as defined by s.6(2)); (2) an administrative receivership; and (3) an administration. In Scotland, the rules apply in every "insolvent" winding up, administrative receivership and administration. Interim returns are also prescribed, to be made when the liquidation, receivership or administration runs for more than six months. Fines may be imposed on an office-holder who fails to comply.

An office-holder's report to the Secretary of State under this section is not privileged and the respondent is entitled to disclosure (*Secretary of State for Trade & Industry v Baker* [1998] Ch. 356; [1998] 1 B.C.L.C. 16, not following *Secretary of State for Trade & Industry v Sananes* [1994] B.C.C. 375). The Insolvency Service's policy in dealing with requests for disclosure of reports and decisions made under these rules to directors, third parties and regulatory authorities is explained in *Dear IP*, December 2011, p.10.35.

An office-holder may disclose to the Secretary of State for the purpose of director disqualification proceedings the transcripts of interviews conducted and documents provided under IA 1986 s.235 even when he has given assurances that the information given and documents provided will be used only for the purposes of the administration, for such disclosure is "for the purposes of the administration" (*Re Polly Peck International plc Ex p. the joint administrators* [1994] B.C.C. 15).

S.7(4)

The two sets of rules referred to above also provide for the enforcement of the obligations here set out by a court order, which may include a direction that the liquidator or other office-holder pay the costs personally.

Documents in the custody of an administrative receiver or other office-holder were not "in the power of" the Secretary of State by virtue of this subsection so that he could be compelled to make discovery [disclosure] of them under RSC Ord.24 [CPR Pt 31]: *Re Lombard Shipping & Forwarding Ltd* [1992] B.C.C. 700.

In *Re Pantmaenog Timber Co Ltd, Official Receiver v Wadge Rapps & Hunt (a firm)* [2003] UKHL 49; [2004] 1 A.C. 158; [2003] B.C.C. 659 the official receiver was liquidator of the company, and (acting on behalf of the Secretary of State) had commenced disqualification proceedings against one of its directors. He sought an order of the court under IA 1986 s.236 requiring the company's solicitors and accountants to produce documents relating to the company for use as evidence in the disqualification proceedings. The House of Lords, overruling the Court of Appeal, held that the official receiver could seek disclosure of documents under s.236 for this purpose, and that he might do so even if he were not the liquidator of the company and even if this was his sole purpose.

It has also been held that it is not objectionable for a police officer to attend disqualification proceedings in order to gain information which may be useful in a proposed criminal prosecution (*Re Priority Stainless (UK) Ltd, Secretary of State for Trade and Industry v Crane* [2004] B.C.C. 825).

In appropriate circumstances, an order may be made under CPR r.31.17(3) against a third party that he should disclose documents in his possession, if they are likely to be material to the case: *Re Howglen Ltd* [2001] B.C.C. 245 (company's banker); *Re Skyward Builders plc* [2002] 2 B.C.L.C. 750 (accountants).

8   Disqualification after investigation of company

8(1)   [Application by Secretary of State] If it appears to the Secretary of State from investigative material that it is expedient in the public interest that a disqualification order should be made against a person who is, or has been, a director or shadow director of a company, he may apply to the court for such an order.

8(1A)   ["Investigative material" in s.8(1)] "Investigative material" means–

    (a)   a report made by inspectors under–

        (i)   section 437 of the Companies Act 1985, or

        (ii)   section 167, 168, 169 or 284 of the Financial Services and Markets Act 2000; and

(but see section 22D(2)).

    (b)   information or documents obtained under–

        (i)   section 437, 446E, 447, 448, 451A or 453A of the Companies Act 1985;

        (ii)   section 2 of the Criminal Justice Act 1987;

        (iii)   section 28 of the Criminal Law (Consolidation)(Scotland) Act 1995;

        (iv)   section 83 of the Companies Act 1989; or

        (v)   section 165, 171, 172, 173 or 175 of the Financial Services and Markets Act 2000.

8(2)   [Court's power] The court may make a disqualification order against a person where, on an application under this section, it is satisfied that his conduct in relation to the company makes him unfit to be concerned in the management of a company.

8(2A)   [Acceptance of undertaking] Where it appears to the Secretary of State from such report, information or documents that, in the case of a person who has offered to give him a disqualification undertaking–

    (a)   the conduct of the person in relation to a company of which the person is or has been a director or shadow director makes him unfit to be concerned in the management of a company, and

    (b)   it is expedient in the public interest that he should accept the undertaking (instead of applying, or proceeding with an application, for a disqualification order),

he may accept the undertaking.

8(3)   ["The court"] In this section **"the court"** means the High Court or, in Scotland, the Court of Session.

8(4)   [Maximum period] The maximum period of disqualification under this section is 15 years.

GENERAL NOTE

Section 8(1) was substituted and s.8(1A) inserted by the Financial Services and Markets Act 2000 (Consequential Amendments and Repeals) Order 2001 (SI 2001/3649) as from December 1, 2001. Section 2A was inserted by IA 2000 s.6(1), (4) as from April 2, 2001. The reference to CA 1985 s.453A was inserted by the Companies (Audit, Investigations and Community Enterprise) Act 2004 Sch.2 para.28 as from April 6, 2005, and the reference to ss.437, 446E and 451A by CA 2006 s.1039 as from October 1, 2007. Minor textual amendments were made and the reference to s.22D(2) inserted by the Companies Act 2006 (Consequential Amendments, Transitional Provisions and Savings) Order 2009 (SI 2009/1941) art.2(1) and Sch.1 para.85(4) as from October 1, 2009.

S.8(1)
The Secretary of State has powers under CA 1985 ss.431–441 to appoint inspectors to investigate the affairs of companies in a number of situations, e.g.:

    •   on the application of the company itself or a section of its members (s.431);

- if the court so orders (s.432(1)); or

- of his own motion, if it appears to him that there are circumstances suggesting fraud or irregularity (s.432(2)).

Under ss.447, 448, he may also require production to him of books or papers relating to a company, and ask for an explanation of them to be given. [These provisions are unaffected by CA 2006.]

The present section gives the court power to make a disqualification order on the application of the Secretary of State, if it appears from a report made to him or from information or documents obtained by him under the above provisions that it is expedient in the public interest that an order should be made against a director or former director of any company. Although ss.6 and 8 are broadly based on the same criterion of "unfitness", there are some differences between the two. Under s.6, if unfitness is found, the court has no discretion to decline to make an order, and there is a minimum period of disqualification of two years. The official receiver has no standing to apply under s.8, and the county court has no jurisdiction. The Statutes of Limitation do not apply, and there is no requirement that any of the companies concerned should have been insolvent. (See *Re JA Chapman & Co Ltd* [2003] 2 B.C.L.C. 206.) In *Secretary of State for Trade and Industry v Hollier* [2006] EWHC 1804; [2007] B.C.C. 11 Etherton J. expressed reservations on the question whether the principles and approach applicable to cases under s.6 should also apply under s.8, but did not pursue the matter. In *Secretary of State for Business, Enterprise and Regulatory Reform v Sullman* [2008] EWHC 3179 (Ch); [2009] B.C.C. 500 Norris J., while accepting that disqualification under s.8 was discretionary and not mandatory as under s.6 (see above) nevertheless felt that the protection of the public and the need to deter other directors justified a seven-year disqualification in the case before him. On open-ended investment companies, see s.22D(2).

Cases where orders have been made under s.8 include: *Re Samuel Sherman plc* [1991] 1 W.L.R. 1070; [1991] B.C.C. 699 (ultra vires use of public company's assets and failure to comply with statutory obligations: five-year disqualification); *Re Looe Fish Ltd* [1993] B.C.C. 348 (improper allotment of shares to manipulate voting: two and a half years); *Re Aldermanbury Trust plc* [1993] B.C.C. 598 (breaches of company law, City Code and fiduciary duty, "seriously flawed" commercial judgments: seven years). In *Ghassemian v Secretary of State for Trade and Industry* [2006] EWHC 1715 (Ch); [2007] B.C.C. 229 the Secretary of State had written to the defendant saying that he was not satisfied that it was expedient that a disqualification order should be made against him but had then proceeded instead to petition for a winding-up order on public interest grounds. He later brought disqualification proceedings on the basis of investigative material procured for the winding-up application. The court held that the indication given to the defendant in the earlier letter did not stand in the way of the making of a disqualification order.

In *Re TransTec plc (No.2)* [2006] EWHC 2110 (Ch); [2007] 2 B.C.L.C. 495 the respondent had been acquitted on charges of fraud but it was held competent for the Secretary of State to bring proceedings under s.8, and for the court to make a disqualification order, on the basis of the same facts, because there were significant differences between the two sets of proceedings and their underlying purpose and, in particular, the standard of proof was the less demanding civil standard.

In *Re Aldermanbury Trust plc* (above) it was held that the court could properly adopt the shortened form of procedure approved in *Re Carecraft Construction Co Ltd* (see the note to s.7(2) above), and avoid a full hearing. But there will be little cause to follow this course in the future, for (by virtue of the new s.8(2A)) the alternative of a disqualification undertaking in lieu of a court order is available in cases under s.8: see the notes to s.1A.

In *R. v Secretary of State for Trade & Industry Ex p. Lonrho plc* [1992] B.C.C. 325 an application for judicial review of the Secretary of State's decision not to seek a disqualification order under this section was unsuccessful. In *R. v Secretary of State for Trade & Industry Ex p. McCormick* [1998] B.C.C. 379 the Court of Appeal, affirming Rimer J., refused a similar application brought following the ruling of the European Court of Human Rights in *Saunders v UK* (1997) 23 E.H.R.R. 313; [1997] B.C.C. 872, where it had been held that the use in criminal proceedings of evidence obtained under compulsion was an infringement of the right against self-incrimination and accordingly rendered the trial unfair and in violation of art.6(1) of the European Convention for the Protection of Human Rights and Fundamental Freedoms. The director argued that the use of a report made by inspectors to the Secretary of State under CA 1985 s.437 and transcripts of the director's interviews with the inspectors should similarly not have been used in disqualification proceedings brought against him. However the court ruled that these proceedings were civil and not criminal in nature and that the report and transcripts were relevant, admissible and not privileged; and that their use was not unfair. (See further the Introductory note to CDDA 1986 at p.2 above.)

S.8(2)

The court must also be satisfied that the conduct of the director in relation to the company (but not, it appears, other companies) makes him unfit to be concerned in the management of a company. But the phrase "conduct in relation to" the company is not to be construed narrowly. In *Secretary of State for Business, Enterprise and Regulatory Reform v Sullman* (above) it was argued unsuccessfully that it was necessary that the company should have been the victim of the conduct in question. Norris J. held that it was sufficient that the person's conduct as a director had a bearing upon the company's business or affairs, whether that conduct occasioned prejudice to the company itself or its shareholders, customers, funders or anyone else with whom it had commercial relationships. The notes to ss.6(1) and 9 will be generally relevant in the present context.

The court's power here is discretionary rather than mandatory.

S.8(2A)
On disqualification undertakings, see the note to s.1A.

S.8(3)
The procedure before the High Court takes the same form as in an application under s.6. See the note to s.7(1) above.

S.8(4)
There is no minimum disqualification period under this section.

8A   Variation etc. of disqualification undertaking

8A(1)   [Reduction, etc. of undertaking] The court may, on the application of a person who is subject to a disqualification undertaking–

(a)   reduce the period for which the undertaking is to be in force, or

(b)   provide for it to cease to be in force.

8A(2)   [Duty of Secretary of State to appear] On the hearing of an application under subsection (1), the Secretary of State shall appear and call the attention of the court to any matters which seem to him to be relevant, and may himself give evidence or call witnesses.

8A(2A)   [Non-application of s.8(2)] Subsection (2) does not apply to an application in the case of an undertaking given under section 9B, and in such a case on the hearing of the application whichever of the OFT or a specified regulator (within the meaning of section 9E) accepted the undertaking–

(a)   must appear and call the attention of the court to any matters which appear to it or him (as the case may be) to be relevant;

(b)   may give evidence or call witnesses.

8A(3)   ["The court"] In this section **"the court"**–

(a)   in the case of an undertaking given under section 9B means the High Court or (in Scotland) the Court of Session;

(b)   in any other case has the same meaning as in section 7(2) or 8 (as the case may be).

S.8A(1), (2)
Section 8A was introduced by IA 2000 as part of the new disqualification undertaking regime. It may be assumed that its purpose is to allay concerns that persons facing disqualification proceedings might be unfairly induced to give undertakings (e.g. as a result of undue pressure or without having had matters of mitigation taken fully into account); and that without some form of appeal or review by the courts, the new legislation could be held to contravene the Human Rights legislation. It is to be noted that the scope of the section is restricted in two ways. First, only the disqualified person may apply to the court; the Secretary of State has no standing to seek a variation (though he is required by s.8A(2) to appear and put his case). Secondly, the court may only vary the undertaking in the applicant's favour, or terminate it altogether: there is no power to increase the period. As an alternative, application may be made to the court under s.17 for leave to act notwithstanding the undertaking.

On procedure see the *Practice Direction* (reproduced as App.VI to the *Guide*).

In *Re I.N.S. Realisations Ltd* [2006] EWHC 135 (Ch); [2006] B.C.C. 307, Hart J. examined the nature of the jurisdiction under this section. The court should treat the applicant's statement of agreed facts given at the time of the undertaking as prima facie binding on the applicant, subject to any factor which would be sufficient to discharge a private law contract or some ground of public interest. Nevertheless, the court's jurisdiction was unfettered; and on the special facts of the case (namely, that the Secretary of State had decided not to continue with disqualification proceedings against another director, the person principally concerned in the alleged misconduct) the applicant's undertaking should cease to be in force. However, there was no power under s.8A to annul the undertaking from the start.

S.8A(2A)

Subsection (2A) was inserted by the Enterprise Act 2002 s.204(1), (4) and SI 2003/1397 (C. 60) arts 1, 2(1) and Sch., as from June 20, 2003. On competition undertakings, see s.9B: the undertaking in these cases is given to the OFT or one of the regulators specified in s.9E(2), and not to the Secretary of State.

S.8A(3).

Subsection (3) was substituted by the Enterprise Act 2002 s.204(1), (5) and SI 2003/1397 (C. 60) arts 1, 2(1) and Sch., as from June 20, 2003, specifying in more detail the competent court for the present purpose.

9   Matters for determining unfitness of directors

9(1)   **[Matters in Sch.1]** Where it falls to a court to determine whether a person's conduct as a director of any particular company or companies makes him unfit to be concerned in the management of a company, the court shall, as respects his conduct as a director of that company or, as the case may be, each of those companies, have regard in particular–

    (a)   to the matters mentioned in Part I of Schedule 1 to this Act, and

    (b)   where the company has become insolvent, to the matters mentioned in Part II of that Schedule;

and references in that Schedule to the director and the company are to be read accordingly.

9(1A)   **[Matters in Sch.1 Pt I, II]** In determining whether he may accept a disqualification undertaking from any person the Secretary of State shall, as respects the person's conduct as a director of any company concerned, have regard in particular–

    (a)   to the matters mentioned in Part I of Schedule 1 to this Act, and

    (b)   where the company has become insolvent, to the matters mentioned in Part II of that Schedule;

and references in that Schedule to the director and the company are to be read accordingly.

9(2)   **[Application of s.6(2)]** Section 6(2) applies for the purposes of this section and Schedule 1 as it applies for the purposes of sections 6 and 7 and in this section and that Schedule **"director"** includes a shadow director.

9(3)   [Omitted by the Companies Act 2006 (Consequential Amendments, Transitional Provisions and Savings) Order 2009 (SI 2009/1941) art.2(1) and Sch.1 para.85(5) as from October 1, 2009.]

9(4)   **[Modification of Sch.1]** The Secretary of State may by order modify any of the provisions of Schedule 1; and such an order may contain such transitional provisions as may appear to the Secretary of State necessary or expedient.

9(5)   **[Power exercisable by statutory instrument etc.]** The power to make orders under this section is exercisable by statutory instrument subject to annulment in pursuance of a resolution of either House of Parliament.

S.9(1)

Under the repealed CA 1985 s.300 (the forerunner of the present s.6), the question of a director's unfitness was a matter for the court to determine in its own judgment. In contrast, CDDA 1986 prescribes in this section and Sch.1 a list of matters to which the court is directed to have particular regard in assessing the question of unfitness. The same factors are to be considered by the Secretary of State in determining whether to accept a disqualification undertaking in lieu of seeking a court order (s.9(1A)). Schedule 1 is not applicable in competition disqualification cases (s.9A(5)(c)).

    The statutory criteria are set out in Sch.1 in two Parts: Pt I applies in all cases, and Pt II applies in addition to Pt I where the company in question has "become insolvent" (as that phrase is defined in s.6(2)). Where the matter falls under s.6, it will always be the case that the "lead company" (the company in respect of which the charge is brought) has "become insolvent", so that both Parts of the Schedule will be relevant. If the director's conduct in relation to other companies is brought into the reckoning under s.6(1)(b), it will be necessary for the court or the Secretary of State to determine whether any of those companies has (or had) "become insolvent" in order to see whether Pt II applies; and this inquiry will always be necessary in a case under s.8. It should be noted, however, that where the company has become insolvent the court may have regard to the matters listed in Pt II of the Schedule even though these matters were not the cause of the insolvency (*Re AG (Manchester) Ltd* [2008] EWHC 64 (Ch); [2008] 1 B.C.L.C. 321).

Much of what is set out in Sch.1 is not new: it merely restates and serves to reinforce the duties of directors under the general statutory and common law rules; and there is even some overlap with the other "disqualification" provisions of this Act—e.g. in regard to persistent failure to file company returns. Read as a whole, Sch.1 does not impose new duties on directors or demand higher standards; rather, it makes it possible to impose a salutary penalty for breaches of duty which went largely unpunished before the present Act because of inadequacies in the law enforcement process.

The matters set out in Sch.1 are not an exhaustive list of directors' obligations, but only guidelines for the court, which may treat any other conduct as evidencing unfitness: *Re Amaron Ltd* [1998] B.C.C. 264. This is so even where there is a statutory provision which might be applied to the conduct of the director (e.g. the giving of a preference to a particular creditor, or the re-use of a defunct company's name in contravention of IA 1986 s.216): the court is not bound by the statutory language but may take a broader view and have regard to the concept in general terms (*Re Sykes (Butchers) Ltd* [1998] B.C.C. 484; *Re Migration Services International Ltd* [2000] B.C.C. 1,095).

In *Re Bath Glass Ltd* (1988) 4 B.C.C. 130 at 133, Peter Gibson J. said: "To reach a finding of unfitness the court must be satisfied that the director has been guilty of a serious failure or serious failures, whether deliberately or through incompetence, to perform those duties of directors which are attendant on the privilege of trading through companies with limited liability. Any misconduct of the respondent qua director may be relevant, even if it does not fall within a specific section of the Companies Act or the Insolvency Act". The court denied in *Cathie v Secretary of State for Business, Innovation and Skills* [2011] EWHC 3026 (Ch) that once a finding of misconduct had been proved the director had to show exceptional circumstances in order to avoid a determination of unfitness.

In *Re Lo-Line Electric Motors Ltd* [1988] Ch. 447 at 496; (1988) 4 B.C.C. 415 at 419; Browne-Wilkinson V.C. said: "Ordinary commercial misjudgment is in itself not sufficient to justify disqualification. In the normal case, the conduct complained of must display a lack of commercial probity although I have no doubt that in an extreme case of gross negligence or total incompetence disqualification could be appropriate".

In *Re Polly Peck International plc, Secretary of State for Trade & Industry v Ellis (No.2)* [1993] B.C.C. 890 at 894, Lindsay J. said that he would "pay regard to the clear thread derived from the authorities that whatever else is required of a respondent's conduct if he is to be disqualified, it must at least be 'serious'".

However, it should be borne in mind that in *Re Sevenoaks Stationers (Retail) Ltd* [1991] Ch. 164 at 176; [1990] B.C.C. 765 at 773 (the leading case on disqualification for "unfitness") Dillon L.J. warned against treating such statements as "judicial paraphrases of the words of the statute, which fall to be construed as a matter of law in lieu of the words of the statute".

In *Re Landhurst Leasing plc* [1999] 1 B.C.L.C. 286 at 344, Park J. observed that in disqualification cases the relevant standard of conduct "is more frequently described as a standard of 'probity' and 'competence' than stated in the traditional terms of care, skill and diligence". The standard may vary depending upon the nature and size of the company and the role which the defendant played in its affairs. Where it has been established that a defendant's conduct has fallen below the standard of probity and competence, a disqualification order must be made, even though this is not thought necessary in the public interest: *Re Grayan Building Services Ltd* [1995] Ch. 241; [1995] B.C.C. 554. The question for the court to determine is whether the director's conduct, *as shown by the evidence*, demonstrates unfitness—not whether, at the time of the hearing, the person is or continues to be unfit.

The fact that the director himself honestly believed that what he was doing was not wrong does not excuse him, if on an objective view his conduct justifies a finding of unfitness: *Goldberg v Secretary of State for Trade and Industry* [2003] EWHC 2843 (Ch); [2004] 1 B.C.L.C. 597.

In the leading Scottish case, *Secretary of State for Trade and Industry v Blackwood*, 2003 S.L.T. 120 the court stressed that a failure to act reasonably (e.g. in deciding to continue to trade) did not necessarily lead to the conclusion that the person concerned was unfit to be a director. In such circumstances directors could not be expected to have wholly dispassionate minds, but might tend to cling to hope.

A number of reported cases have been concerned with a particular issue: the failure by a company and its directors to set aside sufficient funds to meet Crown debts for PAYE, NIC and VAT, in effect using this money as working capital as insolvency looms. The views expressed by different judges in these cases have ranged between treating such Crown debts as "quasi-trust moneys" (Harman J., *Re Wedgecraft Ltd* (unreported, March 7, 1986)), on the one hand, to a refusal to draw any distinction between these and other debts (Hoffmann J., in *Re Dawson Print Group Ltd* (1987) 3 B.C.C. 322), on the other. Prior to the ruling of the Court of Appeal in *Re Sevenoaks Stationers (Retail) Ltd* (above), a consensus had emerged among the judges in the Chancery Division which took a middle line between these extremes, holding that the failure to pay such moneys over to the Crown was, though not a breach of trust, "more serious" and "more culpable" than the non-payment of commercial debts (*Re Stanford Services Ltd* (1987) 3

B.C.C. 326; *Re Lo-Line Electric Motors Ltd* [1988] Ch. 477; (1988) 4 B.C.C. 415). However, in the *Sevenoaks Stationers* case passages from the judgment of Hoffmann J. in *Dawson Print* were approved, and the ruling given that non-payment of a Crown debt cannot automatically be treated as evidence of unfitness; it is necessary to look more closely in each case to see what the significance, if any, of the non-payment of the Crown debt is. In more recent cases, emphasis has been put on another factor: that the company has pursued a policy of deliberately discriminating between creditors. This may be seen as evidence of unfitness regardless of the status of those who are discriminated against but, in the nature of things, it is very often the Crown which is disadvantaged by such a policy. (See *Secretary of State for Trade and Industry v McTighe* [1997] B.C.C. 224, and contrast *Official Receiver v Dhaliwall* [2006] 1 B.C.L.C. 285, where non-payment was held, in the circumstances, not to amount to unfitness.) The fact that there has been correspondence or negotiations with the Revenue authorities may count in the director's favour, and its absence weigh against him: *Re Funtime Ltd* [2000] 1 B.C.L.C. 247; *Re Structural Concrete Ltd* [2001] B.C.C. 578; *Re Amaron Ltd* [1998] B.C.C. 264; *Re Hopes (Heathrow) Ltd* [2001] 1 B.C.L.C. 575 at 581; *Cathie v Secretary of State for Business, Innovation and Skills* [2011] EWHC 3026 (Ch).

One item in Sch.1 para.7, perhaps deserves some comment: "the extent of the director's responsibility for any failure by the company to supply any goods or services which have been paid for (in whole or in part)". This reflects the general anxiety (especially in consumer circles) about the lack of protection given by the law to members of the public who have made payments to a company (e.g. for goods on mail-order) and find that they rank as mere unsecured creditors if it goes into liquidation, perhaps losing everything. Attempts to secure preferential treatment by law for such prepayments were defeated during the debates on the Insolvency Bill in 1985, but the present provision was inserted instead, so that the courts can use disqualification as a sanction against the irresponsible use of such prepayments to boost a company's ailing cash-flow—as was the case in *Re City Pram & Toy Co Ltd* [1998] B.C.C. 537. But the practice was held not to be improper in *Re Uno plc* [2004] EWHC 933 (Ch); [2006] B.C.C. 725.

Other types of conduct which have been held to be evidence of "unfitness" include:

- failure to keep proper books of account and/or to make statutory returns (*Re Rolus Properties Ltd* (1988) 4 B.C.C. 446; *Re Western Welsh International System Buildings Ltd* (1988) 4 B.C.C. 449; *Re T & D Services (Timber Preservation & Damp Proofing Contractors) Ltd* [1990] B.C.C. 592; *Re Chartmore Ltd* [1990] B.C.L.C. 673; *Re Carecraft Construction Co Ltd* [1994] 1 W.L.R. 172; [1993] B.C.C. 336; *Re Synthetic Technology Ltd, Secretary of State for Trade & Industry v Joiner* [1993] B.C.C. 549; *Re New Generation Engineers Ltd* [1993] B.C.L.C. 435; *Re A & C Group Services Ltd* [1993] B.C.L.C. 1297; *Re Pamstock Ltd* [1994] B.C.C. 264; *Re Firedart Ltd* [1994] 2 B.C.L.C. 340; *Re Park House Properties Ltd* [1998] B.C.C. 847; *Official Receiver v Stern (No.2)* [2001] EWCA Civ 1787; [2004] B.C.C. 581);

- trading or continuing to draw remuneration while insolvent (*Re Western Welsh International System Buildings Ltd* (above)); *Re Ipcon Fashions Ltd* (1989) 5 B.C.C. 773; *Re Melcast (Wolverhampton) Ltd* [1991] B.C.L.C. 288; *Re Cargo Agency Ltd* [1992] B.C.C. 388; *Re City Investment Centres Ltd* [1992] B.C.L.C. 956; *Re Synthetic Technology Ltd, Secretary of State for Trade & Industry v Joiner* (above); *Re Firedart Ltd* (above); *Secretary of State for Trade & Industry v McTighe* [1997] B.C.C. 224; *Re Park House Properties Ltd* (above); *Re City Pram & Toy Co Ltd* (above); *Secretary of State for Trade & Industry v Van Hengel* [1995] B.C.C. 173; *Re Amaron Ltd* [1998] B.C.C. 264; *Official Receiver v Stern (No.2)* (above)); *Re Vintage Hallmark plc* [2006] EWHC 2761 (Ch); [2007] 1 B.C.L.C. 788;

- inadequate capitalisation (*Re Chartmore Ltd* (above); *Re Austinsuite Furniture Ltd* [1992] B.C.L.C. 1047; *Re Pamstock Ltd* (above)); or trading (as a public company) in breach of the statutory minimum capital requirements (*Secretary of State for Trade and Industry v Hollier* [2006] EWHC 1804 (Ch); [2007] B.C.C. 11;

- trading with succession of "phoenix" companies and/or using a prohibited company name (*Re Travel Mondial Ltd* [1991] B.C.C. 224; *Re Swift 736 Ltd* [1993] B.C.C. 312; *Re Linvale Ltd* [1993] B.C.L.C. 654; *Re Migration Services International Ltd* [2000] B.C.C. 1095);

- issuing false invoices or other financial statements: *Kappler v Secretary of State for Trade and Industry* [2006] B.C.C. 845; *Re Trans Tec plc (No.2)* [2006] EWHC 2110 (Ch); [2007] 2 B.C.L.C. 495;

- making misrepresentations to customers, suppliers of funds and others: *Secretary of State for Business, etc. v Sullman* [2008] EWHC 3179 (Ch); [2010] B.C.C. 500;

- generating fictitious funds by manipulating ("kiting") cheques (*Secretary of State for Trade and Industry v Swan (No.2)* [2005] EWHC 603 (Ch); [2005] B.C.C. 596); *Re City Truck Group Ltd (No.2)* [2007] EWHC 350 (Ch); [2008] B.C.C. 76;

- misapplication of company's funds or property (*Re Keypak Homecare Ltd (No.2)* [1990] B.C.C. 117; *Re Tansoft Ltd* [1991] B.C.L.C. 339; *Re City Investment Centres Ltd* (above); *Re Austinsuite Furniture Ltd* (above); *Re Synthetic Technology Ltd, Secretary of State for Trade & Industry v Joiner* (above); *Re Park House Properties Ltd* (above); *Secretary of State for Trade and Industry v Blunt* [2006] B.C.C. 112); *Re Mea Corp Ltd* [2006] EWHC 1846 (Ch); [2007] B.C.C. 288; *Secretary of State for Business, Innovation and Skills v Doffman* [2010] EWHC 3175 (Ch);

- irresponsible intra-group loans, etc. (*Re Continental Assurance Co of London plc* [1996] B.C.C. 888; *Re Dominion International Group plc (No.2)* [1996] 1 B.C.L.C. 572; *Official Receiver v Stern (No.2)* (above));

- drawing excessive remuneration (*Re Synthetic Technology Ltd, Secretary of State for Trade & Industry v Joiner* (above); *Re A & C Group Services Ltd* (above));

- irresponsible delegation (*Re Burnham Marketing Services Ltd, Secretary of State for Trade & Industry v Harper* [1993] B.C.C. 518);

- continuing to incur liabilities after trading had ceased (*Re McNulty's Interchange Ltd* (1988) 4 B.C.C. 533; *Re Ipcon Fashions Ltd* (above));

- dishonesty, deception and self-dealing (*Re Godwin Warren Control Systems plc* [1992] B.C.C. 557; *Official Receiver v Doshi* [2001] 2 B.C.L.C. 235; *Re Bunting Electric Manufacturing Co Ltd* [2005] EWHC 3345 (Ch); [2006] 1 B.C.L.C. 550; *Re City Truck Group Ltd* (above); it is immaterial whether the director's dishonesty has been towards the company itself or its clients or creditors: *Re JA Chapman & Co Ltd* [2003] EWHC 532 (Ch); [2003] 2 B.C.L.C. 206);

- breach of trust or fiduciary duty (*Secretary of State for Trade & Industry v Van Hengel* (above); *Re Dominion International Group plc (No.2)* (above));

- giving a preference to a particular creditor or paying creditors selectively (*Re Living Images Ltd* [1996] B.C.C. 112; *Secretary of State for Trade & Industry v McTighe* (above); *Re Funtime Ltd* [2000] 1 B.C.L.C. 247; *Re Structural Concrete Ltd* [2001] B.C.C. 578);

- failure to co-operate with official receiver or the FSA, lack of frankness with the court, or dishonesty as a witness; *Re JA Chapman & Co Ltd* [2003] EWHC 532 (Ch); [2003] 2 B.C.L.C. 206 (*Re Tansoft Ltd* (above); *Re Godwin Warren Control Systems plc* (above); *Secretary of State for Trade & Industry v Reynard* [2002] B.C.C. 813); *Ghassemian v Secretary of State for Trade and Industry* [2006] EWHC 1715 (Ch); [2007] B.C.C. 229;

- entering into a transaction at an undervalue, contrary to s.238 or giving financial assistance, contrary to CA 2006: *Re Genosyis Technology Management Ltd* [2006] EWHC 989 (Ch); [2007] 1 B.C.L.C. 208; *Secretary of State for Business, Enterprise and Regulatory Reform v Poulter* [2009] B.C.C. 608.

Of course, in many cases several of these features will have been present at the same time. Other considerations, such as the number of companies involved, their size, the extent of their losses, the position of the individual concerned in the managerial hierarchy and his experience (or lack of it), and whether there has been a lack of probity, may also go towards deciding whether unfitness has been established or determining the length of the order to be made.

Factors which have weighed with the court in deciding that a disqualification order should not be made, or that a reduced period of disqualification would be appropriate, have included the following:

- acting on professional advice (*Re Bath Glass Ltd* (1988) 4 B.C.C. 130; *Re McNulty's Interchange Ltd* (1988) 4 B.C.C. 533; *Re Douglas Construction Services Ltd* (1988) 4 B.C.C. 553; *Re C U Fittings Ltd* (1989) 5 B.C.C. 210; *Re Cladrose Ltd* [1990] B.C.C. 11; *Re Bradcrown Ltd* [2001] 1 B.C.L.C. 547);

- employing a qualified company secretary or finance director (*Re Rolus Properties Ltd* (1988) 4 B.C.C. 446; *Re Douglas Construction Services Ltd* (above));

- absence of dishonesty (*Re Bath Glass Ltd* (1988) 4 B.C.C. 130; *Re Lo-Line Electric Motors Ltd* [1988] Ch. 477; (1988) 4 B.C.C. 415; *Re D J Matthews (Joinery Design) Ltd* (1988) 4 B.C.C. 513; *Re Burnham Marketing Services Ltd* [1993] B.C.C. 518);

- readiness to make a personal financial commitment to the company or the fact that the respondent has sustained heavy personal loss (*Re Bath Glass Ltd* (above); *Re Douglas Construction Services Ltd* (above); *Re Swift 736 Ltd* [1993] B.C.C. 312);

- reliance on regular budgets and forecasts (even though subsequently shown to be inaccurate) (*Re Bath Glass Ltd* (above));

- the fact that events outside the director's control contributed to the company's misfortunes (*Re Bath Glass Ltd* (above); *Re Cladrose Ltd* (above));

- evidence that the same company or other companies have been successfully and properly run by the respondent (*Re D J Matthews (Joinery Design) Ltd* (above); *Re A & C Group Services Ltd* [1993] B.C.L.C. 1297; *Re Pamstock Ltd* [1994] B.C.C. 264);

- the fact that the business was kept going on assurances of help from others (*Re C U Fittings Ltd* (above));

- the respondent's relative youth and inexperience (*Re Chartmore Ltd* [1990] B.C.L.C. 673; *Re Austinsuite Furniture Ltd* [1992] B.C.L.C. 1047);

- the fact that the director was fully occupied as the company's production manager and had left board matters to others (ibid.);

- the fact that the proceedings have been a long time coming to a hearing and that the respondent has already been under a disqualification by reason of bankruptcy (*Re A & C Group Services Ltd* (above));

- the fact that the respondent has admitted his responsibility (*Re Carecraft Construction Co Ltd* [1994] 1 W.L.R. 172; [1993] B.C.C. 336; *Re Aldermanbury Trust plc* [1993] B.C.C. 598).

In *Re Melcast (Wolverhampton) Ltd* [1991] B.C.L.C. 288 the court held that a ten-year disqualification was merited, but reduced the term to seven years on account of the respondent's age (68). Where other directors have also been disqualified, the court may take into account the period of disqualification imposed on them for the purpose of comparison, but should not be over-influenced by this fact (*Re Swift 736 Ltd* (above)).

One or two cases have been reported in which the court has found that the defendant's conduct was not such as to warrant a finding of unfitness. These include *Re Stephenson Cobbold Ltd* [2001] B.C.C. 38; *Re Cubelock Ltd* [2001] B.C.C. 523; and *Secretary of State for Trade and Industry v Creegan* [2002] 1 B.C.L.C. 99.

The wording of Sch.1 appears to be directed primarily at those directors who have taken an active part in the company's affairs, rather than those whose role has been nominal or who have involved themselves only intermittently; but such passive conduct may also in itself justify a finding of unfitness. Even a non-executive director of a small family company is liable to disqualification if he merely stands by, or is content to remain in ignorance, while those who are actively managing the company run up losses or allow accounts, records and returns to fall into disarray: see *Re Peppermint Park Ltd* [1998] B.C.C. 23; *Re Park House Properties Ltd* [1998] B.C.C. 847; *Re Galeforce Pleating Ltd* [1999] 2 B.C.L.C. 704; *Official Receiver v Stern (No.2)* [2001] EWCA Civ 1787; [2001] 1 B.C.L.C. 119; *Re Bradcrown Ltd* [2002] B.C.C. 428; *Secretary of State for Trade and Industry v Thornbury* [2007] EWHC 3202 (Ch); [2008] 1 B.C.L.C. 139; *Re AG (Manchester) Ltd* [2008] EWHC 64 (Ch); [2008] 1 B.C.L.C. 321; *Secretary of State for Trade and Industry v Thornbury* [2007] EWHC 3202 (Ch); [2008] B.C.C. 768. In *Re City Truck Group Ltd (No.2)* [2007] EWHC 350 (Ch); [2008] B.C.C. 76 a director who passively acquiesced in a fraud perpetrated by a co-director was disqualified for the same period as the principal offender (12 years). The courts in these cases have stressed that the title "director" is not to be accepted by any person without a corresponding assumption of responsibility—the more so if he is paid remuneration.

On the other hand, it has been a factor counting against a director that he held a high position in the company: the greater the status and its rewards, the higher the standard for measuring its responsibilities (*Re Barings plc, Secretary of State for Trade & Industry v Baker* [1998] B.C.C. 583; *Re Barings plc (No.5)* [1999] 1 B.C.L.C. 433 (affirmed on appeal [2001] B.C.C. 273); and see *Secretary of State for Trade and Industry v Swan (No.2)* [2005] EWHC 603 (Ch); [2005] B.C.C. 596). On similar reasoning individuals whose business consisted of acting as nominee directors of large numbers of "offshore" companies for remuneration have been severely dealt with: see *Re Kaytech International plc* [1999] B.C.C. 390; and *Official Receiver v Vass* [1999] B.C.C. 516. The fact that the respondent relied on his fellow-directors may be relevant, but only if it is shown that he was justified in doing so, and for this purpose evidence on his part of his perception of their reliability is material: *Secretary of State for Trade & Industry v Dawes* [1997] B.C.C. 121. In *Re Landhurst Leasing plc* [1999] 1 B.C.L.C. 286, relatively junior directors were held to have been justified in relying on their more experienced co-directors. The court held that a proper degree of delegation and division of responsibility by the board (not amounting to a total abrogation of responsibility by any individual director or directors) was permissible. An absentee director will not necessarily be excused: *Re Peppermint Park Ltd* [1998] B.C.C. 23. The position of a director who dissented from or opposed the course of conduct being followed by his colleagues as disaster loomed has brought a mixed reaction from the judges. Plainly, much depends on the circumstances. In *Re Peppermint Park Ltd* (above) it was said ([1996] B.C.C. 23 at 26) that the director in question should, at least, have resigned his directorship. However in *Secretary of State for Trade & Industry v Taylor, Re C S Holidays Ltd* [1997] 1 W.L.R. 407; [1997] B.C.C. 172 the fact that a director whose protests went unheeded did not resign was not held to be fatal.

On the topic of unfitness, see further Walters and Davis-White, *Directors' Disqualification & Insolvency Restrictions*, Ch.5; and Totty and Moss, *Insolvency*, B1–18 et seq.

S.9(2)
This incorporates the definition of "becomes insolvent" from s.6(2).

S.9(4). (5)
Power is given to the Secretary of State to revise the statutory criteria of unfitness by subordinate legislation.

Disqualification for competition infringements

9A   Competition disqualification order

9A(1)   [Court's power] The court must make a disqualification order against a person if the following two conditions are satisfied in relation to him.

9A(2)   [First condition] The first condition is that an undertaking which is a company of which he is a director commits a breach of competition law.

9A(3)   [Second condition] The second condition is that the court considers that his conduct as a director makes him unfit to be concerned in the management of a company.

9A(4)   [Breach of competition law] An undertaking commits a breach of competition law if it engages in conduct which infringes any of the following–

(a)   the Chapter 1 prohibition (within the meaning of the Competition Act 1998) (prohibition on agreements, etc. preventing, restricting or distorting competition);

(b)   the Chapter 2 prohibition (within the meaning of that Act) (prohibition on abuse of a dominant position);

(c)   Article 81 of the Treaty establishing the European Community (prohibition on agreements, etc. preventing, restricting or distorting competition);

(d)   Article 82 of that Treaty (prohibition on abuse of a dominant position).

9A(5)   [Decision as to unfitness] For the purpose of deciding under subsection (3) whether a person is unfit to be concerned in the management of a company the court–

(a)   must have regard to whether subsection (6) applies to him;

(b)   may have regard to his conduct as a director of a company in connection with any other breach of competition law;

(c)   must not have regard to the matters mentioned in Schedule 1.

9A(6)   [Application of s.9A(6)] This subsection applies to a person if as a director of the company–

(a)   his conduct contributed to the breach of competition law mentioned in subsection (2);

(b)   his conduct did not contribute to the breach but he had reasonable grounds to suspect that the conduct of the undertaking constituted the breach and he took no steps to prevent it;

(c)   he did not know but ought to have known that the conduct of the undertaking constituted the breach.

9A(7)   [Knowledge of breach immaterial] For the purposes of subsection (6)(a) it is immaterial whether the person knew that the conduct of the undertaking constituted the breach.

9A(8)   [Conduct of an undertaking] For the purposes of subsection (4)(a) or (c) references to the conduct of an undertaking are references to its conduct taken with the conduct of one or more other undertakings.

9A(9) **[Maximum disqualification period]** The maximum period of disqualification under this section is 15 years.

9A(10) **[Who may make application]** An application under this section for a disqualification order may be made by the OFT or by a specified regulator.

9A(11) **[Application of Competition Act 1998 s.60]** Section 60 of the Competition Act 1998 (c. 41) (consistent treatment of questions arising under United Kingdom and Community law) applies in relation to any question arising by virtue of subsection (4)(a) or (b) above as it applies in relation to any question arising under Part 1 of that Act.

GENERAL NOTE

Sections 9A–9E were inserted into CDDA 1986 by the Enterprise Act 2002 s.204, introducing the novel regime of competition disqualification orders (CDOs) and competition disqualification undertakings (CDUs). This reform took effect from June 20, 2003: see the Enterprise Act 2002 (Commencement No.3, Transitional and Transitory Provisions and Savings) Order 2003 (SI 2003/1397 (C. 60)) arts 1, 2(1) and Sch.1. Under s.9A the court is empowered to make a disqualification order against a person who is or has been a director or shadow director of a company which has committed a breach of competition law where the court considers that his conduct as a director, taken together with his conduct in relation to one or more other undertakings, makes him unfit to be concerned in the management of a company. In parallel with s.6 of the Act, if there is a finding of unfitness the obligation to make an order is mandatory, and the period of disqualification runs to a maximum of 15 years. However, in contrast with s.6, no minimum period is specified. Application to the court may be made by the Office of Fair Trading or by a number of regulators who are specified in s.9E(2). Section 9B makes provision for the Office of Fair Trading or a specified regulator to accept a CDU instead of a CDO. Powers of investigation of suspected breaches of competition law are conferred on these authorities by s.9C. The court may give a disqualified person leave to act as with other disqualification orders and undertakings; and s.8A has been extended by the insertion of s.8A(2A) so as to give the court power to reduce the length of a CDU or discharge it altogether, as with an undertaking accepted under s.1A.

Guidance notes on this regime and its scope and procedure have been published by the Office of Fair Trading and were republished in revised form on June 29, 2010.

S.9A(1)–(3)
A CDO may be made only against a person who is or was at the time of the breach a director or shadow director (s.9E(5)). On analogy with orders made under s.6, the present section would probably be construed as applying also to a de facto director. But note that it is not necessary that the person should himself have committed a breach of competition law, still less have been convicted of one. What is relevant is whether his company (and possibly also other undertakings—see s.9A(8)) have committed such a breach. If that is so, and he is or was at the relevant time a director, the statutory conditions are satisfied.

"The court" for the purpose of the present provisions is the High Court or, in Scotland, the Court of Session (s.9E(3)). "Conduct" includes omission: see s.9E(4).

S.9A(4), (11)
The breaches of competition law which may lead to a CDO or CDU are specified in this subsection, and include both the domestic and EU competition regimes. The Competition Act 1998 did not deal with the law relating to mergers, but the competition aspects of this topic were later reformed by the Enterprise Act 2002 Pt 3. This Act does not include any measure making CDOs or CDUs available for breaches of Pt 3.

S.9A(5)–(8)
Although a finding of unfitness is at the heart of both ss.6–8 and s.9A, the criteria relevant in the two cases are different. In particular, no reference may be made to Sch.1 when considering a case for a competition order or undertaking, and the question of the company's solvency is of no concern. As with ss.6–8, the conduct of the person as a director of another company may be brought into account, but only in so far as it involves a breach of competition law. Section 9A(6) makes it plain that it may not be necessary to show any causal connection between the director's conduct and the breach: indeed, this and the succeeding subsections, together with s.9E(4), arguably go further in penalising ignorance and inaction than the common law has so far done, or in cases under s.6 such as *Re Barings plc (No.5)* [1999] 1 B.C.L.C. 433. Subsections (5)(b) and (8) extend the picture so that account may be taken of breaches of competition law committed by companies other than the "lead" company: the former deals with the individual's conduct as a director of those other companies, while in the latter case it is the conduct of the lead company taken together with the conduct of other undertakings (including, but not necessarily confined to, its

subsidiaries) which is referred to. Where subs.(8) is invoked, the individual need not be a director of these other companies.

S.9A(9)
Curiously, although the court must make an order if unfitness is found, no minimum period is specified. This is confirmed by s.1(2).

S.9A(10)
For the specified regulators, see s.9E(2).

9B   Competition undertakings

9B(1)   [Application of s.9B] This section applies if–

   (a)   the OFT or a specified regulator thinks that in relation to any person an undertaking which is a company of which he is a director has committed or is committing a breach of competition law,

   (b)   the OFT or the specified regulator thinks that the conduct of the person as a director makes him unfit to be concerned in the management of a company, and

   (c)   the person offers to give the OFT or the specified regulator (as the case may be) a disqualification undertaking.

9B(2)   [Acceptance of undertaking] The OFT or the specified regulator (as the case may be) may accept a disqualification undertaking from the person instead of applying for or proceeding with an application for a disqualification order.

9B(3)   [Disqualification undertaking] A disqualification undertaking is an undertaking by a person that for the period specified in the undertaking he will not–

   (a)   be a director of a company;

   (b)   act as receiver of a company's property;

   (c)   in any way, whether directly or indirectly, be concerned or take part in the promotion, formation or management of a company;

   (d)   act as an insolvency practitioner.

9B(4)   [Undertaking not apply where leave of court] But a disqualification undertaking may provide that a prohibition falling within subsection (3)(a) to (c) does not apply if the person obtains the leave of the court.

9B(5)   [Maximum disqualification period] The maximum period which may be specified in a disqualification undertaking is 15 years.

9B(6)   [Concurrent disqualification periods] If a disqualification undertaking is accepted from a person who is already subject to a disqualification undertaking under this Act or to a disqualification order the periods specified in those undertakings or the undertaking and the order (as the case may be) run concurrently.

9B(7)   [Application of s.9A(4)–(8)] Subsections (4) to (8) of section 9A apply for the purposes of this section as they apply for the purposes of that section but in the application of subsection (5) of that section the reference to the court must be construed as a reference to the OFT or a specified regulator (as the case may be).

GENERAL NOTE

Both the Office of Fair Trading and the regulators specified in s.9E(2) are empowered to accept competition undertakings in lieu of a disqualification order made by the court. Undertakings are to all intents and purposes the same as orders. As is the case under s.1A, the OFT or regulator is not required to accept the offer of an undertaking, but may take the matter to court. Undertakings are recorded on the public register kept under s.18. The notes to s.1A are generally applicable.

S.9B(4)
An application for leave is made under s.17. Note also that a person who has given an undertaking is entitled to apply to the court under s.8A to have the undertaking discharged or its period reduced, in which case s.8A(2A) applies. "The court" here means the High Court or, in Scotland, the Court of Session (s.8A(3)(a)).

S.9B(5)
There is no minimum period.

S.9B(6)
Compare ss.1(3) and 1A(3).

9C Competition investigations

9C(1) [Power to investigate] If the OFT or a specified regulator has reasonable grounds for suspecting that a breach of competition law has occurred it or he (as the case may be) may carry out an investigation for the purpose of deciding whether to make an application under section 9A for a disqualification order.

9C(2) [Application of Competition Act 1998 ss.26–30] For the purposes of such an investigation sections 26 to 30 of the Competition Act 1998 (c. 41) apply to the OFT and the specified regulators as they apply to the OFT for the purposes of an investigation under section 25 of that Act.

9C(3) [Application of s.9C(4)] Subsection (4) applies if as a result of an investigation under this section the OFT or a specified regulator proposes to apply under section 9A for a disqualification order.

9C(4) [Duty to notify before application] Before making the application the OFT or regulator (as the case may be) must–

(a) give notice to the person likely to be affected by the application, and

(b) give that person an opportunity to make representations.

General Note

Under the Competition Act 1998 the OFT has wide powers of investigation. This section makes it plain that comparable powers may be used for the purpose of deciding whether to make an application for a competition disqualification order or accept an undertaking in lieu, and also confers similar powers of investigation on a specified regulator.

S.9C(4)
The application referred to means the application to the court. There is no statutory obligation to give notice before carrying out the investigation.

9D Co-ordination

9D(1) [Power to make regulations] The Secretary of State may make regulations for the purpose of co-ordinating the performance of functions under sections 9A to 9C (relevant functions) which are exercisable concurrently by two or more persons.

9D(2) [Application of Competition Act 1998 s.54(5)–(7)] Section 54(5) to (7) of the Competition Act 1998 (c. 41) applies to regulations made under this section as it applies to regulations made under that section and for that purpose in that section–

(a) references to Part 1 functions must be read as references to relevant functions;

(b) references to a regulator must be read as references to a specified regulator;

(c) a competent person also includes any of the specified regulators.

9D(3)   **[Procedure for regulations]** The power to make regulations under this section must be exercised by statutory instrument subject to annulment in pursuance of a resolution of either House of Parliament.

9D(4)   **[Scope of regulations]** Such a statutory instrument may–

    (a)   contain such incidental, supplemental, consequential and transitional provision as the Secretary of State thinks appropriate;

    (b)   make different provision for different cases.

General Note

No regulations appear to have yet been made under this section.

9E   Interpretation

9E(1)   **[Application of s.9E]** This section applies for the purposes of sections 9A to 9D.

9E(2)   **[The specified regulators]** Each of the following is a specified regulator for the purposes of a breach of competition law in relation to a matter in respect of which he or it has a function–

    (a)   the Office of Communications;

    (b)   the Gas and Electricity Markets Authority;

    (c)   the Water Services Regulation Authority;

    (d)   the Office of Rail Regulation;

    (e)   the Civil Aviation Authority.

9E(3)   **[The court]** The court is the High Court or (in Scotland) the Court of Session.

9E(4)   **[Conduct]** Conduct includes omission.

9E(5)   **[Shadow director]** Director includes shadow director.

General Note

The regulators specified for the purposes of ss.9A–9D are listed in s.9E(2).

Section 9E(2)(a) was amended by the Communications Act 2003 s.406(1) and Sch.17 para.83 as from December 29, 2003 (see the Office of Communications Act 2002 (Commencement No.3 and Communications Act 2003 (Commencement No.2) Order 2003 (SI 2003/3142) art.3(1) and Sch.1). The reference was formerly to the Director General of Telecommunications.

S.9E(3)

The county court has no jurisdiction in relation to competition orders and undertakings.

Other cases of disqualification

10   Participation in wrongful trading

10(1)   **[Court's power]** Where the court makes a declaration under section 213 or 214 of the Insolvency Act 1986 that a person is liable to make a contribution to a company's assets, then, whether or not an application for such an order is made by any person, the court may, if it thinks fit, also make a disqualification order against the person to whom the declaration relates.

10(2)   **[Maximum period]** The maximum period of disqualification under this section is 15 years.

General Note

The sections referred to relate to fraudulent trading as well as wrongful trading. The court is empowered to make a disqualification order in addition to imposing personal liability on the person concerned (who, in the case of fraudulent trading, will not necessarily have been a director or shadow director). This it may do of its own motion, or on the application of any person. The section appears to assume that the disqualification order will be made in the same proceedings as the declaration of liability, but conceivably it could be the subject of a separate, later application.

According to a note in [1990] I.L. & P. 72 at 73, the respondent in *Re Purpoint Ltd* [1991] B.C.C. 121 was disqualified under this section for two years, as well as being ordered to pay compensation under s.214. See also *Re Brian D Pierson (Contractors) Ltd* [1999] B.C.C. 26 in which in an addendum to the judgment the respondents were disqualified under s.10 for five and two years respectively. In *Re Idessa (UK) Ltd* [2011] EWHC 804 (Ch) the judge did not deal with the disqualification issue but referred the matter to the Secretary of State.

11   Undischarged bankrupts

11(1)   [Offences] It is an offence for a person to act as director of a company or directly or indirectly to take part in or be concerned in the promotion, formation or management of a company, without the leave of the court, at a time when–

(a)   he is an undischarged bankrupt,

(aa)   a moratorium period under a debt relief order applies in relation to him, or

(b)   a bankruptcy restrictions order or a debt relief restrictions order is in force in respect of him.

11(2)   ["The court"] "The court" for this purpose is the court by which the person was adjudged bankrupt or, in Scotland, sequestration of his estates was awarded.

11(3)   [Requirements for leave of court] In England and Wales, the leave of the court shall not be given unless notice of intention to apply for it has been served on the official receiver; and it is the latter's duty, if he is of opinion that it is contrary to the public interest that the application should be granted, to attend on the hearing of the application and oppose it.

11(4)   ["Company"] In this section "company" includes a company incorporated outside Great Britain that has an established place of business in Great Britain.

GENERAL NOTE

The ban here imposed on an undischarged bankrupt (or person subject to a BRO or BRU) is analogous in many ways to a disqualification order. Some of the notes to s.1 are relevant to this section. See also IR 1986 rr.6.203, 6.251 et seq., the Enterprise Act 2002 (Disqualification from Office: General) Order 2006 (SI 2006/1722) and the Education (Disqualification Provisions: Bankruptcy and Mental Health) (England) Regulations 2006 (SI 2006/2198).

Section 11(1) was altered so as to include para.(1)(b) by the Enterprise Act 2002 s.257(2) Sch.21 para.5, as from April 1, 2004: see the Enterprise Act 2002 (Commencement No.4 and Transitional Provisions and Savings) Order 2003 (SI 2003/2093 (C. 85)) art.2(2) and Sch.2. The reference to a bankruptcy restrictions order includes a bankruptcy restrictions undertaking (IA 1986 Sch.4A para.8). Section 11(1)(aa) was inserted, and s.11(1)(b) amended, by the Tribunals, Courts and Enforcement Act 2007 s.108(3) and Sch.20 para.16(1)–(3) as from April 6, 2009. Section 11(4) was inserted by the Companies Act 2006 (Consequential Amendments, Transitional Provisions and Savings) Order 2009 (SI 2009/1941) art.2(1) and Sch.1 para.85(7) as from October 1, 2009.

The offence of acting as a director while an undischarged bankrupt under this section is an absolute offence: there is no requirement of mens rea: *R. v Doring* [2002] EWCA Crim 1695; [2002] B.C.C. 838. It is no defence that the defendant genuinely believes that he has been discharged from his bankruptcy: *R. v Brockley* [1994] B.C.C. 131. A bankrupt who acts as a director in contravention of s.11 continues to be criminally liable even if the bankruptcy is later annulled (because his debts have been paid in full) or discharged: *Inland Revenue Commissioners v McEntaggart* [2004] EWHC 3431 (Ch); [2007] 1 B.C.C. 260.

A contract made by a company which is being unlawfully managed in breach of s.11 is not unenforceable on the grounds of illegality: *Hill v Secretary of State for the Environment, Food and Rural Affairs* [2005] EWHC 696 (Ch); [2006] 1 B.C.L.C. 601. The judgment in this case also contains a discussion of the expression "concerned in the management" of a company.

An undischarged bankrupt is also disqualified from acting as trustee of a charity and from serving on various other bodies, under provisions analogous to those which apply to a person subject to a disqualification order: see the note to s.1 above.

41

For cases where a bankrupt sought the leave of the court under this, or an equivalent, provision see *Re McQuillan* (1989) 5 B.C.C. 137; *Re Altim Pty Ltd* [1968] 2 N.S.W.R. 762.

12   Failure to pay under county court administration order

12(1)   **[Effect of s.12(2)]** The following has effect where a court under section 429 of the Insolvency Act 1986 revokes an administration order under Part VI of the County Courts Act 1984.

12(2)   **[Restriction on person]** A person to whom that section applies by virtue of the order under section 429(2)(b) shall not, except with the leave of the court which made the order, act as director or liquidator of, or directly or indirectly take part or be concerned in the promotion, formation or management of, a company.

GENERAL NOTE

The "administration order" here referred to relates to an individual debtor and has no connection with an administration order made in respect of an insolvent company under IA 1985 s.8 or Sch.B1. The *Practice Direction: Directors Disqualification Proceedings* [2007] B.C.C. 862 (reproduced as App.VI to this *Guide*) applies to applications under s.12(2). Note prospective amendment by TCEA 2007 s.106 and Sch.16 para.5.

12A   Northern Irish disqualification orders

12A   A person subject to a disqualification order under the Company Directors Disqualification (Northern Ireland) Order 2002–

(a)   shall not be a director of a company, act as receiver of a company's property or in any way, whether directly or indirectly, be concerned or take part in the promotion, formation or management of a company unless (in each case) he has the leave of the High Court of Northern Ireland, and

(b)   shall not act as an insolvency practitioner.

GENERAL NOTE

This provision was inserted into CDDA 1986 by IA 2000 s.7(1), with effect from April 2, 2001. In consequence, a disqualification order made by a court in Northern Ireland will have the same effect as one made by a court in the rest of the United Kingdom, and a contravention of a Northern Ireland order will carry the same civil and criminal liabilities and penalties: see ss.13–15.

12B   Northern Irish disqualification undertakings

12B   A person subject to a disqualification undertaking under the Company Directors Disqualification (Northern Ireland) Order 2002–

(a)   shall not be a director of a company, act as receiver of a company's property or in any way, whether directly or indirectly, be concerned or take part in the promotion, formation or management of a company unless (in each case) he has the leave of the High Court of Northern Ireland, and

(b)   shall not act as an insolvency practitioner.

GENERAL NOTE

Section 7(2) and (3) of IA 2000 anticipated that legislation would be introduced for Northern Ireland allowing a person to give a disqualification undertaking in lieu of a disqualification order made by a court. This has been done by the Company Directors Disqualification (Northern Ireland) Order 2002 (SI 2002/3150 (NI 4)), and recognition of such undertakings throughout the UK is given effect by the present section, which was inserted into the Act by the Insolvency Act 2000 (Company Directors Disqualification Undertakings) Order 2004 (SI 2004/1941), operative from September 1, 2004. Other sections of the Act have been amended (but not retrospectively) to reflect this change in the law.

Consequences of contravention

13 Criminal penalties

13 If a person acts in contravention of a disqualification order or disqualification undertaking or in contravention of section 12(2), 12A or 12B, or is guilty of an offence under section 11, he is liable–

(a) on conviction on indictment, to imprisonment for not more than 2 years or a fine or both; and

(b) on summary conviction, to imprisonment for not more than 6 months or a fine not exceeding the statutory maximum, or both.

GENERAL NOTE

The reference to s.12B was inserted by the Insolvency Act 2002 (Company Directors Disqualification Undertakings) Order 2004 (SI 2004/1941) art.2(2), as from September 1, 2004.

The breach of a disqualification order or of the analogous ban on an undischarged bankrupt is a criminal offence, as well as potentially attracting civil sanctions under s.15.

Reported prosecutions under this section include *R. v Theivendran* (1992) 13 Cr. App. R. (S) 601; *R. v Brockley* [1994] B.C.C. 131; *R. v Teece* (1994) 15 Cr. App. R. 302. Conviction may lead to a confiscation order, assessed by reference to the benefit that the offender has personally received: *R. v Seager & Blatch* [2009] EWCA Crim 1303; [2010] 1 W.L.R. 815; [2012] B.C.C. 124; *Hill v Department for Business, Innovation and Skills* [2011] EWHC 3436 (Admin); [2012] B.C.C. 151.

On the "statutory maximum", and penalties generally, see IA 1986 s.430 and Sch.10.

14 Offences by body corporate

14(1) **[Offence re officer]** Where a body corporate is guilty of an offence of acting in contravention of a disqualification order or disqualification undertaking or in contravention of section 12A, and it is proved that the offence occurred with the consent or connivance of, or was attributable to any neglect on the part of any director, manager, secretary or other similar officer of the body corporate, or any person who was purporting to act in any such capacity he, as well as the body corporate, is guilty of the offence and liable to be proceeded against and punished accordingly.

14(2) **[Where managers are members]** Where the affairs of a body corporate are managed by its members, subsection (1) applies in relation to the acts and defaults of a member in connection with his functions of management as if he were a director of the body corporate.

GENERAL NOTE

This is a standard provision, equivalent to IA 1986 s.432.

"Body corporate" and "officer" are defined in CA 2006 s.1173(1), and these definitions are incorporated into the present Act by s.22(6). A body corporate includes a company incorporated elsewhere than in Great Britain, but excludes a corporation sole and a Scottish firm. On the meaning of "officer", see the note to IA 1986 s.206(3).

15 Personal liability for company's debts where person acts while disqualified

15(1) **[Personal liability]** A person is personally responsible for all the relevant debts of a company if at any time–

(a) in contravention of a disqualification order or disqualification undertaking or in contravention of section 11, 12A, or 12B of this Act he is involved in the management of the company, or

(b) as a person who is involved in the management of the company, he acts or is willing to act on instructions given without the leave of the court by a person whom he knows at that time–

   (i) to be the subject of a disqualification order made or disqualification undertaking accepted under this Act or under the Company Directors Disqualification (Northern Ireland) Order 2002, or

   (ii) to be an undischarged bankrupt.

15(2)   [Joint and several liability] Where a person is personally responsible under this section for the relevant debts of a company, he is jointly and severally liable in respect of those debts with the company and any other person who, whether under this section or otherwise, is so liable.

15(3)   [Relevant debts of company] For the purposes of this section the relevant debts of a company are–

(a)   in relation to a person who is personally responsible under paragraph (a) of subsection (1), such debts and other liabilities of the company as are incurred at a time when that person was involved in the management of the company, and

(b)   in relation to a person who is personally responsible under paragraph (b) of that subsection, such debts and other liabilities of the company as are incurred at a time when that person was acting or was willing to act on instructions given as mentioned in that paragraph.

15(4)   [Person involved in management] For the purposes of this section, a person is involved in the management of a company if he is a director of the company or if he is concerned, whether directly or indirectly, or takes part, in the management of the company.

15(5)   [Presumption] For the purposes of this section a person who, as a person involved in the management of a company, has at any time acted on instructions given without the leave of the court by a person whom he knew at that time–

(a)   to be the subject of a disqualification order made or disqualification undertaking accepted under this Act or under the Company Directors Disqualification (Northern Ireland) Order 2002, or

(b)   to be an undischarged bankrupt,

is presumed, unless the contrary is shown, to have been willing at any time thereafter to act on any instructions given by that person.

General Note

The references to s.12B in s.15(1) and to the 2002 Order in s.15(1) and (2) were inserted by the Insolvency Act 2002 (Company Directors Disqualification Undertakings) Order 2004 (SI 2004/1941) art.2(5), as from September 1, 2004. Section 15(1)(b) and (5) were substituted by the Companies Act 2006 (Consequential Amendments, Transitional Provisions and Savings) Order 2009 (SI 2009/1941) art.2(1) and Sch.1 para.85(9) as from October 1, 2009.

This section makes a person personally liable, without limit, for the debts of a company if he is involved in its management in breach of a disqualification order or undertaking or while he is an undischarged bankrupt or subject to a BRO or BRU. It is very closely analogous to IA 1986 s.217, which deals with the reuse of the name of a former insolvent company—indeed, the two sections are both derived from the same source.

In *Re Prestige Grindings Ltd* [2006] B.C.C. 421 the liquidator sought a declaration that a director and former director of the company were in breach of a disqualification order and an order under s.15 that they should pay the relevant debts of the company. H.H.J. Norris Q.C. ruled (i) that the right conferred by s.15(1) was a right conferred on the creditors concerned and not on the liquidator, so that it was inappropriate to make an order under the CPR appointing him to represent those creditors, and (ii) that the company had a separate right of action (enforceable by her as liquidator) against the defendants for contribution arising out of their joint and several liability for the relevant debts under s.15(2).

For further comment, see the note to IA 1986 s.217.

In *Inland Revenue Commissioners v McEntaggart* [2004] EWHC 3431 (Ch); [2006] 1 B.C.L.C. 476 liability under s.15(1)(a) and (b) was held to continue even after the bankruptcy in question had been annulled (because all the bankruptcy debts had been paid in full).

Supplementary provisions

16   Application for disqualification order

16(1)   [Notice, appearance, etc.] A person intending to apply for the making of a disqualification order by the court having jurisdiction to wind up a company shall give not less than 10 days' notice of his intention to the person against whom the order is sought; and on the hearing of the application the last-mentioned person may appear and himself give evidence or call witnesses.

16(2) [Applicants] An application to a court with jurisdiction to wind up companies for the making against any person of a disqualification order under any of sections 2 to 4 may be made by the Secretary of State or the official receiver, or by the liquidator or any past or present member or creditor of any company in relation to which that person has committed or is alleged to have committed an offence or other default.

16(3) [Appearance etc. of applicant] On the hearing of any application under this Act made by a person falling within subsection (4), the applicant shall appear and call the attention of the court to any matters which seem to him to be relevant, and may himself give evidence or call witnesses.

16(4) [Applicant in s.16(3)] The following fall within this subsection–

(a) the Secretary of State;

(b) the official receiver;

(c) the OFT;

(d) the liquidator;

(e) a specified regulator (within the meaning of section 9E).

GENERAL NOTE

The procedural provisions set out in s.16(1) apply only where application is made to the court having jurisdiction to wind up the company. They will not apply in those cases where the court is empowered of its own motion to make an order (see, e.g. ss.2, 10), "although doubtless the rules of natural justice will require that the person should be given some notice that the court is contemplating making a disqualification order": (*Secretary of State for Trade & Industry v Langridge, Re Cedac Ltd* [1991] Ch. 402 at 414; [1991] B.C.C. 148 at 155). Again, no notice has to be served (although again the rules of natural justice will have effect) where the proceedings are before a court other than that which has winding-up jurisdiction, e.g. in a case brought under s.5 (ibid.)

The requirement that an intended respondent should be given ten days' notice of the intention to apply for an order is directory rather than mandatory. Failure to give proper notice is a procedural irregularity which does not nullify the application (*Secretary of State for Trade & Industry v Langridge, Re Cedac Ltd*, above). This decision (by a majority) of the Court of Appeal effectively overrules the earlier decision of Harman J. in *Re Jaymar Management Ltd* [1990] B.C.C. 303, but leaves undisturbed the ruling given in the latter case that "ten days' notice" means ten clear days, i.e. exclusive of both the date on which notice is given and that on which the proceedings are issued. See also *Secretary of State for Business, Enterprise and Regulatory Reform v Smith* [2009] B.C.C. 497.

There is no obligation to state in the notice the grounds upon which the application will be made (*Secretary of State for Trade and Industry v Langridge, Re Cedac Ltd* (above) at 414; 155) or to specify which is the "lead" company in relation to which it is made or which (if any) "collateral" companies will be included in the proceedings (*Re Surrey Leisure Ltd* [1999] B.C.C. 847 at 853). However, it is clear from cases such as *Re Finelist Ltd* [2003] EWHC 170 (Ch); [2004] B.C.C. 877; and *Secretary of State for Trade and Industry v Gill* [2004] EWHC 175 (Ch); [2005] B.C.C. 24 that in the proceedings themselves the respondent must be given a clear statement of the charges which are brought against him and the evidence in support, and generally an opportunity before the proceedings are begun to proffer explanations for his conduct: see the note to s.7(1).

Although the second part of s.16(1) appears to suggest that the respondent may call oral evidence at the hearing, it is clear from the rules that (exceptional cases apart) evidence must be presented in the form of affidavits and in keeping with the time limits imposed by the rules (*Re Rex Williams Leisure plc* [1994] Ch. 1; [1993] B.C.C. 79 at 83; affirmed [1994] Ch. 350; [1994] B.C.C. 551). It follows that if he wishes to make a submission of no case to answer he must do so when he has seen and considered the applicant's affidavit evidence and that he cannot wait until after the close of the applicant's case at the hearing (ibid.).

Section 16(3) was amended and subs.(4) inserted by the Enterprise Act 2002 s.204(1), (6) and (7), as from June 20, 2003: see the Enterprise Act 2002 (Commencement No.3, Transitional and Transitory Provisions and Savings) Order 2003 (SI 2003/1397 (C. 60)) arts 1, 2(1) and Sch., in keeping with the introduction of competition disqualification orders and undertakings.

17 Application for leave under an order or undertaking

17(1) [Disqualification order by court with jurisdiction to wind up] Where a person is subject to a disqualification order made by a court having jurisdiction to wind up companies, any application for leave for the purposes of section 1(1)(a) shall be made to that court.

17(2) [Disqualification orders made under s.2 or 5] Where–

(a) a person is subject to a disqualification order made under section 2 by a court other than a court having jurisdiction to wind up companies, or

(b) a person is subject to a disqualification order made under section 5,

any application for leave for the purposes of section 1(1)(a) shall be made to any court which, when the order was made, had jurisdiction to wind up the company (or, if there is more than one such company, any of the companies) to which the offence (or any of the offences) in question related.

17(3) [Disqualification undertaking accepted under s.7 or 8] Where a person is subject to a disqualification undertaking accepted at any time under section 7 or 8, any application for leave for the purposes of section 1A(1)(a) shall be made to any court to which, if the Secretary of State had applied for a disqualification order under the section in question at that time, his application could have been made.

17(3A) [Disqualification undertaking accepted under s.9B] Where a person is subject to a disqualification undertaking accepted at any time under section 9B any application for leave for the purposes of section 9B(4) must be made to the High Court or (in Scotland) the Court of Session.

17(4) [Persons subject to two or more disqualification orders] But where a person is subject to two or more disqualification orders or undertakings (or to one or more disqualification orders and to one or more disqualification undertakings), any application for leave for the purposes of section 1(1)(a), 1A(1)(a) or 9B(4) shall be made to any court to which any such application relating to the latest order to be made, or undertaking to be accepted, could be made.

17(5) [Duty of Secretary of State to appear] On the hearing of an application for leave for the purposes of section 1(1)(a) or 1A(1)(a), the Secretary of State shall appear and call the attention of the court to any matters which seem to him to be relevant, and may himself give evidence or call witnesses.

17(6) [Non-application of s.17(5)] Subsection (5) does not apply to an application for leave for the purposes of section 1(1)(a) if the application for the disqualification order was made under section 9A.

17(7) [Duty of OFT and specified regulator to appear etc.] In such a case and in the case of an application for leave for the purposes of section 9B(4) on the hearing of the application whichever of the OFT or a specified regulator (within the meaning of section 9E) applied for the order or accepted the undertaking (as the case may be)–

(a) must appear and draw the attention of the court to any matters which appear to it or him (as the case may be) to be relevant;

(b) may give evidence or call witnesses.

General Note

This section deals with the procedural aspects of an application to the court, by a person who is subject to a disqualification order, for leave to act in relation to the management, etc. of a company during the currency of the order. In consequence of amendments made by IA 2000, it also deals with applications for leave to act during the currency of a disqualification undertaking.

Subsection (4) was amended and subss.(3A), (6) and (7) inserted by the Enterprise Act 2002 s.204(1); (8)–(10), as from June 20, 2003: see the Enterprise Act 2002 (Commencement No.3, Transitional and Transitory Provisions and Savings) Order 2003 (SI 2003/1397 (C. 60)) arts 1, 2(1) and Sch., in keeping with the introduction of competition disqualification orders and undertakings.

On the substantive issues relating to the grant of leave, see the note to s.1(1) above, and see generally T. Clench, (2008) 21 Insolv. Int. 113 and on certain problems of timing, S. Frieze (2009) 22 Insolv. Int. 179.

The *Practice Direction: Directors Disqualification Proceedings* [2007] B.C.C. 862, Pt 4 (reproduced as App.VI to this *Guide*) applies to applications under s.17 and also to analogous applications (e.g. those made under s.12(2)). Subject to ss.12 and 17(2), applications may be made by Practice Form N. 208 under CPR Pt 8, or by application notice in an existing disqualification application. The claim form or application notice and all affidavits and other documents in the application must be served on the Secretary of State.

Evidence in support of an application is by affidavit. However, in relation to disqualification orders made following the *Carecraft* procedure (see the note to s.1 above), it was said in *Re TLL Realisations Ltd* [2000] B.C.C. 998 that the use of affidavit evidence going over matters included in the *Carecraft* statement would not normally be expected and that the parties should be confined to the facts recorded in the statement unless the court required them to be amplified or clarified. Similarly, on an application for leave to act notwithstanding a disqualification undertaking, the applicant may not seek to dispute the correctness of the facts accepted in the undertaking: *Re Morija plc* [2007] EWHC 3055 (Ch); [2008] 2 B.C.L.C. 313. The Court of Appeal in *Re Westmid Packing Services Ltd, Secretary of State for Trade and Industry v Griffiths* [1998] 2 All E.R. 124; [1998] B.C.C. 836 gave guidelines on what is relevant and admissible evidence for the purposes of an application under s.17.

It is common for an application for leave to be made at the time of the original hearing when the order is made. In *Re Dicetrade Ltd, Secretary of State for Trade & Industry v Worth* [1994] B.C.C. 371 at 373, Dillon L.J. said that this course was "desirable" and "in everyone's interests"; and in *Re TLL Realisations Ltd* (above) the Court of Appeal stated that it was highly desirable that a person who faced the possibility of disqualification and in that event might wish to seek leave to act should make application early enough so that the same judge would consider both the application for disqualification and the application for leave. Although some applicants might hope to derive a tactical advantage from isolating the two, since the former would inevitably highlight their misconduct while the latter would tend to focus on mitigation, the interests of justice overall were more likely to be served (and waste avoided) if both aspects of the case were investigated together; and where this tactic was adopted the judge at the second hearing would be entitled to view the evidence with "a proper degree of healthy scepticism".

If an application for leave to act notwithstanding disqualification is made at the same time as the hearing for the disqualification order and does not take up a substantial part of the time of that hearing, it is convenient not to make a separate order in respect of the costs of that application. However, where a separate application for leave is made some time later, it is to be regarded as free-standing for the purposes of costs. The Secretary of State may then be entitled to his costs on a standard basis: alternatively, if he simply intimates to the applicant (or to his solicitors) any particular points that are relied on so that they can be drawn to the attention of the court, but states that he does not oppose the grant of the relief sought, it may be appropriate to make no order as to costs (*Re Dicetrade Ltd* (above)). Despite this observation, in *Re TLL Realisations Ltd* (above) attention was drawn to the fact that the Secretary of State is placed in a special position by s.17(2) and that this can be attributed to the misconduct of the applicant; and so, it was said, it should be the ordinary consequence that he be allowed his costs.

An order granting leave to act may be made on an interim basis (e.g. pending the hearing of an appeal) and may also be made for a finite period—for instance, to enable the director to sort out matters pertinent to the company's business before the disqualification takes full effect (*Re Amaron Ltd* [1998] B.C.C. 264).

18   Register of disqualification orders and undertakings

18(1)   [Regulations re furnishing information] The Secretary of State may make regulations requiring officers of courts to furnish him with such particulars as the regulations may specify of cases in which–

(a)   a disqualification order is made, or

(b)   any action is taken by a court in consequence of which such an order or a disqualification undertaking is varied or ceases to be in force, or

(c)   leave is granted by a court for a person subject to such an order to do any thing which otherwise the order prohibits him from doing; or

(d)   leave is granted by a court for a person subject to such an undertaking to do anything which otherwise the undertaking prohibits him from doing;

and the regulations may specify the time within which, and the form and manner in which, such particulars are to be furnished.

18(2) **[Register of orders]** The Secretary of State shall, from the particulars so furnished, continue to maintain the register of orders, and of cases in which leave has been granted as mentioned in subsection (1)(c).

18(2A) **[Particulars to be included in register]** The Secretary of State must include in the register such particulars as he considers appropriate of–

    (a)   disqualification undertakings accepted by him under section 7 or 8;

    (b)   disqualification undertakings accepted by the OFT or a specified regulator under section 9B;

    (c)   cases in which leave has been granted as mentioned in subsection (1)(d).

18(3) **[Deletion of orders no longer in force]** When an order or undertaking of which entry is made in the register ceases to be in force, the Secretary of State shall delete the entry from the register and all particulars relating to it which have been furnished to him under this section or any previous corresponding provision and, in the case of a disqualification undertaking, any other particulars he has included in the register.

18(4) **[Inspection of register]** The register shall be open to inspection on payment of such fee as may be specified by the Secretary of State in regulations.

18(4A) **[Extension of s.18]** Regulations under this section may extend the preceding provisions of this section, to such extent and with such modifications as may be specified in the regulations, to disqualification orders or disqualification undertakings made under the Company Directors Disqualification (Northern Ireland) Order 2002.

18(5) **[Regulations by statutory instrument etc.]** Regulations under this section shall be made by statutory instrument subject to annulment in pursuance of a resolution of either House of Parliament.

GENERAL NOTE

Section 18(2), (4A) amended by the Companies Act 2006 (Consequential Amendments, Transitional Provisions and Savings) Order 2009 (SI 2009/1941) art.2(1) and Sch.1 para.85(10) as from October 1, 2009.

The Secretary of State, acting through the registrar of companies, has kept a register of disqualification orders since first being required to do so by CA 1976 s.29. The register, which also records cases where the court has given leave to act, is open to public inspection. It is possible to access without charge extracts from the register on the Companies House website at the internet address *http://www.companieshouse.gov.uk* where names of individual directors can be keyed in to determine if they appear on the register. This section provides for the continuation of the register, and brings forward from the pre-consolidation Acts other rules relating to the register.

This section has been extensively amended in order to accommodate the introduction of disqualification undertakings and competition disqualification orders and undertakings: see generally the notes to ss.1A, 7 and 9A–9E.

In *Cathie v Secretary of State for Business, Innovation and Skills* [2011] EWHC 2234 (Ch) the court granted a stay (pending an appeal against a disqualification order) directing the registrar of companies to withhold recording the order where publication could give rise to irreversible reputational damage to the applicant.

Where a confidentiality order under CA 1985 ss.732B–732F is in force, prohibiting disclosure of a director's home address, the prohibition applies to this register: see the Companies (Disqualification Orders) (Amendment) Regulations 2002 (SI 2002/689, effective April 2, 2002). [CA 2006 has no equivalent to these sections.]

S.18(1)

The regulations currently in force are the Companies (Disqualification Orders) Regulations 2009 (SI 2009/2471), which prescribe forms on which the relevant officers of the courts are to make returns.

The Department of Trade and Industry (now the DBIS) in January 1998 set up a rogue director telephone hotline intended to assist in catching directors and undischarged bankrupts who are acting in breach of the disqualification legislation. The number of the hotline, which is open 24 hours a day, is 0845 601 3546, email: intelligence.live@insolvency.gsi.gov.uk.

S.18(2A)

No forms are prescribed in which particulars of undertakings were to be recorded, corresponding to the forms on which court officers are to notify details of disqualification orders. Instead, it is left to the discretion of the Secretary of State to determine what particulars are appropriate.

Subsection (2A) was modified by the insertion of para.(b) by the Enterprise Act 2002 (Commencement No.3, etc.) Order 2003 (SI 2003/1397 (C. 60) arts 1, 2(1) and Sch., as from June 20, 2003.

S.18(4A)

Disqualification orders made by the courts in Northern Ireland were made effective throughout the rest of the United Kingdom from April 2, 2001 by s.12A: see the note to that section. This subsection allows for provision to be made to enable details of such disqualification orders to be recorded on the register. This was done by the Companies (Disqualification Orders) Regulations 2001 (SI 2001/967) art.9, effective April 6, 2001, and has since been extended so as to include disqualification undertakings by an amendment made to s.18(4A) by the Insolvency Act 2000 (Company Directors Disqualification Undertakings) Order 2004 (SI 2004/1941) art.2(6), as from September 1, 2004.

19 Special savings from repealed enactments

19 Schedule 2 to this Act has effect–

(a) in connection with certain transitional cases arising under sections 93 and 94 of the Companies Act 1981, so as to limit the power to make a disqualification order, or to restrict the duration of an order, by reference to events occurring or things done before those sections came into force,

(b) to preserve orders made under section 28 of the Companies Act 1976 (repealed by the Act of 1981), and

(c) to preclude any applications for a disqualification order under section 6 or 8, where the relevant company went into liquidation before 28th April 1986.

GENERAL NOTE

This section, read in conjunction with Sch.2, makes transitional arrangements, preserving existing disqualification orders and making it clear that the new grounds of disqualification introduced by IA 1985 do not apply retrospectively to events before April 28, 1986, the date when the relevant provisions of that Act become operative.

Miscellaneous and general

20 Admissibility in evidence of statements

20(1) **[General rule on admissibility of statements]** In any proceedings (whether or not under this Act), any statement made in pursuance of a requirement imposed by or under sections 6 to 10, 15 or 19(c) of, or Schedule 1 to, this Act, or by or under rules made for the purposes of this Act under the Insolvency Act 1986, may be used in evidence against any person making or concurring in making the statement.

20(2) **[Limits on use of statement in criminal proceedings]** However, in criminal proceedings in which any such person is charged with an offence to which this subsection applies

(a) no evidence relating to the statement may be adduced, and

(b) no question relating to it may be asked,

by or on behalf of the prosecution, unless evidence relating to it is adduced, or a question relating to it is asked, in the proceedings by or on behalf of that person.

20(3) **[Offences to which s.20(2) applies]** Subsection (2) applies to any offence other than–

(a) an offence which is–

(i) created by rules made for the purposes of this Act under the Insolvency Act 1986, and

(ii) designated for the purposes of this subsection by such rules or by regulations made by the Secretary of State;

(b) an offence which is–

(i) created by regulations made under any such rules, and

      (ii) designated for the purposes of this subsection by such regulations;

  (c) an offence under section 5 of the Perjury Act 1911 (false statements made otherwise than on oath); or

  (d) an offence under section 44(2) of the Criminal Law (Consolidation) (Scotland) Act 1995 (false statements made otherwise than on oath).

20(4)   **[Procedure for making regulations]** Regulations under subsection (3)(a)(ii) shall be made by statutory instrument and, after being made, shall be laid before each House of Parliament.

GENERAL NOTE

This section is similar to IA 1986 s.433, and is derived from the same source. Both sections were amended by the Youth Justice and Criminal Evidence Act 1999 s.59 and Sch.3 para.8, with effect from April 14, 2000, by adding new subss.(2) to (4). This was part of a general reform imposing restrictions on the use in criminal proceedings of statements given under compulsion, following rulings of the European Court of Human Rights. A similar amendment was made to IA 1986 s.219 by IA 2000 s.11. See the notes to IA 1986 ss.219 and 433. The enactment of s.20(2) should in most cases avoid the need to defer the hearing of disqualification applications until criminal proceedings based on the same facts have been disposed of: see *Secretary of State for Trade and Industry v Crane* [2001] 2 B.C.L.C. 222.

    Note that there is no similar restriction on the use of such statements in proceedings for disqualification orders: see the Introductory note to CDDA 1986 at p.1 above.

20A   Legal professional privilege

20A   In proceedings against a person for an offence under this Act nothing in this Act is to be taken to require any person to disclose any information that he is entitled to refuse to disclose on grounds of legal professional privilege (in Scotland, confidentiality of communications).

GENERAL NOTE

Section 20A was inserted by the Companies Act 2006 (Consequential Amendments etc.) Order 2008 (SI 2008/948) art.3(1) and Sch.1 para.106(3) as from April 6, 2008.

21   Interaction with Insolvency Act 1986

21(1)   **[Reference to official receiver]** References in this Act to the official receiver, in relation to the winding up of a company or the bankruptcy of an individual, are to any person who, by virtue of section 399 of the Insolvency Act 1986, is authorised to act as the official receiver in relation to that winding up or bankruptcy; and, in accordance with section 401(2) of that Act, references in this Act to an official receiver includes a person appointed as his deputy.

21(2)   **[Insolvency Act Pts I to VII]** Sections 1A, 6 to 10, 13, 14, 15, 19(c) and 20 of, and Schedule 1 to, this Act and sections 1 and 17 of this Act as they apply for the purposes of those provisions are deemed included in Parts I to VII of the Insolvency Act 1986 for the purposes of the following sections of that Act–

    section 411 (power to make insolvency rules);

    section 414 (fees orders);

    section 420 (orders extending provisions about insolvent companies to insolvent partnerships);

    section 422 (modification of such provisions in their application to recognised banks).

21(3)   **[Application of Insolvency Act s.434]** Section 434 of that Act (Crown application) applies to sections 1A, 6 to 10, 13, 14, 15, 19(c) and 20 of, and Schedule 1 to, this Act and sections 1 and 17 of this Act as they apply for the purposes of those provisions as it does to the provisions of that Act which are there mentioned.

21(4) **[Summary proceedings in Scotland]** For the purposes of summary proceedings in Scotland, section 431 of that Act applies to summary proceedings for an offence under section 11 or 13 of this Act as it applies to summary proceedings for an offence under Parts I to VII of that Act.

GENERAL NOTE

This section requires a reader of this Act to make extensive cross-references to IA 1986. Most of the matters referred to are administrative or procedural in nature, but the extension of the company director disqualification regime so that it applies to the former members of insolvent partnerships is both bold and surprising. The justification for the imposition of a director disqualification order is invariably stated to be that the delinquent director has abused the privilege of limited liability (see, e.g. the Cork Committee's *Report*, para.1807). To extend this penalty to partners, whose personal liability is necessarily unlimited, is anomalous.

The IR 1986, and in particular the review and appeal procedures prescribed by IR 1986 rr.7.47, 7.49A, apply to orders made under this Act: *Re Tasbian Ltd (No.2)* [1992] B.C.C. 322; *Re Probe Data Systems Ltd (No.3)* [1992] B.C.C. 110.

S.21(2)
In regard to the entry for s.411 see the Insolvent Companies (Reports on Conduct of Directors) Rules 1996 (SI 1996/1909, as amended by SI 2001/764 and 2003/2096) and the Insolvent Companies (Reports on Conduct of Directors) (Scotland) Rules 1996 (SI 1996/1910 (S 154), as amended by SI 2001/768).

In regard to the entry for s.420, reference should be made to the Insolvent Partnerships Order 1994 (SI 1994/2421, as amended).

Regulations relating to LLPs have been made under the LLP Act 2000 ss.14, 15: see the LLPR 2001 (SI 2001/1090) reg.4 (as amended).

S.21(3)
The Crown is not bound generally, but only in relation to matters specified in paras (a)–(e) of IA 1986 s.434. See the note to that section.

21A   Bank insolvency

21A   Section 121 of the Banking Act 2009 provides for this Act to apply in relation to bank insolvency as it applies in relation to liquidation.

GENERAL NOTE

Section 21A was inserted by the Banking Act 2009 (C. 1) s.121, as from February 21, 2009. This section applies in the case where a failing bank is the subject of government intervention. See Vol.1, p.6.

21B   Bank administration

21B   Section 155 of the Banking Act 2009 provides for this Act to apply in relation to bank administration as it applies in relation to liquidation.

GENERAL NOTE

Section 21B was inserted by the Banking Act 2009 (C. 1) s.155(4), as from February 21, 2009. This section applies in the case where a failing bank is the subject of government intervention. See Vol.1, p.6.

21C   Building society insolvency and special administration

21C   Section 90E of the Building Societies Act 1986 provides for this Act to apply in relation to building society insolvency and building society special administration as it applies in relation to liquidation.

GENERAL NOTE

Section 21C was inserted by the Building Societies (Insolvency and Special Administration) Order 2009 (SI 2009/805) art.12, as from March 29, 2009. It applies in the case where a failing building society is the subject of government intervention. See Vol.1, p.6.

22 Interpretation

22(1) **[Effect]** This section has effect with respect to the meaning of expressions used in this Act, and applies unless the context otherwise requires.

22(2) **["Company"] "Company"** means–

(a) a company registered under the Companies Act 2006 in Great Britain, or

(b) a company that may be wound up under Part 5 of the Insolvency Act 1986 (unregistered companies).

22(3) **[Application of Insolvency Act ss.247, 251]** Section 247 in Part VII of the Insolvency Act 1986 (interpretation for the first Group of Parts of that Act) applies as regards references to a company's insolvency and to its going into liquidation; and **"administrative receiver"** has the meaning given by section 251 of that Act and references to acting as an insolvency practitioner are to be read in accordance with section 388 of that Act.

22(4) **["Director"] "Director"** includes any person occupying the position of director, by whatever name called.

22(5) **["Shadow director"] "Shadow director"**, in relation to a company, means a person in accordance with whose directions or instructions the directors of the company are accustomed to act (but so that a person is not deemed a shadow director by reason only that the directors act on advice given by him in a professional capacity).

22(6) **["Body corporate" and "officer"] "Body corporate"** and **"officer"** have the same meaning as in the Companies Acts (see section 1173(1) of the Companies Act 2006).

22(7) **["The Companies Acts"] "The Companies Acts"** has the meaning given by section 2(1) of the Companies Act 2006.

22(8) **[References to former legislation]** Any reference to provisions, or a particular provision, of the Companies Acts or the Insolvency Act 1986 includes the corresponding provisions or provision of corresponding earlier legislation.

22(9) **[Application of Companies Acts]** Subject to the provisions of this section, expressions that are defined for the purposes of the Companies Acts (see section 1174 of, and Schedule 8 to, the Companies Act 2006) have the same meaning in this Act.

22(10) **[References to acting as receiver]** Any reference to acting as receiver–

(a) includes acting as manager or as both receiver and manager, but

(b) does not include acting as administrative receiver;

and **"receivership"** is to be read accordingly.

GENERAL NOTE

This section largely borrows or reproduces definitions from other Acts, notably CA 1985 and IA 1985. Further comment on the particular terms listed may be located by reference to App.I.

    Section 22(7), (8) and (9) were amended by the Companies Act 2006 (Consequential Amendments etc.) Order 2008 (SI 2008/948) art.3(1) and Sch.1 para.106(4), as from April 6, 2008. Section 22(2), (6), (7), (8) were substituted, and s.22(9) amended, by the Companies Act 2006 (Consequential Amendments, Transitional Provisions and Savings) Order 2009 (SI 2009/1941) art.2(1) and Sch.1 para.85(11) as from October 1, 2009.

S.22(2)

On the term "unregistered company", see the note to IA 1986 s.220. But the question whether the Act applies to all such bodies is not free from doubt. That it applies to foreign companies has been settled by such cases as *Re Eurostem Maritime Ltd* [1987] P.C.C. 190; and *Official Receiver v Brady* [1999] B.C.C. 258. So far as concerns building societies, incorporated friendly societies, insolvent partnerships, NHS Foundation Trusts, EEIGs, open-ended investment companies and limited liability partnerships the position is covered by specific legislation: see ss.22A–22D, IA 1986 s.420 and the Introductory note on p.1. It is in relation to other bodies not specifically dealt with by such legislation that the situation is unclear, e.g. unincorporated friendly societies and industrial and provident societies. It could quite reasonably be argued (for example) that since the legislation has considered it necessary to make specific provision for *incorporated* friendly societies, unincorporated friendly societies are excluded. On industrial and provident societies, see the argument of C. Mills, (1997) 13 I.L. & P. 182 and the note on p.1.

S.22(4)
A provision to this effect is standard in companies legislation. The intention is to include the case where a corporate body uses such labels as "governor" or "trustee" for members of its board.

In addition to ss.6–9, some other sections of the Act extend to shadow directors (and de facto directors), e.g. s.10 (participation in wrongful trading).

S.22(5)
The definition of a shadow director is the same as that in IA 1986 s.251 and similar to that in CA 2006 s.251(1), (2): see the note to IA 1986 s.251. The term obviously covers the case where a puppet board is set up which acts on the dictates of a non-director who masterminds the company's activities from behind the scene. However, it could also apply to a holding company which exercises a degree of control over decision-making by the board of its subsidiary. In *Re Hydrodan (Corby) Ltd* [1994] B.C.C. 161 at 163 Millett J. said:

> "What is needed is, first, a board of directors claiming and purporting to act as such; and, secondly, a pattern of behaviour in which the board did not exercise any discretion or judgment of its own, but acted in accordance with the directions of others."

A bank, also, might be caught within the definition if it had given "directions or instructions" to a client company (as distinct from giving professional advice, or merely imposing conditions upon which it was prepared to make or continue a loan) at a time when insolvency was threatening: *Re a Company (No.005009 of 1987)* (1988) 4 B.C.C. 424. In *Re Tasbian Ltd (No.3)* [1992] B.C.C. 358 the Court of Appeal held that there was an arguable case, sufficient to allow the issue to go to trial, that an accountant who had been brought in on the initiative of a debenture holder as a consultant and "company doctor" to advise and assist in the recovery of an ailing company was a shadow director, having allegedly gone further than merely acting as a watch-dog or adviser.

In *Secretary of State for Trade and Industry v Deverell* [2001] Ch. 340; [2000] B.C.C. 1,057 the law was summarised by Morritt L.J. in a number of propositions, including the following:

(1)   The term is to be construed in the normal way, and not more strictly because it may have penal consequences.

(2)   It is not necessary that the person's influence should be exercised over the whole field of the company's activities.

(3)   Whether any particular communication is to be construed as a direction or instruction is to be objectively ascertained by the court: the parties' own understanding or description of its nature may be relevant but cannot be conclusive.

(4)   Non-professional advice may come within the statutory description: the concepts of "direction" and "instruction" do not exclude the concept of "advice".

(5)   It is not necessary (though probably sufficient) to show that the properly appointed directors or some of them cast themselves in a subservient role or surrendered their own discretions.

On this basis two so-called "consultants" were held to be shadow directors.

The judgment of Finn J. in the Australian case *ASC v AS Nominees Ltd* (1995) 133 A.L.R. 1 at 51–53 examines the concept of "shadow director" in some detail. Here it was held that a person employed in a managerial role fell within the definition despite denials by directors that they acted on his directions or instructions, and even though the board did not always follow his advice. The evidence showed that this advice exceeded what would normally fall within the proper performance of his managerial duties.

In a later Australian case, *Buzzle Operations Pty Ltd (in liq.) v Apple Computer Australia Pty Ltd* [2011] NSWCA 109, which appears likely to be cited by the English courts, the New South Wales Supreme Court considered that "in accordance" required a causal connection between the instruction or wishes and the action, and "accustomed" meant a pattern of compliance over a period of time. The instructions or wishes must be in relation to board activities and not just managerial decisions, the distinction being one of fact. However, they do not have to be in relation to every board activity and one must approach this subject with an eye to the ultimate question: who is effectively making board decisions? The following propositions were drawn from the leading authorities:

(1) Not every person whose advice is in fact heeded as a general rule by the board is to be classed as a shadow (or de facto) director.

(2) If a person has a genuine interest of his or her own in giving advice to the board (e.g. as a bank or mortgagee), the mere fact that the board will tend to take that advice to preserve it from the person's wrath will not make the person a shadow director.

(3) The vital factor is that the shadow director has the potentiality of control: the fact that he or she does not seek to control every facet of the company or the fact that from time to time the board disregards the advice is of little moment.

(4) Millett J.'s proposition (in *Hydrodan*) that the evidence must show "something more" than just being in a position of control must be shown. The whole of the facts of the case must be shown to see whether that power to control was put into practice.

(5) Although there are problems with cases where the board of the company splits into a majority and minority faction, so long as the influence controls the real decision makers, the person providing the influence may be a shadow director.

In *Secretary of State for Trade and Industry v Becker* [2002] EWHC 2200 (Ch); [2003] 1 B.C.L.C. 555 it was alleged that the respondent was a shadow director of the company because its sole director had acted on his directions or instructions on one occasion. It was held that this was not sufficient: there had to be proof of a pattern of conduct.

A shadow director is to be distinguished from a de facto director. In *Re Hydrodan* (above), Millett J. continued at 163:

"A de facto director is a person who assumes to act as a director. He is held out as a director by the company, and claims and purports to be a director, although never actually or validly appointed as such. To establish that a person was a de facto director of a company it is necessary to plead and prove that he undertook functions in relation to the company which could properly be discharged only by a director. It is not sufficient to show that he was concerned in the management of the company's affairs or undertook tasks in relation to its business which can properly be performed by a manager below board level."

This passage was cited by Lord Hope in *Holland v HM Revenue and Customs (Re Paycheck Services 3 Ltd)* [2010] UKSC 51; [2011] B.C.C. 1, where the concepts of "shadow director" and "de facto director" were considered for the first time by the Supreme Court.

In *Re Hydrodan* Millett J. had expressed the view that the two terms "did not overlap" and "were mutually exclusive". However, Lewison J. in *Re Mea Corp Ltd* [2006] EWHC 1846 (Ch); [2007] B.C.C. 288 expressed the view that there is no conceptual difficulty in concluding that a person could be both a shadow director and a de facto director simultaneously, and in *Re Paycheck Services 3 Ltd* Lord Hope agreed. It had already been held that it is not improper for the Secretary of State to allege as alternatives that a respondent was one or the other: *Re H Laing Demolition Building Contractors Ltd* [1998] B.C.C. 561.

It had been said on more than one occasion that there is no single test of de facto directorship (*Secretary of State for Trade and Industry v Tjolle* [1998] B.C.C. 282 at 290; *Re Kaytech International plc* [1999] B.C.C. 390 at 402), and in *Re Paycheck Services 3 Ltd* this view was endorsed by all the members of the Supreme Court, who did not attempt to redefine the concept of de facto director afresh, but were generally content to cite passages from the judgments delivered in the lower courts in the cases discussed below, with express or tacit approval and very little qualification.

The following have emerged as among the factors which may be relevant in determining whether a person should be categorised as a de facto director:

- whether he was part of the company's "governing structure";

- whether he was "truly in a position to exercise the powers and discharge the functions of a director" of the company;

- whether he had "assumed the status and functions of a company director" or "assumed to act as a director of the company".

The "degree of control" which the person exercised over the affairs of the company has also been regarded as material. There is no doubt also that the judges have regard to the objectives of the legislation—in disqualification cases, for example, the protection of the public.

In *Re Richborough Furniture Ltd* [1996] B.C.C. 155, the respondent's acts were consistent with directorship, but they were also tasks which could have been done by a professional or employee, or by someone performing consultancy services. He escaped liability, as did a person whose role was primarily that of accountant and company secretary in *Secretary of State for Trade and Industry v Hickling* [1996] B.C.C. 678; and a woman described as only "a manager and a compliant and dutiful wife" in *Re Red Label Fashions Ltd* [1999] B.C.C. 308; cf. *Re Paycheck Services 3 Ltd* [2009] B.C.C. 37 (wife performed clerical tasks and also signed cheques, but no "real influence" in corporate governance); *Gemma Ltd v Davies* [2008] EWHC 546 (Ch); [2008] 2 B.C.L.C. 281 (similar facts). In contrast, the respondent in *Secretary of State for Trade and Industry v Jones* [1999] B.C.C. 336, who had acted as management consultant to the company and was also a 50 per cent shareholder, and had (inter alia) signed cheques and dealt with a major customer, was held to have stepped over the borderline and become a de facto director. In several cases, a person who was an undischarged bankrupt or already subject to a disqualification order and who had run the company's business while using a "front man" as a nominee director has been held to have acted as a de facto director: see *Re Moorgate Metals Ltd* [1995] B.C.C. 143; *Re BPR Ltd* [1998] B.C.C. 259; *Re Kaytech International plc* [1999] B.C.C. 390; *Official Receiver v Vass* [1999] B.C.C. 516. (For further discussion of the concept of de facto director, see the Australian case *ASC v AS Nominees Ltd* (1995) 133 A.L.R. 1; and A Dodsworth, (1995) 11 I.L. & P. 176.) See also *Re Mea Corp Ltd* [2006] EWHC 1846 (Ch); [2007] B.C.C. 288; *Primlake Ltd v Matthews Associates* [2006] EWHC 1227 (Ch); [2007] 1 B.C.L.C. 666 (defendant allowed to perform all management functions apart from giving instructions to banks and signing cheques); *Shepherds Investments Ltd v Walters* [2006] EWHC 836 (Ch); [2007] 2 B.C.L.C. 202 (person held out by both the company and himself as a director); *Statek Corp v Alford* [2008] EWHC 32 (Ch); [2008] B.C.C. 266 (defendant told he would be appointed a director and acted as such, although did not receive accounts and minutes of directors' meetings); *Re Idessa (UK) Ltd* [2011] EWHC 804 (Ch) (defendant had "acted on an equal footing" with the company's sole de jure director and had "exercised real influence" over the company's affairs).

A person who has resigned as a director or ceased to hold office may be held to be a de facto director if he continues qua shareholder to take management decisions: *Re Windows West Ltd* [2002] B.C.C. 760; cf. *Re Promwalk Services Ltd* [2002] EWHC 2688 (Ch); [2003] 2 B.C.L.C. 305 (where in fact the purported resignation was held to have been ineffective). In *Secretary of State for Business, Enterprise and Regulatory Reform v Poulter* [2009] B.C.C. 608 Mrs Registrar Derrett said that, at least where the person concerned remained in management, the evidential burden in practice moved to him to show that his role and functions had changed, so that he was no longer acting as director.

The use by a person of the description director (e.g. as a courtesy title) does not necessarily mean that he or she is a de facto director or has been held out as such; *Secretary of State for Trade and Industry v Tjolle* [1998] B.C.C. 282.

Where one company is a director (whether de jure or de facto) of another, it does not follow that the directors of the former are shadow directors or de facto directors of the latter. The ruling of the Supreme Court in *Re Paycheck Services 3 Ltd* makes it very clear that to make such an allegation good it must be shown that they (or the individual director in question) became such by their (or his) own actions. In *Re Paycheck Services 3 Ltd* the defendant was the only active director of the principal company in a group and effectively the "directing mind and will" of all the group companies, one of which was the corporate director of the subject company. The majority held that, even in this extreme situation, the principle of the separate corporate personality should apply and that unless the defendant had played some direct part in the affairs of the subject company he was not a de facto director of it. (See also *Secretary of State for Trade and Industry v Laing* [1996] 2 B.C.L.C. 324.) Similarly, where a person was the sole director of a company which had set up a subsidiary to provide corporate directors for numerous subject companies, he was held to be neither a shadow director nor a de facto director of the subject companies. He had not played any part in their management at any stage or given instructions to its salaried directors, or taken any step which indicated that either he or his company had assumed the status and functions of a director. (*Secretary of State for Trade and Industry v Hall* [2006] EWHC 1995 (Ch); [2009] B.C.C. 190.)

On this topic, see further Walters and Davis-White, *Directors' Disqualification & Insolvency Restrictions*, Ch.3 and S. Griffin (2011) 24 Insolv. Int. 44.

The Act also applies to shadow directors of building societies (see s.22A(3)), but not to shadow directors of incorporated friendly societies (s.22B(3)).

22A   Application of Act to building societies

22A(1)   [To building societies as to companies] This Act applies to building societies as it applies to companies.

22A(2)   [Interpretation] References in this Act to a company, or to a director or an officer of a company include, respectively, references to a building society within the meaning of the Building Societies Act 1986 or to a director or officer, within the meaning of that Act, of a building society.

22A(3)   ["Shadow director"] In relation to a building society the definition of "shadow director" in section 22(5) applies with the substitution of "building society" for "company".

22A(4)   [Schedule 1] In the application of Schedule 1 to the directors of a building society, references to provisions of the Companies Act 2006 or the Insolvency Act 1986 include references to the corresponding provisions of the Building Societies Act 1986.

GENERAL NOTE

Section 22A(4) was amended by the Companies Act 2006 (Consequential Amendments etc.) Order 2008 (SI 2008/948) art.3(1) and Sch.1 para.106(5) as from April 6, 2008.

22B   Application of Act to incorporated friendly societies

22B(1)   [Application as to companies] This Act applies to incorporated friendly societies as it applies to companies.

22B(2)   [Interpretation] References in this Act to a company, or to a director or an officer of a company include, respectively, references to an incorporated friendly society within the meaning of the Friendly Societies Act 1992 or to a member of the committee of management or officer, within the meaning of that Act, of an incorporated friendly society.

22B(3)   [Shadow directors] In relation to an incorporated friendly society every reference to a shadow director shall be omitted.

22B(4)   [Schedule 1] In the application of Schedule 1 to the members of the committee of management of an incorporated friendly society, references to provisions of the Companies Act 2006 or the Insolvency Act 1986 include references to the corresponding provisions of the Friendly Societies Act 1992.

GENERAL NOTE

Section 22B(4) was amended by the Companies Act 2006 (Consequential Amendments etc.) Order 2008 (SI 2008/948) art.3(1) and Sch.1 para.106(6), as from April 6, 2008.

S.22B(3)
Contrast the position as regards shadow directors of building societies: see s.22A(3). In regard to unincorporated friendly societies, see the note to s.22(2).

22C   Application of Act to NHS foundation trusts

22C(1)   [Application of Act to NHS foundation trusts] This Act applies to NHS foundation trusts as it applies to companies within the meaning of this Act.

22C(2)   [References to company or director] References in this Act to a company, or to a director or officer of a company, include, respectively, references to an NHS foundation trust or to a director or officer of the trust; but references to shadow directors are omitted.

22C(3)   [Application of Sch.1] In the application of Schedule 1 to the directors of an NHS foundation trust, references to the provisions of the Companies Act 2006 or the Insolvency Act 1986 include references to the corresponding provisions of Chapter 5 of Part 2 of the National Health Service Act 2006.

GENERAL NOTE

This provision is inserted by the Health and Social Care (Community Care and Standards) Act 2003 s.34 and Sch.4 paras 67, 68, as from April 1, 2004. Section 22C(3) was amended by the National Health Service (Consequential Provisions) Act 2006 s.2 and Sch.1 para.92, as from March 1, 2007; and by the Companies Act 2006 (Consequential Amendments etc.) Order 2008 (SI 2008/948) art.3(1) and Sch.1 para.106(7), as from April 6, 2008.

22D   Application of Act to open-ended investment companies

22D(1)   [Application subject to modifications] This Act applies to open-ended investment companies with the following modifications.

22D(2)   [Investigative material in s.8(1)] In section 8(1) (disqualification after investigation), the reference to investigative material shall be read as including a report made by inspectors under regulations made by virtue of section 262(2)(k) of the Financial Services and Markets Act 2000.

22D(3)   [Application of Sch.1 Pt 1 re director of OEIC] In the application of Part 1 of Schedule 1 (matters for determining unfitness of directors: matters applicable in all cases) in relation to a director of an open-ended investment company, a reference to a provision of the Companies Act 2006 is to be taken to be a reference to the corresponding provision of the Open-Ended Investment Companies Regulations 2001 or of rules made under regulation 6 of those Regulations.

22D(4)   ["Open-ended investment company"] In this section "open-ended investment company" has the meaning given by section 236 of the Financial Services and Markets Act 2000.

History
Section 22D inserted by the Companies Act 2006 (Consequential Amendments, Transitional Provisions and Savings) Order 2009 (SI 2009/1941) art.2(1) and Sch.1 para.85(13) as from October 1, 2009. Note prospective insertion of s.22E by the Co-operative and Community Benefit Societies and Credit Unions Act 2010 s.3.

23   Transitional provisions, savings, repeals

23(1)   [Schedule 3] The transitional provisions and savings in Schedule 3 to this Act have effect, and are without prejudice to anything in the Interpretation Act 1978 with regard to the effect of repeals.

23(2)   [Schedule 4] The enactments specified in the second column of Schedule 4 to this Act are repealed to the extent specified in the third column of that Schedule.

GENERAL NOTE

This section gives force to the repeals, transitional provisions and savings listed in the Schedules referred to.
   Nothing in Sch.4 is repealed that is not re-enacted in the consolidation, apart from the transitional provisions of IA 1985.

24   Extent

24(1)   [England, Wales, Scotland] This Act extends to England and Wales and to Scotland.

24(2)   [Northern Ireland] Nothing in this Act extends to Northern Ireland.

GENERAL NOTE

The disqualification regime in Northern Ireland is now contained in the Companies (Disqualification Orders) Regulations 2010 (SR 2010/184), consolidating all the previous legislation with effect from June 18, 2010.

S.24(2)
Although Northern Ireland has its own legislation relating to director disqualification, IA 2000 made changes to the present Act which give effect to orders of the Northern Ireland courts throughout the rest of the United Kingdom: see the notes to s.12A.

25 Commencement

25 This Act comes into force simultaneously with the Insolvency Act 1986.

GENERAL NOTE

The date of commencement was December 29, 1986: see IA 1986 s.443 and SI 1986/1924 (C. 71), but most of the reforms introduced by IA 1985 which were consolidated into the present Act were brought into force on April 28, 1986: see SI 1986/463 (C. 14).

26 Citation

26 This Act may be cited as the Company Directors Disqualification Act 1986.

SCHEDULES

SCHEDULE 1

MATTERS FOR DETERMINING UNFITNESS OF DIRECTORS

Section 9

PART I

MATTERS APPLICABLE IN ALL CASES

1 Any misfeasance or breach of any fiduciary or other duty by the director in relation to the company, including in particular any breach by the director of a duty under Chapter 2 of Part 10 of the Companies Act 2006 (general duties of directors) owed to the company.

2 Any misapplication or retention by the director of, or any conduct by the director giving rise to an obligation to account for, any money or other property of the company.

3 The extent of the director's responsibility for the company entering into any transaction liable to be set aside under Part XVI of the Insolvency Act 1986 (provisions against debt avoidance).

4 The extent of the director's responsibility for any failure by the company to comply with any of the following provisions of the Companies Act 2006–

(a) section 113 (register of members);

(b) section 114 (register to be kept available for inspection);

(c) section 162 (register of directors);

(d) section 165 (register of directors' residential addresses);

(e) section 167 (duty to notify registrar of changes: directors);

(f) section 275 (register of secretaries);

(g) section 276 (duty to notify registrar of changes: secretaries);

(h) section 386 (duty to keep accounting records);

(i) section 388 (where and for how long accounting records to be kept);

(j) section 854 (duty to make annual returns);

(k) section 860 (duty to register charges);

(l) section 878 (duty to register charges: companies registered in Scotland).

5 The extent of the director's responsibility for any failure by the directors of the company to comply with the following provisions of the Companies Act 2006–

(a) section 394 or 399 (duty to prepare annual accounts);

(b) section 414 or 450 (approval and signature of abbreviated accounts); or

(c) section 433 (name of signatory to be stated in published copy of accounts).

5A [Omitted].

PART II

MATTERS APPLICABLE WHERE COMPANY HAS BECOME INSOLVENT

6 The extent of the director's responsibility for the causes of the company becoming insolvent.

7 The extent of the director's responsibility for any failure by the company to supply any goods or services which have been paid for (in whole or in part).

8 The extent of the director's responsibility for the company entering into any transaction or giving any preference, being a transaction or preference–

(a) liable to be set aside under section 127 or sections 238 to 240 of the Insolvency Act 1986, or

(b) challengeable under section 242 or 243 of that Act or under any rule of law in Scotland.

9 The extent of the director's responsibility for any failure by the directors of the company to comply with section 98 of the Insolvency Act 1986 (duty to call creditors' meeting in creditors' voluntary winding up).

10 Any failure by the director to comply with any obligation imposed on him by or under any of the following provisions of the Insolvency Act 1986–

(a) paragraph 47 of Schedule B1 (company's statement of affairs in administration);

(b) section 47 (statement of affairs to administrative receiver);

(c) section 66 (statement of affairs in Scottish receivership);

(d) section 99 (directors' duty to attend meeting; statement of affairs in creditors' voluntary winding up);

(e) section 131 (statement of affairs in winding up by the court);

(f) section 234 (duty of any one with company property to deliver it up);

(g) section 235 (duty to co-operate with liquidator, etc.).

[For notes, see s.9. Paragraph 5A was inserted by SI 1996/2827, as from January 6, 1997 and amended by SI 2001/1228, as from December 1, 2001. Paragraph 10(a) was amended by substituting "paragraph 47 of Schedule B1" for the words "section 22" following the introduction of the new administration regime by EA 2002 (see the Enterprise Act 2002 (Insolvency) Order 2003 (SI 2003/2096) arts 1, 4 and Sch. para.12, effective September 15, 2003). However, the former wording continues to apply to companies and other bodies in relation to which administration orders have been made under the original Pt II: see generally the notes to IA 1986 Pt II and Sch.B1. Paragraphs 4, 5 and 5A were amended, and para.4A inserted, by the Companies Act 2006 (Consequential Amendments etc.) Order 2008 (SI 2008/948) art.3(1) and Sch.1 para.106(8), as from April 6, 2008. Paragraphs 1, 2, 8, 9 and 10 amended, 4A and 5A deleted and 4 substituted, by the Companies Act 2006 (Consequential Amendments, Transitional Provisions and Savings) Order 2009 (SI 2009/1941) art.2(1) and Sch.1 para.85(14) as from October 1, 2009. On open-ended investment companies, see s.22D(3).]

59

SCHEDULE 2

SAVINGS FROM COMPANIES ACT 1981 ss. 93, 94, AND INSOLVENCY ACT 1985 SCHEDULE 9

SCHEDULE 3

TRANSITIONAL PROVISIONS AND SAVINGS

SCHEDULE 4

REPEALS

[Schedules 2, 3 and 4, which for practical purposes may be regarded as spent, are not reproduced. For notes, see ss.19 and 23.]

Insolvency Act 1986 (original Part II)

(1986 Chapter 45)

[**Note**: The original Pt II of the 1986 Act, together with the associated rules, have been relocated here for reasons of space. The original Pt II will continue to apply to any administrations commenced before September 15, 2003 and to building societies and to those companies to which EA 2002 s.249 applies (see Vol.1, p.41). All other administrations are now governed by IA 1986 Sch.B1.]

ARRANGEMENT OF SECTIONS

ORIGINAL PART II

ADMINISTRATION ORDERS

Introductory note to the original Part II

The company administration procedure was introduced for the first time by the legislation of 1985–86. The provisions in the Act were based on the recommendations of the Cork Committee (*Report*, Ch.9). The Committee thought that there was a need for a new procedure, similar to a receivership, to meet the case where a company was in difficulties but it was not possible to mount a rescue operation by having a receiver appointed because it had not given any creditor a floating charge over its undertaking. Ironically, the wheel has now come full circle. One of the principal aims of EA 2002 was to disallow the use of administrative receivership in the great majority of cases and oblige floating charge holders to place the company into administration instead. In consequence of this change, there has been a shift of emphasis: whereas the primary concern of a receiver is to protect the interest of the charge holder (in most cases by realising sufficient of the company's assets to pay off the secured debt), and he has only very limited duties vis-à-vis other stakeholders in the company, an administrator is bound to have regard to the interests of *all* the company's creditors and members. The rights of the secured creditor are no longer paramount. And although receivership can sometimes result in the survival of some or all of the company's business as a going concern (either because a buyer is found to take it over, in whole or in part, or because the company is allowed to continue to trade until its financial difficulties are resolved), administration is more naturally envisaged as a "rescue" procedure and, indeed, it is this purpose which is now ranked foremost among the objectives for which, under the new regime, an administrator is obliged to perform his functions. Under the original Pt II, however, this is merely one of several objectives.

It should be borne in mind that both the Cork Committee and the Government in its White Paper thought it important that a board of directors which found that its company was in financial difficulties should seek outside help promptly and, if appropriate, hand over control of the company to experienced professional hands. (See the note to s.214 ("wrongful trading").) An administration is plainly a proper step which a board might take in such a situation.

The timetable envisaged by the original Pt II is leisurely (a matter of several months), and the procedure is costly, elaborate and formal, requiring a court order in all cases. This was undoubtedly one of the reasons why administration did not prove as successful in practice as had been expected. The relative unpopularity of the procedure at that time can be gauged from the fact that only 643 administration orders were made in the year 2002, compared with some 16,000 insolvent liquidations and 1,541 receiverships.

These considerations of delay and expense were not the only reason why the number of administrations was relatively low, prior to the introduction of the new regime. Where the company had given a floating charge to its bank or some other creditor over all or substantially all of its assets, the charge holder was given a statutory right to veto the appointment of an administrator and install an administrative receiver himself instead. Since a receiver could act more speedily, flexibly and cheaply, and was bound by law to give precedence to the interests of the secured creditor who had appointed him, it was not surprising that more often than not a charge holder availed himself of this statutory right.

The EA 2002 has (except in a limited number of special cases) abrogated the power of a secured creditor to appoint an administrative receiver, although not with retrospective effect so as to affect the holders of floating charges created prior to September 15, 2003 (IA 1986 ss.72A et seq.). Administration has thus become the standard procedure for the enforcement of a floating charge as well as for an attempt to achieve the rescue of a company's business where it is insolvent or nearly so—except in the case of an eligible small company, where a CVA may be preferred. The charge holder's position has, however, been alleviated to some extent: (a) by allowing such a creditor to appoint an administrator directly, by-passing the need for a court order (IA 1986 Sch.B1 para.14); (b) by giving him the right to intervene and have an insolvency practitioner of his own choice appointed where an administration is proposed by some other person (para.36); and (c) by specifying as one of the objectives for which an administration order can be made "realising property in order to make a distribution to one or more secured or preferential creditors" (para.3(1)(c)). Even so, this latter objective is subordinated to the primary aim of rescuing the company as a going concern, where the administrator thinks that this is practicable.

The Insolvency (Amendment) Rules 2010 (SI 2010/686, effective April 6, 2010) have introduced numerous changes to the procedure relating to the original Pt II, many of which are retrospective in that they affect existing administrations. See the note preceding the original IR 1986 Pt 2, below at p.97.

The statutory text (with annotations) which follows is that of the original IA 1986 Pt II. For the new Pt II, see Sch.B1, Vol.1, pp.533 et seq.

The topic of administration under the original regime is discussed in Totty and Moss, *Insolvency*, Ch.C2 and, under the new regime, at paras C2–36 et seq.

Making, etc. of administration order

8   *Power of court to make order*

8(1)   *[**Administration order**] Subject to this section, if the court–*

    (a)   *is satisfied that a company is or is likely to become unable to pay its debts (within the meaning given to that expression by section 123 of this Act), and*

    (b)   *considers that the making of an order under this section would be likely to achieve one or more of the purposes mentioned below,*

the court may make an administration order in relation to the company.

8(1A)   *[**In petition by FSA**] For the purposes of a petition presented by the Financial Services Authority alone or together with any other party, an authorised deposit taker who defaults in an obligation to pay any sum due and payable in respect of a relevant deposit is deemed to be unable to pay its debts as mentioned in subsection (1).*

8(1B)   *[**Definitions for s.8(1A)**] In subsection (1A)–*

    (a)   *"**authorised deposit taker**" means a person who has permission under Part 4 of the Financial Services and Markets Act 2000 to accept deposits, but excludes a person who has such permission only for the purpose of carrying on another regulated activity in accordance with that permission; and*

    (b)   *"**relevant deposit**" must be read with–*

(i)   *section 22 of the Financial Services and Markets Act 2000,*

(ii)   *any relevant order under that section, and*

(iii)   *Schedule 2 to that Act,*

but any restriction on the meaning of deposit which arises from the identity of the person making it is to be disregarded.

8(2)   **[Definition]** *An administration order is an order directing that, during the period for which the order is in force, the affairs, business and property of the company shall be managed by a person ("**the administrator**") appointed for the purpose by the court.*

8(3)   **[Purposes for order]** *The purposes for whose achievement an administration order may be made are–*

(a)   *the survival of the company, and the whole or any part of its undertaking, as a going concern;*

(b)   *the approval of a voluntary arrangement under Part I;*

(c)   *the sanctioning under Part 26 of the Companies Act 2006 (arrangements and reconstructions) of a compromise or arrangement between the company and any such persons as are mentioned in that section; and*

(d)   *a more advantageous realisation of the company's assets than would be effected on a winding up;*

and the order shall specify the purpose or purposes for which it is made.

8(4)   **[No order if company in liquidation]** *An administration order shall not be made in relation to a company after it has gone into liquidation.*

8(5)   **[Further situations where no order]** *An administration order shall not be made against a company if–*

(a)   *it effects or carries out contracts of insurance, but is not–*

(i)   *exempt from the general prohibition, within the meaning of section 19 of the Financial Services and Markets Act 2000, in relation to effecting or carrying out contracts of insurance, or*

(ii)   *an authorised deposit taker within the meaning given by subsection (1B), and effecting or carrying out contracts of insurance in the course of a banking business;*

(b)   *it continues to have a liability in respect of a deposit which was held by it in accordance with the Banking Act 1979 or the Banking Act 1987, but is not an authorised deposit taker, within the meaning given by subsection (1B).*

8(6)   **[Provisions s.8(5)(a) to be read with]** *Subsection (5)(a) must be read with–*

(a)   *section 22 of the Financial Services and Markets Act 2000;*

(b)   *any relevant order under that section; and*

(c)   *Schedule 2 to that Act.*

8(7)   **[Applicability of EC Regulation]** *In this Part a reference to a company includes a reference to a company in relation to which an administration order may be made by virtue of Article 3 of the EC Regulation.*

GENERAL NOTE

Section 8(1A), (1B), (5) and (6) were inserted, and s.8(4)–(6) substituted, by the Financial Services and Markets Act 2000 (Consequential Amendments and Repeals) Order 2001 (SI 2001/3649) as from December 1, 2001. Section 8(7) was inserted by the Insolvency Act 1986 (Amendment) (No.2) Regulations 2002 (SI 2002/1240) as from May 31, 2002.

S.8(1), (2)

An administration order is defined by s.8(2), as is the "administrator" who may be appointed to manage the affairs, etc. of a company under this section. For the meaning of "affairs" see *Polly Peck International plc v Henry* [1999] 1 B.C.L.C. 407.

The term "company" is not specifically defined for the purposes of this Part (contrast the position under the new regime, Sch.B1 para.111(1A)), and so reference must be made to the general definition contained in CA 2006 ss.1(1), 1171, which applies by virtue of IA 1986 s.251. Accordingly, "company" means a company formed and registered under CA 2006 or an earlier Companies Act. It follows from this definition that an administration order cannot be made in respect of a foreign company (compare *Felixstowe Dock & Railway Co v US Lines Inc* [1989] Q.B. 360). This will be the case also (in the absence of special statutory provision) in relation to bodies other than companies, such as a society incorporated under the Industrial and Provident Societies Act 1965: see the Introductory note to the First Group of Parts preceding s.1. However, in the case of a foreign company, the position is different when a letter of request has been received by an English court from a court in that company's country of incorporation, for s.426, and in particular s.426(5), confers upon the court a jurisdiction wider than it would otherwise have: *Re Dallhold Estates (UK) Pty Ltd* [1992] B.C.C. 394.

Moreover, there has been some relaxation of the territorial limitation described above by virtue of the enactment of s.8(7). Article 3 of the EC Regulation gives jurisdiction to a Member State of the EU to open insolvency proceedings "within the territory of which the centre of the debtor's main interests [COMI] is situated" (in the case of "main" proceedings) and—subject to certain limitations—"if he possesses an establishment within the territory of that… Member State" (in the case of "territorial" proceedings). (See the note to art.3.) The courts have given a broad interpretation to this provision. In *Re BRAC Rent-A-Car International Inc* [2003] B.C.C. 248 it was held that administration proceedings could be opened in the UK (as "main" proceedings) in respect of a company incorporated in Delaware which had conducted its operations almost entirely in the UK (and so had its COMI within this jurisdiction): the scope of the Regulation was not restricted to companies incorporated elsewhere in the EU. In *Re The Salvage Association* [2004] 1 W.L.R. 174; [2003] B.C.C. 504, on the authority of this ruling, Blackburne J. held that the court had jurisdiction to make an administration order (and that a CVA could be implemented) in the case of a body incorporated by Royal Charter whose COMI was within the UK, even though it was not a "company" for the purposes of IA 1986. The decision in *Re The Salvage Association* did not, however, find favour in Whitehall and steps were taken to reverse it by incorporating a revised definition of "company" in s.1 and Sch.B1 para.111. (See the notes to those provisions. It was not, apparently, thought necessary to make a similar change for the purposes of the present section.) It follows that a UK body other than one incorporated under the Companies Acts cannot now be the subject of a CVA or put into administration.

Questions of jurisdiction to petition for an administration order normally need to be resolved before an order is made; but the Act has to be interpreted realistically and, since administration orders often have to be made urgently, it may sometimes be necessary to make an order without settling (at least finally) a dispute as to locus standi or jurisdiction: *Re MTI Trading Systems Ltd* [1997] B.C.C. 703 (the Court of Appeal refused leave to appeal against this decision [1998] B.C.C. 400).

The prerequisites for the operation of the court's jurisdiction are set out in s.8(1). The court must (1) be "satisfied" (on a balance of probabilities: *Re Colt Telecom Group plc (No.2)* [2002] EWHC 2815 (Ch); [2003] B.P.I.R. 324) that the company is, or is likely to become, "unable to pay its debts" (in the statutory sense of this expression, as defined by s.123), and (2) consider that an administration order would be likely to achieve one or more of the purposes specified in s.8(3). The Act gives no guidance as to the nature of the evidence on which a ruling on the second of these issues is to be made; and the matter was at first the subject of some judicial controversy. It is now well settled that the requirements of s.8(3) are satisfied if the court considers that there is "a real prospect" that one or more of the statutory purposes might be achieved—a test lower than "a balance of probabilities" (*Re Harris Simons Construction Ltd* [1989] 1 W.L.R. 386; (1989) 5 B.C.C. 11; *Re Lomax Leisure Ltd* [2000] B.C.C. 352).

The order must specify the purpose or purposes for which it is made (s.8(3)). Accordingly, the court must consider separately, in relation to each proposed purpose, whether the test of likelihood has been satisfied: see *Re S C L Building Services Ltd* (1989) 5 B.C.C. 746 at 747.

In part, the evidence on which the court bases its decision will be supplied by the affidavit filed in support of the petition under IR 1986 r.2.3. In addition, the rules contemplate that a report by an independent person (i.e. someone not already connected with the company as a director, etc.) will be prepared for the assistance of the court (r.2.2). This is not obligatory, but if a report has not been prepared, the court must be given an explanation (r.2(3), (6)). (On the content of the report and the recommended practice in relation to such reports, see the discussion of the *Practice Note* of 1994 in the notes to r.2.2, below.) It is obviously appropriate to have the report prepared by the insolvency practitioner whose appointment as administrator is being proposed, and in the great majority of cases this will be the best way of providing the court with the evidence on which it can act. Where the petitioner is a creditor, however, it is unlikely that he will have access to as much evidence as the court would like to have, and this may give rise to difficulties.

Insolvency, for the purposes of s.8(1)(a), is at least primarily to be determined on a liquidity or "cash flow" basis (that is, on the company's ability to pay its current debts) rather than on a "balance sheet" basis (i.e. whether it is likely to have a surplus after a realisation of all its assets); but since, for this purpose, the provisions of s.123 are relevant, the latter test is made a legitimate alternative by s.123(2), and such a test was applied in *Re Dianoor Jewels Ltd* [2001] 1 B.C.L.C. 450. In *Re Imperial Motors (UK) Ltd* (1989) 5 B.C.C. 214 the court was prepared to find that the company was unable to pay its debts even though it appeared to be solvent on a balance-sheet basis. This was also the case in *Re Business Properties Ltd* (1988) 4 B.C.C. 684. However, Harman J. there expressed the view that in such a situation the court will not normally exercise its discretion to appoint an administrator when the essential ground for seeking relief is deadlock and a breakdown of trust and confidence between the members of the company: the more appropriate remedy is winding up. An administrator, he said, has wide powers for a "short-term, intensive-care" operation, but cannot achieve the realisation and distribution required to conclude the company's affairs.

If the conditions in s.8(1)(a) and (b) are satisfied, the court then has a discretion whether to make an administration order. As Peter Gibson J. observed in *Re Consumer & Industrial Press Ltd* (1988) 4 B.C.C. 68, this is a complete discretion, in which account must be taken of all material circumstances, and is not limited by the wording of s.8(1)(a) and (b). The judge's task may not be at all an easy one, for his decision may benefit some creditors at the expense of others. For example, if an administration is preferred to a winding up, debts which would rank as preferential in a liquidation have no preferential status under the original Pt II. Another factor which weighed with the judge in that case, but was not held to be decisive, was that a liquidator had wider powers to investigate the conduct of directors (e.g. in regard to fraudulent and wrongful trading) than an administrator.

The court has, on occasion, exercised its discretion to make an administration order despite the opposition of a majority creditor which has stated its determination to oppose any proposals: see, e.g. *Re Structures & Computers Ltd* [1998] B.C.C. 348. In this case the majority creditor was allowed its costs as part of the administration.

Re Imperial Motors (UK) Ltd (above) is a further illustration of the exercise of the court's discretion. Here, the court took the view that the interests of the company's secured creditors should weigh more lightly in the scales than those of its unsecured creditors, because they did not stand to lose so much. In *Re Arrows Ltd (No.3)* [1992] B.C.C. 131 a majority of the creditors opposed the making of an order. Hoffmann J. held that, while the court had a discretion to make an order in spite of such opposition, the fact that the proposals were unlikely to be approved by a creditors' meeting if an order were made would weigh strongly against making an order. See further *Re Far East Abrasives Ltd* [2003] B.P.I.R. 375.

The fact that the genuine claims of a third party may be thwarted by putting the company into administration is not a reason for refusing an order: indeed, where the company is insolvent, an order ensures that the interests and claims of the company's creditors are not prejudiced by the outsider's claim: *Re Dianoor Jewels Ltd* [2001] 1 B.C.L.C. 450.

Section 8(2) refers to "the period for which the order is in force". Although it would not appear to follow necessarily from this that an order should be expressed to be made for a fixed period, the courts have so interpreted the provision, and a period of three months has become the standard. (This, of course, ties in with the obligation to report to creditors under IA 1986 s.23, within the same period.) In *Re Newport County Association Football Club Ltd* (1987) 3 B.C.C. 635, Harman J. held that the company had standing to apply for an extension of this period, but expressed the view that such an application would be better made by the administrator. An order for extension was made in *Re Top Marques Car Rental* [2006] EWHC 746 (Ch); [2006] B.P.I.R. 1328.

On the making of a winding-up order, time ceases to run for the purposes of the statutes of limitation against the company's creditors (other than a petitioning creditor): *Re Cases of Taff's Well Ltd* [1992] Ch. 179; [1991] B.C.C. 582. However, the making of an administration order does not prevent time from running: *Re Maxwell Fleet and Facilities Management Ltd* [1999] 2 B.C.L.C. 712; *Re Leyland Printing Co Ltd* [2010] EWHC 2105 (Ch); [2011] B.C.C. 358; cf. *Re Cases of Taff's Well Ltd* (above) at 195, 589.

S.8(3)

If the court makes an administration order, it must specify which of the purposes mentioned in s.8(3) the order seeks to achieve. This requirement clearly limits the functions and powers of the administrator to acts which are consistent with the purpose or purposes stated. However, there is power under s.18(1) to have the order varied so that it states an additional purpose.

Section 8(3) sets out under four headings the purposes which, separately or in combination, an administration order may seek to achieve. Headings (a) and (d) may not be altogether compatible with each other, although in practice they are commonly combined in the same petition or order. (In consequence, the decisive say as to the course which the administration should pursue is then left to the creditors at their meeting.) In *Re Rowbotham Baxter Ltd*

[1990] B.C.C. 113 at 115, Harman J. stated that a proposal involving the sale of a "hived-down" company formed to take over part of the company's business could not be brought within para.(a) ("the survival of the company and part of its undertaking as a going concern"); but it is submitted that it could plainly come within para.(d). In *Re Maxwell Communications Corporation plc* [1992] B.C.C. 372, Hoffmann J. held that the fact that Ch.11 proceedings, affecting a substantial proportion of the company's assets, were pending in the US was relevant to the chances of the survival of the company and all or part of its business. Although in a normal case administration under the original Pt II in itself is not an appropriate procedure for making a distribution to the company's unsecured creditors (see *Rolph v A Y Bank Ltd* [2002] B.P.I.R. 1231; *Re The Designer Room Ltd* [2004] EWHC 720 (Ch); [2004] 3 All E.R. 679; [2004] B.C.C. 904 and *Re Lune Metal Products Ltd* [2006] EWCA Civ 1720; [2007] B.C.C. 217), heading (b) may conveniently be invoked where it is proposed to make a distribution to creditors involving some modification of their rights, in a way which binds dissentients (see *Re St Ives Windings Ltd* [1987] 3 B.C.C. 634), or where a moratorium is sought and the company is not eligible for one under Sch.A1, and heading (c) gives the opportunity to combine an administration with a scheme of arrangement under CA 2006 Pt 26, so establishing a moratorium which prevents individual creditors from enforcing their rights while the necessary formalities of the scheme are completed.

The court will be concerned to see that any proposed CVA or Pt 26 scheme is consistent with insolvency law: *Re T & N Ltd* [2004] EWHC 2361 (Ch); [2005] 2 B.C.L.C. 488.

S.8(5)–(6)
On insurers, banks and other "authorised institutions", see the Introductory note to the new Pt II, following the new s.8, in Vol.1.

The administration procedure may not be used if the company is already in liquidation. (For a general discussion of the relationship between winding up and administration orders, see the note to s.10.)

S.8(7)
See the notes to s.8(1), (2) above and to the EC Regulation art.3.

9   Application for order

9(1)   [Application to court] *An application to the court for an administration order shall be by petition presented either by the company or the directors, or by a creditor or creditors (including any contingent or prospective creditor or creditors), or by a justices' chief executive in the exercise of the power conferred by section 87A of the Magistrates' Courts Act 1980 (enforcement of fines imposed on companies) or by all or any of those parties, together or separately.*

9(2)   [On presentation of petition to court] *Where a petition is presented to the court–*

(a) *notice of the petition shall be given forthwith to any person who has appointed, or is or may be entitled to appoint, an administrative receiver of the company, and to such other persons as may be prescribed, and*

(b) *the petition shall not be withdrawn except with the leave of the court.*

9(3)   [Duties of court] *Where the court is satisfied that there is an administrative receiver of the company, the court shall dismiss the petition unless it is also satisfied either–*

(a) *that the person by whom or on whose behalf the receiver was appointed has consented to the making of the order, or*

(b) *that, if an administration order were made, any security by virtue of which the receiver was appointed would–*

(i) *be liable to be released or discharged under sections 238 to 240 in Part VI (transactions at an undervalue and preferences),*

(ii) *be avoided under section 245 in that Part (avoidance of floating charges), or*

(iii) *be challengeable under section 242 (gratuitous alienations) or 243 (unfair preferences) in that Part, or under any rule of law in Scotland.*

9(4) **[Court powers on hearing petition]** *Subject to subsection (3), on hearing a petition the court may dismiss it, or adjourn the hearing conditionally or unconditionally, or make an interim order or any other order that it thinks fit.*

9(5) **[Extent of interim order]** *Without prejudice to the generality of subsection (4), an interim order under that subsection may restrict the exercise of any powers of the directors or of the company (whether by reference to the consent of the court or of a person qualified to act as an insolvency practitioner in relation to the company, or otherwise).*

General Note

Under the original Pt II, an administration order can be made only in consequence of an application made by petition under this section.

For details of the procedure for making an application, see IR 1986 *Pt 2* (below).

S.9(1)

This list of persons who are eligible to apply for an administration order should be compared with those who may petition for a winding up under s.124(1): see the comment to that subsection. The significant difference between the two is that the right of a member or members to seek an administration order is excluded. (This is in keeping with the rule in regard to winding up, laid down in *Re Rica Gold Washing Co* (1879) 11 Ch. D. 36, that a member has no standing to present a winding-up petition where the company is insolvent. Applying this principle, Harman J. in *Re Chelmsford City Football Club (1980) Ltd* [1991] B.C.C. 133 ruled that members should not be given leave under IR 1986 r.2.9(1)(g) to oppose an application for an administration order.) There is also no counterpart to ss.124(4) and 124A, or to s.124(5), which respectively empower the Secretary of State, in specified circumstances, and the official receiver to petition for a winding up. Note also that under s.7(4)(b) the supervisor of a CVA is included among the persons who may apply to the court for an administration order.

Where the purpose of an administration order is the approval of a CVA under Pt I (see s.8(3)(a)), it will be necessary for the directors to take steps to initiate the CVA proceedings at the same time as the petition is presented under s.9 (unless the CVA is already in being), since they alone will be competent to do so.

Contingent and prospective creditors are given standing to petition under s.9(1), as they are for a winding-up order (see s.124(1)). This contrasts with the position in regard to CVAs: see the note to s.1(1). (On the meaning of "creditor", see the notes to s.1(1) and r.13.12.)

Where a company (or an insolvent partnership) is, or has been, an "authorised person" or "authorised representative" under FSMA 2000, or is or has been carrying on a "regulated activity" (e.g. an investment business) in contravention of s.19 of that Act, the Financial Services Authority may present a petition under this section: FSMA 2000 s.359. For this purpose, there is a special provision in s.359(3) setting out circumstances (presumably, in addition to those contained in IA 1986 s.123) in which such a body is to be deemed unable to pay its debts. If any other person is the petitioner, the FSA is empowered to participate in the proceedings (s.362).

An application by the directors must be made by all the directors (*Re Instrumentation Electrical Services Ltd* (1988) 4 B.C.C. 301). This could, it is submitted, be done by all the directors acting informally (even where there is not an enabling article along the lines of Table A art.93): see *Charterhouse Investment Trust Ltd v Tempest Diesels Ltd* (1985) 1 B.C.C. 99,544 at 99,551; *Runciman v Walter Runciman plc* [1993] B.C.C. 223 at 230. An application can also be made in the name of all the directors once a proper resolution of the board of directors has been passed, for it then becomes the duty of all the directors, including those who took no part in the deliberations of the board and even those who voted against the resolution, to implement it: see *Re Equiticorp International plc* [1989] 1 W.L.R. 1010; (1989) 5 B.C.C. 599.

A petition presented by the supervisor of a CVA, or by the directors, is to be treated for all purposes as the petition of the company (IR 1986 rr.2.1(4), 2.4(3)). A supervisor should petition in the name of the company: see the note to s.7(4).

Although s.9(2) requires notice of the petition to be given to a charge holder, and the rules contemplate that copies of the petition shall be served on specified persons and that they and others may appear and be represented at the hearing of the petition (IR 1986 rr.2.6, 2.9), the court has on occasion been prepared to make an administration order without notice and even, in cases of extreme urgency, to do so against an undertaking by counsel that a petition will be presented in the immediate future. Initially, Harman J. in *Re Rowbotham Baxter Ltd* [1990] B.C.C. 113 at 114 expressed the view that this was "an undesirable practice which should not continue". He said: "The danger is that the court hears one side only, the court has not the advantage of adversarial argument to draw its attention to points which may weigh one way or the other; and this leads… to a serious risk of injustice being done". However, the same judge in the later case of *Re Cavco Floors Ltd* [1990] B.C.C. 589 qualified his earlier remarks by saying that, although it is undesirable for the court to act before presentation of the petition, it is a procedure which may need to be adopted in some cases; and in that case he did make an immediate order. See also *Re Shearing & Loader Ltd* [1991] B.C.C. 232; and *Re Gallidoro Trawlers Ltd* [1991] B.C.C. 691, and compare the "pre-pack" administration which has developed under the new Pt 2, discussed in the note to Sch.B1 para.2. Again, in *Re Chancery plc* [1991] B.C.C. 171, an administration order was made ex parte in the case of a banking company, where the judge also took the unusual course of hearing the application in camera.

There is no provision in the Act or the rules for a petition for an administration order to be advertised.

In many applications for an administration order, and in all applications made without notice, the only evidence before the court will be that submitted by the applicant company and its officers, and the insolvency practitioner's report under IR 1986 r.2.2, which will be based on the same information. In *Re Sharps of Truro Ltd* [1990] B.C.C. 94 and also in *Astor Chemical Ltd v Synthetic Technology Ltd* [1990] B.C.C. 97 at 107–108, the court laid stress on the importance of ensuring that all relevant information was put before the court. "All facts relevant to the exercise of the discretion to appoint an administrator must be revealed, even though to do so may be embarrassing to the applicant" (ibid.). If some material fact emerges after the making of the order, it is the duty of those who learn of it to explain it to the administrator and to put it before the court; and it is proper in such circumstances for the administrator to apply to the court for the discharge of the order, or to seek directions whether he should apply for a discharge.

The hearing of an application for an administration order is normally conducted on the basis of written evidence, and an order for disclosure of documents or the cross-examination of witnesses will be made only in exceptional circumstances: *Re Colt Telecom Group plc (No.1)* [2002] EWHC 2503 (Ch); [2003] B.P.I.R. 311.

S.9(2)
The holder of a floating charge who has power to appoint a receiver of the whole or substantially the whole of the company's property has the power (provided that his security is not successfully challenged under s.9(3)(b)) to block the making of an administration order by putting the company into receivership (s.9(3)). The notice required to be given to him by the present subsection will enable him to take this step if he wishes or, alternatively, to give his consent under s.9(3)(a). In order to ensure that a debenture holder has the power to put in a receiver in these circumstances, it is necessary that express provision should be made in any floating charge drawn up after the Act came into force. In relation to instruments created before the commencement of the Act, there is a transitional measure in Sch.11 para.1, which deems such a provision to be included.

For the "other persons" prescribed by the rules as being entitled to notice of a petition, see IR 1986 r.2.6.

The term "forthwith" has no precise meaning: "it must be done as soon as possible in the circumstances, the nature of the act to be done being taken into account" (Halsbury's *Laws of England*, 4th edn, Vol.45, para.1148). In the present context, it would probably be construed as "as soon as practicable" (*Sameen v Abeyewickrema* [1963] A.C. 597) or "as soon as reasonably practicable" (*Re Seagull Manufacturing Co Ltd (in liq.)* [1993] Ch. 345 at 359; [1993] B.C.C. 241 at 249) rather than the peremptory "at once" (*Re Muscovitch* [1939] Ch. 694) or the lax "at any reasonable time thereafter" (*Hillingdon London Borough Council v Cutler* [1968] 1 Q.B. 124).

The stipulation that a petition for an administration order shall not be withdrawn except with the leave of the court will naturally discourage irresponsible applications, and in particular the use of the procedure by a creditor for the purpose of putting pressure on a debtor company. On the other hand, it is clearly not improper for a petition to be presented under this section in order to secure a moratorium in connection with a CVA (where this is not available under Sch.A1) or a formal scheme of arrangement under CA 2006 Pt 26, see the note to s.8(3).

S.9(3)
This is the first occasion in the Act where the term "administrative receiver" is used. In broad terms, it may be taken as meaning "a receiver or manager of the whole (or substantially the whole) of a company's property". The full statutory definition appears in ss.29(2) and 251.

Although company law generally is able to accommodate the notion that more than one receivership can operate at the same time, or a receivership co-exist with a liquidation, the legislation rules out the idea that there can be an administrator and an administrative receiver in office at the same time. To resolve the matter, the security-holder who has appointed, or has power to appoint, an administrative receiver is given the decisive say. If he has already appointed a receiver when the petition for an administration order is presented, the petition must be dismissed unless the charge holder consents to the making of an order (s.9(3)) and the consequent vacation of the receivership (s.11(1)(b)). If he has not then appointed a receiver, he may do so before the application is heard (s.10(2)(b)), and so bring about the dismissal of the petition under the present subsection. In order to enable the charge holder to assess the position, the rules provide for him to be given five clear days' notice of the date fixed for the hearing of the application (IR 1986 rr.2.6(2)(a), 2.7(1)). The court has power to abridge this period of notice in an appropriate case (*Re a Company (No.00175 of 1987)* (1987) 3 B.C.C. 124). (Note that, although s.72A now imposes a general ban on the appointment of an administrative receiver by a floating charge holder, this provision does not apply retrospectively to charges created before September 15, 2003, and it is also subject to a number of exceptions set out in ss.72B et seq. There is a considerable overlap between the companies to which these exceptions apply and those specified in EA 2002 s.249 which continue to be governed by the original Pt II.)

In the same case, the company urged the court to grant an adjournment of the application in order that the company could arrange to pay off the charge. This would have led to the termination of the receivership and so (it was argued) have enabled an administration order to be made without violation of s.9(3). However, Vinelott J. held that he had no jurisdiction to take this course: the wording of s.9(3) was mandatory and he had no alternative but to dismiss the application.

The superior claims of the charge holder will not survive if an attack is successfully mounted upon the validity of the security on any of the grounds listed under para.(b)—i.e. that it is a transaction at an undervalue or preference within the scope of ss.238–240, or a floating charge that is liable to be avoided under s.245, or is challengeable under the equivalent Scottish provisions (ss.242, 243). It has also been suggested that a creditor taking security might seek to clothe what is essentially a fixed charge with the appearance of a floating charge, or to combine it with a meaningless floating charge, in order to obtain the power under s.9(3) to block an administration order by the purported appointment of an administrative receiver. An argument challenging the genuineness of a floating charge along these lines failed in *Re Croftbell Ltd* [1990] B.C.C. 781: the court held that a charge which was expressed to extend to future assets was to be treated as a floating charge even though at the time of its creation the company had no assets of the class in question.

Paragraph (b) of the subsection is likely to raise procedural and evidentiary difficulties. The terms of the section make it clear that the validity or invalidity of the security may be settled in the course of the hearing of the application for an order, rather than in separate proceedings. It is plain also that the onus of satisfying the court is on the petitioner. Yet he is unlikely to have at his disposal all the evidence that an administrator or liquidator would later have when proceeding under ss.238–240 or s.245. Fairly obviously, the matter cannot be determined without the security-holder as well as the company being made a party (for which, indeed provision is made by IR 1986 r.*2.9*). However, there are still difficult questions which the legislation does not address: is there any guarantee that the case will be properly put for the company (which, in the case of a creditor's petition, may well be opposed to the application)? There will not yet be anyone in office equivalent to the "office-holder" whose role it is to prosecute the proceedings under ss.238–239. Suppose that a decision under the present subsection is reached in favour of the security-holder: will the matter be res judicata if a winding-up order or an unrelated administration order is later made?

There is a further difficulty which may arise under s.9(3)(b), in reckoning the statutory period during which the security must have been created if it is to be avoided. There will be no problem in the case of ss.238–240 and 245, since the "relevant time" will be calculated from the date when the petition for an administration order was *presented* (see ss.240(3)(a), 245(5)(a)); but the significant date for ss.242, 243 (under the original wording of IA 1986, which continues to apply in this context) is the date of the making of the administration *order*, and this will set the court the impossible task of ascribing a real date to a hypothetical order.

A receiver who is not an administrative receiver (e.g. a receiver of part only of the company's property, or (probably) a receiver appointed by the court) is not obliged to vacate office unless required to do so by the administrator: s.11(2).

S.9(4), (5)

The powers of the court, especially to make interim orders, are expressed in the widest terms, and include power to subject the decision-making powers of the corporate organs to its own supervision, or to delegate that function to a qualified insolvency practitioner. It is submitted, however, that orders made under this section can affect only the company and, presumably, such creditors as have been made parties to the application. The position as regards other creditors is dealt with in s.10, below. One question which is not at all clear is whether an interim order under s.9(4) and (5) could restrict the exercise of powers by a security-holder or an administrative receiver pending the determination of a question as to the validity of the security under s.9(3)(b): compare s.10(2)(b), (c).

An interim order under s.9(4) is not an administration order for the purposes of CDDA 1986 s.6(2)(b), so that time does not begin to run for the purposes of the two-year limitation prescribed by CDDA 1986 s.7(2) until an administration order under s.8(3) is made: *Secretary of State for Trade and Industry v Palmer* [1994] B.C.C. 990.

There is no power under the Act for the court to appoint an interim administrator; but in an appropriate case (e.g. where the company's property is in jeopardy) it can appoint the intended administrator or another appropriate person to take control of the property and manage the company's affairs pending the final determination of the hearing: *Re a Company (No.00175 of 1987)* (1987) 3 B.C.C. 124. Such an appointment would be analogous to the appointment of a receiver of disputed property or of property which is in jeopardy. In *Re Gallidoro Trawlers Ltd* [1991] B.C.C. 691 the court, instead of appointing an interim manager, made an order restricting the powers of the company's directors prior to the hearing of the petition.

Where a petition for an administration order is not proceeded with and a winding-up order is made, the court may in a proper case allow the costs of the petition to be treated as costs in the winding up: *Re Gosscott (Groundworks) Ltd* (1988) 4 B.C.C. 372; but there have been other cases where it has been ordered that costs should be borne by the directors personally: see *Re W F Fearman Ltd (No.2)* (1988) 4 B.C.C. 1411; *Taylor v Pace Developments Ltd* [1991] B.C.C. 406; and *Re Stallton Distribution Ltd* [2002] B.C.C. 486. In *Re Land & Property Trust Co plc; Re Andromache Properties Ltd* [1991] B.C.C. 446, Harman J. at first instance made a similar order, but his ruling was reversed on appeal (*Re Land & Property Trust Co plc (No.2)* [1993] B.C.C. 462). In *Re Tajik Air Ltd* [1996] B.C.C. 368 the court declared that directors would not usually be ordered to pay costs in these circumstances unless it could be established summarily that they had acted for an improper purpose, such as concealing their own wrongdoings. It was to be assumed that a report under IR 1986 r.2.2 (if one had been obtained) was a serious and objective assessment of the company's prospects of satisfying one of the statutory purposes, and that the directors were justified in acting in reliance on it, as they would be on legal advice—even if such advice was unrealistic, or wrong.

10   *Effect of application*

10(1)   [Limitations] *During the period beginning with the presentation of a petition for an administration order and ending with the making of such an order or the dismissal of the petition–*

(a)   *no resolution may be passed or order made for the winding up of the company;*

(aa) *no landlord or other person to whom rent is payable may exercise any right of forfeiture by peaceable re-entry in relation to premises let to the company in respect of a failure by the company to comply with any term or condition of its tenancy of such premises, except with the leave of the court and subject to such terms as the court may impose,*

(b)   *no steps may be taken to enforce any security over the company's property, or to repossess goods in the company's possession under any hire-purchase agreement, except with the leave of the court and subject to such terms as the court may impose; and*

(c)   *no other proceedings and no execution or other legal process may be commenced or continued, and no distress may be levied, against the company or its property except with the leave of the court and subject to such terms as aforesaid.*

10(2)   [Where leave not required] *Nothing in subsection (1) requires the leave of the court–*

(a)   *for the presentation of a petition for the winding up of the company,*

(b)   *for the appointment of an administrative receiver of the company, or*

(c)   *for the carrying out by such a receiver (whenever appointed) of any of his functions.*

10(3)   [Period in s.10(1)] *Where–*

(a)   *a petition for an administration order is presented at a time when there is an administrative receiver of the company, and*

(b)   *the person by or on whose behalf the receiver was appointed has not consented to the making of the order,*

the period mentioned in subsection (1) is deemed not to begin unless and until that person so consents.

10(4)   [Hire-purchase agreements] *References in this section and the next to hire-purchase agreements include conditional sale agreements, chattel leasing agreements and retention of title agreements.*

10(5)   [Scotland] *In the application of this section and the next to Scotland, references to execution being commenced or continued include references to diligence being carried out or continued, and references to distress being levied shall be omitted.*

S.10(1)

Unless the company is already in the hands of an administrative receiver (in which case s.10(3) applies), the presentation of a petition for an administration order imposes an automatic moratorium, which prevents certain legal acts and processes from being performed or continued until the application is finally disposed of. The company cannot be put into voluntary liquidation, nor can a winding-up order be made (although a winding-up petition may be *presented*: s.10(2)(a)); and unless the court gives leave, the enforcement of a security, the repossession of goods held under hire-purchase and similar agreements, and the commencement and prosecution of legal proceedings, etc. may not be proceeded with. (Some exceptions are listed in s.10(2), discussed below.) The court's discretion in granting leave under paras (b) and (c) appears to be unrestricted.

Subparagraph 10(1)(aa) was inserted by IA 2000 s.9 with effect from April 2, 2001 to resolve doubts on the question whether the leave of the court was required where a landlord sought to exercise his right of re-entry for non-payment of rent or breach of any other covenant. On this, and more generally on the meaning of the term "security" in this context, see the note to s.11(3)(c).

In *Re a Company (No.001448 of 1989)* (1989) 5 B.C.C. 706 Millett J. held that, even though s.10(1)(c) cannot be invoked until a petition for an administration order has been presented, the court has power under its *quia timet* jurisdiction to restrain the advertisement of a winding-up petition if counsel for the company has given an undertaking that a petition will be presented.

The rules provide that notice of the presentation of a petition for an administration order be given to anyone known to be issuing execution or other legal process or distraining against the company (IR 1986 r.2.6A), in order to avoid the risk of inadvertent contraventions of s.10(1)(c).

Section 10(1)(b) does not apply in relation to the enforcement of "market charges" (as defined by CA 1989 s.173): see s.175 of that Act (as qualified by the Financial Markets and Insolvency Regulations 1991 (SI 1991/880)). It is also disapplied in relation to payment and securities settlement systems by the Finality Regulations reg.19. (See the introductory notes at Vol.1, pp.1–3.)

In relation to the financial markets, nothing in s.10(1)(c) affects any action taken by an exchange or clearing house for the purpose of its default proceedings: CA 1989 s.161(4).

S.10(2)

Although no winding-up order may be *made* while the hearing of an application for an administration order is pending, a petition for winding up may be *presented*. It may well be the case that a creditor will wish to oppose an application for an administration order and argue instead that the company should be put into liquidation. If he has not already presented a winding-up petition, s.10(2)(a) confirms that he is free to do so; and in any case it is open to the court to combine the hearing of the two applications—an obviously convenient course. The leave of the court under s.10(1)(c) may, however, be necessary for such a joinder of proceedings; and if liquidation is in due course to be ordered the application for an administration order must first be dismissed (s.10(1)(a)), and vice versa (s.11(1)(a)).

In *Re a Company (No.001992 of 1988)* (1988) 4 B.C.C. 451 the court ruled that it was proper not to proceed to advertise a winding-up petition until after determination of the application for an administration order; but in later proceedings (reported as *Re Manlon Trading Ltd* (1988) 4 B.C.C. 455) Harman J. ruled that this course should only be taken when a petition for an administration order had actually been presented or an undertaking given to the court to present one: it was not sufficient to act on affidavit evidence that administration was being contemplated.

The Act is silent on the question whether it is possible, at least without leave, to present a second administration petition specifying a different purpose (e.g. a realisation of assets rather than a voluntary arrangement, or vice versa).

S.10(3)

If an administrative receiver is already in office when a petition for an administration order is presented, the earlier "moratorium" provisions of this section do not apply, unless and until the debenture holder gives his consent to the making of an administration order (thereby signalling his willingness to vacate the receivership in favour of the proposed administratorship). There is no corresponding provision dealing with the case where the holder of the charge puts in an administrative receiver *after* the petition for an administration order is presented: the moratorium which will already be in force as regards all the company's other creditors apparently continues until the petition is disposed of in one way or another.

S.10(4)

Of the four categories of agreement mentioned in this section, "hire-purchase agreement" and "conditional sale agreement" are defined (by reference to the Consumer Credit Act 1974) in s.436 and "chattel leasing agreement" and "retention of title agreement" in s.251. In each of these transactions the ownership of the goods concerned remains vested in the bailor or seller, and they do not become the company's property; but the Act for many purposes treats them as if the company has become the owner and the other party has retained only a security interest. See further the notes to ss.15 and 43.

S.10(5)

This provision assimilates the rules contained in the subsections above to the position under Scots law.

11 Effect of order

11(1) **[On making of administration order]** *On the making of an administration order–*

(a) *any petition for the winding up of the company shall be dismissed, and*

(b) *any administrative receiver of the company shall vacate office.*

11(2) **[Vacation of office by receiver]** *Where an administration order has been made, any receiver of part of the company's property shall vacate office on being required to do so by the administrator.*

11(3) **[Limitations]** *During the period for which an administration order is in force–*

(a) *no resolution may be passed or order made for the winding up of the company;*

(b) *no administrative receiver of the company may be appointed;*

(ba) *no landlord or other person to whom rent is payable may exercise any right of forfeiture by peaceable re-entry in relation to premises let to the company in respect of a failure by the company to comply with any term or condition of its tenancy of such premises, except with the consent of the administrator or the leave of the court and subject (where the court gives leave) to such terms as the court may impose;*

(c) *no other steps may be taken to enforce any security over the company's property, or to repossess goods in the company's possession under any hire-purchase agreement, except with the consent of the administrator or the leave of the court and subject (where the court gives leave) to such terms as the court may impose; and*

(d) *no other proceedings and no execution or other legal process may be commenced or continued, and no distress may be levied, against the company or its property except with the consent of the administrator or the leave of the court and subject (where the court gives leave) to such terms as aforesaid.*

11(4) **[Where vacation of office under s.11(1)(b), (2)]** *Where at any time an administrative receiver of the company has vacated office under subsection (1)(b), or a receiver of part of the company's property has vacated office under subsection (2)–*

(a) *his remuneration and any expenses properly incurred by him, and*

(b) *any indemnity to which he is entitled out of the assets of the company,*

shall be charged on and (subject to subsection (3) above) paid out of any property of the company which was in his custody or under his control at that time in priority to any security held by the person by or on whose behalf he was appointed.

11(5) **[Sections 40, 59]** *Neither an administrative receiver who vacates office under subsection (1)(b) nor a receiver who vacates office under subsection (2) is required on or after so vacating office to take any steps for the purpose of complying with any duty imposed on him by section 40 or 59 of this Act (duty to pay preferential creditors).*

GENERAL NOTE

On the making of an administration order, the suspension of the rights of creditors and security-holders imposed by s.10 becomes a total ban, and the administrative receiver, if there has been one in office, must give way to the administrator.

S.11(1)

If a petition for winding up has been presented, whether before or after the presentation of the petition for an administration order, the petitioner should take all possible steps to ensure that his case is heard before, or simultaneously with, the winding-up application: see the note to s.10(2).

An administrative receiver will be required to vacate office under this provision only if his appointor has consented to the making of the administration order or if his security is found liable to be invalidated under s.9(3)(b). On the effects of his vacating office, see the note to s.11(2).

S.11(2)

A receiver of part (i.e. not "substantially the whole") of the company's property is not an administrative receiver: see s.29(2). He is not required automatically to vacate office—the administrator has a discretion; but any steps that he may take to enforce the security will need the consent of the administrator or the leave of the court under s.11(3)(c).

The full implications of the vacation of office by a receiver under this section are not clearly spelt out in the Act. The appointment of the receiver, when it was made, will have crystallised the charge, in so far as it was a floating charge, so that the assets affected will have been subject to a fixed charge throughout the subsistence of the receivership. Section 11(4) grants the receiver a charge on the assets for his fees, etc. and in some circumstances the right to have them paid, and both this subsection and s.15(1) confirm that the debenture-holder's security continues in force during the period when the administrator is in office. Presumably it does so as a fixed charge and is not decrystallised, for otherwise s.15(4) would make little sense. This is not likely to be a point of great significance, however, for under the statutory definition it will be treated for all the purposes of the Act as if it were still a floating charge: see s.251 and the notes to ss.175(2)(b) and 245. The creditors entitled to preference in the receivership will lose all claims against the discharged receiver (s.11(5)) and will have no claim against the administrator (s.15(1)). However, presumably it is intended that they will retain some form of priority over the debenture holder himself by virtue of s.15(4). This is by no means a foregone conclusion, however, for (1) if the administration order is discharged without a winding up, the debenture holder will have to appoint a receiver afresh in order to enforce his security, and this will mean a new "relevant date" for the purposes of s.387 and different "assets coming to the hands of the receiver" for the purposes of s.40(2) or s.59(1); while (2) if the company is put into liquidation immediately upon the discharge of the administration order, s.175 will apply to the exclusion of s.40 or s.59, and under s.387(3)(a) a quite different list of preferential debts would need to be drawn up.

Section 11(2) does not apply in relation to a receiver appointed to enforce a "market charge" (as defined by CA 1989 s.173): see s.175 of that Act (as qualified by the Financial Markets and Insolvency Regulations 1991 (SI 1991/880)). It is also disapplied in relation to payment and securities settlement systems by the Finality Regulations reg.19. (See the introductory notes at Vol.1, pp.1–3.)

In relation to the financial markets, nothing in s.11(3) affects any action taken by an exchange or clearing house for the purpose of its default proceedings: CA 1989 s.161(4).

S.11(3)

This subsection spells out the full details of the restrictions on the enforcement of claims and securities against the company which apply once the administration order becomes operative. In one respect, the ban is strengthened: it is no longer possible to appoint an administrative receiver. In another respect, it is slightly relaxed: the acts mentioned in paras (c) and (d) may now be authorised by the administrator as an alternative to seeking the leave of the court.

In *Air Ecosse Ltd v Civil Aviation Authority* (1987) 3 B.C.C. 492, the Court of Session ruled that the term "proceedings" in s.11(3) was confined in its scope to the activities of the company's creditors in seeking to enforce their debts, and did not extend to quasi-judicial and extra-judicial proceedings such as an application made by a competitor of the company for the revocation of an aviation licence. But this view has been much criticised, and cannot now be regarded as a correct statement of the law. It has since been held that leave is required for an application by an employee to an industrial tribunal complaining that he had been unfairly selected for redundancy (*Carr v British International Helicopters Ltd* [1993] B.C.C. 855; and see *Re Divine Solutions (UK) Ltd* [2004] B.C.C. 325); for an application for the revocation of a patent (*Re Axis Genetics Ltd* [2000] B.C.C. 943); and even for the bringing of criminal proceedings against the company (*Re Rhondda Waste Disposal Ltd, Environment Agency v Clark (Administrator of Rhondda Waste Disposal Ltd)* [2001] Ch. 57; [2000] B.C.C. 653). In *A Straume (UK) Ltd v Bradlor Developments Ltd* [2000] B.C.C. 333 the reference of a dispute arising under a building contract to a statutory adjudication procedure was held to be a quasi-legal proceeding akin to arbitration which required leave, even though further proceedings would be needed to enforce any award that might be made. In contrast with these decisions, the Court of Appeal has ruled in *Re Railtrack plc* [2002] 2 B.C.L.C. 755 that the determination by the Rail Regulator of an application by a train operator under the Railways Act 1993 for permission to use the railway network was not "proceedings" or a "legal process" within s.11.

It is only in exceptional cases that the court will give leave to a creditor to commence proceedings in order to resolve a dispute relating to his claim rather than allow the administration to run its course: *AES Barry Ltd v TXU Europe Energy Trading Ltd* [2004] EWHC 1757 (Ch); [2005] 2 B.C.L.C. 22.

The phrases "any security over the company's property" and "execution or other legal process" contained in paras (c) and (d) have also been the subject of judicial rulings in a number of contexts. In *Bristol Airport plc v Powdrill*

[1990] Ch. 744 (reported as *Re Paramount Airways Ltd* [1990] B.C.C. 130) the Court of Appeal, affirming Harman J., held that for the purposes of s.11(3)(c) and (d): (i) aircraft held by the company on lease was "property" of the company; and (ii) the statutory right of an airport to detain aircraft pursuant to s.88 of the Civil Aviation Act 1982 for failure to pay outstanding airport charges was a "lien or other security" (within the extended definition of "security" contained in IA 1986 s.248) which could not be exercised without the leave of the court.

However, the insertion of para.(ba) into s.11(3) (and correspondingly of para.(aa) into s.10(1)) with effect from April 2, 2001 has laid to rest an issue on which there had been much controversy and conflicting judicial opinion, namely whether a landlord's right of re-entry for non-payment of rent or the breach of any other covenant in the lease constituted a "security" or "the commencement of a legal process" which fell within s.11(c) or (d). The differing judicial views are collected and analysed in the latest of the reported cases, *Re Lomax Leisure Ltd* [2000] B.C.C. 352, in which Neuberger J. concluded that the balance of opinion was in favour of the view that leave was not required, and that this was indirectly supported by observations of the House of Lords in *Re Park Air Services plc* [2000] 2 A.C. 172; [1999] B.C.C. 135. The legislative amendments have therefore reversed this position. However, the views expressed in some of these cases will continue to be relevant in situations analogous to the landlord's right of re-entry which are not covered by the new subsections. In *Re Olympia & York Canary Wharf Ltd, American Express Europe Ltd v Adamson* [1993] B.C.C. 154 Millett J. said that "legal process" means a process which requires the assistance of the court, and that it does not include such steps as the serving of a notice by a party to a contract making time of the essence, or the acceptance by such a party of a repudiatory breach of contract. Similarly, in *Bristol Airport plc v Powdrill* (above) at 766; 153 Browne-Wilkinson V.C. plainly doubted whether the serving of a counter-notice claiming a new tenancy under the Landlord and Tenant Act 1954 could be regarded as a "proceeding".

An application for an extension of time for the registration of a charge cannot be described as "proceedings against a company or its property" within s.11(3)(d): *Re Barrow Borough Transport Ltd* [1990] Ch. 227; (1989) 5 B.C.C. 646. However, once an administration order has been made and it has become clear that administration will result in the insolvent liquidation of the company, the court's discretion should be exercised against granting an extension of time for registration (ibid.).

Section 11 does not affect the substantive rights of the parties: it is concerned merely with procedure. It imposes a moratorium on the enforcement of creditors' rights, but does not destroy those rights. The legal right of a security holder to enforce his security, and that of an owner of goods to immediate possession of his goods, and the causes of action based on such rights, remain vested in that party. If he seeks and obtains the leave of the court to enforce his rights, the grant of leave does not alter the parties' legal rights, but merely grants the applicant liberty to enforce his rights: *Barclays Mercantile Business Finance Ltd v Sibec Developments Ltd (Re Sibec Developments Ltd)* [1992] 1 W.L.R. 1253; [1993] B.C.C. 148.

It was held in *Carr v British International Helicopters Ltd* (above) that a proceeding (such as an application to an industrial tribunal) commenced without leave is not a nullity and that the proceeding could be adjourned while consent or leave is sought. This ruling might once have been thought open to question in the light of the decision of the House of Lords in *Seal v Chief Constable of South Wales Police* [2007] EWHL 31; [2007] 1 W.L.R. 1910: but see now the note to s.285(3), (4).

Section 11(3)(c) does not apply in relation to the enforcement of "market charges" (as defined by CA 1989 s.173): see s.175 of that Act (as qualified by the Financial Markets and Insolvency Regulations 1991 (SI 1991/880)). It is also disapplied in relation to payment and securities settlement systems by the Finality Regulations reg.19. (See the introductory notes at Vol.1, pp.1–3.)

Section 11(3)(d) is similar to s.130(2), which applies in a winding up, and decisions under that section may give guidance as to how the discretion under s.11(3)(d) will be exercised.

Note that the reference to "any hire-purchase agreement" in para.(c) includes also conditional sale agreements, chattel leasing agreements and retention of title agreements: see s.10(4). Section 11(3)(c) extends to goods which are the subject of a hire-purchase or similar agreement even where the agreement has been terminated before the presentation of the petition for an administration order, provided that the goods remain in the company's possession: *Re David Meek Plant Ltd; Re David Meek Access Ltd* [1993] B.C.C. 175. The landmark decision of the Court of Appeal in *Re Atlantic Computer Systems plc* [1992] Ch. 505; [1990] B.C.C. 859 contains a number of important rulings on the jurisdiction conferred by s.11, and guidance on the principles governing the exercise of the court's discretion under the section. The company's business was leasing computers, a substantial number of which it held on hire-purchase or long lease from banks and other financial institutions (referred to in the judgment as "the funders"). Two funders applied to the court contending that the administrators, having received payments from the sub-lessees, were obliged to pay the rentals due under the head leases. Alternatively, the funders sought leave under s.11 to repossess the computer equipment. The trial judge, applying an analogy from winding-up law, held that where leased property was used for the purposes of an administration, the rent or hire charges due to the lessor should rank as an expense of the administration and as such be payable in priority to the company's other creditors; but the Court of Appeal considered that a more appropriate analogy was with administrative receivership, where such charges would not have the same priority. The court expressed the view that, in any case, the discretionary jurisdiction conferred by s.11 should be exercised on the broadest basis and should not be allowed to become fettered by rigid rules of automatic application. However, it went on to hold that the computers remained "goods in the company's possession", notwithstanding the sub-leases, so that the discretionary powers conferred by s.11(3)(c) could be invoked; that lessors and other owners of property in the position of the funders should not be compelled to leave it in the company's hands against their will but should ordinarily be allowed to repossess it; and that this should normally be a matter where the administrator would be expected to give his consent, thus obviating the need to make application to the court for leave.

The judgment concludes with a statement giving guidance on the principles to be applied on applications for the grant of leave under s.11. These principles, which are set out at length (see [1992] Ch. 505 at 542–544; [1990] B.C.C. 859 at 879–882), also serve as guidelines to an administrator in determining whether to grant consent, and may be summarised as follows:

(1)   The person seeking leave has always to make out a case.

(2)   If granting leave to an owner of land or goods to exercise his proprietary rights as lessor and repossess his land or goods is unlikely to impede the achievement of the purpose of the administration, leave should normally be given.

(3)   In other cases where a lessor seeks possession, the court has to carry out a balancing exercise, weighing the legitimate interests of the lessor against those of the company's other creditors.

(4)   In carrying out the balancing exercise, great importance is normally to be given to the lessor's proprietary interests: an administration for the benefit of unsecured creditors should not be conducted at the expense of those who have proprietary rights.

(5)   It will normally be a sufficient ground for the grant of leave that significant loss would be caused to the lessor by a refusal. However if substantially greater loss would be caused to others by the grant of leave, that may outweigh the loss to the lessor caused by a refusal.

(6)–(8)   These paragraphs list the various factors to which the court will have regard in assessing the respective losses under heading (5). These include: the financial position of the company, its ability to pay the interest, rentals or other charges (both arrears and continuing charges), the administrator's proposals and the end result sought to be achieved by the administration, the period for which the administration has already been in force and that for which it is expected to continue, the prospects of success of the administration, the likely loss to the applicant if leave is refused, and the conduct of the parties.

(9)   The above considerations may be relevant not only to the decision whether or not to grant leave, but also to a decision to impose terms if leave is granted.

(10)   The court may, in effect, impose conditions if leave is refused (for instance, by giving directions to the administrator), in which case the above considerations will also be applicable.

(11)   A broadly similar approach will apply in many applications for leave to enforce a security.

(12)   The court will not, on a leave application, seek to adjudicate upon a dispute over the existence, validity or nature of a security unless the issue raises a short point of law which it is convenient to determine without further ado.

See also the judgment of Peter Gibson J. in *Re Meesan Investments Ltd* (1988) 4 B.C.C. 788, where it was observed that the fact that enforcement of the security independently of the administration would increase costs was a factor that the court might take into account in refusing leave.

Although the statement above was directed primarily to the question of giving leave to enforce a security under s.11(3)(c), parts of it may give some guidance to the court in exercising its jurisdiction to grant leave to commence proceedings under para.(d): see *Re Polly Peck International plc (in admin.) (No.4)* [1997] 2 B.C.L.C. 630.

In *Euro Commercial Leasing Ltd v Cartwright & Lewis* [1995] B.C.C. 830 it was accepted on all sides that the remedy for a breach of s.11(3)(c) should be a claim in damages. However, in the case itself, which concerned a solicitors' lien, no damage had resulted from the breach.

Other cases concerning the grant of leave under s.11 include *Re Carter Commercial Developments Ltd* [2002] B.C.C. 803 (enforcement of solicitors' lien); *Re City Logistics Ltd* [2002] 2 B.C.L.C. 103 (costs); *London Flight Centre (Stansted) Ltd v Osprey Aviation Ltd* [2002] B.P.I.R. 1115; *Joinery Plus Ltd v Laing Ltd* [2003] B.P.I.R. 890 (overpayment); and *Sinai Securities Ltd v Hooper* [2004] B.C.C. 973 (appointment of non-administrative receiver).

The guidelines formulated in the *Atlantic Computers* case were adopted and applied in *Innovate Logistics Ltd v Sunberry Properties Ltd* [2008] EWCA Civ 1321; [2009] B.C.C. 164, where leave was sought (but refused) under the corresponding provision of the new administration regime (Sch.B1 para.43(6)). See the note to that provision.

S.11(4)

An administrative receiver automatically vacates office when an order is made (s.11(1)(b)), and any other receiver may be required by the administrator to do so (s.11(2)). This subsection seeks to secure the receiver's right to remuneration, and any entitlement to an indemnity that he may have, ahead of the claims of the security-holder who appointed him. However, (like every other creditor) he cannot receive actual payment of this claim or take steps to enforce it except with the administrator's consent or the court's leave under s.11(3).

S.11(5)

Under the sections mentioned, it is the duty of a receiver who is appointed to enforce a floating charge to pay the company's preferential debts "out of the assets coming into his hands". This subsection makes it clear that the assets must be surrendered to the administrator by the receiver when he vacates office, without regard to this obligation, and also that he is thereafter discharged from that duty.

On "preferential debts", see the notes to ss.386 and 387; and see also the discussion at s.11(2) above.

Note that there is no provision in the original Pt II giving priority to preferential debts in a company administration, unless either a winding up follows immediately on the discharge of the administration order (s.387(3)(a)) or the administration coincides with a voluntary arrangement (s.387(2)(a)). However in appropriate circumstances the court may make an order which reflects the rights which such creditors would have in a winding up—or even puts them in a better position: see *Re WBSL Realisations 1992 Ltd* [1995] B.C.C. 1118 and the note to s.18(2).

12   Notification of order

12(1)   [Information in invoices etc.] *Every invoice, order for goods or business letter which, at a time when an administration order is in force in relation to a company, is issued by or on behalf of the company or the administrator, being a document on or in which the company's name appears, shall also contain the administrator's name and a statement that the affairs, business and property of the company are being managed by the administrator.*

12(2)   [Penalty on default] *If default is made in complying with this section, the company and any of the following persons who without reasonable excuse authorises or permits the default, namely, the administrator and any officer of the company, is liable to a fine.*

S.12(1)

This is a parallel provision to those requiring notification of the appointment of a receiver (ss.39, 64) and notification that a company is in liquidation (s.188).

S.12(2)

The policy reasons for making the company itself liable for this offence are not obvious. Note that the *company* is strictly liable, while any of the other persons named is liable only if he "without reasonable excuse authorises or permits the default". This language may be contrasted with that of ss.39, 64 and 188: "who knowingly and wilfully authorises or permits the default".

On penalties, see s.430 and Sch.10.

Administrators

13   Appointment of administrator

13(1)   [Appointment] *The administrator of a company shall be appointed either by the administration order or by an order under the next subsection.*

13(2)   [Court may fill vacancy] *If a vacancy occurs by death, resignation or otherwise in the office of the administrator, the court may by order fill the vacancy.*

13(3)   [Application for s.13(2) order] *An application for an order under subsection (2) may be made–*

  (a) by any continuing administrator of the company; or

(b) where there is no such administrator, by a creditors' committee established under section 26 below; or

(c) where there is no such administrator and no such committee, by the company or the directors or by any creditor or creditors of the company.

GENERAL NOTE

These provisions deal with the appointment of an administrator and with vacancies in the office of administrator.

It is apparent from s.13(3)(a) and s.231 that two or more persons may be appointed joint administrators.

There is no power under this or any other provision for the court to appoint an interim administrator: see the note to s.9(4).

An administrator must be an insolvency practitioner and qualified to act in relation to the particular company: see s.230(1).

S.13(3)

On "the company" and "the directors", see the note to s.124(1).

14   General powers

14(1)   [Powers of administrator] The administrator of a company–

(a) may do all such things as may be necessary for the management of the affairs, business and property of the company, and

(b) without prejudice to the generality of paragraph (a), has the powers specified in Schedule 1 to this Act;

and in the application of that Schedule to the administrator of a company the words "he" and "him" refer to the administrator.

14(2)   [Extra powers] The administrator also has power–

(a) to remove any director of the company and to appoint any person to be a director of it, whether to fill a vacancy or otherwise, and

(b) to call any meeting of the members or creditors of the company.

14(3)   [Application for directions] The administrator may apply to the court for directions in relation to any particular matter arising in connection with the carrying out of his functions.

14(4)   [Conflict with other powers] Any power conferred on the company or its officers, whether by this Act or the Companies Acts or by the company's articles, which could be exercised in such a way as to interfere with the exercise by the administrator of his powers is not exercisable except with the consent of the administrator, which may be given either generally or in relation to particular cases.

14(5)   [Administrator agent] In exercising his powers the administrator is deemed to act as the company's agent.

14(6)   [Third party] A person dealing with the administrator in good faith and for value is not concerned to inquire whether the administrator is acting within his powers.

S.14(1)

The powers of an administrator are stated in the broadest terms in para.(a), and extend to anything which was within the powers of the directors before the administration order was made—e.g. appointing a trustee to an employees' pension scheme (*Denny v Yeldon* [1995] 1 B.C.L.C. 560; and *Polly Peck International plc v Henry* [1999] 1 B.C.L.C. 407). In addition, some specific powers, common to both administrators and administrative receivers, are set out in more detail in Sch.1. These powers are not restricted to the management of the company's business (as is normally the case with the board of directors). This is indicated by the use of the word "affairs" and appears also from some of the particular matters mentioned in this section and the schedule, e.g. the power to remove directors (s.14(2)).

Although the powers of an administrator are similar in many respects to those of an administrative receiver, there are also important differences, and the analogy cannot be pressed too far. An administrator is appointed to manage the affairs of the company; an administrative receiver's role is to realise the company's assets primarily for the benefit of a particular creditor: *Astor Chemical Ltd v Synthetic Technology Ltd* [1990] B.C.C. 97 at 105–106. A receiver may decline to perform certain contracts which an administrator has no power to disown (ibid.). And, unlike a liquidator, an administrator has no statutory power of disclaimer (*Re P & C and R & T (Stockport) Ltd* [1991] B.C.C. 98 at 104).

The powers of an administrator do not extend to acts which the company itself is not competent to perform: *Re Home Treat Ltd* [1991] B.C.C. 165. In this case, the company's objects as stated in its memorandum did not extend to the running of a nursing home (the company's actual business which the administrators wished to continue pending a sale). The court managed to circumvent this difficulty by a somewhat indulgent ruling that there had been a de facto alteration of the objects clause by an informal resolution of the shareholders at an earlier stage.

For the administrator's special power to deal with charged property, see s.15.

S.14(2)

The power given to an administrator to appoint and remove directors has no parallel elsewhere in company law, apart of course from the statutory power conferred upon the company in general meeting. (During the currency of an administration order, these powers of the general meeting will not be exercisable without the consent of the administrator: see s.14(4).)

If the removal of a director amounts to a breach of his service contract, the company will be liable in damages, even though the removal was in exercise of a statutory power: *Southern Foundries (1926) Ltd v Shirlaw* [1940] A.C. 701; *Shindler v Northern Raincoat Co Ltd* [1960] 1 W.L.R. 1038.

Section 14(2) does not empower the administrator to dispense with the board of directors entirely: CA 2006 s.154 (which prescribes a minimum of two directors for every public company, and one for a private company) will still apply to a company that is subject to an administration order. See further the note to s.14(4), below.

S.14(3)

A similar provision applies to the supervisor of a CVA (s.7(4)) and the liquidator in a winding up by the court (s.168(3)).

The powers of an administrator under ss.14(1)(a) and 17(2) to "manage the affairs, business and property of the company" are wide enough to make it unnecessary in many cases for an administrator to seek directions from the court, so that he may, e.g. sell a substantial asset in a proper case even before the creditors' meeting has been held: see, however, the note to s.17(2). For examples of applications for directions under s.14(3), see *Re British & Commonwealth Holdings plc (No.3)* [1992] 1 W.L.R. 672; [1992] B.C.C. 58; and *Re Maxwell Communications Corporation plc (No.3)* [1993] 1 W.L.R. 1402; [1993] B.C.C. 369—cases which contain important rulings on the effectiveness of debt subordination arrangements created (respectively) by trust deed and by contract; and *Re Lewis's of Leicester Ltd* [1995] B.C.C. 514, where the court was asked to rule whether moneys which had been paid to the company by concession-holders and held in segregated accounts were the subject of a trust or, alternatively, whether the arrangements were open to challenge as preferences or transactions at an undervalue. The court will not normally interfere with a commercial decision of an administrator, and will do so only if what is proposed is wrong in law or is conspicuously unfair to a particular creditor or person dealing with the company: *Re CE King Ltd* [2000] 2 B.C.L.C. 297.

The power of the court to give directions to the administrator under s.14(3) is limited by the words "in connection with the carrying out of his functions". The court cannot go beyond the purposes for which the order was made, and so the power (or any comparable residual or inherent power) cannot be invoked to authorise the making of a distribution to creditors: *Re Lune Metal Products Ltd* [2006] EWCA Civ 1720; [2007] B.C.C. 217.

In *Re TBL Realisations Ltd* [2004] B.C.C. 81 the company's administrators proposed to continue the administration while implementing a CVA with themselves acting as supervisors. The question arose how a judgment debt which had been obtained by certain creditors was to be dealt with, having regard to the fact that this debt was not within the scope of the CVA. The Court of Appeal held that it was proper for directions to be given to the administrators under s.14(3), and ruled that the administrators should make payments to the judgment creditors on a pro rata basis to those to be made to the CVA creditors. The section was also invoked in *Re TXU UK Ltd* [2002] EWHC 2784 (Ch); [2003] B.P.I.R. 1062 to authorise administrators to settle a claim, in reliance either on the court's inherent jurisdiction or on the powers contained in Sch.1 paras 13 and 18.

S.14(4)

On the appointment of an administrator, the directors remain in office, and both the board of directors and the shareholders in general meeting retain their roles as organs of the company under the articles of association and the Companies Act—although their powers will, of course, be severely restricted by the provisions of this section. The directors' statutory and common-law duties will continue to apply to them—including the duty to hold annual meetings, prepare accounts and make returns to the registrar.

S.14(5)

This provision in part echoes the terms on which a receiver is customarily appointed to enforce a debenture holder's security—terms which are now given statutory expression in s.44(1) of this Act. However, the subsection has only a limited effect: it does not make the administrator the company's agent in any full sense, nor even say (as does s.44(1)) that he shall be deemed to *be* the agent of the company; only deemed to be *acting* as its agent in exercising his powers, although the difference in wording may not be material. He is not, like a normal agent, subject to control and direction by the company as his principal (see s.14(4)); his actual authority is virtually unlimited (see s.14(1)), and his ostensible authority completely so (see s.14(6)).

The main object of this provision is to try to ensure that the administrator, at least in the normal case, incurs no personal liability on any contract or other obligation that he may enter into on the company's behalf. (Contrast the position of an administrative receiver (s.44(1)).

Like an agent, the administrator will also owe the usual fiduciary duties to the company, and will be entitled to be indemnified out of its assets for obligations that he incurs.

S.14(6)

This provision is probably inserted out of caution only, since such a third party would almost certainly be protected by the ordinary rules of agency.

15   *Power to deal with charged property, etc.*

15(1)   ***[Power of disposal etc.]*** *The administrator of a company may dispose of or otherwise exercise his powers in relation to any property of the company which is subject to a security to which this subsection applies as if the property were not subject to the security.*

15(2)   ***[Court orders, on application by administrator]*** *Where, on an application by the administrator, the court is satisfied that the disposal (with or without other assets) of–*

   (a)   any property of the company subject to a security to which this subsection applies, or

   (b)   any goods in the possession of the company under a hire-purchase agreement,

would be likely to promote the purpose or one or more of the purposes specified in the administration order, the court may by order authorise the administrator to dispose of the property as if it were not subject to the security or to dispose of the goods as if all rights of the owner under the hire-purchase agreement were vested in the company.

15(3)   ***[Application of s.15(1), (2)]*** *Subsection (1) applies to any security which, as created, was a floating charge; and subsection (2) applies to any other security.*

15(4)   ***[Effect of security where property disposed of]*** *Where property is disposed of under subsection (1), the holder of the security has the same priority in respect of any property of the company directly or indirectly representing the property disposed of as he would have had in respect of the property subject to the security.*

15(5)   ***[Conditions for s.15(2) order]*** *It shall be a condition of an order under subsection (2) that–*

   (a)   the net proceeds of the disposal, and

   (b)   where those proceeds are less than such amount as may be determined by the court to be the net amount which would be realised on a sale of the property or goods in the open market by a willing vendor, such sums as may be required to make good the deficiency,

shall be applied towards discharging the sums secured by the security or payable under the hire-purchase agreement.

15(6)   ***[Where s.15(5) condition re two or more securities]*** *Where a condition imposed in pursuance of subsection (5) relates to two or more securities, that condition requires the net proceeds of the disposal and, where paragraph (b) of that subsection applies, the sums mentioned in that paragraph to be applied towards discharging the sums secured by those securities in the order of their priorities.*

15(7) *[**Copy of s.15(2) order to registrar***] A copy of an order under subsection (2) shall, within 14 days after the making of the order, be sent by the administrator to the registrar of companies.*

15(8) *[**Non-compliance with s.15(7)**] If the administrator without reasonable excuse fails to comply with subsection (7), he is liable to a fine and, for continued contravention, to a daily default fine.*

15(9) *[**Interpretation**] References in this section to hire-purchase agreements include conditional sale agreements, chattel leasing agreements and retention of title agreements.*

GENERAL NOTE

This section gives to the administrator unique powers to override the rights of the holder of a security over the company's property or the owner of property held by the company under a hire-purchase or similar agreement, and to dispose of the property in question as if it were owned by the company itself unencumbered. This he may do without the consent of the chargee or owner of the property, but the authorisation of the court will be needed unless the security is (or was originally) a floating charge. The section includes provisions designed to ensure that rights roughly analogous to those previously enjoyed by the charge holder or owner are preserved.

The power conferred by this section will be of particular value when an administrator wishes to dispose of the business of the company, or some part of it, as a going concern, and a security-holder or property-owner is not willing to co-operate. A similar power is given to an administrative receiver by s.43.

Some guidance as to the operation of the section is given by the judgment in *Re A R V Aviation Ltd* (1988) 4 B.C.C. 708, where the holder of a charge over land owned by the company opposed the administrators' application to be authorised to dispose of it. The charge holder contended, inter alia, that the administrators were basing their application on an over-optimistic valuation of the land in question. The court ruled that a bona fide dispute as to value would clearly call into operation the discretion of the court under s.15(2), and stated that in principle it was desirable for the court to have proper valuation evidence before being asked to exercise that jurisdiction. It also ruled: (i) that "the sums secured by the security" in s.15(5) covered interest and (subject to the court's overriding discretion) the charge holder's costs, as well as the principal sum secured; and (ii) that it was not necessary at the time of making an order for disposal under s.15(2) to assess the amount of the deficiency to which the secured creditor might be entitled under s.15(5): this could be determined at a later hearing.

Note that nothing in this section or s.16 is to be taken as prejudicing the right of a creditor or member to apply to the court for relief under s.27: see s.27(5).

Section 15(1) and (2) do not apply in relation to the enforcement of "market charges" (as defined by CA 1989 s.173): see s.175 of that Act (as qualified by the Financial Markets and Insolvency Regulations 1991 (SI 1991/880)). It is also disapplied in relation to payment and securities settlement systems by the Finality Regulations reg.19. (See the introductory notes in Vol.1, pp.1–3.)

S.15(1), (3), (4)
These subsections, taken together, deal with the case where property of the company is subject to a floating charge. The administrator is empowered to dispose of or deal with the property without the consent of the chargee and without seeking a court order. This is so even though the charge may have crystallised on or before the making of the administration order (s.15(3), and see the note to s.11(2)); but where the same obligation is secured by both a fixed and a floating charge, s.15(2) will apply to such assets as are covered by the fixed charge.

The meaning of s.15(4) is obscure. It seems to be intended to ensure that any dealing by the administrator with the property of the company will not prejudice the chargee's security rights. However, instead of providing that the *security* shall extend to the price or other property acquired by the company in substitution for the asset disposed of, it speaks merely of "priority". This could give rise to many difficult questions. For example, will the charge holder be entitled to claim security over such substituted property if the administration is brought to a successful conclusion and the order discharged? Suppose that the company trades its way back into a sound financial position, though still with a modest overdraft, and control is handed back to the directors: what security will the bank have?

It is also far from clear whether the "priority" referred to means priority in the ranking of one charge vis-à-vis another, or priority in the order that the company's various debts are paid, or priority in some other sense. The uncertainty as to the position of those creditors whose debts would have been entitled to preferential payment in a receivership has been discussed elsewhere (see the note to s.11(2)).

S.15(2), (5), (6)
Property which is subject to a fixed charge (excluding a charge which was originally a floating charge but has since become fixed: see s.15(3)) may be disposed of by the administrator under these subsections without the consent of the charge holder, but only (1) with the authorisation of the court; and (2) on terms that the whole of the net proceeds

of the sale (or the open market value of the property if it is sold for less) is applied in discharge of the amount secured—not necessarily, of course, the whole of the company's indebtedness to the particular creditor. These provisions extend also to goods in the possession of the company under a hire-purchase agreement (or a conditional sale agreement, chattel leasing agreement or retention of title agreement: see s.15(9)): the administrator may sell the goods without the owner's consent, but must apply the realised amount (or open market value) towards discharging the sums payable to the owner under the agreement.

The phrase "payable under the agreement" (s.15(5)) may cause some difficulty, since not all of the agreements listed in s.15(9) will contain an express provision making the company accountable to the owner for the value of the property or the proceeds of sale in the event of a (possibly wrongful) sale to a third party. If, for instance, in regard to a chattel leasing agreement, the administrator sells the chattel unencumbered to a third party under s.15(2) at a time when only one month's rental is outstanding, it would appear to be only the latter sum, and not the full value of the lessor's interest in the property, that must be accounted for under s.15(5). If this is so, the lessor may have only an unsecured claim for money had and received against the company in respect of the balance of the proceeds of sale, or a right to seek relief under s.27. No claim in tort (e.g. for wrongful interference with goods) would appear to lie against either the administrator or the company for action taken under s.15(2); and it must be a matter of doubt whether the court can make an order subject to conditions other than that specified in s.15(5).

If more is realised on the sale than is needed to discharge the sums in question, the balance will go into the general company funds held by the administrator (subject to what is said above). If less, the shortfall will remain due to the chargee or owner as an unsecured debt, unless the sale has been at below the market value and s.15(5)(b) applies.

The administrator must satisfy the court as to the need for the sale, in the terms of s.15(2); and the court is also charged by s.15(5)(b) with the task of settling the open market value of the property, where that provision applies.

If the administrator and the chargee or owner of the property are willing to collaborate, of course, the property may be disposed of much more simply and cheaply under s.11(3)(c).

In *Re Consumer & Industrial Press Ltd (No.2)* (1988) 4 B.C.C. 72 it was held that the court would not, except in "quite exceptional circumstances", authorise an administrator under s.15(2) to dispose of assets before the administrator's proposals had been considered by a creditors' meeting. However, it is now well established that in cases of urgency an administrator may be justified in proceeding with such a sale—even a sale of the company's entire undertaking—without waiting for a creditors' meeting, and that he may do so without seeking the leave of the court: see the note to s.17(2), below. In any event, in an appropriate case, he could enter into an agreement with an intended purchaser conditionally upon the approval of the creditors or the leave of the court.

The administrators in *Re Newman Shopfitters (Cleveland) Ltd* [1991] B.C.L.C. 407 sought the court's authority to retain the proceeds of the sale of mortgaged property in a special bank account until they had reached a decision whether to challenge the validity of the mortgage. However the court held that it had no such power under s.15. If, on the other hand, proceedings to challenge the mortgage had been commenced, appropriate interim relief could have been sought in that action.

S.15(6)

This deals with the application of s.15(5) to the case where an item of property is subject to more than one charge: the normal priorities are preserved.

S.15(7), (8)

The purpose of these provisions is, no doubt, to ensure that the register of charges kept by the registrar under CA 2006 s.860 is kept up to date, for the benefit of people searching. However, the subsections affect all forms of security, and not merely registrable charges, and extend to hire-purchase agreements, etc. which are not charges at all.

Where charges are recorded in a register other than the Companies Registry (e.g. land, ships), it will no doubt be necessary to file a copy of the order in that register also in order to confirm that the transferee will take an unencumbered title.

S.15(9)

See the note to s.10(4). Of course if, under a retention of title agreement, the company has been authorised to deal with the contract goods and the seller has not withdrawn that authority, the administrator may sell the goods on without any need to rely on s.15: *Sandhu v Jet Star Retail Ltd* [2011] EWCA Civ 459.

16   *Operation of s.15 in Scotland*

16(1) **[*Administrator's duty*]** *Where property is disposed of under section 15 in its application to Scotland, the administrator shall grant to the disponee an appropriate document of transfer or conveyance of the property, and–*

(a) *that document, or*

(b) *where any recording, intimation or registration of the document is a legal requirement for completion of title to the property, that recording, intimation or registration,*

has the effect of disencumbering the property of or, as the case may be, freeing the property from the security.

16(2) [Disposal of goods on hire-purchase etc.] *Where goods in the possession of the company under a hire-purchase agreement, conditional sale agreement, chattel leasing agreement or retention of title agreement are disposed of under section 15 in its application to Scotland, the disposal has the effect of extinguishing, as against the disponee, all rights of the owner of the goods under the agreement.*

GENERAL NOTE

This section provides for the disponee who takes property under s.15 to have such evidence as may be required under Scots law to effect or confirm the disencumbering of the property and to extinguish any claim of the previous owner of goods held under hire-purchase and similar agreements.

17   General duties

17(1)   [Control of company property] *The administrator of a company shall, on his appointment, take into his custody or under his control all the property to which the company is or appears to be entitled.*

17(2)   [Management of affairs etc.] *The administrator shall manage the affairs, business and property of the company–*

(a) *at any time before proposals have been approved (with or without modifications) under section 24 below, in accordance with any directions given by the court, and*

(b) *at any time after proposals have been so approved, in accordance with those proposals as from time to time revised, whether by him or a predecessor of his.*

17(3)   [Summoning of creditors' meeting] *The administrator shall summon a meeting of the company's creditors if–*

(a) *he is requested, in accordance with the rules, to do so by one-tenth, in value, of the company's creditors, or*

(b) *he is directed to do so by the court.*

GENERAL NOTE

The position of an administrator is in many ways broadly comparable with that of an administrative receiver, as is confirmed by the fact that by Sch.1 they are given identical statutory powers; but there is an important difference in their roles. A receiver, representing a single secured creditor, is entitled to give priority to the interests of that creditor. An administrator, in contrast, like a liquidator, has no particular interest to which he should give priority. In the context of a sale of company property, a receiver acting in good faith may effect an immediate sale whether or not that is calculated to realise the best price, though he must take reasonable care to obtain a proper price for the property at the moment he chooses to sell it. However an administrator is under a duty to take reasonable care to obtain the best price that the circumstances (as he reasonably perceives them to be) permit, and this means that he must take reasonable care in choosing the time at which to sell the property. The conduct of an administrator is to be judged by the standards of a professional insolvency practitioner of ordinary skill. (See *Re Charnley Davies Ltd* [1990] B.C.C. 605 at 618.)

S.17(1)
This will include property that is encumbered and property owned by another person but in the possession of the company under a hire-purchase or similar agreement: see ss.11 and 15. An administrative receiver will have vacated office under s.11(1)(b). Exceptionally, a receiver of *part* of the company's property may be allowed by the administrator to remain in office, but he may not deal with the property in question without the consent of the administrator or the leave of the court (s.11(2), (3)(d)).

S.17(2)

The administrator's role is to seek to secure the financial rehabilitation of the company or one of the other purposes specified in s.8(3); but the Act does not leave him entirely free to set about his task at once, or to do so on his own initiative. He must call for a statement of affairs (s.22), formulate a set of proposals to define (and, by implication, to limit) the strategy he is to adopt (s.23), and put these proposals before a specially summoned creditors' meeting for approval. This process may take a period of several months; hence the need to give him interim powers to act under s.17(2)(a), subject to any directions that he may be given by the court.

These directions may be sought by the administrator himself or may be part of the relief granted on the application of a creditor or member under s.27.

In an unreported hearing involving the company Charnley Davies Ltd in January 1987, Vinelott J. confirmed advice given to its administrator by counsel that this section is wide enough to empower an administrator to sell the entire undertaking of the company in advance of the creditors' meeting if he considers that such a course is in the best interests of the company and its creditors, and that the administrator does not need the sanction of the court to do so. He ruled that the words "any directions" in s.17(2)(a) mean "the directions, if any". (See *Re Charnley Davies Ltd* [1990] B.C.C. 605 at 610–611.) In *Re N S Distribution Ltd* [1990] B.C.L.C. 169 Harman J. took a similar view, in relation to the sale of a single asset. However these rulings, which might have encouraged administrators to act on their own initiative in such a situation, were tempered by the strongly expressed opinion of Peter Gibson J. in *Re Consumer & Industrial Press Ltd (No.2)* (1988) 4 B.C.C. 72 that to take such action without giving the creditors the opportunity to consider the administrator's proposals would frustrate the purposes of the Act. In consequence, it was thought prudent for administrators to seek the leave of the court in cases of doubt. But in more recent cases, culminating with the fully reasoned judgment of Neuberger J. in *Re T & D Industries plc* [2000] 1 W.L.R. 646; [2000] B.C.C. 956, the view originally put by Vinelott J. has been confirmed, and administrators should now have cause to feel less inhibited by Peter Gibson J.'s qualms, and feel free to back their own judgment in cases of urgency. A similar construction has been put on the corresponding provision in the new administration regime: see the note to Sch.B1 para.68. An alternative course, adverted to by Neuberger J. and acceded to by Rattee J. in *Re Harris Bus Co Ltd* [2000] B.C.C. 1,151, is for the administrator to ask the court to direct the summoning of a meeting of the creditors at short notice under s.17(3) in order to seek their approval.

Paragraph (b) makes it plain that, after the creditors' meeting, the administrator's freedom to act is limited by the terms of the "proposals" approved by the creditors under ss.24 or 25. However, in exceptional circumstances (e.g. where the delay involved in summoning a creditors' meeting to consider a revised scheme could cause substantial loss) the court has a residual jurisdiction under s.14(3) to authorise an administrator to depart from an approved scheme: *Re Smallman Construction Ltd* (1988) 4 B.C.C. 784.

S.17(3)

This provision corresponds to s.168(2), which relates to a liquidator in a compulsory winding up. It is not necessary for the Act to provide in similar terms for the requisitioning of a shareholders' meeting, since the members' rights to do so under CA 2006 s.303 will not be affected by an administration order.

For the rules relating to this section, see IR 1986 rr.*2.21* et seq.

18   *Discharge or variation of administration order*

18(1)   **[Application to court by administrator]** *The administrator of a company may at any time apply to the court for the administration order to be discharged, or to be varied so as to specify an additional purpose.*

18(2)   **[Duty to make application]** *The administrator shall make an application under this section if–*

   (a)   *it appears to him that the purpose or each of the purposes specified in the order either has been achieved or is incapable of achievement, or*

   (b)   *he is required to do so by a meeting of the company's creditors summoned for the purpose in accordance with the rules.*

18(3)   **[Court order]** *On the hearing of an application under this section, the court may by order discharge or vary the administration order and make such consequential provision as it thinks fit, or adjourn the hearing conditionally or unconditionally, or make an interim order or any other order it thinks fit.*

18(4) [Copy of order to registrar] *Where the administration order is discharged or varied the administrator shall, within 14 days after the making of the order effecting the discharge or variation, send a copy of that order to the registrar of companies.*

18(5) [Non-compliance with s.18(4)] *If the administrator without reasonable excuse fails to comply with subsection (4), he is liable to a fine and, for continued contravention, to a daily default fine.*

S.18(1), (2)

Where the purpose of an administration order is the rehabilitation of the company, an administrator will seek to have an order discharged in two contrasting situations—triumph and disaster. If the company's survival has been ensured, his discharge will enable control of the company's affairs to be restored to its directors and shareholders. If the administrator (or a meeting of the creditors) decides that the purpose is unattainable, the administration order may be discharged and a winding-up order may then be made (very likely on the administrator's own application) if this is appropriate.

The court has no jurisdiction to make a winding-up order otherwise than on a petition lodged under s.124—although Sch.B1 para.13(1)(e) now makes an exception. Accordingly, it is not possible for a winding-up order to be made on an application for the discharge of an administration order under the present section: *Re Brooke Marine Ltd* [1988] B.C.L.C. 546.

This Part of the Act (in contrast with the new Pt II) does not make provision for a company to go into voluntary liquidation following the discharge of an administration order—a choice which may commend itself on the grounds of cost—although it is no doubt within the powers of the court to sanction such a course. Particular difficulties which have to be overcome if this method is chosen include (i) s.11(3)(a), which forbids the passing of the necessary winding-up resolution while an administration order is in force; and (ii) the fact that some creditors entitled to preferential payment may be disadvantaged because a different "relevant date" will apply: see s.387(3)(a), (c). In practice, the first of these difficulties is overcome by making the order for discharge conditional on the passing of the winding-up resolution (or resolutions), or alternatively by directing that the orders for discharge shall not be drawn up until copies of the resolutions have been lodged in the court office: see *Re Powerstore (Trading) Ltd* [1998] B.C.C. 305 at 307. An alternative procedure, which was adopted in *Powerstore* and also in *Re Mark One (Oxford Street) plc* [1998] B.C.C. 984, was for the company to pass a conditional resolution for winding up which remained inchoate until the court had made an order discharging the administration order. But this course is not to be recommended, since in *Re Norditrack (UK) Ltd* [2000] 1 W.L.R. 343; [2000] B.C.C. 441 Arden J. ruled that, in the light of established authority, it was not competent for a company to pass such a conditional resolution. The second difficulty was, until the *Powerstore* case, commonly met by an order under s.18(3), directing the liquidator in the future liquidation to make payments to the creditors in question as if they were preferential creditors. However, in that case Lightman J. ruled that s.18(3) gave the court no such power. In the years following it was held in a number of first-instance cases (notably in *Re Mark One (Oxford Street) plc* [1988] B.C.L.C. 984) that it was possible for the court to authorise the administrators to make a distribution to preferential creditors followed by a voluntary liquidation, while judges in a minority of other cases (e.g. *Re The Designer Room* Ltd [2004] B.C.C. 904) held to the contrary. In *Re Cromptons Leisure Machines Ltd* [2006] EWHC 3583 (Ch); [2007] B.C.C. 214 Lewison J. declared that the time had come for all courts at first instance to follow the majority. However, in the same week the issue came before the Court of Appeal, which held otherwise: there is no power either under s.14(3) or in its inherent jurisdiction to sanction such a payment: *Re Lune Metal Products Ltd* [2006] EWCA Civ 1720; [2007] B.C.C. 217. But happily a way forward was found. It was held that the court has power under s.18(3) to make such an order, but only in the context of an application under s.18(1) to discharge an administration order. Leave was accordingly given for an application to be made for a discharge, on the basis that there should first be made a distribution to pay the preferential creditors in full and then a distribution on a pro rata basis to the unsecured creditors, leaving the company as an empty shell. This could be followed, not by a voluntary winding up but by a striking off of the company under CA 2006 s.1000. A similar course was taken in *Re Beauvale Group Ltd* [2006] B.C.C. 912, where it was orders were made that sums which it had been agreed should be paid to the company's preferential creditors should not be returned to the control of the directors but paid by the administrators to themselves as trustees for those creditors.

The court has no power under s.18 to authorise the administrator to make payments to creditors whose debts have become statute-barred: *Re Leyland Printing Co Ltd* [2010] EWHC 2105 (Ch); [2011] B.C.C. 358.

In *Re Polly Peck International plc* (unreported, February 8, 1999, noted by Brier, (1999) 15 I.L.&P. 44) the administrators had largely completed a realisation of the company's assets and a scheme of arrangement had been approved which allowed the scheme supervisors to make distributions to creditors. Although it might have been thought appropriate for the administration to give way to a winding up, the court ordered that the company should continue under administration: it was impracticable to put the company into voluntary liquidation because the shareholders were numerous and widely scattered, and if a compulsory winding-up order were made all future realisations would have to be paid into the Insolvency Services Account where they would earn a poor rate of interest. This justified the continuation of the administration.

In *Re Roches Leisure Services Ltd* [2005] EWHC 3148 (Ch); [2006] B.P.I.R. 453 an order was made discharging an administration order which had expired some years previously, with a view to exit via a compulsory liquidation.

If the purpose of an administration order is simply the approval of a CVA (see s.8(3)(b)), the functions of the administrator will be completed and he will be entitled to a discharge as soon as the proposal for the arrangement has been approved. It is the supervisor, and not the administrator, who will administer the CVA (though these may well be the same person). Similar considerations will apply where an administration order is made in conjunction with a statutory scheme of compromise or arrangement under CA 2006 Pt 26 (see s.8(3)(c)).

The fourth of the "purposes" specified in s.8(3) is "a more advantageous realisation of the company's assets than would be effected on a winding up". When the administrator has achieved this object, it would seem that a liquidation is bound to follow if at the end of the exercise the company is insolvent. However, if there is a surplus, there is no reason why control should not be handed back to the company's own organs, so that they may make their own decision about its future.

An administrator who intends to apply for an administration order to be discharged before he has sent a statement of his proposals to the company's creditors under s.23(1) must comply with IR 1986 r.*2.16(2)*. It appears from *Re Consumer & Industrial Press Ltd (No.2)* (1988) 4 B.C.C. 72 that the court will be reluctant to grant a discharge before the creditors have had an opportunity to consider the proposals. See, however, *Re Charnley Davies Business Services Ltd* (1987) 3 B.C.C. 408, and the note to s.23(1).

The court is also empowered under this section to vary the original order by specifying an additional purpose (but not, apparently, a *substituted* purpose), from among those listed in s.8(3).

In *Re St Ives Windings Ltd* (1987) 3 B.C.C. 634 an administrator who had achieved an advantageous realisation of assets applied under this section to have the administration order varied by specifying the approval of a voluntary arrangement as an additional purpose. It was then possible for the creditors to sanction proposals for the distribution of the proceeds in a way which was binding on a dissenting minority.

In *Re Sharps of Truro Ltd* [1990] B.C.C. 94 at 95 the view was expressed (obiter) that the only person who can apply to set aside an administration order is the administrator himself. While it may be true that the only person competent to apply to the court under the present section is the administrator, the Court of Appeal held in *Cornhill Insurance plc v Cornhill Finance Services Ltd* [1992] B.C.C. 818 that a creditor aggrieved by an administration order could apply to the court under IR 1986 r.7.47 to have the order rescinded on the ground that it was an order that ought not to have been made.

On the discharge of an administration order, the administrator vacates office: s.19(2)(b).

S.18(3)
Consequential directions may well be needed if the affairs of the company are to be handed back to its shareholders and directors, since the Act gives no detailed guidance on this. The position of some secured creditors may need to be redefined: see the note to s.15(4).

S.18(4)
Notice of the making of the administration order will have been sent to the registrar under s.21(2).

S.18(5)
On penalties, see s.430 and Sch.10.

19   *Vacation of office*

19(1)   [Removal or resignation] The administrator of a company may at any time be removed from office by order of the court and may, in the prescribed circumstances, resign his office by giving notice of his resignation to the court.

19(2)   [Vacation of office etc.] The administrator shall vacate office if–

(a)   he ceases to be qualified to act as an insolvency practitioner in relation to the company, or

(b)   the administration order is discharged.

19(3)   [Ceasing to be administrator] Where at any time a person ceases to be administrator, the following subsections apply.

19(4) **[Remuneration and expenses]** *His remuneration and any expenses properly incurred by him shall be charged on and paid out of any property of the company which is in his custody or under his control at that time in priority to any security to which section 15(1) then applies.*

19(5) **[Debts or liabilities re contracts entered into]** *Any sums payable in respect of debts or liabilities incurred, while he was administrator, under contracts entered into by him or a predecessor of his in the carrying out of his or the predecessor's functions shall be charged on and paid out of any such property as is mentioned in subsection (4) in priority to any charge arising under that subsection.*

19(6) **[Debts or liabilities re contracts of employment adopted]** *Any sums payable in respect of liabilities incurred, while he was administrator, under contracts of employment adopted by him or a predecessor of his in the carrying out of his or the predecessor's functions shall, to the extent that the liabilities are qualifying liabilities, be charged on and paid out of any such property as is mentioned in subsection (4) and enjoy the same priority as any sums to which subsection (5) applies.*

For this purpose, the administrator is not to be taken to have adopted a contract of employment by reason of anything done or omitted to be done within 14 days after his appointment.

19(7) **[Interpretation of s.19(6)]** *For the purposes of subsection (6), a liability under a contract of employment is a qualifying liability if–*

    (a) it is a liability to pay a sum by way of wages or salary or contribution to an occupational pension scheme, and

    (b) it is in respect of services rendered wholly or partly after the adoption of the contract.

19(8) **[Liability disregarded for s.19(6)]** *There shall be disregarded for the purposes of subsection (6) so much of any qualifying liability as represents payment in respect of services rendered before the adoption of the contract.*

19(9) **[Interpretation of s.19(7), (8)]** *For the purposes of subsections (7) and (8)–*

    (a) wages or salary payable in respect of a period of holiday or absence from work through sickness or other good cause are deemed to be wages or (as the case may be) salary in respect of services rendered in that period, and

    (b) a sum payable in lieu of holiday is deemed to be wages or (as the case may be) salary in respect of services rendered in the period by reference to which the holiday entitlement arose.

19(10) **[Interpretation of s.19(9)(a)]** *In subsection (9)(a), the reference to wages or salary payable in respect of a period of holiday includes any sums which, if they had been paid, would have been treated for the purposes of the enactments relating to social security as earnings in respect of that period.*

GENERAL NOTE

This section was extensively amended by IA 1994, which received Royal Assent on March 25, 1994 (but not retrospectively so as to affect contracts of employment adopted by an administrator before March 15, 1994). This Act also affects the position of administrative receivers: see the notes to ss.44 and 57, in Vol.1.

The reform was enacted in order to allay doubts and fears following the decision of the Court of Appeal in *Powdrill v Watson; Re Paramount Airways Ltd (No.3)* [1994] 2 All E.R. 513; [1994] B.C.C. 172 (which was later varied by the House of Lords on appeal: see *Powdrill v Watson* [1995] 2 A.C. 394; [1995] B.C.C. 319, discussed below). The effect of the Court of Appeal's interpretation of s.19(5), as it was formerly worded, was to subordinate the administrator's claim to remuneration and the reimbursement of his expenses to a wide range of possible claims by employees and former employees of the company, as explained below.

The statutory reforms of 1994 were enacted before the appeal to the House of Lords in *Powdrill v Watson* had been heard and, despite powerful arguments by pressure groups, the amendments were not made retrospective (as noted above). It follows that contracts of employment adopted by an administrator before March 15, 1994 are governed by the unamended law, as interpreted by the House of Lords. This is also the case with administrative receiverships, since the House of Lords' ruling in *Powdrill v Watson* dealt also with an appeal in the *Leyland DAF* case (reported as *Talbot v Cadge*, also at [1995] 2 A.C. 395; [1995] B.C.C. 319): the former law applies to contracts of employment adopted by administrative receivers before March 15, 1994 (see the note to s.44). Non-administrative receiverships were not included in the amending legislation of 1994 and accordingly the House of Lords' decision is applicable to all contracts of employment in such receiverships, whether adopted before or after that date (see the note to s.37).

S.19(1)

The circumstances in which an administrator may resign his office are prescribed by IR 1986 r.*2.53*. Whether a resignation is effective as soon as notice is given to the court is not made clear by the rules. The usual understanding is that it will be so effective and that, once given, it cannot be unilaterally withdrawn (see *Glossop v Glossop* [1907] 2 Ch. 370). The present position may be contrasted with that applicable to a liquidator (s.171(5)), where a resignation is not effective unless it has been accepted: see IR 1986 rr.4.108–4.110.

The death of an administrator should also be notified to the court: see s.20(1)(a), and IR 1986 r.*2.54*.

S.19(2)

An administrator will cease to be "qualified to act" as an insolvency practitioner "in relation to the company" if he fails to meet any of the criteria set out in s.390.

On the discharge of an administration order, see s.18.

S.19(3)–(6)

These subsections rather oddly address the question of debts and expenses incurred by an administrator only in the context of the position when he ceases to hold office. However, in the *Paramount Airways* case (above), Dillon L.J. said ([1994] 2 All E.R. 513 at 522; [1994] B.C.C. 172 at 180):

> "Although strictly sums payable are, under s.19(5), only payable when the administrator vacates office, it is well understood that administrators will, in the ordinary way, pay expenses of the administration including the salaries and other payments to employees as they arise during the continuance of the administration. There is no need to wait until the end, and it would be impossible as a practical matter to do that. What is picked up at the end are those matters which fall within the phrase, but have not been paid". (See also *Re Salmet International Ltd* [2001] B.C.C. 796.)

The subsections provide that the administrator's remuneration and expenses and all the contractual debts and liabilities that have been incurred while he was in office are to be paid in priority to the claims of any creditor whose debt is secured by a *floating* charge (including a charge which, as created, was a floating charge but has since become fixed: see s.15(1) and (3)). The payments under s.19(5) and 19(6) rank in priority to those under s.19(4). There is no mention of the preferential creditors whose claims would have ranked ahead of the holder of the floating charge in a receivership. (On the question whether these preferential claims survive the appointment of an administrator, see the comment to s.15(4).) If a liquidation follows the administration, the administrator's costs will have priority by virtue of s.19(4) over all claims in the winding up other than those mentioned in s.19(5): *Re Sheridan Securities Ltd* (1988) 4 B.C.C. 200. Where land or goods in the company's possession under a lease or hire-purchase agreement, existing at the commencement of an administration, are used for the purposes of the administration, it was held in *Re Atlantic Computer Systems plc* [1990] B.C.C. 859 that such rent or hire charges would not automatically rank as "expenses of the administration", but whether they did so or not would be for the court in its discretion to determine. This reasoning was rejected in *Re Toshoku Finance UK plc* [2002] UKHL 6; [2002] 1 W.L.R. 671; [2002] B.C.C. 110 in so far as it applied in the context of a liquidation, and has since been held not to apply to administrations under Sch.B1 (*Exeter City Council v Bairstow* [2007] EWHC 400 (Ch); [2007] B.C.C. 236); but it continues to be applicable to administrations under the original Pt II (see *Exeter CC v Bairstow* at [29]–[30]). (See further the note to IR 1986 r.2.67.)

Section 19(4) says nothing about priority as between the administrator's remuneration and administration expenses (apart from those dealt with in s.19(5)): it is up to the administrator to decide how and in what order he should discharge the obligations arising in the course of managing the company's business, including any liabilities arising under pre-administration contracts (*Re Salmet International Ltd* (above)).

In *Re GP Stores Ltd* (July 24, 2004, unreported, but noted by Sharp, (2005) 18 Insolv. Int. 8) an administration was followed by a liquidation but there were insufficient free funds available to pay the liquidator's remuneration and expenses. It fell to the liquidator to discharge the debts owed to the administration expense creditors to the extent that the realised assets would allow. An order was made giving priority to the liquidator's remuneration and expenses over these claims.

In relation to payment and securities settlement systems, where "collateral security" (as defined in the Finality Regulations reg.2(1)) has been provided by a company to which those regulations apply, the claim of a participant or central bank to such security must be paid in priority to the administrator's expenses and remuneration, unless the terms on which the security was provided expressly state that the expenses and remuneration shall have priority (Finality Regulations reg.14(5), (6)). (See the introductory note at Vol.1, p.3.)

Section 19(5) is confined to *contractual* debts and liabilities. This would include damages claims arising out of contracts entered into by the company while the administrator was in office, but not, e.g. any liabilities of the company in tort. In *Centre Reinsurance International Co v Freakley* [2006] UKHL 45; [2006] 1 W.L.R. 2863; [2006] B.C.C. 971 the company had incurred insurance claims handling expenses on the instructions of reinsurers during the administration, pursuant to a contract entered into by the company before it went into administration. The House of Lords, allowing an appeal by the administrators, held that these expenses had not been incurred by the administrators in carrying out their functions and so had no priority over the costs of the administration.

It should be noted that the above decisions depend on the construction of s.19 and the applicable rules. The position is different under the new administration regime, as pointed out by Lord Hoffmann in the *Centre Reinsurance* case at [6] and by David Richards J. in *Exeter City Council v Bairstow* [2007] EWHC 400 (Ch); [2007] B.C.C. 236 (the *"Trident Fashions"* case). (See the discussion of this case and the later legislation dealing with this and related questions in the notes to Sch.B1 para.99 and IR 1986 r.2.67.)

The costs of an administration petition and of the accompanying report under IR 1986 r.2.2, although commonly ordered by the court in its discretion to be costs in the administration, are not "expenses properly incurred by the administrator" so as to attract the priority conferred by s.19(4) or (5): *Re a Company (No.005174 of 1999)* [2000] B.C.C. 698.

S.19(5)–(10)

Section 19(5) gives priority over the administrator's remuneration and expenses to claims in respect of debts and liabilities under contracts entered into by him (or a predecessor) in the carrying out of his functions. Section 19(6) gives the same priority to "qualifying liabilities" (for definition, see below) under contracts of employment "adopted" by him (or a predecessor). However nothing done by the administrator within the first 14 days following his appointment is to be taken as "adopting" a contract of employment.

The making of an administration order does not terminate the company's existing contracts of employment or, for that matter, any other contract of a continuing nature; and so, strictly speaking, no affirmative act on the part of the administrator is needed to keep any such contract in being. This formerly led to much speculation and to differences of judicial opinion as to the meaning of the word "adopt", in relation to a contract of employment, as it appears in this section (and also in ss.37 and 44, in relation to non-administrative and administrative receivers). In *Powdrill v Watson* (above), a definitive ruling was given on the construction of the term for the purposes of these provisions. It was held: (i) that a contract of employment is either adopted as a whole or not; it is not open to an administrator or receiver to "cherry-pick", i.e. choose to accept some liabilities under the contract and not others; and (ii) that a contract of employment "is inevitably adopted if the administrator or receiver causes the company to continue the employment for more than 14 days after his employment" ([1995] 2 A.C. 394 at 450; [1995] B.C.C. 319 at 335). In the case itself, the administrators (following a practice which was widely employed at the time) had written to the employees within the first 14 days after their appointment stating that they "did not and would not at any future time adopt or assume personal liability" in respect of the contracts of employment. The Court of Appeal and House of Lords held that such a disclaimer had no effect: "adoption is a matter not merely of words but of fact" (per Dillon L.J. [1994] 2 All E.R. 513 at 521; [1994] B.C.C. 172 at 180). Earlier judicial views as to the meaning of "adopted" (e.g. that of Evans-Lombe J. at first instance in *Powdrill v Watson* [1993] B.C.C. 662 at 671, "procured the company to continue to carry out", and that of McPherson J. in *Re Diesels & Components Pty Ltd* (1985) 2 A.C.L.C. 555 at 557, "refrained from repudiating") are accordingly no longer authoritative.

In *Powdrill v Watson*, the joint administrators were held to have impliedly "adopted" the contracts of employment of two airline pilots when they had continued, after the 14-day period, to employ them and pay them in accordance with their previous contracts. Their pilots were later dismissed, and in this action successfully claimed various sums, including pay in lieu of notice, unpaid holiday pay and pension contributions. (Certain so-called "loyalty bonuses", which had been separately agreed with the administrators, were held to be outside the contracts of employment and not recoverable.) It followed that, under the unamended s.19(4), the employees' claims were entitled to priority over the administrators' own remuneration and expenses.

The potential consequences of the Court of Appeal's ruling in *Paramount Airways* were far-reaching, for the decision could have led to the reopening of many administrations stretching back to the commencement of the Act in 1986, and the possibility that administrators would be obliged to make restitution of their fees and remuneration in order to meet the claims of former employees, including perhaps claims for substantial "golden handshakes" by senior executives. However, happily for administrators, the House of Lords was able to find a "middle way", which reduced their risk of exposure to such very large claims. It was held that the priority under the section was restricted to liabilities under the adopted contracts incurred by the administrators during their tenure of office, and did not extend to liabilities which had accrued prior to that time. The liabilities in the former category were not limited to those incurred for services actually rendered for the benefit of the administration, but included liability for wages accruing during the contractual period of notice (or damages for failure to give such notice) and pension contributions in respect of the notice period. On the other hand, holiday pay entitlements referable to periods of service expiring before the appointment of the administrators fell into the latter category and did not attract the statutory priority. This ruling governs all contracts of employment adopted by administrators prior to March 15, 1994.

In *Re Antal International Ltd* [2003] EWHC 1339 (Ch); [2003] 2 B.C.L.C. 406 the administrators became aware of the existence of certain contracts of employment only 16 days after the commencement of the administration and immediately took steps ... that nothing that they had done constituted an adoption of the contracts.

In regard to contract... (as amended) makes it plain that the liability of an admi... of employment is to be limited to "qualifying liabilities"... wages, salaries and occupational pension contributions... 9(9), (10)), but only in respect of services rendered whe... nd, in the case where services are rendered partly after t... y as represents payment in respect of services rendered b... istrator can therefore now continue to retain the services ... itment to them is only in respect of current liabilities.

The priority accord... er contracts of employment" and "a liability to pay a sum... ms payable in respect of PAYE and NIC contributions re...] B.C.C. 663. Payments of salary to teachers during the... of services rendered" during the immediately preced... f holiday" within s.19(9)(a), in *Re a Company (No.0051...*

Although the mat... r the purposes of the Limitation Acts, the claims of emplo... istration (unless, of course, they have been met during th... is subject to a limitation period of six years from that da... d of 12 years: *Re Maxwell Fleet & Facilities Management Ltd* [1999] 2 B.C.L.C.

The administrators in *Powdrill v Watson* in their letter to the employees also stated that they disclaimed any personal liability in respect of the contracts of employment. This would appear to have been superfluous, since in the House of Lords Lord Browne-Wilkinson said ([1995] 2 A.C. 394 at 448; [1995] B.C.C. 319 at 333) that there was no question that an administrator accepted personal liability under s.19.

The question whether an administrator, in negotiating a fresh contract with an employee (as distinct from adopting the existing one) could contract out of the statutory rules of priority laid down by s.19(5) was expressly left open by the Court of Appeal, and was not referred to in the House of Lords.

In *Powdrill v Watson*, interest on the sums due to the employees was also awarded.

20   *Release of administrator*

20(1)   *[Time of release] A person who has ceased to be the administrator of a company has his release with effect from the following time, that is to say–*

    (a)   *in the case of a person who has died, the time at which notice is given to the court in accordance with the rules that he has ceased to hold office;*

    (b)   *in any other case, such time as the court may determine.*

20(2)   *[Discharge from liability, etc.] Where a person has his release under this section, he is, with effect from the time specified above, discharged from all liability both in respect of acts or omissions of his in the administration and otherwise in relation to his conduct as administrator.*

20(3)   *[Section 212] However, nothing in this section prevents the exercise, in relation to a person who has had his release as above, of the court's powers under section 212 in Chapter X of Part IV (summary remedy against delinquent directors, liquidators, etc.).*

S.20(1)

Except in the case of the death of an administrator, for which specific provision is made in para.(a), an administrator is to have his release only from such time as the court determines. The relevant rule for the purpose of para.(a) is IR 1986 r.*2.54.*

In *Re Sibec Developments Ltd; Barclays Mercantile Finance Ltd v Sibec Developments Ltd* [1992] 1 W.L.R. 1253; [1993] B.C.C. 148, Millett J. held that the administrators should not be released (and, indeed, that an administration order should not have been discharged) while there was a proper claim against them outstanding which ought to be tried. For a case where the court postponed the administrator's release because his conduct appeared to call for investigation, see *Re Sheridan Securities Ltd* (1988) 4 B.C.C. 200. See also *Re Exchange Travel (Holdings) Ltd* [1992] B.C.C. 954, where the order for release was made to take effect after three months, to give an opportunity for steps to be taken to have the past conduct of the administrators investigated.

S.20(2), (3)
The release of an administrator discharges him from all liability, except that s.20(3) preserves his liability to account to the company under the "misfeasance" provisions of s.212. Although all references to administrators have now been deleted from s.212 by EA 2002, the former wording survives for administrations conducted under the original Pt II (see the Enterprise Act 2002 (Commencement No.4 and Transitional Provisions and Savings) Order 2003 (SI 2003/2093, effective September 15, 2003) art.3). This section applies only in a winding up. There is something of a paradox here: the section appears to grant the office-holder a discharge, as a matter of substance, from all possible liabilities in the most comprehensive terms, and yet at the same time to preserve the court's powers under s.212—a section which has always been understood to be purely procedural in nature.

In *Re Newscreen Media Ltd* [2009] EWHC 944 (Ch); [2009] 2 B.C.L.C. 353 the judge was prepared to assume that the court had jurisdiction to set aside orders for the discharge of an administration and release of the administrator under ss.18 and 20, at least in the case of fraud, but held that only the company concerned or its liquidator would have standing to apply. In *Parkinson Engineering Services plc v Swan* [2009] EWCA Civ 1366; [2010] 1 B.C.L.C. 163 the court allowed an amendment to a claim, brought in the name of the company, substituting the liquidator as claimant, so that a s.212 action against the company's former administrators (which would otherwise have been barred by s.20) could proceed.

Ascertainment and investigation of company's affairs

21   Information to be given by administrator

21(1)   [Duties of administrator] *Where an administration order has been made, the administrator shall–*

(a)   *as soon as reasonably practicable send to the company and publish in the prescribed manner a notice of the order, and*

(b)   *within 28 days after the making of the order, unless the court otherwise directs, send such a notice to all creditors of the company (so far as he is aware of their addresses).*

21(2)   [Copy of order to registrar] *Where an administration order has been made, the administrator shall also, within 14 days after the making of the order, send a copy of the order to the registrar of companies and to such other persons as may be prescribed.*

21(3)   [Penalty for non-compliance] *If the administrator without reasonable excuse fails to comply with this section, he is liable to a fine and, for continued contravention, to a daily default fine.*

S.21(1), (2)
It is the administrator's duty to see that the making of the administration order is:

- notified to the company;

- published (i.e. advertised, both in the *Gazette* and an appropriate newspaper (IR 1986 r.*2.10(2)*));

- notified to all known creditors; and

- registered with the registrar of companies.

Notice must also be given to any person who has appointed an administrative receiver of the company, or is entitled to do so, to any administrative receiver who has been appointed, to the petitioner under any pending winding-up petition, and to any provisional liquidator (IR 1986 r.*2.10(3)*). The section fixes various time limits.

For the relevant rules and forms prescribed for the purposes of this section, see IR 1986 r.*2.10*.

S.21(3)
On penalties, see s.430 and Sch.10.

22 Statement of affairs to be submitted to administrator

22(1) *[Duty of administrator] Where an administration order has been made, the administrator shall forthwith require some or all of the persons mentioned below to make out and submit to him a statement in the prescribed form as to the affairs of the company.*

22(2) *[Contents of statement] The statement shall be verified by affidavit by the persons required to submit it and shall show–*

(a) *particulars of the company's assets, debts and liabilities;*

(b) *the names and addresses of its creditors;*

(c) *the securities held by them respectively;*

(d) *the dates when the securities were respectively given; and*

(e) *such further or other information as may be prescribed.*

22(3) *[Persons in s.22(1)] The persons referred to in subsection (1) are–*

(a) *those who are or have been officers of the company;*

(b) *those who have taken part in the company's formation at any time within one year before the date of the administration order;*

(c) *those who are in the company's employment or have been in its employment within that year, and are in the administrator's opinion capable of giving the information required;*

(d) *those who are or have been within that year officers of or in the employment of a company which is, or within that year was, an officer of the company.*

In this subsection "employment" includes employment under a contract for services.

22(4) *[Time for submitting statement] Where any persons are required under this section to submit a statement of affairs to the administrator, they shall do so (subject to the next subsection) before the end of the period of 21 days beginning with the day after that on which the prescribed notice of the requirement is given to them by the administrator.*

22(5) *[Powers re release, extension of time] The administrator, if he thinks fit, may–*

(a) *at any time release a person from an obligation imposed on him under subsection (1) or (2), or*

(b) *either when giving notice under subsection (4) or subsequently, extend the period so mentioned; and where the administrator has refused to exercise a power conferred by this subsection, the court, if it thinks fit, may exercise it.*

22(6) *[Penalty for non-compliance] If a person without reasonable excuse fails to comply with any obligation imposed under this section, he is liable to a fine and, for continued contravention, to a daily default fine.*

GENERAL NOTE

In this and the following sections there is set out the procedure to be followed once the administrator has been appointed. While this lengthy and formal routine may be desirable if the purpose of the administration order is to secure the rehabilitation of the company, it seems less appropriate when the object of the administration is simply to smooth the path for the approval of a CVA or the sanctioning of a statutory scheme under CA 2006 Pt 26 (see s.8(3)(b), (c)). However, the Act seems to offer no alternative, unless possibly the court is empowered to dispense with the statutory requirements under the broad wording of s.9(4).

The "statement of affairs" has long been a feature of the liquidation procedure in a compulsory winding up (see s.131). Its use is extended by this Act to this and a number of other analogous situations. For further comment, see the notes to s.131.

For the relevant rules and forms prescribed for the purpose of this section, see IR 1986 rr.*2.11* et seq. and, on enforcement, r.7.20.

S.22(1)–(5)
On the meaning of the term "forthwith", see the note to s.9(2).

The expression "officer", in relation to a company, includes a director, manager or secretary (CA 2006 s.1173) and at least in some contexts may extend to the holders of other offices: see the note to s.206(3). The wide definition of "employment" used here could include professionals such as the company's auditors and bankers.

S.22(6)
On penalties, see s.430 and Sch.10.

Administrator's proposals

23   Statement of proposals

23(1)   *[Duties of administrator] Where an administration order has been made, the administrator shall, within 3 months (or such longer period as the court may allow) after the making of the order–*

    (a)   *send to the registrar of companies and (so far as he is aware of their addresses) to all creditors a statement of his proposals for achieving the purpose or purposes specified in the order, and*

    (b)   *lay a copy of the statement before a meeting of the company's creditors summoned for the purpose on not less than 14 days' notice.*

23(2)   *[Copies of statement] The administrator shall also, within 3 months (or such longer period as the court may allow) after the making of the order, either–*

    (a)   *send a copy of the statement (so far as he is aware of their addresses) to all members of the company, or*

    (b)   *publish in the prescribed manner a notice stating an address to which members of the company should write for copies of the statement to be sent to them free of charge.*

23(3)   *[Penalty for non-compliance] If the administrator without reasonable excuse fails to comply with this section, he is liable to a fine and, for continued contravention, to a daily default fine.*

S.23(1)
In the light of the information given to him in the statement of affairs which he has requisitioned under s.22, the administrator must draw up his "proposals"—his strategy for achieving the purpose or purposes specified in the administration order—and summon a meeting of the company's creditors to consider them. A copy of the proposals must be sent to the registrar of companies for registration, and also to every known creditor. (The "statement" referred to in this section is the administrator's statement of his proposals, not the statement of the company's affairs.)

A careful reading of para.(b) reveals that the creditors' meeting must be *held*, and not merely summoned, within the specified period of three months.

A meeting under this section cannot be held for purposes other than the consideration of the administrator's proposals, e.g. to consider whether the company should petition for its own winding up: *Re Charnley Davies Business Services Ltd* (1987) 3 B.C.C. 408. In this case, exceptionally, Harman J. discharged the administration order before a s.23 meeting had been held because action already taken by the administrator on his own initiative had left the meeting with nothing that it could usefully do. On the question of discharge, see further the note to s.18(1), (2).

For the procedure for summoning the creditors' meeting, see IR 1986 rr.*2.18* et seq.

S.23(2)
A copy of the statement of proposals must either be sent to all members of the company individually, or advertised as being available to members free on request. This must be done within (and not at the end of) three months: (*Re Charnley Davies Business Services Ltd*, above) although the court may grant an extension of time. (The members have little say in, or control over, the conduct of the administration—see s.14(4); but if a member is "unfairly prejudiced" by it, he is given a statutory remedy under s.27, and so there is a need that members should be kept broadly in the picture.)

The rules prescribed for the purpose of s.23(2)(b) require the notice to be gazetted: see IR 1986 r.*2.17*.

S.23(3)
On penalties, see s.430 and Sch.10.

24   *Consideration of proposals by creditors' meeting*

24(1)   *[Creditors' meeting to decide] A meeting of creditors summoned under section 23 shall decide whether to approve the administrator's proposals.*

24(2)   *[Approval, modifications] The meeting may approve the proposals with modifications, but shall not do so unless the administrator consents to each modification.*

24(3)   *[Meeting in accordance with rules] Subject as above, the meeting shall be conducted in accordance with the rules.*

24(4)   *[Report and notice by administrator] After the conclusion of the meeting in accordance with the rules, the administrator shall report the result of the meeting to the court and shall give notice of that result to the registrar of companies and to such persons as may be prescribed.*

24(5)   *[If meeting does not approve] If a report is given to the court under subsection (4) that the meeting has declined to approve the administrator's proposals (with or without modifications), the court may by order discharge the administration order and make such consequential provision as it thinks fit, or adjourn the hearing conditionally or unconditionally, or make an interim order or any other order that it thinks fit.*

24(6)   *[Where administration order discharged] Where the administration order is discharged, the administrator shall, within 14 days after the making of the order effecting the discharge, send a copy of that order to the registrar of companies.*

24(7)   *[Penalty for non-compliance] If the administrator without reasonable excuse fails to comply with subsection (6), he is liable to a fine and, for continued contravention, to a daily default fine.*

S.24(1), (2)

The administrator's freedom to act in the exercise of his functions is limited by the scope of the proposals, once approved (see s.17(2)(b))—apart from "insubstantial" deviations (s.25(1)(b)); and so it is important, from his point of view, that they should not be too restrictively drawn—indeed, in *Re Dana (UK) Ltd* [1999] 2 B.C.L.C. 239 Neuberger J. thought that it would make good sense for the proposals put before a s.23 meeting to include a mechanism empowering the largest and/or representative creditors to approve future decisions or variations of decisions of the administrator. In any event, the court may, in exceptional circumstances, authorise the administrator to depart from the scheme, e.g. where there is insufficient time to convene a meeting of the creditors under s.25 to approve a revision of the scheme: see the note to s.25(1), below.

S.24(3)

For the rules governing the conduct of the meeting, see IR 1986 rr.*2.18* et seq. The rules invalidate any resolution of the creditors which is opposed by a majority of the creditors who are not "connected with" the company: see IR 1986 r.*2.28(1A)* and, on the meaning of "connected with", see s.249.

S.24(4)

The administrator is required to report the result of the meeting to the court and to notify the persons specified. If the meeting has approved the proposals, the report to the court seems to be a purely administrative matter: the administrator may, without more formality, get on with his duties under s.17(2)(b).

For the persons prescribed for the purposes of this subsection, see IR 1986 r.*2.30.*

S.24(5)

If the meeting does not approve the proposals, the initiative reverts to the court, acting in its judicial capacity. The administration meantime continues provisionally under s.17(2)(a).

S.24(6), (7)

These subsections repeat the corresponding provisions in s.18(4), (5).

On penalties, see s.430 and Sch.10.

25   *Approval of substantial revisions*

25(1)   *[Application] This section applies where–*

    (a) proposals have been approved (with or without modifications) under section 24, and

(b)   the administrator proposes to make revisions of those proposals which appear to him substantial.

25(2)   [Duties of administrator] The administrator shall–

(a)   send to all creditors of the company (so far as he is aware of their addresses) a statement in the prescribed form of his proposed revisions, and

(b)   lay a copy of the statement before a meeting of the company's creditors summoned for the purpose on not less than 14 days' notice;

and he shall not make the proposed revisions unless they are approved by the meeting.

25(3)   [Copies of statement] The administrator shall also either–

(a)   send a copy of the statement (so far as he is aware of their addresses) to all members of the company, or

(b)   publish in the prescribed manner a notice stating an address to which members of the company should write for copies of the statement to be sent to them free of charge.

25(4)   [Approval, modifications] The meeting of creditors may approve the proposed revisions with modifications, but shall not do so unless the administrator consents to each modification.

25(5)   [Meeting in accordance with rules] Subject as above, the meeting shall be conducted in accordance with the rules.

25(6)   [Notification to registrar, et al.] After the conclusion of the meeting in accordance with the rules, the administrator shall give notice of the result of the meeting to the registrar of companies and to such persons as may be prescribed.

S.25(1)

Once his proposals have been approved, the administrator is bound to adhere to the course of action that they prescribe (except that he may, apparently, make "insubstantial" deviations: see para.(b)). If he wishes to work to a different strategy, he must go back to the creditors for approval of revised proposals. However, in exceptional circumstances (e.g. where the delay involved in summoning a creditors' meeting to consider a revised scheme could cause substantial loss) the court has a residual jurisdiction under s.14(3) to authorise an administrator to depart from an approved scheme: see *Re Smallman Construction Ltd* (1988) 4 B.C.C. 784; and *Re Dana (UK) Ltd* [1999] 2 B.C.L.C. 239.

S.25(2)–(5)

These provisions are effectively the same as ss.23(1), (2) and 24(2), (3), except that there is no time limit prescribed and no obligation to send a copy of the statement of revised proposals to the registrar of companies.

S.25(6)

This subsection echoes s.24(4), except that under that provision it is necessary also to report the result of the meeting to the court.

   If the meeting declines to approve the revised proposals, it would appear that the administrator has the following options:

- to continue to act under the old proposals;
- to draw up a new set of revised proposals and summon a further creditors' meeting under this section;
- to apply to the court under s.18(1) to have the purpose specified in the administration order varied; or
- to apply to the court for a discharge of the order under s.18(2), on the ground that the purpose of the order is incapable of achievement.

For more detailed comment, see the various sections referred to.

Miscellaneous

26   Creditors' committee

26(1)   [Meeting may establish committee] Where a meeting of creditors summoned under section 23 has approved the administrator's proposals (with or without modifications), the meeting may, if it thinks *fit, establish a committee ("**the creditors' committee**") to exercise the functions conferred on it by or under this Act.*

26(2) **[Committee may summon administrator]** *If such a committee is established, the committee may, on giving not less than 7 days' notice, require the administrator to attend before it at any reasonable time and furnish it with such information relating to the carrying out of his functions as it may reasonably require.*

GENERAL NOTE

Once the meeting of creditors has approved a statement of proposals, so that the administrator is empowered to act under s.17(2)(b), it may appoint a committee of creditors under this section. Corresponding provisions are made in the case of an administrative receivership (see ss.49 and 68) and in a winding up (where the committee was formerly called the "committee of inspection" and is now termed the "liquidation committee": see ss.101, 141 and 142).

It is submitted that the phrase "conferred on it" in s.26(1) means "conferred on the committee" and not "conferred on the meeting of creditors", as might appear on a first reading.

For the rules relating to the creditors' committee and its functions, see IR 1986 rr.2.32 et seq.

27 *Protection of interests of creditors and members*

27(1) **[Application by creditor or member]** *At any time when an administration order is in force, a creditor or member of the company may apply to the court by petition for an order under this section on the ground–*

(a) *that the company's affairs, business and property are being or have been managed by the administrator in a manner which is unfairly prejudicial to the interests of its creditors or members generally, or of some part of its creditors or members (including at least himself), or*

(b) *that any actual or proposed act or omission of the administrator is or would be so prejudicial.*

27(2) **[Court order]** *On an application for an order under this section the court may, subject as follows, make such order as it thinks fit for giving relief in respect of the matters complained of, or adjourn the hearing conditionally or unconditionally, or make an interim order or any other order that it thinks fit.*

27(3) **[Limits of order]** *An order under this section shall not prejudice or prevent–*

(a) *the implementation of a voluntary arrangement approved under section 4 in Part I, or any compromise or arrangement sanctioned under Part 26 of the Companies Act 2006; or*

(b) *where the application for the order was made more than 28 days after the approval of any proposals or revised proposals under section 24 or 25, the implementation of those proposals or revised proposals.*

27(4) **[Contents of order]** *Subject as above, an order under this section may in particular–*

(a) *regulate the future management by the administrator of the company's affairs, business and property;*

(b) *require the administrator to refrain from doing or continuing an act complained of by the petitioner, or to do an act which the petitioner has complained he has omitted to do;*

(c) *require the summoning of a meeting of creditors or members for the purpose of considering such matters as the court may direct;*

(d) *discharge the administration order and make such consequential provision as the court thinks fit.*

27(5) **[Sections 15, 16]** *Nothing in sections 15 or 16 is to be taken as prejudicing applications to the court under this section.*

27(6) **[Copy of discharge order to registrar]** *Where the administration order is discharged, the administrator shall, within 14 days after the making of the order effecting the discharge, send a copy of that order to the registrar of companies; and if without reasonable excuse he fails to comply with this subsection, he is liable to a fine and, for continued contravention, to a daily default fine.*

S.27(1)

This section, like s.6, is based broadly on the provisions of CA 1985 s.459 [now CA 2006 s.994]. As with s.6, it is arguable that a court might rule that a member's or creditor's *only* judicial remedy if he has any complaint against the administrator is to have recourse to the procedure under this section: this would be consistent with the apparent purpose of s.27(3)(b). (This would not, of course, rule out proceedings brought by the company itself, or its liquidator.) However, in *Cornhill Insurance plc v Cornhill Financial Services Ltd* [1992] B.C.C. 818 the Court of Appeal held that a creditor who was aggrieved by an administration order which was unfairly prejudicial to it and accordingly ought not to have been made could invoke the jurisdiction of the court under IR 1986 r.7.47 to have the order rescinded. The present provision differs from s.6 in an important respect: it is concerned with the actual management of the company's affairs, etc. by the administrator, whereas s.6 deals only with events prior to the time when the supervisor of an arrangement takes office. It may also be contrasted with CA 2006 s.994 in that a creditor as well as a member may petition.

The scope of s.27 is discussed in detail in the case of *Re Charnley Davies Ltd* [1990] B.C.C. 605, where it was held that a negligent sale by an administrator of a company's assets at an undervalue would be insufficient without more to establish a claim for relief under the section. The appropriate procedure in such a situation is to have the administration order discharged, the company put into compulsory liquidation, an insolvency practitioner other than the administrator appointed liquidator, and a claim brought by the liquidator against the administrator under IA 1986 s.212. The court in *Re Charnley Davies Ltd* declined to endorse suggestions proffered by counsel as to the meaning of the words "unfairly prejudicial": "it would be wrong to substitute different language for that chosen by Parliament, if the substituted language means the same it is not helpful, and if it means something different it distorts the intention of Parliament" ([1990] B.C.C. 605 at 624). "An allegation that the acts complained of are unlawful or infringe the petitioner's legal rights is not a necessary averment in a s.27 petition. [It] is not a sufficient averment either. The petitioner must allege and prove that they are evidence or instances of the management of the company's affairs by the administrator in a manner which is unfairly prejudicial to the petitioner's interests" (ibid., at 624–625). Where the complaint may be adequately redressed by the remedy provided by law, it is unnecessary to assume the additional burden of proving unfairly prejudicial conduct. However, that burden must be assumed—but not necessarily that of proving unlawful conduct as well—if a wider remedy under s.27 is sought.

An administrator, save in exceptional cases, does not owe duties to an individual creditor on the basis of which a claim in negligence will lie, either under this provision or at common law. If the complaint is based on a breach of duty in the conduct of the administration and the company has gone into liquidation, a claim (in the nature of a class action) may be brought under s.212, and if the administrator has had his release, the leave of the court is required under s.20(2): *Kyrris v Oldham* [2003] 1 B.C.L.C. 35.

The courts are in principle unwilling to review commercial decisions, and discourage the use of the procedure under s.27 for this purpose: *MTI Trading Systems Ltd v Winter* [1998] B.C.C. 591.

S.27(3)(a)

An application for an administration order may be made in conjunction with a proposed CVA or a scheme of compromise or arrangement under CA 2006 Pt 26. A member or creditor who objects to a scheme under either of these procedures has his separate remedies under ss.6 and 7(3) above and a right of objection under CA 2006 s.899, and if he has not availed himself of these rights or has done so unsuccessfully, it is reasonable that the arrangement or scheme should stand.

S.27(3)(b)

Under this provision, the court may upset the administration scheme itself only if an application is made within the 28-day period. After that, it may still grant the applicant other forms of relief, but the scheme itself will no longer be open to challenge.

S.27(4)

This is modelled on CA 1985 s.461(2) [CA 2006 s.996(2)]; but paras (c) and (d) have no counterpart in that section.

S.27(5)

The two sections referred to empower the administrator to deal with charged property, in some circumstances with the authorisation of the court. The fact that an act of the administrator has the backing of a court order should not prejudice an application under the present section, since members and creditors will generally have had no standing to be heard when the order was made.

S.27(6)

This is equivalent to s.18(4), (5) and also to s.24(6), (7).

Insolvency Rules 1986 (original Part 2)

(SI 1986/1925)

[**Note**: The rules which follow apply only to administrations established under the original IA 1986 Pt II. For all other administrations, see the new IR 1986 Pt 2 (Vol.1, p.734).

The Insolvency (Amendment) Rules 2010 (SI 2010/686, effective April 6, 2010) introduced numerous changes to the procedure relating to the original Pt 2 of the Rules, some of which are retrospective in that they affect existing administrations. The changes affecting special administration regimes and old administrations (that is, those relating to utilities, building societies and the other bodies specified in the Enterprise Act 2002 s.249(1), and administrations which commenced before September 15, 2003) are specifically dealt with in Sch.5 to the 2010 Rules. This schedule is not a model of clarity and it would take much space to attempt to explain all of its provisions in detail. Briefly we may say that:

- the amending rules do not apply in any respect that is inconsistent with the original Pt II of the Act;

- the "general parts" of the Rules (Pt 0 and Pts 7–13) apply in their amended form (including the new Pt 12A) to administrations commencing on or after April 6, 2010;

- a long list of specified rules in the general parts apply also to administrations existing on that date: these include the use of documents and communications in electronic form for various purposes (rr.12A.6–12A.12, 12A.29–12.30), remote attendance at meetings (rr.12A.20–25), and modified prescribed forms (r.12.28);

- the replacement of affidavits by witness statements verified by a statement of truth (or, in the case of an affidavit of service, by a certificate of service) and the disuse of such terms as "*ex parte*".

Paragraph 4(1) of Sch.5 states:

Where a Rule (other than Rule 2.8) in Part 2 of the former Rules refers to an affidavit, the swearing of an affidavit or the deponent to an affidavit, it is to be read as referring to a witness statement verified by a statement of truth in accordance with Part 22 of the Civil Procedure Rules 1998, the making of such a witness statement or a person making such a witness statement respectively.

In the light of this, the text of the rules which follows has not been altered and continues to follow the original wording, but the reader is reminded in a note to make the mental adjustment.

Account has also been taken of the changes made by the Insolvency (Amendment) (No.2) Rules 2010 (SI 2010/734).]

ARRANGEMENT OF RULES

ORIGINAL PART 2

ADMINISTRATION PROCEDURE

CHAPTER 1

APPLICATION FOR, AND MAKING OF, THE ORDER

2.1 *Affidavit to support petition*

2.1(1)   **[Affidavit required]** *Where it is proposed to apply to the court by petition for an administration order to be made in relation to a company, an affidavit complying with Rule 2.3 below must be prepared and sworn, with a view to its being filed in court in support of the petition.*

[FORM 2.1]

2.1(2)   **[Petition presented by company or directors]** *If the petition is to be presented by the company or by the directors, the affidavit must be made by one of the directors, or the secretary of the company, stating himself to make it on behalf of the company or, as the case may be, on behalf of the directors.*

2.1(3)   **[Creditor's petition]** *If the petition is to be presented by creditors, the affidavit must be made by a person acting under the authority of them all, whether or not himself one of their number. In any case* there must be stated in the affidavit the nature of his authority and the means of his knowledge of the matters to which the affidavit relates.

2.1(4) **[Supervisor's petition]** *If the petition is to be presented by the supervisor of a voluntary arrangement under Part I of the Act, it is to be treated as if it were a petition by the company.*

(See General Note after r.2.3.)

2.2   Independent report on company's affairs

2.2(1) **[Report that administrator's appointment expedient]** *There may be prepared, with a view to its being exhibited to the affidavit in support of the petition, a report by an independent person to the effect that the appointment of an administrator for the company is expedient.*

2.2(2) **[Who may report]** *The report may be by the person proposed as administrator, or by any other person having adequate knowledge of the company's affairs, not being a director, secretary, manager, member, or employee of the company.*

2.2(3) **[Report to specify purpose of order]** *The report shall specify the purposes which, in the opinion of the person preparing it, may be achieved for the company by the making of an administration order, being purposes particularly specified in section 8(3).*

(See General Note after r.2.3.)

2.3   Contents of affidavit

2.3(1) **[Statements in affidavit]** *The affidavit shall state–*

(a) *the deponent's belief that the company is, or is likely to become, unable to pay its debts and the grounds of that belief;*

(b) *which of the purposes specified in section 8(3) is expected to be achieved by the making of an administration order; and*

(c) *whether, in the opinion of the deponent, (i) the EC Regulation will apply and (ii) if so, whether the proceedings will be main proceedings, secondary proceedings or territorial proceedings.*

2.3(2) **[Company's financial position]** *There shall in the affidavit be provided a statement of the company's financial position, specifying (to the best of the deponent's knowledge and belief) assets and liabilities, including contingent and prospective liabilities.*

2.3(3) **[Details of creditors' security]** *Details shall be given of any security known or believed to be held by creditors of the company, and whether in any case the security is such as to confer power on the holder to appoint an administrative receiver. If an administrative receiver has been appointed, that fact shall be stated.*

2.3(4) **[Details of winding-up petition]** *If any petition has been presented for the winding up of the company, details of it shall be given in the affidavit, so far as within the immediate knowledge of the deponent.*

2.3(5) **[Other matters]** *If there are other matters which, in the opinion of those intending to present the petition for an administration order, will assist the court in deciding whether to make such an order, those matters (so far as lying within the knowledge or belief of the deponent) shall also be stated.*

2.3(6) **[Rule 2.2 report]** *If a report has been prepared for the company under Rule 2.2, that fact shall be stated. If not, an explanation shall be provided why not.*

GENERAL NOTE TO rr.*2.1–2.3*

These rules give guidance as to the evidence required in support of a petition for an administration order.

As directed by I(A)R 2010 Sch.5, a witness statement verified by a statement of truth is to be used in place of an affidavit, and the text should be read accordingly.

It is not obligatory to obtain the report of an independent person under r.*2.2*, but the absence of such a report must be explained (r.*2.3(6)*). It is customary for the report to cover such matters as: the qualifications of the independent person and the fact of his independence; how far he is relying on his own work and judgment and how far on the work and opinions of others; the company's insolvency; the factors influencing his opinion in favour of recommending the making of an order and the factors against it; which of the statutory purposes are likely to be achieved; and proposals for the provision of working capital during the administration.

The Vice-Chancellor in a *Practice Note* dated January 17, 1994 (*Practice Note (Administration order applications: content of independent reports*) [1994] 1 W.L.R. 160; [1994] B.C.C. 35) stressed the importance of ensuring that the primary aim of administration orders (namely, to facilitate the rescue and rehabilitation of insolvent companies) is not frustrated by expense, and urged that the costs of obtaining an administration order should not operate as a disincentive or put the process out of the reach of smaller companies.

Accordingly, the *Note* states that the contents of a r.*2(2)* report should not be unnecessarily elaborate and detailed. While the extent of the necessary investigation and the amount of material to be provided must be a matter of judgment for the person concerned and will vary from case to case, what is ordinarily required is a concise assessment of the company's situation and of the prospects of an order achieving one or more of the statutory purposes, normally including an explanation of the availability of any finance required during administration. Where the court finds that it has insufficient material on which to base a decision, the proposed administrator, if he is in court, may offer to supplement the material by giving oral evidence, and later filing a supplemental report covering this extra information.

In suitable cases the court may appoint an administrator but require him to report back to the court within a short time so that the court can consider whether to allow the administration to continue or to discharge the order. In some cases the court may require the administrator to hold a meeting of creditors before reporting back to the court, both within a relatively short period.

The *Note* concludes by reminding practitioners that there may be straightforward cases in which a report is not necessary.

The *Practice Note* referred to above has been supplemented by the *Practice Statement: Administration Orders—Reports* [2002] B.C.C. 354, which deals with the right to inspect reports on the court file. See also the note to r.7.31A.

The significance of the report was stressed by Harman J. in *Re Newport County Association Football Club Ltd* (1987) 3 B.C.C. 635 at 635 in the following passage: "Such a report, which is of course an objective assessment by persons with no axe to grind (using that phrase non-pejoratively), that is to say by persons not having any reason to wish a particular result or to be optimistic about a particular outcome, is one which very much influences the court, because it is prepared by experienced people who are detached from the emotions raised by failure ..., and can make a serious and objective assessment of the chances". This may be compared with *Re W F Fearman Ltd* (1988) 4 B.C.C. 139, where the absence of a report of making an order was regarded as fatal to the application. The witness statement which has to be made under r.*2(3)* calls for full and frank disclosure of those matters which are likely to be relevant at the hearing of the petition, and deliberate concealment of the true position may also be fatal: *Re West Park Golf & Country Club* [1997] 1 B.C.L.C. 20. In *Re Digginwell Plant & Construction Ltd* [2002] B.P.I.R. 299 some creditors had expressed the view that opinions in the report were over-optimistic. The court granted an administration order, but directed the administrators to report back to the court quickly if these fears proved to be true.

In *Re Colt Telecom Group plc (No.2)* [2002] EWHC 2815 (Ch); [2003] B.P.I.R. 324, Jacob J. stressed the fact that an insolvency practitioner giving a r.*2.2* report did so as an expert, and as such is subject to the rules in CPR Pt 35. He emphasised that when an administration petition was likely to be contested, the practitioner should first re-read Pt 35 and the Code of Guidance on Expert Evidence of the Working Party of the Civil Justice Council; should not propose himself as administrator; must be careful not to give or appear to give opinion evidence on matters (e.g. on the valuation of assets) in respect of which he is not an expert; and should not allow his opinions to be misrepresented. A solicitor advising the practitioner should ensure that he is given a copy of Pt 35. Even in an uncontested case, where the practitioner routinely offers to act as administrator, he should be particularly careful to be objective because of the slight conflict of interest involved.

The reference to "all" the creditors in r.*2.1(3)* is to all the petitioning creditors (if there are more than one), and not to all the creditors of the company: compare r.*2.4(4)*.

Paragraph (c) was inserted into r.*2.3(1)* by the Insolvency (Amendment) Rules 2002 (SI 2002/1307, effective May 31, 2002). See the notes to the EC Regulation art.3.

It is customary for the court, when making an administration order, to direct that the costs of the petition and of the r.*2.2* report should be costs in the administration. In *Re a Company (No.005174 of 1999)* [2000] B.C.C. 698 Neuberger J. observed that such an order could in some circumstances be unsatisfactory as it gives no guidance as to how these costs should rank. He went on to say that, although they could not be "expenses properly incurred by the administrator" or "debts or liabilities while he was administrator" so as to come within s.19(4) or (5), the court's jurisdiction under the Act was sufficiently flexible for a judge to be able to rule where such costs should rank, and he expressed the view that they should normally fall to be paid after the fixed-charge creditors and ahead of all other liabilities.

2.4   Form of petition

2.4(1)   [Petition presented by company or directors] *If presented by the company or by the directors, the petition shall state the name of the company and its address for service, which (in the absence of special reasons to the contrary) is that of the company's registered office.*

2.4(2)   [Single creditor's petition] *If presented by a single creditor, the petition shall state his name and address for service.*

2.4(3)   [Director's petition] *If the petition is presented by the directors, it shall state that it is so presented under section 9; but from and after presentation it is to be treated for all purposes as the petition of the company.*

2.4(4)   [Creditors' petition] *If the petition is presented by two or more creditors, it shall state that it is so presented (naming them); but from and after presentation it is to be treated for all purposes as the petition of one only of them, named in the petition as petitioning on behalf of himself and other creditors. An address for service for that one shall be specified.*

2.4(5)   [Specification of proposed administrator] *The petition shall specify the name and address of the person proposed to be appointed as administrator; and it shall be stated that, to the best of the petitioner's knowledge and belief, the person is qualified to act as an insolvency practitioner in relation to the company.*

2.4(6)   [Documents to be exhibited] *There shall be exhibited to the affidavit in support of the petition–*

   (a)   a copy of the petition;

   (b)   a written consent by the proposed administrator to accept appointment, if an administration order is made; and

[FORM 2.2]

   (c)   if a report has been prepared under Rule 2.2, a copy of it.

(See General Note after r.2.8.)

2.5   Filing of petition

2.5(1)   [Filing in court] *The petition and affidavit shall be filed in court, with a sufficient number of copies for service and use as provided by Rule 2.6.*

2.5(2)   [Sealed copies] *Each of the copies delivered shall have applied to it the seal of the court and be issued to the petitioner; and on each copy there shall be endorsed the date and time of filing.*

2.5(3)   [Venue for hearing] *The court shall fix a venue for the hearing of the petition and this also shall be endorsed on each copy of the petition issued under paragraph (2).*

2.5(4)   [After petition filed] *After the petition is filed, it is the duty of the petitioner to notify the court in writing of any winding-up petition presented against the company, as soon as he becomes aware of it.*

(See General Note after r.2.8.)

2.6   Service of petition

2.6(1)   [Interpretation] *In the following paragraphs of this Rule, references to the petition are to a copy of the petition issued by the court under Rule 2.5(2) together with the affidavit in support of it and the documents (other than the copy petition) exhibited to the affidavit.*

2.6(2)   *[Persons to be served] The petition shall be served–*

  (a)   *on any person who has appointed, or is or may be entitled to appoint, an administrative receiver for the company;*

  (b)   *if an administrative receiver has been appointed, on him;*

  (ba)   *if a member State liquidator has been appointed in main proceedings in relation to the company, on him;*

  (c)   *if there is pending a petition for the winding up of the company, on the petitioner (and also on the provisional liquidator, if any); and*

  (d)   *on the person proposed as administrator.*

2.6(3)   *[Creditors' petition] If the petition for the making of an administration order is presented by creditors of the company, the petition shall be served on the company.*

(See General Note after r.2.8.)

2.6A   Notice to sheriff, etc.

2.6A   *The petitioner shall as soon as reasonably practicable after filing the petition give notice of its presentation to–*

  (a)   *any sheriff or other officer who to his knowledge is charged with an execution or other legal process against the company or its property, and*

  (b)   *any person who to his knowledge has distrained against the company or its property.*

(See General Note after r.2.8.)

2.7   Manner in which service to be effected

2.7(1)   *[Person to effect service] Service of the petition in accordance with Rule 2.6 shall be effected by the petitioner, or his solicitor, or by a person instructed by him or his solicitor, not less than 5 days before the date fixed for the hearing.*

2.7(2)   *[How effected] Service shall be effected as follows–*

  (a)   *on the company (subject to paragraph (3) below), by delivering the documents to its registered office;*

  (b)   *on any other person (subject to paragraph (4)), by delivering the documents to his proper address;*

  (c)   *in either case, in such other manner as the court may direct.*

2.7(3)   *[Service to registered office not practicable] If delivery to the company's registered office is not practicable, service may be effected by delivery to its last known principal place of business in England and Wales.*

2.7(4)   *[Proper address under r.2.7(2)(b)] Subject to paragraph (4A), for the purposes of paragraph (2)(b), a person's proper address is any which he has previously notified as his address for service; but if he has not notified any such address, service may be effected by delivery to his usual or last known address.*

2.7(4A)   *[Other person re rr.2.7(2)(b), 2.7(4)] In the case of a person who–*

  (a)   *is an authorised deposit-taker or former authorised deposit-taker,*

  (b)   *has appointed, or is or may be entitled to appoint, an administrative receiver of the company, and*

  (c)   *has not notified an address for service,*

the proper address is the address of an office of that person where, to the knowledge of the petitioner, the company maintains a bank account or, where no such office is known to the petitioner, the registered office of that person, or, if there is no such office, his usual or last known address.

2.7(5) **[What constitutes delivery]** *Delivery of documents to any place or address may be made by leaving them there, or sending them by first class post.*

(See General Note after r.2.8.)

2.8 Proof of service

2.8(1) **[Verifying certificate of service]** *Service of the application must be verified by a certificate of service.*

2.8(1A) **[Contents]** *The certificate of service must be sufficient to identify the application served and must specify–*

(a) the name and registered number of the company or society,

(b) the address of the registered office of the company or society,

(c) the name of the applicant,

(d) the court to which the application was made and the court reference number,

(e) the date of the application,

(f) whether the copy served was a sealed copy,

(g) the date on which service was effected, and

(h) the manner in which service was effected.

[FORM 2.3]

2.8(2) **[Filing in court]** *The certificate of service shall be filed in court as soon as reasonably practicable after service, and in any event not less than one day before the hearing of the petition.*

GENERAL NOTE TO RR.*2.4–2.8*

Here are set out the requirements regarding the form, filing and service of the petition.

Rule *2.8(1)* substituted and r.*2.8(1A)* inserted by I(A)R 2010 (SI 2010/686) Sch.5 para.4(2) as from April 6, 2010 (with retrospective effect).

As directed by I(A)R 2010 Sch.5, a witness statement verified by a statement of truth is to be used in place of an affidavit, and the text in all these rules should be read accordingly.

A petition by the directors (r.*2.4(1), (3)*) must be presented by all the directors: see the note to IA 1986 s.9(1).

The court has power to abridge the period of five days specified by r.*2.7(1)*: *Re a Company (No.00175 of 1987)* (1987) 3 B.C.C. 124.

Although the rules plainly contemplate that the proceedings for an administration order shall be by way of hearing on notice to interested parties, the courts are willing in a case of urgency to make an order without notice (and indeed, before the presentation of the petition), against suitable undertakings by counsel: see the note to s.9(1) and the cases there cited.

Paragraph (ba) was inserted into r.*2.6(2)* by the Insolvency (Amendment) Rules 2002 (SI 2002/1307, effective May 31, 2002). Rule 2.7(4A)(a) was substituted by the Financial Services and Markets Act 2000 (Consequential Amendments and Repeals) Order 2001 (SI 2001/3649) as from December 1, 2001. The phrase "as soon as reasonably practicable" was substituted for the word "forthwith" in rr.*2.6A* and *2.8(2)* by I(A)R 2009 (SI 2009/642) r.5 as from April 6, 2009.

Rule *2.6A* seeks to prevent executions, etc. from being proceeded with in innocent contravention of IA 1986 s.11(3)(d). It does not appear that the reference to "sheriffs" has been changed: cf. the new r.2.7.

Rule *2.7(4A)* is intended to ensure that notice to the company's bank is given at a place where its account can most easily be traced.

It is normal practice for the court to order that the costs of the petition should be costs in the administration. On the ranking of such costs, see the note to r.*2.2*.

2.9   The hearing

2.9(1)   [Appearances] *At the hearing of the petition, any of the following may appear or be represented–*

(a)   *the petitioner;*

(b)   *the company;*

(c)   *any person who has appointed, or is or may be entitled to appoint, an administrative receiver of the company;*

(d)   *if an administrative receiver has been appointed, he;*

(e)   *any person who has presented a petition for the winding up of the company;*

(f)   *the person proposed for appointment as administrator;*

(fa)   *if a member State liquidator has been appointed in main proceedings in relation to the company, he;*

(g)   *with the permission of the court, any other person who appears to have an interest justifying his appearance.*

2.9(2)   [Costs] *If the court makes an administration order, the costs of the petitioner, and of any person appearing whose costs are allowed by the court, are payable as an expense of the administration.*

[FORM 2.4]

GENERAL NOTE

This rule ensures that all those likely to have an interest in the outcome of the proceedings may be heard, but those not particularly specified in paras (a)–(f) of r.*2.9(1)* need the leave of the court. This would include a member, a director or an unsecured creditor.

On the willingness of the courts in special cases to hear applications without notice to other parties, see the note to rr.*2.4–2.8.*

The court will not normally give members of the company, qua members, leave to be heard under this rule, at least where the company is plainly insolvent, notwithstanding the possibility that if the administration achieves its purpose they may have some interest in the outcome: *Re Chelmsford City Football Club (1980) Ltd* [1991] B.C.C. 133. However, discretion was exercised enabling shareholders to appear in *Re Farnborough-Aircraft.com Ltd* [2002] EWHC 1224 (Ch); [2002] 2 B.C.L.C. 641.

Paragraph (fa) was inserted into r.*2.9(1)* by the Insolvency (Amendment) Rules 2002 (SI 2002/1307, effective May 31, 2002).

2.10   Notice and advertisement of administration order

2.10(1)   [Court to give notice] *If the court makes an administration order, it shall as soon as reasonably practicable give notice to the person appointed as administrator.*

[FORM 2.4A]

2.10(2)   [Advertisement] *As soon as reasonably practicable after the order is made, the administrator shall advertise its making once in the Gazette, and once in such newspaper as he thinks most appropriate for ensuring that the order comes to the notice of the company's creditors.*

[FORM 2.5]

2.10(3)   [Administrator to give notice] *The administrator shall also as soon as reasonably practicable give notice of the making of the order–*

(a)   *to any person who has appointed, or is or may be entitled to appoint, an administrative receiver of the company;*

(b)   *if an administrative receiver has been appointed, to him;*

(c)   *if there is pending a petition for the winding up of the company, to the petitioner (and also to the provisional liquidator, if any); and*

(d) to the registrar of companies.

[FORM 2.6]

2.10(4) [Sealed copies] *Two sealed copies of the order shall be sent by the court to the administrator, one of which shall be sent by him to the registrar of companies in accordance with section 21(2).*

[FORM 2.7]

2.10(5) [Directions under s.9(4)] *If under section 9(4) the court makes any other order, it shall give directions as to the persons to whom, and how, notice of it is to be given.*

GENERAL NOTE

This rule dealing with the notification and publicity of the administration order is supplemented by IA 1986 s.12, which requires notification on the company's business letters, etc.

There is no power under the Act or the rules for the court to appoint an interim administrator, although if the court is satisfied that the assets or business of a company are in jeopardy and that there exists a prima facie case for the making of an administration order, it can under its inherent jurisdiction appoint a person to take control of the property of the company and manage its affairs pending the hearing of the application. Such an appointment is analogous to the appointment of a receiver of a disputed property which is in jeopardy (*Re a Company (No.00175 of 1987)* (1987) 3 B.C.C. 124). An alternative course, where a petition for winding up has also been presented, is for the court to appoint a provisional liquidator.

The phrase "as soon as reasonably practicable" was substituted for the word "forthwith" in r.*2.10(1)–(3)* by I(A)R 2009 (SI 2009/642) r.5 as from April 6, 2009. The amending rules allow the administrator under the new Pt 2 to exercise a discretion as to whether any publication in addition to gazetting is required, and the methods which may be utilised to do so (see r.*2.27*), but no similar amendment has been made to r.*2.10(2)*.

CHAPTER 2

STATEMENT OF AFFAIRS AND PROPOSALS TO CREDITORS

2.11 Notice requiring statement of affairs

2.11(1) [Notice] *Where the administrator determines to require a statement of the company's affairs to be made out and submitted to him in accordance with section 22, he shall send notice to each of the persons whom he considers should be made responsible under that section, requiring them to prepare and submit the statement.*

[FORM 2.8]

2.11(2) ["The deponents"] *The persons to whom the notice is sent are referred to in this Chapter as "the deponents".*

2.11(3) [Contents of notice] *The notice shall inform each of the deponents–*

(a) of the names and addresses of all others (if any) to whom the same notice has been sent;

(b) of the time within which the statement must be delivered;

(c) of the effect of section 22(6) (penalty for non-compliance); and

(d) of the application to him, and to each of the other deponents, of section 235 (duty to provide information, and to attend on the administrator if required).

2.11(4) [Instructions for preparation of statement] *The administrator shall, on request, furnish each deponent with the forms required for the preparation of the statement of affairs.*

(See General Note after r.2.15.)

2.12   *Verification and filing*

2.12(1)   [Form and verification] *The statement of affairs shall be in Form 2.9, shall contain all the particulars required by that form and shall be verified by affidavit by the deponents (using the same form).*

[FORM 2.9]

2.12(2)   [Affidavits of concurrence] *The administrator may require any of the persons mentioned in section 22(3) to submit an affidavit of concurrence, stating that he concurs in the statement of affairs.*

2.12(3)   [Affidavit may be qualified] *An affidavit of concurrence may be qualified in respect of matters dealt with in the statement of affairs, where the maker of the affidavit is not in agreement with the deponents, or he considers the statement to be erroneous or misleading, or he is without the direct knowledge necessary for concurring with it.*

2.12(4)   [Delivery of statement to administrator] *The statement of affairs shall be delivered to the administrator by the deponent making the affidavit of verification (or by one of them, if more than one), together with a copy of the verified statement.*

2.12(5)   [Delivery of affidavit of concurrence] *Every affidavit of concurrence shall be delivered by the person who makes it, together with a copy.*

2.12(6)   [Filing in court] *The administrator shall file the verified copy of the statement, and the affidavits of concurrence (if any) in court.*

(See General Note after r.2.15.)

2.13   *Limited disclosure*

2.13(1)   [Administrator may apply to court] *Where the administrator thinks that it would prejudice the conduct of the administration for the whole or part of the statement of affairs to be disclosed, he may apply to the court for an order of limited disclosure in respect of the statement, or any specified part of it.*

2.13(2)   [Powers of court] *The court may on the application order that the statement or, as the case may be, the specified part of it, be not filed in court, or that it is to be filed separately and not be open to inspection otherwise than with permission of the court.*

2.13(3)   [Directions] *The court's order may include directions as to the delivery of documents to the registrar of companies and the disclosure of relevant information to other persons.*

(See General Note after r.2.15.)

2.14   *Release from duty to submit statement of affairs; extension of time*

2.14(1)   [Exercise of s.22(5) power] *The power of the administrator under section 22(5) to give a release from the obligation imposed by that section, or to grant an extension of time, may be exercised at the administrator's own discretion, or at the request of any deponent.*

2.14(2)   [Deponent may apply to court] *A deponent may, if he requests a release or extension of time and it is refused by the administrator, apply to the court for it.*

2.14(3)   [Court may dismiss application etc.] *The court may, if it thinks that no sufficient cause is shown for the application, dismiss it; but it shall not do so unless the applicant has had an opportunity to attend the court for a hearing without notice to any other party, of which he has been given at least 7 days' notice.*

If the application is not dismissed under this paragraph, the court shall fix a venue for it to be heard, and give notice to the deponent accordingly.

2.14(4)   [Deponent to send notice to administrator] *The deponent shall, at least 14 days before the hearing, send to the administrator a notice stating the venue and accompanied by a copy of the application, and of any evidence which he (the deponent) intends to adduce in support of it.*

2.14(5) **[Appearance etc. by administrator]** *The administrator may appear and be heard on the application; and, whether or not he appears, he may file a written report of any matters which he considers ought to be drawn to the court's attention.*

If such a report is filed, a copy of it shall be sent by the administrator to the deponent, not later than 5 days before the hearing.

2.14(6) **[Sealed copies of order]** *Sealed copies of any order made on the application shall be sent by the court to the deponent and the administrator.*

2.14(7) **[Applicant's costs]** *On any application under this Rule the applicant's costs shall be paid in any event by him and, unless the court otherwise orders, no allowance towards them shall be made out of the assets.*

(See General Note after r.2.15.)

2.15 Expenses of statement of affairs

2.15(1) **[Payment of expenses]** *A deponent making the statement of affairs and affidavit shall be allowed, and paid by the administrator out of his receipts, any expenses incurred by the deponent in so doing which the administrator considers reasonable.*

2.15(2) **[Appeal to court]** *Any decision by the administrator under this Rule is subject to appeal to the court.*

2.15(3) **[Effect of Rule]** *Nothing in this Rule relieves a deponent from any obligation with respect to the preparation, verification and submission of the statement of affairs, or to the provision of information to the administrator.*

GENERAL NOTE TO RR.*2.11–2.15*

These rules give details regarding the statement of affairs, which must in this case follow a prescribed form (r.*2.12*).

As directed by I(A)R 2010 Sch.5, a witness statement verified by a statement of truth is to be used in place of an affidavit, and the text should be read accordingly.

2.16 Statement to be annexed to proposals

2.16(1) **[Contents of statement]** *There shall be annexed to the administrator's proposals, when sent to the registrar of companies under section 23 and laid before the creditors' meeting to be summoned under that section, a statement by him showing–*

    (a) details relating to his appointment as administrator, the purposes for which an administration order was applied for and made, and any subsequent variation of those purposes;

    (b) the names of the directors and secretary of the company;

    (c) an account of the circumstances giving rise to the application for an administration order;

    (d) if a statement of affairs has been submitted, a copy or summary of it, with the administrator's comments, if any;

    (e) if no statement of affairs has been submitted, details of the financial position of the company at the latest practicable date (which must, unless the court otherwise orders, be a date not earlier than that of the administration order);

    (f) the manner in which the affairs and business of the company–

        (i) have, since the date of the administrator's appointment, been managed and financed;

        (ii) will, if the administrator's proposals are approved, continue to be managed and financed;

    (fa) whether (i) the EC Regulation applies and (ii) if so, whether the proceedings are main proceedings, secondary proceedings or territorial proceedings; and

(g) such other information (if any) as the administrator thinks necessary to enable creditors to decide whether or not to vote for the adoption of the proposals.

2.16(2) [Where s.18 application] *Where the administrator intends to apply to the court under section 18 for the administration order to be discharged at a time before he has sent a statement of his proposals to creditors in accordance with section 23(1), he shall, at least 10 days before he makes such an application, send to all creditors of the company (so far as he is aware of their addresses) a report containing the information required by paragraph (1)(a)–(f)(i) of this Rule.*

(See General Note after r.2.17.)

2.17 Notice to members of proposals to creditors

2.17 *The manner of publishing–*

(a) *under section 23(2)(b), notice to members of the administrator's proposals to creditors, and*

(b) *under section 25(3)(b), notice to members of substantial revisions of the proposals,*

shall be by gazetting; and the notice shall also in either case be advertised once in the newspaper in which the administration order was advertised.

GENERAL NOTE TO RR.*2.16–2.17*

The administrator's proposals must be sent to the registrar of companies and to every known creditor individually (IA 1986 s.*23(2)*). The administrator must also send copies of the statement directly to members; or alternatively, by virtue of s.*23(2)(b)* and r.*2.17*, he may publish in the *Gazette* an address to which members should write for copies. Rules 12A.6–12A.12 now allow for notices and other documents to be sent to creditors and members by electronic means or the use of websites. It appears that the administrator has no discretion to dispense with the requirement to advertise in the newspaper: see the note to r.*2.10(2)*. Paragraph (fa) was inserted into r.*2.16(1)* by the Insolvency (Amendment) Rules 2002 (SI 2002/1307, effective May 31, 2002). See the notes to the EC Regulation art.3.

CHAPTER 3

CREDITORS' AND COMPANY MEETINGS

Section A: creditors' meetings

2.18 Meeting to consider administrator's proposals

2.18(1) [Notice of s.23(1) meeting] *Notice of the creditors' meeting to be summoned under section 23(1) shall be given to all the creditors of the company who are identified in the statement of affairs, or are known to the administrator and had claims against the company at the date of the administration order.*

2.18(2) [Newspaper advertisement] *Notice of the meeting shall also (unless the court otherwise directs) be given by advertisement in the newspaper in which the administration order was advertised.*

2.18(3) [Notice to directors etc.] *Notice to attend the meeting shall be sent out at the same time to any directors or officers of the company (including persons who have been directors or officers in the past) whose presence at the meeting is, in the administrator's opinion, required.*

[FORM 2.10]

2.18(4) [Adjournment of meeting] *If at the meeting there is not the requisite majority for approval of the administrator's proposals (with modifications, if any), the chairman may, and shall if a resolution is passed to that effect, adjourn the meeting for not more than 14 days.*

(See General Note after r.2.29.)

2.19   Creditors' meetings generally

2.19(1)   [Application of Rule] *This Rule applies to creditors' meetings summoned by the administrator under–*

(a)   *section 14(2)(b) (general power to summon meetings of creditors);*

(b)   *section 17(3) (requisition by creditors; direction by the court);*

(c)   *section 23(1) (to consider administrator's proposals); or*

(d)   *section 25(2)(b) (to consider substantial revisions).*

2.19(2)   [Convenience of venue] *In fixing the venue for the meeting, the administrator shall have regard to the convenience of creditors.*

2.19(3)   [Time of meeting] *The meeting shall be summoned for commencement between 10.00 and 16.00 hours on a business day, unless the court otherwise directs.*

2.19(4)   [Notice] *Notice of the meeting shall be given to all creditors who are known to the administrator and had claims against the company at the date of the administration order; and the notice shall specify the purpose of the meeting and contain a statement of the effect of Rule 2.22(1) (entitlement to vote).*

[FORM 2.11]
[FORM 2.22]

2.19(4A)   [Period of notice] *Except in relation to a meeting summoned under section 23(1) or 25(2), at least 21 days' notice of the meeting shall be given.*

2.19(5)   [Forms of proxy] *With the notice summoning the meeting there shall be sent out forms of proxy.*
[FORM 8.2]

2.19(6)   [Adjournment if no chairman] *If within 30 minutes from the time fixed for commencement of the meeting there is no person present to act as chairman, the meeting stands adjourned to the same time and place in the following week or, if that is not a business day, to the business day immediately following.*

2.19(7)   [Further adjournments] *The meeting may from time to time be adjourned, if the chairman thinks fit, but not for more than 14 days from the date on which it was fixed to commence.*

(See General Note after r.2.29.)

2.20   The chairman at meetings

2.20(1)   [Administrator or his nominee to be chairman] *At any meeting of creditors summoned by the administrator, either he shall be chairman, or a person nominated by him in writing to act in his place.*

2.20(2)   [Nominee chairman] *A person so nominated must be either–*

(a)   *one who is qualified to act as an insolvency practitioner in relation to the company, or*

(b)   *an employee of the administrator or his firm who is experienced in insolvency matters.*

(See General Note after r.2.29.)

2.21   Meeting requisitioned by creditors

2.21(1)   [Documents to accompany request] *Any request by creditors to the administrator for a meeting of creditors to be summoned shall be accompanied by–*

   (a)   a list of the creditors concurring with the request, showing the amounts of their respective claims in the administration;

   (b)   from each creditor concurring, written confirmation of his concurrence; and

   (c)   a statement of the purpose of the proposed meeting.

This paragraph does not apply if the requisitioning creditor's debt is alone sufficient, without the concurrence of other creditors.

2.21(2)   *[Fixing of venue]* The administrator shall, if he considers the request to be properly made in accordance with section 17(3), fix a venue for the meeting, not more than 35 days from his receipt of the request, and give at least 21 days' notice of the meeting to creditors.

2.21(3)   *[Expenses]* The expenses of summoning and holding a meeting at the instance of any person other than the administrator shall be paid by that person, who shall deposit with the administrator security for their payment.

2.21(4)   *[Deposit under r.2.21(3)]* The sum to be deposited shall be such as the administrator may determine, and he shall not act without the deposit having been made.

2.21(5)   *[Resolution of meeting re expenses]* The meeting may resolve that the expenses of summoning and holding it are to be payable out of the assets of the company, as an expense of the administration.

2.21(6)   *[Repayment of deposit]* To the extent that any deposit made under this Rule is not required for the payment of expenses of summoning and holding the meeting, it shall be repaid to the person who made it.

(See General Note after r.2.29.)

2.22   Entitlement to vote

2.22(1)   *[Conditions for voting]* Subject as follows, at a meeting of creditors in administration proceedings a person is entitled to vote only if–

   (a)   he has given to the administrator, not later than 12.00 hours on the business day before the day fixed for the meeting, details in writing of the debt which

      (i)   he claims to be due to him from the company, or

      (ii)   in relation to a member State liquidator, is claimed to be due to creditors in proceedings in relation to which he holds office,

   and the claim has been duly admitted under the following provisions of this Rule, and

   (b)   there has been lodged with the administrator any proxy which he intends to be used on his behalf.

Details of the debt must include any calculation for the purposes of Rules 2.24 to 2.27.

2.22(2)   *[Failure to comply with r.2.22(1)(a)]* The chairman of the meeting may allow a creditor to vote, notwithstanding that he has failed to comply with paragraph (1)(a), if satisfied that the failure was due to circumstances beyond the creditor's control.

2.22(3)   *[Production of documents]* The administrator or, if other, the chairman of the meeting may call for any document or other evidence to be produced to him, where he thinks it necessary for the purpose of substantiating the whole or any part of the claim.

2.22(4)   *[Calculation of votes]* Votes are calculated according to the amount of a creditor's debt as at the date of the administration order, deducting any amounts paid in respect of the debt after that date.

2.22(5)   *[Limitation on voting] A creditor shall not vote in respect of a debt for an unliquidated amount, or any debt whose value is not ascertained, except where the chairman agrees to put upon the debt an estimated minimum value for the purpose of entitlement to vote and admits the claim for that purpose.*

2.22(6)   *[Further limitation] No vote shall be cast by virtue of a claim more than once on any resolution put to the meeting.*

2.22(7)   *[Creditor's vote] Where–*

     (a)   *a creditor is entitled to vote under this Rule,*

     (b)   *has lodged his claim in one or more sets of other proceedings, and*

     (c)   *votes (either in person or by proxy) on a resolution put to the meeting,*

only the creditor's vote shall be counted.

2.22(8)   *[Lodging of claim] Where–*

     (a)   *a creditor has lodged his claim in more than one set of other proceedings, and*

     (b)   *more than one member State liquidator seeks to vote by virtue of that claim,*

the entitlement to vote by virtue of that claim is exercisable by the member State liquidator in main proceedings, whether or not the creditor has lodged his claim in the main proceedings.

2.22(9)   *[Single claim] For the purposes of paragraph (6), the claim of a creditor and of any member State liquidator in relation to the same debt are a single claim.*

2.22(10)   *["Other proceedings"] For the purposes of paragraphs (7) and (8),* **"other proceedings"** *means main proceedings, secondary proceedings or territorial proceedings in another member State.*

(See General Note after r.2.29.)

2.23   Admission and rejection of claims

2.23(1)   *[Power of chairman] At any creditors' meeting the chairman has power to admit or reject a creditor's claim for the purpose of his entitlement to vote; and the power is exercisable with respect to the whole or any part of the claim.*

2.23(2)   *[Appeal from chairman's decision] The chairman's decision under this Rule, or in respect of any matter arising under Rule 2.22, is subject to appeal to the court by any creditor.*

2.23(3)   *[Voting subject to objection] If the chairman is in doubt whether a claim should be admitted or rejected, he shall mark it as objected to and allow the creditor to vote, subject to his vote being subsequently declared invalid if the objection to the claim is sustained.*

2.23(4)   *[If chairman's decision reversed etc.] If on an appeal the chairman's decision is reversed or varied, or a creditor's vote is declared invalid, the court may order that another meeting be summoned, or make such other order as it thinks just.*

2.23(5)   *[In case of s.23 meeting] In the case of the meeting summoned under section 23 to consider the administrator's proposals, an application to the court by way of appeal under this Rule against a decision of the chairman shall not be made later than 28 days after the delivery of the administrator's report in accordance with section 24(4).*

2.23(6)   *[Costs of appeal] Neither the administrator nor any person nominated by him to be chairman is personally liable for costs incurred by any person in respect of an appeal to the court under this Rule, unless the court makes an order to that effect.*

(See General Note after r.2.29.)

2.24   Secured creditors

2.24   *At a meeting of creditors a secured creditor is entitled to vote only in respect of the balance (if any) of his debt after deducting the value of his security as estimated by him.*

(See General Note after r.2.29.)

2.25   Holders of negotiable instruments

2.25   *A creditor shall not vote in respect of a debt on, or secured by, a current bill of exchange or promissory note, unless he is willing–*

     (a)   *to treat the liability to him on the bill or note of every person who is liable on it antecedently to the company, and against whom a bankruptcy order has not been made (or, in the case of a company, which has not gone into liquidation), as a security in his hands, and*

     (b)   *to estimate the value of the security and, for the purpose of his entitlement to vote, to deduct it from his claim.*

(See General Note after r.2.29.)

2.26   Retention of title creditors

2.26   *For the purpose of entitlement to vote at a creditors' meeting in administration proceedings, a seller of goods to the company under a retention of title agreement shall deduct from his claim the value, as estimated by him, of any rights arising under that agreement in respect of goods in possession of the company.*

(See General Note after r.2.29.)

2.27   Hire-purchase, conditional sale and chattel leasing agreements

2.27(1)   *[Entitlement to vote] Subject as follows, an owner of goods under a hire-purchase or chattel leasing agreement, or a seller of goods under a conditional sale agreement, is entitled to vote in respect of the amount of the debt due and payable to him by the company as at the date of the administration order.*

2.27(2)   *[Calculating amount of debt] In calculating the amount of any debt for this purpose, no account shall be taken of any amount attributable to the exercise of any right under the relevant agreement, so far as the right has become exercisable solely by virtue of the presentation of the petition for an administration order or any matter arising in consequence of that, or of the making of the order.*

(See General Note after r.2.29.)

2.28   Resolutions and minutes

2.28(1)   *[Resolution passed by majority in value] Subject to paragraph (1A), at a creditors' meeting in administration proceedings, a resolution is passed when a majority (in value) of those present and voting, in person or by proxy, have voted in favour of it.*

2.28(1A)   *[Resolution invalid] Any resolution is invalid if those voting against it include more than half in value of the creditors to whom notice of the meeting was sent and who are not, to the best of the chairman's belief, persons connected with the company.*

2.28(2)   *[Minute book] The chairman of the meeting shall cause minutes of its proceedings to be entered in the company's minute book.*

2.28(3) *[**Contents of minutes**] The minutes shall include a list of the creditors who attended (personally or by proxy) and, if a creditors' committee has been established, the names and addresses of those elected to be members of the committee.*

(See General Note after r.2.29.)

2.29 Reports and notices under ss.23 and 25

2.29 *Any report or notice by the administrator of the result of a creditors' meeting held under section 23 or 25 shall have annexed to it details of the proposals which were considered by the meeting and of the revisions and modifications to the proposals which were so considered.*

GENERAL NOTE TO RR.*2.18–2.29*

These are the rules governing the summoning and conduct of creditors' meetings. Rules 12A.20–12A.25 now allow "meetings" to be held without the physical attendance of the participants. A meeting may be summoned either by the administrator himself or on the requisition of one-tenth in value of the creditors (IA 1986 s.17(3)(b)). A creditor is required to prove his debt prior to the meeting (r.*2.22(1)(a)*), although the chairman has a limited discretion to make exceptions (r.*2.22(2)*). In contrast, a creditor is not required to lodge his proxy in advance of the meeting but may do so at any time prior to the taking of the vote: *Re Philip Alexander Securities & Futures Ltd* [1998] B.C.C. 819. The "rule against double proof" applies in this context, as it does in all insolvency situations: see *Re Polly Peck International plc* [1996] B.C.C. 486, and the notes to r.12.3. Voting is prima facie by a simple majority in value of those creditors present and voting (including proxy votes): r.*2.28(1)*; but r.*2.28(1A)* prevents a resolution from being carried against the wish of a majority of the non-connected creditors. On the meaning of "connected with", see IA 1986 s.249, and compare IR 1986 r.1.19(4).

Rule *2.22(5)*, like r.1.17(3), assumes that a claimant for an unliquidated amount or for a sum whose value is not ascertained may be regarded as a "creditor" for the purposes of an administration. There is, perhaps, more support for this in the case of an administration than in a voluntary arrangement, since s.9(1) gives contingent and prospective creditors the right to present a petition. See the notes to s.1(1) and rr.1.13–1.21; and contrast the position in a winding up (rr.12.3(1), 13.12).

On the meaning of "agrees", see the note to r.1.17(3), but note that there is here no equivalent to r.1.49(3) fixing a sum of £1 in the absence of an agreement by the chairman to fix a higher value.

A creditor may, if he wishes, split the vote to which he is entitled so as to cast his vote as to £x in value in one way and as to £y in value in the other, provided that £x + £y does not exceed the total debt in respect of which he is qualified to vote under r.*2.22*: *Re Polly Peck International plc* [1991] B.C.C. 503. Accordingly, a trustee for debenture holders can give effect to the wishes of the debenture holders where they differ among themselves, or are at variance with those of the trustee as a creditor in its own right.

Paragraph (1)(a) was also amended, and paras (6)–(10) inserted, into r.*2.22* by SI 2002/1307. The EC Regulation art.32(2) and (3) authorises the "liquidator" in both main and secondary proceedings which have been opened in other Member States to prove in secondary proceedings here in respect of claims which have already been lodged in their own proceedings, and to represent their own creditors by (e.g.) attending creditors' meetings. The amendments to r.*2.22* are designed to ensure that a debt which has been proved in more than one set of proceedings is treated as a single claim, and that no creditor's vote is counted twice. See the notes to the EC Regulation art.32 and, on the different types of proceedings, art.3.

2.30 Notices to creditors

2.30(1) *[**Notice of result of meeting**] Within 14 days of the conclusion of a meeting of creditors to consider the administrator's proposals or revised proposals, the administrator shall send notice of the result of the meeting (including, where appropriate, details of the proposals as approved) to every creditor who received notice of the meeting under the Rules, and to any other creditor of whom the administrator has since become aware.*

[FORM 2.12]

2.30(2) *[**Administrator's report**] Within 14 days of the end of every period of 6 months beginning with the date of approval of the administrator's proposals or revised proposals, the administrator shall send to all creditors of the company a report on the progress of the administration.*

2.30(3)   *[Administrator vacating office]* On vacating office the administrator shall send to creditors a report on the administration up to that time.

This does not apply where the administration is immediately followed by the company going into liquidation, nor when the administrator is removed from office by the court or ceases to be qualified as an insolvency practitioner.

GENERAL NOTE

The result of the meeting must be notified to all known creditors. Rules 12A.6–12A.12 now allow for notices and other documents to be sent to creditors and members by electronic means or the use of websites.

Section B: company meetings

2.31   Venue and conduct of company meeting

2.31(1)   *[Fixing of venue]* Where the administrator summons a meeting of members of the company, he shall fix a venue for it having regard to their convenience.

2.31(2)   *[Chairman]* The chairman of the meeting shall be the administrator or a person nominated by him in writing to act in his place.

2.31(3)   *[Nominee chairman]* A person so nominated must be either–

(a)   one who is qualified to act as an insolvency practitioner in relation to the company, or

(b)   an employee of the administrator or his firm who is experienced in insolvency matters.

2.31(4)   *[Adjournment if no chairman]* If within 30 minutes from the time fixed for commencement of the meeting there is no person present to act as chairman, the meeting stands adjourned to the same time and place in the following week or, if that is not a business day, to the business day immediately following.

2.31(5)   *[Summoning and conduct of meeting]* Subject as above, the meeting shall be summoned and conducted as if it were a general meeting of the company summoned under the company's articles of association, and in accordance with the applicable provisions of the Companies Act.

2.31(5A)   *[Limitation of r.2.31(5)]* Paragraph (5) does not apply where the laws of a member State and not the laws of England and Wales apply in relation to the conduct of the meeting.

2.31(5B)   *[Application of r.2.31(5A)]* Where paragraph (5A) applies, subject as above, the meeting shall be summoned and conducted in accordance with the constitution of the company and the laws of the member State referred to in that paragraph shall apply to the conduct of the meeting.

2.31(6)   *[Minutes]* The chairman of the meeting shall cause minutes of its proceedings to be entered in the company's minute book.

GENERAL NOTE

Any meeting of the shareholders held during the currency of an administration order is summoned and conducted in accordance with the articles of association, but where it is summoned by the administrator, it is he or his nominee who takes the chair. Rules 12A.21–12A.27 now allow "meetings" to be held without the physical attendance of the participants.

Paragraphs (5A) and (5B) were inserted into r.*2.31* by the Insolvency (Amendment) Rules 2002 (SI 2002/1307, effective May 31, 2002). By an amendment made to IA 1986 s.8 it is now possible for a UK court to make an administration order against a company incorporated in another Member State, if its "centre of main interests" is located within the UK. The amendments to r.*2.31* make it plain that the conduct of shareholders' meetings in such a case are to be governed by the law of incorporation. See further the notes to s.8 and to the EC Regulation art.3, and note the considerations regarded as relevant to the exercise of the court's discretion expressed in *Re TXU Europe German Finance BV* [2005] B.C.C. 90.

No doubt r.*2.31(5B)* would be applied by analogy in a case where the company was incorporated outside the EU but has its centre of main interests within the UK, so giving a UK court jurisdiction (see *Re BRAC Rent-a-Car International Inc* [2003] EWHC 128 (Ch); [2003] B.C.C. 248).

CHAPTER 4

THE CREDITORS' COMMITTEE

2.32 Constitution of committee

2.32(1) *[Three–five creditors] Where it is resolved by a creditors' meeting to establish a creditors' committee for the purposes of the administration, the committee shall consist of at least 3 and not more than 5 creditors of the company elected at the meeting.*

2.32(2) *[Eligibility of creditors] Any creditor of the company is eligible to be a member of the committee, so long as his claim has not been rejected for the purpose of his entitlement to vote.*

2.32(3) *[Body corporate as member] A body corporate may be a member of the committee, but it cannot act as such otherwise than by a representative appointed under Rule 2.37 below.*

(See General Note after r.2.46A.)

2.33 Formalities of establishment

2.33(1) *[Certificate of due constitution] The creditors' committee does not come into being, and accordingly cannot act, until the administrator has issued a certificate of its due constitution.*

2.33(2) *[Agreement to act] No person may act as a member of the committee unless and until he has agreed to do so and, unless the relevant proxy or authorisation contains a statement to the contrary, such agreement may be given by his proxy-holder or representative under section 375 of the Companies Act present at the meeting establishing the committee.*

2.33(2A) *[Issue of administrator's certificate] The administrator's certificate of the committee's due constitution shall not issue unless and until at least 3 of the persons who are to be members of the committee have agreed to act.*

2.33(3) *[Amended certificate] As and when the others (if any) agree to act, the administrator shall issue an amended certificate.*

2.33(4) *[Filing of certificates] The certificate, and any amended certificate, shall be filed in court by the administrator.*

[FORM 2.13]

2.33(5) *[Change in membership] If after the first establishment of the committee there is any change in its membership, the administrator shall report the change to the court.*

[FORM 2.14]

(See General Note after r.2.46A.)

2.34 Functions and meetings of the committee

2.34(1) *[Functions] The creditors' committee shall assist the administrator in discharging his functions, and act in relation to him in such manner as may be agreed from time to time.*

2.34(2) *[Holding of meetings] Subject as follows, meetings of the committee shall be held when and where determined by the administrator.*

2.34(3) *[First and subsequent meetings] The administrator shall call a first meeting of the committee not later than 3 months after its first establishment; and thereafter he shall call a meeting–*

115

(a) if so requested by a member of the committee or his representative (the meeting then to be held within 21 days of the request being received by the administrator), and

(b) for a specified date, if the committee has previously resolved that a meeting be held on that date.

2.34(4) [Notice of venue] *The administrator shall give 7 days' written notice of the venue of any meeting to every member of the committee (or his representative designated for that purpose), unless in any case the requirement of notice has been waived by or on behalf of any member.*
  Waiver may be signified either at or before the meeting.

(See General Note after r.2.46A.)

2.35 The chairman at meetings

2.35(1) [Administrator to be chairman] *Subject to Rule 2.44(3), the chairman at any meeting of the creditors' committee shall be the administrator or a person nominated by him in writing to act.*

2.35(2) [Other nominated chairman] *A person so nominated must be either–*

(a) one who is qualified to act as an insolvency practitioner in relation to the company, or

(b) an employee of the administrator or his firm who is experienced in insolvency matters.

(See General Note after r.2.46A.)

2.36 Quorum

2.36 *A meeting of the committee is duly constituted if due notice of it has been given to all the members, and at least 2 members are present or represented.*

(See General Note after r.2.46A.)

2.37 Committee-members' representatives

2.37(1) [Representation] *A member of the committee may, in relation to the business of the committee, be represented by another person duly authorised by him for that purpose.*

2.37(2) [Letter of authority] *A person acting as a committee-member's representative must hold a letter of authority entitling him so to act (either generally or specially) and signed by or on behalf of the committee-member, and for this purpose any proxy or any authorisation under section 375 of the Companies Act in relation to any meeting of creditors of the company shall, unless it contains a statement to the contrary, be treated as a letter of authority to act generally signed by or on behalf of the committee-member.*

2.37(3) [Production of letter of authority] *The chairman at any meeting of the committee may call on a person claiming to act as a committee-member's representative to produce his letter of authority, and may exclude him if it appears that his authority is deficient.*

2.37(4) [Who may not be a representative] *No member may be represented by a body corporate, or by a person who is an undischarged bankrupt, or is subject to a composition or arrangement with his creditors.*

2.37(5) [No dual representation] *No person shall–*

(a) on the same committee, act at one and the same time as representative of more than one committee-member, or

(b) act both as a member of the committee and as representative of another member.

2.37(6) [Signing as representative] *Where a member's representative authenticates any document on the member's behalf, the fact that he so authenticates must be stated below his authentication.*

(See General Note after r.2.46A.)

2.38   Resignation

2.38   *A member of the committee may resign by notice in writing delivered to the administrator.*

(See General Note after r.2.46A.)

2.39   Termination of membership

2.39(1)   [Automatic termination] *Membership of the creditors' committee is automatically terminated if the member–*

(a) *becomes bankrupt, or compounds or arranges with his creditors, or*

(b) *at 3 consecutive meetings of the committee is neither present nor represented (unless at the third of those meetings it is resolved that this Rule is not to apply in his case), or*

(c) *ceases to be, or is found never to have been, a creditor.*

2.39(2)   [Termination on bankruptcy] *However, if the cause of termination is the member's bankruptcy, his trustee in bankruptcy replaces him as a member of the committee.*

(See General Note after r.2.46A.)

2.40   Removal

2.40   *A member of the committee may be removed by resolution at a meeting of creditors, at least 14 days' notice having been given of the intention to move that resolution.*

(See General Note after r.2.46A.)

2.41   Vacancies

2.41(1)   [Application of Rule] *The following applies if there is a vacancy in the membership of the creditors' committee.*

2.41(2)   [Agreement not to fill vacancy] *The vacancy need not be filled if the administrator and a majority of the remaining members of the committee so agree, provided that the total number of members does not fall below the minimum required under Rule 2.32.*

2.41(3)   [Filling vacancy] *The administrator may appoint any creditor (being qualified under the Rules to be a member of the committee) to fill the vacancy, if a majority of the other members of the committee agree to the appointment, and the creditor concerned consents to act.*

(See General Note after r.2.46A.)

2.42   Procedure at meetings

2.42(1)   [Votes and passing of resolutions] *At any meeting of the creditors' committee, each member of it (whether present himself, or by his representative) has one vote; and a resolution is passed when a majority of the members present or represented have voted in favour of it.*

2.42(2)   [Record of resolutions] *Every resolution passed shall be recorded in writing, either separately or as part of the minutes of the meeting.*

2.42(3)   [Signing of records etc.] *A record of each resolution shall be authenticated by the chairman and placed in the company's minute book.*

(See General Note after r.2.46A.)

2.43 Resolutions by post

2.43(1) **[Proposed resolution sent to members]** *In accordance with this Rule, the administrator may seek to obtain the agreement of members of the creditors' committee to a resolution by sending to every member (or his representative designated for the purpose) a copy of the proposed resolution.*

2.43(2) **[Copy of proposed resolution]** *Where the administrator makes use of the procedure allowed by this Rule, he shall send out to members of the committee or their representatives (as the case may be) a copy of any proposed resolution on which a decision is sought, which shall be set out in such a way that agreement with or dissent from each separate resolution may be indicated by the recipient on the copy so sent.*

2.43(3) **[Member may require meeting]** *Any member of the committee may, within 7 business days from the date of the administrator sending out a resolution, require him to summon a meeting of the committee to consider the matters raised by the resolution.*

2.43(4) **[Deemed passing of resolution]** *In the absence of such a request, the resolution is deemed to have been passed by the committee if and when the administrator is notified in writing by a majority of the members that they concur with it.*

2.43(5) **[Copy resolution etc. in minute book]** *A copy of every resolution passed under this Rule, and a note that the committee's concurrence was obtained, shall be placed in the company's minute book.*

(See General Note after r.2.46A.)

2.44 Information from administrator

2.44(1) **[Notice to administrator]** *Where the committee resolves to require the attendance of the administrator under section 26(2), the notice to him shall be in writing signed by the majority of the members of the committee for the time being. A member's representative may sign for him.*

2.44(2) **[Time and place of meeting]** *The meeting at which the administrator's attendance is required shall be fixed by the committee for a business day, and shall be held at such time and place as he determines.*

2.44(3) **[Chairman]** *Where the administrator so attends, the members of the committee may elect any one of their number to be chairman of the meeting, in place of the administrator or a nominee of his.*

(See General Note after r.2.46A.)

2.45 Expenses of members

2.45(1) **[Expenses defrayed out of assets]** *Subject as follows, the administrator shall out of the assets of the company defray any reasonable travelling expenses directly incurred by members of the creditors' committee or their representatives in relation to their attendance at the committee's meetings, or otherwise on the committee's business, as an expense of the administration.*

2.45(2) **[Non-application of r.2.45(1)]** *Paragraph (1) does not apply to any meeting of the committee held within 3 months of a previous meeting, unless the meeting in question is summoned at the instance of the administrator.*

(See General Note after r.2.46A.)

2.46 Members' dealings with the company

2.46(1) **[Effect of membership]** *Membership of the committee does not prevent a person from dealing with the company while the administration order is in force, provided that any transactions in the course of such dealings are in good faith and for value.*

2.46(2)   ***[Court may set aside transaction]*** *The court may, on the application of any person interested, set aside any transaction which appears to it to be contrary to the requirements of this Rule, and may give such consequential directions as it thinks fit for compensating the company for any loss which it may have incurred in consequence of the transaction.*

(See General Note after r.2.46A.)

2.46A   Formal defects

2.46A   *The acts of the creditors' committee established for any administration are valid notwithstanding any defect in the appointment, election or qualifications of any member of the committee or any committee-member's representative or in the formalities of its establishment.*

GENERAL NOTE TO RR.*2.32–2.46A*

The IA 1986 s.26 provides for the establishment of a creditors' committee, corresponding to the liquidation committee in a liquidation. These rules deal with its constitution and functioning. Rules *2.33(2)* and *2.37(2)* are intended to make it easier for insolvency practitioners to convene committee meetings immediately after the creditors' meeting. Rule *2.46A* (and rr.3.30A, 4.172A and 6.156(7)) is in standard form, although one would normally expect to find such a provision in the substantive legislation rather than the rules.

Rules 12A.6–12A.13 now allow for notices and other documents to be sent by or to creditors and members by electronic means or the use of websites, and rr.12A.21–12A.27 allow "meetings" to be held without the physical attendance of the participants.

Rule *2.32* envisages that the election to membership of the creditors' committee will be conducted by a single ballot, with the five creditors who attract the greatest number of votes by value being chosen to form the committee: *Re Polly Peck International plc* [1991] B.C.C. 503.

CHAPTER 5

THE ADMINISTRATOR

2.47   Fixing of remuneration

2.47(1)   ***[Entitlement to remuneration]*** *The administrator is entitled to receive remuneration for his services as such.*

2.47(2)   ***[How fixed]*** *The remuneration shall be fixed either–*

  (a)   *as a percentage of the value of the property with which he has to deal, or*

  (b)   *by reference to the time properly given by the insolvency practitioner (as administrator) and his staff in attending to matters arising in the administration.*

2.47(3)   ***[Determination under r.2.47(2)]*** *It is for the creditors' committee (if there is one) to determine whether the remuneration is to be fixed under paragraph (2)(a) or (b) and, if under paragraph (2)(a), to determine any percentage to be applied as there mentioned.*

2.47(4)   ***[Matters relevant to r.2.47(3) determination]*** *In arriving at that determination, the committee shall have regard to the following matters–*

  (a)   *the complexity (or otherwise) of the case,*

  (b)   *any respects in which, in connection with the company's affairs, there falls on the administrator any responsibility of an exceptional kind or degree,*

  (c)   *the effectiveness with which the administrator appears to be carrying out, or to have carried out, his duties as such, and*

  (d)   *the value and nature of the property with which he has to deal.*

2.47(5) **[If no committee or determination]** *If there is no creditors' committee, or the committee does not make the requisite determination, the administrator's remuneration may be fixed (in accordance with paragraph (2)) by a resolution of a meeting of creditors; and paragraph (4) applies to them as it does to the creditors' committee.*

2.47(6) **[Fixed by court]** *If not fixed as above, the administrator's remuneration shall, on his application, be fixed by the court.*

2.47(7) **[Where joint administrators]** *Where there are joint administrators, it is for them to agree between themselves as to how the remuneration payable should be apportioned. Any dispute arising between them may be referred–*

(a) to the court, for settlement by order, or

(b) to the creditors' committee or a meeting of creditors, for settlement by resolution.

2.47(8) **[Where administrator solicitor]** *If the administrator is a solicitor and employs his own firm, or any partner in it, to act on behalf of the company, profit costs shall not be paid unless this is authorised by the creditors' committee, the creditors or the court.*

(See General Note after r.2.55.)

2.48 Recourse to meeting of creditors

2.48 *If the administrator's remuneration has been fixed by the creditors' committee, and he considers the rate or amount to be insufficient, he may request that it be increased by resolution of the creditors.*

(See General Note after r.2.55.)

2.49 Recourse to the court

2.49(1) **[Administrator may apply to court]** *If the administrator considers that the remuneration fixed for him by the creditors' committee, or by resolution of the creditors, is insufficient, he may apply to the court for an order increasing its amount or rate.*

2.49(2) **[Notice to committee members etc.]** *The administrator shall give at least 14 days' notice of his application to the members of the creditors' committee; and the committee may nominate one or more members to appear or be represented, and to be heard, on the application.*

2.49(3) **[Where no committee]** *If there is no creditors' committee, the administrator's notice of his application shall be sent to such one or more of the company's creditors as the court may direct, which creditors may nominate one or more of their number to appear or be represented.*

2.49(4) **[Costs of application]** *The court may, if it appears to be a proper case, order the costs of the administrator's application, including the costs of any member of the creditors' committee appearing or being represented on it, or any creditor so appearing or being represented, to be paid as an expense of the administration.*

(See General Note after r.2.55.)

2.50 Creditors' claim that remuneration is excessive

2.50(1) **[Creditor may apply to court]** *Any creditor of the company may, with the concurrence of at least 25 per cent. in value of the creditors (including himself), apply to the court for an order that the administrator's remuneration be reduced, on the grounds that it is, in all the circumstances, excessive.*

2.50(2) **[Power of court to dismiss etc.]** *The court may, if it thinks that no sufficient cause is shown for a reduction, dismiss the application; but it shall not do so unless the applicant has had an opportunity to attend the court for an* ex parte *hearing, of which he has been given at least 7 days' notice.*

If the application is not dismissed under this paragraph, the court shall fix a venue for it to be heard, and given notice to the applicant accordingly.

2.50(3)   *[Notice to administrator] The applicant shall, at least 14 days before the hearing, send to the administrator a notice stating the venue and accompanied by a copy of the application, and of any evidence which the applicant intends to adduce in support of it.*

2.50(4)   *[Court order] If the court considers the application to be well-founded, it shall make an order fixing the remuneration at a reduced amount or rate.*

2.50(5)   *[Costs of application] Unless the court orders otherwise, the costs of the application shall be paid by the applicant, and are not payable as an expense of the administration.*

(See General Note after r.2.55.)

2.51   Disposal of charged property, etc.

2.51(1)   *[Application of Rule] The following applies where the administrator applies to the court under section 15(2) for authority to dispose of property of the company which is subject to a security, or goods in the possession of the company under an agreement, to which that subsection relates.*

2.51(2)   *[Venue and notice] The court shall fix a venue for the hearing of the application, and the administrator shall as soon as reasonably practicable give notice of the venue to the person who is the holder of the security or, as the case may be, the owner under the agreement.*

2.51(3)   *[Notice of s.15(2) order] If an order is made under section 15(2), the administrator shall as soon as reasonably practicable give notice of it to that person or owner.*

2.51(4)   *[Sealed copies of order] The court shall send 2 sealed copies of the order to the administrator, who shall send one of them to that person or owner.*

(See General Note after r.2.55.)

2.52   Abstract of receipts and payments

2.52(1)   *[Administrator to send accounts etc.] The administrator shall–*

    (a)   *within 2 months after the end of 6 months from the date of his appointment, and of every subsequent period of 6 months, and*

    (b)   *within 2 months after he ceases to act as administrator,*

send to the court, and to registrar of companies, and to each member of the creditors' committee, the requisite accounts of the receipts and payments of the company.

[FORM 2.15]

2.52(2)   *[Extension of time] The court may, on the administrator's application, extend the period of 2 months mentioned above.*

2.52(3)   *[Form of abstract] The accounts are to be in the form of an abstract showing–*

    (a)   *receipts and payments during the relevant period of 6 months, or*

    (b)   *where the administrator has ceased to act, receipts and payments during the period from the end of the last 6-month period to the time when he so ceased (alternatively, if there has been no previous abstract, receipts and payments in the period since his appointment as administrator).*

2.52(4)   *[Penalty on default] If the administrator makes default in complying with this Rule, he is liable to a fine and, for continued contravention, to a daily default fine.*

(See General Note after r.2.55.)

2.53   Resignation

2.53(1)   [Grounds for resignation] *The administrator may give notice of his resignation on grounds of ill health or because–*

[FORM 2.16]

    (a) *he intends ceasing to be in practice as an insolvency practitioner, or*

    (b) *there is some conflict of interest, or change of personal circumstances, which precludes or makes impracticable the further discharge by him of the duties of administrator.*

2.53(2)   [Other grounds] *The administrator may, with the leave of the court, give notice of his resignation on grounds other than those specified in paragraph (1).*

[FORM 2.17]

2.53(3)   [Notice to specified persons] *The administrator must give to the persons specified below at least 7 days' notice of his intention to resign, or to apply for the court's leave to do so–*

    (a) *if there is a continuing administrator of the company, to him;*

    (b) *if there is no such administrator, to the creditors' committee; and*

    (c) *if there is no such administrator and no creditors' committee, to the company and its creditors.*

2.53(4)   [Notice] *Where the administrator gives notice under paragraph (3), he must also give notice to a member State liquidator, if such a person has been appointed in relation to the company.*

(See General Note after r.2.55.)

2.54   Administrator deceased

2.54(1)   [Notice to court] *Subject as follows, where the administrator has died, it is the duty of his personal representatives to give notice of the fact to the court, specifying the date of the death.*
    This does not apply if notice has been given under any of the following paragraphs of this Rule.

2.54(2)   [Notice by partner etc.] *If the deceased administrator was a partner in a firm, notice may be given by a partner in the firm who is qualified to act as an insolvency practitioner, or is a member of any body recognised by the Secretary of State for the authorisation of insolvency practitioners.*

2.54(3)   [Notice by others] *Notice of the death may be given by any person producing to the court the relevant death certificate or a copy of it.*

(See General Note after r.2.55.)

2.55   Order filling vacancy

2.55   *Where the court makes an order filling a vacancy in the office of administrator, the same provisions apply in respect of giving notice of, and advertising, the order as in the case of the administration order.*

GENERAL NOTE TO RR.2.47–2.55

Here are found miscellaneous rules in regard to the administrator's remuneration, his power to deal with charged property, his duties as regards accounting, and vacancies in the office resulting from his resignation, death, etc. On the fixing and approval of the administrator's remuneration, see *Practice Direction: Insolvency Proceedings* [2012] B.C.C. 265 (reproduced as App.IV to this *Guide*), Pt 5.
    Note that there has been no amendment to the original Pt 2 of the rules corresponding to new r.2.67A (providing for the payment of pre-administration costs) or r.2.106(2)(c) (allowing the administrator's remuneration to be determined as a set amount). The law as it stood before April 6, 2010 will continue to apply.
    Rules 12A.6–12A.12 now allow for notices and other documents to be sent by or to creditors and members by electronic means or the use of websites.

The phrase "as soon as reasonably practicable" was substituted for the word "forthwith" in r.*2.51(3)* by I(A)R 2009 (SI 2009/642) r.5 as from April 6, 2009.

CHAPTER 6

VAT BAD DEBT RELIEF

2.56   Issue of certificate of insolvency

2.56(1)   [Duty of administrator] In accordance with this Rule, it is the duty of the administrator to issue a certificate in the terms of paragraph (b) of section 22(3) of the Value Added Tax Act 1983 (which specifies the circumstances in which a company is deemed insolvent for the purposes of that section) as soon as reasonably practicable upon his forming the opinion described in that paragraph.

2.56(2)   [Contents of certificate] There shall in the certificate be specified–

   (a)   the name of the company and its registered number;

   (b)   the name of the administrator and the date of his appointment;

   (c)   the date on which the certificate is issued.

2.56(3)   [Title of certificate] The certificate shall be intituled "CERTIFICATE OF INSOLVENCY FOR THE PURPOSES OF SECTION 22(3)(b) OF THE VALUE ADDED TAX ACT 1983".

GENERAL NOTE

Bad debt relief was available under the Value Added Tax Act 1983 only where the debtor had become insolvent. The FA 1985 s.32 amended that section so as to include the case where an administrator or administrative receiver is appointed. This rule and r.3.36 provide the necessary machinery for these cases.

   In February 1998 HM Customs and Excise Commissioners issued an extra-statutory concession disapplying the clawback provisions of the Value Added Tax Act 1994 s.36(4A) (which applies to supplies made after November 26, 1996). Under this concession, subject to certain conditions, insolvency practitioners will not be required to repay input tax already claimed in respect of purchases which are subject to a bad debt claim by the supplier.

2.57   Notice to creditors

2.57(1)   [Time for giving notice] Notice of the issue of the certificate shall be given by the administrator within 3 months of his appointment or within 2 months of issuing the certificate, whichever is the later, to all of the company's unsecured creditors of whose address he is then aware and who have, to his knowledge, made supplies to the company, with a charge to value added tax, at any time before his appointment.

2.57(2)   [Later notice] Thereafter, he shall give the notice to any such creditor of whose address and supplies to the company he becomes aware.

2.57(3)   [No obligation re certificate] He is not under obligation to provide any creditor with a copy of the certificate.

2.58   Preservation of certificate with company's records

2.58(1)   [Retention of certificate] The certificate shall be retained with the company's accounting records, and section 222 of the Companies Act (where and for how long records are to be kept) shall apply to the certificate as it applies to those records.

2.58(2)   [Duty of administrator] It is the duty of the administrator, on vacating office, to bring this Rule to the attention of the directors or (as the case may be) any successor of his as administrator.

CHAPTER 7

EC REGULATION—CONVERSION OF ADMINISTRATION INTO WINDING UP

2.59 Application for conversion into winding up

2.59(1) [Documents] Where a member State liquidator proposes to apply to the court for the conversion under Article 37 of the EC Regulation (conversion of earlier proceedings) of an administration into a winding up, an affidavit complying with Rule 2.60 must be prepared and sworn, and filed in court in support of the application.

2.59(2) [Originating application] An application under this Rule shall be by originating application.

2.59(3) [Service] The application and the affidavit required under this Rule shall be served upon–

    (a)   the company; and

    (b)   the administrator.

(See General Note after r.2.61.)

2.60 Contents of affidavit

2.60(1) [Contents] The affidavit shall state–

    (a)   that main proceedings have been opened in relation to the company in a member State other than the United Kingdom;

    (b)   the deponent's belief that the conversion of the administration into a winding up would prove to be in the interests of the creditors in the main proceedings;

    (c)   the deponent's opinion as to whether the company ought to enter voluntary winding up or be wound up by the court; and

    (d)   all other matters that, in the opinion of the member State liquidator, would assist the court–

        (i)   in deciding whether to make such an order, and

        (ii)   if the court were to do so, in considering the need for any consequential provision that would be necessary or desirable.

2.60(2) [Procedure] An affidavit under this Rule shall be sworn by, or on behalf of, the member State liquidator.

(See General Note after r.2.61.)

2.61 Power of court

2.61(1) [Powers of court] On hearing the application for conversion into winding up the court may make such order as it thinks fit.

2.61(2) [Consequential provisions] If the court makes an order for conversion into winding up the order may contain all such consequential provisions as the court deems necessary or desirable.

2.61(3) [Effect of order made under r.2.61(1)] Without prejudice to the generality of paragraph (1), an order under that paragraph may provide that the company be wound up as if a resolution for voluntary winding up under section 84 were passed on the day on which the order is made.

GENERAL NOTE TO RR.2.59–2.61

Rules *2.59–2.61* were added by the Insolvency (Amendment) Rules 2002 (SI 2002/1307, effective May 31, 2002). Article 37 of the EC Regulation empowers the "liquidator" in main proceedings to apply to the court to have "territorial" proceedings (not being winding-up proceedings) which have already been opened in another Member

State converted into winding-up proceedings. These rules deal with the procedure and the powers of the court applicable where it is sought to have administration proceedings so converted. Although the rules confer a wide discretion on the court (including the power to decline to make an order), art.37 is expressed in terms which appear to give the liquidator the right to an order on request. Even so, the choice between deeming the winding up to be compulsory or voluntary rests with the court. Rule 2.61(3), being expressed in permissive terms, would not rule out the court choosing a different date—e.g. the date when the administration order was made—but this will ordinarily be of little significance because provisions such as IA 1986 ss.240(3), 247(3) and 387(3) deal explicitly with the consequential issues which would otherwise follow. See further the notes to the EC Regulation arts 3 and 37.

As directed by I(A)R 2010 Sch.5, a witness statement verified by a statement of truth is to be used in place of an affidavit, and the text in these rules should be read accordingly.

There is no provision corresponding to art.37 in the CBIR.

CHAPTER 8

EC REGULATION—MEMBER STATE LIQUIDATOR

2.62 Interpretation of creditor and notice to member State liquidator

2.62(1) **[Application]** This Rule applies where a member State liquidator has been appointed in relation to the company.

2.62(2) **[Member state liquidator deemed to be creditor]** For the purposes of the Rules referred to in paragraph (3) the member State liquidator is deemed to be a creditor.

2.62(3) **[Rules referred to in r.2.62(2)]** The Rules referred to in paragraph (2) are Rules 2.18(1) (notice of creditors' meeting), 2.19(4) (creditors' meeting), 2.21 (requisitioning of creditors' meeting), 2.22 (entitlement to vote), 2.23 (admission and rejection of claims), 2.24 (secured creditors), 2.25 (holders of negotiable instruments), 2.26 (retention of title creditors), 2.27 (hire-purchase, conditional sale and chattel leasing agreements), 2.30 (notice of result of creditors' meeting), 2.32(2) (creditors' committee), 2.39(1)(b) and (c) (termination of membership of creditors' committee), 2.41(3) (vacancies in creditors' committee), 2.49(3) (administrator's remuneration—recourse to court) and 2.50 (challenge to administrator's remuneration).

2.62(4) **[Exercise of creditors' rights]** Paragraphs (2) and (3) are without prejudice to the generality of the right to participate referred to in paragraph 3 of Article 32 of the EC Regulation (exercise of creditors' rights).

2.62(5) **[Notice, copies]** Where the administrator is obliged to give notice to, or provide a copy of a document (including an order of court) to, the court, the registrar of companies or the official receiver, the administrator shall give notice or provide copies, as the case may be, to the member State liquidator.

2.62(6) **[Duty to cooperate and communicate information]** Paragraph (5) is without prejudice to the generality of the obligations imposed by Article 31 of the EC Regulation (duty to cooperate and communicate information).

GENERAL NOTE

Chapter 8 was added to the rules by the Insolvency (Amendment) Rules 2002 (SI 2002/1307, effective May 31, 2002). Article 32(2) and (3) of the EC Regulation states that the "liquidators" in the main and any secondary proceedings may (and, indeed, subject to certain conditions, *shall*) lodge in other proceedings claims which have already been lodged in the proceedings for which they have been appointed, and that such a liquidator may participate in other proceedings on the same basis as a creditor, in particular by attending creditors' meetings. The new rule spells out the rights of such a liquidator in more detail, and (by para.5) ensures that he will receive notice of various documents, over and above those which would come to him as a deemed creditor.

EC Regulation on Insolvency Proceedings 2000

Introductory note to the Regulation

The EC Regulation on Insolvency Proceedings ("the Regulation") was adopted by the Council of the European Union on May 29, 2000. Being a Regulation (as distinct from a Convention or Directive), it had force throughout the EU (apart from Denmark, which has exercised its right to an opt-out) immediately upon its enactment, without the need for ratification or implementation by domestic legislation in the Member States. (References to the EU hereafter should not normally be taken as including Denmark.) The Regulation became operative on May 31, 2002. On the same date, a number of statutory instruments were brought into force, amending the existing insolvency legislation, Rules and prescribed forms in order to facilitate the integration of the Regulation with our own law and practice. (These changes have been noted at the appropriate places in this *Guide*. To the extent that insolvency is a devolved matter, it falls to the devolved administrations to make corresponding amendments.)

The Regulation has introduced an ordered regime governing the administration of the affairs of an insolvent which extend into more than one Member State of the EU. It makes major advances in such areas as ensuring the recognition without further formality throughout the Community of a court order in bankruptcy or an order or resolution for winding up, and defining the respective roles of the office-holders where more than one set of insolvency proceedings involving the same debtor have been instituted in different Member States.

The Regulation had a long and chequered history, having begun life initially in the 1960s as part of the proposals for reciprocal recognition and enforcement of foreign judgments which eventually became the Brussels Convention. But the two projects were severed at an early stage and the Draft Bankruptcy Convention (as it was then known) ran into considerable opposition, partly because its aims were over-ambitious and partly because it was over-complex and ineptly drafted. The project was quietly dropped in the 1980s. Meantime, a new initiative got under way under the aegis of the Council of Europe, which began with rather modest aims but as discussions progressed became more comprehensive and elaborate. In 1990 a final text was agreed, and the Convention was opened for signature in Istanbul in June of that year. The Istanbul Convention, as it is generally known, has been signed by a number of States (not including the UK), but has not attracted enough ratifications to come into force. So far as concerns the UK and its relationship with the rest of the EU, it is now a dead letter: art.44(k) of the EC Regulation provides that the Regulation supersedes the Istanbul Convention in this respect.

The real significance of the Istanbul Convention is that its success in reaching the stage of a final text agreed by all participants acted as a catalyst to get the negotiations for an EC Convention restarted. A fresh working party began to work on a revived project in May 1989, and by November 1995 a finalised text had been agreed and was opened for signature and, in the next few months, signed by all the EU Member States except the UK. Regrettably, the UK failed to do so (in the wake of the "beef ban") and the entire project ran out of time and the draft convention lapsed. However, all was not lost because the text, in virtually identical form, was revived (but in the form of a Regulation, and not a Convention) and following a joint initiative by Germany and Finland in 1999 was duly adopted by the Council of Ministers in the following May.

As noted above, the Regulation has effect as primary legislation in its own right, and thus automatically repeals any existing legislation and supersedes any rule of law that is inconsistent with its provisions. The main area where this is likely to be seen is in relation to the wide jurisdiction which our courts have traditionally asserted over foreign nationals and companies to make bankruptcy and winding-up orders: from now on, in any case where the "centre of main interests" (COMI) of the individual or company concerned is in another Member State, this jurisdiction will be curtailed. In contrast, in some respects our courts are given wider powers under the Regulation than they have under the domestic legislation, e.g. to make administration orders in respect of foreign companies and other bodies which have their COMI within the UK: see the note to art.3.

For the purposes of the Regulation, the UK is regarded as one jurisdiction, and includes Gibraltar. It applies only where the debtor's COMI is situated in a Member State (other than Denmark). If the debtor is primarily based outside the EU, matters will continue to be governed by the existing domestic law, even as regards issues arising between EU jurisdictions *inter se*. And the Regulation has nothing to say about assets or creditors based outside the EU, or insolvency proceedings that have been instituted in a non-EU jurisdiction, even in a case where the debtor's COMI is in a Member State. And, of course, it applies only where the individual or company concerned is insolvent.

While the Regulation aims for a substantial degree of "universality" (i.e. the recognition throughout the Community of proceedings that have been instituted in any Member State), it does not attempt to achieve "unity" (i.e. a regime which gives a single insolvency administration the sole and exclusive management of all the insolvent estate for the benefit of all the insolvent's creditors, in whatever parts of the EU it may be situated). The Regulation envisages a hierarchy of judicial competence, having one (and only one) "main" proceeding in one Member State (where the debtor's COMI is located), with the possibility of there being any number of "secondary" or "territorial" proceedings in any other jurisdictions where there are assets. (The term "territorial proceedings" refers to ancillary proceedings instituted *before* main proceedings have been opened, and "secondary proceedings" to those instituted subsequently.) A creditor based anywhere in the EU is free to prove in the main proceedings and also in any secondary proceedings (subject to safeguards to avoid his getting more than his share), and the proceedings in each State and the authority of its office-holder are to be automatically recognised with no special formalities throughout the Community. Recognition of the competence of main proceedings brings about a moratorium on the enforcement of claims applicable in all Member States, and there is provision for communication and co-operation between the officeholders in related insolvency proceedings. In principle, assets situated outside the jurisdiction of main proceedings can be removed from there to form part of the main estate; however, there is provision for a certain degree of ring-fencing so that the claims of local creditors, and particularly those entitled to preferential treatment, can be satisfied before anything is remitted to the main jurisdiction.

The Regulation does not seek to harmonise the substantive insolvency laws of the various Member States: by and large, it enshrines the general principle that the applicable law shall be that of the State in which the particular insolvency proceedings (whether main, secondary or territorial) are being conducted. However, it does deal with certain questions in the conflict of laws, declaring that a different law shall be applicable law in specified cases (so that, for instance, set-off shall be allowed even though it is not recognised by the law of the proceedings). This is likely to reduce the occasions on which difficult issues of jurisdiction may arise in an insolvency context—as happened, for instance, in *Re Hayward* [1997] Ch. 45; and *Pollard v Ashurst* [2001] B.P.I.R. 131: see the note to IA 1986 s.314.

The Regulation applies to both individual and corporate insolvencies. (But it should be noted that it does not apply to *solvent* liquidations: cross-border issues in these proceedings are governed by Council Regulation EC 44/2001 of December 22, 2000 on jurisdiction and the recognition and enforcement of judgments in civil and commercial matters (the "Judgments Regulation", formerly the Brussels Convention).) In its scope it is capable of including insolvency procedures such as CVAs and administrations as well as bankruptcies and liquidations (although not in secondary proceedings). But it does not extend to schemes of reconstruction and arrangement under CA 1986 Pt 26 (*Re Rodenstock GmbH* [2011] EWHC 1104 (Ch); [2011] Bus.L.R. 1245). It includes creditors' voluntary liquidations (after formal confirmation by the court), but not any form of receivership. Although neither insolvent partnerships nor the estates of persons dying insolvent are specified as being within the Regulation, this has been assumed to be the case in the accompanying subordinate legislation.

There is a specific exclusion of insolvency proceedings concerning insurance undertakings, banks and other credit institutions, and collective and other investment undertakings, since these have their own special legislative or regulatory regimes. See the note to the Preamble para.9.

The Regulation has its own special vocabulary, which calls for some mental adjustment by an English reader. In particular, it may be necessary to issue a warning in relation to terms such as "liquidator" (a word used to describe the office-holder in any form of insolvency proceeding, even a trustee in bankruptcy), the "opening" of insolvency proceedings (see the note to art.2(f)), and the terms "judgment" and "court", which by a mind-boggling feat are stretched so as to include the passing of a resolution for voluntary winding up by the shareholders at a general meeting!

One aspect of the Regulation which may be open to criticism is an underlying assumption that the debtor is (and continues to be) in business of some kind and that it is a creditor who will be the initiator of the insolvency proceedings. This can be seen, for instance, in art.3(2), where secondary proceedings can be opened only in a Member State if the debtor "*possesses* an establishment" within that State (present tense); in art.2(h), defining "establishment" as a "place of operations where the debtor *carries on* a non-transitory *economic* activity with human means and goods"; and in art.3(4)(b), which restricts the right to open "territorial" proceedings to a creditor whose debt arises from the operation of that establishment. A non-trading individual (or a former trader who had ceased to carry on business) with an outstanding tax debt who wished to petition for his own bankruptcy in secondary or territorial proceedings could well have difficulty in surmounting the various hurdles imposed by these definitions.

Another aspect of the Regulation which has also been the subject of criticism is the fact that it makes no special provision for the insolvency of corporate groups, where members of the group are incorporated in different Member States. It is contended that this may lead to a number of separate insolvency procedures without the co-ordination or even the co-operation which could lead to a more harmonious and efficient outcome. The authoritative decision of the European Court in *Re Eurofood IFSC Ltd* [2006] B.C.C. 397 makes no concessions here: it emphatically stresses the separate personality of the constituent member companies in ruling that "parental control" of a subsidiary, without more, should not be determinative of its COMI. Of course, if it can be established on the evidence that the COMI of the subsidiary companies is in the jurisdiction of the holding company, the court in that State can make orders in respect of the subsidiaries that enable all the insolvency administrations to be co-ordinated—as happened in the *Daisytek* and *Crisscross* cases: see Fletcher, (2005) 18 Insolv. Int. 85. Similar co-ordination was achieved in the insolvency of the MG Rover Group: see *Re MG Rover España SA* [2006] B.C.C. 599 and *Re MG Rover Belux SA/NV* [2007] B.C.C. 446, where the courts were able to give effect indirectly to the local laws of foreign subsidiaries.

Mention should also be made of the "Virgós-Schmit Report" (July 8, 1996), a commentary on the text of the Convention which preceded the Regulation. Although this report does not refer directly to the Regulation and has never been officially adopted, it contains useful background material and has been referred to in a number of judgments in this country. The text is conveniently reproduced as an Appendix in Moss, Fletcher and Isaacs, *The EC Regulation on Insolvency Proceedings* (2nd edn, 2009); and in Roy Goode, *Principles of Corporate Insolvency Law* (4th edn, 2011); and is available online at *http://aei.pitt.edu/952*.

Note also the European Communication and Cooperation Guidelines for Cross-Border Insolvency (commonly known as the "Coco Guidelines") which were published in October 2007, establishing a non-binding set of standards for co-operation by insolvency practitioners in cross-border insolvency cases which are subject to the EC Regulation. The Guidelines are discussed by B. Wessels, (2011) 24 Insolv. Int. 65.

The statutory instruments enacted to make the legislation and Rules compatible with the Regulation are as follows. All except the first came into force on May 31, 2002. Attention is drawn also to the Insolvency Service's Guidance Note, referred to in the General note to arts 39–42 below.

The Insolvency Act 1986 (Amendment) Regulations 2002 (SI 2002/1037, effective May 3, 2002)

The Insolvency Act 1986 (Amendment) (No.2) Regulations 2002 (SI 2002/1240)

The Insolvency (Amendment) Rules 2002 (SI 2002/1307)

The Insolvent Partnerships (Amendment) Order 2002 (SI 2002/1308)

The Administration of Insolvent Estates of Deceased Persons Order 2002 (SI 2002/1309)

By the Treaty of Accession of April 16, 2003 (see [2003] O.J. L236/711), 10 new Member States were admitted to the EU, and consequential amendments to the Regulation were made by EC Council Regulation 603/2005 (see [2005] O.J. L100/1), as well as by the Treaty itself. Some of the existing Member States (including the UK) took the opportunity to make minor changes to the Regulation. Further changes were made by EC Council Regulation 694/2006 ([2006] O.J. L121/1) as from May 7, 2006 and again by EC Council Regulation 681/2007 ([2007] O.J. L159/1), in order to accommodate the expansion of EU membership so as to include Bulgaria and Romania and to incorporate amendments notified by other Member States. These changes took effect from June 21, 2007 and January 1, 2008). Annexes A and B were amended by Regulation 788/2008 as from July 24, 2008. Further amendments to the entries for Belgium in Annexes A, B and C were effected by Regulation 210/2010 as from April 2, 2010, and to the entries for Austria and Latvia by Regulation 583/2011 as from July 8, 2011.

The EC Regulation is discussed in Totty and Moss, *Insolvency*, paras H9–18.1 et seq.

The Model Law on Cross-Border Insolvency, agreed by UNCITRAL in 1997, closely follows the scheme of the EC Regulation in many respects and uses some of the same terminology. It has been enacted for Britain by the Cross-Border Insolvency Regulations 2006 (SI 2006/1030), which are included, with annotation, below. Article 3 of Sch.1 to the 2006 Regulations provides that to the extent that the Model Law conflicts with an obligation of the United Kingdom under the EC Regulation, the requirements of the latter shall prevail. It follows that where an insolvency concerns a debtor who has interests in more than one EU Member State and a COMI within the EU, cross-border issues concerning those interests will normally fall to be determined by the EC Regulation. However, there is not a complete overlap: in *Stocznia Gdynia SA v Bud-Bank Leasing sp z oo* [2010] B.C.C. 255 an application to the UK court concerning statutory compensation proceedings in a Polish insolvency was held to have been correctly brought under the CBIR rather than the EC Regulation because the compensation proceedings satisfied the requirements for recognition under the CBIR but not those of the Regulation.

Council Regulation (EC) No 1346/2000 of 29 May 2000 on Insolvency Proceedings

[Preamble]

THE COUNCIL OF THE EUROPEAN UNION,

Having regard to the Treaty establishing the European Community, and in particular Articles 61(c) and 67(1) thereof,

Having regard to the initiative of the Federal Republic of Germany and the Republic of Finland,

Having regard to the opinion of the European Parliament,

Having regard to the opinion of the Economic and Social Committee,

Whereas:

(1) The European Union has set out the aim of establishing an area of freedom, security and justice.

(2) The proper functioning of the internal market requires that cross-border insolvency proceedings should operate efficiently and effectively and this Regulation needs to be adopted in order to achieve this objective which comes within the scope of judicial cooperation in civil matters within the meaning of Article 65 of the Treaty.

(3) The activities of undertakings have more and more cross-border effects and are therefore increasingly being regulated by Community law. While the insolvency of such undertakings also affects the proper functioning of the internal market, there is a need for a Community act requiring coordination of the measures to be taken regarding an insolvent debtor's assets.

(4) It is necessary for the proper functioning of the internal market to avoid incentives for the parties to transfer assets or judicial proceedings from one Member State to another, seeking to obtain a more favourable legal position (forum shopping).

(5) These objectives cannot be achieved to a sufficient degree at national level and action at Community level is therefore justified.

(6) In accordance with the principle of proportionality this Regulation should be confined to provisions governing jurisdiction for opening insolvency proceedings and judgments which are delivered directly on the basis of the insolvency proceedings and are closely connected with such proceedings. In addition, this Regulation should contain provisions regarding the recognition of those judgments and the applicable law which also satisfy that principle.

(7) Insolvency proceedings relating to the winding-up of insolvent companies or other legal persons, judicial arrangements, compositions and analogous proceedings are excluded from the scope of the 1968 Brussels Convention on Jurisdiction and the Enforcement of Judgments in Civil and Commercial Matters, as amended by the Conventions on Accession to this Convention.

(8) In order to achieve the aim of improving the efficiency and effectiveness of insolvency proceedings having cross-border effects, it is necessary, and appropriate, that the provisions on jurisdiction, recognition and applicable law in this area should be contained in a Community law measure which is binding and directly applicable in Member States.

(9) This Regulation should apply to insolvency proceedings, whether the debtor is a natural person or a legal person, a trader or an individual. The insolvency proceedings to which this Regulation applies are listed in the Annexes. Insolvency proceedings concerning insurance undertakings, credit institutions, investment undertakings holding funds or securities for third parties and collective investment undertakings should be excluded from the scope of this Regulation. Such undertakings should not be covered by this Regulation since they are subject to special arrangements and, to some extent, the national supervisory authorities have extremely wide-ranging powers of intervention.

(10) Insolvency proceedings do not necessarily involve the intervention of a judicial authority; the expression "court" in this Regulation should be given a broad meaning and include a person or body empowered by national law to open insolvency proceedings. In order for this Regulation to apply, proceedings (comprising acts and formalities set down in law) should not only have to comply with the provisions of this Regulation, but they should also be officially recognised and

legally effective in the Member State in which the insolvency proceedings are opened and should be collective insolvency proceedings which entail the partial or total divestment of the debtor and the appointment of a liquidator.

(11) This Regulation acknowledges the fact that as a result of widely differing substantive laws it is not practical to introduce insolvency proceedings with universal scope in the entire Community. The application without exception of the law of the State of opening of proceedings would, against this background, frequently lead to difficulties. This applies, for example, to the widely differing laws on security interests to be found in the Community. Furthermore, the preferential rights enjoyed by some creditors in the insolvency proceedings are, in some cases, completely different. This Regulation should take account of this in two different ways. On the one hand, provision should be made for special rules on applicable law in the case of particularly significant rights and legal relationships (e.g. rights in rem and contracts of employment). On the other hand, national proceedings covering only assets situated in the State of opening should also be allowed alongside main insolvency proceedings with universal scope.

(12) This Regulation enables the main insolvency proceedings to be opened in the Member State where the debtor has the centre of his main interests. These proceedings have universal scope and aim at encompassing all the debtor's assets. To protect the diversity of interests, this Regulation permits secondary proceedings to be opened to run in parallel with the main proceedings. Secondary proceedings may be opened in the Member State where the debtor has an establishment. The effects of secondary proceedings are limited to the assets located in that State. Mandatory rules of coordination with the main proceedings satisfy the need for unity in the Community.

(13) The "centre of main interests" should correspond to the place where the debtor conducts the administration of his interests on a regular basis and is therefore ascertainable by third parties.

(14) This Regulation applies only to proceedings where the centre of the debtor's main interests is located in the Community.

(15) The rules of jurisdiction set out in this Regulation establish only international jurisdiction, that is to say, they designate the Member State the courts of which may open insolvency proceedings. Territorial jurisdiction within that Member State must be established by the national law of the Member State concerned.

(16) The court having jurisdiction to open the main insolvency proceedings should be enabled to order provisional and protective measures from the time of the request to open proceedings. Preservation measures both prior to and after the commencement of the insolvency proceedings are very important to guarantee the effectiveness of the insolvency proceedings. In that connection this Regulation should afford different possibilities. On the one hand, the court competent for the main insolvency proceedings should be able also to order provisional protective measures covering assets situated in the territory of other Member States. On the other hand, a liquidator temporarily appointed prior to the opening of the main insolvency proceedings should be able, in the Member States in which an establishment belonging to the debtor is to be found, to apply for the preservation measures which are possible under the law of those States.

(17) Prior to the opening of the main insolvency proceedings, the right to request the opening of insolvency proceedings in the Member State where the debtor has an establishment should be limited to local creditors and creditors of the local establishment or to cases where main proceedings cannot be opened under the law of the Member State where the debtor has the centre of his main interest. The reason for this restriction is that cases where territorial insolvency proceedings are requested before the main insolvency proceedings are intended to be limited to what is absolutely necessary. If the main insolvency proceedings are opened, the territorial proceedings become secondary.

(18) Following the opening of the main insolvency proceedings, the right to request the opening of insolvency proceedings in a Member State where the debtor has an establishment is not restricted by this Regulation. The liquidator in the main proceedings or any other person empowered under the national law of that Member State may request the opening of secondary insolvency proceedings.

(19) Secondary insolvency proceedings may serve different purposes, besides the protection of local interests. Cases may arise where the estate of the debtor is too complex to administer as a unit or where differences in the legal systems concerned are so great that difficulties may arise from the extension of effects deriving from the law of the State of the opening to the other States where the assets are located. For this reason the liquidator in the main proceedings may request the opening of secondary proceedings when the efficient administration of the estate so requires.

(20) Main insolvency proceedings and secondary proceedings can, however, contribute to the effective realisation of the total assets only if all the concurrent proceedings pending are coordinated. The main condition here is that the various liquidators must cooperate closely, in particular by exchanging a sufficient amount of information. In order to ensure the dominant role of the main insolvency proceedings, the liquidator in such proceedings should be given several possibilities for intervening in secondary insolvency proceedings which are pending at the same time. For example, he should be able to propose a restructuring plan or composition or apply for realisation of the assets in the secondary insolvency proceedings to be suspended.

(21) Every creditor, who has his habitual residence, domicile or registered office in the Community, should have the right to lodge his claims in each of the insolvency proceedings pending in the Community relating to the debtor's assets. This should also apply to tax authorities and social insurance institutions. However, in order to ensure equal treatment of creditors, the distribution of proceeds must be coordinated. Every creditor should be able to keep what he has received in the course of insolvency proceedings but should be entitled only to participate in the distribution of total assets in other proceedings if creditors with the same standing have obtained the same proportion of their claims.

(22) This Regulation should provide for immediate recognition of judgments concerning the opening, conduct and closure of insolvency proceedings which come within its scope and of judgments handed down in direct connection with such insolvency proceedings. Automatic recognition should therefore mean that the effects attributed to the proceedings by the law of the State in which the proceedings were opened extend to all other Member States. Recognition of judgments delivered by the courts of the Member States should be based on the principle of mutual trust. To that end, grounds for non-recognition should be reduced to the minimum necessary. This is also the basis on which any dispute should be resolved where the courts of two Member States both claim competence to open the main insolvency proceedings. The decision of the first court to open proceedings should be recognised in the other Member States without those Member States having the power to scrutinise the court's decision.

(23) This Regulation should set out, for the matters covered by it, uniform rules on conflict of laws which replace, within their scope of application, national rules of private international law. Unless otherwise stated, the law of the Member State of the opening of the proceedings should be applicable (lex concursus). This rule on conflict of laws should be valid both for the main proceedings and for local proceedings; the lex concursus determines all the effects of the insolvency proceedings, both procedural and substantive, on the persons and legal relations concerned. It governs all the conditions for the opening, conduct and closure of the insolvency proceedings.

(24) Automatic recognition of insolvency proceedings to which the law of the opening State normally applies may interfere with the rules under which transactions are carried out in other Member States. To protect legitimate expectations and the certainty of transactions in Member States other

than that in which proceedings are opened, provisions should be made for a number of exceptions to the general rule.

(25) There is a particular need for a special reference diverging from the law of the opening State in the case of rights in rem, since these are of considerable importance for the granting of credit. The basis, validity and extent of such a right in rem should therefore normally be determined according to the lex situs and not be affected by the opening of insolvency proceedings. The proprietor of the right in rem should therefore be able to continue to assert his right to segregation or separate settlement of the collateral security. Where assets are subject to rights in rem under the lex situs in one Member State but the main proceedings are being carried out in another Member State, the liquidator in the main proceedings should be able to request the opening of secondary proceedings in the jurisdiction where the rights in rem arise if the debtor has an establishment there. If a secondary proceeding is not opened, the surplus on sale of the asset covered by rights in rem must be paid to the liquidator in the main proceedings.

(26) If a set-off is not permitted under the law of the opening State, a creditor should nevertheless be entitled to the set-off if it is possible under the law applicable to the claim of the insolvent debtor. In this way, set-off will acquire a kind of guarantee function based on legal provisions on which the creditor concerned can rely at the time when the claim arises.

(27) There is also a need for special protection in the case of payment systems and financial markets. This applies for example to the position-closing agreements and netting agreements to be found in such systems as well as to the sale of securities and to the guarantees provided for such transactions as governed in particular by Directive 98/26/EC of the European Parliament and of the Council of 19 May 1998 on settlement finality in payment and securities settlement systems. For such transactions, the only law which is material should thus be that applicable to the system or market concerned. This provision is intended to prevent the possibility of mechanisms for the payment and settlement of transactions provided for in the payment and set-off systems or on the regulated financial markets of the Member States being altered in the case of insolvency of a business partner. Directive 98/26/EC contains special provisions which should take precedence over the general rules in this Regulation.

(28) In order to protect employees and jobs, the effects of insolvency proceedings on the continuation or termination of employment and on the rights and obligations of all parties to such employment must be determined by the law applicable to the agreement in accordance with the general rules on conflict of law. Any other insolvency-law questions, such as whether the employees' claims are protected by preferential rights and what status such preferential rights may have, should be determined by the law of the opening State.

(29) For business considerations, the main content of the decision opening the proceedings should be published in the other Member States at the request of the liquidator. If there is an establishment in the Member State concerned, there may be a requirement that publication is compulsory. In neither case, however, should publication be a prior condition for recognition of the foreign proceedings.

(30) It may be the case that some of the persons concerned are not in fact aware that proceedings have been opened and act in good faith in a way that conflicts with the new situation. In order to protect such persons who make a payment to the debtor because they are unaware that foreign proceedings have been opened when they should in fact have made the payment to the foreign liquidator, it should be provided that such a payment is to have a debt-discharging effect.

(31) This Regulation should include Annexes relating to the organisation of insolvency proceedings. As these Annexes relate exclusively to the legislation of Member States, there are specific and substantiated reasons for the Council to reserve the right to amend these Annexes in order to take account of any amendments to the domestic law of the Member States.

(32) The United Kingdom and Ireland, in accordance with Article 3 of the Protocol on the position of the United Kingdom and Ireland annexed to the Treaty on European Union and the Treaty establishing the European Community, have given notice of their wish to take part in the adoption and application of this Regulation.

(33) Denmark, in accordance with Articles 1 and 2 of the Protocol on the position of Denmark annexed to the Treaty on European Union and the Treaty establishing the European Community, is not participating in the adoption of this Regulation, and is therefore not bound by it nor subject to its application,

HAS ADOPTED THIS REGULATION:

GENERAL NOTE

This lengthy Preamble (typical of many pieces of EC legislation) gives rise to a number of problems, some of which are discussed by Professor Rajak in [2000] C.F.I.L.R. 180. It has been accepted by the European Court of Justice that a Preamble may be referred to where the text in the body of a Regulation is unclear or imprecise (*Schweizerische Lactina Panchaud AG (Bundesamt für Ernährung und Forstwirtschaft) v Germany (No.346/88)* [1991] 2 C.M.L.R. 283), and this approach reflects that of our own courts to recitals and similar "background" statements. But this Preamble, like many of its kind, goes much further: in some parts, it does simply set out the background, context and aims of the Regulation; in others, it does no more than duplicate substantive provisions in the various articles of the substantive text; and in yet others (e.g. para.15) it goes out of its way to exhort Member States to take supporting action at a domestic level. However, there are other paragraphs which plainly have legislative effect (e.g. para.14: "This Regulation applies only to proceedings where the centre of the debtor's main interests is located in the Community"); and also many passages (characterised by the word "should") where it is unclear whether the intention is to go beyond the normal function of a Preamble and actually to formulate substantive rules which one would expect to find in the body of the legislation itself. So, e.g. para.9 states that the Regulation "should apply" to insolvency proceedings, "whether the debtor is a natural person or a legal person, a trader or an individual", without any corresponding provision in the articles which follow; and the definition of a debtor's "centre of main interests" is largely set out in para.13 ("the 'centre of main interests' should correspond to the place where the debtor conducts the administration of his interests on a regular basis and is therefore ascertainable by third parties"), but is not repeated where one would expect to find it, in art.3(1).

Para.3

The term "activities" is not used in the body of the Regulation, but is found in other EC legislation, e.g. in Directive 80/987 of October 20, 1980 on the approximation of the laws of the Member States relating to the protection of employees in the insolvency of their employer. In this context it is not necessary that the undertaking concerned should have a branch or fixed establishment in the State concerned, so long as it has a "stable economic presence" there: *Sweden v Holmqvist* (C-310/07).

Paras 6, 7

The "Brussels Convention" referred to in para.7 of the Preamble has been replaced by EC Regulation 44/2001 on jurisdiction and the recognition and enforcement of judgments in civil and commercial matters ([2001] O.J. L12/1), commonly known as the "Judgments Regulation" or "Jurisdiction and Judgments Regulation". Insolvency matters are excluded from the scope of the Brussels Convention and the successor Regulation (see art.1(2)(b) of the latter Regulation). (But not winding-up proceedings as such; thus, matters arising in a members' voluntary winding up are within the Convention: *Re Cover Europe Ltd* [2002] 2 B.C.L.C. 61.) However, that Regulation is declared to apply to certain judgments handed down by a court in the course or "closure" of insolvency proceedings, and compositions approved by a court in such a context, by art.25 of the present Regulation: see the note to art.25, below.

Some rulings on the scope of the two Regulations and the boundary between their jurisdictions are discussed in the notes to arts 7–15 and 25, below. In *Byers v Yacht Bull Corp* [2010] EWHC 133 (Ch); [2010] B.C.C. 368 a claim brought by English liquidators as to the beneficial ownership of a yacht was held to fall under the general law and have no close or direction with the winding up; accordingly the Judgments Regulation (which gave the French courts jurisdiction) applied. The mere fact that the claimants in the proceedings were insolvency office-holders was not sufficient to disapply that Regulation. See also *Citigate Dewe Rogerson Ltd v Artaban Public Affairs SPRL* [2009] EWHC 1689 (Ch); [2009] B.P.I.R. 1355; *Gibraltar Residential Properties Ltd v Gibralcon 2004 SA* [2010] EWHC 2595 (TCC); and contrast *Polymer Vision R&D Ltd v Van Dooren* [2011] EWHC 2951 (Comm). Neither the EU Regulation nor the Judgments Regulation restricts the jurisdiction of the courts in this country in relation to the sanctioning of schemes of arrangement concerning solvent companies: *Re Rodenstock GmbH* [2011] EWHC 1104 (Ch).

The relationship between the Insolvency Regulation and EC Regulation 1393/2007 of November 13, 2007 on the service in Member States of judicial and extrajudicial documents in civil or commercial matters (the Service Regulation) is unclear (*Re Anderson Owen Ltd* [2009] EWHC 2837 (Ch); [2010] B.P.I.R. 37).

"Judgment", for the purposes of the Regulation, has an extended meaning: see the note to art.2(e).

Para.9

There is no counterpart to the first sentence of this paragraph in the body of the Regulation. This is of no significance so far as concerns debtors based in the UK, since our domestic legislation covers all the categories that are mentioned; but it could be material in some civil-law jurisdictions where traditionally bankruptcy has not been available to non-trading individuals.

Although it would appear both from the second sentence of this paragraph and from art.2(a) that the application of the Regulation is confined to those forms of proceedings listed in the Annexes, we must infer that this is not so, for this would exclude the winding up, etc. of insolvent partnerships and the administration of the estates of persons dying insolvent—each of which comes within the general rubric laid down by art.1, and which has been the subject of specific supporting legislation (see the Insolvent Partnerships (Amendment) Order 2002 (SI 2002/1308) and the Administration of Insolvent Estates of Deceased Persons (Amendment) Order 2002 (SI 2002/1309), both effective May 31, 2002).

The exclusion of insurance undertakings, etc. is confirmed by art.1(2). These bodies have their own special legislative or regulatory regimes and are the subject of separate EC Directives and domestic legislation: see EC Directives 2001/17 (insurance undertakings) and 2001/24 (credit institutions). The former has been implemented by the Insurance (Reorganisation and Winding up) Regulations 2004 (SI 2004/353, replacing SI 2003/1102, effective February 18, 2004), and separately, for Lloyd's, by SI 2005/1998, as from August 10, 2005. The latter has been implemented by the Credit Institutions (Reorganisation and Winding up) Regulations 2004 (SI 2004/1045), effective May 5, 2004. The broad effect of the Insurance Regulations is that a UK court will not be able to make an administration or winding-up order or appoint a provisional liquidator to an insurance undertaking which is authorised in another EEA Member State, and such an insurer cannot enter into a voluntary arrangement under UK law. In the winding up of UK insurance undertakings, priority is now given to insurance claims over other debts. However, the focus of the relevant directive is primarily on direct insurance, rather than reinsurance, and the Regulations do not apply to undertakings engaged purely in reinsurance. Note that both the Insurance Regulations and the Credit Institutions Regulations apply throughout the EEA, in contrast with the EC Regulation which is restricted to the EC (excluding Denmark). The Credit Institutions Regulations were successfully invoked by the representative in Icelandic insolvency proceedings, applying Icelandic law to the exclusion of the rules applicable under IA 1986 in Scottish administration proceedings, in *Landsbanki Islands hf v Mills* [2010] CSOH 100; [2011] 2 B.C.L.C. 437. Accordingly, the extinguishment of a claim pursuant to the Icelandic proceedings debarred the claimant from initiating proceedings in Scotland to recover the debt. However, on appeal (*Heritable Bank plc v Winding-up Board of Landsbanki Islands HF* [2011] CSIH 61) it was held that this ruling only prevented the claimant from taking *positive* action: it was still open to it to plead its claim by way of set-off in Scottish insolvency proceedings. See also *Rawlinson & Hunter Trustees SA v Kaupthing Bank HF* [2011] EWHC 566 (Comm); [2011] 2 B.C.L.C. 682 (where it was held that the Regulations did not apply and that English law should apply to the proceedings) and *Re Phoenix Kapitaldienst GmbH* [2012] EWHC 62 (Ch).

The jurisdiction of a UK court to sanction a scheme of arrangement under CA 2006 Pt 26 depends on whether the company or companies concerned are "liable to be wound up" under IA 1986. If the company concerned is solvent, no question under the EC Regulation arises: *Re Rodenstock GmbH* [2011] EWHC 1104 (Ch); [2011] Bus.L.R. 1245. The impact of the EC Regulation and other EC and domestic legislation on this question in relation to foreign-based insurance and reinsurance companies is closely examined in *Re la Mutuelles du Mans Assurances IARD* [2005] EWHC 1599 (Ch); [2006] B.C.C. 11; and *Re DAP Holding NV* [2005] EWHC 2092 (Ch); [2006] B.C.C. 48.

Para.10

See the note to art.2(d) and (e): the terms "court" and "judgment" are given extended definitions so as to extend to (e.g.) a shareholders' meeting and the passing at such a meeting of a resolution for voluntary winding up.

Para.11

As is explained in the Introductory note to the Regulation on p.126, the Regulation does not aim to harmonise the substantive insolvency laws of the Member States or to achieve an insolvency regime on the principle of "unity", where there would be only one proceeding in which the whole of the debtor's assets situated in all the Member States would be administered for the benefit of all the creditors in the Community. Instead, its principal object is to establish an ordered system of administration which allows for separate proceedings to be instituted in several Member States concurrently, with appropriate provisions for mutual recognition, co-operation and co-ordination designed to ensure that they do not compete with one another. Each of the separate proceedings is primarily to be governed by its national law (art.4), but this is subject to certain overriding rules dealing with security interests, contracts of employment, etc. (arts 5–15). In addition, the Regulation allows each separate jurisdiction a degree of ring-fencing, so that (for instance) the rights of creditors or particular classes of creditor in that jurisdiction are respected.

Paras 12, 13

On "main" and "secondary" proceedings, see the note to art.3, and for the definition of "establishment", art.2(h). There is no definition of a debtor's "centre of main interests" in the body of the Regulation (apart from the presumptive rule that, in the case of a company or legal person, this is to be the place of its registered office: art.3(1)); and so we must assume that para.13 applies. The concluding words indicate that this is to be determined objectively. See further the note to art.3(1).

Para.14

The entire focus is on the debtor's centre of main interests. There is no reference to the nationality, domicile, residence or physical presence of an individual debtor or to the place of incorporation of a company (except that this is linked with the presumption in art.3(1)). It is plain from this statement that the Regulation does not apply to a debtor whose centre of main interests is outside the EU: in that event, the courts of the UK may continue to assert their traditional wide jurisdiction (see the notes to IA 1986 ss.220 and 265); and in such a case the Regulation will not apply even where there are contemporaneous insolvency proceedings in more than one Member State. On the other hand, if the COMI is within the UK, the Regulation applies even where the debtor is a national of a non-EU country or a company incorporated in such a country (see *Re BRAC Rent-a-Car International Inc* [2003] EWHC 128 (Ch); [2003] B.C.C. 249, discussed in the note to art.3 below); while if the COMI is in another Member State, any proceedings instituted in the UK can only be "territorial" or "secondary" proceedings and the jurisdiction will be limited as prescribed by art.3(2)–(4).

Where the debtor has interests in more than one Member State and there is doubt or a dispute as to which is the centre of main interests, para.22 of the Preamble indicates that this should be settled on a "first seised" basis. The Irish High Court faced a conflict on this issue in *Re Eurofood IFSC Ltd* [2004] B.C.C. 383, in relation to the Irish subsidiary of the Italian Parmalat group of companies. After a provisional liquidator had been appointed to the subsidiary but before the hearing of the winding-up petition an Italian court made an order purporting to put it into "extraordinary administration", declaring that the subsidiary's COMI was in Italy. At the time when the provisional liquidator was appointed, all the evidence had pointed unquestionably to its COMI being in Ireland, but steps had since been taken by the holding company's administrator to appoint Italian directors in an attempt to move its COMI to Italy, and the Italian court was persuaded that this had been achieved. The Irish court nevertheless made a winding-up order, declaring that the appointment of the provisional liquidator constituted the "opening" of proceedings, which were main proceedings. The later purported decisions of the Italian court could not alter the fact that main proceedings (which under the Regulation were bound to be recognised throughout the EU) had already been opened. The Supreme Court of Ireland upheld this ruling [2004] IESC 45; [2005] B.C.C. 999, but primarily on the grounds that the Italian court had not followed fair procedures, with the consequence that its decision should not be recognised on public policy grounds.

The case was referred to the European Court of Justice (C-341/04), where the Advocate General's opinion is reported at [2005] B.C.C. 1,021 and the judgment of the Court at [2006] B.C.C. 397. In upholding the decisions of the Irish courts, the ECJ has firmly endorsed the "first seised" principle. It ruled not only that the Italian court was out of order in purporting to override the Irish court's finding that the COMI of Eurofoods was in Ireland and that in consequence its proceedings were "main" proceedings, but also that any challenge to this decision could only be brought before the Irish court itself and not in any other Member State. (Compare *Re Eurodis Electron plc* [2011] EWHC 1025 (Ch), where a company whose COMI was in England had (it appeared wrongly) been wound up and dissolved in Belgium: the court in England had no power to declare that the Belgian court's winding-up order was invalid.)

The "first seised" principle also applies under the "Judgments Regulation" (44/2001, the successor to the Brussels Convention of 1968: see the note to para.6, 7 above). For a case under this Regulation, see *Kolden Holdens Ltd v Rodette Commerce Ltd* [2008] EWCA Civ 10; [2008] 1 B.C.L.C. 481.

Para.15

Once it is settled that the courts of a Member State have jurisdiction under the Regulation, it is still necessary to satisfy the requirements of the national law.

Para.16

This paragraph contemplates the making of "provisional and protective measures" in rather convoluted language, which is fortunately clarified by the substantive provision in art.38. See the note to that article.

Para.17

This refers forward to the remarkably restrictive conditions laid down for the opening of insolvency proceedings, other than main proceedings, by art.3(2)–(4): see the note to that article.

Paras 18, 19

These paragraphs, confirmed by art.29, are intended to ensure that the office-holder in "main" proceedings may himself institute secondary proceedings in any other Member State where the debtor has assets.

Para.20

Where there are several insolvency proceedings, the office-holders are urged to co-operate, but with the proviso that whoever has charge of the main proceedings has the whip-hand. Articles 31 and 33–34 give effect to these aims.

Para.21

See the notes to arts 20, 32 and 39, which contain the corresponding substantive provisions.

Para.22

The automatic recognition throughout the Community of the orders and judgments of the courts of a Member State and of the authority of the office-holder in any insolvency proceedings is one of the central principles of the Regulation. Articles 16–17, 19 and 25 carry this objective into effect.

Paras 23–28

The rules relating to the applicable law in insolvency proceedings which have a cross-border dimension within the Community are set out in arts 4 et seq. The basic rule is that the law of the State under which the proceedings have been instituted is prima facie to be applied, presumably including its own conflict of laws rules (art.4); but arts 5–15 contain a uniform set of rules prescribing exceptions to this general rule. A security interest (such as a mortgage), for instance, over an asset situated in another Member State is to be governed by the law of that State rather than that of the proceedings; and a debtor who is entitled to a right of set-off under the law applicable to his claim may assert that right even where such a right is not recognised by the law governing the insolvency proceedings. For more detailed comments, see the notes to arts 5–15.

Paras 29–30

Articles 21–24 give substantive effect to requirements regarding publicity and notice contained in these paragraphs.

Paras 32–33

The UK (including Gibraltar) and Ireland have opted in to the Regulation, but Denmark has opted out, at least for the time being.

CHAPTER I—GENERAL PROVISIONS

Article 1

[Scope]

1(1)   [Application] This Regulation shall apply to collective insolvency proceedings which entail the partial or total divestment of a debtor and the appointment of a liquidator.

1(2)   [Non-application] This Regulation shall not apply to insolvency proceedings concerning insurance undertakings, credit institutions, investment undertakings which provide services involving the holding of funds or securities for third parties, or to collective investment undertakings.

GENERAL NOTE

The scope of the Regulation is defined by this article, as amplified by art.2 and Annex A. So far as concerns UK insolvency procedures, it is clear that all forms of receivership are excluded, since receivership is not a "collective" procedure administered for the benefit of all concerned, or even all creditors. There might have been some doubt whether administration and voluntary arrangements were included (since neither involves the "divestment" of the debtor, except in the sense that the debtor loses some control of his assets), but for the fact that they are listed in Annex A. The use of the word "shall" in art.2(a) might suggest that the list in Annex A is definitive, but that it is not appears to be confirmed by the fact that statutory instruments supplementing the Regulation have been made in relation to insolvent partnerships and the insolvent estates of deceased persons (see the note to the Preamble para.9). Amendments made to Annexes A–C by EC Council Regulation 603/2005, as from April 21, 2005 remove any doubts that administrations where the administrator is appointed out of court, and companies to which a provisional liquidator has been appointed, are within the Regulation, but oddly the opportunity was not taken to add these other categories of insolvency as well.

Winding up subject to the supervision of the court has, of course, been abolished in the UK.

The Regulation throughout makes the fundamental assumption that its application is confined to "insolvency" proceedings; but there is nowhere any definition of "insolvency" or an equivalent term, and no guidance given as to how it is to be determined whether a debtor is insolvent. One area in which this issue may arise is where a company has been ordered to be wound up by the court on the "just and equitable" ground under IA 1986 s.122(1)(g). However, if the petition is brought on public interest grounds under IA 1986 s.124A (or a corresponding provision in other legislation), the Regulation does not apply, even if the company concerned is insolvent: *Re Marann Brooks CSV Ltd* [2003] B.C.C. 239.

The term "liquidator" is used in a wide sense, to include the insolvency practitioner who administers any of the forms of insolvency proceedings covered by the Regulation: see the note to art.2(b).

On the exclusion of the bodies listed in art.1(2), see the note to the Preamble para.9. In *Financial Services Authority v Dobb, White & Co* [2003] EWHC 3146 (Ch); [2004] B.P.I.R. 479 it was held that the reference in art.2(1) to "undertakings for collective investment in transferable securities" is limited to undertakings authorised under Council Directive 611/85. In *Byers v Yacht Bull Corp* [2010] EWHC 133 (Ch); [2010] B.C.C. 368 it was held that the exclusion for investment undertakings related not to such undertakings generally but only to undertakings which provided "services involving the holding of funds or securities for third parties".

Article 2

[Definitions]

2   For the purposes of this Regulation:

(a)   **"insolvency proceedings"** shall mean the collective proceedings referred to in Article 1(1). These proceedings are listed in Annex A;

(b)   **"liquidator"** shall mean any person or body whose function is to administer or liquidate assets of which the debtor has been divested or to supervise the administration of his affairs. Those persons and bodies are listed in Annex C;

(c)   **"winding-up proceedings"** shall mean insolvency proceedings within the meaning of point (a) involving realising the assets of the debtor, including where the proceedings have been closed by a composition or other measure terminating the insolvency, or closed by reason of the insufficiency of the assets. Those proceedings are listed in Annex B;

(d)   **"court"** shall mean the judicial body or any other competent body of a Member State empowered to open insolvency proceedings or to take decisions in the course of such proceedings;

(e)   **"judgment"** in relation to the opening of insolvency proceedings or the appointment of a liquidator shall include the decision of any court empowered to open such proceedings or to appoint a liquidator;

(f)   **"the time of the opening of proceedings"** shall mean the time at which the judgment opening proceedings becomes effective, whether it is a final judgment or not;

(g)   **"the Member State in which assets are situated"** shall mean, in the case of:

–   tangible property, the Member State within the territory of which the property is situated,

–   property and rights ownership of or entitlement to which must be entered in a public register, the Member State under the authority of which the register is kept,

–   claims, the Member State within the territory of which the third party required to meet them has the centre of his main interests, as determined in Article 3(1);

(h)   **"establishment"** shall mean any place of operations where the debtor carries out a non-transitory economic activity with human means and goods.

This article contains the definitions of most of the terms that are used in a technical sense in the Regulation. Note also, however, the meaning given to the phrase "the debtor's centre of main interests" by the Preamble, para.13.

Art.2(a)
See the notes to the Preamble para.9 and art.1(1).

Art.2(b)
The term "liquidator" is used in a wide sense, to include the insolvency practitioner who administers any of the forms of insolvency proceedings covered by the Regulation. Some mental effort will be required to accept that the term "liquidator" extends to a trustee in bankruptcy!

As noted in the comment to art.1(1), the list of persons and bodies set out in Annex C cannot be considered exhaustive, in the light of the provision made by domestic legislation for insolvent partnerships and the insolvent estates of deceased persons. On the other hand, the judgment of the ECJ in *Re Eurofoods Ltd* (C-341/04) [2006] B.C.C. 397 is careful to state, on every occasion that there is a reference to a provisional liquidator, that such an office-holder is "referred to in Annex C to the Regulation". It is a matter for speculation whether the court would have reached the same conclusion if Annex C did not specifically mention a provisional liquidator. Fortunately, the UK list in Annex C has been amended to make good this omission.

Art.2(c)
The comments made above apply also to this definition. What is clearly intended is the exclusion of any form of rehabilitation or rescue proceedings, e.g. an administration, IVA or CVA.

Art.2(d), (e)
Reference should be made to the Preamble para.10, which makes it plain that the expression "court" is to be given a broad meaning, reflecting the fact that insolvency proceedings do not necessarily involve the intervention of a judicial authority, and is to include "a person or body empowered by national law to open insolvency proceedings". Accordingly, a creditors' voluntary winding up is within the Regulation, and in that context "court" means the members in general meeting (for it is that body, and not the meeting of creditors, whose resolution is determinative); and "judgment" must be read as meaning the resolution.

Articles 16(1) and 19 declare that a "judgment opening insolvency proceedings" and a "liquidator's appointment" shall be accorded recognition without further formality in all other Member States. Article 16(1) unhelpfully refers to such a judgment being "handed down by a court"; but any difficulty that this phrase might create is met by the requirement in Annexes A and B that a creditors' voluntary winding up should be confirmed by the court (plainly, "court" is here to be understood in its normal sense). Provision is made for such confirmation by IR 1986 r.7.62. But the court's confirmation serves only an evidentiary purpose; it is the members' resolution that is the "judgment opening the insolvency proceedings".

On similar reasoning, the body which is to be taken as the "court" for the purposes of a CVA or IVA is the creditor's meeting: see IA 1986 ss.5(2)(a) and 260(2)(a), and the resolution as the "judgment": see *Re The Salvage Association* [2003] EWHC 1028 (Ch); [2003] B.C.C. 504, at 19 et seq. There is no mention in the Regulation of any need to have such a resolution confirmed by the court: presumably it is assumed that since the outcome of the creditors' meeting will have been reported to the court, it will be possible for a certificate sufficient to meet the purposes of the Regulation to be issued by the court without the formality of confirmation. It would have been helpful if some provision dealing with this point had been included in the Rules.

Similar comments apply to administration, where a company is put into administration by the holder of a floating charge or the company or its directors without a court order under IA 1986 Sch.B1 paras 14 or 22. The "court" will be the person or persons making the appointment, and the "judgment" will be the filing of the notice of appointment under paras 18 or 29, as the case may be: this will also determine the time of the opening of the insolvency proceedings (paras 19, 31). Again, there is no reference in the legislation to any need for confirmation by the court. Some disquiet has been expressed at the lack of clear legislative guidance on these points and in consequence it has been suggested that, in order to avoid uncertainty and misunderstanding in other EU jurisdictions (and a fortiori in foreign jurisdictions not covered by the Regulation), it may be prudent to have the administrator appointed by the court rather than under paras 14 or 22. However, so far as concerns other Member States, the recent amendment of Annexes A and B to include specific mention of out-of-court appointments should allay any doubts. Even so, it is likely to be helpful to foreign office-holders and creditors for the court to provide a supplementary order (as was done in *Re MG Rover España SA* [2006] B.C.C. 599), explaining the nature of the insolvency proceeding and the powers of the office-holder. (This case is important also for the view expressed that Sch.B1 para.66 can empower administrators to make payments to employees under the national laws of EU Member States over and above any entitlement they might have under English law, so possibly avoiding the need to open secondary proceedings in each national territory (which would necessarily be winding-up proceedings).) See also *Re Collins & Aikman Europe Ltd* [2006] EWHC 1343 (Ch); [2006] B.C.C. 861 and *Re Nortel Networks SA (No.2)* [2009] EWHC 1482 (Ch); [2010] B.C.C. 21.

Art.2(f)

This definition throws light on the meaning of the expression "the opening of proceedings", which could well be a source of confusion. It is to be taken as referring to whatever step in the proceedings marks the effective beginning of the particular insolvency regime: liquidation, bankruptcy, administration, etc. Subject to the caveat below, it should not be confused with any earlier act, such as the filing in court of a petition for winding up or a bankruptcy or administration order, or with the "commencement" of a winding up as defined by IA 1986 ss.86, 129. It follows that the event which counts should be the court order or, in the case of a voluntary winding up, CVA or IVA, the resolution of the appropriate body. In an administration where the appointment is made out of court, it will be the time of the filing of the notice of appointment under IA 1986 Sch.B1 paras 18 or 29, as noted above. In *Re Eurofood IFSC Ltd* (C-341/04) [2006] Ch. 508; [2006] B.C.C. 397 the appointment of a provisional liquidator was held to constitute the "opening" of proceedings—confirmed by the phrase in art.2(f) "whether it is a final judgment or not". The one exceptional case would appear to be the insolvent estate of a deceased person, where the court's order is related back to the date of death (Administration of Insolvent Estates of Deceased Persons Order 1986 Sch.1 Pt II para.12).

However, the above interpretation of art.2(f) should be read subject to the caveat that in the opinion of the Advocate General in the *Eurofood* case ([2006] Ch. 508 at 511; [2005] B.C.C. 1,021) the time of the opening of proceedings might be taken to be the time filing of a winding-up petition because that is the key factor in the definition of the "commencement" of the winding up in IA 1986 s.129(2). (The ECJ found it unnecessary to rule on this point.) It is submitted that this is an unwarranted confusion and that the contention cannot be correct (see the note to IA 1986 s.129(2)), in view of the fact that the presentation of a petition does not of itself involve any divestment of the debtor company's assets, even retrospectively.

The concept of the "opening" of insolvency proceedings is critically examined by Gabriel Moss Q.C. in [2008] 21 Insolv. Int. 1.

See also the ruling of the Dutch court in *Re BenQ Mobile Holding BV* [2008] B.C.C. 489, noted by Paulus, (2007) 20 Insolv. Int. 87.

There may be some significance in the use of the word "time", rather than "date": see the note to IA 1986 s.86.

Art.2(g)

Although this paragraph may not cover all possible forms of property (e.g. some non-registrable intangibles), it should avoid many conflict of laws questions that might otherwise arise.

Art.2(h)

This term is of paramount importance where it is sought to open insolvency proceedings in a Member State other than that in which the debtor has his centre of main interests (see art.3(2)–(4)). It is probably not necessary to give too literal a meaning to the word "goods": it is frequently used in EC documents in the more general sense of "assets". What is more surprising, and likely to prove an unwelcome limitation, is the stress placed on an *economic* activity carried on by the debtor. This could well create an obstacle to the opening of territorial or secondary insolvency proceedings in the case of a non-trader or a retired person who may have both assets and debts, but not his home, in a Member State but does not carry on any form of business there.

In *Telia AB v Hillcourt (Docklands) Ltd* [2002] EWHC 3277 (Ch); [2003] B.C.C. 856 Park J. declined to hold that the business premises of the UK subsidiary of a Swedish company whose COMI was in Sweden constituted an "establishment" of the latter in England. This would follow from the basic rule that a subsidiary, being a separate corporate entity, carries on its own business and not, in the absence of evidence to that effect, that of its holding company, and is consistent with the ECJ's decision respecting the separate personality of a subsidiary company in *Re Eurofood IFSC Ltd* (C-341/04) [2006] Ch. 508; [2006] B.C.C. 397. In contrast, in *Shierson v Vlieland-Boddy* [2005] EWCA Civ 974; [2005] B.C.C. 949 the court "lifted the veil" of incorporation and held that where a company, as owner of a property, was carrying on an economic activity with human means and goods here, this company was only a front or nominee for an individual debtor and that in consequence he had an "establishment" within the jurisdiction.

Article 3

[International jurisdiction]

3(1)   [Main insolvency proceedings] The courts of the Member State within the territory of which the centre of a debtor's main interests is situated shall have jurisdiction to open insolvency proceedings. In the case of a company or legal person, the place of the registered office shall be presumed to be the centre of its main interests in the absence of proof to the contrary.

3(2) **[Territorial insolvency proceedings]** Where the centre of a debtor's main interests is situated within the territory of a Member State, the courts of another Member State shall have jurisdiction to open insolvency proceedings against that debtor only if he possesses an establishment within the territory of that other Member State. The effects of those proceedings shall be restricted to the assets of the debtor situated in the territory of the latter Member State.

3(3) **[Secondary proceedings]** Where insolvency proceedings have been opened under paragraph 1, any proceedings opened subsequently under paragraph 2 shall be secondary proceedings. These latter proceedings must be winding-up proceedings.

3(4) **[Territorial proceedings prior to main proceedings]** Territorial insolvency proceedings referred to in paragraph 2 may be opened prior to the opening of main insolvency proceedings in accordance with paragraph 1 only:

    (a)   where insolvency proceedings under paragraph 1 cannot be opened because of the conditions laid down by the law of the Member State within the territory of which the centre of the debtor's main interests is situated; or

    (b)   where the opening of territorial insolvency proceedings is requested by a creditor who has his domicile, habitual residence or registered office in the Member State within the territory of which the establishment is situated, or whose claim arises from the operation of that establishment.

GENERAL NOTE

The Regulation only applies where the centre of the debtor's main interests is located in the EU—although he need not be an EU national: see the Preamble para.14. It also applies only where the debtor has assets (and, usually, creditors) in more than one Member State. And it has nothing to say about assets situated outside the EU, or creditors resident or domiciled outside the Community. In any of the situations not covered by the Regulation, a Member State is free to apply its national law (including, in the case of the UK, the CBIR).

Article 3(1) deals with the jurisdiction to open "main" proceedings and art.3(2)–(4) with the jurisdiction for "secondary" and "territorial" proceedings. Non-main proceedings are "secondary" if they are opened after the opening of main proceedings, and "territorial" if they precede the opening of main proceedings. (But arts 31–35 dealing with secondary proceedings are made to apply also to territorial proceedings by art.36.)

The reference in art.3(1) and (2) to "the courts of a Member State" could give rise to difficulties where it is sought to put a company into creditors' voluntary liquidation where the company is incorporated in one State but has its centre of main interests in another. The resolution would have to be passed by the company's shareholders in accordance with the law of the State of incorporation, but even assuming that the meeting was held in the "main" Member State it would call for some ingenuity to construe "the court of that Member State" as meaning that meeting. Some of these questions arose in *Re TXU Europe German Finance BV* [2005] B.C.C. 90. Two companies registered respectively in Ireland and the Netherlands had their COMIs in England. Being satisfied that the law of both Ireland and the Netherlands made provision for a procedure equivalent to a special resolution and that the counterparts to the registrar of companies in each country were willing to recognise the winding up for the purposes of the dissolution of their companies, Mr Registrar Baister, in exercise of the discretion conferred by IR 1986 r.7.62(5), made an order confirming resolutions which had been passed for a voluntary winding up of the two companies (which, in the circumstances, was a creditors' winding up). The court accepted that the liquidations would be conducted in accordance with English insolvency law, but did so only on the basis of assurances given by the liquidator that foreign creditors would be treated fairly.

Article 27 provides that the fact that main proceedings have been opened is to be taken as conclusive evidence of the debtor's insolvency in any later secondary proceedings.

Art.3(1)

Apart from the (rebuttable) presumption set out in the second sentence, there is nothing in the substantive parts of the Regulation to help in determining the debtor's "centre of main interests"; but the Preamble para.13, does throw some light on the meaning of the phrase. The "centre of main interests", it is stated, "should correspond to the place where the debtor conducts the administration of his interests on a regular basis and is therefore ascertainable by third parties". Unlike the definition of "establishment" in art.2(h), there is here no express reference to a business or "economic" activity.

The meaning of the term "centre of main interests" has been the subject of judicial consideration in a number of cases. (See the series of articles by Professor I.F. Fletcher in (2005) 18 Insolv. Int. 49, 68, 85, which include a discussion of some unreported cases, and the wide-ranging review by G. McCormack in [2009] Cambridge L.J. 169.) In *Skjevesland v Geveran Trading Co Ltd* [2002] EWHC 2898 (Ch); [2003] B.C.C. 391; affirming [2003] B.C.C. 209, the debtor was a banker domiciled in Switzerland who had homes in several European countries but had last lived in England over two years ago. He divided his time for business purposes between Switzerland and Spain and, although he spent more time in Spain, about 90 per cent of his economic activities were carried out in Switzerland. It was held that his centre of main interests was in Switzerland. The judge referred to the Virgós-Schmit Report (EC Council document 6500/DRS 8 (CFC)), a commentary on the draft EC Bankruptcy Convention (the forerunner of the EC Regulation), where the importance was emphasised of jurisdiction in international insolvency matters being based "on a place known to the debtor's potential creditors". The finding that the COMI was in Switzerland (and accordingly not within the EU) meant that the Regulation did not apply. A bankruptcy order could therefore be made under IA 1986 s.265(1)(c), based on his residence here within the past three years. On the same reasoning, if the COMI of a company is in Denmark, the English court will have jurisdiction to make a winding-up order, since Denmark has opted out of the Regulation: *Re The Arena Corporation Ltd* [2003] EWHC 3032 (Ch); [2004] B.P.I.R. 375 (at first instance, a point not raised on appeal [2004] EWCA Civ 371; [2004] B.P.I.R. 415). In *Re Daisytek-ISA Ltd* [2003] B.C.C. 562 administration orders were made in respect of the English subsidiary of a US parent company (Daisytek) and its own subsidiaries incorporated respectively in England, Germany and France. Although the foreign subsidiaries had their registered offices and conducted their business abroad, they were managed to a large extent from Daisytek's head office in Bradford. In ruling that all of the European subsidiaries had their centre of main interests in England, the court had regard to various factors: the location of banking activities and the keeping of financial records, the degree of independence in making purchases (approval by the parent was required for purchases over €5000), policy in the recruitment of senior employees, the provision of services to customers, control of corporate identity and branding, and responsibility for corporate strategy. The scale and importance of the subsidiaries' interests carried out was greater in the UK than in the subsidiaries' own countries. Again, it was stressed that the most important "third parties" concerned with identifying the centre of main interests were the various companies' potential creditors—their financiers and trade suppliers. The evidence was that a large majority of these would have looked to Bradford in this regard. As a decision dealing with insolvency in a group-company context, this case is similar to *Re Aim Underwriting Agencies (Ireland) Ltd* (July 2, 2004, noted (March 2005) Sweet & Maxwell's *Insolvency Bulletin* 10); but may be contrasted with *Re Eurofood IFSC Ltd* (C-341/04) [2006] B.C.C. 397, where none of these factors was present: the ECJ held that the mere fact of "parental control" was not sufficient to put the subsidiary's COMI into the jurisdiction of the holding company. (It should be noted that the reasoning of the ECJ is based not so much on an examination of the facts in isolation, but rather on whether they are sufficiently strong to displace the presumption that the subsidiary's COMI is that of its place of its registered office.) *Daisytek* was followed on finely-balanced facts in *Re Parkside Flexibles SA* [2006] B.C.C. 589. (The Court of Appeal of Versailles (September 4, 2003, reported as *Klempka v ISA Daisytek SA* [2003] B.C.C. 984), in a robust judgment, subsequently endorsed this ruling, and their judgment has been affirmed by the Court of Cassation: *French Republic v Klempka* [2006] B.C.C. 841.) See also *Re MPOTEC GmbH* [2006] B.C.C. 681; *Re Lennox Holdings plc* [2009] B.C.C. 155 and the ruling of the Dutch court in *Re BenQ Mobile Holding BV* [2008] B.C.C. 489, noted by Paulus, (2007) 20 Insolv. Int. 87. It appears from *Interedil Srl v Fallimento Interedil Srl* (C-396/09, October 20, 2011) that where a company had moved its registered office from one jurisdiction to another but had then ceased to have a registered office anywhere, the presumption is applied by reference to the last place where it was registered.

In *Shierson v Vlieland-Boddy* [2004] EWHC 2572 (Ch); [2005] B.C.C. 416, at first instance, the view was taken that the question of the location of the COMI should be decided as at the date of judgment and not at any earlier time. However, on appeal [2005] EWCA Civ 974; [2005] B.C.C. 949, it was held that this issue should be determined by reference to the time when the court is first required to decide whether to open the insolvency proceedings: this would normally be at the date of the hearing but occasionally at an earlier point, such as when an application had been made for leave to serve a bankruptcy petition out of the jurisdiction. This might also be appropriate in regard to any application for interim relief. It was conceded in this case that a debtor must be free to change his COMI from time, and even to do so when he is insolvent (although the court should "look critically" at the facts where this appears to have been done for the purpose of "forum-shopping") (para.[46]). These questions were explored further by the ECJ in *Re Staubitz-Schreiber* (C-1/04) [2006] B.C.C. 639; where the debtor had changed her COMI from Germany to Spain after her application to open insolvency proceedings had been filed but before the case had been heard. The Advocate General, in his opinion, which was endorsed by the European Court, stated that art.3(1) of the Regulation should be interpreted as meaning that the court of the Member State of the territory where the debtor's COMI is situated at the time when the request to open insolvency proceedings retains the jurisdiction to open those proceedings notwithstanding a subsequent move of the COMI by the debtor. As is pointed out by Petkovich, (2006) 22 I.L. & P.76, this places the time for determination of the COMI even earlier than *Shierson v Vlieland-Boddy*, where it was the date of first hearing rather than the lodging of the request that was considered to be the relevant time.

For the purposes of the Regulation, a company must have a COMI, and only one. Its COMI may be moved from one jurisdiction to another, but it does not change simply because (e.g.) its principal director moves from one place to another. It will continue to have a COMI even after it has ceased trading (not necessarily the same as it had before): *Re Ci4net.com Inc* [2004] EWHC 1941 (Ch); [2005] B.C.C. 277. In *Re Hellas Telecommunications (Luxembourg) II SCA* [2009] EWHC 3199 (Ch); [2010] B.C.C. 295 the court was satisfied on the evidence that the company had moved its COMI from Luxembourg (where it was incorporated) to England some three months before the hearing, so giving the English court jurisdiction. See also *Re European Directories (DH6) BV* [2010] EWHC 3472 (Ch); [2012] B.C.C. 46 and M. Rutstein and L. Bloomberg [2010] C.R. & I. 156.

An important concept in the law of a number of civil-law countries is the "seat" of a company. This is very similar to that of the COMI which is fundamental for the purposes of establishing jurisdiction under the EC Regulation, and in those countries the two will coincide. However, it is not possible as a matter of law in those countries for a company to move its seat from one jurisdiction to another without winding up in the place of origin and re-incorporating in the new one (*Cartesio Oktató és Szolgáltató bt* (C-210/06) [2009] B.C.C. 232). This is not a problem in other jurisdictions of the EU, so far as concerns the COMI: the location of the COMI is a matter of fact, and it can be moved from one country to another without any legal restriction.

Although it would appear to follow that there can only be one set of "main" proceedings in respect of the same debtor (as, indeed, is the view expressed in the Virgós-Schmit Report, para.73), it was held in *Re Ultra Motor Homes International Ltd* [2005] EWHC 872 (Ch); [2006] B.C.C. 57 at [34] that this is not the case where both sets of proceedings are in the same Member State—e.g. where a CVA and a liquidation involving the same company are current and subsisting at the same time.

A provision in the domestic law of a Member State which would deprive the courts of another Member State of jurisdiction to open main insolvency proceedings where the company concerned has its COMI is ineffective: *Rastelli David e C. Snc v Hidoux* (C-191/10, December 15, 2011).

Note that it is not necessary that the debtor should be domiciled (or, if a company, incorporated) within the EU. In *Re BRAC Rent-a-Car International Inc* [2003] EWHC 128 (Ch); [2003] 1 W.L.R. 1421; [2003] B.C.C. 248 an administration order was made in respect of a company incorporated in Delaware, on the basis of a finding that its centre of main interests was within the UK. Perhaps more controversially, in *Re 3T Telecom Ltd* [2005] EWHC 275 (Ch); [2006] 2 B.C.L.C. 137 it was held that an English court had jurisdiction to make an administration order in relation to a company incorporated in Northern Ireland on the basis that its COMI was in England, notwithstanding IA 1986 s.441(2). (The Regulation, in contrast with the CBIR reg.7, has no provision dealing with cross-border issues between the separate jurisdictions of the UK.)

The use of the present tense (*is* situated), if taken literally, would rule out the opening of insolvency proceedings in some cases where this plainly cannot have been intended—e.g. an insolvent deceased estate. The courts would surely give a purposive construction to the phrase in such a case (i.e. "the place where the debtor formerly had his centre of main interests is situated"). On the other hand, it must be understood literally where the debtor has moved his COMI from one Member State to another: only the latter would have jurisdiction.

The case-law on the COMI question continues to develop. Among recent decisions may be listed: *Re Parkside Flexibles SA* [2006] B.C.C. 589 (Polish subsidiary, member of English group, factors evenly balanced but regarded as decisive that creditors were having recourse to England, so COMI held to be in England); *Re Collins & Aikman Group Corp* [2005] EWHC 1754 (Ch); [2006] B.C.C. 606 (COMI of 24 European members of US group held to be in England and not in jurisdictions of their respective EU registered offices); *Re Sendo Ltd* [2005] EWHC 1604 (Ch); [2006] 1 B.C.L.C. 395 (wholly-owned Cayman Islands subsidiary of English company held to have COMI in England); *Cross Construction Sussex Ltd v Tseliki* [2006] EWHC 1056 (Ch); [2006] B.P.I.R. 888 (evidence insufficient to establish English COMI); *Energotech SARL* [2007] B.C.C. 123 (Polish-registered company held by French court to have COMI in France); *Re Lennox Holdings plc* [2009] B.C.C. 155 (all "head office functions" of Spanish subsidiaries located in England, where holding company was based: held that their COMI was in England); *Official Receiver v Mitterfellner* [2009] B.P.I.R. 1075 (insufficient evidence that COMI had been changed from Germany to England). In *Hans Brochier Holdings Ltd v Exner* [2006] EWHC 2594 (Ch); [2007] B.C.C. 127 administrators were appointed out of court to a company registered in England in the belief, backed by credible evidence, that its COMI was in England. Later the same day a German court appointed a preliminary administrator on the basis that the COMI was in Germany, but this would not be formalised (and accordingly not "opened" for the purposes of the Regulation) until some time later. On further investigation, the administrators concluded that the COMI was in fact in Germany. Warren J. held that the English appointment could not in the circumstances give rise to a main proceeding, although conceivably it could be effective as a territorial proceeding. In *Stojevic v Official Receiver* [2007] B.P.I.R. 141 the position was similar: the applicant had been made bankrupt by a court in Austria in January 2004, unaware of the fact that a bankruptcy order against him had been made in this country in March 2003. Investigation revealed that his COMI was in Austria. The Court granted an annulment of the English order. In *Re Eurodis Electron plc* [2011] EWHC 1025 (Ch); [2012] B.C.C. 57 a company incorporated in Belgium had its COMI in England. Notwithstanding this, it had been wound up and dissolved by a Belgian court, purportedly in main proceedings. It was ruled that the Regulation did not empower the courts in one country to determine that the orders of a court of another jurisdiction were invalid, so that the Belgian order had to stand. This did not prevent the English court from making a winding-up order under s.221(5)(a).

Decisions under the CBIR may also be relevant for the purposes of the EC Regulation, since both share the concept of the COMI. See, e.g. *Re Stanford International Bank Ltd* [2009] EWHC 1441; [2009] EWHC 1661; [2009] B.P.I.R. 1157; affirmed on appeal [2010] EWCA Civ 137; [2011] B.C.C. 211 (presumption that COMI was in jurisdiction of registered office supported by balance of evidence).

On the possibility that more than one Member State may claim the right to open main proceedings, see the note to the Preamble, para.14 and para.22.

Decisions in other EU jurisdictions on the COMI and related questions have been noted in English journals. These include *Parmalat Slovakia* (Hungary, 2004, (2004) 18 Insolv. Int. 31); *Stojevic* (Austria, 2003, (2005) 18 Insolv. Int. 141); and *Schefenacker*, *Deutsche Nickel* and *Hans Brochier* (Germany) 22 Insolv. Int. 25, 26; and see also the saga of the MG Rover subsidiaries recounted in (2005) 21 I.L. & P 91, 159. Many cases are accessible on the database *http://www.eir-database.com*.

Note that the term "centre of main interests" is of no relevance to the determination of issues of jurisdiction within the UK.

Art.3(2)–(3)
The prerequisites for the opening of secondary proceedings in a particular Member State are:

– main proceedings have already been opened in the State where the debtor has his COMI;

– the debtor must possess an establishment within that Member State;

– there must be assets of the debtor situated within that Member State;

– the proceedings must be for winding up (and not rehabilitation or rescue).

Again, the use of the present tense is disturbing, particularly since "possesses" must necessarily refer to the current position (in contrast with "is situated", which in the context of art.3(1) is arguably ambiguous). It may well have been intended that if a debtor has ceased to possess an establishment in a particular jurisdiction, everything is to be administered in the main proceedings; but this would prevent any ring-fencing of the local assets for the benefit of local creditors and could cost preferential creditors their priority.

The liquidator in the main proceedings is given considerable powers to intervene in the administration of the secondary proceedings: see arts 33 et seq.

Art.3(4)
Where no main proceedings have been opened in the Member State where the debtor has his COMI, "territorial" proceedings may be opened in another Member State. Unlike secondary proceedings, these need not be winding-up proceedings but could take the form of an administration or a CVA or IVA. But the jurisdiction to open territorial proceedings is restricted not only by art.2(2), which requires the debtor to possess an establishment within the jurisdiction and confines the effect of the proceedings to assets situated there, but also more severely by art.3(4) to the two situations set out in subparas (a) and (b). Paragraph (4)(a) presupposes that the "main" Member State cannot exercise jurisdiction but that the "territorial" State can: this might be (e.g.) because the debtor is a non-trader or minor or foreign national who cannot be bankrupted under the law of the main State. Paragraph (4)(b) requires the applicant to be a creditor based in the "territorial" Member State who seeks to have the debtor put into insolvency on the basis of a trading debt incurred by the debtor in running his establishment. For this reason the Court of Appeal of Paris held, in *EcoJet Ltd v Selafa MJA* [2005] B.C.C. 979, that it was not competent for a French court to open territorial proceedings of its own motion. In *Procurer-generaal bij het Hof van Bereoep te Antwerpen v Zaza Retail* (C-112/10, November 20, 2011) the European Court of Justice ruled that the conditions for the opening of territorial proceedings must be interpreted strictly: the restrictions in art.3(4)(a) are to be construed objectively and do not depend on the circumstances of the individual applicant; and the term "creditor" in art.3(4)(b) does not include a person acting on behalf of the creditors as a body. These limitations would not only rule out an individual from petitioning for his own bankruptcy in a State other than that of his COMI, but also a resolution for the (creditors') voluntary winding up of a company incorporated here but having its COMI in another Member State, or an administration initiated by such a

company or its directors; and it would appear to put obstacles in the way of setting up an IVA or CVA for a debtor who is a British national or UK-registered company with a COMI elsewhere in the Community.

If main proceedings are subsequently opened in the State where the COMI is situated, the liquidator in those proceedings has, by virtue of art.36, the extensive powers of intervention set out in arts 31–35, and also the right conferred by art.37 to request that the proceedings be converted into winding-up proceedings if they do not already take that form.

Article 4

[Law applicable]

4(1) **["State of the opening of proceedings"]** Save as otherwise provided in this Regulation, the law applicable to insolvency proceedings and their effects shall be that of the Member State within the territory of which such proceedings are opened, hereafter referred to as the **"State of the opening of proceedings"**.

4(2) **[Conditions for the opening of proceedings]** The law of the State of the opening of proceedings shall determine the conditions for the opening of those proceedings, their conduct and their closure. It shall determine in particular:

(a) against which debtors insolvency proceedings may be brought on account of their capacity;

(b) the assets which form part of the estate and the treatment of assets acquired by or devolving on the debtor after the opening of the insolvency proceedings;

(c) the respective powers of the debtor and the liquidator;

(d) the conditions under which set-offs may be invoked;

(e) the effects of insolvency proceedings on current contracts to which the debtor is party;

(f) the effects of the insolvency proceedings on proceedings brought by individual creditors, with the exception of lawsuits pending;

(g) the claims which are to be lodged against the debtor's estate and the treatment of claims arising after the opening of insolvency proceedings;

(h) the rules governing the lodging, verification and admission of claims;

(i) the rules governing the distribution of proceeds from the realisation of assets, the ranking of claims and the rights of creditors who have obtained partial satisfaction after the opening of insolvency proceedings by virtue of a right in rem or through a set-off;

(j) the conditions for and the effects of closure of insolvency proceedings, in particular by composition;

(k) creditors' rights after the closure of insolvency proceedings;

(l) who is to bear the costs and expenses incurred in the insolvency proceedings;

(m) the rules relating to the voidness, voidability or unenforceability of legal acts detrimental to all the creditors.

GENERAL NOTE

Article 4 applies to all forms of insolvency proceedings, whether main, secondary or territorial. Subject to arts 5 et seq., each jurisdiction is to apply its own laws and rules of procedure. To remove doubt, many of the respects to which this basic principle is to apply are spelt out in detail in subpara.(2). It follows that, once it is established that the UK has jurisdiction under art.3 (whether in main, territorial or secondary proceedings), the rules of law and practice and the powers of the office-holder will be the same as those in a domestic insolvency, and these will apply subject only to any limitations specifically set out elsewhere in the Regulation: see *Alitalia Linee Aeree Italiane SpA, Connock v Fantozzi* [2011] EWHC 15 (Ch); [2011] 1 W.L.R. 2049; [2011] B.C.C. 579.

Paragraph 4(1) is expressed in categorical terms. It is submitted that, even in the case where a certificate confirming a creditors' voluntary winding up is denied, the jurisdiction conferred on the local court by this article will apply: see the note to r.7.62(5).

Art.4(2)(b)

In *German Graphics v Alice van der Schee* (C-292/08, September 10, 2009) judgment had been given by a German court in favour of the claimant against a Dutch purchaser on the basis of a reservation of title. The latter went into liquidation in Holland and its liquidator sought to resist enforcement of the judgment on the ground that under art.4(2) the goods formed part of the insolvent estate. The ECJ rejected this contention: the case was governed by the Judgments Regulation 44/2001 to the exclusion of the Insolvency Regulation and (apart from the fact that the liquidator was a party to the proceedings) there was no link with the insolvency proceedings. (Note, however, that had there been any dispute as to the validity of the retention of title claim the Dutch court would have had jurisdiction to determine this issue under art.4(2)(m): contrast *SCT Industri AB v Alpenblume AB* (C-111/08, July 2, 2009, where the property had been sold by the liquidator under powers conferred on him by insolvency law).) See also *Re Ultra Motorhomes International Ltd* [2005] EWHC 872 (Ch); [2006] B.C.C. 57 (dispute concerning the ownership of a motor vehicle held not to be "closely connected" with liquidation proceedings so as to give the court of the liquidation jurisdiction).

Art.4(2)(e), (f)

An apparent inconsistency between paras (2)(e) and (2)(f) was discussed by Clarke J. in *Elektrim SA v Vivendi Universal SA* [2008] EWHC 2155 (Comm); [2008] 2 Lloyd's Rep. 636. See the note to art.15.

Art.4(2)(j), (k)

This provision would appear to put it beyond doubt that a discharge in bankruptcy or a composition which is effective under the law of any competent Member State will be recognised throughout the Community as extinguishing all the debts of the insolvent (or at least those comprehended by the composition), wherever incurred, but in territorial or secondary proceedings art.17(2) imposes a qualification, empowering creditors who have not consented to the discharge to pursue any assets of the debtor that are situated in another State. (See, however, the *Global* case, discussed in the note to art.25.)

Art.4(2)(m)

The law of the opening of the proceedings was applied by the Court of Appeal of Versailles in *Becheret Thierry v Industrie Guido Malvestio SpA* [2005] B.C.C. 974.

Article 5

[Third parties' rights in rem]

5(1) [Proceedings not to affect third party rights in rem] The opening of insolvency proceedings shall not affect the rights in rem of creditors or third parties in respect of tangible or intangible, moveable or immoveable assets—both specific assets and collections of indefinite assets as a whole which change from time to time—belonging to the debtor which are situated within the territory of another Member State at the time of the opening of proceedings.

5(2) [Rights referred to in art. 5(1)] The rights referred to in paragraph 1 shall in particular mean:

    (a) the right to dispose of assets or have them disposed of and to obtain satisfaction from the proceeds of or income from those assets, in particular by virtue of a lien or a mortgage;

    (b) the exclusive right to have a claim met, in particular a right guaranteed by a lien in respect of the claim or by assignment of the claim by way of a guarantee;

    (c) the right to demand the assets from, and/or to require restitution by, anyone having possession or use of them contrary to the wishes of the party so entitled;

    (d) a right in rem to the beneficial use of assets.

5(3) [Recorded rights] The right, recorded in a public register and enforceable against third parties, under which a right in rem within the meaning of paragraph 1 may be obtained, shall be considered a right in rem.

5(4) [Actions for voidness, voidability or unenforceability not precluded] Paragraph 1 shall not preclude actions for voidness, voidability or unenforceability as referred to in Article 4(2)(m).

GENERAL NOTE

This is the first of the exceptions to the general rule that the administration of insolvency proceedings (whether main, secondary or territorial) in a particular Member State shall be governed by the law of those proceedings: all rights in rem (including security rights of a proprietary nature) in respect of assets situated outside the territory of that State are to be determined by reference to the law ordinarily applicable to such rights under conflict of laws rules. Lawyers in common-law jurisdictions (and Scotland) will be relieved to see that the security of a floating charge is specifically included.

Article 6

[Set-off]

6(1) [Proceedings not to affect creditors' set-off rights] The opening of insolvency proceedings shall not affect the right of creditors to demand the set-off of their claims against the claims of the debtor, where such a set-off is permitted by the law applicable to the insolvent debtor's claim.

6(2) [Actions for voidness, voidability or unenforceability not precluded] Paragraph 1 shall not preclude actions for voidness, voidability or unenforceability as referred to in Article 4(2)(m).

GENERAL NOTE

The right of set-off referred to relates to the position between the debtor and a creditor whose claim arises in a jurisdiction other than that of the Member State in which the insolvency proceedings are being administered. This, as regards a claim governed by English law, will not be a right of set-off in insolvency under IA 1986 s.323 or IR 1986 r.4.90 but a right arising independently of the insolvency under the rules of common law or equity. See further the note to r.4.90.

Article 7

[Reservation of title]

7(1) [Proceedings not to affect seller's title reservation rights] The opening of insolvency proceedings against the purchaser of an asset shall not affect the seller's rights based on a reservation of title where at the time of the opening of proceedings the asset is situated within the territory of a Member State other than the State of opening of proceedings.

7(2) [Insufficient grounds for rescission or termination] The opening of insolvency proceedings against the seller of an asset, after delivery of the asset, shall not constitute grounds for rescinding or terminating the sale and shall not prevent the purchaser from acquiring title where at the time of the opening of proceedings the asset sold is situated within the territory of a Member State other than the State of the opening of proceedings.

7(3) [Actions for voidness, voidability or unenforceability not precluded] Paragraphs 1 and 2 shall not preclude actions for voidness, voidability or unenforceability as referred to in Article 4(2)(m).

(See General Note after art.15.)

Article 8

[Contracts relating to immoveable property]

8 The effects of insolvency proceedings on a contract conferring the right to acquire or make use of immoveable property shall be governed solely by the law of the Member State within the territory of which the immoveable property is situated.

(See General Note after art.15.)

Article 9

[Payment systems and financial markets]

9(1) **[Law of Member State applicable]** Without prejudice to Article 5, the effects of insolvency proceedings on the rights and obligations of the parties to a payment or settlement system or to a financial market shall be governed solely by the law of the Member State applicable to that system or market.

9(2) **[Actions for voidness, voidability or unenforceability not precluded]** Paragraph 1 shall not preclude any action for voidness, voidability or unenforceability which may be taken to set aside payments or transactions under the law applicable to the relevant payment system or financial market.

(See General Note after art.15.)

Article 10

[Contracts of employment]

10 The effects of insolvency proceedings on employment contracts and relationships shall be governed solely by the law of the Member State applicable to the contract of employment.

(See General Note after art.15.)

Article 11

[Effects on rights subject to registration]

11 The effects of insolvency proceedings on the rights of the debtor in immoveable property, a ship or an aircraft subject to registration in a public register shall be determined by the law of the Member State under the authority of which the register is kept.

(See General Note after art.15.)

Article 12

[Community patents and trade marks]

12 For the purposes of this Regulation, a Community patent, a Community trade mark or any other similar right established by Community law may be included only in the proceedings referred to in Article 3(1).

(See General Note after art.15.)

Article 13

[Detrimental acts]

13 Article 4(2)(m) shall not apply where the person who benefited from an act detrimental to all the creditors provides proof that:

   – the said act is subject to the law of a Member State other than that of the State of the opening of proceedings, and

   – that law does not allow any means of challenging that act in the relevant case.

(See General Note after art.15.)

Article 14

[Protection of third-party purchasers]

14 Where, by an act concluded after the opening of insolvency proceedings, the debtor disposes, for consideration, of:

— an immoveable asset, or

— a ship or an aircraft subject to registration in a public register, or

— securities whose existence presupposes registration in a register laid down by law,

the validity of that act shall be governed by the law of the State within the territory of which the immoveable asset is situated or under the authority of which the register is kept.

(See General Note after art.15.)

Article 15

[Effects of insolvency proceedings on lawsuits pending]

15 The effects of insolvency proceedings on a lawsuit pending concerning an asset or a right of which the debtor has been divested shall be governed solely by the law of the Member State in which that lawsuit is pending.

GENERAL NOTE TO ARTS 7–15

Here are set out the remaining situations where the law of the State in which insolvency proceedings have been opened is to give way to the rules of the local law or those of some other jurisdiction.

Art.9
Provision is made for the disapplication of the rules of insolvency law in payment and settlement systems and transactions on the financial markets by the Finality Directive and by CA 1989 Pt VII, respectively: see the notes at Vol.1 pp.1–3. This article ensures that a similar disapplication will apply where the insolvency proceedings have been opened in a Member State other than that whose law is applicable to the system or market in question.

Art.12
The effect of this article is that Community patents and trade marks cannot be dealt with at all in secondary or territorial proceedings, even (in the latter case) where no main proceedings have been opened.

Art.13
Article 4(2)(m) gives jurisdiction to the State of the opening of the proceedings in the application of "the rules relating to the voidness, voidability or unenforceability of legal acts detrimental to all the creditors" which would include provisions relating to preferences, transactions at an undervalue, etc. (For examples, see the judgment of the Court of Appeal of Versailles in *Becheret Thierry v Industrie Guido Malvestio SpA* [2005] B.C.C. 974; and *Seagon v Deko Marty Belgium NV* (C-339/07) [2009] 1 W.L.R. 2168; [2009] B.C.C. 347.) Article 13 disapplies this rule where (1) the person who benefited from the transaction in question shows that the proper law would, apart from art.4(2)(m), be that of another Member State; and (2) the transaction would not be open to challenge at all under that law. It would follow that the transaction cannot be avoided or held to be void or unenforceable in the court where proceedings have been opened. Where, however, the transaction would be open to challenge under its proper law but the two laws differ in any respect, art.4(2)(m) will apply.

Art.15
In *Elektrim SA v Vivendi Universal SA* [2008] EWHC 2155 (Comm); [2008] 2 Lloyd's Rep. 636 an arbitration under English law between the parties had commenced in London but had not been heard when one of them was declared bankrupt by a Polish court. Polish insolvency law provided that in the event of bankruptcy any arbitration clause concluded by the bankrupt should lose its legal effect, and any pending arbitration proceedings should be discontinued. Clarke J. held that under art.15 English law should prevail on the basis that the arbitration was a "lawsuit pending", with the consequence that the arbitration had not been annulled; and further that in so far as art.4(2)(e) might be construed as nullifying the arbitration clause in a "current contract" and the ensuing proceedings it should give way to the clear intention of the legislator as expressed in art.15. This decision was affirmed by the

Court of Appeal (sub nom. *Syska v Vivendi Universal SA*) [2009] EWCA Civ 677; [2009] 2 All E.R. (Comm) 891; [2010] B.C.C. 348. The position would be otherwise, however (and the general provisions of art.4 would prevail) where arbitration proceedings had not been begun before the date of commencement of the insolvency.

CHAPTER II

RECOGNITION OF INSOLVENCY PROCEEDINGS

Introductory note to Chapter II

"Recognition" in this chapter has two aspects: first, recognition of the "judgment" (i.e. the order of a national court or act of any other person or body which has effect as the "opening" of insolvency proceedings); and, secondly, recognition of the authority of the office-holder (the "liquidator") in such proceedings. In each case the validity of the judgment and the liquidator's authority is to be accepted without the need for a court order in the nature of an exequatur or any other formality in the other Member State. All that is needed is a certified copy of the liquidator's appointment (accompanied by a translation, where appropriate). The only additional requirement is that, in the case of a creditors' voluntary winding up, a certificate of confirmation must be obtained from a court in the host country.

Article 16

[Principle]

16(1)   [Judgment pursuant to art.3 recognised] Any judgment opening insolvency proceedings handed down by a court of a Member State which has jurisdiction pursuant to Article 3 shall be recognised in all the other Member States from the time that it becomes effective in the State of the opening of proceedings.

This rule shall also apply where, on account of his capacity, insolvency proceedings cannot be brought against the debtor in other Member States.

16(2)   [Recognition not to preclude secondary proceedings] Recognition of the proceedings referred to in Article 3(1) shall not preclude the opening of the proceedings referred to in Article 3(2) by a court in another Member State. The latter proceedings shall be secondary insolvency proceedings within the meaning of Chapter III.

(See General Note after art.17.)

Article 17

[Effects of recognition]

17(1)   [Judgment opening proceedings where no secondary proceedings] The judgment opening the proceedings referred to in Article 3(1) shall, with no further formalities, produce the same effects in any other Member State as under this law of the State of the opening of proceedings, unless this Regulation provides otherwise and as long as no proceedings referred to in Article 3(2) are opened in that other Member State.

17(2)   [No challenge to secondary proceedings] The effects of the proceedings referred to in Article 3(2) may not be challenged in other Member States. Any restriction of the creditors' rights, in particular a stay or discharge, shall produce effects vis-à-vis assets situated within the territory of another Member State only in the case of those creditors who have given their consent.

GENERAL NOTE TO ARTS 16, 17

Article 16 applies to all forms of insolvency proceedings, whether main proceedings under art.3(1), or secondary or territorial proceedings under art.3(2)–(4). "Court" and "judgment" have the wider meanings given by art.2(d), (e), so that (e.g.) "judgment" includes a resolution for creditors' voluntary winding up or the appointment of an administrator made out of court: see the notes to that article. A creditors' voluntary winding up requires to be confirmed by the court, following the procedure set out in IR 1986 r.7.62.

The concluding sentence of art.16(1) ensures that an insolvency proceeding opened in a Member State which has jurisdiction will be recognised in another Member State even where the debtor could not be the subject of insolvency proceedings in the latter—e.g. if its bankruptcy law does not extend to a debtor who is a minor.

In art.17(1) "this law" appears to be an error for "the law". The effect of art.17(1) is that once main proceedings have been opened in the State of the debtor's centre of main interests, its insolvency law is to apply automatically throughout the rest of the Community. So, in *MG Probud Gdynia sp z oo* (C-444/07) [2010] B.C.C. 453 the ECJ ruled that once main proceedings had been opened in Poland, the jurisdiction of the company's COMI, it was not competent for a creditor to attach assets in Germany, this being contrary to Polish law. Article 17(1) is subject to two exceptions: (i) if territorial proceedings have already been opened, or secondary proceedings are subsequently opened, in another State, the insolvency law of the latter will apply in that State; and (ii) where special provision is made elsewhere in the Regulation (as, e.g. under art.24), and in particular where arts 5–15 apply, the law of the insolvency proceedings in question will be displaced. Although art.17(2), which applies to territorial and secondary proceedings, also accords general recognition to such proceedings throughout the EU, it adds a caveat which reflects the limitation of the effects such proceedings may have on assets situated in the territory of the State concerned (art.3(2)). So, for instance, if territorial proceedings in the UK were to result in a compromise under which every creditor accepted a 50 per cent payment in full satisfaction of his debt, this would not prevent an individual creditor from pursuing a claim for the balance in another Member State where the debtor had assets, unless he had agreed otherwise.

Article 18

[Powers of the liquidator]

18(1) [Extent of powers] The liquidator appointed by a court which has jurisdiction pursuant to Article 3(1) may exercise all the powers conferred on him by the law of the State of the opening of proceedings in another Member State, as long as no other insolvency proceedings have been opened there nor any preservation measure to the contrary has been taken there further to a request for the opening of insolvency proceedings in that State. He may in particular remove the debtor's assets from the territory of the Member State in which they are situated, subject to Articles 5 and 7.

18(2) [Power concerning moveable property] The liquidator appointed by a court which has jurisdiction pursuant to Article 3(2) may in any other Member State claim through the courts or out of court that moveable property was removed from the territory of the State of the opening of proceedings to the territory of that other Member State after the opening of the insolvency proceedings. He may also bring any action to set aside which is in the interests of the creditors.

18(3) [Liquidator to comply with local law] In exercising his powers, the liquidator shall comply with the law of the Member State within the territory of which he intends to take action, in particular with regard to procedures for the realisation of assets. Those powers may not include coercive measures or the right to rule on legal proceedings or disputes.

(See General Note after art.19.)

Article 19

[Proof of the liquidator's appointment]

19 The liquidator's appointment shall be evidenced by a certified copy of the original decision appointing him or by any other certificate issued by the court which has jurisdiction.

A translation into the official language or one of the official languages of the Member State within the territory of which he intends to act may be required. No legalisation or other similar formality shall be required.

GENERAL NOTE TO ARTS 18, 19

Article 18: note the qualification "so long as no other proceedings have been opened there". In *Re Alitalia Linee Aeree Italiane SpA* [2011] EWHC 15 (Ch); [2011] B.C.C. 579 main proceedings had been opened in Italy and secondary proceedings in England. The Italian liquidator wished to make certain payments to employees out of funds in England which would have a preferential ranking under Italian law, but it was held that the funds had to be applied in accordance with English law under which the employees were unsecured creditors with no priority.

Article 19 ensures that the authority of an office-holder shall be recognised throughout the Community with the minimum of formality and with no additional requirement in any Member State apart from possibly a translation into the local language.

In main proceedings, the powers of the "liquidator" are extensive and, indeed, are restricted only if territorial or secondary proceedings have been opened in another Member State or if a moratorium or similar interim measure has come into operation there in anticipation of the opening of such proceedings. But whereas the liquidator in main proceedings has a general power to gather up assets that are situated in other Member States (art.18(1)), that of a liquidator in territorial or secondary proceedings is limited to repatriating assets that have been removed abroad after those proceedings have been opened—and in this regard it is submitted that "opened" in a winding up by the court refers to the court order (or possibly, some other event), but not the petition: see the note to IA 1986 s.129(2).

The local law and procedures must in all cases be respected (art.18(3)).

IR 1986 r.2.133 may apply.

Article 20

[Return and imputation]

20(1)   [Creditor to return assets obtained outside Member State] A creditor who, after the opening of the proceedings referred to in Article 3(1) obtains by any means, in particular through enforcement, total or partial satisfaction of his claim on the assets belonging to the debtor situated within the territory of another Member State, shall return what he has obtained to the liquidator, subject to Articles 5 and 7.

20(2)   [Equal distribution of dividends to creditors] In order to ensure equal treatment of creditors a creditor who has, in the course of insolvency proceedings, obtained a dividend on his claim shall share in distributions made in other proceedings only where creditors of the same ranking or category have, in those other proceedings, obtained an equivalent dividend.

GENERAL NOTE

Article 20(1) empowers the liquidator in main proceedings to require any creditor who has recovered part or all of his debt by proceeding against assets of the debtor situated in another Member State to disgorge what he has received. This would not normally be possible under UK national law unless the creditor sought to prove in the insolvency, in which case he would be required to surrender his gains under the principle of hotchpot. Article 20(2), in contrast, does not oblige a creditor who has been paid a dividend in other insolvency proceedings to part with what he has received: it is only if he chooses to prove in the second insolvency that he must bring that sum into account and participate on a pari passu basis.

Article 21

[Publication]

21(1)   [Liquidator may request publication of appointment] The liquidator may request that notice of the judgment opening insolvency proceedings and, where appropriate, the decision appointing him, be published in any other Member State in accordance with the publication procedures provided for in that State. Such publication shall also specify the liquidator appointed and whether the jurisdiction rule applied is that pursuant to Article 3(1) or Article 3(2).

21(2)   [Where publication mandatory] However, any Member State within the territory of which the debtor has an establishment may require mandatory publication. In such cases, the liquidator or any authority empowered to that effect in the Member State where the proceedings referred to in Article 3(1) are opened shall take all necessary measures to ensure such publication.

(See General Note after art.23.)

Article 22

[Registration in a public register]

22(1)   **[Registration of judgment opening proceedings]** The liquidator may request that the judgment opening the proceedings referred to in Article 3(1) be registered in the land register, the trade register and any other public register kept in the other Member States.

22(2)   **[Where registration mandatory]** However, any Member State may require mandatory registration. In such cases, the liquidator or any authority empowered to that effect in the Member State where the proceedings referred to in Article 3(1) have been opened shall take all necessary measures to ensure such registration.

(See General Note after art.23.)

Article 23

[Costs]

23 The costs of the publication and registration provided for in Articles 21 and 22 shall be regarded as costs and expenses incurred in the proceedings.

GENERAL NOTE TO ARTS 21–23

No legislation has been enacted in this country requiring mandatory publication or registration under arts 21(2) or 22(2). Where this is requested by the liquidator, the ordinary procedures to be followed under IA 1986 and the Rules will be applicable. No special forms have been prescribed.

On the advantages of registration even though this is not mandatory, see the article by G. Flannery in [2005] 21 I.L. & P. 57.

Article 24

[Honouring of an obligation to a debtor]

24(1)   **[Deemed discharge of obligation]** Where an obligation has been honoured in a Member State for the benefit of a debtor who is subject to insolvency proceedings opened in another Member State, when it should have been honoured for the benefit of the liquidator in those proceedings, the person honouring the obligation shall be deemed to have discharged it if he was unaware of the opening of proceedings.

24(2)   **[Effect of publication]** Where such an obligation is honoured before the publication provided for in Article 21 has been effected, the person honouring the obligation shall be presumed, in the absence of proof to the contrary, to have been unaware of the opening of insolvency proceedings; where the obligation is honoured after such publication has been effected, the person honouring the obligation shall be presumed, in the absence of proof to the contrary, to have been aware of the opening of proceedings.

GENERAL NOTE

This article gives protection to a creditor, based in a Member State other than that in which the insolvency proceedings have been opened, who has paid a debt in ignorance of the existence of the proceedings. The liquidator will thus be unable to have the payment set aside as a preference or declared void under IA 1986 s.127, for instance. Note the different rules as to the onus of proof in art.24(2).

Article 25

[Recognition and enforceability of other judgments]

25(1)   **[Course and closure without further formality]** Judgments handed down by a court whose judgment concerning the opening of proceedings is recognised in accordance with Article 16 and which concern the course and closure of insolvency proceedings, and compositions approved by that court shall also be recognised with no further formalities. Such judgments shall be enforced in accordance with Articles 31 to 51, with the exception of Article 34(2), of the Brussels Convention on Jurisdiction and the Enforcement of Judgments in Civil and Commercial Matters, as amended by the Conventions of Accession to this Convention.

The first subparagraph shall also apply to judgments deriving directly from the insolvency proceedings and which are closely linked with them, even if they were handed down by another court.

The first subparagraph shall also apply to judgments relating to preservation measures taken after the request for the opening of insolvency proceedings.

25(2) **[Other judgments]** The recognition and enforcement of judgments other than those referred to in paragraph 1 shall be governed by the Convention referred to in paragraph 1, provided that that Convention is applicable.

25(3) **[Exceptions]** The Member States shall not be obliged to recognise or enforce a judgment referred to in paragraph 1 which might result in a limitation of personal freedom or postal secrecy.

GENERAL NOTE

As noted in the Preamble para.7, insolvency proceedings are specifically excluded from the scope of the Brussels Convention (now superseded by the Judgments Regulation (EC Regulation 44/2001)). However, this article brings back within its ambit the judgments and compositions referred to in para.(1), so as to make them enforceable in other Member States in the same way as other judgments of the courts. So, for instance, an order that a creditor return a payment on the ground that it was a preference under IA 1986 s.239 will now be enforceable under the Judgments Regulation in another Member State. The object of para.2 was, presumably, to make it clear that nothing in the present Regulation was intended to qualify or restrict the operation of the Convention. The scope of art.25 and the delimitation between it and the Judgments Regulation is the subject of a detailed article by B. Wessels, (2008) 21 Insolv. Int. 135.

An order made by the English court in bankruptcy proceedings requiring a Dutch company to disclose information was held enforceable under art.25 in *Re France* (March 18, 2011, Supreme Court of the Netherlands).

A members' voluntary winding up, not being insolvency proceedings, was held to be within the Brussels Convention in *Re Cover Europe Ltd* [2002] 2 B.C.L.C. 61.

Article 25(1) would appear to make the discharge of a debt in another EC jurisdiction binding throughout the Community. This makes all the more anomalous the ruling in *Global Distressed Alpha Fund 1 LLP v PT Bakrie Investindo* [2011] EWHC 256 (Comm); [2011] B.P.I.R. 644 (not involving the EC Regulation) where it was held that a foreign discharge was not effective where the underlying contract is governed by English law. See further the note to IA 1986 s.426.

See further the notes to the Preamble para.7 and arts 7–15.

Article 26

[Public policy]

26   Any Member State may refuse to recognise insolvency proceedings opened in another Member State or to enforce a judgment handed down in the context of such proceedings where the effects of such recognition or enforcement would be manifestly contrary to that State's public policy, in particular its fundamental principles or the constitutional rights and liberties of the individual.

GENERAL NOTE

No doubt the inclusion of this provision was considered an important safeguard when the representatives of the Member States agreed to the final text.

One thing which is not spelt out is the way in which the objecting State is to declare its refusal—whether by an organ of government, a court, or an office-holder. In the Irish case *Re Eurofood IFSC Ltd* [2004] B.C.C. 383 the judge relied on public policy as one of the grounds for refusing to recognise a ruling of an Italian court that main proceedings had effectively been opened in Italy so as to oust his own jurisdiction, and this view was affirmed on appeal by the Irish Supreme Court [2004] IESC 47; [2005] B.C.C. 999, primarily because the Italian court had not given the provisional liquidator a fair opportunity to present his case. The ECJ (*Re Eurofood IFSC Ltd* (C-341/04)

[2006] B.C.C. 397), whilst upholding this decision, stressed that recourse to the public policy clause should be reserved for exceptional cases (in keeping with existing ECJ case law on the Brussels Convention (now the Judgments Regulation), which it said was "transposable" to art.6 of the Regulation). (See also *French Republic v Klempka* [2006] B.C.C. 841.)

Of interest also is the ruling of the Commercial Court of Nanterre in *Re SAS Rover France* (May 19, 2005, unreported: see Haravon, (2005) 18 Insolv. Int. 118 at 120), concerning a French subsidiary of the MG Rover Group Ltd which had been put into administration in England. The French Public Prosecutor claimed that the English decision should not be recognised on public policy grounds, in effect arguing that safeguards imposed by French employment and social security legislation might be jeopardised. The Commercial Court held that the English court order should be recognised under art.16 and accepted undertakings offered by the administrators that these safeguards would be respected. The Court of Appeal in Versailles has upheld this ruling (see (2006) 19 Insolv. Int. 31).

However, one rule of public policy has been expressly abrogated by the Regulation. This is the widely accepted principle that the courts will not enforce the fiscal laws of another State. Article 39 explicitly includes the claims of the tax and social security authorities of Member States among the debts for which proofs may be lodged. But a State's penal laws are not accorded the same concession, and so it will be open to a liquidator to reject an attempt by the authorities of another State to prove for a fine imposed by a court in the latter.

CHAPTER III

SECONDARY INSOLVENCY PROCEEDINGS

Article 27

[Opening of proceedings]

27   The opening of the proceedings referred to in Article 3(1) by a court of a Member State and which is recognised in another Member State (main proceedings) shall permit the opening in that other Member State, a court of which has jurisdiction pursuant to Article 3(2), of secondary insolvency proceedings without the debtor's insolvency being examined in that other State. These latter proceedings must be among the proceedings listed in Annex B. Their effects shall be restricted to the assets of the debtor situated within the territory of that other Member State.

(See General Note after art.30.)

Article 28

[Applicable law]

28   Save as otherwise provided in this Regulation, the law applicable to secondary proceedings shall be that of the Member State within the territory of which the secondary proceedings are opened.

(See General Note after art.30.)

Article 29

[Right to request the opening of proceedings]

29   The opening of secondary proceedings may be requested by:

   (a) the liquidator in the main proceedings;

   (b) any other person or authority empowered to request the opening of insolvency proceedings under the law of the Member State within the territory of which the opening of secondary proceedings is requested.

(See General Note after art.30.)

Article 30

[Advance payment of costs and expenses]

30   Where the law of the Member State in which the opening of secondary proceedings is requested requires that the debtor's assets be sufficient to cover in whole or in part the costs and expenses of the proceedings, the court may, when it receives such a request, require the applicant to make an advance payment of costs or to provide appropriate security.

GENERAL NOTE TO ARTS 27–30

"Secondary" insolvency proceedings are proceedings opened *after* the opening of "main" insolvency proceedings in a Member State other than that of the debtor's centre of main interests. The corresponding term for proceedings opened *prior* to main proceedings is "territorial" proceedings (art.3(4)). Secondary proceedings are subject to a number of limitations. In particular:

–   the debtor must possess an "establishment" within the State;

–   the effects of the proceedings are limited to assets situated within the State;

–   the proceedings must be "winding-up" proceedings (see Annex B), and cannot be for the rehabilitation or rescue of the debtor.

In addition, secondary proceedings are subject to the wide powers of intervention conferred on the liquidator in the main proceedings by arts 33 et seq. On the other hand, once secondary proceedings have been opened in another State, the powers of the "main" liquidator and the scope of the law of the "main" jurisdiction have to yield to those of the secondary proceedings: see *Alitalia Linee Aeree Italiane SpA, Connock v Fantozzi* [2011] EWHC 15 (Ch); [2011] B.C.C. 579 (law of secondary proceedings in England prevailed over Italian law, the jurisdiction of main proceedings).

Art.27
Note that the fact that main insolvency proceedings have been opened is to be taken as proof of the debtor's insolvency in any secondary proceedings.

Art.29
Even where no secondary proceedings have been opened, it may be in the interests of the main proceedings for its liquidator to open secondary proceedings in another State, e.g. to take advantage of "claw-back" provisions in the law of the latter. Article 29(a) gives him locus standi to set such proceedings in motion. IA 1986 s.124(1) has been amended to confirm this. The administrators in *Re Nortel Networks SA (No.2)* [2009] EWHC 1482 (Ch); [2010] B.C.C. 21 received the court's blessing to institute secondary proceedings in France in order to achieve savings in time and costs.

Article 31

[Duty to cooperate and communicate information]

31(1)   [Duty of liquidators to communicate] Subject to the rules restricting the communication of information, the liquidator in the main proceedings and the liquidators in the secondary proceedings shall be duty bound to communicate information to each other. They shall immediately communicate any information which may be relevant to the other proceedings, in particular the progress made in lodging and verifying claims and all measures aimed at terminating the proceedings.

31(2)   [Duty of liquidators to cooperate] Subject to the rules applicable to each of the proceedings, the liquidator in the main proceedings and the liquidators in the secondary proceedings shall be duty bound to cooperate with each other.

31(3)   [Duty of liquidator in secondary proceedings] The liquidator in the secondary proceedings shall give the liquidator in the main proceedings an early opportunity of submitting proposals on the liquidation or use of the assets in the secondary proceedings.

GENERAL NOTE

This article directs the liquidators in all the proceedings in quite peremptory terms to communicate information to each other and to co-operate with each other. That it applies between the liquidators in secondary proceedings *inter se* appears from the use of "the liquidators" in the plural. The secondary liquidator's obligation to receive proposals under para.3 is more than a matter of mere courtesy: it is backed by the extensive powers of intervention conferred on the main liquidator by arts 33 et seq. In *Re Nortel Networks SA* [2009] EWHC 206 (Ch); [2009] B.C.C. 343 it was accepted that the duty to co-operate imposed on office-holders by art.31(1) has been treated by the courts of Member States as incorporating a wider obligation extending to the courts which have the control of insolvency procedures. Accordingly, Patten J. at the request of the administrators of main proceedings in this jurisdiction issued letters of request to the courts of other Member States asking those courts to put in place arrangements under which the administrators would be given notice of any request or application for the opening of secondary proceedings there and giving the administrators an opportunity to be heard on any such application, so that they could explain to the foreign court why such proceedings would not be in the interests of the creditors. However, the obligation to co-operate does not extend to requiring a liquidator to apply assets otherwise than in accordance with the Regulation: *Re Alitalia Linee Aeree Italiane SpA* [2011] EWHC 15 (Ch); [2011] B.C.C. 579.

Article 32

[Exercise of creditors' rights]

32(1)   [Lodgement of claim] Any creditor may lodge his claim in the main proceedings and in any secondary proceedings.

32(2)   [Lodgement in other proceedings] The liquidators in the main and any secondary proceedings shall lodge in other proceedings claims which have already been lodged in the proceedings for which they were appointed, provided that the interests of creditors in the latter proceedings are served thereby, subject to the right of creditors to oppose that or to withdraw the lodgement of their claims where the law applicable so provides.

32(3)   [Liquidator's power] The liquidator in the main or secondary proceedings shall be empowered to participate in other proceedings on the same basis as a creditor, in particular by attending creditors' meetings.

GENERAL NOTE

There is an inconsistency here with the Preamble para.21, which states that every creditor "who has his habitual residence, domicile or registered office in the Community" should have the right to lodge a claim in each of the insolvency proceedings pending in the Community relating to the debtor's assets—a formula which is repeated in art.39. It may well be that art.32 should be read also subject to this restriction, so that a non-EU creditor could not claim to be entitled to prove by virtue of this provision. However, the point will not arise in UK proceedings, since the domestic law has always allowed foreign creditors to prove, wherever they are based.

The right of liquidators to participate in each others' proceedings on the same basis as a creditor, and in particular to prove on behalf of their own creditors in such proceedings, has been confirmed by changes to the Rules: see IR 1986 rr.2.133, 7.64. Rules 4.84 and 6.106 provide for the withdrawal of a proof in liquidation and bankruptcy proceedings.

Article 33

[Stay of liquidation]

33(1)   [Court to stay secondary proceedings on liquidator's request] The court, which opened the secondary proceedings, shall stay the process of liquidation in whole or in part on receipt of a request from the liquidator in the main proceedings, provided that in that event it may require the liquidator in the main proceedings to take any suitable measure to guarantee the interests of the creditors in the secondary proceedings and of individual classes of creditors. Such a request from the liquidator may be rejected only if it is manifestly of no interest to the creditors in the main proceedings. Such a stay of the process of liquidation may be ordered for up to three months. It may be continued or renewed for similar periods.

33(2) **[Termination of stay]** The court referred to in paragraph 1 shall terminate the stay of the process of liquidation:

– at the request of the liquidator in the main proceedings,

– of its own motion, at the request of a creditor or at the request of the liquidator in the secondary proceedings if that measure no longer appears justified, in particular, by the interests of creditors in the main proceedings or in the secondary proceedings.

GENERAL NOTE

Although this article uses the word "shall", the court is in fact given a considerable amount of discretion in deciding whether or not to grant a stay, in particular to secure the position of local creditors.

Article 34

[Measures ending secondary insolvency proceedings]

34(1) **[Liquidator's power to propose closure of secondary proceedings]** Where the law applicable to secondary proceedings allows for such proceedings to be closed without liquidation by a rescue plan, a composition or a comparable measure, the liquidator in the main proceedings shall be empowered to propose such a measure himself.

Closure of the secondary proceedings by a measure referred to in the first subparagraph shall not become final without the consent of the liquidator in the main proceedings; failing his agreement, however, it may become final if the financial interests of the creditors in the main proceedings are not affected by the measure proposed.

34(2) **[Creditors' consent required to restrictions]** Any restriction of creditors' rights arising from a measure referred to in paragraph 1 which is proposed in secondary proceedings, such as a stay of payment or discharge of debt, may not have effect in respect of the debtor's assets not covered by those proceedings without the consent of all the creditors having an interest.

34(3) **[Position during stay]** During a stay of the process of liquidation ordered pursuant to Article 33, only the liquidator in the main proceedings or the debtor, with the former's consent, may propose measures laid down in paragraph 1 of this Article in the secondary proceedings; no other proposal for such a measure shall be put to the vote or approved.

(See General Note after art.35.)

Article 35

[Assets remaining in the secondary proceedings]

35 If by the liquidation of assets in the secondary proceedings it is possible to meet all claims allowed under those proceedings, the liquidator appointed in those proceedings shall immediately transfer any assets remaining to the liquidator in the main proceedings.

GENERAL NOTE TO ARTS 34, 35

Although secondary proceedings may be *opened* only in the form of winding-up proceedings (a term which includes bankruptcy and sequestration: see Annex B), art.34 contemplates that such proceedings may be terminated by a rescue plan or composition—e.g. a CVA or IVA, an administration or a scheme of arrangement under CA 2006 Pt 26. The liquidator in the main proceedings may himself propose such an outcome, while the concluding sentence in art.34 gives him a limited power of veto where it is proposed by anyone else. He alone (or the debtor with his consent) may make such a proposal if the liquidation has been stayed under art.33.

On art.34(2), see the note to art.17(2).

Art.35

While secondary proceedings are operative in a Member State, the liquidator in the main proceedings is debarred from using his normal power to remove assets from that jurisdiction to his own under art.18(1). Where there is a surplus after meeting the claims of local creditors, art.35 does not merely reinstate that right, but directs the secondary liquidator to remit the assets to him.

Article 36

[Subsequent opening of the main proceedings]

36 Where the proceedings referred to in Article 3(1) are opened following the opening of the proceedings referred to in Article 3(2) in another Member State, Articles 31 to 35 shall apply to those opened first, in so far as the progress of those proceedings so permits.

(See General Note after art.37.)

Article 37

[Conversion of earlier proceedings]

37 The liquidator in the main proceedings may request that proceedings listed in Annex A previously opened in another Member State be converted into winding-up proceedings if this proves to be in the interests of the creditors in the main proceedings.

The court with jurisdiction under Article 3(2) shall order conversion into one of the proceedings listed in Annex B.

GENERAL NOTE TO ARTS 36, 37

These articles deal with the position where main proceedings are opened in the State of the debtor's centre of main interests at a time when territorial proceedings are already under way in another State. Article 36 brings into play the provisions of arts 31–35, subject to any necessary modifications. Article 37 is more radical, giving the main liquidator the power to apply to have the territorial proceedings converted into winding-up (or bankruptcy) proceedings, so bringing the situation into line with secondary proceedings. Although it would appear from a reading of art.37 that the court has no option but to accede to such a request from the main liquidator (or, at the very most, require to be satisfied that conversion will be in the interests of the creditors in the main proceedings), the amendments made to the Rules assume that the court is entitled in its discretion to take account of "all other matters" that may be considered relevant in deciding whether or not to make an order (see IR 1986 rr.1.31–1.33, *2.59–2.61,* 2.130–2.132, 5.31A–5.33).

Article 38

[Preservation measures]

38 Where the court of a Member State which has jurisdiction pursuant to Article 3(1) appoints a temporary administrator in order to ensure the preservation of the debtor's assets, that temporary administrator shall be empowered to request any measures to secure and preserve any of the debtor's assets situated in another Member State, provided for under the law of that State, for the period between the request for the opening of insolvency proceedings and the judgment opening the proceedings.

GENERAL NOTE

Article 38 applies only in main proceedings, and deals with the position before a moratorium would come into force automatically under art.17(1). The "temporary administrator" who is empowered to request a stay, etc. in other Member States would plainly include a provisional liquidator. Whether art.38 could be invoked to enforce the moratorium which comes into force after a petition or application for an administration order has been presented (IA 1986 s.10(1), Sch.B1 para.44), notice of intention to appoint an administrator has been given under Sch.B1 paras 26, 44(2), or an interim order has been made pending the approval of an IVA (s.252) is doubtful, since neither involves the appointment of a person to act as "temporary administrator". However, if the court in such a case were to appoint an interim manager or a receiver (see the note to IA 1986 s.9(4), (5)), this difficulty could perhaps be overcome.

CHAPTER IV

PROVISION OF INFORMATION FOR CREDITORS AND LODGEMENT OF THEIR CLAIMS

Article 39

[Right to lodge claims]

39 Any creditor who has his habitual residence, domicile or registered office in a Member State other than the State of the opening of proceedings, including the tax authorities and social security authorities of Member States, shall have the right to lodge claims in the insolvency proceedings in writing.

(See General Note after art.42.)

Article 40

[Duty to inform creditors]

40(1) **[Notification of proceedings to creditors in other Member States]** As soon as insolvency proceedings are opened in a Member State, the court of that State having jurisdiction or the liquidator appointed by it shall immediately inform known creditors who have their habitual residences, domiciles or registered offices in the other Member States.

40(2) **[Content of notice]** That information, provided by an individual notice, shall in particular include time limits, the penalties laid down in regard to those time limits, the body or authority empowered to accept the lodgement of claims and the other measures laid down. Such notice shall also indicate whether creditors whose claims are preferential or secured in rem need lodge their claims.

(See General Note after art.42.)

Article 41

[Content of the lodgement of a claim]

41 A creditor shall send copies of supporting documents, if any, and shall indicate the nature of the claim, the date on which it arose and its amount, as well as whether he alleges preference, security in rem or a reservation of title in respect of the claim and what assets are covered by the guarantee he is invoking.

(See General Note after art.42.)

Article 42

[Languages]

42(1) **[Information in official language]** The information provided for in Article 40 shall be provided in the official language or one of the official languages of the State of the opening of proceedings. For that purpose a form shall be used bearing the heading "Invitation to lodge a claim. Time limits to be observed" in all the official languages of the institutions of the European Union.

42(2) **[Lodgement of claim in official language]** Any creditor who has his habitual residence, domicile or registered office in a Member State other than the State of the opening of proceedings may lodge his claim in the official language or one of the official languages of that other State. In that event, however, the lodgement of his claim shall bear the heading "Lodgement of claim" in the official language or one of the official languages of the State of the opening of proceedings. In addition, he may be required to provide a translation into the official language or one of the official languages of the State of the opening of proceedings.

GENERAL NOTE TO ARTS 39–42

These articles apply in all forms of insolvency proceedings, whether main, secondary or territorial.

Art.39

As noted in the comment to art.32(1), there is some inconsistency between these two articles. It would appear that a creditor must be based in the Community before he can assert the right under the Regulation to prove in another Member State, but that this would not rule out the right given to any other foreign creditor to prove in an insolvency under the domestic law of the particular proceedings (see art.4(2)(g)). The express inclusion of the tax and social security authorities among the permitted claimants is a remarkable change from the traditional position—although some other Crown debts, such as fines, will continue to be unenforceable abroad.

Art.40

Note the link with art.42(1), which requires the information to be given on a form bearing a heading in all the official languages of the institutions of the EU. See the note to art.42(1).

Art.41

New forms of proof of debt for use in winding-up and bankruptcy proceedings (Forms 4.25, 6.37) have been prescribed. No forms are prescribed for use in other insolvency proceedings, but the requirements of this article should be noted.

Art.42

Note the requirement that the form giving the information required by art.40 must bear a heading in *all* the official languages of the institutions of the EU (presumably including Danish, even though Denmark is not within the Regulation). This must be strictly observed: *R Jung GmbH v SIFA* [2006] B.C.C. 678. The Insolvency Service has published a list of all these headings in the 23 official languages of the EU (and also in Russian): see *Dear IP*, July 2009, p.17.120, Schedule A. (Also available on *http://ec.europa.eu/education/languages/languages-of-europe/doc135_en.htm*.) Some of the foreign scripts may present a challenge! Also set out on p.17.122, Schedule B are the phrases equivalent to "Lodgement of claim" in all of these languages, required by art.42(2); but in this case the heading need only be in *one* language, viz. an official language of the State of the opening of proceedings.

CHAPTER V

TRANSITIONAL AND FINAL PROVISIONS

Article 43

[Applicability in time]

43 The provisions of this Regulation shall apply only to insolvency proceedings opened after its entry into force. Acts done by a debtor before the entry into force of this Regulation shall continue to be governed by the law which was applicable to them at the time they were done.

(See General Note after art.44.)

Article 44

[Relationship to Conventions]

44(1) **[Conventions replaced]** After its entry into force, this Regulation replaces, in respect of the matters referred to therein, in the relations between Member States, the Conventions concluded between two or more Member States, in particular:

(a) the Convention between Belgium and France on Jurisdiction and the Validity and Enforcement of Judgments, Arbitration Awards and Authentic Instruments, signed at Paris on 8 July 1899;

(b) the Convention between Belgium and Austria on Bankruptcy, Winding-up, Arrangements, Compositions and Suspension of Payments (with Additional Protocol of 13 June 1973), signed at Brussels on 16 July 1969;

(c)   the Convention between Belgium and the Netherlands on Territorial Jurisdiction, Bankruptcy and the Validity and Enforcement of Judgments, Arbitration Awards and Authentic Instruments, signed at Brussels on 28 March 1925;

(d)   the Treaty between Germany and Austria on Bankruptcy, Winding-up, Arrangements and Compositions, signed at Vienna on 25 May 1979;

(e)   the Convention between France and Austria on Jurisdiction, Recognition and Enforcement of Judgments on Bankruptcy, signed at Vienna on 27 February 1979;

(f)   the Convention between France and Italy on the Enforcement of Judgments in Civil and Commercial Matters, signed at Rome on 3 June 1930;

(g)   the Convention between Italy and Austria on Bankruptcy, Winding-up, Arrangements and Compositions, signed at Rome on 12 July 1977;

(h)   the Convention between the Kingdom of the Netherlands and the Federal Republic of Germany on the Mutual Recognition and Enforcement of Judgments and other Enforceable Instruments in Civil and Commercial Matters, signed at The Hague on 30 August 1962;

(i)   the Convention between the United Kingdom and the Kingdom of Belgium providing for the Reciprocal Enforcement of Judgments in Civil and Commercial Matters, with Protocol, signed at Brussels on 2 May 1934;

(j)   the Convention between Denmark, Finland, Norway, Sweden and Iceland on Bankruptcy, signed at Copenhagen on 7 November 1933;

(k)   the European Convention on Certain International Aspects of Bankruptcy, signed at Istanbul on 5 June 1990.

(l)   the Convention between the Federative People's Republic of Yugoslavia and the Kingdom of Greece on the Mutual Recognition and Enforcement of Judgments, signed at Athens on 18 June 1959;

(m) the Agreement between the Federative People's Republic of Yugoslavia and the Republic of Austria on the Mutual Recognition and Enforcement of Arbitral Awards and Arbitral Settlements in Commercial Matters, signed at Belgrade on 18 March 1960;

(n)   the Convention between the Federative People's Republic of Yugoslavia and the Republic of Italy on Mutual Judicial Cooperation in Civil and Administrative Matters, signed at Rome on 3 December 1960;

(o)   the Agreement between the Socialist Federative Republic of Yugoslavia and the Kingdom of Belgium on Judicial Cooperation in Civil and Commercial Matters, signed at Belgrade on 24 September 1971;

(p)   the Convention between the Governments of Yugoslavia and France on the Recognition and Enforcement of Judgments in Civil and Commercial Matters, signed at Paris on 18 May 1971;

(q)   the Agreement between the Czechoslovak Socialist Republic and the Hellenic Republic on Legal Aid in Civil and Criminal Matters, signed at Athens on 22 October 1980, still in force between the Czech Republic and Greece;

(r)   the Agreement between the Czechoslovak Socialist Republic and the Republic of Cyprus on Legal Aid in Civil and Criminal Matters, signed at Nicosia on 23 April 1982, still in force between the Czech Republic and Cyprus;

(s)   the Treaty between the Government of the Czechoslovak Socialist Republic and the Government of the Republic of France on Legal Aid and the Recognition and Enforcement of Judgments in Civil, Family and Commercial Matters, signed at Paris on 10 May 1984, still in force between the Czech Republic and France;

(t) the Treaty between the Czechoslovak Socialist Republic and the Italian Republic on Legal Aid in Civil and Criminal Matters, signed at Prague on 6 December 1985, still in force between the Czech Republic and Italy;

(u) the Agreement between the Republic of Latvia, the Republic of Estonia and the Republic of Lithuania on Legal Assistance and Legal Relationships, signed at Tallinn on 11 November 1992;

(v) the Agreement between Estonia and Poland on Granting Legal Aid and Legal Relations on Civil, Labour and Criminal Matters, signed at Tallinn on 27 November 1998;

(w) the Agreement between the Republic of Lithuania and the Republic of Poland on Legal Assistance and Legal Relations in Civil, Family, Labour and Criminal Matters, signed in Warsaw on 26 January 1993;

(x) the Convention between Socialist Republic of Romania and the Hellenic Republic on legal assistance in civil and criminal matters and its Protocol, signed at Bucharest on 19 October 1972;

(y) the Convention between Socialist Republic of Romania and the French Republic on legal assistance in civil and commercial matters, signed at Paris on 5 November 1974;

(z) the Agreement between the People's Republic of Bulgaria and the Hellenic Republic on Legal Assistance in Civil and Criminal Matters, signed at Athens on 10 April 1976;

(aa) the Agreement between the People's Republic of Bulgaria and the Republic of Cyprus on Legal Assistance in Civil and Criminal Matters, signed at Nicosia on 29 April 1983;

(ab) the Agreement between the Government of the People's Republic of Bulgaria and the Government of the French Republic on Mutual Legal Assistance in Civil Matters, signed at Sofia on 18 January 1989;

(ac) the Treaty between Romania and the Czech Republic on judicial assistance in civil matters, signed at Bucharest on 11 July 1994;

(ad) the Treaty between Romania and Poland on legal assistance and legal relations in civil cases, signed at Bucharest on 15 May 1999.

History
Paragraph 44(1)(l)–(q) inserted by the Act of Accession of 2003 Annex II Ch.18 art.44(1) as from May 1, 2004; para.44(1)(r)–(ad) inserted by EC Regulation 1791/2006 Annex Ch.11 para.A(1)(a) as from January 1, 2007.

44(2)   [Proceedings commenced prior to operation of Regulation] The Conventions referred to in paragraph 1 shall continue to have effect with regard to proceedings opened before the entry into force of this Regulation.

44(3)   [Non-application] This Regulation shall not apply:

(a) in any Member State, to the extent that it is irreconcilable with the obligations arising in relation to bankruptcy from a convention concluded by that State with one or more third countries before the entry into force of this Regulation;

(b) in the United Kingdom of Great Britain and Northern Ireland, to the extent that is irreconcilable with the obligations arising in relation to bankruptcy and the winding-up of insolvent companies from any arrangements with the Commonwealth existing at the time this Regulation enters into force.

GENERAL NOTE TO ARTS 43–44

Articles 43 and 44(2) make it clear that the Regulation is not retrospective, so as to apply to proceedings opened before May 31, 2002. However, it must be borne in mind that the term "opened" refers to the time when the proceedings take effect, and not (e.g.) to the time of presentation of a petition for a bankruptcy or winding-up order (see the note to art.2(f)). In *Re Ultra Motorhomes International Ltd* [2005] EWHC 872 (Ch); [2006] B.C.C. 57 the company had gone into a CVA and later into liquidation. The EC Regulation came into force between these events. The court was concerned with an application made by the supervisor of the CVA, to which the liquidator was not a party. It was held that the Regulation did not apply to these proceedings, which were purely a matter within the CVA.

Art.44

Few will be aware of the Convention referred to in para.1(i): it is not referred to in leading textbooks. Anyway, it is now spent!

The UK has not signed the Istanbul Convention (para.1(k)), which is in any event now superseded within the EU by the present Convention.

The purpose of para.3(b) is obscure. Even if "with the Commonwealth" is to be read as "within the Commonwealth" or as "with other members of the Commonwealth", it has no obvious application, although it may perhaps to be taken as a clumsy and ill-informed allusion to the procedure under IA 1986 s.426.

Article 45

[Amendment of the Annexes]

45 The Council, acting by qualified majority on the initiative of one of its members or on a proposal from the Commission, may amend the Annexes.

GENERAL NOTE

See for example Council Regulation 603/2005.

Article 46

[Reports]

46 No later than 1 June 2012, and every five years thereafter, the Commission shall present to the European Parliament, the Council and the Economic and Social Committee a report on the application of this Regulation. The report shall be accompanied if need be by a proposal for adaptation of this Regulation.

Article 47

[Entry into force]

47 This Regulation shall enter into force on 31 May 2002.

This Regulation shall be binding in its entirety and directly applicable in the Member States in accordance with the Treaty establishing the European Community.

Done at Brussels, 29 May 2000.

Insolvency proceedings referred to in Article 2(a)

BELGIQUE/BELGIË

— Het faillissement/La faillite

— De gerechtelijke reorganisatie door een collectief akkoord/La réorganisation judiciaire par accord collectif

— De gerechtelijke reorganisatie door overdracht onder gerechtelijk gezag/La réorganisation judiciaire par transfert sous autorité de justice

— De collectieve schuldenregeling/Le règlement collectif de dettes

— De vrijwillige vereffening/La liquidation volontaire

— De gerechtelijke vereffening/La liquidation judiciaire

— De voorlopige ontneming van beheer, bepaald in artikel 8 van de faillissementswet/Le dessaisissement provisoire, visé à l'article 8 de la loi sur les faillites

БЪЛГАРИЯ

— Производство по несъстоятелност

ČESKÁ REPUBLIKA

— Konkurs

— Reorganizace

— Oddlužení

DEUTSCHLAND

— Das Konkursverfahren

— Das gerichtliche Vergleichsverfahren

— Das Gesamtvollstreckungsverfahren

— Das Insolvenzverfahren

EESTI

— Pankrotimenetlus

EIRE/IRELAND

— Compulsory winding up by the court

— Bankruptcy

— The administration in bankruptcy of the estate of persons dying insolvent

— Winding-up in bankruptcy of partnerships

— Creditors' voluntary winding up (with confirmation of a court)

— Arrangements under the control of the court which involve the vesting of all or part of the property of the debtor in the Official Assignee for realisation and distribution

— Company examinership

ΕΛΛΑΣ

— Η πτώχευση

— Η ειδική εκκαθάριση

— Η προσωρινή διαχείριση εταιρείας. Η διοίκηση και διαχείριση των πιστωτών

— Η υπαγωγή επιχείρησης υπό επίτροπο με σκοπό τη σύναψη συμβιβασμού με τους πιστωτές

ESPAÑA

— Concurso

FRANCE

— Sauvegarde

— Redressement judiciaire

— Liquidation judiciaire

ITALIA

— Fallimento

— Concordato preventivo

— Liquidazione coatta amministrativa

— Amministrazione straordinaria

ΚΥΠΡΟΣ

— Υποχρεωτική εκκαθάριση από το Δικαστήριο

— Εκούσια εκκαθάριση από πιστωτές κατόπιν Δικαστικού Διατάγματος

— Εκούσια εκκαθάριση από μέλη

— Εκκαθάριση με την εποπτεία του Δικαοτηρίου

— Πτώχευση κατόπιν Δικαοτικού Διατάγματος

— Διαχείριση της περιουσίας προσώπων που απεβίωσαν αφερέγγυα

LATVIJA

— Juridiskās personas maksātnespējas process

— Fiziskās personas maksātnespējas process

LIETUVA

— Įmonės restruktūrizavimo byla

— Įmonės bankroto byla

— Įmonės bankroto procesas ne teismo tvarka

LUXEMBOURG

— Faillite

— Gestion contrôlée

— Concordat préventif de faillite (par abandon d'actif)

— Régime spécial de liquidation du notariat

MAGYARORSZÁG

— Csődeljárás

— Felszámolási eljárás

MALTA

— Xoljiment

— Amministrazzjoni

— Stralċ volontarju mill-membri jew mill-kredituri

— Stralċ mill-Qorti

— Falliment f'każ ta' negozjant

NEDERLAND

— Het faillissement

— De surséance van betaling

— De schuldsaneringsregeling natuurlijke personen

ÖSTERREICH

— Das Konkursverfahren (Insolvenzverfahren)

— Das Sanierungsverfahren ohne Eigenverwaltung (Insolvenzverfahren)

— Das Sanierungsverfahren mit Eigenverwaltung (Insolvenzverfahren)

— Das Schuldenregulierungsverfahren

— Das Abschöpfungsverfahren

— Das Ausgleichsverfahren

POLSKA

— Postępowanie upadłościowe

— Postępowanie układowe

— Upadłość obejmująca likwidację

— Upadłość z możliwością zawarcia układu

PORTUGAL

— Processo de insolvência

— Processo de falência

— Processos especiais de recuperação de empresa, ou seja:

— Concordata

— Reconstituição empresarial

— Reestruturação financeira

— Gestão controlada

ROMÂNIA

— Procedura insolvenţei

— Reorganizarea judiciară

— Procedura falimentului

SLOVENIJA

— Stečajni postopek

— Skrajšani stečajni postopek

— Postopek prisilne poravnave

— Prisilna poravnava v stečaju

SLOVENSKO

— Konkurzné konanie

— Reštrukturalizačné konanie

SUOMI/FINLAND

— Konkurssi/konkurs

— Yrityssaneeraus/företagssanering

SVERIGE

— Konkurs

— Företagsrekonstruktion

UNITED KINGDOM

— Winding up by or subject to the supervision of the court

— Creditors' voluntary winding up (with confirmation by the court)

— Administration, including appointments made by filing prescribed documents with the court

— Voluntary arrangements under insolvency legislation

— Bankruptcy or sequestration

GENERAL NOTE

See the note to arts 1(1) and 2(a). Although art.2(a) suggests that the list of proceedings in Annex A is definitive, it appears that other collective proceedings (e.g. the administration of the insolvent estates of deceased persons, and insolvent partnerships, both of which are listed by Ireland) are not excluded.

Winding up subject to the supervision of the court has been abolished in the UK, but not in Gibraltar.

Entries for the 10 new Member States were added as from May 1, 2004 by the Treaty and Act of Accession of April 16, 2003, Annex 2 s.81.A (see [2003] O.J. L236/711). The text of Annex A was wholly substituted by EC Council Regulation 603/2005 ([2005] O.J. L100/1) as from April 1, 2005, and again by EC Council Regulation 694/2006 ([2006] O.J. L121/1) as from May 7, 2006. The text was again wholly replaced by EC Council Regulation 681/2007 ([2007] O.J. L159/1) in order to accommodate the expansion of EU membership so as to include the insolvency proceedings of Bulgaria and Romania and to incorporate amendments notified by other member States. These changes took effect from June 21, 2007 (apart from certain amendments notified by the Czech Republic, which apply from January 1, 2008). Modifications to the entries for Latvia in Annexes A and B were made by EC Council Regulation 788/2008 ([2008] O.J. L213/1) as from July 24, 2008. Further amendments to the entries for Belgium in Annexes A, B and C were made by Regulation 210/2010 as from April 2, 2010, and to the entries for Austria and Latvia by Regulation 583/2011 as from July 8, 2011. The UK entry now makes it clear that administrations made by an out of court appointment are included.

Annex B

Winding up proceedings referred to in Article 2(c)

BELGIQUE/BELGIË

— Het faillissement/La faillite

— De vrijwillige vereffening/La liquidation volontaire

— De gerechtelijke vereffening/La liquidation judiciaire

— De gerechtelijke reorganisatie door overdracht onder gerechtelijk gezag/La réorganisation judiciaire par transfert sous autorité de justice

БЪЛГАРИЯ

— Производство по несъстоятелност

ČESKÁ REPUBLIKA

— Konkurs

DEUTSCHLAND

— Das Konkursverfahren

— Das Gesamtvollstreckungsverfahren

— Das Insolvenzverfahren

EESTI

— Pankrotimenetlus

EIRE/IRELAND

— Compulsory winding up

— Bankruptcy

— The administration in bankruptcy of the estate of persons dying insolvent

— Winding-up in bankruptcy of partnerships

— Creditors' voluntary winding up (with confirmation of a court)

— Arrangements under the control of the court which involve the vesting of all or part of the property of the debtor in the Official Assignee for realisation and distribution

ΕΛΛΑΣ

— Η πτώχευση

— Η ειδική εκκαθάριση

ESPAÑA

— Concurso

FRANCE

— Liquidation judiciaire

ITALIA

— Fallimento

— Concordato preventivo con cessione dei beni

— Liquidazione coatta amministrativa

— Amministrazione straordinaria con programma di cessione dei complessi aziendali

— Amministrazione straordinaria con programma di ristrutturazione di cui sia parte integrante un concordato con cessione dei beni

ΚΥΠΡΟΣ

— Υποχρεωτική εκκαθάριση από το Δικαστήριο

— Εκκαθάριση με την εποπτεία του Δικαοτηρίου

— Εκούσια εκκαθάριση από πιοτωτές (με την επικύρωση του Δικαοτηρίου)

— Πτώχευση

— Διαχείριση της περιουσίας προσώπων που απεβίωσαν αφερέγγυα

LATVIJA

— Juridiskās personas maksātnespējas process

— Fiziskās personas maksātnespējas process

LIETUVA

— Įmonės bankroto byla

— Įmonės bankroto procesas ne teismo tvarka

LUXEMBOURG

— Faillite

— Régime spécial de liquidation du notariat

MAGYARORSZÁG

— Felszámolási eljárás

MALTA

— Stralċ volontarju

— Stralċ mill-Qorti

— Falliment inkluż il-ħruġ ta' mandat ta' qbid mill-Kuratur f'każ ta' negozjant fallut

NEDERLAND

— Het faillissement

— De schuldsaneringsregeling natuurlijke personen

ÖSTERREICH

— Das Konkursverfahren (Insolvenzverfahren)

POLSKA

— Postępowanie upadłościowe

— Upadłość obejmująca likwidację

PORTUGAL

— Processo de insolvência

— Processo de falência

ROMÂNIA

— Procedura falimentului

SLOVENIJA

— Stečajni postopek

— Skrajšani stečajni postopek

SLOVENSKO

— Konkurzné konanie

SUOMI/FINLAND

— Konkurssi/konkurs

SVERIGE

— Konkurs

UNITED KINGDOM

— Winding up by or subject to the supervision of the court

— Winding up through administration, including appointments made by filing prescribed documents with the court

— Creditors' voluntary winding up (with confirmation by the court)

— Bankruptcy or sequestration

GENERAL NOTE

See the General Note to Annex A. "Winding up through administration" may be a reference to IA 1986 Sch.B1 para.13(1)(e), but the intended meaning is not clear.

Annex C

Liquidators referred to in Article 2(b)

BELGIQUE/BELGIË

— De curator/Le curateur

— De gedelegeerd rechter/Le juge-délégué

— De gerechtsmandataris/Le mandataire de justice

— De schuldbemiddelaar/Le médiateur de dettes

— De vereffenaar/Le liquidateur

— De voorlopige bewindvoerder/ L'administrateur provisoire

БЪЛГАРИЯ

— Назначен предварително временен синдик

— Временен синдик

— (Постоянен) синдик

— Служебен синдик

ČESKÁ REPUBLIKA

— Insolvenční správce

— Předběžný insolvenční správce

— Oddělený insolvenční správce

— Zvláštní insolvenční správce

— Zástupce insolvenčního správce

DEUTSCHLAND

— Konkursverwalter

— Vergleichsverwalter

— Sachwalter (nach der Vergleichsordnung)

— Verwalter

— Insolvenzverwalter

— Sachwalter (nach der Insolvenzordnung)

— Treuhänder

— Vorläufiger Insolvenzverwalter

EESTI

— Pankrotihaldur

— Ajutine pankrotihaldur

— Usaldusisik

EIRE/IRELAND

— Liquidator

— Official Assignee

— Trustee in bankruptcy

— Provisional Liquidator

— Examiner

ΕΛΛΑΣ

— Ο σύνδικος

— Ο προσωρινός διαχειριστής. Η διοικούσα επιτροπή των πιστωτών

— Ο ειδικός εκκαθαριστής

— Ο επίτροπος

ESPAÑA

— Administradores concursales

FRANCE

— Mandataire judiciaire

— Liquidateur

— Administrateur judiciaire

— Commissaire à l'exécution du plan

ITALIA

— Curatore

— Commissario giudiziale

— Commissario straordinario

— Commissario liquidatore

— Liquidatore giudiziale

ΚΥΠΡΟΣ

— Εκκαθαριστής και Προσωρινός Εκκαθαριστής

— Επίσημος Παραλήπτης

— Διαχειριστής της Πτώχευσης

— Εξεταστής

LATVIJA

— Maksātnespējas procesa administrators

LIETUVA

— Bankrutuojančių įmonių administratorius

— Restruktūrizuojamų įmonių administratorius

LUXEMBOURG

— Le curateur

— Le commissaire

— Le liquidateur

— Le conseil de gérance de la section d'assainissement du notariat

MAGYARORSZÁG

— Vagyonfelügyelő

— Felszámoló

MALTA

— Amministratur Proviżorju

— Riċevitur Uffiċjali

— Stralċjarju

— Manager Speċjali

— Kuraturi f'każ ta' proċeduri ta' falliment

NEDERLAND

— De curator in het faillissement

— De bewindvoerder in de surséance van betaling

— De bewindvoerder in de schuldsaneringsregeling natuurlijke personen

ÖSTERREICH

— Masseverwalter

— Sanierungsverwalter

— Ausgleichsverwalter

— Besonderer Verwalter

— Einstweiliger Verwalter

— Sachwalter

— Treuhänder

— Insolvenzgericht

— Konkursgericht

POLSKA

— Syndyk

— Nadzorca sądowy

— Zarządca

PORTUGAL

— Administrador da insolvência

— Gestor judicial

— Liquidatário judicial

— Comissão de credores

ROMÂNIA

— Practician în insolvenţă

— Administrator judiciar

— Lichidator

SLOVENIJA

— Upravitelj prisilne poravnave

— Stečajni upravitelj

— Sodišče, pristojno za postopek prisilne poravnave

— Sodišče, pristojno za stečajni postopek

SLOVENSKO

— Predbežný správca

— Správca

SUOMI/FINLAND

— Pesänhoitaja/boförvaltare

— Selvittäjä/utredare

SVERIGE

— Förvaltare

— Rekonstruktör

UNITED KINGDOM

— Liquidator

— Supervisor of a voluntary arrangement

— Administrator

— Official Receiver

— Trustee

— Provisional Liquidator

— Judicial factor

GENERAL NOTE

See the General Note to Annex A.

UNCITRAL Model Law on Cross-Border Insolvency

Adopted by the UN Commission on International Trade Law (UNCITRAL) on May 30, 1997 and formally agreed by the UN General Assembly on December 15, 1997.

[**Note:** The text of the UNCITRAL Model Law, as formally agreed, is not reproduced here, since it is not part of the law of the UK but has been superseded for this purpose by Sch.1 to the Cross-Border Insolvency Regulations 2006 (below). However, since the Preamble to the Model Law has not been incorporated into Sch.1 and may be relevant for reference as an aid to interpretation of the Regulations, it is set out below.

The following have so far adopted legislation based on the Model Law: Australia, Republic of Korea, Colombia, Eritrea, Japan, Mexico, New Zealand, Poland, Romania, Montenegro, Serbia, South Africa, Great Britain, British Virgin Islands, United States of America, Mauritius, Slovenia, Canada, Greece.]

Preamble

The purpose of the present Law is to provide effective mechanisms for dealing with cases of cross-border insolvency so as to promote the objectives of:

(a) cooperation between the courts and other competent authorities of this State and foreign States involved in cases of cross-border insolvency;

(b) greater legal certainty for trade and investment;

(c) fair and efficient administration or cross-border insolvencies that protects the interests of all creditors and other interested persons, including the debtor;

(d) protection and maximization of the value of the debtor's assets;

(e) facilitation of the rescue of financially troubled businesses, thereby protecting investment and preserving employment.

Cross-Border Insolvency Regulations 2006

(SI 2006/1030)

Made on April 3, 2006 by the Secretary of State with the agreement of the Lord Chancellor and the Scottish Ministers. Operative from April 4, 2006.

Introductory note to the Regulations

These Regulations (the "CBIR") enact legislation for England and Wales and for Scotland based on the provisions of the Model Law on Cross-Border Insolvency which was adopted by the UN Commission on International Trade Law (UNCITRAL) on May 30, 1997 and later, on December 15 of that year, formally agreed by the UN General Assembly. The Preamble to the UNCITRAL Model Law is reproduced above. The original text of the Model Law is to be found in the Official Records of the General Assembly, 52nd Session, Supplement No.17. (For access to this text and related documents, see the note to reg.2.)

Comparable legislation has since been enacted for Northern Ireland: see the Cross-Border Insolvency Regulations (Northern Ireland) 2007 (SR 2007/115, effective April 12, 2007). These Regulations in Sch.1 provide a version of the Model Law as adapted for Northern Ireland.

The Model Law itself has no force either as legislation or as a treaty: instead, it is designed for use as a precedent by the legislative draftsman in any jurisdiction which is seeking to reform its law on cross-border insolvency. But it has the further objective of seeking to bring about the harmonisation of the laws of different countries, as they individually enact legislation based on the same model; and this will be enhanced as the courts in those jurisdictions have regard to judicial rulings and academic writings in other enacting States.

The principal objects of the Model Law are:

- to facilitate the recognition in one jurisdiction of insolvency proceedings which have been instituted in another, and similarly the recognition of the authority of the office-holder in such proceedings;

- to give foreign creditors access to local courts and allow them to participate in local insolvency proceedings;

- where insolvency proceedings have been, or are about to be, instituted in more than one jurisdiction, to establish an orderly regime to regulate the relationship between them;

- to encourage co-operation between the courts, office-holders and other competent authorities involved in cross-border insolvency proceedings.

Provision was made for the adoption of the Model Law in this country in the Insolvency Act 2000 s.14. Regulations with this in view were published in draft form by the Insolvency Service of the DTI on August 22, 2005 as part of a consultation exercise, and revised in the light of responses to that consultation before being put before Parliament in March, 2006, and ultimately enacted as the CBIR on April 3, 2006. Regulation 2 provides that the UNCITRAL Model Law shall have the force of law in Great Britain "in the form set out in Schedule 1" to the Regulations, "which contains the UNCITRAL Model Law with certain modifications to adapt it for application in Great Britain". It is therefore the text of Sch.1 rather than that of the UNCITRAL Model Law that is the primary formulation of the law for this country; but reg.2(2) directs that the latter, together with other relevant UNCITRAL documents, may be considered in ascertaining the meaning or effect of any provision of the CBIR.

The CBIR apply to foreign insolvency proceedings anywhere in the world without any condition of reciprocity— i.e. it is not necessary that the particular foreign State should have enacted comparable legislation before recourse may be had to these Regulations. It follows that the office-holders in foreign proceedings may take full advantage of the CPIR in this country, whereas their counterparts here will be able to do so abroad only to the extent that there is enabling legislation in the relevant foreign country.

There is one limitation on the otherwise universal territorial scope of the Regulations: art.3 of Sch.1 provides that where there is any conflict with an obligation of the UK under the EC Regulation on Insolvency Proceedings, the requirements of the latter shall prevail. So to the extent that any cross-border issues arise between insolvency proceedings in a British jurisdiction and proceedings elsewhere in the EU (apart from Denmark), it is the EC Regulation that will apply. However, the definitions of "insolvency proceedings" for the purposes of the Regulations and the EC Regulation are not identical and in some circumstances the case may fall within the former and not the latter, so that the Regulations alone will apply: see *Re Stocznia Gdynia SA v Bud-Bank Leasing sp z oo* [2010] B.C.C. 255, where statutory compensation proceedings under Polish law were held to be outside the jurisdiction of the EC Regulation but within the Regulations.

On the other hand, the Model Law is to have precedence if there is any conflict between it and UK domestic insolvency law (reg.3(2)). The CBIR do not apply to various utilities, building societies, insurers and credit institutions (Sch.1 art.1.2)).

In many respects, the Model Law has parallels in the EC Regulation, using some of the same concepts and definitions—e.g. those of "centre of main interests" (COMI), "main proceeding" and "establishment". Judicial rulings on those concepts and comments made in the notes to the EC Regulation in this *Guide* may be helpful in understanding parallel provisions in the CBIR. There, however, a number of important differences, including the following:

- The purpose of the CBIR is almost entirely enabling: there is very little in this legislation which restricts the jurisdiction of our own courts or limits their powers. In contrast, much more of the EC Regulation is prescriptive—for instance, where the COMI of the debtor is in another Member State, a British court's powers are limited in the orders which it may make, even if no main insolvency proceedings have been opened in the debtor's home State.

- It is only the UK courts which will have any role in interpreting the legislative text of the CBIR (although, no doubt, the judgments of foreign courts will be of persuasive authority): contrast the overriding powers of the European Court.

- The Regulations have been enacted unilaterally and independently by our own Parliament: there is no superior legislative authority which can countermand them. Even if UNCITRAL were to consider amending the Model Law, this would have no effect within the UK unless the changes were implemented by domestic legislation.

- No distinction is made by the CBIR between what are classified separately by the EC Regulation as "secondary" and "territorial" proceedings. Indeed, until "main" proceedings have been formally recognised in this country under the CBIR Ch.III, any form of insolvency proceeding available under IA 1986 may be commenced here without regard to issues such as whether the debtor's COMI may be in some other jurisdiction or whether main proceedings have been opened elsewhere.

The scope of the CBIR is broadly as follows:

- Chapter II provides for the recognition in this country of foreign office-holders with no special formalities (other than a translation, where needed), and gives them and foreign creditors direct access to courts in Great Britain.

- Chapter III similarly provides for the recognition of foreign insolvency proceedings. These include reorganisation and rescue proceedings as well as bankruptcies and liquidations, but receiverships are excluded by the CBIR for all purposes. The recognition of foreign proceedings as "main" proceedings brings about an automatic stay of proceedings and executions, etc. against the debtor in this country, but does not affect the right to institute the commencement of an insolvency proceeding or to file claims in such a proceeding. A stay or other appropriate relief may also be granted by the court as a matter of discretion following recognition of non-main proceedings. A foreign office-holder is empowered to intervene in proceedings here to which the debtor is a party.

- Chapter IV makes provision for co-operation and direct communication between a British court and foreign courts or office-holders. It should be noted that there is no repeal of IA 1986 s.426. The CBIR is not, like s.426, limited to "designated" countries and territories; and there may be some circumstances where recourse to that provision rather than the CBIR may be considered advantageous or necessary—e.g. where the debtor is an insurance company, or perhaps where it is a company in receivership in (say) Australia.

- Chapter V regulates the position where there are concurrent insolvency proceedings in this and one or more other jurisdictions. The provisions of this Chapter apply only after the foreign proceedings have been recognised under Chapter III. The rules are very similar to those of the EC Regulation. If the foreign proceeding has been recognised as a main proceeding, non-main proceedings may be commenced here only if the debtor has assets here, and are restricted in scope to assets within the jurisdiction. The rule of hotchpot applies where a creditor has received payment in another insolvency abroad.

The plan of the CBIR Sch.1 follows closely that of the UNCITRAL Model Law: in particular, the sequence and numbering of the articles correspond. But the paragraphs within each article sometimes vary considerably from the original model.

Evidence shows that the CBIR is proving useful in practice, although because most appointments are uncontroversial there are few reported cases. Some examples include *Re Phoenix Kapitaldienst GmbH* [2008] B.P.I.R. 1082 (German administrator); *Warner v Verfides* [2008] EWHC 2609 (Ch); [2009] Bus.L.R. 500 (Australian trustee in bankruptcy); *Re Stanford International Bank Ltd* [2010] EWCA Civ 137; [2010] B.P.I.R. 679 (Antiguan liquidator); *Samsun Logix Corp v DEF* [2009] EWHC 576 (Ch); [2010] B.C.C. 556 (insolvency proceedings in Korean court); *Re SwissAir Schweizerische Luftverkehr-Aktiengesellschaft* [2009] EWHC 2099 (Ch); [2010] B.C.C. 667 (Swiss liquidation recognised as main proceeding and English liquidator ordered to remit assets to Swiss liquidator); *Williams v Simpson* [2011] B.P.I.R. 938 (HC, New Zealand, noted in (2011) 24 Insolv. Int. 14: interim relief in the form of a search and seizure order granted by New Zealand court pursuant to request by English trustee in bankruptcy). English courts have, of course, traditionally been well disposed to recognise foreign insolvency proceedings and their representatives (as in *Cambridge Gas Transport Corp v Navigator Holdings plc* [2006] UKPC 26; [2006] B.C.C. 962—see the note to IA 1986 s.426), and these rulings at common law are commonly cited in cases under the CBIR.

1   Citation, commencement and interpretation

1(1)   These Regulations may be cited as the Cross-Border Insolvency Regulations 2006 and shall come into force on the day after the day on which they are made.

1(2)   In these Regulations **"the UNCITRAL Model Law"** means the Model Law on cross-border insolvency as adopted by the United Nations Commission on International Trade Law on 30th May 1997.

1(3)   In these Regulations "overseas company" has the meaning given by section 1044 of the Companies Act 2006 and "establishment", in relation to such a company, has the same meaning as in the Overseas Companies Regulations 2009.

GENERAL NOTE

The effective date is April 4, 2006. Regulation 1(3) inserted by the Companies Act 2006 (Consequential Amendments, Transitional Provisions and Savings) Order 2009 (SI 2009/1941) art.2(1) and Sch.1 para.264, as from October 1, 2009.

2   UNCITRAL Model Law to have force of law

2(1)   The UNCITRAL Model Law shall have the force of law in Great Britain in the form set out in Schedule 1 to these Regulations (which contains the UNCITRAL Model Law with certain modifications to adapt it for application in Great Britain).

2(2)   Without prejudice to any practice of the courts as to the matters which may be considered apart from this paragraph, the following documents may be considered in ascertaining the meaning or effect of any provision of the UNCITRAL Model Law as set out in Schedule 1 to these Regulations–

   (a)   the UNCITRAL Model Law;

   (b)   any documents of the United Nations Commission on International Trade Law and its working group relating to the preparation of the UNCITRAL Model Law; and

   (c)   the Guide to Enactment of the UNCITRAL Model Law (UNCITRAL document A/CN.9/442) prepared at the request of the United Nations Commission on International Trade Law made in May 1997.

GENERAL NOTE

The Model Law as adopted by UNCITRAL and agreed by the UN General Assembly has no legislative force: the source of law so far as concerns Great Britain is that set out in Sch.1, below. However, the Model Law and the other documents mentioned in reg.2(2) may be referred to for the purpose of interpreting Sch.1. The Model Law and the Guide to Enactment may be found at: *http://www.uncitral.org/uncitral/en/uncitral_texts/insolvency/1997Model.html*.

On July 1, 2009 UNCITRAL adopted the Practice Guide on Cross-Border Co-operation, a reference source for insolvency professionals and judges on the practical aspects of co-operation and communication in cross-border cases (discussed by L. Elliott and N. Griffiths [2010] C.R. & I. 12). (See further the note to art.27.) In 2011 a further text entitled "UNCITRAL Model Law on Cross-Border Insolvency: the judicial perspective" was published, offering general guidance to judges on how to approach applications for recognition and relief under the Model Law. This may be accessed under *http://www.uncitral.org.pdf/english/texts/insolven/pre-judicial-perspective.pdf*

The CBIR do not extend to Northern Ireland, but comparable legislation has now been enacted for that jurisdiction: see the Introductory note to the Regulations, preceding reg.1.

The Preamble to the Model Law is not reproduced in Sch.1, although, as noted above, it may be relevant for purposes of interpretation. For this reason the Preamble has been included in this *Guide*, immediately before the text of the CBIR.

The UNCITRAL Guide to Enactment is referred to in the present work by the abbreviation "G to E".

3   Modification of British insolvency law

3(1)   British insolvency law (as defined in article 2 of the UNCITRAL Model Law as set out in Schedule 1 to these Regulations) and Part 3 of the Insolvency Act 1986 shall apply with such modifications as the context requires for the purpose of giving effect to the provisions of these Regulations.

3(2)   In the case of any conflict between any provision of British insolvency law or of Part 3 of the Insolvency Act 1986 and the provisions of these Regulations, the latter shall prevail.

GENERAL NOTE

Regulation 3 confirms that British insolvency law is to be read subject to the CBIR, so that where there is any inconsistency the CBIR is to prevail. "British insolvency law" is defined in art.2 so as to exclude Pt 3 of IA 1986 (Receivership); but for the purposes of this one provision Pt 3 is, in effect, written back into the definition.

4   Procedural matters in England and Wales

4   Schedule 2 to these Regulations (which makes provision about procedural matters in England and Wales in connection with the application of the UNCITRAL Model Law as set out in Schedule 1 to these Regulations) shall have effect.

5   Procedural matters in Scotland

5   Schedule 3 to these Regulations (which makes provision about procedural matters in Scotland in connection with the application of the UNCITRAL Model Law as set out in Schedule 1 to these Regulations) shall have effect.

6   Notices delivered to the registrar of companies

6   Schedule 4 to these Regulations (which makes provision about notices delivered to the registrar of companies under these Regulations) shall have effect.

7   Co-operation between courts exercising jurisdiction in relation to cross-border insolvency

7(1)   An order made by a court in either part of Great Britain in the exercise of jurisdiction in relation to the subject matter of these Regulations shall be enforced in the other part of Great Britain as if it were made by a court exercising the corresponding jurisdiction in that other part.

7(2)   However, nothing in paragraph (1) requires a court in either part of Great Britain to enforce, in relation to property situated in that part, any order made by a court in the other part of Great Britain.

7(3)   The courts having jurisdiction in relation to the subject matter of these Regulations in either part of Great Britain shall assist the courts having the corresponding jurisdiction in the other part of Great Britain.

GENERAL NOTE

These provisions mirror IA 1986 s.426(1), (2) and (4). This avoids any supposition that the UNCITRAL regime should apply as between the three jurisdictions of England and Wales, Scotland and Northern Ireland in consequence of reg.3(2), above.

8 Disapplication of section 388 of the Insolvency Act 1986

8 Nothing in section 388 of the Insolvency Act 1986 applies to anything done by a foreign representative–

(a) under or by virtue of these Regulations;

(b) in relation to relief granted or cooperation or coordination provided under these Regulations.

GENERAL NOTE

IA 1986 s.388 defines the term "act as an insolvency practitioner". The effect of this disapplication is to ensure that an office-holder in foreign insolvency proceedings who is empowered to act under the CBIR is not required to be qualified under British law and will not commit an offence under s.389 (acting as an insolvency practitioner without qualification) when so acting. This may give rise to some practical difficulties (e.g. where the foreign proceedings do not involve the appointment of a "representative"): see D. Marks and G. Jones, (2009) 22 Insolv. Int. 10.

For an early example of the use of the Model Law in this country, see *C Brooks Thurmond III v Rajapaskse* [2008] B.P.I.R. 283, where an income payments order was made against a bankrupt at the request of a foreign trustee.

SCHEDULE 1

Regulation 2(1)

UNCITRAL MODEL LAW ON CROSS-BORDER INSOLVENCY

CHAPTER I

GENERAL PROVISIONS

Article 1. Scope of Application

1 This Law applies where–

(a) assistance is sought in Great Britain by a foreign court or a foreign representative in connection with a foreign proceeding; or

(b) assistance is sought in a foreign State in connection with a proceeding under British insolvency law; or

(c) a foreign proceeding and a proceeding under British insolvency law in respect of the same debtor are taking place concurrently; or

(d) creditors or other interested persons in a foreign State have an interest in requesting the commencement of, or participating in, a proceeding under British insolvency law.

2 This Law does not apply to a proceeding concerning–

(a) a company holding an appointment under Chapter 1 of Part 2 of the Water Industry Act 1991 (water and sewage undertakers) or a qualifying licensed water supplier within the meaning of section 23(6) of that Act (meaning and effect of special administration order);

(b) Scottish Water established under section 20 of the Water Industry (Scotland) Act 2002 (Scottish Water);

(c) a protected railway company within the meaning of section 59 of the Railways Act 1993 (railway administration order) (including that section as it has effect by virtue of section 19 of the Channel Tunnel Rail Link Act 1996 (administration));

(d) a licence company within the meaning of section 26 of the Transport Act 2000 (air traffic services);

(e)   a public private partnership company within the meaning of section 210 of the Greater London Authority Act 1999 (public-private partnership agreement);

(f)   a protected energy company within the meaning of section 154(5) of the Energy Act 2004 (energy administration orders);

(g)   a building society within the meaning of section 119 of the Building Societies Act 1986 (interpretation);

(h)   a UK credit institution or an EEA credit institution or any branch of either such institution as those expressions are defined by regulation 2 of the Credit Institutions (Reorganisation and Winding Up) Regulations 2004 (interpretation);

(i)   a third country credit institution within the meaning of regulation 36 of the Credit Institutions (Reorganisation and Winding Up) Regulations 2004 (interpretation of this Part);

(j)   a person who has permission under or by virtue of Parts 4 or 19 of the Financial Services and Markets Act 2000 to effect or carry out contracts of insurance;

(k)   an EEA insurer within the meaning of regulation 2 of the Insurers (Reorganisation and Winding Up) Regulations 2004 (interpretation);

(l)   a person (other than one included in paragraph 2(j)) pursuing the activity of reinsurance who has received authorisation for that activity from a competent authority within an EEA State; or

(m)   any of the Concessionaires within the meaning of section 1 of the Channel Tunnel Act 1987.

3   In paragraph 2 of this article–

(a)   in sub-paragraph (j) the reference to **"contracts of insurance"** must be construed in accordance with–

(i)   section 22 of the Financial Services and Markets Act 2000 (classes of regulated activity and categories of investment);

(ii)   any relevant order under that section; and

(iii)   Schedule 2 to that Act (regulated activities);

(b)   in sub-paragraph (l) **"EEA State"** means a State, other than the United Kingdom, which is a contracting party to the agreement on the European Economic Area signed at Oporto on 2 May 1992.

4   The court shall not grant any relief, or modify any relief already granted, or provide any co-operation or coordination, under or by virtue of any of the provisions of this Law if and to the extent that such relief or modified relief or cooperation or coordination would–

(a)   be prohibited under or by virtue of–

(i)   Part 7 of the Companies Act 1989;

(ii)   Part 3 of the Financial Markets and Insolvency (Settlement Finality) Regulations 1999; or

(iii)   Part 3 of the Financial Collateral Arrangements (No.2) Regulations 2003;

in the case of a proceeding under British insolvency law; or

(b)   interfere with or be inconsistent with any rights of a collateral taker under Part 4 of the Financial Collateral Arrangements (No.2) Regulations 2003 which could be exercised in the case of such a proceeding.

5   Where a foreign proceeding regarding a debtor who is an insured in accordance with the provisions of the Third Parties (Rights against Insurers) Act 1930 is recognised under this Law, any stay and suspension referred to in article 20(1) and any relief granted by the court under article 19 or 21 shall not apply to or affect–

(a)   any transfer of rights of the debtor under that Act; or

(b)   any claim, action, cause or proceeding by a third party against an insurer under or in respect of rights of the debtor transferred under that Act.

6   Any suspension under this Law of the right to transfer, encumber or otherwise dispose of any of the debtor's assets–

(a)   is subject to section 26 of the Land Registration Act 2002 where owner's powers are exercised in relation to a registered estate or registered charge;

(b)   is subject to section 52 of the Land Registration Act 2002, where the powers referred to in that section are exercised by the proprietor of a registered charge; and

(c)   in any other case, shall not bind a purchaser of a legal estate in good faith for money or money's worth unless the purchaser has express notice of the suspension.

7   In paragraph 6–

(a)   **"owner's powers"** means the powers described in section 23 of the Land Registration Act 2002 and **"registered charge"** and **"registered estate"** have the same meaning as in section 132(1) of that Act; and

(b)   **"legal estate"** and **"purchaser"** have the same meaning as in section 17 of the Land Charges Act 1972.

GENERAL NOTE

This article defines the circumstances in which the CBIR will come into play, and in arts 2.2 et seq. lists various bodies in regard to which the Regulations are excluded.

Art.1.1
The G to E conveniently uses the expressions "inward-bound" and "outward-bound" to describe the various purposes provided for by the Model Law: the former term where someone from abroad seeks to invoke the jurisdiction of a British court or seeks assistance from the office-holder in British insolvency proceedings; the latter where a similar request is made to a foreign court or office-holder for recognition or assistance in connection with an insolvency proceeding in this country. Paragraphs (a) and (d) of art.1.1 are concerned with the "inward-bound" scope of the CBIR, and para.1.1(b) with their "outward-bound" aspects. Paragraph 1.1(c) refers to a third purpose: the co-ordination of matters where insolvency proceedings are taking place at the same time both here and in one or more foreign jurisdictions.

Art.1.2, 1.3
Although in principle the Model Law is formulated to apply generally to all insolvency proceedings, provision is made for the exception of "specially regulated insolvency proceedings", and in particular those concerning banks, insurance companies and public utilities. Those excluded from the application of the CBIR are listed here. It should be noted that there is no general exclusion of any particular category of company (e.g. banks), but each is specified by reference to the definition in a particular enactment or authorisation under it.
   The DBIS has intimated that it will consider the inclusion of credit institutions and insurance undertakings within the Model Law (under IA 2000 s.14) at a later stage. A suggestion that corporate bodies other than companies should be specifically excluded (see the note to IA 1986 s.1(4)–(6)) was rejected.
   The Model Law allows an enacting State to make special provision for the insolvency of debtors who are non-traders or consumers. The UK, in keeping with its own domestic law, has not chosen to make any distinction in respect of these categories.

Art.1.4
There is an exclusion provision here for the various payment and settlement systems where parts of the domestic insolvency legislation is disapplied.

Art.1.5

The rights of third parties under the 1930 Act are preserved by this provision, in the case where the insolvent is insured against liabilities to such parties. (Note potential replacement of this Act by the Third Parties (Rights against Insurers) Act 2010.)

Arts 1.6, 1.7

The sections referred to prevent the title of the disponee, registered proprietor or purchaser from being questioned.

Article 2. Definitions

For the purposes of this Law–

(a) **"British insolvency law"** means–

    (i) in relation to England and Wales, provision extending to England and Wales and made by or under the Insolvency Act 1986 (with the exception of Part 3 of that Act) or by or under that Act as extended or applied by or under any other enactment (excluding these Regulations); and

    (ii) in relation to Scotland, provision extending to Scotland and made by or under the Insolvency Act 1986 (with the exception of Part 3 of that Act), the Bankruptcy (Scotland) Act 1985 or by or under those Acts as extended or applied by or under any other enactment (excluding these Regulations);

GENERAL NOTE

IA 1986 Pt 3 deals with receivership (including administrative receivership) in England and Wales and in Scotland. The 1986 Act does not contain a comprehensive definition of receivership and there is room for doubt whether parts of it apply to particular types of receiver (e.g. court-appointed receivers, Law of Property Act receivers); but there can be no question that they also are outside the CBIR because such receiverships are not "collective" insolvency proceedings within the ambit of the Model Law.

(b) **"British insolvency officeholder"** means–

    (i) the official receiver within the meaning of section 399 of the Insolvency Act 1986 when acting as liquidator, provisional liquidator, trustee, interim receiver or nominee or supervisor of a voluntary arrangement;

    (ii) a person acting as an insolvency practitioner within the meaning of section 388 of that Act but shall not include a person acting as an administrative receiver; and

    (iii) the Accountant in Bankruptcy within the meaning of section 1 of the Bankruptcy (Scotland) Act 1985 when acting as interim or permanent trustee;

(c) **"the court"** except as otherwise provided in articles 14(4) and 23(6)(b), means in relation to any matter the court which in accordance with the provisions of article 4 of this Law has jurisdiction in relation to that matter;

GENERAL NOTE

"Court" is here used in its normal sense, in contrast with the EC Regulation art.2(d), where it is given an extended definition which includes any body competent to open insolvency proceedings (such as a general meeting of shareholders resolving to put their company into liquidation).

(d) **"the EC Insolvency Regulation"** means Council Regulation (EC) No.1346/2000 of 29 May 2000 on Insolvency Proceedings;

(e) **"establishment"** means any place of operations where the debtor carries out a non-transitory economic activity with human means and assets or services;

GENERAL NOTE

This definition has been adopted from the EC Regulation art.2(h), with the substitution of the word "assets" for "goods" (in the context, a better translation). The definition is open to criticism in placing emphasis on the debtor's *economic* activity: as with the EC Regulation, an insolvent individual who is not (and perhaps never has been) in business but has assets and debts in the jurisdiction may be excluded from the scope of the CBIR.

(f) **"foreign court"** means a judicial or other authority competent to control or supervise a foreign proceeding;

GENERAL NOTE

In contrast with the definition of "the court" in para.(c), this term is wider. The G to E, para.74 explains that a foreign proceeding which meets the requisites set out in para.(i) below "should receive the same treatment irrespective of whether it has been commenced or supervised by a judicial body or an administrative body. Therefore, the definition … includes also non-judicial authorities. [The paragraph] follows a similar definition contained in Article 2, subparagraph (d), of the European Convention on Insolvency Proceedings". (The Convention was the precursor to the EC Regulation.)

(g) **"foreign main proceeding"** means a foreign proceeding taking place in the State where the debtor has the centre of its main interests;

(h) **"foreign non-main proceeding"** means a foreign proceeding, other than a foreign main proceeding, taking place in a State where the debtor has an establishment within the meaning of sub-paragraph (e) of this article;

GENERAL NOTE

The terms "main proceeding" and "centre of main interests", like "establishment", have been adopted from the EC Convention on Insolvency Proceedings. The notes to the EC Regulation art.3, will therefore be relevant. The use of the word "its" (and the references to debtors as "companies" in the G to E (e.g. in para.71) is misleading: there is ample reference elsewhere to insolvencies of natural persons (see, e.g. the G to E, para.66).

It should be noted also that the distinction made by the CBIR between "main" and "non-main" proceedings becomes relevant only after the foreign proceeding has been recognised by a British court under Chapter III. Prior to that time, it is of no concern to the court or any party to an insolvency proceeding before a British court to establish the location of the debtor's COMI or to determine whether that proceeding or any current proceeding in a foreign State is "main" or otherwise.

(i) **"foreign proceeding"** means a collective judicial or administrative proceeding in a foreign State, including an interim proceeding, pursuant to a law relating to insolvency in which proceeding the assets and affairs of the debtor are subject to control or supervision by a foreign court, for the purpose of reorganisation or liquidation;

GENERAL NOTE

As noted above, the CBIR do not make a distinction between the categories which in the EC Regulation are termed "territorial" and "secondary" proceedings (see the note to the EC Regulation art.3). Nothing in the CBIR limits proceedings which would fall within the second category to winding-up proceedings, as the EC Regulation does. In *Re Stanford International Bank Ltd* [2010] EWCA Civ 137; [2011] Ch. 33; [2011] B.C.C. 211 a receiver of an insolvent bank, appointed by a court in the United States, was held not to be entitled to recognition as he had not been appointed pursuant to a law relating to insolvency; but liquidators of the same bank appointed in Antigua (the jurisdiction of the bank's COMI) fulfilled this requirement and accordingly the liquidation proceedings were recognised as main proceedings and the liquidators as foreign representatives. In his judgment the Chancellor of the High Court examined in detail the definitions in art.2(g), ("foreign main proceeding"), 2(h) ("foreign non-main proceeding"), 2(i) ("foreign proceeding") and 2(j) ("foreign representative"). See also *Re Stocznia Gdynia SA v Bud-Bank Leasing sp z oo* [2010] B.C.C. 255 (Polish administrator of statutory compensation scheme recognised as representative of insolvency proceedings); *Rubin v Eurofinance SA* [2010] EWCA Civ 895; [2011] B.C.C. 649 (adversary proceedings under US Bankruptcy Code Ch.11 recognised as foreign proceedings, applying common-law principles rather than the CBIR); *Samsun Logix Corp v DEF* [2009] EWHC 576 (Ch); [2010] B.C.C. 556, further proceedings (sub nom. *D/S Norden A/S v Samsun Logix Corp*) [2009] EWHC 2304 (Ch); [2009] B.P.I.R. 1367. Note that "proceeding" is not confined to court proceedings. In *Re New Paragon Investments Ltd* (unreported, November 25, 2011) Mr Registrar Nicholls held that a creditors' voluntary winding up in Hong Kong was a "foreign proceeding" under the CBIR.

(j) **"foreign representative"** means a person or body, including one appointed on an interim basis, authorised in a foreign proceeding to administer the reorganisation or the liquidation of the debtor's assets or affairs or to act as a representative of the foreign proceeding;

GENERAL NOTE

The term "representative" is a happier choice than the word "liquidator" that is used in the EC Regulation. This definition makes it plain that it includes office-holders in reorganisation as well as in winding-up and bankruptcy proceedings (i.e. IVAs, CVAs, administrations), and that interim liquidators, interim receivers (in bankruptcies) and interim trustees (in Scotland) also qualify. The concluding words appear also to contemplate that a foreign court might appoint a person other than the office-holder as the representative here of a foreign proceeding.

(k) **"hire-purchase agreement"** includes a conditional sale agreement, a chattel leasing agreement and a retention of title agreement;

GENERAL NOTE

This definition, added to the CBIR at a late stage, is adopted from IA 1986 Sch.A1 para.1 and Sch. B1 para.111(1).

(l) **"section 426 request"** means a request for assistance in accordance with section 426 of the Insolvency Act 1986 made to a court in any part of the United Kingdom;

(m) **"secured creditor"** in relation to a debtor, means a creditor of the debtor who holds in respect of his debt a security over property of the debtor;

(n) **"security"** means–

(i) in relation to England and Wales, any mortgage, charge, lien or other security; and

(ii) in relation to Scotland, any security (whether heritable or moveable), any floating charge and any right of lien or preference and any right of retention (other than a right of compensation or set off);

GENERAL NOTE

The definitions of this and the preceding expression make it plain that only securities over property are included (and not, e.g. a guarantee of the debt given by a third party); but the security may be proprietary or possessory. A "charge-back" over a sum held by a bank on deposit is arguably not within the definition.

(o) in the application of Articles 20 and 23 to Scotland, **"an individual"** means any debtor within the meaning of the Bankruptcy (Scotland) Act 1985;

(p) in the application of this Law to Scotland, references howsoever expressed to–

(i) **"filing"** an application or claim are to be construed as references to lodging an application or submitting a claim respectively;

(ii) **"relief"** and **"standing"** are to be construed as references to "remedy" and "title and interest" respectively; and

(iii) a **"stay"** are to be construed as references to restraint, except in relation to continuation of actions or proceedings when they shall be construed as a reference to sist; and

(q) references to the law of Great Britain include a reference to the law of either part of Great Britain (including its rules of private international law).

Article 3. International obligations of Great Britain under the EC Insolvency Regulation

To the extent that this Law conflicts with an obligation of the United Kingdom under the EC Insolvency Regulation, the requirements of the EC Insolvency Regulation prevail.

GENERAL NOTE

This article expresses "the principle of international obligations of the enacting State over internal law" (G to E, para.76). It may be that the CBIR are not entirely displaced by the EC Regulation: at the margins the scope of the CBIR may be slightly wider (e.g. the lists of excluded bodies differ in detail in some places).

The EC Regulation applies only in relation to cross-border insolvencies where the debtor's affairs extend into more than one Member State of the EU (other than Denmark) and the debtor's COMI is in one such State; and it is not concerned with assets or creditors of the debtor based outside the EU, or insolvency proceedings that have been instituted in a non-EU jurisdiction. If the application of the EC Regulation is excluded on any of these grounds, the CBIR provides a complementary regime.

Article 4. Competent court

1 The functions referred to in this Law relating to recognition of foreign proceedings and cooperation with foreign courts shall be performed by the High Court and assigned to the Chancery Division, as regards England and Wales and the Court of Session as regards Scotland.

2 Subject to paragraph 1 of this article, the court in either part of Great Britain shall have jurisdiction in relation to the functions referred to in that paragraph if–

(a) the debtor has–

(i) a place of business; or

(ii) in the case of an individual, a place of residence; or

(iii) assets,

situated in that part of Great Britain; or

(b) the court in that part of Great Britain considers for any other reason that it is the appropriate forum to consider the question or provide the assistance requested.

3 In considering whether it is the appropriate forum to hear an application for recognition of a foreign proceeding in relation to a debtor, the court shall take into account the location of any court in which a proceeding under British insolvency law is taking place in relation to the debtor and the likely location of any future proceedings under British insolvency law in relation to the debtor.

GENERAL NOTE

Note that the conditions set out in art.4.2 apply only to determine the court's competence in relation to the recognition of foreign proceedings and co-operation with foreign courts. Competence in any other respect remains to be determined by IA 1986 or any other appropriate law.

Article 5. Authorisation of British insolvency officeholders to act in a foreign State

A British insolvency officeholder is authorised to act in a foreign State on behalf of a proceeding under British insolvency law, as permitted by the applicable foreign law.

GENERAL NOTE

This article provides "outward-bound" facilities for the office-holder in a British insolvency proceeding. Its concern is to ensure that his power to act in a foreign jurisdiction is not open to challenge for want of proper authorisation. It does not, of course, oblige the authorities in the foreign State to recognise him, or confer any particular powers on him: the scope of his powers will depend on the law of that State, but he will at least have the best possible evidence of his authorisation. It is not necessary that the foreign State should itself have enacted the Model Law or some similar legislation.

One further step which might with advantage be taken in some circumstances is illustrated by *Re MG Rover España SA* [2006] B.C.C. 599—to have the court make a supplementary order describing the nature of the proceeding (e.g. a CVA or administration) and the role and powers of the office-holder.

Article 6. Public policy exception

Nothing in this Law prevents the court from refusing to take an action governed by this Law if the action would be manifestly contrary to the public policy of Great Britain or any part of it.

GENERAL NOTE

A similar public policy exception is to be found in the EC Regulation art.26. This was a major factor in the judgment of the Irish Supreme Court in *Re Eurofood IFSC Ltd* [2004] I.E.S.C. 47; [2005] B.C.C. 999, in refusing to recognise the decision of the Italian court. (See also the ruling of the ECJ (*Re Eurofood IFSC Ltd* (C-341/04) [2006] B.C.C. 397 at paras 60–68.) No definition of public policy is given, but both provisions use the phrase "manifestly" contrary to public policy—an expression intended to invite a restrictive interpretation. The fact that foreign proceedings differ from those of this country, e.g. as regards creditors' rights and priorities, is not a ground to refuse recognition or relief: *Re Stocznia Gdynia SA v Bud-Bank Leasing sp z oo* [2010] B.C.C. 255.

Article 7. Additional assistance under other laws

Nothing in this Law limits the power of a court or a British insolvency officeholder to provide additional assistance to a foreign representative under other laws of Great Britain.

GENERAL NOTE

The most obvious "other law" is IA 1986 s.426; but there are also many known instances in which a judge in the UK has co-operated on an informal basis with a another judge administering a foreign insolvency, relying on the court's inherent jurisdiction or considerations of judicial comity, even where s.426 could not be invoked.

Article 8. Interpretation

In the interpretation of this Law, regard is to be had to its international origin and to the need to promote uniformity in its application and the observance of good faith.

GENERAL NOTE

A provision similar to this appears in a number of treaties and other Model Laws. The G to E, para.92, draws attention to the Case Law on International Texts (CLOUT) under which UNCITRAL publishes abstracts of judicial decisions, so facilitating a harmonised interpretation of the Model Law. The CLOUT system is available on the internet home page of UNCITRAL (*http://www.uncitral.org*), and also from the UNCITRAL Secretariat in hard copy.

CHAPTER II

ACCESS OF FOREIGN REPRESENTATIVES AND CREDITORS TO COURTS IN GREAT BRITAIN

Article 9. Right of direct access

A foreign representative is entitled to apply directly to a court in Great Britain.

GENERAL NOTE

This removes any doubt as to the representative's right of access. In practice the courts of the UK have normally been willing to allow such access, with rather less restriction or formality than many other countries.

Article 10. Limited jurisdiction

The sole fact that an application pursuant to this Law is made to a court in Great Britain by a foreign representative does not subject the foreign representative or the foreign assets and affairs of the debtor to the jurisdiction of the courts of Great Britain or any part of it for any purpose other than the application.

GENERAL NOTE

The G to E, para.94, explains that this provision constitutes a "safe conduct" rule aimed at ensuring that the court would not assume jurisdiction over all the assets of the debtor on the sole ground that the foreign representative had made an application for recognition of the foreign proceeding. It also makes it clear that the application alone is not a sufficient ground for the court to assert jurisdiction over the foreign representative in regard to matters unrelated to the insolvency. This does not rule out an assertion of jurisdiction that does not affect the assets of the debtor's estate—e.g. if a tort or misconduct is committed by the foreign representative the court would have grounds for jurisdiction to deal with the consequences of such misconduct. Note also that the court in granting relief under arts 19 et seq. may impose conditions, such as requiring the foreign representative to provide security or caution.

Article 11. Application by a foreign representative to commence a proceeding under British insolvency law

A foreign representative appointed in a foreign main proceeding or foreign non-main proceeding is entitled to apply to commence a proceeding under British insolvency law if the conditions for commencing such a proceeding are otherwise met.

GENERAL NOTE

This article gives the foreign representative procedural standing to commence a proceeding under British insolvency law. It makes it unnecessary for such an office-holder to be specifically listed in such provisions as IA 1986 s.124(1) (presentation of petition for winding up) or s.264(1) (presentation of bankruptcy petition). It is not a precondition for this purpose that the foreign proceeding should have been formally recognised under Chapter III, below. The conditions referred to are only those which would apply in any case (apart from the possible need to furnish a translation of documents under art.15.4): in contrast with art.19, the court is not given a discretion to impose other conditions.

Article 12. Participation of a foreign representative in a proceeding under British insolvency law

Upon recognition of a foreign proceeding, the foreign representative is entitled to participate in a proceeding regarding the debtor under British insolvency law.

GENERAL NOTE

This article gives the representative standing to participate in an insolvency proceeding concerning the debtor that is taking place in this country. It is limited to giving standing and does not vest the representative with any other rights or powers. Nor does it specify the kinds of application that he may make. In contrast with art.11, it is a prerequisite that the foreign proceeding has been recognised. Note that "proceeding" includes extra-judicial proceedings such as an administration or creditors' voluntary winding up.

The Model Law uses the term "participate" here and "intervene" in art.24, in the latter to refer to a case where the representative takes part in an "individual action" by or against the debtor as opposed to a collective insolvency proceeding (see G to E, para.102). It is not suggested that this differentiation is of significance.

Article 13. Access of foreign creditors to a proceeding under British insolvency law

1 Subject to paragraph 2 of this article, foreign creditors have the same rights regarding the commencement of, and participation in, a proceeding under British insolvency law as creditors in Great Britain.

2 Paragraph 1 of this article does not affect the ranking of claims in a proceeding under British insolvency law, except that the claim of a foreign creditor shall not be given a lower priority than that of general unsecured claims solely because the holder of such a claim is a foreign creditor.

3 A claim may not be challenged solely on the grounds that it is a claim by a foreign tax or social security authority but such a claim may be challenged–

(a) on the ground that it is in whole or in part a penalty, or

(b)   on any other ground that a claim might be rejected in a proceeding under British insolvency law.

GENERAL NOTE

There has never been any discrimination against foreign creditors in UK insolvency law (apart from foreign revenue, etc. authorities: see the note to art.13.3 below).

Art.13.2
As well as giving them standing to file claims, this article establishes a minimum ranking for foreign creditors equal to that of the debtor's general unsecured creditors. Of course if they would have a lower priority here for some other reason (e.g. debts owed by a corporate debtor to its shareholders under IA 1986 s.74(2)(f)), the postponement is not affected by the present provision.

Art.13.3
Claims by foreign revenue, etc. authorities have traditionally not been provable debts in this country, but the reversal of this rule by art.13.3 mirrors that in the EC Regulation art.39. Claims by a foreign State on other grounds (e.g. fines) are not affected by this provision.

Article 14. Notification to foreign creditors of a proceeding under British insolvency law

1   Whenever under British insolvency law notification is to be given to creditors in Great Britain, such notification shall also be given to the known creditors that do not have addresses in Great Britain. The court may order that appropriate steps be taken with a view to notifying any creditor whose address is not yet known.

2   Such notification shall be made to the foreign creditors individually, unless–

(a)   the court considers that under the circumstances some other form of notification would be more appropriate; or

(b)   the notification to creditors in Great Britain is to be by advertisement only, in which case the notification to the known foreign creditors may be by advertisement in such foreign newspapers as the British insolvency officeholder considers most appropriate for ensuring that the content of the notification comes to the notice of the known foreign creditors.

3   When notification of a right to file a claim is to be given to foreign creditors, the notification shall–

(a)   indicate a reasonable time period for filing claims and specify the place for their filing;

(b)   indicate whether secured creditors need to file their secured claims; and

(c)   contain any other information required to be included in such a notification to creditors pursuant to the law of Great Britain and the orders of the court.

4   In this article **"the court"** means the court which has jurisdiction in relation to the particular proceeding under British insolvency law under which notification is to be given to creditors.

GENERAL NOTE

See the G to E, paras 106 et seq. The main purpose of notifying foreign creditors is to inform them of the commencement of the insolvency proceeding and of the time-limit to file their claims. The concern of this article is that foreign creditors should be notified as expeditiously as possible and without the delay and expense which the use of letters rogatory and similar formalities would involve. Even where provision is made for the use of such formalities by another legal source, such as the Convention on the Service Abroad of Judicial and Extrajudicial Documents in Civil and Commercial Documents (1965), the G to E expresses the view that since art.14 is even more facilitative than the Convention there is no real conflict. In the last resort, reference could be made to art.3 to resolve any doubt.

Art.14.2
The object of the requirement for individual notification is to ensure that foreign creditors are not at a disadvantage in comparison with local creditors, e.g. where the law of the home jurisdiction allows notification to be made by advertisement in national newspapers, which foreign creditors would not usually see. But where, as is most likely,

individual notification would be costly or impractical, subparas (a) and (b) give the court discretion to direct notification by other means.

CHAPTER III

RECOGNITION OF A FOREIGN PROCEEDING AND RELIEF

Article 15. Application for recognition of a foreign proceeding

1 A foreign representative may apply to the court for recognition of the foreign proceeding in which the foreign representative has been appointed.

2 An application for recognition shall be accompanied by–

    (a) a certified copy of the decision commencing the foreign proceeding and appointing the foreign representative; or

    (b) a certificate from the foreign court affirming the existence of the foreign proceeding and of the appointment of the foreign representative; or

    (c) in the absence of evidence referred to in sub-paragraphs (a) and (b), any other evidence acceptable to the court of the existence of the foreign proceeding and of the appointment of the foreign representative.

3 An application for recognition shall also be accompanied by a statement identifying all foreign proceedings, proceedings under British insolvency law and section 426 requests in respect of the debtor that are known to the foreign representative.

4 The foreign representative shall provide the court with a translation into English of documents supplied in support of the application for recognition.

GENERAL NOTE

Recognition of the foreign proceeding necessarily involves recognition of the foreign representative and the validity of his appointment. The Model Law aims to avoid the need for any formal "legalisation" of the foreign documents submitted as evidence—an aim endorsed by this article, stipulating for no other requirement than a translation where this is needed. The court is entitled to assume that the documents are authentic without further ado (art.16.2), but is not bound to do so. On the meaning of "foreign representative", see the note to art.2(j).

On the procedure, see generally Sch.2 Pt 2, and on notice, Sch.2 paras 21 et seq. The G to E, paras 120–121 points out that the Model Law does not make the issuance of any form of notice mandatory, but stresses the need for a recognition proceeding to be dealt with expeditiously. Mr Registrar Nicholls has issued a helpful note on various aspects of the procedure under arts 15 and 21, reported as *Re Rajapaske (Note)* [2007] B.P.I.R. 99.

Art.15.2

The Model Law uses the term "proceeding" to include insolvencies which are commenced extra-judicially, such as voluntary arrangements, creditors' voluntary liquidations and many administrations, as well as those effected by court order. In such cases, (or rather their foreign equivalents) an English court may be prepared to accept a certified copy of (e.g.) the resolutions of the company's general meeting and creditors by which the company was put into liquidation and the liquidator appointed; but it may be thought preferable to obtain a certificate from the foreign court similar to that prescribed by IR 1986 r.7.62.

It will be recalled that interim foreign proceedings are within the definition (art.2(i)).

Art.15.3

The information prescribed by this provision will be needed by the court not so much for the grant of recognition itself but for any later decision granting relief: it is likely to be important to ensure that such relief is consistent with any other insolvency proceeding, wherever situated, involving the same debtor.

See also art.8, on information that becomes known to the foreign representative after recognition, and art.30, on co-ordination of more than one foreign insolvency proceeding.

Art.15.4

The court is entitled, but not bound, to require a translation (G to E, para.119).

Article 16. Presumptions concerning recognition

1 If the decision or certificate referred to in paragraph 2 of article 15 indicates that the foreign proceeding is a proceeding within the meaning of sub-paragraph (i) of article 2 and that the foreign representative is a person or body within the meaning of sub-paragraph (j) of article 2, the court is entitled to so presume.

2 The court is entitled to presume that documents submitted in support of the application for recognition are authentic, whether or not they have been legalised.

3 In the absence of proof to the contrary, the debtor's registered office, or habitual residence in the case of an individual, is presumed to be the centre of the debtor's main interests.

GENERAL NOTE

These presumptions enable to court to expedite the evidentiary process.

Article 17. Decision to recognise a foreign proceeding

1 Subject to article 6, a foreign proceeding shall be recognised if–

(a)   it is a foreign proceeding within the meaning of sub-paragraph (i) of article 2;

(b)   the foreign representative applying for recognition is a person or body within the meaning of sub-paragraph (j) of article 2;

(c)   the application meets the requirements of paragraphs 2 and 3 of article 15; and

(d)   the application has been submitted to the court referred to in article 4.

2 The foreign proceeding shall be recognised–

(a)   as a foreign main proceeding if it is taking place in the State where the debtor has the centre of its main interests; or

(b)   as a foreign non-main proceeding if the debtor has an establishment within the meaning of sub-paragraph (e) of article 2 in the foreign State.

3 An application for recognition of a foreign proceeding shall be decided upon at the earliest possible time.

4 The provisions of articles 15 to 16, this article and article 18 do not prevent modification or termination of recognition if it is shown that the grounds for granting it were fully or partially lacking or have fully or partially ceased to exist and in such a case, the court may, on the application of the foreign representative or a person affected by recognition, or of its own motion, modify or terminate recognition, either altogether or for a limited time, on such terms and conditions as the court thinks fit.

GENERAL NOTE

The purpose of this article is to indicate that, if the application meets the requirements set out, recognition should be granted as a matter of course and without delay, so ensuring the effective protection of the debtor's assets. The decision to grant recognition should not involve an examination of the merits of the foreign court's decision or the foreign representative's suitability. The only exception is art.6 (public policy).

Art.17.2

Recognition must categorise the foreign proceeding as "main" or "non-main". This is important because the former brings about an automatic stay of proceedings and the freezing of assets under art.20. If the proceeding is deemed to be non-main, the grant of a stay is in the discretion of the court.

It is not permitted to recognise a foreign proceeding as non-main if the debtor has assets but no establishment (as defined in art.2(e)) in the foreign jurisdiction. As noted in the comment to that article, the use of "it" is misleading: the CBIR apply to individual as well as corporate debtors. Non-recognition could not, of course, affect in any way the conduct of that proceeding in its home State; still less restrict the powers of the office-holder in the main proceedings (which could be British insolvency proceedings) from exercising any rights he may have in relation to those assets.

Art.17.4

Examples of the grounds which may justify the modification or termination of recognition include the emergence of new facts, or a change of circumstances such as the termination of the foreign proceeding or a change in its nature (reorganisation giving way to liquidation, or vice versa). The court may also be requested to re-examine whether in the decision-making process the requirements for recognition were observed. The G to E, para.131, stresses that the review of a decision should not involve an inquiry into the merits of the case, any more than the decision itself.

Procedural matters, including appeals, are not dealt with by the Model Law but left to the domestic law of the enacting State.

Article 18. Subsequent information

From the time of filing the application for recognition of the foreign proceeding, the foreign representative shall inform the court promptly of–

(a) any substantial change in the status of the recognised foreign proceeding or the status of the foreign representative's appointment; and

(b) any other foreign proceeding, proceeding under British insolvency law or section 426 request regarding the same debtor that becomes known to the foreign representative.

GENERAL NOTE

"Substantial" changes are to be distinguished from those which are merely technical. As well as the possibility that the foreign proceeding may change from reorganisation to liquidation, or vice versa, the court will wish to be informed if the recognition was of an interim proceeding or the appointment of the representative was on an interim basis and it has since been made permanent.

Art.18(b)

In the light of the new information the court may wish to consider whether the relief already granted should be modified so as to co-ordinate with the other proceeding or s.426 request.

Article 19. Relief that may be granted upon application for recognition of a foreign proceeding

1 From the time of filing an application for recognition until the application is decided upon, the court may, at the request of the foreign representative, where relief is urgently needed to protect the assets of the debtor or the interests of the creditors, grant relief of a provisional nature, including–

(a) staying execution against the debtor's assets;

(b) entrusting the administration or realisation of all or part of the debtor's assets located in Great Britain to the foreign representative or another person designated by the court, in order to protect and preserve the value of assets that, by their nature or because of other circumstances, are perishable, susceptible to devaluation or otherwise in jeopardy; and

(c) any relief mentioned in paragraph 1 (c), (d) or (g) of article 21.

2 Unless extended under paragraph 1(f) of article 21, the relief granted under this article terminates when the application for recognition is decided upon.

3 The court may refuse to grant relief under this article if such relief would interfere with the administration of a foreign main proceeding.

GENERAL NOTE

The provisional relief which may be granted under this provision is discretionary and the circumstances in which it may be granted under para.(b) would appear to be limited to those specified, except for the use of the word "including" in the opening sentence. Note that the power to refuse relief under para.(c) is also discretionary.

It is stressed in the G to E, para.136 that the type of relief which the court is authorised to grant here is that which "is usually available only in collective insolvency proceedings", as opposed to the "individual" relief which may be granted under rules of civil procedure (i.e. measures covering specific assets identified by a creditor).

The recognition of a foreign proceeding could not affect the substantive rights of any party. For instance, it could not give validity to the discharge of a foreign debt which would be regarded as ineffective under English law (as in *Global Distressed Alpha Fund 1 LLP v PT Bakrie Investindo* [2011] EWHC 256 (Comm); [2011] B.P.I.R. 645: see the note to IA 1986 s.426).

Article 20. Effects of recognition of a foreign main proceeding

1 Upon recognition of a foreign proceeding that is a foreign main proceeding, subject to paragraph 2 of this article–

    (a) commencement or continuation of individual actions or individual proceedings concerning the debtor's assets, rights, obligations or liabilities is stayed;

    (b) execution against the debtor's assets is stayed; and

    (c) the right to transfer, encumber or otherwise dispose of any assets of the debtor is suspended.

2 The stay and suspension referred to in paragraph 1 of this article shall be–

    (a) the same in scope and effect as if the debtor, in the case of an individual, had been adjudged bankrupt under the Insolvency Act 1986 or had his estate sequestrated under the Bankruptcy (Scotland) Act 1985, or, in the case of a debtor other than an individual, had been made the subject of a winding-up order under the Insolvency Act 1986; and

    (b) subject to the same powers of the court and the same prohibitions, limitations, exceptions and conditions as would apply under the law of Great Britain in such a case,

and the provisions of paragraph 1 of this article shall be interpreted accordingly.

3 Without prejudice to paragraph 2 of this article, the stay and suspension referred to in paragraph 1 of this article, in particular, does not affect any right–

    (a) to take any steps to enforce security over the debtor's property;

    (b) to take any steps to repossess goods in the debtor's possession under a hire-purchase agreement;

    (c) exercisable under or by virtue of or in connection with the provisions referred to in article 1(4); or

    (d) of a creditor to set off its claim against a claim of the debtor,

being a right which would have been exercisable if the debtor, in the case of an individual, had been adjudged bankrupt under the Insolvency Act 1986 or had his estate sequestrated under the Bankruptcy (Scotland) Act 1985, or, in the case of a debtor other than an individual, had been made the subject of a winding-up order under the Insolvency Act 1986.

4 Paragraph 1(a) of this article does not affect the right to–

    (a) commence individual actions or proceedings to the extent necessary to preserve a claim against the debtor; or

    (b) commence or continue any criminal proceedings or any action or proceedings by a person or body having regulatory, supervisory or investigative functions of a public nature, being an action or proceedings brought in the exercise of those functions.

5   Paragraph 1 of this article does not affect the right to request or otherwise initiate the commencement of a proceeding under British insolvency law or the right to file claims in such a proceeding.

6   In addition to and without prejudice to any powers of the court under or by virtue of paragraph 2 of this article, the court may, on the application of the foreign representative or a person affected by the stay and suspension referred to in paragraph 1 of this article, or of its own motion, modify or terminate such stay and suspension or any part of it, either altogether or for a limited time, on such terms and conditions as the court thinks fit.

GENERAL NOTE

The stay which comes into being under this article follows automatically from the recognition of a foreign proceeding as a main proceeding, and its extent is defined in the later paragraphs. No court order is necessary. Where the foreign law governing the main proceeding provides for a different (possibly less stringent) stay, the stay in this jurisdiction will be that defined by art.20.

Note that the automatic stay will apply even in the case of an "interim" foreign proceeding.

The use of the phrase "or individual proceedings" is intended to include arbitrations, but it is conceded (G to E, para.145) that it may not always be possible, in practical terms, to implement a stay of arbitral proceedings—perhaps an international arbitration taking place under the law of a third jurisdiction. In any case, it may be thought in the interests of the debtor to allow such a proceeding to continue—a course which could be sanctioned by the court under arts 20.2 or 20.6.

The CBIR do not specify what sanctions might apply for breach of a stay.

Article 21 gives the court discretionary powers to grant a stay beyond the scope of art.20, e.g. because the foreign insolvency is a non-main proceeding, or where a wider stay is sought (see art.21.1(a)-(c)). Note the limitations imposed by arts 1.4–1.7.

In *Samsun Logix Corp v DEF* [2009] EWHC 576 (Ch); [2010] B.C.C. 556 the court ruled that a Korean receivership constituted foreign main proceedings, with the consequence that a stay under art.20 came into force.

Art.20.2

Under the Model Law, it is assumed that domestic law provisions such as those referred to may be invoked for the purpose of terminating the stay, for instance if a foreign interim proceeding is discontinued (G to E, para.144); but the CBIR make express provision for this in art.20.6.

Art.20.3

Rights of security, repossession and set-off are not affected, as are the special regimes applicable to payment and settlement systems. "Hire-purchase agreement" has the extended meaning set out in art.2(k).

Arts 20.4, 20.5

Article 20.4(a) is restricted to the *commencing* of proceedings (e.g. to prevent a claim becoming statute-barred under the law of the proper law of the underlying contract). In any event, a foreign claimant might feel assured that by commencing local proceedings his claim would not be prejudiced.

Subparagraph (b), which is not so restricted, would include director disqualification proceedings.

Article 21. Relief that may be granted upon recognition of a foreign proceeding

1   Upon recognition of a foreign proceeding, whether main or non-main, where necessary to protect the assets of the debtor or the interests of the creditors, the court may, at the request of the foreign representative, grant any appropriate relief, including–

    (a)   staying the commencement or continuation of individual actions or individual proceedings concerning the debtor's assets, rights, obligations or liabilities, to the extent they have not been stayed under paragraph 1(a) of article 20;

    (b)   staying execution against the debtor's assets to the extent it has not been stayed under paragraph 1(b) of article 20;

    (c)   suspending the right to transfer, encumber or otherwise dispose of any assets of the debtor to the extent this right has not been suspended under paragraph 1(c) of article 20;

(d) providing for the examination of witnesses, the taking of evidence or the delivery of information concerning the debtor's assets, affairs, rights, obligations or liabilities;

(e) entrusting the administration or realisation of all or part of the debtor's assets located in Great Britain to the foreign representative or another person designated by the court;

(f) extending relief granted under paragraph 1 of article 19; and

(g) granting any additional relief that may be available to a British insolvency officeholder under the law of Great Britain, including any relief provided under paragraph 43 of Schedule B1 to the Insolvency Act 1986.

2 Upon recognition of a foreign proceeding, whether main or non-main, the court may, at the request of the foreign representative, entrust the distribution of all or part of the debtor's assets located in Great Britain to the foreign representative or another person designated by the court, provided that the court is satisfied that the interests of creditors in Great Britain are adequately protected.

3 In granting relief under this article to a representative of a foreign non-main proceeding, the court must be satisfied that the relief relates to assets that, under the law of Great Britain, should be administered in the foreign non-main proceeding or concerns information required in that proceeding.

4 No stay under paragraph 1(a) of this article shall affect the right to commence or continue any criminal proceedings or any action or proceedings by a person or body having regulatory, supervisory or investigative functions of a public nature, being an action or proceedings brought in the exercise of those functions.

GENERAL NOTE

This article deals with "post-recognition" relief; for "pre-recognition" relief, see art.19.

As noted above, the grant of a stay under this provision is discretionary, and may be more extensive than that which comes into being automatically under art.20. But the relief available under this article is entirely general, and not restricted to a stay of proceedings: see paras 1(d)–(g) and (2).

Art.21.1

For examples of the court's exercise of discretion under this provision, see *Picard v FIM Advisers LLP* [2010] EWHC 1299 (Ch); [2011] 1 B.C.L.C. 129 (order granted for production of documents to US administrator of Madoff company); *Re Chesterfield United Inc* [2012] EWHC 244 (Ch) (similar facts); *Larsen v Navios International Inc* [2011] EWHC 878 (Ch) (contractual set-off which would infringe pari passu principle disallowed). In the *Larsen* case the court held that, while art.21 authorises relief to be given by the English court as from the date of recognition, the relevant date for identifying the rights in respect of which the relief is to be afforded is the date of the opening of the foreign proceedings. In *Re Chesterfield United* it was held that art.21(1)(g) sets only minimum standards and that, if the local law (in this case IA 1986 s.236) provided for additional relief a foreign representative could seek that under art.21(1)(g).

Art.21.2

The court's discretion extends to directing the "turnover" of assets to the foreign representative, or to some other person. A number of other provisions of the CBIR also provide safeguards intended to ensure the protection of local interests: see, e.g. arts 22.1, 22.2. In *Re SwissAir Schweizerische Luftverkehr-Aktiengesellschaft* [2009] EWHC 2099 (Ch); [2010] B.C.C. 667 an order was made for the remittal of assets to main proceedings in Switzerland, no conditions being held to be necessary.

In *Cosco Bulk Carrier Shipping Co Ltd v Armada Shipping SA* [2011] EWHC 216 (Ch); [2011] B.P.I.R. 626 Briggs J. exercised the discretion under art.21 to order a stay in a case where the respondent company was in liquidation in Switzerland, on the ground that the issues involved questions of shipping law which could better be considered by expert arbitrators in this country.

Art.21.3

In contrast with the EC Regulation, which is a Community enactment effective in all the Member States (apart from Denmark) the authority of the Model Law cannot be imposed on a foreign jurisdiction by the CBIR or any other external source. It follows that the scope of a foreign non-main proceeding will not be limited to assets situated within its own jurisdiction unless such a restriction is imposed by the local law. Such a limitation can, however, be placed on the relief which the court may grant to a foreign non-main representative ("the law of Great Britain" including, of course, the CBIR). Moreover, if there are also insolvency proceedings current in another foreign State, the court can ensure that any relief granted will not interfere with the administration of those proceedings, in particular the main proceeding.

Article 22. Protection of creditors and other interested persons

1 In granting or denying relief under article 19 or 21, or in modifying or terminating relief under paragraph 3 of this article or paragraph 6 of article 20, the court must be satisfied that the interests of the creditors (including any secured creditors or parties to hire-purchase agreements) and other interested persons, including if appropriate the debtor, are adequately protected.

2 The court may subject relief granted under article 19 or 21 to conditions it considers appropriate, including the provision by the foreign representative of security or caution for the proper performance of his functions.

3 The court may, at the request of the foreign representative or a person affected by relief granted under article 19 or 21, or of its own motion, modify or terminate such relief.

GENERAL NOTE

It is to be noted that there is no reference here to "local" creditors, or indeed any definition of such a term in the CBIR. "The interests of the creditors" would, however, include the priority to which preferential creditors and those entitled to participate in the "prescribed part" under IA 1986 s.176A are entitled. Adequate protection may include the giving of notice to interested parties. This matter is left to be dealt with by the general law and the discretion of the court.

Article 23. Actions to avoid acts detrimental to creditors

1 Subject to paragraphs 6 and 9 of this article, upon recognition of a foreign proceeding, the foreign representative has standing to make an application to the court for an order under or in connection with sections 238, 239, 242, 243, 244, 245, 339, 340, 342A, 343, and 423 of the Insolvency Act 1986 and sections 34, 35, 36, 36A and 61 of the Bankruptcy (Scotland) Act 1985.

2 Where the foreign representative makes such an application (**"an article 23 application"**), the sections referred to in paragraph 1 of this article and sections 240, 241, 341, 342, 342B to 342F, 424 and 425 of the Insolvency Act 1986 and sections 36B and 36C of the Bankruptcy (Scotland) Act 1985 shall apply–

    (a) whether or not the debtor, in the case of an individual, has been adjudged bankrupt or had his estate sequestrated, or, in the case of a debtor other than an individual, is being wound up or is in administration, under British insolvency law; and

    (b) with the modifications set out in paragraph 3 of this article.

3 The modifications referred to in paragraph 2 of this article are as follows–

    (a) for the purposes of sections 241(2A)(a) and 342(2A)(a) of the Insolvency Act 1986, a person has notice of the relevant proceedings if he has notice of the opening of the relevant foreign proceeding;

    (b) for the purposes of sections 240(1) and 245(3) of that Act, the onset of insolvency shall be the date of the opening of the relevant foreign proceeding;

    (c) the periods referred to in sections 244(2), 341(1)(a) to (c) and 343(2) of that Act shall be periods ending with the date of the opening of the relevant foreign proceeding;

(d) for the purposes of sections 242(3)(a), (3)(b) and 243(1) of that Act, the date on which the winding up of the company commences or it enters administration shall be the date of the opening of the relevant foreign proceeding; and

(e) for the purposes of sections 34(3)(a), (3)(b), 35(1)(c), 36(1)(a) and (1)(b) and 61(2) of the Bankruptcy (Scotland) Act 1985, the date of sequestration or granting of the trust deed shall be the date of the opening of the relevant foreign proceeding.

4 For the purposes of paragraph 3 of this article, the date of the opening of the foreign proceeding shall be determined in accordance with the law of the State in which the foreign proceeding is taking place, including any rule of law by virtue of which the foreign proceeding is deemed to have opened at an earlier time.

5 When the foreign proceeding is a foreign non-main proceeding, the court must be satisfied that the article 23 application relates to assets that, under the law of Great Britain, should be administered in the foreign non-main proceeding.

6 At any time when a proceeding under British insolvency law is taking place regarding the debtor–

(a) the foreign representative shall not make an article 23 application except with the permission of–

(i) in the case of a proceeding under British insolvency law taking place in England and Wales, the High Court; or

(ii) in the case of a proceeding under British insolvency law taking place in Scotland, the Court of Session; and

(b) references to **"the court"** in paragraphs 1, 5 and 7 of this article are references to the court in which that proceeding is taking place.

7 On making an order on an article 23 application, the court may give such directions regarding the distribution of any proceeds of the claim by the foreign representative, as it thinks fit to ensure that the interests of creditors in Great Britain are adequately protected.

8 Nothing in this article affects the right of a British insolvency officeholder to make an application under or in connection with any of the provisions referred to in paragraph 1 of this article.

9 Nothing in paragraph 1 of this article shall apply in respect of any preference given, floating charge created, alienation, assignment or relevant contributions (within the meaning of section 342A(5) of the Insolvency Act 1986) made or other transaction entered into before the date on which this Law comes into force.

GENERAL NOTE

This article empowers a foreign representative to make application to a British court for any of the forms of relief listed in para.1 (avoidance of preferences, transactions at an undervalue, etc.) even though the debtor is not the subject of an insolvency proceeding under British law, and where the foreign representative would not otherwise have standing to apply to the court. The article does not create any substantive right regarding the claims in question and is not concerned with any question that may arise under the conflict of laws.

In contrast with the EC Regulation, the foreign representative is not deemed to be a creditor or his position equated with that of a creditor for these or any other purposes under the CBIR.

Article 24. Intervention by a foreign representative in proceedings in Great Britain

Upon recognition of a foreign proceeding, the foreign representative may, provided the requirements of the law of Great Britain are met, intervene in any proceedings in which the debtor is a party.

GENERAL NOTE

Again, this article is concerned to ensure that the foreign representative is accorded standing, even in cases where the relevant legislation does not contemplate his intervention. It applies to representatives in both main and non-main proceedings, and includes extra-judicial proceedings as well as court actions. These will be proceedings between the debtor and a third party (as distinct from intervention or participation in the insolvency itself (on which see art.12)), and can only be those that have not been stayed under arts 20 or 21.

CHAPTER IV

COOPERATION WITH FOREIGN COURTS AND FOREIGN REPRESENTATIVES

Introductory note to Chapter IV

Chapter IV, on co-operation, is described as a "core element" of the Model Law (G to E, para.173). Its objective is to enable courts and insolvency administrators to be efficient and to achieve optimal results, whether in preventing the dissipation of assets, in maximising their value or in finding the best solutions for a reorganisation.

Note the use of the word "may", in contrast with "shall" in art.26. The Model Law itself also uses "shall" in art.25, but the substitution of "may" in the CBIR must be assumed to have been deliberate. Thus the court has a discretion, but an office-holder does not.

It is not a necessary condition for the application of Chapter IV that the foreign proceeding should have been recognised under Chapter III.

Article 25. Cooperation and direct communication between a court of Great Britain and foreign courts or foreign representatives

1 In matters referred to in paragraph 1 of article 1, the court may cooperate to the maximum extent possible with foreign courts or foreign representatives, either directly or through a British insolvency officeholder.

2 The court is entitled to communicate directly with, or to request information or assistance directly from, foreign courts or foreign representatives.

Art.25.1

The substitution of the word "may" (see above) sits oddly with retention of the phrase "to the maximum extent possible"! The extent to which the parties should be involved is a matter for the discretion of the court.

Art.25.2

The use of the word "directly" is intended to encourage the court to forgo the use of formalities, such as involving higher courts, or using letters rogatory or diplomatic or consular channels.

Article 26. Cooperation and direct communication between the British insolvency officeholder and foreign courts or foreign representatives

1 In matters referred to in paragraph 1 of article 1, a British insolvency officeholder shall to the extent consistent with his other duties under the law of Great Britain, in the exercise of his functions and subject to the supervision of the court, cooperate to the maximum extent possible with foreign courts or foreign representatives.

2 The British insolvency officeholder is entitled, in the exercise of his functions and subject to the supervision of the court, to communicate directly with foreign courts or foreign representatives.

GENERAL NOTE

As noted above, this article is mandatory in its terms. The phrase "subject to the supervision of the court" is not intended to require the office-holder to seek approval of his acts on an ad hoc basis in situations where the court's supervisory role under the domestic law is largely nominal (e.g. a CVA or IVA): see G to E, para.180.

Article 27. Forms of cooperation

Cooperation referred to in articles 25 and 26 may be implemented by any appropriate means, including–

    (a)   appointment of a person to act at the direction of the court;

(b) communication of information by any means considered appropriate by the court;

(c) coordination of the administration and supervision of the debtor's assets and affairs;

(d) approval or implementation by courts of agreements concerning the coordination of proceedings;

(e) coordination of concurrent proceedings regarding the same debtor.

GENERAL NOTE

The list of options is not exhaustive. It would not rule out the suspension or termination of local insolvency proceedings, if appropriate. In *Rubin v Eurofinance SA* [2010] EWCA Civ 895; [2011] B.C.C. 649 Ward L.J. (at [64]) expressed concern that the forms of co-operation specifically mentioned in art.27 did not include enforcement (and, indeed, that there was no mention of enforcement anywhere in the CBIR), but he did indicate that in his view co-operation "to the maximum extent possible" would include enforcement.

In furtherance of art.27(d), on July 1, 2009, UNCITRAL adopted a *Practice Guide on Cross-Border Insolvency Cooperation* which was adopted by a resolution of the UN General Assembly on December 16, 2009, and published in 2010. The purpose of the *Practice Guide* is to "to provide information for practitioners and judges on practical aspects of cooperation and communication in cross-border insolvency cases, specifically in cases involving insolvency proceedings in multiple States where the insolvent debtor has assets and cases where some of the debtor's creditors are not from the State in which the insolvency proceedings have commenced". Although it might apply to individual debtors, it is typically aimed at enterprise groups with offices, business activities and assets in multiple States. The *Practice Guide* focuses on the use and negotiation of cross-border insolvency agreements, providing an analysis of a number of written agreements approved by courts and oral arrangements between parties to cross-border insolvency proceedings in the preceding 20 years. The *Practice Guide* is not intended to be prescriptive but to illustrate how resolution of issues and conflicts may be facilitated by the use of such agreements tailored to the specifics of each case and the requirements of applicable law. The *Practice Guide* is available on the Publications section of the UNCITRAL website.

CHAPTER V

CONCURRENT PROCEEDINGS

Article 28. Commencement of a proceeding under British insolvency law after recognition of a foreign main proceeding

After recognition of a foreign main proceeding, the effects of a proceeding under British insolvency law in relation to the same debtor shall, insofar as the assets of that debtor are concerned, be restricted to assets that are located in Great Britain and, to the extent necessary to implement cooperation and coordination under articles 25, 26 and 27, to other assets of the debtor that, under the law of Great Britain, should be administered in that proceeding.

GENERAL NOTE

This is another provision of the CBIR which is expressed in mandatory terms. It applies only after the foreign proceeding has been recognised, *and* recognised as a main proceeding. Before there has been any recognition, or if the foreign proceedings are recognised only as non-main, the law of the relevant British jurisdiction applies to the exclusion of the CBIR. So, for instance, the cases where the court assumed jurisdiction to make an order for the winding up order of a foreign company under IA 1986 Pt V, even when the debtor company had no assets in the UK (e.g. *Re Eloc, etc. BV* [1982] Ch. 43: see IA 1986 s.220) will still be authoritative—unless, of course, the EC Regulation applies. But once a main foreign proceeding has been recognised, any domestic insolvency proceeding is restricted to dealing with local assets.

Does this restriction apply to a proceeding that has already commenced here before recognition? Far from making this clear, the draftsman has left us with an uncertainty. The heading to art.28 plainly confines its scope to the commencement of new proceedings, as does the Model Law ("a proceeding under [British] insolvency law may be commenced only if the debtor has assets in this State"). But the CBIR text alters this to "the effects of a proceeding under British insolvency law ... shall ... be restricted to assets that are located in Great Britain".

Article 28 does not require also (or instead) that the debtor should have an establishment in Britain: contrast art.17.2(b), dealing with the recognition of foreign non-main proceedings.

The concluding words (after "in Great Britain") are designed to cope with exceptional situations, such as where assets of the debtor have been fraudulently moved abroad, or where there is no foreign proceeding necessary or available in the State where the assets are situated; the G to E (para.187) suggests also "where it would be possible to sell the debtor's assets in the enacting State and the assets abroad as a 'going concern'". The words "to the extent necessary to implement co-operation and co-ordination under Articles 25, 26 and 27" limit the potential open-ended application of this provision.

Article 29. Coordination of a proceeding under British insolvency law and a foreign proceeding

Where a foreign proceeding and a proceeding under British insolvency law are taking place concurrently regarding the same debtor, the court may seek cooperation and coordination under articles 25, 26 and 27, and the following shall apply–

    (a)   when the proceeding in Great Britain is taking place at the time the application for recognition of the foreign proceeding is filed–

        (i)   any relief granted under article 19 or 21 must be consistent with the proceeding in Great Britain; and

        (ii)   if the foreign proceeding is recognised in Great Britain as a foreign main proceeding, article 20 does not apply;

    (b)   when the proceeding in Great Britain commences after the filing of the application for recognition of the foreign proceeding–

        (i)   any relief in effect under article 19 or 21 shall be reviewed by the court and shall be modified or terminated if inconsistent with the proceeding in Great Britain;

        (ii)   if the foreign proceeding is a foreign main proceeding, the stay and suspension referred to in paragraph 1 of article 20 shall be modified or terminated pursuant to paragraph 6 of article 20, if inconsistent with the proceeding in Great Britain; and

        (iii)   any proceedings brought by the foreign representative by virtue of paragraph 1 of article 23 before the proceeding in Great Britain commenced shall be reviewed by the court and the court may give such directions as it thinks fit regarding the continuance of those proceedings; and

    (c)   in granting, extending or modifying relief granted to a representative of a foreign non-main proceeding, the court must be satisfied that the relief relates to assets that, under the law of Great Britain, should be administered in the foreign non-main proceeding or concerns information required in that proceeding.

GENERAL NOTE

Again, the words "shall apply" indicate that this provision is mandatory. The commencement of a local proceeding is not to prevent or terminate the recognition of a foreign proceeding, but the article maintains a pre-eminence of the local proceeding in various ways, e.g. by providing that:

- any relief granted to the foreign proceeding must be consistent with the local proceeding;

- any relief granted previously to the foreign proceeding must be reviewed and modified or terminated to ensure such consistency;

- if the foreign proceeding is a main proceeding, there must be a review of the effects of the automatic stay;

- where a local proceeding is pending at the time when a foreign proceeding is recognised as a main proceeding, no automatic stay ensues.

However, art.29 avoids establishing a rigid hierarchy between the different proceedings.

Art.29(c)

This provision incorporates the principle expressed also in arts 19.4, 21.3 and 30.

Article 30. Coordination of more than one foreign proceeding

In matters referred to in paragraph 1 of article 1, in respect of more than one foreign proceeding regarding the same debtor, the court may seek cooperation and coordination under articles 25, 26 and 27, and the following shall apply–

(a) any relief granted under article 19 or 21 to a representative of a foreign non-main proceeding after recognition of a foreign main proceeding must be consistent with the foreign main proceeding;

(b) if a foreign main proceeding is recognised after the filing of an application for recognition of a foreign non-main proceeding, any relief in effect under article 19 or 21 shall be reviewed by the court and shall be modified or terminated if inconsistent with the foreign main proceeding; and

(c) if, after recognition of a foreign non-main proceeding, another foreign non-main proceeding is recognised, the court shall grant, modify or terminate relief for the purpose of facilitating coordination of the proceedings.

GENERAL NOTE

This provision applies whether or not an insolvency proceeding is pending in Britain: but if it has already commenced, art.29 governs the position as between the home and any foreign proceeding. However, where there are proceedings here and also in two or more foreign jurisdictions, this article applies as between those foreign proceedings. If one of the latter is a main proceeding, this provision gives that proceeding primacy—unlike art.29, which gives the local proceeding priority. In other respects, it mirrors art.29.

Article 31. Presumption of insolvency based on recognition of a foreign main proceeding

In the absence of evidence to the contrary, recognition of a foreign main proceeding is, for the purpose of commencing a proceeding under British insolvency law, proof that the debtor is unable to pay its debts or, in relation to Scotland, is apparently insolvent within the meaning given to those expressions under British insolvency law.

GENERAL NOTE

The presumption created by this provision is rebuttable. It does not apply where the foreign proceeding is a non-main proceeding. Where applicable, it displaces the requirements of IA 1986 s.268 (proof of "inability to pay" in bankruptcy proceedings) and "apparently insolvent" in the Bankruptcy (Scotland) Act 1985 s.7.

Article 32. Rule of payment in concurrent proceedings

Without prejudice to secured claims or rights in rem, a creditor who has received part payment in respect of its claim in a proceeding pursuant to a law relating to insolvency in a foreign State may not receive a payment for the same claim in a proceeding under British insolvency law regarding the same debtor, so long as the payment to the other creditors of the same class is proportionately less than the payment the creditor has already received.

GENERAL NOTE

The principle of hotchpot applies in regard to the claims of unsecured creditors in concurrent insolvency proceedings.

SCHEDULE 2

Regulation 4

PROCEDURAL MATTERS IN ENGLAND AND WALES

Introductory note to Schedule 2
The notes to Sch.1 will generally be applicable. Schedule 3 contains corresponding provisions for Scotland.

1 Interpretation

1(1) In this Schedule–

"the 1986 Act" means the Insolvency Act 1986;

"article 21 relief application" means an application to the court by a foreign representative under article 21(1) or (2) of the Model Law for relief;

"business day" means any day other than a Saturday, a Sunday, Christmas Day, Good Friday or a day which is a bank holiday in England and Wales under or by virtue of the Banking and Financial Dealings Act 1971;

"CPR" means the Civil Procedure Rules 1998 and **"CPR"** followed by a Part or rule by number means the Part or rule with that number in those Rules;

"enforcement officer" means an individual who is authorised to act as an enforcement officer under the Courts Act 2003;

"file in court" and **"file with the court"** means deliver to the court for filing;

"the Gazette" means the London Gazette;

"interim relief application" means an application to the court by a foreign representative under article 19 of the Model Law for interim relief;

"main proceedings" means proceedings opened in accordance with Article 3(1) of the EC Insolvency Regulation and falling within the definition of insolvency proceedings in Article 2(a) of the EC Insolvency Regulation;

"member State liquidator" means a person falling within the definition of liquidator in Article 2(b) of the EC Insolvency Regulation appointed in proceedings to which it applies in a member State other than the United Kingdom;

"the Model Law" means the UNCITRAL Model Law as set out in Schedule 1 to these Regulations;

"modification or termination order" means an order by the court pursuant to its powers under the Model Law modifying or terminating recognition of a foreign proceeding, the stay and suspension referred to in article 20(1) or any part of it or any relief granted under article 19 or 21 of the Model Law;

"originating application" means an application to the court which is not an application in pending proceedings before the court;

"ordinary application" means any application to the court other than an originating application;

"practice direction" means a direction as to the practice and procedure of any court within the scope of the CPR;

"recognition application" means an application to the court by a foreign representative in accordance with article 15 of the Model Law for an order recognising the foreign proceeding in which he has been appointed;

"recognition order" means an order by the court recognising a proceeding the subject of a recognition application as a foreign main proceeding or foreign non-main proceeding, as appropriate;

"relevant company" means a company that is–

(a) registered under the Companies Act 2006,

(b) subject to a requirement imposed by regulations under section 1043 of that Act 2006 (unregistered UK companies) to deliver any documents to the registrar of companies, or

(c) subject to a requirement imposed by regulations under section 1046 of that Act (overseas companies) to deliver any documents to the registrar of companies;

"review application" means an application to the court for a modification or termination order;

"the Rules" means the Insolvency Rules 1986 and **"Rule"** followed by a number means the rule with that number in those Rules;

"secondary proceedings" means proceedings opened in accordance with Articles 3(2) and 3(3) of the EC Insolvency Regulation and falling within the definition of winding up proceedings in Article 2(c) of the EC Insolvency Regulation;

"territorial proceedings" means proceedings opened in accordance with Articles 3(2) and 3(4) of the EC Insolvency Regulation and falling within the definition of insolvency proceedings in Article 2(a) of the EC Insolvency Regulation.

1(2) Expressions defined in the Model Law have the same meaning when used in this Schedule.

1(3) In proceedings under these Regulations, **"Registrar"** means–

(a) a Registrar in Bankruptcy of the High Court; and

(b) where the proceedings are in a district registry, the district judge.

1(4) References to the **"venue"** for any proceedings or attendance before the court, are to the time, date and place for the proceedings or attendance.

1(5) References in this Schedule to ex parte hearings shall be construed as references to hearings without notice being served on any other party, and references to applications made ex parte as references to applications made without notice being served on any other party; and other references which include the expression **"ex parte"** shall be similarly construed.

1(6) References in this Schedule to a debtor who is of interest to the Financial Services Authority are references to a debtor who–

(a) is, or has been, an authorised person within the meaning of section 31 of the Financial Services and Markets Act 2000 (authorised persons);

(b) is, or has been, an appointed representative within the meaning of section 39 (exemption of appointed representatives) of that Act; or

(c) is carrying on, or has carried on, a regulated activity in contravention of the general prohibition.

1(7) In sub-paragraph (6) **"the general prohibition"** has the meaning given by section 19 of the Financial Services and Markets Act 2000 and the reference to a **"regulated activity"** must be construed in accordance with–

(a) section 22 of that Act (classes of regulated activity and categories of investment);

(b) any relevant order under that section; and

(c) Schedule 2 to that Act (regulated activities).

1(8) References in this Schedule to a numbered form are to the form that bears that number in Schedule 5.

GENERAL NOTE

Definition of "relevant company" inserted into para.1(1) by the Companies Act 2006 (Consequential Amendments, Transitional Provisions and Savings) Order 2009 (SI 2009/1941) art.2(1) and Sch.1 para.264(3)(a) as from October 1,

2009. A company incorporated under an earlier Companies Act is deemed to be "registered under" CA 2006 by s.1(1) of that Act.

PART 2

APPLICATIONS TO COURT FOR RECOGNITION OF FOREIGN PROCEEDINGS

2 Affidavit in support of recognition application

2 A recognition application shall be in Form ML 1 and shall be supported by an affidavit sworn by the foreign representative complying with paragraph 4.

3 Form and content of application

3 The application shall state the following matters–

    (a)   the name of the applicant and his address for service within England and Wales;

    (b)   the name of the debtor in respect of which the foreign proceeding is taking place;

    (c)   the name or names in which the debtor carries on business in the country where the foreign proceeding is taking place and in this country, if other than the name given under sub-paragraph (b);

    (d)   the principal or last known place of business of the debtor in Great Britain (if any) and, in the case of an individual, his usual or last known place of residence in Great Britain (if any);

    (e)   any registered number allocated to the debtor under the Companies Act 2006;

    (f)   brief particulars of the foreign proceeding in respect of which recognition is applied for, including the country in which it is taking place and the nature of the proceeding;

    (g)   that the foreign proceeding is a proceeding within the meaning of article 2(i) of the Model Law;

    (h)   that the applicant is a foreign representative within the meaning of article 2(j) of the Model Law;

    (i)   the address of the debtor's centre of main interests and, if different, the address of its registered office or habitual residence, as appropriate; and

    (j)   if the debtor does not have its centre of main interests in the country where the foreign proceeding is taking place, whether the debtor has an establishment within the meaning of article 2(e) of the Model Law in that country, and if so, its address.

GENERAL NOTE

An application for recognition (using Form ML 1) must contain the matters listed in this paragraph, and must be supported by affidavit evidence complying with para.4.

Para.3(g), (h)
The foreign proceeding must be a collective proceeding (including an interim proceeding) but may be for reorganisation or rehabilitation as well as liquidation or bankruptcy. It appears that the representative need not necessarily be the office-holder in the foreign proceeding.

Para.3(i), (j)
Recognition involves classifying the foreign proceeding as "main" or "non-main", hence the need for this information. If the debtor does not have an establishment in the country concerned, recognition as a non-main proceeding is not possible.

4 Contents of affidavit in support

4(1) There shall be attached to the application an affidavit in support which shall contain or have exhibited to it–

200

(a) the evidence and statement required under article 15(2) and (3) respectively of the Model Law;

(b) any other evidence which in the opinion of the applicant will assist the court in deciding whether the proceeding the subject of the application is a foreign proceeding within the meaning of article 2(i) of the Model Law and whether the applicant is a foreign representative within the meaning of article 2(j) of the Model Law;

(c) evidence that the debtor has its centre of main interests or an establishment, as the case may be, within the country where the foreign proceeding is taking place; and

(d) any other matters which in the opinion of the applicant will assist the court in deciding whether to make a recognition order.

4(2) The affidavit shall state whether, in the opinion of the applicant, the EC Insolvency Regulation applies to any of the proceedings identified in accordance with article 15(3) of the Model Law and, if so, whether those proceedings are main proceedings, secondary proceedings or territorial proceedings.

4(3) The affidavit shall also have exhibited to it the translations required under article 15(4) of the Model Law and a translation in English of any other document exhibited to the affidavit which is in a language other than English.

4(4) All translations referred to in sub-paragraph (3) must be certified by the translator as a correct translation.

Para.4(2)

The reference is to proceedings other than that for which recognition is being sought: the court will wish to know of all insolvency proceedings relating to the same debtor, so as to have a complete picture.

5 The hearing and powers of court

5(1) On hearing a recognition application the court may in addition to its powers under the Model Law to make a recognition order–

(a) dismiss the application;

(b) adjourn the hearing conditionally or unconditionally;

(c) make any other order which the court thinks appropriate.

5(2) If the court makes a recognition order, it shall be in Form ML 2.

6 Notification of subsequent information

6(1) The foreign representative shall set out any subsequent information required to be given to the court under article 18 of the Model Law in a statement which he shall attach to Form ML 3 and file with the court.

6(2) The statement shall include–

(a) details of the information required to be given under article 18 of the Model Law; and

(b) in the case of any proceedings required to be notified to the court under that article, a statement as to whether, in the opinion of the foreign representative, any of those proceedings are main proceedings, secondary proceedings or territorial proceedings under the EC Insolvency Regulation.

6(3) The foreign representative shall send a copy of the Form ML 3 and attached statement filed with the court to the following–

(a) the debtor; and

(b) those persons referred to in paragraph 26(3).

GENERAL NOTE

Article 18 requires the court to be informed of any changes in the position occurring or becoming known after the application for recognition has been filed.

PART 3

APPLICATIONS FOR RELIEF UNDER THE MODEL LAW

7 Application for interim relief—affidavit in support

7(1) An interim relief application must be supported by an affidavit sworn by the foreign representative stating–

(a) the grounds on which it is proposed that the interim relief applied for should be granted;

(b) details of any proceeding under British insolvency law taking place in relation to the debtor;

(c) whether, to the foreign representative's knowledge, an administrative receiver or receiver or manager of the debtor's property is acting in relation to the debtor;

(d) an estimate of the value of the assets of the debtor in England and Wales in respect of which relief is applied for;

(e) whether, to the best of the knowledge and belief of the foreign representative, the interests of the debtor's creditors (including any secured creditors or parties to hire-purchase agreements) and any other interested parties, including if appropriate the debtor, will be adequately protected;

(f) whether, to the best of the foreign representative's knowledge and belief, the grant of any of the relief applied for would interfere with the administration of a foreign main proceeding; and

(g) all other matters that in the opinion of the foreign representative will assist the court in deciding whether or not it is appropriate to grant the relief applied for.

GENERAL NOTE

"Interim relief" is relief sought under art.19 while an application for recognition is pending; after recognition, art.21 applies. The applicant may be the representative of either main or non-main proceedings in the foreign jurisdiction.

8 Service of interim relief application not required

8 Unless the court otherwise directs, it shall not be necessary to serve the interim relief application on, or give notice of it to, any person.

9 The hearing and powers of court

9 On hearing an interim relief application the court may in addition to its powers under the Model Law to make an order granting interim relief under article 19 of the Model Law–

(a) dismiss the application;

(b) adjourn the hearing conditionally or unconditionally;

(c) make any other order which the court thinks appropriate.

10 Application for relief under article 21 of the Model Law—affidavit in support

10 An article 21 relief application must be supported by an affidavit sworn by the foreign representative stating–

(a) the grounds on which it is proposed that the relief applied for should be granted;

(b) an estimate of the value of the assets of the debtor in England and Wales in respect of which relief is applied for;

(c) in the case of an application by a foreign representative who is or believes that he is a representative of a foreign non-main proceeding, the reasons why the applicant believes that the relief relates to assets that, under the law of Great Britain, should be administered in the foreign non-main proceeding or concerns information required in that proceeding;

(d) whether, to the best of the knowledge and belief of the foreign representative, the interests of the debtor's creditors (including any secured creditors or parties to hire-purchase agreements) and any other interested parties, including if appropriate the debtor, will be adequately protected; and

(e) all other matters that in the opinion of the foreign representative will assist the court in deciding whether or not it is appropriate to grant the relief applied for.

GENERAL NOTE

Once again, the applicant may be the representative of either main or non-main proceedings, but in the former case he will already have the benefit of a general stay of proceedings. The types of relief available under art.21 range very widely, from the grant of a freezing injunction to an order for the examination of witnesses.

11   The hearing and powers of court

11   On hearing an article 21 relief application the court may in addition to its powers under the Model Law to make an order granting relief under article 21 of the Model Law–

(a) dismiss the application;

(b) adjourn the hearing conditionally or unconditionally;

(c) make any other order which the court thinks appropriate.

PART 4

REPLACEMENT OF FOREIGN REPRESENTATIVE

12   Application for confirmation of status of replacement foreign representative

12(1)   This paragraph applies where following the making of a recognition order the foreign representative dies or for any other reason ceases to be the foreign representative in the foreign proceeding in relation to the debtor.

12(2)   In this paragraph **"the former foreign representative"** shall mean the foreign representative referred to in sub-paragraph (1).

12(3)   If a person has succeeded the former foreign representative or is otherwise holding office as foreign representative in the foreign proceeding in relation to the debtor, that person may apply to the court for an order confirming his status as replacement foreign representative for the purpose of proceedings under these Regulations.

13   Contents of application and affidavit in support

13(1)   An application under paragraph 12(3) shall in addition to the matters required to be stated by paragraph 19(2) state the following matters–

(a) the name of the replacement foreign representative and his address for service within England and Wales;

(b)   details of the circumstances in which the former foreign representative ceased to be foreign representative in the foreign proceeding in relation to the debtor (including the date on which he ceased to be the foreign representative);

(c)   details of his own appointment as replacement foreign representative in the foreign proceeding (including the date of that appointment).

13(2)   The application shall be accompanied by an affidavit in support sworn by the applicant which shall contain or have attached to it–

(a)   a certificate from the foreign court affirming–

     (i)   the cessation of the appointment of the former foreign representative as foreign representative; and

     (ii)   the appointment of the applicant as the foreign representative in the foreign proceeding; or

(b)   in the absence of such a certificate, any other evidence acceptable to the court of the matters referred to in paragraph (a); and

(c)   a translation in English of any document exhibited to the affidavit which is in a language other than English.

13(3)   All translations referred to in paragraph (c) must be certified by the translator as a correct translation.

14   The hearing and powers of court

14(1)   On hearing an application under paragraph 12(3) the court may–

(a)   make an order confirming the status of the replacement foreign representative as foreign representative for the purpose of proceedings under these Regulations;

(b)   dismiss the application;

(c)   adjourn the hearing conditionally or unconditionally;

(d)   make an interim order;

(e)   make any other order which the court thinks appropriate, including in particular an order making such provision as the court thinks fit with respect to matters arising in connection with the replacement of the foreign representative.

14(2)   If the court dismisses the application, it may also if it thinks fit make an order terminating recognition of the foreign proceeding and–

(a)   such an order may include such provision as the court thinks fit with respect to matters arising in connection with the termination; and

(b)   paragraph 15 shall not apply to such an order.

PART 5

REVIEWS OF COURT ORDERS

15   Reviews of court orders—where court makes order of its own motion

15(1)   The court shall not of its own motion make a modification or termination order unless the foreign representative and the debtor have either–

(a)   had an opportunity of being heard on the question; or

(b)   consented in writing to such an order.

15(2)   Where the foreign representative or the debtor desires to be heard on the question of such an order, the court shall give all relevant parties notice of a venue at which the question will be considered and may give directions as to the issues on which it requires evidence.

15(3)   For the purposes of sub-paragraph (2), all relevant parties means the foreign representative, the debtor and any other person who appears to the court to have an interest justifying his being given notice of the hearing.

15(4)   If the court makes a modification or termination order, the order may include such provision as the court thinks fit with respect to matters arising in connection with the modification or termination.

16   Review application—affidavit in support

16   A review application must be supported by an affidavit sworn by the applicant stating–

(a)   the grounds on which it is proposed that the relief applied for should be granted;

(b)   whether, to the best of the knowledge and belief of the applicant, the interests of the debtor's creditors (including any secured creditors or parties to hire-purchase agreements) and any other interested parties, including if appropriate the debtor, will be adequately protected; and

(c)   all other matters that in the opinion of the applicant will assist the court in deciding whether or not it is appropriate to grant the relief applied for.

17   Hearing of review application and powers of the court

17   On hearing a review application, the court may in addition to its powers under the Model Law to make a modification or termination order–

(a)   dismiss the application;

(b)   adjourn the hearing conditionally or unconditionally;

(c)   make an interim order;

(d)   make any other order which the court thinks appropriate, including an order making such provision as the court thinks fit with respect to matters arising in connection with the modification or termination.

PART 6

COURT PROCEDURE AND PRACTICE WITH REGARD TO PRINCIPAL APPLICATIONS AND ORDERS

18   Preliminary and interpretation

18(1)   This Part applies to–

(a)   any of the following applications made to the court under these Regulations–

(i)   a recognition application;

(ii)   an article 21 relief application;

(iii)   an application under paragraph 12(3) for an order confirming the status of a replacement foreign representative;

(iv)   a review application; and

(b)   any of the following orders made by the court under these Regulations–

(i)   a recognition order;

(ii)   an order granting interim relief under article 19 of the Model Law;

(iii)   an order granting relief under article 21 of the Model Law;

(iv)   an order confirming the status of a replacement foreign representative; and

(v)   a modification or termination order.

GENERAL NOTE

The procedure for an application for recognition is provided for separately in paras 2–6. The applicant will not necessarily be the foreign representative, e.g. under para.18(a)(iv) it could be another interested party.

19   Form and contents of application

19(1)   Subject to sub-paragraph (4) every application to which this Part applies shall be an ordinary application and shall be in Form ML 5.

19(2)   Each application shall be in writing and shall state–

(a)   the names of the parties;

(b)   the nature of the relief or order applied for or the directions sought from the court;

(c)   the names and addresses of the persons (if any) on whom it is intended to serve the application;

(d)   the names and addresses of all those persons on whom these Regulations require the application to be served (so far as known to the applicant); and

(e)   the applicant's address for service.

19(3)   The application must be signed by the applicant if he is acting in person, or, when he is not so acting, by or on behalf of his solicitor.

19(4)   This paragraph does not apply to a recognition application.

20   Filing of application

20(1)   The application (and all supporting documents) shall be filed with the court, with a sufficient number of copies for service and use as provided by paragraph 21(2).

20(2)   Each of the copies filed shall have applied to it the seal of the court and be issued to the applicant; and on each copy there shall be endorsed the date and time of filing.

20(3)   The court shall fix a venue for the hearing of the application and this also shall be endorsed on each copy of the application issued under sub-paragraph (2).

21   Service of the application

21(1)   In sub-paragraph (2), references to the application are to a sealed copy of the application issued by the court together with any affidavit in support of it and any documents exhibited to the affidavit.

21(2)   Unless the court otherwise directs, the application shall be served on the following persons, unless they are the applicant–

(a)   on the foreign representative;

(b)   on the debtor;

(c)   if a British insolvency officeholder is acting in relation to the debtor, on him;

(d) if any person has been appointed an administrative receiver of the debtor or, to the knowledge of the foreign representative, as a receiver or manager of the property of the debtor in England and Wales, on him;

(e) if a member State liquidator has been appointed in main proceedings in relation to the debtor, on him;

(f) if to the knowledge of the foreign representative a foreign representative has been appointed in any other foreign proceeding regarding the debtor, on him;

(g) if there is pending in England and Wales a petition for the winding up or bankruptcy of the debtor, on the petitioner;

(h) on any person who to the knowledge of the foreign representative is or may be entitled to appoint an administrator of the debtor under paragraph 14 of Schedule B1 to the 1986 Act (appointment of administrator by holder of qualifying floating charge); and

(i) if the debtor is a debtor who is of interest to the Financial Services Authority, on that Authority.

22   Manner in which service to be effected

22(1)   Service of the application in accordance with paragraph 21(2) shall be effected by the applicant, or his solicitor, or by a person instructed by him or his solicitor, not less than 5 business days before the date fixed for the hearing.

22(2)   Service shall be effected by delivering the documents to a person's proper address or in such other manner as the court may direct.

22(3)   A person's proper address is any which he has previously notified as his address for service within England and Wales; but if he has not notified any such address or if for any reason service at such address is not practicable, service may be effected as follows–

(a) (subject to sub-paragraph (4)) in the case of a company incorporated in England and Wales, by delivery to its registered office;

(b) in the case of any other person, by delivery to his usual or last known address or principal place of business in Great Britain.

22(4)   If delivery to a company's registered office is not practicable, service may be effected by delivery to its last known principal place of business in Great Britain.

22(5)   Delivery of documents to any place or address may be made by leaving them there or sending them by first class post in accordance with the provisions of paragraphs 70 and 75(1).

23   Proof of service

23(1)   Service of the application shall be verified by an affidavit of service in Form ML 6, specifying the date on which, and the manner in which, service was effected.

23(2)   The affidavit of service, with a sealed copy of the application exhibited to it, shall be filed with the court as soon as reasonably practicable after service, and in any event not less than 1 business day before the hearing of the application.

24   In case of urgency

24   Where the case is one of urgency, the court may (without prejudice to its general power to extend or abridge time limits)–

(a) hear the application immediately, either with or without notice to, or the attendance of, other parties; or

(b)   authorise a shorter period of service than that provided for by paragraph 22(1),

and any such application may be heard on terms providing for the filing or service of documents, or the carrying out of other formalities, as the court thinks fit.

25   The hearing

25(1)   At the hearing of the application, the applicant and any of the following persons (not being the applicant) may appear or be represented–

(a)   the foreign representative;

(b)   the debtor and, in the case of any debtor other than an individual, any one or more directors or other officers of the debtor, including–

    (i)   where applicable, any person specified in particulars registered under section 1046 of the Companies Act 2006 (overseas companies) as authorised to represent the debtor;

    (ii)   in the case of a debtor which is a partnership, any person who is an officer of the partnership within the meaning of article 2 of the Insolvent Partnerships Order 1994;

(c)   if a British insolvency officeholder is acting in relation to the debtor, that person;

(d)   if any person has been appointed an administrative receiver of the debtor or as a receiver or manager of the property of the debtor in England and Wales, that person;

(e)   if a member State liquidator has been appointed in main proceedings in relation to the debtor, that person;

(f)   if a foreign representative has been appointed in any other foreign proceeding regarding the debtor, that person;

(g)   any person who has presented a petition for the winding up or bankruptcy of the debtor in England and Wales;

(h)   any person who is or may be entitled to appoint an administrator of the debtor under paragraph 14 of Schedule B1 to the 1986 Act (appointment of administrator by holder of qualifying floating charge);

(i)   if the debtor is a debtor who is of interest to the Financial Services Authority, that Authority; and

(j)   with the permission of the court, any other person who appears to have an interest justifying his appearance.

GENERAL NOTE

Paragraph 25(1)(b)(i) substituted by the Companies Act 2006 (Consequential Amendments, Transitional Provisions and Savings) Order 2009 (SI 2009/1941) art.2(1) and Sch.1 para.264(3)(c) as from October 1, 2009.

26   Notification and advertisement of order

26(1)   If the court makes any of the orders referred to in paragraph 18(1)(b), it shall as soon as reasonably practicable send two sealed copies of the order to the foreign representative.

26(2)   The foreign representative shall send a sealed copy of the order as soon as reasonably practicable to the debtor.

26(3)   The foreign representative shall, as soon as reasonably practicable after the date of the order give notice of the making of the order–

(a)   if a British insolvency officeholder is acting in relation to the debtor, to him;

(b)   if any person has been appointed an administrative receiver of the debtor or, to the knowledge of the foreign representative, as a receiver or manager of the property of the debtor, to him;

(c)   if a member State liquidator has been appointed in main proceedings in relation to the debtor, to him;

(d)   if to his knowledge a foreign representative has been appointed in any other foreign proceeding regarding the debtor, that person;

(e)   if there is pending in England and Wales a petition for the winding up or bankruptcy of the debtor, to the petitioner;

(f)   to any person who to his knowledge is or may be entitled to appoint an administrator of the debtor under paragraph 14 of Schedule B1 to the 1986 Act (appointment of administrator by holder of qualifying floating charge);

(g)   if the debtor is a debtor who is of interest to the Financial Services Authority, to that Authority;

(h)   to such other persons as the court may direct.

26(4)   In the case of an order recognising a foreign proceeding in relation to the debtor as a foreign main proceeding, or an order under article 19 or 21 of the Model Law staying execution, distress or other legal process against the debtor's assets, the foreign representative shall also, as soon as reasonably practicable after the date of the order give notice of the making of the order–

(a)   to any enforcement officer or other officer who to his knowledge is charged with an execution or other legal process against the debtor or its property; and

(b)   to any person who to his knowledge is distraining against the debtor or its property.

26(5)   In the application of sub-paragraphs (3) and (4) the references to property shall be taken as references to property situated within England and Wales.

26(6)   Where the debtor is a relevant company, the foreign representative shall send notice of the making of the order to the registrar of companies before the end of the period of 5 business days beginning with the date of the order. The notice to the registrar of companies shall be in Form ML 7.

26(7)   The foreign representative shall advertise the making of the following orders once in the Gazette and once in such newspaper as he thinks most appropriate for ensuring that the making of the order comes to the notice of the debtor's creditors–

(a)   a recognition order;

(b)   an order confirming the status of a replacement foreign representative; and

(c)   a modification or termination order which modifies or terminates recognition of a foreign proceeding,

and the advertisement shall be in Form ML 8.

Para.26(6)
On notices to the registrar of companies, see Sch.4.

27   Adjournment of hearing; directions

27(1)   This paragraph applies in any case where the court exercises its power to adjourn the hearing of the application.

27(2)   The court may at any time give such directions as it thinks fit as to–

(a)   service or notice of the application on or to any person, whether in connection with the venue of a resumed hearing or for any other purpose;

(b)   the procedure on the application;

(c)   the manner in which any evidence is to be adduced at a resumed hearing and in particular as to–

    (i)   the taking of evidence wholly or in part by affidavit or orally;

    (ii)   the cross-examination on the hearing in court or in chambers, of any deponents to affidavits;

(d)   the matters to be dealt with in evidence.

PART 7

APPLICATIONS TO THE CHIEF LAND REGISTRAR

28   Applications to Chief Land Registrar following court orders

28(1)   Where the court makes any order in proceedings under these Regulations which is capable of giving rise to an application or applications under the Land Registration Act 2002, the foreign representative shall, as soon as reasonably practicable after the making of the order or at the appropriate time, make the appropriate application or applications to the Chief Land Registrar.

28(2)   In sub-paragraph (1) an appropriate application is–

(a)   in any case where–

    (i)   a recognition order in respect of a foreign main proceeding or an order suspending the right to transfer, encumber or otherwise dispose of any assets of the debtor is made, and

    (ii)   the debtor is the registered proprietor of a registered estate or registered charge and holds it for his sole benefit,

an application under section 43 of the Land Registration Act 2002 for a restriction of the kind referred to in sub-paragraph (3) to be entered in the relevant registered title; and

(b)   in any other case, an application under the Land Registration Act 2002 for such an entry in the register as shall be necessary to reflect the effect of the court order under these Regulations.

28(3)   The restriction referred to in sub-paragraph (2)(a) is a restriction to the effect that no disposition of the registered estate or registered charge (as appropriate) by the registered proprietor of that estate or charge is to be completed by registration within the meaning of section 27 of the Land Registration Act 2002 except under a further order of the court.

GENERAL NOTE

See art.1.6.

PART 8

MISFEASANCE

29   Misfeasance by foreign representative

29(1)   The court may examine the conduct of a person who–

(a)   is or purports to be the foreign representative in relation to a debtor; or

(b)   has been or has purported to be the foreign representative in relation to a debtor.

29(2)   An examination under this paragraph may be held only on the application of–

(a)   a British insolvency officeholder acting in relation to the debtor;

(b)   a creditor of the debtor; or

210

(c) with the permission of the court, any other person who appears to have an interest justifying an application.

29(3) An application under sub-paragraph (2) must allege that the foreign representative–

(a) has misapplied or retained money or other property of the debtor;

(b) has become accountable for money or other property of the debtor;

(c) has breached a fiduciary or other duty in relation to the debtor; or

(d) has been guilty of misfeasance.

29(4) On an examination under this paragraph into a person's conduct the court may order him–

(a) to repay, restore or account for money or property;

(b) to pay interest;

(c) to contribute a sum to the debtor's property by way of compensation for breach of duty or misfeasance.

29(5) In sub-paragraph (3) **"foreign representative"** includes a person who purports or has purported to be a foreign representative in relation to a debtor.

GENERAL NOTE

This provision corresponds with IA 1986 s.212 and Sch.B1 para.75.

PART 9

GENERAL PROVISION AS TO COURT PROCEDURE AND PRACTICE

30 Principal court rules and practice to apply with modifications

30(1) The CPR and the practice and procedure of the High Court (including any practice direction) shall apply to proceedings under these Regulations in the High Court with such modifications as may be necessary for the purpose of giving effect to the provisions of these Regulations and in the case of any conflict between any provision of the CPR and the provisions of these Regulations, the latter shall prevail.

30(2) All proceedings under these Regulations shall be allocated to the multi-track for which CPR Part 29 (the multi-track) makes provision, and accordingly those provisions of the CPR which provide for allocation questionnaires and track allocation shall not apply.

31 Applications other than the principal applications—preliminary

31 Paragraphs 32 to 37 of this Part apply to any application made to the court under these Regulations, except any of the applications referred to in paragraph 18(1)(a).

GENERAL NOTE

"Principal applications" refers to the applications specified in para.18(1)(a).

32 Form and contents of application

32(1) Every application shall be in the form appropriate to the application concerned. Forms ML 4 and ML 5 shall be used for an originating application and an ordinary application respectively under these Regulations.

32(2)   Each application shall be in writing and shall state–

    (a)   the names of the parties;

    (b)   the nature of the relief or order applied for or the directions sought from the court;

    (c)   the names and addresses of the persons (if any) on whom it is intended to serve the application or that no person is intended to be served;

    (d)   where these Regulations require that notice of the application is to be given to specified persons, the names and addresses of all those persons (so far as known to the applicant); and

    (e)   the applicant's address for service.

32(3)   An originating application shall set out the grounds on which the applicant claims to be entitled to the relief or order sought.

32(4)   The application must be signed by the applicant if he is acting in person or, when he is not so acting, by or on behalf of his solicitor.

33   Filing and service of application

33(1)   The application shall be filed in court, accompanied by one copy and a number of additional copies equal to the number of persons who are to be served with the application.

33(2)   Subject as follows in this paragraph and in paragraph 34, or unless the court otherwise orders, upon the presentation of the documents mentioned in sub-paragraph (1), the court shall fix a venue for the application to be heard.

33(3)   Unless the court otherwise directs, the applicant shall serve a sealed copy of the application, endorsed with the venue of the hearing, on the respondent named in the application (or on each respondent if more than one).

33(4)   The court may give any of the following directions–

    (a)   that the application be served upon persons other than those specified by the relevant provision of these Regulations;

    (b)   that the giving of notice to any person may be dispensed with;

    (c)   that notice be given in some way other than that specified in sub-paragraph (3).

33(5)   Subject to sub-paragraph (6), the application must be served at least 10 business days before the date fixed for the hearing.

33(6)   Where the case is one of urgency, the court may (without prejudice to its general power to extend or abridge time limits)–

    (a)   hear the application immediately, either with or without notice to, or the attendance of, other parties; or

    (b)   authorise a shorter period of service than that provided for by sub-paragraph (5);

and any such application may be heard on terms providing for the filing or service of documents, or the carrying out of other formalities, as the court thinks fit.

34   Other hearings *ex parte*

34(1)   Where the relevant provisions of these Regulations do not require service of the application on, or notice of it to be given to, any person, the court may hear the application *ex parte*.

34(2)   Where the application is properly made *ex parte*, the court may hear it forthwith, without fixing a venue as required by paragraph 33(2).

34(3) Alternatively, the court may fix a venue for the application to be heard, in which case paragraph 33 applies (so far as relevant).

35 Use of affidavit evidence

35(1) In any proceedings evidence may be given by affidavit unless the court otherwise directs; but the court may, on the application of any party, order the attendance for cross-examination of the person making the affidavit.

35(2) Where, after such an order has been made, the person in question does not attend, his affidavit shall not be used in evidence without the permission of the court.

36 Filing and service of affidavits

36(1) Unless the court otherwise allows–

    (a) if the applicant intends to rely at the first hearing on affidavit evidence, he shall file the affidavit or affidavits (if more than one) in court and serve a copy or copies on the respondent, not less than 10 business days before the date fixed for the hearing; and

    (b) where a respondent to an application intends to oppose it and to rely for that purpose on affidavit evidence, he shall file the affidavit or affidavits (if more than one) in court and serve a copy or copies on the applicant, not less than 5 business days before the date fixed for the hearing.

36(2) Any affidavit may be sworn by the applicant or by the respondent or by some other person possessing direct knowledge of the subject matter of the application.

37 Adjournment of hearings; directions

37 The court may adjourn the hearing of an application on such terms (if any) as it thinks fit and in the case of such an adjournment paragraph 27(2) shall apply.

38 Transfer of proceedings within the High Court

38(1) The High Court may, having regard to the criteria in CPR rule 30.3(2), order proceedings in the Royal Courts of Justice or a district registry, or any part of such proceedings (such as an application made in the proceedings), to be transferred–

    (a) from the Royal Courts of Justice to a district registry; or

    (b) from a district registry to the Royal Courts of Justice or to another district registry.

38(2) The High Court may order proceedings before a district registry for the detailed assessment of costs to be transferred to another district registry if it is satisfied that the proceedings could be more conveniently or fairly taken in that other district registry.

38(3) An application for an order under sub-paragraph (1) or (2) must, if the claim is proceeding in a district registry, be made to that registry.

38(4) A transfer of proceedings under this paragraph may be ordered–

    (a) by the court of its own motion; or

    (b) on the application of a person appearing to the court to have an interest in the proceedings.

38(5) Where the court orders proceedings to be transferred, the court from which they are to be transferred must give notice of the transfer to all the parties.

38(6) An order made before the transfer of the proceedings shall not be affected by the order to transfer.

39   Transfer of proceedings—actions to avoid acts detrimental to creditors

39(1)   If–

(a)   in accordance with article 23(6) of the Model Law, the court grants a foreign representative permission to make an application in accordance with paragraph 1 of that article; and

(b)   the relevant proceedings under British insolvency law taking place regarding the debtor are taking place in the county court,

the court may also order those proceedings to be transferred to the High Court.

39(2)   Where the court makes an order transferring proceedings under sub-paragraph (1)–

(a)   it shall send sealed copies of the order to the county court from which the proceedings are to be transferred, and to the official receivers attached to that court and the High Court respectively; and

(b)   the county court shall send the file of the proceedings to the High Court.

39(3)   Following compliance with this paragraph, if the official receiver attached to the court to which the proceedings are transferred is not already, by virtue of directions given by the Secretary of State under section 399(6)(a) of the 1986 Act, the official receiver in relation to those proceedings, he becomes, in relation to those proceedings, the official receiver in place of the official receiver attached to the other court concerned.

GENERAL NOTE

General jurisdiction under the Regulations is conferred on the High Court (art.4). If a foreign representative wishes to participate in proceedings that are already current in the county court, it is likely to be thought appropriate that they be transferred to the High Court.

40   Shorthand writers

40(1)   The judge may in writing nominate one or more persons to be official shorthand writers to the court.

40(2)   The court may, at any time in the course of proceedings under these Regulations, appoint a shorthand writer to take down the evidence of a person examined in pursuance of a court order under article 19 or 21 of the Model Law.

40(3)   The remuneration of a shorthand writer appointed in proceedings under these Regulations shall be paid by the party at whose instance the appointment was made or otherwise as the court may direct.

40(4)   Any question arising as to the rates of remuneration payable under this paragraph shall be determined by the court in its discretion.

41   Enforcement procedures

41   In any proceedings under these Regulations, orders of the court may be enforced in the same manner as a judgment to the same effect.

42   Title of proceedings

42(1)   Every proceeding under these Regulations shall, with any necessary additions, be intituled "IN THE MATTER OF…(naming the debtor to which the proceedings relate) AND IN THE MATTER OF THE CROSS-BORDER INSOLVENCY REGULATIONS 2006".

42(2)   Sub-paragraph (1) shall not apply in respect of any form prescribed under these Regulations.

43 Court records

43 The court shall keep records of all proceedings under these Regulations, and shall cause to be entered in the records the taking of any step in the proceedings, and such decisions of the court in relation thereto, as the court thinks fit.

44 Inspection of records

44(1) Subject as follows, the court's records of proceedings under these Regulations shall be open to inspection by any person.

44(2) If in the case of a person applying to inspect the records the Registrar is not satisfied as to the propriety of the purpose for which inspection is required, he may refuse to allow it. That person may then apply forthwith and *ex parte* to the judge, who may refuse the inspection or allow it on such terms as he thinks fit.

44(3) The decision of the judge under sub-paragraph (2) is final.

45 File of court proceedings

45(1) In respect of all proceedings under these Regulations, the court shall open and maintain a file for each case; and (subject to directions of the Registrar) all documents relating to such proceedings shall be placed on the relevant file.

45(2) No proceedings under these Regulations shall be filed in the Central Office of the High Court.

46 Right to inspect the file

46(1) In the case of any proceedings under these Regulations, the following have the right, at all reasonable times, to inspect the court's file of the proceedings–

   (a) the Secretary of State;

   (b) the person who is the foreign representative in relation to the proceedings;

   (c) if a foreign representative has been appointed in any other foreign proceeding regarding the debtor to which the proceedings under these Regulations relate, that person;

   (d) if a British insolvency officeholder is acting in relation to the debtor to which the proceedings under these Regulations relate, that person;

   (e) any person stating himself in writing to be a creditor of the debtor to which the proceedings under these Regulations relate;

   (f) if a member State liquidator has been appointed in relation to the debtor to which the proceedings under these Regulations relate, that person; and

   (g) the debtor to which the proceedings under these Regulations relate, or, if that debtor is a company, corporation or partnership, every person who is, or at any time has been–

      (i) a director or officer of the debtor;

      (ii) a member of the debtor; or

      (iii) where applicable, any person specified in particulars registered under section 1046 of the Companies Act 2006 (overseas companies) as authorised to represent the debtor.

46(2) The right of inspection conferred as above on any person may be exercised on his behalf by a person properly authorised by him.

46(3) Any person may, by leave of the court, inspect the file.

46(4)   The right of inspection conferred by this paragraph is not exercisable in the case of documents, or parts of documents, as to which the court directs (either generally or specially) that they are not to be made open to inspection without the court's permission. An application for a direction of the court under this sub-paragraph may be made by the foreign representative or by any party appearing to the court to have an interest.

46(5)   If, for the purpose of powers conferred by the 1986 Act or the Rules, the Secretary of State or the official receiver wishes to inspect the file of any proceedings under these Regulations, and requests the transmission of the file, the court shall comply with such request (unless the file is for the time being in use for the court's purposes).

46(6)   Paragraph 44(2) and (3) apply in respect of the court's file of any proceedings under these Regulations as they apply in respect of court records.

46(7)   Where these Regulations confer a right for any person to inspect documents on the court's file of proceedings, the right includes that of taking copies of those documents on payment of the fee chargeable under any order made under section 92 of the Courts Act 2003.

GENERAL NOTE

Paragraph 46(1)(g)(iii) substituted by the Companies Act 2006 (Consequential Amendments, Transitional Provisions and Savings) Order 2009 (SI 2009/1941) art.2(1) and Sch.1 para.264(3)(d) as from October 1, 2009.

47   Copies of court orders

47(1)   In any proceedings under these Regulations, any person who under paragraph 46 has a right to inspect documents on the court file also has the right to require the foreign representative in relation to those proceedings to furnish him with a copy of any court order in the proceedings.

47(2)   Sub-paragraph (1) does not apply if a copy of the court order has been served on that person or notice of the making of the order has been given to that person under other provisions of these Regulations.

48   Filing of Gazette notices and advertisements

48(1)   In any court in which proceedings under these Regulations are pending, an officer of the court shall file a copy of every issue of the Gazette which contains an advertisement relating to those proceedings.

48(2)   Where there appears in a newspaper an advertisement relating to proceedings under these Regulations pending in any court, the person inserting the advertisement shall file a copy of it in that court.

The copy of the advertisement shall be accompanied by, or have endorsed on it, such particulars as are necessary to identify the proceedings and the date of the advertisement's appearance.

48(3)   An officer of any court in which proceedings under these Regulations are pending shall from time to time file a memorandum giving the dates of, and other particulars relating to, any notice published in the Gazette, and any newspaper advertisements, which relate to proceedings so pending.

The officer's memorandum is prima facie evidence that any notice or advertisement mentioned in it was duly inserted in the issue of the newspaper or the Gazette which is specified in the memorandum.

49   Persons incapable of managing their affairs—introductory

49(1)   Paragraphs 50 to 52 apply where in proceedings under these Regulations it appears to the court that a person affected by the proceedings is one who is incapable of managing and administering his property and affairs either–

(a)   by reason of mental disorder within the meaning of the Mental Health Act 1983; or

(b)   due to physical affliction or disability.

49(2)   The person concerned is referred to as **"the incapacitated person"**.

GENERAL NOTE

Reference might also have been made to the Mental Capacity Act 2005 Pt I.

50   Appointment of another person to act

50(1)   The court may appoint such person as it thinks fit to appear for, represent or act for the incapacitated person.

50(2)   The appointment may be made either generally or for the purpose of any particular application or proceeding, or for the exercise of particular rights or powers which the incapacitated person might have exercised but for his incapacity.

50(3)   The court may make the appointment either of its own motion or on application by–

(a)   a person who has been appointed by a court in the United Kingdom or elsewhere to manage the affairs of, or to represent, the incapacitated person; or

(b)   any relative or friend of the incapacitated person who appears to the court to be a proper person to make the application; or

(c)   in any case where the incapacitated person is the debtor, the foreign representative.

50(4)   Application under sub-paragraph (3) may be made *ex parte*; but the court may require such notice of the application as it thinks necessary to be given to the person alleged to be incapacitated, or any other person, and may adjourn the hearing of the application to enable the notice to be given.

51   Affidavit in support of application

51   An application under paragraph 50(3) shall be supported by an affidavit of a registered medical practitioner as to the mental or physical condition of the incapacitated person.

52   Service of notices following appointment

52   Any notice served on, or sent to, a person appointed under paragraph 50 has the same effect as if it had been served on, or given to, the incapacitated person.

53   Rights of audience

53   Rights of audience in proceedings under these Regulations are the same as obtain in proceedings under British insolvency law.

54   Right of attendance

54(1)   Subject as follows, in proceedings under these Regulations, any person stating himself in writing, in records kept by the court for that purpose, to be a creditor of the debtor to which the proceedings relate, is entitled at his own cost, to attend in court or in chambers at any stage of the proceedings.

54(2)   Attendance may be by the person himself, or his solicitor.

54(3)   A person so entitled may request the court in writing to give him notice of any step in the proceedings; and, subject to his paying the costs involved and keeping the court informed as to his address, the court shall comply with the request.

54(4)   If the court is satisfied that the exercise by a person of his rights under this paragraph has given rise to costs for the estate of the debtor which would not otherwise have been incurred and ought not, in the circumstances, to fall on that estate, it may direct that the costs be paid by the person concerned, to an amount specified.

The rights of that person under this paragraph shall be in abeyance so long as those costs are not paid.

54(5)   The court may appoint one or more persons to represent the creditors of the debtor to have the rights conferred by this paragraph, instead of the rights being exercised by any or all of them individually.

If two or more persons are appointed under this paragraph to represent the same interest, they must (if at all) instruct the same solicitor.

GENERAL NOTE

In keeping with the emphasis which the Model Law places generally on the need for speed and informality, a person claiming to be a creditor needs only to state the fact in writing to obtain standing. Note the provision in para.54(5) empowering all the creditors to act by a representative.

55   Right of attendance for member State liquidator

55   For the purposes of paragraph 54(1), a member State liquidator appointed in relation to a debtor subject to proceedings under these Regulations shall be deemed to be a creditor.

56   British insolvency officeholder's solicitor

56   Where in any proceedings the attendance of the British insolvency officeholder's solicitor is required, whether in court or in chambers, the British insolvency officeholder himself need not attend, unless directed by the court.

57   Formal defects

57   No proceedings under these Regulations shall be invalidated by any formal defect or by any irregularity, unless the court before which objection is made considers that substantial injustice has been caused by the defect or irregularity, and that the injustice cannot be remedied by any order of the court.

58   Restriction on concurrent proceedings and remedies

58   Where in proceedings under these Regulations the court makes an order staying any action, execution or other legal process against the property of a debtor, service of the order may be effected by sending a sealed copy of the order to whatever is the address for service of the claimant or other party having the carriage of the proceedings to be stayed.

59   Affidavits

59(1)   Where in proceedings under these Regulations, an affidavit is made by any British insolvency officeholder acting in relation to the debtor, he shall state the capacity in which he makes it, the position which he holds and the address at which he works.

59(2)   Any officer of the court duly authorised in that behalf, may take affidavits and declarations.

59(3)   Subject to sub-paragraph (4), where these Regulations provide for the use of an affidavit, a witness statement verified by a statement of truth may be used as an alternative.

59(4)   Sub-paragraph (3) does not apply to paragraphs 4 (affidavit in support of recognition application), 7 (affidavit in support of interim relief application), 10 (affidavit in support of article 21 relief application), 13 (affidavit in support of application regarding status of replacement foreign representative) and 16 (affidavit in support of review application).

GENERAL NOTE

A witness statement may be used as an alternative to an affidavit, except in the cases specified in para.59(4).

60   Security in court

60(1)   Where security has to be given to the court (otherwise than in relation to costs), it may be given by guarantee, bond or the payment of money into court.

60(2)   A person proposing to give a bond as security shall give notice to the party in whose favour the security is required, and to the court, naming those who are to be sureties to the bond.

60(3)   The court shall forthwith give notice to the parties concerned of a venue for the execution of the bond and the making of any objection to the sureties.

60(4)   The sureties shall make an affidavit of their sufficiency (unless dispensed with by the party in whose favour the security is required) and shall, if required by the court, attend the court to be cross-examined.

61   Further information and disclosure

61(1)   Any party to proceedings under these Regulations may apply to the court for an order–

(a)   that any other party–

(i)   clarify any matter which is in dispute in the proceedings; or

(ii)   give additional information in relation to any such matter,

in accordance with CPR Part 18 (further information); or

(b)   to obtain disclosure from any other party in accordance with CPR Part 31 (disclosure and inspection of documents).

61(2)   An application under this paragraph may be made without notice being served on any other party.

62   Office copies of documents

62(1)   Any person who has under these Regulations the right to inspect the court file of proceedings may require the court to provide him with an office copy of any document from the file.

62(2)   A person's right under this paragraph may be exercised on his behalf by his solicitor.

62(3)   An office copy provided by the court under this paragraph shall be in such form as the Registrar thinks appropriate, and shall bear the court's seal.

63   "The court"

63(1)   Anything to be done in proceedings under these Regulations by, to or before the court may be done by, to or before a judge of the High Court or a Registrar.

63(2)   Where these Regulations require or permit the court to perform an act of a formal or administrative character, that act may be performed by a court officer.

PART 10

COSTS AND DETAILED ASSESSMENT

64   Requirement to assess costs by the detailed procedure

64   In any proceedings before the court, the court may order costs to be decided by detailed assessment.

65   Costs of officers charged with execution of writs or other process

65(1)   Where by virtue of article 20 of the Model Law or a court order under article 19 or 21 of the Model Law an enforcement officer, or other officer, charged with execution of the writ or other process–

(a)   is required to deliver up goods or money; or

(b)   has deducted costs from the proceeds of an execution or money paid to him,

the foreign representative may require in writing that the amount of the enforcement officer's or other officer's bill of costs be decided by detailed assessment.

65(2)   Where such a requirement is made, if the enforcement officer or other officer does not commence detailed assessment proceedings within 3 months of the requirement under sub-paragraph (1), or within such further time as the court, on application, may permit, any claim by the enforcement officer or other officer in respect of his costs is forfeited by such failure to commence proceedings.

65(3)   Where, in the case of a deduction of costs by the enforcement officer or other officer, any amount deducted is disallowed at the conclusion of the detailed assessment proceedings, the enforcement officer or other officer shall forthwith pay a sum equal to that disallowed to the foreign representative for the benefit of the debtor.

66   Final costs certificate

66(1)   A final costs certificate of the costs officer is final and conclusive as to all matters which have not been objected to in the manner provided for under the rules of the court.

66(2)   Where it is proved to the satisfaction of a costs officer that a final costs certificate has been lost or destroyed, he may issue a duplicate.

PART 11

APPEALS IN PROCEEDINGS UNDER THESE REGULATIONS

67   Appeals from court orders

67(1)   An appeal from a decision of a Registrar of the High Court in proceedings under these Regulations lies to a single judge of the High Court; and an appeal from a decision of that judge on such an appeal lies, with the permission of the Court of Appeal, to the Court of Appeal.

67(2)   An appeal from a decision of a judge of the High Court in proceedings under these Regulations which is not a decision on an appeal made to him under sub-paragraph (1) lies, with the permission of that judge or the Court of Appeal, to the Court of Appeal.

GENERAL NOTE

These rules correspond to those applicable generally to decisions of the High Court in matters of insolvency. See IR 1986 rr.7.47 et seq. and the *Practice Direction: Insolvency Proceedings* [2012] B.C.C. 265 (reproduced as App.IV to this *Guide*), Pt 4.

68   Procedure on appeals

68(1)   Subject as follows, CPR Part 52 (appeals to the Court of Appeal) and its practice direction apply to appeals in proceedings under these Regulations.

68(2)   The provisions of Part 4 of the practice direction on Insolvency Proceedings supporting CPR Part 49 relating to first appeals (as defined in that Part) apply in relation to any appeal to a single judge of the High Court under paragraph 67, with any necessary modifications.

68(3)   In proceedings under these Regulations, the procedure under CPR Part 52 is by ordinary application and not by appeal notice.

PART 12

GENERAL

69 Notices

69(1) All notices required or authorised by or under these Regulations to be given must be in writing, unless it is otherwise provided, or the court allows the notice to be given in some other way.

69(2) Where in proceedings under these Regulations a notice is required to be sent or given by any person, the sending or giving of it may be proved by means of a certificate by that person that he posted the notice, or instructed another person (naming him) to do so.

69(3) A certificate under this paragraph may be endorsed on a copy or specimen of the notice to which it relates.

70 "Give notice" etc.

70(1) A reference in these Regulations to giving notice, or to delivering, sending or serving any document, means that the notice or document may be sent by post.

70(2) Subject to paragraph 75, any form of post may be used.

70(3) Personal service of a document is permissible in all cases.

70(4) Notice of the venue fixed for an application may be given by service of the sealed copy of the application under paragraph 33(3).

71 Notice, etc. to solicitors

71 Where in proceedings under these Regulations a notice or other document is required or authorised to be given to a person, it may, if he has indicated that his solicitor is authorised to accept service on his behalf, be given instead to the solicitor.

72 Notice to joint British insolvency officeholders

72 Where two or more persons are acting jointly as the British insolvency officeholder in proceedings under British insolvency law, delivery of a document to one of them is to be treated as delivery to them all.

73 Forms for use in proceedings under these Regulations

73(1) The forms contained in Schedule 5 to these Regulations shall be used in, and in connection with, proceedings under these Regulations.

73(2) The forms shall be used with such variations, if any, as the circumstances may require.

74 Time limits

74(1) The provisions of CPR Rule 2.8 (time) apply, as regards computation of time, to anything required or authorised to be done by these Regulations.

74(2) The provisions of CPR rule 3.1(2)(a) (the court's general powers of management) apply so as to enable the court to extend or shorten the time for compliance with anything required or authorised to be done by these Regulations.

75 Service by post

75(1) For a document to be properly served by post, it must be contained in an envelope addressed to the person on whom service is to be effected, and pre-paid for first class post.

75(2)   A document to be served by post may be sent to the last known address of the person to be served.

75(3)   Where first class post is used, the document is treated as served on the second business day after the date of posting, unless the contrary is shown.

75(4)   The date of posting is presumed, unless the contrary is shown, to be the date shown in the post-mark on the envelope in which the document is contained.

76   General provisions as to service and notice

76   Subject to paragraphs 22, 75 and 77, CPR Part 6 (service of documents) applies as regards any matter relating to the service of documents and the giving of notice in proceedings under these Regulations.

77   Service outside the jurisdiction

77(1)   Sections III and IV of CPR Part 6 (service out of the jurisdiction and service of process of foreign court) do not apply in proceedings under these Regulations.

77(2)   Where for the purposes of proceedings under these Regulations any process or order of the court, or other document, is required to be served on a person who is not in England and Wales, the court may order service to be effected within such time, on such person, at such place and in such manner as it thinks fit, and may also require such proof of service as it thinks fit.

77(3)   An application under this paragraph shall be supported by an affidavit stating–

(a)   the grounds on which the application is made; and

(b)   in what place or country the person to be served is, or probably may be found.

78   False claim of status as creditor

78(1)   Rule 12.18 (false claim of status as creditor, etc) shall apply with any necessary modifications in any case where a person falsely claims the status of a creditor of a debtor, with the intention of obtaining a sight of documents whether on the court's file or in the hands of the foreign representative or other person, which he has not under these Regulations any right to inspect.

78(2)   Rule 21.21 and Schedule 5 of the Rules shall apply to an offence under Rule 12.18 as applied by sub-paragraph (1) as they apply to an offence under Rule 12.18.

79   The Gazette

79(1)   A copy of the Gazette containing any notice required by these Regulations to be gazetted is evidence of any fact stated in the notice.

79(2)   In the case of an order of the court notice of which is required by these Regulations to be gazetted, a copy of the Gazette containing the notice may in any proceedings be produced as conclusive evidence that the order was made on the date specified in the notice.

SCHEDULE 3

Regulation 5

PROCEDURAL MATTERS IN SCOTLAND

Introductory note to Schedule 3
This Schedule is the counterpart for Scotland of Sch.2, but is less elaborate and detailed. General competence in matters under the Regulations is conferred on the Court of Session by art.4 of Sch.1.

PART 1

INTERPRETATION

1   Interpretation

1(1)   In this Schedule–

"the 1986 Act" means the Insolvency Act 1986;

"article 21 remedy application" means an application to the court by a foreign representative under article 21(1) or (2) of the Model Law for remedy;

"business day" means any day other than a Saturday, a Sunday, Christmas Day, Good Friday or a day which is a bank holiday in Scotland under or by virtue of the Banking and Financial Dealings Act 1971;

"the Gazette" means the Edinburgh Gazette;

"main proceedings" means proceedings opened in accordance with Article 3(1) of the EC Insolvency Regulation and falling within the definition of insolvency proceedings in Article 2(a) of the EC Insolvency Regulation;

"member State liquidator" means a person falling within the definition of liquidator in Article 2(b) of the EC Insolvency Regulation appointed in proceedings to which it applies in a member State other than the United Kingdom;

"the Model Law" means the UNCITRAL Model Law as set out in Schedule 1 to these Regulations;

"modification or termination order" means an order by the court pursuant to its powers under the Model Law modifying or terminating recognition of a foreign proceeding, the sist, restraint or suspension referred to in article 20(1) or any part of it or any remedy granted under article 19 or 21 of the Model Law;

"recognition application" means an application to the court by a foreign representative in accordance with article 15 of the Model Law for an order recognising the foreign proceeding in which he has been appointed;

"recognition order" means an order by the court recognising a proceeding the subject of a recognition application as a foreign main proceeding or foreign non-main proceeding, as appropriate;

"relevant company" [Redefined by SI 2009/1941 in identical terms as for England and Wales: see above, p.198.]

"review application" means an application to the court for a modification or termination order.

1(2)   Expressions defined in the Model Law have the same meaning when used in this Schedule.

1(3)   References in this Schedule to a debtor who is of interest to the Financial Services Authority are references to a debtor who–

(a)   is, or has been, an authorised person within the meaning of section 31 of the Financial Services and Markets Act 2000 (authorised persons);

(b)   is, or has been, an appointed representative within the meaning of section 39 (exemption of appointed representatives) of that Act; or

(c)   is carrying, or has carried on, a regulated activity in contravention of the general prohibition.

1(4)   In sub-paragraph (3) **"the general prohibition"** has the meaning given by section 19 of the Financial Services and Markets Act 2000 and the reference to a **"regulated activity"** must be construed in accordance with–

(a)   section 22 of that Act (classes of regulated activity and categories of investment);

(b)   any relevant order under that section; and

(c)   Schedule 2 to that Act (regulated activities).

1(5)   References in this Schedule to a numbered form are to the form that bears that number in Schedule 5.

PART 2

THE FOREIGN REPRESENTATIVE

2   Application for confirmation of status of replacement foreign representative

2(1)   This paragraph applies where following the making of a recognition order the foreign representative dies or for any other reason ceases to be the foreign representative in the foreign proceedings in relation to the debtor.

2(2)   In this paragraph **"the former foreign representative"** means the foreign representative referred to in sub-paragraph (1).

2(3)   If a person has succeeded the former foreign representative or is otherwise holding office as foreign representative in the foreign proceeding in relation to the debtor, that person may apply to the court for an order confirming his status as replacement foreign representative for the purpose of proceedings under these Regulations.

2(4)   If the court dismisses an application under sub-paragraph (3) then it may also, if it thinks fit, make an order terminating recognition of the foreign proceeding and–

(a)   such an order may include such provision as the court thinks fit with respect to matters arising in connection with the termination; and

(b)   paragraph 5 shall not apply to such an order.

3   Misfeasance by a foreign representative

3(1)   The court may examine the conduct of a person who–

(a)   is or purports to be the foreign representative in relation to a debtor, or

(b)   has been or has purported to be the foreign representative in relation to a debtor.

3(2)   An examination under this paragraph may be held only on the application of–

(a)   a British insolvency officeholder acting in relation to the debtor,

(b)   a creditor of the debtor, or

(c)   with the permission of the court, any other person who appears to have an interest justifying an application.

3(3)   An application under sub-paragraph (2) must allege that the foreign representative–

(a)   has misapplied or retained money or other property of the debtor,

(b)   has become accountable for money or other property of the debtor,

(c)   has breached a fiduciary duty or other duty in relation to the debtor, or

(d)   has been guilty of misfeasance.

3(4)   On an examination under this paragraph into a person's conduct the court may order him–

(a)   to repay, restore or account for money or property;

(b)   to pay interest;

(c)   to contribute a sum to the debtor's property by way of compensation for breach of duty or misfeasance.

3(5)   In sub-paragraph (3), **"foreign representative"** includes a person who purports or has purported to be a foreign representative in relation to a debtor.

Part 3

Court Procedure And Practice

4   Preliminary and interpretation

4(1)   This Part applies to–

(a)   any of the following applications made to the court under these Regulations–

　(i)   a recognition application;

　(ii)   an article 21 remedy application;

　(iii)   an application under paragraph 2(3) for an order confirming the status of a replacement foreign representative;

　(iv)   a review application; and

(b)   any of the following orders made by the court under these Regulations–

　(i)   a recognition order;

　(ii)   an order granting interim remedy under article 19 of the Model Law;

　(iii)   an order granting remedy under article 21 of the Model Law;

　(iv)   an order confirming the status of a replacement foreign representative; or

　(v)   a modification or termination order.

General Note

There is no separate provision in the Scottish procedural rules for recognition applications corresponding with Sch.2 paras 2–6.

5   Reviews of court orders—where court makes order of its own motion

5(1)   The court shall not of its own motion make a modification or termination order unless the foreign representative and the debtor have either–

(a)   had an opportunity of being heard on the question, or

(b)   consented in writing to such an order.

5(2)   If the court makes a modification or termination order, the order may include such provision as the court thinks fit with respect to matters arising in connection with the modification or termination.

6   The hearing

6(1)   At the hearing of the application, the applicant and any of the following persons (not being the applicant) may appear or be represented–

   (a)   the foreign representative;

   (b)   the debtor and, in the case of any debtor other than an individual, any one or more directors or other officers of the debtor, including–

      (i)   where applicable, any person specified in particulars registered under section 1046 of the Companies Act 2006 (overseas companies) as authorised to represent the debtor;

      (ii)   in the case of a debtor which is a partnership, any person who is a member of the partnership;

   (c)   if a British insolvency officeholder is acting in relation to the debtor, that person;

   (d)   if any person has been appointed an administrative receiver of the debtor or as a receiver or manager of the property of the debtor, that person;

   (e)   if a member State liquidator has been appointed in main proceedings in relation to the debtor, that person;

   (f)   if a foreign representative has been appointed in any other foreign proceeding regarding the debtor, that person;

   (g)   any person who has presented a petition for the winding up or sequestration of the debtor in Scotland;

   (h)   any person who is or may be entitled to appoint an administrator of the debtor under paragraph 14 of Schedule B1 to the 1986 Act (appointment of administrator by holder of qualifying floating charge);

   (i)   if the debtor is a debtor who is of interest to the Financial Services Authority, that Authority; and

   (j)   with the permission of the court, any other person who appears to have an interest justifying his appearance.

GENERAL NOTE

Paragraph 6(1)(b)(i) substituted by the Companies Act 2006 (Consequential Amendments, Transitional Provisions and Savings) Order 2009 (SI 2009/1941) art.2(1) and Sch.1 para.264(4)(b) as from October 1, 2009.

7   Notification and advertisement of order

7(1)   This paragraph applies where the court makes any of the orders referred to in paragraph 4(1)(b).

7(2)   The foreign representative shall send a certified copy of the interlocutor as soon as reasonably practicable to the debtor.

7(3)   The foreign representative shall, as soon as reasonably practicable after the date of the order, give notice of the making of the order–

   (a)   if a British insolvency officeholder is acting in relation to the debtor, to him;

   (b)   if any person has been appointed an administrative receiver of the debtor or, to the knowledge of the foreign representative, as a receiver or manager of the property of the debtor, to him;

   (c)   if a member State liquidator has been appointed in main proceedings in relation to the debtor, to him;

   (d)   if to his knowledge a foreign representative has been appointed in any other foreign proceeding regarding the debtor, that person;

(e) if there is pending in Scotland a petition for the winding up or sequestration of the debtor, to the petitioner;

(f) to any person who to his knowledge is or may be entitled to appoint an administrator of the debtor under paragraph 14 of Schedule B1 to the 1986 Act (appointment of administrator by holder of qualifying floating charge);

(g) if the debtor is a debtor who is of interest to the Financial Services Authority, to that Authority; and

(h) to such persons as the court may direct.

7(4) Where the debtor is a relevant company, the foreign representative shall send notice of the making of the order to the registrar of companies before the end of the period of 5 business days beginning with the date of the order. The notice to the registrar of companies shall be in Form ML 7.

7(5) The foreign representative shall advertise the making of the following orders once in the Gazette and once in such newspaper as he thinks most appropriate for ensuring that the making of the order comes to the notice of the debtor's creditors–

(a) a recognition order,

(b) an order confirming the status of a replacement foreign representative, and

(c) a modification or termination order which modifies or terminates recognition of a foreign proceeding,

and the advertisement shall be in Form ML 8.

Para.7(4)
On notices to the registrar of companies, see Sch.4.

8 Registration of court order

8(1) Where the court makes a recognition order in respect of a foreign main proceeding or an order suspending the right to transfer, encumber or otherwise dispose of any assets of the debtor being heritable property, the clerk of the court shall send forthwith a certified copy of the order to the keeper of the register of inhibitions and adjudications for recording in that register.

8(2) Recording under sub-paragraph (1) or (3) shall have the effect as from the date of the order of an inhibition and of a citation in an adjudication of the debtor's heritable estate at the instance of the foreign representative.

8(3) Where the court makes a modification or termination order, the clerk of the court shall send forthwith a certified copy of the order to the keeper of the register of inhibitions and adjudications for recording in that register.

8(4) The effect mentioned in sub-paragraph (2) shall expire–

(a) on the recording of a modification or termination order under sub-paragraph (3); or

(b) subject to sub-paragraph (5), if the effect has not expired by virtue of paragraph (a), at the end of the period of 3 years beginning with the date of the order.

8(5) The foreign representative may, if recognition of the foreign proceeding has not been modified or terminated by the court pursuant to its powers under the Model Law, before the end of the period of 3 years mentioned in sub-paragraph (4)(b), send a memorandum in a form prescribed by the Court of Session by act of sederunt to the keeper of the register of inhibitions and adjudications for recording in that register, and such recording shall renew the effect mentioned in sub-paragraph (2); and thereafter the said effect shall continue to be preserved only if such memorandum is so recorded before the expiry of every subsequent period of 3 years.

9 Right to inspect court process

9(1) In the case of any proceedings under these Regulations, the following have the right, at all reasonable times, to inspect the court process of the proceedings–

    (a) the Secretary of State;

    (b) the person who is the foreign representative in relation to the proceedings;

    (c) if a foreign representative has been appointed in any other foreign proceeding regarding the debtor, that person;

    (d) if a British insolvency officeholder is acting in relation to the debtor, that person;

    (e) any person stating himself in writing to be a creditor of the debtor to which the proceedings under these Regulations relate;

    (f) if a member State liquidator has been appointed in relation to a debtor which is subject to proceedings under these Regulations, that person; and

    (g) the debtor to which the proceedings under these Regulations relate, or, if that debtor is a company, corporation or partnership, every person who is, or at any time has been–

        (i) a director or officer of the debtor,

        (ii) a member of the debtor, or

        (iii) where applicable, any person specified in particulars registered under section 1046 of the Companies Act 2006 (overseas companies) as authorised to represent the debtor.

9(2) The right of inspection conferred as above on any person may be exercised on his behalf by a person properly authorised by him.

GENERAL NOTE

Paragraph 9(1)(g)(iii) substituted by the Companies Act 2006 (Consequential Amendments, Transitional Provisions and Savings) Order 2009 (SI 2009/1941) art.2(1) and Sch.1 para.264(3)(c) as from October 1, 2009.

10 Copies of court orders

10(1) In any proceedings under these Regulations, any person who under paragraph 9 has a right to inspect documents in the court process also has the right to require the foreign representative in relation to those proceedings to furnish him with a copy of any court order in the proceedings.

10(2) Sub-paragraph (1) does not apply if a copy of the court order has been served on that person or notice of the making of the order has been given to that person under other provisions of these Regulations.

11 Transfer of proceedings—actions to avoid acts detrimental to creditors

11 If, in accordance with article 23(6) of the Model Law, the court grants a foreign representative permission to make an application in accordance with paragraph (1) of that article, it may also order the relevant proceedings under British insolvency law taking place regarding the debtor to be transferred to the Court of Session if those proceedings are taking place in Scotland and are not already in that court.

PART 3

GENERAL

12 Giving of notices, etc

12(1) All notices required or authorised by or under these Regulations to be given, sent or delivered must be in writing, unless it is otherwise provided, or the court allows the notice to be sent or given in some other way.

12(2) Any reference in these Regulations to giving, sending or delivering a notice or any such document means, without prejudice to any other way and unless it is otherwise provided, that the notice or document may be sent by post, and that, subject to paragraph 13, any form of post may be used. Personal service of the notice or document is permissible in all cases.

12(3) Where under these Regulations a notice or other document is required or authorised to be given, sent or delivered by a person (**"the sender"**) to another (**"the recipient"**), it may be given, sent or delivered by any person duly authorised by the sender to do so to any person duly authorised by the recipient to receive or accept it.

12(4) Where two or more persons are acting jointly as the British insolvency officeholder in proceedings under British insolvency law, the giving, sending or delivering of a notice or document to one of them is to be treated as the giving, sending or delivering of a notice or document to each or all.

13 Sending by post

13(1) For a document to be properly sent by post, it must be contained in an envelope addressed to the person to whom it is to be sent, and pre-paid for either first or second class post.

13(2) Any document to be sent by post may be sent to the last known address of the person to whom the document is to be sent.

13(3) Where first class post is used, the document is to be deemed to be received on the second business day after the date of posting, unless the contrary is shown.

13(4) Where second class post is used, the document is to be deemed to be received on the fourth business day after the date of posting, unless the contrary is shown.

14 Certificate of giving notice, etc

14(1) Where in any proceedings under these Regulations a notice or document is required to be given, sent or delivered by any person, the date of giving, sending or delivery of it may be proved by means of a certificate by that person that he gave, posted or otherwise sent or delivered the notice or document on the date stated in the certificate, or that he instructed another person (naming him) to do so.

14(2) A certificate under this paragraph may be endorsed on a copy of the notice to which it relates.

14(3) A certificate purporting to be signed by or on behalf of the person mentioned in sub-paragraph (1) shall be deemed, unless the contrary is shown, to be sufficient evidence of the matters stated therein.

15 Forms for use in proceedings under these Regulations

15(1) Forms ML 7 and ML 8 contained in Schedule 5 to these Regulations shall be used in, and in connection with, proceedings under these Regulations.

15(2) The forms shall be used with such variations, if any, as the circumstances may require.

SCHEDULE 4

Regulation 6

NOTICES DELIVERED TO THE REGISTRAR OF COMPANIES

1 Interpretation

1(1) In this Schedule–

"**electronic communication**" means the same as in the Electronic Communications Act 2000;

"**Model Law notice**" means a notice delivered to the registrar of companies under paragraph 26(6) of Schedule 2 or paragraph 7(4) of Schedule 3.

1(2) Expressions defined in the Model Law or Schedule 2 or 3, as appropriate, have the same meaning when used in this Schedule.

1(3) References in this Schedule to delivering a notice include sending, forwarding, producing or giving it.

2 Functions of the registrar of companies

2(1) Where a Model Law notice is delivered to the registrar of companies in respect of a relevant company, the registrar shall enter a note in the register relating to that company.

2(2) The note referred to in sub-paragraph (1) shall contain the following particulars, in each case as stated in the notice delivered to the registrar–

(a) brief details of the court order made;

(b) the date of the court order; and

(c) the name and address for service of the person who is the foreign representative in relation to the company.

3 Registrar of companies to whom notices to be delivered

3 [Omitted by the Companies Act 2006 (Consequential Amendments, Transitional Provisions and Savings) Order 2009 (SI 2009/1941) art.2(1) and Sch.1 para.264(5)(b) as from October 1, 2009.]

4 Delivery to registrar of notices

4(1) Electronic communications may be used for the delivery of any Model Law notice, provided that such delivery is in such form and manner as is directed by the registrar.

4(2) Where the Model Law notice is required to be signed, it shall instead be authenticated in such manner as is directed by the registrar.

4(3) If a Model Law notice is delivered to the registrar which does not comply with the requirements of these Regulations, he may serve on the person by whom the notice was delivered (or, if there are two or more such persons, on any of them) a notice (a non-compliance notice) indicating the respect in which the Model Law notice does not comply.

4(4) Where the registrar serves a non-compliance notice, then, unless a replacement Model Law notice–

(a) is delivered to him within 14 days after the service of the non-compliance notice, and

(b) complies with the requirements of these Regulations or is not rejected by him for failure to comply with those requirements,

the original Model Law notice shall be deemed not to have been delivered to him.

5   Enforcement of foreign representative's duty to give notice to registrar

5(1)   If a foreign representative, having made default in complying with paragraph 26(6) of Schedule 2 or paragraph 7(4) of Schedule 3 fails to make good the default within 14 days after the service of a notice on the foreign representative requiring him to do so, the court may, on an application made to it by any creditor, member, director or other officer of the debtor or by the registrar of companies, make an order directing the foreign representative to make good the default within such time as may be specified in the order.

5(2)   The court's order may provide that all costs of and incidental to the application shall be borne by the foreign representative.

6   Rectification of the register under court order

6(1)   The registrar shall remove from the register any note, or part of a note–

(a)   that relates to or is derived from a court order that the court has declared to be invalid or ineffective, or

(b)   that the court declares to be factually inaccurate or derived from something that is factually inaccurate or forged,

and that the court directs should be removed from the register.

6(2)   The court order must specify what is to be removed from the register and indicate where on the register it is and the registrar shall carry out his duty under sub-paragraph (1) within a reasonable time of receipt by him of the relevant court order.

SCHEDULE 5

FORMS

[Not reproduced.]

Ancillary Statutes

Debtors Act 1869

(32 & 33 Vict. Chapter 62)

An Act for the Abolition of Imprisonment for Debt, for the punishment of fraudulent debtors, and for other purposes.

[*August 9, 1869*]

[**Note**: Changes made by the Bankruptcy Act 1883, the Statute Law Revision (No.2) Act 1893, the Supreme Court of Judicature (Consolidation) Act 1925, the Theft Act 1968, the Civil Procedure (Modification of Enactments) Order 2002 (SI 2002/439) and the Statute Law (Repeals) Act 2004 have been incorporated into the text (in the case of pre-1996 legislation without annotation). See also the Debtors Act 1878, below.]

Preliminary

1 Short title

1 This Act may be cited for all purposes as "The Debtors Act 1869".

2 Extent of Act

2 This Act shall not extend to Scotland or Ireland.

3 Commencement and construction of Act

3 Words and expressions defined or explained in the Bankruptcy Act 1869 shall have the same meaning in this Act.

PART I

ABOLITION OF IMPRISONMENT FOR DEBT

4 Abolition of imprisonment for debt, with exceptions

4 With the exceptions herein-after mentioned, no person shall be arrested or imprisoned for making default in payment of a sum of money.

There shall be excepted from the operation of the above enactment:

(1) Default in payment of a penalty, or sum in the nature of a penalty, other than a penalty in respect of any contract:

(2) Default in payment of any sum recoverable summarily before a justice or justices of the peace:

(3) Default by a trustee or person acting in a fiduciary capacity and ordered to pay by a court of equity any sum in his possession or under his control:

(4) Default by a solicitor in payment of costs when ordered to pay costs for misconduct as such, or in payment of a sum of money when ordered to pay the same in his character of an officer of the court making the order:

(5) Default in payment for the benefit of creditors of any portion of a salary or other income in respect of the payment of which any court having jurisdiction in bankruptcy is authorized to make an order:

(6) Default in payment of sums in respect of the payment of which orders are in this Act authorized to be made:

Provided, first, that no person shall be imprisoned in any case excepted from the operation of this section for a longer period than one year; and, secondly, that nothing in this section shall alter the effect of any judgment or order of any court for payment of money except as regards the arrest and imprisonment of the person making default in paying such money.

5 Saving of power of committal for small debts

5 Subject to the provisions herein-after mentioned, and to the prescribed rules, any court may commit to prison for a term not exceeding six weeks, or until payment of the sum due, any person who makes default in payment of any debt or instalment of any debt due from him in pursuance of any order or judgment of that or any other competent court.

Provided–

(1) That the jurisdiction by this section given of committing a person to prison shall, in the case of any court other than the superior courts of law and equity, be exercised only subject to the following restrictions; that is to say,

    (a) Be exercised only by a judge or his deputy, and by an order made in open court and showing on its face the ground on which it is issued:

    (b) [Repealed by the Bankruptcy Act 1883 s.169(1) and Sch.5.]

    (c) Be exercised only as respects a judgment of a county court by a county court judge or his deputy.

(2) That such jurisdiction shall only be exercised where it is proved to the satisfaction of the court that the person making default either has or has had since the date of the order or judgment the means to pay the sum in respect of which he has made default, and has refused or neglected, or refuses or neglects, to pay the same.

Proof of the means of the person making default may be given in such manner as the court thinks just.

For the purpose of considering whether to commit a debtor to prison under this section, the debtor may be summoned in accordance with the prescribed rules.

Any jurisdiction by this section given to the superior courts may be exercised by a judge sitting in chambers, or otherwise, in the prescribed manner.

Persons committed under this section by a superior court may be committed to the prison in which they would have been confined if arrested on a writ of capias ad satisfaciendum, and every order of committal by any superior court shall, subject to the prescribed rules, be issued, obeyed, and executed in the like manner as such writ.

No imprisonment under this section shall operate as a satisfaction or extinguishment of any debt or demand or course of action, or deprive any person of any right to take out execution against the lands, goods, or chattels of the person imprisoned, in the same manner as if such imprisonment had not taken place.

Any person imprisoned under this section shall be discharged out of custody upon a certificate signed in the prescribed manner to the effect that he has satisfied the debt or instalment of a debt in respect of which he was imprisoned, together with the prescribed costs (if any).

History
Seventh (originally the fifth) paragraph of proviso (2) deleted by the Statute Law (Repeals) Act 2004 Sch.1 Pt 17, as from July 22, 2004.

6   Power under certain circumstances to arrest defendant about to quit England

6   Where the plaintiff in any action in the High Court in which, if brought before the commencement of this Act, the defendant would have been liable to arrest, proves at any time before final judgment by evidence on oath, to the satisfaction of a judge of the High Court, that the plaintiff has good cause of action against the defendant to the amount of fifty pounds or upwards, and that there is probable cause for believing that the defendant is about to quit England unless he be apprehended, and that the absence of the defendant from England will materially prejudice the plaintiff in the prosecution of his action such judge may in the prescribed manner order such defendant to be arrested and imprisoned for a period not exceeding six months, unless and until he has sooner given the prescribed security, not exceeding the amount claimed in the action, that he will not go out of England without the leave of the court.

Where the action is for a penalty or sum in the nature of a penalty other than a penalty in respect of any contract, it shall not be necessary to prove that the absence of the defendant from England will materially prejudice the plaintiff in the prosecution of his action, and the security given (instead of being that the defendant will not go out of England) shall be to the effect that any sum recovered against the defendant in the action shall be paid, or that the defendant shall be rendered to prison.

7   [Repealed by the Statute Law Revision Act 1883.]

8   Saving for sequestration against property

8   Sequestration against the property of a debtor may be issued by any court of equity in the same manner as if such debtor had been actually arrested.

9   [Repealed by the Statute Law Revision (No.2) Act 1893.]

10   Definition of "prescribed"

10   In this part of this Act–

"prescribed", where it appears other than as part of the expression "the prescribed rules", means prescribed by rules of court; and

"the prescribed rules" means rules of court.

PART II

PUNISHMENT OF FRAUDULENT DEBTORS

11, 12   [Repealed by the Bankruptcy Act 1914 s.168 and Sch.6.]

13   Penalty on fraudulently obtaining credit, etc.

13   Any person shall in each of the cases following be deemed guilty of a misdemeanour, and on conviction thereof shall be liable to be imprisoned for any time not exceeding one year; that is to say,

(1) [Repealed by the Theft Act 1968 ss.33(3), 35 and Sch.3 Pt I.]

(2) If he has with intent to defraud his creditors, or any of them, made or caused to be made any gift, delivery, or transfer of or any charge on his property:

(3) If he has, with intent to defraud his creditors, concealed or removed any part of his property since or within two months before the date of any unsatisfied judgment or order for payment of money obtained against him.

Debtors Act 1878

(41 & 42 Vict. Chapter 54)

An Act to amend the Debtors Act 1869, and the Debtors Act (Ireland) 1872.

[*13th August 1878*]

1 Court or Judge to have discretion in cases within exceptions 3 and 4 in 32 & 33 Vict. c.62. s. 4, and 35 & 36 Vict. c.57. s. 5, respectively

1 In any case coming within the exceptions numbered three and four in the fourth section of the Debtors Act 1869, and in the fifth section of the Debtors Act (Ireland) 1872, respectively, or within either of those exceptions, any court or judge, making the order for payment, or having jurisdiction in the action or proceeding in which the order for payment is made, may inquire into the case, and (subject to the provisoes contained in the said sections respectively) may grant or refuse, either absolutely or upon terms, any process or order of arrest or imprisonment, and any application to stay the operation of any such process, or order, or for discharge from arrest or imprisonment thereunder.

History
Section 1 amended by the Statute Law (Repeals) Act 2004 Sch.1 Pt 17, as from July 22, 2004.

2 Short title and construction

2 This Act may be cited as the Debtors Act 1878, and shall be construed as one with the Debtors Act 1869, as regards England, and as one with the Debtors Act (Ireland) 1872, as regards Ireland; and the Debtors Act 1869, and this Act may be cited as the Debtors Acts 1869 and 1878; and the Debtors Act (Ireland) 1872, and this Act may be cited as the Debtors Acts (Ireland) 1872 and 1878.

Law of Property Act 1925

(15 & 16 Geo. 5 Chapter 20)

ARRANGEMENT OF SECTIONS

An Act to consolidate the enactments relating to conveyancing and the law of property in England and Wales.

[*9th April 1925*]

[**Note**: Changes made by the Insolvency Act 1985, the Agricultural Tenancies Act 1995, the Trusts of Land and Appointment of Trustees Act 1996 and the Commonhold and Leasehold Reform Act 2002 have been incorporated into the text (without annotation).]

PART III

MORTGAGES, RENTCHARGES, AND POWERS OF ATTORNEY

Mortgages

98 Actions for possession by mortgagors

98(1) A mortgagor for the time being entitled to the possession or receipt of the rents and profits of any land, as to which the mortgagee has not given notice of his intention to take possession or to enter into the receipt of the rents and profits thereof, may sue for such possession, or for the recovery of such rents or profits, or to prevent or recover damages in respect of any trespass or other wrong relative thereto, in his own name only, unless the cause of action arises upon a lease or other contract made by him jointly with any other person.

98(2) This section does not prejudice the power of a mortgagor independently of this section to take proceedings in his own name only, either in right of any legal estate vested in him or otherwise.

98(3) This section applies whether the mortgage was made before or after the commencement of this Act.

99 Leasing powers of mortgagor and mortgagee in possession

99(1) A mortgagor of land while in possession shall, as against every incumbrancer, have power to make from time to time any such lease of the mortgaged land, or any part thereof, as is by this section authorised.

99(2) A mortgagee of land while in possession shall, as against all prior incumbrancers, if any, and as against the mortgagor, have power to make from time to time any such lease as aforesaid.

99(3)   The leases which this section authorises are–

(i)   agricultural or occupation leases for any term not exceeding twenty-one years, or, in the case of a mortgage made after the commencement of this Act, fifty years; and

(ii)   building leases for any term not exceeding ninety-nine years, or, in the case of a mortgage made after the commencement of this Act, nine hundred and ninety-nine years.

99(4)   Every person making a lease under this section may execute and do all assurances and things necessary or proper in that behalf.

99(5)   Every such lease shall be made to take effect in possession not later than twelve months after its date.

99(6)   Every such lease shall reserve the best rent that can reasonably be obtained, regard being had to the circumstances of the case, but without any fine being taken.

99(7)   Every such lease shall contain a covenant by the lessee for payment of the rent, and a condition of re-entry on the rent not being paid within a time therein specified not exceeding thirty days.

99(8)   A counterpart of every such lease shall be executed by the lessee and delivered to the lessor, of which execution and delivery the execution of the lease by the lessor shall, in favour of the lessee and all persons deriving title under him, be sufficient evidence.

99(9)   Every such building lease shall be made in consideration of the lessee, or some person by whose direction the lease is granted, having erected, or agreeing to erect within not more than five years from the date of the lease, buildings, new or additional, or having improved or repaired buildings, or agreeing to improve or repair buildings within that time, or having executed, or agreeing to execute within that time, on the land leased, an improvement for or in connexion with building purposes.

99(10)   In any such building lease a peppercorn rent, or a nominal or other rent less than the rent ultimately payable, may be made payable for the first five years, or any less part of the term.

99(11)   In case of a lease by the mortgagor, he shall, within one month after making the lease, deliver to the mortgagee, or, where there are more than one, to the mortgagee first in priority, a counterpart of the lease duly executed by the lessee, but the lessee shall not be concerned to see that this provision is complied with.

99(12)   A contract to make or accept a lease under this section may be enforced by or against every person on whom the lease if granted would be binding.

99(13)   Subject to subsection (13A) below, this section applies only if and as far as a contrary intention is not expressed by the mortgagor and mortgagee in the mortgage deed, or otherwise in writing, and has effect subject to the terms of the mortgage deed or of any such writing and to the provisions therein contained.

99(13A)   Subsection (13) of this section–

(a)   shall not enable the application of any provision of this section to be excluded or restricted in relation to any mortgage of agricultural land made after 1st March 1948 but before 1st September 1995, and

(b)   shall not enable the power to grant a lease of an agricultural holding to which, by virtue of section 4 of the Agricultural Tenancies Act 1995, the Agricultural Holdings Act 1986 will apply, to be excluded or restricted in relation to any mortgage of agricultural land made on or after 1st September 1995.

99(13B)   In subsection (13A) of this section–

"agricultural holding" has the same meaning as in the Agricultural Holdings Act 1986; and

"agricultural land" has the same meaning as in the Agriculture Act 1947.

99(14)   The mortgagor and mortgagee may, by agreement in writing, whether or not contained in the mortgage deed, reserve to or confer on the mortgagor or the mortgagee, or both, any further or other powers of leasing or having reference to leasing; and any further or other powers so reserved or conferred shall be exercisable, as far as may be, as if they were conferred by this Act, and with all the like incidents, effects, and consequences:

Provided that the powers so reserved or conferred shall not prejudicially affect the rights of any mortgagee interested under any other mortgage subsisting at the date of the agreement, unless that mortgagee joins in or adopts the agreement.

99(15)   Nothing in this Act shall be construed to enable a mortgagor or mortgagee to make a lease for any longer term or on any other conditions than such as could have been granted or imposed by the mortgagor, with the concurrence of all the incumbrancers, if this Act and the enactments replaced by this section had not been passed:

Provided that, in the case of a mortgage of leasehold land, a lease granted under this section shall reserve a reversion of not less than one day.

99(16)   Subject as aforesaid, this section applies to any mortgage made after the thirty-first day of December, eighteen hundred and eighty-one, but the provisions thereof, or any of them, may, by agreement in writing made after that date between mortgagor and mortgagee, be applied to a mortgage made before that date, so nevertheless that any such agreement shall not prejudicially affect any right or interest of any mortgagee not joining in or adopting the agreement.

99(17)   The provisions of this section referring to a lease shall be construed to extend and apply, as far as circumstances admit, to any letting, and to an agreement, whether in writing or not, for leasing or letting.

99(18)   For the purposes of this section **"mortgagor"** does not include an incumbrancer deriving title under the original mortgagor.

99(19)   The powers of leasing conferred by this section shall, after a receiver of the income of the mortgaged property or any part thereof has been appointed by a mortgagee under his statutory power, and so long as the receiver acts, be exercisable by such mortgagee instead of by the mortgagor, as respects any land affected by the receivership, in like manner as if such mortgagee were in possession of the land, and the mortgagee may, by writing, delegate any of powers to the receiver.

100   Powers of mortgagor and mortgagee in possession to accept surrenders of leases

100(1)   For the purpose only of enabling a lease authorised under the last preceding section, or under any agreement made pursuant to that section, or by the mortgage deed (in this section referred to as an authorised lease) to be granted, a mortgagor of land while in possession shall, as against every incumbrancer, have, by virtue of this Act, power to accept from time to time a surrender of any lease of the mortgaged land or any part thereof comprised in the lease, with or without an exception of or in respect of all or any of the mines and minerals therein, and, on a surrender of the lease so far as it comprises part only of the land or mines and minerals leased, the rent may be apportioned.

100(2)   For the same purpose, a mortgagee of land while in possession shall, as against all prior or other incumbrancers, if any, and as against the mortgagor, have, by virtue of this Act, power to accept from time to time any such surrender as aforesaid.

100(3)   On a surrender of part only of the land or mines and minerals leased, the original lease may be varied, provided that the lease when varied would have been valid as an authorised lease if granted by the person accepting the surrender; and, on a surrender and the making of a new or other lease, whether for the same or for any extended or other term, and whether subject or not to the same or to any other covenants, provisions, or conditions, the value of the lessee's interest in the lease surrendered may, subject to the provisions of this section, be taken into account in the determination of the amount of the rent to be reserved, and of the nature of the covenants, provisions, and conditions to be inserted in the new or other lease.

100(4)   Where any consideration for the surrender, other than an agreement to accept an authorised lease, is given by or on behalf of the lessee to or on behalf of the person accepting the surrender, nothing in this section authorises a surrender to a mortgagor without the consent of the incumbrancers, or authorises a surrender to a second or subsequent incumbrancer without the consent of every prior incumbrancer.

100(5)   No surrender shall, by virtue of this section, be rendered valid unless–

(a)   An authorised lease is granted of the whole of the land or mines and minerals comprised in the surrender to take effect in possession immediately or within one month after the date of the surrender; and

(b)   The term certain or other interest granted by the new lease is not less in duration than the unexpired term or interest which would have been subsisting under the original lease if that lease had not been surrendered; and

(c)   Where the whole of the land mines and minerals originally leased has been surrendered, the rent reserved by the new lease is not less than the rent which would have been payable under the original lease if it had not been surrendered; or where part only of the land or mines and minerals has been surrendered, the aggregate rents respectively remaining payable or reserved under the original lease and new lease are not less than the rent which would have been payable under the original lease if not partial surrender had been accepted.

100(6)   A contract to make or accept a surrender under this section may be enforced by or against every person on whom the surrender, if completed, would be binding.

100(7)   This section applies only if and as far as a contrary intention is not expressed by the mortgagor and mortgagee in the mortgage deed, or otherwise in writing, and shall have effect subject to the terms of the mortgage deed or of any such writing and to the provisions therein contained.

100(8)   This section applies to a mortgage made after the thirty-first day of December, nineteen hundred and eleven, but the provisions of this section, or any of them, may, by agreement in writing made after that date, between mortgagor and mortgagee, be applied to a mortgage made before that date, so nevertheless that any such agreement shall not prejudicially affect any right or interest of any mortgagee not joining in or adopting the agreement.

100(9)   The provisions of this section referring to a lease shall be construed to extend and apply, as far as circumstances admit, to any letting, and to an agreement, whether in writing or not, for leasing or letting.

100(10) The mortgagor and mortgagee may, by agreement in writing, whether or not contained in the mortgage deed, reserve or confer on the mortgagor or mortgagee, or both, any further or other powers relating to the surrender of leases; and any further or other powers so conferred or reserved shall be exercisable, as far as may be, as if they were conferred by this Act, and with all the like incidents, effects and consequences:

Provided that the powers so reserved or conferred shall not prejudicially affect the rights of any mortgagee interested under any other mortgage subsisting at the date of the agreement, unless that mortgagee joins in or adopts the agreement.

100(11)   Nothing in this section operates to enable a mortgagor or mortgagee to accept a surrender which could not have been accepted by the mortgagor with the concurrence of all the incumbrancers if this Act and the enactments replaced by this section had not been passed.

100(12)   For the purposes of this section **"mortgagor"** does not include an incumbrancer deriving title under the original mortgagor.

100(13)   The powers of accepting surrenders conferred by this section shall, after a receiver of the income of the mortgaged property or any part thereof has been appointed by the mortgagee, under the statutory power, and so long as the receiver acts, be exercisable by such mortgagee instead of by the mortgagor, as respects any land affected by the receivership, in like manner as if such mortgagee were in possession of the land; and the mortgagee may, by writing, delegate any of such powers to the receiver.

101   Powers incident to estate or interest of mortgagee

101(1)   A mortgagee, where the mortgage is made by deed, shall, by virtue of this Act, have the following powers, to the like extent as if they had been in terms conferred by the mortgage deed, but not further (namely):

(i)   A power, when the mortgage money has become due, to sell, or to concur with any other person in selling, the mortgaged property, or any part thereof, either subject to prior charges or not, and either together or in lots, by public auction or by private contract, subject to such conditions respecting title, or evidence of title, or other matter, as the mortgagee thinks fit, with power to vary any contract for sale, and to buy in at an auction, or to rescind any contract for sale, and to re-sell, without being answerable for any loss occasioned thereby; and

(ii)   A power, at any time after the date of the mortgage deed, to insure and keep insured against loss or damage by fire any building, or any effects or property of an insurable nature, whether affixed to the freehold or not, being or forming part of the property which or an estate or interest wherein is mortgaged, and the premiums paid for any such insurance shall be a charge on the mortgaged property or estate or interest, in addition to the mortgage money, and with the same priority, and with interest at the same rate, as the mortgage money; and

(iii)   A power, when the mortgage money has become due, to appoint a receiver of the income of the mortgaged property, or any part thereof; or, if the mortgaged property consists of an interest in income, or of a rentcharge or an annual or other periodical sum, a receiver of that property or any part thereof; and

(iv)   A power, while the mortgagee is in possession, to cut and sell timber and other trees ripe for cutting, and not planted or left standing for shelter or ornament, or to contract for any such cutting and sale, to be completed within any time not exceeding twelve months from the making of the contract.

101(1A)   Subsection (1)(i) is subject to section 21 of the Commonhold and Leasehold Reform Act 2002 (no disposition of part-units).

101(2)   Where the mortgage deed is executed after the thirty-first day of December, nineteen hundred and eleven, the power of sale aforesaid includes the following powers as incident thereto (namely)–

(i)   A power to impose or reserve or make binding, as far as the law permits, by covenant, condition, or otherwise, on the unsold part of the mortgaged property or any part thereof, or on the purchaser and any property sold, any restriction or reservation with respect to building on or other user of land, or with respect to mines and minerals, or for the purpose of the more beneficial working thereof, or with respect to any other thing:

(ii)   A power to sell the mortgaged property, or any part thereof, or all or any mines and minerals apart from the surface–

(a)   With or without a grant or reservation of rights of way, rights of water, easements, rights, and privileges for or connected with building or other purposes in relation to the property remaining in mortgage or any part thereof, or to any property sold: and

(b)   With or without an exception or reservation of all or any of the mines and minerals in or under the mortgaged property, and with or without a grant or reservation of powers or working, wayleaves, or rights of way, rights of water and drainage and other powers, easements, rights, and privileges for or connected with mining purposes in relation to the property remaining unsold or any part thereof, or to any property sold: and

(c)   With or without covenants by the purchaser to expend money on the land sold.

101(3)   The provisions of this Act relating to the foregoing powers, comprised either in this section, or in any other section regulating the exercise of those powers, may be varied or extended by the mortgage deed, and, as so varied or extended, shall, as far as may be, operate in the like manner and with all the like incidents, effects, and consequences, as if such variations or extensions were contained in this Act.

101(4)   This section applies only if and as far as a contrary intention is not expressed in the mortgage deed, and has effect subject to the terms of the mortgage deed and to the provisions therein contained.

101(5)   Save as otherwise provided, this section applies where the mortgage deed is executed after the thirty-first day of December, eighteen hundred and eighty-one.

101(6)   The power of sale conferred by this section includes such power of selling the estate in fee simple or any leasehold reversion as is conferred by the provisions of this Act relating to the realisation of mortgages.

102   Provision as to mortgages of undivided shares in land

102(1)   A person who was before the commencement of this Act a mortgagee of an undivided share in land shall have the same power to sell his interest under the trust to which the land is subject, as, independently of this Act, he would have had in regard to the share in the land; and shall also have a right to require the trustees in whom the land is vested to account to him for the income attributable to that share or to appoint a receiver to receive the same from such trustees corresponding to the right which, independently of this Act, he would have had to take possession or to appoint a receiver of the rents and profits attributable to the same share.

102(2)   The powers conferred by this section are exercisable by the persons deriving title under such mortgagee.

103   Regulation of exercise of power of sale

103   A mortgagee shall not exercise the power of sale conferred by this Act unless and until–

(i)   Notice requiring payment of the mortgage money has been served on the mortgagor or one of two or more mortgagors, and default has been made in payment of the mortgage money, or of part thereof, for three months after such service; or

(ii)   Some interest under the mortgage is in arrear and unpaid for two months after becoming due; or

(iii)   There has been a breach of some provision contained in the mortgage deed or in this Act, or in an enactment replaced by this Act, and on the part of the mortgagor, or of some person concurring in making the mortgage, to be observed or performed, other than and besides a covenant for payment of the mortgage money or interest thereon.

104   Conveyance on sale

104(1)   A mortgagee exercising the power of sale conferred by this Act shall have power, by deed, to convey the property sold, for such estate and interest therein as he is by this Act authorised to sell or convey or may be the subject of the mortgage, freed from all estates, interests, and rights to which the mortgage has priority, but subject to all estates, interests, and rights which have priority to the mortgage.

104(2)   Where a conveyance is made in exercise of the power of sale conferred by this Act, or any enactment replaced by this Act, the title of the purchaser shall not be impeachable on the ground–

(a)   that no case had arisen to authorise the sale; or

(b) that due notice was not given; or

(c) where the mortgage is made after the commencement of this Act, that leave of the court, when so required, was not obtained; or

(d) whether the mortgage was made before or after such commencement, that the power was otherwise improperly or irregularly exercised;

and a purchaser is not, either before or on conveyance, concerned to see or inquire whether a case has arisen to authorise the sale, or due notice has been given, or the power is otherwise properly and regularly exercised; but any person damnified by an unauthorised, or improper, or irregular exercise of the power shall have his remedy in damages against the person exercising the power.

104(3) A conveyance on sale by a mortgagee, made after the commencement of this Act, shall be deemed to have been made in exercise of the power of sale conferred by this Act unless a contrary intention appears.

105 Application of proceeds of sale

105 The money which is received by the mortgagee, arising from the sale, after discharge of prior incumbrances to which the sale is not made subject, if any, or after payment into court under this Act of a sum to meet any prior incumbrance, shall be held by him in trust to be applied by him, first, in payment of all costs, charges, and expenses properly incurred by him as incident to the sale or any attempted sale, or otherwise; and secondly, in discharge of the mortgage money, interest, and costs, and other money, if any, due under the mortgage; and the residue of the money so received shall be paid to the person entitled to the mortgaged property, or authorised to give receipts for the proceeds of the sale thereof.

106 Provisions as to exercise of power of sale

106(1) The power of sale conferred by this Act may be exercised by any person for the time being entitled to receive and give a discharge for the mortgage money.

106(2) The power of sale conferred by this Act does not affect the right of foreclosure.

106(3) The mortgagee shall not be answerable for any involuntary loss happening in or about the exercise or execution of the power of sale conferred by this Act, or of any trust connected therewith, or, where the mortgage is executed after the thirty-first day of December, nineteen hundred and eleven, of any power or provision contained in the mortgage deed.

106(4) At any time after the power of sale conferred by this Act has become exercisable, the person entitled to exercise the power may demand and recover from any person, other than a person having in the mortgaged property an estate, interest, or right in priority to the mortgage, all the deeds and documents relating to the property, or to the title thereto, which a purchaser under the power of sale would be entitled to demand and recover from him.

107 Mortgagee's receipts, discharges, etc.

107(1) The receipt in writing of a mortgagee shall be a sufficient discharge for any money arising under the power of sale conferred by this Act, or for any money or securities comprised in his mortgage, or arising thereunder; and a person paying or transferring the same to the mortgagee shall not be concerned to inquire whether any money remains due under the mortgage.

107(2) Money received by a mortgagee under his mortgage or from the proceeds of securities comprised in his mortgage shall be applied in like manner as in this Act directed respecting money received by him arising from a sale under the power of sale conferred by this Act, but with this variation, that the costs, charges, and expenses payable shall include the costs, charges, and expenses properly incurred of recovering and receiving the money or securities, and of conversion of securities into money, instead of those incident to sale.

108   Amount and application of insurance money

108(1)   The amount of an insurance effected by a mortgagee against loss or damage by fire under the power in that behalf conferred by this Act shall not exceed the amount specified in the mortgage deed, or, if no amount is therein specified, two third parts of the amount that would be required, in case of total destruction, to restore the property insured.

108(2)   An insurance shall not, under the power conferred by this Act, be effected by a mortgagee in any of the following cases (namely):

(i)   Where there is a declaration in the mortgage deed that no insurance is required:

(ii)   Where an insurance is kept up by or on behalf of the mortgagor in accordance with the mortgage deed:

(iii)   Where the mortgage deed contains no stipulation respecting insurance, and an insurance is kept up by or on behalf of the mortgagor with the consent of the mortgagee to the amount to which the mortgagee is by this Act authorised to insure.

108(3)   All money received on an insurance of mortgaged property against loss or damage by fire or otherwise effected under this Act, or any enactment replaced by this Act, or on an insurance for the maintenance of which the mortgagor is liable under the mortgage deed, shall, if the mortgagee so requires, be applied by the mortgagor in making good the loss or damage in respect of which the money is received.

108(4)   Without prejudice to any obligation to the contrary imposed by law, or by special contract, a mortgagee may require that all money received on an insurance of mortgaged property against loss or damage by fire or otherwise effected under this Act, or any enactment replaced by this Act, or on an insurance for the maintenance of which the mortgagor is liable under the mortgage deed, be applied in or towards the discharge of the mortgage money.

109   Appointment, powers, remuneration and duties of receiver

109(1)   A mortgagee entitled to appoint a receiver under the power in that behalf conferred by this Act shall not appoint a receiver until he has become entitled to exercise the power of sale conferred by this Act, but may then, by writing under his hand, appoint such person as he thinks fit to be receiver.

109(2)   A receiver appointed under the powers conferred by this Act, or any enactment replaced by this Act, shall be deemed to be the agent of the mortgagor; and the mortgagor shall be solely responsible for the receiver's acts or defaults unless the mortgage deed otherwise provides.

109(3)   The receiver shall have power to demand and recover all the income of which he is appointed receiver, by action, distress, or otherwise, in the name either of the mortgagor or of the mortgagee, to the full extent of the estate or interest which the mortgagor could dispose of, and to give effectual receipts accordingly for the same, and to exercise any powers which may have been delegated to him by the mortgagee pursuant to this Act.

[**Note:** The prospective amendment by TCEA 2007 s.86 and Sch.14 para.22.]

109(4)   A person paying money to the receiver shall not be concerned to inquire whether any case has happened to authorise the receiver to act.

109(5)   The receiver may be removed, and a new receiver may be appointed, from time to time by the mortgagee by writing under his hand.

109(6)   The receiver shall be entitled to retain out of any money received by him, for his remuneration, and in satisfaction of all costs, charges, and expenses incurred by him as receiver, a commission at such rate, not exceeding five per centum on the gross amount of all money received, as is specified in his appointment, and if no rate is so specified, then at the rate of five per centum on that gross amount, or at such other rate as the court thinks fit to allow, on application made by him for that purpose.

109(7)   The receiver shall, if so directed in writing by the mortgagee, insure to the extent, if any, to which the mortgagee might have insured and keep insured against loss or damage by fire, out of the money received by him, any building, effects, or property comprised in the mortgage, whether affixed to the freehold or not, being of an insurable nature.

109(8)   Subject to the provisions of this Act as to the application of insurance money, the receiver shall apply all money received by him as follows, namely:

(i)   In discharge of all rents, taxes, rates, and outgoings whatever affecting the mortgaged property; and

(ii)   In keeping down all annual sums or other payments, and the interest on all principal sums, having priority to the mortgage in right where of he is receiver; and

(iii)   In payment of his commission, and of the premiums on fire, life, or other insurances, if any, properly payable under the mortgage deed or under this Act, and the cost of executing necessary or proper repairs directed in writing by the mortgagee; and

(iv)   In payment of the interest accruing due in respect of any principal money due under the mortgage; and

(v)   In or towards discharge of the principal money if so directed in writing by the mortgagee;

and shall pay the residue, if any, of the money received by him to the person who, but for the possession of the receiver, would have been entitled to receive the income of which he is appointed receiver, or who is otherwise entitled to the mortgaged property.

110   Effect of bankruptcy of the mortgagor on the power to sell or appoint a receiver

110(1)   Where the statutory or express power for a mortgagee either to sell or to appoint a receiver is made exercisable by reason of the mortgagor being adjudged a bankrupt, such power shall not be exercised only on account of the adjudication, without the leave of the court.

110(2)   This section applies only where the mortgage deed is executed after the commencement of this Act.

Third Parties (Rights Against Insurers) Act 1930

(20 & 21 Geo. 5 Chapter 25)

An Act to confer on third parties rights against insurers of third-party risks in the event of the insured becoming insolvent, and in certain other events.

[*10th July 1930*]

Special note

The Third Parties (Rights against Insurers) Act 2010 received the Royal Assent on March 25, 2010. This Act, when brought into force, will repeal and completely replace the 1930 Act. However, at the time of going to press it has not been brought into force, and it is uncertain whether this will occur during the currency of the present edition. In the circumstances we have decided to include the text of both Acts. Readers should check on the position in order to be sure which text to use. For the 2010 Act, see below, p.494.

[**Note**: Changes made by the Supreme Court of Judicature (Consolidation) Act 1925, the Statute Law Revision Act 1950, the Bankruptcy (Scotland) Act 1985, the Insolvency Acts 1985 and 1986, the Limited Liability Partnerships Regulations 2001 (SI 2001/1090) and the Enterprise Act 2002 (Insolvency) Order 2003 (SI 2003/2096) have been incorporated into the text (in the case of pre-2003 legislation without annotation). References to administration petitions, orders, etc. have been adapted throughout, following the introduction of the new administration regime, pursuant to the Enterprise Act 2002 (Insolvency) Order 2003 (SI 2003/2096), as from September 15, 2003.]

1   Rights of third parties against insurers on bankruptcy, etc. of the insured

1(1)   Where under any contract of insurance a person (hereinafter referred to as the insured) is insured against liabilities to third parties which he may incur, then–

(a)   in the event of the insured becoming bankrupt or making a composition or arrangement with his creditors; or

(b)   in the case of the insured being a company, in the event of a winding-up order being made, or a resolution for a voluntary winding-up being passed, with respect to the company, or of the company entering administration, or of a receiver or manager of the company's business or undertaking being duly appointed, or of possession being taken, by or on behalf of the holders of any debentures secured by a floating charge, of any property comprised in or subject to the charge or of a voluntary arrangement proposed for the purposes of Part I of the Insolvency Act 1986 being approved under that Part;

if, either before or after that event, any such liability as aforesaid is incurred by the insured, his rights against the insurer under the contract in respect of the liability shall, notwithstanding anything in any Act or rule of law to the contrary, be transferred to and vest in the third party to whom the liability was so incurred.

1(2)   Where the estate of any person falls to be administered in accordance with an order under section 421 of the Insolvency Act 1986, then, if any debt provable in bankruptcy (in Scotland, any claim accepted in the sequestration)is owing by the deceased in respect of a liability against which he was insured under a contract of insurance as being a liability to a third party, the deceased debtor's rights against the insurer under the contract in respect of that liability shall, notwithstanding anything in any such order, be transferred to and vest in the person to whom the debt is owing.

1(3)   In so far as any contract of insurance made after the commencement of this Act in respect of any liability of the insured to third parties purports, whether directly or indirectly, to avoid the contract or to alter the rights of the parties thereunder upon the happening to the insured of any of the events specified

246

in paragraph (a) or paragraph (b) of subsection (1) of this section or upon the estate of any person falling to be administered in accordance with an order under section 421 of the Insolvency Act 1986, the contract shall be of no effect.

1(4) Upon a transfer under subsection (1) or subsection (2) of this section, the insurer shall, subject to the provisions of section three of this Act, be under the same liability to the third party as he would have been under to the insured, but–

(a) if the liability of the insurer to the insured exceeds the liability of the insured to the third party, nothing in this Act shall affect the rights of the insured against the insurer in respect of the excess; and

(b) if the liability of the insurer to the insured is less than the liability of the insured to the third party, nothing in this Act shall affect the rights of the third party against the insured in respect of the balance.

1(5) For the purposes of this Act, the expression **"liabilities to third parties"**, in relation to a person insured under any contract of insurance, shall not include any liability of that person in the capacity of insurer under some other contract of insurance.

1(6) This Act shall not apply–

(a) where a company is wound up voluntarily merely for the purposes of reconstruction or of amalgamation with another company; or

(b) to any case to which subsections (1) and (2) of section seven of the Workmen's Compensation Act 1925, applies.

2 Duty to give necessary information to third parties

2(1) In the event of any person becoming bankrupt or making a composition or arrangement with his creditors, or in the event of the estate of any person falling to be administered in accordance with an order under section 421 of the Insolvency Act 1986, or in the event of a winding-up order being made, or a resolution for a voluntary winding-up being passed, with respect to any company or of the company entering administration or of a receiver or manager of the company's business or undertaking being duly appointed or of possession being taken by or on behalf of the holders of any debentures secured by a floating charge of any property comprised in or subject to the charge it shall be the duty of the bankrupt, debtor, personal representative of the deceased debtor or company, and, as the case may be, of the trustee in bankruptcy, trustee, liquidator, administrator, receiver, or manager, or person in possession of the property to give at the request of any person claiming that the bankrupt, debtor, deceased debtor, or company is under a liability to him such information as may reasonably be required by him for the purpose of ascertaining whether any rights have been transferred to and vested in him by this Act and for the purpose of enforcing such rights, if any, and any contract of insurance, in so far as it purports, whether directly or indirectly, to avoid the contract or to alter the rights of the parties thereunder upon the giving of any such information in the events aforesaid or otherwise to prohibit or prevent the giving thereof in the said events shall be of no effect.

2(1A) The reference in subsection (1) of this section to a trustee includes a reference to the supervisor of a voluntary arrangement proposed for the purposes of, and approved under, Part I or Part VIII of the Insolvency Act 1986.

2(2) If the information given to any person in pursuance of subsection (1) of this section discloses reasonable ground for supposing that there have or may have been transferred to him under this Act rights against any particular insurer, that insurer shall be subject to the same duty as is imposed by the said subsection on the persons therein mentioned.

2(3) The duty to give information imposed by this section shall include a duty to allow all contracts of insurance, receipts for premiums, and other relevant documents in the possession or power of the person on whom the duty is so imposed to be inspected and copies thereof to be taken.

3   Settlement between insurers and insured persons

3 Where the insured has become bankrupt or where in the case of the insured being a company, a winding-up order or an administration order has been made or a resolution for a voluntary winding-up has been passed, with respect to the company, no agreement made between the insurer and the insured after liability has been incurred to a third party and after the commencement of the bankruptcy or winding-up or the day of the making of the administration order, as the case may be, nor any waiver, assignment, or other disposition made by, or payment made to the insured after the commencement or day aforesaid shall be effective to defeat or affect the rights transferred to the third party under this Act, but those rights shall be the same as if no such agreement, waiver, assignment, disposition or payment had been made.

[**Note:** No amendments corresponding to those made to s.2 appear to have been made to this section.]

3A   Application to limited liability partnerships

3A(1) This Act applies to limited liability partnerships as it applies to companies.

3A(2) In its application to limited liability partnerships, references to a resolution for a voluntary winding-up being passed are references to a determination for a voluntary winding-up being made.

4   Application to Scotland

4 In the application of this Act to Scotland–

  (a) [Repealed by the Bankruptcy (Scotland) Act 1985 s.75(1), (2) and Sch.7 para.6(2)(a), Sch.8.]

  (b) any reference to an estate falling to be administered in accordance with an order under section 421 of the Insolvency Act 1986, shall be deemed to include a reference to an award of sequestration of the estate of a deceased debtor, and a reference to an appointment of a judicial factor, under section 11A of the Judicial Factors (Scotland) Act 1889, on the insolvent estate of a deceased person.

5   Short title

5 This Act may be cited as the Third Parties (Rights Against Insurers) Act 1930.

Industrial and Provident Societies Act 1965

(1965 Chapter 12)

An Act to consolidate certain enactments relating to industrial and provident societies, being those enactments as they apply in Great Britain and the Channel Islands with corrections and improvements made under the Consolidation of Enactments (Procedure) Act 1949.

[*2nd June 1965*]

[**Note**: Changes made by the Insolvency Act 1986, the Financial Services and Markets Act 2000 (Mutual Societies) Order 2001 (SI 2001/2617), the Financial Services and Markets Act 2000 (Consequential Amendments and Repeals) Order 2001 (SI 2001/3649), the Companies Act 2006 (Consequential Amendments, Transitional Provisions and Savings) Order 2009 (SI 2009/1941) and the Legislative Reform (Industrial and Provident Societies and Credit Unions) Order 2011 (SI 2011/2687) have been incorporated into the text (in the case of pre-2003 legislation without annotation). References to the appropriate registrar, that registrar or the chief registrar have been substituted throughout by references to the Authority (i.e. the Financial Services Authority), pursuant to SI 2001/2617 art.13(1) and Sch.3 Pt III paras 214, 215, 229 and Sch.4 as from December 1, 2001. Note that this Act is to be renamed (or more accurately, "may be cited") as the Co-operative and Community Benefit and Credit Unions Act 1965 when the Co-operative and Community Benefit and Credit Unions Act 2010 comes into force: see s.2 of the latter Act.]

Dissolution of society

55   Dissolution of society

55(1)   A registered society may be dissolved–

(a)   on its being wound up in pursuance of an order or resolution made as is directed in the case of companies registered under the Companies Acts, or

(b)   in accordance with section 58 of this Act, by an instrument of dissolution–

    (i)   to which not less than three-fourths of the members of the society have given their consent testified by their signatures to the instrument;

    (ii)   in the case of a dormant society which is not a credit union, which has been approved by a special resolution of the society; or

    (iii)   in the case of a credit union, which has been approved by a special resolution of the society and confirmed by the Authority.

55(1A)   In subsection (1)(b) above **"special resolution"** has the same meaning as in section 50 of this Act.

55(1B)   In subsection (1)(b)(ii) above a society is **"dormant"** if its accounts for the current year of account and the two years of account immediately preceding the current year of account show no accounting transactions other than–

(a)   fees paid to the Authority;

(b)   payment of dividends; or

(c)   payment of interest;

and it has notified the Authority that it is dormant.

55(1C)   For the purposes of subsection (1)(b)(iii) above the Authority shall be deemed to have confirmed a special resolution if, within twenty one days of the credit union sending a copy of that special resolution to the Authority, the Authority has not notified the credit union in writing to the contrary.

55(2)   The provisions relating to the winding up of companies registered under the Companies Acts have effect in relation to a registered society as if the society were such a company, subject to the following modifications–

(a)   any reference to the registrar of companies shall be read as a reference to the Authority;

(b)   any reference to a company registered in Scotland shall be read as a reference to a society registered under this Act whose registered office is situated in Scotland;

(c)   if the society is wound up in Scotland, the court having jurisdiction is the sheriff court within whose jurisdiction the society's registered office is situated.

55(3)   A copy of any resolution passed for the voluntary winding up of a registered society must be sent by the society to the Authority within 15 days after it is passed.

For the purposes of section 62 of this Act (offences by officers etc) as it applies in relation to a failure to comply with this subsection, a liquidator of the society shall be treated as an officer of it.

55(4)   A copy of any resolution passed for the voluntary winding up of a registered society must be annexed to every copy of the registered rules of the society issued after the passing of the resolution.

55(5)   This section has effect subject to section 59 of this Act (restriction on dissolution or cancellation of registration).

History

Section 55 substituted and ss.57, 58(1) amended by the Companies Act 2006 (Consequential Amendments, Transitional Provisions and Savings) Order 2009 (SI 2009/1941) art.2(1) and Sch.1 para.14(8) as from October 1, 2009. Section 55(1)(b) amended and s.55(1A)–(1C) inserted by the Legislative Reform (Industrial and Provident Societies and Credit Unions) Order 2011 (SI 2011/2687) art.9(1), (2) as from January 8, 2012.

56   Power of Authority to petition for winding up

56   In the case of a society to which section 4 of this Act applies which was registered or deemed to be registered under the Act of 1893 before 26th July 1938, a petition for the winding up of the society may be presented to the court by the Authority if it appears to the Authority–

(a)   that neither of the conditions specified in section 1(2) of this Act is fulfilled in the case of that society; and

(b)   that it would be in the interests of persons who have invested or deposited money with the society or of any other person that the society should be wound up.

57   Liability of members in winding up

57   Where a registered society is wound up by virtue of section 55(1)(a) of this Act, the liability of a present or past member of the society to contribute for payment of the debts and liabilities of the society, the expenses of winding up, and the adjustment of the rights of contributories amongst themselves, shall be qualified as follows, that is to say–

(a)   no person who ceased to be a member not less than one year before the beginning of the winding up shall be liable to contribute;

(b)   no person shall be liable to contribute in respect of any debt or liability contracted after he ceased to be a member;

(c)   no person who is not a member shall be liable to contribute unless it appears to the court that the contributions of the existing members are insufficient to satisfy the just demands on the society;

(d)   no contribution shall be required from any person exceeding the amount, if any, unpaid on the shares in respect of which he is liable as a past or present member;

(e)   in the case of a withdrawable share which has been withdrawn, a person shall be taken to have ceased to be a member in respect of that share as from the date of the notice or application for withdrawal.

58   Instrument of dissolution

58(1)   The following provisions of this section shall have effect where a society is to be dissolved by an instrument of dissolution under section 55(1)(b) of this Act.

58(2)   The instrument of dissolution shall set forth–

(a)   the liabilities and assets of the society in detail;

(b)   the number of the members and the nature of their respective interests in the society;

(c)   the claims of creditors, if any, and the provision to be made for their payment; and

(d)   unless stated in the instrument of dissolution to be left to the award of the Authority, the intended appropriation or division of the funds and property of the society.

58(3)   Alterations in the instrument of dissolution may be made by the consent of not less than three-fourths of the members of the society testified by their signatures to the alteration or, if the instrument was approved by a special resolution of the society, by a further special resolution.

58(4)   The instrument of dissolution shall be sent to the Authority accompanied by a statutory declaration made by three members and the secretary of the society that all relevant provisions of this Act have been complied with; and any person knowingly making a false or fraudulent declaration in the matter shall be guilty of a misdemeanour or, in Scotland, an offence.

58(5)   The instrument of dissolution and any alterations thereto shall be registered in like manner as an amendment of the rules of the society and shall be binding upon all the members of the society, but shall not be so registered until the Authority has received such a final return from the society as is referred to in section 39(4) of this Act.

58(5A)   Subsection (5) of this section does not apply to an instrument which pursuant to section 55(1)(b)(iii) above is not confirmed by the Authority.

58(5B)   A copy of every special resolution for the purposes of section 55(1)(b) of this Act or subsection (3) of this section, signed by the chairman of the meeting at which the resolution was confirmed and countersigned by the secretary of the society, shall be sent to the Authority before the end of the period of fourteen days beginning with the day on which the resolution was confirmed.

58(5C)   The Authority shall register any copy of a special resolution sent to it in accordance with subsection (5B) of this section at the same time as it registers the instrument of dissolution and any alterations thereto.

58(6) The Authority shall cause notice of the dissolution to be advertised in the Gazette and in some newspaper circulating in or about the locality in which the society's registered office is situated; and unless–

(a)   within three months from the date of the Gazette in which that advertisement appears a member or other person interested in or having any claim on the funds of the society commences in the county court, or in Scotland before the sheriff, having jurisdiction in that locality proceedings to set aside the dissolution of the society; and

(b)   that dissolution is set aside accordingly,

then, subject to subsection (7) of this section, the society shall be legally dissolved from the date of the advertisement and the requisite consents to, or approval of, the instrument of dissolution shall be deemed to have been duly obtained without proof of the signatures thereto or of the special resolution, as the case may be.

58(7)   If the certificate referred to in section 59 of this Act has not been lodged with the Authority by the date of the advertisement referred to in subsection (6) of this section, the society shall be legally dissolved only from the date when that certificate is so lodged.

58(8)   Notice of any proceedings to set aside the dissolution of a society shall be sent to the Authority by the person taking those proceedings not later than seven days after they are commenced or not later than the expiration of the period of three months referred to subsection (6) of this section, whichever is the earlier; and notice of any order setting the dissolution aside shall be sent by the society to the Authority within seven days after the making of the order.

58(9)   In the application of this section to a society which for the time being consists solely of two registered societies, the reference in subsection (4) thereof to three members shall be construed as a reference to both members.

58(10)   In this section "special resolution" has the same meaning as in section 50 of this Act.

History
Section 58(3), (6) amended and s.58(5A)–(5C), (10) inserted by the Legislative Reform (Industrial and Provident Societies and Credit Unions) Order 2011 (SI 2011/2687) art.9(3) as from January 8, 2012.

Special restriction on dissolution, etc.

59   Restriction on dissolution or cancellation of registration of society

59   Where a registered society is to be dissolved in accordance with section 55 of this Act, or where a registered society's engagements are transferred under section 51 or 52 of this Act, the society shall not be dissolved, and the registration of the society shall not be cancelled, until there has been lodged with the Authority a certificate signed by the liquidator or by the secretary or some other officer of the society approved by the Authority that all property vested in the society has been duly conveyed or transferred by the society to the persons entitled.

Administration of Justice Act 1970

(1970 Chapter 31)

An Act to make further provision about the courts (including assizes), their business, jurisdiction and procedure; to enable a High Court judge to accept appointment as arbitrator or umpire under an arbitration agreement; to amend the law respecting the enforcement of debt and other liabilities; to amend section 106 of the Rent Act 1968; and for miscellaneous purposes connected with the administration of justice.

[29th May 1970]

[**Note**: Changes made by the Social Security Act 1973, the Consumer Credit Act 1974, the Social Security Pensions Act 1975, the Social Security (Consequential Provisions) Acts 1975 and 1992, the Magistrates' Courts Act 1980, and the Pension Schemes Act 1993 have been incorporated into the text without annotation.]

PART II

ENFORCEMENT OF DEBT

Provisions restricting sanction of imprisonment

11   Restriction on power of committal under Debtors Act

11   The jurisdiction given by section 5 of the Debtors Act 1869 to commit to prison a person who makes default in payment of a debt, or instalment of a debt, due from him in pursuance of an order or judgment shall be exercisable only–

(a)   by the High Court in respect of a High Court maintenance order; and

(b)   by a county court in respect of–

(i)   a High Court or a county court maintenance order; or

(ii)   a judgment or order which is enforceable by a court in England and Wales and is for the payment of any of the taxes, contributions or liabilities specified in Schedule 4 to this Act.

[**Note**: A prospective amendment to be made by the Social Security Act 1973 s.100 and Sch.27 para.85 from a day to be appointed is now considered unlikely to be brought into force.]

PART IV

ACTIONS BY MORTGAGEES FOR POSSESSION

36   Additional powers of court in action by mortgagee for possession of dwelling-house

36(1)   Where the mortgagee under a mortgage of land which consists of or includes a dwelling-house brings an action in which he claims possession of the mortgaged property, not being an action for foreclosure in which a claim for possession of the mortgaged property is also made, the court may exercise any of the powers conferred on it by subsection (2) below if it appears to the court that in the event of its exercising the power the mortgagor is likely to be able within a reasonable period to pay any sums due under the mortgage or to remedy a default consisting of a breach of any other obligation arising under or by virtue of the mortgage.

36(2)   The court–

(a)   may adjourn the proceedings, or

(b)   on giving judgment, or making an order, for delivery of possession of the mortgaged property, or at any time before the execution of such judgment or order, may–

     (i)   stay or suspend execution of the judgment or order, or

     (ii)   postpone the date for delivery of possession, for such period or periods as the court thinks reasonable.

36(3)   Any such adjournment, stay, suspension or postponement as is referred to in subsection (2) above may be made subject to such conditions with regard to payment by the mortgagor of any sum secured by the mortgage or the remedying of any default as the court thinks fit.

36(4)   The court may from time to time vary or revoke any condition imposed by virtue of this section.

36(5)   [Repealed by the Statute Law (Repeals) Act 2004 Sch.1 Pt 12, as from July 22, 2004.]

36(6)   In the application of this section to Northern Ireland, **"the court"** means a judge of the High Court in Northern Ireland, and in subsection (1) the words from "not being" to "made" shall be omitted.

37, 38   [Repealed by the County Courts Act 1984 s.148(3) and Sch.4.]

38A   This Part of this Act shall not apply to a mortgage securing an agreement which is a regulated agreement within the meaning of the Consumer Credit Act 1974.

39   Interpretation of Part IV

39(1)   In this Part of this Act–

"dwelling-house" includes any building or part thereof which is used as a dwelling;

"mortgage" includes a charge and **"mortgagor"** and **"mortgagee"** shall be construed accordingly;

"mortgagor" and **"mortgagee"** includes any person deriving title under the original mortgagor or mortgagee.

39(2)   The fact that part of the premises comprised in a dwelling-house is used as a shop or office or for business, trade or professional purposes shall not prevent the dwelling-house from being a dwelling-house for the purposes of this Part of this Act.

SCHEDULE 4

TAXES, SOCIAL INSURANCE CONTRIBUTIONS, ETC SUBJECT TO SPECIAL
ENFORCEMENT PROVISIONS IN PART II

Sections 11, 12, 14

1 Income tax or any other tax or liability recoverable under section 65, 66 or 68 of the Taxes Management Act 1970.

2 [Repealed by the Statute Law Repeals Act 1989.]

3 Contributions equivalent premiums under Part III of the Pension Schemes Act 1993.

3A Class 1, 2 and 4 contributions under Part I of the Social Security Contributions and Benefits Act 1992.

4 [Repealed by the Social Security Act 1973 s.100 and Sch.28 Pt I.]

Attachment of Earnings Act 1971

(1971 Chapter 32)

An Act to consolidate the enactments relating to the attachment of earnings as a means of enforcing the discharge of monetary obligations.

[12th May 1971]

[**Note**: Changes made by the Social Security Pensions Act 1975, the Insolvency Act 1976, the Administration of Justice Act 1977, the Merchant Shipping Acts 1979 and 1995, the Magistrates' Courts Act 1980, the Contempt of Court Act 1981, the Criminal Justice Acts 1982 and 1991, the Administration of Justice Act 1982, the County Courts Act 1984, the Social Security Act 1985, the Courts and Legal Services Act 1990, the Maintenance Enforcement Act 1991, the Attachment of Earnings (Employer's Deduction) Order 1991 (SI 1991/356), the Transfer of Functions (Science) Order 1992 (SI 1992/1296), the Pension Schemes Act 1993, the Transfer of Functions (Science) Order 1995 (SI 1995/2985), the Reserve Forces Act 1998 (Consequential Provisions, etc.) Regulations 1998 (SI 1998/3086), the Access to Justice Act 1999, the Tax Credits Act 2002, the Criminal Defence Service Act 2006, the Collection of Fines (Final Scheme) Order 2006 (SI 2006/1737) and the Civil Jurisdiction and Judgments (Maintenance) Regulations 2011 (SI 2011/1484) have been incorporated into the text (in the case of pre-2003 legislation without annotation). (See also history note to s.1). References to "justices' clerks" have been changed to "designated officers" (formerly "justices' chief executives") and other corresponding changes have been made pursuant to the Access to Justice Act 1999 s.90(1) and Sch.13 paras 64 et seq., as from April 1, 2001, and the Courts Act 2003 s.109(1) and Sch.8 paras 141 et seq., as from September 1, 2004. The government has announced that the prospective amendment of this Act to be effected by TCEA 2007 ss.91, 92 and Sch.15 will not now be brought into force.]

Cases in which attachment is available

1   Courts with power to attach earnings

1(1)   The High Court may make an attachment of earnings order to secure payments under a High Court maintenance order.

1(2)   A county court may make an attachment of earnings order to secure–

(a)   payments under a High Court or a county court maintenance order;

(b)   the payment of a judgment debt, other than a debt of less than £5 or such other sum as may be prescribed by county court rules; or

(c)   payments under an administration order.

1(3)   A magistrates' court may make an attachment of earnings order to secure–

(a)   payments under a magistrates' court maintenance order; or

(b)   …

(c)   the payment of any sum required to be paid by an order under section 17(2) of the Access to Justice Act 1999 or under regulations under section 17A(1) of that Act.

1(4)   …

1(5)   Any power conferred by this Act to make an attachment of earnings order includes a power to make such an order to secure the discharge of liabilities arising before the coming into force of this Act.

History
Subsection (1)(3)(c) amended by the Criminal Defence Service Act 2006 s.4(1), as from October 2, 2006. Subsections (3)(b) and (4) omitted by the Collection of Fines (Final Scheme) Order 2006 (SI 2006/1737) arts 34, 35 as from July 3, 2006. Previously, these and other similar amendments to the Act (noted below) had been made by the Collection of Fines (Pilot Scheme) and Discharge of Fines by Unpaid Work (Pilot Schemes) (Amendment) Order 2006 (SI 2006/502) art.6, as from March 27, 2006 (one of several schemes for piloting the provisions of Sch.5 (collection of fines) to the Courts Act 2003).

1A   Orders to which this Act applies

1A   The   following provisions of this Act apply, except where otherwise stated, to attachment of earnings orders made, or to be made, by any court under this Act or under Schedule 5 to the Courts Act 2003, or by a fines officer under that Schedule.

2   Principal definitions

2   In this Act–

(a)   **"maintenance order"** means any order, decision, settlement or instrument specified in Schedule 1 to this Act and includes one such an order which has been discharged or has otherwise ceased to operate if any arrears are recoverable thereunder;

(b)   **"High Court maintenance order"**, **"county court maintenance order"** and **"magistrates' court maintenance order"** mean respectively a maintenance order enforceable by the High Court, a county court and a magistrates' court;

   (c) **"judgment debt"** means a sum payable under–

      (i) a judgment or order enforceable by a court in England and Wales (not being a magistrates' court);

      (ii) an order of a magistrates' court for the payment of money recoverable summarily as a civil debt; or

      (iii) an order of any court which is enforceable as if it were for the payment of money so recoverable,

but does not include any sum payable under a maintenance order or an administration order;

   (d) **"the relevant adjudication"**, in relation to any payment secured or to be secured by an attachment of earnings order, means the conviction, judgment, order or other adjudication from which there arises the liability to make the payment; and

   (e) **"the debtor"**, in relation to an attachment of earnings order, or to proceedings in which a court has power to make an attachment of earnings order, or to proceedings arising out of such an order, means the person by whom payment is required by the relevant adjudication to be made.

History
Definition of "maintenance order" amended by the Civil Jurisdiction and Judgments (Maintenance) Regulations 2011 (SI 2011/1484) Sch.7 para.4(2) as from June 18, 2011.

3 Application for order and conditions of court's power to make it

3(A1) This section shall not apply to an attachment of earnings order to be made under Schedule 5 to the Courts Act 2003.

3(1) The following persons may apply for an attachment of earnings order–

   (a) the person to whom payment under the relevant adjudication is required to be made (whether directly or through an officer of any court);

   (b) where the relevant adjudication is an administration order, any one of the creditors scheduled to the order;

   (c) without prejudice to paragraph (a) above, where the application is to a magistrates' court for an order to secure maintenance payments, and there is in force an order under section 59 of the Magistrates' Courts Act 1980, or section 19(2) of the Maintenance Orders Act 1950, that those payments be made to the designated officer for a magistrates' court, that officer;

   (d) in the following cases the debtor–

      (i) where the application is to a magistrates' court; or

      (ii) where the application is to the High Court or a county court for an order to secure maintenance payments.

3(2) [Repealed by the Maintenance Enforcement Act 1991 s.11 and Sch.2 para.1 and Sch.3.]

3(3) Subject to subsection (3A) below for an attachment of earnings order to be made on the application of any person other than the debtor it must appear to the court that the debtor has failed to make one or more payments required by the relevant adjudication.

3(3A) Subsection (3) above shall not apply where the relevant adjudication is a maintenance order.

3(3B) …

3(3C) …

3(4)   Where proceedings are brought–

  (a) in the High Court or a county court for the enforcement of a maintenance order by committal under section 5 of the Debtors Act 1869; or

  (b) in a magistrates' court for the enforcement of a maintenance order under section 76 of the Magistrates' Courts Act 1980 (distress or committal),

then the court may make an attachment of earnings order to secure payments under the maintenance order, instead of dealing with the case under section 5 of the said Act of 1869 or, as the case may be, section 76 of the said Act of 1980.

3(5)   [Repealed by the Maintenance Enforcement Act 1991 s.11 and Sch.2 para.1 and Sch.3.]

3(6)   Where proceedings are brought in a county court for an order of committal under section 5 of the Debtors Act 1869 in respect of a judgment debt for any of the taxes, contributions or liabilities specified in Schedule 2 to this Act, the court may, in any circumstances in which it has power to make such an order, make instead an attachment of earnings order to secure the payment of the judgment debt.

3(7)   A county court shall not make an attachment of earnings order to secure the payment of a judgment debt if there is in force an order or warrant for the debtor's committal, under section 5 of the Debtors Act 1869, in respect of that debt; but in any such case the court may discharge the order or warrant with a view to making an attachment of earnings order instead.

History
Subsection (A1) inserted, and subss.(3A) and (3B) omitted, by the Collection of Fines (Final Scheme) Order 2006 (SI 2006/1737) arts 34, 37, as from July 3, 2006. (See also History note to s.1.) Previously, subss.(3B) and (3C) inserted by the Criminal Procedure and Investigations Act 1996 s.33, as regards fines imposed and compensation orders made on convictions for offences committed on or after October 1, 1996; and s.3(3C)(a) modified by the Powers of Criminal Courts (Sentencing) Act 2000 s.165(1) and Sch.9 para.44 as from August 25, 2000.
  Prospective amendment to subs.(6) made by the Social Security Act 1973 s.100 and Sch.27 Pt I para.88 is now considered unlikely to be brought into force.

Administration orders in the county court

4   Extension of power to make administration order

4(1)   Where, on an application to a county court for an attachment of earnings order to secure the payment of a judgment debt, it appears to the court that the debtor also has other debts, the court–

  (a) shall consider whether the case may be one in which all the debtor's liabilities should be dealt with together and that for that purpose an administration order should be made; and

  (b) if of opinion that it may be such a case, shall have power (whether or not it makes the attachment of earnings order applied for), with a view to making an administration order, to order the debtor to furnish to the court a list of all his creditors and the amounts which he owes to them respectively.

4(2)   If, on receipt of the list referred to in subsection (1)(b) above, it appears to the court that the debtor's whole indebtedness amounts to not more than the amount which for the time being is the county court limit for the purposes of section 112 of the County Courts Act 1984 (limit of total indebtedness governing county court's power to make administration order on application of debtor), the court may make such an order in respect of the debtor's estate.

4(2A)   Subsection (2) above is subject to section 112(3) and (4) of the County Courts Act 1984 (which require that, before an administration order is made, notice is to be given to all the creditors and thereafter restricts the right of any creditor to institute bankruptcy proceedings).

4(3)   [Repealed by the Insolvency Act 1976 ss.13(1), 14(4) and Sch.3.]

4(4)   Nothing in this section is to be taken as prejudicing any right of a debtor to apply, under section 112 of the County Courts Act 1984 for an administration order.

5   Attachment of earnings to secure payments under administration order

5(1)   Where a county court makes an administration order in respect of a debtor's estate, it may also make an attachment of earnings order to secure the payments required by the administration order.

5(2)   At any time when an administration order is in force a county court may (with or without an application) make an attachment of earnings order to secure the payments required by the administration order, if it appears to the court that the debtor has failed to make any such payment.

5(3)   The power of a county court under this section to make an attachment of earnings order to secure the payments required by an administration order shall, where the debtor is already subject to an attachment of earnings order to secure the payment of a judgment debt, include power to direct that the last-mentioned order shall take effect (with or without variation under section 9 of this Act) as an order to secure the payments required by the administration order.

Consequences of attachment order

6   Effect and contents of order

6(1)   An attachment of earnings order shall be an order directed to a person who appears to the court, or as the case may be the fines officer, making the order to have the debtor in his employment and shall operate as an instruction to that person–

    (a)   to make periodical deductions from the debtor's earnings in accordance with Part I of Schedule 3 to this Act; and

    (b)   at such times as the order may require, or as the court, or where the order is made under Schedule 5 to the Courts Act 2003, as the court or the fines officer as the case may be, may allow, to pay the amounts deducted to the collecting officer of the court, as specified in the order.

6(2)   For the purposes of this Act, the relationship of employer and employee shall be treated as subsisting between two persons if one of them as a principal and not as a servant or agent, pays to the other any sums defined as earnings by section 24 of this Act.

6(3)   An attachment of earnings order shall contain prescribed particulars enabling the debtor to be identified by the employer.

6(4)   Except where it is made to secure maintenance payments, the order shall specify the whole amount payable under the relevant adjudication (or so much of that amount as remains unpaid), including any relevant costs.

6(5)   Subject to subsection (5A) below, the order shall specify–

    (a)   the normal deduction rate, that is to say, the rate (expressed as a sum of money per week, month or other period) at which the court thinks it reasonable for the debtor's earnings to be applied to meeting his liability under the relevant adjudication; and

    (b)   the protected earnings rate, that is to say the rate (so expressed) below which, having regard to the debtor's resources and needs, the court thinks it reasonable that the earnings actually paid to him should not be reduced.

6(5A)   If the order is made under Schedule 5 to the Courts Act 2003 then it shall specify the percentage deduction rate in accordance with fines collection regulations made under that Schedule.

6(6)   In the case of an order made to secure payments under a maintenance order (not being an order for the payment of a lump sum), the normal deduction rate–

(a) shall be determined after taking account of any right or liability of the debtor to deduct income tax when making the payments; and

(b) shall not exceed the rate which appears to the court necessary for the purpose of–

(i) securing payment of the sums falling due from time to time under the maintenance order, and

(ii) securing payment within a reasonable period of any sums already due and unpaid under the maintenance order.

6(7) For the purposes of an attachment of earnings order, the collecting officer of the court shall be (subject to later variation of the order under section 9 of this Act)–

(a) in the case of an order made by the High Court, either–

(i) the proper officer of the High Court, or

(ii) the appropriate officer of such county court as the order may specify;

(b) in the case of an order made by a county court, the appropriate officer of that court; and

(c) in the case of an order made by a magistrates' court, the designated officer for that court or for another magistrates' court specified in the order.

6(8) In subsection (7) above **"appropriate officer"** means an officer designated by the Lord Chancellor.

Note
Subsection (5A) inserted, and subss.(1) and (5) amended, by the Collection of Fines (Final Scheme) Order 2006 (SI 2006/1737) arts 34, 38, as from July 3, 2006. (See also history note to s.1.)

Prospective amendment, inserting new s.6(9)–(12), by the Courts and Legal Services Act 1990 s.125(2) and Sch.17 para.5 from a day to be appointed, has not yet been brought into force.

7 Compliance with order by employer

7(1) Where an attachment of earnings order has been made, the employer shall, if he has been served with the order, comply with it; but he shall be under no liability for non-compliance before seven days have elapsed since the service.

7(2) Where a person is served with an attachment of earnings order directed to him and he has not the debtor in his employment, or the debtor subsequently ceases to be in his employment, he shall (in either case), within ten days from the date of service or, as the case may be, the cesser, give notice of that fact to the court.

7(3) Part II of Schedule 3 to this Act shall have effect with respect to the priority to be accorded as between two or more attachment of earnings orders directed to a person in respect of the same debtor.

7(4) On any occasion when the employer makes, in compliance with the order, a deduction from the debtor's earnings–

(a) he shall be entitled to deduct, in addition, £1.00, or such other sum as may be prescribed by order made by the Lord Chancellor, towards his clerical and administrative costs; and

(b) he shall give to the debtor a statement in writing of the total amount of the deduction.

7(5) An order of the Lord Chancellor under subsection (4)(a) above–

(a) may prescribe different sums in relation to different classes of cases;

(b) may be varied or revoked by a subsequent order made under that paragraph; and

(c) shall be made by statutory instrument subject to annulment by resolution of either House of Parliament.

8   Interrelation with alternative remedies open to creditor

8(1)   Where an attachment of earnings order has been made to secure maintenance payments, no order or warrant of commitment shall be issued in consequence of any proceedings for the enforcement of the related maintenance order begun before the making of the attachment of earnings order.

8(2)   Where a county court has made an attachment of earnings order to secure the payment of a judgment debt–

(a)   no order or warrant of commitment shall be issued in consequence of any proceedings for the enforcement of the debt begun before the making of the attachment of earnings order; and

(b)   so long as the order is in force, no execution for the recovery of the debt shall issue against any property of the debtor without the leave of the county court.

8(3)   An attachment of earnings order made to secure maintenance payments shall cease to have effect upon the making of an order of commitment or the issue of a warrant of commitment for the enforcement of the related maintenance order, or upon the exercise for that purpose of the power conferred on a magistrates' court by section 77(2) of the Magistrates' Courts Act 1980 to postpone the issue of such a warrant.

8(4)   An attachment of earnings order made to secure the payment of a judgment debt shall cease to have effect on the making of an order of commitment or the issue of a warrant of commitment for the enforcement of the debt.

8(5)   An attachment of earnings order made to secure—

(a)   any payment mentioned in section 1(3)(c) of this Act; or

(b)   the payment of any sum mentioned in paragraph 1 of Schedule 5 to the Courts Act 2003,

shall cease to have effect on the issue of a warrant committing the debtor to prison for default in making that payment.

Note
Subsection (5) substituted by the Collection of Fines (Final Scheme) Order 2006 (SI 2006/1737) arts 34, 39, as from July 3, 2006. (See also history note to s.1.)

Subsequent proceedings

9   Variation, lapse and discharge of orders

9(1)   The court, or where an attachment of earnings order is made under Schedule 5 to the Courts Act 2003, as the court or the fines officer as the case may be, may make an order discharging or varying an attachment of earnings order.

9(2)   Where an order is varied, the employer shall, if he has been served with notice of the variation, comply with the order as varied; but he shall be under no liability for non-compliance before seven days have elapsed since the service.

9(3)   Rules of court may make provision–

(a)   as to the circumstances in which an attachment of earnings order made under this Act may be varied or discharged by the court of its own motion;

(aa)   as to the circumstances in which an attachment of earnings order made under Schedule 5 to the Courts Act 2003 may be varied or discharged by the court or the fines officer of its or his own motion;

(b)   in the case of an attachment of earnings order made by a magistrates' court, for enabling a single justice, on an application made by the debtor on the ground of a material change in his resources and needs since the order was made or last varied, to vary the order for a period of not more than four weeks by an increase of the protected earnings rate.

9(4)   Where an attachment of earnings order has been made and the person to whom it is directed ceases to have the debtor in his employment, the order shall lapse (except as respects deduction from earnings paid after the cesser and payment to the collecting officer of amounts deducted at any time) and be of no effect unless and until the court, or where the order was made under Schedule 5 to the Courts Act 2003, unless and until the court or the fines officer as the case may be, again directs it to a person (whether the same as before or another) who appears to the court or the fines officer (as the case may be) to have the debtor in his employment.

9(5)   The lapse of an order under subsection (4) above shall not prevent its being treated as remaining in force for other purposes.

Note
Subparagraph (3)(ii)(aa) inserted, and subsections (1), (3) and (4) amended, by the Collection of Fines (Final Scheme) Order 2006 (SI 2006/1737) arts 34, 40, as from July 3, 2006. (See also history note to s.1.)

10   Normal deduction rate to be reduced in certain cases

10(1)   The following provisions shall have effect, in the case of an attachment of earnings order made to secure maintenance payments, where it appears to the collecting officer of the court that–

(a)   the aggregate of the payments made for the purposes of the related maintenance order by the debtor (whether under the attachment of earnings order or otherwise) exceeds the aggregate of the payments required up to that time by the maintenance order; and

(b)   the normal deduction rate specified by the attachment of earnings order (or, where two or more such orders are in force in relation to the maintenance order, the aggregate of the normal deduction rates specified by those orders) exceeds the rate of payments required by the maintenance order; and

(c)   no proceedings for the variation or discharge of the attachment of earnings order are pending.

10(2)   In the case of an order made by the High Court or a county court, the collecting officer shall give the prescribed notice to the person to whom he is required to pay sums received under the attachment of earnings order, and to the debtor; and the court shall make the appropriate variation order, unless the debtor requests it to discharge the attachment of earnings order, or to vary it in some other way, and the court thinks fit to comply with the request.

10(3)   In the case of an order made by a magistrates' court, the collecting officer shall apply to the court for the appropriate variation order; and the court shall grant the application unless the debtor appears at the hearing and requests the court to discharge the attachment of earnings order, or to vary it in some other way, and the court thinks fit to comply with the request.

10(4)   In this section, **"the appropriate variation order"** means an order varying the attachment of earnings order in question by reducing the normal deduction rate specified thereby so as to secure that that rate (or, in the case mentioned in subsection (1)(b) above, the aggregate of the rates therein mentioned)–

(a)   is the same as the rate of payments required by the maintenance order; or

(b)   is such lower rate as the court thinks fit having regard to the amount of the excess mentioned in subsection (1)(a).

11   Attachment order in respect of maintenance payments to cease to have effect on the occurrence of certain events

11(1)   An attachment of earnings order made to secure maintenance payments shall cease to have effect–

(a) upon the grant of an application for registration of the related maintenance order under section 2 of the Maintenance Orders Act 1958 (which provides for the registration in a magistrates' court of a High Court or county court maintenance order, and for registration in the High Court of a magistrates' court maintenance order);

(b) where the related maintenance order is registered under Part I of the said Act of 1958, upon the giving of notice with respect thereto under section 5 of that Act (notice with view to cancellation of registration);

(c) subject to subsection (3) below, upon the discharge of the related maintenance order while it is not registered under Part I of the said Act of 1958;

(d) upon the related maintenance order ceasing to be registered in a court in England or Wales, or becoming registered in a court in Scotland or Northern Ireland, under Part II of the Maintenance Orders Act 1950.

11(2) Subsection (1)(a) above shall have effect, in the case of an application for registration under section 2(1) of the said Act of 1958, notwithstanding that the grant of the application may subsequently become void under subsection (2) of that section.

11(3) Where the related maintenance order is discharged as mentioned in subsection (1)(c) above and it appears to the court discharging the order that arrears thereunder will remain to be recovered after the discharge, that court may, if it thinks fit, direct that subsection (1) shall not apply.

12 Termination of employer's liability to make deductions

12(1) Where an attachment of earnings order ceases to have effect under section 8 or 11 of this Act, the proper officer of the prescribed court shall give notice of the cesser to the person to whom the order was directed.

12(2) Where, in the case of an attachment of earnings order made otherwise than to secure maintenance payments, the whole amount payable under the relevant adjudication has been paid, and also any relevant costs, the court shall give notice to the employer that no further compliance with the order is required.

12(3) Where an attachment of earnings order–

(a) ceases to have effect under section 8 or 11 of this Act; or

(b) is discharged under section 9,

the person to whom the order has been directed shall be under no liability in consequence of his treating the order as still in force at any time before the expiration of seven days from the date on which the notice required by subsection (1) above or, as the case may be, a copy of the discharging order is served on him.

Administrative provisions

13 Application of sums received by collecting officer

13(1) Subject to subsection (3) below, the collecting officer to whom a person makes payments in compliance with an attachment of earnings order shall, after deducting such court fees, if any, in respect of proceedings for or arising out of the order, as are deductible from those payments, deal with the sums paid in the same way as he would if they had been paid by the debtor to satisfy the relevant adjudication.

13(2) Any sums paid to the collecting officer under an attachment of earnings order made to secure maintenance payments shall, when paid to the person entitled to receive those payments, be deemed to be payments made by the debtor (with such deductions, if any, in respect of income tax as the debtor is entitled or required to make) so as to discharge–

(a) first, any sums for the time being due and unpaid under the related maintenance order (a sum due at an earlier date being discharged before a sum due at a later date); and

(b) secondly, any costs incurred in proceedings relating to the related maintenance order which were payable by the debtor when the attachment of earnings order was made or last varied.

13(3) Where a county court makes an attachment of earnings order to secure the payment of a judgment debt and also, under section 4(1) of this Act, orders the debtor to furnish to the court a list of all his creditors, sums paid to the collecting officer in compliance with the attachment of earnings order shall not be dealt with by him as mentioned in subsection (1) above, but shall be retained by him pending the decision of the court whether or not to make an administration order and shall then be dealt with by him as the court may direct.

14 Power of court to obtain statements of earnings etc.

14(1) Where in any proceedings a court has power under this Act or under Schedule 5 to the Courts Act 2003, or a fines officer has power under that Schedule, to make an attachment of earnings order, the court or the fines officer, as the case may be, may–

(a) order the debtor to give to the court or the fines officer, as the case may be, within a specified period, a statement signed by him of–

(i) the name and address of any person by whom earnings are paid to him;

(ii) specified particulars as to his earnings and anticipated earnings, and as to his resources and needs; and

(iii) specified particulars for the purpose of enabling the debtor to be identified by any employer of his;

(b) order any person appearing to the court or the fines officer, as the case may be, to have the debtor in his employment to give to the court, or the fines officer, as the case may be within a specified period, a statement signed by him or on his behalf of specified particulars of the debtor's earnings and anticipated earnings.

14(2) Where an attachment of earnings order has been made, the court or the fines officer, as the case may be, may at any time thereafter while the order is in force

(a) make such an order as is described in subsection (1)(a) or (b) above; and

(b) order the debtor to attend before the court on a day and at a time specified in the order to give the information described in subsection (1)(a) above.

14(3) In the case of an application to a magistrates' court for an attachment of earnings order, or for the variation or discharge of such an order, the power to make an order under subsection (1) or (2) above shall be exercisable also, before the hearing of the application, by a single justice.

14(4) Without prejudice to subsections (1) to (3) above, rules of court may provide that where notice of an application for an attachment of earnings order is served on the debtor, it shall include a requirement that he shall give to the court, within such period and in such manner as may be prescribed, a statement in writing of the matters specified in subsection (1)(a) above and of any other prescribed matters which are, or may be, relevant under section 6 of this Act to the determination of the normal deduction rate and the protected earnings rate to be specified in any order made on the application. This subsection does not apply to an attachment of earnings order to be made under Schedule 5 to the Courts Act 2003.

14(5) In any proceedings in which a court has power under this Act or under Schedule 5 to the Courts Act 2003, or a fines officer has power under that Schedule, to make an attachment of earnings order, and in any proceedings for the making, variation or discharge of such an order, a document purporting to be a statement given to the court or the fines officer, as the case may be, in compliance with an order under subsection (1)(a) or (b) above, or with any such requirement of a notice of application for an attachment of earnings order as is mentioned in subsection (4) above, shall, in the absence of proof to the contrary, be deemed to be a statement so given and shall be evidence of the facts stated therein.

Note
Subsections (1), (2), (4), (5) amended by the Collection of Fines (Final Scheme) Order 2006 (SI 2006/1737) arts 34, 41, as from July 3, 2006. (See also history note to s.1.)

15   Obligation of debtor and his employers to notify changes of employment and earnings

15(1)   While an attachment of earnings order is in force–

(a)   the debtor shall from time to time notify the court in writing of every occasion on which he leaves any employment, or becomes employed or re-employed, not later (in each case) than seven days from the date on which he did so;

(b)   the debtor shall, on any occasion when he becomes employed or re-employed, include in his notification under paragraph (a) above particulars of his earnings and anticipated earnings from the relevant employment; and

(c)   any person who becomes the debtor's employer and knows that the order is in force and by, or (if the order was made by a fines officer) for, which court it was made shall, within seven days of his becoming the debtor's employer or of acquiring that knowledge (whichever is the later) notify that court in writing that he is the debtor's employer, and include in his notification a statement of the debtor's earnings and anticipated earnings.

15(2)   In the case of an attachment of earnings order made by a fines officer, the reference to "the court" in subsection (1)(a) above shall mean the court for which that order was made.

Note
Subsection (1) amended, and subsection (2) inserted, by the Collection of Fines (Final Scheme) Order 2006 (SI 2006/1737) arts 34, 42, as from July 3, 2006. (See also history note to s.1.)

16   Power of court to determine whether particular payments are earnings

16(1)   Where an attachment of earnings order is in force, the court shall, on the application of a person specified in subsection (2) below, determine whether payments to the debtor of a particular class or description specified by the application are earnings for the purposes of the order; and the employer shall be entitled to give effect to any determination for the time being in force under this section.

16(2)   The persons referred to in subsection (1) above are–

(a)   the employer;

(b)   the debtor;

(c)   the person to whom payment under the relevant adjudication is required to be made (whether directly or through an officer of any court); and

(d)   without prejudice to paragraph (c) above, where the application is in respect of an attachment of earnings order made to secure payments under a magistrates' court maintenance order, the collecting officer.

16(3)   Where an application under this section is made by the employer, he shall not incur any liability for non-compliance with the order as respects any payments of the class or description specified by the application which are made by him to the debtor while the application, or any appeal in consequence thereof, is pending; but this subsection shall not, unless the court otherwise orders, apply as respects such payments if the employer subsequently withdraws the application or, as the case may be, abandons the appeal.

17   Consolidated attachment orders

17(1)   The powers of a county court under sections 1 and 3 of this Act shall include power to make an attachment of earnings order to secure the payment of any number of judgment debts; and the powers of a magistrates' court under those sections or under Schedule 5 to the Courts Act 2003, and the powers of a fines officer under that Schedule, shall include power to make an attachment of earnings order to secure the discharge of any number of such liabilities as are specified in section 1(3) of this Act and paragraph 1 of Schedule 5 to the Courts Act 2003.

17(2)   An attachment of earnings order made by virtue of this section shall be known as a consolidated attachment order.

17(3)   The power to make a consolidated attachment order shall be exercised subject to and in accordance with rules of court; and rules made for the purposes of this section may provide–

(a)   for the transfer from one court to another or (where Schedule 5 to the Courts Act 2003 applies) from a court or a fines officer, as the case may be, acting in one local justice area, to a court or a fines officer, as the case may be, acting in another local justice area–

   (i)   of an attachment of earnings order, or any proceedings for or arising out of such an order; and

   (ii)   of functions relating to the enforcement of any liability capable of being secured by attachment of earnings;

(b)   for enabling a court or a fines officer, as the case may be, to which or to whom any order, proceedings or functions have been transferred under the rules to vary or discharge an attachment of earnings order made by another court or fines officer and to replace it (if the court, or fines officer as the case may be, thinks fit) with a consolidated attachment order;

(c)   for the cases in which any power exercisable under this section or the rules may be exercised by a court or a fines officer, as the case may be, of its or his own motion or on the application of a prescribed person;

(d)   for requiring the officer of a court who receives payments made to him in compliance with an attachment of earnings order, instead of complying with section 13 of this Act, to deal with them as directed by the court or the rules; and

(e)   for modifying or excluding provisions of this Act or Part III of the Magistrates' Courts Act 1980, but only so far as may be necessary or expedient for securing conformity with the operation of rules made by virtue of paragraphs (a) to (d) of this subsection.

Note
Subparagraph (3)(d) substituted, and subss.(1), (3) amended, by the Collection of Fines (Final Scheme) Order 2006 (SI 2006/1737) arts 34, 43, as from July 3, 2006. (See also history note to s.1.)

Special provisions with respect to magistrates' courts

18   Certain action not to be taken by collecting officer except on request

18(1)   A designated officer for a magistrates' court who is entitled to receive payments under a maintenance order for transmission to another person shall not–

(a)   apply for an attachment of earnings order to secure payments under the maintenance order; or

(b)   except as provided by section 10(3) of this Act, apply for an order discharging or varying such an attachment of earnings order; or

(c)   apply for a determination under section 16 of this Act,

unless he is requested in writing to do so by a person entitled to receive the payments through him.

18(2)   Where the designated officer for a magistrates' court is so requested–

(a)   he shall comply with the request unless it appears to him unreasonable in the circumstances to do so; and

(b)   the person by whom the request was made shall have the same liabilities for all the costs properly incurred in or about any proceedings taken in pursuance of the request as if the proceedings had been taken by that person.

18(3)   For the purposes of subsection (2)(b) above, any application made by the designated officer for a magistrates' court as required by section 10(3) of this Act shall be deemed to be made on the request of the person in whose favour the attachment of earnings order in question was made.

19   Procedure on applications

19(1)   Subject to rules of court made by virtue of the following subsection, an application to a magistrates' court for an attachment of earnings order, or an order discharging or varying an attachment of earnings order, shall be made by complaint.

19(2)   Rules of court may make provision excluding subsection (1) in the case of such an application as is referred to in section 9(3)(b) of this Act.

19(3)   An application to a magistrates' court for a determination under section 16 of this Act shall be made by complaint.

19(4)   For the purposes of section 51 of the Magistrates' Courts Act 1980 (which provides for the issue of a summons directed to the person against whom an order may be made in pursuance of a complaint)–

(a)   the power to make an order in pursuance of a complaint by the debtor for an attachment of earnings order, or the discharge or variation of such an order, shall be deemed to be a power to make an order against the person to whom payment under the relevant adjudication is required to be made (whether directly or through an officer of any court); and

(b)   the power to make an attachment of earnings order, or an order discharging or varying an attachment of earnings order, in pursuance of a complaint by any other person (including a complaint in proceedings to which section 3(4)(b) of this Act applies) shall be deemed to be a power to make an order against the debtor.

19(5)   A complaint for an attachment of earnings order may be heard notwithstanding that it was not made within the six months allowed by section 127(1) of the Magistrates' Courts Act 1980.

20   Jurisdiction in respect of persons residing outside England and Wales

20(1)   It is hereby declared that a magistrates' court has jurisdiction to hear a complaint by or against a person residing outside England and Wales for the discharge or variation of an attachment of earnings order made by a magistrates' court to secure maintenance payments; and where such a complaint is made, the following provisions shall have effect.

20(2)   If the person resides in Scotland or Northern Ireland, section 15 of the Maintenance Orders Act 1950 (which relates to the service of process on persons residing in those countries) shall have effect in relation to the complaint as it has effect in relation to the proceedings therein mentioned.

20(3)   Subject to the following subsection, if the person resides outside the United Kingdom and does not appear at the time and place appointed for the hearing of the complaint, the court may, if it thinks it reasonable in all the circumstances to do so, proceed to hear and determine the complaint at the time and place appointed for the hearing, or for any adjourned hearing, in like manner as if the person had then appeared.

20(4)   Subsection (3) above shall apply only if it is proved to the satisfaction of the court, on oath or in such other manner as may be prescribed, that the complainant has taken such steps as may be prescribed to give to the said person notice of the complaint and of the time and place appointed for the hearing of it.

21   Costs on application under s.16

21(1)   On making a determination under section 16 of this Act, a magistrates' court may in its discretion make such order as it thinks just and reasonable for payment by any of the persons mentioned in subsection (2) of that section of the whole or any part of the costs of the determination (but subject to section 18(2)(b) of this Act).

21(2)   Costs ordered to be paid under this section shall–

(a)   in the case of costs to be paid by the debtor to the person in whose favour the attachment of earnings order in question was made, be deemed–

    (i)   if the attachment of earnings order was made to secure maintenance payments, to be a sum due under the related maintenance order, and

    (ii)   otherwise, to be a sum due to the designated officer for the magistrates' court; and

(b)   in any other case, be enforceable as a civil debt.

Miscellaneous provisions

22   Persons employed under the Crown

22(1)   The fact that an attachment of earnings order is made at the suit of the Crown shall not prevent its operation at any time when the debtor is in the employment of the Crown.

22(2)   Where a debtor is in the employment of the Crown and an attachment of earnings order is made in respect of him, then for the purposes of this Act–

(a)   the chief officer for the time being of the department, office or other body in which the debtor is employed shall be treated as having the debtor in his employment (any transfer of the debtor from one department, office or body to another being treated as a change of employment); and

(b)   any earnings paid by the Crown or a Minister of the Crown, or out of the public revenue of the United Kingdom, shall be treated as paid by the said chief officer.

22(3)   If any question arises, in proceedings for or arising out of an attachment of earnings order, as to what department, office or other body is concerned for the purposes of this section, or as to who for those purposes is the chief officer thereof, the question shall be referred to and determined by the Minister for the Civil Service; but that Minister shall not be under any obligation to consider a reference under this subsection unless it is made by the court.

22(4)   A document purporting to set out a determination of the said Minister under subsection (3) above and to be signed by an official of the Office of Public Service shall, in any such proceedings as are mentioned in that subsection, be admissible in evidence and be deemed to contain an accurate statement of such a determination unless the contrary is shown.

22(5)   This Act shall have effect notwithstanding any enactment passed before 29th May 1970 and preventing or avoiding the attachment or diversion of sums due to a person in respect of service under the Crown, whether by way of remuneration, pension or otherwise.

23   Enforcement provisions

23(1)   If, after being served with notice of an application to a county court for an attachment of earnings order or for the variation of such an order or with an order made under section 14(2)(b) above, the debtor fails to attend on the day and at the time specified for any hearing of the application or specified in the order, the court may adjourn the hearing and order him to attend at a specified time on another day; and if the debtor–

(a)   fails to attend at that time on that day; or

(b)   attends, but refuses to be sworn or give evidence,

he may be ordered by the judge to be imprisoned for not more than fourteen days.

23(1A)   In any case where the judge has power to make an order of imprisonment under subsection (1) for failure to attend, he may, in lieu of or in addition to making that order, order the debtor to be arrested and brought before the court either forthwith or at such time as the judge may direct.

23(2)   Subject to this section, a person commits an offence if–

(a)   being required by section 7(1) or 9(2) of this Act to comply with an attachment of earnings order, he fails to do so; or

(b)   being required by section 7(2) of this Act to give a notice for the purposes of that subsection, he fails to give it, or fails to give it within the time required by that subsection; or

(c)   he fails to comply with an order under section 14(1) of this Act or with any such requirement of a notice of application for an attachment of earnings order as is mentioned in section 14(4), or fails (in either case) to comply within the time required by the order or notice; or

(d)   he fails to comply with section 15 of this Act; or

(e)   he gives a notice for the purposes of section 7(2) of this Act, or a notification for the purposes of section 15, which he knows to be false in a material particular, or recklessly gives such a notice or notification which is false in a material particular; or

(f)   in purported compliance with section 7(2) or 15 of this Act, or with an order under section 14(1), or with any such requirement of a notice of application for an attachment of earnings order as is mentioned in section 14(4), he makes any statement which he knows to be false in a material particular, or recklessly makes any statement which is false in a material particular.

23(3)   Where a person commits an offence under subsection (2) above in relation to proceedings in, or to an attachment of earnings order made by, the High Court or a county court, he shall be liable on summary conviction to a fine of not more than level 2 on the standard scale or he may be ordered by a judge of the High Court or the county court judge (as the case may be) to pay a fine of not more than £250 or, in the case of an offence specified in subsection (4) below, to be imprisoned for not more than fourteen days; and where a person commits an offence under subsection (2) otherwise than as mentioned above in this subsection, he shall be liable on summary conviction to a fine of not more than level 2 on the standard scale.

23(4)   The offences referred to above in the case of which a judge may impose imprisonment are–

(a)   an offence under subsection (2)(c) or (d), if committed by the debtor; and

(b)   an offence under subsection (2)(e) or (f), whether committed by the debtor or any other person.

23(5)   It shall be a defence–

(a)   for a person charged with an offence under subsection (2)(a) above to prove that he took all reasonable steps to comply with the attachment of earnings order in question;

(b)   for a person charged with an offence under subsection (2)(b) to prove that he did not know, and could not reasonably be expected to know, that the debtor was not in his employment, or (as the case may be) had ceased to be so, and that he gave the required notice as soon as reasonably practicable after the fact came to his knowledge.

23(6)   Where a person is convicted or dealt with for an offence under subsection (2)(a), the court may order him to pay, to whoever is the collecting officer of the court for the purposes of the attachment of earnings order in question, any sums deducted by that person from the debtor's earnings and not already paid to the collecting officer.

23(7)   Where under this section a person is ordered by a judge of the High Court or a county court judge to be imprisoned, the judge may at any time revoke the order and, if the person is already in custody, order his discharge.

23(8)   Any fine imposed by a judge of the High Court under subsection (3) above and any sums ordered by the High Court to be paid under subsection (6) above shall be recoverable in the same way as a fine imposed by that court in the exercise of its jurisdiction to punish for contempt of court; section 129 of the County Courts Act 1984 (enforcement of fines) shall apply to payment of a fine imposed by a county court judge under subsection (3) and of any sums ordered by a county court judge to be paid under subsection (6); and any sum ordered by a magistrates' court to be paid under subsection (6) shall be recoverable as a sum adjudged to be paid on a conviction by that court.

23(9)   For the purposes of section 13 of the Administration of Justice Act 1960 (appeal in cases of contempt of court), subsection (3) above shall be treated as an enactment enabling the High Court or a county court to deal with an offence under subsection (2) above as if it were contempt of court.

23(10)   In this section references to proceedings in a court are to proceedings in which that court has power to make an attachment of earnings order or has made such an order.

23(11)   A district judge, assistant district judge or deputy district judge shall have the same powers under this section as a judge of a county court.

24   Meaning of "earnings"

24(1)   For the purposes of this Act, but subject to the following subsection, **"earnings"** are any sums payable to a person–

- (a) by way of wages or salary (including any fees, bonus, commission, overtime pay or other emoluments payable in addition to wages or salary or payable under a contract of service);

- (b) by way of pension (including an annuity in respect of past services, whether or not rendered to the person paying the annuity, and including periodical payments by way of compensation for the loss, abolition or relinquishment, or diminution in the emoluments, of any office or employment);

- (c) by way of statutory sick pay.

24(2)   The following shall not be treated as earnings–

- (a) sums payable by any public department of the Government of Northern Ireland or of a territory outside the United Kingdom;

- (b) pay or allowances payable to the debtor as a member of Her Majesty's forces other than pay or allowances payable by his employer to him as a special member of a reserve force (within the meaning of the Reserve Forces Act 1996);

- (ba) a tax credit (within the meaning of the Tax Credits Act 2002);

- (c) pension, allowances or benefit payable under any enactment relating to social security;

- (d) pension or allowances payable in respect of disablement or disability;

- (e) except in relation to a maintenance order wages payable to a person as a seaman, other than wages payable to him as a seaman of a fishing boat.

- (f) guaranteed minimum pension within the meaning of the Pension Schemes Act 1993.

24(3) In subsection (2)(e) above–

"fishing boat" means a vessel of whatever size, and in whatever way propelled, which is for the time being employed in sea fishing or in the sea-fishing service;

"seaman" includes every person (except masters and pilots) employed or engaged in any capacity on board any ship; and

"wages" includes emoluments.

25   General interpretation

25(1) In this Act, except where the context otherwise requires–

"administration order" means an order made under, and so referred to in, Part VI of the County Courts Act 1984;

"the court", in relation to an attachment of earnings order, means the court which made the order, subject to rules of court as to the venue for, and the transfer of, proceedings in county courts and magistrates' courts;

"debtor" and **"relevant adjudication"** have the meanings given by section 2 of this Act;

"the employer", in relation to an attachment of earnings order, means the person who is required by the order to make deductions from earnings paid by him to the debtor;

"the fines officer", in relation to a debtor who is subject to a collection order made under Schedule 5 to the Courts Act 2003, means any fines officer working at the fines office specified in that order;

"judgment debt" has the meaning given by section 2 of this Act;

"maintenance order" has the meaning given by section 2 of this Act;

"maintenance payments" means payments required under a maintenance order;

"prescribed" means prescribed by rules of court.

25(2) Any reference in this Act to sums payable under a judgment or order, or to the payment of such sums, includes a reference to costs and the payment of them; and the references in sections 6(4) and 12(2) to relevant costs are to any costs of the proceedings in which the attachment of earnings order in question was made, being costs which the debtor is liable to pay.

25(3) References in sections 6(5)(b), 9(3)(b) and 14(1)(a) of this Act to the debtor's needs include references to the needs of any person for whom he must, or reasonably may, provide.

25(4) [Repealed by the Dock Work Act 1989 s.7(1) and Sch. Pt I.]

25(5) Any power to make rules which is conferred by this Act is without prejudice to any other power to make rules of court.

25(6) This Act, so far as it relates to magistrates' courts, and Part III of the Magistrates' Courts Act 1980 shall be construed as if this Act were contained in that Part.

25(7) References in this Act to any enactment include references to that enactment as amended by or under any other enactment, including this Act.

History

Definition of "the fines officer" inserted by the Collection of Fines (Final Scheme) Order 2006 (SI 2006/1737) arts 34, 44, as from July 3, 2006. (See also history note to s.1.)

Definition of "rules of court" in subs.(1) deleted by the Courts Act 2003 s.109(1), (3) and Sch.8 para.145 and Sch.10, as from September 1, 2004 (see SI 2004/2066 (C. 88) art.2(c)(vii), (d)(ii)).

General

26 Transitional provision

26(1)   As from the appointed day, an attachment of earnings order made before that day under Part II of the Maintenance Orders Act 1958 (including an order made under that Part of that Act as applied by section 46 or 79 of the Criminal Justice Act 1967) shall take effect as an attachment of earnings order made under the corresponding power in this Act, and the provisions of this Act shall apply to it accordingly, so far as they are capable of doing so.

26(2)   Rules of court may make such provision as the rule-making authority considers requisite–

(a)   for enabling an attachment of earnings order to which subsection (1) above applies to be varied so as to bring it into conformity, as from the appointed day, with the provisions of this Act, or to be replaced by an attachment of earnings order having effect as if made under the corresponding power in this Act;

(b)   to secure that anything required or authorised by this Act to be done in relation to an attachment of earnings order made thereunder is required or, as the case may be, authorised to be done in relation to an attachment of earnings order to which the said subsection (1) applies.

26(3)   In this section, **"the appointed day"** means the day appointed under section 54 of the Administration of Justice Act 1970 for the coming into force of Part II of that Act.

[**Note**: The "appointed day" referred to was August 2, 1971.]

27 Consequential amendment of enactments

27(1)   In consequence of the repeals effected by this Act, section 20 of the Maintenance Orders Act 1958 (which contains certain provisions about magistrates' courts and their procedure), except subsection (6) of that section (which amends section 52(3) of the Magistrates' Courts Act 1952), shall have effect as set out in Schedule 5 to this Act.

27(2)   [Repealed by the Insolvency Act 1976 s.14(4) and Sch.3.]

27(3)   [Amended the Merchant Shipping Act 1970 s.95(4), now repealed.]

28   [Repealed by the Northern Ireland Constitution Act 1973 s.41(1) and Sch.6 Pt I.]

29 Citation, repeal, extent and commencement

29(1)   This Act may be cited as the Attachment of Earnings Act 1971.

29(2)   The enactments specified in Schedule 6 to this Act are hereby repealed to the extent specified in the third column of that Schedule.

29(3)   This Act, except section 20(2), does not extend to Scotland and, except section 20(2) does not extend to Northern Ireland.

29(4)   This Act shall come into force on the day appointed under section 54 of the Administration of Justice Act 1970 for the coming into force of Part II of that Act.

SCHEDULE 1

MAINTENANCE ORDERS TO WHICH THIS ACT APPLIES

Section 2

1   An order for alimony, maintenance or other payments made, or having effect as if made, under Part II of the Matrimonial Causes Act 1965 (ancillary relief in actions for divorce etc.).

2   An order for payments to or in respect of a child, being an order made, or having effect as if made, under Part III of the said Act of 1965 (maintenance of children following divorce, etc.).

3   An order for periodical or other payments made, or having effect as if made under Part II of the Matrimonial Causes Act 1973.

4   An order for maintenance or other payments to or in respect of a spouse or child, being an order made under Part I of the Domestic Proceedings and Magistrates' Courts Act 1978.

5   An order for periodical or other payments made or having effect as if made under Schedule 1 to the Children Act 1989.

6   [Repealed by the Family Law Reform Act 1987 s.33(1), (4) and Sch.2 para.44(b) and Sch.3 paras 1, 6 and Sch.4.]

7   An order under paragraph 23 of Schedule 2 to the Children Act 1989 section 23 of the Ministry of Social Security Act 1966, section 18 of the Supplementary Benefits Act 1976 or section 106 of the Social Security Administration Act 1992 (various provisions for obtaining contributions from a person whose dependants are assisted or maintained out of public funds).

8   [Repealed by the Health and Social Care Act 2008 s.166 and Sch.15 Pt 5.]

9   An order to which section 16 of the Maintenance Orders Act 1950 applies by virtue of subsection (2)(b) or (c) of that section (that is to say an order made by a court in Scotland or Northern Ireland and corresponding to one of those specified in the foregoing paragraphs) and which has been registered in a court in England and Wales under Part II of that Act.

10   A maintenance order within the meaning of the Maintenance Orders (Facilities for Enforcement) Act 1920 (Commonwealth orders enforceable in the United Kingdom) registered in, or confirmed by, a court in England and Wales under that Act.

11   A maintenance order within the meaning of Part I of the Maintenance Orders (Reciprocal Enforcement) Act 1972 registered in a magistrates' court under the said Part I.

12   An order under section 34(1)(b) of the Children Act 1975 (payments of maintenance in respect of a child to his custodian).

13   A maintenance order within the meaning of Part I of the Civil Jurisdiction and Judgments Act 1982 which is registered in a magistrates' court under that Part.

14   A maintenance judgment within the meaning of Council Regulation (EC) No. 44/2001 of 22nd December 2000 on jurisdiction and the recognition and enforcement of judgments in civil and commercial matters, as amended from time to time and as applied by the Agreement made on 19th October 2005 between the European Community and the Kingdom of Denmark on jurisdiction and the recognition and enforcement of judgments in civil and commercial matters (OJ No.L 299 16.11.2005 at p.62), which is registered in a magistrates' court under that Regulation.

14A(1)   A decision, court settlement or authentic instrument which falls to be enforced by a magistrates' court by virtue of the Maintenance Regulation and the Civil Jurisdiction and Judgments (Maintenance) Regulations 2011.

14A(2)   In this paragraph–

"the Maintenance Regulation" means Council Regulation (EC) No 4/2009 including as applied in relation to Denmark by virtue of the Agreement made on 19th October 2005 between the European Community and the Kingdom of Denmark;

"decision", "court settlement" and "authentic instrument" have the meanings given by Article 2 of that Regulation.

History
Paragraph 14 amended by the Civil Jurisdiction and Judgments Regulations 2007 (SI 2007/1655) reg.5 and Sch.
para.7.
  Paragraph 14A added by Civil Jurisdiction and Judgments (Maintenance) Regulations 2011 (SI 2011/1484) Sch.7
para.4(3) as from June 18, 2011.

SCHEDULE 2

TAXES, SOCIAL SECURITY CONTRIBUTIONS ETC. RELEVANT FOR PURPOSES OF SECTION 3(6)

Section 3

1 Income tax or any other tax or liability recoverable under section 65, 66 or 68 of the Taxes
Management Act 1970.

2 [Repealed by Statute Law (Repeals) Act 1989.]

3 Contributions equivalent premiums under Part III of the Pension Schemes Act 1993.

3A Class 1, 2 and 4 contributions under Part I of the Social Security Contributions and Benefits Act
1992.

4 [Repealed by Social Security Act 1973 s.100(2) and Sch.28 Pt I.]

SCHEDULE 3

DEDUCTIONS BY EMPLOYER UNDER ATTACHMENT OF EARNINGS ORDER

Sections 6 and 7

PART I

SCHEME OF DEDUCTIONS

Preliminary definitions

1 The following three paragraphs have effect for defining and explaining, for purposes of this Schedule,
expressions used therein.

2 **"Pay-day"**, in relation to earnings paid to a debtor, means an occasion on which they are paid.

3 **"Attachable earnings"**, in relation to a pay-day, are the earnings which remain payable to the debtor
on that day after deduction by the employer of–

  (a) income tax;

  (b) [Repealed by the Social Security Pensions Act 1975 s.65(3) and Sch.5.]

  (bb) primary class 1 contributions under Part I of the Social Security Act 1975;

  (c) amounts deductible under any enactment, or in pursuance of a request in writing by the debtor, for
       the purposes of a superannuation scheme, namely any enactment, rules, deed or other instrument
       providing for the payment of annuities or lump sums–

    (i) to the persons with respect to whom the instrument has effect on their retirement at a
         specified age or on becoming incapacitated at some earlier age, or

    (ii) to the personal representatives or the widows, relatives or dependants of such persons on
         their death or otherwise,

whether with or without any further or other benefits.

4(1)   On any pay-day–

(a) **"the normal deduction"** is arrived at by applying the normal deduction rate (as specified in the relevant attachment of earnings order) with respect to the relevant period; and

(b) **"the protected earnings"** are arrived at by applying the protected earnings rate (as so specified) with respect to the relevant period.

4(2)   For the purposes of this paragraph the relevant period in relation to any pay-day is the period beginning–

(a) if it is the first pay-day of the debtor's employment with the employer, with the first pay day of the employment; or

(b) if on the last pay-day earnings were paid in respect of a period falling wholly or partly after that pay-day, with the first day after the end of that period; or

(c) in any other case, with the first day after the last pay-day, and ending–

(i) where earnings are paid in respect of a period falling wholly or partly after the pay-day, with the last day of that period; or

(ii) in any other case, with the pay-day.

Employer's deduction (judgment debts and administration orders)

5   In the case of an attachment of earnings order made to secure the payment of a judgment debt or payments under an administration order, the employer shall on any pay-day–

(a) if the attachable earnings exceed the protected earnings, deduct from the attachable earnings the amount of the excess or the normal deduction, whichever is the less;

(b) make no deduction if the attachable earnings are equal to, or less than, the protected earnings.

Employer's deduction (other cases)

6(1)   The following provision shall have effect in the case of an attachment of earnings order to which paragraph 5 above and paragraph 6A below do not apply.

6(2)   If on a pay-day the attachable earnings exceed the sum of–

(a) the protected earnings; and

(b) so much of any amount by which the attachable earnings on any previous pay-day fell short of the protected earnings as has not been made good by virtue of this sub-paragraph on another previous pay-day,

then, in so far as the excess allows, the employer shall deduct from the attachable earnings the amount specified in the following sub-paragraph.

6(3)   The said amount is the sum of–

(a) the normal deduction; and

(b) so much of the normal deduction on any previous pay-day as was not deducted on that day and has not been paid by virtue of this sub-paragraph on any other previous pay-day.

6(4)   No deduction shall be made on any pay-day when the attachable earnings are equal to, or less than, the protected earnings.

6A   In the case of an attachment of earnings order made under Schedule 5 to the Courts Act 2003, the employer shall make deductions from the debtor's earnings in accordance with fines collection regulations made under that Schedule.

Note

Subparagraph (6A) inserted by the Collection of Fines (Final Scheme) Order 2006 (SI 2006/1737) arts 34, 45, as from July 3, 2006. (See also history note to s.1.)

PART II

PRIORITY AS BETWEEN ORDERS

7 Where the employer is required to comply with two or more attachment of earnings orders in respect of the same debtor, all or none of which orders are made to secure either the payment of judgment debts or payments under an administration order, then on any pay-day the employer shall, for the purpose of complying with Part I of this Schedule,–

(a) deal with the orders according to the respective dates on which they were made, disregarding any later order until an earlier one has been dealt with;

(b) deal with any later order as if the earnings to which it relates were the residue of the debtor's earnings after the making of any deduction to comply with any earlier order.

8 Where the employer is required to comply with two or more attachment of earnings orders, and one or more (but not all) of those orders are made to secure either the payment of judgment debts or payments under an administration order, then on any pay-day the employer shall, for the purpose of complying with Part I of this Schedule–

(a) deal first with any order which is not made to secure the payment of a judgment debt or payments under an administration order (complying with paragraph 7 above if there are two or more such orders); and

(b) deal thereafter with any order which is made to secure the payment of a judgment debt or payments under an administration order as if the earnings to which it relates were the residue of the debtor's earnings after the making of any deduction to comply with an order having priority by virtue of sub-paragraph (a) above; and

(c) if there are two or more orders to which sub-paragraph (b) above applies, comply with paragraph 7 above in respect of those orders.

SCHEDULE 4

[Repealed by the Social Security Act 1986 s.86(2) and Sch.11.]

SCHEDULE 5

SECTION 20 OF MAINTENANCE ORDERS ACT 1958 AS HAVING EFFECT IN CONSEQUENCE OF THIS ACT

Section 27

[Not reproduced.]

SCHEDULE 6

ENACTMENTS REPEALED

Section 29

[Not reproduced.]

Matrimonial Causes Act 1973

(1973 Chapter 18)

An Act to consolidate certain enactments relating to matrimonial proceedings, maintenance agreements, and declarations of legitimacy, validity of marriage and British nationality, with amendments to give effect to recommendations of the Law Commission.

[*23rd May 1973*]

[**Note:** Changes made by the Statute Law (Repeals) Act 1977 and the Insolvency Acts 1985 and 1986 have been incorporated, without annotation.]

39 Settlement, etc. made in compliance with a property adjustment order may be avoided on bankruptcy of settlor

39 The fact that a settlement or transfer of property had to be made in order to comply with a property adjustment order shall not prevent that settlement or transfer from being a transaction in respect of which an order may be made under section 339 or 340 of the Insolvency Act 1986 (transactions at an undervalue and preferences.)

55 Citation, commencement and extent

55(1) This Act may be cited as the Matrimonial Causes Act 1973.

55(2) This Act shall come into force on such day as the Lord Chancellor may appoint by order made by statutory instrument.

55(3) Subject to the provisions of paragraphs 3(2) of Schedule 2 below, this Act does not extend to Scotland or Northern Ireland.

[**Note:** the day appointed pursuant to s.45(2) was January 1, 1974: see the Matrimonial Causes Act 1973 (Commencement) Order 1973 (SI 1973/1972).]

Administration of Justice Act 1977

(1977 Chapter 38)

[*29th July 1977*]

PART I

GENERAL

7 Extent of powers of receivers and managers in respect of companies

7(1) A receiver appointed under the law of any part of the United Kingdom in respect of the whole or part of any property or undertaking of a company and in consequence of the company having created a charge which, as created, was a floating charge may exercise his powers in any other part of the United Kingdom so far as their exercise is not inconsistent with the law applicable there.

7(2) In subsection (1) above **"receiver"** includes a manager and a person who is appointed both receiver and manager.

Charging Orders Act 1979

(1979 Chapter 53)

An Act to make provision for imposing charges to secure payment of money due, or to become due, under judgments or orders of court; to provide for restraining and prohibiting dealings with, and the making of payments in respect of, certain securities; and for connected purposes.

[*6th December 1979*]

[**Note**: Changes made by the Supreme Court Act 1981, the Administration of Justice Act 1982, the County Courts Act 1984, the Building Societies Act 1986, the Land Registration Act 2002 and the Civil Procedure (Modification of Enactments) Order 2002 (SI 2002/439) have been incorporated into the text (in the case of pre-2003 legislation without annotation). The government has announced that the prospective amendment of this Act to be effected by TCEA 2007 ss.91, 92 and Sch.15 will not now be brought into force.]

Charging orders

1 Charging orders

1(1) Where, under a judgment or order of the High Court or a county court, a person (the **"debtor"**) is required to pay a sum of money to another person (the **"creditor"**) then, for the purpose of enforcing that judgment or order, the appropriate court may make an order in accordance with the provisions of this Act imposing on any such property of the debtor as may be specified in the order a charge for securing the payment of any money due or to become due under the judgment or order.

1(2) The appropriate court is–

(a) in a case where the property to be charged is a fund in court, the court in which that fund is lodged;

(b) in a case where paragraph (a) above does not apply and the order to be enforced is a maintenance order of the High Court, the High Court or a county court;

(c) in a case where neither paragraph (a) nor paragraph (b) above applies and the judgment or order to be enforced is a judgment or order of the High Court for a sum exceeding the county court limit, the High Court or a county court; and

(d) in any other case, a county court.

In this section **"county court limit"** means the county court limit for the time being specified in an Order in Council under section 145 of the County Courts Act 1984 as the county court limit for the purposes of this section and **"maintenance order"** has the same meaning as in section 2(a) of the Attachment of Earnings Act 1971.

1(3) An order under subsection (1) above is referred to in this Act as a **"charging order"**.

1(4) Where a person applies to the High Court for a charging order to enforce more than one judgment or order, that court shall be the appropriate court in relation to the application if it would be the appropriate court, apart from this subsection, on an application relating to one or more of the judgments or orders concerned.

1(5) In deciding whether to make a charging order the court shall consider all the circumstances of the case and, in particular, any evidence before it as to–

    (a) the personal circumstances of the debtor, and

    (b) whether any other creditor of the debtor would be likely to be unduly prejudiced by the making of the order.

2 Property which may be charged

2(1) Subject to subsection (3) below, a charge may be imposed by a charging order only on–

    (a) any interest held by the debtor beneficially–

        (i) in any asset of a kind mentioned in subsection (2) below, or

        (ii) under any trust; or

    (b) any interest held by a person as trustee of a trust (**"the trust"**), if the interest is in such an asset or is an interest under another trust and–

        (i) the judgment or order in respect of which a charge is to be imposed was made against that person as trustee of the trust, or

        (ii) the whole beneficial interest under the trust is held by the debtor unencumbered and for his own benefit, or

        (iii) in a case where there are two or more debtors all of whom are liable to the creditor for the same debt, they together hold the whole beneficial interest under the trust unencumbered and for their own benefit.

2(2) The assets referred to in subsection (1) above are–

    (a) land,

    (b) securities of any of the following kinds–

        (i) government stock,

        (ii) stock of any body (other than a building society) incorporated within England and Wales,

        (iii) stock of any body incorporated outside England and Wales or of any state or territory outside the United Kingdom, being stock registered in a register kept at any place within England and Wales,

        (iv) units of any unit trust in respect of which a register of the unit holders is kept at any place within England and Wales, or

    (c) funds in court.

2(3) In any case where a charge is imposed by a charging order on any interest in an asset of a kind mentioned in paragraph (b) or (c) of subsection (2) above, the court making the order may provide for the charge to extend to any interest or dividend payable in respect of the asset.

3 Provisions supplementing sections 1 and 2

3(1) A charging order may be made either absolutely or subject to conditions as to notifying the debtor or as to the time when the charge is to become enforceable, or as to other matters.

3(2)   The Land Charges Act 1972 and the Land Registration Act 2002 shall apply in relation to charging orders as they apply in relation to other orders or writs issued or made for the purpose of enforcing judgments.

3(3)   [Repealed.]

3(4)   Subject to the provisions of this Act, a charge imposed by a charging order shall have the like effect and shall be enforceable in the same courts and in the same manner as an equitable charge created by the debtor by writing under his hand.

3(5)   The court by which a charging order was made may at any time, on the application of the debtor or of any person interested in any property to which the order relates, make an order discharging or varying the charging order.

3(6)   Where a charging order has been protected by an entry registered under the Land Charges Act 1972 or the Land Registration Act 2002, an order under subsection (5) above discharging the charging order may direct that the entry be cancelled.

3(7)   The Lord Chancellor may by order made by statutory instrument amend section 2(2) of this Act by adding to, or removing from, the kinds of asset for the time being referred to there, any asset of a kind which in his opinion ought to be so added or removed.

3(8)   Any order under subsection (7) above shall be subject to annulment in pursuance of a resolution of either House of Parliament.

4   [Repealed by the Insolvency Act 1985 s.235 and Sch.10 Pt III.]

Stop orders and notices

5   Stop orders and notices

5(1)   In this section–

"**stop order**" means an order of the court prohibiting the taking, in respect of any of the securities specified in the order, of any of the steps mentioned in subsection (5) below;

"**stop notice**" means a notice requiring any person or body on whom it is duly served to refrain from taking, in respect of any of the securities specified in the notice, any of those steps without first notifying the person by whom, or on whose behalf, the notice was served; and

"**prescribed securities**" means securities (including funds in court) of a kind prescribed by rules of court made under this section.

5(2)   The power to make rules of court under section 1 of, and Schedule 1 to, the Civil Procedure Act 1997 shall include power by any such rules to make provision–

(a)   for the High Court to make a stop order on the application of any person claiming to be entitled to an interest in prescribed securities; and

(b)   for the service of a stop notice by any person claiming to be entitled to an interest in prescribed securities.

5(3)   [Repealed.]

5(4)   Rules of court made by virtue of subsection (2) above shall prescribe the person or body on whom a copy of any stop order or a stop notice is to be served.

5(5)   The steps mentioned in subsection (1) above are–

(a)   the registration of any transfer of the securities;

(b) in the case of funds in court, the transfer, sale, delivery out, payment or other dealing with the funds, or of the income thereon;

(c) the making of any payment by way of dividend, interest or otherwise in respect of the securities; and

(d) in the case of units of a unit trust, any acquisition of or other dealing with the units by any person or body exercising functions under the trust.

5(6) Any rules of court made by virtue of this section may include such incidental, supplemental and consequential provisions as the authority making them consider necessary or expedient, and may make different provision in relation to different cases or classes of case.

Supplemental

6 Interpretation

6(1) In this Act–

"**building society**" has the same meaning as in the Building Societies Act 1986;

"**charging order**" means an order made under section 1(1) of this Act;

"**debtor**" and "**creditor**" have the meanings given by section 1(1) of this Act;

"**dividend**" includes any distribution in respect of any unit of a unit trust;

"**government stock**" means any stock issued by Her Majesty's government in the United Kingdom or any funds of, or annuity granted by, that government;

"**stock**" includes shares, debentures and any securities of the body concerned, whether or not constituting a charge on the assets of that body;

"**unit trust**" means any trust established for the purpose, or having the effect, of providing, for persons having funds available for investment, facilities for the participation by them, as beneficiaries under the trust, in any profits or income arising from the acquisition, holding, management or disposal of any property whatsoever.

6(2) For the purposes of section 1 of this Act references to a judgment or order of the High Court or a county court shall be taken to include references to a judgment, order, decree or award (however called) of any court or arbitrator (including any foreign court or arbitrator) which is or has become enforceable (whether wholly or to a limited extent) as if it were a judgment or order of the High Court or a county court.

6(3) References in section 2 of this Act to any securities include references to any such securities standing in the name of the Accountant General.

7 Consequential amendment, repeals and transitional provisions

7(1) [Repealed by the County Courts Act 1984 s.148(3) and Sch.4.]

7(2) [Repealed by the Supreme Court Act 1981 s.152(4) and Sch.7, and the County Courts Act 1984 s.148(3) and Sch.4.]

7(3) Any order made or notice given under any enactment repealed by this Act or under any rules of court revoked by rules of court made under this Act (the "new rules") shall, if still in force when the provisions of this Act or, as the case may be, the new rules come into force, continue to have effect as if made under this Act, or, as the case may be, under the new rules.

7(4) [Repealed.]

8 Short title, commencement and extent

8(1)   This Act may be cited as the Charging Orders Act 1979.

8(2)   This Act comes into force on such day as the Lord Chancellor may appoint by order made by statutory instrument.

8(3)   This Act does not extend to Scotland or Northern Ireland.

County Courts Act 1984

(1984 Chapter 28)

An Act to consolidate certain enactments relating to county courts.

[26th June 1984]

[**Note**: Changes made by the Insolvency Act 1985 and the Civil Procedure Act 1997 have been incorporated into the text (in the case of pre-2003 legislation without annotation). Prospective amendments made by the Courts and Legal Services Act 1990 s.13 as from a day to be appointed are now thought unlikely to be brought into force and have not been included. Note prospective amendment by TCEA 2007 s.106 and Sch.16.]

PART VI

ADMINISTRATION ORDERS

112 Power to make administration order

112(1) Where a debtor–

(a) is unable to pay forthwith the amount of a judgment obtained against him; and

(b) alleges that his whole indebtedness amounts to a sum not exceeding the county court limit, inclusive of the debt for which the judgment was obtained;

a county court may make an order providing for the administration of his estate.

112(2) In this Part of this Act–

"administration order" means an order under this section; and

"the appropriate court", in relation to an administration order, means the court which has the power to make the order.

112(3) Before an administration order is made, the appropriate court shall, in accordance with rules of court, send to every person whose name the debtor has notified to the appropriate court as being a creditor of his, a notice that that person's name has been so notified.

112(4) So long as an administration order is in force, a creditor whose name is included in the schedule to the order shall not, without the leave of the appropriate court, be entitled to present, or join in, a bankruptcy petition against the debtor unless–

(a) his name was so notified; and

(b) the debt by virtue of which he presents, or joins in, the petition, exceeds £1,500; and

(c) the notice given under subsection (3) was received by the creditor within 28 days immediately preceding the day on which the petition is presented.

112(5)   An administration order shall not be invalid by reason only that the total amount of the debts is found at any time to exceed the county court limit, but in that case the court may, if it thinks fit, set aside the order.

112(6)   An administration order may provide for the payment of the debts of the debtor by instalments or otherwise, and either in full or to such extent as appears practicable to the court under the circumstances of the case, and subject to any conditions as to his future earnings or income which the court may think just.

112(7)   The Secretary of State may by regulations increase or reduce the sum for the time being specified in subsection (4)(b); but no such increase in the sum so specified shall affect any case in which the bankruptcy petition was presented before the coming into force of the increase.

112(8)   The power to make regulations under subsection (7) shall be exercisable by statutory instrument; and no such regulations shall be made unless a draft of them has been approved by resolution of each House of Parliament.

Note
The "county court limit" is £5000: County Courts (Administration Order Jurisdiction) Order 1981 (SI 1981/1122) art.2.

113   Notice of order and proof of debts

113   Where an administration order has been made–

(a)   notice of the order–

    (i)   [Repealed by the Administration of Justice Act 1985 s.67(2) and Sch.8 Pt II as from December 30, 1985.]

    (ii)   shall be posted in the office of the county court for the district in which the debtor resides, and

    (iii)   shall be sent to every person whose name the debtor has notified to the appropriate court as being a creditor of his or who has proved;

(b)   any creditor of the debtor, on proof of his debt before the registrar, shall be entitled to be scheduled as a creditor of the debtor for the amount of his proof;

(c)   any creditor may object in the prescribed manner to any debt scheduled, or to the manner in which payment is directed to be made by instalments;

(d)   any person who, after the date of the order, becomes a creditor of the debtor shall, on proof of his debt before the registrar, be scheduled as a creditor of the debtor for the amount of his proof, but shall not be entitled to any dividend under the order until the creditors who are scheduled as having been creditors before the date of the order have been paid to the extent provided by the order.

114   Effect of administration order

114(1)   Subject to sections 115 and 116, when an administration order is made, no creditor shall have any remedy against the person or property of the debtor in respect of any debt–

(a)   of which the debtor notified the appropriate court before the administration order was made; or

(b)   which has been scheduled to the order,

except with the leave of the appropriate court, and on such terms as that court may impose.

114(2)   Subject to subsection (3), any county court in which proceedings are pending against the debtor in respect of any debt so notified or scheduled shall, on receiving notice of the administration order, stay the proceedings, but may allow costs already incurred by the creditor, and such costs may, on application, be added to the debt.

114(3)   The requirement to stay proceedings shall not operate as a requirement that a county court in which proceedings in bankruptcy against the debtor are pending shall stay those proceedings.

115   Execution by registrar

115(1)   Where it appears to the registrar of the appropriate court at any time while an administration order is in force that property of the debtor exceeds in value the minimum amount, he shall, at the request of any creditor, and without fee, issue execution against the debtor's goods.

115(1A)   In subsection (1) above **"the minimum amount"** means £50 or such other amount as the Lord Chancellor may by order specify instead of that amount or the amount for the time being specified in such an order; and an order under this subsection shall be made by statutory instrument subject to annulment in pursuance of a resolution of either House of Parliament.

115(2)   Section 89 applies on an execution under this section as it applies on an execution under Part V.

116   Right of landlord to distrain notwithstanding order

116   A landlord or other person to whom any rent is due from a debtor in respect of whom an administration order is made, may at any time, either before or after the date of the order, distrain upon the goods or effects of the debtor for the rent due to him from the debtor, with this limitation, that if the distress for rent is levied after the date of the order, it shall be available only for six months' rent accrued due prior to the date of the order and shall not be available for rent payable in respect of any period subsequent to the date when the distress was levied, but the landlord or other person to whom the rent may be due from the debtor may prove under the order for the surplus due for which the distress may not have been available.

117   Appropriation of money paid under order and discharge of order

117(1)   Money paid into court under an administration order shall be appropriated–

    (a)   first in satisfaction of the costs of administration (which shall not exceed 10 pence in the pound on the total amount of the debts); and

    (b)   then in liquidation of debts in accordance with the order.

117(2)   Where the amount received is sufficient to pay–

    (a)   each creditor scheduled to the order to the extent provided by the order;

    (b)   the costs of the plaintiff in the action in respect of which the order was made; and

    (c)   the costs of the administration,

the order shall be superseded, and the debtor shall be discharged from his debts to the scheduled creditors.

Council Regulation (EEC No.2137/85) of July 25, 1985 on the European Economic Interest Grouping (EEIG)

[Relevant provisions of the Regulation (which has legislative force in the UK) are reproduced in Sch.1 to the European Economic Interest Grouping Regulations 1989 (SI 1989/638), below.]

Building Societies Act 1986

(1986 Chapter 53)

ARRANGEMENT OF SECTIONS

An Act to make fresh provision with respect to building societies and further provision with respect to conveyancing services.

[25th July 1986]

[**Note**: Changes made by the Companies Act 1989, the Insolvency (Northern Ireland) Order 1989 (SI 1989/2405), the Building Societies Act 1997, the Financial Services and Markets Act 2000 (Mutual Societies) Order 2001 (SI 2001/2617), the Financial Services and Markets Act 2000 (Consequential Amendments and Repeals) Order 2001 (SI 2001/3649), the Building Societies (Insolvency and Special Administration) Order 2009 (SI 2009/805) and the Companies Act 2006 (Consequential Amendments, Transitional Provisions and Savings) Order 2009 (SI 2009/1941) have been incorporated into the text (in the case of pre-2003 legislation without annotation). Former references to the Commission and to the central office have been replaced throughout by references to the Authority (i.e. the Financial Services Authority) or to the Treasury and references to the Investor Protection Board by references to the scheme manager, pursuant to the Financial Services and Markets Act 2000 (Mutual Societies) Order 2001 (SI 2001/2617) Pt II as from December 1, 2001.

Note that where a building society receives financial assistance from the Bank of England or has entered into an agreement for assistance or received an offer of such an agreement, these regulations are modified pursuant to the Banking (Special Provisions) Act 2008 s.11 and the Building Societies (Financial Assistance) Order 2008 (SI 2008/1427), effective June 5, 2008. The Act is also modified extensively by the Banking Act 2009 and the Building Societies (Insolvency and Special Administration) Order 2009 (SI 2009/805) to deal with the case where a failing building society is the subject of government intervention: see Vol.1, p.6.]

PART I

FUNCTIONS OF THE AUTHORITY

1 Functions of the Financial Services Authority in relation to building societies

1(1) The Financial Services Authority (**"the Authority"**) has the following functions under this Act in relation to building societies–

(a) to secure that the principal purpose of building societies remains that of making loans which are secured on residential property and are funded substantially by their members;

(b) to administer the system of regulation of building societies provided for by or under this Act; and

(c) to advise and make recommendations to the Treasury and other government departments on any matter relating to building societies.

1(2) The Authority also has, in relation to such societies, the other functions conferred on it by or under this Act or any other enactment.

PART X

DISSOLUTION, WINDING UP, MERGERS AND TRANSFERS OF BUSINESS

Dissolution and winding up

86 Modes of dissolution and winding up

86(1) A building society–

(a) may be dissolved by consent of the members, or

(b) may be wound up voluntarily or by the court,

in accordance with this Part; and a building society may not, except where it is dissolved by virtue of section 93(5), 94(10) or 97(9), or following building society insolvency or building society special administration, be dissolved or wound up in any other manner.

86(2) A building society which is in the course of dissolution by consent, or is being wound up voluntarily, may be wound up by the court.

History
Section 86 amended by the Building Societies (Insolvency and Special Administration) Order 2009 (SI 2009/805) art.7, as from March 29, 2009.

87 Dissolution by consent

87(1) A building society may be dissolved by an instrument of dissolution, with the consent (testified by their signature of that instrument) of three-quarters of the members of the society, holding not less than two-thirds of the number of shares in the society.

87(2) An instrument of dissolution under this section shall set out–

(a) the liabilities and assets of the society in detail;

(b) the number of members, and the amount standing to their credit in the accounting records of the society;

(c) the claims of depositors and other creditors, and the provision to be made for their payment;

(d) the intended appropriation or division of the funds and property of the society;

(e) the names of one or more persons to be appointed as trustees for the purposes of the dissolution, and their remuneration.

87(3) An instrument of dissolution made with consent given and testified as mentioned in subsection (1) above may be altered with the like consent, testified in the like manner.

87(4) The provisions of this Act shall continue to apply in relation to a building society as if the trustees appointed under the instrument of dissolution were the board of directors of the society.

87(5) The trustees, within 15 days of the necessary consent being given and testified (in accordance with subsection (1) above) to–

(a) an instrument of dissolution, or

(b) any alteration to such an instrument,

shall give notice to the Authority of the fact and, except in the case of an alteration to an instrument, of the date of commencement of the dissolution, enclosing a copy of the instrument or altered instrument, as the case may be; and if the trustees fail to comply with this subsection they shall each be liable on summary conviction to a fine not exceeding level 3 on the standard scale.

87(6) An instrument of dissolution under this section or an alteration to such an instrument, shall be binding on all members of the society as from the date on which the copy of the instrument or altered instrument, as the case may be, is placed in the public file of the society under subsection (10) below.

87(7) The trustees shall, within 28 days from the termination of the dissolution, give notice to the Authority of the fact and the date of the termination, enclosing an account and balance sheet signed and certified by them as correct, and showing the assets and liabilities of the society at the commencement of the dissolution, and the way in which those assets and liabilities have been applied and discharged; and, if they fail to do so they shall each be liable on summary conviction–

(a) to a fine not exceeding level 2 on the standard scale, and

(b) in the case of a continuing offence, to an additional fine not exceeding £10 for every day during which the offence continues.

87(8) Except with the consent of the Authority, no instrument of dissolution, or alteration of such an instrument, shall be of any effect if the purpose of the proposed dissolution or alteration is to effect or facilitate the transfer of the society's engagements to any other society or the transfer of its business to a company.

87(9) Any provision in a resolution or document that members of a building society proposed to be dissolved shall accept investments in a company or another society (whether in shares, deposits or any other form) in or towards satisfaction of their rights in the dissolution shall be conclusive evidence of such a purpose as is mentioned in subsection (8) above.

87(10) The Authority shall keep in the public file of the society any notice or other document received by it under subsection (5) or (7) above and shall record in that file the date on which the notice or document is placed in it.

88 Voluntary winding up

88(1) A building society may be wound up voluntarily under the applicable winding up legislation if it resolves by special resolution that it be wound up voluntarily, but a resolution may not be passed if–

(a) the conditions in section 90D are not satisfied, or

(b) the society is in building society insolvency or building society special administration.

88(1A) A resolution under subsection (1) shall have no effect without the prior approval of the court.

88(2)   A copy of any special resolution passed for the voluntary winding up of a building society shall be sent by the society to the Authority within 15 days after it is passed; and the Authority shall keep the copy in the public file of the society.

88(3)   A copy of any such resolution shall be annexed to every copy of the memorandum or of the rules issued after the passing of the resolution.

88(4)   If a building society fails to comply with subsection (2) or (3) above the society shall be liable on summary conviction to a fine not exceeding level 3 on the standard scale and so shall any officer who is also guilty of the offence.

88(5)   For the purposes of this section, a liquidator of the society shall be treated as an officer of it.

History
Section 88(1) modified by the Building Societies (Insolvency and Special Administration) Order 2009 (SI 2009/805) art.4, as from March 29, 2009.

89   Winding up by court: grounds and petitioners

89(1)   A building society may be wound up under the applicable winding up legislation by the court on any of the following grounds in addition to the grounds referred to or specified in section 37(1), that is to say, if–

 (a)   the society has by special resolution resolved that it be wound up by the court;

 (b)   the number of members is reduced below ten;

 (c)   the number of directors is reduced below two;

 (d)   being a society registered as a building society under this Act or the repealed enactments, the society has not been given permission under Part IV of the Financial Services and Markets Act 2000 to accept deposits and more than three years has expired since it was so registered;

 (e)   the society's permission under Part IV of the Financial Services and Markets Act 2000 to accept deposits has been cancelled (and no such permission has subsequently been given to it);

 (f)   the society exists for an illegal purpose;

 (g)   the society is unable to pay its debts; or

 (h)   the court is of the opinion that it is just and equitable that the society should be wound up.

89(2)   Except as provided by subsection (3) below, section 37 or the applicable winding up legislation, a petition for the winding up of a building society may be presented by–

 (a)   the Authority,

 (b)   the building society or its directors,

 (c)   any creditor or creditors (including any contingent or any prospective creditor), or

 (d)   any contributory or contributories,

or by all or any of those parties, together or separately.

89(3)   A contributory may not present a petition unless either–

 (a)   the number of members is reduced below ten, or

 (b)   the share in respect of which he is a contributory has been held by him, or has devolved to him on the death of a former holder and between them been held, for at least six months before the commencement of the winding up.

89(4) For the purposes of this section, in relation to a building society–

(a) [Repealed by the Financial Services and Markets Act 2000 (Mutual Societies) Order (SI 2001/2617) art.13(2) and Sch.4 as from December 1, 2001.]

(b) the reference to its existing for an illegal purpose includes a reference to its existing after it has ceased to comply with the requirement imposed by section 5(1)(a) (purpose or principal purpose).

89(5) In this section, **"contributory"** has the same meaning as in paragraph 9(2) or, as the case may be, paragraph 37(2) of Schedule 15 to this Act.

89A Building society insolvency as alternative order

89A(1) On a petition for a winding up order or an application for an administration order in respect of a building society the court may, instead, make a building society insolvency order (under section 94 of the Banking Act 2009 as applied by section 90C below).

89A(2) A building society insolvency order may be made under subsection (1) only–

(a) on the application of the Authority made with the consent of the Bank of England, or

(b) on the application of the Bank of England.

History
Section 89A inserted by the Building Societies (Insolvency and Special Administration) Order 2009 (SI 2009/805) art.5, as from March 29, 2009.

90 Application of winding up legislation to building societies

90(1) In this section **"the companies winding up legislation"** means the enactments applicable in relation to England and Wales, Scotland or Northern Ireland which are specified in paragraph 1 of Schedule 15 to this Act (including any enactment which creates an offence by any person arising out of acts or omissions occurring before the commencement of the winding up).

90(2) In its application to the winding up of a building society, by virtue of section 88(1) or 89(1), the companies winding up legislation shall have effect with the modifications effected by Parts I to III of Schedule 15 to this Act; and the supplementary provisions of Part IV of that Schedule shall also have effect in relation to such a winding up.

90(3) In sections 37, 88, 89, and 103, **"the applicable winding up legislation"** means the companies winding up legislation as so modified.

90A Application of other companies insolvency legislation to building societies

90A For the purpose of–

(a) enabling voluntary arrangements to be approved in relation to building societies,

(b) enabling administration orders to be made in relation to building societies, and

(c) making provision with respect to persons appointed in England and Wales or Northern Ireland as receivers and managers of building societies' property,

the enactments specified in paragraph 1(2) of Schedule 15A to this Act shall apply in relation to building societies with the modifications specified in that Schedule.

History
Note prospective insertion of s.90B by the Building Societies (Funding) and Mutual Societies (Transfers) Act 2007 s.2.

90C   Application of bank insolvency and administration legislation to building societies

90C(1)   Parts 2 (Bank Insolvency) and 3 (Bank Administration) of the Banking Act 2009 shall apply in relation to building societies with any modifications specified in an order made under section 130 or 158 of that Act and with the modifications specified in subsection (2) below.

90C(2)   In the application of Parts 2 and 3 of that Act to building societies–

(a)   references to "bank" (except in the term "bridge bank" and the terms specified in paragraphs (b) and (c)) have effect as references to "building society";

(b)   references to "bank insolvency", "bank insolvency order", "bank liquidation" and "bank liquidator" have effect as references to "building society insolvency", "building society insolvency order", "building society liquidation" and "building society liquidator";

(c)   references to "bank administration", "bank administration order" and "bank administrator" have effect as references to "building society special administration", "building society special administration order" and "building society special administrator".

History
Section 90C inserted by the Building Societies (Insolvency and Special Administration) Order 2009 (SI 2009/805) art.2, as from March 29, 2009.

90D   Notice to the Authority of preliminary steps

90D(1)   An application for an administration order in respect of a building society may not be determined unless the conditions below are satisfied.

90D(2)   A petition for a winding up order in respect of a building society may not be determined unless the conditions below are satisfied.

90D(3)   A resolution for voluntary winding up of a building society may not be passed unless the conditions below are satisfied.

90D(4)   An administrator of a building society may not be appointed unless the conditions below are satisfied.

90D(5)   Condition 1 is that the Authority has been notified–

(a)   by the applicant for an administration order, that the application has been made,

(b)   by the petitioner for a winding up order, that the petition has been presented,

(c)   by the building society, that a resolution for voluntary winding up may be passed, or

(d)   by the person proposing to appoint an administrator, of the proposed appointment.

90D(6)   Condition 2 is that a copy of the notice complying with Condition 1 has been filed with the court (and made available for public inspection by the court).

90D(7)   Condition 3 is that–

(a)   the period of 2 weeks, beginning with the day on which the notice is received, has ended, or

(b)   both–

(i)   the Authority has informed the person who gave the notice that it does not intend to apply for a building society insolvency order (under section 95 of the Banking Act 2009 as applied by section 90C above), and

(ii)   the Bank of England has informed the person who gave the notice that it does not intend to apply for a building society insolvency order or to exercise a stabilisation power under Part 1 of the Banking Act 2009.

90D(8)   Condition 4 is that no application for a building society insolvency order is pending.

90D(9)   Arranging for the giving of notice in order to satisfy Condition 1 can be a step with a view to minimising the potential loss to a building society's creditors for the purpose of section 214 of the Insolvency Act 1986 (wrongful trading) or Article 178 (wrongful trading) of the Insolvency (Northern Ireland) Order 1989 as applied in relation to building societies by section 90 of, and Schedule 15 to, this Act.

90D(10)   Where the Authority receives notice under Condition 1–

(a)   the Authority shall inform the Bank of England,

(b)   the Authority shall inform the person who gave the notice, within the period in Condition 3(a), whether it intends to apply for a building society insolvency order, and

(c)   if the Bank of England decides to apply for a building society insolvency order or to exercise a stabilisation power under Part 1 of the Banking Act 2009, the Bank shall inform the person who gave the notice, within the period in Condition 3(a).

History
Section 90D inserted by the Building Societies (Insolvency and Special Administration) Order 2009 (SI 2009/805) art.6, as from March 29, 2009.

90E   Disqualification of directors

90E(1)   In this section **"the Disqualification Act"** means the Company Directors Disqualification Act 1986.

90E(2)   In the Disqualification Act–

(a)   a reference to liquidation includes a reference to building society insolvency and a reference to building society special administration,

(b)   a reference to winding up includes a reference to making or being subject to a building society insolvency order and a reference to making or being subject to a building society special administration order,

(c)   a reference to becoming insolvent includes a reference to becoming subject to a building society insolvency order and a reference to becoming subject to a building society special administration order, and

(d)   a reference to a liquidator includes a reference to a building society liquidator and a reference to a building society special administrator.

90E(3)   For the purposes of the application of section 7(3) of the Disqualification Act (disqualification order or undertaking) to a building society which is subject to a building society insolvency order, the responsible office-holder is the building society liquidator

90E(4)   For the purposes of the application of that section to a building society which is subject to a building society special administration order, the responsible office-holder is the building society special administrator.

90E(5)   In the application of this section to Northern Ireland, references to the Disqualification Act are to the Company Directors Disqualification (Northern Ireland) Order 2002 and the reference in subsection (3) to section 7(3) of the Disqualification Act is a reference to Article 10(4) of that Order (disqualification order or undertaking; and reporting provisions).

History
Section 90E inserted by the Building Societies (Insolvency and Special Administration) Order 2009 (SI 2009/805) art.6, as from March 29, 2009.

91   Power of court to declare dissolution of building society void

91(1)   Where a building society has been dissolved under section 87 or following a winding up, building society insolvency or building society special administration, the High Court or, in relation to a society whose principal office was in Scotland, the Court of Session, may, at any time within 12 years after the date on which the society was dissolved, make an order under this section declaring the dissolution to have been void.

91(2)   An order under this section may be made, on such terms as the court thinks fit, on an application by the trustees under section 87 or the liquidator, building society liquidator or building society special administrator, as the case may be, or by any other person appearing to the Court to be interested.

91(3)   When an order under this section is made, such proceedings may be taken as might have been taken if the society had not been dissolved.

91(4)   The person on whose application the order is made shall, within seven days of its being so made, or such further time as the Court may allow, furnish the Authority with a copy of the order; and the Authority shall keep the copy in the public file of the society.

91(5)   If a person fails to comply with subsection (4) above, he shall be liable on summary conviction–

    (a)   to a fine not exceeding level 3 on the standard scale, and

    (b)   in the case of a continuing offence, to an additional fine not exceeding £40 for every day during which the offence continues.

History
Section 91(1), (2) amended by the Building Societies (Insolvency and Special Administration) Order 2009 (SI 2009/805) art.8, as from March 29, 2009.

92   Supplementary

92   Where at any time a building society is being wound up or dissolved by consent, or is in building society insolvency or building society special administration, a borrowing member shall not be liable to pay any amount other than one which, at that time, is payable under the mortgage or other security by which his indebtedness to the society in respect of the loan is secured.

History
Section 92 amended by the Building Societies (Insolvency and Special Administration) Order 2009 (SI 2009/805) art.9, as from March 29, 2009.

PART XI

MISCELLANEOUS AND SUPPLEMENTARY AND CONVEYANCING SERVICES

119   Interpretation

119(1)   In this Act, except where the context otherwise requires–

[...]

"building society" means a building society incorporated (or deemed to be incorporated) under this Act;

"building society insolvency", **"building society insolvency order"** and **"building society liquidator"** shall be construed in accordance with Part 2 of the Banking Act 2009 as applied with modifications by section 90C above;

"building society special administration", **"building society special administration order"** and **"building society special administrator"** shall be construed in accordance with Part 3 of the Banking Act 2009 as applied with modifications by section 90C above;

"the Companies Acts" has the meaning given by section 2(1) of the Companies Act 2006;

[...]

History
Definition of "the Companies Acts" inserted by the Companies Act 2006 (Consequential Amendments, Transitional Provisions and Savings) Order 2009 (SI 2009/1941) Sch.1 para.87 as from October 1, 2009.

SCHEDULE 15

APPLICATION OF COMPANIES WINDING UP LEGISLATION TO BUILDING SOCIETIES

Section 90

PART I

GENERAL MODE OF APPLICATION

1   The enactments which comprise the companies winding up legislation (referred to in this Schedule as **"the enactments"**) are the provisions of–

(a)   Parts IV, VI, VII and, XII and XIII of the Insolvency Act 1986, or

(b)   Articles 5 to 8 of Part I and Parts V, VII and XI of the Insolvency (Northern Ireland) Order 1989; or,

in so far as they relate to offences under any such enactment, sections 430 and 432 of, and Schedule 10 to, the Insolvency Act 1986 or Articles 2(6) and 373 of, and Schedule 7 to, the Insolvency (Northern Ireland) Order 1989.

2   Subject to the following provisions of this Schedule, the enactments apply to the winding up of building societies as they apply to the winding up of companies limited by shares and registered under the Companies Act 2006 in England and Wales or Scotland or (as the case may be) in Northern Ireland.

3(1)   The enactments shall, in their application to building societies, have effect with the substitution–

(a)   for "company" of "building society";

(b)   for "the registrar of companies" or "the registrar" of "the Financial Services Authority";

(c)   for "the articles" of "the rules"; and

(d)   for "registered office" of "principal office".

3(2)   In the application of the enactments to building societies–

(aa)   every reference to a company registered in Scotland shall have effect as a reference to a building society whose principal office is situated in Scotland;

(a)   every reference to the officers, or to a particular officer, of a company shall have effect as a reference to the officers, or to the corresponding officer, of the building society and as including a person holding himself out as such an officer; and

(b)   every reference to an administrative receiver shall be omitted.

4(1)   Where any of the enactments as applied to building societies requires a notice or other document to be sent to the Authority, it shall have effect as if it required the Authority to keep the notice or document in the public file of the society concerned and to record in that file the date on which the notice or document is placed in it.

4(2)   Where any of the enactments, as so applied, refers to the registration, or to the date of registration, of such a notice or document, that enactment shall have effect as if it referred to the placing of the notice or document in the public file or (as the case may be) to the date on which it was placed there.

5   Any enactment which specifies a money sum altered by order under section 416 of the Insolvency Act 1986, or, as the case may be, Article 362 of the Insolvency (Northern Ireland) Order 1989, (powers to alter monetary limits) applies with the effect of the alteration.

PART II

MODIFIED APPLICATION OF INSOLVENCY ACT 1986 PARTS IV AND XII

Preliminary

6   In this Part of this Schedule, Part IV of the Insolvency Act 1986 is referred to as "Part IV"; and that Act is referred to as "the Act".

Members of a building society as contributories in winding up

7(1)   Section 74 (liability of members) of the Act is modified as follows.

7(2)   In subsection (1), the reference to any past member shall be omitted.

7(3)   Paragraphs (a) to (d) of subsection (2) shall be omitted; and so shall subsection (3).

7(4)   The extent of the liability of a member of a building society in a winding up shall not exceed the extent of his liability under paragraph 6 of Schedule 2 to this Act.

8   Sections 75 to 78 and 83 in Chapter I of Part IV (miscellaneous provisions not relevant to building societies) do not apply.

9(1)   Section 79 (meaning of "contributory") of the Act does not apply.

9(2)   In the enactments as applied to a building society, **"contributory"**–

    (a)   means every person liable to contribute to the assets of the society in the event of its being wound up, and

    (b)   for the purposes of all proceedings for determining, and all proceedings prior to the determination of, the persons who are to be deemed contributories, includes any person alleged to be a contributory, and

    (c)   includes persons who are liable to pay or contribute to the payment of–

        (i)   any debt or liability of the building society being wound up, or

        (ii)   any sum for the adjustment of rights of members among themselves, or

        (iii)   the expenses of the winding up;

    but does not include persons liable to contribute by virtue of a declaration by the court under section 213 (imputed responsibility for fraudulent trading) or section 214 (wrongful trading) of the Act.

Voluntary winding up

10(1)   Section 84 of the Act does not apply.

10(2)   In the enactments as applied to a building society, the expression **"resolution for voluntary winding up"** means a resolution passed under section 88(1) of this Act.

11 In subsection (1) of section 101 (appointment of liquidation committee) of the Act, the reference to functions conferred on a liquidation committee by or under that Act shall have effect as a reference to its functions by or under that Act as applied to building societies.

12(1) Section 107 (distribution of property) of the Act does not apply; and the following applies in its place.

12(2) Subject to the provisions of Part IV relating to preferential payments, a building society's property in a voluntary winding up shall be applied in satisfaction of the society's liabilities to creditors *pari passu* and, subject to that application, in accordance with the rules of the society.

13 Sections 110 and 111 (liquidator accepting shares, etc. as consideration for sale of company property) of the Act do not apply.

14 Section 116 (saving for certain rights) of the Act shall also apply in relation to the dissolution by consent of a building society as it applies in relation to its voluntary winding up.

Winding up by the court

15 In sections 117 (High Court and county court jurisdiction) and 120 (Court of Session and sheriff court jurisdiction) of the Act, each reference to a company's share capital paid up or credited as paid up shall have effect as a reference to the amount standing to the credit of shares in a building society as shown by the latest balance sheet.

16 Section 122 (circumstances in which company may be wound up by the court) of the Act does not apply.

17 Section 124 (application for winding up) of the Act does not apply.

18(1) In section 125 (powers of court on hearing of petition) of the Act, subsection (1) applies with the omission of the words from "but the court" to the end of the subsection.

18(2) The conditions which the court may impose under section 125 of the Act include conditions for securing–

(a) that the building society be dissolved by consent of its members under section 87, or

(b) that the society amalgamates with, or transfers its engagements to, another building society under section 93 or 94, or

(c) that the society transfers its business to a company under section 97,

and may also include conditions for securing that any default which occasioned the petition be made good and that the costs, or in Scotland the expenses, of the proceedings on that petition be defrayed by the person or persons responsible for the default.

19 Section 126 (power of court, between petition and winding-up order, to stay or restrain proceedings against company) of the Act has effect with the omission of subsection (2).

20 If, before the presentation of a petition for the winding up by the court of a building society, an instrument of dissolution under section 87 is placed in the society's public file, section 129(1) (commencement of winding up by the court) of the Act shall also apply in relation to the date on which the instrument is so placed and to any proceedings in the course of the dissolution as it applies to the commencement date for, and proceedings in, a voluntary winding up.

21(1) Section 130 of the Act (consequences of winding-up order) shall have effect with the following modifications.

21(2) Subsections (1) and (3) shall be omitted.

21(3) A building society shall, within 15 days of a winding-up order being made in respect of it, give notice of the order to the Authority; and the Authority shall keep the notice in the public file of the society.

21(4) If a building society fails to comply with sub-paragraph (3) above, it shall be liable on summary conviction to a fine not exceeding level 3 on the standard scale; and so shall any officer who is also guilty of the offence.

22 Section 140 (appointment of liquidator by court in certain circumstances) of the Act does not apply.

23 In the application of sections 141(1) and 142(1) (liquidation committees), of the Act to building societies, the references to functions conferred on a liquidation committee by or under that Act shall have effect as references to its functions by or under that Act as so applied.

24 The conditions which the court may impose under section 147 (power to stay or sist winding up) of the Act shall include those specified in paragraph 18(2) above.

25 Section 154 (adjustment of rights of contributories) of the Act shall have effect with the modification that any surplus is to be distributed in accordance with the rules of the society.

26 [Repealed by the Companies Act 2006 (Commencement No.3, Consequential Amendments, Transitional Provisions and Savings) Order 2007 SI 2007/2194 (C.84), art.10(1) and Sch.4 para.49(1), as from October 1, 2007.]

Winding up: general

27 Section 187 (power to make over assets to employees) of the Act does not apply.

28(1) In section 201 (dissolution: voluntary winding up) of the Act, subsection (2) applies without the words from "and on the expiration" to the end of the subsection and, in subsection (3), the word "However" shall be omitted.

28(2) Sections 202 to 204 (early dissolution) of the Act do not apply.

29 In section 205 (dissolution: winding up by the court) of the Act, subsection (2) applies with the omission of the words from "and, subject" to the end of the subsection; and in subsections (3) and (4) references to the Secretary of State shall have effect as references to the Authority.

Penal provisions

30 Sections 216 and 217 of the Act (restriction on re-use of name) do not apply.

31(1) Sections 218 and 219 (prosecution of delinquent officers) of the Act do not apply in relation to offences committed by members of a building society acting in that capacity.

31(2) Sections 218(5) of the Act and subsections (1) and (2) of section 219 of the Act do not apply.

31(3) The references in subsections (3) and (4) of section 219 of the Act to the Secretary of State shall have effect as references to the Authority; and the reference in subsection (3) to section 218 of the Act shall have effect as a reference to that section as supplemented by paragraph 32 below.

32(1) Where a report is made to the prosecuting authority (within the meaning of section 218) under section 218(4) of the Act, in relation to an officer of a building society, he may, if he thinks fit, refer the matter to the Authority for further enquiry.

32(2) On such a reference to it the Authority shall exercise its power under section 55(1) of this Act to appoint one or more investigators to investigate and report on the matter.

32(3) An answer given by a person to a question put to him in exercise of the powers conferred by section 55 on a person so appointed may be used in evidence against the person giving it.

33 Section 387 (meaning in Schedule 6 of **"the relevant date"**) of the Act applies with the omission of subsections (2) and (4) to (6).

PART III

MODIFIED APPLICATION OF THE INSOLVENCY (NORTHERN IRELAND) ORDER 1989, PARTS V AND XI

[Not reproduced.]

PART IV

DISSOLUTION OF BUILDING SOCIETY WOUND UP (ENGLAND AND WALES, SCOTLAND AND NORTHERN IRELAND)

56(1) Where a building society has been wound up voluntarily, it is dissolved as from 3 months from the date of the placing in the public file of the society of the return of the final meetings of the society and its creditors made by the liquidator under–

(a) section 94 or (as the case may be) 106 of the Insolvency Act 1986 (as applied to building societies), or on such other date as is determined in accordance with section 201 of that Act, or

(b) Article 80 or (as the case may be) 92 of the Insolvency (Northern Ireland) Order 1989 (as so applied), or on such other date as is determined in accordance with that Article,

as the case may be.

56(2) Where a building society has been wound up by the court, it is dissolved as from 3 months from the date of the placing in the public file of the society of–

(a) the liquidator's notice under section 172(8) of the Insolvency Act 1986 (as applied to building societies), or, as the case may be, Article 146(7) of the Insolvency (Northern Ireland) Order 1989 (as applied to building societies), or

(b) the notice of the completion of the winding up from the official receiver or the official receiver for Northern Ireland for company liquidations,

or on such other date as is determined in accordance with section 205 of that Act or Article 169 of that Order, as the case may be.

57(1) Sections 1012 to 1023 and 1034 of the Companies Act 2006 (property of dissolved company) apply in relation to the property of a dissolved building society (whether dissolved under section 87 or following its winding up) as they apply in relation to the property of a dissolved company.

57(2) Paragraph 3(1) above shall apply to those sections for the purpose of their application to building societies.

57(3) Any reference in those sections to restoration to the register shall be read as a reference to the effect of an order under section 91 of this Act.

57(4) [Omitted.]

History
Paragraph 57(1), (3) substituted and para.57(4) omitted by the Companies Act 2006 (Consequential Amendments, Transitional Provisions and Savings) Order 2009 (SI 2009/1941) art.2(1) and Sch.1 para.87(11)(b), (c) as from October 1, 2009.

Insolvency rules and fees: England and Wales and Scotland

58(1)   Rules may be made under section 411 of the Insolvency Act for the purpose of giving effect, in relation to building societies, to the provisions of the applicable winding up legislation.

58(2)   An order made by the competent authority under section 414 of the Insolvency Act 1986 may make provision for fees to be payable under that section in respect of proceedings under the applicable winding up legislation and the performance by the official receiver or the Secretary of State of functions under it.

Insolvency rules and fees: Northern Ireland

59(1)   Rules may be made under Article 359 the Insolvency (Northern Ireland) Order 1989 for the purpose of giving effect in relation to building societies, to the provisions of the applicable winding up legislation.

59(2)   An order made by the Department of Economic Development under Article 361 of the Insolvency (Northern Ireland) Order 1989 may make provision for fees to be payable under that Article in respect of proceedings under the applicable winding-up legislation and the performance by the official receiver for Northern Ireland or that Department of functions under it.

Schedule 15A

Application of Other Companies Insolvency Legislation to Building Societies

Section 90A

Part I

General Mode of Application

1(1)   Subject to the provisions of this Schedule, the enactments specified in sub-paragraph (2) below (referred to in this Schedule as **"the enactments"**) apply in relation to building societies as they apply in relation to companies limited by shares and registered under the Companies Act 2006 in England and Wales or Scotland or (as the case may be) in Northern Ireland.

1(2)   The enactments referred to in sub-paragraph (1) above are–

    (a)   Parts I (except section 1A) and II, Chapter I of Part III, Parts VI, VII, XII and XIII, section 434 and Part XVIII of the Insolvency Act 1986, or

    (b)   Parts I to IV, VII, XI and XII and Article 378 of the Insolvency (Northern Ireland) Order 1989, and, in so far as they relate to offences under any such enactment, sections 430 and 432 of, and Schedule 10 to, the Insolvency Act 1986 or Article 2(6) and 373 of, and Schedule 7 to, the Insolvency (Northern Ireland) Order 1989.

2(1)   The enactments shall, in their application to building societies, have effect with the substitution–

    (a)   for "company" of "building society";

    (b)   for "the registrar of companies" or "the registrar" of "the Financial Services Authority";

    (c)   for "the articles" of "the rules"; and

    (d)   for "registered office" of "principal office".

2(2)   In the application of the enactments to building societies–

    (aa) every reference to a company registered in Scotland shall have effect as a reference to a building society whose principal office is situated in Scotland;

(a) every reference to the officers, or to a particular officer, of a company shall have effect as a reference to the officers, or to the corresponding officer, of the building society and as including a person holding himself out as such an officer; and

(b) every reference to an administrative receiver shall be omitted.

3(1) Where any of the enactments as applied to building societies requires a notice or other document to be sent to the Authority, it shall have effect as if it required the Authority to keep the notice or document in the public file of the society concerned and to record in that file the date on which the notice or document is placed in it.

3(2) Where any of the enactments, as so applied, refers to the registration, or to the date of registration, of such a notice or document, that enactment shall have effect as if it referred to the placing of the notice or document in the public file or (as the case may be) to the date on which it was placed there.

4(1) Rules may be made under section 411 of the Insolvency Act 1986 or, as the case may be, Article 359 of the Insolvency (Northern Ireland) Order 1989 for the purpose of giving effect, in relation to building societies, to the provisions of the enactments.

4(2) An order made by the competent authority under section 414 of the Insolvency Act 1986 may make provision for fees to be payable under that section in respect of proceedings under the enactments and the performance by the official receiver or the Secretary of State of functions under them.

4(3) An order made by the Department of Economic Development under Article 361 of the Insolvency (Northern Ireland) Order 1989 may make provision for fees to be payable under that Article in respect of proceedings under the enactments and the performance by the official receiver or that Department of functions under them.

5 Any enactment which specifies a money sum altered by order under section 416 of the Insolvency Act 1986, or, as the case may be, Article 362 of the Insolvency (Northern Ireland) Order 1989, (powers to alter monetary limits) applies with the effect of the alteration.

5A In this Schedule, **"scheme manager"** has the same meaning as in the Financial Services and Markets Act 2000.

PART II

MODIFIED APPLICATION OF PARTS I AND II AND CHAPTER I OF PART III OF INSOLVENCY ACT 1986

Preliminary

6 In this Part of this Schedule, the Insolvency Act 1986 is referred to as **"the Act"**.

Voluntary arrangements

7 Section 1 of the Act (proposals for voluntary arrangements) has effect as if–

(a) it required any proposal under Part I of the Act to be so framed as to enable a building society to comply with the requirements of this Act; and

(b) any reference to debts included a reference to liabilities owed to the holders of shares in a building society.

8 In section 2 (procedure where nominee is not liquidator or administrator) and section 3 (summoning of meetings) of the Act as applied to a building society, any reference to a meeting of the society is a reference to–

(a) a meeting of both shareholding and borrowing members of the society; and

(b)   a meeting of shareholding members alone,

and subsection (1) of section 2 shall have effect with the omission of the words from "and the directors" to the end.

8A   In subsection (2) of section 4A of the Act (approval of arrangement) as applied to a building society, paragraph (b) and the word "or" immediately preceding that paragraph are omitted.

9   In section 6 of the Act (challenge of decisions) as applied to a building society, **"contributory"**–

(a)   means every person liable to contribute to the assets of the society in the event of its being wound up, and

(b)   for the purposes of all proceedings for determining, and all proceedings prior to the determination of, the persons who are to be deemed contributories, includes any person alleged to be a contributory, and

(c)   includes persons who are liable to pay or contribute to the payment of–

(i)   any debt or liability of the building society being wound up, or

(ii)   any sum for the adjustment of rights of members among themselves, or

(iii)   the expenses of the winding up;

but does not include persons liable to contribute by virtue of a declaration by the court under section 213 (imputed responsibility for fraudulent trading) or section 214 (wrongful trading) of the Act.

9A   In section 7A of the Act (prosecution of delinquent officers) as applied to a building society–

(a)   in subsection (2), for paragraphs (i) and (ii) there is substituted "the Authority",

(b)   subsections (3) to (7) are omitted,

(c)   in subsection (8), for "Secretary of State" there is substituted "Authority".

Administration orders

10(1)   Section 8 of the Act (power of court to make administration order) has effect as if it included provision that, where–

(a)   an application for an administration order to be made in relation to a building society is made by the Authority (with or without other parties); and

(b)   the society has defaulted in an obligation to pay any sum due and payable in respect of any deposit or share,

the society shall be deemed for the purposes of subsection (1) to be unable to pay its debts.

10(2)   In subsection (3) of that section, paragraph (c) and, in subsection (4) of that section, the words from "nor where" to the end are omitted.

11(1)   Subsection (1) of section 9 of the Act (application for administration order) as applied to a building society has effect as if–

(a)   it enabled an application to the court for an administration order to be by petition presented, with or without other parties, by the Authority or by a shareholding member entitled under section 89(3) of this Act to petition for the winding up of the society; and

(b)   the words from "or by the clerk" to "on companies)" were omitted.

11(2) In subsection (2)(a) of that section as so applied, the reference to any person who has appointed, or is or may be entitled to appoint, an administrative receiver of the society is a reference to the Authority (unless it is a petitioner).

11(3) Subsection (3) of that section, and in subsection (4) of that section, the words "Subject to subsection (3)," are omitted.

12 In section 10 of the Act (effect of application for administration order), the following are omitted, namely–

(a) in subsection (2), paragraphs (b) and (c); and

(b) subsection (3).

13 In section 11 of the Act (effect of administration order), the following are omitted, namely–

(a) in subsection (1), paragraph (b) and the word "and" immediately preceding that paragraph;

(b) in subsection (3), paragraph (b);

(c) in subsection (4), the words "an administrative receiver of the company has vacated office under subsection (1)(b), or"; and

(d) subsection (5).

14 In subsection (1) of section 12 of the Act (notification of administration order), the reference to every invoice, order for goods or business letter is a reference to every statement of account, order for goods or services, business letter or advertisement.

15 Subsection (3) of section 13 of the Act (appointment of administrator) has effect as if it enabled an application for an order under subsection (2) of that section to be made by the Authority.

16(1) Subject to sub-paragraph (2) below, section 14 of the Act (general powers of administrator) has effect as if it required the administrator of a building society, in exercising his powers under that section–

(a) to ensure compliance with the provisions of this Act; and

(b) not to appoint to be a director any person who is not a fit and proper person to hold that position.

16(2) Sub-paragraph (1)(a) above does not apply in relation to section 5, 6 or 7 of this Act.

16(3) In subsection (4) of that section as applied to a building society, the reference to any power conferred by the Act or the Companies Acts or by the company's articles is a reference to any power conferred by this Act or by the society's memorandum or rules.

16(4) [Repealed.]

17(1) Subject to sub-paragraph (3) below, paragraph 16 of Schedule 1 to the Act (powers of administrators) as applied to a building society has effect as if it conferred power to transfer liabilities in respect of deposits with or shares in the society.

17(2) No transfer under that paragraph shall be a transfer of engagements for the purposes of Part X of this Act.

17(3) No transfer under that paragraph which, apart from sub-paragraph (2) above, would be a transfer of engagements for the purposes of that Part shall be made unless it is approved by the court, or by meetings summoned under section 23(1) or 25(2) of the Act (as modified by paragraph 21 or 23 below).

18 In section 15 of the Act (power to deal with charged property etc.)–

(a) subsection (1) is omitted; and

(b) for subsections (3) and (4) there is substituted the following subsection–

   "**(3)** Subsection (2) applies to any security other than one which, as created, was a floating charge."

19(1)   Section 17 of the Act (general duties of administrator) has effect as if, instead of the requirement imposed by subsection (3), it required the administrator of a building society to summon a meeting of the society's creditors if–

(a)   he is requested, in accordance with the rules, to do so by 500 of the society's creditors, or by one-tenth, in number or value, of those creditors, or

(b)   he is directed to do so by the court.

19(2)   That section also has effect as if it required the administrator of a building society to summon a meeting of the society's shareholding members if–

(a)   he is requested, in accordance with the rules, to do so by 500 of the society's shareholding members, or by one-tenth, in number, of those members, or

(b)   he is directed to do so by the court.

20   In subsection (4) of section 19 of the Act (vacation of office) as applied to a building society, the words "in priority to any security to which section 15(1) then applies" are omitted.

21(1)   Subsection (1) of section 23 of the Act (statement of proposals) as applied to a building society has effect as if–

(a)   the reference to the Authority included a reference to the scheme manager;

(b)   the reference to all creditors included a reference to all holders of shares in the society; and

(c)   the reference to a meeting of the society's creditors included a reference to a meeting of holders of shares in the society.

21(2)   In subsection (2) of that section as so applied, references to members of the society do not include references to holders of shares in the society.

22   Section 24 of the Act (consideration of proposals by creditors' meeting) as applied to a building society has effect as if any reference to a meeting of creditors included a reference to a meeting of holders of shares in the society.

23(1)   Section 25 of the Act (approval of substantial revisions) as applied to a building society has effect as if–

(a)   subsection (2) required the administrator to send a statement in the prescribed form of his proposed revisions to the Authority and to the scheme manager; and

(b)   the reference in that subsection to a meeting of creditors included a reference to a meeting of holders of shares in the society.

23(2)   In subsection (3) of that section as so applied, references to members of the society do not include references to holders of shares in the society.

24   Subsection (1) of section 27 of the Act (protection of interests of creditors and members) has effect–

(a)   as if it enabled the Authority or the scheme manager to apply to the court by petition for an order under that section; and

(b)   in relation to an application by the Authority or the scheme manager, as if the words "(including at least himself)" were omitted.

Receivers and managers

25   In section 38 of the Act (receivership accounts), **"prescribed"** means prescribed by regulations made by statutory instrument by the Treasury.

26 In subsection (1) of section 39 of the Act (notification that receiver or manager appointed), the reference to every invoice, order for goods or business letter is a reference to every statement of account, order for goods or services, business letter or advertisement.

27 Section 40 (payment of debts out of assets subject to floating charge) and sections 42 to 49 (administrative receivers) of the Act are omitted.

PART III

MODIFIED APPLICATION OF PARTS II, III AND IV OF INSOLVENCY (NORTHERN IRELAND) ORDER 1989

[Applies to Northern Ireland only; not reproduced.]

Companies Act 1989

(1989 Chapter 40)

ARRANGEMENT OF SECTIONS

An Act to amend the law relating to company accounts; to make new provision with respect to the persons eligible for appointment as company auditors; to amend the Companies Act 1985 and certain other enactments with respect to investigations and powers to obtain information and to confer new powers exercisable to assist overseas regulatory authorities; to make new provision with respect to the registration of company charges and otherwise to amend the law relating to companies; to amend the Fair Trading Act 1973; to enable provision to be made for the payment of fees in connection with the exercise by the Secretary of State, the Director General of Fair Trading and the Monopolies and Mergers Commission of their functions under Part V of that Act; to make provision for safeguarding the operation of certain financial markets; to amend the Financial Services Act 1986; to enable provision to be made for the recording and transfer of title to securities without a written instrument; to amend the Company Directors Disqualification Act 1986, the Company Securities (Insider Dealing) Act 1985, the Policyholders Protection Act 1975 and the law relating to building societies; and for connected purposes.

[*16th November 1989*]

[**Note**: Changes made by the Transfer of Functions (Financial Services) Order 1992 (SI 1992/1315), the Bank of England Act 1998, the Financial Markets and Insolvency Regulations 1998 (SI 1998/1748), the Financial Services and Markets Act 2000 (Consequential Amendments and Repeals) Order 2001 (SI 2001/3649), the Civil Jurisdiction and Judgments Regulations 2007 (SI 2007/1655), the Financial Services and Insolvency Regulations 2009 (SI 2009/853) and the Enterprise Act 2002 have been incorporated into the text (in the case of pre-2003 legislation without annotation). Former references to the Secretary of State have been replaced throughout by references to the Authority (i.e. the Financial Services Authority) and/or the Treasury, and references to the Financial Services Act 1986 by references to the Financial Services and Markets Act 2000, pursuant to the Financial Services and Markets Act 2000 (Consequential Amendments and Repeals) Order 2001 (SI 2001/3649) as from December 1, 2001. Note prospective amendment by TCEA 2007 s.62(3) and Sch.13.]

PART VII

FINANCIAL MARKETS AND INSOLVENCY

Introduction

154 Introduction

154 This Part has effect for the purposes of safeguarding the operation of certain financial markets by provisions with respect to–

(a) the insolvency, winding up or default of a person party to transactions in the market (sections 155 to 172),

(b) the effectiveness or enforcement of certain charges given to secure obligations in connection with such transactions (sections 173 to 176), and

(c) rights and remedies in relation to certain property provided as cover for margin in relation to such transactions or as default fund contribution, or subject to such a charge (sections 177 to 181).

History
Section 154(c) amended by the Financial Markets and Insolvency Regulations 2009 (SI 2009/853) reg.2(1), (2) as from June 15, 2009.

Recognised investment exchanges and clearing houses

155 Market contracts

155(1) [**"Market contracts"**] This Part applies to the following descriptions of contract connected with a recognised investment exchange or recognised clearing house.
  The contracts are referred to in this Part as **"market contracts"**.

155(2) [**Recognised investment exchange**] Except as provided in subsection (2A), in relation to a recognised investment exchange this Part applies to–

(a) contracts entered into by a member or designated non-member of the exchange with a person other than the exchange which are either

  (i) contracts made on the exchange or on an exchange to whose undertaking the exchange has succeeded whether by amalgamation, merger or otherwise; or

  (ii) contracts in the making of which the member or designated non-member was subject to the rules of the exchange or of an exchange to whose undertaking the exchange has succeeded whether by amalgamation, merger or otherwise;

(b) contracts entered into by the exchange, in its capacity as such, with a member of the exchange or with a recognised clearing house or with another recognised investment exchange for the purpose of enabling the rights and liabilities of that member or clearing house or other investment exchange under a transaction to be settled; and

(c) contracts entered into by the exchange with a member of the exchange or with a recognised clearing house or with another recognised investment exchange for the purpose of providing central counterparty clearing services to that member or clearing house or other investment exchange.

A **"designated non-member"** means a person in respect of whom action may be taken under the default rules of the exchange but who is not a member of the exchange.

History
Section 155(2)(b) substituted, and s.155(2)(c) inserted, by the Financial Markets and Insolvency Regulations 2009 (SI 2009/853) reg.2(1), (3)(a) as from June 15, 2009.

155(2A)   [Recognised overseas investment exchange] Where the exchange in question is a recognised overseas investment exchange, this Part does not apply to a contract that falls within paragraph (a) of subsection (2) (unless it also falls within subsection (3)).

History
Section 155(2A) substituted by the Financial Markets and Insolvency Regulations 2009 (SI 2009/853) reg.2(1), (3)(b) as from June 15, 2009.

155(3)   [Recognised clearing house] In relation to a recognised clearing house this Part applies to–

(a) contracts entered into by the clearing house, in its capacity as such, with a member of the clearing house or with a recognised investment exchange or with another recognised clearing house for the purpose of enabling the rights and liabilities of that member or investment exchange or other clearing house under a transaction to be settled; and

(b) contracts entered into by the clearing house with a member of the clearing house or with a recognised investment exchange or with another recognised clearing house for the purpose of providing central counterparty clearing services to that member or investment exchange or other clearing house.

History
Section 155(3) substituted by the Financial Markets and Insolvency Regulations 2009 (SI 2009/853) reg.2(1), (3)(c) as from June 15, 2009.

155(3A)   ["Central counterparty clearing services"] In this section "central counterparty clearing services" means–

(a) the services provided by a recognised investment exchange or a recognised clearing house to the parties to a transaction in connection with contracts between each of the parties and the investment exchange or clearing house (in place of, or as an alternative to, a contract directly between the parties),

(b) the services provided by a recognised clearing house to a recognised investment exchange or to another recognised clearing house in connection with contracts between them, or

(c) the services provided by a recognised investment exchange to a recognised clearing house or to another recognised investment exchange in connection with contracts between them.

History
Section 155(3A) inserted by the Financial Markets and Insolvency Regulations 2009 (SI 2009/853) reg.2(1), (3)(d) as from June 15, 2009.

155(4)   [Regulations] The Secretary of State may by regulations make further provision as to the contracts to be treated as "market contracts", for the purposes of this Part, in relation to a recognised investment exchange or recognised clearing house.

155(5) **[Scope of regulations]** The regulations may add to, amend or repeal the provisions of subsections (2) and (3) above.

156 Additional requirements for recognition: default rules, etc.

156 [Repealed by the Financial Services and Markets Act 2000 (Consequential Amendments and Repeals) Order 2001 (SI 2001/3649) arts 1, 75(e) as from December 1, 2001.]

157 Change in default rules

157(1) **[Notice of proposed amendment]** A recognised UK investment exchange or recognised UK clearing house shall give the Authority at least 14 days' notice of any proposal to amend, revoke or add to its default rules; and the Authority may within 14 days from receipt of the notice direct the exchange or clearing house not to proceed with the proposal, in whole or in part.

157(2) **[Direction]** A direction under this section may be varied or revoked.

157(3) **[Breach of direction]** Any amendment or revocation of, or addition to, the default rules of an exchange or clearing house in breach of a direction under this section is ineffective.

158 Modifications of the law of insolvency

158(1) **[Effect of ss.159–165]** The general law of insolvency has effect in relation to market contracts, and action taken under the rules of a recognised investment exchange or recognised clearing house with respect to such contracts, subject to the provisions of sections 159 to 165.

158(2) **[Relevant insolvency proceedings]** So far as those provisions relate to insolvency proceedings in respect of a person other than a defaulter, they apply in relation to–

(a) proceedings in respect of a recognised investment exchange or a member or designated non-member of a recognised investment exchange,

(aa) proceedings in respect of a recognised clearing house or a member of a recognised clearing house, and

(b) proceedings in respect of a party to a market contract begun after a recognised investment exchange or recognised clearing house has taken action under its default rules in relation to a person party to the contract as principal,

but not in relation to any other insolvency proceedings, notwithstanding that rights or liabilities arising from market contracts fall to be dealt with in the proceedings.

History
Section 158(2)(a) substituted, and s.158(2)(aa) inserted, by the Financial Markets and Insolvency Regulations 2009 (SI 2009/853) reg.2(1), (4) as from June 15, 2009.

158(3) **[Beginning of insolvency proceedings]** The reference in subsection (2)(b) to the beginning of insolvency proceedings is to–

(a) the presentation of a bankruptcy petition or a petition for sequestration of a person's estate, or

(b) the application for an administration order or the presentation of a winding-up petition or the passing of a resolution for voluntary winding up, or

(c) the appointment of an administrative receiver.

History
Section 158(3)(b) substituted by the Enterprise Act 2002 s.248(3) Sch.17 paras 43, 44(a) as from September 15, 2003 (see the Enterprise Act 2002 (Commencement No.4 and Transitional Provisions and Savings) Order 2003 (SI 2003/2093 (C. 85)) art.2(1) Sch.1), subject to transitional provisions in SI 2003/2093 (C. 85) art.3. The amendment has no effect in relation to certain companies by virtue of the Enterprise Act 2002 s.249(1).

158(3A)   [Reference to an application for an administration order in s.158(3)(b)] In subsection (3)(b) the reference to an application for an administration order shall be taken to include a reference to–

(a)   in a case where an administrator is appointed under paragraph 14 or 22 of Schedule B1 to the Insolvency Act 1986 (appointment by floating charge holder, company or directors) following filing with the court of a copy of a notice of intention to appoint under that paragraph, the filing of the copy of the notice, and

(b)   in a case where an administrator is appointed under either of those paragraphs without a copy of a notice of intention to appoint having been filed with the court, the appointment of the administrator.

History
Section 158(3A) inserted by the Enterprise Act 2002 s.248(3) Sch.17 paras 43, 44(b) as from September 15, 2003 (see the Enterprise Act 2002 (Commencement No.4 and Transitional Provisions and Savings) Order 2003 (SI 2003/2093 (C. 85)) art.2(1) Sch.1), subject to transitional provisions in SI 2003/2093 (C. 85) art.3. The amendment has no effect in relation to certain companies by virtue of the Enterprise Act 2002 s.249(1).

158(4)   [Regulations] The Secretary of State may make further provision by regulations modifying the law of insolvency in relation to the matters mentioned in subsection (1).

158(5)   [Scope of regulations] The regulations may add to, amend or repeal the provisions mentioned in subsection (1), and any other provisions of this Part as it applies for the purposes of those provisions, or provide that those provisions have effect subject to such additions, exceptions or adaptations as are specified in the regulations.

159   Proceedings of exchange or clearing house take precedence over insolvency procedures

159(1)   [Matters not invalidated on insolvency] None of the following shall be regarded as to any extent invalid at law on the ground of inconsistency with the law relating to the distribution of the assets of a person on bankruptcy, winding up or sequestration, or in the administration of a company or other body or in the administration of an insolvent estate–

(a)   a market contract,

(b)   the default rules of a recognised investment exchange or recognised clearing house,

(c)   the rules of a recognised investment exchange or recognised clearing house as to the settlement of market contracts not dealt with under its default rules.

159(2)   [Office-holder's powers] The powers of a relevant office-holder in his capacity as such, and the powers of the court under the Insolvency Act 1986 or the Bankruptcy (Scotland) Act 1985 shall not be exercised in such a way as to prevent or interfere with–

(a)   the settlement in accordance with the rules of a recognised investment exchange or recognised clearing house of a market contract not dealt with under its default rules, or

(b)   any action taken under the default rules of such an exchange or clearing house.

This does not prevent a relevant office-holder from afterwards seeking to recover any amount under section 163(4) or 164(4) or prevent the court from afterwards making any such order or decree as is mentioned in section 165(1) or (2) (but subject to subsections (3) and (4) of that section).

159(3)   [Effect of following provisions] Nothing in the following provisions of this Part shall be construed as affecting the generality of the above provisions.

159(4)   [Proof, set-off disallowed] A debt or other liability arising out of a market contract which is the subject of default proceedings may not be proved in a winding up or bankruptcy or in the administration of a company or other body, or in Scotland claimed in a winding up or sequestration or in the administration of a company or other body, until the completion of the default proceedings.

A debt or other liability which by virtue of this subsection may not be proved or claimed shall not be taken into account for the purposes of any set-off until the completion of the default proceedings.

159(4A) **[Proof prior to completion of default proceedings]** However, prior to the completion of default proceedings–

(a) where it appears to the chairman of the meeting of creditors that a sum will be certified under section 162(1) to be payable, subsection (4) shall not prevent any proof or claim including or consisting of an estimate of that sum which has been lodged or, in Scotland, submitted, from being admitted or, in Scotland, accepted, for the purpose only of determining the entitlement of a creditor to vote at a meeting of creditors; and

(b) a creditor whose claim or proof has been lodged and admitted or, in Scotland, submitted and accepted, for the purpose of determining the entitlement of a creditor to vote at a meeting of creditors and which has not been subsequently wholly withdrawn, disallowed or rejected, is eligible as a creditor to be a member of a liquidation committee or, in bankruptcy proceedings in England and Wales or in the administration of a company or other body, a creditors' committee.

159(5) **[Completion of default proceedings]** For the purposes of subsections (4) and (4A) the default proceedings shall be taken to be completed in relation to a person when a report is made under section 162 stating the sum (if any) certified to be due to or from him.

History
Section 159(1), (4), (4A) amended by the Financial Markets and Insolvency Regulations 2009 (SI 2009/853) reg.2(1), (5) as from June 15, 2009.

160 Duty to give assistance for purposes of default proceedings

160(1) **[Assistance reasonably required]** It is the duty of–

(a) any person who has or had control of any assets of a defaulter, and

(b) any person who has or had control of any documents of or relating to a defaulter,

to give a recognised investment exchange or recognised clearing house such assistance as it may reasonably require for the purposes of its default proceedings.

This applies notwithstanding any duty of that person under the enactments relating to insolvency.

160(2) **[Legal professional privilege]** A person shall not under this section be required to provide any information or produce any document which he would be entitled to refuse to provide or produce on grounds of legal professional privilege in proceedings in the High Court or on grounds of confidentiality as between client and professional legal adviser in proceedings in the Court of Session.

160(3) **[Original documents]** Where original documents are supplied in pursuance of this section, the exchange or clearing house shall return them forthwith after the completion of the relevant default proceedings, and shall in the meantime allow reasonable access to them to the person by whom they were supplied and to any person who would be entitled to have access to them if they were still in the control of the person by whom they were supplied.

160(4) **[Office-holder's expenses]** The expenses of a relevant office-holder in giving assistance under this section are recoverable as part of the expenses incurred by him in the discharge of his duties; and he shall not be required under this section to take any action which involves expenses which cannot be so recovered, unless the exchange or clearing house undertakes to meet them.

There shall be treated as expenses of his such reasonable sums as he may determine in respect of time spent in giving the assistance and for the purpose of determining the priority in which his expenses are payable out of the assets, sums in respect of time spent shall be treated as his remuneration and other sums shall be treated as his disbursements or, in Scotland, outlays.

160(5) **[Regulations]** The Secretary of State may by regulations make further provision as to the duties of persons to give assistance to a recognised investment exchange or recognised clearing house for the purposes of its default proceedings, and the duties of the exchange or clearing house with respect to information supplied to it.

The regulations may add to, amend or repeal the provisions of subsections (1) to (4) above.

160(6) **["Document"]** In this section **"document"** includes information recorded in any form.

161 Supplementary provisions as to default proceedings

161(1) **[Dissipation of assets]** If the court is satisfied on an application by a relevant office-holder that a party to a market contract with a defaulter intends to dissipate or apply his assets so as to prevent the office-holder recovering such sums as may become due upon the completion of the default proceedings, the court may grant such interlocutory relief (in Scotland, such interim order) as it thinks fit.

161(2) **[Reserve in respect of claims]** A liquidator, administrator or trustee of a defaulter or, in Scotland, a permanent trustee on the sequestrated estate of the defaulter shall not–

(a)   declare or pay any dividend to the creditors, or

(b)   return any capital to contributories,

unless he has retained what he reasonably considers to be an adequate reserve in respect of any claims arising as a result of the default proceedings of the exchange or clearing house concerned.

161(3) **[Court order]** The court may on an application by a relevant office-holder make such order as it thinks fit altering or dispensing from compliance with such of the duties of his office as are affected by the fact that default proceedings are pending or could be taken, or have been or could have been taken.

161(4) **[Disapplication of Insolvency Act 1986 provisions]** Nothing in section 126, 128, 130, 185 or 285 of, or paragraph 40, 41, 42 or 43 (including those paragraphs as applied by paragraph 44) of Schedule B1 to, the Insolvency Act 1986 (which restrict the taking of certain legal proceedings and other steps), and nothing in any rule of law in Scotland to the like effect as the said section 285, in the Bankruptcy (Scotland) Act 1985 or in the Debtors (Scotland) Act 1987 as to the effect of sequestration, shall affect any action taken by an exchange or clearing house for the purpose of its default proceedings.

History
Section 161(4) amended by the Enterprise Act 2002 s.248(3) and Sch.17 paras 43, 45 and further amended by the Financial Markets and Insolvency Regulations 2009 (SI 2009/853) reg.2(1), (6)(a), (b) as from June 15, 2009. The former amendment has no effect in relation to certain companies by virtue of the Enterprise Act 2002 s.249(1), and so the original wording of s.161(4) continues to apply to them, subject to a minor amendment made by reg.6(c); this now reads "Nothing in section 10, 11, 126, 128, 130, 185 or 285 of the Insolvency Act 1986 [etc.]".

Note
See note after s.182.

162 Duty to report on completion of default proceedings

162(1) **[Report to Authority]** Subject to subsection (1A), a recognised investment exchange or recognised clearing house shall, on the completion of proceedings under its default rules, report to the Authority on its proceedings stating in respect of each creditor or debtor the sum certified by them to be payable from or to the defaulter or, as the case may be, the fact that no sum is payable.

162(1A) **[When report not required]** A recognised overseas investment exchange or recognised overseas clearing house shall not be subject to the obligation under subsection (1) unless it has been notified by the Authority that a report is required for the purpose of insolvency proceedings in any part of the United Kingdom.

162(2) [Report or reports] The exchange or clearing house may make a single report or may make reports from time to time as proceedings are completed with respect to the transactions affecting particular persons.

162(3) [Copy report] The exchange or clearing house shall supply a copy of every report under this section to the defaulter and to any relevant office-holder acting in relation to him or his estate.

162(4) [Publication] When a report under this section is received by the Authority, it shall publish notice of that fact in such manner as it thinks appropriate for bringing the report to the attention of creditors and debtors of the defaulter.

162(5) [Inspection] An exchange or clearing house shall make available for inspection by a creditor or debtor of the defaulter so much of any report by it under this section as relates to the sum (if any) certified to be due to or from him or to the method by which that sum was determined.

162(6) [Fee for copy] Any such person may require the exchange or clearing house, on payment of such reasonable fee as the exchange or clearing house may determine, to provide him with a copy of any part of a report which he is entitled to inspect.

163 Net sum payable on completion of default proceedings

163(1) [Application] The following provisions apply with respect to the net sum certified by a recognised investment exchange or recognised clearing house, upon proceedings under its default rules being duly completed in accordance with this Part, to be payable by or to a defaulter.

163(2) [Debt in England and Wales] If, in England and Wales, a bankruptcy or winding-up or administration order has been made, or a resolution for voluntary winding up has been passed, the debt–

(a) is provable in the bankruptcy or winding up or administration or, as the case may be, is payable to the relevant office-holder, and

(b) shall be taken into account, where appropriate, under section 323 of the Insolvency Act 1986 (mutual dealings and set-off) or the corresponding provision applicable in the case of winding up or administration,

in the same way as a debt due before the commencement of the bankruptcy, the date on which the body corporate goes into liquidation (within the meaning of section 247 of the Insolvency Act 1986), or enters administration or, in the case of a partnership, the date of the winding-up order or the date on which the partnership enters administration.

163(3) [Scotland] If, in Scotland, an award of sequestration or a winding-up or administration order has been made, or a resolution for voluntary winding up has been passed, the debt–

(a) may be claimed in the sequestration, winding up or administration or, as the case may be, is payable to the relevant office-holder, and

(b) shall be taken into account for the purposes of any rule of law relating to set-off applicable in sequestration, winding up or administration,

in the same way as a debt due before the date of sequestration (within the meaning of section 73(1) of the Bankruptcy (Scotland) Act 1985) or the commencement of the winding up (within the meaning of section 129 of the Insolvency Act 1986) or the date on which the body corporate enters administration.

163(3A) [Making of an administration order in s.163(2), (3)] In subsections (2) and (3), a reference to the making of an administration order shall be taken to include a reference to the appointment of an administrator under–

(a) paragraph 14 of Schedule B1 to the Insolvency Act 1986 (appointment by holder of qualifying floating charge); or

(b) paragraph 22 of that Schedule (appointment by company or directors).

163(4) **[Notice]** However, where (or to the extent that) a sum is taken into account by virtue of subsection (2)(b) or (3)(b) which arises from a contract entered into at a time when the creditor had notice–

(a) that a bankruptcy petition or, in Scotland, a petition for sequestration was pending,

(b) that a meeting of creditors had been summoned under section 98 of the Insolvency Act 1986 or that a winding-up petition was pending, or

(c) that an application for an administration order was pending or that any person had given notice of intention to appoint an administrator,

the value of any profit to him arising from the sum being so taken into account (or being so taken into account to that extent) is recoverable from him by the relevant office-holder unless the court directs otherwise.

163(5) **[Non-application of s.163(4)]** Subsection (4) does not apply in relation to a sum arising from a contract effected under the default rules of a recognised investment exchange or recognised clearing house.

163(6) **[Priority]** Any sum recoverable by virtue of subsection (4) ranks for priority, in the event of the insolvency of the person from whom it is due, immediately before preferential or, in Scotland, preferred debts.

History
Section 163(2), (3) amended, and s.163(3A), (4)(c) inserted, by the Financial Markets and Insolvency Regulations 2009 (SI 2009/853) reg.2(1), (7) as from June 15, 2009.

Note
See note after s.182.

164 Disclaimer of property, rescission of contracts, etc.

164(1) **[Disapplication of Insolvency Act 1986 ss.178, 186, 315, 345]** Sections 178, 186, 315 and 345 of the Insolvency Act 1986 (power to disclaim onerous property and court's power to order rescission of contracts, etc.) do not apply in relation to–

(a) a market contract, or

(b) a contract effected by the exchange or clearing house for the purpose of realising property provided as margin in relation to market contracts or as default fund contribution.

In the application of this subsection in Scotland, the reference to sections 178, 315 and 345 shall be construed as a reference to any rule of law having the like effect as those sections.

164(2) **[Scotland]** In Scotland, a permanent trustee on the sequestrated estate of a defaulter or a liquidator is bound by any market contract to which that defaulter is a party and by any contract as is mentioned in subsection (1)(b) above notwithstanding section 42 of the Bankruptcy (Scotland) Act 1985 or any rule of law to the like effect applying in liquidations.

164(3) **[Disapplication of Insolvency Act 1986 ss.127, 284]** Sections 127 and 284 of the Insolvency Act 1986 (avoidance of property dispositions effected after commencement of winding up or presentation of bankruptcy petition), and section 32(8) of the Bankruptcy (Scotland) Act 1985 (effect of dealing with debtor relating to estate vested in permanent trustee), do not apply to–

(a) a market contract, or any disposition of property in pursuance of such a contract,

(b) the provision of margin in relation to market contracts, (ba) the provision of default fund contribution to the exchange or clearing house,

(c) a contract effected by the exchange or clearing house for the purpose of realising property provided as margin in relation to a market contract or as default fund contribution, or any disposition of property in pursuance of such a contract, or

(d) any disposition of property in accordance with the rules of the exchange or clearing house as to the application of property provided as margin or as default fund contribution.

164(4)   [Notice] However, where–

(a) a market contract is entered into by a person who has notice that a petition has been presented for the winding up or bankruptcy or sequestration of the estate of the other party to the contract, or

(b) margin in relation to a market contract or default fund contribution is accepted by a person who has notice that such a petition has been presented in relation to the person by whom or on whose behalf the margin or default fund contribution is provided,

the value of any profit to him arising from the contract or, as the case may be, the amount or value of the margin or default fund contribution is recoverable from him by the relevant office-holder unless the court directs otherwise.

164(5)   [Non-application of s.164(4)] Subsection (4)(a) does not apply where the person entering into the contract is a recognised investment exchange or recognised clearing house acting in accordance with its rules, or where the contract is effected under the default rules of such an exchange or clearing house; but subsection (4)(b) applies in relation to the provision of margin in relation to such a contract or of default fund contribution.

164(6)   [Priority] Any sum recoverable by virtue of subsection (4) ranks for priority, in the event of the insolvency of the person from whom it is due, immediately before preferential or, in Scotland, preferred debts.

History
Section 164(1), (3), (4), (5) amended by the Financial Markets and Insolvency Regulations 2009 (SI 2009/853) reg.2(1), (8) as from June 15, 2009.

Note
See note after s.182.

165   Adjustment of prior transactions

165(1)   [Disapplication of Insolvency Act 1986 provisions] No order shall be made in relation to a transaction to which this section applies under–

(a) section 238 or 339 of the Insolvency Act 1986 (transactions at an under-value),

(b) section 239 or 340 of that Act (preferences), or

(c) section 423 of that Act (transactions defrauding creditors).

165(2)   [Scotland] As respects Scotland, no decree shall be granted in relation to any such transaction–

(a) under section 34 or 36 of the Bankruptcy (Scotland) Act 1985 or section 242 or 243 of the Insolvency Act 1986 (gratuitous alienations and unfair preferences), or

(b) at common law on grounds of gratuitous alienations or fraudulent preferences.

165(3)   [Application] This section applies to–

(a) a market contract to which a recognised investment exchange or recognised clearing house is a party or which is entered into under its default rules, and

(b) a disposition of property in pursuance of such a market contract.

165(4) **[Margin]** Where margin is provided in relation to a market contract and (by virtue of subsection (3)(a) or otherwise) no such order or decree as is mentioned in subsection (1) or (2) has been, or could be, made in relation to that contract, this section applies to–

(a) the provision of the margin,

(b) any contract effected by the exchange or clearing house in question for the purpose of realising the property provided as margin, and

(c) any disposition of property in accordance with the rules of the exchange or clearing house in question as to the application of property provided as margin.

165(5) **[Further application]** This section also applies to–

(a) the provision of default fund contribution to a recognised investment exchange or recognised clearing house,

(b) any contract effected by a recognised investment exchange or recognised clearing house for the purpose of realising the property provided as default fund contribution, and

(c) any disposition of property in accordance with the rules of the recognised investment exchange or recognised clearing house as to the application of property provided as default fund contribution.

History
Section 165(4)(c) amended, and s.165(5) inserted, by the Financial Markets and Insolvency Regulations 2009 (SI 2009/853) reg.2(1), (9) as from June 15, 2009.

166   Powers of Secretary of State to give directions

166(1) **[Application]** The powers conferred by this section are exercisable in relation to a recognised UK investment exchange or recognised UK clearing house.

166(2) **[No action under default rules]** Where in any case an exchange or clearing house has not taken action under its default rules–

(a) if it appears to the Authority that it could take action, the Authority may direct it to do so, and

(b) if it appears to the Authority that it is proposing to take or may take action, the Authority may direct it not to do so.

166(3) **[Consultation]** Before giving such a direction the Authority shall consult the exchange or clearing house in question; and it shall not give a direction unless it is satisfied, in the light of that consultation–

(a) in the case of a direction to take action, that failure to take action would involve undue risk to investors or other participants in the market, or

(b) in the case of a direction not to take action, that the taking of action would be premature or otherwise undesirable in the interests of investors or other participants in the market.

166(4) **[Direction]** A direction shall specify the grounds on which it is given.

166(5) **[Duration of direction]** A direction not to take action may be expressed to have effect until the giving of a further direction (which may be a direction to take action or simply revoking the earlier direction).

166(6) **[Effect of insolvency]** No direction shall be given not to take action if, in relation to the person in question–

(a) a bankruptcy order or an award of sequestration of his estate has been made, or an interim receiver or interim trustee has been appointed, or

(b)   a winding up order has been made, a resolution for voluntary winding up has been passed or an administrator, administrative receiver or provisional liquidator has been appointed;

and any previous direction not to take action shall cease to have effect on the making or passing of any such order, award or appointment.

166(7)   **[Action under default rules]** Where an exchange or clearing house has taken or been directed to take action under its default rules, the Authority may direct it to do or not to do such things (being things which it has power to do under its default rules) as are specified in the direction.

The Authority shall not give such a direction unless it is satisfied that the direction will not impede or frustrate the proper and efficient conduct of the default proceedings.

166(8)   **[Enforcement]** A direction under this section is enforceable, on the application of the Authority, by injunction or, in Scotland, by an order under section 45 of the Court of Session Act 1988; and where an exchange or clearing house has not complied with a direction, the court may make such order as it thinks fit for restoring the position to what it would have been if the direction had been complied with.

Note
See note after s.167.

167   Application to determine whether default proceedings to be taken

167(1)   **[Application]** This section applies where a relevant insolvency event has occurred in the case of–

(a)   a recognised investment exchange or a member or designated non-member of a recognised investment exchange, or

(b)   a recognised clearing house or a member of a recognised clearing house.

The investment exchange, member, designated non-member or clearing house in whose case a relevant insolvency event has occurred is referred to below as **"the person in default"**.

167(1A)   **["Relevant insolvency event"]** For the purposes of this section a "relevant insolvency event" occurs where–

(a)   a bankruptcy order is made,

(b)   an award of sequestration is made,

(c)   an order appointing an interim receiver is made,

(d)   an administration or winding up order is made,

(e)   an administrator is appointed under paragraph 14 of Schedule B1 to the Insolvency Act 1986 (appointment by holder of qualifying floating charge) or under paragraph 22 of that Schedule (appointment by company or directors),

(f)   a resolution for voluntary winding up is passed, or

(g)   an order appointing a provisional liquidator is made.

167(1B)   **[Application by office-holder]** Where in relation to a person in default a recognised investment exchange or a recognised clearing house ("the responsible exchange or clearing house")–

(a)   has power under its default rules to take action in consequence of the relevant insolvency event or the matters giving rise to it, but

(b)   has not done so,

a relevant office-holder appointed in connection with or in consequence of the relevant insolvency event may apply to the Authority.

History
Section 167(1A) inserted by the Enterprise Act 2002 s.248(3), Sch.17 paras 43, 46 as from September 15, 2003 subject to transitional provisions in SI 2003/2093 (C. 85) art.3. The amendment has no effect in relation to certain companies by virtue of the Enterprise Act 2002 s.249(1). Section 167(1), (1A) amended, and s.167(1B) inserted, by the Financial Markets and Insolvency Regulations 2009 (SI 2009/853) reg.2(1), (10)(a) as from June 15, 2009.

167(2) **[Contents of application]** The application shall specify the responsible exchange or clearing house and the grounds on which it is made.

167(3) **[Authority's duty]** On receipt of the application the Authority shall notify the responsible exchange or clearing house, and unless within three business days after the day on which the notice is received the responsible exchange or clearing house–

(a)   takes action under its default rules, or

(b)   notifies the Authority that it proposes to do so forthwith,

then, subject as follows, the provisions of sections 158 to 165 above do not apply in relation to market contracts to which the person in default is a party or to anything done by the responsible exchange or clearing house for the purposes of, or in connection with, the settlement of any such contract.

For this purpose a **"business day"** means any day which is not a Saturday or Sunday, Christmas Day, Good Friday or a bank holiday in any part of the United Kingdom under the Banking and Financial Dealings Act 1971.

167(4) **[Application of ss.158–165]** The provisions of sections 158 to 165 are not disapplied if before the end of the period mentioned in subsection (3) the Authority gives the responsible exchange or clearing house a direction under section l66(2)(a) (direction to take action under default rules).

No such direction may be given after the end of that period.

167(5) **[Enforcement]** If the responsible exchange or clearing house notifies the Authority that it proposes to take action under its default rules forthwith, it shall do so; and that duty is enforceable, on the application of the Authority, by injunction or, in Scotland, by an order under section 45 of the Court of Session Act 1988.

History
Section 167(2)–(5) amended by the Financial Markets and Insolvency Regulations 2009 (SI 2009/853) reg.2(1), (10)(b)–(d) as from June 15, 2009.

168   Delegation of functions to designated agency

168   [Repealed by the Financial Services and Markets Act 2000 (Consequential Amendments and Repeals) Order 2001 (SI 2001/3649) arts 1, 75(f) as from December 1, 2001.]

169   Supplementary provisions

169(1)   [Repealed by the Financial Services and Markets Act 2000 (Consequential Amendments and Repeals) Order 2001 (SI 2001/3649) arts 1, 75(g) as from December 1, 2001.]

169(2)   **[Application of ss.296, 297 of Financial Services and Markets Act 2000]** Sections 296 and 297 of the Financial Services and Markets Act 2000 apply in relation to a failure by a recognised investment exchange or recognised clearing house to comply with an obligation under this Part as to a failure to comply with an obligation under that Act.

History
In s.169(2) the words "Sections 296 and 297 of the Financial Services and Markets Act 2000 apply" substituted by the Financial Services and Markets Act 2000 (Consequential Amendments and Repeals) Order 2001 (SI 2001/3649) arts 1, 83(1), (2) as from December 1, 2001.

169(3)   **[Revocation of recognition]** Where the recognition of an investment exchange or clearing house is revoked under the Financial Services and Markets Act 2000, the appropriate authority may, before or after the revocation order, give such directions as it thinks fit with respect to the continued application of the provisions of this Part, with such exceptions, additions and adaptations as may be specified in the direction, in relation to cases where a relevant event of any description specified in the directions occurred before the revocation order takes effect.

169(3A) **["The appropriate authority"]** **"The appropriate authority"** means–

(a)   in the case of an overseas investment exchange or clearing house, the Treasury; and

(b)   in the case of a UK investment exchange or clearing house, the Authority.

169(4)   [Repealed by the Financial Services and Markets Act 2000 (Consequential Amendments and Repeals) Order 2001 (SI 2001/3649) arts 1, 75(g) as from December 1, 2001.]

169(5)   **[Application of s.414 regulations]** Regulations under section 414 of the Financial Services and Markets Act 2000 (service of notices) may make provision in relation to a notice, direction or other document required or authorised by or under this Part to be given to or served on any person other than the Treasury or the Authority.

Other exchanges and clearing houses

170   Certain overseas exchanges and clearing houses

170(1)   **[Regulations]** The Secretary of State and the Treasury may by regulations provide that this Part applies in relation to contracts connected with an overseas investment exchange or overseas clearing house which–

(a)   is not a recognised investment exchange or recognised clearing house, but

(b)   is approved by the Treasury in accordance with such requirements as may be so specified,

as it applies in relation to contracts connected with a recognised investment exchange or recognised clearing house.

History
Section 170(1) substituted by the Financial Markets and Insolvency Regulations 2009 (SI 2009/853) reg.2(1), (11) as from June 15, 2009.

170(2)   **[Approval by Treasury]** The Treasury shall not approve an overseas investment exchange or clearing house unless they are satisfied–

(a)   that the rules and practices of the body, together with the law of the country in which the body's head office is situated, provide adequate procedures for dealing with the default of persons party to contracts connected with the body, and

(b)   that it is otherwise appropriate to approve the body.

170(3)   **[Section 170(2)(a) default]** The reference in subsection (2)(a) to default is to a person being unable to meet his obligations.

170(4)   **[Application of Financial Services and Markets Act]** The regulations may apply in relation to the approval of a body under this section such of the provisions of the Financial Services and Markets Act 2000 as the Secretary of State considers appropriate.

170(5)   **[Scope of regulations]** The Secretary of State may make regulations which, in relation to a body which is so approved–

(a)   apply such of the provisions of the Financial Services and Markets Act 2000 as the Secretary of State considers appropriate, and

(b)   provide that the provisions of this Part apply with such exceptions, additions and adaptations as appear to the Secretary of State to be necessary or expedient;

and different provision may be made with respect to different bodies or descriptions of body.

170(6) **[Modification of Financial Services Act 2000 provisions]** Where the regulations apply any provisions of the Financial Services Act 2000, they may provide that those provisions apply with such exceptions, additions and adaptations as appear to the Secretary of State to be necessary or expedient.

Note
Section 170 not in force with rest of Part.

171 Certain money market institutions

171 [Repealed by the Financial Services and Markets Act 2000 (Consequential Amendments and Repeals) Order 2001 (SI 2001/3649) arts 1, 75(h) as from December 1, 2001.]

172 Settlement arrangements provided by the Bank of England

172(1) **[Regulations]** The Secretary of State may by regulations provide that this Part applies to contracts of any specified description in relation to which settlement arrangements are provided by the Bank of England, as it applies to contracts connected with a recognised investment exchange or recognised clearing house.

172(2) **[Modification of provisions]** Regulations under this section may provide that the provisions of this Part apply with such exceptions, additions and adaptations as appear to the Secretary of State to be necessary or expedient.

172(3) **[Consultation]** Before making any regulations under this section, the Secretary of State and the Treasury shall consult the Bank of England.

Note
Section 172 not in force with rest of Part.

Market charges

173 Market charges

173(1) **["Market charge"]** In this Part **"market charge"** means a charge, whether fixed or floating, granted–

(a) in favour of a recognised investment exchange, for the purpose of securing debts or liabilities arising in connection with the settlement of market contracts;

(aa) in favour of The Stock Exchange, for the purpose of securing debts or liabilities arising in connection with short term certificates;

(b) in favour of a recognised clearing house, for the purpose of securing debts or liabilities arising in connection with their ensuring the performance of market contracts; or

(c) in favour of a person who agrees to make payments as a result of the transfer or allotment of specified securities made through the medium of a computer-based system established by the Bank of England and The Stock Exchange, for the purpose of securing debts or liabilities of the transferee or allottee arising in connection therewith.

173(2) **[Specified purposes]** Where a charge is granted partly for purposes specified in subsection (1)(a), (aa), (b) or (c) and partly for other purposes, it is a "market charge" so far as it has effect for the specified purposes.

173(3) **[Definitions]** In subsection (1)–

"short term certificate" means an instrument issued by The Stock Exchange undertaking to procure the transfer of property of a value and description specified in the instrument to or to the order of the person to whom the instrument is issued or his endorsee or to a person acting on behalf of either of them and also undertaking to make appropriate payments in cash, in the event that the obligation to procure the transfer of property cannot be discharged in whole or in part; "**specified securities**" means securities for the time being specified in the list in Schedule 1 to the Stock Transfer Act 1982, and includes any right to such securities; and "**transfer**", in relation to any such securities or right, means a transfer of the beneficial interest.

173(4)   [Regulations] The Secretary of State may by regulations make further provision as to the charges granted in favour of any such person as is mentioned in subsection (1)(a), (b) or (c) which are to be treated as "market charges" for the purposes of this Part; and the regulations may add to, amend or repeal the provisions of subsections (1) to (3) above.

173(5)   [Scope of regulations] The regulations may provide that a charge shall or shall not be treated as a market charge if or to the extent that it secures obligations of a specified description, is a charge over property of a specified description or contains provisions of a specified description.

173(6)   [Consultation] Before making regulations under this section in relation to charges granted in favour of a person within subsection (1)(c), the Secretary of State and the Treasury shall consult the Bank of England.

174   Modifications of the law of insolvency

174(1)   [Application] The general law of insolvency has effect in relation to market charges and action taken in enforcing them subject to the provisions of section 175.

174(2)   [Regulations] The Secretary of State may by regulations make further provision modifying the law of insolvency in relation to the matters mentioned in subsection (1).

174(3)   [Scope of regulations] The regulations may add to, amend or repeal the provisions mentioned in subsection (1), and any other provision of this Part as it applies for the purposes of those provisions, or provide that those provisions have effect with such exceptions, additions or adaptations as are specified in the regulations.

174(4)   [Different provision for different cases] The regulations may make different provision for cases defined by reference to the nature of the charge, the nature of the property subject to it, the circumstances, nature or extent of the obligations secured by it or any other relevant factor.

174(5)   [Consultation] Before making regulations under this section in relation to charges granted in favour of a person within section 173(1)(c), the Secretary of State and the Treasury shall consult the Bank of England.

175   Administration orders, etc.

175(1)   [Disapplication of Insolvency Act 1986 Sch.B1 paras 43(2), (3), 70–72] The following provisions of Schedule B1 to the Insolvency Act 1986 (administration) do not apply in relation to a market charge–

(a)   paragraph 43(2) and (3) (restriction on enforcement of security or repossession of goods) (including that provision as applied by paragraph 44 (interim moratorium)), and

(b)   paragraphs 70, 71 and 72 (power of administrator to deal with charged or hire-purchase property).

175(1A)   [Disapplication of Insolvency Act 1986 Sch.B1 para.41(2)] Paragraph 41(2) of that Schedule (receiver to vacate office at request of administrator) does not apply to a receiver appointed under a market charge.

175(2)   [Enforcing market charge] However, where a market charge falls to be enforced after the occurrence of an event to which subsection (2A) applies, and there exists another charge over some or all of the same property ranking in priority to or *pari passu* with the market charge, on the application of any person interested the court may order that there shall be taken after enforcement of the market charge such steps as the court may direct for the purpose of ensuring that the chargee under the other charge is not prejudiced by the enforcement of the market charge.

175(2A)   [Application of s.175(2A)] This subsection applies to–

(a) making an administration application under paragraph 12 of Schedule B1 to the Insolvency Act 1986,

(b) appointing an administrator under paragraph 14 or 22 of that Schedule (appointment by floating charge holder, company or directors),

(c) filing with the court a copy of notice of intention to appoint an administrator under either of those paragraphs.

175(3)   [Disapplication of Insolvency Act 1986 ss.43, 61] The following provisions of the Insolvency Act 1986 (which relate to the powers of receivers) do not apply in relation to a market charge–

(a) section 43 (power of administrative receiver to dispose of charged property), and

(b) section 61 (power of receiver in Scotland to dispose of an interest in property).

175(4)   [Disposition of property] Sections 127 and 284 of the Insolvency Act 1986 (avoidance of property dispositions effected after commencement of winding up or presentation of bankruptcy petition), and section 32(8) of the Bankruptcy (Scotland) Act 1985 (effect of dealing with debtor relating to estate vested in permanent trustee), do not apply to a disposition of property as a result of which the property becomes subject to a market charge or any transaction pursuant to which that disposition is made.

175(5)   [Notice] However, if a person (other than the chargee under the market charge) who is party to a disposition mentioned in subsection (4) has notice at the time of the disposition that a petition has been presented for the winding up or bankruptcy or sequestration of the estate of the party making the disposition, the value of any profit to him arising from the disposition is recoverable from him by the relevant office-holder unless the court directs otherwise.

175(6)   [Priority] Any sum recoverable by virtue of subsection (5) ranks for priority, in the event of the insolvency of the person from whom it is due, immediately before preferential or, in Scotland, preferred debts.

175(7)   [Application of s.164(4)] In a case falling within both subsection (4) above (as a disposition of property as a result of which the property becomes subject to a market charge) and section 164(3) (as the provision of margin in relation to a market contract), section 164(4) applies with respect to the recovery of the amount or value of the margin and subsection (5) above does not apply.

History
Section 175(1), (1A) substituted, s.175(2) amended, and s.175(2A) inserted, by the Enterprise Act 2002 s.248(3) and Sch.17 paras 43, 47 as from September 15, 2003 (see the Enterprise Act 2002 (Commencement No.4 and Transitional and Savings) Order 2003 (SI 2003/2093 (C. 85) art.2(1) and Sch.1), subject to transitional provisions in SI 2003/2093 (C. 85) art.3. The amendments have no effect in relation to certain companies by virtue of the Enterprise Act 2002 s.249(1), and so the original wording of s.175 continues to apply to them (as amended, however, by the Financial Markets and Insolvency Regulations 2009 (SI 2009/853) reg.2(1), (12) as from June 15, 2009). Section 175(1) for this purpose now reads:

"(1) The following provisions of the Insolvency Act 1986 (which relate to administration orders and administrators) do not apply in relation to a market charge–

(a) sections 10 and 11 (effect of application for administration order and of an administration order), and

(b) section 15(1), (2) and (3) (power of administrator to deal with charged property)."

Note
Re s.175(2), (5) see Act of Sederunt (Applications under Part VII of the Companies Act 1989) 1991 (SI 1991/145 (S 10)).
    See also note after s.182.

176   Power to make provision about certain other charges

176(1)   [Regulations] The Secretary of State may by regulations provide that the general law of insolvency has effect in relation to charges of such descriptions as may be specified in the regulations, and action taken in enforcing them, subject to such provisions as may be specified in the regulations.

176(2)   [Kinds of charge] The regulations may specify any description of charge granted in favour of–

(a)   a body approved under section 170 (certain overseas exchanges and clearing houses),

(b)   a person included in the list maintained by the Authority for the purposes of section 301 of the Financial Services and Markets Act 2000 (certain money market institutions),

(c)   the Bank of England,

(d)   a person who has permission under Part 4 of the Financial Services and Markets Act 2000 to carry on a relevant regulated activity, or

(e)   an international securities self-regulating organisation approved for the purposes of an order made under section 22 of the Financial Services and Markets Act 2000,

for the purpose of securing debts or liabilities arising in connection with or as a result of the settlement of contracts or the transfer of assets, rights or interests on a financial market.

176(3)   [Other charges] The regulations may specify any description of charge granted for that purpose in favour of any other person in connection with exchange facilities or clearing services provided by a recognised investment exchange or recognised clearing house or by any such body, person, authority or organisation as is mentioned in subsection (2).

176(4)   [Where charge granted partly for s.176(2) purpose] Where a charge is granted partly for the purpose specified in subsection (2) and partly for other purposes, the power conferred by this section is exercisable in relation to the charge so far as it has effect for that purpose.

176(5)   [Scope of regulations] The regulations may–

(a)   make the same or similar provision in relation to the charges to which they apply as is made by or under sections 174 and 175 in relation to market charges, or

(b)   apply any of those provisions with such exceptions, additions or adaptations as are specified in the regulations.

176(6)   [Consultation] Before making regulations under this section relating to a description of charges defined by reference to their being granted in favour of a person included in the list maintained by the Authority for the purposes of section 301 of the Financial Services and Markets Act 2000, or in connection with exchange facilities or clearing services provided by a person included in that list, the Secretary of State and the Treasury shall consult the Authority and the Bank of England.

176(6A)   [Consultation] Before making regulations under this section relating to a description of charges defined by reference to their being granted in favour of the Bank of England, or in connection with settlement arrangements provided by the Bank, the Secretary of State and the Treasury shall consult the Bank.

176(7)   [Further provisions] Regulations under this section may provide that they apply or do not apply to a charge if or to the extent that it secures obligations of a specified description, is a charge over property of a specified description or contains provisions of a specified description.

176(8) **["Relevant regulated activity" in s.176(2)(d)]** For the purposes of subsection (2)(d), **"relevant regulated activity"** means–

(a) dealing in investments as principal or as agent;

(b) arranging deals in investments;

(ba) operating a multilateral trading facility;

(c) managing investments;

(d) safeguarding and administering investments;

(e) sending dematerialised instructions; or

(f) establishing etc. a collective investment scheme.

176(9) **[Provisions s.176(8) to be read with]** Subsection (8) must be read with–

(a) section 22 of the Financial Services and Markets Act 2000;

(b) any relevant order under that section; and

(c) Schedule 2 to that Act.

Market property

177 Application of margin or default fund contribution not affected by certain other interests

177(1) **[Property held as margin or default fund contribution]** The following provisions have effect with respect to the application by a recognised investment exchange or recognised clearing house of property (other than land) held by the exchange or clearing house as margin in relation to a market contract or as default fund contribution.

177(2) **[Prior interest]** So far as necessary to enable the property to be applied in accordance with the rules of the exchange or clearing house, it may be so applied notwithstanding any prior equitable interest or right, or any right or remedy arising from a breach of fiduciary duty, unless the exchange or clearing house had notice of the interest, right or breach of duty at the time the property was provided as margin or as default fund contribution.

177(3) **[Subsequent right]** No right or remedy arising subsequently to the property being provided as margin or as default fund contribution may be enforced so as to prevent or interfere with the application of the property by the exchange or clearing house in accordance with its rules.

177(4) **[Disponee]** Where an exchange or clearing house has power by virtue of the above provisions to apply property notwithstanding an interest, right or remedy, a person to whom the exchange or clearing house disposes of the property in accordance with its rules takes free from that interest, right or remedy.

History
Section 177 amended by the Financial Markets and Insolvency Regulations 2009 (SI 2009/853) reg.2(1), (13) as from June 15, 2009.

178 Priority of floating market charge over subsequent charges

178(1) **[Regulations]** The Secretary of State may by regulations provide that a market charge which is a floating charge has priority over a charge subsequently created or arising, including a fixed charge.

178(2) **[Different provision for different cases]** The regulations may make different provision for cases defined, as regards the market charge or the subsequent charge, by reference to the description of charge, its terms, the circumstances in which it is created or arises, the nature of the charge, the person in favour of whom it is granted or arises or any other relevant factor.

Note
Section 178 not in force with rest of Part.

179 Priority of market charge over unpaid vendor's lien

179 Where property subject to an unpaid vendor's lien becomes subject to a market charge, the charge has priority over the lien unless the chargee had actual notice of the lien at the time the property became subject to the charge.

180 Proceedings against market property by unsecured creditors

180(1) **[No legal proceedings]** Where property (other than land) is held by a recognised investment exchange or recognised clearing house as margin in relation to market contracts or as default fund contribution or is subject to a market charge, no execution or other legal process for the enforcement of a judgment or order may be commenced or continued, and no distress may be levied, against the property by a person not seeking to enforce any interest in or security over the property, except with the consent of–

    (a) in the case of property provided as cover for margin or as default fund contribution, the investment exchange or clearing house in question, or

    (b) in the case of property subject to a market charge, the person in whose favour the charge was granted.

180(2) **[Consent]** Where consent is given the proceedings may be commenced or continued notwithstanding any provision of the Insolvency Act 1986 or the Bankruptcy (Scotland) Act 1985.

180(3) **[Limit on ancillary relief]** Where by virtue of this section a person would not be entitled to enforce a judgment or order against any property, any injunction or other remedy granted with a view to facilitating the enforcement of any such judgment or order shall not extend to that property.

180(4) **[Scotland]** In the application of this section to Scotland, the reference to execution being commenced or continued includes a reference to diligence being carried out or continued, and the reference to distress being levied shall be omitted.

History
Section 180(1) amended by the Financial Markets and Insolvency Regulations 2009 (SI 2009/853) reg.2(1), (14) as from June 15, 2009.

[Note prospective amendment of s.180(1) by the Tribunals, Courts and Enforcement Act 2007 s.62(3) and Sch.13 para.91.]

181 Power to apply provisions to other cases

181(1) **[Power to apply ss.177–180]** A power to which this subsection applies includes the power to apply sections 177 to 180 to any description of property provided as cover for margin in relation to contracts in relation to which the power is exercised or, as the case may be, property subject to charges in relation to which the power is exercised.

History
In s.181(1) the words "A power to which this subsection applies includes the" substituted by the Financial Services and Markets Act 2000 (Consequential Amendments and Repeals) Order 2001 (SI 2001/3649) arts 1, 86(1), (2) as from December 1, 2001.

181(2) **[Modification of ss.177–180 by regulations]** The regulations may provide that those sections apply with such exceptions, additions and adaptations as may be specified in the regulations.

181(3) **[Application of s.181(1)]** Subsection (1) applies to the powers of the Secretary of State and the Treasury to act jointly under–

(a)   sections 170, 172 and 176 of this Act; and

(b)   section 301 of the Financial Services and Markets Act 2000 (supervision of certain contracts).

Supplementary provisions

182   Powers of court in relation to certain proceedings begun before commencement

182(1)   [Relevant persons] The powers conferred by this section are exercisable by the court where insolvency proceedings in respect of–

(a)   a member of a recognised investment exchange or a recognised clearing house, or

(b)   a person by whom a market charge has been granted,

are begun on or after 22nd December 1988 and before the commencement of this section.

That person is referred to in this section as **"the relevant person"**.

182(2)   ["Insolvency proceedings"] For the purposes of this section **"insolvency proceedings"** means proceedings under Part II, IV, V or IX of the Insolvency Act 1986 (administration, winding up and bankruptcy) or under the Bankruptcy (Scotland) Act 1985; and references in this section to the beginning of such proceedings are to–

(a)   the presentation of a petition on which an administration order, winding-up order, bankruptcy order or award of sequestration is made, or

(b)   the passing of a resolution for voluntary winding up.

182(3)   [Insolvent estate of deceased person] This section applies in relation to–

(a)   in England and Wales, the administration of the insolvent estate of a deceased person, and

(b)   in Scotland, the administration by a judicial factor appointed under section 11A of the Judicial Factors (Scotland) Act 1889 of the insolvent estate of a deceased person,

as it applies in relation to insolvency proceedings.

In such a case references to the beginning of the proceedings shall be construed as references to the death of the relevant person.

182(4)   [Court order] The court may on an application made, within three months after the commencement of this section, by–

(a)   a recognised investment exchange or recognised clearing house, or

(b)   a person in whose favour a market charge has been granted,

make such order as it thinks fit for achieving, except so far as assets of the relevant person have been distributed before the making of the application, the same result as if the provisions of Schedule 22 had come into force on 22nd December 1988.

182(5)   [Schedule 22] The provisions of that Schedule (**"the relevant provisions"**) reproduce the effect of certain provisions of this Part as they appeared in the Bill for this Act as introduced into the House of Lords and published on that date.

182(6)   [Court's powers] The court may in particular–

(a)   require the relevant person or a relevant office-holder–

(i)   to return property provided as cover for margin or which was subject to a market charge, or to pay to the applicant or any other person the proceeds of realisation of such property, or

(ii)   to pay to the applicant or any other person such amount as the court estimates would have been payable to that person if the relevant provisions had come into force on 22nd December

1988 and market contracts had been settled in accordance with the rules of the recognised investment exchange or recognised clearing house, or a proportion of that amount if the property of the relevant person or relevant office-holder is not sufficient to meet the amount in full;

(b)   provide that contracts, rules and dispositions shall be treated as not having been void;

(c)   modify the functions of a relevant office-holder, or the duties of the applicant or any other person, in relation to the insolvency proceedings, or indemnify any such person in respect of acts or omissions which would have been proper if the relevant provisions had been in force;

(d)   provide that conduct which constituted an offence be treated as not having done so;

(e)   dismiss proceedings which could not have been brought if the relevant provisions had come into force on 22nd December 1988, and reverse the effect of any order of a court which could not, or would not, have been made if those provisions had come into force on that date.

182(7)   [Office-holder's remuneration] An order under this section shall not be made against a relevant office-holder if the effect would be that his remuneration, costs and expenses could not be met.

Note
For meaning of "the court" and description of insolvency applications in ss.161, 163, 164, 175 and 182 see the Financial Markets and Insolvency Regulations 1991 (SI 1991/880) reg.19.

183   Insolvency proceedings in other jurisdictions

183(1)   [Corresponding foreign law] The references to insolvency law in section 426 of the Insolvency Act 1986 (co-operation with courts exercising insolvency jurisdiction in other jurisdictions) include, in relation to a part of the United Kingdom, the provisions made by or under this Part and, in relation to a relevant country or territory within the meaning of that section, so much of the law of that country or territory as corresponds to any provisions made by or under this Part.

183(2)   [Where foreign order prohibited in UK] A court shall not, in pursuance of that section or any other enactment or rule of law, recognise or give effect to–

(a)   any order of a court exercising jurisdiction in relation to insolvency law in a country or territory outside the United Kingdom, or

(b)   any act of a person appointed in such a country or territory to discharge any functions under insolvency law,

in so far as the making of the order or the doing of the act would be prohibited in the case of a court in the United Kingdom or a relevant office-holder by provisions made by or under this Part.

183(3)   [Civil Jurisdiction and Judgments Act 1982] Subsection (2) does not affect the recognition or enforcement of a judgment required to be recognised or enforced under or by virtue of the Civil Jurisdiction and Judgments Act 1982 or Council Regulation (EC) No.44/2001 of 22nd December 2000 on jurisdiction and the recognition and enforcement of judgments in civil and commercial matters, as amended from time to time and as applied by the Agreement made on 19th October 2005 between the European Community and the Kingdom of Denmark on jurisdiction and the recognition and enforcement of judgments in civil and commercial matters (OJ No. L 299 16.11.2005 at p.62).

History
Section 183(3) amended by the Civil Jurisdiction and Judgments Regulations 2007 (SI 2007/1655) reg.5 and Sch. para.15, as from July 1, 2007.

184   Indemnity for certain acts, etc.

184(1)   [Office-holder's negligence excepted] Where a relevant office-holder takes any action in relation to property of a defaulter which is liable to be dealt with in accordance with the default rules of a recognised investment exchange or recognised clearing house, and believes and has reasonable grounds for believing that he is entitled to take that action, he is not liable to any person in respect of any loss or damage resulting from his action except in so far as the loss or damage is caused by the office-holder's own negligence.

184(2)   **[Compliance with rules]** Any failure by a recognised investment exchange or recognised clearing house to comply with its own rules in respect of any matter shall not prevent that matter being treated for the purposes of this Part as done in accordance with those rules so long as the failure does not substantially affect the rights of any person entitled to require compliance with the rules.

184(3)   **[Bad faith]** No recognised investment exchange or recognised clearing house, nor any officer or servant or member of the governing body of a recognised investment exchange or recognised clearing house, shall be liable in damages for anything done or omitted in the discharge or purported discharge of any functions to which this subsection applies unless the act or omission is shown to have been in bad faith.

184(4)   **[Section 184(3) functions]** The functions to which subsection (3) applies are the functions of the exchange or clearing house so far as relating to, or to matters arising out of–

(a)   its default rules, or

(b)   any obligations to which it is subject by virtue of this Part.

184(5)   **[Limit on liability in damages]** No person to whom the exercise of any function of a recognised investment exchange or recognised clearing house is delegated under its default rules, nor any officer or servant of such a person, shall be liable in damages for anything done or omitted in the discharge or purported discharge of those functions unless the act or omission is shown to have been in bad faith.

185   Power to make further provision by regulations

185(1)   **[Regulations]** The Secretary of State may by regulations make such further provision as appears to him necessary or expedient for the purposes of this Part.

185(2)   **[Particular provisions]** Provision may, in particular, be made–

(a)   for integrating the provisions of this Part with the general law of insolvency, and

(b)   for adapting the provisions of this Part in their application to overseas investment exchanges and clearing houses.

185(3)   **[Scope of regulations]** Regulations under this section may add to, amend or repeal any of the provisions of this Part or provide that those provisions have effect subject to such additions, exceptions or adaptations as are specified in the regulations.

185(4)   **[Section 301 of Financial Services and Markets Act]** References in this section to the provisions of this Part include any provision made under section 301 of the Financial Services and Markets Act 2000.

Note
See the Financial Markets and Insolvency Regulations 1991 (SI 1991/880) and the Financial Markets and Insolvency Regulations 1998 (SI 1998/1748).

186   Supplementary provisions as to regulations

186(1)   **[Different provision for cases]** Regulations under this Part may make different provision for different cases and may contain such incidental, transitional and other supplementary provisions as appear to the Secretary of State to be necessary or expedient.

186(2) **[Regulations by statutory instrument]** Regulations under this Part shall be made by statutory instrument which shall be subject to annulment in pursuance of a resolution of either House of Parliament.

187 Construction of references to parties to market contracts

187(1) **[Different capacities]** Where a person enters into market contracts in more than one capacity, the provisions of this Part apply (subject as follows) as if the contracts entered into in each different capacity were entered into by different persons.

187(2) **[Agency]** References in this Part to a market contract to which a person is a party include (subject as follows, and unless the context otherwise requires) contracts to which he is party as agent.

187(3) **[Regulations]** The Secretary of State may by regulations–

(a) modify or exclude the operation of subsections (1) and (2), and

(b) make provision as to the circumstances in which a person is to be regarded for the purposes of those provisions as acting in different capacities.

188 Meaning of "default rules" and related expressions

188(1) **["Default rules"]** In this Part **"default rules"** means rules of a recognised investment exchange or recognised clearing house which provide for the taking of action in the event of a person (including another recognised investment exchange or recognised clearing house) appearing to be unable, or likely to become unable, to meet his obligations in respect of one or more market contracts connected with the exchange or clearing house.

188(2) **["Defaulter"]** References in this Part to a **"defaulter"** are to a person in respect of whom action has been taken by a recognised investment exchange or recognised clearing house under its default rules, whether by declaring him to be a defaulter or otherwise; and references in this Part to "default" shall be construed accordingly.

188(3) **["Default proceedings"]** In this Part **"default proceedings"** means proceedings taken by a recognised investment exchange or recognised clearing house under its default rules.

188(3A) **[Default fund contribution]** In this Part "default fund contribution" means–

(a) contribution by a member or designated non-member of a recognised investment exchange to a fund which–

    (i) is maintained by that exchange for the purpose of covering losses arising in connection with defaults by any of the members of the exchange, or defaults by any of the members or designated non-members of the exchange, and

    (ii) may be applied for that purpose under the default rules of the exchange;

(b) contribution by a member of a recognised clearing house to a fund which–

    (i) is maintained by that clearing house for the purpose of covering losses arising in connection with defaults by any of the members of the clearing house, and

    (ii) may be applied for that purpose under the default rules of the clearing house;

(c) contribution by a recognised clearing house to a fund which–

    (i) is maintained by a recognised investment exchange or another recognised clearing house (A) for the purpose of covering losses arising in connection with defaults by recognised clearing houses or recognised investment exchanges other than A or by any of their members, and

    (ii) may be applied for that purpose under A's default rules; or

    (d)   contribution by a recognised investment exchange to a fund which–

        (i)   is maintained by a recognised clearing house or another recognised investment exchange (A) for the purpose of covering losses arising in connection with defaults by recognised investment exchanges or recognised clearing houses other than A or by any of their members, and

        (ii)   may be applied for that purpose under A's default rules.

History
Section 188(3A) inserted by the Financial Markets and Insolvency Regulations 2009 (SI 2009/853) reg.2(1), (15) as from June 15, 2009.

188(4)   **[Action under default rules]** If an exchange or clearing house takes action under its default rules in respect of a person, all subsequent proceedings under its rules for the purposes of or in connection with the settlement of market contracts to which the defaulter is a party shall be treated as done under its default rules.

189   Meaning of "relevant office-holder"

189(1)   **[Office-holders]** The following are relevant office-holders for the purposes of this Part–

    (a)   the official receiver,

    (b)   any person acting in relation to a company as its liquidator, provisional liquidator, administrator or administrative receiver,

    (c)   any person acting in relation to an individual (or, in Scotland, any debtor within the meaning of the Bankruptcy (Scotland) Act 1985) as his trustee in bankruptcy or interim receiver of his property or as permanent or interim trustee in the sequestration of his estate,

    (d)   any person acting as administrator of an insolvent estate of a deceased person.

189(2)   **["Company" in s.189(1)(b)]** In subsection (1)(b) **"company"** means any company, society, association, partnership or other body which may be wound up under the Insolvency Act 1986.

190   Minor definitions

190(1)   **[Definitions]** In this Part–

"administrative receiver" has the meaning given by section 251 of the Insolvency Act 1986;

"the Authority" means the Financial Services Authority;

"charge" means any form of security, including a mortgage and, in Scotland, a heritable security;

"interim trustee" and **"permanent trustee"** have the same meaning as in the Bankruptcy (Scotland) Act 1985;

"overseas", in relation to an investment exchange or clearing house, means having its head office outside the United Kingdom;

"recognised clearing house" and **"recognised investment exchange"** have the same meaning as in the Financial Services and Markets Act 2000;

"set-off", in relation to Scotland, includes compensation;

"The Stock Exchange" means the London Stock Exchange Limited;

"UK", in relation to an investment exchange or clearing house, means having its head office in the United Kingdom.

190(2) **[Settlement]** References in this Part to settlement in relation to a market contract are to the discharge of the rights and liabilities of the parties to the contract, whether by performance, compromise or otherwise.

190(3) **["Margin", "cover for margin"]** In this Part the expressions **"margin"** and **"cover for margin"** have the same meaning.

190(4) [Repealed by the Financial Services and Markets Act 2000 (Consequential Amendments and Repeals) Order 2001 (SI 2001/3649) arts 1, 89(1), (6) as from December 1, 2001.]

190(5) **[Notice]** For the purposes of this Part a person shall be taken to have notice of a matter if he deliberately failed to make enquiries as to that matter in circumstances in which a reasonable and honest person would have done so.

This does not apply for the purposes of a provision requiring "actual notice".

190(6) **[Insolvency law]** References in this Part to the law of insolvency include references to every provision made by or under the Insolvency Act 1986 or the Bankruptcy (Scotland) Act 1985; and in relation to a building society references to insolvency law or to any provision of the Insolvency Act 1986 are to that law or provision as modified by the Building Societies Act 1986.

190(7) **[Scotland]** In relation to Scotland, references in this Part–

(a)   to sequestration include references to the administration by a judicial factor of the insolvent estate of a deceased person, and

(b)   to an interim or permanent trustee include references to a judicial factor on the insolvent estate of a deceased person,

unless the context otherwise requires.

191   Index of defined expressions

191   The following Table shows provisions defining or otherwise explaining expressions used in this Part (other than provisions defining or explaining an expression used only in the same section or paragraph)–

administrative receiver	section 190(1)
the Authority	section 190(1)
charge	section 190(1)
cover for margin	section 190(3)
default fund contribution	section 188(3A)
default rules (and related expressions)	section 188
designated non-member	section 155(2)
insolvency law (and similar expressions)	section 190(6)
interim trustee	section 190(1) and (7)(b)
margin	section 190(3)
market charge	section 173
market contract	section 155
notice	section 190(5)
overseas (in relation to an investment exchange or clearing house)	section 190(1)
party (in relation to a market contract)	section 187
permanent trustee	section 190(1) and (7)(b)
recognised clearing house and recognised investment exchange	section 190(1)
relevant office-holder	section 189
sequestration	section 190(7)(a)
set off (in relation to Scotland)	section 190(1)
settlement and related expressions (in relation to a market contract)	section 190(2)

The Stock Exchange   section 190(1)

trustee, interim or permanent (in relation to Scotland)   section 190(7)(b)

UK (in relation to an investment exchange or clearing house)   section 190(1)

History

The entry for "default fund contribution" inserted by the Financial Markets and Insolvency Regulations 2009 (SI 2009/853) reg.2(1), (16) as from June 15, 2009.

Social Security Administration Act 1992

(1992 Chapter 5)

An Act to consolidate certain enactments relating to the administration of social security and related matters with amendments to give effect to recommendations of the Law Commission and the Scottish Law Commission.

[13th February 1992]

[**Note**: These two sections were inserted by the Social Security Act 1998 s.64. The text is shown as amended by the Social Security (Transfer of Functions, etc.) Act 1999 and the Transfer of Tribunal Functions, etc. Order 2009 (SI 2009/56).]

PART VI

ENFORCEMENT

Unpaid contributions etc

121C Liability of directors etc. for company's contributions

121C(1)   This section applies to contributions which a body corporate is liable to pay, where–

(a) the body corporate has failed to pay the contributions at or within the time prescribed for the purpose; and

(b) the failure appears to the Inland Revenue to be attributable to fraud or neglect on the part of one or more individuals who, at the time of the fraud or neglect, were officers of the body corporate ("culpable officers").

121C(2)   The Inland Revenue may issue and serve on any culpable officer a notice (a "personal liability notice")–

(a) specifying the amount of the contributions to which this section applies ("the specified amount");

(b) requiring the officer to pay to the Inland Revenue–

 (i) a specified sum in respect of that amount; and

 (ii) specified interest on that sum; and

(c) where that sum is given by paragraph (b) of subsection (3) below, specifying the proportion applied by the Inland Revenue for the purposes of that paragraph.

121C(3)   The sum specified in the personal liability notice under subsection (2)(b)(i) above shall be–

(a) in a case where there is, in the opinion of the Inland Revenue, no other culpable officer, the whole of the specified amount; and

(b) in any other case, such proportion of the specified amount as, in the opinion of the Inland Revenue, the officer's culpability for the failure to pay that amount bears to that of all the culpable officers taken together.

121C(4)   In assessing an officer's culpability for the purposes of subsection (3)(b) above, the Inland Revenue may have regard both to the gravity of the officer's fraud or neglect and to the consequences of it.

121C(5)   The interest specified in the personal liability notice under subsection (2)(b)(ii) above shall be at the prescribed rate and shall run from the date on which the notice is issued.

121C(6)   An officer who is served with a personal liability notice shall be liable to pay to the Inland Revenue the sum and the interest specified in the notice under subsection (2)(b) above.

121C(7)   Where, after the issue of one or more personal liability notices, the amount of contributions to which this section applies is reduced by a payment made by the body corporate–

    (a)   the amount that each officer who has been served with such a notice is liable to pay under this section shall be reduced accordingly;

    (b)   the Inland Revenue shall serve on each such officer a notice to that effect; and

    (c)   where the reduced liability of any such officer is less than the amount that he has already paid under this section, the difference shall be repaid to him together with interest on it at the prescribed rate.

121C(8)   Any amount paid under a personal liability notice shall be deducted from the liability of the body corporate in respect of the specified amount.

121C(8A)   The amount which an officer is liable to pay under this section is to be recovered in the same manner as a Class 1 contribution to which regulations under paragraph 6 of Schedule 1 to the Contributions and Benefits Act apply and for this purpose references in those regulations to Class 1 contributions are to be construed accordingly.

121C(9)   In this section–

"contributions" includes any interest or penalty in respect of contributions; "officer", in relation to a body corporate, means–

    (a)   any director, manager, secretary or other similar officer of the body corporate, or any person purporting to act as such; and

    (b)   in a case where the affairs of the body corporate are managed by its members, any member of the body corporate exercising functions of management with respect to it or purporting to do so;

"the prescribed rate" means the rate from time to time prescribed by regulations under section 178 of the Finance Act 1989 for the purposes of the corresponding provision of Schedule 1 to the Contributions and Benefits Act, that is to say–

    (a)   in relation to subsection (5) above, paragraph 6(2)(a);

    (b)   in relation to subsection (7) above, paragraph 6(2)(b).

History
Section 121C(8A) inserted by the National Insurance Contributions and Statutory Payments Act 2004 s.5(3).

121D   Appeals in relation to personal liability notices

121D(1)   No appeal shall lie in relation to a personal liability notice except as provided by this section.

121D(2)   An individual who is served with a personal liability notice may appeal against the Inland Revenue's decision as to the issue and content of the notice on the ground that–

    (a)   the whole or part of the amount specified under subsection (2)(a) of section 121C above (or the amount so specified as reduced under subsection (7) of that section) does not represent contributions to which that section applies;

    (b)   the failure to pay that amount was not attributable to any fraud or neglect on the part of the individual in question;

(c) the individual was not an officer of the body corporate at the time of the alleged fraud or neglect; or

(d) the opinion formed by the Inland Revenue under subsection (3)(a) or (b) of that section was unreasonable.

121D(3) The Inland Revenue shall give a copy of any notice of an appeal under this section, within 28 days of the giving of the notice, to each other individual who has been served with a personal liability notice.

121D(4) On an appeal under this section, the burden of proof as to any matter raised by a ground of appeal shall be on the Inland Revenue.

121D(5) Where an appeal under this section–

(a) is brought on the basis of evidence not considered by the Inland Revenue, or on the ground mentioned in subsection (2)(d) above; and

(b) is not allowed on some other basis or ground,

and is notified to the tribunal, the tribunal shall either dismiss the appeal or remit the case to the Inland Revenue, with any recommendations the tribunal sees fit to make, for the Inland Revenue to consider whether to vary their decision as to the issue and content of the personal liability notice.

121D(6) In this section–

"officer", in relation to a body corporate, has the same meaning as in section 121C above;

"personal liability notice" has the meaning given by subsection (2) of that section;

"tribunal" means the First-tier Tribunal or, where determined under Tribunal Procedure Rules, the Upper Tribunal;

"vary" means vary under regulations made under section 10 of the Social Security Contributions (Transfer of Functions, etc.) Act 1999.

History
Section 121D(2), (5), (6) amended by the Transfer of Tribunal Functions, etc. Order 2009 (SI 2009/56) art.3(1) and Sch.1 paras 170, 171 as from April 1, 2009.

Friendly Societies Act 1992

(1992 Chapter 40)

An Act to make further provision for friendly societies; to provide for the cessation of registration under the Friendly Societies Act 1974; to make provision about disputes involving friendly societies or other bodies registered under the Friendly Societies Act 1974 and about the functions of the Chief Registrar of friendly societies; and for connected purposes.

[16th March 1992]

[**Note**: Changes made by the Financial Institutions (Prudential Supervision) Regulations 1996 (SI 1996/1669) and the Financial Services and Markets Act 2000 (Mutual Societies) Order 2001 (SI 2001/2617) have been incorporated into the text, without annotation. Former references to the Commission, the central office and various registrars have been replaced throughout by references to the Authority (i.e. the Financial Services Authority) or the Treasury pursuant to SI 2001/2617 art.13(1) and Sch.3 Pt I, as from December 1, 2001.]

PART I

FUNCTIONS OF THE AUTHORITY

1 Functions of the Financial Services Authority in relation to friendly societies

1(1) The Financial Services Authority (**"the Authority"**) has the following functions under this Act and the 1974 Act in relation to friendly societies–

(a) to secure that the purposes of each friendly society are inconformity with this Act and any other enactment regulating the purposes of friendly societies;

(b) to administer the system of regulation of the activities of friendly societies provided for by or under this Act and the 1974 Act; and

(c) to advise and make recommendations to the Treasury and other government departments on any matter relating to friendly societies.

1(2) The Authority also has, in relation to such societies, the other functions conferred on it by or under this Act or any other enactment.

PART II

Dissolution and winding up

19   Modes of dissolution and winding up

19(1)   An incorporated friendly society–

(a)   may be dissolved by consent of the members; or

(b)   may be wound up voluntarily or by the court,

in accordance with this Part of this Act; and an incorporated friendly society may not, except where it is dissolved by virtue of section 85(4), 86(5) or 90(9) below, be dissolved or wound up in any other manner.

19(2)   An incorporated friendly society which is in the course of dissolution by consent, or is being wound up voluntarily, may be wound up by the court.

20   Dissolution by consent

20(1)   An incorporated friendly society may be dissolved by an instrument of dissolution.

20(2)   An instrument of dissolution shall only have effect if it is approved by special resolution.

20(3)   An instrument of dissolution shall set out–

(a)   the liabilities and assets of the society in detail;

(b)   the number of members, and the nature of their interests in the society;

(c)   the claims of creditors, and the provision to be made for their payment;

(d)   the intended appropriation or division of the funds and property of the society;

(e)   the names of one or more persons to be appointed as trustees for the purposes of the dissolution, and their remuneration.

20(4)   An instrument of dissolution may be altered, but the alteration shall only have effect if it is approved by special resolution.

20(5)   The provisions of this Act shall continue to apply in relation to an incorporated friendly society as if the trustees appointed under the instrument of dissolution were the committee of management of the society.

20(6)   The trustees shall–

(a)   within 15 days of the passing of a special resolution approving an instrument of dissolution, give notice to the Authority of the fact and the date of commencement of the dissolution, enclosing a copy of the instrument; and

(b)   within 15 days of the passing of a special resolution approving an alteration of such an instrument, give notice to the Authority of the fact, enclosing a copy of the altered instrument;

and if the trustees fail to comply with this subsection, they shall each be guilty of an offence and liable on summary conviction to a fine not exceeding level 3 on the standard scale.

20(7)   An instrument of dissolution or an alteration to such an instrument shall be binding on all members of the society as from the date on which the copy of the instrument or altered instrument, as the case may be, is placed on the public file of the society under subsection (12) below.

20(8)   The trustees shall, within 28 days from the termination of the dissolution, give notice to the Authority of the fact and the date of the termination, enclosing an account and balance sheet signed and certified by them as correct, and showing–

(a)   the assets and liabilities of the society at the commencement of the dissolution; and

(b)   the way in which those assets and liabilities have been applied and discharged.

20(9)   If the trustees fail to comply with subsection (8) above they shall each be guilty of an offence and liable on summary conviction–

(a)   to a fine not exceeding level 2 on the standard scale; and

(b)   in the case of a continuing offence, to an additional fine not exceeding one-tenth of that level for every day during which the offence continues.

20(10)   Except with the consent of the Authority, no instrument of dissolution or alteration to such an instrument shall be of any effect if the purpose of the proposed dissolution or alteration is to effect or facilitate the transfer of the society's engagements to any other friendly society or to a company.

20(11)   Any provision in a resolution or document that members of an incorporated friendly society proposed to be dissolved shall accept membership of some other body in or towards satisfaction of their rights in the dissolution shall be conclusive evidence of such purpose as is mentioned in subsection (10) above.

20(12)   The Authority shall keep in the public file of the society any notice or other document received by it under subsection (6) or (8) above and shall record in that file the date on which the notice or document is placed in it.

21   Voluntary winding up

21(1)   An incorporated friendly society may be wound up voluntarily under the applicable winding up legislation if it resolves by special resolution that it be wound up voluntarily.

21(2)   A copy of any special resolution passed for the voluntary winding up of an incorporated friendly society shall be sent by the society to the Authority within 15 days after it is passed; and the Authority shall keep the copy in the public file of the society.

21(3)   A copy of any such resolution shall be annexed to every copy of the memorandum or of the rules issued after the passing of the resolution.

21(4)   If an incorporated friendly society fails to comply with subsection (2) or (3) above, the society shall be guilty of an offence and liable on summary conviction to a fine not exceeding level 3 on the standard scale.

21(5)   For the purposes of this section, a liquidator of the society shall be treated as an officer of it.

22   Winding up by court: grounds and petitioners

22(1)   An incorporated friendly society may be wound up under the applicable winding up legislation by the court on any of the following grounds, that is to say, if–

(a)   the society has by special resolution resolved that it be wound up by the court;

(b)   the number of members is reduced below 7;

(c)   the number of members of the committee of management is reduced below 2;

(d)   the society has not commenced business within a year from its incorporation or has suspended its business for a whole year;

(e)   the society exists for an illegal purpose;

(f)   the society is unable to pay its debts; or

(g)   the court is of the opinion that it is just and equitable that the society should be wound up.

22(2)   Except as provided by subsection (3) below or the applicable winding up legislation, a petition for the winding up of an incorporated friendly society may be presented by–

(a)   the Authority;

(b)   the society or its committee of management;

(c)   any creditor or creditors (including any contingent or any prospective creditor); or

(d)   any contributory or contributories,

or by all or any of those parties, together or separately.

22(3)   A contributory may not present a petition unless the number of members is reduced below 7 or he has been a contributory for at least six months before the winding up.

22(4)   In this section **"contributory"** has the meaning assigned to it by paragraph 9 of Schedule 10 to this Act.

23   Application of winding up legislation to incorporated friendly societies

23(1)   In this section **"the companies winding up legislation"** means the enactments applicable in relation to England and Wales, Scotland and Northern Ireland which are specified in paragraph 1 of Schedule 10 to this Act (including any enactment which creates an offence by any person arising out of acts or omissions occurring before the commencement of the winding up).

23(2)   In its application to the winding up of an incorporated friendly society, by virtue of section 21(1) or 22(1) above, the companies winding up legislation shall have effect with the modifications effected by Parts I to III of Schedule 10 to this Act; and the supplementary provisions of Part IV of that Schedule also have effect in relation to such a winding up and in relation to a dissolution by consent.

23(3)   In section 21 and 22 above **"the applicable winding up legislation"** means the companies winding up legislation as so modified.

24   Continuation of long term business

24(1)   This section has effect in relation to the winding up of an incorporated friendly society which carries on long term business (including any reinsurance business).

24(2)   The liquidator shall, unless the court otherwise orders, carry on the long term business of the society with a view to its being transferred as a going concern under this Act; and, in carrying on that business, the liquidator may agree to the variation of any contracts of insurance in existence when the winding up order is made but shall not effect any new contracts of insurance.

24(3)   If the liquidator is satisfied that the interests of the creditors in respect of liabilities of the society attributable to its long term business require the appointment of a special manager of the society's long term business, he may apply to the court, and the court may on such application appoint a special manager of that business to act during such time as the court may direct, with such powers (including any of the powers of a receiver or manager) as may be entrusted to him by the court.

24(4)   Section 177(5) of the Insolvency Act 1986 or, as the case may be, Article 151 of the Insolvency (Northern Ireland) Order 1989 shall apply to a special manager appointed under subsection (3) above as it applies to a special manager appointed under that section or that Article.

24(5)   The court may, if it thinks fit and subject to such conditions (if any) as it may determine, reduce the amount of the contracts made by the society in the course of carrying on its long term business.

24(6) The court may, on the application of the liquidator, a special manager appointed under subsection (3) above or the Authority appoint an independent actuary to investigate the long term business of the society and to report to the liquidator, the special manager or the Authority, as the case may be, on the desirability or otherwise of that business being continued and on any reduction in the contracts made in the course of carrying on that business that may be necessary for its successful continuation.

25 Power of court to declare dissolution void

25(1) Where an incorporated friendly society has been dissolved under section 20 above or following a winding up, the court may, at any time within 12 years after the date on which the society was dissolved, make an order under this section declaring the dissolution to have been void.

25(2) An order under this section may be made, on such terms as the court thinks fit, on an application by the trustees under section 20 above or the liquidator, as the case may be, or by any other person appearing to the court to be interested.

25(3) When an order under this section is made, such proceedings may be taken as might have been taken if the society had not been dissolved.

25(4) The person on whose application the order is made shall, within 7 days of its being so made, or such further time as the court may allow, furnish the Authority with a copy of the order; and the Authority shall keep the copy in the public file of the society.

25(5) If a person fails to comply with subsection (4) above, he shall be guilty of an offence and liable on summary conviction–

    (a) to a fine not exceeding level 3 on the standard scale; and

    (b) in the case of a continuing offence, to an additional fine not exceeding one-tenth of that level for every day during which the offence continues.

25(6) In this section **"the court"** means–

    (a) in relation to a society whose registered office is in England and Wales, the High Court;

    (b) in relation to a society whose registered office is in Scotland, the Court of Session; and

    (c) in relation to a society whose registered office is in Northern Ireland, the High Court in Northern Ireland.

26 Cancellation of registration

26(1) Where the Authority is satisfied that an incorporated friendly society has been dissolved under section 20 above or following a winding up, it shall cancel the society's registration under this Act.

26(2) Where the Authority is satisfied, with respect to an incorporated friendly society–

    (a) that a certificate of incorporation has been obtained for the society by fraud or mistake; or

    (b) that the society has ceased to exist; or

    (c) in the case of a society to which section 37(2) or (3) below applies, that the principal place of business of the society is outside the United Kingdom,

it may cancel the registration of the society.

26(3) Without prejudice to subsection (2) above, the Authority may, if it thinks fit, cancel the registration of an incorporated friendly society at the request of the society, evidenced in such manner as the Authority may direct.

26(4) Before cancelling the registration of an incorporated friendly society under subsection (2) above, the Authority shall give to the society not less than two months' previous notice, specifying briefly the grounds of the proposed cancellation.

26(5) Where the registration of an incorporated friendly society is cancelled under subsection (2) above, the society may appeal–

(a) where the registered office of the society is situated in England and Wales, to the High Court;

(b) where that office is situated in Scotland, to the Court of Session; or

(c) where that office is situated in Northern Ireland, to the High Court in Northern Ireland;

and on any such appeal the court may, if it thinks it just to do so, set aside the cancellation.

26(6) Where the registration of a society is cancelled under subsection (2) or (3) above, then, subject to the right of appeal under subsection (5) above, the society, so far as it continues to exist, shall cease to be a society incorporated under this Act.

26(7) Subsection (6) above shall not affect any liability actually incurred by an incorporated friendly society; and any such liability may be enforced against the society as if the cancellation had not taken place.

26(8) Any cancellation of the registration of an incorporated friendly society under this section shall be effected by written notice given by the Authority to the society.

26(9) As soon as practicable after the cancellation of the registration of an incorporated friendly society under this section the Authority shall cause notice thereof to be published in the London Gazette, the Edinburgh Gazette or the Belfast Gazette according to the situation of the society's registered office, and if it thinks fit, in one or more newspapers.

SCHEDULE 10

APPLICATION OF COMPANIES WINDING UP LEGISLATION TO INCORPORATED FRIENDLY SOCIETIES

Section 23

PART I

GENERAL MODE OF APPLICATION

1 The enactments which comprise the companies winding up legislation (referred to in this Schedule as **"the enactments"**) are the provisions of–

(a) Parts IV, VI, VII, XII and XIII of the Insolvency Act 1986, or

(b) Parts V, VI, XI and XII of the Insolvency (Northern Ireland) Order 1989,

and, in so far as they relate to offences under any such enactment, sections 430 and 432 of, and Schedule 10 to, that Act or Article 373 of, and Schedule 7 to, that Order.

2 Subject to the following provisions of this Schedule, the enactments apply to the winding up of incorporated friendly societies as they apply to the winding up of companies registered under the Companies Act 2006.

3(1) Subject to the following provisions of this Schedule, the enactments shall, in their application to incorporated friendly societies, have effect with the substitution–

(a) for "company" of "incorporated friendly society";

(b) for "directors" of "committee of management";

(c) for "the registrar of companies" or "the registrar" of "the Financial Services Authority"; and

(d) for "the articles" of "the rules".

3(2) Subject to the following provisions of this Schedule in the application of the enactments to incorporated friendly societies–

(aa) every reference to a company registered in Scotland shall have effect as a reference to an incorporated friendly society whose registered office is situated in Scotland;

(a) every reference to the officers, or to a particular officer, of a company shall have effect as a reference to the officers, or to the corresponding officer, of the incorporated friendly society and as including a person holding himself out as such an officer;

(b) every reference to a director of a company shall be construed as a reference to a member of the committee of management; and

(c) every reference to an administrator, an administration order, an administrative receiver, a shadow director or a voluntary arrangement shall be omitted.

4(1) Where any of the enactments as applied to incorporated friendly societies requires a notice or other document to be sent to the Authority, it shall have effect as if it required the Authority to keep the notice or document in the public file of the society and to record in that file the date on which the notice or document is placed in it.

4(2) Where any of the enactments, as so applied, refers to the registration, or to the date of registration, of such a notice or document, that enactment shall have effect as if it referred to the placing of the notice or document in the public file or (as the case may be) to the date on which it was placed there.

5 Any enactment which specifies a sum altered by order under section 416 of the Insolvency Act 1986 or Article 362 of the Insolvency (Northern Ireland) Order 1989 (powers to alter monetary limits) applies with the effect of the alteration.

PART II

MODIFIED APPLICATION OF INSOLVENCY ACT 1986 PARTS IV AND XII

Preliminary

6 In this Part of this Schedule, Part IV of the Insolvency Act 1986 is referred to as **"Part IV"**; and that Act is referred to as **"the Act"**.

Members of a friendly society as contributories in winding up

7(1) Section 74 (liability of members) of the Act is modified as follows.

7(2) In subsection (1), the reference to any past member shall be omitted.

7(3) Paragraphs (a) to (d) of subsection (2) shall be omitted; and so shall subsection (3).

7(4) The extent of the liability of a member of an incorporated friendly society in a winding up shall not exceed the extent of his liability under paragraph 8 of Schedule 3 to this Act.

8 Sections 75 to 78 and 83 in Chapter I of Part IV (miscellaneous provisions not relevant to incorporated friendly societies) do not apply.

9(1) Section 79 (meaning of "contributory") of the Act does not apply.

9(2) In the enactments as applied to an incorporated friendly society, **"contributory"**–

(a) means every person liable to contribute to the assets of the society in the event of its being wound up; and

(b) for the purposes of all proceedings for determining, and all proceedings prior to the determination of, the persons who are to be deemed contributories, includes any person alleged to be a contributory; and

(c) includes persons who are liable to pay or contribute to the payment of–

(i) any debt or liability of the incorporated friendly society being wound up; or

(ii) any sum for the adjustment of rights of members among themselves; or

(iii) the expenses of the winding up;

but does not include persons liable to contribute by virtue of a declaration by the court under section 213 (imputed responsibility for fraudulent trading) or section 214 (wrongful trading) of the Act.

Voluntary winding up

10(1) Section 84 of the Act does not apply.

10(2) In the enactments as applied to an incorporated friendly society, the expression **"resolution for voluntary winding up"** means a resolution passed under section 21(1) above.

11 Section 88 shall have effect with the omission of the words from the beginning to "and".

12(1) Subsection (1) of section 89 shall have effect as if for the words from the beginning to "meeting" there were substituted the words–

"**(1)** Where it is proposed to wind up an incorporated friendly society voluntarily, the committee of management (or, in the case of an incorporated friendly society whose committee of management has more than two members, the majority of them) may at a meeting of the committee".

12(2) The reference to the directors in subsection (2) shall be construed as a reference to members of the committee of management.

13 Section 90 shall have effect as if for the words "directors statutory declaration under section 89" there were substituted the words "statutory declaration made under section 89 by members of the committee of management".

14 Sections 95(1) and 96 shall have effect as if the word "directors" were omitted from each of them.

15 In subsection (1) of section 101 (appointment of liquidation committee) of the Act, the reference to functions conferred on a liquidation committee by or under that Act shall have effect as a reference to its functions by or under that Act as applied to incorporated friendly societies.

16(1) Section 107 (distribution of property) of the Act does not apply; and the following applies in its place.

16(2) Subject to the provisions of Part IV relating to preferential payments, an incorporated friendly society's property in a voluntary winding up shall be applied in satisfaction of the society's liabilities to creditors pari passu and, subject to that application, in accordance with the rules of the society.

17 Sections 110 and 111 (liquidator accepting shares, etc. as consideration for sale of company property) of the Act do not apply.

Winding up by the court

18 In sections 117 (High Court and county court jurisdiction) and 120 (Court of Session and sheriff court jurisdiction) of the Act, each reference to a company's share capital paid up or credited as paid up shall have effect as a reference to the amount of the contribution or subscription income of an incorporated friendly society as shown by the latest balance sheet.

19   Section 122 (circumstances in which company may be wound up by the court) of the Act does not apply.

20   Section 124 (application for winding up) of the Act does not apply.

21(1)   In section 125 (powers of court on hearing of petition) of the Act, subsection (1) applies with the omission of the words from "but the court" to the end of the subsection.

21(2)   The conditions which the court may impose under section 125 of the Act include conditions for securing–

(a)   that the incorporated friendly society be dissolved by consent of its members under section 20 above; or

(b)   that the society amalgamates with, or transfers all or any of its engagements to, another friendly society under section 85 or 86 above, or

(c)   that the society converts itself into a company under section 91 above,

and may also include conditions for securing that any default which occasioned the petition be made good and that the costs, or in Scotland the expenses, of the proceedings on that petition be defrayed by the person or persons responsible for the default.

22   Section 126 (power of court, between petition and winding-up order, to stay or restrain proceedings against company) of the Act has effect with the omission of subsection (2).

23   If, before the presentation of a petition for the winding up by the court of an incorporated friendly society, an instrument of dissolution under section 20 above is placed in the society's public file, section 129(1) (commencement of winding up by the court) of the Act shall also apply in relation to the date on which the notice is so placed and to any proceedings in the course of the dissolution as it applies to the commencement date for, and proceedings in, a voluntary winding up.

24(1)   Section 130 of the Act (consequences of winding-up order) shall have effect with the following modifications.

24(2)   Subsections (1) and (3) shall be omitted.

24(3)   An incorporated friendly society shall, within 15 days of a winding-up order being made in respect of it, give notice of the order to the Authority; and the Authority shall keep the notice in the public file of the society.

24(4)   If an incorporated friendly society fails to comply with sub-paragraph (3) above, it shall be guilty of an offence and liable on summary conviction to a fine not exceeding level 3 on the standard scale.

25   Section 140 (appointment of liquidator by court in certain circumstances) of the Act does not apply.

26   In the application of sections 141(1) and 142(1) to incorporated friendly societies, the references to functions conferred on a liquidation committee by or under that Act shall have effect as references to its functions by or under that Act as so applied.

27   The conditions which the court may impose under section 147 (power to stay or sist winding up) of the Act shall include those specified in paragraph 21(2) above.

28   Section 154 (adjustment of rights of contributories) of the Act shall have effect with the modification that any surplus is to be distributed in accordance with the rules of the society.

29   [Repealed by the Companies Act 2006 (Commencement No.3, Consequential Amendments, Transitional Provisions and Savings) Order 2007 (SI 2007/2194) Sch.5 para.71(1) as from October 1, 2007.]

Winding up: general

30 Section 187 (power to make over assets to employees) of the Act does not apply.

31(1) In section 201 (dissolution: voluntary winding up) of the Act, subsection (2) applies without the words from "and on the expiration" to the end of the subsection and, in subsection (3), the word "However" shall be omitted.

31(2) Sections 202 to 204 (early dissolution) of the Act do not apply.

32 In section 205 (dissolution: winding up by the court) of the Act, subsection (2) applies with the omission of the words from "and, subject" to the end of the subsection; and in subsections (3) and (4) references to the Secretary of State shall have effect as references to the Authority.

Penal provisions

33 Sections 216 and 217 of the Act (restriction on re-use of name) do not apply.

34(1) Sections 218 and 219 (prosecution of delinquent officers) of the Act do not apply in relation to offences committed by members of an incorporated friendly society acting in that capacity.

34(2) Sections 218(5) of the Act and subsections (1) and (2) of section 219 of the Act do not apply.

34(3) The references in subsections (3) and (4) of section 219 of the Act to the Secretary of State shall have effect as references to the Authority; and the reference in subsection (3) to section 218 of the Act shall have effect as a reference to that section as supplemented by paragraph 35 below.

35(1) Where a report is made to the prosecuting authority (within the meaning of section 218) under section 218(4) of the Act, in relation to an officer of an incorporated friendly society, he may, if he thinks fit, refer the matter to the Authority for further enquiry.

35(2) On such a reference to it the Authority shall exercise its power under section 65(1) above to appoint one or more investigators to investigate and report on the matter.

35(3) An answer given by a person to a question put to him, in exercise of the powers conferred by section 65 above on a person so appointed, may be used in evidence against the person giving it.

Preferential debts

36 Section 387 (meaning in Schedule 6 of "the relevant date") of the Act applies with the omission of subsections (2) and (4) to (6).

PART III

MODIFIED APPLICATION OF INSOLVENCY (NORTHERN IRELAND) ORDER 1989

[Applies to Northern Ireland only; not reproduced.]

PART IV

SUPPLEMENTARY

Dissolution of incorporated friendly society after winding up

67(1) Where an incorporated friendly society has been wound up voluntarily, it is dissolved as from 3 months from the date of the placing in the public file of the society of the return of the final meetings of the society and its creditors made by the liquidator under–

(a)   section 94 or 106 of the Insolvency Act 1986 (as applied to incorporated friendly societies), or on such other date as is determined in accordance with section 201 of that Act; or

(b)   Article 80 or 92 of the Insolvency (Northern Ireland) Order 1989 (as so applied), or on such other date as is determined in accordance with Article 166 of that Order.

67(2)   Where an incorporated friendly society has been wound up by the court, it is dissolved as from 3 months from the date of the placing in the public file of the society of the liquidator's notice under–

(a)   section 172(8) of the Insolvency Act 1986 (as applied to incorporated friendly societies) or on such other date as is determined in accordance with section 205 of that Act; or

(b)   Article 146(7) of the Insolvency (Northern Ireland) Order 1989 (as so applied) or on such other date as is determined in accordance with Article 169 of that Order.

68(1)   Sections 1012 to 1023 and 1034 of the Companies Act 2006 (property of dissolved company) apply in relation to the property of a dissolved incorporated friendly society (whether dissolved under section 20 or following its winding up) as they apply in relation to the property of a dissolved company.

68(2)   Paragraph 3(1) above shall apply to those sections for the purpose of their application to incorporated friendly societies.

68(3)   Any reference in those sections to restoration to the register shall be read as a reference to the effect of an order under section 25 of this Act.

68(4)   [Deleted.]

History
Paragraph 68(1), (3) substituted, and para.(4) deleted by the Companies Act 2006 (Consequential Amendments, Transitional Provisions and Savings) Order 2009 (SI 2009/1941) art.2(1) and Sch.1 para.133(7)(b) as from October 1, 2009.

Insolvency rules and fees

69(1)   Rules may be made under–

(a)   section 411 of the Insolvency Act 1986; or

(b)   Article 359 of the Insolvency (Northern Ireland) Order 1989,

for the purpose of giving effect, in relation to incorporated friendly societies, to the provisions of the applicable winding up legislation.

69(2)   An order made by the competent authority under section 414 of the Insolvency Act 1986 may make provision for fees to be payable under that section in respect of proceedings under the applicable winding-up legislation and the performance by the official receiver or the Secretary of State of functions under it.

69(3)   An order made by the competent authority under Article 361 of the Insolvency (Northern Ireland) Order 1989 may make provisions for fees to be payable under that section in respect of proceedings under the applicable winding-up legislation and the performance by the official receiver in Northern Ireland or the Department of Economic Development in Northern Ireland of functions under it.

Pension Schemes Act 1993

(1993 Chapter 48)

[5th November 1993]

[**Note:** Changes made by the Pensions Act 1995, the Employment Rights Act 1996, the Welfare Reform, the Pensions Act 1999, the Pensions Act 2004 and the National Insurance Contributions Act 2008 have been incorporated into the text (in the case of pre-2003 changes without annotation). References to administration orders, etc. have been altered appropriately throughout pursuant to changes made by the Enterprise Act 2002.]

PART VII

INSOLVENCY OF EMPLOYERS

CHAPTER II

PAYMENT BY SECRETARY OF STATE OF UNPAID SCHEME CONTRIBUTIONS

123 Interpretation of Chapter II

123(1) **[Insolvency of employer for purposes of Ch.II]** For the purposes of this Chapter, an employer shall be taken to be insolvent if, but only if, in England and Wales–

(a) he has been adjudged bankrupt or has made a composition or arrangement with his creditors;

(b) he has died and his estate falls to be administered in accordance with an order under section 421 of the Insolvency Act 1986; or

(c) where the employer is a company–

　(i) a winding-up order is made or a resolution for voluntary winding up is passed with respect to it or the company enters administration,

　(ii) a receiver or manager of its undertaking is duly appointed,

　(iii) possession is taken, by or on behalf of the holders of any debentures secured by a floating charge, of any property of the company comprised in or subject to the charge, or

　(iv) a voluntary arrangement proposed for the purpose of Part I of the Insolvency Act 1986 is approved under that Part.

123(2)   [Insolvency of employer in Scotland for purposes of Ch.II] For the purposes of this Chapter, an employer shall be taken to be insolvent if, but only if, in Scotland–

(a)   sequestration of his estate is awarded or he executes a trust deed for his creditors or enters into a composition contract;

(b)   he has died and a judicial factor appointed under section 11A of the Judicial Factors (Scotland) Act 1889 is required by that section to divide his insolvent estate among his creditors; or

(c)   where the employer is a company–

   (i)   a winding-up order is made or a resolution for voluntary winding up is passed with respect to it or the company enters administration,

   (ii)   a receiver of its undertaking is duly appointed, or

   (iii)   a voluntary arrangement proposed for the purpose of Part I of the Insolvency Act 1986 is approved under that Part.

123(3)   [Definitions] In this Chapter–

"contract of employment", "employee", "employer" and "employment" and other expressions which are defined in the Employment Rights Act 1996 have the same meaning as in that Act;

"holiday pay" means–

(a)   pay in respect of holiday actually taken; or

(b)   any accrued holiday pay which under the employee's contract of employment would in the ordinary course have become payable to him in respect of the period of a holiday if his employment with the employer had continued until he became entitled to a holiday;

123(4)   [Repealed]

123(5)   [Resources of a scheme] Any reference in this Chapter to the resources of a scheme is a reference to the funds out of which the benefits provided by the scheme are from time to time payable.

History
Definition of "occupational pension scheme" and s.123(4) repealed by Pensions Act 2004 Sch.13 para.1 as from September 22, 2005.

124   Duty of Secretary of State to pay unpaid contributions to schemes

124(1)   [Duty of Secretary of State] If, on an application made to him in writing by the persons competent to act in respect of an occupational pension scheme or a personal pension scheme, the Secretary of State is satisfied–

(a)   that an employer has become insolvent; and

(b)   that at the time he did so there remained unpaid relevant contributions falling to be paid by him to the scheme,

then, subject to the provisions of this section and section 125, the Secretary of State shall pay into the resources of the scheme the sum which in his opinion is payable in respect of the unpaid relevant contributions.

124(2)   [Relevant contributions] In this section and section 125 **"relevant contributions"** means contributions falling to be paid by an employer to an occupational pension scheme or a personal pension scheme, either on his own account or on behalf of an employee. and for the purposes of this section a contribution shall not he treated as falling to be paid on behalf of an employee unless a sum equal to that amount has been deducted from the pay of the employee by way of a contribution from him.

124(3) **[Sum payable by employer re unpaid contributions]** Subject to subsection (3A), the sum payable under this section in respect of unpaid contributions of an employer on his own account to an occupational pension scheme or a personal pension scheme shall be the least of the following amounts–

(a) the balance of relevant contributions remaining unpaid on the date when he became insolvent and payable by the employer on his own account to the scheme in respect of the 12 months immediately preceding that date;

(b) the amount certified by an actuary to be necessary for the purpose of meeting the liability of the scheme on dissolution to pay the benefits provided by the scheme to or in respect of the employees of the employer;

(c) an amount equal to 10 per cent of the total amount of remuneration paid or payable to those employees in respect of the 12 months immediately preceding the date on which the employer became insolvent.

124(3A) **[Sum payable into money purchase scheme]** Where the scheme in question is a money purchase scheme, the sum payable under this section by virtue of subsection (3) shall be the lesser of the amounts mentioned in paragraphs (a) and (c) of that subsection.

124(4) **[Remuneration]** For the purposes of subsection (3)(c), **"remuneration"** includes holiday pay, statutory sick pay, statutory maternity pay under Part V of the Social Security Act 1986 or Part XII of the Social Security Contributions and Benefits Act 1992, and any payment such as is referred to in section 184(2) of the Employment Rights Act 1996.

124(5) **[Limit on payment of unpaid contributions]** Any sum payable under this section in respect of unpaid contributions on behalf of an employee shall not exceed the amount deducted from the pay of the employee in respect of the employee's contributions to the scheme during the 12 months immediately preceding the date on which the employer became insolvent.

124(6) **["On his own account"]** In this section **"on his own account"**, in relation to an employer, means on his own account but to fund benefits for, or in respect of, one or more employees.

History
Section 124(6) inserted by Pensions Act 2004 Sch.12 para.20 as from September 22, 2005.

125   Certification of amounts payable under section 124 by insolvency officers

125(1) **[Application of s.125(1)]** This section applies where one of the officers mentioned in subsection (2) (**"the relevant officer"**) has been or is required to be appointed in connection with an employer's insolvency.

125(2) **[Officers referred to in s.125(1)]** The officers referred to in subsection (1) are–

(a) a trustee in bankruptcy;

(b) a liquidator;

(c) an administrator;

(d) a receiver or manager; or

(e) a trustee under a composition or arrangement between the employer and his creditors or under a trust deed for his creditors executed by the employer;

and in this subsection **"trustee"**, in relation to a composition or arrangement, includes the supervisor of a voluntary arrangement proposed for the purposes of and approved under Part I or VIII of the Insolvency Act 1986.

125(3) **[Payment under s.124 on receipt of statement by relevant officer]** Subject to subsection (5), where this section applies the Secretary of State shall not make any payment under section 124 in respect of unpaid relevant contributions until he has received a statement from the relevant officer of the amount of relevant contributions which appear to have been unpaid on the date on which the employer became insolvent and to remain unpaid; and the relevant officer shall on request by the Secretary of State provide him as soon as reasonably practicable with such a statement.

125(4) **[Amount payable]** Subject to subsection (5), an amount shall be taken to be payable, paid or deducted as mentioned in subsection (3)(a) or (c) or (5) of section 124 only if it is so certified by the relevant officer.

125(5) **[Power of Secretary of State to make payment]** If the Secretary of State is satisfied–

(a)   that he does not require a statement under subsection (3) in order to determine the amount of relevant contributions that was unpaid on the date on which the employer became insolvent and remains unpaid, or

(b)   that he does not require a certificate under subsection (4) in order to determine the amounts payable, paid or deducted as mentioned in subsection (3)(a) or (c) or (5) of section 124,

he may make a payment under that section in respect of the contributions in question without having received such a statement or, as the case may be, such a certificate.

126   Complaint to industrial tribunal

126(1) **[Persons acting re pension schemes]** Any persons who are competent to act in respect of an occupational pension scheme or a personal pension scheme and who have applied for a payment to be made under section 124 into the resources of the scheme may present a complaint to an employment tribunal that–

(a)   the Secretary of State has failed to make any such payment; or

(b)   any such payment made by him is less than the amount which should have been paid.

126(2) **[Entitlement to complaint]** Such a complaint must be presented within the period of three months beginning with the date on which the decision of the Secretary of State on that application was communicated to the persons presenting it or, if that is not reasonably practicable, within such further period as is reasonable.

126(3) **[Declaration of tribunal]** Where an employment tribunal finds that the Secretary of State ought to make a payment under section 124, it shall make a declaration to that effect and shall also declare the amount of any such payment which it finds that the Secretary of State ought to make.

127   Transfer to Secretary of State of rights and remedies

127(1) **[Where Secretary of State makes s.124 payment]** Where in pursuance of section 124 the Secretary of State makes any payment into the resources of an occupational pension scheme or a personal pension scheme in respect of any contributions to the scheme, any rights and remedies in respect of those contributions belonging to the persons competent to act in respect of the scheme shall, on the making of the payment, become rights and remedies of the Secretary of State.

127(2) **[Extent of rights and remedies re s.127(1)]** Where the Secretary of State makes any such payment as is mentioned in subsection (1) and the sum (or any part of the sum) falling to be paid by the employer on account of the contributions in respect of which the payment is made constitutes–

(a)   a preferential debt within the meaning of the Insolvency Act 1986 for the purposes of any provision of that Act (including any such provision as applied by an order made under that Act) or any provision of the Companies Acts (as defined in section 2(1) of the Companies Act 2006); or

(b)   a preferred debt within the meaning of the Bankruptcy (Scotland) Act 1985 for the purposes of any provision of that Act (including any such provision as applied by section 11A of the Judicial Factors (Scotland) Act 1889), then, without prejudice to the generality of subsection (1), there shall be included among the rights and remedies which become rights and remedies of the Secretary of State in accordance with that subsection any right arising under any such provision by reason of the status of that sum (or that part of it) as a preferential or preferred debt.

127(3)   [Computation of claims in s.127(2)(a)] In computing for the purposes of any provision referred to in subsection (2)(a) or (b) the aggregate amount payable in priority to other creditors of the employer in respect of–

(a)   any claim of the Secretary of State to be so paid by virtue of subsection (2); and

(b)   any claim by the persons competent to act in respect of the scheme, any claim falling within paragraph (a) shall be treated as if it were a claim of those persons; but the Secretary of State shall be entitled, as against those persons, to be so paid in respect of any such claim of his (up to the full amount of the claim) before any payment is made to them in respect of any claim falling within paragraph (b).

CHAPTER III

PRIORITY IN BANKRUPTCY

128   Priority in bankruptcy etc.

128   Schedule 4 shall have effect for the purposes of paragraph 8 of Schedule 6 to the Insolvency Act 1986 and paragraph 4 of Schedule 3 to the Bankruptcy (Scotland) Act 1985 (by virtue of which sums to which Schedule 4 to this Act applies are preferential or, as the case may be, preferred debts in cases of insolvency).

SCHEDULE 4

PRIORITY IN BANKRUPTCY ETC

Section 128

Earner's contributions to occupational pension scheme

1   This Schedule applies to any sum owed on account of an earner's contributions to an occupational pension scheme being contributions deducted from earnings paid in the period of four months immediately preceding the relevant date or otherwise due in respect of earnings paid or payable in that period.

Employer's contributions to occupational pension scheme

2(1)   This Schedule applies to any sum owed on account of an employer's contributions to a salary related contracted-out scheme which were payable in the period of 12 months immediately preceding the relevant date.

2(1A)   The amount of the debt having priority by virtue of sub-paragraph (1) shall be taken to be an amount equal to the appropriate amount.

2(2)   This Schedule applies to any sum owed on account of an employer's minimum payments to a money purchase contracted-out scheme falling to be made in the period of 12 months immediately preceding the relevant date.

2(3)   In so far as payments cannot from the terms of the scheme be identified as falling within sub-paragraph (2), the amount of the debt having priority by virtue of that sub-paragraph shall be taken to be an amount equal to the appropriate amount.

2(3A) In sub-paragraph (1A) or (3) **"the appropriate amount"** means the aggregate of–

(a) the percentage for non-contributing earners of the total reckonable earnings paid or payable, in the period of 12 months referred to in sub-paragraph (1) or (2) (as the case may be), to or for the benefit of non-contributing earners; and

(b) the percentage for contributing earners of the total reckonable earnings paid or payable, in that period, to or for the benefit of contributing earners.

2(4) For the purposes of sub-paragraph (3A)–

(a) the earnings to be taken into account as reckonable earnings are those paid or payable to or for the benefit of earners in employment which is contracted-out by reference to the scheme in the whole or any part of the period of 12 months there mentioned; and

(b) earners are to be identified as contributing or non-contributing in relation to service of theirs in employment which is contracted-out by reference to the scheme according to whether or not in the period in question they were liable under the terms of the scheme to contribute in respect of that service towards the provision of pensions under the scheme.

2(5) In this paragraph–

"appropriate flat-rate percentage" has the same meaning as in section 42A;

"employer" shall be construed in accordance with regulations made under section 181(2); and

"the percentage for contributing earners" means–

(a) in relation to a salary related contracted-out scheme, 3 per cent, and

(b) in relation to a money purchase contracted-out scheme, the percentage which is the appropriate flat-rate percentage for secondary Class 1 contributions,

"the percentage for non-contributing earners" means–

(a) in relation to a salary related contracted-out scheme, 4.8 per cent, and

(b) in relation to a money purchase contracted-out scheme, a percentage equal to the sum of the appropriate flat-rate percentages for primary and secondary Class 1 contributions;

"reckonable earnings", in relation to any employment, means the earner's earnings from that employment so far as those earnings–

(a) were comprised in any payment of earnings made to him or for his benefit at a time when the employment was contracted-out employment; and

(b) exceeded the current lower earnings limit but not the upper accrual point.

History
Definition of "reckonable earnings" amended by the National Insurance Contributions Act 2008 Sch.1 para.13(2).

State scheme premiums

3(1) This Schedule applies to any sum owed on account of a contributions equivalent premium payable at any time before, or in consequence of; a person going into liquidation or being adjudged bankrupt, or in Scotland, the sequestration of a debtor's estate, or (in the case of a company not in liquidation)–

(a) the appointment of a receiver as mentioned in section 40 of the Insolvency Act 1986 (debenture-holders secured by floating charge), or

(b) the appointment of a receiver under section 53(6) or 54(5) of that Act (Scottish company with property subject to floating charge), or

(c)   the taking of possession by debenture-holders (so secured) as mentioned in section 754 of the Companies Act 2006.

3(2)   Where any such premium is payable in respect of a period of service of more than 12 months (taking into account any previous linked qualifying service), the amount to be paid in priority by virtue of this paragraph shall be limited to the amount of the premium that would have been payable if the service had been confined to the last 12 months taken into account in fixing the actual amount of the premium.

3(3)   Where–

(a)   by virtue of this paragraph the whole or part of a premium is required to be paid in priority to other debts of the debtor or his estate; and

(b)   the person liable for the payment would be entitled to recover the whole or part of any sum paid on account of it from another person either under section 61 or under any provision made by the relevant scheme for the purposes of that section or otherwise,

then, subject to sub-paragraph (4), that other person shall be liable for any part of the premium for the time being unpaid.

3(4)   No person shall be liable by virtue of sub-paragraph (3) for an amount in excess of the sum which might be so recovered from him if the premium had been paid in full by the person liable for it, after deducting from that sum any amount which has been or may be recovered from him in respect of any part of that payment paid otherwise than under that sub-paragraph.

3(5)   The payment under sub-paragraph (3) of any amount in respect of a premium shall have the same effect on the rights and liabilities of the person making it (other than his liabilities under that sub-paragraph) as if it had been a payment of that amount on account of the sum recoverable from him in respect of a premium as mentioned in sub-paragraph (3)(b).

History
Paragraphs 3(1)(c) and 4(1)(a) amended by the Companies Act 2006 (Consequential Amendments etc.) Order 2008 (SI 2008/948) art.3(1) and Sch.1 para.194(3), as from April 6, 2008.

Interpretation

4(1)   In this Schedule–

(a)   in its application in England and Wales, section 754(3) of the Companies Act 2006 and section 387 of the Insolvency Act 1986 apply as regards the meaning of the expression "the relevant date"; and

(b)   in its application in Scotland, that expression has the same meaning as in Part I of Schedule 3 to the Bankruptcy (Scotland) Act 1985.

4(2)   In this Schedule references to a contracted-out scheme, contracted-out employment and a state scheme premium include references to a contracted-out scheme, contracted out employment and a state scheme premium (other than a personal pension protected rights premium) within the meaning of any provisions in force in Northern Ireland and corresponding to the provisions of this Act.

History
See note after para.3.

Employment Rights Act 1996

(1996 Chapter 18)

ARRANGEMENT OF SECTIONS

[22nd May 1996]

[**Note:** Changes made by the Employment Rights (Dispute Resolution) Act 1998, the Employment Rights (Increase of Limits) Order 2011 (SI 2011/3006), the Enterprise Act 2002 and the Tribunals, Courts and Enforcement Act 2007 have been incorporated into the text. References to administration orders, etc. have been altered appropriately throughout, pursuant to changes made by the Enterprise Act 2002. References to "industrial tribunals" have been altered throughout to "employment tribunals" pursuant to the Employment Rights (Dispute Resolution) Act 1998.]

PART XII

INSOLVENCY OF EMPLOYERS

182   Employee's rights on insolvency of employer

182   If, on an application made to him in writing by an employee, the Secretary of State is satisfied that–

(a)   the employee's employer has become insolvent,

(b)   the employee's employment has been terminated, and

(c)   on the appropriate date the employee was entitled to be paid the whole or part of any debt to which this Part applies,

the Secretary of State shall, subject to section 186, to pay the employee out of the National Insurance Fund the amount to which, in the opinion of the Secretary of State, the employee is entitled in respect of the debt.

183   Insolvency

183(1)   [Insolvency of employer] An employer has become insolvent for the purposes of this Part–

(a)   where the employer is an individual, if (but only if) subsection (2) is satisfied,

(b)   where the employer is a company, if (but only if) subsection (3) is satisfied, and

(c)   where the employer is a limited liability partnership, if (but only if) subsection (4) is satisfied.

183(2)   [Insolvent individual employer] This subsection is satisfied in the case of an employer who is an individual–

(a)   in England and Wales if–

(ai)   a moratorium period under a debt relief order applies in relation to him,

(i)   he has been adjudged bankrupt or has made a composition or arrangement with his creditors, or

(ii) he has died and his estate falls to be administered in accordance with an order under section 421 of the Insolvency Act 1986, and

(b) in Scotland if–

(i)   sequestration of his estate has been awarded or he has executed a trust deed for his creditors or has entered into a composition contract, or

(ii) he has died and a judicial factor appointed under section 11A of the Judicial Factors (Scotland) Act 1889 is required by that section to divide his insolvent estate among his creditors.

183(3) **[Insolvent company employer]** This subsection is satisfied in the case of an employer which is a company–

(a) if a winding up order has been made, or a resolution for voluntary winding up has been passed, with respect to the company,

(aa) if the company is in administration for the purposes of the Insolvency Act 1986,

(b) if a receiver or (in England and Wales only) a manager of the company's undertaking has been duly appointed, or (in England and Wales only) possession has been taken, by or on behalf of the holders of any debentures secured by a floating charge, of any property of the company comprised in or subject to the charge, or

(c) if a voluntary arrangement proposed in the case of the company for the purposes of Part I of the Insolvency Act 1986 has been approved under that Part of that Act.

183(4) **[Insolvent limited liability partnership]** This subsection is satisfied in the case of an employer which is a limited liability partnership–

(a) if a winding-up order, an administration order or a determination for a voluntary winding-up has been made with respect to the limited liability partnership,

(b) if a receiver or (in England and Wales only) a manager of the undertaking of the limited liability partnership has been duly appointed, or (in England and Wales only) possession has been taken, by or on behalf of the holders of any debentures secured by a floating charge, of any property of the limited liability partnership comprised in or subject to the charge, or

(c) if a voluntary arrangement proposed in the case of the limited liability partnership for the purposes of Part I of the Insolvency Act 1986 has been approved under that Part of that Act.

History
Section 183(2)(ai) inserted by the Tribunals, Courts and Employment Act 2007 s.108(3) and Sch.20 para.17 as from April 6, 2009. Section 183(1)(c), (4) inserted by the Limited Liability Partnerships Regulations 2001 (SI 2001/1090) reg.5 and Sch.5 para.19(1), (3) as from April 6, 2001.

184   Debts to which Part applies

184(1) **[Application of Pt XII]** This Part applies to the following debts–

(a) any arrears of pay in respect of one or more (but not more than eight) weeks,

(b) any amount which the employer is liable to pay the employee for the period of notice required by section 86(1) or (2) or for any failure of the employer to give the period of notice required by section 86(1),

(c) any holiday pay–

(i) in respect of a period or periods of holiday not exceeding six weeks in all, and

(ii) to which the employee became entitled during the twelve months ending with the appropriate date,

(d) any basic award of compensation for unfair dismissal or so much of an award under a designated dismissal procedures agreement as does not exceed any basic award of compensation for unfair dismissal to which the employee would be entitled but for the agreement, and

(e) any reasonable sum by way of reimbursement of the whole or part of any fee or premium paid by an apprentice or articled clerk.

184(2) [Arrears of pay for s.184(1)(a)] For the purposes of subsection (1)(a) the following amounts shall be treated as arrears of pay–

(a) a guarantee payment,

(b) any payment for time off under Part VI of this Act or section 169 of the Trade Union and Labour Relations (Consolidation) Act 1992 (payment for time off for carrying out trade union duties etc.),

(c) remuneration on suspension on medical grounds under section 64 of this Act and remuneration on suspension on maternity grounds under section 68 of this Act, and

(d) remuneration under a protective award under section 189 of the Trade Union and Labour Relations (Consolidation) Act 1992.

184(3) ["Holiday pay" in s.184(1)(c)] In subsection (1)(c) **"holiday pay"**, in relation to an employee, means–

(a) pay in respect of a holiday actually taken by the employee, or

(b) any accrued holiday pay which, under the employee's contract of employment, would in the ordinary course have become payable to him in respect of the period of a holiday if his employment with the employer had continued until he became entitled to a holiday.

184(4) [Reasonable sum under s.184(1)(e)] A sum shall be taken to be reasonable for the purposes of subsection (1)(e) in a case where a trustee in bankruptcy, or (in Scotland) a permanent or interim trustee (within the meaning of the Bankruptcy (Scotland) Act 1985), or liquidator has been or is required to be appointed–

(a) as respects England and Wales, if it is admitted to be reasonable by the trustee in bankruptcy or liquidator under section 348 of the Insolvency Act 1986 (effect of bankruptcy on apprenticeships etc.), whether as originally enacted or as applied to the winding up of a company by rules under section 411 of that Act, and

(b) as respects Scotland, if it is accepted by the permanent or interim trustee or liquidator for the purposes of the sequestration or winding up.

185 The appropriate date

185 In this Part **"the appropriate date"**–

(a) in relation to arrears of pay (not being remuneration under a protective award made under section 189 of the Trade Union and Labour Relations (Consolidation) Act 1992) and to holiday pay, means the date on which the employer became insolvent,

(b) in relation to a basic award of compensation for unfair dismissal and to remuneration under a protective award so made, means whichever is the latest of–

(i) the date on which the employer became insolvent,

(ii) the date of the termination of the employee's employment, and

(iii) the date on which the award was made, and

(c) in relation to any other debt to which this Part applies, means whichever is the later of–

(i) the date on which the employer became insolvent, and

(ii) the date of the termination of the employee's employment.

186 Limit on amount payable under section 182

186(1) [Maximum amount for Pt XII] The total amount payable to an employee in respect of any debt to which this Part applies, where the amount of the debt is referable to a period of time, shall not exceed–

(a) £430 in respect of any one week, or

(b) in respect of a shorter period, an amount bearing the same proportion to £430 as that shorter period bears to a week.

History
In s.186(1), the figure "£430" substituted for the former figure "£400" by the Employment Rights (Increase of Limits) Order 2011 (SI 2011/3006) art.3 and Sch. where the appropriate date falls on or after February 1, 2012. Previously, the following substitutions took effect: £400 for £380 (SI 2010/2926), from February 1, 2011; £380 for £350 (SI 2009/1903), from October 1, 2009; £350 for £330 (SI 2008/3055), from February 1, 2009; £330 for £310 (SI 2007/3570, from February 1, 2008); £310 for £290 (SI 2006/3045, from February 1, 2007); £290 for £280 (SI 2005/3352, from February 1, 2006); £280 for £270 (SI 2004/3379, from February 1, 2005); £270 for £260 (SI 2003/3038, from February 1, 2004); £260 for £250 (SI 2002/2297, from February 1, 2003); £250 for £240 (SI 2002/10, from February 1, 2002); £240 for £230 (SI 2001/21, from February 1, 2001); £230 for £220 (SI 1999/3375, from February 1, 2000); £220 for £210 (SI 1998/924, from April 1, 1998).

Note
The figures in s.186(1)(a) and (b) may be varied by the Secretary of State (see Employment Relations Act 1999 s.34(1)(d)).

186(2) [Repealed by Employment Relations Act 1999 ss.36(1)(a), 44 and Sch.9 Pt 10 with effect from December 17, 1999 (see Employment Relations Act 1999 (Commencement No.3 and Transitional Provision) Order 1999 (SI 1999/3374 (C. 90) art.2 and Sch.).]

187 Role of relevant officer

187(1) [No payment until statement received] Where a relevant officer has been, or is required to be, appointed in connection with an employer's insolvency, the Secretary of State shall not make a payment under section 182 in respect of a debt until he has received a statement from the relevant officer of the amount of that debt which appears to have been owed to the employee on the appropriate date and to remain unpaid.

187(2) [Power of Secretary of State to make payment] If the Secretary of State is satisfied that he does not require a statement under subsection (1) in order to determine the amount of a debt which was owed to the employee on the appropriate date and remains unpaid, he may make a payment under section 182 in respect of the debt without having received such a statement.

187(3) [Duty of relevant officer to provide statement] A relevant officer shall, on request by the Secretary of State, provide him with a statement for the purposes of subsection (1) as soon as is reasonably practicable.

187(4) [Relevant officers for purposes of s.187] The following are relevant officers for the purposes of this section–

(a) a trustee in bankruptcy or a permanent or interim trustee (within the meaning of the Bankruptcy (Scotland) Act 1985),

(b) a liquidator,

   (c)   an administrator,

   (d)   a receiver or manager,

   (e)   a trustee under a composition or arrangement between the employer and his creditors, and

   (f)   a trustee under a trust deed for his creditors executed by the employer.

187(5)   **["Trustee" in s.187(4)(e)]** In subsection (4)(e) **"trustee"** includes the supervisor of a voluntary arrangement proposed for the purposes of, and approved under, Part I or VIII of the Insolvency Act 1986.

188   Complaints to employment tribunals

188(1)   **[Entitlement to present complaint]** A person who has applied for a payment under section 182 may present a complaint to an employment tribunal–

   (a)   that the Secretary of State has failed to make any such payment, or

   (b)   that any such payment made by him is less than the amount which should have been paid.

188(2)   **[Time-limit for presentation of complaint]** An employment tribunal shall not consider a complaint under subsection (1) unless it is presented–

   (a)   before the end of the period of three months beginning with the date on which the decision of the Secretary of State on the application was communicated to the applicant, or

   (b)   within such further period as the tribunal considers reasonable in a case where it is not reasonably practicable for the complaint to be presented before the end of that period of three months.

188(3)   **[Declaration by tribunal]** Where an employment tribunal finds that the Secretary of State ought to make a payment under section 182, the tribunal shall–

   (a)   make a declaration to that effect, and

   (b)   declare the amount of any such payment which it finds the Secretary of State ought to make.

189   Transfer to Secretary of State of rights and remedies

189(1)   **[Where s.182 payment made to employee]** Where, in pursuance of section 182, the Secretary of State makes a payment to an employee in respect of a debt to which this Part applies–

   (a)   on the making of the payment any rights and remedies of the employee in respect of the debt (or, if the Secretary of State has paid only part of it, in respect of that part) become rights and remedies of the Secretary of State, and

   (b)   any decision of an employment tribunal requiring an employer to pay that debt to the employee has the effect that the debt (or the part of it which the Secretary of State has paid) is to be paid to the Secretary of State.

189(2)   **[Extent of rights and remedies re s.182]** Where a debt (or any part of a debt) in respect of which the Secretary of State has made a payment in pursuance of section 182 constitutes–

   (a)   a preferential debt within the meaning of the Insolvency Act 1986 for the purposes of any provision of that Act (including any such provision as applied by any order made under that Act) or any provision of the Companies Act 2006, or–

   (b)   a preferred debt within the meaning of the Bankruptcy (Scotland) Act 1985 for the purposes of any provision of that Act (including any such provision as applied by section 11A of the Judicial Factors (Scotland) Act 1889),

the rights which become rights of the Secretary of State in accordance with subsection (1) include any right arising under any such provision by reason of the status of the debt (or that part of it) as a preferential or preferred debt.

189(3) **[Computation of debts in s.189(2)]** In computing for the purposes of any provision mentioned in subsection (2)(a) or (b) the aggregate amount payable in priority to other creditors of the employer in respect of–

(a) any claim of the Secretary of State to be paid in priority to other creditors of the employer by virtue of subsection (2), and

(b) any claim by the employee to be so paid made in his own right,

any claim of the Secretary of State to be so paid by virtue of subsection (2) shall be treated as if it were a claim of the employee.

189(4) [Omitted and repealed by the Enterprise Act 2002 s.248(3) Sch.17 para.49(1), (4) and s.278(2) Sch.26 as from September 15, 2003 subject to transitional provisions.]

189(5) **[Sum recovered to be paid into National Insurance Fund]** Any sum recovered by the Secretary of State in exercising any right, or pursuing any remedy, which is his by virtue of this section shall be paid into the National Insurance Fund.

190 Power to obtain information

190(1) **[Power of Secretary of State on application]** Where an application is made to the Secretary of State under section 182 in respect of a debt owed by an employer, the Secretary of State may require–

(a) the employer to provide him with such information as he may reasonably require for the purpose of determining whether the application is well-founded, and

(b) any person having the custody or control of any relevant records or other documents to produce for examination on behalf of the Secretary of State any such document in that person's custody or under his control which is of such a description as the Secretary of State may require.

190(2) **[Requirement by notice, etc.]** Any such requirement–

(a) shall be made by notice in writing given to the person on whom the requirement is imposed, and

(b) may be varied or revoked by a subsequent notice so given.

190(3) **[Penalty for refusal, etc.]** If a person refuses or wilfully neglects to furnish any information or produce any document which he has been required to furnish or produce by a notice under this section he is guilty of an offence and liable on summary conviction to a fine not exceeding level 3 on the standard scale.

190(4) **[Penalty for false statement]** If a person, in purporting to comply with a requirement of a notice under this section, knowingly or recklessly makes any false statement he is guilty of an offence and liable on summary conviction to a fine not exceeding level 5 on the standard scale.

190(5) **[Offence by body corporate and officers under s.190]** Where an offence under this section committed by a body corporate is proved–

(a) to have been committed with the consent or connivance of, or

(b) to be attributable to any neglect on the part of,

any director, manager, secretary or other similar officer of the body corporate, or any person who was purporting to act in any such capacity, he (as well as the body corporate) is guilty of the offence and liable to be proceeded against and punished accordingly.

190(6) **[Application of s.190(5)]** Where the affairs of a body corporate are managed by its members, subsection (5) applies in relation to the acts and defaults of a member in connection with his functions of management as if he were a director of the body corporate.

Financial Services and Markets Act 2000

(2000 Chapter 8)

ARRANGEMENT OF SECTIONS

An Act to make provision about the regulation of financial services and markets; to provide for the transfer of certain statutory functions relating to building societies, friendly societies, industrial and provident societies and certain other mutual societies; and for connected purposes.

[14th June 2000]

[**Note**: Changes made by the Insolvency Act 2000, the Enterprise Act 2002, the Dormant Bank and Building Society Accounts Act 2008, the Banking Act 2009, the Financial Services Act 2010, the Companies Act 2006 (Consequential Amendments etc.) Order 2008 (SI 2008/948), the Building Societies (Insolvency and Special Administration) Order 2009 (SI 2009/805) and by the Undertakings for Collective Investment in Transferable Securities Regulations 2011 (SI 2011/1613) have been incorporated into the text (in the case of pre-2003 legislation without annotation). References to administration orders, etc. have been altered appropriately throughout pursuant to changes made by the Enterprise Act 2002. The provisions of this Act which apply to limited liability partnerships are noted at the appropriate places.]

PART XV

THE FINANCIAL SERVICES COMPENSATION SCHEME

The scheme manager

212   The scheme manager

212(1)   [Duty of Authority] The Authority must establish a body corporate (**"the scheme manager"**) to exercise the functions conferred on the scheme manager by or under this Part.

212(2)   [Manager capable of exercising Part XV or 15A functions] The Authority must take such steps as are necessary to ensure that the scheme manager is, at all times, capable of exercising those functions and the functions conferred on it by or under Part 15A.

212(3)   [Constitution] The constitution of the scheme manager must provide for it to have–

(a)   a chairman; and

(b)   a board (which must include the chairman) whose members are the scheme manager's directors.

212(4)   [Membership of board] The chairman and other members of the board must be persons appointed, and liable to removal from office, by the Authority (acting, in the case of the chairman, with the approval of the Treasury).

212(5)   [Independence of board members] But the terms of their appointment (and in particular those governing removal from office) must be such as to secure their independence from the Authority in the operation of the compensation scheme.

212(6)   [Manager not exercising functions for Crown] The scheme manager is not to be regarded as exercising functions on behalf of the Crown.

212(7)   [Manager's staff, etc. not Crown servants] The scheme manager's board members, officers and staff are not to be regarded as Crown servants.

History
Section 212(2) amended by the Financial Services Act 2010 Sch.2 para.21 as from October 12, 2010.

The scheme

213   The compensation scheme

213(1)   [Establishment of scheme] The Authority must by rules establish a scheme for compensating persons in cases where relevant persons are unable, or are likely to be unable, to satisfy claims against them.

213(2)   [The compensation scheme] The rules are to be known as the Financial Services Compensation Scheme (but are referred to in this Act as " **the compensation scheme**").

213(3)   [Provision for scheme manager to assess compensation, etc.] The compensation scheme must, in particular, provide for the scheme manager–

(a)   to assess and pay compensation, in accordance with the scheme, to claimants in respect of claims made in connection with regulated activities carried on (whether or not with permission) by relevant persons; and

(b)   to have power to impose levies on authorised persons, or any class of authorised person, for the purpose of meeting its expenses (including in particular expenses incurred, or expected to be incurred, in paying compensation, borrowing or insuring risks).

213(4)   [Power of scheme manager to impose levies] The compensation scheme may provide for the scheme manager to have power to impose levies on authorised persons, or any class of authorised person, for the purpose of recovering the cost (whenever incurred) of establishing the scheme.

213(5)   [Duty of Authority re s.213(3)(b)] In making any provision of the scheme by virtue of subsection (3)(b), the Authority must take account of the desirability of ensuring that the amount of the levies imposed on a particular class of authorised person reflects, so far as practicable, the amount of the claims made, or likely to be made, in respect of that class of person.

213(6)   [Recovery of levies as debts due] An amount payable to the scheme manager as a result of any provision of the scheme made by virtue of subsection (3)(b) or (4) may be recovered as a debt due to the scheme manager.

213(7)   [Application of ss.214–217] Sections 214 to 217 make further provision about the scheme but are not to be taken as limiting the power conferred on the Authority by subsection (1).

213(8)   ["Specified"] In those sections **"specified"** means specified in the scheme.

213(9)   ["Relevant person"] In this Part (except in sections 219, 220 or 224) **"relevant person"** means a person who was–

(a)   an authorised person at the time the act or omission giving rise to the claim against him took place; or

(b)   an appointed representative at that time.

213(10)   [Qualification for authorisation under Sch.3] But a person who, at that time–

(a)   qualified for authorisation under Schedule 3, and

(b)   fell within a prescribed category in relation to any authorised activities,

is not to be regarded as a relevant person in relation to those activities, unless the person had elected to participate in the scheme in relation to those activities at that time.

213(11) **["Authorised activities" in s.213(10)]** In subsection (10) "authorised activities", in relation to a person, means activities for which the person had, at the time mentioned in that subsection, permission as a result of any provision of, or made under, Schedule 3.

History

Section 213(10) substituted and s.213(11) inserted by the Undertakings for Collective Investment in Transferable Securities Regulations 2011 (SI 2011/1613) reg.2 from July 1, 2011.

Note

See the Financial Services and Markets Act 2000 (Compensation Scheme: Electing Participants) Regulations 2001 (SI 2001/1783). Note prospective amendment of ss.213(7), and 218(1), (2)(b) and insertion of new s.214A by the Banking Act 2009 s.170(2).

Provisions of the scheme

214 General

214(1) **[Provisions of the scheme]** The compensation scheme may, in particular, make provision–

(a) as to the circumstances in which a relevant person is to be taken (for the purposes of the scheme) to be unable, or likely to be unable, to satisfy claims made against him;

(b) for the establishment of different funds for meeting different kinds of claim;

(c) for the imposition of different levies in different cases;

(d) limiting the levy payable by a person in respect of a specified period;

(e) for repayment of the whole or part of a levy in specified circumstances;

(f) for a claim to be entertained only if it is made by a specified kind of claimant;

(g) for a claim to be entertained only if it falls within a specified kind of claim;

(h) as to the procedure to be followed in making a claim;

(i) for the making of interim payments before a claim is finally determined;

(j) limiting the amount payable on a claim to a specified maximum amount or a maximum amount calculated in a specified manner;

(k) for payment to be made, in specified circumstances, to a person other than the claimant.

214(1A) **[Procedural rules in s.214(1)(h) allow for deemed claims]** Rules by virtue of subsection (1)(h) may, in particular, allow the scheme manager to treat persons who are or may be entitled to claim under the scheme as if they had done so.

214(1B) **[Reference to enactment or instrument to include deemed claims]** A reference in any enactment or instrument to a claim or claimant under this Part includes a reference to a deemed claim or claimant in accordance with subsection (1A).

214(1C) **[Power to settle claims subject to maximum in s.214(1)(j)]** Rules by virtue of subsection (1)(j) may, in particular, allow, or be subject to rules which allow, the scheme manager to settle a class of claim by payment of sums fixed without reference to, or by modification of, the normal rules for calculation of maximum entitlement for individual claims.

History

In s.214 subss.(1A), (1B) and (1C) were inserted by Banking Act 2009 (C. 1) s.174, as from February 21, 2009.

Note

For the application of rules made under s.214(1) to credit unions, see the Financial Services and Markets Act 2000 (Consequential Amendments and Transitional Provisions) (Credit Unions) Order 2002 (SI 2002/1501).

214(2)   [Variability of provisions] Different provision may be made with respect to different kinds of claim.

214(3)   [Provision for manager to determine, etc. scheme matters] The scheme may provide for the determination and regulation of matters relating to the scheme by the scheme manager.

214(4)   [Scope of scheme] The scheme, or particular provisions of the scheme, may be made so as to apply only in relation to–

(a)   activities carried on,

(b)   claimants,

(c)   matters arising, or

(d)   events occurring,

in specified territories, areas or localities.

214(5)   [Persons qualified for authorisation under Sch.3] The scheme may provide for a person who–

(a)   qualifies for authorisation under Schedule 3, and

(b)   falls within a prescribed category,

to elect to participate in the scheme in relation to some or all of the activities for which he has permission as a result of any provision of, or made under, that Schedule.

214(6)   [Power of scheme manager where entitlement to payment under other scheme, etc.] The scheme may provide for the scheme manager to have power–

(a)   in specified circumstances,

(b)   but only if the scheme manager is satisfied that the claimant is entitled to receive a payment in respect of his claim–

(i)   under a scheme which is comparable to the compensation scheme, or

(ii)   as the result of a guarantee given by a government or other authority,

to make a full payment of compensation to the claimant and recover the whole or part of the amount of that payment from the other scheme or under that guarantee.

Note

See the Financial Services and Markets Act 2000 (Compensation Scheme: Electing Participants) Regulations 2001 (SI 2001/1783).

Note prospective insertion of new s.214A by the Banking Act 2009 s.170(2).

214B   Contribution to costs of special resolution regime

214B(1)   [Application] This section applies if–

(a)   a stabilisation power under Part 1 of the Banking Act 2009 has been exercised in respect of a bank, building society or credit union within the meaning of that Part (**"the institution"**); and

(b)   the Treasury think that the institution was or was likely to have been, or but for the exercise of the power would have become, unable to satisfy claims against it.

214B(2)   [Scheme manager to make payments for expenses] The Treasury may require the scheme manager to make payments (to the Treasury or any other person) in respect of expenses of a prescribed description incurred (by the Treasury or that person) in connection with the exercise of the power.

214B(3)   [Limit on s.216B(2) payments] Subsection (2) is subject to section 214C (limit on amount of special resolution regime payments).

214B(4) **["Expenses" in s.214B(2) includes interest]** In subsection (2) **"expenses"** includes interest at a specified rate on the difference, at any time, between–

(a) the total amount of expenses (including interest) incurred at or before that time; and

(b) the total amount recovered, or received from the scheme manager, in respect of the institution, at or before that time, by–

    (i) the Treasury; and

    (ii) any other person who has incurred expenses in connection with the exercise of the power that are of a description prescribed under subsection (2).

214B(5) **[Treatment of s.214B payments]** Any payment made by the scheme manager under subsection (2) is to be treated for the purposes of this Part as an expense under the compensation scheme.

214B(6) **["Specified rate" in ss.214B, 214C]** In this section and section 214C **"specified rate"** means a rate specified by the Treasury.

214B(7) **[Different rates]** Different rates may be specified under different provisions or for different periods.

214B(8) **[Setting of rate]** A rate may be specified by reference to a rate set (from time to time) by any person.

214C Limit on amount of special resolution regime payments

214C(1) **[Maximum amount]** The total amount of special resolution regime payments required to be made in respect of a person (**"the institution"**) may not exceed–

(a) notional net expenditure (see subsection (3)), minus

(b) actual net expenditure (see subsection (4)).

214C(2) **["Special resolution regime payment"]** A **"special resolution regime payment"** is–

(a) a payment under section 214B(2); or

(b) a payment required to be made by the scheme manager by virtue of section 61 of the Banking Act 2009 (special resolution regime: compensation).

214C(3) **[Notional net expenditure]** Notional net expenditure is–

(a) the total amount of expenses that would have been incurred under the compensation scheme in respect of the institution if the stabilisation power had not been exercised and the institution had been unable to satisfy claims against it, minus

(b) the total amount that would have been likely, at the time when the power was exercised, to be recovered by the scheme manager in respect of the institution in those circumstances.

214C(4) **[Actual net expenditure]** Actual net expenditure is–

(a) the total amount of expenses (other than special resolution regime payments) actually incurred by the scheme manager in respect of the institution, minus

(b) the total amount actually recovered by the scheme manager in respect of the institution.

214C(5) **["Expenses" in s.214C(3)(a) includes interest]** In subsection (3)(a) **"expenses"** includes interest at a specified rate on the difference, at any time, between–

(a) the total amount of expenses (including interest) that would have been incurred as mentioned in subsection (3)(a) at or before that time; and

   (b)   the total amount that would have been likely to have been recovered as mentioned in subsection (3)(b) at or before that time.

214C(6)   **["Expenses" in s.214C(4)(a) includes interest]** In subsection (4)(a) **"expenses"** includes interest at a specified rate on the difference, at any time, between–

   (a)   the total amount of expenses (including special resolution regime payments and interest) actually incurred by the scheme manager in respect of the institution at or before that time; and

   (b)   the total amount actually recovered by the scheme manager in respect of the institution at or before that time.

214C(7)   **[Amounts recovered in s.214C(3)(b), (4)(b), (5b), (6)(b)]** In paragraph (b) of subsections (3) to (6) references to amounts recovered (or likely to have been recovered) by the scheme manager do not include any levy received (or likely to have been received) by it.

214D   Contributions under section 214B: supplementary

214D(1)   **[Scope]** This section supplements sections 214B and 214C.

214D(2)   **[Scheme manager duty re s.214C(3)(a) expenses]** The scheme manager must determine–

   (a)   the amounts of expenses (other than interest) that would have been incurred as mentioned in section 214C(3)(a); and

   (b)   the time or times at which those amounts would have been likely to have been incurred.

214D(3)   **[Appointment of valuer duty re s.214C(3)(b) amounts recoverable]** The Treasury, or a person designated by the Treasury, must in accordance with regulations appoint a person (**"the valuer"**) to determine–

   (a)   the amounts that would have been likely, at the time when the stabilisation power was exercised, to be recovered as mentioned in section 214C(3)(b); and

   (b)   the time or times at which those amounts would have been likely to be recovered.

The person appointed under this subsection may be the person appointed as valuer under section 54 of the Banking Act 2009 in respect of the exercise of the stabilisation power.

214D(4)   **[Regulations for principles re s.214D(2), (3)]** Regulations may enable the Treasury to specify principles to be applied by–

   (a)   the scheme manager when exercising functions under subsection (2); or

   (b)   the valuer when exercising functions under subsection (3).

214D(5)   **[Particular matters in regulations]** The regulations may in particular enable the Treasury to require the scheme manager or valuer–

   (a)   to use, or not to use, specified methods;

   (b)   to take specified matters into account in a specified manner; or

   (c)   not to take specified matters into account.

214D(6)   **[Verification in regulations]** Regulations–

   (a)   must provide for independent verification of expenses within section 214B(2);

   (b)   may provide for the independent verification of other matters; and

   (c)   may contain provision about the appointment and payment of an auditor.

214D(7)   **[Regulations re valuer decision and payment]** Regulations–

   (a)   must contain provision enabling the valuer to reconsider a decision;

(b) must provide a right of appeal to a court or tribunal against any decision of the valuer;

(c) may provide for payment of the valuer; and

(d) may apply (with or without modifications) or make provision corresponding to–

(i) any provision of sections 54 to 56 of the Banking Act 2009; or

(ii) any provision made, or that could be made, by virtue of any of those sections.

214D(8) **[Provision for early payments under s.214B(2)]** Regulations may make provision for payments under section 214B(2) to be made–

(a) before any verification required by the regulations is undertaken, and

(b) before the limit imposed by section 214C is calculated,

subject to any necessary later adjustment.

214D(9) **[No expectation for repayment after verification etc.]** If they do so they must provide that the amount of any payment required by virtue of subsection (8) must not be such as to give rise to an expectation that an amount will be required to be repaid to the scheme manager (once any necessary verification has been undertaken and the limit imposed by section 214C has been calculated).

214D(10) **[Further provisions in regulations]** Regulations may–

(a) make provision supplementing section 214B or 214C or this section;

(b) make further provision about the method by which amounts to be paid under section 214B(2) are to be determined;

(c) make provision about timing;

(d) make provision about procedures to be followed;

(e) provide for discretionary functions to be exercised by a specified body or by persons of a specified class; and

(f) make provision about the resolution of disputes (which may include provision conferring jurisdiction on a court or tribunal).

214D(11) **["Regulations"]** **"Regulations"** means regulations made by the Treasury.

214D(12) **[Source of s.214D payments by Treasury]** Any payment made by the Treasury by virtue of this section is to be met out of money provided by Parliament.

214D(13) **[Compensation scheme provisions for s.214B(2) payments and levies]** The compensation scheme may make provision about payments under section 214B(2) and levies in connection with such payments (except provision inconsistent with any provision made by or under section 214B or 214C or this section).

History
Section 214B substituted and s.214C, 214D inserted by the Financial Services Act 2010 s.16(1) as from April 8, 2010. Previously s.214B was inserted by Banking Act 2009 (C. 1) Pt 4 s.171, as from February 21, 2009.
    For the relevant regulations, see the Financial Services and Markets Act 2000 (Contribution to Costs of Special Resolution Regime) Regulations 2009 (SI 2009/807).

215 **Rights of the scheme in insolvency**

215(1) **[Provisions of the scheme]** The compensation scheme may make provision–

(a) about the effect of a payment of compensation under the scheme on rights or obligations arising out of matters in connection with which the compensation was paid;

(b) giving the scheme manager a right of recovery in respect of those rights or obligations.

215(2) [Right of recovery in event of insolvency] Such a right of recovery conferred by the scheme does not, in the event of a person's insolvency, exceed such right (if any) as the claimant would have had in that event.

215(3) [Manager's rights equivalent to Authority's under s.362] If a person other than the scheme manager makes an administration application under Schedule B1 to the 1986 Act or presents a petition under Article 22 of the 1989 Order in relation to a company or partnership which is a relevant person, the scheme manager has the same rights as are conferred on the Authority by section 362.

215(3A) [Making an administration application in s.215(3)] In subsection (3) the reference to making an administration application includes a reference to–

(a) appointing an administrator under paragraph 14 or 22 of Schedule B1 to the 1986 Act, or

(b) filing with the court a copy of notice of intention to appoint an administrator under either of those paragraphs.

215(4) [Manager's rights equivalent to Authority's under s.371] If a person other than the scheme manager presents a petition for the winding up of a body which is a relevant person, the scheme manager has the same rights as are conferred on the Authority by section 371.

215(5) [Manager's rights equivalent to Authority's under s.374] If a person other than the scheme manager presents a bankruptcy petition to the court in relation to an individual who, or an entity which, is a relevant person, the scheme manager has the same rights as are conferred on the Authority by section 374.

215(6) [Power to make insolvency rules] Insolvency rules may be made for the purpose of integrating any procedure for which provision is made as a result of subsection (1) into the general procedure on the administration of a company or partnership or on a winding-up, bankruptcy or sequestration.

Note
Section 215(3), (4) and (6) apply to limited liability partnerships by virtue of the Limited Liability Partnerships Regulations 2001 (SI 2001/1090) regs 1, 6(1) as from April 6, 2001 subject to reg.6(2).

215(7) ["Bankruptcy petition"] "Bankruptcy petition" means a petition to the court–

(a) under section 264 of the 1986 Act or Article 238 of the 1989 Order for a bankruptcy order to be made against an individual;

(b) under section 5 of the 1985 Act for the sequestration of the estate of an individual; or

(c) under section 6 of the 1985 Act for the sequestration of the estate belonging to or held for or jointly by the members of an entity mentioned in subsection (1) of that section.

215(8) ["Insolvency rules"] "Insolvency rules" are–

(a) for England and Wales, rules made under sections 411 and 412 of the 1986 Act;

(b) for Scotland, rules made by order by the Treasury, after consultation with the Scottish Ministers, for the purposes of this section; and

(c) for Northern Ireland, rules made under Article 359 of the 1989 Order and section 55 of the Judicature (Northern Ireland) Act 1978.

215(9) [Interpretation] "The 1985 Act", "the 1986 Act", "the 1989 Order" and **"court"** have the same meaning as in Part XXIV.

History
Section 215(1) amended by the Banking Act 2009 s.175 as from February 21, 2009.

216   Continuity of long-term insurance policies

216(1)   [Duty of scheme manager] The compensation scheme may, in particular, include provision requiring the scheme manager to make arrangements for securing continuity of insurance for policyholders, or policyholders of a specified class, of relevant long-term insurers.

216(2)   ["Relevant long-term insurers"] **"Relevant long-term insurers"** means relevant persons who–

(a)   have permission to effect or carry out contracts of long-term insurance; and

(b)   are unable, or likely to be unable, to satisfy claims made against them.

216(3)   [Transfer of policies to another authorised person, etc.] The scheme may provide for the scheme manager to take such measures as appear to him to be appropriate–

(a)   for securing or facilitating the transfer of a relevant long-term insurer's business so far as it consists of the carrying out of contracts of long-term insurance, or of any part of that business, to another authorised person;

(b)   for securing the issue by another authorised person to the policyholders concerned of policies in substitution for their existing policies.

216(4)   [Payments to policyholders] The scheme may also provide for the scheme manager to make payments to the policyholders concerned–

(a)   during any period while he is seeking to make arrangements mentioned in subsection (1);

(b)   if it appears to him that it is not reasonably practicable to make such arrangements.

216(5)   [Section 213(3)(b)–further powers] A provision of the scheme made by virtue of section 213(3)(b) may include power to impose levies for the purpose of meeting expenses of the scheme manager incurred in–

(a)   taking measures as a result of any provision of the scheme made by virtue of subsection (3);

(b)   making payments as a result of any such provision made by virtue of subsection (4).

217   Insurers in financial difficulties

217(1)   [Measures to safeguard policyholders] The compensation scheme may, in particular, include provision for the scheme manager to have power to take measures for safeguarding policyholders, or policyholders of a specified class, of relevant insurers.

217(2)   ["Relevant insurers"] **"Relevant insurers"** means relevant persons who–

(a)   have permission to effect or carry out contracts of insurance; and

(b)   are in financial difficulties.

217(3)   [Measures to transfer insurance business, etc.] The measures may include such measures as the scheme manager considers appropriate for–

(a)   securing or facilitating the transfer of a relevant insurer's business so far as it consists of the carrying out of contracts of insurance, or of any part of that business, to another authorised person;

(b)   giving assistance to the relevant insurer to enable it to continue to effect or carry out contracts of insurance.

217(4)   [Further provisions re s.217(3) measures, etc.] The scheme may provide–

(a)   that if measures of a kind mentioned in subsection (3)(a) are to be taken, they should be on terms appearing to the scheme manager to be appropriate, including terms reducing, or deferring payment of, any of the things to which any of those who are eligible policyholders in relation to the relevant insurer are entitled in their capacity as such;

(b)   that if measures of a kind mentioned in subsection (3)(b) are to be taken, they should be conditional on the reduction of, or the deferment of the payment of, the things to which any of those who are eligible policyholders in relation to the relevant insurer are entitled in their capacity as such;

(c)   for ensuring that measures of a kind mentioned in subsection (3)(b) do not benefit to any material extent persons who were members of a relevant insurer when it began to be in financial difficulties or who had any responsibility for, or who may have profited from, the circumstances giving rise to its financial difficulties, except in specified circumstances;

(d)   for requiring the scheme manager to be satisfied that any measures he proposes to take are likely to cost less than it would cost to pay compensation under the scheme if the relevant insurer became unable, or likely to be unable, to satisfy claims made against him.

217(5)   **[Provision for power of Authority]** The scheme may provide for the Authority to have power–

(a)   to give such assistance to the scheme manager as it considers appropriate for assisting the scheme manager to determine what measures are practicable or desirable in the case of a particular relevant insurer;

(b)   to impose constraints on the taking of measures by the scheme manager in the case of a particular relevant insurer;

(c)   to require the scheme manager to provide it with information about any particular measures which the scheme manager is proposing to take.

217(6)   **[Provision to make interim payments, etc.]** The scheme may include provision for the scheme manager to have power–

(a)   to make interim payments in respect of eligible policyholders of a relevant insurer;

(b)   to indemnify any person making payments to eligible policyholders of a relevant insurer.

217(7)   **[Imposition of levies to meet expenses]** A provision of the scheme made by virtue of section 213(3)(b) may include power to impose levies for the purpose of meeting expenses of the scheme manager incurred in–

(a)   taking measures as a result of any provision of the scheme made by virtue of subsection (1);

(b)   making payments or giving indemnities as a result of any such provision made by virtue of subsection (6).

217(8)   **[Interpretation]** **"Financial difficulties"** and **"eligible policyholders"** have such meanings as may be specified.

Note
Note prospective amendment of s.217(3) by the Banking Act 2009 s.170(2).

Annual report

218   Annual report

218(1)   **[Duty of scheme manager]** At least once a year, the scheme manager must make a report to the Authority on the discharge of its functions.

218(2)   **[Content, etc. of report]** The report must–

(a)   include a statement setting out the value of each of the funds established by the compensation scheme; and

(b) comply with any requirements specified in rules made by the Authority.

218(3)   [Publication] The scheme manager must publish each report in the way it considers appropriate.

Note
Note prospective amendment of s.218(1), (2)(b) by the Banking Act 2009 s.170(2).

Information and documents

218A   Authority's power to require information

218A(1)   [Rule-making power] The Authority may make rules enabling the Authority to require authorised persons to provide information, which may then be made available to the scheme manager by the Authority.

218A(2)   [Required information to be of use to scheme manager] A requirement may be imposed only if the Authority thinks the information is of a kind that may be of use to the scheme manager in connection with functions in respect of the scheme.

218A(3)   [Application of requirement] A requirement under this section may apply–

(a) to authorised persons generally or only to specified persons or classes of person;

(b) to the provision of information at specified periods, in connection with specified events or in other ways.

218A(4)   [Section 165 notice] In addition to requirements under this section, a notice under section 165 may relate to information or documents which the Authority thinks are reasonably required by the scheme manager in connection with the performance of functions in respect of the scheme; and section 165(4) is subject to this subsection.

218A(5)   [Rules in s.218A(1)] Rules under subsection (1) shall be prepared, made and treated in the same way as (and may be combined with) the Authority's general rules.

History
Section 218A inserted by Banking Act 2009 s.176(1), as from February 21, 2009.

219   Scheme manager's power to require information

219(1)   [Power of scheme manager] The scheme manager may, by notice in writing require a person–

(a) to provide specified information or information of a specified description; or

(b) to produce specified documents or documents of a specified description.

219(1A)   [Persons who may be required to provide information etc.] A requirement may be imposed only–

(a) on a person (P) against whom a claim has been made under the scheme,

(b) on a person (P) who is unable or likely to be unable to satisfy claims under the scheme against P,

(c) on a person ("the Third Party") whom the scheme manager thinks was knowingly involved in matters giving rise to a claim against another person (P) under the scheme, or

(d) on a person ("the Third Party") whom the scheme manager thinks was knowingly involved in matters giving rise to the actual or likely inability of another person (P) to satisfy claims under the scheme.

219(1B)   [Determination of P satisfying claims in s.219(1A)(b), (d)] For the purposes of subsection (1A)(b) and (d) whether P is unable or likely to be unable to satisfy claims shall be determined in accordance with provision to be made by the scheme (which may, in particular–

(a) apply or replicate, with or without modifications, a provision of an enactment;

(b) confer discretion on a specified person).

219(2) **[Form, etc. of information]** The information or documents must be provided or produced–

(a) before the end of such reasonable period as may be specified; and

(b) in the case of information, in such manner or form as may be specified.

219(3) **[Application of section]** This section applies only to information and documents the provision or production of which the scheme manager considers to be necessary (or likely to be necessary) for the fair determination of claims which have been or may be made against P.

219(3A) **[Power to require information for determining s.214D(2) matters]** Where a stabilisation power under Part 1 of the Banking Act 2009 has been exercised in respect of a bank, building society or credit union, the scheme manager may by notice in writing require the bank, building society or credit union, or the Bank of England to provide information that the scheme manager requires for the purpose of determining the matters mentioned in section 214D(2)(a) and (b) above.

219(4) **[Power to take copies, etc. of documents]** If a document is produced in response to a requirement imposed under this section, the scheme manager may–

(a) take copies or extracts from the document; or

(b) require the person producing the document to provide an explanation of the document.

219(5) **[Failure to produce documents]** If a person who is required under this section to produce a document fails to do so, the scheme manager may require the person to state, to the best of his knowledge and belief, where the document is.

219(6) **[Limitation of section in case of insolvency]** If P is insolvent, no requirement may be imposed under this section on a person to whom section 220 or 224 applies.

219(7) **[Lien claimed]** If a person claims a lien on a document, its production under this Part does not affect the lien.

219(8) [...]

219(9) **["Specified"]** "Specified" means specified in the notice given under subsection (1).

219(10) [...]

History
Subsections (1), (3) and (6) amended, subs.(3A) inserted and subs.(8) and (10) omitted by the Banking Act 2009 s.176, as from February 21, 2009. Subsection (3A) amended by the Financial Services Act 2010 s.21(8)(a), (b) and Sch.2 para.22 as from April 8, 2010.

220   Scheme manager's power to inspect information held by liquidator etc.

220(1) **[Inspection of relevant documents]** For the purpose of assisting the scheme manager to discharge its functions in relation to a claim made in respect of an insolvent relevant person, a person to whom this section applies must permit a person authorised by the scheme manager to inspect relevant documents.

220(2) **[Extracts, etc. from documents]** A person inspecting a document under this section may take copies of, or extracts from, the document.

220(3) **[Application to section]** This section applies to–

(a) the administrative receiver, administrator, liquidator, bank liquidator, building society liquidator or trustee in bankruptcy of an insolvent relevant person;

(b)   the permanent trustee, within the meaning of the Bankruptcy (Scotland) Act 1985, on the estate of an insolvent relevant person.

220(4)   [Scope of section] This section does not apply to a liquidator, administrator or trustee in bankruptcy who is–

(a)   the Official Receiver;

(b)   the Official Receiver for Northern Ireland; or

(c)   the Accountant in Bankruptcy.

220(5)   ["Relevant person"] "Relevant person" has the same meaning as in section 224.

History
Section 220(3) amended by the Banking Act 2009 s.123(3) as from February 21, 2009 and by the Building Societies (Insolvency and Special Administration) Order 2009 (SI 2009/805) art.15 as from March 29, 2009.

221   Powers of court where information required

221(1)   [Power of court] If a person ("the defaulter")–

(a)   fails to comply with a requirement imposed under section 219, or

(b)   fails to permit documents to be inspected under section 220,

the scheme manager may certify that fact in writing to the court and the court may enquire into the case.

221(2)   [Penalty] If the court is satisfied that the defaulter failed without reasonable excuse to comply with the requirement (or to permit the documents to be inspected), it may deal with the defaulter (and, in the case of a body corporate, any director or officer) as if he were in contempt; and " officer", in relation to a limited liability partnership, means a member of the limited liability partnership.

221(3)   ["Court"] "Court" means–

(a)   the High Court;

(b)   in Scotland, the Court of Session.

Miscellaneous

221A   Delegation of functions

221A(1)   [Delegation to scheme agent] The scheme manager may arrange for any of its functions to be discharged on its behalf by another person (a "scheme agent").

221A(2)   [Conditions re scheme agent] Before entering into arrangements the scheme manager must be satisfied that the scheme agent–

(a)   is competent to discharge the function, and

(b)   has been given sufficient directions to enable the agent to take any decisions required in the course of exercising the function in accordance with policy determined by the scheme manager.

221A(3)   [Payments to scheme agent] Arrangements may include provision for payments to be made by the scheme manager to the scheme agent (which payments are management expenses of the scheme manager except where the function in question is one under Part 15A).

History
Section 221A inserted by the Banking Act 2009 s.179(1), as from February 21, 2009. Section 221A(3) amended by the Financial Services Act 2010 Sch.2 para.23 as from October 12, 2010.

222   Statutory immunity

222(1)   **[Immunity of scheme manager, etc.]** Neither the scheme manager nor any person who is, or is acting as, its board member, officer, scheme agent or member of staff is to be liable in damages for anything done or omitted in the discharge, or purported discharge, of the scheme manager's functions.

222(2)   **[Non-application of s.222(1)]** Subsection (1) does not apply–

   (a)   if the act or omission is shown to have been in bad faith; or

   (b)   so as to prevent an award of damages made in respect of an act or omission on the ground that the act or omission was unlawful as a result of section 6(1) of the Human Rights Act 1998.

History
Section 222(1) amended by the Banking Act 2009 s.179(2) as from February 21, 2009.

223   Management expenses

223(1)   **[Limit on expenses]** The amount which the scheme manager may recover, from the sums levied under the scheme, as management expenses attributable to a particular period may not exceed such amount as may be fixed by the scheme as the limit applicable to that period.

223(2)   **[Calculation of levy]** In calculating the amount of any levy to be imposed by the scheme manager, no amount may be included to reflect management expenses unless the limit mentioned in subsection (1) has been fixed by the scheme.

223(3)   **["Management expenses"]** "Management expenses" means expenses incurred, or expected to be incurred, by the scheme manager in connection with its functions under this Act other than those incurred–

   (a)   in paying compensation;

   (b)   as a result of any provision of the scheme made by virtue of section 216(3) or (4) or 217(1) or (6);

   (c)   under section 214B or 214D;

   (d)   under Part 15A.

History
Section 222(3)(c) inserted by the Banking Act 2009 s.171(2) as from February 21, 2009. Section 223(3)(c) amended and s.223(3)(d) inserted by the Financial Services Act 2010 Sch.2 para.24(2), (3) as from October 12, 2010.
   Note prospective insertion of s.223A by the Banking Act 2009 s.172.

223B   Borrowing from National Loans Fund

223B(1)   The scheme manager may request a loan from the National Loans Fund for the purpose of funding expenses incurred or expected to be incurred under the scheme.

223B(2)   The Treasury may arrange for money to be paid out of the National Loans Fund in pursuance of a request under subsection (1).

223B(3)   The Treasury shall determine–

   (a)   the rate of interest on a loan, and

   (b)   other terms and conditions.

223B(4)   The Treasury may make regulations–

   (a)   about the amounts that may be borrowed under this section;

   (b)   permitting the scheme manager to impose levies under section 213 for the purpose of meeting expenses in connection with loans under this section (and the regulations may have effect despite any provision of this Act);

(c)   about the classes of person on whom those levies may be imposed;

(d)   about the amounts and timing of those levies.

223B(5)   The compensation scheme may include provision about borrowing under this section provided that it is not inconsistent with regulations under this section.

History
Section 223B inserted by Banking Act 2009 s.173, as from February 21, 2009.

223C   Payments in error

223C(1)   **[Provision by levy in ss.213, 214A, 214B, 223B]** Payments made by the scheme manager in error may be provided for in setting a levy by virtue of section 213, 214A, 214B or 223B.

223C(2)   **[Non-application to payments in bad faith]** This section does not apply to payments made in bad faith.

History
Section 223C inserted by Banking Act 2009 s.177, as from February 21, 2009.

224   Scheme manager's power to inspect documents held by Official Receiver etc.

224(1)   **[Duty of Official Receiver, etc. re inspection of documents]** If, as a result of the insolvency or bankruptcy of a relevant person, any documents have come into the possession of a person to whom this section applies, he must permit any person authorised by the scheme manager to inspect the documents for the purpose of establishing–

(a)   the identity of persons to whom the scheme manager may be liable to make a payment in accordance with the compensation scheme; or

(b)   the amount of any payment which the scheme manager may be liable to make.

224(2)   **[Extracts, etc. from documents]** A person inspecting a document under this section may take copies or extracts from the document.

224(3)   **["Relevant person"]** In this section **"relevant person "** means a person who was–

(a)   an authorised person at the time the act or omission which may give rise to the liability mentioned in subsection (1)(a) took place; or

(b)   an appointed representative at that time.

224(4)   **[Persons qualified for authorisation under Sch.3]** But a person who, at that time–

(a)   qualified for authorisation under Schedule 3, and

(b)   fell within a prescribed category,

is not to be regarded as a relevant person for the purposes of this section in relation to any activities for which he had permission as a result of any provision of, or made under, that Schedule unless he had elected to participate in the scheme in relation to those activities at that time.

Note
See the Financial Services and Markets Act 2000 (Compensation Scheme: Electing Participants) Regulations 2001 (SI 2001/1783).

224(5)   **[Application of section]** This section applies to–

(a)   the Official Receiver;

(b)   the Official Receiver for Northern Ireland; and

(c)   the Accountant in Bankruptcy.

224A   Functions under the Banking Act 2009

224A(1)   [Reference in Pt 15 to functions of scheme manager] A reference in this Part to functions of the scheme manager (including a reference to functions conferred by or under this Part) includes a reference to functions conferred by or under the Banking Act 2009.

224A(2)   [Special resolution regime compensation payments treated as expense] Any payment required to be made by the scheme manager by virtue of section 61 of that Act (special resolution regime: compensation) is to be treated for the purposes of this Part as an expense under the compensation scheme.

History
Section 224A inserted by Banking Act 2009 s.180, as from February 21, 2009 and s.224A(2) inserted by the Financial Services Act 2010 Sch.2 para.25 as from October 12, 2010.

PART XVA

POWER TO REQUIRE FSCS MANAGER TO ACT IN RELATION TO OTHER SCHEMES

Introduction

224B   Meaning of "relevant scheme" etc

224B(1)   [Application for Pt XVA] The following provisions apply for the purposes of this Part.

224B(2)   ["Relevant scheme"] "**Relevant scheme**" means a scheme or arrangement (other than the FSCS) for the payment of compensation (in certain cases) to customers of persons who provide financial services or carry on a business connected with the provision of such services.

224B(3)   [References to manager] References to the manager of a relevant scheme are to the person who administers it or (if there is no such person) the person responsible for making payments under it.

224B(4)   ["The FSCS"] "**The FSCS**" means the Financial Services Compensation Scheme (see section 213(2)).

224B(5)   ["The FSCS manager"] "**The FSCS manager**" means the scheme manager as defined by section 212(1).

224B(6)   ["Expense"] "**Expense**" includes anything that, if incurred in relation to the FSCS, would amount to an expense for the purposes of the FSCS.

224B(7)   ["Notice"] "**Notice**" means a notice in writing.

224B(8)   ["Customers", "persons", provision of financial services in s.224B(2)] In subsection (2)–

(a)   "**customers**" includes customers outside the United Kingdom;

(b)   "**persons**" includes persons outside the United Kingdom;

(c)   references to the provision of financial services include the provision outside the United Kingdom of such services.

224B(9)   [Application where manager is Treasury or Minister] This Part applies to cases where the manager of the relevant scheme is the Treasury or any other Minister of the Crown as it applies to cases where that manager is any other person.

History
See note after s.224F

224C   Power to require FSCS manager to act on behalf of manager of relevant scheme

224C(1)   [Application of section] This section applies if compensation is payable under a relevant scheme.

224C(2)   [FSCS manager required to exercise specified functions] The Treasury may by notice require the FSCS manager to exercise (on behalf of the manager of the relevant scheme) specified functions in respect of specified claims for compensation under the relevant scheme.

224C(3)   [Notice requires scheme manager consent] A notice may be given only with the consent of the manager of the relevant scheme.

224C(4)   ["Specified" in s.224C(2)] In subsection (2) "specified" means specified, or of a description specified, in the notice.

224C(5)   [Claims] Claims or descriptions of claims may be specified by reference to the persons or description of persons whose claims they are.

History
See note after s.224F.

224D   Cases where FSCS manager may decline to act

224D(1)   [Application of section] This section applies where a notice under section 224C(2) (a "section 224C notice") has been given in respect of a relevant scheme.

224D(2)   [Where no duty to comply with s.224C] The FSCS manager is not under a duty to comply with the section 224C notice if, as soon as reasonably practicable after receiving it, the FSCS manager gives a notice to the Treasury stating that a ground set out in section 224E applies.

224D(3)   [Recovery of expenses] Where a notice under subsection (2) is given, the FSCS manager may recover from the manager of the relevant scheme an amount equal to the total expenses incurred by the FSCS manager in connection with the relevant scheme in the period–

(a)   beginning with the giving of the section 224C notice; and

(b)   ending with the giving of the notice under subsection (2).

224D(4)   [Cessation of duty to comply with s.224C notice] The duty to comply with the section 224C notice ceases if, after starting to comply with it, the FSCS manager gives a notice to the Treasury and the manager of the relevant scheme stating that a ground set out in section 224E applies.

224D(5)   [FSCS manager to inform Treasury where s.224D(4) given] Where a notice under subsection (4) is given, the FSCS manager must give the Treasury such information connected with the FSCS manager's exercise of functions in relation to the relevant scheme as the Treasury may reasonably require.

224D(6)   [Notice in s.224D] Any notice under this section–

(a)   may be given only if, before giving it, the FSCS manager has taken reasonable steps to deal with anything that is causing the ground or grounds in question to apply; and

(b)   must contain details of those steps.

History
See note after s.224F.

224E   Grounds for declining to act

224E(1)   [Grounds in s.224D(2), (4)] This section sets out the grounds referred to in section 224D(2) and (4).

224E(2)   **[First ground: inability to obtain information]** The first ground is that the FSCS manager is not satisfied that it will be able to obtain any information required in order to comply with the section 224C notice.

224E(3)   **[Second ground: inability to obtain advice etc.]** The second ground is that the FSCS manager is not satisfied that it will be able to obtain any advice or other assistance from the manager of the relevant scheme that is required in order to comply with the section 224C notice.

224E(4)   **[Third ground: expenses not paid]** The third ground is–

   (a)   that the FSCS manager has not received an amount at least equal to the total expenses it expects to incur in connection with its relevant scheme functions; and

   (b)   either–

      (i)   that there are no arrangements for the provision of funds to the FSCS manager to enable it to exercise those functions and meet those expenses; or

      (ii)   that the FSCS manager considers that any such arrangements are unsatisfactory.

224E(5)   **[Fourth ground: s.224C notice compliance detrimental]** The fourth ground is that the FSCS manager considers that complying with the section 224C notice would detrimentally affect the exercise of its functions under the FSCS.

224E(6)   **[Fifth ground: no undertaking not to bring proceedings]** The fifth ground is–

   (a)   that there is no undertaking from the manager of the relevant scheme not to bring proceedings against the FSCS manager; or

   (b)   that the FSCS manager considers that the terms of any such undertaking are unsatisfactory.

224E(7)   **[Sixth ground: no reimbursement of expenses]** The sixth ground is–

   (a)   that there are no arrangements for the reimbursement of any expenses incurred by the FSCS manager in connection with any proceedings brought against it in respect of its relevant scheme functions (including expenses incurred in meeting any award of damages made against it); or

   (b)   that the FSCS manager considers that any such arrangements are unsatisfactory.

224E(8)   **[Undertaking in s.224E(6)]** In subsection (6) references to an undertaking of the kind mentioned there are to an undertaking not to bring proceedings in respect of the FSCS manager's relevant scheme functions except proceedings in respect of an act or omission of the FSCS manager that is alleged to have been in bad faith.

224E(9)   **["Proceedings"]** In this section "**proceedings**" includes proceedings outside the United Kingdom.

History
See note after s.224F.

Rules

224F   Rules about relevant schemes

224F(1)   **[Power of Authority to make rules]** The Authority may by rules make provision in connection with the exercise by the FSCS manager of functions in respect of relevant schemes.

224F(2)   **[Corresponding provision in FSCS]** The provision that may be made by the rules includes any provision corresponding to provision that could be contained in the FSCS; but this is subject to subsections (3) and (4).

224F(3)   [Power to impose levies to meet management expenses] The rules may confer on the FSCS manager a power to impose levies on authorised persons (or any class of authorised persons) for the purpose of meeting its management expenses incurred in connection with its functions in respect of relevant schemes.

224F(4)   [Reimbursement of expenses from scheme manager] But if the rules confer such a power they must provide that the power may be exercised in relation to expenses incurred in connection with a relevant scheme only if the FSCS manager has tried its best to obtain reimbursement of the expenses from the manager of the relevant scheme.

224F(5)   [Rules may apply FSCS provisions] The rules may apply any provision of the FSCS, with or without modifications.

224F(6)   [Management expenses recoverable as a debt] An amount payable to the FSCS manager as a result of any provision of the rules made by virtue of subsection (3) may be recovered as a debt due to the FSCS manager.

224F(7)   ["Management expenses"] References to the FSCS manager's **"management expenses"** are to its expenses incurred otherwise than in paying compensation.

History
Sections 224B–224F inserted by the Financial Services Act 2010 s.17 as from October 12, 2010.

Part XXIV

Insolvency

Interpretation

355   Interpretation of this Part

355(1)   [Interpretation] In this Part–

   "the 1985 Act" means the Bankruptcy (Scotland) Act 1985;

   "the 1986 Act" means the Insolvency Act 1986;

   "the 1989 Order" means the Insolvency (Northern Ireland) Order 1989;

   "body" means a body of persons–

   (a)   over which the court has jurisdiction under any provision of, or made under, the 1986 Act (or the 1989 Order); but

   (b)   which is not a building society, a friendly society or an industrial and provident society;

   and **"court"** means–

   (a)   the court having jurisdiction for the purposes of the 1985 Act or the 1986 Act; or

   (b)   in Northern Ireland, the High Court.

355(2)   ["Insurer"] In this Part **"insurer"** has such meaning as may be specified in an order made by the Treasury.

Note
For the definition of "insurer" for the purpose of Pt XXIV, see the Financial Services and Markets Act 2000 (Insolvency) (Definition of "Insurer") Order 2001 (SI 2001/2634) arts 1, 2 as from December 1, 2001 (as amended by the Financial Services and Markets Act 2000 (Administration Orders Relating to Insurers) Order 2002 (SI 2002/1242) arts 1, 2 as from May 31, 2002).

Voluntary arrangements

356 Authority's powers to participate in proceedings: company voluntary arrangements

356(1) [Application of the 1986 Act] Where a voluntary arrangement has effect under Part I of the 1986 Act in respect of a company or insolvent partnership which is an authorised person, the Authority may apply to the court under section 6 or 7 of that Act.

356(2) [Application of the 1989 Order] Where a voluntary arrangement has been approved under Part II of the 1989 Order in respect of a company or insolvent partnership which is an authorised person, the Authority may apply to the court under Article 19 or 20 of that Order.

356(3) [Authority's right of audience] If a person other than the Authority makes an application to the court in relation to the company or insolvent partnership under any of those provisions, the Authority is entitled to be heard at any hearing relating to the application.

History
Section 356(1), (2) substituted, and s.356(3) amended, by the Insolvency Act 2000 s.15(3)(c) as from January 1, 2003 (see the Insolvency Act 2000 (Commencement No.3 and Transitional Provisions) Order 2002 (SI 2002/2711 (C. 83)) arts 1, 2).

Note
Section 356 applies to limited liability partnerships by virtue of the Limited Liability Partnerships Regulations 2001 (SI 2001/1090) regs 1, 6(1) as from April 6, 2001 subject to reg.6(2).

357 Authority's powers to participate in proceedings: individual voluntary arrangements

357(1) [Authority's right of audience] The Authority is entitled to be heard on an application by an individual who is an authorised person under section 253 of the 1986 Act (or Article 227 of the 1989 Order).

357(2) [Application of s.357(3)–(6)] Subsections (3) to (6) apply if such an order is made on the application of such a person.

357(3) [Meetings of creditors] A person appointed for the purpose by the Authority is entitled to attend any meeting of creditors of the debtor summoned under section 257 of the 1986 Act (or Article 231 of the 1989 Order).

357(4) [Duty of chairman of meeting] Notice of the result of a meeting so summoned is to be given to the Authority by the chairman of the meeting.

357(5) [Application to court] The Authority may apply to the court–

(a) under section 262 of the 1986 Act (or Article 236 of the 1989 Order); or

(b) under section 263 of the 1986 Act (or Article 237 of the 1989 Order).

357(6) [Authority's right of audience] If a person other than the Authority makes an application to the court under any provision mentioned in subsection (5), the Authority is entitled to be heard at any hearing relating to the application.

358 Authority's powers to participate in proceedings: trust deeds for creditors in Scotland

358(1) [Application of section] This section applies where a trust deed has been granted by or on behalf of a debtor who is an authorised person.

358(2) [Duty of trustee] The trustee must, as soon as practicable after he becomes aware that the debtor is an authorised person, send to the Authority–

(a) in every case, a copy of the trust deed;

(b) where any other document or information is sent to every creditor known to the trustee in pursuance of paragraph 5(1)(c) of Schedule 5 to the 1985 Act, a copy of such document or information.

358(3)   [Application of Bankruptcy (Scotland) Act 1985 Sch.5 para.7] Paragraph 7 of that Schedule applies to the Authority as if it were a qualified creditor who has not been sent a copy of the notice as mentioned in paragraph 5(1)(c) of the Schedule.

358(4)   [Notice to be given to Authority] The Authority must be given the same notice as the creditors of any meeting of creditors held in relation to the trust deed.

358(5)   [Authority's right to attend, etc. meeting] A person appointed for the purpose by the Authority is entitled to attend and participate in (but not to vote at) any such meeting of creditors as if the Authority were a creditor under the deed.

358(6)   [Rights of Authority as creditor unaffected] This section does not affect any right the Authority has as a creditor of a debtor who is an authorised person.

358(7)   [Interpretation] Expressions used in this section and in the 1985 Act have the same meaning in this section as in that Act.

Administration orders

359   Administration order

359(1)   [Power to make administration application] The Authority may make an administration application under Schedule B1 to the 1986 Act (or present a petition under Article 22 of the 1989 Order) in relation to a company or insolvent partnership which–

(a) is or has been an authorised person,

(b) is or has been an appointed representative, or

(c) is carrying on or has carried on a regulated activity in contravention of the general prohibition.

359(2)   [Application of s.359(3)] Subsection (3) applies in relation to an administration application made (or a petition presented) by the Authority by virtue of this section.

359(3)   [Inability to pay debts] Any of the following shall be treated for the purpose of paragraph 11(a) of Schedule B1 to the 1986 Act (or Article 21(1)(a) of the 1989 Order) as unable to pay its debts–

(a) a company or partnership in default on an obligation to pay a sum due and payable under an agreement,

(b) an authorised deposit taker in default on an obligation to pay a sum due and payable in respect of a relevant deposit, and

(c) an authorised reclaim fund in default on an obligation to pay a sum payable as a result of a claim made by virtue of section 1(2)(b) or 2(2)(b) of the Dormant Bank and Building Society Accounts Act 2008.

359(4)   ["Agreement", "authorised deposit taker", "company ", "relevant deposit"] In this section–

"agreement" means an agreement the making or performance of which constitutes or is part of a regulated activity carried on by the company or partnership,

"authorised deposit taker" means a person with a Part IV permission to accept deposits (but not a person who has a Part IV permission to accept deposits only for the purpose of carrying on another regulated activity in accordance with that permission),

"authorised reclaim fund" means a reclaim fund within the meaning given by section 5(1) of the Dormant Bank and Building Society Accounts Act 2008 that is authorised for the purposes of this Act;

"company" means a company–

(a)   in respect of which an administrator may be appointed under Schedule B1 to the 1986 Act, or

(b)   to which Article 21 of the 1989 Order applies, and

"relevant deposit" shall, ignoring any restriction on the meaning of deposit arising from the identity of the person making the deposit, be construed in accordance with–

(a)   section 22,

(b)   any relevant order under that section, and

(c)   Schedule 2.

359(5)   ["Authorised deposit taker" in s.359(4)] The definition of "authorised deposit taker" in subsection (4) shall be construed in accordance with–

(a)   section 22,

(b)   any relevant order under that section, and

(c)   Schedule 2.

History
See note after s.362A. Section 359(3)(c) inserted and s.359(4) amended by the Dormant Bank and Building Society Accounts Act 2008 Sch.2 para.6 as from March 12, 2009.

Note
Section 359(1)–(4) applies to limited liability partnerships by virtue of the Limited Liability Partnerships Regulations 2001 (SI 2001/1090) regs 1, 6(1) as from April 6, 2001 subject to reg.6(2). See the Enterprise Act 2002 (Commencement No.4 and Transitional Provisions and Savings) Order 2003 (SI 2003/2093 (C. 85)) art.3(1), (3) for transitional saving.

360   Insurers

360(1)   [Power of Treasury to make order] The Treasury may by order provide that such provisions of Part II of the 1986 Act (or Part III of the 1989 Order) as may be specified are to apply in relation to insurers with such modifications as may be specified.

360(2)   [Provisions, etc. of s.360 order] An order under this section–

(a)   may provide that such provisions of this Part as may be specified are to apply in relation to the administration of insurers in accordance with the order with such modifications as may be specified; and

(b)   requires the consent of the Secretary of State.

360(3)   ["Specified"] "Specified" means specified in the order.

Note
The definition of "insurer" for these purposes is that contained in the Financial Services and Markets Act 2000 (Insolvency) (Definition of "Insurer") Order 2001 (SI 2001/2634) art.2, as extended to apply to s.360 by virtue of the Financial Services and Markets Act 2000 (Administration Orders Relating to Insurers) Order 2002 (SI 2002/1242) arts 1(1), 2 as from May 31, 2002. The 2001 definition does not extend so as to include Lloyd's, but separate provision is now made for Lloyd's by the Insurers (Reorganisation and Winding Up) (Lloyd's) Regulations 2005 (SI 2005/1998) which, by reg.2(4), disapplies s.360. For Northern Ireland, see the Financial Services and Markets Act 2000 (Administration Orders Relating to Insurers) (Northern Ireland) Order 2007 (SI 2007/846), effective April 6, 2007.

361   Administrator's duty to report to Authority

361(1)   [Application of s.361] This section applies where a company or partnership is–

(a)   in administration within the meaning of Schedule B1 to the 1986 Act, or

(b)   the subject of an administration order under Part III of the 1989 Order.

361(2)   [Duty of administrator] If the administrator thinks that the company or partnership is carrying on or has carried on a regulated activity in contravention of the general prohibition, he must report to the Authority without delay.

361(3)   [Non-application of s.361(3)] Subsection (2) does not apply where the administration arises out of an administration order made on an application made or petition presented by the Authority.

History
See note after s.362A.

Note
Section 361 applies to limited liability partnerships by virtue of the Limited Liability Partnerships Regulations 2001 (SI 2001/1090) regs 1, 6(1) as from April 6, 2001 subject to reg.6(2). See the Enterprise Act 2002 (Commencement No.4 and Transitional Provisions and Savings) Order 2003 (SI 2003/2093 (C. 85)) arts 3(1), (3) for transitional saving.

362   Authority's powers to participate in proceedings

362(1)   [Application of section] This section applies if a person other than the Authority makes an administration application under Schedule B1 to the 1986 Act (or presents a petition under Article 22 of the 1989 Order) in relation to a company or partnership which–

(a)   is, or has been, an authorised person;

(b)   is, or has been, an appointed representative; or

(c)   is carrying on, or has carried on, a regulated activity in contravention of the general prohibition.

362(1A)   [Further application of section] This section also applies in relation to–

(a)   the appointment under paragraph 14 or 22 of Schedule B1 to the 1986 Act of an administrator of a company of a kind described in subsection (1)(a) to (c), or

(b)   the filing with the court of a copy of notice of intention to appoint an administrator under either of those paragraphs.

362(2)   [Authority's right of audience] The Authority is entitled to be heard–

(a)   at the hearing of the administration application or the petition; and

(b)   at any other hearing of the court in relation to the company or partnership under Part II of the 1986 Act (or Part III of the 1989 Order).

362(3)   [Notices, etc.] Any notice or other document required to be sent to a creditor of the company or partnership must also be sent to the Authority.

362(4)   [Applications under Insolvency Act 1986 Sch.B1 para.74 etc.] The Authority may apply to the court under paragraph 74 of Schedule B1 to the 1986 Act (or Article 39 of the 1989 Order).

362(4A)   [Application under s.362(4)] In respect of an application under subsection (4)–

(a)   paragraph 74(1)(a) and (b) shall have effect as if for the words " harm the interests of the applicant (whether alone or in common with some or all other members or creditors)" there were substituted the words " harm the interests of some or all members or creditors", and

(b)   Article 39 of the 1989 Order shall have effect with the omission of the words "(including at least himself)".

362(5)   [Attendance at meetings] A person appointed for the purpose by the Authority is entitled–

(a)   to attend any meeting of creditors of the company or partnership summoned under any enactment;

(b) to attend any meeting of a committee established under paragraph 57 of Schedule B1 to the 1986 Act (or Article 38 of the 1989 Order); and

(c) to make representations as to any matter for decision at such a meeting.

362(6) [Applications under Companies Act 2006 Pt 26] If, during the course of the administration of a company, a compromise or arrangement is proposed between the company and its creditors, or any class of them, the Authority may apply to the court under section 896 or 899 of the Companies Act 2006.

History
See note after s.362A. Sections 362(6), 365(7) and 371(5) amended by the Companies Act 2006 (Consequential Amendments etc.) Order 2008 (SI 2008/948) art.3(1) and Sch.1 para.211 as from April 6, 2008.

Note
Section 362 applies to limited liability partnerships by virtue of the Limited Liability Partnerships Regulations 2001 (SI 2001/1090) regs 1, 6(1) as from April 6, 2001 subject to reg.6(2).

362A Administrator appointed by company or directors

362A(1) [Application of s.362A] This section applies in relation to a company of a kind described in section 362(1)(a) to (c).

362A(2) [Consent of Authority for appointment of administrator] An administrator of the company may not be appointed under paragraph 22 of Schedule B1 to the 1986 Act without the consent of the Authority.

362A(3) [Form of consent] Consent under subsection (2)–

(a) must be in writing, and

(b) must be filed with the court along with the notice of intention to appoint under paragraph 27 of that Schedule.

362A(4) [Where no notice of intention to appoint required] In a case where no notice of intention to appoint is required–

(a) subsection (3)(b) shall not apply, but

(b) consent under subsection (2) must accompany the notice of appointment filed under paragraph 29 of that Schedule.

History
Sections 359, 361 and 362(4), (4A) substituted, s.362(1), (2)(a), (5)(b) amended, and ss.362(1A), 362A inserted by the Enterprise Act 2002 s.248(3) Sch.17 paras 53, 55–58 as from September 15, 2003 (see the Enterprise Act 2002 (Commencement No.4 and Transitional Provisions and Savings) Order 2003 (SI 2003/2093 (C. 85)) art.2(1) Sch.1), subject to transitional provisions in SI 2003/2093 (C. 85) art.3. The amendments have no effect in relation to certain companies by virtue of the Enterprise Act 2002 s.249(1).

Receivership

363 Authority's powers to participate in proceedings

363(1) [Application of section] This section applies if a receiver has been appointed in relation to a company which–

(a) is, or has been, an authorised person;

(b) is, or has been, an appointed representative; or

(c) is carrying on, or has carried on, a regulated activity in contravention of the general prohibition.

363(2) [Authority's right of audience] The Authority is entitled to be heard on an application made under section 35 or 63 of the 1986 Act (or Article 45 of the 1989 Order).

363(3) **[Applications to court]** The Authority is entitled to make an application under section 41(1)(a) or 69(1)(a) of the 1986 Act (or Article 51(1)(a) of the 1989 Order).

363(4) **[Reports]** A report under section 48(1) or 67(1) of the 1986 Act (or Article 58(1) of the 1989 Order) must be sent by the person making it to the Authority.

363(5) **[Attendance at meetings]** A person appointed for the purpose by the Authority is entitled–

(a) to attend any meeting of creditors of the company summoned under any enactment;

(b) to attend any meeting of a committee established under section 49 or 68 of the 1986 Act (or Article 59 of the 1989 Order); and

(c) to make representations as to any matter for decision at such a meeting.

Note
Section 363 applies to limited liability partnerships by virtue of the Limited Liability Partnerships Regulations 2001 (SI 2001/1090) regs 1, 6(1) as from April 6, 2001 subject to reg.6(2).

364 Receiver's duty to report to Authority

364 If–

(a) a receiver has been appointed in relation to a company, and

(b) it appears to the receiver that the company is carrying on, or has carried on, a regulated activity in contravention of the general prohibition,

the receiver must report the matter to the Authority without delay.

Note
Section 364 applies to limited liability partnerships by virtue of the Limited Liability Partnerships Regulations 2001 (SI 2001/1090) regs 1, 6(1) as from April 6, 2001 subject to reg.6(2).

Voluntary winding up

365 Authority's powers to participate in proceedings

365(1) **[Application of section]** This section applies in relation to a company which–

(a) is being wound up voluntarily;

(b) is an authorised person; and

(c) is not an insurer effecting or carrying out contracts of long-term insurance.

365(2) **[Applications to court under Insolvency Act 1986 s.112]** The Authority may apply to the court under section 112 of the 1986 Act (or Article 98 of the 1989 Order) in respect of the company.

365(3) **[Authority's right of audience]** The Authority is entitled to be heard at any hearing of the court in relation to the voluntary winding up of the company.

365(4) **[Notices, etc.]** Any notice or other document required to be sent to a creditor of the company must also be sent to the Authority.

365(5) **[Attendance at meetings]** A person appointed for the purpose by the Authority is entitled–

(a) to attend any meeting of creditors of the company summoned under any enactment;

(b) to attend any meeting of a committee established under section 101 of the 1986 Act (or Article 87 of the 1989 Order); and

(c) to make representations as to any matter for decision at such a meeting.

365(6)   [Voluntary winding-up of company] The voluntary winding up of the company does not bar the right of the Authority to have it wound up by the court.

365(7)   [Applications under Companies Act 2006 Pt 26] If, during the course of the winding up of the company, a compromise or arrangement is proposed between the company and its creditors, or any class of them, the Authority may apply to the court under section 896 or 899 of the Companies Act 2006.

Note
Section 365 applies to limited liability partnerships by virtue of the Limited Liability Partnerships Regulations 2001 (SI 2001/1090) regs 1, 6(1) as from April 6, 2001 subject to reg.6(2).

366   Insurers effecting or carrying out long-term contracts of insurance

366(1)   [Voluntary winding-up] An insurer effecting or carrying out contracts of long-term insurance may not be wound up voluntarily without the consent of the Authority.

366(2)   [Notice of general meeting] If notice of a general meeting of such an insurer is given, specifying the intention to propose a resolution for voluntary winding up of the insurer, a director of the insurer must notify the Authority as soon as practicable after he becomes aware of it.

366(3)   [Offence, penalty] A person who fails to comply with subsection (2) is guilty of an offence and liable on summary conviction to a fine not exceeding level 5 on the standard scale.

366(4)   [No written resolution or by meeting at short notice] A winding up resolution may not be passed–

(a)   as a written resolution (in accordance with Chapter 2 of Part 13 of the Companies Act 2006), or

(b)   at a meeting called in accordance with section 307(4) to (6) or 337(2) of that Act (agreement of members to calling of meeting at short notice).

366(5)   [Copies of winding-up resolutions] A copy of a winding-up resolution forwarded to the registrar of companies in accordance with section 30 of the Companies Act 2006 must be accompanied by a certificate issued by the Authority stating that it consents to the voluntary winding up of the insurer.

366(6)   [Compliance with s.366(5)] If subsection (5) is complied with, the voluntary winding up is to be treated as having commenced at the time the resolution was passed.

366(7)   [Non-compliance with s.366(5)] If subsection (5) is not complied with, the resolution has no effect.

366(8)   ["Winding-up resolution"] **"Winding-up resolution"** means a resolution for voluntary winding up of an insurer effecting or carrying out contracts of long-term insurance.

Winding up by the court

367   Winding-up petitions

367(1)   [Power of Authority re petition for winding-up] The Authority may present a petition to the court for the winding up of a body which–

(a)   is, or has been, an authorised person;

(b)   is, or has been, an appointed representative; or

(c)   is carrying on, or has carried on, a regulated activity in contravention of the general prohibition.

367(2)   ["Body"] In subsection (1) **"body"** includes any partnership.

367(3)   [Power of court] On such a petition, the court may wind up the body if–

(a)   the body is unable to pay its debts within the meaning of section 123 or 221 of the 1986 Act (or Article 103 or 185 of the 1989 Order); or

(b)   the court is of the opinion that it is just and equitable that it should be wound up.

367(4)   [Body in default of obligation under agreement] If a body is in default on an obligation to pay a sum due and payable under an agreement, it is to be treated for the purpose of subsection (3)(a) as unable to pay its debts.

367(5)   ["Agreement"] "Agreement" means an agreement the making or performance of which constitutes or is part of a regulated activity carried on by the body concerned.

367(6)   [Application of s.367(7)] Subsection (7) applies if a petition is presented under subsection (1) for the winding up of a partnership–

(a)   on the ground mentioned in subsection (3)(b); or

(b)   in Scotland, on a ground mentioned in subsection (3)(a) or (b).

367(7)   [Jurisdiction of court] The court has jurisdiction, and the 1986 Act (or the 1989 Order) has effect, as if the partnership were an unregistered company as defined by section 220 of that Act (or Article 184 of that Order).

Note
Section 367 applies to limited liability partnerships by virtue of the Limited Liability Partnerships Regulations 2001 (SI 2001/1090) regs 1, 6(1) as from April 6, 2001 subject to reg.6(2).

368   Winding-up petitions: EEA and Treaty firms

368   The Authority may not present a petition to the court under section 367 for the winding up of–

(a)   an EEA firm which qualifies for authorisation under Schedule 3, or

(b)   a Treaty firm which qualifies for authorisation under Schedule 4,

unless it has been asked to do so by the home state regulator of the firm concerned.

369   Insurers: service of petition etc. on Authority

369(1)   [Petition for winding-up—persons other than Authority]   If a person other than the Authority presents a petition for the winding up of an authorised person with permission to effect or carry out contracts of insurance, the petitioner must serve a copy of the petition on the Authority.

369(2)   [Appointment of liquidator—persons other than Authority]   If a person other than the Authority applies to have a provisional liquidator appointed under section 135 of the 1986 Act (or Article 115 of the 1989 Order) in respect of an authorised person with permission to effect or carry out contracts of insurance, the applicant must serve a copy of the application on the Authority.

369A   Reclaim funds: service of petition etc on Authority

369A(1)   [Copy of winding-up petition on Authority] If a person other than the Authority presents a petition for the winding up of an authorised reclaim fund, the petitioner must serve a copy of the petition on the Authority.

369A(2)   [Copy of application for provisional liquidator on Authority] If a person other than the Authority applies to have a provisional liquidator appointed under section 135 of the 1986 Act (or Article 115 of the 1989 Order) in respect of an authorised reclaim fund, the applicant must serve a copy of the application on the Authority.

369A(3)   ["Authorised reclaim fund"] In this section **"authorised reclaim fund"** means a reclaim fund within the meaning given by section 5(1) of the Dormant Bank and Building Society Accounts Act 2008 that is authorised for the purposes of this Act.

History
Section 369A inserted by the Dormant Bank and Building Society Accounts Act 2008 Sch.2 para.7 as from March 12, 2009.

370   Liquidator's duty to report to Authority

370   If–

    (a) a company is being wound up voluntarily or a body is being wound up on a petition presented by a person other than the Authority, and

    (b) it appears to the liquidator that the company or body is carrying on, or has carried on, a regulated activity in contravention of the general prohibition,

the liquidator must report the matter to the Authority without delay.

Note
Section 370 applies to limited liability partnerships by virtue of the Limited Liability Partnerships Regulations 2001 (SI 2001/1090) regs 1, 6(1) as from April 6, 2001 subject to reg.6(2).

371   Authority's powers to participate in proceedings

371(1)   **[Application of section]** This section applies if a person other than the Authority presents a petition for the winding up of a body which–

    (a) is, or has been, an authorised person;

    (b) is, or has been, an appointed representative; or

    (c) is carrying on, or has carried on, a regulated activity in contravention of the general prohibition.

371(2)   **[Authority's right of audience]** The Authority is entitled to be heard–

    (a) at the hearing of the petition; and

    (b) at any other hearing of the court in relation to the body under or by virtue of Part IV or V of the 1986 Act (or Part V or VI of the 1989 Order).

371(3)   **[Notice, etc.]** Any notice or other document required to be sent to a creditor of the body must also be sent to the Authority.

371(4)   **[Attendance at meetings]** A person appointed for the purpose by the Authority is entitled–

    (a) to attend any meeting of creditors of the body;

    (b) to attend any meeting of a committee established for the purposes of Part IV or V of the 1986 Act under section 101 of that Act or under section 141 or 142 of that Act;

    (c) to attend any meeting of a committee established for the purposes of Part V or VI of the 1989 Order under Article 87 of that Order or under Article 120 of that Order; and

    (d) to make representations as to any matter for decision at such a meeting.

371(5)   **[Applications under Companies Act 2006 Pt 26]** If, during the course of the winding up of a company, a compromise or arrangement is proposed between the company and its creditors, or any class of them, the Authority may apply to the court under section 896 or 899 of the Companies Act 2006.

Note
Section 371 applies to limited liability partnerships by virtue of the Limited Liability Partnerships Regulations 2001 (SI 2001/1090) regs 1, 6(1) as from April 6, 2001 subject to reg.6(2).

Bankruptcy

372   Petitions

372(1)   [Power of Authority] The Authority may present a petition to the court–

(a)   under section 264 of the 1986 Act (or Article 238 of the 1989 Order) for a bankruptcy order to be made against an individual; or

(b)   under section 5 of the 1985 Act for the sequestration of the estate of an individual.

372(2)   [Grounds for presentation of petition] But such a petition may be presented only on the ground that–

(a)   the individual appears to be unable to pay a regulated activity debt; or

(b)   the individual appears to have no reasonable prospect of being able to pay a regulated activity debt.

372(3)   [Companies in default of obligation under agreement] An individual appears to be unable to pay a regulated activity debt if he is in default on an obligation to pay a sum due and payable under an agreement.

372(4)   [Ability to pay regulated activity debt] An individual appears to have no reasonable prospect of being able to pay a regulated activity debt if–

(a)   the Authority has served on him a demand requiring him to establish to the satisfaction of the Authority that there is a reasonable prospect that he will be able to pay a sum payable under an agreement when it falls due;

(b)   at least three weeks have elapsed since the demand was served; and

(c)   the demand has been neither complied with nor set aside in accordance with rules.

372(5)   [Demands made under s.372(4)(a)] A demand made under subsection (4)(a) is to be treated for the purposes of the 1986 Act (or the 1989 Order) as if it were a statutory demand under section 268 of that Act (or Article 242 of that Order).

372(6)   [Section 372(1)(b) petitions] For the purposes of a petition presented in accordance with subsection (1)(b)–

(a)   the Authority is to be treated as a qualified creditor; and

(b)   a ground mentioned in subsection (2) constitutes apparent insolvency.

372(7)   ["Individual"] "Individual" means an individual–

(a)   who is, or has been, an authorised person; or

(b)   who is carrying on, or has carried on, a regulated activity in contravention of the general prohibition.

372(8)   ["Agreement"] "Agreement" means an agreement the making or performance of which constitutes or is part of a regulated activity carried on by the individual concerned.

372(9)   ["Rules"] "Rules" means–

(a)   in England and Wales, rules made under section 412 of the 1986 Act;

(b)   in Scotland, rules made by order by the Treasury, after consultation with the Scottish Ministers, for the purposes of this section; and

(c)   in Northern Ireland, rules made under Article 359 of the 1989 Order.

373   Insolvency practitioner's duty to report to Authority

373(1)   [Duty of insolvency practitioner] If–

(a)   a bankruptcy order or sequestration award is in force in relation to an individual by virtue of a petition presented by a person other than the Authority, and

(b)   it appears to the insolvency practitioner that the individual is carrying on, or has carried on, a regulated activity in contravention of the general prohibition,

the insolvency practitioner must report the matter to the Authority without delay.

373(2)   ["Bankruptcy order"] "Bankruptcy order" means a bankruptcy order under Part IX of the 1986 Act (or Part IX of the 1989 Order).

373(3)   ["Sequestration award"] "Sequestration award" means an award of sequestration under section 12 of the 1985 Act.

373(4)   ["Individual"] "Individual" includes an entity mentioned in section 374(1)(c).

374   Authority's powers to participate in proceedings

374(1)   [Application of section] This section applies if a person other than the Authority presents a petition to the court–

(a)   under section 264 of the 1986 Act (or Article 238 of the 1989 Order) for a bankruptcy order to be made against an individual;

(b)   under section 5 of the 1985 Act for the sequestration of the estate of an individual; or

(c)   under section 6 of the 1985 Act for the sequestration of the estate belonging to or held for or jointly by the members of an entity mentioned in subsection (1) of that section.

374(2)   [Authority's right of audience] The Authority is entitled to be heard–

(a)   at the hearing of the petition; and

(b)   at any other hearing in relation to the individual or entity under–

    (i)   Part IX of the 1986 Act;

    (ii)   Part IX of the 1989 Order; or

    (iii)   the 1985 Act.

374(3)   [Insolvency Act 1986 s.274, etc. report—copy to Authority] A copy of the report prepared under section 274 of the 1986 Act (or Article 248 of the 1989 Order) must also be sent to the Authority.

374(4)   [Attendance at meetings] A person appointed for the purpose by the Authority is entitled–

(a)   to attend any meeting of creditors of the individual or entity;

(b)   to attend any meeting of a committee established under section 301 of the 1986 Act (or Article 274 of the 1989 Order);

(c)   to attend any meeting of commissioners held under paragraph 17 or 18 of Schedule 6 to the 1985 Act; and

(d)   to make representations as to any matter for decision at such a meeting.

374(5)   ["Individual"] "Individual" means an individual who–

(a)   is, or has been, an authorised person; or

(b)   is carrying on, or has carried on, a regulated activity in contravention of the general prohibition.

374(6) **["Entity"] "Entity"** means an entity which–

(a) is, or has been, an authorised person; or

(b) is carrying on, or has carried on, a regulated activity in contravention of the general prohibition.

Provisions against debt avoidance

375   Authority's right to apply for an order

375(1) **[Insolvency Act 1986 s.423, etc.—application]** The Authority may apply for an order under section 423 of the 1986 Act (or Article 367 of the 1989 Order) in relation to a debtor if–

(a) at the time the transaction at an undervalue was entered into, the debtor was carrying on a regulated activity (whether or not in contravention of the general prohibition); and

(b) a victim of the transaction is or was party to an agreement entered into with the debtor, the making or performance of which constituted or was part of a regulated activity carried on by the debtor.

375(2) **[Treatment of s.375(1)(b) applications]** An application made under this section is to be treated as made on behalf of every victim of the transaction to whom subsection (1)(b) applies.

375(3) **[Interpretation]** Expressions which are given a meaning in Part XVI of the 1986 Act (or Article 367, 368 or 369 of the 1989 Order) have the same meaning when used in this section.

Supplemental provisions concerning insurers

376   Continuation of contracts of long-term insurance where insurer in liquidation

376(1) **[Application of section]** This section applies in relation to the winding up of an insurer which effects or carries out contracts of long-term insurance.

376(2) **[Duty of liquidator]** Unless the court otherwise orders, the liquidator must carry on the insurer's business so far as it consists of carrying out the insurer's contracts of long-term insurance with a view to its being transferred as a going concern to a person who may lawfully carry out those contracts.

376(3) **[Duty of liquidator—carrying on the business]** In carrying on the business, the liquidator–

(a) may agree to the variation of any contracts of insurance in existence when the winding up order is made; but

(b) must not effect any new contracts of insurance.

376(4) **[Appointment of special manager]** If the liquidator is satisfied that the interests of the creditors in respect of liabilities of the insurer attributable to contracts of long-term insurance effected by it require the appointment of a special manager, he may apply to the court.

376(5) **[Power of court]** On such an application, the court may appoint a special manager to act during such time as the court may direct.

376(6) **[Powers of special manager]** The special manager is to have such powers, including any of the powers of a receiver or manager, as the court may direct.

376(7) **[Application of Insolvency Act 1986 s.177(5), etc.]** Section 177(5) of the 1986 Act (or Article 151(5) of the 1989 Order) applies to a special manager appointed under subsection (5) as it applies to a special manager appointed under section 177 of the 1986 Act (or Article 151 of the 1989 Order).

376(8) **[Company contracts—reduction of value]** If the court thinks fit, it may reduce the value of one or more of the contracts of long-term insurance effected by the insurer.

376(9) **[Terms, etc. of reduction]** Any reduction is to be on such terms and subject to such conditions (if any) as the court thinks fit.

376(10)   [Appointment of independent actuary] The court may, on the application of an official, appoint an independent actuary to investigate the insurer's business so far as it consists of carrying out its contracts of long-term insurance and to report to the official–

(a) on the desirability or otherwise of that part of the insurer's business being continued; and

(b) on any reduction in the contracts of long-term insurance effected by the insurer that may be necessary for successful continuation of that part of the insurer's business.

376(11)   ["Official"] "Official" means–

(a) the liquidator;

(b) a special manager appointed under subsection (5); or

(c) the Authority.

376(12)   [Applications by liquidator] The liquidator may make an application in the name of the insurer and on its behalf under Part VII without obtaining the permission that would otherwise be required by section 167 of, and Schedule 4 to, the 1986 Act (or Article 142 of, and Schedule 2 to, the 1989 Order).

377   Reducing the value of contracts instead of winding up

377(1)   [Application of section] This section applies in relation to an insurer which has been proved to be unable to pay its debts.

377(2)   [Power of court] If the court thinks fit, it may reduce the value of one or more of the insurer's contracts instead of making a winding up order.

377(3)   [Terms, etc. of reduction] Any reduction is to be on such terms and subject to such conditions (if any) as the court thinks fit.

378   Treatment of assets on winding up

378(1)   [Power of Treasury to make regulations] The Treasury may by regulations provide for the treatment of the assets of an insurer on its winding up.

378(2)   [Content of regulations] The regulations may, in particular, provide for–

(a) assets representing a particular part of the insurer's business to be available only for meeting liabilities attributable to that part of the insurer's business;

(b) separate general meetings of the creditors to be held in respect of liabilities attributable to a particular part of the insurer's business.

Note
See the Financial Services and Markets Act 2000 (Treatment of Assets of Insurers on Winding Up) Regulations 2001 (SI 2001/2968).

379   Winding-up rules

379(1)   [Content] Winding-up rules may include provision–

(a) for determining the amount of the liabilities of an insurer to policyholders of any class or description for the purpose of proof in a winding up; and

(b) generally for carrying into effect the provisions of this Part with respect to the winding up of insurers.

379(2)   [Further contents] Winding-up rules may, in particular, make provision for all or any of the following matters–

   (a)   the identification of assets and liabilities;

   (b)   the apportionment, between assets of different classes or descriptions, of–

      (i)   the costs, charges and expenses of the winding up; and

      (ii)   any debts of the insurer of a specified class or description;

   (c)   the determination of the amount of liabilities of a specified description;

   (d)   the application of assets for meeting liabilities of a specified description;

   (e)   the application of assets representing any excess of a specified description.

379(3)   **["Specified"] "Specified"** means specified in winding-up rules.

379(4)   **["Winding-up rules"] "Winding-up rules"** means rules made under section 411 of the 1986 Act (or Article 359 of the 1989 Order).

379(5)   **[Winding-up rules under Insolvency Act 1986, etc.]** Nothing in this section affects the power to make winding-up rules under the 1986 Act or the 1989 Order.

Note
See the Insurers (Winding Up) Rules 2001 (SI 2001/3635).

Limited Liability Partnerships Act 2000

(2000 Chapter 12)

An Act to make provision for limited liability partnerships.

[20th July 2000]

Regulations

14   Insolvency and winding up

14(1)   [Regulations to apply or incorporate Parts of Insolvency Act 1986] Regulations shall make provision about the insolvency and winding up of limited liability partnerships by applying or incorporating, with such modifications as appear appropriate–

(a)   in relation to a limited liability partnership registered in Great Britain, Parts 1 to 4, 6 and 7 of the Insolvency Act 1986;

(b)   in relation to a limited liability partnership registered in Northern Ireland, Parts 2 to 5 and 7 of the Insolvency (Northern Ireland) Order 1989, and so much of Part 1 of that Order as applies for the purposes of those Parts.

14(2)   [Other regulations] Regulations may make other provision about the insolvency and winding up of limited liability partnerships, and provision about the insolvency and winding up of oversea limited liability partnerships, by–

(a)   applying or incorporating, with such modifications as appear appropriate, any law relating to the insolvency or winding up of companies or other corporations which would not otherwise have effect in relation to them, or

(b)   providing for any law relating to the insolvency or winding up of companies or other corporations which would otherwise have effect in relation to them not to apply to them or to apply to them with such modifications as appear appropriate.

14(3)   ["Oversea limited liability partnership"] In this Act **"oversea limited liability partnership"** means a body incorporated or otherwise established outside the United Kingdom and having such connection with the United Kingdom, and such other features, as regulations may prescribe.

History
Section 14(1), (3) amended by the Limited Liability Partnerships (Application of Companies Act 2006) Regulations 2009 (SI 2009/1804) Sch.3 para.6 as from October 1, 2009.

15   Application of company law etc.

15   Regulations may make provision about limited liability partnerships and oversea limited liability partnerships (not being provision about insolvency or winding up) by–

(a)   applying or incorporating, with such modifications as appear appropriate, any law relating to companies or other corporations which would not otherwise have effect in relation to them,

(b)   providing for any law relating to companies or other corporations which would otherwise have effect in relation to them not to apply to them or to apply to them with such modifications as appear appropriate, or

(c)   applying or incorporating, with such modifications as appear appropriate, any law relating to partnerships.

Note
See the Limited Liability Partnerships Regulations 2001 (SI 2001/1090), below.

Proceeds of Crime Act 2002

(2002 Chapter 29)

An Act to establish the Assets Recovery Agency and make provision about the appointment of its Director and his functions (including Revenue functions), to provide for confiscation orders in relation to persons who benefit from criminal conduct and for restraint orders to prohibit dealing with property, to allow the recovery of property which is or represents property obtained through unlawful conduct or which is intended to be used in unlawful conduct, to make provision about money laundering, to make provision about investigations relating to benefit from criminal conduct or to property which is or represents property obtained through unlawful conduct or to money laundering, to make provision to give effect to overseas requests and orders made where property is found or believed to be obtained through criminal conduct, and for connected purposes.

[24th July 2002]

[**Note**: Part 9 was brought into force by the Proceeds of Crime Act 2002 (Commencement No.5, Transitional Provisions, Savings and Amendment) Order 2003 (SI 2003/333) art.2 and Sch., as from March 24, 2003, subject to transitional provisions and savings. Changes made by the Serious Crime Act 2007 have been incorporated into the text. Note prospective amendment of the sections extracted below by the Policing and Crime Act 2009 Sch.7 paras 80 et seq. and Sch.8 Pt 4 from a date to be appointed.]

PART 9

INSOLVENCY ETC.

Bankruptcy in England and Wales

417 Modifications of the 1986 Act

417(1) This section applies if a person is adjudged bankrupt in England and Wales.

417(2) The following property is excluded from his estate for the purposes of Part 9 of the 1986 Act–

(a) property for the time being subject to a restraint order which was made under section 41, 120 or 190 before the order adjudging him bankrupt;

(b)   any property in respect of which an order under section 50 is in force;

(c)   any property in respect of which an order under section 128(3) is in force;

(d)   any property in respect of which an order under section 198 is in force.

417(3)   Subsection (2)(a) applies to heritable property in Scotland only if the restraint order is recorded in the General Register of Sasines or registered in the Land Register of Scotland before the order adjudging the person bankrupt.

417(4)   If in the case of a debtor an interim receiver stands at any time appointed under section 286 of the 1986 Act and any property of the debtor is then subject to a restraint order made under section 41, 120 or 190 the powers conferred on the receiver by virtue of that Act do not apply to property then subject to the restraint order.

History
See note after s.430.

418   Restriction of powers

418(1)   If a person is adjudged bankrupt in England and Wales the powers referred to in subsection (2) must not be exercised in relation to the property referred to in subsection (3).

418(2)   These are the powers–

(a)   the powers conferred on a court by sections 41 to 67 and the powers of a receiver appointed under section 48 or 50;

(b)   the powers conferred on a court by sections 120 to 136 and Schedule 3 and the powers of an administrator appointed under section 125 or 128(3);

(c)   the powers conferred on a court by sections 190 to 215 and the powers of a receiver appointed under section 196 or 198.

418(3)   This is the property–

(a)   property which is for the time being comprised in the bankrupt's estate for the purposes of Part 9 of the 1986 Act;

(b)   property in respect of which his trustee in bankruptcy may (without leave of the court) serve a notice under section 307, 308 or 308A of the 1986 Act (after-acquired property, tools, tenancies etc);

(c)   property which is to be applied for the benefit of creditors of the bankrupt by virtue of a condition imposed under section 280(2)(c) of the 1986 Act;

(d)   in a case where a confiscation order has been made under section 6 or 156 of this Act, any sums remaining in the hands of a receiver appointed under section 50 or 198 of this Act after the amount required to be paid under the confiscation order has been fully paid;

(e)   in a case where a confiscation order has been made under section 92 of this Act, any sums remaining in the hands of an administrator appointed under section 128 of this Act after the amount required to be paid under the confiscation order has been fully paid.

418(4)   But nothing in the 1986 Act must be taken to restrict (or enable the restriction of) the powers referred to in subsection (2).

418(5)   In a case where a petition in bankruptcy was presented or a receiving order or adjudication in bankruptcy was made before 29 December 1986 (when the 1986 Act came into force) this section has effect with these modifications–

(a)   for the reference in subsection (3)(a) to the bankrupt's estate for the purposes of Part 9 of that Act substitute a reference to the property of the bankrupt for the purposes of the 1914 Act;

    (b)   omit subsection (3)(b);

    (c)   for the reference in subsection (3)(c) to section 280(2)(c) of the 1986 Act substitute a reference to section 26(2) of the 1914 Act;

    (d)   for the reference in subsection (4) to the 1986 Act substitute a reference to the 1914 Act.

History
See note after s.430.

419 Tainted gifts

419(1)   This section applies if a person who is adjudged bankrupt in England and Wales has made a tainted gift (whether directly or indirectly).

419(2)   No order may be made under section 339, 340 or 423 of the 1986 Act (avoidance of certain transactions) in respect of the making of the gift at any time when–

    (a)   any property of the recipient of the tainted gift is subject to a restraint order under section 41, 120 or 190, or

    (b)   there is in force in respect of such property an order under section 50, 128(3) or 198.

419(3)   Any order made under section 339, 340 or 423 of the 1986 Act after an order mentioned in subsection (2)(a) or (b) is discharged must take into account any realisation under Part 2, 3 or 4 of this Act of property held by the recipient of the tainted gift.

419(4)   A person makes a tainted gift for the purposes of this section if he makes a tainted gift within the meaning of Part 2, 3 or 4.

419(5)   In a case where a petition in bankruptcy was presented or a receiving order or adjudication in bankruptcy was made before 29 December 1986 (when the 1986 Act came into force) this section has effect with the substitution for a reference to section 339, 340 or 423 of the 1986 Act of a reference to section 27, 42 or 44 of the 1914 Act.

History
See note after s.430.

Winding up in England and Wales and Scotland

426 Winding up under the 1986 Act

426(1)   In this section **"company"** means any company which may be wound up under the 1986 Act.

426(2)   If an order for the winding up of a company is made or it passes a resolution for its voluntary winding up, the functions of the liquidator (or any provisional liquidator) are not exercisable in relation to the following property–

    (a)   property for the time being subject to a restraint order which was made under section 41, 120 or 190 before the relevant time;

    (b)   any property in respect of which an order under section 50 is in force;

    (c)   any property in respect of which an order under section 128(3) is in force;

    (d)   any property in respect of which an order under section 198 is in force.

426(3)   Subsection (2)(a) applies to heritable property in Scotland only if the restraint order is recorded in the General Register of Sasines or registered in the Land Register of Scotland before the relevant time.

426(4)   If an order for the winding up of a company is made or it passes a resolution for its voluntary winding up the powers referred to in subsection (5) must not be exercised in the way mentioned in subsection (6) in relation to any property–

(a) which is held by the company, and

(b) in relation to which the functions of the liquidator are exercisable.

426(5) These are the powers–

(a) the powers conferred on a court by sections 41 to 67 and the powers of a receiver appointed under section 48 or 50;

(b) the powers conferred on a court by sections 120 to 136 and Schedule 3 and the powers of an administrator appointed under section 125 or 128(3);

(c) the powers conferred on a court by sections 190 to 215 and the powers of a receiver appointed under section 196 or 198.

426(6) The powers must not be exercised–

(a) so as to inhibit the liquidator from exercising his functions for the purpose of distributing property to the company's creditors;

(b) so as to prevent the payment out of any property of expenses (including the remuneration of the liquidator or any provisional liquidator) properly incurred in the winding up in respect of the property.

426(7) But nothing in the 1986 Act must be taken to restrict (or enable the restriction of) the exercise of the powers referred to in subsection (5).

426(8) For the purposes of the application of Parts 4 and 5 of the 1986 Act (winding up) to a company which the Court of Session has jurisdiction to wind up, a person is not a creditor in so far as any sum due to him by the company is due in respect of a confiscation order made under section 6, 92 or 156.

426(9) The relevant time is–

(a) if no order for the winding up of the company has been made, the time of the passing of the resolution for voluntary winding up;

(b) if such an order has been made, but before the presentation of the petition for the winding up of the company by the court such a resolution has been passed by the company, the time of the passing of the resolution;

(c) if such an order has been made, but paragraph (b) does not apply, the time of the making of the order.

426(10) In a case where a winding up of a company commenced or is treated as having commenced before 29 December 1986, this section has effect with the following modifications–

(a) in subsections (1) and (7) for "the 1986 Act" substitute "the Companies Act 1985";

(b) in subsection (8) for "Parts 4 and 5 of the 1986 Act" substitute "Parts 20 and 21 of the Companies Act 1985".

History
See note after s.430.

427 Tainted gifts

427(1) In this section **"company"** means any company which may be wound up under the 1986 Act.

427(2) This section applies if–

(a) an order for the winding up of a company is made or it passes a resolution for its voluntary winding up, and

(b) it has made a tainted gift (whether directly or indirectly).

427(3) No order may be made under section 238, 239 or 423 of the 1986 Act (avoidance of certain transactions) and no decree may be granted under section 242 or 243 of that Act (gratuitous alienations and unfair preferences), or otherwise, in respect of the making of the gift at any time when–

(a) any property of the recipient of the tainted gift is subject to a restraint order under section 41, 120 or 190, or

(b) there is in force in respect of such property an order under section 50, 128(3) or 198.

427(4) Any order made under section 238, 239 or 423 of the 1986 Act or decree granted under section 242 or 243 of that Act, or otherwise, after an order mentioned in subsection (3)(a) or (b) is discharged must take into account any realisation under Part 2, 3 or 4 of this Act of property held by the recipient of the tainted gift.

427(5) A person makes a tainted gift for the purposes of this section if he makes a tainted gift within the meaning of Part 2, 3 or 4.

427(6) In a case where the winding up of a company commenced or is treated as having commenced before 29 December 1986 this section has effect with the substitution–

(a) for references to section 239 of the 1986 Act of references to section 615 of the Companies Act 1985 (c. 6);

(b) for references to section 242 of the 1986 Act of references to section 615A of the Companies Act 1985;

(c) for references to section 243 of the 1986 Act of references to section 615B of the Companies Act 1985.

History
See note after s.430.

Floating charges

430 Floating charges

430(1) In this section **"company"** means a company which may be wound up under–

(a) the 1986 Act, or

(b) the 1989 Order.

430(2) If a company holds property which is subject to a floating charge, and a receiver has been appointed by or on the application of the holder of the charge, the functions of the receiver are not exercisable in relation to the following property–

(a) property for the time being subject to a restraint order which was made under section 41, 120 or 190 before the appointment of the receiver;

(b) any property in respect of which an order under section 50 is in force;

(c) any property in respect of which an order under section 128(3) is in force;

(d) any property in respect of which an order under section 198 is in force.

430(3) Subsection (2)(a) applies to heritable property in Scotland only if the restraint order is recorded in the General Register of Sasines or registered in the Land Register of Scotland before the appointment of the receiver.

430(4) If a company holds property which is subject to a floating charge, and a receiver has been appointed by or on the application of the holder of the charge, the powers referred to in subsection (5) must not be exercised in the way mentioned in subsection (6) in relation to any property–

(a) which is held by the company, and

(b) in relation to which the functions of the receiver are exercisable.

430(5) These are the powers–

(a) the powers conferred on a court by sections 41 to 67 and the powers of a receiver appointed under section 48 or 50;

(b) the powers conferred on a court by sections 120 to 136 and Schedule 3 and the powers of an administrator appointed under section 125 or 128(3);

(c) the powers conferred on a court by sections 190 to 215 and the powers of a receiver appointed under section 196 or 198.

430(6) The powers must not be exercised–

(a) so as to inhibit the receiver from exercising his functions for the purpose of distributing property to the company's creditors;

(b) so as to prevent the payment out of any property of expenses (including the remuneration of the receiver) properly incurred in the exercise of his functions in respect of the property.

430(7) But nothing in the 1986 Act or the 1989 Order must be taken to restrict (or enable the restriction of) the exercise of the powers referred to in subsection (5).

430(8) In this section **"floating charge"** includes a floating charge within the meaning of section 462 of the Companies Act 1985 (c. 6).

History
Sections 417, 418, 419, 426, and 427 amended (by the deletion of references to repealed sections) by the Serious Crime Act 2007 s.74(2) and Sch.8, as from April 6, 2008.

Limited liability partnerships

431   Limited liability partnerships

431(1) In sections 426, 427 and 430 **"company"** includes a limited liability partnership which may be wound up under the 1986 Act.

431(2) A reference in those sections to a company passing a resolution for its voluntary winding up is to be construed in relation to a limited liability partnership as a reference to the partnership making a determination for its voluntary winding up.

Insolvency practitioners

432   Insolvency practitioners

432(1) Subsections (2) and (3) apply if a person acting as an insolvency practitioner seizes or disposes of any property in relation to which his functions are not exercisable because–

(a) it is for the time being subject to a restraint order made under section 41, 120 or 190, or

(b) it is for the time being subject to a property freezing order made under section 245A, an interim receiving order made under section 246, a prohibitory property order made under section 255A or an interim administration order made under section 256,

and at the time of the seizure or disposal he believes on reasonable grounds that he is entitled (whether in pursuance of an order of a court or otherwise) to seize or dispose of the property.

432(2) He is not liable to any person in respect of any loss or damage resulting from the seizure or disposal, except so far as the loss or damage is caused by his negligence.

432(3)   He has a lien on the property or the proceeds of its sale–

(a)   for such of his expenses as were incurred in connection with the liquidation, bankruptcy, sequestration or other proceedings in relation to which he purported to make the seizure or disposal, and

(b)   for so much of his remuneration as may reasonably be assigned to his acting in connection with those proceedings.

432(4)   Subsection (2) does not prejudice the generality of any provision of the 1985 Act, the 1986 Act, the 1989 Order or any other Act or Order which confers protection from liability on him.

432(5)   Subsection (7) applies if–

(a)   property is subject to a restraint order made under section 41, 120 or 190,

(b)   a person acting as an insolvency practitioner incurs expenses in respect of property subject to the restraint order, and

(c)   he does not know (and has no reasonable grounds to believe) that the property is subject to the restraint order.

432(6)   Subsection (7) also applies if–

(a)   property is subject to a restraint order made under section 41, 120 or 190,

(b)   a person acting as an insolvency practitioner incurs expenses which are not ones in respect of property subject to the restraint order, and

(c)   the expenses are ones which (but for the effect of the restraint order) might have been met by taking possession of and realising property subject to it.

432(7)   Whether or not he has seized or disposed of any property, he is entitled to payment of the expenses under–

(a)   section 54(2) or 55(3) if the restraint order was made under section 41;

(b)   section 130(3) or 131(3) if the restraint order was made under section 120;

(c)   section 202(2) or 203(3) if the restraint order was made under section 190.

432(8)   Subsection (10) applies if–

(a)   property is subject to a property freezing order made under section 245A, an interim receiving order made under section 246, a prohibitory property order made under section 255A or an interim administration order made under section 256,

(b)   a person acting as an insolvency practitioner incurs expenses in respect of property subject to the order, and

(c)   he does not know (and has no reasonable grounds to believe) that the property is subject to the order.

432(9)   Subsection (10) also applies if–

(a)   property is subject to a property freezing order made under section 245A, an interim receiving order made under section 246, a prohibitory property order made under section 255A or an interim administration order made under section 256,

(b)   a person acting as an insolvency practitioner incurs expenses which are not ones in respect of property subject to the order, and

(c)   the expenses are ones which (but for the effect of the order) might have been met by taking possession of and realising property subject to it.

432(10)   Whether or not he has seized or disposed of any property, he is entitled to payment of the expenses under section 280.

History
Section 432(1)(b), (8)(a) and (9)(a) amended by the Serious Organised Crime and Police Act 2005 s.109 and Sch.6 para.23 as from January 1, 2006. Section 432(7) amended (by the deletion of references to repealed sections) by the Serious Crime Act 2007 s.74(2) and Sch.8, as from April 6, 2008.

433   Meaning of insolvency practitioner

433(1)   This section applies for the purposes of section 432.

433(2)   A person acts as an insolvency practitioner if he so acts within the meaning given by section 388 of the 1986 Act or Article 3 of the 1989 Order; but this is subject to subsections (3) to (5).

433(3)   The expression "person acting as an insolvency practitioner" includes the official receiver acting as receiver or manager of the property concerned.

433(4)   In applying section 388 of the 1986 Act under subsection (2) above–

(a)   the reference in section 388(2)(a) to a permanent or interim trustee in sequestration must be taken to include a reference to a trustee in sequestration;

(b)   section 388(5) (which includes provision that nothing in the section applies to anything done by the official receiver or the Accountant in Bankruptcy) must be ignored.

433(5)   In applying Article 3 of the 1989 Order under subsection (2) above, paragraph (5) (which includes provision that nothing in the Article applies to anything done by the official receiver) must be ignored.

Interpretation

434   Interpretation

434(1)   The following paragraphs apply to references to Acts or Orders–

(a)   the 1913 Act is the Bankruptcy (Scotland) Act 1913 (c. 20);

(b)   the 1914 Act is the Bankruptcy Act 1914 (c. 59);

(c)   the 1985 Act is the Bankruptcy (Scotland) Act 1985 (c. 66);

(d)   the 1986 Act is the Insolvency Act 1986 (c. 45);

(e)   the 1989 Order is the Insolvency (Northern Ireland) Order 1989 (S.I. 1989/2405 (N.I. 19)).

434(2)   An award of sequestration is made on the date of sequestration within the meaning of section 12(4) of the 1985 Act.

434(3)   This section applies for the purposes of this Part.

Companies (Audit, Investigations and Community Enterprise) Act 2004

(2004 Chapter 27)

[*28th October 2004*]

PART 2

COMMUNITY INTEREST COMPANIES

Requirements

31 Distribution of assets on winding up

31(1) [Distributions on winding up] Regulations may make provision for and in connection with the distribution, on the winding up of a community interest company, of any assets of the company which remain after satisfaction of the company's liabilities.

31(2) [Modification of enactments] The regulations may, in particular, amend or modify the operation of any enactment or instrument.

Supervision by Regulator

50 Petition for winding up

50(1) [Petition for winding up] The Regulator may present a petition for a community interest company to be wound up if the court is of the opinion that it is just and equitable that the company should be wound up.

50(2) [Non-application of s.50(1)] Subsection (1) does not apply if the company is already being wound up by the court.

50(3) [Insertion of s.124(4A) in 1986 Act] In section 124 of the Insolvency Act 1986 (c. 45) (application for winding up), after subsection (4) insert–

"**(4A)** A winding-up petition may be presented by the Regulator of Community Interest Companies in a case falling within section 50 of the Companies (Audit, Investigations and Community Enterprise) Act 2004."

51 Dissolution and striking off

51(1) [Restoration to the register] If a community interest company has been–

(a) dissolved, or

(b) struck off the register under section 1000 or 1001 of the Companies Act 2006, the Regulator may apply to the court under section 1029 of that Act for an order restoring the company's name to the register.

51(2)   [Omitted.]

51(3)   **[Copy of application for striking off to Regulator]** If an application under section 1003 of the Companies Act 2006 (striking off on application by company) is made on behalf of a community interest company, section 1006 of the Companies Act 2006 (persons to be notified of application) is to be treated as also requiring a copy of the application to be given to the Regulator.

History
Section 51(3) amended by the Companies Act 2006 (Commencement No.2, Consequential Amendments, Transitional Provisions and Savings) Order 2007 (SI 2007/1093 (C. 49)) art.6(2) and Sch.4 para.17, as from April 6, 2007. Section 51(2) substituted, s.51(2) omitted and s.51(3) amended by the Companies Act 2006 (Consequential Amendments, Transitional Provisions and Savings) Order 2009 (SI 2009/1941) art.2(1) and Sch.1 para.234 as from October 1, 2009.

Pensions Act 2004

(2004 Chapter 35)

An Act to make provision relating to pensions and financial planning for retirement and provision relating to entitlement to bereavement payments, and for connected purposes.

[*18th November 2004*]

[**Note**: The provisions of Pt 2 of this Act are modified in their application to multi-employer pensions schemes by the Pension Protection Fund (Multi-employer Schemes) (Modification) Regulations 2005 (SI 2005/441), effective April 6, 2005.]

PART 2

THE BOARD OF THE PENSION PROTECTION FUND

CHAPTER 2

INFORMATION RELATING TO EMPLOYER'S INSOLVENCY ETC.

Insolvency events

120 Duty to notify insolvency events in respect of employers

120(1) This section applies where, in the case of an occupational pension scheme, an insolvency event occurs in relation to the employer.

120(2) The insolvency practitioner in relation to the employer must give a notice to that effect within the notification period to–

(a) the Board,

(b) the Regulator, and

(c) the trustees or managers of the scheme.

120(3) For the purposes of subsection (2) the **"notification period"** is the prescribed period beginning with the later of–

(a) the insolvency date, and

(b) the date the insolvency practitioner becomes aware of the existence of the scheme.

120(4) A notice under this section must be in such form and contain such information as may be prescribed.

121 Insolvency event, insolvency date and insolvency practitioner

121(1) In this Part each of the following expressions has the meaning given to it by this section–

"insolvency event"

"insolvency date"

"insolvency practitioner".

121(2) An insolvency event occurs in relation to an individual where–

(a) he is adjudged bankrupt or sequestration of his estate has been awarded;

(b) the nominee in relation to a proposal for a voluntary arrangement under Part 8 of the Insolvency Act 1986 (c. 45) submits a report to the court under section 256(1) or 256A(3) of that Act which states that in his opinion a meeting of the individual's creditors should be summoned to consider the debtor's proposal;

(c) a deed of arrangement made by or in respect of the affairs of the individual is registered in accordance with the Deeds of Arrangement Act 1914 (c. 47);

(d) he executes a trust deed for his creditors or enters into a composition contract;

(e) he has died and–

(i) an insolvency administration order is made in respect of his estate in accordance with an order under section 421 of the Insolvency Act 1986, or

(ii) a judicial factor appointed under section 11A of the Judicial Factors (Scotland) Act 1889 (c. 39) is required by that section to divide the individual's estate among his creditors.

121(3) An insolvency event occurs in relation to a company where–

(a) the nominee in relation to a proposal for a voluntary arrangement under Part 1 of the Insolvency Act 1986 submits a report to the court under section 2 of that Act (procedure where nominee is not the liquidator or administrator) which states that in his opinion meetings of the company and its creditors should be summoned to consider the proposal;

(b) the directors of the company file (or in Scotland lodge) with the court documents and statements in accordance with paragraph 7(1) of Schedule A1 to that Act (moratorium where directors propose voluntary arrangement);

(c) an administrative receiver within the meaning of section 251 of that Act is appointed in relation to the company;

(d) the company enters administration within the meaning of paragraph 1(2)(b) of Schedule B1 to that Act;

(e) a resolution is passed for a voluntary winding up of the company without a declaration of solvency under section 89 of that Act;

(f) a meeting of creditors is held in relation to the company under section 95 of that Act (creditors' meeting which has the effect of converting a members' voluntary winding up into a creditors' voluntary winding up);

(g) an order for the winding up of the company is made by the court under Part 4 or 5 of that Act.

121(4)   An insolvency event occurs in relation to a partnership where–

(a)   an order for the winding up of the partnership is made by the court under any provision of the Insolvency Act 1986 (c. 45) (as applied by an order under section 420 of that Act (insolvent partnerships));

(b)   sequestration is awarded on the estate of the partnership under section 12 of the Bankruptcy (Scotland) Act 1985 (c. 66) or the partnership grants a trust deed for its creditors;

(c)   the nominee in relation to a proposal for a voluntary arrangement under Part 1 of the Insolvency Act 1986 (as applied by an order under section 420 of that Act) submits a report to the court under section 2 of that Act (procedure where nominee is not the liquidator or administrator) which states that in his opinion meetings of the members of the partnership and the partnership's creditors should be summoned to consider the proposal;

(d)   the members of the partnership file with the court documents and statements in accordance with paragraph 7(1) of Schedule A1 to that Act (moratorium where directors propose voluntary arrangement) (as applied by an order under section 420 of that Act);

(e)   the partnership enters administration within the meaning of paragraph 1(2)(b) of Schedule B1 to that Act (as applied by an order under section 420 of that Act).

121(5)   An insolvency event also occurs in relation to a person where an event occurs which is a prescribed event in relation to such a person.

121(6)   Except as provided by subsections (2) to (5), for the purposes of this Part an event is not to be regarded as an insolvency event in relation to a person.

121(7)   The Secretary of State may by order amend subsection (4)(e) to make provision consequential upon any order under section 420 of the Insolvency Act 1986 (insolvent partnerships) applying the provisions of Part 2 of that Act (administration) as amended by the Enterprise Act 2002 (c. 40).

121(8)   **"Insolvency date"**, in relation to an insolvency event, means the date on which the event occurs.

121(9)   **"Insolvency practitioner"**, in relation to a person, means–

(a)   a person acting as an insolvency practitioner, in relation to that person, in accordance with section 388 of the Insolvency Act 1986;

(b)   in such circumstances as may be prescribed, a person of a prescribed description.

121(10)   In this section–

"company" means a company as defined in section 1(1) of the Companies Act 2006 or a company which may be wound up under Part 5 of the Insolvency Act 1986 (c. 45) (unregistered companies);

"person acting as an insolvency practitioner", in relation to a person, includes the official receiver acting as receiver or manager of any property of that person.

121(11)   In applying section 388 of the Insolvency Act 1986 under subsection (9) above–

(a)   the reference in section 388(2)(a) to a permanent or interim trustee in sequestration must be taken to include a reference to a trustee in sequestration, and

(b)   section 388(5) (which includes provision that nothing in the section applies to anything done by the official receiver or the Accountant in Bankruptcy) must be ignored.

History
Section 121(4)(e) substituted by the Pension Protection Fund (Insolvent Partnerships) (Amendment of Insolvency Events) Order 2005 (SI 2005/2893) art.2, as from November 10, 2005.

Status of scheme

122 Insolvency practitioner's duty to issue notices confirming status of scheme

122(1) This section applies where an insolvency event has occurred in relation to the employer in relation to an occupational pension scheme.

122(2) An insolvency practitioner in relation to the employer must–

(a) if he is able to confirm that a scheme rescue is not possible, issue a notice to that effect (a **"scheme failure notice"**), or

(b) if he is able to confirm that a scheme rescue has occurred, issue a notice to that effect (a **"withdrawal notice"**).

122(3) Subsection (4) applies where–

(a) in prescribed circumstances, insolvency proceedings in relation to the employer are stayed or come to an end, or

(b) a prescribed event occurs.

122(4) If a person who was acting as an insolvency practitioner in relation to the employer immediately before this subsection applies has not been able to confirm in relation to the scheme–

(a) that a scheme rescue is not possible, or

(b) that a scheme rescue has occurred,

he must issue a notice to that effect.

122(5) For the purposes of this section–

(a) a person is able to confirm that a scheme rescue has occurred in relation to an occupational pension scheme if, and only if, he is able to confirm such matters as are prescribed for the purposes of this paragraph, and

(b) a person is able to confirm that a scheme rescue is not possible, in relation to such a scheme if, and only if, he is able to confirm such matters as are prescribed for the purposes of this paragraph.

122(6) Where an insolvency practitioner or former insolvency practitioner in relation to the employer issues a notice under this section, he must give a copy of that notice to–

(a) the Board,

(b) the Regulator, and

(c) the trustees or managers of the scheme.

122(7) A person must comply with an obligation imposed on him by subsection (2), (4) or (6) as soon as reasonably practicable.

122(8) Regulations may require notices issued under this section–

(a) to be in a prescribed form;

(b) to contain prescribed information.

123 Approval of notices issued under section 122

123(1) This section applies where the Board receives a notice under section 122(6) (**"the section 122 notice"**).

123(2) The Board must determine whether to approve the section 122 notice.

123(3)   The Board must approve the section 122 notice if, and only if, it is satisfied–

(a)   that the insolvency practitioner or former insolvency practitioner who issued the notice was required to issue it under that section, and

(b)   that the notice complies with any requirements imposed by virtue of subsection (8) of that section.

123(4)   Where the Board makes a determination for the purposes of subsection (2), it must issue a determination notice and give a copy of that notice to–

(a)   the Regulator,

(b)   the trustees or managers of the scheme,

(c)   the insolvency practitioner or the former insolvency practitioner who issued the section 122 notice,

(d)   any insolvency practitioner in relation to the employer (who does not fall within paragraph (c)), and

(e)   if there is no insolvency practitioner in relation to the employer, the employer.

123(5)   In subsection (4) **"determination notice"** means a notice which is in the prescribed form and contains such information about the determination as may be prescribed.

Board's duties

124   Board's duty where there is a failure to comply with section 122

124(1)   This section applies where in relation to an occupational pension scheme–

(a)   the Board determines under section 123 not to approve a notice issued under section 122 by an insolvency practitioner or former insolvency practitioner in relation to the employer, or

(b)   an insolvency practitioner or former insolvency practitioner in relation to the employer fails to issue a notice under section 122 and the Board is satisfied that such a notice ought to have been issued under that section.

124(2)   The obligations on the insolvency practitioner or former insolvency practitioner imposed by subsections (2) and (4) of section 122 are to be treated as obligations imposed on the Board and the Board must accordingly issue a notice as required under that section.

124(3)   Subject to subsections (4) and (5), where a notice is issued under section 122 by the Board by virtue of this section, it has effect as if it were a notice issued under section 122 by an insolvency practitioner or, as the case may be, former insolvency practitioner in relation to the employer.

124(4)   Where a notice is issued under section 122 by virtue of this section, section 122(6) does not apply and the Board must, as soon as reasonably practicable, give a copy of the notice to–

(a)   the Regulator,

(b)   the trustees or managers of the scheme,

(c)   the insolvency practitioner or former insolvency practitioner mentioned in subsection (1),

(d)   any insolvency practitioner in relation to the employer (who does not fall within paragraph (c)), and

(e)   if there is no insolvency practitioner in relation to the employer, the employer.

124(5)   Where the Board–

(a)   is required to issue a notice under section 122 by virtue of this section, and

(b)   is satisfied that the notice ought to have been issued at an earlier time,

it must specify that time in the notice and the notice is to have effect as if it had been issued at that time.

125   Binding notices confirming status of scheme

125(1)   Subject to subsection (2), for the purposes of this Part, a notice issued under section 122 is not binding until–

(a)   the Board issues a determination notice under section 123 approving the notice,

(b)   the period within which the issue of the determination notice under that section may be reviewed by virtue of Chapter 6 has expired, and

(c)   if the issue of the determination notice is so reviewed–

   (i)   the review and any reconsideration,

   (ii)   any reference to the PPF Ombudsman in respect of the issue of the notice, and

   (iii)   any appeal against his determination or directions,

has been finally disposed of and the determination notice has not been revoked, varied or substituted.

125(2)   Where a notice is issued under section 122 by the Board by virtue of section 124, the notice is not binding until–

(a)   the period within which the issue of the notice may be reviewed by virtue of Chapter 6 has expired, and

(b)   if the issue of the notice is so reviewed–

   (i)   the review and any reconsideration,

   (ii)   any reference to the PPF Ombudsman in respect of the issue of the notice, and

   (iii)   any appeal against his determination or directions,

has been finally disposed of and the notice has not been revoked, varied or substituted.

125(3)   Where a notice issued under section 122 becomes binding, the Board must as soon as reasonably practicable give a notice to that effect together with a copy of the binding notice to–

(a)   the Regulator,

(b)   the trustees or managers of the scheme,

(c)   the insolvency practitioner or former insolvency practitioner who issued the notice under section 122 or, where that notice was issued by the Board by virtue of section 124, the insolvency practitioner or former insolvency practitioner mentioned in subsection (1) of that section,

(d)   any insolvency practitioner in relation to the employer (who does not fall within paragraph (c)), and

(e)   if there is no insolvency practitioner in relation to the employer, the employer.

125(4)   A notice under subsection (3)–

(a)   must be in the prescribed form and contain such information as may be prescribed, and

(b)   where it is given in relation to a withdrawal notice issued under section 122(2)(b) which has become binding, must state the time from which the Board ceases to be involved with the scheme (see section 149).

Fraud Act 2006

(2006 Chapter 35)

An Act to make provision for, and in connection with, criminal liability for fraud and obtaining services dishonestly.

[*8th November 2006*]

[**Note**: Changes made by the Companies Act 2006 (Commencement No.3, Consequential Amendments, Transitional Provisions and Savings) Order 2007 (SI 2007/2194 (C. 84)) have been incorporated into the text.]

9   Participating in fraudulent business carried on by sole trader etc.

9(1)   A person is guilty of an offence if he is knowingly a party to the carrying on of a business to which this section applies.

9(2)   This section applies to a business which is carried on–

(a)   by a person who is outside the reach of section 993 of the Companies Act 2006 (offence of fraudulent trading); and

(b)   with intent to defraud creditors of any person or for any other fraudulent purpose.

9(3)   The following are within the reach of that section–

(a)   a company (as defined in section 1(1) of the Companies Act 2006);

(b)   a person to whom that section applies (with or without adaptations or modifications) as if the person were a company;

(c)   a person exempted from the application of that section.

9(4)   [Repealed.]

9(5)   "Fraudulent purpose" has the same meaning as in that section.

9(6)   A person guilty of an offence under this section is liable–

(a)   on summary conviction, to imprisonment for a term not exceeding 12 months or to a fine not exceeding the statutory maximum (or to both);

(b)   on conviction on indictment, to imprisonment for a term not exceeding 10 years or to a fine (or to both).

9(7)   Subsection (6)(a) applies in relation to Northern Ireland as if the reference to 12 months were a reference to 6 months.

History
Section 9(2), (3), and (5) amended, and s.9(4) repealed, by the Companies Act 2006 (Commencement No.3, Consequential Amendments, Transitional Provisions and Savings) Order 2007 (SI 2007/2194 (C. 84)) art.10(1), (3) and Sch.4 para.111 and Sch.5, as from October 1, 2007.

Companies Act 2006

(2006 Chapter 46)

ARRANGEMENT OF SECTIONS

An Act to reform company law and restate the greater part of the enactments relating to companies; to make other provision relating to companies and other forms of business organisation; to make provision about directors' disqualification, business names, auditors and actuaries; to amend Part 9 of the Enterprise Act 2002; and for connected purposes.

[8th November 2006]

[**Note:** Changes made by the Companies (Mergers and Divisions of Public Companies) (Amendment) Regulations 2008 (SI 2008/690), by the Companies Act 2006 (Consequential Amendments etc.) Order 2008 (SI 2008/948), by the Companies Act 2006 (Consequential Amendments and Transitional Provisions) Order 2011 (SI 2011/1265) and by the Companies (Reporting Requirements in Mergers and Divisions) Regulations 2011 (SI 2011/1606) have been incorporated into the text. The following sections of CA 2006 apply to limited liability partnerships by virtue of the Limited Liability Partnerships (Application of Companies Act 2006) Regulations 2009 (SI 2009/1804) as from October 1, 2009 (subject to the modifications set out in those regulations and, in the case of ss.1012–1023, to the transitional provisions in the Companies Act 2006 and Limited Liability Partnerships (Transitional Provisions and Savings) (Amendment) Regulations 2009 (SI 2009/2476): ss.754, 860–892, 895–900, 993, 1000–1034.]

PART 10

A COMPANY'S DIRECTORS

CHAPTER 4

TRANSACTIONS WITH DIRECTORS REQUIRING APPROVAL OF MEMBERS

Substantial property transactions

190 Substantial property transactions: requirement of members' approval

190(1) [Requirement for members' approval] A company may not enter into an arrangement under which–

(a) a director of the company or of its holding company, or a person connected with such a director, acquires or is to acquire from the company (directly or indirectly) a substantial non-cash asset, or

(b) the company acquires or is to acquire a substantial non-cash asset (directly or indirectly) from such a director or a person so connected,

unless the arrangement has been approved by a resolution of the members of the company or is conditional on such approval being obtained.

For the meaning of "substantial non-cash asset" see section 191.

190(2)   [Directors of company's holding company] If the director or connected person is a director of the company's holding company or a person connected with such a director, the arrangement must also have been approved by a resolution of the members of the holding company or be conditional on such approval being obtained.

190(3)   [No liability for failure to obtain approval] A company shall not be subject to any liability by reason of a failure to obtain approval required by this section.

190(4)   [Non-UK registered companies; wholly owned subsidiaries] No approval is required under this section on the part of the members of a body corporate that–

(a) is not a UK-registered company, or

(b) is a wholly-owned subsidiary of another body corporate.

190(5)   [Arrangements involving more than one non-cash asset] For the purposes of this section–

(a) an arrangement involving more than one non-cash asset, or

(b) an arrangement that is one of a series involving non-cash assets,

shall be treated as if they involved a non-cash asset of a value equal to the aggregate value of all the non-cash assets involved in the arrangement or, as the case may be, the series.

190(6)   [Disapplication of section] This section does not apply to a transaction so far as it relates–

(a) to anything to which a director of a company is entitled under his service contract, or

(b) to payment for loss of office as defined in section 215 (payments requiring members' approval).

193   Exception in case of company in winding up or administration

193(1)   [Application of section] This section applies to a company–

(a) that is being wound up (unless the winding up is a members' voluntary winding up), or

(b) that is in administration within the meaning of Schedule B1 to the Insolvency Act 1986 (c. 45) or the Insolvency (Northern Ireland) Order 1989 (S.I. 1989/2405 (N.I. 19)).

193(2)   [Approval not required] Approval is not required under section 190 (requirement of members' approval for substantial property transactions)–

(a) on the part of the members of a company to which this section applies, or

(b) for an arrangement entered into by a company to which this section applies.

PART 19

DEBENTURES

Supplementary provisions

754   Priorities where debentures secured by floating charge

754(1)   [Application in England and Wales or Northern Ireland] This section applies where debentures of a company registered in England and Wales or Northern Ireland are secured by a charge that, as created, was a floating charge.

754(2)   [Priority of preferential creditors] If possession is taken, by or on behalf of the holders of the debentures, of any property comprised in or subject to the charge, and the company is not at that time in the course of being wound up, the company's preferential debts shall be paid out of assets coming to the hands of the persons taking possession in priority to any claims for principal or interest in respect of the debentures.

754(3)   ["Preferential debts", "the relevant date"] "Preferential debts" means the categories of debts listed in Schedule 6 to the Insolvency Act 1986 (c. 45) or Schedule 4 to the Insolvency (Northern Ireland) Order 1989 (S.I. 1989/2405 (N.I. 19)).

For the purposes of those Schedules "**the relevant date**" is the date of possession being taken as mentioned in subsection (2)

754(4)   [Recoupment of payment from company assets] Payments under this section shall be recouped, as far as may be, out of the assets of the company available for payment of general creditors.

PART 25

COMPANY CHARGES

CHAPTER 1

COMPANIES REGISTERED IN ENGLAND AND WALES OR IN NORTHERN IRELAND

Requirement to register company charges

860   Charges created by a company

860(1)   [Deliver of particulars of charge to registrar] A company that creates a charge to which this section applies must deliver the prescribed particulars of the charge, together with the instrument (if any) by which the charge is created or evidenced, to the registrar for registration before the end of the period allowed for registration.

860(2)   [Registration of charge] Registration of a charge to which this section applies may instead be effected on the application of a person interested in it.

860(3)   [Fees for registration] Where registration is effected on the application of some person other than the company, that person is entitled to recover from the company the amount of any fees properly paid by him to the registrar on registration.

860(4)   [Offence] If a company fails to comply with subsection (1), an offence is committed by–

(a)   the company, and

(b)   every officer of it who is in default.

860(5)   [Offence] A person guilty of an offence under this section is liable–

(a)   on conviction on indictment, to a fine;

(b)   on summary conviction, to a fine not exceeding the statutory maximum.

860(6)   [Disapplication of subs.(4)] Subsection (4) does not apply if registration of the charge has been effected on the application of some other person.

860(7)   [Application of section] This section applies to the following charges–

(a)   a charge on land or any interest in land, other than a charge for any rent or other periodical sum issuing out of land,

(b) a charge created or evidenced by an instrument which, if executed by an individual, would require registration as a bill of sale,

(c) a charge for the purposes of securing any issue of debentures,

(d) a charge on uncalled share capital of the company,

(e) a charge on calls made but not paid,

(f) a charge on book debts of the company,

(g) a floating charge on the company's property or undertaking,

(h) a charge on a ship or aircraft, or any share in a ship,

(i) a charge on goodwill or on any intellectual property.

861 Charges which have to be registered: supplementary

861(1) [Holding of debentures] The holding of debentures entitling the holder to a charge on land is not, for the purposes of section 860(7)(a), an interest in the land.

861(2) [Location of land] It is immaterial for the purposes of this Chapter where land subject to a charge is situated.

861(3) [Deposit by way of security of negotiable instrument] The deposit by way of security of a negotiable instrument given to secure the payment of book debts is not, for the purposes of section 860(7)(f), a charge on those book debts.

861(4) ["Intellectual property"] For the purposes of section 860(7)(i), "intellectual property" means–

(a) any patent, trade mark, registered design, copyright or design right;

(b) any licence under or in respect of any such right.

861(5) [Interpretation] In this Chapter–

"charge" includes mortgage, and

"company" means a company registered in England and Wales or in Northern Ireland.

862 Charges existing on property acquired

862(1) [Application of section] This section applies where a company acquires property which is subject to a charge of a kind which would, if it had been created by the company after the acquisition of the property, have been required to be registered under this Chapter.

862(2) [Delivery of particulars of charge to registrar] The company must deliver the prescribed particulars of the charge, together with a certified copy of the instrument (if any) by which the charge is created or evidenced, to the registrar for registration.

862(3) [Timing of compliance] Subsection (2) must be complied with before the end of the period allowed for registration.

862(4) [Offence] If default is made in complying with this section, an offence is committed by–

(a) the company, and

(b) every officer of it who is in default.

862(5) [Penalty] A person guilty of an offence under this section is liable–

(a) on conviction on indictment, to a fine;

(b) on summary conviction, to a fine not exceeding the statutory maximum.

863   Charge in series of debentures

863(1)   [Delivery of details of charge to registrar] Where a series of debentures containing, or giving by reference to another instrument, any charge to the benefit of which debenture holders of that series are entitled *pari passu* is created by a company, it is for the purposes of section 860(1) sufficient if the required particulars, together with the deed containing the charge (or, if there is no such deed, one of the debentures of the series), are delivered to the registrar before the end of the period allowed for registration.

863(2)   [Required particulars] The following are the required particulars–

(a)   the total amount secured by the whole series, and

(b)   the dates of the resolutions authorising the issue of the series and the date of the covering deed (if any) by which the series is created or defined, and

(c)   a general description of the property charged, and

(d)   the names of the trustees (if any) for the debenture holders.

863(3)   [Particulars of date and amount of each issue of debentures] Particulars of the date and amount of each issue of debentures of a series of the kind mentioned in subsection (1) must be sent to the registrar for entry in the register of charges.

863(4)   [Effect of failure to comply] Failure to comply with subsection (3) does not affect the validity of the debentures issued.

863(5)   [Application of s.860(2)–(6)] Subsections (2) to (6) of section 860 apply for the purposes of this section as they apply for the purposes of that section, but as if references to the registration of a charge were references to the registration of a series of debentures.

864   Additional registration requirement for commission etc in relation to debentures

864(1)   [Amount or rate per cent of commission, discount or allowance] Where any commission, allowance or discount has been paid or made either directly or indirectly by a company to a person in consideration of his–

(a)   subscribing or agreeing to subscribe, whether absolutely or conditionally, for debentures in a company, or

(b)   procuring or agreeing to procure subscriptions, whether absolute or conditional, for such debentures,

the particulars required to be sent for registration under section 860 shall include particulars as to the amount or rate per cent. of the commission, discount or allowance so paid or made.

864(2)   [Deposit of debentures as security for a debt] The deposit of debentures as security for a debt of the company is not, for the purposes of this section, treated as the issue of debentures at a discount.

864(3)   [Effect of failure to comply] Failure to comply with this section does not affect the validity of the debentures issued.

865   Endorsement of certificate on debentures

865(1)   [Duty to endorse] The company shall cause a copy of every certificate of registration given under section 869 to be endorsed on every debenture or certificate of debenture stock which is issued by the company, and the payment of which is secured by the charge so registered.

865(2)   [Endorsement before charge created] But this does not require a company to cause a certificate of registration of any charge so given to be endorsed on any debenture or certificate of debenture stock issued by the company before the charge was created.

865(3)   [Offence] If a person knowingly and wilfully authorises or permits the delivery of a debenture or certificate of debenture stock which under this section is required to have endorsed on it a copy of a certificate of registration, without the copy being so endorsed upon it, he commits an offence.

865(4)   [Penalty] A person guilty of an offence under this section is liable on summary conviction to a fine not exceeding level 3 on the standard scale.

Charges in other jurisdictions

866   Charges created in, or over property in, jurisdictions outside the United Kingdom

866(1)   [Effect of delivery to registrar of verified copy of instrument] Where a charge is created outside the United Kingdom comprising property situated outside the United Kingdom, the delivery to the registrar of a verified copy of the instrument by which the charge is created or evidenced has the same effect for the purposes of this Chapter as the delivery of the instrument itself.

866(2)   [Registration of charge under s.860] Where a charge is created in the United Kingdom but comprises property outside the United Kingdom, the instrument creating or purporting to create the charge may be sent for registration under section 860 even if further proceedings may be necessary to make the charge valid or effectual according to the law of the country in which the property is situated.

867   Charges created in, or over property in, another United Kingdom jurisdiction

867(1)   [Application of section] Subsection (2) applies where–

(a)   a charge comprises property situated in a part of the United Kingdom other than the part in which the company is registered, and

(b)   registration in that other part is necessary to make the charge valid or effectual under the law of that part of the United Kingdom.

867(2)   [Delivery to registrar of verified copy of instrument] The delivery to the registrar of a verified copy of the instrument by which the charge is created or evidenced, together with a certificate stating that the charge was presented for registration in that other part of the United Kingdom on the date on which it was so presented has, for the purposes of this Chapter, the same effect as the delivery of the instrument itself.

868   [Applies to Northern Ireland: not reproduced.]

The register of charges

869   Register of charges to be kept by registrar

869(1)   [Duty to keep register] The registrar shall keep, with respect to each company, a register of all the charges requiring registration under this Chapter.

869(2)   [Charges to benefit of holders of series of debentures] In the case of a charge to the benefit of which holders of a series of debentures are entitled, the registrar shall enter in the register the required particulars specified in section 863(2).

869(3)   [Charges imposed by Enforcement of Judgments Office] In the case of a charge imposed by the Enforcement of Judgments Office under Article 46 of the Judgments Enforcement (Northern Ireland) Order 1981, the registrar shall enter in the register the date on which the charge became effective.

869(4) [Other charges] In the case of any other charge, the registrar shall enter in the register the following particulars–

(a) if it is a charge created by a company, the date of its creation and, if it is a charge which was existing on property acquired by the company, the date of the acquisition,

(b) the amount secured by the charge,

(c) short particulars of the property charged, and

(d) the persons entitled to the charge.

869(5) [Certificate of registration] The registrar shall give a certificate of the registration of any charge registered in pursuance of this Chapter, stating the amount secured by the charge.

869(6) [Requirements for certificate] The certificate–

(a) shall be signed by the registrar or authenticated by the registrar's official seal, and

(b) is conclusive evidence that the requirements of this Chapter as to registration have been satisfied.

869(7) [Register open to inspection] The register kept in pursuance of this section shall be open to inspection by any person.

870 The period allowed for registration

870(1) [Charges created by company] The period allowed for registration of a charge created by a company is–

(a) 21 days beginning with the day after the day on which the charge is created, or

(b) if the charge is created outside the United Kingdom, 21 days beginning with the day after the day on which the instrument by which the charge is created or evidenced (or a copy of it) could, in due course of post (and if despatched with due diligence) have been received in the United Kingdom.

870(2) [Charges to which property acquired by company subject to] The period allowed for registration of a charge to which property acquired by a company is subject is–

(a) 21 days beginning with the day after the day on which the acquisition is completed, or

(b) if the property is situated and the charge was created outside the United Kingdom, 21 days beginning with the day after the day on which the instrument by which the charge is created or evidenced (or a copy of it) could, in due course of post (and if despatched with due diligence) have been received in the United Kingdom.

870(3) [Particulars of a series of debentures] The period allowed for registration of particulars of a series of debentures as a result of section 863 is–

(a) if there is a deed containing the charge mentioned in section 863(1), 21 days beginning with the day after the day on which that deed is executed, or

(b) if there is no such deed, 21 days beginning with the day after the day on which the first debenture of the series is executed.

871 Registration of enforcement of security

871(1) [Notice to registrar of appointment of receiver etc.] If a person obtains an order for the appointment of a receiver or manager of a company's property, or appoints such a receiver or manager under powers contained in an instrument, he shall within 7 days of the order or of the appointment under those powers, give notice of the fact to the registrar.

871(2) **[Notice to registrar of cessation of appointment]** Where a person appointed receiver or manager of a company's property under powers contained in an instrument ceases to act as such receiver or manager, he shall, on so ceasing, give the registrar notice to that effect.

871(3) **[Entry of facts notified in register]** The registrar must enter a fact of which he is given notice under this section in the register of charges.

871(4) **[Offence]** A person who makes default in complying with the requirements of this section commits an offence.

871(5) **[Penalty]** A person guilty of an offence under this section is liable on summary conviction to a fine not exceeding level 3 on the standard scale and, for continued contravention, a daily default fine not exceeding one-tenth of level 3 on the standard scale.

872 Entries of satisfaction and release

872(1) **[Application of section]** Subsection (2) applies if a statement is delivered to the registrar verifying with respect to a registered charge–

(a) that the debt for which the charge was given has been paid or satisfied in whole or in part, or

(b) that part of the property or undertaking charged has been released from the charge or has ceased to form part of the company's property or undertaking.

872(2) **[Registration of memorandum of satisfaction]** The registrar may enter on the register a memorandum of satisfaction in whole or in part, or of the fact part of the property or undertaking has been released from the charge or has ceased to form part of the company's property or undertaking (as the case may be).

872(3) **[Copy of memorandum of satisfaction]** Where the registrar enters a memorandum of satisfaction in whole, the registrar shall if required send the company a copy of it.

873 Rectification of register of charges

873(1) **[Application of section]** Subsection (2) applies if the court is satisfied–

(a) that the failure to register a charge before the end of the period allowed for registration, or the omission or mis-statement of any particular with respect to any such charge or in a memorandum of satisfaction–

(i) was accidental or due to inadvertence or to some other sufficient cause, or

(ii) is not of a nature to prejudice the position of creditors or shareholders of the company, or

(b) that on other grounds it is just and equitable to grant relief.

873(2) **[Court power to order rectification of register]** The court may, on the application of the company or a person interested, and on such terms and conditions as seem to the court just and expedient, order that the period allowed for registration shall be extended or, as the case may be, that the omission or mis-statement shall be rectified.

Avoidance of certain charges

874 Consequence of failure to register charges created by a company

874(1) **[Void charges]** If a company creates a charge to which section 860 applies, the charge is void (so far as any security on the company's property or undertaking is conferred by it) against–

(a) a liquidator of the company,

(b)   an administrator of the company, and

(c)   a creditor of the company,

unless that section is complied with.

874(2)   [Subsection (1) subject to provisions of Chapter] Subsection (1) is subject to the provisions of this Chapter.

874(3)   [Effect on contract or obligation for repayment of money secured by charge] Subsection (1) is without prejudice to any contract or obligation for repayment of the money secured by the charge; and when a charge becomes void under this section, the money secured by it immediately becomes payable.

Companies' records and registers

875   Companies to keep copies of instruments creating charges

875(1)   [Duty to keep copies available for inspection] A company must keep available for inspection a copy of every instrument creating a charge requiring registration under this Chapter, including any document delivered to the company under section 868(3)(b) (Northern Ireland: orders imposing charges affecting land).

875(2)   [Series of uniform debentures] In the case of a series of uniform debentures, a copy of one of the debentures of the series is sufficient.

876   Company's register of charges

876(1)   [Duty to keep register of charges available for inspection] Every limited company shall keep available for inspection a register of charges and enter in it–

(a)   all charges specifically affecting property of the company, and

(b)   all floating charges on the whole or part of the company's property or undertaking.

876(2)   [Description of charge] The entry shall in each case give a short description of the property charged, the amount of the charge and, except in the cases of securities to bearer, the names of the persons entitled to it.

876(3)   [Offence] If an officer of the company knowingly and wilfully authorises or permits the omission of an entry required to be made in pursuance of this section, he commits an offence.

876(4)   [Penalty] A person guilty of an offence under this section is liable–

(a)   on conviction on indictment, to a fine;

(b)   on summary conviction, to a fine not exceeding the statutory maximum.

877   Instruments creating charges and register of charges to be available for inspection

877(1)   [Application of section] This section applies to–

(a)   documents required to be kept available for inspection under section 875 (copies of instruments creating charges), and

(b)   a company's register of charges kept in pursuance of section 876.

877(2)   [Availability for inspection] The documents and register must be kept available for inspection–

(a)   at the company's registered office, or

(b)   at a place specified in regulations under section 1136.

877(3) [Notice to registrar] The company must give notice to the registrar–

(a) of the place at which the documents and register are kept available for inspection, and

(b) of any change in that place,

unless they have at all times been kept at the company's registered office.

877(4) [Right to inspect] The documents and register shall be open to the inspection–

(a) of any creditor or member of the company without charge, and

(b) of any other person on payment of such fee as may be prescribed.

877(5) [Offence] If default is made for 14 days in complying with subsection (3) or an inspection required under subsection (4) is refused, an offence is committed by–

(a) the company, and

(b) every officer of the company who is in default.

877(6) [Penalty] A person guilty of an offence under this section is liable on summary conviction to a fine not exceeding level 3 on the standard scale and, for continued contravention, a daily default fine not exceeding one-tenth of level 3 on the standard scale.

877(7) [Court order compelling inspection] If an inspection required under subsection (4) is refused the court may by order compel an immediate inspection.

CHAPTER 2

COMPANIES REGISTERED IN SCOTLAND

Charges requiring registration

878 Charges created by a company

878(1) [Delivery of documents for registration] A company that creates a charge to which this section applies must deliver the prescribed particulars of the charge, together with a copy certified as a correct copy of the instrument (if any) by which the charge is created or evidenced, to the registrar for registration before the end of the period allowed for registration.

878(2) [Registration on application of interested person] Registration of a charge to which this section applies may instead be effected on the application of a person interested in it.

878(3) [Recovery of registration fees] Where registration is effected on the application of some person other than the company, that person is entitled to recover from the company the amount of any fees properly paid by him to the registrar on the registration.

878(4) [Offence] If a company fails to comply with subsection (1), an offence is committed by–

(a) the company, and

(b) every officer of the company who is in default.

878(5) [Penalty] A person guilty of an offence under this section is liable–

(a) on conviction on indictment, to a fine;

(b) on summary conviction, to a fine not exceeding the statutory maximum.

878(6) [Disapplication of subs.(4)] Subsection (4) does not apply if registration of the charge has been effected on the application of some other person.

878(7) **[Application of section]** This section applies to the following charges–

(a) a charge on land or any interest in such land, other than a charge for any rent or other periodical sum payable in respect of the land,

(b) a security over incorporeal moveable property of any of the following categories–

(i) goodwill,

(ii) a patent or a licence under a patent,

(iii) a trademark,

(iv) a copyright or a licence under a copyright,

(v) a registered design or a licence in respect of such a design,

(vi) a design right or a licence under a design right,

(vii) the book debts (whether book debts of the company or assigned to it), and

(viii) uncalled share capital of the company or calls made but not paid,

(c) a security over a ship or aircraft or any share in a ship,

(d) a floating charge.

879 Charges which have to be registered: supplementary

879(1) **[Heritable securities]** A charge on land, for the purposes of section 878(7)(a), includes a charge created by a heritable security within the meaning of section 9(8) of the Conveyancing and Feudal Reform (Scotland) Act 1970 (c. 35).

879(2) **[Holdings of debentures]** The holding of debentures entitling the holder to a charge on land is not, for the purposes of section 878(7)(a), deemed to be an interest in land.

879(3) **[Location of land]** It is immaterial for the purposes of this Chapter where land subject to a charge is situated.

879(4) **[Deposit by way of security of negotiable instrument]** The deposit by way of security of a negotiable instrument given to secure the payment of book debts is not, for the purposes of section 878(7)(b)(vii), to be treated as a charge on those book debts.

879(5) **[Date of creation of charge]** References in this Chapter to the date of the creation of a charge are–

(a) in the case of a floating charge, the date on which the instrument creating the floating charge was executed by the company creating the charge, and

(b) in any other case, the date on which the right of the person entitled to the benefit of the charge was constituted as a real right.

879(6) **["Company"]** In this Chapter "company" means an incorporated company registered in Scotland.

880 Duty to register charges existing on property acquired

880(1) **[Application of section]** Subsection (2) applies where a company acquires any property which is subject to a charge of any kind as would, if it had been created by the company after the acquisition of the property, have been required to be registered under this Chapter.

880(2) **[Delivery of prescribed particulars to registrar]** The company must deliver the prescribed particulars of the charge, together with a copy (certified to be a correct copy) of the instrument (if any) by which the charge was created or is evidenced, to the registrar for registration before the end of the period allowed for registration.

880(3)   [Offence] If default is made in complying with this section, an offence is committed by–

(a)   the company, and

(b)   every officer of it who is in default.

880(4)   [Penalty] A person guilty of an offence under this section is liable–

(a)   on conviction on indictment, to a fine;

(b)   on summary conviction, to a fine not exceeding the statutory maximum.

881   Charge by way of ex facie absolute disposition, etc

881(1)   [Availability of charge as security for indebtedness] For the avoidance of doubt, it is hereby declared that, in the case of a charge created by way of an ex facie absolute disposition or assignation qualified by a back letter or other agreement, or by a standard security qualified by an agreement, compliance with section 878(1) does not of itself render the charge unavailable as security for indebtedness incurred after the date of compliance.

881(2)   [Increase of amount secured] Where the amount secured by a charge so created is purported to be increased by a further back letter or agreement, a further charge is held to have been created by the ex facie absolute disposition or assignation or (as the case may be) by the standard security, as qualified by the further back letter or agreement.

881(3)   [Application of provisions to further charges] In that case, the provisions of this Chapter apply to the further charge as if–

(a)   references in this Chapter (other than in this section) to a charge were references to the further charge, and

(b)   references to the date of the creation of a charge were references to the date on which the further back letter or agreement was executed.

Special rules about debentures

882   Charge in series of debentures

882(1)   [Compliance with s.878] Where a series of debentures containing, or giving by reference to any other instrument, any charge to the benefit of which the debenture-holders of that series are entitled *pari passu*, is created by a company, it is sufficient for purposes of section 878 if the required particulars, together with a copy of the deed containing the charge (or, if there is no such deed, of one of the debentures of the series) are delivered to the registrar before the end of the period allowed for registration.

882(2)   [Required particulars] The following are the required particulars–

(a)   the total amount secured by the whole series,

(b)   the dates of the resolutions authorising the issue of the series and the date of the covering deed (if any) by which the security is created or defined,

(c)   a general description of the property charged,

(d)   the names of the trustees (if any) for the debenture-holders, and

(e)   in the case of a floating charge, a statement of any provisions of the charge and of any instrument relating to it which prohibit or restrict or regulate the power of the company to grant further securities ranking in priority to, or *pari passu* with, the floating charge, or which vary or otherwise regulate the order of ranking of the floating charge in relation to subsisting securities.

882(3) **[More than one issue of debentures in series]** Where more than one issue is made of debentures in the series, particulars of the date and amount of each issue of debentures of the series must be sent to the registrar for entry in the register of charges.

882(4) **[Effect of failure to comply]** Failure to comply with subsection (3) does not affect the validity of any of those debentures.

882(5) **[Application of s.878(2)–(6)]** Subsections (2) to (6) of section 878 apply for the purposes of this section as they apply for the purposes of that section but as if for the reference to the registration of the charge there was substituted a reference to the registration of the series of debentures.

883 Additional registration requirement for commission etc in relation to debentures

883(1) **[Commission, allowances or discounts paid]** Where any commission, allowance or discount has been paid or made either directly or indirectly by a company to a person in consideration of his–

(a) subscribing or agreeing to subscribe, whether absolutely or conditionally, for debentures in a company, or

(b) procuring or agreeing to procure subscriptions, whether absolute or conditional, for such debentures,

the particulars required to be sent for registration under section 878 shall include particulars as to the amount or rate per cent. of the commission, discount or allowance so paid or made.

883(2) **[Deposit of debentures as security for debt]** The deposit of debentures as security for a debt of the company is not, for the purposes of this section, treated as the issue of debentures at a discount.

883(3) **[Effect of failure to comply]** Failure to comply with this section does not affect the validity of the debentures issued.

Charges on property outside the United Kingdom

884 Charges on property outside United Kingdom

884 Where a charge is created in the United Kingdom but comprises property outside the United Kingdom, the copy of the instrument creating or purporting to create the charge may be sent for registration under section 878 even if further proceedings may be necessary to make the charge valid or effectual according to the law of the country in which the property is situated.

The register of charges

885 Register of charges to be kept by registrar

885(1) **[Duty to keep register]** The registrar shall keep, with respect to each company, a register of all the charges requiring registration under this Chapter.

885(2) **[Charge to benefit of holders in series of debentures]** In the case of a charge to the benefit of which holders of a series of debentures are entitled, the registrar shall enter in the register the required particulars specified in section 882(2).

885(3) **[Other charges]** In the case of any other charge, the registrar shall enter in the register the following particulars–

(a) if it is a charge created by a company, the date of its creation and, if it is a charge which was existing on property acquired by the company, the date of the acquisition,

   (b)   the amount secured by the charge,

   (c)   short particulars of the property charged,

   (d)   the persons entitled to the charge, and

   (e)   in the case of a floating charge, a statement of any of the provisions of the charge and of any instrument relating to it which prohibit or restrict or regulate the company's power to grant further securities ranking in priority to, or *pari passu* with, the floating charge, or which vary or otherwise regulate the order of ranking of the floating charge in relation to subsisting securities.

885(4)   **[Certificate of registration]** The registrar shall give a certificate of the registration of any charge registered in pursuance of this Chapter, stating–

   (a)   the name of the company and the person first-named in the charge among those entitled to the benefit of the charge (or, in the case of a series of debentures, the name of the holder of the first such debenture issued), and

   (b)   the amount secured by the charge.

885(5)   **[Content of certificate]** The certificate–

   (a)   shall be signed by the registrar or authenticated by the registrar's official seal, and

   (b)   is conclusive evidence that the requirements of this Chapter as to registration have been satisfied.

885(6)   **[Register open to inspection]** The register kept in pursuance of this section shall be open to inspection by any person.

886   The period allowed for registration

886(1)   **[Charges created by company]** The period allowed for registration of a charge created by a company is–

   (a)   21 days beginning with the day after the day on which the charge is created, or

   (b)   if the charge is created outside the United Kingdom, 21 days beginning with the day after the day on which a copy of the instrument by which the charge is created or evidenced could, in due course of post (and if despatched with due diligence) have been received in the United Kingdom.

886(2)   **[Charges to which property acquired by company is subject to]** The period allowed for registration of a charge to which property acquired by a company is subject is–

   (a)   21 days beginning with the day after the day on which the transaction is settled, or

   (b)   if the property is situated and the charge was created outside the United Kingdom, 21 days beginning with the day after the day on which a copy of the instrument by which the charge is created or evidenced could, in due course of post (and if despatched with due diligence) have been received in the United Kingdom.

886(3)   **[Registration of particulars in series of debentures]** The period allowed for registration of particulars of a series of debentures as a result of section 882 is–

   (a)   if there is a deed containing the charge mentioned in section 882(1), 21 days beginning with the day after the day on which that deed is executed, or

   (b)   if there is no such deed, 21 days beginning with the day after the day on which the first debenture of the series is executed.

887   Entries of satisfaction and relief

887(1)   **[Application of section]** Subsection (2) applies if a statement is delivered to the registrar verifying with respect to any registered charge–

(a) that the debt for which the charge was given has been paid or satisfied in whole or in part, or

(b) that part of the property charged has been released from the charge or has ceased to form part of the company's property.

887(2) [Floating charge] If the charge is a floating charge, the statement must be accompanied by either–

(a) a statement by the creditor entitled to the benefit of the charge, or a person authorised by him for the purpose, verifying that the statement mentioned in subsection (1) is correct, or

(b) a direction obtained from the court, on the ground that the statement by the creditor mentioned in paragraph (a) could not be readily obtained, dispensing with the need for that statement.

887(3) [Memorandum of satisfaction] The registrar may enter on the register a memorandum of satisfaction (in whole or in part) regarding the fact contained in the statement mentioned in subsection (1).

887(4) [Copy of memorandum] Where the registrar enters a memorandum of satisfaction in whole, he shall, if required, furnish the company with a copy of the memorandum.

887(5) [Requirements where property disposed of] Nothing in this section requires the company to submit particulars with respect to the entry in the register of a memorandum of satisfaction where the company, having created a floating charge over all or any part of its property, disposes of part of the property subject to the floating charge.

888 Rectification of register of charges

888(1) [Application of section] Subsection (2) applies if the court is satisfied–

(a) that the failure to register a charge before the end of the period allowed for registration, or the omission or mis-statement of any particular with respect to any such charge or in a memorandum of satisfaction–

(i) was accidental or due to inadvertence or to some other sufficient cause, or

(ii) is not of a nature to prejudice the position of creditors or shareholders of the company, or

(b) that on other grounds it is just and equitable to grant relief.

888(2) [Court power to order rectification] The court may, on the application of the company or a person interested, and on such terms and conditions as seem to the court just and expedient, order that the period allowed for registration shall be extended or, as the case may be, that the omission or mis-statement shall be rectified.

Avoidance of certain charges

889 Charges void unless registered

889(1) [Void charges] If a company creates a charge to which section 878 applies, the charge is void (so far as any security on the company's property or any part of it is conferred by the charge) against–

(a) the liquidator of the company,

(b) an administrator of the company, and

(c) any creditor of the company

unless that section is complied with.

889(2) [Effect on contract or obligation for repayment of money secured] Subsection (1) is without prejudice to any contract or obligation for repayment of the money secured by the charge; and when a charge becomes void under this section the money secured by it immediately becomes payable.

890 Copies of instruments creating charges to be kept by company

890(1) **[Duty to keep copies available for inspection]** Every company shall cause a copy of every instrument creating a charge requiring registration under this Chapter to be kept available for inspection.

890(2) **[Series of uniform debentures]** In the case of a series of uniform debentures, a copy of one debenture of the series is sufficient.

891 Company's register of charges

891(1) **[Duty to keep register of charges available for inspection]** Every company shall keep available for inspection a register of charges and enter in it all charges specifically affecting property of the company, and all floating charges on any property of the company.

891(2) **[Description of charge]** There shall be given in each case a short description of the property charged, the amount of the charge and, except in the case of securities to bearer, the names of the persons entitled to it.

891(3) **[Offence]** If an officer of the company knowingly and wilfully authorises or permits the omission of an entry required to be made in pursuance of this section, he commits an offence.

891(4) **[Penalty]** A person guilty of an offence under this section is liable–

(a) on conviction on indictment, to a fine;

(b) on summary conviction, to a fine not exceeding the statutory maximum.

892 Instruments creating charges and register of charges to be available for inspection

892(1) **[Application of section]** This section applies to–

(a) documents required to be kept available for inspection under section 890 (copies of instruments creating charges), and

(b) a company's register of charges kept in pursuance of section 891.

892(2) **[Location of documents and register]** The documents and register must be kept available for inspection–

(a) at the company's registered office, or

(b) at a place specified in regulations under section 1136.

892(3) **[Notice to registrar of location]** The company must give notice to the registrar–

(a) of the place at which the documents and register are kept available for inspection, and

(b) of any change in that place,

unless they have at all times been kept at the company's registered office.

892(4) **[Right to inspect]** The documents and register shall be open to the inspection–

(a) of any creditor or member of the company without charge, and

(b) of any other person on payment of such fee as may be prescribed.

892(5) **[Offence]** If default is made for 14 days in complying with subsection (3) or an inspection required under subsection (4) is refused, an offence is committed by–

(a) the company, and

(b) every officer of the company who is in default.

892(6) **[Penalty]** A person guilty of an offence under this section is liable on summary conviction to a fine not exceeding level 3 on the standard scale and, for continued contravention, a daily default fine not exceeding one-tenth of level 3 on the standard scale.

892(7) **[Court order compelling inspection]** If an inspection required under subsection (4) is refused the court may by order compel an immediate inspection.

CHAPTER 3

POWERS OF THE SECRETARY OF STATE

893   Power to make provision for effect of registration in special register

893(1) **["Special register"]** In this section a "special register" means a register, other than the register of charges kept under this Part, in which a charge to which Chapter 1 or Chapter 2 applies is required or authorised to be registered.

893(2) **[Power to make regulations for information-sharing arrangements]** The Secretary of State may by order make provision for facilitating the making of information-sharing arrangements between the person responsible for maintaining a special register ("the responsible person") and the registrar that meet the requirement in subsection (4).

"Information-sharing arrangements" are arrangements to share and make use of information held by the registrar or by the responsible person.

893(3) **[Power to make regulations for registration in special register]** If the Secretary of State is satisfied that appropriate information-sharing arrangements have been made, he may by order provide that–

(a) the registrar is authorised not to register a charge of a specified description under Chapter 1 or Chapter 2,

(b) a charge of a specified description that is registered in the special register within a specified period is to be treated as if it had been registered (and certified by the registrar as registered) in accordance with the requirements of Chapter 1 or, as the case may be, Chapter 2, and

(c) the other provisions of Chapter 1 or, as the case may be, Chapter 2 apply to a charge so treated with specified modifications.

893(4) **[Awareness of existence of charges in special register]** The information-sharing arrangements must ensure that persons inspecting the register of charges–

(a) are made aware, in a manner appropriate to the inspection, of the existence of charges in the special register which are treated in accordance with provision so made, and

(b) are able to obtain information from the special register about any such charge.

893(5) **[Scope of regulations]** An order under this section may–

(a) modify any enactment or rule of law which would otherwise restrict or prevent the responsible person from entering into or giving effect to information-sharing arrangements,

(b) authorise the responsible person to require information to be provided to him for the purposes of the arrangements,

(c) make provision about–

(i) the charging by the responsible person of fees in connection with the arrangements and the destination of such fees (including provision modifying any enactment which would otherwise apply in relation to fees payable to the responsible person), and

(ii) the making of payments under the arrangements by the registrar to the responsible person,

(d) require the registrar to make copies of the arrangements available to the public (in hard copy or electronic form).

893(6)   **["Specified"]** In this section "specified" means specified in an order under this section.

893(7)   **[Description of charge]** A description of charge may be specified, in particular, by reference to one or more of the following–

(a) the type of company by which it is created,

(b) the form of charge which it is,

(c) the description of assets over which it is granted,

(d) the length of the period between the date of its registration in the special register and the date of its creation.

893(8)   **[Registers maintained outside UK]** Provision may be made under this section relating to registers maintained under the law of a country or territory outside the United Kingdom.

893(9)   **[Negative resolution procedure]** An order under this section is subject to negative resolution procedure.

894   General power to make amendments to this Part

894(1)   **[Power to amend provisions]** The Secretary of State may by regulations under this section–

(a) amend this Part by altering, adding or repealing provisions,

(b) make consequential amendments or repeals in this Act or any other enactment (whether passed or made before or after this Act).

894(2)   **[Affirmative resolution procedure]** Regulations under this section are subject to affirmative resolution procedure.

PART 26

ARRANGEMENTS AND RECONSTRUCTIONS

Application of this Part

895   Application of this Part

895(1)   **[Proposed compromise or arrangement between creditors or members]** The provisions of this Part apply where a compromise or arrangement is proposed between a company and–

(a) its creditors, or any class of them, or

(b) its members, or any class of them.

895(2)   **["Arrangement", "company"]** In this Part–

"arrangement" includes a reorganisation of the company's share capital by the consolidation of shares of different classes or by the division of shares into shares of different classes, or by both of those methods; and "company"–

(a) in section 900 (powers of court to facilitate reconstruction or amalgamation) means a company within the meaning of this Act, and

(b) elsewhere in this Part means any company liable to be wound up under the Insolvency Act 1986 (c. 45) or the Insolvency (Northern Ireland) Order 1989 (S.I. 1989/2405 (N.I. 19)).

895(3) [Part 26 subject to application of Pt 27] The provisions of this Part have effect subject to Part 27 (mergers and divisions of public companies) where that Part applies (see sections 902 and 903).

Meeting of creditors or members

896 Court order for holding of meeting

896(1) [Power of court to order meeting on application] The court may, on an application under this section, order a meeting of the creditors or class of creditors, or of the members of the company or class of members (as the case may be), to be summoned in such manner as the court directs.

896(2) [Who may make application] An application under this section may be made by–

(a) the company,

(b) any creditor or member of the company,

(c) if the company is being wound up, the liquidator, or

(d) if the company is in administration, the administrator.

896(3) [Application of s.323 re corporate representation] Section 323 (representation of corporations at meetings) applies to a meeting of creditors under this section as to a meeting of the company (references to a member of the company being read as references to a creditor).

History
Section 896(2)(c) substituted and s.896(2)(d) and (3) inserted by the Companies Act 2006 (Consequential Amendments etc.) Order 2008 (SI 2008/948) Sch.1 para.249 as from April 6, 2008.

897 Statement to be circulated or made available

897(1) [Explanatory statement with notice summoning meeting] Where a meeting is summoned under section 896–

(a) every notice summoning the meeting that is sent to a creditor or member must be accompanied by a statement complying with this section, and

(b) every notice summoning the meeting that is given by advertisement must either–

(i) include such a statement, or

(ii) state where and how creditors or members entitled to attend the meeting may obtain copies of such a statement.

897(2) [Contents of statement] The statement must–

(a) explain the effect of the compromise or arrangement, and

(b) in particular, state–

(i) any material interests of the directors of the company (whether as directors or as members or as creditors of the company or otherwise), and

435

(ii)   the effect on those interests of the compromise or arrangement, in so far as it is different from the effect on the like interests of other persons.

897(3)   [Where compromise or arrangement affects debenture holder rights] Where the compromise or arrangement affects the rights of debenture holders of the company, the statement must give the like explanation as respects the trustees of any deed for securing the issue of the debentures as it is required to give as respects the company's directors.

897(4)   [Explanatory statement free of charge] Where a notice given by advertisement states that copies of an explanatory statement can be obtained by creditors or members entitled to attend the meeting, every such creditor or member is entitled, on making application in the manner indicated by the notice, to be provided by the company with a copy of the statement free of charge.

897(5)   [Offence] If a company makes default in complying with any requirement of this section, an offence is committed by–

(a)   the company, and

(b)   every officer of the company who is in default. This is subject to subsection (7) below.

897(6)   [Officers of the company re offence] For this purpose the following are treated as officers of the company–

(a)   a liquidator or administrator of the company, and

(b)   a trustee of a deed for securing the issue of debentures of the company.

897(7)   [Defence] A person is not guilty of an offence under this section if he shows that the default was due to the refusal of a director or trustee for debenture holders to supply the necessary particulars of his interests.

897(8)   [Penalty] A person guilty of an offence under this section is liable–

(a)   on conviction on indictment, to a fine;

(b)   on summary conviction, to a fine not exceeding the statutory maximum.

898   Duty of directors and trustees to provide information

898(1)   [Notice of director or trustee re explanatory statement] It is the duty of–

(a)   any director of the company, and

(b)   any trustee for its debenture holders,

to give notice to the company of such matters relating to himself as may be necessary for the purposes of section 897 (explanatory statement to be circulated or made available).

898(2)   [Offence] Any person who makes default in complying with this section commits an offence.

898(3)   [Penalty] A person guilty of an offence under this section is liable on summary conviction to a fine not exceeding level 3 on the standard scale.

Court sanction for compromise or arrangement

899   Court sanction for compromise or arrangement

899(1) [Majority required before sanction] If a majority in number representing 75% in value of the creditors or class of creditors or members or class of members (as the case may be), present and voting either in person or by proxy at the meeting summoned under section 896, agree a compromise or arrangement, the court may, on an application under this section, sanction the compromise or arrangement.

899(2) **[Who may apply to court for sanction]** An application under this section may be made by–

(a) the company,

(b) any creditor or member of the company, or

(c) if the company is being wound up, the liquidator, or

(d) if the company is in administration, the administrator.

899(3) **[Who sanction binding on]** A compromise or arrangement sanctioned by the court is binding on–

(a) all creditors or the class of creditors or on the members or class of members (as the case may be), and

(b) the company or, in the case of a company in the course of being wound up, the liquidator and contributories of the company.

899(4) **[Court order to registrar]** The court's order has no effect until a copy of it has been delivered to the registrar.

899(5) **[Application of s.323 re corporate representation]** Section 323 (representation of corporations at meetings) applies to a meeting of creditors under this section as to a meeting of the company (references to a member of the company being read as references to a creditor).

History

Section 899(2)(c) substituted and s.899(2)(d) and (5) inserted by the Companies Act 2006 (Consequential Amendments etc.) Order 2008 (SI 2008/948) Sch.1 para.250 as from April 6, 2008. Section 899(3) amended by the Companies Act 2006 (Consequential Amendments and Transitional Provisions) Order 2011 (SI 2011/1265) art.28(3) as from May 12, 2011.

Reconstructions and amalgamations

900   **Powers of court to facilitate reconstruction or amalgamation**

900(1) **[Application to court]** This section applies where application is made to the court under section 899 to sanction a compromise or arrangement and it is shown that–

(a) the compromise or arrangement is proposed for the purposes of, or in connection with, a scheme for the reconstruction of any company or companies, or the amalgamation of any two or more companies, and

(b) under the scheme the whole or any part of the undertaking or the property of any company concerned in the scheme ("a transferor company") is to be transferred to another company ("the transferee company").

900(2) **[Provision in court order]** The court may, either by the order sanctioning the compromise or arrangement or by a subsequent order, make provision for all or any of the following matters–

(a) the transfer to the transferee company of the whole or any part of the undertaking and of the property or liabilities of any transferor company;

(b) the allotting or appropriation by the transferee company of any shares, debentures, policies or other like interests in that company which under the compromise or arrangement are to be allotted or appropriated by that company to or for any person;

(c)   the continuation by or against the transferee company of any legal proceedings pending by or against any transferor company;

(d)   the dissolution, without winding up, of any transferor company;

(e)   the provision to be made for any persons who, within such time and in such manner as the court directs, dissent from the compromise or arrangement;

(f)   such incidental, consequential and supplemental matters as are necessary to secure that the reconstruction or amalgamation is fully and effectively carried out.

900(3)   **[Order for transfer of property or liabilities]** If an order under this section provides for the transfer of property or liabilities–

(a)   the property is by virtue of the order transferred to, and vests in, the transferee company, and

(b)   the liabilities are, by virtue of the order, transferred to and become liabilities of that company.

900(4)   **[Property to vest free of any charge]** The property (if the order so directs) vests freed from any charge that is by virtue of the compromise or arrangement to cease to have effect.

900(5)   **["Property", "liabilities"]** In this section–

"**property**" includes property, rights and powers of every description; and

"**liabilities**" includes duties.

900(6)   **[Copy of order to registrar]** Every company in relation to which an order is made under this section must cause a copy of the order to be delivered to the registrar within seven days after its making.

900(7)   **[Offence]** If default is made in complying with subsection (6) an offence is committed by–

(a)   the company, and

(b)   every officer of the company who is in default.

900(8) [Penalty] A person guilty of an offence under subsection (7) is liable on summary conviction to a fine not exceeding level 3 on the standard scale and, for continued contravention, a daily default fine not exceeding one-tenth of level 3 on the standard scale.

Obligations of company with respect to articles etc

901   Obligations of company with respect to articles etc

901(1)   **[Application of s.901]** This section applies–

(a)   to any order under section 899 (order sanctioning compromise or arrangement), and

(b)   to any order under section 900 (order facilitating reconstruction or amalgamation) that alters the company's constitution.

901(2)   **[Copy of amended articles or resolution to registrar]** If the order amends–

(a)   the company's articles, or

(b)   any resolution or agreement to which Chapter 3 of Part 3 applies (resolution or agreement affecting a company's constitution),

the copy of the order delivered to the registrar by the company under section 899(4) or section 900(6) must be accompanied by a copy of the company's articles, or the resolution or agreement in question, as amended.

901(3)   [Subsequent issue of articles accompanied by order] Every copy of the company's articles issued by the company after the order is made must be accompanied by a copy of the order, unless the effect of the order has been incorporated into the articles by amendment.

901(4)   [References to effect or order, articles] In this section–

(a)   references to the effect of the order include the effect of the compromise or arrangement to which the order relates; and

(b)   in the case of a company not having articles, references to its articles shall be read as references to the instrument constituting the company or defining its constitution.

901(5)   [Offence] If a company makes default in complying with this section an offence is committed by–

(a)   the company, and

(b)   every officer of the company who is in default.

901(6)   [Penalty] A person guilty of an offence under this section is liable on summary conviction to a fine not exceeding level 3 on the standard scale.

PART 27

MERGERS AND DIVISIONS OF PUBLIC COMPANIES

CHAPTER 1

INTRODUCTORY

902   Application of this Part

902(1)   [Compromise for reconstruction involving merger or division] This Part applies where–

(a)   a compromise or arrangement is proposed between a public company and–

(i)   its creditors or any class of them, or

(ii)   its members or any class of them,

for the purposes of, or in connection with, a scheme for the reconstruction of any company or companies or the amalgamation of any two or more companies,

(b)   the scheme involves–

(i)   a merger (as defined in section 904), or

(ii)   a division (as defined in section 919), and

(c)   the consideration for the transfer (or each of the transfers) envisaged is to be shares in the transferee company (or one or more of the transferee companies) receivable by members of the transferor company (or transferor companies), with or without any cash payment to members.

902(2)   ["New company", "existing company"] In this Part–

(a)   a "new company" means a company formed for the purposes of, or in connection with, the scheme, and

(b)   an "existing company" means a company other than one formed for the purposes of, or in connection with, the scheme.

439

902(3) **[No application of Pt 27 in winding up]** This Part does not apply where the company in respect of which the compromise or arrangement is proposed is being wound up.

903 Relationship of this Part to Part 26

903(1) **[No sanction under Pt 26 unless Pt 27 complied with]** The court must not sanction the compromise or arrangement under Part 26 (arrangements and reconstructions) unless the relevant requirements of this Part have been complied with.

903(2) **[Requirements applicable to merger]** The requirements applicable to a merger are specified in sections 905 to 914.

Certain of those requirements, and certain general requirements of Part 26, are modified or excluded by the provisions of sections 915 to 918A.

903(3) **[Requirements applicable to decision]** The requirements applicable to a division are specified in sections 920 to 930.

Certain of those requirements, and certain general requirements of Part 26, are modified or excluded by the provisions of sections 931 to 934.

History
Section 903(2) amended by the Companies (Reporting Requirements in Mergers and Divisions) Regulations 2011 (SI 2011/1606) reg.4 as from August 1, 2011.

CHAPTER 2

MERGER

Introductory

904 Mergers and merging companies

904(1) **[Requirements under the scheme]** The scheme involves a merger where under the scheme–

(a) the undertaking, property and liabilities of one or more public companies, including the company in respect of which the compromise or arrangement is proposed, are to be transferred to another existing public company (a "merger by absorption"), or

(b) the undertaking, property and liabilities of two or more public companies, including the company in respect of which the compromise or arrangement is proposed, are to be transferred to a new company, whether or not a public company, (a "merger by formation of a new company").

904(2) **["The merging companies"]** References in this Part to "the merging companies" are–

(a) in relation to a merger by absorption, to the transferor and transferee companies;

(b) in relation to a merger by formation of a new company, to the transferor companies.

Requirements applicable to merger

905 Draft terms of scheme (merger)

905(1) **[Draft adopted by directors of merging companies]** A draft of the proposed terms of the scheme must be drawn up and adopted by the directors of the merging companies.

905(2) **[Particulars of draft terms]** The draft terms must give particulars of at least the following matters–

(a) in respect of each transferor company and the transferee company–

(i)   its name,

(ii)   the address of its registered office, and

(iii)   whether it is a company limited by shares or a company limited by guarantee and having a share capital;

(b)   the number of shares in the transferee company to be allotted to members of a transferor company for a given number of their shares (the "share exchange ratio") and the amount of any cash payment;

(c)   the terms relating to the allotment of shares in the transferee company;

(d)   the date from which the holding of shares in the transferee company will entitle the holders to participate in profits, and any special conditions affecting that entitlement;

(e)   the date from which the transactions of a transferor company are to be treated for accounting purposes as being those of the transferee company;

(f)   any rights or restrictions attaching to shares or other securities in the transferee company to be allotted under the scheme to the holders of shares or other securities in a transferor company to which any special rights or restrictions attach, or the measures proposed concerning them;

(g)   any amount of benefit paid or given or intended to be paid or given–

(i)   to any of the experts referred to in section 909 (expert's report), or

(ii)   to any director of a merging company,

and the consideration for the payment of benefit.

905(3)   [Requirements in s.905(2)(b), (c), (d) not required under s.915] The requirements in subsection (2)(b), (c) and (d) are subject to section 915 (circumstances in which certain particulars not required).

906   Publication of draft terms by registrar (merger)

906(1)   [Copy draft terms to registrar] The directors of each of the merging companies must deliver a copy of the draft terms to the registrar.

906(2)   [Registrar to publish receipt in Gazette] The registrar must publish in the Gazette notice of receipt by him from that company of a copy of the draft terms.

906(3)   [Time limit for publication in Gazette] That notice must be published at least one month before the date of any meeting of that company summoned for the purpose of approving the scheme.

906(4)   [Requirements subject to s.906A] The requirements in this section are subject to section 906A (publication of draft terms on company website).

History
Heading amended and s.906(4) inserted by the Companies (Reporting Requirements in Mergers and Divisions) Regulations 2011 (SI 2011/1606) reg.5 as from August 1, 2011.

906A   Publication of draft terms on company website (merger)

906A(1)   [When s.906 not applicable] Section 906 does not apply in respect of a company if the conditions in subsections (2) to (6) are met.

906A(2)   [First condition: draft terms on website] The first condition is that the draft terms are made available on a website which–

(a)   is maintained by or on behalf of the company, and

(b)   identifies the company.

906A(3)   [Second condition: availability free] The second condition is that neither access to the draft terms on the website nor the supply of a hard copy of them from the website is conditional on payment of a fee or otherwise restricted.

906A(4)   [Third condition: notice to registrar of website] The third condition is that the directors of the company deliver to the registrar a notice giving details of the website.

906A(5)   [Fourth condition: gazetting] The fourth condition is that the registrar publishes the notice in the Gazette at least one month before the date of any meeting of the company summoned for the purpose of approving the scheme.

906A(6)   [Fifth condition: minimum period on website] The fifth condition is that the draft terms remain available on the website throughout the period beginning one month before, and ending on, the date of any such meeting.

History
Section 906A inserted by the Companies (Reporting Requirements in Mergers and Divisions) Regulations 2011 (SI 2011/1606) reg.6 as from August 1, 2011.

907   Approval of members of merging companies

907(1)   [Requisite majority] The scheme must be approved by a majority in number, representing 75% in value, of each class of members of each of the merging companies, present and voting either in person or by proxy at a meeting.

907(2)   [Approval subject to ss.916, 917, 918] This requirement is subject to sections 916, 917 and 918 (circumstances in which meetings of members not required).

908   Directors' explanatory report (merger)

908(1)   [Duty of directors] The directors of each of the merging companies must draw up and adopt a report.

908(2)   [Contents of report] The report must consist of–

(a)   the statement required by section 897 (statement explaining effect of compromise or arrange- ment), and

(b)   insofar as that statement does not deal with the following matters, a further statement–

    (i)   setting out the legal and economic grounds for the draft terms, and in particular for the share exchange ratio, and

    (ii)   specifying any special valuation difficulties.

908(3)   [Requirement subject to ss.915, 915A, 918A] The requirement in this section is subject to section 915 (circumstances in which reports not required), section 915A (other circumstances in which reports and inspection not required) and section 918A (agreement to dispense with reports etc).

History
Section 908(3) amended by the Companies (Reporting Requirements in Mergers and Divisions) Regulations 2011 (SI 2011/1606) reg.7 as from August 1, 2011.

909   Expert's report (merger)

909(1)   [Requirement for expert's report] An expert's report must be drawn up on behalf of each of the merging companies.

909(2) **[Report on draft terms]** The report required is a written report on the draft terms to the members of the company.

909(3) **[Single report by joint expert]** The court may on the joint application of all the merging companies approve the appointment of a joint expert to draw up a single report on behalf of all those companies.

If no such appointment is made, there must be a separate expert's report to the members of each merging company drawn up by a separate expert appointed on behalf of that company.

909(4) **[The expert]** The expert must be a person who–

    (a)   is eligible for appointment as a statutory auditor (see section 1212), and

    (b)   meets the independence requirement in section 936.

909(5) **[Contents of expert's report]** The expert's report must–

    (a)   indicate the method or methods used to arrive at the share exchange ratio;

    (b)   give an opinion as to whether the method or methods used are reasonable in all the circumstances of the case, indicate the values arrived at using each such method and (if there is more than one method) give an opinion on the relative importance attributed to such methods in arriving at the value decided on;

    (c)   describe any special valuation difficulties that have arisen;

    (d)   state whether in the expert's opinion the share exchange ratio is reasonable; and

    (e)   in the case of a valuation made by a person other than himself (see section 935), state that it appeared to him reasonable to arrange for it to be so made or to accept a valuation so made.

909(6) **[Rights of expert to documents and information]** The expert (or each of them) has–

    (a)   the right of access to all such documents of all the merging companies, and

    (b)   the right to require from the companies' officers all such information,

as he thinks necessary for the purposes of making his report.

909(7) **[Requirement for report subject to ss.915, 915A, 918A]** The requirement in this section is subject to section 915 (circumstances in which reports not required), section 915A (other circumstances in which reports and inspection not required) and section 918A (agreement to dispense with expert's report).

History
Section 909(7) amended by the Companies (Mergers and Divisions of Public Companies) (Amendment) Regulations 2008 (SI 2008/690) reg.2 as from April 6, 2008 and further amended by the Companies (Reporting Requirements in Mergers and Divisions) Regulations 2011 (SI 2011/1606) reg.8 as from August 1, 2011.

910 Supplementary accounting statement (merger)

910(1) **[Application of section]** This section applies if the last annual accounts of any of the merging companies relate to a financial year ending before–

    (a)   the date seven months before the first meeting of the company summoned for the purposes of approving the scheme, or

    (b)   if no meeting of the company is required (by virtue of any of sections 916 to 918), the date six months before the directors of the company adopt the draft terms of the scheme.

910(1A)   **[Half-yearly financial report not made public]** If the company has not made public a half-yearly financial report relating to a period ending on or after the date mentioned in subsection (1), the directors of the company must prepare a supplementary accounting statement.

910(2)   **[Statement to consist of balance sheet]** That statement must consist of–

(a)   a balance sheet dealing with the state of affairs of the company as at a date not more than three months before the draft terms were adopted by the directors, and

(b)   where the company would be required under section 399 to prepare group accounts if that date were the last day of a financial year, a consolidated balance sheet dealing with the state of affairs of the company and the undertakings that would be included in such a consolidation.

910(3)   **[Requirements as to balance sheet]** The requirements of this Act (and where relevant Article 4 of the IAS Regulation) as to the balance sheet forming part of a company's annual accounts, and the matters to be included in notes to it, apply to the balance sheet required for an accounting statement under this section, with such modifications as are necessary by reason of its being prepared otherwise than as at the last day of a financial year.

910(4)   **[Signing and approval of balance sheet]** The provisions of section 414 as to the approval and signing of accounts apply to the balance sheet required for an accounting statement under this section.

910(5)   **["Half-yearly financial report"]** In this section **"half-yearly financial report"** means a report of that description required to be made public by rules under section 89A of the Financial Services and Markets Act 2000 (transparency rules).

910(6)   **[Section 910 requirement subject to ss.915A, 918A]** The requirement in this section is subject to section 915A (other circumstances in which reports and inspection not required) and section 918A (agreement to dispense with reports etc).

History
Section 910(1) amended and s.910(1A), (5), (6) inserted by the Companies (Reporting Requirements in Mergers and Divisions) Regulations 2011 (SI 2011/1606) reg.9 as from August 1, 2011.

911   **Inspection of documents (merger)**

911(1)   **[Rights of members]** The members of each of the merging companies must be able, during the period specified below–

(a)   to inspect at the registered office of that company copies of the documents listed below relating to that company and every other merging company, and

(b)   to obtain copies of those documents or any part of them on request free of charge.

911(2)   **[Specified period]** The period referred to above is the period–

(a)   beginning one month before, and

(b)   ending on the date of,

the first meeting of the members, or any class of members, of the company for the purposes of approving the scheme.

911(3)   **[Kind of documents]** The documents referred to above are–

(a)   the draft terms;

(b)   the directors' explanatory report;

(c)   the expert's report;

(d) the company's annual accounts and reports for the last three financial years ending on or before the first meeting of the members, or any class of members, of the company summoned for the purposes of approving the scheme;

(e) any supplementary accounting statement required by section 910; and

(f) if no statement is required by section 910 because the company has made public a recent half-yearly financial report (see subsection (1A) of that section), that report.

911(3A) [Inspection at registered office subject to s.911A(1)] The requirement in subsection (1)(a) is subject to section 911A(1) (publication of documents on company website).

911(4) [Requirements of s.311(3)(b), (c) subject to s.915] The requirements of subsection (3)(b) and (c) are subject to section 915 (circumstances in which reports not required) and section 918A (agreement to dispense with reports etc).

911(5) [No right to free hard copy under s.1145] Section 1145 (right to hard copy) does not apply to a document sent or supplied in accordance with subsection (1)(b) to a member who has consented to information being sent or supplied by the company by electronic means and has not revoked that consent.

911(6) [Website communications not applicable re s.911(1)(b)] Part 4 of Schedule 5 (communications by means of a website) does not apply for the purposes of subsection (1)(b) (but see section 911A(5)).

911(7) [Inspection requirements subject to s.915A] The requirements in this section are subject to section 915A (other circumstances in which reports and inspection not required).

History
Section 911(3), (4) amended and s.911(3A), (5)–(7) inserted by the Companies (Reporting Requirements in Mergers and Divisions) Regulations 2011 (SI 2011/1606) reg.10 as from August 1, 2011.

911A Publication of documents on company website (merger)

911A(1) [When inspection of documents at registered office not applicable] Section 911(1)(a) does not apply to a document if the conditions in subsections (2) to (4) are met in relation to that document. This is subject to subsection (6).

911A(2) [First condition: availability on website] The first condition is that the document is made available on a website which–

(a) is maintained by or on behalf of the company, and

(b) identifies the company.

911A(3) [Second condition: no fee] The second condition is that access to the document on the website is not conditional on payment of a fee or otherwise restricted.

911A(4) [Third condition: minimum period of availability] The third condition is that the document remains available on the website throughout the period beginning one month before, and ending on, the date of any meeting of the company summoned for the purpose of approving the scheme.

911A(5) [Obtaining copy of documents under s.911A(2)–(4) conditions] A person is able to obtain a copy of a document as required by section 911(1)(b) if–

(a) the conditions in subsections (2) and (3) are met in relation to that document, and

(b) the person is able, throughout the period specified in subsection (4)–

(i) to retain a copy of the document as made available on the website, and

(ii) to produce a hard copy of it.

911A(6)   **[Continuing right of inspection]** Where members of a company are able to obtain copies of a document only as mentioned in subsection (5), section 911(1)(a) applies to that document even if the conditions in subsections (2) to (4) are met.

History
Section 911A inserted by the Companies (Reporting Requirements in Mergers and Divisions) Regulations 2011 (SI 2011/1606) reg.11 as from August 1, 2011.

911B   **Report on material changes of assets of merging companies**

911B(1)   **[Duty of merging companies' directors to report]** The directors of each of the merging companies must report–

(a)   to every meeting of the members, or any class of members, of that company summoned for the purpose of agreeing to the scheme, and

(b)   to the directors of every other merging company,

any material changes in the property and liabilities of that company between the date when the draft terms were adopted and the date of the meeting in question.

911B(2)   **[Duty of other merging companies' directors to report]** The directors of each of the other merging companies must in turn–

(a)   report those matters to every meeting of the members, or any class of members, of that company summoned for the purpose of agreeing to the scheme, or

(b)   send a report of those matters to every member entitled to receive notice of such a meeting.

911B(3)   **[Duty subject to ss.915A and 918A]** The requirement in this section is subject to section 915A (other circumstances in which reports and inspection not required) and section 918A (agreement to dispense with reports etc).

History
Section 911B inserted by the Companies (Reporting Requirements in Mergers and Divisions) Regulations 2011 (SI 2011/1606) reg.12 as from August 1, 2011.

912   **Approval of articles of new transferee company (merger)**

912   In the case of a merger by formation of a new company, the articles of the transferee company, or a draft of them, must be approved by ordinary resolution of each of the transferor companies.

History
Section 912 amended by the Companies (Reporting Requirements in Mergers and Divisions) Regulations 2011 (SI 2011/1606) reg.13 as from August 1, 2011.

913   **Protection of holders of securities to which special rights attached (merger)**

913(1)   **[Scheme to provide]** The scheme must provide that where any securities of a transferor company (other than shares) to which special rights are attached are held by a person otherwise than as a member or creditor of the company, that person is to receive rights in the transferee company of equivalent value.

913(2)   **[Non-application of s.913(1)]** Subsection (1) does not apply if–

(a)   the holder has agreed otherwise, or

(b) - the holder is, or under the scheme is to be, entitled to have the securities purchased by the transferee company on terms that the court considers reasonable.

914   No allotment of shares to transferor company or transferee company (merger)

914   The scheme must not provide for any shares in the transferee company to be allotted to–

(a)   a transferor company (or its nominee) in respect of shares in the transferor company held by the transferor company itself (or its nominee); or

(b)   the transferee company (or its nominee) in respect of shares in a transferor company held by the transferee company (or its nominee).

History
Section 914 substituted by the Companies (Cross-Border Mergers and Divisions of Public Companies) (Amendment) Regulations 2008 (SI 2008/690) reg.3 as from April 6, 2008.

Exceptions where shares of transferor company held by transferee company

915   Circumstances in which certain particulars and reports not required (merger)

915(1) [Application of s.915] This section applies in the case of a merger by absorption where all of the relevant securities of the transferor company (or, if there is more than one transferor company, of each of them) are held by or on behalf of the transferee company.

915(2)   [Draft terms] The draft terms of the scheme need not give the particulars mentioned in section 905(2)(b), (c) or (d) (particulars relating to allotment of shares to members of transferor company).

915(3)   [Circulation of explanatory statement] Section 897 (explanatory statement to be circulated or made available) does not apply.

915(4)   [Directors' explanatory report, expert's report] The requirements of the following sections do not apply–

section 908 (directors' explanatory report),

section 909 (expert's report).

915(5)   [Inspection of certain reports subject to ss.915 and 918A] The requirements of section 911 (inspection of documents) so far as relating to any document required to be drawn up under the provisions mentioned in subsection (4) above do not apply.

915(6)   ["Relevant securities"] In this section "relevant securities", in relation to a company, means shares or other securities carrying the right to vote at general meetings of the company.

History
Section 915(5) amended by the Companies Act 2006 (Consequential Amendments and Transitional Provisions) Order 2011 (SI 2011/1265) art.28(4) as from May 12, 2011.

915A   Other circumstances in which reports and inspection not required (merger)

915A(1)   [Applicability of s.915A in merger by absorption] This section applies in the case of a merger by absorption where 90% or more (but not all) of the relevant securities of the transferor company (or, if there is more than one transferor company, of each of them) are held by or on behalf of the transferee company.

915A(2)   [Disapplication of ss.908, 909, 910, 911, 911B requirements] If the conditions in subsections (3) and (4) are met, the requirements of the following sections do not apply–

(a)   section 908 (directors' explanatory report),

(b)   section 909 (expert's report),

(c)   section 910 (supplementary accounting statement),

(d)   section 911 (inspection of documents), and

(e)   section 911B (report on material changes of assets of merging company).

915A(3)   [First condition: right to require acquisition of securities] The first condition is that the scheme provides that every other holder of relevant securities has the right to require the transferee company to acquire those securities.

915A(4)   [Second condition: consideration to be fair and reasonable] The second condition is that, if a holder of securities exercises that right, the consideration to be given for those securities is fair and reasonable.

915A(5)   [Power of court to determine consideration for securities] The powers of the court under section 900(2) (power to facilitate reconstruction or amalgamation) include the power to determine, or make provision for the determination of, the consideration to be given for securities acquired under this section.

915A(6)   ["Other holder", "relevant securities"] In this section–

"other holder" means a person who holds securities of the transferor company otherwise than on behalf of the transferee company (and does not include the transferee company itself);

"relevant securities", in relation to a company, means shares or other securities carrying the right to vote at general meetings of the company.

History
Section 915A inserted by the Companies (Reporting Requirements in Mergers and Divisions) Regulations 2011 (SI 2011/1606) reg.14 as from August 1, 2011.

916   Circumstances in which meeting of members of transferee company not required (merger)

916(1)   [Application of s.916] This section applies in the case of a merger by absorption where 90% or more (but not all) of the relevant securities of the transferor company (or, if there is more than one transferor company, of each of them) are held by or on behalf of the transferee company.

916(2)   [Court satisfied conditions complied with] It is not necessary for the scheme to be approved at a meeting of the members, or any class of members, of the transferee company if the court is satisfied that the following conditions have been complied with.

916(3)   First condition: s.916(3A), (3B) satisfied] The first condition is that either subsection (3A) or subsection (3B) is satisfied.

916(3A)   [Registrar's publication of notice of receipt of draft terms] This subsection is satisfied if publication of notice of receipt of the draft terms by the registrar took place in respect of the transferee company at least one month before the date of the first meeting of members, or any class of members, of the transferor company summoned for the purpose of agreeing to the scheme.

916(3B)   [Publication of draft terms on website etc.] This subsection is satisfied if–

(a)   the conditions in section 906A(2) to (4) are met in respect of the transferee company,

(b)   the registrar published the notice mentioned in subsection (4) of that section in the Gazette at least one month before the date of the first meeting of members, or any class of members, of the transferor company summoned for the purpose of agreeing to the scheme, and

(c)   the draft terms remained available on the website throughout the period beginning one month before, and ending on, that date.

916(4)   [Second condition: s.916(4A), (4B) satisfied] The second condition is that subsection (4A) or (4B) is satisfied for each of the documents listed in the applicable paragraphs of section 911(3)(a) to (f) relating to the transferee company and the transferor company (or, if there is more than one transferor company, each of them).

916(4A) **[Inspection of document at transferee's registered office]** This subsection is satisfied for a document if the members of the transferee company were able during the period beginning one month before, and ending on, the date mentioned in subsection (3A) to inspect that document at the registered office of that company.

916(4B) **[Document available on website free of charge]** This subsection is satisfied for a document if–

(a) the document is made available on a website which is maintained by or on behalf of the transferee company and identifies the company,

(b) access to the document on the website is not conditional on the payment of a fee or otherwise restricted, and

(c) the document remains available on the website throughout the period beginning one month before, and ending on, the date mentioned in subsection (3A).

916(4C) **[Third condition: minimum period of free availability]** The third condition is that the members of the transferee company were able to obtain copies of the documents mentioned in subsection (4), or any part of those documents, on request and free of charge, throughout the period beginning one month before, and ending on, the date mentioned in subsection (3A).

916(4D) **[Application of s.911A(5) on website for s.916(4C)]** For the purposes of subsection (4C)–

(a) section 911A(5) applies as it applies for the purposes of section 911(1)(b), and

(b) Part 4 of Schedule 5 (communications by means of a website) does not apply.

916(5) **[Fourth condition: no minority requisition of meeting]** The fourth condition is that–

(a) one or more members of the transferee company, who together held not less than 5% of the paid-up capital of the company which carried the right to vote at general meetings of the company (excluding any shares in the company held as treasury shares) would have been able, during that period, to require a meeting of each class of members to be called for the purpose of deciding whether or not to agree to the scheme, and

(b) no such requirement was made.

916(6) **["Relevant securities"]** In this section "relevant securities", in relation to a company, means shares or other securities carrying the right to vote at general meetings of the company.

History
Section 916(3)–(4D) substituted and s.916(5) amended by the Companies (Reporting Requirements in Mergers and Divisions) Regulations 2011 (SI 2011/1606) reg.15 as from August 1, 2011.

917 Circumstances in which no meetings required (merger)

917(1) **[Application of s.917]** This section applies in the case of a merger by absorption where all of the relevant securities of the transferor company (or, if there is more than one transferor company, of each of them) are held by or on behalf of the transferee company.

917(2) **[Court satisfied conditions complied with]** It is not necessary for the scheme to be approved at a meeting of the members, or any class of members, of any of the merging companies if the court is satisfied that the following conditions have been complied with.

917(3) **[First condition: s.917(3A), (3B) satisfied]** The first condition is that either subsection (3A) or subsection (3B) is satisfied.

917(3A) **[Registrar's publication of notice of receipt of draft terms]** This subsection is satisfied if publication of notice of receipt of the draft terms by the registrar took place in respect of all the merging companies at least one month before the date of the court's order.

917(3B)   [Publication of draft terms on website etc.] This subsection is satisfied if–

(a)   the conditions in section 906A(2) to (4) are met in respect of each of the merging companies,

(b)   in each case, the registrar published the notice mentioned in subsection (4) of that section in the Gazette at least one month before the date of the court's order, and

(c)   the draft terms remained available on the website throughout the period beginning one month before, and ending on, that date.

917(4)   [Second condition: s.917(4A), (4B) satisfied] The second condition is that subsection (4A) or (4B) is satisfied for each of the documents listed in the applicable paragraphs of section 911(3)(a) to (f) relating to the transferee company and the transferor company (or, if there is more than one transferor company, each of them).

917(4A)   [Inspection of document at transferee's registered office] This subsection is satisfied for a document if the members of the transferee company were able during the period beginning one month before, and ending on, the date mentioned in subsection (3A) to inspect that document at the registered office of that company.

917(4B)   [Document available on website free of charge] This subsection is satisfied for a document if–

(a)   the document is made available on a website which is maintained by or on behalf of the transferee company and identifies the company,

(b)   access to the document on the website is not conditional on the payment of a fee or otherwise restricted, and

(c)   the document remains available on the website throughout the period beginning one month before, and ending on, the date mentioned in subsection (3A).

917(4C)   [Third condition: minimum period of free copies] The third condition is that the members of the transferee company were able to obtain copies of the documents mentioned in subsection (4), or any part of those documents, on request and free of charge, throughout the period beginning one month before, and ending on, the date mentioned in subsection (3A).

917(4D)   [Application of s.911A(5) on website for s.917(4C)] For the purposes of subsection (4C)–

(a)   section 911A(5) applies as it applies for the purposes of section 911(1)(b), and

(b)   Part 4 of Schedule 5 (communications by means of a website) does not apply.

917(5)   [Fourth condition: no minority requisition of meeting] The fourth condition is that–

(a)   one or more members of the transferee company, who together held not less than 5% of the paid-up capital of the company which carried the right to vote at general meetings of the company (excluding any shares in the company held as treasury shares) would have been able, during that period, to require a meeting of each class of members to be called for the purpose of deciding whether or not to agree to the scheme, and

(b)   no such requirement was made.

917(6)   ["Relevant securities"] In this section "relevant securities", in relation to a company, means shares or other securities carrying the right to vote at general meetings of the company.

History
Section 917(3)–(4D) substituted and s.917(5) amended by the Companies (Reporting Requirements in Mergers and Divisions) Regulations 2011 (SI 2011/1606) reg.16 as from August 1, 2011.

918   Other circumstances in which meeting of members of transferee company not required (merger)

918(1)   [Court satisfied conditions complied with] In the case of any merger by absorption, it is not necessary for the scheme to be approved by the members of the transferee company if the court is satisfied that the following conditions have been complied with.

918(2)   [First condition: s.918(2A), (2B) satisfied] The first condition is that either subsection (2A) or subsection (2B) is satisfied.

918(2A)   [Registrar's publication of notice of receipt of draft terms] This subsection is satisfied if publication of notice of receipt of the draft terms by the registrar took place in respect of the transferee company at least one month before the date of the first meeting of members, or any class of members, of the transferor company (or, if there is more than one transferor company, any of them) summoned for the purposes of agreeing to the scheme.

918(2B)   [Publication of draft terms on website etc.] This subsection is satisfied if–

(a)   the conditions in section 906A(2) to (4) are met in respect of the transferee company,

(b)   the registrar published the notice mentioned in subsection (4) of that section in the Gazette at least one month before the date of the first meeting of members, or any class of members, of the transferor company (or, if there is more than one transferor company, any of them) summoned for the purposes of agreeing to the scheme, and

(c)   the draft terms remained available on the website throughout the period beginning one month before, and ending on, that date.

918(3)   [Second condition: s.918(3A), (3B) satisfied] The second condition is that subsection (3A) or (3B) is satisfied for each of the documents listed in the applicable paragraphs of section 911(3) relating to the transferee company and the transferor company (or, if there is more than one transferor company, each of them).

918(3A)   [Inspection of document at transferee's registered office] This subsection is satisfied for a document if the members of the transferee company were able during the period beginning one month before, and ending on, the date of any such meeting as is mentioned in subsection (2A) to inspect that document at the registered office of that company.

918(3B)   [Document available on website free of charge] This subsection is satisfied for a document if–

(a)   the document is made available on a website which is maintained by or on behalf of the transferee company and identifies the company,

(b)   access to the document on the website is not conditional on the payment of a fee or otherwise restricted, and

(c)   the document remains available on the website throughout the period beginning one month before, and ending on, the date of any such meeting as is mentioned in subsection (2A).

918(3C)   [Third condition: minimum period of free copies] The third condition is that the members of the transferee company were able to obtain copies of the documents mentioned in subsection (3), or any part of those documents, on request and free of charge, throughout the period beginning one month before, and ending on, the date of any such meeting as is mentioned in subsection (2A).

918(3D)   [Application of s.911A(5) on website for s.918(3C)] For the purposes of subsection (3C)–

(a)   section 911A(5) applies as it applies for the purposes of section 911(1)(b), and

(b) Part 4 of Schedule 5 (communications by means of a website) does not apply.

918(4) **[Fourth condition: no minority requisition of meeting]** The fourth condition is that–

(a) one or more members of that company, who together held not less than 5% of the paid-up capital of the company which carried the right to vote at general meetings of the company (excluding any shares in the company held as treasury shares) would have been able, during that period, to require a meeting of each class of members to be called for the purpose of deciding whether or not to agree to the scheme, and

(b) no such requirement was made.

History
Section 918(2)–(3D) substituted and s.918(4) amended by the Companies (Reporting Requirements in Mergers and Divisions) Regulations 2011 (SI 2011/1606) reg.17 as from August 1, 2011.

918A   Agreement to dispense with reports etc (merger)

918A(1) **[Agreement of members of merging companies]** If all members holding shares in, and all persons holding other securities of, the merging companies, being shares or securities that carry a right to vote in general meetings of the company in question, so agree, the following requirements do not apply.

918A(1A) **[Dispensation of ss.908, 909, 910, 911, 911B requirements]** The requirements that may be dispensed with under this section are–

(a) the requirements of–

(i) section 908 (directors' explanatory report),

(ii) section 909 (expert's report),

(iii) section 910 (supplementary accounting statement), and

(iv) section 911B (report on material changes of assets of merging company); and

(b) the requirements of section 911 (inspection of documents) so far as relating to any document required to be drawn up under sections 908, 909 or 910.

918A(2) **[Date for determining members etc. and voting rights]** For the purposes of this section–

(a) the members, or holders of other securities, of a company, and

(b) whether shares or other securities carry a right to vote in general meetings of the company,

are determined as at the date of the application to the court under section 896.

History
Section 918A inserted by the Companies (Cross-Border Mergers and Divisions of Public Companies) (Amendment) Regulations 2008 (SI 2008/690) reg.2(2) as from April 6, 2008. Section 918A(1) and the heading amended and s.918A(1A) inserted by the Companies (Reporting Requirements in Mergers and Divisions) Regulations 2011 (SI 2011/1606) reg.18 as from August 1, 2011.

CHAPTER 3

DIVISION

Introductory

919   Divisions and companies involved in a division

919(1) **[Requirements under the scheme]** The scheme involves a division where under the scheme the undertaking, property and liabilities of the company in respect of which the compromise or arrangement is proposed are to be divided among and transferred to two or more companies each of which is either–

(a)   an existing public company, or

(b)   a new company (whether or not a public company).

919(2)   [Companies involved in the division] References in this Part to the companies involved in the division are to the transferor company and any existing transferee companies.

Requirements to be complied with in case of division

920   Draft terms of scheme (division)

920(1)   [Draft adopted by directors of companies involved] A draft of the proposed terms of the scheme must be drawn up and adopted by the directors of each of the companies involved in the division.

920(2)   [Contents of draft terms] The draft terms must give particulars of at least the following matters–

(a)   in respect of the transferor company and each transferee company–

    (i)   its name,

    (ii)   the address of its registered office, and

    (iii)   whether it is a company limited by shares or a company limited by guarantee and having a share capital;

(b)   the number of shares in a transferee company to be allotted to members of the transferor company for a given number of their shares (the "share exchange ratio") and the amount of any cash payment;

(c)   the terms relating to the allotment of shares in a transferee company;

(d)   the date from which the holding of shares in a transferee company will entitle the holders to participate in profits, and any special conditions affecting that entitlement;

(e)   the date from which the transactions of the transferor company are to be treated for accounting purposes as being those of a transferee company;

(f)   any rights or restrictions attaching to shares or other securities in a transferee company to be allotted under the scheme to the holders of shares or other securities in the transferor company to which any special rights or restrictions attach, or the measures proposed concerning them;

(g)   any amount of benefit paid or given or intended to be paid or given–

    (i)   to any of the experts referred to in section 924 (expert's report), or

    (ii)   to any director of a company involved in the division,

and the consideration for the payment of benefit.

920(3)   [Further contents] The draft terms must also–

(a)   give particulars of the property and liabilities to be transferred (to the extent that these are known to the transferor company) and their allocation among the transferee companies;

(b)   make provision for the allocation among and transfer to the transferee companies of any other property and liabilities that the transferor company has acquired or may subsequently acquire; and

(c)   specify the allocation to members of the transferor company of shares in the transferee companies and the criteria upon which that allocation is based.

921   Publication of draft terms by registrar (division)

921(1)   [Duty of directors to deliver copy to registrar] The directors of each company involved in the division must deliver a copy of the draft terms to the registrar.

921(2)   [Registrar to publish receipt in the Gazette] The registrar must publish in the Gazette notice of receipt by him from that company of a copy of the draft terms.

921(3)   [Time limit for publication of notice] That notice must be published at least one month before the date of any meeting of that company summoned for the purposes of approving the scheme.

921(4)   [Publication requirements subject to ss.921A, 934] The requirements in this section are subject to section 921A (publication of draft terms on company website) and section 934 (power of court to exclude certain requirements).

History
Section 921(4) and the heading amended by the Companies (Reporting Requirements in Mergers and Divisions) Regulations 2011 (SI 2011/1606) reg.19 as from August 1, 2011.

921A   Publication of draft terms on company website (division)

921A(1)   [Non-application of s.921A subject to conditions] Section 921 does not apply in respect of a company if the conditions in subsections (2) to (6) are met.

921A(2)   [First condition: draft terms on website] The first condition is that the draft terms are made available on a website which–

    (a)   is maintained by or on behalf of the company, and

    (b)   identifies the company.

921A(3)   [Second condition: availability free] The second condition is that neither access to the draft terms on the website nor the supply of a hard copy of them from the website is conditional on payment of a fee or otherwise restricted.

921A(4)   [Third condition: notice to registrar of website] The third condition is that the directors of the company deliver to the registrar a notice giving details of the website.

921A(5)   [Fourth condition: gazetting] The fourth condition is that the registrar publishes the notice in the Gazette at least one month before the date of any meeting of the company summoned for the purpose of approving the scheme.

921A(6)   [Fifth condition: minimum period available on website] The fifth condition is that the draft terms remain available on the website throughout the period beginning one month before, and ending on, the date of any such meeting.

History
Section 921A inserted by the Companies (Reporting Requirements in Mergers and Divisions) Regulations 2011 (SI 2011/1606) reg.20 as from August 1, 2011.

922   Approval of members of companies involved in the division

922(1)   [Requisite majority for approval] The compromise or arrangement must be approved by a majority in number, representing 75% in value, of each class of members of each of the companies involved in the division, present and voting either in person or by proxy at a meeting.

922(2)   [Approval subject to ss.931, 932] This requirement is subject to sections 931 and 932 (circumstances in which meeting of members not required).

923   Directors' explanatory report (division)

923(1)   [Duty of directors to adopt report] The directors of the transferor and each existing transferee company must draw up and adopt a report.

923(2)   [Contents of report] The report must consist of–

(a)   the statement required by section 897 (statement explaining effect of compromise or arrangement), and

(b)   insofar as that statement does not deal with the following matters, a further statement–

    (i)   setting out the legal and economic grounds for the draft terms, and in particular for the share exchange ratio and for the criteria on which the allocation to the members of the transferor company of shares in the transferee companies was based, and

    (ii)   specifying any special valuation difficulties.

923(3)   [Valuation of non-cash consideration for shares] The report must also state–

(a)   whether a report has been made to any transferee company under section 593 (valuation of non-cash consideration for shares), and

(b)   if so, whether that report has been delivered to the registrar of companies.

923(4)   [Dispensing with report] The requirement in this section is subject to section 933 (agreement to dispense with reports etc) and section 933A (certain requirements excluded where shareholders given proportional rights).

History
Section 923(4) amended by the Companies (Reporting Requirements in Mergers and Divisions) Regulations 2011 (SI 2011/1606) reg.21 as from August 1, 2011.

924   Expert's report (division)

924(1)   [Requirement for expert's report] An expert's report must be drawn up on behalf of each company involved in the division.

924(2)   [Report on draft terms] The report required is a written report on the draft terms to the members of the company.

924(3)   [Single report by joint expert] The court may on the joint application of the companies involved in the division approve the appointment of a joint expert to draw up a single report on behalf of all those companies.

If no such appointment is made, there must be a separate expert's report to the members of each company involved in the division drawn up by a separate expert appointed on behalf of that company.

924(4)   [The expert] The expert must be a person who–

(a)   is eligible for appointment as a statutory auditor (see section 1212), and

(b)   meets the independence requirement in section 936.

924(5)   [Content of expert's report] The expert's report must–

(a)   indicate the method or methods used to arrive at the share exchange ratio;

(b)   give an opinion as to whether the method or methods used are reasonable in all the circumstances of the case, indicate the values arrived at using each such method and (if there is more than one method) give an opinion on the relative importance attributed to such methods in arriving at the value decided on;

(c)   describe any special valuation difficulties that have arisen;

(d)   state whether in the expert's opinion the share exchange ratio is reasonable; and

(e)   in the case of a valuation made by a person other than himself (see section 935), state that it appeared to him reasonable to arrange for it to be so made or to accept a valuation so made.

924(6)   [Rights of expert to documents and information] The expert (or each of them) has–

(a)   the right of access to all such documents of the companies involved in the division, and

(b)   the right to require from the companies' officers all such information,

as he thinks necessary for the purposes of making his report.

924(7)   [Agreement to dispense with report] The requirement in this section is subject to section 933 (agreement to dispense with reports etc) and section 933A (certain requirements excluded where shareholders given proportional rights).

History
Section 924(7) amended by the Companies (Reporting Requirements in Mergers and Divisions) Regulations 2011 (SI 2011/1606) reg.22 as from August 1, 2011.

925   Supplementary accounting statement (division)

925(1)   [Application of s.925] This section applies if the last annual accounts of a company involved in the division relate to a financial year ending before–

(a)   the date seven months before the first meeting of the company summoned for the purposes of approving the scheme, or

(b)   if no meeting of the company is required (by virtue of section 931 or 932), the date six months before the directors of the company adopt the draft terms of the scheme.

925(1A)   [Statement if half-yearly financial report not made] If the company has not made public a half-yearly financial report relating to a period ending on or after the date mentioned in subsection (1), the directors of the company must prepare a supplementary accounting statement.

925(2)   [Statement to consist of balance sheet] That statement must consist of–

(a)   a balance sheet dealing with the state of affairs of the company as at a date not more than three months before the draft terms were adopted by the directors, and

(b)   where the company would be required under section 399 to prepare group accounts if that date were the last day of a financial year, a consolidated balance sheet dealing with the state of affairs of the company and the undertakings that would be included in such a consolidation.

925(3)   [Requirements as to balance sheet] The requirements of this Act (and where relevant Article 4 of the IAS Regulation) as to the balance sheet forming part of a company's annual accounts, and the matters to be included in notes to it, apply to the balance sheet required for an accounting statement under this section, with such modifications as are necessary by reason of its being prepared otherwise than as at the last day of a financial year.

925(4)   [Signing and approval of balance sheet] The provisions of section 414 as to the approval and signing of accounts apply to the balance sheet required for an accounting statement under this section.

925(4A) **["Half-yearly financial report"]** In this section **"half-yearly financial report"** means a report of that description required to be made public by rules under section 89A of the Financial Services and Markets Act 2000 (transparency rules).

925(5) **[Agreement to dispense with report]** The requirement in this section is subject to section 933 (agreement to dispense with reports etc) and section 933A (certain requirements excluded where shareholders given proportional rights).

History
Section 925(1) substituted, s.925(5) amended and s.925(1A), (4A) inserted by the Companies (Reporting Requirements in Mergers and Divisions) Regulations 2011 (SI 2011/1606) reg.23 as from August 1, 2011.

926 Inspection of documents (division)

926(1) **[Rights of members]** The members of each company involved in the division must be able, during the period specified below–

(a) to inspect at the registered office of that company copies of the documents listed below relating to that company and every other company involved in the division, and

(b) to obtain copies of those documents or any part of them on request free of charge.

926(2) **[Specified period]** The period referred to above is the period–

(a) beginning one month before, and

(b) ending on the date of,

the first meeting of the members, or any class of members, of the company for the purposes of approving the scheme.

926(3) **[Kind of documents]** The documents referred to above are–

(a) the draft terms;

(b) the directors' explanatory report;

(c) the expert's report;

(d) the company's annual accounts and reports for the last three financial years ending on or before the first meeting of the members, or any class of members, of the company summoned for the purposes of approving the scheme;

(e) any supplementary accounting statement required by section 925; and

(f) if no statement is required by section 925 because the company has made public a recent half-yearly financial report (see subsection (1A) of that section), that report.

926(3A) **[Rights of inspection/copies subject to website availability]** The requirement in subsection (1)(a) is subject to section 926A(1) (publication of documents on company website).

926(4) **[Requirements of s.927(3)(b), (c), (e) subject to ss.933, 933A, 934]** The requirements in subsection (3)(b), (c) and (e) are subject to section 933 (agreement to dispense with reports etc), section 933A (certain requirements excluded where shareholders given proportional rights) and section 934 (power of court to exclude certain requirements).

926(5) **[No right to free hard copy under s.1145]** Section 1145 (right to hard copy) does not apply to a document sent or supplied in accordance with subsection (1)(b) to a member who has consented to information being sent or supplied by the company by electronic means and has not revoked that consent.

926(6)   [Website communications not applicable re s.926(1)(b)] Part 4 of Schedule 5 (communications by means of a website) does not apply for the purposes of subsection (1)(b) (but see section 926A(5)).

History
Section 926(3)(e), (4) amended and s.926((3)(f), (3A), (5), (6) inserted by the Companies (Reporting Requirements in Mergers and Divisions) Regulations 2011 (SI 2011/1606) reg.24 as from August 1, 2011.

926A   Publication of documents on company website (division)

926A(1)   [No inspection of documents subject to conditions] Section 926(1)(a) does not apply to a document if the conditions in subsections (2) to (4) are met in relation to that document.
This is subject to subsection (6).

926A(2)   [First condition: document available on website] The first condition is that the document is made available on a website which–

(a)   is maintained by or on behalf of the company, and

(b)   identifies the company.

926A(3)   [Second condition: availability free] The second condition is that access to the document on the website is not conditional on payment of a fee or otherwise restricted.

926A(4)   [Third condition: minimum period on website] The third condition is that the document remains available on the website throughout the period beginning one month before, and ending on, the date of any meeting of the company summoned for the purpose of approving the scheme.

926A(5)   [Ability to obtain copy] A person is able to obtain a copy of a document as required by section 926(1)(b) if–

(a)   the conditions in subsections (2) and (3) are met in relation to that document, and

(b)   the person is able, throughout the period specified in subsection (4)–

    (i)   to retain a copy of the document as made available on the website, and

    (ii)   to produce a hard copy of it.

926A(6)   [Inspection where ability to obtain copy under s.926A(5)] Where members of a company are able to obtain copies of a document only as mentioned in subsection (5), section 926(1)(a) applies to that document even if the conditions in subsections (2) to (4) are met.

History
Section 926A inserted by the Companies (Reporting Requirements in Mergers and Divisions) Regulations 2011 (SI 2011/1606) reg.25 as from August 1, 2011.

927   Report on material changes of assets of transferor company (division)

927(1)   [Duty of directors of transferor company] The directors of the transferor company must report–

(a)   to every meeting of the members, or any class of members, of that company summoned for the purpose of agreeing to the scheme, and

(b)   to the directors of each existing transferee company,

any material changes in the property and liabilities of the transferor company between the date when the draft terms were adopted and the date of the meeting in question.

927(2) **[Duty of directors of each transferee company]** The directors of each existing transferee company must in turn–

(a) report those matters to every meeting of the members, or any class of members, of that company summoned for the purpose of agreeing to the scheme, or

(b) send a report of those matters to every member entitled to receive notice of such a meeting.

927(3) **[Agreement to dispense with report]** The requirement in this section is subject to section 933 (agreement to dispense with reports etc) and section 933A (certain requirements excluded where shareholders given proportional rights).

History
Section 927(3) amended by the Companies (Reporting Requirements in Mergers and Divisions) Regulations 2011 (SI 2011/1606) reg.26 as from August 1, 2011.

928 Approval of articles of new transferee company (division)

928 The articles of every new transferee company, or a draft of them, must be approved by ordinary resolution of the transferor company.

929 Protection of holders of securities to which special rights attached (division)

929(1) **[Scheme to provide]** The scheme must provide that where any securities of the transferor company (other than shares) to which special rights are attached are held by a person otherwise than as a member or creditor of the company, that person is to receive rights in a transferee company of equivalent value.

929(2) **[Non-application of s.929(1)]** Subsection (1) does not apply if–

(a) the holder has agreed otherwise, or

(b) the holder is, or under the scheme is to be, entitled to have the securities purchased by a transferee company on terms that the court considers reasonable.

930 No allotment of shares to transferor company or to transferee company (division)

930 The scheme must not provide for any shares in a transferee company to be allotted to–

(a) the transferor company (or its nominee) in respect of shares in the transferor company held by the transferor company itself (or its nominee); or

(b) a transferee company (or its nominee) in respect of shares in the transferor company held by the transferee company (or its nominee).

History
Section 930 substituted by the Companies (Cross-Border Mergers and Divisions of Public Companies) (Amendment) Regulations 2008 (SI 2008/690) reg.4 as from April 6, 2008.

Exceptions where shares of transferor company held by transferee company

931 Circumstances in which meeting of members of transferor company not required (division)

931(1) **[Application of s.931]** This section applies in the case of a division where all of the shares or other securities of the transferor company carrying the right to vote at general meetings of the company are held by or on behalf of one or more existing transferee companies.

931(2) **[Court satisfied conditions complied with]** It is not necessary for the scheme to be approved by a meeting of the members, or any class of members, of the transferor company if the court is satisfied that the following conditions have been complied with.

931(3) **[First condition: s.931(3A), (3B) satisfied]** The first condition is that either subsection (3A) or subsection (3B) is satisfied.

931(3A) **[Registrar's publication of notice of receipt of draft terms]** This subsection is satisfied if publication of notice of receipt of the draft terms by the registrar took place in respect of all the companies involved in the division at least one month before the date of the court's order.

931(3B) **[Availability on website etc.]** This subsection is satisfied if–

(a) the conditions in section 921A(2) to (4) are met in respect of each of the companies involved in the division,

(b) in each case, the registrar published the notice mentioned in subsection (4) of that section in the Gazette at least one month before the date of the court's order, and

(c) the draft terms remained available on the website throughout the period beginning one month before, and ending on, that date.

931(4) **[Second condition: s.931(4A), (4B) satisfied]** The second condition is that subsection (4A) or (4B) is satisfied for each of the documents listed in the applicable paragraphs of section 926(3) relating to every company involved in the division.

931(4A) **[Inspection by members at registered office]** This subsection is satisfied for a document if the members of every company involved in the division were able during the period beginning one month before, and ending on, the date of the court's order to inspect that document at the registered office of their company.

931(4B) **[Document available on website free of charge]** This subsection is satisfied for a document if–

(a) the document is made available on a website which is maintained by or on behalf of the company to which it relates and identifies the company,

(b) access to the document on the website is not conditional on payment of a fee or otherwise restricted, and

(c) the document remains available on the website throughout the period beginning one month before, and ending on, the date of the court's order.

931(4C) **[Third condition: minimum period of free copies]** The third condition is that the members of every company involved in the division were able to obtain copies of the documents mentioned in subsection (4), or any part of those documents, on request and free of charge, throughout the period beginning one month before, and ending on, the date of the court's order.

931(4D) **[Application of s.926A(5) on website for s.931(4C)]** For the purposes of subsection (4C)–

(a) section 926A(5) applies as it applies for the purposes of section 926(1)(b), and

(b) Part 4 of Schedule 5 (communications by means of a website) does not apply.

931(5) [Omitted.]

931(6) **[Fourth condition]** The fourth condition is that the directors of the transferor company have sent–

(a) to every member who would have been entitled to receive notice of a meeting to agree to the scheme (had any such meeting been called), and

(b) to the directors of every existing transferee company,

a report of any material change in the property and liabilities of the transferor company between the date when the terms were adopted by the directors and the date one month before the date of the court's order.

History

Section 931(3), (4) substituted, s.931(4A)–(4D) inserted and s.931(5) omitted by the Companies (Reporting Requirements in Mergers and Divisions) Regulations 2011 (SI 2011/1606) reg.27 as from August 1, 2011.

Other exceptions

932 Circumstances in which meeting of members of transferee company not required (division)

932(1) **[Court satisfied conditions complied with]** In the case of a division, it is not necessary for the scheme to be approved by the members of a transferee company if the court is satisfied that the following conditions have been complied with in relation to that company.

932(2) **[First condition: s.932(2A), (2B) satisfied]** The first condition is that either subsection (2A) or subsection (2B) is satisfied.

932(2A) **[Registrar's publication of notice of receipt of draft terms]** This subsection is satisfied if publication of notice of receipt of the draft terms by the registrar took place in respect of the transferee company at least one month before the date of the first meeting of members of the transferor company summoned for the purposes of agreeing to the scheme.

932(2B) **[Availability on website etc.]** This subsection is satisfied if–

(a) the conditions in section 921A(2) to (4) are met in respect of the transferee company,

(b) the registrar published the notice mentioned in subsection (4) of that section in the Gazette at least one month before the date of the first meeting of members of the transferor company summoned for the purposes of agreeing to the scheme, and

(c) the draft terms remained available on the website throughout the period beginning one month before, and ending on, that date.

932(3) **[Second condition: s.932(3A), (3B) satisfied]** The second condition is that subsection (3A) or (3B) is satisfied for each of the documents listed in the applicable paragraphs of section 926(3) relating to the transferee company and every other company involved in the division.

932(3A) **[Inspection be transferee's members at registered office]** This subsection is satisfied for a document if the members of the transferee company were able during the period beginning one month before, and ending on, the date mentioned in subsection (2A) to inspect that document at the registered office of that company.

932(3B) **[Availability on website free of charge etc.]** This subsection is satisfied for a document if–

(a) the document is made available on a website which is maintained by or on behalf of the transferee company and identifies the company,

(b) access to the document on the website is not conditional on payment of a fee or otherwise restricted, and

(c) the document remains available on the website throughout the period beginning one month before, and ending on, the date mentioned in subsection (2A).

932(3C) **[Third condition: minimum period of free copies]** The third condition is that the members of the transferee company were able to obtain copies of the documents mentioned in subsection (3), or any part of those documents, on request and free of charge, throughout the period beginning one month before, and ending on, the date mentioned in subsection (2A).

932(3D)   **[Application of s.926A(5) on website for s.932(3C)]** For the purposes of subsection (3C)–

(a)   section 926A(5) applies as it applies for the purposes of section 926(1)(b), and

(b)   Part 4 of Schedule 5 (communications by means of a website) does not apply.

932(4)   **[Fourth condition: no minority requisition of meeting]** The fourth condition is that–

(a)   one or more members of that company, who together held not less than 5% of the paid-up capital of the company which carried the right to vote at general meetings of the company (excluding any shares in the company held as treasury shares) would have been able, during that period, to require a meeting of each class of members to be called for the purpose of deciding whether or not to agree to the scheme, and

(b)   no such requirement was made.

932(5)   **[Exclusion of first, second and third conditions]** The first, second and third conditions above are subject to section 934 (power of court to exclude certain requirements).

History

Section 932(2), (3) substituted and s.932(4), (5) amended by the Companies (Reporting Requirements in Mergers and Divisions) Regulations 2011 (SI 2011/1606) reg.28 as from August 1, 2011.

933   Agreement to dispense with reports etc (division)

933(1)   **[Agreements of all members and holders of securities]** If all members holding shares in, and all persons holding other securities of, the companies involved in the division, being shares or securities that carry a right to vote in general meetings of the company in question, so agree, the following requirements do not apply.

933(2)   **[Requirements to be dispensed with]** The requirements that may be dispensed with under this section are–

(a)   the requirements of–

     (i)   section 923 (directors' explanatory report),

     (ii)   section 924 (expert's report),

     (iii)   section 925 (supplementary accounting statement), and

     (iv)   section 927 (report on material changes in assets of transferor company); and

(b)   the requirements of section 926 (inspection of documents) so far as relating to any document required to be drawn up under the provisions mentioned in paragraph (a)(i), (ii) or (iii) above.

933(3)   **[Date for determination of members and security holders]** For the purposes of this section–

(a)   the members, or holders of other securities, of a company, and

(b)   whether shares or other securities carry a right to vote in general meetings of the company,

are determined as at the date of the application to the court under section 896.

933A   Certain requirements excluded where shareholders given proportional rights (division)

933A(1) [Application where each transferee a new company] This section applies in the case of a division where each of the transferee companies is a new company.

933A(2) [Where proportional allotment rights] If all the shares in each of the transferee companies are to be allotted to the members of the transferor company in proportion to their rights in the allotted share capital of the transferor company, the following requirements do not apply.

933A(3) [Disapplication of ss.923 , 924, 925, 926, 927] The requirements which do not apply are–

    (a)   the requirements of–

        (i)   section 923 (directors' explanatory report),

        (ii)   section 924 (expert's report),

        (iii)   section 925 (supplementary accounting statement), and

        (iv)   section 927 (report on material changes in assets of transferor company); and

    (b)   the requirements of section 926 (inspection of documents) so far as relating to any document required to be drawn up under the provisions mentioned in paragraph (a)(i), (ii) or (iii) above.

History

Section 933A inserted by the Companies (Reporting Requirements in Mergers and Divisions) Regulations 2011 (SI 2011/1606) reg.29 as from August 1, 2011.

934   Power of court to exclude certain requirements (division)

934(1)   [Court satisfied condition complied with] In the case of a division, the court may by order direct that–

    (a)   in relation to any company involved in the division, the requirements of–

        (i)   section 921 (publication of draft terms), and

        (ii)   section 926 (inspection of documents),

    do not apply, and

    (b)   in relation to an existing transferee company, section 932 (circumstances in which meeting of members of transferee company not required) has effect with the omission of the first, second and third conditions specified in that section,

if the court is satisfied that the following conditions will be fulfilled in relation to that company.

934(2)   [First condition: members' free copies within time period] The first condition is that the members of that company will have received, or will have been able to obtain free of charge, copies of the documents listed in section 926–

    (a)   in time to examine them before the date of the first meeting of the members, or any class of members, of that company summoned for the purposes of agreeing to the scheme, or

    (b)   in the case of an existing transferee company where in the circumstances described in section 932 no meeting is held, in time to require a meeting as mentioned in subsection (4) of that section.

934(3)   [Second condition: creditors' free copies within time period] The second condition is that the creditors of that company will have received or will have been able to obtain free of charge copies of the draft terms in time to examine them–

    (a)   before the date of the first meeting of the members, or any class of members, of the company summoned for the purposes of agreeing to the scheme, or

    (b)   in the circumstances mentioned in subsection (2)(b) above, at the same time as the members of the company.

934(4)   [Third condition: order not to prejudice to any members or creditors] The third condition is that no prejudice would be caused to the members or creditors of the transferor company or any transferee company by making the order in question.

History
Section 934(1)(b) amended by the Companies (Reporting Requirements in Mergers and Divisions) Regulations 2011 (SI 2011/1606) reg.30 as from August 1, 2011.

CHAPTER 4

SUPPLEMENTARY PROVISIONS

Expert's report and related matters

935 Expert's report: valuation by another person

935(1) [Power of expert to delegate valuation] Where it appears to an expert–

(a) that a valuation is reasonably necessary to enable him to draw up his report, and

(b) that it is reasonable for that valuation, or part of it, to be made by (or for him to accept a valuation made by) another person who–

(i) appears to him to have the requisite knowledge and experience to make the valuation or that part of it, and

(ii) meets the independence requirement in section 936,

he may arrange for or accept such a valuation, together with a report which will enable him to make his own report under section 909 or 924.

935(2) [Disclosure in expert's report] Where any valuation is made by a person other than the expert himself, the latter's report must state that fact and must also–

(a) state the former's name and what knowledge and experience he has to carry out the valuation, and

(b) describe so much of the undertaking, property and liabilities as was valued by the other person, and the method used to value them, and specify the date of the valuation.

936 Experts and valuers: independence requirement

936(1) [Requirement for independence] A person meets the independence requirement for the purposes of section 909 or 924 (expert's report) or section 935 (valuation by another person) only if–

(a) he is not–

(i) an officer or employee of any of the companies concerned in the scheme, or

(ii) a partner or employee of such a person, or a partnership of which such a person is a partner;

(b) he is not–

(i) an officer or employee of an associated undertaking of any of the companies concerned in the scheme, or

(ii) a partner or employee of such a person, or a partnership of which such a person is a partner; and

(c) there does not exist between–

(i) the person or an associate of his, and

(ii) any of the companies concerned in the scheme or an associated undertaking of such a company, a connection of any such description as may be specified by regulations made by the Secretary of State.

936(2) **[Auditor not officer or employee of company]** An auditor of a company is not regarded as an officer or employee of the company for this purpose.

936(3) **[Definitions]** For the purposes of this section–

(a) the "companies concerned in the scheme" means every transferor and existing transferee company;

(b) "associated undertaking", in relation to a company, means–

(i) a parent undertaking or subsidiary undertaking of the company, or

(ii) a subsidiary undertaking of a parent undertaking of the company; and

(c) "associate" has the meaning given by section 937.

936(4) **[Regulations subject to negative resolution procedure]** Regulations under this section are subject to negative resolution procedure.

937 Experts and valuers: meaning of "associate"

937(1) **[Definition of associate]** This section defines "associate" for the purposes of section 936 (experts and valuers: independence requirement).

937(2) **["Associate" re individual]** In relation to an individual, "associate" means–

(a) that individual's spouse or civil partner or minor child or step-child,

(b) any body corporate of which that individual is a director, and

(c) any employee or partner of that individual.

937(3) **["Associate" re body corporate]** In relation to a body corporate, "associate" means–

(a) any body corporate of which that body is a director,

(b) any body corporate in the same group as that body, and

(c) any employee or partner of that body or of any body corporate in the same group.

937(4) **["Associate" re partnership that is a legal person]** In relation to a partnership that is a legal person under the law by which it is governed, "associate" means–

(a) any body corporate of which that partnership is a director,

(b) any employee of or partner in that partnership, and

(c) any person who is an associate of a partner in that partnership.

937(5) **["Associate" re partnership that is not a legal person]** In relation to a partnership that is not a legal person under the law by which it is governed, "associate" means any person who is an associate of any of the partners.

937(6) **[Meanings for limited liability partnership]** In this section, in relation to a limited liability partnership, for "director" read "member".

938   Power of court to summon meeting of members or creditors of existing transferee company

938(1)   [Power of court] The court may order a meeting of–

(a)   the members of an existing transferee company, or any class of them, or

(b)   the creditors of an existing transferee company, or any class of them,

to be summoned in such manner as the court directs.

938(2)   [Who may make application to court] An application for such an order may be made by–

(a)   the company concerned,

(b)   a member or creditor of the company, or

(c)   if the company is being wound up, the liquidator, or

(d)   if the company is in administration, the administrator.

938(3)   [Creditors' meeting covered by s.323] Section 323 (representation of corporations at meetings) applies to a meeting of creditors under this section as to a meeting of the company (references to a member being read as references to a creditor).

History
Section 938(3) inserted by the Companies Act 2006 (Consequential Amendments, etc.) Order 2008 (SI 2008/948) arts 2(1), (2), 3(1) and Sch.1 Pt 2 para.251 as from April 6, 2008. Section 938(c), (d) inserted by the Companies Act 2006 (Consequential Amendments, Transitional Provisions and Savings) Order 2009 (SI 2009/1941) Sch.1 para.260(5) as from October 1, 2009.

939   Court to fix date for transfer of undertaking etc of transferor company

939(1)   [Duty of court] Where the court sanctions the compromise or arrangement, it must–

(a)   in the order sanctioning the compromise or arrangement, or

(b)   in a subsequent order under section 900 (powers of court to facilitate reconstruction or amalgamation),

fix a date on which the transfer (or transfers) to the transferee company (or transferee companies) of the undertaking, property and liabilities of the transferor company is (or are) to take place.

939(2)   [Where order provides for dissolution of transferor company] Any such order that provides for the dissolution of the transferor company must fix the same date for the dissolution.

939(3)   [Where transferor company to take steps re transfer] If it is necessary for the transferor company to take steps to ensure that the undertaking, property and liabilities are fully transferred, the court must fix a date, not later than six months after the date fixed under subsection (1), by which such steps must be taken.

939(4)   [Power of court to postpone dissolution] In that case, the court may postpone the dissolution of the transferor company until that date.

939(5)   [Postponement when transferor company to take steps] The court may postpone or further postpone the date fixed under subsection (3) if it is satisfied that the steps mentioned cannot be completed by the date (or latest date) fixed under that subsection.

Liability of transferee companies

940 Liability of transferee companies for each other's defaults

940(1) **[Joint and several liability]** In the case of a division, each transferee company is jointly and severally liable for any liability transferred to any other transferee company under the scheme to the extent that the other company has made default in satisfying that liability.
This is subject to the following provisions.

940(2) **[Non-application of s.940(1) re liability to creditors]** If a majority in number representing 75% in value of the creditors or any class of creditors of the transferor company, present and voting either in person or by proxy at a meeting summoned for the purposes of agreeing to the scheme, so agree, subsection (1) does not apply in relation to the liabilities owed to the creditors or that class of creditors.

940(3) **[Maximum liability of transferee]** A transferee company is not liable under this section for an amount greater than the net value transferred to it under the scheme. The "net value transferred" is the value at the time of the transfer of the property transferred to it under the scheme less the amount at that date of the liabilities so transferred.

Disruption of websites

940A Disregard of website failures beyond control of company

940A(1) **[Conditions for not making information available under s.940A(2)]** A failure to make information or a document available on the website throughout a period specified in any of the provisions mentioned in subsection (2) is to be disregarded if–

(a) it is made available on the website for part of that period, and

(b) the failure to make it available throughout that period is wholly attributable to circumstances that it would not be reasonable to have expected the company to prevent or avoid.

940A(2) **[Provisions referred to in s.940A(1)]** The provisions referred to above are–

(a) section 906A(6),

(b) section 911A(4),

(c) section 916(3B) and (4B)

(d) section 917(3B) and (4B),

(e) section 918(2B) and (3B),

(f) section 921A(6),

(g) section 926A(4),

(h) section 931(3B) and (4B), and

(i) section 932(2B) and (3B).

History
Section 940A inserted by the Companies (Reporting Requirements in Mergers and Divisions) Regulations 2011 (SI 2011/1606) reg.31 as from August 1, 2011.

Interpretation

941 Meaning of "liabilities" and "property"

941 In this Part–

"liabilities" includes duties;

"property" includes property, rights and powers of every description.

993　Offence of fraudulent trading

993(1)　[Offence] If any business of a company is carried on with intent to defraud creditors of the company or creditors of any other person, or for any fraudulent purpose, every person who is knowingly a party to the carrying on of the business in that manner commits an offence.

993(2)　[Whether or not company in winding up] This applies whether or not the company has been, or is in the course of being, wound up.

993(3)　[Penalty] A person guilty of an offence under this section is liable–

(a)　on conviction on indictment, to imprisonment for a term not exceeding ten years or a fine (or both);

(b)　on summary conviction–

    (i)　in England and Wales, to imprisonment for a term not exceeding twelve months or a fine not exceeding the statutory maximum (or both);

    (ii)　in Scotland or Northern Ireland, to imprisonment for a term not exceeding six months or a fine not exceeding the statutory maximum (or both).

Registrar's power to strike off defunct company

1000　Power to strike off company not carrying on business or in operation

1000(1)　[Inquiry as to whether company carrying on business] If the registrar has reasonable cause to believe that a company is not carrying on business or in operation, the registrar may send to the company by post a letter inquiring whether the company is carrying on business or in operation.

1000(2)　Failure to respond to inquiry] If the registrar does not within one month of sending the letter receive any answer to it, the registrar must within 14 days after the expiration of that month send to the company by post a registered letter referring to the first letter, and stating–

(a)　that no answer to it has been received, and

(b)　that if an answer is not received to the second letter within one month from its date,

a notice will be published in the Gazette with a view to striking the company's name off the register.

1000(3)　[Publication on notice of striking off and dissolution] If the registrar–

(a)　receives an answer to the effect that the company is not carrying on business or in operation, or

(b)　does not within one month after sending the second letter receive any answer, the registrar may publish in the Gazette, and send to the company by post, a notice that at the expiration of three months from the date of the notice the name of the company mentioned in it will, unless cause is shown to the contrary, be struck off the register and the company will be dissolved.

1000(4)   [Power to strike name off register] At the expiration of the time mentioned in the notice the registrar may, unless cause to the contrary is previously shown by the company, strike its name off the register.

1000(5)   [Notice in Gazette] The registrar must publish notice in the Gazette of the company's name having been struck off the register.

1000(6)   [Dissolution] On the publication of the notice in the Gazette the company is dissolved.

1000(7)   [Directors' liabilities; Court power to wind-up] However–

(a)   the liability (if any) of every director, managing officer and member of the company continues and may be enforced as if the company had not been dissolved, and

(b)   nothing in this section affects the power of the court to wind up a company the name of which has been struck off the register.

1001   Duty to act in case of company being wound up

1001(1)   [Extent of duty] If, in a case where a company is being wound up–

(a)   the registrar has reasonable cause to believe–

(i)   that no liquidator is acting, or

(ii)   that the affairs of the company are fully wound up, and

(b)   the returns required to be made by the liquidator have not been made for a period of six consecutive months,

the registrar must publish in the Gazette and send to the company or the liquidator (if any) a notice that at the expiration of three months from the date of the notice the name of the company mentioned in it will, unless cause is shown to the contrary, be struck off the register and the company will be dissolved.

1001(2)   [Power to strike name off register] At the expiration of the time mentioned in the notice the registrar may, unless cause to the contrary is previously shown by the company, strike its name off the register.

1001(3)   [Publication of notice in Gazette] The registrar must publish notice in the Gazette of the company's name having been struck off the register.

1001(4)   [Dissolution of company] On the publication of the notice in the Gazette the company is dissolved.

1001(5)   [Directors' liabilities; Court power to wind-up] However–

(a)   the liability (if any) of every director, managing officer and member of the company continues and may be enforced as if the company had not been dissolved, and

(b)   nothing in this section affects the power of the court to wind up a company the name of which has been struck off the register.

1002   Supplementary provisions as to service of letter or notice

1002(1)   [Service at company's registered office] A letter or notice to be sent under section 1000 or 1001 to a company may be addressed to the company at its registered office or, if no office has been registered, to the care of some officer of the company.

1002(2)   [Service where officer's details are not known] If there is no officer of the company whose name and address are known to the registrar, the letter or notice may be sent to each of the persons who subscribed the memorandum (if their addresses are known to the registrar).

1002(3)   [Notice to liquidator] A notice to be sent to a liquidator under section 1001 may be addressed to him at his last known place of business.

Voluntary striking off

1003   Striking off on application by company

1003(1)   [Power to strike off] On application by a company, the registrar of companies may strike the company's name off the register.

1003(2)   [Requirements for application] The application–

(a)   must be made on the company's behalf by its directors or by a majority of them, and

(b)   must contain the prescribed information.

1003(3)   [Timing of striking off] The registrar may not strike a company off under this section until after the expiration of three months from the publication by the registrar in the Gazette of a notice–

(a)   stating that the registrar may exercise the power under this section in relation to the company, and

(b)   inviting any person to show cause why that should not be done.

1003(4)   [Publication of notice in Gazette] The registrar must publish notice in the Gazette of the company's name having been struck off.

1003(5)   [Dissolution of company] On the publication of the notice in the Gazette the company is dissolved.

1003(6)   [Directors' liabilities; Court power to wind-up] However–

(a)   the liability (if any) of every director, managing officer and member of the company continues and may be enforced as if the company had not been dissolved, and

(b)   nothing in this section affects the power of the court to wind up a company the name of which has been struck off the register.

1004   Circumstances in which application not to be made: activities of company

1004(1)   [Activities restricting applications] An application under section 1003 (application for voluntary striking off) on behalf of a company must not be made if, at any time in the previous three months, the company has–

(a)   changed its name,

(b)   traded or otherwise carried on business,

(c)   made a disposal for value of property or rights that, immediately before ceasing to trade or otherwise carry on business, it held for the purpose of disposal for gain in the normal course of trading or otherwise carrying on business, or

(d)   engaged in any other activity, except one which is–

(i)   necessary or expedient for the purpose of making an application under that section, or deciding whether to do so,

(ii)   necessary or expedient for the purpose of concluding the affairs of the company,

(iii) necessary or expedient for the purpose of complying with any statutory requirement, or

(iv) specified by the Secretary of State by order for the purposes of this sub-paragraph.

1004(2)   [Trading or carrying on business] For the purposes of this section, a company is not to be treated as trading or otherwise carrying on business by virtue only of the fact that it makes a payment in respect of a liability incurred in the course of trading or otherwise carrying on business.

1004(3)   [Amendment of subs.(1) by order] The Secretary of State may by order amend subsection (1) for the purpose of altering the period in relation to which the doing of the things mentioned in paragraphs (a) to (d) of that subsection is relevant.

1004(4)   [Negative resolution procedure] An order under this section is subject to negative resolution procedure.

1004(5)   [Offence] It is an offence for a person to make an application in contravention of this section.

1004(6)   [Defence] In proceedings for such an offence it is a defence for the accused to prove that he did not know, and could not reasonably have known, of the existence of the facts that led to the contravention.

1004(7)   [Penalty] A person guilty of an offence under this section is liable–

(a)   on conviction on indictment, to a fine;

(b)   on summary conviction, to a fine not exceeding the statutory maximum.

1005   Circumstances in which application not to be made: other proceedings not concluded

1005(1)   [Circumstances where application not to be made] An application under section 1003 (application for voluntary striking off) on behalf of a company must not be made at a time when–

(a)   an application to the court under Part 26 has been made on behalf of the company for the sanctioning of a compromise or arrangement and the matter has not been finally concluded;

(b)   a voluntary arrangement in relation to the company has been proposed under Part 1 of the Insolvency Act 1986 (c. 45) or Part 2 of the Insolvency (Northern Ireland) Order 1989 (S.I. 1989/2405 (N.I. 19)) and the matter has not been finally concluded;

(c)   the company is in administration under Part 2 of that Act or Part 3 of that Order;

(d)   paragraph 44 of Schedule B1 to that Act or paragraph 45 of Schedule B1 to that Order applies (interim moratorium on proceedings where application to the court for an administration order has been made or notice of intention to appoint administrator has been filed);

(e)   the company is being wound up under Part 4 of that Act or Part 5 of that Order, whether voluntarily or by the court, or a petition under that Part for winding up of the company by the court has been presented and not finally dealt with or withdrawn;

(f)   there is a receiver or manager of the company's property;

(g)   the company's estate is being administered by a judicial factor.

1005(2)   [Matters considered concluded: subs.(1)(a)] For the purposes of subsection (1)(a), the matter is finally concluded if–

(a)   the application has been withdrawn,

(b)   the application has been finally dealt with without a compromise or arrangement being sanctioned by the court, or

(c)   a compromise or arrangement has been sanctioned by the court and has, together with anything required to be done under any provision made in relation to the matter by order of the court, been fully carried out.

1005(3)   [Matters considered concluded: subs.(1)(b)] For the purposes of subsection (1)(b), the matter is finally concluded if–

(a)   no meetings are to be summoned under section 3 of the Insolvency Act 1986 (c. 45) or Article 16 of the Insolvency (Northern Ireland) Order 1989,

(b)   meetings summoned under that section or Article fail to approve the arrangement with no, or the same, modifications,

(c)   an arrangement approved by meetings summoned under that section, or in consequence of a direction under section 6(4)(b) of that Act or Article 19(4)(b) of that Order, has been fully implemented, or

(d)   the court makes an order under section 6(5) of that Act or Article 19(5) of that Order revoking approval given at previous meetings and, if the court gives any directions under section 6(6) of that Act or Article 19(6) of that Order, the company has done whatever it is required to do under those directions.

1005(4)   [Offence] It is an offence for a person to make an application in contravention of this section.

1005(5)   [Defence] In proceedings for such an offence it is a defence for the accused to prove that he did not know, and could not reasonably have known, of the existence of the facts that led to the contravention.

1005(6)   [Penalty] A person guilty of an offence under this section is liable–

(a)   on conviction on indictment, to a fine;

(b)   on summary conviction, to a fine not exceeding the statutory maximum.

1006   Copy of application to be given to members, employees, etc

1006(1)   [Duty to provide copies] A person who makes an application under section 1003 (application for voluntary striking off) on behalf of a company must secure that, within seven days from the day on which the application is made, a copy of it is given to every person who at any time on that day is–

(a)   a member of the company,

(b)   an employee of the company,

(c)   a creditor of the company,

(d)   a director of the company,

(e)   a manager or trustee of any pension fund established for the benefit of employees of the company, or

(f)   a person of a description specified for the purposes of this paragraph by regulations made by the Secretary of State.

Regulations under paragraph (f) are subject to negative resolution procedure.

1006(2)   [Director who is party to application] Subsection (1) does not require a copy of the application to be given to a director who is a party to the application.

1006(3)   [Withdrawn applications] The duty imposed by this section ceases to apply if the application is withdrawn before the end of the period for giving the copy application.

1006(4) **[Offence]** A person who fails to perform the duty imposed on him by this section commits an offence.

If he does so with the intention of concealing the making of the application from the person concerned, he commits an aggravated offence.

1006(5) **[Defence]** In proceedings for an offence under this section it is a defence for the accused to prove that he took all reasonable steps to perform the duty.

1006(6) **[Penalty]** A person guilty of an offence under this section (other than an aggravated offence) is liable–

(a) on conviction on indictment, to a fine;

(b) on summary conviction, to a fine not exceeding the statutory maximum.

1006(7) **[Penalty: aggravated offence]** A person guilty of an aggravated offence under this section is liable–

(a) on conviction on indictment, to imprisonment for a term not exceeding seven years or a fine (or both);

(b) on summary conviction–

    (i) in England and Wales, to imprisonment for a term not exceeding twelve months or to a fine not exceeding the statutory maximum (or both);

    (ii) in Scotland or Northern Ireland, to imprisonment for a term not exceeding six months, or to a fine not exceeding the statutory maximum (or both).

1007 Copy of application to be given to new members, employees, etc

1007(1) **[Application of section]** This section applies in relation to any time after the day on which a company makes an application under section 1003 (application for voluntary striking off) and before the day on which the application is finally dealt with or withdrawn.

1007(2) **[Duty to supply copy of application]** A person who is a director of the company at the end of a day on which a person (other than himself) becomes–

(a) a member of the company,

(b) an employee of the company,

(c) a creditor of the company,

(d) a director of the company,

(e) a manager or trustee of any pension fund established for the benefit of employees of the company, or

(f) a person of a description specified for the purposes of this paragraph by regulations made by the Secretary of State,

must secure that a copy of the application is given to that person within seven days from that day.

Regulations under paragraph (f) are subject to negative resolution procedure.

1007(3) **[Withdrawn application]** The duty imposed by this section ceases to apply if the application is finally dealt with or withdrawn before the end of the period for giving the copy application.

1007(4) **[Offence]** A person who fails to perform the duty imposed on him by this section commits an offence.

If he does so with the intention of concealing the making of the application from the person concerned, he commits an aggravated offence.

1007(5) **[Defence]** In proceedings for an offence under this section it is a defence for the accused to prove–

(a) that at the time of the failure he was not aware of the fact that the company had made an application under section 1003, or

(b) that he took all reasonable steps to perform the duty.

1007(6) **[Penalty]** A person guilty of an offence under this section (other than an aggravated offence) is liable–

(a) on conviction on indictment, to a fine;

(b) on summary conviction, to a fine not exceeding the statutory maximum.

1007(7) **[Penalty: aggravated offence]** A person guilty of an aggravated offence under this section is liable–

(a) on conviction on indictment, to imprisonment for a term not exceeding seven years or a fine (or both);

(b) on summary conviction–

 (i) in England and Wales, to imprisonment for a term not exceeding twelve months or to a fine not exceeding the statutory maximum (or both);

 (ii) in Scotland or Northern Ireland, to imprisonment for a term not exceeding six months, or to a fine not exceeding the statutory maximum (or both).

1008 Copy of application: provisions as to service of documents

1008(1) **[Effect of provisions]** The following provisions have effect for the purposes of–

section 1006 (copy of application to be given to members, employees, etc), and

section 1007 (copy of application to be given to new members, employees, etc).

1008(2) **[Service of documents]** A document is treated as given to a person if it is–

(a) delivered to him, or

(b) left at his proper address, or

(c) sent by post to him at that address.

1008(3) **[Proper address]** For the purposes of subsection (2) and section 7 of the Interpretation Act 1978 (c. 30) (service of documents by post) as it applies in relation to that subsection, the proper address of a person is–

(a) in the case of a firm incorporated or formed in the United Kingdom, its registered or principal office;

(b) in the case of a firm incorporated or formed outside the United Kingdom–

 (i) if it has a place of business in the United Kingdom, its principal office in the United Kingdom, or

 (ii) if it does not have a place of business in the United Kingdom, its registered or principal office;

(c) in the case of an individual, his last known address.

1008(4) **[Creditors]** In the case of a creditor of the company a document is treated as given to him if it is left or sent by post to him–

(a)   at the place of business of his with which the company has had dealings by virtue of which he is a creditor of the company, or

(b)   if there is more than one such place of business, at each of them.

1009   Circumstances in which application to be withdrawn

1009(1)   [Application of section] This section applies where, at any time on or after the day on which a company makes an application under section 1003 (application for voluntary striking off) and before the day on which the application is finally dealt with or withdrawn–

(a)   the company–

    (i)   changes its name,

    (ii)   trades or otherwise carries on business,

    (iii)   makes a disposal for value of any property or rights other than those which it was necessary or expedient for it to hold for the purpose of making, or proceeding with, an application under that section, or

    (iv)   engages in any activity, except one to which subsection (4) applies;

(b)   an application is made to the court under Part 26 on behalf of the company for the sanctioning of a compromise or arrangement;

(c)   a voluntary arrangement in relation to the company is proposed under Part 1 of the Insolvency Act 1986 (c. 45) or Part 2 of the Insolvency (Northern Ireland) Order 1989 (S.I. 1989/2405 (N.I. 19));

(d)   an application to the court for an administration order in respect of the company is made under paragraph 12 of Schedule B1 to that Act or paragraph 13 of Schedule B1 to that Order;

(e)   an administrator is appointed in respect of the company under paragraph 14 or 22 of Schedule B1 to that Act or paragraph 15 or 23 of Schedule B1 to that Order, or a copy of notice of intention to appoint an administrator of the company under any of those provisions is filed with the court;

(f)   there arise any of the circumstances in which, under section 84(1) of that Act or Article 70 of that Order, the company may be voluntarily wound up;

(g)   a petition is presented for the winding up of the company by the court under Part 4 of that Act or Part 5 of that Order;

(h)   a receiver or manager of the company's property is appointed; or

(i)   a judicial factor is appointed to administer the company's estate.

1009(2)   [Director's duty to withdraw application] A person who, at the end of a day on which any of the events mentioned in subsection (1) occurs, is a director of the company must secure that the company's application is withdrawn forthwith.

1009(3)   [Company not treated as trading] For the purposes of subsection (1)(a), a company is not treated as trading or otherwise carrying on business by virtue only of the fact that it makes a payment in respect of a liability incurred in the course of trading or otherwise carrying on business.

1009(4)   [Excepted activities] The excepted activities referred to in subsection (1)(a)(iv) are–

(a)   any activity necessary or expedient for the purposes of–

    (i)   making, or proceeding with, an application under section 1003 (application for voluntary striking off),

    (ii)   concluding affairs of the company that are outstanding because of what has been necessary or expedient for the purpose of making, or proceeding with, such an application, or

    (iii) complying with any statutory requirement;

  (b) any activity specified by the Secretary of State by order for the purposes of this subsection.

An order under paragraph (b) is subject to negative resolution procedure.

1009(5)   **[Offence]** A person who fails to perform the duty imposed on him by this section commits an offence.

1009(6)   **[Defence]** In proceedings for an offence under this section it is a defence for the accused to prove–

  (a) that at the time of the failure he was not aware of the fact that the company had made an application under section 1003, or

  (b) that he took all reasonable steps to perform the duty.

1009(7)   **[Penalty]** A person guilty of an offence under this section is liable–

  (a) on conviction on indictment, to a fine;

  (b) on summary conviction, to a fine not exceeding the statutory maximum.

1010   Withdrawal of application

1010   An application under section 1003 is withdrawn by notice to the registrar.

1011   Meaning of "creditor"

1011   In this Chapter "creditor" includes a contingent or prospective creditor.

CHAPTER 2

PROPERTY OF DISSOLVED COMPANY

Property vesting as bona vacantia

1012   Property of dissolved company to be bona vacantia

1012(1)   **[Property and rights deemed bona vacantia]** When a company is dissolved, all property and rights whatsoever vested in or held on trust for the company immediately before its dissolution (including leasehold property, but not including property held by the company on trust for another person) are deemed to be *bona vacantia* and–

  (a) accordingly belong to the Crown, or to the Duchy of Lancaster or to the Duke of Cornwall for the time being (as the case may be), and

  (b) vest and may be dealt with in the same manner as other *bona vacantia* accruing to the Crown, to the Duchy of Lancaster or to the Duke of Cornwall.

1012(2)   **[Restoration to register]** Subsection (1) has effect subject to the possible restoration of the company to the register under Chapter 3 (see section 1034).

1013   Crown disclaimer of property vesting as bona vacantia

1013(1)   **[Crown disclaimer of property]** Where property vests in the Crown under section 1012, the Crown's title to it under that section may be disclaimed by a notice signed by the Crown representative, that is to say the Treasury Solicitor, or, in relation to property in Scotland, the Queen's and Lord Treasurer's Remembrancer.

1013(2)   [Right to execute notice of disclaimer] The right to execute a notice of disclaimer under this section may be waived by or on behalf of the Crown either expressly or by taking possession.

1013(3)   [Time limit for execution] A notice of disclaimer must be executed within three years after–

(a)   the date on which the fact that the property may have vested in the Crown under section 1012 first comes to the notice of the Crown representative, or

(b)   if ownership of the property is not established at that date, the end of the period reasonably necessary for the Crown representative to establish the ownership of the property.

1013(4)   [Time limit for execution where application for decision made] If an application in writing is made to the Crown representative by a person interested in the property requiring him to decide whether he will or will not disclaim, any notice of disclaimer must be executed within twelve months after the making of the application or such further period as may be allowed by the court.

1013(5)   [Execution outside time limit] A notice of disclaimer under this section is of no effect if it is shown to have been executed after the end of the period specified by subsection (3) or (4).

1013(6)   [Delivery of notice to registrar] A notice of disclaimer under this section must be delivered to the registrar and retained and registered by him.

1013(7)   [Publication of copy in Gazette] Copies of it must be published in the Gazette and sent to any persons who have given the Crown representative notice that they claim to be interested in the property.

1013(8)   [Application of section] This section applies to property vested in the Duchy of Lancaster or the Duke of Cornwall under section 1012 as if for references to the Crown and the Crown representative there were respectively substituted references to the Duchy of Lancaster and to the Solicitor to that Duchy, or to the Duke of Cornwall and to the Solicitor to the Duchy of Cornwall, as the case may be.

1014   Effect of Crown disclaimer

1014(1)   [Effect of notice of disclaimer] Where notice of disclaimer is executed under section 1013 as respects any property, that property is deemed not to have vested in the Crown under section 1012.

1014(2)   [Application of other sections to Crown disclaimer] The following sections contain provisions as to the effect of the Crown disclaimer–

sections 1015 to 1019 apply in relation to property in England and Wales or Northern Ireland;

sections 1020 to 1022 apply in relation to property in Scotland.

Effect of Crown disclaimer: England and Wales and Northern Ireland

1015   General effect of disclaimer

1015(1)   [General effect of disclaimer] The Crown's disclaimer operates so as to terminate, as from the date of the disclaimer, the rights, interests and liabilities of the company in or in respect of the property disclaimed.

1015(2)   [Exemption] It does not, except so far as is necessary for the purpose of releasing the company from any liability, affect the rights or liabilities of any other person.

1016   Disclaimer of leaseholds

1016(1)   [Effect of disclaimer of leaseholds] The disclaimer of any property of a leasehold character does not take effect unless a copy of the disclaimer has been served (so far as the Crown representative is aware of their addresses) on every person claiming under the company as underlessee or mortgagee, and either–

(a) no application under section 1017 (power of court to make vesting order) is made with respect to that property before the end of the period of 14 days beginning with the day on which the last notice under this paragraph was served, or

(b) where such an application has been made, the court directs that the disclaimer shall take effect.

1016(2) **[Fixtures, tenant's improvements, etc.]** Where the court gives a direction under subsection (1)(b) it may also, instead of or in addition to any order it makes under section 1017, make such order as it thinks fit with respect to fixtures, tenant's improvements and other matters arising out of the lease.

1016(3) **["Crown representative"]** In this section the "Crown representative" means–

(a) in relation to property vested in the Duchy of Lancaster, the Solicitor to that Duchy;

(b) in relation to property vested in the Duke of Cornwall, the Solicitor to the Duchy of Cornwall;

(c) in relation to property in Scotland, the Queen's and Lord Treasurer's Remembrancer;

(d) in relation to other property, the Treasury Solicitor.

1017 Power of court to make vesting order

1017(1) **[Power to make order]** The court may on application by a person who–

(a) claims an interest in the disclaimed property, or

(b) is under a liability in respect of the disclaimed property that is not discharged by the disclaimer,

make an order under this section in respect of the property.

1017(2) **[Nature of order]** An order under this section is an order for the vesting of the disclaimed property in, or its delivery to–

(a) a person entitled to it (or a trustee for such a person), or

(b) a person subject to such a liability as is mentioned in subsection (1)(b) (or a trustee for such a person).

1017(3) **[Justification for making order]** An order under subsection (2)(b) may only be made where it appears to the court that it would be just to do so for the purpose of compensating the person subject to the liability in respect of the disclaimer.

1017(4) **[Terms of order]** An order under this section may be made on such terms as the court thinks fit.

1017(5) **[Effect of order]** On a vesting order being made under this section, the property comprised in it vests in the person named in that behalf in the order without conveyance, assignment or transfer.

1018 Protection of persons holding under a lease

1018(1) **[Requirement for terms]** The court must not make an order under section 1017 vesting property of a leasehold nature in a person claiming under the company as underlessee or mortgagee except on terms making that person–

(a) subject to the same liabilities and obligations as those to which the company was subject under the lease, or

(b) if the court thinks fit, subject to the same liabilities and obligations as if the lease had been assigned to him.

1018(2) **[Orders relating to part of property]** Where the order relates to only part of the property comprised in the lease, subsection (1) applies as if the lease had comprised only the property comprised in the vesting order.

1018(3)   [Declination of order on terms set] A person claiming under the company as underlessee or mortgagee who declines to accept a vesting order on such terms is excluded from all interest in the property.

1018(4)   [Acceptance of order on terms set] If there is no person claiming under the company who is willing to accept an order on such terms, the court has power to vest the company's estate and interest in the property in any person who is liable (whether personally or in a representative character, and whether alone or jointly with the company) to perform the lessee's covenants in the lease.

1018(5)   [Vesting in person freed from estates, etc.] The court may vest that estate and interest in such a person freed and discharged from all estates, incumbrances and interests created by the company.

1019   Land subject to rentcharge

1019   Where in consequence of the disclaimer land that is subject to a rentcharge vests in any person, neither he nor his successors in title are subject to any personal liability in respect of sums becoming due under the rentcharge, except sums becoming due after he, or some person claiming under or through him, has taken possession or control of the land or has entered into occupation of it.

Effect of Crown disclaimer: Scotland

1020   General effect of disclaimer

1020(1)   [General effect of disclaimer] The Crown's disclaimer operates to determine, as from the date of the disclaimer, the rights, interests and liabilities of the company, and the property of the company, in or in respect of the property disclaimed.

1020(2)   [Exception] It does not (except so far as is necessary for the purpose of releasing the company and its property from liability) affect the rights or liabilities of any other person.

1021   Power of court to make vesting order

1021(1)   [Extent of power] The court may–

(a) on application by a person who either claims an interest in disclaimed property or is under a liability not discharged by this Act in respect of disclaimed property, and

(b) on hearing such persons as it thinks fit,

make an order for the vesting of the property in or its delivery to any persons entitled to it, or to whom it may seem just that the property should be delivered by way of compensation for such liability, or a trustee for him.

1021(2)   [Terms of order] The order may be made on such terms as the court thinks fit.

1021(3)   [Vesting of property] On a vesting order being made under this section, the property comprised in it vests accordingly in the person named in that behalf in the order, without conveyance or assignation for that purpose.

1022   Protection of persons holding under a lease

1022(1)   [Requirement for terms] Where the property disclaimed is held under a lease the court must not make a vesting order in favour of a person claiming under the company, whether–

(a) as sub-lessee, or

(b) as creditor in a duly registered or (as the case may be) recorded heritable security over a lease,

except on the following terms.

1022(2) **[Terms]** The person must by the order be made subject–

(a) to the same liabilities and obligations as those to which the company was subject under the lease in respect of the property, or

(b) if the court thinks fit, only to the same liabilities and obligations as if the lease had been assigned to him.

In either event (if the case so requires) the liabilities and obligations must be as if the lease had comprised only the property comprised in the vesting order.

1022(3) **[Declination of order on terms set]** A sub-lessee or creditor declining to accept a vesting order on such terms is excluded from all interest in and security over the property.

1022(4) **[Acceptance of order on terms set]** If there is no person claiming under the company who is willing to accept an order on such terms, the court has power to vest the company's estate and interest in the property in any person liable (either personally or in a representative character, and either alone or jointly with the company) to perform the lessee's obligations under the lease.

1022(5) **[Vesting in person freed from estates, etc.]** The court may vest that estate and interest in such a person freed and discharged from all interests, rights and obligations created by the company in the lease or in relation to the lease.

1022(6) **[Heritable securities]** For the purposes of this section a heritable security–

(a) is duly recorded if it is recorded in the Register of Sasines, and

(b) is duly registered if registered in accordance with the Land Registration (Scotland) Act 1979 (c. 33).

Supplementary provisions

1023 Liability for rentcharge on company's land after dissolution

1023(1) **[Application of section]** This section applies where on the dissolution of a company land in England and Wales or Northern Ireland that is subject to a rentcharge vests by operation of law in the Crown or any other person ("the proprietor").

1023(2) **[Personal liability of proprietor]** Neither the proprietor nor his successors in title are subject to any personal liability in respect of sums becoming due under the rentcharge, except sums becoming due after the proprietor, or some person claiming under or through him, has taken possession or control of the land or has entered into occupation of it.

1023(3) **[Body corporate]** In this section "company" includes any body corporate.

CHAPTER 3

RESTORATION TO THE REGISTER

Administrative restoration to the register

1024 Application for administrative restoration to the register

1024(1) **[Right to apply]** An application may be made to the registrar to restore to the register a company that has been struck off the register under section 1000 or 1001 (power of registrar to strike off defunct company).

1024(2) **[Dissolved companies]** An application under this section may be made whether or not the company has in consequence been dissolved.

1024(3) **[Former directors or members]** An application under this section may only be made by a former director or former member of the company.

1024(4) **[Time limit]** An application under this section may not be made after the end of the period of six years from the date of the dissolution of the company.

For this purpose an application is made when it is received by the registrar.

1025 Requirements for administrative restoration

1025(1) **[Requirement for conditions to be met]** On an application under section 1024 the registrar shall restore the company to the register if, and only if, the following conditions are met.

1025(2) **[Carrying on business]** The first condition is that the company was carrying on business or in operation at the time of its striking off.

1025(3) **[Bona vacantia property]** The second condition is that, if any property or right previously vested in or held on trust for the company has vested as *bona vacantia*, the Crown representative has signified to the registrar in writing consent to the company's restoration to the register.

1025(4) **[Consent of Crown representative]** It is the applicant's responsibility to obtain that consent and to pay any costs (in Scotland, expenses) of the Crown representative–

(a)　in dealing with the property during the period of dissolution, or

(b)　in connection with the proceedings on the application,

that may be demanded as a condition of giving consent.

1025(5) **[Delivery of documents; payment of penalties]** The third condition is that the applicant has–

(a)　delivered to the registrar such documents relating to the company as are necessary to bring up to date the records kept by the registrar, and

(b)　paid any penalties under section 453 or corresponding earlier provisions (civil penalty for failure to deliver accounts) that were outstanding at the date of dissolution or striking off.

1025(6) **["Crown representative"]** In this section the "Crown representative" means–

(a)　in relation to property vested in the Duchy of Lancaster, the Solicitor to that Duchy;

(b)　in relation to property vested in the Duke of Cornwall, the Solicitor to the Duchy of Cornwall;

(c)　in relation to property in Scotland, the Queen's and Lord Treasurer's Remembrancer;

(d)　in relation to other property, the Treasury Solicitor.

1026 Application to be accompanied by statement of compliance

1026(1) **[Requirement for statement of compliance]** An application under section 1024 (application for administrative restoration to the register) must be accompanied by a statement of compliance.

1026(2) **[Nature of statement]** The statement of compliance required is a statement–

(a)　that the person making the application has standing to apply (see subsection (3) of that section), and

(b)　that the requirements for administrative restoration (see section 1025) are met.

1026(3) **[Evidence of contents]** The registrar may accept the statement of compliance as sufficient evidence of those matters.

1027   Registrar's decision on application for administrative restoration

1027(1)   [Duty to give notice] The registrar must give notice to the applicant of the decision on an application under section 1024 (application for administrative restoration to the register).

1027(2)   [Restoration to register] If the decision is that the company should be restored to the register, the restoration takes effect as from the date that notice is sent.

1027(3)   [Publication of entry in Gazette] In the case of such a decision, the registrar must–

(a)   enter on the register a note of the date as from which the company's restoration to the register takes effect, and

(b)   cause notice of the restoration to be published in the Gazette.

1027(4)   [Content of notice] The notice under subsection (3)(b) must state–

(a)   the name of the company or, if the company is restored to the register under a different name (see section 1033), that name and its former name,

(b)   the company's registered number, and

(c)   the date as from which the restoration of the company to the register takes effect.

1028   Effect of administrative restoration

1028(1)   [General effect] The general effect of administrative restoration to the register is that the company is deemed to have continued in existence as if it had not been dissolved or struck off the register.

1028(2)   [Penalties under s.453] The company is not liable to a penalty under section 453 or any corresponding earlier provision (civil penalty for failure to deliver accounts) for a financial year in relation to which the period for filing accounts and reports ended–

(a)   after the date of dissolution or striking off, and

(b)   before the restoration of the company to the register.

1028(3)   [Court directions] The court may give such directions and make such provision as seems just for placing the company and all other persons in the same position (as nearly as may be) as if the company had not been dissolved or struck off the register.

1028(4)   [Timing of application for court directions] An application to the court for such directions or provision may be made any time within three years after the date of restoration of the company to the register.

Restoration to the register by the court

1029   Application to court for restoration to the register

1029(1)   [Scope of application] An application may be made to the court to restore to the register a company–

(a)   that has been dissolved under Chapter 9 of Part 4 of the Insolvency Act 1986 (c. 45) or Chapter 9 of Part 5 of the Insolvency (Northern Ireland) Order 1989 (S.I. 1989/2405 (N.I. 19)) (dissolution of company after winding up),

(b)   that is deemed to have been dissolved under paragraph 84(6) of Schedule B1 to that Act or paragraph 85(6) of Schedule B1 to that Order (dissolution of company following administration), or

(c)   that has been struck off the register–

(i)   under section 1000 or 1001 (power of registrar to strike off defunct company), or

(ii)   under section 1003 (voluntary striking off),

whether or not the company has in consequence been dissolved.

1029(2)   [Entitlement to make application] An application under this section may be made by–

(a)   the Secretary of State,

(b)   any former director of the company,

(c)   any person having an interest in land in which the company had a superior or derivative interest,

(d)   any person having an interest in land or other property–

(i)   that was subject to rights vested in the company, or

(ii)   that was benefited by obligations owed by the company,

(e)   any person who but for the company's dissolution would have been in a contractual relationship with it,

(f)   any person with a potential legal claim against the company,

(g)   any manager or trustee of a pension fund established for the benefit of employees of the company,

(h)   any former member of the company (or the personal representatives of such a person),

(i)   any person who was a creditor of the company at the time of its striking off or dissolution,

(j)   any former liquidator of the company,

(k)   where the company was struck off the register under section 1003 (voluntary striking off), any person of a description specified by regulations under section 1006(1)(f) or 1007(2)(f) (persons entitled to notice of application for voluntary striking off),

or by any other person appearing to the court to have an interest in the matter.

1030   When application to the court may be made

1030(1)   [Timing of application] An application to the court for restoration of a company to the register may be made at any time for the purpose of bringing proceedings against the company for damages for personal injury.

1030(2)   [Limitation provisions of other enactments] No order shall be made on such an application if it appears to the court that the proceedings would fail by virtue of any enactment as to the time within which proceedings must be brought.

1030(3)   [Power to disregard time periods] In making that decision the court must have regard to its power under section 1032(3) (power to give consequential directions etc) to direct that the period between the dissolution (or striking off) of the company and the making of the order is not to count for the purposes of any such enactment.

1030(4)   [Six-year limit] In any other case an application to the court for restoration of a company to the register may not be made after the end of the period of six years from the date of the dissolution of the company, subject as follows.

1030(5)   [Timing following refusal of administrative restoration to register] In a case where–

(a)   the company has been struck off the register under section 1000 or 1001 (power of registrar to strike off defunct company),

(b)   an application to the registrar has been made under section 1024 (application for administrative restoration to the register) within the time allowed for making such an application, and

(c) the registrar has refused the application,

an application to the court under this section may be made within 28 days of notice of the registrar's decision being issued by the registrar, even if the period of six years mentioned in subsection (4) above has expired.

1030(6) **[Interpretation]** For the purposes of this section–

(a) "personal injury" includes any disease and any impairment of a person's physical or mental condition; and

(b) references to damages for personal injury include–

   (i) any sum claimed by virtue of section 1(2)(c) of the Law Reform (Miscellaneous Provisions) Act 1934 (c. 41) or section 14(2)(c) of the Law Reform (Miscellaneous Provisions) Act (Northern Ireland) 1937 (1937 c. 9 (N.I.)) (funeral expenses)), and

   (ii) damages under the Fatal Accidents Act 1976 (c. 30), the Damages (Scotland) Act 1976 (c. 13) or the Fatal Accidents (Northern Ireland) Order 1977 (S.I. 1977/1251 (N.I. 18)).

1031 **Decision on application for restoration by the court**

1031(1) **[Power to order restoration to register[** On an application under section 1029 the court may order the restoration of the company to the register–

(a) if the company was struck off the register under section 1000 or 1001 (power of registrar to strike off defunct companies) and the company was, at the time of the striking off, carrying on business or in operation;

(b) if the company was struck off the register under section 1003 (voluntary striking off) and any of the requirements of sections 1004 to 1009 was not complied with;

(c) if in any other case the court considers it just to do so.

1031(2) **[Effect of court order]** If the court orders restoration of the company to the register, the restoration takes effect on a copy of the court's order being delivered to the registrar.

1031(3) **[Publication of notice in Gazette]** The registrar must cause to be published in the Gazette notice of the restoration of the company to the register.

1031(4) **[Content of notice]** The notice must state–

(a) the name of the company or, if the company is restored to the register under a different name (see section 1033), that name and its former name,

(b) the company's registered number, and

(c) the date on which the restoration took effect.

1032 **Effect of court order for restoration to the register**

1032(1) **[General effect]** The general effect of an order by the court for restoration to the register is that the company is deemed to have continued in existence as if it had not been dissolved or struck off the register.

1032(2) **[Penalties under s.453]** The company is not liable to a penalty under section 453 or any corresponding earlier provision (civil penalty for failure to deliver accounts) for a financial year in relation to which the period for filing accounts and reports ended–

(a) after the date of dissolution or striking off, and

(b) before the restoration of the company to the register.

1032(3)   [Power of court to give directions] The court may give such directions and make such provision as seems just for placing the company and all other persons in the same position (as nearly as may be) as if the company had not been dissolved or struck off the register.

1032(4)   [Scope of directions] The court may also give directions as to–

(a)   the delivery to the registrar of such documents relating to the company as are necessary to bring up to date the records kept by the registrar,

(b)   the payment of the costs (in Scotland, expenses) of the registrar in connection with the proceedings for the restoration of the company to the register,

(c)   where any property or right previously vested in or held on trust for the company has vested as *bona vacantia*, the payment of the costs (in Scotland, expenses) of the Crown representative–

(i)   in dealing with the property during the period of dissolution, or

(ii)   in connection with the proceedings on the application.

1032(5)   ["Crown representative"] In this section the "Crown representative" means–

(a)   in relation to property vested in the Duchy of Lancaster, the Solicitor to that Duchy;

(b)   in relation to property vested in the Duke of Cornwall, the Solicitor to the Duchy of Cornwall;

(c)   in relation to property in Scotland, the Queen's and Lord Treasurer's Remembrancer;

(d)   in relation to other property, the Treasury Solicitor.

Supplementary provisions

1033   Company's name on restoration

1033(1)   [Name on restoration] A company is restored to the register with the name it had before it was dissolved or struck off the register, subject to the following provisions.

1033(2)   [Name where previous name not permitted] If at the date of restoration the company could not be registered under its former name without contravening section 66 (name not to be the same as another in the registrar's index of company names), it must be restored to the register–

(a)   under another name specified–

(i)   in the case of administrative restoration, in the application to the registrar, or

(ii)   in the case of restoration under a court order, in the court's order, or

(b)   as if its registered number was also its name.

References to a company's being registered in a name, and to registration in that context, shall be read as including the company's being restored to the register.

1033(3)   [Restoration under name specified in application] If a company is restored to the register under a name specified in the application to the registrar, the provisions of–

section 80 (change of name: registration and issue of new certificate of incorporation), and

section 81 (change of name: effect),

apply as if the application to the registrar were notice of a change of name.

1033(4)   [Restoration under name specified in court order] If a company is restored to the register under a name specified in the court's order, the provisions of–

section 80 (change of name: registration and issue of new certificate of incorporation), and section 81 (change of name: effect),

apply as if the copy of the court order delivered to the registrar were notice of a change a name.

1033(5) **[Restoration under registered number]** If the company is restored to the register as if its registered number was also its name–

    (a)   the company must change its name within 14 days after the date of the restoration,

    (b)   the change may be made by resolution of the directors (without prejudice to any other method of changing the company's name),

    (c)   the company must give notice to the registrar of the change, and

    (d)   sections 80 and 81 apply as regards the registration and effect of the change.

1033(6) **[Offence]** If the company fails to comply with subsection (5)(a) or (c) an offence is committed by–

    (a)   the company, and

    (b)   every officer of the company who is in default.

1033(7) **[Penalty]** A person guilty of an offence under subsection (6) is liable on summary conviction to a fine not exceeding level 5 on the standard scale and, for continued contravention, a daily default fine not exceeding one-tenth of level 5 on the standard scale.

1034   Effect of restoration to the register where property has vested as bona vacantia

1034(1) **[Right to dispose property]** The person in whom any property or right is vested by section 1012 (property of dissolved company to be *bona vacantia*) may dispose of, or of an interest in, that property or right despite the fact that the company may be restored to the register under this Chapter.

1034(2) **[Effect of restoration on disposition]** If the company is restored to the register–

    (a)   the restoration does not affect the disposition (but without prejudice to its effect in relation to any other property or right previously vested in or held on trust for the company), and

    (b)   the Crown or, as the case may be, the Duke of Cornwall shall pay to the company an amount equal to–

        (i)   the amount of any consideration received for the property or right or, as the case may be, the interest in it, or

        (ii)   the value of any such consideration at the time of the disposition,

or, if no consideration was received an amount equal to the value of the property, right or interest disposed of, as at the date of the disposition

1034(3) **[Crown representative's costs]** There may be deducted from the amount payable under subsection (2)(b) the reasonable costs of the Crown representative in connection with the disposition (to the extent that they have not been paid as a condition of administrative restoration or pursuant to a court order for restoration).

1034(4) **[Duchy of Lancaster]** Where a liability accrues under subsection (2) in respect of any property or right which before the restoration of the company to the register had accrued as *bona vacantia* to the Duchy of Lancaster, the Attorney General of that Duchy shall represent Her Majesty in any proceedings arising in connection with that liability.

1034(5) **[Duchy of Cornwall]** Where a liability accrues under subsection (2) in respect of any property or right which before the restoration of the company to the register had accrued as *bona vacantia* to the Duchy of Cornwall, such persons as the Duke of Cornwall (or other possessor for the time being of the

Duchy) may appoint shall represent the Duke (or other possessor) in any proceedings arising out of that liability.

1034(6)   ["Crown representative"] In this section the "Crown representative" means–

(a)   in relation to property vested in the Duchy of Lancaster, the Solicitor to that Duchy;

(b)   in relation to property vested in the Duke of Cornwall, the Solicitor to the Duchy of Cornwall;

(c)   in relation to property in Scotland, the Queen's and Lord Treasurer's Remembrancer;

(d)   in relation to other property, the Treasury Solicitor.

PART 34

OVERSEAS COMPANIES

Other requirements

1052   Company charges

1052(1)   [Power to make regulations] The Secretary of State may by regulations make provision about the registration of specified charges over property in the United Kingdom of a registered overseas company.

1052(2)   [Scope of power] The power in subsection (1) includes power to make provision about–

(a)   a registered overseas company that–

(i)   has particulars registered in more than one part of the United Kingdom;

(ii)   has property in more than one part of the United Kingdom;

(b)   the circumstances in which property is to be regarded, for the purposes of the regulations, as being, or not being, in the United Kingdom or in a particular part of the United Kingdom;

(c)   the keeping by a registered overseas company of records and registers about specified charges and their inspection;

(d)   the consequences of a failure to register a charge in accordance with the regulations;

(e)   the circumstances in which a registered overseas company ceases to be subject to the regulations.

1052(3)   [Company charges] The regulations may for this purpose apply, with or without modifications, any of the provisions of Part 25 (company charges).

1052(4)   [Modification of Pt 25] The regulations may modify any reference in an enactment to Part 25, or to a particular provision of that Part, so as to include a reference to the regulations or to a specified provision of the regulations.

1052(5)   [Negative resolution procedure] Regulations under this section are subject to negative resolution procedure.

1052(6)   [Interpretation] In this section–

"registered overseas company" means an overseas company that has registered particulars under section 1046(1), and

"specified" means specified in the regulations.

[Note insertion of new ss.1170A (receiver or manager and certain related references), 1170B (meaning of "contributory") by SI 2009/1941 s.2(1) and Sch.1 para.260(8) as from October 1, 2009.]

Introductory

1182   Persons subject to foreign restrictions

1182(1)   **[Scope of section]** This section defines what is meant by references in this Part to a person being subject to foreign restrictions.

1182(2)   **[Persons subject to foreign restrictions]** A person is subject to foreign restrictions if under the law of a country or territory outside the United Kingdom–

    (a)   he is, by reason of misconduct or unfitness, disqualified to any extent from acting in connection with the affairs of a company,

    (b)   he is, by reason of misconduct or unfitness, required–

        (i)   to obtain permission from a court or other authority, or

        (ii)   to meet any other condition,

    before acting in connection with the affairs of a company, or

    (c)   he has, by reason of misconduct or unfitness, given undertakings to a court or other authority of a country or territory outside the United Kingdom–

        (i)   not to act in connection with the affairs of a company, or

        (ii)   restricting the extent to which, or the way in which, he may do so.

1182(3)   **[Actions in connection with company's affairs]** The references in subsection (2) to acting in connection with the affairs of a company are to doing any of the following–

    (a)   being a director of a company,

    (b)   acting as receiver of a company's property, or

    (c)   being concerned or taking part in the promotion, formation or management of a company.

1182(4)   **[Interpretation]** In this section–

    (a)   "company" means a company incorporated or formed under the law of the country or territory in question, and

    (b)   in relation to such a company–

"director" means the holder of an office corresponding to that of director of a UK company; and

"receiver" includes any corresponding officer under the law of that country or territory.

1183   Meaning of "the court" and "UK company"

1183   In this Part–

"the court" means–

    (a)   in England and Wales, the High Court or a county court;

    (b)   in Scotland, the Court of Session or the sheriff court;

    (c)   in Northern Ireland, the High Court;

"UK company" means a company registered under this Act.

1184   Disqualification of persons subject to foreign restrictions

1184(1)   [Power to make regulations] The Secretary of State may make provision by regulations disqualifying a person subject to foreign restrictions from–

(a)   being a director of a UK company,

(b)   acting as receiver of a UK company's property, or

(c)   in any way, whether directly or indirectly, being concerned or taking part in the promotion, formation or management of a UK company.

1184(2)   [Scope of regulations] The regulations may provide that a person subject to foreign restrictions–

(a)   is disqualified automatically by virtue of the regulations, or

(b)   may be disqualified by order of the court on the application of the Secretary of State.

1184(3)   [Power of Secretary of State to accept undertakings] The regulations may provide that the Secretary of State may accept an undertaking (a "disqualification undertaking") from a person subject to foreign restrictions that he will not do anything which would be in breach of a disqualification under subsection (1).

1184(4)   ["Person disqualified under this Part"] In this Part–

(a)   a "person disqualified under this Part" is a person–

   (i)   disqualified as mentioned in subsection (2)(a) or (b), or

   (ii)   who has given and is subject to a disqualification undertaking;

(b)   references to a breach of a disqualification include a breach of a disqualification undertaking.

1184(5)   [Applications to court for permission to act] The regulations may provide for applications to the court by persons disqualified under this Part for permission to act in a way which would otherwise be in breach of the disqualification.

1184(6)   [Cessation of disqualification] The regulations must provide that a person ceases to be disqualified under this Part on his ceasing to be subject to foreign restrictions.

1184(7)   [Affirmative resolution procedure] Regulations under this section are subject to affirmative resolution procedure.

1185   Disqualification regulations: supplementary

1185(1)   [Scope of regulation under s.1184] Regulations under section 1184 may make different provision for different cases and may in particular distinguish between cases by reference to–

(a)   the conduct on the basis of which the person became subject to foreign restrictions;

(b)   the nature of the foreign restrictions;

(c)   the country or territory under whose law the foreign restrictions were imposed.

1185(2)   [Scope of regulations under s.1184(2)(b)] Regulations under section 1184(2)(b) or (5) (provision for applications to the court)–

(a)   must specify the grounds on which an application may be made;

(b)   may specify factors to which the court shall have regard in determining an application.

1185(3)   [Factors to be taken into consideration] The regulations may, in particular, require the court to have regard to the following factors–

(a)   whether the conduct on the basis of which the person became subject to foreign restrictions would, if done in relation to a UK company, have led a court to make a disqualification order on an application under the Company Directors Disqualification Act 1986 (c. 46) or the Company Directors Disqualification (Northern Ireland) Order 2002 (S.I. 2002/3150 (N.I. 4));

(b)   in a case in which the conduct on the basis of which the person became subject to foreign restrictions would not be unlawful if done in relation to a UK company, the fact that the person acted unlawfully under foreign law;

(c)   whether the person's activities in relation to UK companies began after he became subject to foreign restrictions;

(d)   whether the person's activities (or proposed activities) in relation to UK companies are undertaken (or are proposed to be undertaken) outside the United Kingdom.

1185(4)   [Scope of regulations under s.1184(3)] Regulations under section 1184(3) (provision as to undertakings given to the Secretary of State) may include provision allowing the Secretary of State, in determining whether to accept an undertaking, to take into account matters other than criminal convictions notwithstanding that the person may be criminally liable in respect of those matters.

1185(5)   [Scope of regulations under s.1184(5)] Regulations under section 1184(5) (provision for application to court for permission to act) may include provision–

(a)   entitling the Secretary of State to be represented at the hearing of the application, and

(b)   as to the giving of evidence or the calling of witnesses by the Secretary of State at the hearing of the application.

1186   Offence of breach of disqualification

1186(1)   [Offence] Regulations under section 1184 may provide that a person disqualified under this Part who acts in breach of the disqualification commits an offence.

1186(2)   [Penalty] The regulations may provide that a person guilty of such an offence is liable–

(a)   on conviction on indictment, to imprisonment for a term not exceeding two years or a fine (or both);

(b)   on summary conviction–

(i)   in England and Wales, to imprisonment for a term not exceeding twelve months or to a fine not exceeding the statutory maximum (or both);

(ii)   in Scotland or Northern Ireland, to imprisonment for a term not exceeding six months, or to a fine not exceeding the statutory maximum (or both).

1186(3)   [Offences committed before commencement of s.154(1) of 2003 Act] In relation to an offence committed before the commencement of section 154(1) of the Criminal Justice Act 2003 (c. 44), for "twelve months" in subsection (2)(b)(i) substitute "six months".

Power to make persons liable for company's debts

1187   Personal liability for debts of company

1187(1)   [Persons subject to foreign restrictions] The Secretary of State may provide by regulations that a person who, at a time when he is subject to foreign restrictions–

(a)   is a director of a UK company, or

(b)   is involved in the management of a UK company,

is personally responsible for all debts and other liabilities of the company incurred during that time.

1187(2)   [Joint and several liability] A person who is personally responsible by virtue of this section for debts and other liabilities of a company is jointly and severally liable in respect of those debts and liabilities with–

(a)   the company, and

(b)   any other person who (whether by virtue of this section or otherwise) is so liable.

1187(3)   [Persons involved in management of company] For the purposes of this section a person is involved in the management of a company if he is concerned, whether directly or indirectly, or takes part, in the management of the company.

1187(4)   [Different provisions for different cases] The regulations may make different provision for different cases and may in particular distinguish between cases by reference to–

(a)   the conduct on the basis of which the person became subject to foreign restrictions;

(b)   the nature of the foreign restrictions;

(c)   the country or territory under whose law the foreign restrictions were imposed.

1187(5)   [Affirmative resolution procedure] Regulations under this section are subject to affirmative resolution procedure.

Power to require statements to be sent to the registrar of companies

1188   Statements from persons subject to foreign restrictions

1188(1)   [Power to make regulations] The Secretary of State may make provision by regulations requiring a person who–

(a)   is subject to foreign restrictions, and

(b)   is not disqualified under this Part,

to send a statement to the registrar if he does anything that, if done by a person disqualified under this Part, would be in breach of the disqualification.

1188(2)   [Contents of statement] The statement must include such information as may be specified in the regulations relating to–

(a)   the person's activities in relation to UK companies, and

(b)   the foreign restrictions to which the person is subject.

1188(3)   [Specification of time limit] The statement must be sent to the registrar within such period as may be specified in the regulations.

1188(4)   [Different provisions for different cases] The regulations may make different provision for different cases and may in particular distinguish between cases by reference to–

(a)   the conduct on the basis of which the person became subject to foreign restrictions;

(b)   the nature of the foreign restrictions;

(c)   the country or territory under whose law the foreign restrictions were imposed.

1188(5)   [Affirmative resolution procedure] Regulations under this section are subject to affirmative resolution procedure.

1189   Statements from persons disqualified

1189(1)   [Power to make regulations] The Secretary of State may make provision by regulations requiring a statement or notice sent to the registrar of companies under any of the provisions listed below that relates (wholly or partly) to a person who–

(a)   is a person disqualified under this Part, or

(b)   is subject to a disqualification order or disqualification undertaking under the Company Directors Disqualification Act 1986 (c. 46) or the Company Directors Disqualification (Northern Ireland) Order 2002 (S.I. 2002/3150 (N.I. 4)),

to be accompanied by an additional statement.

1189(2)   [Specified provisions] The provisions referred to above are–

(a)   section 12 (statement of a company's proposed officers),

(b)   section 167(2) (notice of person having become director), and

(c)   section 276 (notice of a person having become secretary or one of joint secretaries).

1189(3)   [Additional statement] The additional statement is a statement that the person has obtained permission from a court, on an application under section 1184(5) or (as the case may be) for the purposes of section 1(1)(a) of the Company Directors Disqualification Act 1986 (c. 46) or Article 3(1) of the Company Directors Disqualification (Northern Ireland) Order 2002 (S.I. 2002/3150 (N.I. 4)), to act in the capacity in question.

1189(4)   [Affirmative resolution procedure] Regulations under this section are subject to affirmative resolution procedure.

1190   Statements: whether to be made public

1190(1)   [Regulations may require statement to be public] Regulations under section 1188 or 1189 (statements required to be sent to registrar) may provide that a statement sent to the registrar of companies under the regulations is to be treated as a record relating to a company for the purposes of section 1080 (the companies register).

1190(2)   [Provision for withholding from public inspection] The regulations may make provision as to the circumstances in which such a statement is to be, or may be–

(a)   withheld from public inspection, or

(b)   removed from the register.

1190(3)   [Conditions for withholding from public inspection] The regulations may, in particular, provide that a statement is not to be withheld from public inspection or removed from the register unless the person to whom it relates provides such information, and satisfies such other conditions, as may be specified.

1190(4)   [Disapplication of s.1081] The regulations may provide that section 1081 (note of removal of material from the register) does not apply, or applies with such modifications as may be specified, in the case of material removed from the register under the regulations.

1190(5)   ["Specified"] In this section "specified" means specified in the regulations.

1191   Offences

1191(1)   [Offence] Regulations under section 1188 or 1189 may provide that it is an offence for a person–

(a)   to fail to comply with a requirement under the regulations to send a statement to the registrar;

(b) knowingly or recklessly to send a statement under the regulations to the registrar that is misleading, false or deceptive in a material particular.

1191(2)   [Penalty] The regulations may provide that a person guilty of such an offence is liable–

(a) on conviction on indictment, to imprisonment for a term not exceeding two years or a fine (or both);

(b) on summary conviction–

    (i)   in England and Wales, to imprisonment for a term not exceeding twelve months or to a fine not exceeding the statutory maximum (or both);

    (ii) in Scotland or Northern Ireland, to imprisonment for a term not exceeding six months, or to a fine not exceeding the statutory maximum (or both).

1191(3)   [Offences committed before commencement of s.154(1) of 2003 Act] In relation to an offence committed before the commencement of section 154(1) of the Criminal Justice Act 2003 (c. 44), for "twelve months" in subsection (2)(b)(i) substitute "six months".

Third Parties (Rights against Insurers) Act 2010

(2010 Chapter 10)

An Act to make provision about the rights of third parties against insurers of liabilities to third parties in the case where the insured is insolvent, and in certain other cases.

[*25th March 2010*]

Special note

At the time when this edition went to press, this Act had not been brought into force, and until it becomes effective the Third Parties (Rights against Insurers) Act 1930 (above, p.246) will be the applicable law. Readers should check on the position in order to be sure what text to use.

Transfer of rights to third parties

1 Rights against insurer of insolvent person etc

1(1) This section applies if–

(a) a relevant person incurs a liability against which that person is insured under a contract of insurance, or

(b) a person who is subject to such a liability becomes a relevant person.

1(2) The rights of the relevant person under the contract against the insurer in respect of the liability are transferred to and vest in the person to whom the liability is or was incurred (the **"third party"**).

1(3) The third party may bring proceedings to enforce the rights against the insurer without having established the relevant person's liability; but the third party may not enforce those rights without having established that liability.

494

1(4) For the purposes of this Act, a liability is established only if its existence and amount are established; and, for that purpose, **"establish"** means establish–

(a) by virtue of a declaration under section 2 or a declarator under section 3,

(b) by a judgment or decree,

(c) by an award in arbitral proceedings or by an arbitration, or

(d) by an enforceable agreement.

1(5) In this Act–

(a) references to an **"insured"** are to a person who incurs or who is subject to a liability to a third party against which that person is insured under a contract of insurance;

(b) references to a **"relevant person"** are to a person within sections 4 to 7;

(c) references to a **"third party"** are to be construed in accordance with subsection (2);

(d) references to **"transferred rights"** are to rights under a contract of insurance which are transferred under this section.

2 Establishing liability in England and Wales and Northern Ireland

2(1) This section applies where a person (P)–

(a) claims to have rights under a contract of insurance by virtue of a transfer under section 1, but

(b) has not yet established the insured's liability which is insured under that contract.

2(2) P may bring proceedings against the insurer for either or both of the following–

(a) a declaration as to the insured's liability to P;

(b) a declaration as to the insurer's potential liability to P.

2(3) In such proceedings P is entitled, subject to any defence on which the insurer may rely, to a declaration under subsection (2)(a) or (b) on proof of the insured's liability to P or (as the case may be) the insurer's potential liability to P.

2(4) Where proceedings are brought under subsection (2)(a) the insurer may rely on any defence on which the insured could rely if those proceedings were proceedings brought against the insured in respect of the insured's liability to P.

2(5) Subsection (4) is subject to section 12(1).

2(6) Where the court makes a declaration under this section, the effect of which is that the insurer is liable to P, the court may give the appropriate judgment against the insurer.

2(7) Where a person applying for a declaration under subsection (2)(b) is entitled or required, by virtue of the contract of insurance, to do so in arbitral proceedings, that person may also apply in the same proceedings for a declaration under subsection (2)(a).

2(8) In the application of this section to arbitral proceedings, subsection (6) is to be read as if "tribunal" were substituted for "court" and "make the appropriate award" for "give the appropriate judgment".

2(9) When bringing proceedings under subsection (2)(a), P may also make the insured a defendant to those proceedings.

2(10) If (but only if) the insured is a defendant to proceedings under this section (whether by virtue of subsection (9) or otherwise), a declaration under subsection (2) binds the insured as well as the insurer.

2(11)   In this section, references to the insurer's potential liability to P are references to the insurer's liability in respect of the insured's liability to P, if established.

3   Establishing liability in Scotland

3(1)   This section applies where a person (P)–

   (a)   claims to have rights under a contract of insurance by virtue of a transfer under section 1, but

   (b)   has not yet established the insured's liability which is insured under that contract.

3(2)   P may bring proceedings against the insurer for either or both of the following–

   (a)   a declarator as to the insured's liability to P;

   (b)   a declarator as to the insurer's potential liability to P.

3(3)   Where proceedings are brought under subsection (2)(a) the insurer may rely on any defence on which the insured could rely if those proceedings were proceedings brought against the insured in respect of the insured's liability to P.

3(4)   Subsection (3) is subject to section 12(1).

3(5)   Where the court grants a declarator under this section, the effect of which is that the insurer is liable to P, the court may grant the appropriate decree against the insurer.

3(6)   Where a person applying for a declarator under subsection (2)(b) is entitled or required, by virtue of the contract of insurance, to do so in an arbitration, that person may also apply in the same arbitration for a declarator under subsection (2)(a).

3(7)   In the application of this section to an arbitration, subsection (5) is to be read as if "tribunal" were substituted for "court" and "make the appropriate award" for "grant the appropriate decree".

3(8)   When bringing proceedings under subsection (2)(a), P may also make the insured a defender to those proceedings.

3(9)   If (but only if) the insured is a defender to proceedings under this section (whether by virtue of subsection (8) or otherwise), a declarator under subsection (2) binds the insured as well as the insurer.

3(10)   In this section, the reference to the insurer's potential liability to P is a reference to the insurer's liability in respect of the insured's liability to P, if established.

Relevant persons

4   Individuals

4(1)   An individual is a relevant person if any of the following is in force in respect of that individual in England and Wales–

   (a)   a deed of arrangement registered in accordance with the Deeds of Arrangement Act 1914,

   (b)   an administration order made under Part 6 of the County Courts Act 1984,

   (c)   an enforcement restriction order made under Part 6A of that Act,

   (d)   subject to subsection (4), a debt relief order made under Part 7A of the Insolvency Act 1986,

   (e)   a voluntary arrangement approved in accordance with Part 8 of that Act, or

   (f)   a bankruptcy order made under Part 9 of that Act.

4(2)   An individual is a relevant person if any of the following is in force in respect of that individual (or, in the case of paragraph (a) or (b), that individual's estate) in Scotland–

(a)   an award of sequestration made under section 5 of the Bankruptcy (Scotland) Act 1985,

(b)   a protected trust deed within the meaning of that Act, or

(c)   a composition approved in accordance with Schedule 4 to that Act.

4(3)   An individual is a relevant person if any of the following is in force in respect of that individual in Northern Ireland–

(a)   an administration order made under Part 6 of the Judgments Enforcement (Northern Ireland) Order 1981 (S.I. 1981/226 (N.I. 6)),

(b)   a deed of arrangement registered in accordance with Chapter 1 of Part 8 of the Insolvency (Northern Ireland) Order 1989 (S.I. 1989/2405 (N.I. 19)),

(c)   a voluntary arrangement approved under Chapter 2 of Part 8 of that Order, or

(d)   a bankruptcy order made under Part 9 of that Order.

4(4)   If an individual is a relevant person by virtue of subsection (1)(d), that person is a relevant person for the purposes of section 1(1)(b) only.

4(5)   Where an award of sequestration made under section 5 of the Bankruptcy (Scotland) Act 1985 is recalled or reduced, any rights which were transferred under section 1 as a result of that award are re-transferred to and vest in the person who became a relevant person as a result of the award.

4(6)   Where an order discharging an individual from an award of sequestration made under section 5 of the Bankruptcy (Scotland) Act 1985 is recalled or reduced under paragraph 17 or 18 of Schedule 4 to that Act, the order is to be treated for the purposes of this section as never having been made.

5   Individuals who die insolvent

5(1)   An individual who dies insolvent is a relevant person for the purposes of section 1(1)(b) only.

5(2)   For the purposes of this section an individual (D) is to be regarded as having died insolvent if, following D's death–

(a)   D's estate falls to be administered in accordance with an order under section 421 of the Insolvency Act 1986 or Article 365 of the Insolvency (Northern Ireland) Order 1989 (S.I. 1989/2405 (N. I. 19)),

(b)   an award of sequestration is made under section 5 of the Bankruptcy (Scotland) Act 1985 in respect of D's estate and the award is not recalled or reduced, or

(c)   a judicial factor is appointed under section 11A of the Judicial Factors (Scotland) Act 1889 in respect of D's estate and the judicial factor certifies that the estate is absolutely insolvent within the meaning of the Bankruptcy (Scotland) Act 1985.

5(3)   Where a transfer of rights under section 1 takes place as a result of an insured person being a relevant person by virtue of this section, references in this Act to an insured are, where the context so requires, to be read as references to the insured's estate.

6   Corporate bodies etc

6(1)   A body corporate or an unincorporated body is a relevant person if–

(a)   a compromise or arrangement between the body and its creditors (or a class of them) is in force, having been sanctioned in accordance with section 899 of the Companies Act 2006, or

(b)   the body has been dissolved under section 1000, 1001 or 1003 of that Act, and the body has not been–

(i)   restored to the register by virtue of section 1025 of that Act, or

   (ii)   ordered to be restored to the register by virtue of section 1031 of that Act.

6(2)   A body corporate or an unincorporated body is a relevant person if, in England and Wales or Scotland–

   (a)   a voluntary arrangement approved in accordance with Part 1 of the Insolvency Act 1986 is in force in respect of it,

   (b)   an administration order made under Part 2 of that Act is in force in respect of it,

   (c)   there is a person appointed in accordance with Part 3 of that Act who is acting as receiver or manager of the body's property (or there would be such a person so acting but for a temporary vacancy),

   (d)   the body is, or is being, wound up voluntarily in accordance with Chapter 2 of Part 4 of that Act,

   (e)   there is a person appointed under section 135 of that Act who is acting as provisional liquidator in respect of the body (or there would be such a person so acting but for a temporary vacancy), or

   (f)   the body is, or is being, wound up by the court following the making of a winding-up order under Chapter 6 of Part 4 of that Act or Part 5 of that Act.

6(3)   A body corporate or an unincorporated body is a relevant person if, in Scotland–

   (a)   an award of sequestration has been made under section 6 of the Bankruptcy (Scotland) Act 1985 in respect of the body's estate, and the body has not been discharged under that Act,

   (b)   the body has been dissolved and an award of sequestration has been made under that section in respect of its estate,

   (c)   a protected trust deed within the meaning of the Bankruptcy (Scotland) Act 1985 is in force in respect of the body's estate, or

   (d)   a composition approved in accordance with Schedule 4 to that Act is in force in respect of the body.

6(4)   A body corporate or an unincorporated body is a relevant person if, in Northern Ireland–

   (a)   a voluntary arrangement approved in accordance with Part 2 of the Insolvency (Northern Ireland) Order 1989 (S.I. 1989/2405 (N. I. 19)) is in force in respect of the body,

   (b)   an administration order made under Part 3 of that Order is in force in respect of the body,

   (c)   there is a person appointed in accordance with Part 4 of that Order who is acting as receiver or manager of the body's property (or there would be such a person so acting but for a temporary vacancy),

   (d)   the body is, or is being, wound up voluntarily in accordance with Chapter 2 of Part 5 of that Order,

   (e)   there is a person appointed under Article 115 of that Order who is acting as provisional liquidator in respect of the body (or there would be such a person so acting but for a temporary vacancy), or

   (f)   the body is, or is being, wound up by the court following the making of a winding-up order under Chapter 6 of Part 5 of that Order or Part 6 of that Order.

6(5)   A body within subsection (1)(a) is not a relevant person in relation to a liability that is transferred to another body by the order sanctioning the compromise or arrangement.

6(6)   Where a body is a relevant person by virtue of subsection (1)(a), section 1 has effect to transfer rights only to a person on whom the compromise or arrangement is binding.

6(7)   Where an award of sequestration made under section 6 of the Bankruptcy (Scotland) Act 1985 is recalled or reduced, any rights which were transferred under section 1 as a result of that award are re-transferred to and vest in the person who became a relevant person as a result of the award.

6(8)   Where an order discharging a body from an award of sequestration made under section 6 of the Bankruptcy (Scotland) Act 1985 is recalled or reduced under paragraph 17 or 18 of Schedule 4 to that Act, the order is to be treated for the purposes of this section as never having been made.

6(9)   In this section–

(a)   a reference to a person appointed in accordance with Part 3 of the Insolvency Act 1986 includes a reference to a person appointed under section 101 of the Law of Property Act 1925;

(b)   a reference to a receiver or manager of a body's property includes a reference to a receiver or manager of part only of the property and to a receiver only of the income arising from the property or from part of it;

(c)   for the purposes of subsection (3) "body corporate or unincorporated body" includes any entity, other than a trust, the estate of which may be sequestrated under section 6 of the Bankruptcy (Scotland) Act 1985;

(d)   a reference to a person appointed in accordance with Part 4 of the Insolvency (Northern Ireland) Order 1989 (S.I. 1989/2405 (N. I. 19)) includes a reference to a person appointed under section 19 of the Conveyancing Act 1881.

7   Scottish trusts

7(1)   A trustee of a Scottish trust is, in respect of a liability of that trustee that falls to be met out of the trust estate, a relevant person if–

(a)   an award of sequestration has been made under section 6 of the Bankruptcy (Scotland) Act 1985 in respect of the trust estate, and the trust has not been discharged under that Act,

(b)   a protected trust deed within the meaning of that Act is in force in respect of the trust estate, or

(c)   a composition approved in accordance with Schedule 4 to that Act is in force in respect of the trust estate.

7(2)   Where an award of sequestration made under section 6 of the Bankruptcy (Scotland) Act 1985 is recalled or reduced any rights which were transferred under section 1 as a result of that award are re-transferred to and vest in the person who became a relevant person as a result of the award.

7(3)   Where an order discharging an individual, body or trust from an award of sequestration made under section 6 of the Bankruptcy (Scotland) Act 1985 is recalled or reduced under paragraph 17 or 18 of Schedule 4 to that Act, the order is to be treated for the purposes of this section as never having been made.

7(4)   In this section "Scottish trust" means a trust the estate of which may be sequestrated under section 6 of the Bankruptcy (Scotland) Act 1985.

Transferred rights: supplemental

8   Limit on rights transferred

8   Where the liability of an insured to a third party is less than the liability of the insurer to the insured (ignoring the effect of section 1), no rights are transferred under that section in respect of the difference.

9   Conditions affecting transferred rights

9(1)   This section applies where transferred rights are subject to a condition (whether under the contract of insurance from which the transferred rights are derived or otherwise) that the insured has to fulfil.

9(2)   Anything done by the third party which, if done by the insured, would have amounted to or contributed to fulfilment of the condition is to be treated as if done by the insured.

9(3) The transferred rights are not subject to a condition requiring the insured to provide information or assistance to the insurer if that condition cannot be fulfilled because the insured is–

(a) an individual who has died, or

(b) a body corporate that has been dissolved.

9(4) A condition requiring the insured to provide information or assistance to the insurer does not include a condition requiring the insured to notify the insurer of the existence of a claim under the contract of insurance.

9(5) The transferred rights are not subject to a condition requiring the prior discharge by the insured of the insured's liability to the third party.

9(6) In the case of a contract of marine insurance, subsection (5) applies only to the extent that the liability of the insured is a liability in respect of death or personal injury.

9(7) In this section–

"contract of marine insurance" has the meaning given by section 1 of the Marine Insurance Act 1906;

"dissolved" means dissolved under–

(a) Chapter 9 of Part 4 of the Insolvency Act 1986,

(b) section 1000, 1001 or 1003 of the Companies Act 2006, or

(c) Chapter 9 of Part 5 of the Insolvency (Northern Ireland) Order 1989 (S.I. 1989/2405 (N. I. 19));

"personal injury" includes any disease and any impairment of a person's physical or mental condition.

10 Insurer's right of set off

10(1) This section applies if–

(a) rights of an insured under a contract of insurance have been transferred to a third party under section 1,

(b) the insured is under a liability to the insurer under the contract ("the insured's liability"), and

(c) if there had been no transfer, the insurer would have been entitled to set off the amount of the insured's liability against the amount of the insurer's own liability to the insured.

10(2) The insurer is entitled to set off the amount of the insured's liability against the amount of the insurer's own liability to the third party in relation to the transferred rights.

Provision of information etc

11 Information and disclosure for third parties

11 Schedule 1 (information and disclosure for third parties) has effect.

Enforcement of transferred rights

12 Limitation and prescription

12(1) Subsection (2) applies where a person brings proceedings for a declaration under section 2(2)(a), or for a declarator under section 3(2)(a), and the proceedings are started or, in Scotland, commenced–

(a) after the expiry of a period of limitation applicable to an action against the insured to enforce the insured's liability, or of a period of prescription applicable to that liability, but

(b) while such an action is in progress.

12(2)   The insurer may not rely on the expiry of that period as a defence unless the insured is able to rely on it in the action against the insured.

12(3)   For the purposes of subsection (1), an action is to be treated as no longer in progress if it has been concluded by a judgment or decree, or by an award, even if there is an appeal or a right of appeal.

12(4)   Where a person who has already established an insured's liability to that person brings proceedings under this Act against the insurer, nothing in this Act is to be read as meaning–

(a)   that, for the purposes of the law of limitation in England and Wales, that person's cause of action against the insurer arose otherwise than at the time when that person established the liability of the insured,

(b)   that, for the purposes of the law of prescription in Scotland, the obligation in respect of which the proceedings are brought became enforceable against the insurer otherwise than at that time, or

(c)   that, for the purposes of the law of limitation in Northern Ireland, that person's cause of action against the insurer arose otherwise than at the time when that person established the liability of the insured.

13   Jurisdiction within the United Kingdom

13(1)   Where a person (P) domiciled in a part of the United Kingdom is entitled to bring proceedings under this Act against an insurer domiciled in another part, P may do so in the part where P is domiciled or in the part where the insurer is domiciled (whatever the contract of insurance may stipulate as to where proceedings are to be brought).

13(2)   The following provisions of the Civil Jurisdiction and Judgments Act 1982 (relating to determination of domicile) apply for the purposes of subsection (1)–

(a)   section 41(2), (3), (5) and (6) (individuals);

(b)   section 42(1), (3), (4) and (8) (corporations and associations);

(c)   section 45(2) and (3) (trusts);

(d)   section 46(1), (3) and (7) (the Crown).

13(3)   In Schedule 5 to that Act (proceedings excluded from general provisions as to allocation of jurisdiction within the United Kingdom) at the end add–

"*Proceedings by third parties against insurers*

11   Proceedings under the Third Parties (Rights against Insurers) Act 2010."

Enforcement of insured's liability

14   Effect of transfer on insured's liability

14(1)   Where rights in respect of an insured's liability to a third party are transferred under section 1, the third party may enforce that liability against the insured only to the extent (if any) that it exceeds the amount recoverable from the insurer by virtue of the transfer.

14(2)   Subsection (3) applies if a transfer of rights under section 1 occurs because the insured person is a relevant person by virtue of–

(a)   section 4(1)(a) or (e), (2)(b) or (3)(b) or (c),

(b)   section 6(1)(a), (2)(a), (3)(c) or (4)(a), or

(c)   section 7(1)(b).

14(3)   If the liability is subject to the arrangement, trust deed or compromise by virtue of which the insured is a relevant person, the liability is to be treated as subject to that arrangement, trust deed or compromise only to the extent that the liability exceeds the amount recoverable from the insurer by virtue of the transfer.

14(4)   Subsection (5) applies if a transfer of rights under section 1 occurs in respect of a liability which, after the transfer, becomes one that is subject to a composition approved in accordance with Schedule 4 to the Bankruptcy (Scotland) Act 1985.

14(5)   The liability is to be treated as subject to the composition only to the extent that the liability exceeds the amount recoverable from the insurer by virtue of the transfer.

14(6)   For the purposes of this section the amount recoverable from the insurer does not include any amount that the third party is unable to recover as a result of–

    (a)   a shortage of assets on the insurer's part, in a case where the insurer is a relevant person, or

    (b)   a limit set by the contract of insurance on the fund available to meet claims in respect of a particular description of liability of the insured.

14(7)   Where a third party is eligible to make a claim in respect of the insurer's liability under or by virtue of rules made under Part 15 of the Financial Services and Markets Act 2000 (the Financial Services Compensation Scheme)–

    (a)   subsection (6)(a) applies only if the third party has made such a claim, and

    (b)   the third party is to be treated as being able to recover from the insurer any amount paid to, or due to, the third party as a result of the claim.

Application of Act

15   Reinsurance

15   This Act does not apply to a case where the liability referred to in section 1(1) is itself a liability incurred by an insurer under a contract of insurance.

16   Voluntarily-incurred liabilities

16   It is irrelevant for the purposes of section 1 whether or not the liability of the insured is or was incurred voluntarily.

17   Avoidance

17(1)   A contract of insurance to which this section applies is of no effect in so far as it purports, whether directly or indirectly, to avoid or terminate the contract or alter the rights of the parties under it in the event of the insured–

    (a)   becoming a relevant person, or

    (b)   dying insolvent (within the meaning given by section 5(2)).

17(2)   A contract of insurance is one to which this section applies if the insured's rights under it are capable of being transferred under section 1.

18   Cases with a foreign element

18   Except as expressly provided, the application of this Act does not depend on whether there is a connection with a part of the United Kingdom; and in particular it does not depend on–

(a) whether or not the liability (or the alleged liability) of the insured to the third party was incurred in, or under the law of, England and Wales, Scotland or Northern Ireland;

(b) the place of residence or domicile of any of the parties;

(c) whether or not the contract of insurance (or a part of it) is governed by the law of England and Wales, Scotland or Northern Ireland;

(d) the place where sums due under the contract of insurance are payable.

Supplemental

19   Power to amend Act

19(1)   The Secretary of State may by order made by statutory instrument amend section 4, 5 or 6 so as to–

(a) substitute a reference to a provision of Northern Ireland legislation with a reference to a different provision of Northern Ireland legislation, or

(b) add a reference to a provision of a description within subsection (2).

19(2)   A provision is within this subsection if–

(a) it is made by or under Northern Ireland legislation, and

(b) in the opinion of the Secretary of State, it corresponds with a provision under the law of England and Wales or the law of Scotland that is referred to in the section being amended.

19(3)   An order under this section may include consequential, incidental, supplementary, transitional, transitory or saving provision.

19(4)   An order under this section may not be made unless a draft of the statutory instrument containing the order has been laid before, and approved by a resolution of, each House of Parliament.

20   Amendments, transitionals, repeals, etc

20(1)   Schedule 2 (amendments) has effect.

20(2)   Schedule 3 (transitory, transitional and saving provisions) has effect.

20(3)   Schedule 4 (repeals and revocations) has effect.

21   Short title, commencement and extent

21(1)   This Act may be cited as the Third Parties (Rights against Insurers) Act 2010.

21(2)   This Act comes into force on such day as the Secretary of State may by order made by statutory instrument appoint.

21(3)   This Act extends to England and Wales, Scotland and Northern Ireland, subject as follows.

21(4)   Section 2 and paragraphs 3 and 4 of Schedule 1 do not extend to Scotland.

21(5)   Section 3 extends to Scotland only.

21(6)   Any amendment, repeal or revocation made by this Act has the same extent as the provision to which it relates.

SCHEDULE 1

INFORMATION AND DISCLOSURE FOR THIRD PARTIES

Notices requesting information

1(1)　If a person (A) reasonably believes that–

(a)　another person (B) has incurred a liability to A, and

(b)　B is a relevant person,

A may, by notice in writing, request from B such information falling within sub-paragraph (3) as the notice specifies.

1(2)　If a person (A) reasonably believes that–

(a)　a liability has been incurred to A,

(b)　the person who incurred the liability is insured against it under a contract of insurance,

(c)　rights of that person under the contract have been transferred to A under section 1, and

(d)　there is a person (C) who is able to provide information falling within sub-paragraph (3),

A may, by notice in writing, request from C such information falling within that sub-paragraph as the notice specifies.

1(3)　The following is the information that falls within this sub-paragraph–

(a)　whether there is a contract of insurance that covers the supposed liability or might reasonably be regarded as covering it;

(b)　if there is such a contract–

(i)　who the insurer is;

(ii)　what the terms of the contract are;

(iii)　whether the insured has been informed that the insurer has claimed not to be liable under the contract in respect of the supposed liability;

(iv)　whether there are or have been any proceedings between the insurer and the insured in respect of the supposed liability and, if so, relevant details of those proceedings;

(v)　in a case where the contract sets a limit on the fund available to meet claims in respect of the supposed liability and other liabilities, how much of it (if any) has been paid out in respect of other liabilities;

(vi)　whether there is a fixed charge to which any sums paid out under the contract in respect of the supposed liability would be subject.

1(4)　For the purpose of sub-paragraph (3)(b)(iv), relevant details of proceedings are–

(a)　in the case of court proceedings–

(i)　the name of the court;

(ii)　the case number;

(iii)　the contents of all documents served in the proceedings in accordance with rules of court or orders made in the proceedings, and the contents of any such orders;

(b)　in the case of arbitral proceedings or, in Scotland, an arbitration–

(i)　the name of the arbitrator;

504

(ii)   information corresponding with that mentioned in paragraph (a)(iii).

1(5)   In sub-paragraph (3)(b)(vi), in its application to Scotland, "fixed charge" means a fixed security within the meaning given by section 47(1) of the Bankruptcy and Diligence etc (Scotland) Act 2007 (asp 3).

1(6)   A notice given by a person under this paragraph must include particulars of the facts on which that person relies as entitlement to give the notice.

Provision of information where notice given under paragraph 1

2(1)   A person (R) who receives a notice under paragraph 1 must, within the period of 28 days beginning with the day of receipt of the notice–

(a)   provide to the person who gave the notice any information specified in it that R is able to provide;

(b)   in relation to any such information that R is not able to provide, notify that person why R is not able to provide it.

2(2)   Where–

(a)   a person (R) receives a notice under paragraph 1,

(b)   there is information specified in the notice that R is not able to provide because it is contained in a document that is not in R's control,

(c)   the document was at one time in R's control, and

(d)   R knows or believes that it is now in another person's control,

R must, within the period of 28 days beginning with the day of receipt of the notice, provide the person who gave the notice with whatever particulars R can as to the nature of the information and the identity of that other person.

2(3)   If R fails to comply with a duty imposed on R by this paragraph, the person who gave R the notice may apply to court for an order requiring R to comply with the duty.

2(4)   No duty arises by virtue of this paragraph in respect of information as to which a claim to legal professional privilege or, in Scotland, to confidentiality as between client and professional legal adviser could be maintained in legal proceedings.

Notices requiring disclosure: defunct bodies

3(1)   If–

(a)   a person (P) has started proceedings under this Act against an insurer in respect of a liability that P claims has been incurred to P by a body corporate, and

(b)   the body is defunct,

P may by notice in writing require a person to whom sub-paragraph (2) applies to disclose to P any documents that are relevant to that liability.

3(2)   This sub-paragraph applies to a person if–

(a)   immediately before the time of the alleged transfer under section 1, that person was an officer or employee of the body, or

(b)   immediately before the body became defunct, that person was–

    (i)   acting as an insolvency practitioner in relation to the body (within the meaning given by section 388(1) of the Insolvency Act 1986 or Article 3 of the Insolvency (Northern Ireland) Order 1989 (S.I. 1989/2405 N.I. 19)), or

    (ii) acting as the official receiver in relation to the winding up of the body.

3(3)   A notice under this paragraph must be accompanied by–

    (a)   a copy of the particulars of claim required to be served in connection with the proceedings mentioned in sub-paragraph (1), or

    (b)   where those proceedings are arbitral proceedings, the particulars of claim that would be required to be so served if they were court proceedings.

3(4)   For the purposes of this paragraph a body corporate is defunct if, subject to sub-paragraph (5), it has been dissolved under–

    (a)   Chapter 9 of Part 4 of the Insolvency Act 1986,

    (b)   Chapter 9 of Part 5 of the Insolvency (Northern Ireland) Order 1989 (S.I. 1989/2405 N.I. 19)), or

    (c)   section 1000, 1001 or 1003 of the Companies Act 2006.

3(5)   But a body corporate is not defunct for the purposes of this paragraph if the body has been–

    (a)   restored to the register by virtue of section 1025 of the Companies Act 2006, or

    (b)   ordered to be restored to the register by virtue of section 1031 of that Act.

Disclosure and inspection where notice given under paragraph 3

4(1)   Subject to the provisions of this paragraph and to any necessary modifications–

    (a)   the duties of disclosure of a person who receives a notice under paragraph 3, and

    (b)   the rights of inspection of the person giving the notice,

are the same as the corresponding duties and rights under Civil Procedure Rules of parties to court proceedings in which an order for standard disclosure has been made.

4(2)   In sub-paragraph (1), in its application to Northern Ireland–

    (a)   the reference to Civil Procedure Rules is–

       (i)   in the case of proceedings in the High Court, to be read as a reference to the Rules of the Court of Judicature (Northern Ireland) 1980 (S.R. 1980 No. 346), and

       (ii) in the case of proceedings in the county court, to be read as a reference to the County Court Rules (Northern Ireland) 1981 (S.R. 1981 No. 225), and

    (b)   the reference to an order for standard disclosure is to be read as a reference to an order for discovery.

4(3)   A person who by virtue of sub-paragraph (1) or (2) has to serve a list of documents must do so within the period of 28 days beginning with the day of receipt of the notice.

4(4)   A person who has received a notice under paragraph 3 and has served a list of documents in response to it is not under a duty of disclosure by reason of that notice in relation to documents that the person did not have when the list was served.

Avoidance

5 A contract of insurance is of no effect in so far as it purports, whether directly or indirectly–

(a) to avoid or terminate the contract or alter the rights of the parties under it in the event of a person providing information, or giving disclosure, that the person is required to provide or give by virtue of a notice under paragraph 1 or 3, or

(b) otherwise to prohibit, prevent or restrict a person from providing such information or giving such disclosure.

Other rights to information etc

6 Rights to information, or to inspection of documents, that a person has by virtue of paragraph 1 or 3 are in addition to any such rights as the person has apart from that paragraph.

Interpretation

7 For the purposes of this Schedule–

(a) a person is able to provide information only if–

(i) that person can obtain it without undue difficulty from a document that is in that person's control, or

(ii) where that person is an individual, the information is within that person's knowledge;

(b) a document is in a person's control if it is in that person's possession or if that person has a right to possession of it or to inspect or take copies of it.

[Schedules 2–4 not reproduced.]

Charities Act 2011

(2011 Chapter 25)

[*14th March 2012*]

PART 6

CY-PRÈS POWERS AND ASSISTANCE AND SUPERVISION OF CHARITIES BY COURT AND COMMISSION

Legal proceedings relating to charities

113 Petitions for winding up charities under Insolvency Act

113(1) This section applies where a charity may be wound up by the High Court under the Insolvency Act 1986.

113(2) A petition for the charity to be wound up under the 1986 Act by any court in England or Wales having jurisdiction may be presented by the Attorney General, as well as by any person authorised by that Act.

113(3) Such a petition may also be presented by the Commission if, at any time after it has instituted an inquiry under section 46 with respect to the charity, it is satisfied either as mentioned in section 76(1)(a) (misconduct or mismanagement etc.) or as mentioned in section 76(1)(b) (need to protect property etc.).

113(4) The power exercisable by the Commission by virtue of this section is exercisable–

(a) by the Commission of its own motion, but

(b) only with the agreement of the Attorney General on each occasion.

PART 11

CHARITABLE INCORPORATED ORGANISATIONS (CIOS)

CHAPTER 5

SUPPLEMENTARY

245 Regulations about winding up, insolvency and dissolution

245(1) CIO regulations may make provision about–

(a) the winding up of CIOs,

(b) their insolvency,

(c) their dissolution, and

(d) their revival and restoration to the register following dissolution.

245(2) The regulations may, in particular, make provision–

(a) about the transfer on the dissolution of a CIO of its property and rights (including property and rights held on trust for the CIO) to the official custodian or another person or body;

(b)   requiring any person in whose name any stocks, funds or securities are standing in trust for a CIO to transfer them into the name of the official custodian or another person or body;

(c)   about the disclaiming, by the official custodian or other transferee of a CIO's property, of title to any of that property;

(d)   about the application of a CIO's property cy-près;

(e)   about circumstances in which charity trustees may be personally liable for contributions to the assets of a CIO or for its debts;

(f)   about the reversal on a CIO's revival of anything done on its dissolution.

245(3)   The regulations may–

(a)   apply any enactment which would not otherwise apply, either without modification or with modifications specified in the regulations,

(b)   disapply, or modify (in ways specified in the regulations) the application of, any enactment which would otherwise apply.

245(4)   In subsection (3), "enactment" includes a provision of subordinate legislation within the meaning of the Interpretation Act 1978.

EC Regulation 2157/2001

Council Regulation (EC) No 2157/2001 of 8 October 2001 on the Statute for a European company (SE)

[Preamble]

THE COUNCIL OF THE EUROPEAN UNION,

Having regard to the Treaty establishing the European Community, and in particular Article 308 thereof,

Having regard to the proposal from the Commission,

Having regard to the opinion of the European Parliament,

Having regard to the opinion of the Economic and Social Committee,

Whereas:

(20) This Regulation does not cover other areas of law such as taxation, competition, intellectual property or insolvency. The provisions of the Member States' law and of Community law are therefore applicable in the above areas and in other areas not covered by this Regulation.

TITLE I

GENERAL PROVISIONS

Article 7

7 [Registered office] The registered office of an SE shall be located within the Community, in the same Member State as its head office. A Member State may in addition impose on SEs registered in its territory the obligation of locating their head office and their registered office in the same place.

Article 10

10 [Treatment of SE as public limited-liability company] Subject to this Regulation, an SE shall be treated in every Member State as if it were a public limited-liability company formed in accordance with the law of the Member State in which it has its registered office.

TITLE V

WINDING UP, LIQUIDATION, INSOLVENCY AND CESSATION OF PAYMENTS

Article 63

63 [Applicable law] As regards winding up, liquidation, insolvency, cessation of payments and similar procedures, an SE shall be governed by the legal provisions which would apply to a public limited-liability company formed in accordance with the law of the Member State in which its registered office is situated, including provisions relating to decision-making by the general meeting.

Article 64

64(1) [Infringement by SE of art.7] When an SE no longer complies with the requirement laid down in Article 7, the Member State in which the SE's registered office is situated shall take appropriate measures to oblige the SE to regularise its position within a specified period either:

(a) by re-establishing its head office in the Member State in which its registered office is situated or

(b) by transferring the registered office by means of the procedure laid down in Article 8.

64(2) **[Liquidation for failure to rectify infringement]** The Member State in which the SE's registered office is situated shall put in place the measures necessary to ensure that an SE which fails to regularise its position in accordance with paragraph 1 is liquidated.

64(3) **[Judicial remedy for infringement]** The Member State in which the SE's registered office is situated shall set up a judicial remedy with regard to any established infringement of Article 7. That remedy shall have a suspensory effect on the procedures laid down in paragraphs 1 and 2.

64(4) **[Notification of infringement]** Where it is established on the initiative of either the authorities or any interested party that an SE has its head office within the territory of a Member State in breach of Article 7, the authorities of that Member State shall immediately inform the Member State in which the SE's registered office is situated.

Article 65

65 **[Publication of insolvency proceedings]** Without prejudice to provisions of national law requiring additional publication, the initiation and termination of winding up, liquidation, insolvency or cessation of payment procedures and any decision to continue operating shall be publicised in accordance with Article 13.

Note
Article 13 refers to Directive 68/151, which has been implemented for this purpose in the UK by CA 1985 s.711 [now CA 2006 ss.1064, 1077 et seq.].

Article 66

66(1) **[Conversion to public limited-liability company]** An SE may be converted into a public limited-liability company governed by the law of the Member State in which its registered office is situated. No decision on conversion may be taken before two years have elapsed since its registration or before the first two sets of annual accounts have been approved.

66(2) **[Legal implications of conversion]** The conversion of an SE into a public limited-liability company shall not result in the winding up of the company or in the creation of a new legal person.

66(3) **[Draft terms of conversion]** The management or administrative organ of the SE shall draw up draft terms of conversion and a report explaining and justifying the legal and economic aspects of the conversion and indicating the implications of the adoption of the public limited-liability company for the shareholders and for the employees.

66(4) **[Publication of draft terms]** The draft terms of conversion shall be publicised in the manner laid down in each Member State's law in accordance with Article 3 of Directive 68/151/EEC at least one month before the general meeting called to decide thereon.

66(5) **[Expert examination of draft terms]** Before the general meeting referred to in paragraph 6, one or more independent experts appointed or approved, in accordance with the national provisions adopted in implementation of Article 10 of Directive 78/855/EEC, by a judicial or administrative authority in the Member State to which the SE being converted into a public limited-liability company is subject shall certify that the company has assets at least equivalent to its capital.

66(6) **[Approval of draft terms by general meeting]** The general meeting of the SE shall approve the draft terms of conversion together with the statutes of the public limited-liability company. The decision of the general meeting shall be passed as laid down in the provisions of national law adopted in implementation of Article 7 of Directive 78/855/EEC.

Ancillary Statutory Instruments

Land Registration Rules 1925

(SR & O 1925/1093 (L. 28))

Made on 3 November, 1925, by the Lord Chancellor under the Land Registration Act 1925 s.144.
Operative from January 1, 1926.

ARRANGEMENT OF RULES

[**Note**: Changes made by the Land Registration (Companies and Insolvency) Rules 1986 (SI 1986/2116), the Land Registration No.2 Rules 1995 (SI 1995/1354), the Land Registration Rules 2002 (SI 2002/2539 (L. 11)) and the Enterprise Act 2002 (Insolvency) Order 2003 (SI 2003/2096) have been incorporated into the text (in the case of pre-2003 legislation without annotation).]

PART III

REGISTERED DEALINGS WITH REGISTERED LAND

Transmissions of Land and Charges
(ii) On Bankruptcy or Liquidation

174   Registration of Official Receiver

174(1)   The Official Receiver may be registered as proprietor in place of the bankrupt on production to the Registrar of–

(a)   an office copy of a bankruptcy order relating to the bankrupt, and

(b)   a certificate signed by the Official Receiver that the land or charge is comprised in the bankrupt's estate.

174(2)   The Official Receiver may be registered as proprietor in place of a deceased proprietor on production of such evidence as the Registrar may require.

174(3)   Nothing in these rules shall affect the provisions of section 103 of the Settled Land Act 1925.

175   Registration of trustee in bankruptcy in place of Official Receiver

175   Where the Official Receiver has been registered as proprietor and some other person is subsequently appointed trustee, such person may be registered as proprietor in the place of the Official Receiver on production of the evidence required by rule 176(1)(b).

176   Original registration of trustee in bankruptcy

176(1)   If the Official Receiver has not been registered as proprietor and some other person has been appointed trustee of the bankrupt's estate, such person may be registered as proprietor in the place of the bankrupt on production to the Registrar of–

(a)   an office copy of a bankruptcy order relating to the bankrupt made by a court having jurisdiction in insolvency,

(b)   either copy of his certificate of appointment as trustee by the meeting of the bankrupt's creditors duly certified by the trustee or his solicitor as being a true copy of the original or a copy of his certificate of appointment as trustee by the Secretary of State or an office copy of the order of the Court of his appointment as trustee, and

(c)   a certificate signed by the trustee that the land or charge is comprised in the bankrupt's estate.

176(2)   A trustee in bankruptcy may be registered as proprietor in place of a deceased proprietor on production of such evidence as the Registrar may require.

177   Words added in register

177   Where the Official Receiver or trustee in bankruptcy is registered as proprietor, the words "Official Receiver" or "Trustee in bankruptcy of [*name*]" shall be added in the register.

178   Registration of a trustee under a scheme of arrangement

178   [Revoked by the Land Registration (Companies and Insolvency) Rules 1986 (SI 1986/2116) r.5, as from December 29, 1986.]

179   Creditors' notice

179(1)   A creditors' notice shall be entered in the Proprietorship Register in the following form–

"CREDITORS' NOTICE entered under section 61(1) of the Land Registration Act 1925 to protect the rights of all creditors, as the title of the proprietor of the land appears to be affected by a petition in bankruptcy against [*name of debtor*], presented in the [*name*] Court (Court Reference Number...) (Land Charges Reference Number PA...).".

179(2)   A creditors' notice shall be entered in the Charges Register in the following form–

"CREDITORS' NOTICE entered under section 61(1) of the Land Registration Act 1925 to protect the rights of all creditors, as the title of the proprietor of the charge dated... referred to above appears to be affected by a petition in bankruptcy against [*name of debtor*], presented in the [*name*] Court (Court Reference Number...) (Land Charges Reference Number PA...).".

179(3)   Notice of any such entry made in the Proprietorship Register shall be given to the proprietor of the land and notice of any such entry made in the Charges Register shall be given to the proprietor of the charge referred to in the entry.

180   Bankruptcy inhibition

180(1)   A bankruptcy inhibition shall be entered in the Proprietorship Register in the following form–

"BANKRUPTCY INHIBITION entered under section 61(3) of the Land Registration Act 1925, as the title of the proprietor of the land appears to be affected by a bankruptcy order made by the [*name*]

Court (Court Reference Number…) against [*name of debtor*] (Land Charges Reference Number WO…).

No disposition by the proprietor of the land or transmission is to be registered until the trustee in bankruptcy of the property of the bankrupt is registered.".

180(2)   A bankruptcy inhibition shall be entered in the Charges Register in the following form–

"BANKRUPTCY INHIBITION entered under section 61(3) of the Land Registration Act 1925, as the title of the proprietor of the charge dated… referred to above appears to be affected by a bankruptcy order made by the [*name*] Court (Court Reference Number…) against [*name of debtor*] (Land Charges Reference Number WO…).

No disposition or transmission of the charge is to be registered until the trustee in bankruptcy of the property of the bankrupt is registered.".

180(3)   Notice of any such entry made in the Proprietorship Register shall be given to the proprietor of the land and notice of any such entry made in the Charges Register shall be given to the proprietor of the charge referred to in the entry.

181   Action of the Registrar under Section 62 of the Act (bankruptcy)

181   Where–

(a)   any doubt arises as to the identity of the debtor, or

(b)   the registration of a pending action in respect of a petition in bankruptcy is vacated, or

(c)   the bankruptcy order is annulled, or

(d)   the bankruptcy proceedings do not affect or have ceased to affect the statutory powers of the bankrupt under the Act,

the Registrar shall, as soon as practicable after receiving notice thereof and after making such enquiry and giving such notices (if any) as he shall deem necessary, take such action in the matter as he shall think advisable.

182   Mistake in a bankruptcy order

182   Where a mistake has occurred in a bankruptcy order or where any amendment in the register appears to be required, it shall be the duty of the Official Receiver or the trustee in bankruptcy, as soon as it comes to his knowledge, to notify such mistake or to suggest such amendment to the Registrar, who shall thereupon, after making such enquiries and giving such notices (if any) as he shall deem necessary, make such amendment in the register as may be necessary.

183   Trustee in bankruptcy vacating office

183   When a trustee in bankruptcy who has been registered as proprietor vacates his office as trustee because he ceases to be a person who is qualified to act as an insolvency practitioner under the Insolvency Act 1986 or any Act amending or replacing that Act or by release, resignation, death, removal from office or any other cause, the Official Receiver may be registered as proprietor; or, if some other person be appointed trustee, such person may be registered as proprietor on production of the evidence required by rule 176(1).

184   Where property becomes divested

184(1)   Where the Official Receiver or a trustee has been registered as proprietor, and, by reason of any act or omission or order, his estate and interest in the property has become divested, he may give notice to the Registrar in Form 58.

184(2)   The notice shall be entered on the register, together with a general restriction against dealings until further order.

184(3)   On such entry being made the Official Receiver or trustee shall be exonerated from all such liability (if any) as may affect him in respect of the property by reason of his name being entered on the register as proprietor thereof.

184(4)   Where such notice has been entered on the register an entry may be made under these rules without notice to the proprietor, or inquiry as to his execution of a transfer.

185   Administration orders and liquidation of a company

185(1)   When a company enters administration under the provisions of the Insolvency Act 1986 the order or the notice of appointment and the appointment of the administrator named therein shall on his application and on production of an office copy thereof be noted on the register.

185(2)   When a company is in liquidation, any order, appointment or resolution appointing a liquidator shall be noted in the register on his application and on production of either an office copy of the order or a copy of the appointment or resolution certified by the liquidator or his solicitor as being a true copy of the original together with such other evidence as the Registrar may require.

History
Rule 185 amended by the Enterprise Act 2002 (Insolvency) Order 2003 (SI 2003/2096) art.4 and Sch. para.41, as from September 15, 2003.

185A   Proceedings under the EC Regulation on insolvency proceedings

185A(1)   Any relevant person may apply for a note of a judgment opening insolvency proceedings to be entered in the register.

185A(2)   An application under paragraph (1) must be accompanied by such evidence as the Registrar may reasonably require.

185A(3)   Following an application under paragraph (1) if the Registrar is satisfied that the judgment opening insolvency proceedings has been made he may enter a note of the judgment in the register.

185A(4)   In this rule–

"judgment opening insolvency proceedings" means a judgment opening proceedings within the meaning of article 3(1) of the Regulation;

"relevant person" means any person or body authorised under the provisions of article 22 of the Regulation to request or require an entry to be made in the register in respect of the judgment opening insolvency proceedings the subject of the application;

"Regulation" means Council Regulation (EC) No 1346/2000.

Insolvency Practitioners Tribunal (Conduct of Investigations) Rules 1986

(SI 1986/952)

Made on 5 June 1986 by the Secretary of State for Trade and Industry under para.4(4) of Sch.1 to the Insolvency Act 1985 after consulting the Council on Tribunals in accordance with s.10 of the Tribunals and Inquiries Act 1971. Operative from 1 July 1986.

[**Note:** These Rules apply (with modifications) to limited liability partnerships by virtue of the Limited Liability Partnerships Regulations 2001 (SI 2001/1090) regs 1, 10(1) and Sch.6 Pt II para.9 as from April 6, 2001. Although these Rules were made under the former Insolvency Act 1985 they continue for the purposes of the consolidated legislation—see Sch.7 para.4(4) to the Insolvency Act 1986.]

1   Citation commencement and interpretation

1(1)   These Rules may be cited as the Insolvency Practitioners Tribunal (Conduct of Investigations) Rules 1986 and shall come into force on 1st July 1986.

1(2)   In these Rules:

   (a)   references to **"the Act"** are references to the Insolvency Act 1985;

   (b)   **"the applicant"** means an applicant for authorisation under section 5 of the Act or, where it is proposed to withdraw an authorisation granted under that section, the holder of the authorisation;

   (c)   **"Treasury Solicitor"** means the Solicitor for the affairs of Her Majesty's Treasury as provided in the Treasury Solicitor Act 1876; and

   (d)   **"a Scottish case"** means any case where at the time of the reference of the case to the Tribunal the applicant is either habitually resident in or has his principal place of business in Scotland.

2   Reference to the tribunal

2(1)   On referring a case to the tribunal under section 8(2) of the Act the relevant authority shall–

   (a)   send to the tribunal a copy of the written notice served by it on the applicant in pursuance of section 6(2) of the Act, together with a copy of the notification by the applicant that he wishes the case to be referred to the tribunal, and

   (b)   give notice to the applicant of the date on which the case has been referred by it to the tribunal and of the address to which any statement notice or other document required by these Rules to be given or sent to the tribunal is to be given or sent.

2(2)   Within 21 days of referring the case to the tribunal the relevant authority shall send to the tribunal such further information and copies of such other documents and records as it considers would be of assistance to the tribunal and shall, at the same time, send to the applicant such further information and copies of such other documents and records; or, if there is no such information or copies, the relevant authority shall within the said period notify the tribunal and the applicant to that effect.

3   Statement of the applicant

3(1)   Within 21 days after the relevant authority has sent to the applicant the material mentioned in Rule 2(2) or, as the case may be, after it has sent to him the notification mentioned in that Rule, the applicant shall send to the tribunal a statement of his grounds for requiring the case to be investigated by the tribunal specifying–

(a)   which matters of fact (if any) contained in the written notice served on him under section 6(2) of the Act he disputes,

(b)   any other matters which he considers should be drawn to the attention of the tribunal, and

(c)   the names and addresses of any witnesses whose evidence he wishes the tribunal to hear.

3(2)   The applicant shall, on sending the statement referred to in paragraph (1) of this Rule to the tribunal, send a copy to the relevant authority.

4   Appointment of solicitors and counsel to the tribunal

4   At any time after the case has been referred to it the tribunal may appoint the Treasury Solicitor and Counsel, or, in Scottish cases, may request the Treasury Solicitor to appoint a solicitor and may appoint Counsel, to exercise the functions of:

(a)   assisting the tribunal in seeking and presenting evidence in accordance with the requirements of the tribunal; and

(b)   representing the public interest in relation to the matters before the tribunal.

5   Investigation by the tribunal

5   After the receipt of the statement referred to in Rule 3 or, if no such statement is received, after the expiry of the period referred to in that Rule the tribunal shall investigate the case and make a report by carrying out such inquiries as it thinks appropriate for that purpose into and concerning the information, documents, records and matters placed before it under the provisions of Rules 2 and 3 above; and in carrying out such inquiries the requirements set out in the following Rules shall apply.

6   Methods of inquiry by the tribunal

6(1)   As soon as practicable after the tribunal has considered the subject matter of the investigation it shall notify the relevant authority and the applicant of the manner in which it proposes to conduct its inquiries and in particular whether oral evidence is to be taken.

6(2)   The tribunal shall give the relevant authority and the applicant a reasonable opportunity of making representations on the manner in which it proposes to conduct its inquiries and such representations may be made orally or in writing at the option of the relevant authority or the applicant as the case may be.

6(3)   After considering any representations that may be made under paragraph (2) above the tribunal shall notify the relevant authority and the applicant whether and, if so, in what respects, it has decided to alter the manner in which it proposes to carry out its inquiries.

6(4)   If at any subsequent stage in the investigation the tribunal proposes to make any material change in the manner in which its inquiries are to be carried out it shall notify the relevant authority and the applicant and the provisions of paragraphs (2) and (3) above shall apply accordingly.

7   Taking of evidence

7   When in the carrying out of its inquiries the tribunal:

(a)   wishes to examine a witness orally:

   (i)   it shall give notice to the applicant and the relevant authority of the time and place at which the examination will be held, and

   (ii)   the applicant and the relevant authority shall be entitled to be present at the examination by the tribunal of any witness and to put such additional questions to him as may appear to the tribunal to be relevant to the subject matter of the investigation; or

(b) takes into consideration documentary evidence or evidence in the form of computer or other non documentary records not placed before the tribunal under the provisions of Rules 2 and 3 above, the tribunal shall give the applicant and the relevant authority an opportunity of inspecting that evidence and taking copies or an appropriate record thereof.

8   Final representations

8   After the tribunal has completed the taking of such evidence as it considers necessary for the purpose of the investigation it shall give the applicant and the relevant authority a reasonable opportunity of making representations on the evidence and on the subject matter of the investigation generally. Such representations may be made orally or in writing at the option of the applicant or, as the case may be, of the relevant authority.

9   Representation at a hearing

9   At the hearing of oral representations or the taking of oral evidence–

(a) the applicant may be represented by Counsel or solicitor, or by any other person allowed by the tribunal to appear on his behalf; and

(b) the relevant authority may be represented by Counsel or solicitor or by any officer of the relevant authority.

10   Service of written representations

10   Where the relevant authority or the applicant makes any written representations to the tribunal in the course of its investigation the relevant authority or, as the case may be, the applicant shall send a copy of such representations to the other.

11   Hearings in public or in private

11(1)   The tribunal shall conduct its investigation in private and, save to the extent that these Rules provide for the hearing of oral representations or for the taking of oral evidence and the applicant requests that any such hearing be in public, no person other than those specified in Rule 9 above or having the leave of the tribunal shall be entitled to be present at any such hearing.

11(2)   Nothing in this Rule shall prevent a member of the Council on Tribunals or of its Scottish Committee from attending in his capacity as such a member any such hearing.

12   Notices

12   Any notice or other document required by these Rules to be given or sent may be given or sent by first class post.

13   Time limits

13   The tribunal may in any investigation permit the relevant authority or the applicant to send any document or perform any act after the time prescribed in the Rules for so sending or performing and such permission may be granted after any such time has expired.

14   Powers of chairman

14   Anything required or authorised to be done by the tribunal in the course of an investigation may be done by the chairman except–

(a) the settling of the manner in which the tribunal is to conduct its investigation,

(b) the hearing or consideration of any representations made by the relevant authority or the applicant, and

(c)   the taking of evidence, whether orally or in the form of documents or non-documentary records.

15   Period within which report to be made

15(1)   The tribunal shall make its report on the case to the relevant authority no later than four months after the date on which the case is referred to it under section 8(2) of the Act unless the relevant authority, on the application of the tribunal, permits the report to be made within such further period as the relevant authority may notify in writing to the tribunal.

15(2)   The relevant authority may only permit the report to be made within the further period referred to in paragraph (1) above where it appears to that authority that, through exceptional circumstances, the tribunal will be unable to make its report within the period of four months referred to in paragraph (1) above.

16   Scottish cases

16   Any hearing or oral representations under Rule 6(2) or 8 or any examination of a witness under Rule 7(a) in a Scottish case shall be made or held in Scotland unless the applicant consents to any such hearing or examination taking place elsewhere.

Insolvency (Scotland) Rules 1986

(SI 1986/1915 (S 139))

Made on 10 November 1986 by the Secretary of State under s.411 of the Insolvency Act 1986. Operative from 29 December 1986.

[**Note**: Changes made by the Insolvency (Scotland) Amendment Rules 2002 (SI 2002/2709 (S 10)), the Enterprise Act 2002 (Consequential Amendments) (Prescribed Part) (Scotland) Order 2003 (SI 2003/2108 (S 7)), the Insolvency (Scotland) Regulations 2003 (SI 2003/2109 (S 8)), the Insolvency (Scotland) Amendment Rules 2003 (SI 2003/2111 (S 9)), the Insolvency (Scotland) Amendment Rules 2006 (SI 2006/734 (S 6)), the Insolvency (Scotland) Amendment Rules 2007 (SI 2007/2537 (S 5)), the Act of Sederunt (Sheriff Court Rules) (Miscellaneous Amendments) 2008 (SI 2008/223), the Insolvency (Scotland) Rules 1986 Amendment Rules 2008 (SI 2008/393), the Insolvency (Scotland) Amendments Rules 2008 (SI 2008/662 (S 4)), the Bank Insolvency (Scotland) Rules 2009 (SI 2009/351), the Insolvency (Scotland) Amendment Rules 2009 (SI 2009/662 (S 1)) and the Insolvency (Scotland) Amendment Rules 2010 (SI 2010/688 (S 2)) have been incorporated into the text (in the case of pre-2003 legislation without annotation. In relation to modifications for financial collateral arrangements, see the Financial Collateral Arrangements (No.2) Regulations 2003 (SI 2003/3226) (below). References to the registrar of companies have been substituted throughout (or, on occasion, supplemented) by references to the Accountant in Bankruptcy, pursuant to the Scotland Act 1998 (Consequential Modifications) (No.2) Order 1999 (1999/1820) arts 1(2), 4 and Sch.2 para.141 and the Scotland Act 1998 (Commencement) Order 1998 (SI 1998/3178) art.3; and references to administration petitions, orders, etc. similarly adapted pursuant to the introduction of the new administration regime, by the Insolvency (Scotland) Regulations 2003 (SI 2003/2109 (S 8)) reg.6 and Sch.2 para.1, as from September 15, 2003. Any references to a "messenger-at-arms", a "sheriff officer" and an "officer of court" are to be construed as references to a judicial officer: see the Bankruptcy and Diligence etc. (Scotland) Act 2007 s.60. Pursuant to the Insolvency (Scotland) (Amendment) Rules 2009 (SI 2009/662 S1)) r.2 and Sch. para.1 the phrase "as soon as reasonably practicable" has been substituted for the word "forthwith" throughout Pt 1, as from April 6, 2009.]

ARRANGEMENT OF RULES

INTRODUCTORY PROVISIONS

0.1   Citation and commencement

0.1   These Rules may be cited as the Insolvency (Scotland) Rules 1986 and shall come into operation on 29th December 1986.

0.2   Interpretation

0.2(1)   In these Rules

"**the Act**" means the Insolvency Act 1986;

"**the Companies Act**" means the Companies Act 1985;

"**the Banking Act**" means the Banking Act 1987;

"**the Bankruptcy Act**" means the Bankruptcy (Scotland) Act 1985;

"**the Rules**" means the Insolvency (Scotland) Rules 1986;

"**accounting period**" in relation to the winding up of a company, shall be construed in accordance with section 52(1) and (6) of the Bankruptcy Act as applied by Rule 4.68;

"**authorised person**" is a reference to a person who is authorised pursuant to section 389A of the Act to act as nominee or supervisor of a voluntary arrangement proposed or approved under Part I or Part VIII of the Act.

"business day" means any day other than a Saturday, a Sunday, Christmas Day, Good Friday or a day which is a bank holiday in any part of Great Britain;

"centre of main interests" has the same meaning as in the EC Regulation;

"company" means a company which the courts in Scotland have jurisdiction to wind up;

"EC Regulation" means Council Regulation (EC) No. 1346/2000 of 29th May 2000 on insolvency proceedings;

"establishment" has the meaning given by Article 2(h) of the EC Regulation;

"insolvency proceedings" means any proceedings under the first group of Parts in the Act or under these Rules;

"main proceedings" means proceedings opened in accordance with Article 3(1) of the EC Regulation and falling within the definition of insolvency proceedings in Article 2(a) of the EC Regulation, and

    (a)   in relation to England and Wales and Scotland set out in Annex A to the EC Regulation under the heading "United Kingdom"; and

    (b)   in relation to another member State, set out in Annex A to the EC Regulation under the heading relating to that member State;

"member State liquidator" means a person falling within the definition of liquidator in Article 2(b) of the EC Regulation appointed in proceedings to which it applies in a member State other than the United Kingdom;

"prescribed part" has the same meaning as it does in section 176A(2)(a) of the Act;

"proxy-holder" shall be construed in accordance with Rule 7.14;

"receiver" means a receiver appointed under section 51 (Receivers (Scotland)); and

"responsible insolvency practitioner" means, in relation to any insolvency proceedings, the person acting as supervisor of a voluntary arrangement under Part I of the Act, or as administrator, receiver, liquidator or provisional liquidator;

"secondary proceedings" means proceedings opened in accordance with Articles 3(2) and 3(3) of the EC Regulation and falling within the definition of winding-up proceedings in Article 2(c) of the EC Regulation, and

    (a)   in relation to England and Wales and Scotland, set out in Annex B to the EC Regulation under the heading "United Kingdom"; and

    (b)   in relation to another member State, set out in Annex B to the EC Regulation under the heading relating to that member State;

"standard content" means—

    (a)   in relation to a notice to be published or advertised in the Edinburgh Gazette, the contents specified in Rule 7.21A; and

    (b)   in relation to a notice to be advertised in any other way, the contents specified in Rule 7.21B;

"territorial proceedings" means proceedings opened in accordance with Articles 3(2) and 3(4) of the EC Regulation and falling within the definition of insolvency proceedings in Article 2(a) of the EC Regulation, and

    (a)   in relation to England and Wales and Scotland, set out in Annex A to the EC Regulation under the heading "United Kingdom"; and

    (b)   in relation to another member State, set out in Annex A to the EC Regulation under the heading relating to that member State.

History

In r.0.2(1) the definition of "standard content" inserted by the Insolvency (Scotland) Amendment Rules 2010 (SI 2010/688 (S 2)) art.3 and Sch.1 para.1 as from April 6, 2010, subject to transitional provisions in art.4.

Previously in r.0.2(1) the definition of "prescribed part" inserted by the Enterprise Act 2002 (Consequential Amendments) (Prescribed Part) (Scotland) Order 2003 (SI 2003/2108 (S 7)) arts 2, 3 as from September 15, 2003.

Previously in r.0.2(1) the definitions of "centre of main interests", "EC Regulation", "establishment", "main proceedings", "member State liquidator", "secondary proceedings" and "territorial proceedings" inserted by the Insolvency (Scotland) Regulations 2003 (SI 2003/2109 (S 8)) regs 23, 24 as from September 8, 2003.

Previous to that in r.0.2(1) the definition of "authorised person" inserted by the Insolvency (Scotland) Amendment Rules 2002 (SI 2002/2709 (S 10)) rr.1, 3 as from January 1, 2003.

0.2(2) In these Rules, unless the context otherwise requires, any reference–

(a) to a section is a reference to a section of the Act;

(b) to a Rule is a reference to a Rule of the Rules;

(c) to a Part or a Schedule is a reference to a Part of, or Schedule to, the Rules;

(d) to a Chapter is a reference to a Chapter of the Part in which that reference is made.

0.2(3) A document or information given, delivered or sent in hard copy form under any Rule in Parts 1 and 2, or any other Rule applied by those parts, is sufficiently authenticated if it is signed by the person sending or supplying it.

History
See history note after r.0.2(4).

0.2(4) A document or information given, delivered or sent in electronic form under any Rule in Parts 1 and 2, or any other Rule applied by those parts, is sufficiently authenticated–

(a) if the identity of the sender is confirmed in a manner specified by the recipient, or

(b) where no such manner has been specified by the recipient, if the communication contains or is accompanied by a statement of the identity of the sender and the recipient has no reason to doubt the truth of that statement.

History
Rule 0.2(3), (4) inserted by the Insolvency (Scotland) Amendment Rules 2010 (SI 2010/688 (S 2)) art.3 and Sch.1 para.2 as from April 6, 2010, in all cases (see art.5).

0.3 Application

0.3 These Rules apply–

(a) to receivers appointed, and

(b) to all other insolvency proceedings which are commenced, on or after the date on which the Rules come into operation.

PART 1

COMPANY VOLUNTARY ARRANGEMENTS

CHAPTER 1

PRELIMINARY

1.1 Scope of this Part; interpretation

1.1(1) The Rules in this Part apply where, pursuant to Part I of the Act, it is intended to make and there is made a proposal to a company and to its creditors for a voluntary arrangement, that is to say, a composition in satisfaction of its debts or a scheme of arrangement of its affairs.

1.1(2)   In this Part–

   (a)   Chapter 2 applies where the proposal for the voluntary arrangement is made by the directors of the company and

     (i)   the company is neither in liquidation nor is in administration; and

     (ii)   no steps have been taken to obtain a moratorium under Schedule A1 to the Act in connection with the proposal;

   (b)   Chapter 3 applies where the company is in liquidation or administration and the proposal is made by the liquidator or (as the case may be) the administrator, he in either case being the nominee for the purposes of the proposal;

   (c)   Chapter 4 applies in the same case as Chapter 3, but where the nominee is not the liquidator or administrator;

   (d)   Chapters 5, 6, and 8 apply in all the three cases mentioned in sub-paragraphs (a) to (c) above; and

   (e)   Chapter 7 applies where the proposal is made by the directors of an eligible company with a view to obtaining a moratorium.

History

In r.1.1(2)(d) the figures "5, 6 and 8" substituted for "5 and 6" by the Insolvency (Scotland) Regulations 2003 (SI 2003/2109 (S 8)) regs 23, 25 as from September 8, 2003.

    Previous to that in r.1.1(2) subpara.(a) substituted for the same and subparas (c), (d) and (e) substituted for the former text of (c) and (d) by the Insolvency (Scotland) Amendment Rules 2002 (SI 2002/2709 (S 10)) rr.1, 4(1) and Sch. Pt 1 para.1(1)(a), (b) as from January 1, 2003 subject to transitional provisions contained in r.4(2).

1.1(3)   In Chapters 3, 4 and 5 the liquidator or the administrator is referred to as the **"responsible insolvency practitioner"**.

1.1(4)   In this Part, a reference to an **"eligible company"** is to a company that is eligible for a moratorium in accordance with paragraph 2 of Schedule A1 to the Act.

History

Rule 1.1(4) inserted by the Insolvency (Scotland) Amendment Rules 2002 (SI 2002/2709 (S 10)) rr.1, 4(1) and Sch. Pt 1 para.1(1)(c) as from January 1, 2003 subject to transitional provisions contained in r.4(2).

CHAPTER 1A

THE GIVING OF NOTICE AND THE SUPPLY OF DOCUMENTS

1.1A   Application

1.1A(1)   Subject to paragraph (2), this Chapter applies where a notice or other document is required to be given, delivered or sent under this Part of these Rules.

1.1A(2)   This Chapter does not apply to–

   (a)   the lodging of any application, or other document, with the court;

   (b)   the service of any application, or other document, lodged with the court;

   (c)   the service of any order of the court; or

   (d)   the submission of documents to the registrar of companies.

History

See history note after r.1.1D.

1.1B Electronic delivery

1.1B(1) Unless in any particular case some other form of delivery is required by the Act or these Rules or any order of the court, a notice or other document may be given, delivered or sent by electronic means provided that the intended recipient of the notice or other document has–

(a) consented (whether in the specific case or generally) to electronic delivery (and has not revoked that consent); and

(b) provided an electronic address for delivery.

1.1B(2) Where a nominee or supervisor gives, sends or delivers a notice or other document to any person by electronic means, it must contain or be accompanied by a statement that the recipient may request a hard copy of the notice or document, and specify a telephone number, e-mail address and postal address that may be used to make such a request.

1.1B(3) Where a hard copy of the notice or other document is requested it must be sent within 5 business days of receipt of the request by the nominee or supervisor, who may not make a charge for sending it in that form.

1.1B(4) In the absence of evidence to the contrary, a notice or other document shall be presumed to have been delivered where–

(a) the sender can produce a copy of the electronic message which–

(i) contained the notice or other document, or to which the notice or other document was attached; and

(ii) shows the time and date the message was sent; and

(b) that electronic message was sent to the address supplied under paragraph (1)(b).

1.1B(5) A message sent electronically is deemed to have been delivered to the recipient no later than 9.00 am on the next business day after it was sent.

History
See history note after r.1.1D.

1.1C Use of websites by nominee or supervisor

1.1C(1) This Rule applies for the purpose of section 246B.

1.1C(2) A nominee or supervisor required to give, deliver or send a document to any person may (other than in a case where personal service is required) satisfy that requirement by sending that person a notice–

(a) stating that the document is available for viewing and downloading on a website;

(b) specifying the address of that website together with any password necessary to view and download the document from that website; and

(c) containing a statement that the recipient of the notice may request a hard copy of the document, and specifying a telephone number, e-mail address and postal address which may be used to make such a request.

1.1C(3) Where a notice to which this Rule applies is sent, the document to which it relates must–

(a) be available on the website for a period of not less than 3 months after the date on which the notice is sent; and

(b) be in such a format as to enable it to be downloaded from the website within a reasonable time of an electronic request being made for it to be downloaded.

1.1C(4) Where a hard copy of the document is requested it must be sent within 5 business days of the receipt of the request by the nominee or supervisor, who may not make a charge for sending it in that form.

1.1C(5) Where a document is given, delivered or sent to a person by means of a website in accordance with this Rule, it is deemed to have been delivered–

(a) when the document was first made available on the website, or

(b) if later, when the notice under paragraph (2) was delivered to that person.

History
See history note after r.1.1D.

1.1D   Special provision on account of expense as to website use

1.1D(1) Where the court is satisfied that the expense of sending notices in accordance with Rule 1.1C would, on account of the number of persons entitled to receive them, be disproportionate to the benefit of sending notices in accordance with that Rule, it may order that the requirement to give, deliver or send a relevant document to any person may (other than in a case where personal service is required) be satisfied by the nominee or supervisor sending each of those persons a notice–

(a) stating that all relevant documents will be made available for viewing and downloading on a website;

(b) specifying the address of that website together with any password necessary to view and download a relevant document from that site; and

(c) containing a statement that the person to whom the notice is given, delivered or sent may at any time request that hard copies of all, or specific, relevant documents are sent to that person, and specifying a telephone number, e-mail address and postal address which may be used to make that request.

1.1D(2) A document to which this Rule relates must–

(a) be available on the website for a period of not less than 12 months from the date when it was first made available on the website or, if later, from the date upon which the notice was sent, and

(b) be in such a format as to enable it to be downloaded from the website within a reasonable time of an electronic request being made for it to be downloaded.

1.1D(3) Where hard copies of relevant documents have been requested, they must be sent by the nominee or supervisor–

(a) within 5 business days of the receipt by the nominee or supervisor of the request to be sent hard copies, in the case of relevant documents first appearing on the website before the request was received, or

(b) within 5 business days from the date a relevant document first appears on the website, in all other cases.

1.1D(4) A nominee or supervisor must not require a person making a request under paragraph (3) to pay a fee for the supply of the document.

1.1D(5) Where a relevant document is given, delivered or sent to a person by means of a website in accordance with this Rule, it is deemed to have been delivered–

(a) when the relevant document was first made available on the website, or

(b) if later, when the notice under paragraph (1) was delivered to that person.

1.1D(6)   In this Rule a relevant document means any document which the nominee or supervisor is first required to give, deliver or send to any person after the court has made an order under paragraph (1).

History
Rules 1.1A–1.1D inserted by the Insolvency (Scotland) Amendment Rules 2010 (SI 2010/688 (S 2)) art.3 and Sch.1 para.3 as from April 6, 2010, in all cases (see art.5).

CHAPTER 2

PROPOSAL BY DIRECTORS

1.2   Preparation of proposal

1.2   [Omitted by the Insolvency (Scotland) Amendment Rules 2010 (SI 2010/688 (S 2)) art.3 and Sch.1 para.4 as from April 6, 2010, in all cases (see art.5).]

1.3   Contents of proposal

1.3(1)   The directors' proposal shall provide a short explanation why, in their opinion, a voluntary arrangement under Part I of the Act is desirable, and give reasons why the company's creditors may be expected to concur with such an arrangement.

1.3(2)   The following matters shall be stated, or otherwise dealt with, in the directors' proposal–

(a) the following matters, so far as within the directors' immediate knowledge–

    (i)   the company's assets, with an estimate of their respective values;

    (ii) the extent (if any) to which the assets are subject to any security in favour of any creditors;

    (iii) the extent (if any) to which particular assets of the company are to be excluded from the voluntary arrangement;

(b) particulars of any property other than assets of the company itself, which is proposed to be included in the arrangement, the source of such property and the terms on which it is to be made available for inclusion;

(c) the nature and amount of the company's liabilities (so far as within the directors' immediate knowledge), the manner in which they are proposed to be met, modified, postponed or otherwise dealt with by means of the arrangement, and (in particular)–

    (i)   how it is proposed to deal with preferential creditors (defined in section 386) and creditors who are, or claim to be, secured;

    (ii) how persons connected with the company (being creditors) are proposed to be treated under the arrangement; and

    (iii) whether there are, to the directors' knowledge, any circumstances giving rise to the possibility, in the event that the company should go into liquidation, of claims under–

        section 242 (gratuitous alienations),

        section 243 (unfair preferences),

        section 244 (extortionate credit transactions), or

        section 245 (floating charges invalid);

    and, where any such circumstances are present, whether, and if so how, it is proposed under the voluntary arrangement to make provision for wholly or partly indemnifying the company in respect of such claims;

(ca) to the best of the directors' knowledge and belief–

(i) an estimate of the value of the prescribed part, should the company go into liquidation if the proposal for the voluntary arrangement is not accepted, whether or not section 176A is to be disapplied, and

(ii) an estimate of the value of the company's net property on the date that the estimate is made,

provided that such estimates shall not be required to include any information the disclosure of which could seriously prejudice the commercial interests of the company, but if such information is excluded the estimates shall be accompanied by a statement to that effect;

(d) whether any, and if so what, cautionary obligations (including guarantees) have been given of the company's debts by other persons, specifying which (if any) of the cautioners are persons connected with the company;

(e) the proposed duration of the voluntary arrangement;

(f) the proposed dates of distributions to creditors, with estimates of their amounts;

(fa) how it is proposed to deal with the claim of any person who is bound by the arrangement by virtue of section 5(2)(b)(ii);

(g) the amount proposed to be paid to the nominee (as such) by way of remuneration and expenses;

(h) the manner in which it is proposed that the supervisor of the arrangement should be remunerated and his expenses defrayed;

(i) whether, for the purposes of the arrangement, any cautionary obligations (including guarantees) are to be offered by directors, or other persons, and whether (if so) any security is to be given or sought;

(j) the manner in which funds held for the purposes of the arrangement are to be banked, invested or otherwise dealt with pending distribution to creditors;

(k) the manner in which funds held for the purpose of payment to creditors, and not so paid on the termination of the arrangement, are to be dealt with;

(l) the manner in which the business of the company is being and is proposed to be conducted during the course of the arrangement;

(m) details of any further credit facilities which it is intended to arrange for the company and how the debts so arising are to be paid;

(n) the functions which are to be undertaken by the supervisor of the arrangement;

(o) the name, address and qualification of the person proposed as supervisor of the voluntary arrangement, and confirmation that he is either qualified to act as an insolvency practitioner in relation to the company or is an authorised person in relation to the company;

(p) whether the EC Regulation will apply and, if so, whether the proceedings will be main proceedings or territorial proceedings; and

(q) such other matters (if any) as the directors consider appropriate for ensuring that members and creditors are enabled to reach an informed decision on the proposal.

History
In r.1.3(2) subpara.(q) inserted by the Insolvency (Scotland) Amendment Rules 2010 (SI 2010/688 (S 2)) art.3 and Sch.1 para.5 as from April 6, 2010, subject to art.6.
    Previously in r.1.3(2) subpara.(ca) inserted by the Enterprise Act 2002 (Consequential Amendments) (Prescribed Part) (Scotland) Order 2003 (SI 2003/2108 (S 7)) arts 2, 4 as from September 2003.
    Previously in r.1.3(2) subpara.(p) inserted by the Insolvency (Scotland) Regulations 2003 (SI 2003/2109 (S 8)) regs 23, 25 as from September 8, 2003. In r.1.3(2) subpara.(fa) inserted and subpara.(o) substituted (the DTI has advised that the word "; and" at the end of subpara.(o) is a drafting error and will be corrected in future legislation) by

the Insolvency (Scotland) Amendment Rules 2002 (SI 2002/2709 (S 10)) rr.1, 4(1) and Sch. Pt 1 para.2 as from January 1, 2003 subject to transitional provisions contained in r.4(2).

1.3(3) With the agreement in writing of the nominee, the directors' proposal may be amended at any time up to delivery of the nominee's report to the court under section 2(2).

History
In r.1.3(3) "nominee's" substituted for "former's" by the Insolvency (Scotland) Amendment Rules 2010 (SI 2010/688 (S 2)) art.3 and Sch.1 para.6 as from April 6, 2010, subject to transitional provisions in art.4.

1.4 Notice to intended nominee

1.4(1) The directors shall give to the intended nominee written notice of their proposal.

1.4(2) The notice, accompanied by a copy of the proposal, shall be delivered either to the nominee himself, or to a person authorised to take delivery of documents on his behalf.

1.4(3) If the intended nominee agrees to act, he shall cause a copy of the notice to be endorsed to the effect that it has been received by him on a specified date; and the period of 28 days referred to in section 2(2) then runs from that date.

1.4(4) The copy of the notice so endorsed shall be returned by the nominee as soon as is reasonably practicable to the directors at an address specified by them in the notice for that purpose.

1.5 Statement of affairs

1.5(1) The directors shall, at the same time as the proposal is delivered to the nominee, deliver to the nominee a statement of the company's affairs.

History
Rule 1.5(1) substituted by the Insolvency (Scotland) Amendment Rules 2010 (SI 2010/688 (S 2)) art.3 and Sch.1 para.7 as from April 6, 2010, subject to transitional provisions in art.4.

1.5(2) The statement shall comprise the following particulars (supplementing or amplifying, so far as is necessary for clarifying the state of the company's affairs, those already given in the directors' proposal)–

(a) a list of the company's assets, divided into such categories as are appropriate for easy identification, with estimated values assigned to each category;

(b) in the case of any property on which a claim against the company is wholly or partly secured, particulars of the claim and its amount and of how and when the security was created;

(c) the names and addresses of the company's preferential creditors (defined in section 386), with the amounts of their respective claims;

(d) the names and addresses of the company's unsecured creditors, with the amounts of their respective claims;

(e) particulars of any debts owed by or to the company to or by persons connected with it;

(f) the names and addresses of the company's members and details of their respective shareholdings; and

(g) such other particulars (if any) as the nominee may in writing require to be furnished for the purposes of making his report to the court on the directors' proposal.

1.5(3) The statement of affairs shall be made up to a date not earlier than 2 weeks before the date of the notice given by the directors to the nominee under Rule 1.4. However the nominee may allow an extension of that period to the nearest practicable date (not earlier than 2 months before the date of the notice under Rule 1.4); and if he does so, he shall give his reasons in his report to the court on the directors' proposal.

1.5(4) The statement shall be certified as correct, to the best of the relevant director's knowledge and belief, by one director.

History
In r.1.5(4) "the relevant director's" substituted for "their" and "one director" substituted for "two or more directors of the company or by the company secretary and at least one director (other than the secretary himself)" by the Insolvency (Scotland) Amendment Rules 2010 (SI 2010/688 (S 2)) art.3 and Sch.1 para.8 as from April 6, 2010, subject to transitional provisions in art.4.

1.6 Additional disclosure for assistance of nominee

1.6(1) If it appears to the nominee that he cannot properly prepare his report on the basis of information in the directors' proposal and statement of affairs, he may call on the directors to provide him with–

(a) further and better particulars as to the circumstances in which, and the reasons why, the company is insolvent or (as the case may be) threatened with insolvency;

(b) particulars of any previous proposals which have been made in respect of the company under Part I of the Act;

(c) any further information with respect to the company's affairs which the nominee thinks necessary for the purposes of his report.

1.6(2) The nominee may call on the directors to inform him, with respect to any person who is, or at any time in the 2 years preceding the notice under Rule 1.4 has been, a director or officer of the company, whether and in what circumstances (in those 2 years or previously) that person–

(a) has been concerned in the affairs of any other company (whether or not incorporated in Scotland) which has become insolvent, or

(b) has had his estate sequestrated, granted a trust deed for his creditors, been adjudged bankrupt or compounded or entered into an arrangement with his creditors.

1.6(3) For the purpose of enabling the nominee to consider their proposal and prepare his report on it, the directors must give the nominee such access to the company's accounts and records as the nominee may require.

History
In r.1.6(3) "the nominee such access to the company's accounts and records as the nominee may require" substituted for "him access to the company's accounts and records" by the Insolvency (Scotland) Amendment Rules 2010 (SI 2010/688 (S 2)) art.3 and Sch.1 para.9 as from April 6, 2010, subject to transitional provisions in art.4.

1.7 Nominee's report on the proposal

1.7(1) With his report to the court under section 2 the nominee shall lodge–

(a) a copy of the directors' proposal (with amendments, if any, authorised under Rule 1.3(3));

(b) a copy or summary of the company's statement of affairs.

1.7(2) If the nominee makes known his opinion that the directors' proposal has a reasonable prospect of being approved and implemented and that meetings of the company and its creditors should be summoned under section 3, his report shall have annexed to it his comments on the proposal. If his opinion is otherwise, he shall give his reasons for that opinion.

History
In r.1.7(2) the words "that the directors' proposal has a reasonable prospect of being approved and implemented and" inserted by the Insolvency (Scotland) Amendment Rules 2002 (SI 2002/2709 (S 10)) rr.1, 4(1) and Sch. Pt 1 para.3 as from January 1, 2003 subject to transitional provisions contained in r.4(2).

1.7(3)   The nominee shall send a copy of his report and of his comments (if any) to the company. Any director, member or creditor of the company is entitled, at all reasonable times on any business day, to inspect the report and comments.

1.8   Replacement of nominee

1.8(1)   Where a person other than the nominee intends to apply to the court under section 2(4) for the nominee to be replaced (except in any case where the nominee has died), he shall give to the nominee at least 5 business days' notice of his application.

1.8(2)   Where the nominee intends to apply to the court under section 2(4) to be replaced, he shall give at least 5 business days' notice of his application to the person intending to make the proposal.

[FORM 1.8 (Scot)]

History
In r.1.8(1), (2) "5 business" substituted for "7" by the Insolvency (Scotland) Amendment Rules 2010 (SI 2010/688 (S 2)) art.3 and Sch.1 para.10 as from April 6, 2010, subject to transitional provisions in art.4.

1.8(3)   No appointment of a replacement nominee shall be made by the court unless there is lodged in court a statement by the replacement nominee–

    (a)   indicating his consent to act; and

    (b)   that he is qualified to act as an insolvency practitioner in relation to the company or is an authorised person in relation to the company.

History
Rule 1.8 substituted by the Insolvency (Scotland) Amendment Rules 2002 (SI 2002/2709 (S 10)) rr.1, 4(1) and Sch. Pt 1 para.4 as from January 1, 2003 subject to transitional provisions contained in r.4(2).

1.9   Summoning of meetings under section 3

1.9(1)   If in his report the nominee states that in his opinion meetings of the company and its creditors should be summoned to consider the directors' proposal, the date on which the meetings are to be held shall be not more than 28 days from the date on which he lodged his report in court under section 2.

History
In r.1.9(1) "less than 14, nor" formerly appearing after "shall be" omitted by the Insolvency (Scotland) Amendment Rules 2010 (SI 2010/688 (S 2)) art.3 and Sch.1 para.11 as from April 6, 2010, subject to art.6.

1.9(2)   The notice summoning the meeting shall specify the court in which the nominee's report under section 2 has been lodged and shall state the effect of Rule 1.16A(2) to (4), and with each notice there shall be sent–

    (a)   a copy of the directors' proposal;

    (b)   a copy of the statement of affairs or, if the nominee thinks fit, a summary of it (the summary to include a list of creditors and the amount of their debts);

    (c)   the nominee's comments on the proposal; and

    (d)   forms of proxy.

History
In r.1.9(2) "and shall state the effect of Rule 1.16A(2) to (4)," and subpara.(d) inserted by the Insolvency (Scotland) Amendment Rules 2010 (SI 2010/688 (S 2)) art.3 and Sch.1 paras 12 and 13 as from April 6, 2010, subject to transitional provisions in art.4.

1.9(3)   Notices calling the meetings shall be sent by the nominee at least 14 days before the day fixed for them to be held–

(a) in the case of the creditors' meeting, to all the creditors specified in the statement of affairs, and any other creditors of the company of whose address the nominee is aware; and

(b) in the case of the meeting of members of the company, to all persons who are, to the best of the nominee's belief, members of it.

History
Rule 1.9(3) inserted by the Insolvency (Scotland) Amendment Rules 2010 (SI 2010/688 (S 2)) art.3 and Sch.1 para.14 as from April 6, 2010, subject to transitional provisions in art.4.

CHAPTER 3

PROPOSAL BY ADMINISTRATOR OR LIQUIDATOR WHERE HE IS THE NOMINEE

1.10 Preparation of proposal

1.10 The responsible insolvency practitioner's proposal shall specify–

(a) all such matters as under Rule 1.3 (subject to paragraph (c) below) in Chapter 2 the directors of the company would be required to include in a proposal by them with, in addition, where the company is in administration or liquidation, the names and addresses of the company's preferential creditors (defined in section 386), with the amounts of their respective claims, and

(c) the administrator or liquidator shall include, in place of the estimate referred to in Rule 1.3(2)(ca), a statement which contains–

  (i) to the best of his knowledge and belief–

    (aa) an estimate of the value of the prescribed part (whether or not he proposes to make an application under section 176A(5) or section 176A(3) applies), and

    (bb) an estimate of the value of the company's net property,

    provided that such estimates shall not be required to include any information the disclosure of which could seriously prejudice the commercial interests of the company, but if such information is excluded the estimates shall be accompanied by a statement to that effect, and

  (ii) whether, and, if so, why, he proposes to make an application under section 176A(5).

History
In r.1.10(a) "or liquidation" inserted and subpara.(b) omitted by the Insolvency (Scotland) Amendment Rules 2010 (SI 2010/688 (S 2)) art.3 and Sch.1 para.15 as from April 6, 2010, subject to art.6.
  Previously in r.1.10(a) the words "(subject to paragraph (c) below)" and para.(c) inserted by the Enterprise Act 2002 (Consequential Amendments) (Prescribed Part) (Scotland) Order 2003 (SI 2003/2108 (S 7)) art.4 as from September 15, 2003.

1.11 Summoning of meetings under section 3

1.11(1) Notices calling meetings under section 3(2) shall be sent by the responsible insolvency practitioner at least 14 days before the day fixed for them to be held–

(a) in the case of the creditors' meeting, to all the creditors specified in the statement of affairs, and any other creditors of the company of whose address the responsible insolvency practitioner is aware; and

(b) in the case of the meeting of members of the company, to all persons who are, to the best of the responsible insolvency practitioner's belief, members of it.

History
Rule 1.11(1) substituted by the Insolvency (Scotland) Amendment Rules 2010 (SI 2010/688 (S 2)) art.3 and Sch.1 para.16 as from April 6, 2010, subject to transitional provisions in art.4.

1.11(2) With each notice summoning the meeting, there shall be sent–

(a) a copy of the responsible insolvency practitioner's proposal;

(b) a copy of the company's statement of affairs or, if he thinks fit, a summary of it (the summary to include a list of the creditors and the amount of their debts);

(c) a statement of the effect of Rule 1.16A(2) to (4); and

(d) forms of proxy.

History
Rule 1.11(2)(c), (d) inserted by the Insolvency (Scotland) Amendment Rules 2010 (SI 2010/688 (S 2)) art.3 and Sch.1 para.17 as from April 6, 2010, subject to transitional provisions in art.4.

CHAPTER 4

PROPOSAL BY ADMINISTRATOR OR LIQUIDATOR WHERE ANOTHER INSOLVENCY PRACTITIONER IS THE NOMINEE

1.12 Preparation of proposal and notice to nominee

1.12(1) The responsible insolvency practitioner shall give notice to the intended nominee, and prepare his proposal for a voluntary arrangement, in the same manner as is required of the directors in the case of a proposal by them, under Chapter 2.

1.12(2) Rule 1.2 applies to the responsible insolvency practitioner as it applies to the directors; and Rule 1.4 applies as regards the action to be taken by the nominee.

1.12(3) The content of the proposal shall be as required by Rule 1.10.

1.12(4) Rule 1.6 applies, in respect of the information to be provided to the nominee, reading references to the directors as referring to the responsible insolvency practitioner.

1.12(5) With the proposal the responsible insolvency practitioner shall provide a copy of the company's statement of affairs.

1.12(6) Rules 1.7 to 1.9 apply as regards a proposal under this Chapter as they apply to a proposal under Chapter 2.

CHAPTER 5

MEETINGS

1.13 General

1.13 [Omitted by the Insolvency (Scotland) Amendment Rules 2010 (SI 2010/688 (S 2)) art.3 and Sch.1 para.18 as from April 6, 2010, subject to transitional provisions in art.4.]

1.14 Summoning of meetings

1.14(1) In fixing the date, time and place for the creditors' meeting and the company meeting, the nominee must have regard primarily to the convenience of the creditors.

History
In r.1.14(1) "nominee must" substituted for "person summoning the meetings ("the convenor") shall" by the Insolvency (Scotland) Amendment Rules 2010 (SI 2010/688 (S 2)) art.3 and Sch.1 para.19 as from April 6, 2010, subject to transitional provisions in art.4.

1.14(2)   The meetings may be held on the same day or on different days. If held on the same day, the meetings shall be held in the same place, but in either case the creditors' meeting shall be fixed for a time in advance of the company meeting.

1.14(3)   Where the meetings are not held on the same day, they shall be held within 5 business days of each other.

History

In r.1.14(3) "5 business" substituted for "7" by the Insolvency (Scotland) Amendment Rules 2010 (SI 2010/688 (S 2)) art.3 and Sch.1 para.20 as from April 6, 2010, subject to transitional provisions in art.4.

Previously r.1.14(2) and (3) substituted for the former text of r.1.14(2) by the Insolvency (Scotland) Amendment Rules 2002 (SI 2002/2709 (S 10)) rr.1, 4(1) and Sch. Pt 1 para.5 as from January 1, 2003 subject to transitional provisions contained in r.4(2).

1.14(4)   Meetings shall, in all cases, be summoned for commencement between 10.00 and 16.00 hours on a business day.

History

Rule 1.14(4) inserted by the Insolvency (Scotland) Amendment Rules 2010 (SI 2010/688 (S 2)) art.3 and Sch.1 para.21 as from April 6, 2010, subject to transitional provisions in art.4.

1.14ZA   Remote attendance at meetings

1.14ZA(1)   This Rule applies to a request to the nominee of a meeting under section 246A(9) to specify a place for the meeting.

1.14ZA(2)   The request must be accompanied by–

(a) in the case of a request by creditors, a list of the creditors making (or concurring with) the request and the amounts of those creditors' respective debts in the insolvency proceedings in question,

(b) in the case of a request by members, a list of the members making (or concurring with) the request and those members' voting rights, and

(c) from each person concurring, written confirmation of that person's concurrence.

1.14ZA(3)   The request must be made within 7 business days of the date on which the nominee sent the notice of the meeting in question.

1.14ZA(4)   Where the nominee considers that the request has been properly made in accordance with the Act and these Rules, the nominee must–

(a) give notice (to all those previously given notice of the meeting)–

(i)   that the meeting is to be held at a specified place, and

(ii) whether the date and time of the meeting are to remain the same or not;

(b) specify a time, date and place for the meeting, the date of which must not be more than 28 days after the original date for the meeting; and

(c) give at least 14 days notice of the time, date and place of the meeting (to all those previously given notice of the meeting),

and the notices required by subparagraphs (a) and (c) may be given at the same or different times.

1.14ZA(5)   Where the nominee has specified a place for the meeting in response to a request to which this Rule applies, the chairman of the meeting must attend the meeting by being present in person at that place.

History

Rule 1.14ZA inserted by the Insolvency (Scotland) Amendment Rules 2010 (SI 2010/688 (S 2)) art.3 and Sch.1 para.22 as from April 6, 2010, in all cases (see art.5).

1.14A   The chairman at meetings

1.14A(1)   Subject as follows, at both the creditors' meeting and the company meeting, and at any combined meeting, the convenor shall be chairman.

1.14A(2)   If for any reason he is unable to attend, he may nominate another person to act as chairman in his place; but a person so nominated must be–

     (a)   a person qualified to act as an insolvency practitioner in relation to the company;

     (b)   an authorised person in relation to the company; or

     (c)   an employee of the convenor or his firm who is experienced in insolvency matters.

History
Rule 1.14A inserted by the Insolvency (Scotland) Amendment Rules 2002 (SI 2002/2709 (S 10)) rr.1, 4(1) and Sch. Pt 1 para.6 as from January 1, 2003 subject to transitional provisions contained in r.4(2).

1.14AA   Chairman of meeting as proxy holder

1.14AA   At any meeting, the chairman shall not, by virtue of any proxy held by him, vote to increase or reduce the amount of the remuneration or expenses of the nominee or the supervisor of the proposed arrangement, unless the proxy specifically directs him to vote in that way.

History
Rule 1.14AA inserted by the Insolvency (Scotland) Amendment Rules 2010 (SI 2010/688 (S 2)) art.3 and Sch.1 para.23 as from April 6, 2010, subject to transitional provisions in art.4.

1.15   Attendance by company officers

1.15(1)   At least 14 days' notice to attend the meetings shall be given by the convenor to–

     (a)   all directors of the company, and

     (b)   any persons in whose case the convenor thinks that their presence is required as being officers of the company or as having been directors or officers of it at any time in the 2 years immediately preceding the date of the notice.

1.15(2)   The chairman may, if he thinks fit, exclude any present or former director or officer from attendance at a meeting, either completely or for any part of it; and this applies whether or not a notice under this Rule has been sent to the person excluded.

1.15A   Entitlement to vote (creditors)

1.15A(1)   Subject as follows, every creditor who has notice of the creditors' meeting is entitled to vote at the meeting or any adjournment of it.

1.15A(2)   Votes are calculated according to the amount of the creditor's debt as at the date of the meeting or, where the company is being wound up or is subject to an administration order, the date of its going into liquidation or (as the case may be) of the administration order.

1.15A(3)   A creditor may vote in respect of a debt for an unliquidated amount or any debt whose value is not ascertained and for the purposes of voting (but not otherwise) his debt shall be valued at £1 unless the chairman agrees to put a higher value on it.

1.15A(4)   A creditor is entitled to vote at any meeting if the creditor, either at the meeting or before it, has submitted the creditor's claim to the responsible insolvency practitioner and the creditor's claim has been accepted in whole or in part.

History
Rule 1.15A(4) inserted by the Insolvency (Scotland) Amendment Rules 2010 (SI 2010/688 (S 2)) art.3 and Sch.1 para.24 as from April 6, 2010, subject to transitional provisions in art.4.
     See also history note after r.1.15B.

1.15AA   Entitlement to vote (members)

1.15AA(1)   Members of a company at their meeting shall vote according to the rights attaching to their shares in accordance with the company's articles of association.

1.15AA(2)   Reference in this Rule to a person's shares include any other interests which that person may have as a member of the company.

History
Rule 1.15AA inserted by the Insolvency (Scotland) Amendment Rules 2010 (SI 2010/688 (S 2)) art.3 and Sch.1 para.25 as from April 6, 2010, subject to transitional provisions in art.4.

1.15B   Procedure for admission of creditors' claims for voting purposes

1.15B(1)   Subject as follows, at any creditors' meeting the chairman shall ascertain the entitlement of persons wishing to vote and shall admit or reject their claims accordingly.

1.15B(2)   The chairman may admit or reject a claim in whole or in part.

1.15B(3)   The chairman's decision on any matter under this Rule or under paragraph (3) of Rule 1.15A is subject to appeal to the court by any creditor or member of the company.

1.15B(4)   If the chairman is in doubt whether a claim should be admitted or rejected, he shall mark it as objected to and allow votes to be cast in respect of it, subject to such votes being subsequently declared invalid if the objection to the claim is sustained.

1.15B(5)   If on an appeal the chairman's decision is reversed or varied, or votes are declared invalid, the court may order another meeting to be summoned, or make such order as it thinks just.

The court's power to make an order under this paragraph is exercisable only if it considers that the circumstances giving rise to the appeal give rise to unfair prejudice or material irregularity.

1.15B(6)   An application to the court by way of appeal against the chairman's decision shall not be made after the end of the period of 28 days beginning with the first day on which the report required by section 4(6) has been made to the court.

1.15B(7)   The chairman is not personally liable for any expenses incurred by any person in respect of an appeal under this Rule.

History
Rules 1.15A and 1.15B inserted by the Insolvency (Scotland) Amendment Rules 2002 (SI 2002/2709 (S 10)) rr.1, 4(1) and Sch. Pt 1 para.7 as from January 1, 2003 subject to transitional provisions contained in r.4(2).

1.16   Adjournments

1.16(1)   If the chairman thinks fit, the creditors' meeting and the company meeting may be held together.

1.16(2)   The chairman may, and shall if it is so resolved at the meeting in question, adjourn that meeting for not more than 14 days.

1.16(3)   If there are subsequently further adjournments, the final adjournment shall not be to a day later than 14 days after the date on which the meeting in question was originally held.

1.16(4)   In the case of a proposal by the directors, if the meetings are adjourned under paragraph (2), notice of the fact shall be given by the nominee as soon as is reasonably practicable to the court.

1.16(5)   If following the final adjournment of the creditors' meeting the proposal (with or without modifications) has not been approved by the creditors it is deemed rejected.

1.16(6)   During a meeting, the chairman may, in the chairman's discretion and without an adjournment, declare the meeting suspended for any period up to one hour.

History
Rule 1.16(6) inserted by the Insolvency (Scotland) Amendment Rules 2010 (SI 2010/688 (S 2)) art.3 and Sch.1 para.26 as from April 6, 2010, subject to transitional provisions in art.4.
   Previously r.1.16 substituted by the Insolvency (Scotland) Amendment Rules 2002 (SI 2002/2709 (S 10)) rr.1, 4(1) and Sch. Pt 1 para.8 as from January 1, 2003 subject to transitional provisions contained in r.4(2).

1.16A   Requisite majorities at creditors' meetings

1.16A(1)   Subject to paragraph (2), a resolution is passed at a creditors' meeting when a majority (in value) of those present and voting in person or by proxy have voted in favour of it.

1.16A(2)   A resolution to approve the proposal or a modification is passed when a majority of three quarters or more (in value) of those present and voting in person or by proxy have voted in favour of it.

1.16A(3)   There is to be left out of account a creditor's vote in respect of any claim or part of a claim–

- (a) where written notice of the claim was not given, either at the meeting or before it, to the chairman or nominee;

- (b) where the claim or part is secured;

- (c) where the claim is in respect of a debt wholly or partly on, or secured by, a current bill of exchange or promissory note, unless the creditor is willing–

   - (i) to treat the liability to the creditor on the bill or note of every person who is liable on it antecedently to the company, and who has not been made bankrupt or had their estate sequestrated (or in the case of a company, which has not gone into liquidation), as a security in the creditor's hands; and

   - (ii) to estimate the value of the security and (for the purpose of entitlement to vote, but not of any distribution under the arrangement) to deduct it from the creditor's claim.

1.16A(4)   Any resolution is invalid if those voting against it include more than half in value of the creditors–

- (a) to whom notice of the meeting was sent;

- (b) whose votes are not to be left out of account under paragraph (3); and

- (c) who are not, to the best of the chairman's belief, persons connected with the company.

1.16A(5)   It is for the chairman of the meeting to decide whether under this Rule–

- (a) a vote is to be left out of account in accordance with paragraph (3), and

- (b) a person is a connected person for the purpose of paragraph (4)(c),

and in relation to the second of these two cases the chairman is entitled to rely on the information provided by the company's statement of affairs or otherwise in accordance with this Part of the Rules.

1.16A(6)   If the chairman uses a proxy contrary to Rule 1.14AA the chairman's vote with that proxy does not count towards any majority under this Rule.

1.16A(7)   The chairman's decision on any matter under the Rule is subject to appeal to the court by any creditor and paragraphs (5) to (7) of Rule 1.15B apply as regards such an appeal.

History
See history note after r.1.16E.

1.16B   Requisite majorities at company meetings

1.16B(1)   Subject as follows and to any express provision made in the articles of association of the company, at a meeting of the members of the company any resolution is to be regarded as passed if voted for by more than one-half in value of the members present in person or by proxy and voting on the resolution.

1.16B(2)   The value of members is determined by reference to the number of votes conferred on each member by the company's articles.

1.16B(3)   If the chairman uses a proxy contrary to Rule 1.14AA, the chairman's vote with that proxy does not count towards any majority under this Rule.

History
See history note after r.1.16E.

1.16C   Action where person excluded

1.16C(1)   In this Rule and Rules 1.16D and 1.16E an "excluded person" means a person who–

(a)   has taken all steps necessary to attend a meeting under the arrangements put in place to do so by the convener of the meeting under section 246A(6); and

(b)   those arrangements do not permit that person to attend the whole or part of that meeting.

1.16C(2)   Where the chairman becomes aware during the course of the meeting that there is an excluded person, the chairman may–

(a)   continue the meeting;

(b)   declare the meeting void and convene the meeting again; or

(c)   declare the meeting valid up to the point where the person was excluded and adjourn the meeting.

1.16C(3)   Where the chairman continues the meeting, the meeting is valid unless–

(a)   the chairman decides in consequence of a complaint under Rule 1.16E to declare the meeting void and hold the meeting again; or

(b)   the court directs otherwise.

1.16C(4)   Without prejudice to paragraph (2), where the chairman becomes aware during the course of the meeting of an excluded person, the chairman may, in the chairman's discretion and without an adjournment, declare the meeting suspended for any period up to one hour.

History
See history note after r.1.16E.

1.16D   Indication to excluded person

1.16D(1)   A person who claims to be an excluded person may request an indication of what occurred during the period of that person's claimed exclusion (the "indication").

1.16D(2)   A request under paragraph (1) must be made as soon as reasonably practicable, and, in any event, no later than 4 p.m. on the business day following the day on which the exclusion is claimed to have occurred.

1.16D(3)   A request under paragraph (1) must be made to–

(a)   the chairman, where it is made during the course of the business of the meeting; or

(b)   the nominee or supervisor where it is made after the conclusion of the business of the meeting.

1.16D(4)   Where satisfied that the person making the request is an excluded person, the person to whom the request is made must give the indication as soon as reasonably practicable and, in any event, no later than 4. p.m. on the day following the request in paragraph (1).

1.16E   Complaint

1.16E(1)   Any person who–

     (a)   is, or claims to be, an excluded person; or

     (b)   attends the meeting (in person or by proxy) and considers that they have been adversely affected by a person's actual, apparent or claimed exclusion,

("the complainant") may make a complaint.

1.16E(2)   The person to whom the complaint must be made ("the relevant person") is–

     (a)   the chairman, where it is made during the course of the meeting; or

     (b)   the nominee or supervisor, where it is made after the meeting.

1.16E(3)   The relevant person must–

     (a)   consider whether there is an excluded person;

     (b)   where satisfied that there is an excluded person, consider the complaint; and

     (c)   where satisfied that there has been prejudice, take such action as the relevant person considers fit to remedy the prejudice.

1.16E(4)   Paragraph (5) applies where–

     (a)   the relevant person is satisfied that the complainant is an excluded person;

     (b)   during the period of the person's exclusion–

         (i)   a resolution was put to the meeting; and

         (ii)   voted on; and

     (c)   the excluded person asserts how the excluded person intended to vote on the resolution.

1.16E(5)   Subject to paragraph (6), where satisfied that the effect of the intended vote in paragraph (4), if cast, would have changed the result of the resolution, the relevant person must–

     (a)   count the intended vote as being cast in accordance with the complainant's stated intention;

     (b)   amend the record of the result of the resolution; and

     (c)   where those entitled to attend the meeting have been notified of the result of the resolution, notify them of the change.

1.16E(6)   Where satisfied that more than one complainant in paragraph (4) is an excluded person, the relevant person must have regard to the combined effect of the intended votes.

1.16E(7)   A complaint must be made as soon as reasonably practicable and, in any event, by 4 p.m. on the business day following–

     (a)   the day on which the person was excluded; or

     (b)   where an indication is requested under Rule 1.16D, the day on which the complainant received the indication.

1.16E(8)   The relevant person must notify the complainant in writing of any decision.

1.16E(9)   A complainant who is not satisfied by the action of the relevant person may apply to the court for a direction to be given to the relevant person as to the action to be taken in respect of the complaint, and any application must be made no more than 2 business days from the date of receiving the decision of the relevant person.

History
Rules 1.16A–1.16E inserted by the Insolvency (Scotland) Amendment Rules 2010 (SI 2010/688 (S 2)) art.3 and Sch.1 para.27 as from April 6, 2010, subject to transitional provisions in art.4 (in relation to rr.1.16A and 1.16B) but otherwise (in relation to rr.1.16C–1.16E) in all cases (see art.5).

1.17 Report of meetings

1.17(1) A report of the meetings shall be prepared by the person who was chairman of them.

1.17(2) The report shall–

(a) state whether the proposal for a voluntary arrangement was approved by the creditors of the company alone or by both the creditors and members of the company and in either case whether such approval was with any modifications;

(b) set out the resolutions which were taken at each meeting, and the decision on each one;

(c) list the creditors and members of the company (with their respective values) who were present or represented at the meeting, and how they voted on each resolution;

(ca) state whether, in the opinion of the supervisor–

(i) the EC Regulation applies to the voluntary arrangement; and

(ii) if so, whether the proceedings are main proceedings or territorial proceedings; and

(d) include such further information (if any) as the chairman thinks it appropriate to make known to the court.

History
In r.1.17(2) subpara.(ca) inserted by the Insolvency (Scotland) Regulations 2003 (SI 2003/2109 (S 8)) reg.25 as from September 8, 2003.
Previously r.1.17(2)(a) substituted by the Insolvency (Scotland) Amendment Rules 2002 (SI 2002/2709 (S 10)) rr.1, 4(1) and Sch. Pt 1 para.9(a) as from January 1, 2003 subject to transitional provisions contained in r.4(2).

1.17(3) A copy of the chairman's report shall, within 4 business days of the meetings being held, be lodged in court.

History
In r.1.17(3) "business" inserted by the Insolvency (Scotland) Amendment Rules 2010 (SI 2010/688 (S 2)) art.3 and Sch.1 para.28 as from April 6, 2010, subject to transitional provisions in art.4.

1.17(4) In respect of each of the meetings the persons to whom notice of the result of the meetings is to be sent under section 4(6) are all those who were sent notice of the meeting. The notice shall be sent as soon as reasonably practicable after a copy of the chairman's report is lodged in court under paragraph (3).

History
In r.1.17(4) "as soon as reasonably practicable" substituted for "immediately" by the Insolvency (Scotland) Amendment Rules 2010 (SI 2010/688 (S 2)) art.3 and Sch.1 para.29 as from April 6, 2010, subject to transitional provisions in art.4.

1.17(5) If the decision approving the voluntary arrangement has effect under section 4A (whether or not in the form proposed) the chairman shall as soon as is reasonably practicable send a copy of the report to the registrar of companies.

History
In r.1.17(5) the words "If the decision approving the voluntary arrangement has effect under section 4A" substituted for the former words "If the voluntary arrangement has been approved by the meetings" by the Insolvency (Scotland)

Amendment Rules 2002 (SI 2002/2709 (S 10)) rr.1, 4(1) and Sch. Pt 1 para.9(b) as from January 1, 2003 subject to transitional provisions contained in r.4(2).

CHAPTER 6

IMPLEMENTATION OF THE VOLUNTARY ARRANGEMENT

1.18   Resolutions to follow approval

1.18(1)   If the voluntary arrangement is approved (with or without modifications) by the creditors' meeting, a resolution must be taken by the creditors, where two or more supervisors are appointed, on the question whether acts to be done in connection with the arrangement may be done by any one or more of them, or must be done by all of them.

History
In r.1.18(1) "must" substituted for "may" by the Insolvency (Scotland) Amendment Rules 2010 (SI 2010/688 (S 2)) art.3 and Sch.1 para.30 as from April 6, 2010, subject to transitional provisions in art.4.
   Rule 1.18(1) substituted by the Insolvency (Scotland) Amendment Rules 2002 (SI 2002/2709 (S 10)) rr.1, 4(1) and Sch. Pt 1 para.10(a) as from January 1, 2003 subject to transitional provisions contained in r.4(2).

1.18(2)   [Omitted by the Insolvency (Scotland) Amendment Rules 2002 (SI 2002/2709 (S 10)) rr.1, 4(1) and Sch. Pt 1 para.10(b) as from January 1, 2003 subject to transitional provisions contained in r.4(2).]

1.18(3)   If at either meeting a resolution is moved for the appointment of some person other than the nominee to be supervisor of the arrangement, there must be produced to the chairman, at or before the meeting–

(a)   that person's written consent to act (unless the person is present and then and there signifies his consent), and

(b)   his written confirmation that he is qualified to act as an insolvency practitioner in relation to the company or is an authorised person in relation to the company.

History
In r.1.18(3)(b) the words "or is an authorised person in relation to the company" inserted by the Insolvency (Scotland) Amendment Rules 2002 (SI 2002/2709 (S 10)) rr.1, 4(1) and Sch. Pt 1 para.10(c) as from January 1, 2003 subject to transitional provisions contained in r.4(2).

1.18A   Notice of order made under section 4A(6)

1.18A(1)   This Rule applies where the court makes an order under section 4A(6).

1.18A(2)   The member of the company who applied for the order shall serve certified copies of it on–

(a)   the supervisor of the voluntary arrangement; and

(b)   the directors of the company.

1.18A(3)   Service on the directors may be effected by service of a single copy on the company at its registered office.

1.18A(4)   The directors or (as the case may be) the supervisor shall as soon as is reasonably practicable after receiving a copy of the court's order, give notice of it to all persons who were sent notice of the creditors' or company meetings or who, not having been sent such notice, are affected by the order.

1.18A(5)   The person on whose application the order of the court was made shall, within 5 business days of the order, deliver a certified copy interlocutor to the registrar of companies.

History
In r.1.18A(5) "5 business" substituted for "7" by the Insolvency (Scotland) Amendment Rules 2010 (SI 2010/688 (S 2)) art.3 and Sch.1 para.31 as from April 6, 2010, subject to transitional provisions in art.4.

Rule 1.18A inserted by the Insolvency (Scotland) Amendment Rules 2002 (SI 2002/2709 (S 10)) rr.1, 4(1) and Sch. Pt 1 para.11 as from January 1, 2003 subject to transitional provisions contained in r.4(2).

1.19 Hand-over of property, etc. to supervisor

1.19(1) Where the decision approving the voluntary arrangement has effect under section 4A, the directors or, where–

(a) the company is in liquidation or is in administration, and

(b) a person other than the responsible insolvency practitioner is appointed as supervisor of the voluntary arrangement,

the responsible insolvency practitioner, shall as soon as is reasonably practicable do all that is required for putting the supervisor into possession of the assets included in the arrangement.

History
In r.1.19(1) the words "Where the decision approving the voluntary arrangement has effect under section 4A" substituted for the former words "After the approval of the voluntary arrangement" by the Insolvency (Scotland) Amendment Rules 2002 (SI 2002/2709 (S 10)) rr.1, 4(1) and Sch. Pt 1 para.12 as from January 1, 2003 subject to transitional provisions contained in r.4(2).

1.19(2) Where paragraph 1(a) and (b) applies, the supervisor shall, on taking possession of the assets, discharge any balance due to the responsible insolvency practitioner by way of remuneration or on account of–

(a) fees, costs, charges and expenses properly incurred and payable under the Act or the Rules, and

(b) any advances made in respect of the company, together with interest on such advances at the official rate (within the meaning of Rule 4.66(2)(b)) ruling at the date on which the company went into liquidation or (as the case may be) entered administration.

1.19(3) Alternatively, the supervisor shall, before taking possession, give the responsible insolvency practitioner a written undertaking to discharge any such balance out of the first realisation of assets.

1.19(4) The sums due to the responsible insolvency practitioner as above shall be paid out of the assets included in the arrangement in priority to all other sums payable out of those assets, subject only to the deduction from realisations by the supervisor of the proper costs and expenses of such realisations.

1.19(5) The supervisor shall from time to time out of the realisation of assets discharge all cautionary obligations (including guarantees) properly given by the responsible insolvency practitioner for the benefit of the company and shall pay all the responsible insolvency practitioner's expenses.

1.20 Revocation or suspension of the arrangement

1.20(1) This Rule applies where the court makes an order of revocation or suspension under section 6.

1.20(2) The person who applied for the order shall serve copies of it–

(a) on the supervisor of the voluntary arrangement, and

(b) on the directors of the company or the administrator or liquidator (according to who made the proposal for the arrangement).

Service on the directors may be effected by service of a single copy of the order on the company at its registered office.

1.20(3) If the order includes a direction given by the court, under section 6(4)(b), for any further meetings to be summoned, notice shall also be given by the person who applied for the order to whoever is, in accordance with the direction, required to summon the meetings.

1.20(4)   The directors or (as the case may be) the administrator or liquidator shall–

(a)   as soon as is reasonably practicable after receiving a copy of the court's order, give notice of it to all persons who were sent notice of the creditors' and the company meetings or who, not having been sent that notice, appear to be affected by the order; and

(b)   within 5 business days of their receiving a copy of the order (or within such longer period as the court may allow), give notice to the court whether it is intended to make a revised proposal to the company and its creditors, or to invite re-consideration of the original proposal.

History
See history note after r.1.20(5).

1.20(5)   The person on whose application the order of revocation or suspension was made shall, within 5 business days after the making of the order, deliver a copy of the order to the registrar of companies.

History
In r.1.20(4)(b) and (5) "5 business" substituted for "7" by the Insolvency (Scotland) Amendment Rules 2010 (SI 2010/688 (S 2)) art.3 and Sch.1 para.32 as from April 6, 2010, subject to transitional provisions in art.4.

1.21   Supervisor's accounts

1.21(1)   This Rule applies where the voluntary arrangement authorises or requires the supervisor–

(a)   to carry on the business of the company or trade on its behalf or in its name;

(b)   to realise assets of the company; or

(c)   otherwise to administer or dispose of any of its funds.

1.21(2)   The supervisor must keep accounts and records of the supervisor's acts and dealings in, and in connection with, the arrangement, including in particular records of all receipts and payments of money.

1.21(3)   The supervisor must preserve any accounts and records in paragraph (2) which–

(a)   were kept by any other person who has acted as supervisor of the arrangement; and

(b)   are in the supervisor's possession.

History
See history note after r.1.21.

1.21A   Supervisor's reports

1.21A(1)   Subject to paragraph (2), the supervisor must, in respect of each period of 12 months ending with the anniversary of the commencement of the arrangement, send within 2 months of the end of that period a report on the progress and prospects for the full implementation of the voluntary arrangement to–

(a)   the registrar of companies;

(b)   the company;

(c)   all of the company's creditors who are bound by the voluntary arrangement of whose address the supervisor is aware;

(d)   subject to paragraph (4) below, the members of the company; and

(e)   if the company is not in liquidation, the company's auditors (if any) for the time being.

1.21A(2)   The supervisor is not required to send a report under paragraph (1), if an obligation to send a final report under Rule 1.23 arises in the period of 2 months mentioned in paragraph (1).

1.21A(3)   Where the supervisor is authorised or required to do any of the things mentioned in Rule 1.21 (1)(a) to (c), the report required to be sent pursuant to paragraph (1), must include or be accompanied by–

(a)   an abstract of receipts and payments required to be recorded by virtue of Rule 1.21(2); or

(b)   where there have been no such receipts and payments, a statement to that effect.

1.21A(4)   The court may, on application by the supervisor, dispense with the sending under this Rule of abstracts or reports to members of the company, either altogether or on the basis that the availability of the abstract or report to members is to be advertised by the supervisor in a specified manner.

History
Rules 1.21 and 1.21A substituted for r.1.21 by the Insolvency (Scotland) Amendment Rules 2010 (SI 2010/688 (S 2)) art.3 and Sch.1 para.33 as from April 6, 2010, subject to transitional provisions in art.4.

1.22   Fees, costs, charges and expenses

1.22   The fees, costs, charges and expenses that may be incurred for any of the purposes of a voluntary arrangement are–

(a)   any disbursements made by the nominee prior to the decision approving the arrangement taking effect under section 4A, and any remuneration for his services as is agreed between himself and the company (or, as the case may be, the administrator or liquidator);

(b)   any fees, costs, charges or expenses which–

(i)   are sanctioned by the terms of the arrangement, or

(ii)   would be payable, or correspond to those which would be payable, in an administration or winding up.

History
In r.1.22 the words "decision approving the arrangement taking effect under section 4A" substituted for the former words "approval of the arrangement" by the Insolvency (Scotland) Amendment Rules 2002 (SI 2002/2709 (S 10)) rr.1, 4(1) and Sch. Pt 1 para.13 as from January 1, 2003 subject to transitional provisions contained in r.4(2).

1.23   Completion or termination of the arrangement

1.23(1)   Not more than 28 days after the final completion or termination of the voluntary arrangement, the supervisor shall send to creditors and members of the company who are bound by it a notice that the voluntary arrangement has been fully implemented or (as the case may be) has terminated.

1.23(2)   With the notice there shall be sent to each creditor and member a copy of a report by the supervisor summarising all receipts and payments made by him in pursuance of the arrangement, and explaining in relation to implementation of the arrangement any departure from the proposals as they originally took effect, or (in the case of termination of the arrangement) explaining the reasons why the arrangement has terminated.

[FORM 1.4 (Scot)]

1.23(2A)   In the report under paragraph (2), the supervisor shall include a statement as to the amount paid, if any, to unsecured creditors by virtue of the application of section 176A (prescribed part).

History
Rule 1.23(2A) inserted by the Enterprise Act 2002 (Consequential Amendments) (Prescribed Part) (Scotland) Order 2003 (SI 2003/2108 (S 7)) art.4 as from September 15, 2003.

1.23(3)   The supervisor shall, within the 28 days mentioned above, send to the registrar of companies and to the court a copy of the notice to creditors and members under paragraph (1), together with a copy of the report under paragraph (2), and the supervisor shall not vacate office until after such copies have been sent.

History
Rule 1.23 substituted by the Insolvency (Scotland) Amendment Rules 2002 (SI 2002/2709 (S 10)) rr.1, 4(1) and Sch. Pt 1 para.14 as from January 1, 2003 subject to transitional provisions contained in r.4(2).

1.24 False representations, etc.

1.24 [Rule 1.24 omitted by the Insolvency (Scotland) Amendment Rules 2002 (SI 2002/2709 (S 10)) rr.1, 4(1) and Sch. Pt 1 para.15 as from January 1, 2003 subject to transitional provisions contained in r.4(2).]

CHAPTER 7

OBTAINING A MORATORIUM—PROCEEDINGS DURING A MORATORIUM—NOMINEES—CONSIDERATION OF PROPOSALS WHERE MORATORIUM OBTAINED

History
Chapter 7 inserted by the Insolvency (Scotland) Amendment Rules 2002 (SI 2002/2709 (S 10)) rr.1, 4(1) and Sch. Pt 1 para.16 as from January 1, 2003 subject to transitional provisions contained in r.4(2).

Section A: Obtaining a moratorium

1.25 Preparation of proposal by directors and submission to nominee

1.25(1) The document containing the proposal referred to in paragraph 6(1)(a) of Schedule A1 to the Act shall–

(a) be prepared by the directors;

(b) comply with the requirements of paragraphs (1) and (2) of Rule 1.3 (save that the reference to preferential creditors shall be to preferential creditors within the meaning of paragraph 31(8) of Schedule A1 to the Act); and

(c) state the address to which notice of the consent of the nominee to act and the documents referred to in Rule 1.28 shall be sent.

1.25(2) With the agreement in writing of the nominee, the directors may amend the proposal at any time before submission to them by the nominee of the statement required by paragraph 6(2) of Schedule A1 to the Act.

History
See history note after r.1.45.

1.26 Delivery of documents to the intended nominee etc.

1.26(1) The documents required to be delivered to the nominee pursuant to paragraph 6(1) of Schedule A1 to the Act shall be delivered to the nominee himself or to a person authorised to take delivery of documents on his behalf.

1.26(2) On receipt of the documents, the nominee shall as soon as is reasonably practicable issue an acknowledgement of receipt of the documents to the directors which shall indicate the date on which the documents were received.

History
See history note after r.1.45.

1.27   Statement of affairs

[FORM 1.6 (Scot)]

1.27(1)   The statement of the company's affairs required to be delivered to the nominee pursuant to paragraph 6(1)(b) of Schedule A1 to the Act shall be delivered to the nominee at the same time as the delivery to him of the document setting out the terms of the proposed voluntary arrangement.

History
In r.1.27(1) "at the same time as" substituted for "no later than 7 days after", and "or such longer time as he may allow" formerly appearing at the end omitted, by the Insolvency (Scotland) Amendment Rules 2010 (SI 2010/688 (S 2)) art.3 and Sch.1 para.34 as from April 6, 2010, subject to transitional provisions in art.4.

1.27(2)   The statement of affairs shall comprise the same particulars as required by Rule 1.5(2) (supplementing or amplifying, so far as is necessary for clarifying the state of the company's affairs, those already given in the directors' proposal).

1.27(3)   The statement of affairs shall be made up to a date not earlier than 2 weeks before the date of the delivery of the document containing the proposal for the voluntary arrangement to the nominee under Rule 1.26(1).

However, the nominee may allow an extension of that period to the nearest practicable date (not earlier than 2 months before the date of delivery of the documents referred to in Rule 1.26(1)) and if he does so, he shall give a statement of his reasons in writing to the directors.

1.27(4)   The statement of affairs shall be certified as correct, to the best of the relevant director's knowledge and belief, by one director.

History
In r.1.27(4) "the relevant director's" substituted for "their", and "one director" substituted for "two or more directors of the company, or by the company secretary and at least one director (other than the secretary himself)", by the Insolvency (Scotland) Amendment Rules 2010 (SI 2010/688 (S 2)) art.3 and Sch.1 para.35 as from April 6, 2010, subject to transitional provisions in art.4.
   See history note after r.1.45.

1.28   The nominee's statement

[FORM 1.5 (Scot)]

1.28(1)   The nominee shall submit to the directors the statement required by paragraph 6(2) of Schedule A1 to the Act within 28 days of the submission to him of the document setting out the terms of the proposed voluntary arrangement.

1.28(2)   The statement shall have annexed to it–

   (a)   the nominee's comments on the proposal, unless the statement contains an opinion in the negative on any of the matters referred to in paragraph 6(2)(a) and (b) of Schedule A1 to the Act, in which case he shall instead give his reasons for that opinion, and

[FORM 1.8 (Scot)]

   (b)   where he is willing to act in relation to the proposed arrangement, a statement of his consent to act.

History
See history note after r.1.45.

1.29   Documents submitted to the court to obtain moratorium

[FORMS 1.5 (Scot), 1.6 (Scot), 1.7 (Scot), 1.8 (Scot) and 1.9 (Scot)]

1.29(1)   Where pursuant to paragraph 7 of Schedule A1 to the Act the directors lodge the document and statements referred to in that paragraph in court those documents shall be delivered together with 4 copies of a schedule listing them within 3 working days of the date of the submission to them of the nominee's statement under paragraph 6(2) of Schedule A1 to the Act.

1.29(2)   When the directors lodge the document and statements referred to in paragraph (1), they shall also lodge–

(a)   a copy of any statement of reasons made by the nominee pursuant to Rule 1.27(3); and

(b)   a copy of the nominee's comments on the proposal submitted to them pursuant to Rule 1.28(2).

1.29(3)   The copies of the schedule shall be endorsed by the court with the date on which the documents were lodged in court and 3 copies of the schedule certified by the court shall be returned by the court to the person who lodged the documents in court.

[FORM 1.6 (Scot)]

1.29(4)   The statement of affairs required to be lodged under paragraph 7(1)(b) of Schedule A1 to the Act shall comprise the same particulars as required by Rule 1.5(2).

History
See history note after r.1.45.

1.30   Notice and advertisement of beginning of a moratorium

1.30(1)   After receiving the copies of the schedule endorsed by the court under Rule 1.29(3), the directors shall as soon as is reasonably practicable serve two of them on the nominee and one on the company.

[FORM 1.10 (Scot)]

1.30(2)   On receipt of the copies of the schedule pursuant to paragraph (1), the nominee–

(a)   as soon as is reasonably practicable, shall advertise the coming into force of the moratorium once in the Edinburgh Gazette; and

(b)   may advertise the coming into force of the moratorium in such other manner as the nominee thinks fit.

1.30(2A)   In addition to the standard content, notices published under paragraph (2) must state–

(a)   the nature of the business of the company;

(b)   that a moratorium under section 1A has come into force; and

(c)   the date upon which the moratorium came into force.

History
Rule 1.30(2A) inserted by the Insolvency (Scotland) Amendment Rules 2010 (SI 2010/688 (S 2)) art.3 and Sch.1 para.36 as from April 6, 2010, subject to transitional provisions in art.4.

1.30(3)   The nominee shall as soon as is reasonably practicable notify the registrar of companies, the keeper of the register of inhibitions and adjudications, the company and any petitioning creditor of the company of whose claim and address the nominee is aware of the coming into force of the moratorium and such notification shall specify the date on which the moratorium came into force.

History
In r.1.30(3) "and address the nominee" substituted for "he" by the Insolvency (Scotland) Amendment Rules 2010 (SI 2010/688 (S 2)) art.3 and Sch.1 para.37 as from April 6, 2010, subject to transitional provisions in art.4.

1.30(4)   The nominee shall give notice of the coming into force of the moratorium specifying the date on which it came into force to any messenger-at-arms or sheriff officer who, to his knowledge, is instructed to execute diligence or other legal process against the company or its property.

History
See history note after r.1.45.

1.31 Notice of extension of moratorium

[FORM 1.12 (Scot)]
[FORM 1.13 (Scot)]

1.31(1) The nominee shall as soon as is reasonably practicable notify the registrar of companies, the keeper of the register of inhibitions and adjudications and the court of a decision taking effect pursuant to paragraph 36 of Schedule A1 to the Act to extend or further extend the moratorium and such notice shall specify the new expiry date of the moratorium.

1.31(2) Where an order is made by the court extending or further extending or renewing or continuing a moratorium, the nominee shall as soon as is reasonably practicable after receiving a copy of the same give notice to the registrar of companies and the keeper of the register of inhibitions and adjudications and together with the notice shall send a copy to the registrar of companies.

History
In r.1.31(2) "certified copy interlocutor" substituted for "copy" by the Insolvency (Scotland) Amendment Rules 2010 (SI 2010/688 (S 2)) art.3 and Sch.1 para.38 as from April 6, 2010, subject to transitional provisions in art.4.
　　See history note after r.1.45.

1.32 Notice and advertisement of end of moratorium

[FORM 1.10 (Scot)]

1.32(1) After the moratorium comes to an end, the nominee–

(a) as soon as is reasonably practicable, shall advertise its coming to an end once in the Edinburgh Gazette; and

(b) may advertise its coming to an end in such other manner as the nominee thinks fit;

and such notice shall specify the date on which the moratorium came to an end.

[FORM 1.14 (Scot)] *[FORM 1.15 (Scot)]*

1.32(1A) In addition to the standard content, notices published under paragraph (2) must state–

(a) the nature of the business of the company;

(b) that a moratorium under section 1A has come to an end; and

(c) the date upon which the moratorium came to an end.

History
Rule 1.32(1A) inserted by the Insolvency (Scotland) Amendment Rules 2010 (SI 2010/688 (S 2)) art.3 and Sch.1 para.39 as from April 6, 2010, subject to transitional provisions in art.4.

1.32(2) The nominee shall as soon as is reasonably practicable give notice of the ending of the moratorium to the registrar of companies, the court, the keeper of the register of inhibitions and adjudications, the company and any creditor of the company of whose claim and address the nominee is aware and such notice shall specify the date on which the moratorium came to an end.

History
In r.1.32(2) "the nominee" substituted for "he" by the Insolvency (Scotland) Amendment Rules 2010 (SI 2010/688 (S 2)) art.3 and Sch.1 para.40 as from April 6, 2010, subject to transitional provisions in art.4.
　　See history note after r.1.45.

1.33 Inspection of court file

1.33 Any director, member or creditor of the company is entitled, at all reasonable times on any business day, to inspect the court file.

History
See history note after r.1.45.

Section B: Proceedings during a moratorium

1.34 Disposal of charged property etc. during a moratorium

1.34(1) This Rule applies in any case where the company makes an application to the court under paragraph 20 of Schedule A1 to the Act for leave to dispose of property of the company which is subject to a security, or goods in possession of the company under an agreement to which that paragraph relates.

1.34(2) The court shall fix a venue for the hearing of the application and the company shall as soon as is reasonably practicable give notice of the venue to the person who is the holder of the security or, as the case may be, the owner under the agreement.

1.34(3) If an order is made, the company shall as soon as is reasonably practicable give notice of it to that person or owner.

1.34(4) The court shall send two certified copies of the order to the company, who shall send one of them to that person or owner.

History
See history note after r.1.45.

Section C: Nominees

1.35 Withdrawal of nominee's consent to act

[*FORM 1.16 (Scot)*]
[*FORM 1.17 (Scot)*]

1.35 Where the nominee withdraws his consent to act, he shall, pursuant to paragraph 25(5) of Schedule A1 to the Act, as soon as is reasonably practicable give notice of his withdrawal and the reason for withdrawing his consent to act to–

    (a) the registrar of companies;

    (b) the court;

    (c) the company; and

    (d) any creditor of the company of whose claim and address the nominee is aware.

History
In r.1.35(d) "the nominee" substituted for "he" by the Insolvency (Scotland) Amendment Rules 2010 (SI 2010/688 (S 2)) art.3 and Sch.1 para.41 as from April 6, 2010, subject to transitional provisions in art.4.
   See history note after r.1.45.

1.36 Replacement of nominee by the court

1.36(1) Where the directors intend to make an application to the court under paragraph 28 of Schedule A1 to the Act for the nominee to be replaced, they shall give to the nominee at least 5 business days' notice of their application.

History
See history note after r.1.36(2).

1.36(2) Where the nominee intends to make an application to the court under that paragraph to be replaced, he shall give to the directors at least 5 business days' notice of his application.

[FORM 1.8 (Scot)]

History
In r.1.36(1) and (2) "5 business" substituted for "7" by the Insolvency (Scotland) Amendment Rules 2010 (SI 2010/688 (S 2)) art.3 and Sch.1 para.42 as from April 6, 2010, subject to transitional provisions in art.4.

1.36(3) No appointment of a replacement nominee shall be made by the court unless there is lodged in court a statement by the replacement nominee indicating that the replacement nominee–

(a) consents to act; and

(b) is qualified to act as an insolvency practitioner in relation to the company or is an authorised person in relation to the company.

[FORM 1.18 (Scot)] [FORM 1.19 (Scot)]

History
In r.1.36(3) "that the replacement nominee–
(a) consents to act; and
(b) is qualified to act as an insolvency practitioner in relation to the company or is an authorised person in relation to the company" substituted for "his consent to act" by the Insolvency (Scotland) Amendment Rules 2010 (SI 2010/688 (S 2)) art.3 and Sch.1 para.43 as from April 6, 2010, subject to transitional provisions in art.4.
See history note after r.1.45.

1.37 Notification of appointment of a replacement nominee

1.37 Where a person is appointed as a replacement nominee he shall as soon as is reasonably practicable give notice of his appointment to–

(a) the registrar of companies;

(b) the court (in any case where he was not appointed by the court); and

(c) the person whom he has replaced as nominee.

History
See history note after r.1.45.

1.38 Applications to court under paragraph 26 or 27 of Schedule A1 to the Act

1.38 Where any person intends to make an application to the court pursuant to paragraph 26 or 27 of Schedule A1 to the Act, he shall give to the nominee at least 5 business days' notice of his application.

History
In r.1.38 "5 business" substituted for "7" by the Insolvency (Scotland) Amendment Rules 2010 (SI 2010/688 (S 2)) art.3 and Sch.1 para.44 as from April 6, 2010, subject to transitional provisions in art.4.
See history note after r.1.45.

Section D: Consideration of proposals where moratorium obtained

1.39 General

1.39(1) [Omitted by the Insolvency (Scotland) Amendment Rules 2010 (SI 2010/688 (S 2)) art.3 and Sch.1 para.45 as from April 6, 2010, subject to transitional provisions in art.4.]

1.39(2) Subject to the provisions in this section of this Chapter, Rules 1.14, 1.14ZA, 1.14A, 1.14AA, 1.15, 1.15AA, 1.16A(3) to (7) and 1.16B to 1.16E shall apply with regard to meetings summoned pursuant to paragraph 29(1) of Schedule A1 to the Act as they apply to meetings of the company and creditors which are summoned under section 3 of the Act.

History
Rule 1.39(2) substituted by the Insolvency (Scotland) Amendment Rules 2010 (SI 2010/688 (S 2)) art.3 and Sch.1 para.46 as from April 6, 2010, subject to transitional provisions in art.4.
　　See history note after r.1.45.

1.40　Summoning of meetings; procedure at meetings etc.

1.40(1)　Where the nominee summons meetings of creditors and the company pursuant to paragraph 29(1) of Schedule A1 to the Act, each of those meetings shall be summoned for a date that is not more than 28 days from the date on which the moratorium came into force.

1.40(2)　Notices calling the creditors' meetings shall be sent by the nominee to all creditors specified in the statement of affairs and any other creditors of the company of whose address the nominee is aware at least 14 days before the day fixed for the meeting.

History
In r.1.40(2) "the nominee" substituted for "he" by the Insolvency (Scotland) Amendment Rules 2010 (SI 2010/688 (S 2)) art.3 and Sch.1 para.47 as from April 6, 2010, subject to transitional provisions in art.4.

1.40(3)　Notices calling the company meeting shall be sent by the nominee to all persons who are, to the best of the nominee's belief, members of the company at least 14 days before the day fixed for the meeting.

1.40(4)　Each notice sent under this Rule must–

(a)　in addition to the standard content, specify–

　　(i)　the court in which the documents relating to the obtaining of the moratorium were lodged; and

　　(ii)　the court reference; and

(b)　state the effect of Rule 1.43.

History
See history note after r.1.40(4A).
　　See history note after r.1.45.

1.40(4A)　With each notice there must be sent–

(a)　a copy of the directors' proposal;

(b)　a copy of the statement of the company's affairs or, if the nominee thinks fit, a summary of it (the summary to include a list of creditors and the amount of their debts);

(c)　the nominee's comments on the proposal; and

(d)　forms of proxy.

History
Rule 1.40(4) and (4A) substituted by the Insolvency (Scotland) Amendment Rules 2010 (SI 2010/688 (S 2)) art.3 and Sch.1 para.48 as from April 6, 2010, subject to transitional provisions in art.4.

1.41　Entitlement to vote (creditors)

1.41(1)　Subject as follows, every creditor who has notice of the creditors' meeting is entitled to vote at the meeting or any adjournment of it.

1.41(2)　Votes are calculated according to the amount of the creditor's debt as at the beginning of the moratorium, after deducting any amounts paid in respect of that debt after that date.

1.41(3)   A creditor may vote in respect of a debt for an unliquidated amount or any debt whose value is not ascertained and for the purposes of voting (but not otherwise) his debt shall be valued at £1 unless the chairman agrees to put a higher value on it.

History
See history note after r.1.45.

1.42   Procedure for admission of creditors' claims for voting purposes

1.42(1)   Subject as follows, at any creditors' meeting the chairman shall ascertain the entitlement of persons wishing to vote and shall admit or reject their claims accordingly.

1.42(2)   The chairman may admit or reject a claim in whole or in part.

1.42(3)   The chairman's decision on any matter under this Rule or under paragraph (3) of Rule 1.41 is subject to appeal to the court by any creditor or member of the company.

1.42(4)   If the chairman is in doubt whether a claim should be admitted or rejected, he shall mark it as objected to and allow votes to be cast in respect of it, subject to such votes being subsequently declared invalid if the objection to the claim is sustained.

1.42(5)   If on an appeal the chairman's decision is reversed or varied, or votes are declared invalid, the court may order another meeting to be summoned, or make such order as it thinks just.
    The court's power to make an order under this paragraph is exercisable only if it considers that the circumstances giving rise to the appeal give rise to unfair prejudice or material irregularity.

1.42(6)   An application to the court by way of appeal against the chairman's decision shall not be made after the end of the period of 28 days beginning with the first day on which the report required by paragraph 30(3) of Schedule A1 to the Act has been made to the court.

1.42(7)   The chairman is not personally liable for any expenses incurred by any person in respect of an appeal under this Rule.

History
See history note after r.1.45.

1.43   Requisite majorities (creditors)

1.43(1)   Subject as follows, a resolution is passed at a creditors' meeting when a majority (in value) of those present and voting in person or by proxy have voted in favour of it.

History
See history note after r.1.43(2).

1.43(2)   A resolution to approve the proposal or a modification is passed when a majority of three quarters or more (in value) of those present and voting in person or by proxy have voted in favour of it.

History
Rule 1.43(1) and (2) substituted by the Insolvency (Scotland) Amendment Rules 2010 (SI 2010/688 (S 2)) art.3 and Sch.1 para.49 as from April 6, 2010, subject to transitional provisions in art.4.

1.43(3)   At a meeting of the creditors for any resolution to pass extending (or further extending) a moratorium, or to bring a moratorium to an end before the end of the period of any extension, there must be a majority in excess of three-quarters in value of the creditors present in person or by proxy and voting on the resolution. For this purpose a secured creditor is entitled to vote in respect of the amount of his claim without deducting the value of his security.

History
See history note after r.1.45.

1.44 Proceedings to obtain agreement on the proposal

1.44(1) If the chairman thinks fit, the creditors' meeting and the company meeting may be held together.

1.44(1A) During a meeting, the chairman may, in the chairman's discretion and without an adjournment, declare the meeting suspended for any period up to one hour.

History
Rule 1.44(1A) inserted by the Insolvency (Scotland) Amendment Rules 2010 (SI 2010/688 (S 2)) art.3 and Sch.1 para.50 as from April 6, 2010, subject to transitional provisions in art.4.

1.44(2) The chairman may, and shall if it is so resolved at the meeting in question, adjourn that meeting, but any adjournment shall not be to a day which is more than 14 days after the date on which the moratorium (including any extension) ends.

1.44(3) If the meetings are adjourned under paragraph (2), notice of the fact shall be given by the nominee as soon as is reasonably practicable to the court.

1.44(4) If following the final adjournment of the creditors' meeting the proposal (with or without modifications) has not been approved by the creditors, it is deemed rejected.

History
See history note after r.1.45.

1.45 Implementation of the arrangement

[FORMS 1.1 (Scot), 1.2 (Scot), 1.3 (Scot) and 1.4 (Scot)]

1.45(1) Where a decision approving the arrangement has effect under paragraph 36 of Schedule A1 to the Act, the directors shall as soon as is reasonably practicable do all that is required for putting the supervisor into possession of the assets included in the arrangement.

1.45(2) Subject to paragraph (3), Rules 1.17, 1.18, 1.18A and 1.20 to 1.23 apply.

1.45(3) The provisions referred to in paragraph (2) are modified as follows–

  (a) in paragraph (4) of Rule 1.17 the reference to section 4(6) is to be read as a reference to paragraph 30(3) of Schedule A1 to the Act;

  (b) in paragraph (5) of Rule 1.17 the reference to section 4A is to be read as a reference to paragraph 36 of Schedule A1 to the Act;

  (c) in paragraph (1) of Rule 1.18A the reference to section 4A(6) is to be read as a reference to paragraph 36(5) of Schedule A1 to the Act;

  (d) in paragraph (1) of Rule 1.20 the reference to section 6 is to be read as a reference to paragraph 38 of Schedule A1 to the Act and the references in paragraphs (2) and (4) to the administrator or liquidator shall be ignored;

  (e) in paragraph (3) of Rule 1.20 the reference to section 6(4)(b) is to be read as a reference to paragraph 38(4)(b) of Schedule A1 to the Act; and

  (f) in sub-paragraph (a) of paragraph (1) of Rule 1.22 the reference to section 4A is to be read as a reference to paragraph 36 of Schedule A1 to the Act.

History
Rules 1.25–1.45 inserted by the Insolvency (Scotland) Amendment Rules 2002 (SI 2002/2709 (S 10)) rr.1, 4(1) and Sch. Pt 1 para.16 as from January 1, 2003 subject to transitional provisions contained in r.4(2). Rules 1.30(2), 1.32(1) substituted by the Insolvency (Scotland) (Amendment) Rules 2009 (SI 2009/662 (S 1)) r.2 and Sch. para.2, 3 as from April 6, 2009.

CHAPTER 8

EC REGULATION—CONVERSION OF VOLUNTARY ARRANGEMENT INTO WINDING UP

1.46 Application for conversion into winding up

1.46(1) Where a member State liquidator proposes to apply to the court for conversion of a voluntary arrangement into winding-up proceedings, an affidavit complying with Rule 1.47 must be prepared and filed in court in support of the application.

History
See history not after r.1.46(1A).

1.46(1A) In this Rule, and in Rules 1.47 and 1.48, "conversion into winding-up proceedings" means an order under Article 37 of the EC Regulation (conversion of earlier proceedings) that the voluntary arrangement is converted into–

    (a) administration proceedings whose purposes are limited to the winding up of the company through administration and are to exclude the purpose contained in paragraph 3(1)(a) of Schedule B1 to the Act;

    (b) a creditors' voluntary winding up; or

    (c) a winding up by the court.

History
Rule 1.46(1) and (1A) substituted for former r.1.46(1) by the Insolvency (Scotland) Amendment Rules 2010 (SI 2010/688 (S 2)) art.3 and Sch.1 para.51 as from April 6, 2010, subject to transitional provisions in art.4.

1.46(2) The application and the affidavit required under this Rule shall be served upon–

    (a) the company; and

    (b) the supervisor.

History
See history note after r.1.49.

1.47 Contents of affidavit

1.47(1) The affidavit shall state–

    (a) that main proceedings have been opened in relation to the company in a member State other than the United Kingdom;

    (b) the belief of the person making the statement that the conversion of the voluntary arrangement into winding-up proceedings would prove to be in the interests of the creditors in the main proceedings;

    (c) the opinion of the person making the statement as to whether the company ought to enter voluntary winding up or be wound up by the court; and

    (d) all other matters that, in the opinion of the member State liquidator, would assist the court–

        (i) in deciding whether to make such an order, and

        (ii) if the court were to do so, in considering the need for any consequential provision that would be necessary or desirable.

History
In r.1.47(1)(b) "belief of the person making the statement" substituted for "deponent's belief", and "winding-up proceedings" substituted for "a winding up"; and s.1.47(1)(c) substituted by the Insolvency (Scotland) Amendment Rules 2010 (SI 2010/688 (S 2)) art.3 and Sch.1 paras 52 and 53 as from April 6, 2010, subject to transitional provisions in art.4.

1.47(2)   An affidavit under this Rule shall be sworn by, or on behalf of, the member State liquidator.

History
See history note after r.1.49.

1.48   Power of court

1.48(1)   On hearing the application for conversion into winding-up proceedings, the court may make such order as it thinks fit.

History
See history note after r.1.48(4).

1.48(2)   If the court makes an order for conversion into winding-up proceedings, the order may contain all such consequential provisions as the court deems necessary or desirable.

History
See history note after r.1.48(4).

1.48(3)   Without prejudice to the generality of paragraph (1), an order under that paragraph may provide that the company be wound up as if a resolution for voluntary winding up under section 84 were passed on the day on which the order is made.

1.48(4)   Where the court makes an order for conversion into winding-up proceedings under paragraph (1), any expenses properly incurred as expenses of the administration of the voluntary arrangement in question shall be a first charge on the company's assets.

History
In r.1.48(1), (2) and (4) "winding-up proceedings" substituted for "winding up" by the Insolvency (Scotland) Amendment Rules 2010 (SI 2010/688 (S 2)) art.3 and Sch.1 para.54 as from April 6, 2010, subject to transitional provisions in art.4.
    See history note after r.1.49.

Chapter 9

EC Regulation—Member State Liquidator

1.49   Notice to member State liquidator

1.49(1)   This Rule applies where a member State liquidator has been appointed in relation to the company.

1.49(2)   Where the supervisor is obliged to give notice to, or provide a copy of a document (including an order of court) to, the court or the registrar of companies, the supervisor shall give notice or provide a copy, as appropriate, to the member State liquidator.

1.49(3)   Paragraph (2) is without prejudice to the generality of the obligations imposed by Article 31 of the EC Regulation (duty to co operate and communicate information).

History
Rules 1.46–1.49 inserted by the Insolvency (Scotland) Regulations 2003 (SI 2003/2109 (S 8)) reg.25 as from September 8, 2003.

Chapter 10

1.50   Omission of information from statement of affairs

1.50   The court, on the application of the nominee, the directors or any person appearing to it to have an interest, may direct that specified information may be omitted from any statement of affairs required to be sent to the creditors where the disclosure of such information would be likely to prejudice the conduct of the voluntary arrangement or might reasonably be expected to lead to violence against any person.

History
Rule 1.50 inserted by the Insolvency (Scotland) Amendment Rules 2010 (SI 2010/688 (S 2)) art.3 and Sch.1 para.55 as from April 6, 2010, subject to transitional provisions in art.4.

PART 2

ADMINISTRATION PROCEDURE

[**Note**: The rules which follow apply to administrations under the new regime (i.e. principally to cases where the company entered into administration on or after September 15, 2003). For administrations entered into prior to that date, and also the special cases described in the Introductory note to the new Pt II following IA 1986 s.8, the rules of the original regime continue to apply. These are set out following r.2.60 below.]

CHAPTER 1

PRELIMINARY

2.1   Introductory and interpretation

2.1(1)   In this Part–

(a)   Chapter 2 applies in relation to the appointment of an administrator by the court;

(b)   Chapter 3 applies in relation to the appointment of an administrator by the holder of a qualifying floating charge under paragraph 14;

(c)   Chapter 4 applies in relation to the appointment of an administrator by the company or the directors under paragraph 22;

(d)   The following Chapters apply in all the cases mentioned in sub paragraphs (a) to (c) above:

 –   Chapter 5: Process of administration;

 –   Chapter 5A: The giving of notice and supply of documents;

 –   Chapter 6: Meetings;

 –   Chapter 7: The creditors' committee;

 –   Chapter 8: Functions and remuneration of administrator;

 –   Chapter 8A: Expenses of the administration;

 –   Chapter 9: Distributions to creditors;

 –   Chapter 10: Ending administration;

 –   Chapter 11: Replacing administrator;

 –   Chapter 12: EC Regulation—conversion of administration to winding up;

 –   Chapter 13: EC Regulation—member State liquidator.

History
In r.2.1(1)(d) "– Chapter 5A: The giving of notice and supply of documents;" inserted by the Insolvency (Scotland) Amendment Rules 2010 (SI 2010/688 (S 2)) art.3 and Sch.1 para.56 as from April 6, 2010, subject to transitional provisions in art.4.

2.1(2)   In this Part of these Rules a reference to a numbered paragraph shall, unless the context otherwise requires, be to the paragraph so numbered in Schedule B1 to the Act.

CHAPTER 2

APPOINTMENT OF ADMINISTRATOR BY COURT

2.2 Form of application

2.2(1) Where an application is made by way of petition for an administration order to be made in relation to a company, there shall be lodged together with the petition a Statement of the Proposed Administrator.

2.2(2) In this Part, references to a Statement of the Proposed Administrator are to a statement by each of the persons proposed to be administrator of a company, in the form required by Rule 7.30 and Schedule 5, stating–

    (a) that he consents to accept appointment as administrator of that company;

    (b) details of any prior professional relationship that he has had with that company; and

    (c) his opinion that it is reasonably likely that the purpose of administration will be achieved.

2.2(3) The petition shall state whether, in the opinion of the petitioner, (i) the EC Regulation will apply and (ii) if so, whether the proceedings will be main, secondary or territorial proceedings.

History
See note after r.2.30.

2.3 Service of petition

2.3(1) Notice of a petition under paragraph 12 shall be given by the petitioner to any holder of a qualifying floating charge, and to the following persons–

    (a) an administrative receiver, if appointed;

    (b) a member State liquidator, if one has been appointed in main proceedings in relation to the company;

    (c) if a petition for the winding up of the company has been presented but no order for winding up has yet been made, the petitioner under that petition;

    (d) a provisional liquidator, if appointed;

    (e) the person proposed in the petition to be the administrator;

    (f) the registrar of companies;

    (g) the Keeper of the Register of Inhibitions and Adjudications for recording in that register;

    (h) the company, if the application is made by anyone other than the company; and

    (i) the supervisor of a voluntary arrangement under Part I of the Act, if such has been appointed.

2.3(2) Notice of the petition shall also be given to the persons upon whom the court orders that the petition be served.

2.4 Application to appoint specified person as administrator by holder of qualifying floating charge

2.4(1) This Rule applies where the holder of a qualifying floating charge, who has been given notice of an administration application, applies under paragraph 36(1)(b) to have a specified person appointed as administrator in place of the person proposed in the application.

2.4(2) An application under paragraph 36(1)(b) shall include averments as to the basis upon which the applicant is entitled to make an appointment under paragraph 14, and shall be accompanied by–

(a) the written consent, in accordance with Rule 2.10(5), of all holders of a prior qualifying floating charge;

(b) the Statement of the Proposed Administrator;

(c) a copy of the instrument or instruments by which the relevant floating charge was created, including any relevant instrument of alteration; and

(d) such other documents as the applicant considers might assist the court in determining the application.

2.4(3) If an administration order is made appointing the specified person, the expenses of the original petitioner and of the applicant under this Rule shall, unless the court orders otherwise, be paid as an expense of the administration.

2.5 Application where company in liquidation

2.5(1) Where an administration application is made under paragraph 37 or 38, the petition shall contain, in addition to those averments required in an application under paragraph 12, averments in relation to–

(a) the full details of the existing insolvency proceedings, including the name and address of the liquidator, the date he was appointed and by whom; and

(b) the reasons why administration has subsequently been considered appropriate,

and shall be accompanied by a copy of the order or certificate by which the liquidator was appointed and by such other documents as the petitioner considers might assist the court in determining the application.

2.5(2) Where an administration application is made under paragraph 37, the petition shall contain, in addition to the averments required by paragraph (1) above, averments as to the basis upon which the petitioner is qualified to make an appointment under paragraph 14, and shall be accompanied by a copy of the instrument or instruments by which the relevant floating charge was created, including any relevant instrument of alteration, and by such other documents as the petitioner considers might assist the court in determining the application.

2.6 Expenses

2.6 If the court makes an administration order, the expenses of the petitioner, and of any other party whose expenses are allowed by the court, shall be regarded as expenses of the administration.

2.7 Administration orders where company in liquidation

2.7 Where the court makes an administration order in relation to a company which is in liquidation, the administration order shall contain consequential provisions, including–

(a) in the case of a liquidator in a voluntary winding up, his removal from office;

(b) provisions concerning the release of the liquidator, including his entitlement to recover expenses and to be paid his remuneration;

(c) provision for payment of the costs of the petitioning creditor in the winding-up;

(d) provisions regarding any indemnity given to the liquidator;

(e) provisions regarding the handling or realisation of any of the company's assets under the control of the liquidator; and

(f) such other provisions as the court shall think fit.

2.8   Notice of dismissal of application for an administration order

2.8   If the court dismisses the petition under paragraph 13(1)(b), the petitioner shall as soon as reasonably practicable send notice of the court's order dismissing the petition to all those to whom the petition was notified under Rule 2.3.

CHAPTER 3

APPOINTMENT OF ADMINISTRATOR BY HOLDER OF FLOATING CHARGE

2.9   Notice of intention to appoint

2.9   For the purposes of paragraph 44(2), a notice of intention to appoint shall be in the form required by Rule 7.30 and Schedule 5, and shall be lodged in court at the same time as it is sent in accordance with paragraph 15(1) to the holder of any prior qualifying floating charge.

2.10   Notice of appointment

2.10(1)   The notice of appointment under paragraph 14 shall be in the form required by Rule 7.30 and Schedule 5.

2.10(2)   Subject to Rule 2.12, there shall be lodged together with the notice of appointment–

(a)   the Statement of the Proposed Administrator; and

(b)   either–

    (i)   evidence that the person making the appointment has fulfilled the requirements of paragraph 15(1)(a); or

    (ii)   copies of the written consent of all those required to give consent in accordance with paragraph 15(1)(b).

2.10(3)   The statutory declaration required by paragraph 18(2) shall be made no earlier than 5 days before the notice of appointment is lodged.

2.10(4)   The holder of a prior floating charge may indicate his consent by completing the section provided on the form of notice of intention to appoint and returning to the person making the appointment a copy of that form.

2.10(5)   Where the holder of a prior floating charge does not choose to use the form of notice of intention to appoint to indicate his consent or no such form has been sent to him, his written consent shall include–

(a)   details of the name, registered address and registered number of the company in respect of which the appointment is proposed to be made;

(b)   details of the charge held including the date it was registered and, where applicable, any financial limit and any deeds of priority;

(c)   the name and address of the floating charge holder consenting to the proposed appointment;

(d)   the name and address of the holder of the qualifying floating charge who is proposing to make the appointment;

(e)   the date that notice of intention to appoint was given;

(f)   the name of the proposed administrator; and

(g)   a statement of consent to the proposed appointment.

2.10(6)   Where the holder of a qualifying floating charge receives notice of an administration application and makes an appointment under paragraph 14, he shall as soon as reasonably practicable send a copy of the notice of appointment to the petitioner and to the court in which the petition has been lodged.

2.11   Notice to administrator

2.11   The person making the appointment shall, as soon as reasonably practicable, send to the administrator a copy of the notice of appointment, certified by the clerk of court and endorsed with the date and time of presentation of the principal notice.

2.12   Appointment taking place out of court business hours

2.12(1)   The holder of a qualifying floating charge may lodge a notice of appointment under paragraph 14 in court in accordance with this Rule when (and only when) the court is not open for public business.

2.12(2)   A notice of appointment lodged under this Rule shall be in the form required by Rule 7.30 and Schedule 5.

2.12(3)   The person making the appointment shall lodge the notice by sending it by fax to the court, and shall ensure that a fax transmission report is produced by the sending machine which records the date and time of the fax transmission.

2.12(4)   The person making the appointment shall send to the administrator, as soon as reasonably practicable, a copy of the notice of appointment and of the fax transmission report.

2.12(5)   The appointment shall take effect from the date and time of the fax transmission.

2.12(6)   The person making the appointment shall lodge in court, on the next day that the court is open for public business, the principal notice of appointment together with the documents required by Rule 2.10(2) and–

(a)   the fax transmission report showing the date and time at which the notice was sent; and

(b)   a statement of the full reasons for the out of hours lodging of the notice of appointment, including why it would have been damaging to the company or its creditors not to have so acted.

2.12(7)   The administrator's appointment shall cease to have effect if the requirements of paragraph (6) of this Rule are not met within the time set out in that paragraph.

2.12(8)   Where any question arises in respect of the date and time that the notice of appointment was lodged in court it shall be a presumption capable of rebuttal that the date and time shown on the fax transmission report is the date and time at which the notice was so lodged.

CHAPTER 4

APPOINTMENT OF ADMINISTRATOR BY COMPANY OR DIRECTORS

2.13   Notice of intention to appoint

2.13(1)   A notice of intention to appoint given under paragraph 26 shall be in the form required by Rule 7.30 and Schedule 5 and shall be given by the company or the directors, as the case may be, to any holder of a qualifying floating charge.

2.13(2)   A copy of the notice of intention to appoint shall at the same time be sent–

(a)   to the supervisor of any voluntary arrangement under Part I of the Act; and

(b)   where the notice is given by the directors (other than as agents of the company), to the company.

2.14 Timing of statutory declaration

2.14 The statutory declaration required by paragraph 27(2) shall be made not more than 5 business days before the notice is lodged in court.

2.15 Resolution or decision to appoint

2.15 The person making the appointment shall lodge together with the notice of intention to appoint either a copy of the resolution of the company to appoint an administrator (where the company proposes to make the appointment) or a record of the decision of the directors (where the directors propose to make the appointment).

2.16 Notice of appointment

2.16(1) The notice of appointment referred to in paragraph 29 shall be in the form required by Rule 7.30 and Schedule 5.

2.16(2) The statutory declaration required by paragraph 29(2) shall be made no earlier than 5 days before the notice is lodged.

2.16(3) There shall be lodged together with the notice of appointment the Statement of the Proposed Administrator and, unless the period of notice set out in paragraph 26(1) has expired, the written consent of all those persons to whom notice was given in accordance with that paragraph.

2.17 Appointment where no notice of intention to appoint has been given

2.17 Where a notice of intention to appoint an administrator has not been given, there shall be lodged together with the notice of appointment either a copy of the resolution of the company to appoint an administrator (where the company proposes to make the appointment) or a record of the decision of the directors (where the directors propose to make the appointment).

2.18 Notice to administrator

2.18 The person making the appointment shall, as soon as reasonably practicable, send to the administrator a copy of the notice of appointment, certified by the clerk of court and endorsed with the date and time of presentation of the principal notice.

CHAPTER 5

PROCESS OF ADMINISTRATION

2.19 Notification and advertisement of administrator's appointment

2.19(1) The notice of appointment, which an administrator must publish as soon as is reasonably practicable after his appointment by virtue of paragraph 46(2)(b), shall be advertised in the Edinburgh Gazette and may be advertised in such other manner as the administrator thinks fit.

2.19(1A) In addition to the standard content, notices published under paragraph (1) must state–

    (a) that an administrator has been appointed,

    (b) the date of the appointment; and

    (c) the nature of the business of the company.

History

Rule 2.19(1A) inserted by the Insolvency (Scotland) Amendment Rules 2010 (SI 2010/688 (S 2)) art.3 and Sch.1 para.57 as from April 6, 2010, subject to transitional provisions in art.4.

Thank you for purchasing the 15th edition of **Sealy & Milman: Annotated Guide to the Insolvency Legislation 2012**

ADD SEALY & MILMAN TO YOUR WESTLAW UK SUBSCRIPTION
Sealy & Milman: Annotated Guide to the Insolvency Legislation is now available as an add-on to a Westlaw UK subscription.

QUICKER ACCESS TO MORE UP-TO- DATE INFORMATION
On Westlaw UK, **Sealy & Milman** is updated weekly. Much more than just a copy of the book online, Westlaw UK helps you join-up your research with direct links to primary law and all related materials.

START YOUR FREE TRIAL TODAY
Sign-up for a Free Trial today and see the way that having the most current information can help you make a difference.

Complete your details below and a member of our Customer Training and Support Team will be in touch to discuss your requirements. Please note we are unable to offer free trials to students. If you would like to access Westlaw UK, please contact your Law Librarian.

WESTLAW UK FREE TRIAL
I would like a free trial of:

☐ **Westlaw UK**

☐ **Sealy & Milman: Annotated Guide to the Insolvency Legislation on Westlaw UK**

OTHER SWEET & MAXWELL SERVICES
I am also interested in the following Sweet & Maxwell online services:

☐ **Lawtel**

☐ **Lawtel Precedents**

☐ **I do not wish to receive any information about other relevant Sweet & Maxwell products and services.**

☐ **Please use my email for relevant marketing and informational material**

Title	**Name**
Organisation	
Job title	
Address	
Postcode	
Telephone	
Email	
S&M account number (if known)	

All orders are accepted subject to the terms of this order form and our Terms of Trading (see www.sweetandmaxwell.co.uk). By submitting this order form I confirm that I accept these terms and I am authorised to sign on behalf of the customer.

Signed	**Job Title**
Print Name	**Date**

Thomson Reuters (Professional) UK Limited – Legal Business (Company No. 1679046). 100 Avenue Road, Swiss Cottage, London NW3 EPF. Registered in England and Wales. Registered office: Aldgate House, 33 Aldgate High Street, London EC3N 1DL. Trades using various trading names, a list of which is posted on its website at sweetandmaxwell.co.uk
"Thomson Reuters" and the Thomson Reuters logo are trademarks of Thomson Reuters and its affiliated companies.

(BC004) V9 (04.2012) SH / DA

SWEET & MAXWELL

 THOMSON REUTERS

SWEET & MAXWELL

FREEPOST

PO BOX 2000

ANDOVER

SP10 9AH

UNITED KINGDOM

2.19(2)   The administrator shall at the same time give notice of his appointment to the following persons–

(a)   a receiver, if appointed;

(b)   a petitioner in a petition for the winding up of the company, if that petition is pending;

(c)   any provisional liquidator of the company, if appointed;

(d)   any supervisor of a voluntary arrangement under Part 1 of the Act; and

(e)   the Keeper of the Register of Inhibitions and Adjudications for recording in that register.

2.19(3)   Where, by virtue of a provision of Schedule B1 to the Act or of these Rules, the administrator is required to send a notice of his appointment to any person, he shall satisfy that requirement by sending to that person a notice in the form required by Rule 7.30 and Schedule 5.

History
Rule 2.19(1) substituted by the Insolvency (Scotland) (Amendment) Rules 2009 (SI 2009/662 (S 1)) r.2 and Sch. para.4 as from April 6, 2009.

2.20   Notice requiring statement of affairs

2.20(1)   In this Chapter **"relevant person"** has the meaning given to it in paragraph 47(3).

2.20(2)   Subject to Rule 2.21, the administrator shall send to each relevant person upon whom he decides to make a requirement under paragraph 47 a notice in the form required by Rule 7.30 and Schedule 5 requiring him to provide a statement of the company's affairs.

2.20(3)   The notice shall inform each of the relevant persons–

(a)   of the names and addresses of all others (if any) to whom the same notice has been sent;

(b)   of the time within which the statement must be delivered;

(c)   of the effect of paragraph 48(4) (penalty for non-compliance); and

(d)   of the application to him, and to each other relevant person, of section 235 (duty to provide information, and to attend on the administrator, if required).

2.20(4)   The administrator shall furnish each relevant person upon whom he decides to make a requirement under paragraph 47 with the forms required for the preparation of the statement of affairs.

2.21   Statements of affairs and statements of concurrence

2.21(1)   The statement of the company's affairs shall be in the form required by Rule 7.30 and Schedule 5.

2.21(2)   Where more than one relevant person is required to submit a statement of affairs the administrator may require one or more such persons to submit, in place of a statement of affairs, a statement of concurrence in the form required by Rule 7.30 and Schedule 5; and where the administrator does so, he shall inform the person making the statement of affairs of that fact.

2.21(3)   The person making the statutory declaration in support of a statement of affairs shall send the statement, together with one copy thereof, to the administrator, and a copy of the statement to each of those persons whom the administrator has required to submit a statement of concurrence.

2.21(4)   A person required to submit a statement of concurrence shall deliver to the administrator the statement of concurrence, together with one copy thereof, before the end of the period of 5 business days (or such other period as the administrator may agree) beginning with the day on which the statement of affairs being concurred with is received by him.

2.21(5) A statement of concurrence may be qualified in respect of matters dealt with in the statement of affairs, where the maker of the statement of concurrence is not in agreement with the statement of affairs, he considers that statement to be erroneous or misleading, or he is without the direct knowledge necessary for concurring with it.

2.21(6) Subject to Rule 2.22, the administrator shall, as soon as is reasonably practicable, file a copy of the statement of affairs and any statement of concurrence with the registrar of companies.

2.21(7) Subject to Rule 2.22, the administrator shall insert any statement of affairs submitted to him, together with any statement of concurrence, in the sederunt book.

2.22 Limited disclosure

2.22(1) Where the administrator thinks that it would prejudice the conduct of the administration or might be reasonably expected to lead to violence against any person for the whole or part of the statement of the company's affairs to be disclosed, he may apply to the court for an order of limited disclosure in respect of the statement, or any specified part of it.

History
In r.2.22(1) "or might be reasonably expected to lead to violence against any person" inserted by the Insolvency (Scotland) Amendment Rules 2010 (SI 2010/688 (S 2)) art.3 and Sch.1 para.58 as from April 6, 2010, subject to transitional provisions in art.4.

2.22(2) The court may order that the statement or, as the case may be, the specified part of it, shall not be filed with the registrar of companies or entered in the sederunt book.

2.22(3) The administrator shall as soon as reasonably practicable file a copy of that order with the registrar of companies, and shall place a copy of the order in the sederunt book.

2.22(4) If a creditor seeks disclosure of the statement of affairs or a specified part of it in relation to which an order has been made under this Rule, he may apply to the court for an order that the administrator disclose it or a specified part of it.

2.22(5) The court may attach to an order for disclosure any conditions as to confidentiality, duration and scope of the order in any material change of circumstances, and other matters as it sees fit.

2.22(6) If there is a material change in circumstances rendering the limit on disclosure unnecessary, the administrator shall, as soon as reasonably practicable after the change, apply to the court for the order to be discharged or varied; and upon the discharge or variation of the order the administrator shall, as soon as reasonably practicable–

(a) file a copy of the full statement of affairs (or so much of the statement of affairs as is no longer subject to the order) with the registrar of companies;

(b) where he has previously sent a copy of his proposals to the creditors in accordance with paragraph 49, provide the creditors with a copy of the full statement of affairs (or so much of the statement as is no longer subject to the order) or a summary thereof; and

(c) place a copy of the full statement of affairs (or so much of the statement as is no longer subject to the order) in the sederunt book.

2.23 Release from duty to submit statement of affairs; extension of time

2.23(1) The power of the administrator under paragraph 48(2) to revoke a requirement under paragraph 47(1), or to grant an extension of time, may be exercised at the administrator's own instance, or at the request of any relevant person.

2.23(2) A relevant person whose request under this Rule has been refused by the administrator may apply to the court for a release or extension of time.

2.23(3)   An applicant under this Rule shall bear his own expenses in the application and, unless the court otherwise orders, no allowance towards such expenses shall be made as an expense of the administration of the company.

History
In r.2.23(3) "as an expense of the administration" substituted for "out of the assets" by the Insolvency (Scotland) Amendment Rules 2010 (SI 2010/688 (S 2)) art.3 and Sch.1 para.59 as from April 6, 2010, subject to transitional provisions in art.4.

2.24   Expenses of statement of affairs

2.24(1)   A relevant person who provides to the administrator a statement of affairs of the company or statement of concurrence shall be allowed, and paid by the administrator as an expense of the administration, any expenses incurred by the relevant person in so doing which the administrator considers reasonable.

History
In r.2.24(1) "affairs of the company" substituted for "the company's affairs", and "as an expense of the administration" substituted for "out of his receipts", by the Insolvency (Scotland) Amendment Rules 2010 (SI 2010/688 (S 2)) art.3 and Sch.1 para.60 as from April 6, 2010, subject to transitional provisions in art.4.

2.24(2)   Any decision by the administrator under this Rule is subject to appeal to the court.

2.24(3)   Nothing in this Rule relieves a relevant person from any obligation to provide a statement of affairs or statement of concurrence, or to provide information to the administrator.

2.25   Administrator's proposals

2.25(1)   The statement required to be made by the administrator under paragraph 49 shall include, in addition to the matters set out in that paragraph–

(a)   details of the court which granted the administration order or in which the notice of appointment was lodged, and the relevant court reference number (if any);

(b)   the full name, registered address, registered number and any other trading names of the company;

(c)   details relating to his appointment as administrator, including the date of appointment and the person making the application or appointment, and, where there are joint administrators, a statement of the matters referred to in paragraph 100(2);

(d)   the names of the directors and secretary of the company and details of any shareholdings which they have in the company;

(e)   an account of the circumstances giving rise to the appointment of the administrator;

(f)   if a statement of the company's affairs has been submitted, a copy or summary of it, with the administrator's comments, if any;

(g)   if an order limiting the disclosure of the statement of affairs has been made, a statement of that fact, as well as–

    (i)   details of who provided the statement of affairs;

    (ii)   the date of the order of limited disclosure; and

    (iii)   the details or a summary of the details that are not subject to that order;

(h)   if a full statement of affairs is not provided, the names and addresses of the creditors, and details of the debts owed to, and security held by, each of them;

(i)   if no statement of affairs has been submitted–

    (i)   details of the financial position of the company at the latest practicable date (which must, unless the court otherwise orders, be a date not earlier than that on which the company entered administration);

    (ii)   the names and addresses of the creditors, and details of the debts owed to, and security held by, each of them; and

    (iii)   an explanation as to why there is no statement of affairs;

(j)   the basis upon which it is proposed that the administrator's remuneration should be fixed;

(ka)   a statement complying with paragraph (1B) of any pre-administration costs charged or incurred by the administrator or, to the administrator's knowledge, by any other person qualified to act as an insolvency practitioner;

(k)   except where the administrator proposes a voluntary arrangement in relation to the company–

    (i)   to the best of the administrator's knowledge and belief–

      (aa)   an estimate of the value of the prescribed part (whether or not he proposes to make an application to the court under section 176A(5) and whether or not section 176A(3) applies); and

      (bb)   an estimate of the value of the company's net property,

      provided that such estimates shall not be required to include any information the disclosure of which could serious prejudice the commercial interests of the company, but if such information is excluded the estimates shall be accompanied by a statement to that effect; and

    (ii)   whether and, if so, why the administrator proposes to make an application to the court under section 176A(5);

(l)   a statement (which must comply with paragraph (1C) where that paragraph applies) of how it is envisaged the purpose of the administration will be achieved and how it is proposed that the administration shall end;

(m)   [Omitted by the Insolvency (Scotland) Amendment Rules 2010 (SI 2010/688 (S 2)) art.3 and Sch.1 para.63 as from April 6, 2010, subject to transitional provisions in art.4.]

(n)   where it is proposed to make distributions to creditors in accordance with Chapter 9, the classes of creditors to whom it is proposed that distributions be made and whether or not the administrator intends to make an application to the court under paragraph 65(3);

(o)   where the administrator has decided not to call a meeting of creditors, his reasons;

(p)   the manner in which the affairs and business of the company–

    (i)   have, since the date of the administrator's appointment, been managed and financed; and

    (ii)   will, if the administrator's proposals are approved, continue to be managed and financed;

(q)   whether–

    (i)   the EC Regulation applies; and

    (ii)   if so, whether the proceedings are main, secondary or territorial proceedings; and

(r)   such other information (if any) as the administrator thinks necessary to enable creditors to decide whether or not to vote for the adoption of the proposals.

History

Rule 2.25(1)(ka) inserted, and r.2.25(1)(l) substituted, by the Insolvency (Scotland) Amendment Rules 2010 (SI 2010/688 (S 2)) art.3 and Sch.1 paras 61 and 62 as from April 6, 2010, subject to transitional provisions in art.4. See note after r.2.30.

2.25(1A)   In this Part–

(a) **"pre-administration costs"** are–

(i)   fees charged, and

(ii)   expenses incurred,

by the administrator, or another person qualified to act as an insolvency practitioner, before the company entered administration but with a view to its doing so; and

(b) **"unpaid pre-administration costs"** are pre-administration costs which had not been paid when the company entered administration.

History
See history note after r.2.25(1C).

2.25(1B)   A statement of pre-administration costs complies with this paragraph if it includes–

(a) details of any agreement under which the fees were charged and expenses incurred, including the parties to the agreement and the date on which the agreement was made,

(b) details of the work done for which the fees were charged and expenses incurred,

(c) an explanation of why the work was done before the company entered administration and how it would further the achievement of an objective in sub-paragraph (1) of paragraph 3 in accordance with sub-paragraphs (2) to (4) of that paragraph,

(d) a statement of the amount of the pre-administration costs, setting out separately–

(i)   the fees charged by the administrator,

(ii)   the expenses incurred by the administrator,

(iii)   the fees charged (to the administrator's knowledge) by any other person qualified to act as an insolvency practitioner (and, if more than one, by each separately), and

(iv)   the expenses incurred (to the administrator's knowledge) by any other person qualified to act as an insolvency practitioner (and, if more than one, by each separately),

(e) a statement of the amounts of unpaid pre-administration costs (set out separately as under sub-paragraph (d),

(f) the identity of the person who made the payment or, if more than one person made the payment, the identity of each such person and of the amounts paid by each such person set out separately as under sub-paragraph (d),

(g) a statement of the amounts of unpaid pre-administration costs (set out separately as under sub-paragraph (d)), and

(h) a statement that the payment of unpaid pre-administration costs as an expense of the administration is–

(i)   subject to approval under Rule 2.39C, and

(ii)   not part of the proposals subject to approval under paragraph 53.

History
See history note after r.2.25(1C).

2.25(1C)   This paragraph applies where it is proposed that the administration will end by the company moving to a creditors' voluntary liquidation; and in that case, the statement required by Rule 2.25(1)(l) must include–

(a) details of the proposed liquidator;

  (b)   where applicable, the declaration required by section 231 (appointment to office of two or more persons); and

  (c)   a statement that the creditors may, before the proposals are approved, nominate a different person as liquidator in accordance with paragraph 83(7)(a) and Rule 2.47.

History
Rule 2.25(1A)–(1C) inserted by the Insolvency (Scotland) Amendment Rules 2010 (SI 2010/688 (S 2)) art.3 and Sch.1 para.64 as from April 6, 2010, subject to transitional provisions in art.4.

2.25(2) A copy of the administrator's statement of his proposals shall be sent to the registrar of companies together with a notice in the form required by Rule 7.30 and Schedule 5.

2.25(3) Where the statement of proposals states that the administrator thinks–

  (a)   that the company has sufficient property to enable each creditor of the company to be paid in full;

  (b)   that the company has insufficient property to make a distribution to unsecured creditors other than by virtue of section 176A(2)(a); or

  (c)   that neither of the objectives specified in paragraph 3(1)(a) and (b) can be achieved,

and no meeting has been requisitioned under paragraph 52(2), the administrator's proposals shall be deemed to have been approved by the creditors upon the expiry of the period set out in Rule 2.31.

2.25(3A) Where proposals are deemed under paragraph (3) to have been approved, the administrator must, as soon as reasonably practicable after the expiry of the period set out in Rule 2.31, give notice of the date on which they were deemed to have been approved to the registrar of companies, the court and the creditors in the form required by Rule 7.30 and Schedule 5; and a copy of the proposals must be attached to the notice given to the court and to creditors who have not previously received them.

History
Rule 2.25(3A) inserted by the Insolvency (Scotland) Amendment Rules 2010 (SI 2010/688 (S 2)) art.3 and Sch.1 para.65 as from April 6, 2010, subject to transitional provisions in art.4.

2.25(4) The administrator shall give notice to the creditors of any order varying the period referred to in paragraph 49(5) (which sets out the period during which the administrator shall send out a copy of his statement of proposals).

2.25(5) Where the administrator intends to apply to the court (or to lodge a notice under paragraph 80(2)) for the administration to cease at a time before he has sent a statement of his proposals to creditors in accordance with paragraph 49, he shall, at least 7 business days before he makes such an application or lodges such a notice, send to all creditors of the company (so far as he is aware of their addresses) a report containing the information required by paragraph (1)(a) to (q) of this Rule.

History
In r.2.25(5) "7 business" substituted for "10" by the Insolvency (Scotland) Amendment Rules 2010 (SI 2010/688 (S 2)) art.3 and Sch.1 para.66 as from April 6, 2010, subject to transitional provisions in art.4.

2.25(6) Where the administrator wishes to publish a notice under paragraph 49(6), the notice shall be advertised in such manner as the administrator thinks fit.

2.25(6A) A notice published under Rule 2.25(6) must include the standard content and must state–

  (a)   that members can write to request that a copy of the statement of proposals be provided free of charge; and

  (b)   the address to which to write.

History
Rule 2.25(6A) substituted by the Insolvency (Scotland) Amendment Rules 2010 (SI 2010/688 (S 2)) art.3 and Sch.1 para.67 as from April 6, 2010, subject to transitional provisions in art.4.

2.25(7) A notice under paragraph 49(6) must be published as soon as reasonably practicable after the administrator sends his statement of proposals to the company's creditors and in any case no later than 8 weeks (or such other period as may be agreed by the creditors or ordered by the court) from the date upon which the company entered administration.

History
Rule 2.25(6) substituted and r.2.25(6A) inserted by the Insolvency (Scotland) (Amendment) Rules 2009 (SI 2009/662 (S 1)) r.2 and Sch. paras 5, 6 as from April 6, 2009.

2.25A Limited disclosure of paragraph 49 statement

2.25A(1) Where the administrator thinks that it would prejudice the conduct of the administration or might reasonably be expected to lead to violence against any person for any of the matters specified in Rule 2.25(1)(h) and (i) to be disclosed, the administrator may apply to the court for an order of limited disclosure in respect of any specified part of the statement under paragraph 49 containing such matter.

2.25A(2) The court may, on such application, order that some or all of the specified part of the statement must not be sent to the registrar of companies or to creditors or members of the company as otherwise required by paragraph 49(4).

2.25A(3) The administrator must as soon as reasonably practicable send to the persons specified in paragraph 49(4) the statement under paragraph 49 (to the extent provided by the order) and an indication of the nature of the matter in relation to which the order was made.

2.25A(4) The administrator must also send a copy of the order to the registrar of companies.

2.25A(5) A creditor who seeks disclosure of a part of a statement under paragraph 49 in relation to which an order has been made under this Rule may apply to the court for an order that the administrator disclose it. The application must be supported by written evidence in the form of an affidavit.

2.25A(6) The court may make any order for disclosure subject to any conditions as to confidentiality, duration and scope of the order in the event of any change of circumstances, or other matters as it sees just.

2.25A(7) If there is a material change in circumstances rendering the limit on disclosure or any part of it unnecessary, the administrator must, as soon as reasonably practicable after the change, apply to the court for the order or any part of it to be discharged or varied.

2.25A(8) The administrator must, as soon as reasonably practicable after the making of an order under paragraph (7), send to the persons specified in paragraph 49(4) a copy of the statement under paragraph 49 to the extent provided by the order.

History
See history note after r.2.25E

CHAPTER 5A

THE GIVING OF NOTICE AND SUPPLY OF DOCUMENTS

2.25B Application

2.25B(1) Subject to paragraph (2), this Chapter applies where a notice or other document is required to be given, delivered or sent under this Part of these Rules.

2.25B(2) This Chapter does not apply to–

    (a) the lodging of any application, or other document, with the court;

(b)   the service of any application, or other document, lodged with the court;

(c)   the service of any order of the court; or

(d)   the submission of documents to the registrar of companies.

History
See history note after r.2.25E

2.25C   Electronic delivery

2.25C(1)   Unless in any particular case some other form of delivery is required by the Act or these Rules or any order of the court, a notice or other document may be given, delivered or sent by electronic means provided that the intended recipient of the notice or other document has–

(a)   consented (whether in the specific case or generally) to electronic delivery (and has not revoked that consent); and

(b)   provided an electronic address for delivery.

2.25C(2)   Where an administrator gives, sends or delivers a notice or other document to any person by electronic means, it must contain or be accompanied by a statement that the recipient may request a hard copy of the notice or document, and specify a telephone number, e-mail address and postal address which may be used to make such a request.

2.25C(3)   Where a hard copy of the notice or other document is requested it must be sent within 5 business days of receipt of the request by the administrator, who may not make a charge for sending it in that form.

2.25C(4)   In the absence of evidence to the contrary, a notice or other document shall be presumed to have been delivered where–

(a)   the sender can produce a copy of the electronic message which–

   (i)   contained the notice or other document, or to which the notice or other document was attached; and

   (ii) shows the time and date the message was sent; and

(b)   that electronic message was sent to the address supplied under paragraph (1)(b).

2.25C(5)   A message delivered electronically shall be deemed to have been delivered to the recipient at 9.00 am on the next business day after it was sent.

History
See history note after r.2.25E

2.25D   Use of websites by administrator

2.25D(1)   This Rule applies for the purpose of section 246B.

2.25D(2)   An administrator required to give, deliver or send a document to any person may (other than in a case where personal service is required) satisfy that requirement by sending that person a notice–

(a)   stating that the document is available for viewing and downloading on a website;

(b)   specifying the address of that website together with any password necessary to view and download the document from that website; and

(c)   containing a statement that the recipient of the notice may request a hard copy of the document, and specifying a telephone number, e-mail address and postal address which may be used to make such a request.

2.25D(3)   Where a notice to which this Rule applies is sent, the document to which it relates must–

(a)   be available on the website for a period of not less than 3 months after the date on which the notice is sent; and

(b)   be in such a format as to enable it to be downloaded from the website within a reasonable time of an electronic request being made for it to be downloaded.

2.25D(4)   Where a hard copy of the document is requested it must be sent within 5 business days of the receipt of the request by the administrator, who may not make a charge for sending it in that form.

2.25D(5)   Where a document is given, delivered or sent to a person by means of a website in accordance with this Rule, it is deemed to have been delivered–

(a)   when the document was first made available on the website, or

(b)   if later, when the notice under paragraph (2) was delivered to that person.

History
See history note after r.2.25E

2.25E   Special provision on account of expense as to website use

2.25E(1)   Where the court is satisfied that the expense of sending notices in accordance with Rule 2.25D would, on account of the number of persons entitled to receive them, be disproportionate to the benefit of sending notices in accordance with that Rule, it may order that the requirement to give, deliver or send a relevant document to any person may (other than in a case where personal service is required) be satisfied by the administrator sending each of those persons a notice–

(a)   stating that all relevant documents will be made available for viewing and downloading on a website;

(b)   specifying the address of that website together with any password necessary to view and download the document from that site; and

(c)   containing a statement that the person to whom the notice is given, delivered or sent may at any time request that hard copies of all, or specific, relevant documents are sent to that person, and specifying a telephone number, e-mail address and postal address which may be used to make that request.

2.25E(2)   A document to which this Rule relates must–

(a)   be available on the website for a period of not less than 12 months from the date when it was first made available on the website or, if later, from the date upon which the notice was sent, and

(b)   be in such a format as to enable it to be downloaded from the website within a reasonable time of an electronic request being made for it to be downloaded.

2.25E(3)   Where hard copies of relevant documents have been requested, they must be sent by the administrator–

(a)   within 5 business days of the receipt by the administrator of the request to be sent hard copies, in the case of relevant documents first appearing on the website before the request was received, or

(b)   within 5 business days from the date a relevant document first appears on the website, in all other cases.

2.25E(4)   An administrator must not require a person making a request under paragraph (3) to pay a fee for the supply of the document.

2.25E(5)   Where a relevant document is given, delivered or sent to a person by means of a website in accordance with this Rule, it is deemed to have been delivered–

    (a)   when the relevant document was first made available on the website, or

    (b)   if later, when the notice under paragraph (1) was delivered to that person.

2.25E(6)   In this Rule a relevant document means any document which the administrator is first required to give, deliver or send to any person after the court has made an order under paragraph (1).

History

Rules 2.25A–2.25E inserted by the Insolvency (Scotland) Amendment Rules 2010 (SI 2010/688 (S 2)) art.3 and Sch.1 para.68 as from April 6, 2010, subject to transitional provisions in art.4 (in relation to r.2.25A) but otherwise in all cases (in relation to rr.2.25B–2.25E) (see art.5).

CHAPTER 6

MEETINGS

2.26   General

2.26   The provisions of Chapter 1 of Part 7 (Meetings) shall apply with regard to meetings of the company's creditors or members which are summoned by the administrator, subject to the provisions in this chapter.

2.26A   Notice of meetings

2.26A(1)   The administrator shall publish notice of all meetings of the company's creditors or members in the Edinburgh Gazette and in such other manner as the administrator thinks fit to ensure the meeting comes to the notice of any persons who are entitled to attend.

History

Rule 2.26A(1) substituted for former r.2.26A(1) and (2) by the Insolvency (Scotland) Amendment Rules 2010 (SI 2010/688 (S 2)) art.3 and Sch.1 para.69(a) as from April 6, 2010, subject to transitional provisions in art.4.

2.26A(3)   A notice published under paragraph (1) shall include–

    (a)   the name, registered number and address of the registered office of the company in administration;

    (b)   the venue fixed for the meeting;

    (c)   the date and time of the meeting; and

    (d)   the full name and address of the administrator.

History

In r.2.26A(3) "(1)" substituted for "(1) or (2)" by the Insolvency (Scotland) Amendment Rules 2010 (SI 2010/688 (S 2)) art.3 and Sch.1 para.69(b) as from April 6, 2010.

2.26A(4)   Rule 7.3(3) (notice of meeting) shall not apply to a meeting of creditors summoned by the administrator.

History

Rule 2.26A inserted by the Insolvency (Scotland) (Amendment) Rules 2009 (SI 2009/662 (S 1)) r.2 and Sch. para.7 as from April 6, 2009.

2.26B   Remote attendance at meetings

2.26B(1)   This Rule applies to a request to the administrator under section 246A(9) to specify a place for the meeting.

2.26B(2)   The request must be accompanied by–

    (a)   in the case of a request by creditors, a list of the creditors making (or concurring with) the request and the amounts of those creditors' respective debts in the insolvency proceedings in question,

576

(b)   in the case of a request by members, a list of the members making (or concurring with) the request and those members' voting rights, and

(c)   from each person concurring, written confirmation of that person's concurrence.

2.26B(3)   The request must be made within 7 business days of the date on which the administrator sent the notice of the meeting in question.

2.26B(4)   Where the administrator considers that the request has been properly made in accordance with the Act and these Rules, the administrator must–

(a)   give notice (to all those previously given notice of the meeting)–

   (i)   that the meeting is to be held at a specified place, and

   (ii)   whether the date and time of the meeting are to remain the same or not;

(b)   specify a time, date and place for the meeting, the date of which must not be more than 28 days after the original date for the meeting; and

(c)   give at least 14 days' notice of the time, date and place of the meeting to all those previously given notice of the meeting,

and the notices required by subparagraphs (a) and (c) may be given at the same or different times.

2.26B(5)   Where the administrator has specified a place for the meeting in response to a request to which this Rule applies, the chairman of the meeting must attend the meeting by being present in person at that place.

2.26B(6)   Rule 7.6(4), (5), (6) and (7) (expenses of summoning meetings) as applied by Rule 2.26, do not apply to the summoning and holding of a meeting at a place specified in accordance with section 246A(9).

History
See history note after r.2.26C.

2.26C   Entitlement to vote and draw dividend

2.26C(1)   A creditor, in order to obtain an adjudication as to entitlement–

(a)   to vote at any meeting of the creditors in the administration; or

(b)   to a dividend (so far as funds are available) out of the assets of the company in respect of any accounting period,

must submit a claim to the administrator.

2.26C(2)   A creditor's claim must be submitted–

(a)   at or before the meeting; or, as the case may be,

(b)   not later than 8 weeks before the end of the accounting period.

2.26C(3)   A creditor's claim must–

(a)   be made out by, or under the direction of, the creditor;

(b)   have attached an account or voucher (according to the nature of the debt claimed) which constitutes *prima facie* evidence of the debt; and

(c)   state the following matters–

   (i)   the creditor's name and address;

   (ii)   if the creditor is a company, its registered number;

(iii) the total amount of the creditor's claim (including value added tax) as at the date on which the company entered administration, (or if the company was in liquidation when it entered administration, the date on which it went into liquidation) less any payments that have been made to the creditor after that date in respect of that claim;

(iv) whether or not the claim includes outstanding uncapitalised interest;

(v) particulars of how and when the debt was incurred by the company;

(vi) particulars of any security held, the date on which it was given and the value which the creditor puts on it;

(vii) details of any reservation of title in respect of goods to which the debt refers; and

(viii) the name, address and authority of the person making out the proof, if other than the creditor.

2.26C(4)   The administrator may dispense with any requirement in paragraph (3)(b) in respect of any debt or any class of debt.

2.26C(5)   A claim submitted by a creditor, which has been accepted in whole or in part by the administrator for the purpose of voting at a meeting, or of drawing a dividend in respect of any accounting period, shall be deemed to have been resubmitted for the purpose of obtaining an adjudication as to the creditor's entitlement both to vote at any subsequent meeting and (so far as funds are available) to a dividend in respect of an accounting period or, as the case may be, any subsequent accounting period.

2.26C(6)   A creditor who has submitted a claim, may at any time submit a further claim specifying a different amount for that creditor's claim, provided that a secured creditor shall not be entitled to produce a further claim specifying a different value for the security at any time after the administrator has required the creditor to discharge, convey or assign the security.

2.26C(7)   Where an administration is immediately preceded by a winding up, a creditor who has proved a debt in the winding up is deemed to have proved it in the administration.

History
Rules 2.26B and 2.26C inserted by the Insolvency (Scotland) Amendment Rules 2010 (SI 2010/688 (S 2)) art.3 and Sch.1 para.70 as from April 6, 2010, subject to transitional provisions in art.4 (in relation to r.2.26C), but in all cases in relation to r.2.26B (see art.5).

2.27   Meetings to consider administrator's proposals

2.27(1)   The administrator may, upon giving at least 14 days' notice, require the attendance at a creditors' meeting of any directors or officers of the company (including persons who have been directors or officers in the past) whose presence at the meeting is, in the administrator's opinion, appropriate.

2.27(2)   If at the meeting there is not the requisite majority for approval of the administrator's proposals (with modifications, if any), the chairman may, and shall if a resolution is passed to that effect, adjourn the meeting for not more than 14 days.

History
In r.2.27(2) "once only and" former appearing after "adjourn the meeting" omitted by the Insolvency (Scotland) Amendment Rules 2010 (SI 2010/688 (S 2)) art.3 and Sch.1 para.71 as from April 6, 2010, subject to transitional provisions in art.4.

2.27(3)   The administrator shall give notice to the creditors of any order varying the period referred to in paragraph 51(2) (which sets out the period during which the administrator must set the date for an initial creditors' meeting).

2.27(4)   [Omitted by the Insolvency (Scotland) Amendment Rules 2010 (SI 2010/688 (S 2)) art.3 and Sch.1 para.72 as from April 6, 2010, subject to transitional provisions in art.4.]

2.27A Suspension and adjournment

2.27A(1) This Rule applies to all meetings of creditors, and Rule 7.8 does not apply.

2.27A(2) If within 30 minutes from the time fixed for the commencement of the meeting those persons attending the meeting do not constitute a quorum, the chairman may adjourn the meeting to such time and place as the chairman may appoint.

2.27A(3) Once only in the course of the meeting the chairman may, without an adjournment, declare the meeting suspended for any period up to one hour.

2.27A(4) In the course of any meeting, the chairman may, in the chairman's discretion, and shall, if the meeting so resolves, adjourn it to such date, time and place as seems to the chairman to be appropriate in the circumstances.

2.27A(5) An adjournment under paragraph (4) must not be for a period of more than 14 days, subject to a direction from the court.

2.27A(6) If there are subsequent further adjournments, the final adjournment must not be to a day later than 14 days after the date on which the meeting was originally held.

2.27A(7) Where a meeting is adjourned under this Rule, proxies may be used if lodged at or before the adjourned meeting.

2.27A(8) Where a meeting is adjourned under this Rule, any proxies given for the original meeting may be used at the adjourned meeting.

History
Rule 2.27A inserted by the Insolvency (Scotland) Amendment Rules 2010 (SI 2010/688 (S 2)) art.3 and Sch.1 para.73 as from April 6, 2010, subject to transitional provisions in art.4.

2.28 Correspondence instead of creditors' meetings

2.28(1) This Rule applies where an administrator proposes to conduct the business of a creditors' meeting by correspondence in accordance with paragraph 58.

2.28(2) Notice of the business to be conducted shall be given to all who are entitled to be notified of a creditors' meeting by virtue of paragraph 51.

2.28(3) The administrator may seek to obtain the agreement of the creditors to a resolution by sending to every creditor a copy of the proposed resolution.

2.28(4) The administrator shall send to the creditors a copy of any proposed resolution on which a decision is sought, which shall be set out in such a way that agreement with or dissent from each separate resolution may be indicated by the recipient on the copy so sent.

2.28(5) The administrator shall set a closing date for receipt of votes and comments. The closing date shall be set at the discretion of the administrator, but shall not be less than 14 days from the date of issue of the notice under paragraph (1) of this Rule.

2.28(6) In order to be considered, votes and comments must be received by the administrator by the closing date and must be accompanied by the statement of claim and account or voucher referred to in Rule 2.26C, except where the statement of claim and account or voucher have already been submitted by the creditor to the administrator.

History
In r.2.28(6) "2.26C, except where" to the end substituted for "4.15 as applied by this Part" by the Insolvency (Scotland) Amendment Rules 2010 (SI 2010/688 (S 2)) art.3 and Sch.1 para.74 as from April 6, 2010, subject to transitional provisions in art.4.

2.28(7) For the conduct of business to proceed, the administrator must receive at least one response which satisfies the requirements of paragraph (6) of this Rule.

2.28(8) If no responses are received by the closing date then the administrator shall summon a creditors' meeting.

2.28(9) Any single creditor, or a group of creditors, of the company whose debt(s) amount to at least 10% of the total debts of the company may, within 5 business days from the date of the administrator sending out a resolution or proposals, require him to summon a creditors' meeting to consider the matters raised therein.

2.28(10) If the administrator's proposals or revised proposals are rejected by the creditors pursuant to this Rule, the administrator may summon a creditors' meeting.

2.28(11) A reference in this Part to anything done at a creditors' meeting includes a reference to anything done in the course of correspondence in accordance with this Rule; and Rule 2.35 shall apply to the business of a creditors' meeting conducted by correspondence as it applies to a creditors' meeting.

2.29　Applicable law (company meetings)

2.29 Subject to anything to the contrary in the Act and these Rules, a meeting of the members of the company must be summoned and conducted–

   (a)   in the case of a company incorporated in a part of the United Kingdom in accordance with the law of that part including any applicable provision in or made under the Companies Act 2006;

   (b)   in the case of a company incorporated in an EEA state other than the United Kingdom, in accordance with the law of that state applicable to meetings of the company; or

   (c)   in any other case, in accordance with the law of Scotland, including any provision in or made under the Companies Act 2006 applicable to the company as an overseas company.

History
Rule 2.29 substituted by the Insolvency (Scotland) Amendment Rules 2010 (SI 2010/688 (S 2)) art.3 and Sch.1 para.75 as from April 6, 2010, subject to transitional provisions in art.4.

2.30　Entitlement to vote—member State liquidators

2.30(1) Where–

   (a)   a creditor is entitled to vote at a creditors' meeting;

   (b)   has lodged his claim in one or more sets of other proceedings;

   (c)   votes (either in person or by proxy) on a resolution put to the meeting; and

   (d)   a member State liquidator casts a vote in respect of the same claim,

only the creditor's vote shall be counted.

2.30(2) Where–

   (a)   a creditor has lodged his claim in more than one set of other proceedings; and

   (b)   more than one member State liquidator seeks to vote by virtue of that claim,

the entitlement to vote by virtue of that claim is exercisable by the member State liquidator in main proceedings, whether or not the creditor has lodged his claim in the main proceedings.

2.30(3) For the purposes of this Rule, **"other proceedings"** means main, secondary or territorial proceedings in another member State.

History
Rules 2.2(3), 2.25(1)(q)(ii) and 2.30(3) amended by the Insolvency (Scotland) Amendment Rules 2006 (SI 2006/734 (S 6)), as from April 6, 2006.

2.31 Meeting requisitioned by creditors

2.31 The request for an initial creditors' meeting under paragraph 52(2) must be made within 8 business days of the date upon which the administrator sends out his statement of proposals.

History
In r.2.31 "8 business" substituted for "12" by the Insolvency (Scotland) Amendment Rules 2010 (SI 2010/688 (S 2)) art.3 and Sch.1 para.76 as from April 6, 2010, subject to transitional provisions in art.4.

2.32(1) Rule 7.6(2)(a) and (b) do not apply if the requisitioning creditor's debt alone is sufficient to meet the requirement of paragraph 52(2)(a) or, as the case may be, paragraph 56(1)(a), without the concurrence of other creditors.

History
In r.2.32(1) "and (b) do" substituted for "does" by the Insolvency (Scotland) Amendment Rules 2010 (SI 2010/688 (S 2)) art.3 and Sch.1 para.77 as from April 6, 2010, subject to transitional provisions in art.4.

2.32(2) In its application to initial creditors' meetings in administration, for the period of 35 days referred to in Rule 7.6(3) there is substituted a period of 28 days.

2.32A Notice of meetings by advertisement only

2.23A(1) The court may order that notice of any meeting be given by advertisement and not by individual notice to the persons concerned.

2.23A(2) In considering whether to act under this Rule, the court must have regard to the cost of advertisement, the amount of assets available and the extent of the interest of creditors, members or any particular class of either.

History
Rule 2.32A inserted by the Insolvency (Scotland) Amendment Rules 2010 (SI 2010/688 (S 2)) art.3 and Sch.1 para.78 as from April 6, 2010, subject to transitional provisions in art.4.

2.33 Hire-purchase, conditional sale and hiring agreements

2.33(1) Subject as follows, an owner of goods under a hire-purchase agreement or under an agreement for the hire of goods for more than 3 months, or a seller of goods under a conditional sale agreement, is entitled to vote in respect of the amount of the debt due and payable to him by the company on the date that the company entered administration.

2.33(2) In calculating the amount of any debt for this purpose, no account shall be taken of any amount attributable to the exercise of any right under the relevant agreement, so far as the right has become exercisable solely by virtue of the making of an administration application, a notice of intention to appoint an administrator or any matter' arising as a consequence, or of the company entering administration.

2.34 Revision of the administrator's proposals

2.34(1) A statement of revised proposals under paragraph 54 shall include–

(a) details of the court which granted the administration order or in which the notice of appointment was lodged and the relevant court reference number (if any);

(b) the full name, registered address, registered number and any other trading names of the company;

(c) details relating to the appointment of the administrator, including the date of appointment and the person making the administration application or appointment;

(d) the names of the directors and secretary of the company and details of any shareholdings which they have in the company;

(e)   a summary of the initial proposals and the reason or reasons for proposing a revision;

(f)   details of the proposed revision including details of the administrator's assessment of the likely impact of the proposed revision upon creditors generally or upon each class of creditors (as the case may be);

(g)   where it is proposed, by virtue of the revision, to make distributions to creditors in accordance with Chapter 9, the classes of creditors to whom it is proposed that distributions be made and whether or not the administrator intends to make an application to the court under paragraph 65(3);

(h)   where the revision includes a proposal to move from administration to a creditors' voluntary liquidation–

     (i)   details of the proposed liquidator;

     (ii)   a statement that, in accordance with paragraph 83(7) and Rule 2.47, creditors may nominate another person to act as liquidator;

     (iii)   any other information that the administrator thinks necessary to enable creditors to decide whether or not to vote for the proposed revisions; and

     (iv)   where applicable, the declaration required by section 231.

History

Rule 2.34(1)(h)(iv) inserted by the Insolvency (Scotland) Amendment Rules 2010 (SI 2010/688 (S 2)) art.3 and Sch.1 para.79 as from April 6, 2010, subject to transitional provisions in art.4.

2.34(2)   Subject to paragraph 54(3), within 5 business days of sending out the statement mentioned in paragraph (1) above, the administrator shall send a copy of the statement to every member of the company.

History

In r.2.34(2) "business" inserted by the Insolvency (Scotland) Amendment Rules 2010 (SI 2010/688 (S 2)) art.3 and Sch.1 para.80 as from April 6, 2010, subject to transitional provisions in art.4.

2.34(3)   Where the administrator wishes to publish a notice under paragraph 54(3), the notice shall be advertised in such manner as the administrator thinks fit.

2.34(4)   The notice referred to in paragraph (3) shall–

(a)   state the full name of the company;

(b)   state the name and address of the administrator;

(c)   specify an address to which any member of the company can write to request that a copy of the statement be provided free of charge; and

(d)   be published as soon as is reasonably practicable after the administrator sends the statement to the creditors.

History

Rule 2.34(3) substituted, and r.2.34(4) inserted, by the Insolvency (Scotland) (Amendment) Rules 2009 (SI 2009/662 (S 1)) r.2 and Sch. paras 8, 9 as from April 6, 2009.

2.35   Notices to creditors

2.35(1)   As soon as reasonably practicable after the conclusion of a meeting of creditors to consider the administrator's proposals or revised proposals, or of the conclusion of the business of such a meeting by correspondence in accordance with these Rules, the administrator shall–

(a) send notice of the result of the meeting in the form required by Rule 7.30 and Schedule 5 (including details of any modifications to the proposals that were approved) to every creditor who received notice of the meeting and to the registrar of companies;

(b) lodge in court, and send to any creditors who did not receive notice of the meeting and of whose claim he has become subsequently aware, a copy of the notice of the result of the meeting along with a copy of the proposals which were considered at that meeting; and

(c) place a copy of the notice of the result of the meeting in the sederunt book.

History
In r.2.35(1)(a) "and to the registrar of companies" inserted, and r.2.35(1)(b) "to the registrar of companies and" omitted, by the Insolvency (Scotland) Amendment Rules 2010 (SI 2010/688 (S 2)) art.3 and Sch.1 paras 81 and 82 as from April 6, 2010, subject to transitional provisions in art.4.

2.35(2) Where the business of a creditors' meeting has been carried out by correspondence in accordance with Rule 2.28, for the references in the foregoing paragraph of this Rule to the result of the meeting and notice of the meeting there shall be substituted references to the result of the correspondence and to the correspondence.

2.35A   Action where person excluded

2.35A(1) In this Rule and Rules 2.35B and 2.35C an **"excluded person"** means a person who–

(a) has taken all steps necessary to attend a meeting under the arrangements put in place to do so by the convener of the meeting under section 246A(6); and

(b) those arrangements do not permit that person to attend the whole or part of that meeting.

2.35A(2) Where the chairman becomes aware during the course of the meeting that there is an excluded person, the chairman may–

(a) continue the meeting;

(b) declare the meeting void and convene the meeting again;

(c) declare the meeting valid up to the point where the person was excluded and adjourn the meeting.

2.35A(3) Where the chairman continues the meeting, the meeting is valid unless–

(a) the chairman decides in consequence of a complaint under Rule 2.35C to declare the meeting void and hold the meeting again; or

(b) the court directs otherwise.

2.35A(4) Without prejudice to paragraph (2), where the chairman becomes aware during the course of the meeting of an excluded person, the chairman may, in the chairman's discretion and without an adjournment, declare the meeting suspended for any period up to one hour.

History
See history note after r.2.35C.

2.35B   Indication to excluded person

2.35B(1) A person who claims to be an excluded person may request an indication of what occurred during the period of that person's claimed exclusion (the **"indication"**).

2.35B(2) A request under paragraph (1) must be made as soon as reasonably practicable, and, in any event, no later than 4 p.m. on the business day following the day on which the exclusion is claimed to have occurred.

2.35B(3) A request under paragraph (1) must be made to–

(a) the chairman, where it is made during the course of the business of the meeting; or

(b) the administrator where it is made after the conclusion of the business of the meeting.

2.35B(4)   Where satisfied that the person making the request is an excluded person, the person to whom the request is made must give the indication as soon as reasonably practicable and, in any event, no later than 4. p.m. on the day following the request in paragraph (1).

History
See history note after r.2.35C.

2.35C   Complaint

2.35C(1)   Any person who–

    (a) is, or claims to be, an excluded person; or

    (b) attends the meeting (in person or by proxy) and considers that they have been adversely affected by a person's actual, apparent or claimed exclusion,

(**"the complainant"**) may make a complaint.

2.35C(2)   The person to whom the complaint must be made (**"the relevant person"**) is–

    (a) the chairman, where it is made during the course of the meeting; or

    (b) the administrator, where it is made after the meeting.

2.35C(3)   The relevant person must–

    (a) consider whether there is an excluded person;

    (b) where satisfied that there is an excluded person, consider the complaint; and

    (c) where satisfied that there has been prejudice, take such action as the relevant person considers fit to remedy the prejudice.

2.35C(4)   Paragraph (5) applies where–

    (a) the relevant person is satisfied that the complainant is an excluded person;

    (b) during the period of the person's exclusion–

        (i) a resolution was put to the meeting; and

        (ii) voted on; and

    (c) the excluded person asserts how the excluded person intended to vote on the resolution.

2.35C(5)   Subject to paragraph (6), where satisfied that the effect of the intended vote in paragraph (4), if cast, would have changed the result of the resolution, the relevant person must–

    (a) count the intended vote as being cast in accordance with the complainant's stated intention;

    (b) amend the record of the result of the resolution; and

    (c) where those entitled to attend the meeting have been notified of the result of the resolution, notify them of the change.

2.35C(6)   Where satisfied that more than one complainant in paragraph (4) is an excluded person, the relevant person must have regard to the combined effect of the intended votes.

2.35C(7)   A complaint must be made as soon as reasonably practicable and, in any event, by 4 p.m. on the business day following–

    (a) the day on which the person was excluded; or

(b) where an indication is requested under Rule 2.35B, the day on which the complainant received the indication.

2.35C(8) The relevant person must notify the complainant in writing of any decision.

2.35C(9) A complainant who is not satisfied by the action of the relevant person may apply to the court for a direction to be given to the relevant person as to the action to be taken in respect of the complaint, and any application must be made no more than 2 business days from the date of receiving the decision of the relevant person.

History
Rules 2.35A–2.35C inserted by the Insolvency (Scotland) Amendment Rules 2010 (SI 2010/688 (S 2)) art.3 and Sch.1 para.83 as from April 6, 2010, in all cases (see art.5).

CHAPTER 7

THE CREDITORS' COMMITTEE

2.36 Constitution of committee

2.36(1) Where it is resolved by the creditors' meeting to establish a creditors' committee under paragraph 57, the committee shall consist of at least 3 and not more than 5 creditors of the company elected at the meeting.

2.36(2) A person claiming to be a creditor is entitled to be a member of the committee provided that–

(a) that person's claim has neither been wholly disallowed for voting purposes, nor wholly rejected for the purpose of distribution or dividend; and

(b) the claim mentioned in sub-paragraph (a) is not fully secured.

2.36(3) A body corporate or a partnership may be a member of the committee, but it cannot act as such otherwise than by a representative appointed under Rule 2.36H.

History
See history note after r.2.36R.

2.36A Functions of the committee

2.36A In addition to any functions conferred on the creditors' committee by any provisions of the Act, the creditors' committee shall assist the administrator in discharging the administrator's functions and shall act in relation to the administrator in such manner as may be agreed from time to time.

History
See history note after r.2.36R.

2.36B Formalities of establishment

2.36B(1) The creditors' committee shall not come into being, and accordingly cannot act, until the administrator has issued a certificate of its due constitution.

2.36B(2) If the chairman of the meeting which resolves to establish the committee is not the administrator, the chairman shall, as soon as reasonably practicable, give notice of the resolution to the administrator (or, as the case may be, the person appointed as administrator by the same meeting), and inform the administrator of the names and addresses of the persons elected to be members of the committee.

2.36B(3) No person may act as a member of the committee unless and until that person has agreed to do so and, unless the relevant proxy or authorisation contains a statement to the contrary, such agreement may be given on behalf of the member by that member's proxy-holder who is present at the meeting at which the committee is established or, in the case of a body corporate or partnership, by its duly appointed representative.

2.36B(4) The administrator's certificate of the committee's due constitution shall not be issued before the minimum number of members set out in Rule 2.36(1) elected to be members of the committee have agreed to act, but shall be issued as soon as reasonably practicable thereafter.

2.36B(5) As and when the others elected to be members of the committee (if any) agree to act, the administrator shall issue an amended certificate.

2.36B(6) The certificate (and any amended certificate) shall be sent by the administrator to the registrar of companies.

2.36B(7) If after the first establishment of the committee there is any change in its membership, the administrator shall, as soon as reasonably practicable report the change to the registrar of companies.

History
See history note after r.2.36R.

2.36C   Meetings of the committee

2.36C(1) Subject as follows, meetings of the creditors' committee shall be held when and where determined by the administrator.

2.36C(2) The administrator shall call a first meeting of the committee to take place within 6 weeks of the committee's establishment.

2.36C(3) After the calling of the first meeting, the administrator must call a meeting–

    (a)   if so requested by a member of the committee or a member's representative (the meeting then to be held within 21 days of the request being received by the administrator), and

    (b)   for a specified date, if the committee has previously resolved that a meeting be held on that date.

2.36C(4) Subject to paragraph (5) the administrator shall give 5 business days written notice of the time and place of any meeting to every member of the committee (or a member's representative, if designated for that purpose), unless in any case the requirement of the notice has been waived by or on behalf of any member. Waiver may be signified either at or before the meeting.

2.36C(5) Where the administrator has determined that a meeting should be conducted and held in the manner referred to in Rule 2.36D, the notice period mentioned in paragraph (4) is 7 business days.

History
See history note after r.2.36R.

2.36D   Remote attendance at meetings of creditors' committees

2.36D(1) This Rule applies to any meeting of a creditors' committee held under this Part.

2.36D(2) Where the administrator considers it appropriate, the meeting may be conducted and held in such a way that persons who are not present together at the same place may attend it.

2.36D(3) Where a meeting is conducted and held in the manner referred to in paragraph (2), a person attends the meeting if that person is able to exercise any rights which that person may have to speak and vote at the meeting.

2.36D(4) For the purposes of this Rule–

    (a)   a person is able to exercise the right to speak at a meeting when that person is in a position to communicate to all those attending the meeting, during the meeting, any information or opinions which that person has on the business of the meeting; and

    (b)   a person is able to exercise the right to vote at a meeting when–

(i)   that person is able to vote, during the meeting, on resolutions or determinations put to the vote at the meeting, and

(ii) that person's vote can be taken into account in determining whether or not such resolutions or determinations are passed at the same time as the votes of all the other persons attending the meeting.

2.36D(5)   Where a meeting is to be conducted and held in the manner referred to in paragraph (2), the administrator must make whatever arrangements the administrator considers appropriate to–

(a)   enable those attending the meeting to exercise their rights to speak or vote, and

(b)   ensure the identification of those attending the meeting and the security of any electronic means used to enable attendance.

2.36D(6)   Where in the reasonable opinion of the administrator–

(a)   a meeting will be attended by persons who will not be present together at the same place, and

(b)   it is unnecessary or inexpedient to specify a place for the meeting,

any requirement under these Rules to specify a place for the meeting may be satisfied by specifying the arrangements the administrator proposes to enable persons to exercise their rights to speak or vote.

2.36D(7)   In making the arrangements referred to in paragraph (5) and in forming the opinion referred to in paragraph (6)(b), the administrator must have regard to the legitimate interests of the committee members or their representatives attending the meeting in the efficient despatch of the business of the meeting.

2.36D(8)   If–

(a)   the notice of a meeting does not specify a place for the meeting,

(b)   the administrator is requested in accordance with Rule 2.36E to specify a place for the meeting, and

(c)   that request is made by at least one member of the committee,

the administrator must specify a place for the meeting.

History
See history note after r.2.36R.

2.36E   Procedure for requests that a place for a meeting should be specified under Rule 2.36D

2.36E(1) This Rule applies to a request to the administrator of a meeting under Rule 2.36D to specify a place for the meeting.

2.36E(2) The request must be made within 5 business days of the date on which the administrator sent the notice of the meeting in question.

2.36E(3) Where the administrator considers that the request has been properly made in accordance with this Rule, the administrator must–

(a)   give notice to all those previously given notice of the meeting–

(i)   that it is to be held at a specified place, and

(ii) whether the date and time are to remain the same or not;

(b)   specify a time, date and place for the meeting, the date of which must be not later than 7 business days after the original date for the meeting; and

(c)   give 5 business days' notice of the time, date and place to all those previously given notice of the meeting,

and the notices required by sub-paragraphs (a) and (c) may be given at the same or different times.

2.36E(4)   Where the administrator has specified a place for the meeting in response to a request to which this Rule applies, the chairman of the meeting must attend the meeting by being present in person at that place.

History
See history note after r.2.36R.

2.36F   The chairman at meetings

2.36F(1)   The chairman at any meeting of the creditors' committee must be the administrator, or a person appointed by the administrator in writing to act.

2.36F(2)   A person so appointed must be either–

(a)   a person who is qualified to act as an insolvency practitioner in relation to the company, or

(b)   an employee of the administrator or the administrator's firm who is experienced in insolvency matters.

History
See history note after r.2.36R.

2.36G   Quorum

2.36G   A meeting of the committee is duly constituted if due notice of it has been given to all the members, and at least 2 members are present or represented.

History
See history note after r.2.36R.

2.36H   Committee members' representatives

2.36H(1)   A member of the creditors' committee may, in relation to the business of the committee, be represented by another person duly authorised by the creditor for that purpose.

2.36H(2)   A person acting as a committee member's representative must hold a mandate entitling that person so to act (either generally or specially) and authenticated by or on behalf of the committee member, and for this purpose any proxy in relation to any meeting of creditors of the company shall, unless it contains a statement to the contrary, be treated as such a mandate to act generally authenticated by or on behalf of the committee member.

2.36H(3)   The chairman at any meeting of the committee may call on a person claiming to act as a committee member's representative to produce a mandate and may exclude that person if it appears that the mandate is deficient.

2.36H(4)   No member may be represented by–

(a)   another member of the committee;

(b)   a person who is at the same time representing another committee member;

(c)   a body corporate;

(d)   a partnership;

(e)   a person whose estate is currently sequestrated;

(f)   an undischarged bankrupt;

(g) a person who is subject to a bankruptcy restrictions order, bankruptcy restrictions undertaking or interim bankruptcy restrictions order; or

(h) a disqualified director.

2.36H(5)   Where a member's representative authenticates any document on the member's behalf, the fact that the representative so authenticates must be stated below the representative's signature.

History
See history note after r.2.36R.

2.36I   Resignation

2.36I   A member of the creditors' committee may resign by notice in writing delivered to the administrator.

History
See history note after r.2.36R.

2.36J   Termination of membership

2.36J   Membership of the creditors' committee of any person is automatically terminated if–

(a) the member's estate is sequestrated or the member becomes bankrupt or grants a trust deed for the benefit of, or makes a composition with, creditors,

(b) at 3 consecutive meetings of the committee the member is neither present nor represented (unless at the third of those meetings it is resolved that this Rule is not to apply in the member's case), or

(c) the member ceases to be a creditor and a period of 3 months has elapsed from the date that that member ceased to be a creditor, or the member is found never to have been a creditor.

History
See history note after r.2.36R.

2.36K   Removal

2.36K   A member of the creditors' committee may be removed by resolution at a meeting of creditors. At least 14 days notice must be given of the intention to move such a resolution.

History
See history note after r.2.36R.

2.36L   Vacancies

2.36L(1)   The following applies if there is a vacancy among the members of the creditors' committee.

2.36L(2)   The vacancy need not be filled if the administrator and a majority of the remaining members so agree, provided that the total number of members does not fall below 3.

2.36L(3)   The administrator may appoint any creditor, who is qualified under the Rules to be a member of the committee, to fill the vacancy, if a majority of the other members agree to the appointment, and the creditor concerned consents to act.

2.36L(4)   Alternatively, a meeting of creditors may resolve that a creditor be appointed (with that creditor's consent) to fill the vacancy.

2.36L(5)   Where the vacancy is filled by an appointment made by a creditors' meeting at which the administrator is not present, the chairman of the meeting must report to the administrator the appointment which has been made.

History
See history note after r.2.36R.

2.36M   Voting rights and resolutions

2.36M(1)   At any meeting of the creditors' committee, each member of it (whether present in person or by a member's representative) has one vote; and a resolution is passed when a majority of the members present or represented have voted in favour of it.

2.36M(2)   Every resolution passed must be recorded in writing and authenticated by the chairman, either separately or as part of the minutes of the meeting, and the record must be kept as part of the sederunt book.

History
See history note after r.2.36R.

2.36N   Resolutions otherwise than at a meeting

2.36N(1)   In accordance with this Rule, the administrator may seek to obtain the agreement of members of the creditors' committee to a resolution by sending to every member (or a member's representative designated for the purpose) a copy of the proposed resolution.

2.36N(2)   Where the administrator makes use of the procedure allowed by this Rule, the administrator shall send out to members of the committee or their representatives (as the case may be) a statement incorporating a copy of any proposed resolution on which a decision is sought, which shall be set out in such a way that agreement with or dissent from each separate resolution may be indicated by the recipient on the copy so sent.

2.36N(3)   Any member of the committee may, within 7 business days from the date of the administrator sending out a resolution, require the administrator to summon a meeting of the committee to consider the matters raised by the resolution.

2.36N(4)   In the absence of such a requirement, the resolution is deemed to have been passed by the committee if and when the administrator is notified in writing by a majority of the members that they concur with it.

2.36N(5)   A copy of every resolution passed under this Rule, and a note that the committee's concurrence was obtained, shall be kept in the sederunt book.

History
See history note after r.2.36R.

2.36O   Expenses of members, etc.

2.36O(1)   The administrator shall defray any reasonable travelling expenses directly incurred by members of the creditors' committee or their representatives in respect of their attendance at the committee's meetings, or otherwise on the committee's business, as an expense of the administration.

2.36O(2)   Paragraph (1) does not apply to any meeting of the committee held within 6 weeks of a previous meeting, unless the meeting in question is summoned at the instance of the administrator.

History
See history note after r.2.36R.

2.36P   Formal defects

2.36P   The acts of the creditors' committee established for any administration are valid notwithstanding any defect in the appointment, election or qualifications of any member of the committee or any committee member's representative or in the formalities of its establishment.

History
See history note after r.2.36R.

2.36Q Information from administrator

2.36Q(1) Where the creditors' committee resolves to require the attendance of the administrator under paragraph 57(3), the notice to the administrator shall be in writing and authenticated by the majority of the members of the committee for the time being or their representatives.

2.36Q(2) The meeting at which the administrator's attendance is required shall be fixed by the committee for a business day, and shall be held at such time and place as the administrator determines.

2.36Q(3) Where the administrator so attends, the members of the committee may elect any one of their number to be chairman of the meeting, in place of the administrator or any nominee of the administrator.

History
See history note after r.2.36R.

2.36R Members' dealings with the company

2.36R(1) This Rule applies to–

(a) any member of a creditors' committee;

(b) any committee member's representative;

(c) any person who is an associate of–

(i) a member of the committee, or

(ii) a committee member's representative; and

(d) any person who has been a member of the committee at any time in the last 12 months or who is an associate of such a member.

2.36R(2) A person to whom this Rule applies may deal with the company provided that any transactions in the course of such dealings are in good faith and for value.

History
Rules 2.36–2.36R substituted for former r.2.36 by the Insolvency (Scotland) Amendment Rules 2010 (SI 2010/688 (S 2)) art.3 and Sch.1 para.84 as from April 6, 2010, subject to transitional provisions in art.4.

CHAPTER 8

FUNCTIONS AND REMUNERATION OF ADMINISTRATOR

2.37 Disposal of secured property, etc.

2.37(1) This Rule applies where the administrator applies to the court under paragraph 71 or 72 for authority to dispose of property of the company which is subject to a security (other than a floating charge), or goods in the possession of the company under a hire purchase agreement.

2.37(2) If an order is made under paragraph 71 or 72 the administrator shall as soon as reasonably practicable give notice of it to that person or owner and shall send to that person or owner a copy of the order, certified by the clerk of court.

2.37(3) The administrator shall place in the sederunt book a copy of any order granted under paragraph 71 or 72.

2.38   Progress reports

2.38(1)   The administrator shall

(a)   within six weeks after the end of each accounting period; and

(b)   within six weeks after he ceases to act as administrator,

send to the court and to the registrar of companies, and to each creditor, a progress report.

2.38(2)   For the purposes of this Part, including Rules contained elsewhere in these Rules but applied by this Part, **"accounting period"** in relation to an administration shall be construed as follows:

(a)   the first accounting period is the period of 6 months beginning with the date on which the company entered administration; and

(b)   any subsequent accounting period is the period of 6 months beginning with the end of the last accounting period.

History
Rule 2.38(2) substituted by the Insolvency (Scotland) Amendment Rules 2010 (SI 2010/688 (S 2)) art.3 and Sch.1 para.85 as from April 6, 2010, in all cases (see art.5).

2.38(3)   For the purposes of this Part, **"progress report"** means a report which includes–

(a)   the name of the court which granted the administration order or in which the notice of appointment was lodged, and the court reference number (if any);

(b)   details of the company's name, address and registration number;

(c)   details of the administrator's name and address, date of appointment and, where the administrator was appointed under paragraph 14 or 22, the name and address of the person who made the appointment;

(d)   details of any extensions to the initial period of appointment;

(e)   details of progress to date, including a receipts and payments account which states what assets of the company have been realised, for what value, and what payments have been made to creditors. The account is to be in the form of an abstract showing–

(i)   receipts and payments during the relevant accounting period; or

(ii)   where the administrator has ceased to act, receipts and payments during the period from the end of the last accounting period to the time when he so ceased (or, where he has made no previous progress report, receipts and payments in the period since his appointment as administrator);

(f)   details of what assets remain to be realised;

(g)   where a distribution is to be made in accordance with Chapter 9 in respect of an accounting period, the scheme of division; and

(h)   any other relevant information for the creditors.

2.38(4)   In a receipts and payments account falling within paragraph (3)(e)(ii) above, the administrator shall include a statement as to the amount paid to unsecured creditors by virtue of the application of section 176A (prescribed part).

2.38(5)   The court may, on the application of the administrator, extend the period of six weeks referred to in paragraph (1) of this Rule.

2.38(6)   If the administrator makes default in complying with this Rule, he is liable to a fine and, for continued contravention, to a daily default fine.

2.38(7)   This Rule is without prejudice to the requirements of Chapter 9 (distributions to creditors).

2.39   Determination of outlays and remuneration

2.39(1)   Within 2 weeks after the end of an accounting period, the administrator shall in respect of that period submit to the creditors' committee or, if there is no creditors' committee, to a meeting of creditors–

(a)   his accounts of his intromissions with the company's assets for audit and, where funds are available after making allowance for contingencies, a scheme of division of the divisible funds; and

(b)   a claim for the outlays reasonably incurred by him and for his remuneration.

2.39(2)   The administrator may, at any time before the end of an accounting period, submit to the creditors' committee or, if there is no creditors' committee, a meeting of creditors an interim claim in respect of that period for the outlays reasonably incurred by him and for his remuneration and the creditors' committee or meeting of creditors, as the case may be, may make an interim determination in relation to the amount of the outlays and remuneration payable to the administrator and, where they do so, they shall take into account that interim determination when making their determination under paragraph (3)(a)(ii).

2.39(3)   Within 6 weeks after the end of an accounting period–

(a)   the creditors' committee or, as the case may be, a meeting of creditors–

(i)   may audit the accounts; and

(ii)   shall issue a determination fixing the amount of the outlays and the remuneration payable to the administrator; and

(b)   the administrator shall make the audited accounts, scheme of division and the said determination available for inspection by the members of the company and the creditors.

2.39(4)   The basis for fixing the amount of the remuneration payable to the administrator may be a commission calculated by reference to the value of the company's assets which have been realised by the administrator, but there shall in any event be taken into account–

(a)   the work which, having regard to that value, was reasonably undertaken by him; and

(b)   the extent of his responsibilities in administering the company's assets.

2.39(5)   If the administrator's remuneration and outlays have been fixed by determination of the creditors' committee in accordance with paragraph (3)(a)(ii) and he considers the amount to be insufficient, he may request that it be increased by resolution of the creditors.

2.39(6)   If the creditors' committee fails to issue a determination in accordance with paragraph (3)(a)(ii), the administrator shall submit his claim to a meeting of creditors and they shall issue a determination in accordance with paragraph (3)(a)(ii).

2.39(7)   If the meeting of creditors fails to issue a determination in accordance with paragraph (6) then the administrator shall submit his claim to the court and it shall issue a determination.

2.39(8)   In a case where the administrator has made a statement under paragraph 52(1)(b), a resolution under paragraph (5) or Rule 2.39A(8) shall be taken to be passed if (and only if) passed with the approval of–

(a)   each secured creditor of the company; or

(b)   if the administrator has made, or proposes to make, a distribution to preferential creditors–

(i)   each secured creditor of the company; and

    (ii)   preferential creditors whose debts amount to more than 50% of the preferential debts of the company, disregarding debts of any creditor who does not respond to an invitation to give or withhold approval.

2.39(9)   In a case where the administrator has made a statement under paragraph 52(1)(b), if there is no creditor's committee, or the committee does not make the requisite determination in accordance with paragraphs (2) or (3)(a)(ii), the administrator's remuneration and outlays may be fixed (in accordance with this Rule) by the approval of–

    (a)   each secured creditor of the company; or

    (b)   if the administrator has made, or proposes to make, a distribution to preferential creditors–

        (i)   each secured creditor of the company; and

        (ii)   preferential creditors whose debts amount to more than 50% of the preferential debts of the company, disregarding debts of any creditor who does not respond to an invitation to give or withhold approval.

2.39(10)   In fixing the amount of the administrator's remuneration and outlays in respect of any accounting period, the creditors' committee or, as the case may be, a meeting of creditors may take into account any adjustment which the creditors' committee or meeting of creditors may wish to make in the amount of the remuneration and outlays fixed in respect of any earlier accounting period.

History
See note after r.2.39A.

2.39A   Appeal against fixing of remuneration

2.39A(1)   If the administrator considers that the remuneration or outlays fixed for him by the creditors' committee, or by resolution of the creditors is insufficient, he may apply to the court for an order increasing their amount or rate.

History
In r.2.39A(1) "or outlays" inserted and "their" substituted for "its" by the Insolvency (Scotland) Amendment Rules 2010 (SI 2010/688 (S 2)) art.3 and Sch.1 para.86 as from April 6, 2010, subject to transitional provisions in art.4.

2.39A(2)   The administrator shall give at least 14 days' notice of his application to the members of the creditors' committee; and the committee may nominate one or more members to appear or be represented, and to be heard, on the application.

2.39A(3)   If there is no creditors' committee, the administrator's notice of his application shall be sent to such one or more of the company's creditors as the court may direct, which creditors may nominate one or more of their number to appear or be represented and be heard.

2.39A(4)   The court may, if it appears to be a proper case, order the expenses of the administrator's application, including the expenses of any member of the creditors' committee appearing or being represented on it, or any creditor so appearing or being represented, to be paid as an expense of the administration.

2.39A(5)   If the administrator's remuneration and outlays have been fixed by the creditors' committee or by the creditors, any creditor or creditors of the company representing in value at least 25 percent of the creditors may apply to the court not later than 8 weeks after the end of an accounting period for an order that the administrator's remuneration or outlays be reduced on the grounds that they are, in all the circumstances, excessive.

History
In r.2.39A(5) "and outlays have" substituted for "has" and "or outlays be reduced on the grounds that they are, in all the circumstances, excessive" substituted for "be reduced, on the grounds that it is, in all the circumstances,

excessive" by the Insolvency (Scotland) Amendment Rules 2010 (SI 2010/688 (S 2)) art.3 and Sch.1 para.87 as from April 6, 2010, subject to transitional provisions in art.4.

2.39A(6)   If the court considers the application to be well-founded, it shall make an order fixing the remuneration at a reduced amount or rate.

2.39A(7)   The court may, if it appears to be a proper case, order the expenses of the creditor making the application to be paid as an expense of the administration.

2.39A(8)   Where there are joint administrators–

(a) it is for them to agree between themselves as to how the remuneration payable should be apportioned;

(b) if they cannot agree as to how the remuneration payable should be apportioned, any one of them may refer the issue for determination–

   (i)   by the court; or

   (ii) by resolution of the creditors' committee or a meeting of creditors.

History
Rule 2.39 substituted and r.2.39A inserted by the Insolvency (Scotland) Amendment Rules 2006 (SI 2006/734) r.8 as from April 6, 2006.

CHAPTER 8A

EXPENSES OF THE ADMINISTRATION

2.39B   Expenses of the administration

2.39B(1)   This Rule applies for the purposes of determining the order of priority of the expenses of the administration.

2.39B(2)   Paragraphs (1) and (3) of Rule 4.67 shall apply with regard to the expenses of the administration as they do to a company in liquidation, subject to the modifications specified below.

2.39B(3)   In Rule 4.67(1) and (3) as applied by paragraph (2)–

(a) in paragraph (1)–

   (i)   omit the words "Subject to section 156 and paragraph (2),";

   (ii)   for any reference to liquidator there is substituted a reference to administrator;

   (iii) for any reference to liquidation there is substituted a reference to administration;

   (iv)   omit the words "provisional liquidator or" in sub-paragraph (a) and the words "provisional liquidator," in sub-paragraph (b);

   (v)   omit the words "or special manager" in sub-paragraph (b);

   (vi)   omit sub-paragraphs (c) and (e);

   (vii) for the words "Rule 4.9(1)" in sub-paragraph (f) there is substituted "Rule 2.24(1)"; and

   (viii) for the words "Rule 4.32" in sub-paragraph (h) there is substituted "Rule 2.39" and unpaid pre-administration costs approved under Rule 2.39C; and

(b) in paragraph (3) for the reference to liquidator there is substituted a reference to administrator.

2.39B(4)   The priorities laid down by virtue of paragraph (2) are subject to the power of the court to make orders under paragraph (5) where the assets are insufficient to satisfy the liabilities.

595

2.39B(5)   The court may, in the event of the assets being insufficient to satisfy the liabilities, make an order as to the payment out of the assets of the expenses incurred in the administration in such order of priority as the court thinks just.

2.39B(6)   For the purposes of paragraph 99(3), the former administrator's remuneration and expenses shall comprise all those items set out in Rule 4.67(1) as applied by paragraph (2).

History
In r.2.39B(3)(a)(viii) "and unpaid pre-administration costs approved under Rule 2.39C" inserted by the Insolvency (Scotland) Amendment Rules 2010 (SI 2010/688 (S 2)) art.3 and Sch.1 para.88 as from April 6, 2010, subject to transitional provisions in art.4.

Previously, new Chapter 8A and r.2.39B inserted by the Insolvency (Scotland) Amendment Rules 2008 (SI 2008/662 (S 4)) r.5, as from April 6, 2008.

2.39C   Pre-administration costs

2.39C(1)   Where the administrator has made a statement of pre-administration costs under Rule 2.25(1)(ka), the creditors' committee may determine whether and to what extent the unpaid pre-administration costs set out in the statement are approved for payment.

2.39C(2)   But paragraph (3) applies if–

   (a)   there is no creditors' committee,

   (b)   there is, but it does not make the necessary determination, or

   (c)   it does do so, but the administrator or other insolvency practitioner who has charged fees or incurred expenses as pre-administration costs considers the amount determined to be insufficient.

2.39C(3)   When this paragraph applies, determination of whether and to what extent the unpaid pre-administration costs are approved for payment shall be–

   (a)   by resolution of a meeting of creditors other than in a case falling in sub-paragraph (b), or

   (b)   in a case where the administrator has made a statement under paragraph 52(1)(b)–

      (i)   by the approval of each secured creditor of the company, or

      (ii)   if the administrator has made, or intends to make, a distribution to preferential creditors, by the approval of each secured creditor of the company and preferential creditors whose debts amount to more than 50% of the preferential debts of the company, disregarding debts of any creditor who does not respond to an invitation to give or withhold approval.

2.39C(4)   The administrator must call a meeting of the creditors' committee or of creditors if so requested for the purposes of paragraphs (1) to (3) by another insolvency practitioner who has charged fees or incurred expenses as pre-administration costs; and the administrator must give notice of the meeting within 28 days of receipt of the request.

2.39C(5)   If–

   (a)   there is no determination under paragraph (1) or (3), or

   (b)   there is such a determination but the administrator or other insolvency practitioner who has charged fees or incurred expenses as pre-administration costs considers the amount determined to be insufficient,

the administrator (where the fees were charged or expenses incurred by the administrator) or other insolvency practitioner (where the fees were charged or expenses incurred by that practitioner) may apply to the court for a determination of whether and to what extent the unpaid pre-administration costs are approved for payment.

2.39C(6)   Paragraphs (2) to (4) of Rule 2.39A apply to an application under paragraph (5) of this Rule as they do to an application under paragraph (1) of that Rule (references to the administrator being read as references to the insolvency practitioner who has charged fees or incurred expenses as pre-administration costs).

2.39C(7)   Where the administrator fails to call a meeting of the creditors' committee or of creditors in accordance with paragraph (4), the other insolvency practitioner may apply to the court for an order requiring the administrator to do so.

History
Rule 2.39C inserted by the Insolvency (Scotland) Amendment Rules 2010 (SI 2010/688 (S 2)) art.3 and Sch.1 para.89 as from April 6, 2010, subject to transitional provisions in art.4.

CHAPTER 9

DISTRIBUTIONS TO CREDITORS

2.40(1)   This Chapter applies in any case where the administrator proposes to make a distribution to creditors or any class of them.

2.40(2)   Where the distribution is to a particular class of creditors, references in this Chapter (except Rule 2.41(4)(c)) to creditors shall, so far as the context requires, be references to that class of creditors only.

2.41(1)   Chapter 5 of Part 4 (claims in liquidation) and Chapter 9 of that Part (distribution of company's assets by liquidator) (except Rule 4.67) shall apply with regard to claims to a dividend out of the assets of a company in administration as they do to a company in liquidation, subject to the modifications specified below and to any other necessary modifications.

2.41(1A)   Section 53 of the Bankruptcy Act, as applied by Rule 4.68, shall not apply for the purposes of this Rule.

2.41(2)   Subject to paragraph (5) below, in the said Chapters 5 and 9, or in any provision of the Bankruptcy Act as applied by Rule 4.16 or 4.68–

(a)   for any reference to the liquidator, liquidation, and liquidation committee there shall be substituted a reference to the administrator, the administration and the creditors' committee in the administration; and

(b)   for any reference to the date of commencement of winding up there shall be substituted a reference to the date on which the company entered administration.

2.41(3)   Section 52(3) of the Bankruptcy Act, as applied by Rule 4.68, shall apply subject to paragraph (4) of this Rule.

2.41(4)   The administrator may make a distribution to secured or preferential creditors or, where he has the permission of the court, to unsecured creditors only if–

(a)   he has sufficient funds for the purpose;

(b)   he does not intend to give notice pursuant to paragraph 83;

(c)   his statement of proposals, as approved by the creditors under paragraph 53(1) or 54(5), contains a proposal to make a distribution to the class of creditors in question; and

(d)   the payment of a dividend is consistent with the functions and duties of the administrator and any proposals made by him or which he intends to make.

2.41(5)   Where the administration was immediately preceded by a winding up–

    (a)   in Rule 4.17(2) the reference to administration and the date on which the company entered administration existing but for the application of this Rule shall be construed as a reference to liquidation and the date of commencement of winding up respectively;

    (b)   in Schedule 1 to the Bankruptcy Act, as applied by Rule 4.16, the reference to the date on which the company entered administration in paragraph 1(1) and the second reference to that date in paragraph 1(2) shall be construed as a reference to the date of commencement of winding up within the meaning of section 129; and

    (c)   in Rule 4.66(1)(d) the reference to "date of commencement of the administration" shall be construed as a reference to the date of commencement of winding up.

History
Rule 2.41(5)(c) inserted by the Insolvency (Scotland) Amendment Rules 2010 (SI 2010/688 (S 2)) art.3 and Sch.1 para.90 as from April 6, 2010, subject to transitional provisions in art.4.
    Previously, r.2.41(1A) and (5) inserted, and r.2.41(2) and (3) amended, by the Insolvency (Scotland) Amendment Rules 2006 (SI 2006/734 (S 6)) r.9, as from April 6, 2006. Rule 2.41(1) amended by the Insolvency (Scotland) Amendment Rules 2008 (SI 2008/662 (S 4)) r.6, as from April 6, 2008.

2.41A   Payments of dividends

2.41A(1)   On the final determination of the remuneration under Rules 2.39 and 2.39A, the administrator shall, subject to Rule 2.41, pay to the creditors their dividends in accordance with the scheme of division.

2.41A(2)   Any dividend–

    (a)   allocated to a creditor which is not cashed or uplifted; or

    (b)   dependent on a claim in respect of which an amount has been set aside under subsection (7) or (8) of section 52 of the Bankruptcy Act as applied by Rules 2.41 and 4.68,

shall be deposited by the administrator in an appropriate bank or institution.

2.41A(3)   If a creditor's claim is revalued, the administrator may–

    (a)   in paying any dividend to that creditor, make such adjustment to it as he considers necessary to take account of that revaluation; or

    (b)   require the creditor to repay to him the whole or part of a dividend already paid to him.

2.41A(4)   The administrator shall insert in the sederunt book the audited accounts, the scheme of division and the final determination in relation to the administrator's outlays and remuneration.

2.41A(5)   For the purposes of paragraph 99(3), the former administrator's remuneration and expenses shall comprise all those items set out in Rule 4.67(1) as applied by Rule 2.41.

History
Rule 2.41A inserted by the Insolvency (Scotland) Amendment Rules 2006 (SI 2006/734 (S 6)) r.10, as from April 6, 2006.

2.41B   New administrator appointed

2.41B(1)   If a new administrator is appointed in place of another, the former administrator must, as soon as reasonably practicable, transmit to the new administrator all the creditors' claims which the former administrator has received, together with an itemised list of them.

2.41B(2)   The new administrator must authenticate the list by way of receipt for the creditors' claims and return it to the former administrator.

2.41B(3)   From then on, all creditors' claims must be sent to and retained by the new administrator.

History
Rule 2.41B inserted by the Insolvency (Scotland) Amendment Rules 2010 (SI 2010/688 (S 2)) art.3 and Sch.1 para.91 as from April 6, 2010, subject to transitional provisions in art.4.

CHAPTER 10

ENDING ADMINISTRATION

2.42   Final progress reports

2.42   **"Final progress report"** means a progress report which includes a summary account of–

(a)   the administrator's original proposals;

(b)   any major changes to, or deviations from, those proposals in the course of the administration;

(c)   the steps taken during the administration; and

(d)   the outcome.

2.43   Notice of automatic end of administration

2.43(1)   Where the appointment of an administrator has ceased to have effect, and the administrator is not required by any other Rule to give notice of that fact, he shall, as soon as reasonably practicable, and in any event within 5 business days of the date when the appointment has ceased, lodge in court a notice of automatic end of administration in the form required by Rule 7.30 and Schedule 5, together with a final progress report.

2.43(2)   The administrator shall, as soon as reasonably practicable, send a copy of the notice and accompanying report to the registrar of companies, and to all other persons who received a copy of the administrator's proposals.

History
In r.2.43(2) "other" inserted by the Insolvency (Scotland) Amendment Rules 2010 (SI 2010/688 (S 2)) art.3 and Sch.1 para.92 as from April 6, 2010, in all cases (see art.5).

2.43(3)   If the administrator makes default in complying with this Rule, he is liable to a fine and, for continued contravention, to a daily default fine.

2.44   Applications for extension of administration

2.44(1)   An application to court for an extension of administration shall be accompanied by a progress report for the period since the last progress report (if any).

2.44(2)   A request for an extension of administration by consent of creditors shall be accompanied by a progress report for the period since the administrator's last progress report (if any).

2.44(3)   The administrator shall use the notice of extension of period of administration in the form required by Rule 7.30 and Schedule 5 in all circumstances where he is required to give such notice.

2.45   Notice of end of administration—other than by a creditors' voluntary liquidation under paragraph 83 or by dissolution under paragraph 84

2.45(1)   A notice by the administrator

(a)   that the purpose of administration has been sufficiently achieved; or

(b)   that the court has ordered that the appointment shall cease to have effect,

shall be in the form required by Rule 7.30 and Schedule 5, and shall be accompanied by a final progress report.

2.45(2)   The administrator shall, as soon as reasonably practicable, and (in the case of a notice under paragraph 80(2)) within 5 business days of satisfying the requirements of paragraph 80(2)(a), send a copy of the notice to every creditor of the company of whose claim and address he is aware, to all other persons who were notified of his appointment, and to the company.

History
In r.2.45(2) "other" substituted for "those" by the Insolvency (Scotland) Amendment Rules 2010 (SI 2010/688 (S 2)) art.3 and Sch.1 para.94 as from April 6, 2010 in all cases (see art.5).

2.45(3)   Where the administrator wishes to publish a notice under paragraph 80(5), the notice–

(a)   shall be published in the Edinburgh Gazette; and

(b)   may be advertised in such other manner as the administrator thinks fit.

2.45(4)   A notice published under Rule 2.45(3) shall–

(a)   state the full name of the company;

(b)   state the name and address of the administrator;

(c)   state the date when the administrator's appointment ceased to have effect;

(d)   specify an address to which any creditor of the company can write to request that a copy of the notice be provided; and

(e)   be published within five business days of filing the notice of the end of administration with the court.

History
In the heading to r.2.45 "—other than by a creditors' voluntary liquidation under paragraph 83 or by dissolution under paragraph 84" inserted by the Insolvency (Scotland) Amendment Rules 2010 (SI 2010/688 (S 2)) art.3 and Sch.1 para.93 as from April 6, 2010, subject to transitional provisions in art.4.
    Rule 2.45(3), (4) substituted by the Insolvency (Scotland) (Amendment) Rules 2009 (SI 2009/662 (S 1)) r.2 and Sch. paras 10, 11 as from April 6, 2009.

2.46   Application to court

2.46(1)   An application under paragraph 79 for an order providing for the appointment of an administrator of the company to cease to have effect shall be accompanied by a progress report for the period since the last such report (if any) and a statement indicating what the administrator thinks should be the next steps for the company.

2.46(2)   Where the administrator applies to the court because the creditors' meeting has required him to, his application shall be accompanied by a statement in which he shall indicate (giving reasons) whether or not he agrees with the creditors' requirement that he make the application.

2.46(3)   Where the administrator applies to the court other than at the request of a creditors' meeting, he shall give to–

(a)   the applicant for the administration order under which he was appointed;

(b)   the person by whom he was appointed or to the holder of the floating charge by virtue of which he was appointed (as the case may be); and

(c)   the creditors,

at least 5 business days' written notice of his intention so to apply.

History
In r.2.46(3) "5 business" substituted for "7" by the Insolvency (Scotland) Amendment Rules 2010 (SI 2010/688 (S 2)) art.3 and Sch.1 para.95 as from April 6, 2010, subject to transitional provisions in art.4.

2.46(4) Where the administrator applies to court under paragraph 79 in conjunction with a petition under section 124 for an order to wind up the company, he shall, in addition to the requirements of paragraph (3), notify the creditors of whether he intends to seek appointment as liquidator.

2.47 Moving from administration to creditors' voluntary liquidation

2.47(1) A notice pursuant to paragraph 83(3) shall be in the form required by Rule 7.30 and Schedule 5.

2.47(2) As soon as reasonably practicable after the day on which the registrar registers that notice, the person who has ceased to be the administrator (whether or not that person becomes the liquidator) must send a final progress report (which must include details of the assets to be dealt with in the liquidation) to the registrar and to all other persons who received notice of the administrator's appointment.

2.47(3) For the purposes of paragraph 83(7)(a) a person is nominated by the creditors as liquidator by–

(a) the creditors' approval of the statement of the proposed liquidator in the administrator's proposals or revised proposals, or

(b) the nomination by the creditors of a different person before the creditors' approval of the administrator's proposals or revised proposals.

2.47(4) Where the creditors nominate a different person, the nomination must, where applicable, include the declaration required by section 231 (appointment to office of two or more persons).

History
Rule 2.47 substituted by the Insolvency (Scotland) Amendment Rules 2010 (SI 2010/688 (S 2)) art.3 and Sch.1 para.96 as from April 6, 2010, subject to transitional provisions in art.4.

2.48 Moving from administration to dissolution

2.48(1) The notice required by paragraph 84(1) shall be in the form required by Rule 7.30 and Schedule 5, and shall be accompanied by a final progress report.

2.48(2) As soon as reasonably practicable a copy of the notice and accompanying documents shall be sent to all other persons who received notice of the administrator's appointment.

History
In r.2.48(2) "other persons" substituted for "those" by the Insolvency (Scotland) Amendment Rules 2010 (SI 2010/688 (S 2)) art.3 and Sch.1 para.97 as from April 6, 2010, subject to transitional provisions in art.4.

2.48(3) Where the court makes an order under paragraph 84(7) it shall, where the applicant is not the administrator, give a copy of the order to the administrator.

2.48(4) The notice required by paragraph 84(8) shall be in the form required by Rule 7.30 and Schedule 5.

Chapter 11

Replacing Administrator

2.49 Grounds for resignation

2.49(1) The administrator may give notice of his resignation on grounds of ill health or because–

(a) he intends ceasing to be in practice as an insolvency practitioner; or

(b) there is some conflict of interest, or change of personal circumstances, which precludes or makes impracticable the further discharge by him of the duties of administrator.

2.49(2) The administrator may, with the leave of the court, give notice of his resignation on grounds other than those specified in paragraph (1).

2.50   Notice of intention to resign

2.50(1)   The administrator must give to the persons specified below at least 5 business days' notice of his intention to resign, or to apply for the court's leave to do so

   (a)   if there is a continuing administrator of the company, to him;

   (b)   if there is a creditors' committee, to it; and

   (c)   if there is no such administrator and no creditors' committee, to the company and its creditors.

History
In r.2.50(1) "5 business" substituted for "7" by the Insolvency (Scotland) Amendment Rules 2010 (SI 2010/688 (S 2)) art.3 and Sch.1 para.98 as from April 6, 2010, subject to transitional provisions in art.4.

2.50(2)   Where the administrator gives notice under paragraph (1), he shall also give notice to a member State liquidator, if such a person has been appointed in relation to the company.

2.50(3)   Where the administrator was appointed by the holder of a qualifying floating charge under paragraph 14, the notice of intention to resign shall also be sent to all holders of a qualifying floating charge.

2.50(4)   Where the administrator was appointed by the company or the directors of the company under paragraph 22, a copy of the notice of intention to resign shall also be sent to the company and to all holders of a qualifying floating charge.

2.51   Notice of resignation

2.51(1)   Where the administrator was appointed under an administration order, the notice of resignation shall be lodged in court, and a copy sent to the registrar of companies.

2.51(2)   A copy of the notice of resignation shall be sent, not more than 5 business days after it has been lodged in court, to all other persons to whom notice of intention to resign was sent.

History
In r.2.48(2) "other persons" substituted for "those" by the Insolvency (Scotland) Amendment Rules 2010 (SI 2010/688 (S 2)) art.3 and Sch.1 para.99 as from April 6, 2010, subject to transitional provisions in art.4.

2.51(3)   Where the administrator was appointed by the holder of a qualifying floating charge, a copy of the notice of resignation shall be lodged in court and sent to the registrar of companies, and to anyone else who received notice of intention to resign, within 5 business days of the notice of resignation being sent to the holder of the floating charge by virtue of which the appointment was made.

2.51(4)   Where the administrator was appointed by the company or the directors, a copy of the notice of resignation shall be lodged in court and sent to the registrar of companies, and to anyone else who received the notice of intention to resign, within 5 business days of the notice of resignation being sent to either the company or the directors that made the appointment.

2.52   Incapacity to act, through death or otherwise

2.52(1)   Subject to the following paragraph of this Rule, where the administrator has died, it is the duty of his executors to give notice of that fact to the court and to the registrar of companies, specifying the date of death.

History
In r.2.52(1) "or, where the deceased administrator was a partner in a firm, of a partner of that firm", formerly appearing after "his executors", omitted by the Insolvency (Scotland) Amendment Rules 2010 (SI 2010/688 (S 2)) art.3 and Sch.1 para.100 as from April 6, 2010, subject to transitional provisions in art.4.

2.52(1A)   If the deceased administrator was a partner in or an employee of a firm, notice may be given by a partner in the firm who is qualified to act as an insolvency practitioner, or is a member of any body recognised by the Secretary of State for the authorisation of insolvency practitioners.

History
Rule 2.52(1A) inserted by the Insolvency (Scotland) Amendment Rules 2010 (SI 2010/688 (S 2)) art.3 and Sch.1 para.101 as from April 6, 2010, subject to transitional provisions in art.4.

2.52(2)   Notice of the death may also be given by any person.

2.52(3)   Where an administrator who has ceased to be qualified to act as an insolvency practitioner in relation to the company gives notice in accordance with paragraph 89(2), he shall also give notice to the registrar of companies.

2.53   Application to replace

2.53(1)   Where an application is made to the court under paragraph 91 or 95 to appoint a replacement administrator, the application shall be accompanied by a Statement of the Proposed Administrator.

2.53(2)   Where the original administrator was appointed under an administration order, a copy of the application shall be served on the person who made the application for the administration order.

2.53(3)   Where the court makes an order filling a vacancy in the office of administrator, the same provisions shall apply, subject to such modification as may be necessary, in respect of giving notice of, and advertising, the appointment as in the case of the original appointment of an administrator.

2.54(1)   This Rule applies where any person has appointed an administrator by notice in accordance with these Rules and a replacement administrator is appointed.

2.54(2)   The same provisions apply in respect of giving notice of, and advertising, the replacement appointment as in the case of an initial appointment, and all statements, consents and other documents as required shall also be required in this case.

2.54(3)   All forms and notices shall clearly identify that the appointment is of a replacement administrator.

2.55   Joint or concurrent appointments

2.55(1)   Where a person is appointed in accordance with paragraph 103 to act as administrator jointly or concurrently with the person or persons then acting, the same provisions shall apply, subject to this Rule and to such other modification as may be necessary, in respect of the making of this appointment as in the case of the original appointment of an administrator.

2.55(2)   An appointment made under paragraph 103 shall be notified to the registrar of companies in the form required by Rule 7.30 and Schedule 5.

2.56   Application to court to remove administrator from office

2.56(1)   An application to the court to remove an administrator from office shall be served upon–

(a)   the administrator;

(b)   where the administrator was appointed by the court, the person who made the application for the administration order;

(c)   where the appointment was made by the holder of a qualifying floating charge, the holder of the floating charge by virtue of which the appointment was made;

(d)   where the appointment was made by the directors or by the company, the person who made the appointment;

(e)   the creditors' committee (if any);

(f)   the joint administrator (if any); and

(g) where there is neither a creditor's committee nor a joint administrator, upon the company and the creditors.

2.56(2) An applicant under this Rule shall, within 5 business days of the order being made, send a copy of the order to all those to whom notice of the application was sent, and a notice to the registrar of companies in the form required by Rule 7.30 and Schedule 5.

CHAPTER 12

EC REGULATION—CONVERSION OF ADMINISTRATION TO WINDING UP

2.57 Application for conversion into winding up

2.57(1) Where a member State liquidator proposes to apply to the court for the conversion into winding-up proceedings of an administration, an affidavit complying with Rule 2.58 must be prepared and lodged in court in support of the application.

History
See history note after r.2.57(1A).

2.57(1A) In this Rule, and in Rules 2.58 and 2.59, "conversion into winding-up proceedings" means an order under Article 37 of the EC Regulation (conversion of earlier proceedings) that–

(a) the purposes of the administration are to be limited to the winding up of the company through administration and are to exclude the purpose contained in sub-paragraph (a) of paragraph 3(1);

(b) the administration is converted into a creditors' voluntary winding up; or

(c) the administration is converted into a winding up by the court.

History
Rule 2.57(1) and (1A) substituted for former r.2.57(1) by the Insolvency (Scotland) Amendment Rules 2010 (SI 2010/688 (S 2)) art.3 and Sch.1 para.102 as from April 6, 2010, subject to transitional provisions in art.4.

2.57(2) The application and the affidavit required under this Rule shall be served upon–

(a) the company; and

(b) the administrator.

History
See note after r.2.58.

2.58 Contents of affidavit

2.58(1) The affidavit shall state–

(a) that main proceedings have been opened in relation to the company in a member State other than the United Kingdom;

(b) the deponent's belief that the conversion of the administration into winding-up proceedings would prove to be in the interests of the creditors in the main proceedings;

(c) the deponent's opinion as to whether the company ought to enter voluntary winding up, be wound up by the court or be wound up through the administration; and

(d) all other matters that, in the opinion of the member State liquidator, would assist the court–

    (i) in deciding whether to make such an order; and

    (ii) if the court were to do so, in considering the need for any consequential provision that would be necessary or desirable.

History
In r.2.58(1)(b) "winding-up proceedings" substituted for "a winding up" by the Insolvency (Scotland) Amendment Rules 2010 (SI 2010/688 (S 2)) art.3 and Sch.1 para.103 as from April 6, 2010, subject to transitional provisions in art.4.

2.58(2) An affidavit under this rule shall be sworn by, or on behalf of, the member State liquidator.

History
Rules 2.57(1) and 2.58(1)(c) amended by the Insolvency (Scotland) Amendment Rules 2006 (SI 2006/734 (S 6)) rr.11, 12 as from April 6, 2006.

2.59 Power of court

2.59(1) On hearing the application for conversion into winding-up proceedings the court may make such order as it thinks fit.

History
See history note after r.2.59(2).

2.59(2) If the court makes an order for conversion into winding-up proceedings the order may contain all such consequential provisions as the court deems necessary or desirable.

History
In r.2.59(1) and (2) "winding-up proceedings" substituted for "winding up" by the Insolvency (Scotland) Amendment Rules 2010 (SI 2010/688 (S 2)) art.3 and Sch.1 para.104 as from April 6, 2010, subject to transitional provisions in art.4.

2.59(3) Without prejudice to the generality of paragraph (1) of this Rule, an order under that paragraph may provide that the company be wound up as if a resolution for voluntary winding up under section 84 were passed on the day on which the order is made.

CHAPTER 13

EC REGULATION—MEMBER STATE LIQUIDATOR

2.60 Interpretation of creditor and notice to member State liquidator

2.60(1) This Rule applies where a member State liquidator has been appointed in relation to the company.

2.60(2) For the purposes of Chapters 6, 7 and 8 of these Rules, (and except where the context otherwise requires) the member State liquidator is deemed to be a creditor.

2.60(3) Paragraph (2) of this Rule is without prejudice to the generality of the right to participate referred to in paragraph 3 of Article 32 of the EC Regulation (exercise of creditor's rights).

2.60(4) Where the administrator is obliged to give notice to, or provide a copy of a document (including an order of court) to, the court, the registrar of companies, or a provisional liquidator or liquidator, the administrator shall also give notice or provide copies, as the case may be, to the member State liquidator.

2.60(5) Paragraph (4) is without prejudice to the generality of the obligations imposed by Article 31 of the EC Regulation (duty to co-operate and communicate information).

History of Part 2
Part 2 above substituted by the Insolvency (Scotland) Amendment Rules 2003 (SI 2003/2111 (S 9)) r.3 Sch.1 subject to transitional and savings provisions in r.7 as from September 15, 2003. The original Pt 2 rules continue to apply to administrations entered into prior to September 15, 2003, and also to the special cases described in the Introductory note on the new Pt II following IA 1986 s.8. The original Pt 2 rules read as follows:

ADMINISTRATION PROCEDURE

CHAPTER 1

APPLICATION FOR, AND MAKING OF, THE ORDER

2.1 Independent report on company's affairs

2.1(1) Where it is proposed to apply to the court by way of petition for an administration order to be made under section 8 in relation to a company, there may be prepared in support of the petition a report by an independent person to the effect that the appointment of an administrator for the company is expedient.

2.1(2) The report may be by the person proposed as administrator, or by any other person having adequate knowledge of the company's affairs, not being a director, secretary, manager, member or employee of the company.

2.1(3) The report shall specify which of the purposes specified in section 8(3) may, in the opinion of the person preparing it, be achieved for the company by the making of an administration order in relation to it.

2.2 Notice of petition

2.2(1) Under section 9(2)(a), notice of the petition shall forthwith be given by the petitioner to any person who has appointed, or is or may be entitled to appoint, an administrative receiver, and to the following persons–

(a) an administrative receiver, if appointed;

(b) if a petition for the winding up of the company has been presented but no order for winding up has yet been made, the petitioner under that petition;

(c) a provisional liquidator, if appointed;

(d) the person proposed in the petition to be the administrator;

(e) the registrar of companies;

(f) the Keeper of the Register of Inhibitions and Adjudications for recording in that register; and

(g) the company, if the petition for the making of an administration order is presented by the directors or by a creditor or creditors of the company.

2.2(2) Notice of the petition shall also be given to the persons upon whom the court orders that the petition be served.

2.3 Notice and advertisement of administration order

2.3(1) If the court makes an administration order, it shall forthwith give notice of the order to the person appointed as administrator.

2.3(2) Under section 21(1)(a) the administrator shall forthwith after the order is made, advertise the making of the order once in the Edinburgh Gazette and once in a newspaper circulating in the area where the company has its principal place of business or in such newspapers as he thinks most appropriate for ensuring that the order comes to the notice of the company's creditors.

2.3(3) Under section 21(2), the administrator shall send a notice with a copy of the court's order certified by the clerk of court to the registrar of companies, and in addition shall send a copy of the order to the following persons–

(a) any person who has appointed, or is or may be entitled to appoint, an administrative receiver;

(b) an administrative receiver, if appointed;

(c) a petitioner in a petition for the winding up of the company, if that petition is pending;

(d) any provisional liquidator of the company, if appointed; and

(e)   the Keeper of the Register of Inhibitions and Adjudications for recording in that register.

2.3(4)   *If the court dismisses the petition under section 9(4) or discharges the administration order under section 18(3) or 24(5), the petitioner or, as the case may be, the administrator shall–*

(a)   forthwith send a copy of the court's order dismissing the petition or effecting the discharge to the Keeper of the Register of Inhibitions and Adjudications for recording in that register; and

(b)   within 14 days after the date of making of the order, send a notice with a copy, certified by the clerk of the court, of the court's order dismissing the petition or effecting the discharge to the registrar of companies.

2.3(5)   *Paragraph (4) is without prejudice to any order of the court as to the persons by and to whom, and how, notice of any order made by the court under section 9(4), 18 or 24 is to be given and to section 18(4) or 24(6) (notice by administrator of court's order discharging administration order).*

CHAPTER 2

STATEMENT OF AFFAIRS AND PROPOSALS TO CREDITORS

2.4   Notice requiring statement of affairs

2.4(1)   *This Rule and Rules 2.5 and 2.6 apply where the administrator decides to require a statement as to the affairs of the company to be made out and submitted to him in accordance with section 22.*

2.4(2)   *The administrator shall send to each of the persons upon whom he decides to make such a requirement under section 22, a notice in the form required by Rule 7.30 and Schedule 5 requiring him to make out and submit a statement of affairs.*

2.4(3)   *Any person to whom a notice is sent under this Rule is referred to in this Chapter as "a deponent".*

2.5   Form of the statement of affairs

2.5(1)   *The statement of affairs shall be in the form required by Rule 7.30 and Schedule 5.*

2.5(2)   *The administrator shall insert any statement of affairs submitted to him in the sederunt book.*

2.6   Expenses of statement of affairs

2.6(1)   *A deponent who makes up and submits to the administrator a statement of affairs shall be allowed and be paid by the administrator out of his receipts, any expenses incurred by the deponent in so doing which the administrator considers to be reasonable.*

2.6(2)   *Any decision by the administrator under this Rule is subject to appeal to the court.*

2.6(3)   *Nothing in this Rule relieves a deponent from any obligation to make up and submit a statement of affairs, or to provide information to the administrator.*

2.7   Statement to be annexed to proposals

2.7(1)   *There shall be annexed to the administrator's proposals, when sent to the registrar of companies under section 23 and laid before the creditors' meeting to be summoned under that section, a statement by him showing–*

(a)   details relating to his appointment as administrator, the purposes for which an administration order was applied for and made, and any subsequent variation of those purposes;

(b)   the names of the directors and secretary of the company;

(c)   an account of the circumstances giving rise to the application for an administration order;

(d)   if a statement of affairs has been submitted, a copy or summary of it with the administrator's comments, if any;

(e)   if no statement of affairs has been submitted, details of the financial position of the company at the latest practicable date (which must, unless the court otherwise orders, be a date not earlier than that of the administration order);

607

(f)   the manner in which the affairs and business of the company–

     (i)   have, since the date of the administrator's appointment, been managed and financed, and

     (ii)   will, if the administrator's proposals are approved, continue to be managed and financed;

(fa)   whether–

     (i)   the EC Regulation applies; and

     (ii)   if so, whether the proceedings are main proceedings or territorial proceedings; and

(g)   such other information (if any) as the administrator thinks necessary to enable creditors to decide whether or not to vote for the adoption of the proposals.

History
In r.2.7(1) subpara.(fa) inserted by the Insolvency (Scotland) Regulations 2003 (SI 2003/2109 (S 8)) reg.26 as from September 8, 2003.

2.7(2)   Where the administrator intends to apply to the court under section 18 for the administration order to be discharged at a time before he has sent a statement of his proposals to creditors, in accordance with section 23(1), he shall, at least 10 days before he makes such an application, send to all creditors of the company of whom he is aware, a report containing the information required by paragraph (1)(a) to (f)(i) of this Rule.

2.8   Notices of proposals to members

2.8(1)   Any notice required to be published by the administrator–

(a)   under section 23(2)(b) (notice of address for members of the company to write for a copy of the administrator's statement of proposals), and

(b)   under section 25(3)(b) (notice of address for members of the company to write for a copy of the administrator's statement of proposed revisions to the proposals),

shall be inserted once in the Edinburgh Gazette and once in the newspaper in which the administrator's appointment was advertised.

CHAPTER 3

MEETINGS AND NOTICES

2.9   General

2.9   The provisions of Chapter 1 of Part 7 (Meetings) shall apply with regard to meetings of the company's creditors or members which are summoned by the administrator, subject to the provisions in this Chapter.

2.9A   Applicable law

2.9A(1)   Rule 2.9 does not apply where the laws of a member State (and not the law of Scotland) apply in relation to the conduct of the meeting.

2.9A(2)   Where this Rule applies, subject as above, the meeting shall be summoned and conducted in accordance with the constitution of the company and the laws of the member State referred to in paragraph (1) above shall apply to the conduct of the meeting.

2.9B   Entitlement to vote

2.9B(1)   No vote shall be cast by virtue of a claim more than once on any resolution put to the meeting.

2.9B(2)   Where–

(a)   a creditor is entitled to vote under this Rule,

(b)   has lodged his claim in one or more sets of other proceedings; and

(c)   votes (either in person or by proxy) on a resolution put to the meeting, *only the creditor's vote shall be counted.*

2.9B(3)   *Where–*

(a)   *a creditor has lodged his claim in more than one set of other proceedings, and*

(b)   *more than one member State liquidator seeks to vote by virtue of that claim,*

the entitlement to vote by virtue of that claim is exercisable by the member State liquidator in main proceedings, whether or not the creditor has lodged his claim in the main proceedings.

2.9B(4)   *For the purposes of paragraph (1), the claim of a creditor and of any member State liquidator in relation to the same debt are a single claim.*

2.9B(5)   *For the purposes of paragraphs (2) and (3), "other proceedings" mean main proceedings or territorial proceedings in another member State.*

History
Rules 2.9A and 2.9B inserted by the Insolvency (Scotland) Regulations 2003 (SI 2003/2109 (S 8)) reg.26 as from September 8, 2003.

2.10   Meeting to consider administrator's proposals

2.10(1)   *The administrator shall give at least 14 days' notice to attend the meeting of the creditors under section 23(1) to any directors or officers of the company (including persons who have been directors or officers in the past) whose presence at the meeting is, in the administrator's opinion, required.*

2.10(2)   *If at the meeting there is not the requisite majority for approval of the administrator's proposals (with modifications, if any), the chairman may, and shall if a resolution is passed to that effect, adjourn the meeting for not more than 14 days.*

2.11   Retention of title creditors

2.11   *For the purpose of entitlement to vote at a creditors' meeting in administration proceedings, a seller of goods to the company under a retention of title agreement shall deduct from his claim the value, as estimated by him, of any rights arising under that agreement in respect of goods in the possession of the company.*

2.12   Hire-purchase, conditional sale and hiring agreements

2.12(1)   *Subject as follows, an owner of goods under a hire-purchase agreement or under an agreement for the hire of goods for more than 3 months, or a seller of goods under a conditional sale agreement, is entitled to vote in respect of the amount of the debt due and payable to him by the company as at the date of the administration order.*

2.12(2)   *In calculating the amount of any debt for this purpose, no account shall be taken of any amount attributable to the exercise of any right under the relevant agreement, so far as the right has become exercisable solely by virtue of the presentation of the petition for an administration order or any mater arising in consequence of that or of the making of the order.*

2.13   Report and notice of meetings

2.13   *Any report or notice by the administrator of the result of creditors' meetings held under section 23(1) or 25(2) shall have annexed to it details of the proposals which were considered by the meeting in question and of any revisions and modifications to the proposals which were also considered.*

2.14   Notices to creditors

2.14(1)   *Within 14 days after the conclusion of a meeting of creditors to consider the administrator's proposals or proposed revisions under section 23(1) or 25(2), the administrator shall send notice of the result of the meeting (including, where appropriate, details of the proposals as approved) to every creditor to whom notice of the meeting was sent and to any other creditor of whom the administrator has become aware since the notice was sent.*

2.14(2)   *Within 14 days after the end of every period of 6 months beginning with the date of approval of the administrator's proposals or proposed revisions, the administrator shall send to all creditors of the company a report on the progress of the administration.*

2.14(3)   *On vacating office, the administrator shall send to creditors a report on the administration up to that time. This does not apply where the administration is immediately followed by the company going into liquidation, nor where the administrator is removed from office by the court or ceases to be qualified to act as an insolvency practitioner.*

CHAPTER 4

THE CREDITORS' COMMITTEE

2.15   Application of provisions in Part 3 (receivers)

2.15(1)   *Chapter 3 of Part 3 (The creditors' committee) shall apply with regard to the creditors' committee in the administration as it applies to the creditors' committee in receivership, subject to the modifications specified below and to any other necessary modifications.*

2.15(2)   *For any reference in the said Chapter 3, or in any provision of Chapter 7 of Part 4 as applied by Rule 3.6, to the receiver, receivership or the creditors' committee in receivership, there shall be substituted a reference to the administrator, the administration and the creditors' committee in the administration.*

2.15(3)   *In Rule 3.4(1) and 3.7(1), for the reference to section 68 or 68(2), there shall be substituted a reference to section 26 or 26(2).*

2.15(4)   *For Rule 3.5 there shall be substituted the following Rule–*

   "3.5   Functions of the committee

   3.5   *The creditors' committee shall assist the administrator in discharging his functions and shall act in relation to him in such manner as may be agreed from time to time."*

CHAPTER 5

THE ADMINISTRATOR

2.16   Remuneration

2.16(1)   *The administrator's remuneration shall be determined from time to time by the creditors' committee or, if there is no creditors' committee, by the court, and shall be paid out of the assets as an expense of the administration.*

2.16(2)   *The basis for determining the amount of the remuneration payable to the administrator may be a commission calculated by reference to the value of the company's property with which he has to deal, but there shall in any event be taken into account–*

   (a)   *the work which, having regard to that value, was reasonably undertaken by him; and*

   (b)   *the extent of his responsibilities in administering the company's assets.*

2.16(3)   *Rules 4.32 to 4.34 of Chapter 6 of Part 4 shall apply to an administration as they apply to a liquidation but as if for any reference to the liquidator or the liquidation committee there was substituted a reference to the administrator or the creditors committee.*

2.17   Abstract of receipts and payments

2.17(1)   *The administrator shall–*

   (a)   *within 2 months after the end of 6 months from the date of his appointment, and of every subsequent period of 6 months, and*

   (b)   *within 2 months after he ceases to act as administrator,*

send to the court, and to the registrar of companies, and to each member of the creditors' committee, the requisite accounts of the receipts and payments of the company.

610

2.17(2) *The court may, on the administrator's application, extend the period of 2 months mentioned in paragraph (1).*

2.17(3) *The accounts are to be in the form of an abstract showing–*

(a) receipts and payments during the relevant period of 6 months, or

(b) where the administrator has ceased to act, receipts and payments during the period from the end of the last 6 month period to the time when he so ceased (alternatively, if there has been no previous abstract, receipts and payments in the period since his appointment as administrator).

2.17(4) *If the administrator makes default in complying with this Rule, he is liable to a fine and, for continued contravention, to a daily default fine.*

2.18 Resignation from office

2.18(1) *The administrator may give notice of his resignation on grounds of ill health or because–*

(a) he intends ceasing to be in practice as an insolvency practitioner, or

(b) there is some conflict of interest or change of personal circumstances, which precludes or makes impracticable the further discharge by him of the duties of administrator.

2.18(2) *The administrator may, with the leave of the court, give notice of his resignation on grounds other than those specified in paragraph (1).*

2.18(3) *The administrator must give to the persons specified below at least 7 days' notice of his intention to resign, or to apply for the court's leave to do so–*

(a) if there is a continuing administrator of the company, to him;

(b) if there is no such administrator, to the creditors' committee; and

(c) if there is no such administrator and no creditors' committee, to the company and its creditors.

2.18(4) *Where the administrator gives notice under paragraph (3), he must also give notice to a member State liquidator, if such a person has been appointed in relation to the company.*

History
Rule 2.18 subpara.(4) inserted by the Insolvency (Scotland) Regulations 2003 (SI 2003/2109 (S 8)) reg.26 as from September 8, 2003.

2.19 Administrator deceased

2.19(1) *Subject to the following paragraph, where the administrator has died, it is the duty of his executors or, where the deceased administrator was a partner in a firm, of a partner of that firm to give notice of that fact to the court, specifying the date of the death. This does not apply if notice has been given under the following paragraph.*

2.19(2) *Notice of the death may also be given by any person producing to the court a copy of the death certificate.*

2.20 Order filling vacancy

2.20 *Where the court makes an order filling a vacancy in the office of administrator, the same provisions apply in respect of giving notice of, and advertising, the appointment as in the case of the administration order.*

CHAPTER 6

VAT BAD DEBT RELIEF

2.21 Application of provisions in Part 3 (receivers)

2.21 *Chapter 5 of Part 3 (VAT bad debt relief) shall apply to an administrator as it applies to an administrative receiver, subject to the modification that, for any reference to the administrative receiver, there shall be substituted a reference to the administrator.*

2.22   Application for conversion into winding up

2.22(1)   *Where a member State liquidator proposes to apply to the court for the conversion under Article 37 of the EC Regulation (conversion of earlier proceedings) of an administration into a winding up, an affidavit complying with Rule 2.23 must be prepared and sworn, and lodged in court in support of the application.*

2.22(2)   *The application and the affidavit required under this Rule shall be served upon–*

(a)   *the company; and*

(b)   *the administrator.*

2.23   Contents of affidavit

2.23(1)   *The affidavit shall state–*

(a)   *that main proceedings have been opened in relation to the company in a member State other than the United Kingdom;*

(b)   *the deponent's belief that the conversion of the administration into a winding up would prove to be in the interests of the creditors in the main proceedings;*

(c)   *the deponent's opinion as to whether the company ought to enter voluntary winding up or be wound up by the court; and*

(d)   *all other matters that, in the opinion of the member State liquidator, would assist the court–*

    (i)   *in deciding whether to make such an order, and*

    (ii)   *if the court were to do so, in considering the need for any consequential provision that would be necessary or desirable.*

2.23(2)   *An affidavit under this Rule shall be sworn by, or on behalf of, the member State liquidator.*

2.24   Power of court

2.24(1)   *On hearing the application for conversion into winding up, the court may make such order as it thinks fit.*

2.24(2)   *If the court makes an order for conversion into winding up, the order may contain all such consequential provisions as the court deems necessary or desirable.*

2.24(3)   *Without prejudice to the generality of paragraph (1), an order under that paragraph may provide that the company be wound up as if a resolution for voluntary winding up under section 84 were passed on the day on which the order is made.*

2.25   Interpretation of creditor and notice to member State liquidator

2.25(1)   *This Rule applies where a member State liquidator has been appointed in relation to the company.*

2.25(2)   *For the purposes of the Rules referred to in paragraph (3) the member State liquidator is deemed to be a creditor.*

2.25(3)   *The Rules referred to in paragraph (2) are–*

(a)   *Rule 2.10(1);*

(b)   *Rule 2.11;*

(c)   *Rule 2.12; and*

(d)   *Rule 2.14.*

2.25(4)   *For the purposes of the application by Rule 2.15 of Rule 3.4 with regard to a creditors' committee in an administration, the member State liquidator is deemed to be a creditor.*

2.25(5)   *For the purposes of the application by Rule 2.9 of Rule 7.9(3) insofar as–*

(a)   *Rule 7.9(3) applies Rules 4.15 and 4.16; and*

(b)   *by virtue of its application by Rule 7.9(3), Rule 4.16 applies section 49 of the Bankruptcy Act,*

the member State liquidator is deemed to be a creditor.

2.25(6)   *For the purposes of the application by Rule 2.15 of Chapter 3 of Part 3 and the application by Rule 3.6 of Rules 4.50(b) and 4.52(3), the member State liquidator is deemed to be a creditor.*

2.25(7)   *For the purposes of the application by Rule 2.16 of Rule 4.34(3), the member State liquidator is deemed to be a creditor.*

2.25(8)   *Paragraphs (2) to (7) are without prejudice to the generality of the right to participate referred to in paragraph 3 of Article 32 of the EC Regulation (exercise of creditors' rights).*

2.25(9)   *Where the administrator is obliged to give notice to, or provide a copy of a document (including an order of court) to, the court or the registrar of companies, the administrator shall give notice or provide copies, as the case may be, to the member State liquidator.*

2.25(10)   *Paragraph (9) is without prejudice to the generality of the obligations imposed by Article 31 of the EC Regulation (duty to co operate and communicate information).*

History
Rules 2.22–2.25 inserted by the Insolvency (Scotland) Regulations 2003 (SI 2003/2109 (S 8)) reg.26 as from September 8, 2003.

PART 3

RECEIVERS

CHAPTER 1

APPOINTMENT

3.1   Acceptance of appointment

3.1(1)   Where a person has been appointed a receiver by the holder of a floating charge under section 53, his acceptance (which need not be in writing) of that appointment for the purposes of paragraph (a) of section 53(6) shall be intimated by him to the holder of the floating charge or his agent within the period specified in that paragraph and he shall, as soon as possible after his acceptance, endorse a written docquet to that effect on the instrument of appointment.

3.1(2)   The written docquet evidencing receipt of the instrument of appointment, which is required by section 53(6)(b), shall also be endorsed on the instrument of appointment.

3.1(3)   The receiver shall, as soon as possible after his acceptance of the appointment, deliver a copy of the endorsed instrument of appointment to the holder of the floating charge or his agent.

3.1(4)   This Rule shall apply in the case of the appointment of joint receivers as it applies to the appointment of a receiver, except that, where the docquet of acceptance required by paragraph (1) is endorsed by each of the joint receivers, or two or more of them, on the same instrument of appointment, it is the joint receiver who last endorses his docquet of acceptance who is required to send a copy of the instrument of appointment to the holder of the floating charge or his agent under paragraph (3).

CHAPTER 2

STATEMENT OF AFFAIRS

3.2 Notice requiring statement of affairs

3.2(1) Where the receiver decides to require from any person or persons a statement as to the affairs of the company to be made out and submitted to him in accordance with section 66, he shall send to each of those persons a notice in the form required by Rule 7.30 and Schedule 5 requiring him to make out and submit a statement of affairs in the form prescribed by the Receivers (Scotland) Regulations 1986.

3.2(2) Any person to whom a notice is sent under this Rule is referred to in this Chapter as **"a deponent"**.

3.2(3) The receiver shall insert any statement of affairs submitted to him in the sederunt book.

3.3 Expenses of statement of affairs

3.3(1) A deponent who makes up and submits to the receiver a statement of affairs shall be allowed and be paid by the receiver, as an expense of the receivership, any expenses incurred by the deponent in so doing which the receiver considers to be reasonable.

3.3(2) Any decision by the receiver under this Rule is subject to appeal to the court.

3.3(3) Nothing in this Rule relieves a deponent from any obligation to make up and submit a statement of affairs, or to provide information to the receiver.

CHAPTER 3

THE CREDITORS' COMMITTEE

3.4 Constitution of committee

3.4(1) Where it is resolved by the creditors' meeting to establish a creditors' committee under section 68, the committee shall consist of at least 3 and not more than 5 creditors of the company elected at the meeting.

3.4(2) Any creditor of the company who has lodged a claim is eligible to be a member of the committee, so long as his claim has not been rejected for the purpose of his entitlement to vote.

3.4(3) A body corporate or a partnership may be a member of the committee, but it cannot act as such otherwise than by a representative appointed under Rule 7.20, as applied by Rule 3.6.

3.5 Functions of the committee

3.5 In addition to the functions conferred on it by the Act, the creditors' committee shall represent to the receiver the views of the unsecured creditors and shall act in relation to him in such manner as may be agreed from time to time.

3.6 Application of provisions relating to liquidation committee

3.6(1) Chapter 7 of Part 4 (The liquidation committee) shall apply with regard to the creditors' committee in the receivership and its members as it applies to the liquidation committee and the creditor members thereof, subject to the modifications specified below and to any other necessary modifications.

3.6(2) For any reference in the said Chapter 7 to–

(a) the liquidator or the liquidation committee, there shall be substituted a reference to the receiver or to the creditors' committee;

(b) to the creditor member, there shall be substituted a reference to a creditor,

and any reference to a contributory member shall be disregarded.

3.6(3) In Rule 4.42(3) and 4.52(2), for the reference to Rule 4.41(1), there shall be substituted a reference to Rule 3.4(1).

3.6(4) In Rule 4.57,

(a) for the reference to an expense of the liquidation, there shall be substituted a reference to an expense of the receivership;

(b) at the end of that Rule there shall be inserted the following–

"This does not apply to any meeting of the committee held within 3 months of a previous meeting, unless the meeting in question is summoned at the instance of the receiver.".

3.6(5) The following Rules shall not apply, namely–
Rules 4.40, 4.41, 4.43 to 4.44, 4.53, 4.56, 4.58 and 4.59.

3.7 Information from receiver

3.7(1) Where the committee resolves to require the attendance of the receiver under section 68(2), the notice to him shall be in writing signed by the majority of the members of the committee for the time being or their representatives.

3.7(2) The meeting at which the receiver's attendance is required shall be fixed by the committee for a business day, and shall be held at such time and place as he determines.

3.7(3) Where the receiver so attends, the members of the committee may elect any one of their number to be chairman of the meeting, in place of the receiver or any nominee of his.

3.8 Members' dealings with the company

3.8(1) Membership of the committee does not prevent a person from dealing with the company while the receiver is acting, provided that any transactions in the course of such dealings are entered into on normal commercial terms.

3.8(2) The court may, on the application of any person interested, set aside a transaction which appears to it to be contrary to the requirements of this Rule, and may give such consequential directions as it thinks fit for compensating the company for any loss which it may have incurred in consequence of the transaction.

3.8A Prescribed Part

3.8A Where a receiver is appointed over the whole or any part of the property of a company and section 176A(2) applies, the receiver shall–

(a) where the company is in liquidation or administration, make available to the liquidator or administrator for distribution to unsecured creditors the sums representing the prescribed part, or

(b) in any other case (save where the receiver petitions for the winding up of the company), apply to the court for directions as to the disposal of the prescribed part.

History
Rule 3.8A inserted by the Enterprise Act 2002 (Consequential Amendments) (Prescribed Part) (Scotland) Order 2003 (SI 2003/2108 (S 7)) art.5 as from September 15, 2003.

CHAPTER 4

MISCELLANEOUS

3.9 Abstract of receipts and payments

3.9(1) The receiver shall–

(a) within 2 months after the end of 12 months from the date of his appointment, and of every subsequent period of 12 months, and

(b) within 2 months after he ceases to act as receiver,

send the requisite accounts of his receipts and payments as receiver to–

    (i) the Accountant in Bankruptcy,

    (ii) the holder of the floating charge by virtue of which he was appointed,

    (iii) the members of the creditors' committee (if any),

    (iv) the company or, if it is in liquidation, the liquidator.

3.9(2) The court may, on the receiver's application, extend the period of 2 months referred to in paragraph (1).

3.9(3) The accounts are to be in the form of an abstract showing–

(a) receipts and payments during the relevant period of 12 months, or

(b) where the receiver has ceased to act, receipts and payments during the period from the end of the last 12-month period to the time when he so ceased (alternatively, if there has been no previous abstract, receipts and payments in the period since his appointment as receiver).

3.9(4) This Rule is without prejudice to the receiver's duty to render proper accounts required otherwise than as above.

3.9(5) If the receiver makes default in complying with this Rule, he is liable to a fine and, for continued contravention, to a daily default fine.

3.10 Receiver deceased

3.10 If the receiver dies, the holder of the floating charge by virtue of which he was appointed shall, forthwith on his becoming aware of the death, give notice of it to–

(a) the registrar of companies,

(b) the members of the creditors' committee (if any),

(c) the company or, if it is in liquidation, the liquidator,

(d) the holder of any other floating charge and any receiver appointed by him,

(e) the Accountant in Bankruptcy.

3.11 Vacation of office

3.11 The receiver, on vacating office on completion of the receivership or in consequence of his ceasing to be qualified as an insolvency practitioner, shall, in addition to giving notice to the registrar of companies and the Accountant in Bankruptcy under section 62(5), give notice of his vacating office, within 14 days thereof, to–

(a) the holder of the floating charge by virtue of which he was appointed, (b)　the members of the creditors' committee (if any),

(c)　the company or, if it is in liquidation, the liquidator,

(d)　the holder of any other floating charge and any receiver appointed by him.

CHAPTER 5

VAT BAD DEBT RELIEF

3.12　Issue of certificate of insolvency

3.12(1)　In accordance with this Rule, it is the duty of the administrative receiver to issue a certificate in the terms of paragraph (b) of section 22(3) of the Value Added Tax Act 1983 (which specifies the circumstances in which a company is deemed insolvent for the purposes of that section) forthwith upon his forming the opinion described in that paragraph.

3.12(2)　There shall in the certificate be specified–

(a)　the name of the company and its registered number;

(b)　the name of the administrative receiver and the date of his appointment; and

(c)　the date on which the certificate is issued.

3.12(3)　The certificate shall be entitled "CERTIFICATE OF INSOLVENCY FOR THE PURPOSES OF SECTION 22(3)(b) OF THE VALUE ADDED TAX ACT 1983".

3.13　Notice to creditors

3.13(1)　Notice of the issue of the certificate shall be given by the administrative receiver within 3 months of his appointment or within 2 months of issuing the certificate, whichever is the later, to all of the company's unsecured creditors of whose address he is then aware and who have, to his knowledge, made supplies to the company, with a charge to value added tax, at any time before his appointment.

3.13(2)　Thereafter, he shall give the notice to any such creditor of whose address and supplies to the company he becomes aware.

3.13(3)　He is not under obligation to provide any creditor with a copy of the certificate.

3.14　Preservation of certificate with company's records

3.14(1)　The certificate shall be retained with the company's accounting records, and section 222 of the Companies Act (where and for how long records are to be kept) shall apply to the certificate as it applies to those records.

3.14(2)　It is the duty of the administrative receiver, on vacating office, to bring this Rule to the attention of the directors or (as the case may be) any successor of his as receiver.

PART 4

WINDING UP BY THE COURT

CHAPTER 1

PROVISIONAL LIQUIDATOR

4.1　Appointment of provisional liquidator

4.1(1)　An application to the court for the appointment of a provisional liquidator under section 135 may be made by the petitioner in the winding up, or by a creditor of the company, or by a contributory, or by

617

the company itself, or by any person who under any enactment would be entitled to present a petition for the winding up of the company.

4.1(2) The court shall be satisfied that a person has caution for the proper performance of his functions as provisional liquidator if a statement is lodged in court or it is averred in the winding-up petition that the person to be appointed is an insolvency practitioner, duly qualified under the Act to act as liquidator, and that he consents so to act.

4.2 Order of appointment

4.2(1) The provisional liquidator shall forthwith after the order appointing him is made, give notice of his appointment to–

   (a) the registrar of companies;

   (aa) the Accountant in Bankruptcy;

   (b) the company; and

   (c) any receiver of the whole or any part of the property of the company.

4.2(2) The provisional liquidator shall advertise his appointment in accordance with any directions of the court.

4.3 Caution

4.3 The cost of providing the caution required by the provisional liquidator under the Act shall unless the court otherwise directs be–

   (a) if a winding up order is not made, reimbursed to him out of the property of the company, and the court may make an order against the company accordingly, and

   (b) if a winding up order is made, reimbursed to him as an expense of the liquidation.

4.4 Failure to find or to maintain caution

4.4(1) If the provisional liquidator fails to find or to maintain his caution, the court may remove him and make such order as it thinks fit as to expenses.

4.4(2) If an order is made under this Rule removing the provisional liquidator, or discharging the order appointing him, the court shall give directions as to whether any, and if so what, steps should be taken for the appointment of another person in his place.

4.5 Remuneration

4.5(1) The remuneration of the provisional liquidator shall be fixed by the court from time to time.

4.5(2) Section 53(4) of the Bankruptcy Act shall apply to determine the basis for fixing the amount of the remuneration of the provisional liquidator, subject to the modifications specified in Rule 4.16(2) and to any other necessary modifications.

4.5(3) Without prejudice to any order of the court as to expenses, the provisional liquidator's remuneration shall be paid to him, and the amount of any expenses incurred by him (including the remuneration and expenses of any special manager appointed under section 177) reimbursed–

   (a) if a winding up order is not made, out of the property of the company, and

   (b) if a winding up order is made, as an expense of the liquidation.

4.5(4) Unless the court otherwise directs, in a case falling within paragraph (3)(a) above, the provisional liquidator may retain out of the company's property such sums or property as are or may be required for meeting his remuneration and expenses.

4.6   Termination of appointment

4.6(1)   Except in relation to winding-up petitions under section 124A, the appointment of the provisional liquidator may be terminated by the court on his application, or on that of any of the persons entitled to make application for his appointment under Rule 4.1.

4.6(2)   If the provisional liquidator's appointment terminates, in consequence of the dismissal of the winding up petition or otherwise, the court may give such directions as it thinks fit with respect to–

(a)   the accounts of his administration;

(b)   the expenses properly incurred by the provisional liquidator; or

(c)   any other matters which it thinks appropriate.

4.6(3)   In winding-up petitions under section 124A, the appointment of the provisional liquidator may be terminated by the court on his application, or on that of the Secretary of State.

History
Rule 4.6(1) amended and r.4.6(3) inserted by the Insolvency (Scotland) Amendment Rules 2006 (SI 2006/734 (S 6)) r.13 as from April 6, 2006.

CHAPTER 2

STATEMENT OF AFFAIRS

4.7   Notice requiring statement of affairs

4.7(1)   This Chapter applies where the liquidator or, in a case where a provisional liquidator is appointed, the provisional liquidator decides to require a statement as to the affairs of the company to be made out and submitted to him in accordance with section 131.

4.7(2)   In this Chapter the expression "liquidator" includes "provisional liquidator".

4.7(3)   The liquidator shall send to each of the persons upon whom he decides to make such a requirement under section 131, a notice in the form required by Rule 7.30 and Schedule 5 requiring him to make out and submit a statement of affairs.

4.7(4)   Any person to whom a notice is sent under this Rule is referred to in this Chapter as **"a deponent"**.

4.8   Form of the statement of affairs

4.8(1)   The statement of affairs shall be in the form required by Rule 7.30 and Schedule 5.

4.8(2)   The liquidator shall insert any statement of affairs submitted to him in the sederunt book.

4.9   Expenses of statement of affairs

4.9(1)   At the request of any deponent, made on the grounds that he cannot himself prepare a proper statement of affairs, the liquidator may authorise an allowance towards expenses to be incurred by the deponent in employing some person or persons to be approved by the liquidator to assist the deponent in preparing it.

4.9(2)   Any such request by the deponent shall be accompanied by an estimate of the expenses involved.

4.9(3)   An authorisation given by the liquidator under this Rule shall be subject to such conditions (if any) as he thinks fit to impose with respect to the manner in which any person may obtain access to relevant books and papers.

4.9(4)   Nothing in this Rule relieves a deponent from any obligation to make up and submit a statement of affairs, or to provide information to the liquidator.

4.9(5) Any allowance by the liquidator under this Rule shall be an expense of the liquidation.

4.9(6) The liquidator shall intimate to the deponent whether he grants or refuses his request for an allowance under this Rule and where such request is refused the deponent affected by the refusal may appeal to the court not later than 14 days from the date intimation of such refusal is made to him.

CHAPTER 3

INFORMATION

4.10 Information to creditors and contributories

4.10(1) The liquidator shall report to the creditors and, except where he considers it would be inappropriate to do so, the contributories with respect to the proceedings in the winding up within six weeks after the end of each accounting period or he may submit such a report to a meeting of creditors or of contributories held within such period.

4.10(1A) The report under paragraph (1) shall include–

(a) to the best of the liquidator's knowledge and belief–

  (i) an estimate of the value of the prescribed part (whether or not he proposes to make an application to the court under section 176A(5) or section 176A(3) applies), and

  (ii) an estimate of the value of the company's net property,

  provided that such estimates shall not be required to include any information the disclosure of which could seriously prejudice the commercial interests of the company, but if such information is excluded the estimates shall be accompanied by a statement to that effect, and

(b) whether, and, if so, why, the liquidator proposes to make an application to the court under section 176A(5).

History
Rule 4.10(1A) inserted by the Enterprise Act 2002 (Consequential Amendments) (Prescribed Part) (Scotland) Order 2003 (SI 2003/2108 (S 7)) art.6 as from September 15, 2003.

4.10(2) Any reference in this Rule to creditors is to persons known to the liquidator to be creditors of the company.

4.10(3) Where a statement of affairs has been submitted to him, the liquidator may send out to creditors and contributories with the next convenient report to be made under paragraph (1) a summary of the statement and such observations (if any) as he thinks fit to make with respect to it.

4.10(4) Any person appointed as liquidator of a company under section 140(1) who, following such appointment becomes aware of creditors of the company of whom he was not aware when he was acting as the administrator of the company, shall send to such creditors a copy of any statement or report which was sent by him to creditors under Rule 2.25, with a note to the effect that it is being sent under this Rule.

History
In r.4.10(4) the words "Rule 2.25" substituted for the former words "Rule 2.7" by the Insolvency (Scotland) Amendment Rules 2003/2111 (S 9)) r.6, Sch.2 para.4 subject to transitional and savings provisions in r.7 as from September 15, 2003.

4.11 Information to accountant in bankruptcy

4.11 The statement which section 192 requires the liquidator to send to the Accountant in Bankruptcy if the winding up is not concluded within one year from its commencement, shall be sent not more than 30 days after the expiration of that year and thereafter not more than 30 days after the end of each accounting period which ends after that year until the winding up is concluded in the form required by Rule 7.30 and Schedule 5 and shall contain the particulars specified therein.

CHAPTER 4

MEETINGS OF CREDITORS AND CONTRIBUTORIES

4.12 First meetings in the liquidation

4.12(1) This Rule applies where under section 138(3) or (4) the interim liquidator summons meetings of the creditors and the contributories of the company or, as the case may be, a meeting of the creditors for the purpose of choosing a person to be liquidator of the company in place of the interim liquidator.

4.12(2) Meetings summoned by the interim liquidator under that section are known respectively as **"the first meeting of creditors"** and **"the first meeting of contributories"**, and jointly as **"the first meetings in the liquidation"**.

4.12(2A) Any meetings of creditors or contributories under section 138(3) or (4) shall be summoned for a date not later than 42 days after the date of the winding up order or such longer period as the court may allow.

4.12(3) Subject as follows, no resolutions shall be taken at the first meeting of creditors other than the following–

(a) a resolution to appoint one or more named insolvency practitioners to be liquidator or, as the case may be, joint liquidators and, in the case of joint liquidators, whether any act required or authorised to be done by the liquidator is to be done by both or all of them, or by any one or more;

(b) a resolution to establish a liquidation committee under section 142(1);

(c) unless a liquidation committee is to be established, a resolution specifying the terms on which the liquidator is to be remunerated, or to defer consideration of that matter;

(d) a resolution to adjourn the meeting for not more than 3 weeks;

(e) any other resolution which the chairman considers it right to allow for special reason.

4.12(4) This rule also applies with respect to the first meeting of contributories except that that meeting shall not pass any resolution to the effect of paragraph (3)(c).

4.13 Other meetings

4.13(1) The liquidator shall summon a meeting of the creditors in each year during which the liquidation is in force.

4.13(2) Subject to the above provision, the liquidator may summon a meeting of the creditors or of the contributories at any time for the purpose of ascertaining their wishes in all matters relating to the liquidation.

4.14 Attendance at meetings of company's personnel

4.14(1) This Rule applies to meetings of creditors and to meetings of contributories.

4.14(2) Whenever a meeting is summoned, the liquidator may, if he thinks fit, give at least 21 days' notice to any one or more of the company's personnel that he is or they are required to be present at the meeting or be in attendance.

4.14(3) In this Rule, **"the company's personnel"** means the persons referred to in paragraphs (a) to (d) of section 235(3) (present and past officers, employees, etc.).

4.14(4)   The liquidator may authorise payment to any person whose attendance is requested at a meeting under this Rule of his reasonable expenses incurred in travelling to the meeting and any payment so authorised shall be an expense of the liquidation.

4.14(5)   In the case of any meeting, any of the company's personnel may, if he has given reasonable notice of his wish to be present, be admitted to take part; but this is at the discretion of the chairman of the meeting, whose decision as to what (if any) intervention may be made by any of them is final.

4.14(6)   If it is desired to put questions to any of the company's personnel who are not present, the meeting may be adjourned with a view to obtaining his attendance.

4.14(7)   Where one of the company's personnel is present at a meeting, only such questions may be put to him as the chairman may in his discretion allow.

CHAPTER 5

CLAIMS IN LIQUIDATION

4.15   Submission of claims

4.15(1)   A creditor, in order to obtain an adjudication as to his entitlement–

(a)   to vote at any meeting of the creditors in the liquidation; or

(b)   to a dividend (so far as funds are available) out of the assets of the company in respect of any accounting period,

shall submit his claim to the liquidator–

(a)   at or before the meeting; or, as the case may be,

(b)   not later than 8 weeks before the end of the accounting period.

4.15(2)   A creditor shall submit his claim by producing to the liquidator–

(a)   a statement of claim in the form required by Rule 7.30 and Schedule 5; and

(b)   an account or voucher (according to the nature of the debt claimed) which constitutes *prima facie* evidence of the debt,

but the liquidator may dispense with any requirement of this paragraph in respect of any debt or any class of debt.

4.15(3)   A claim submitted by a creditor, which has been accepted in whole or in part by the liquidator for the purpose of voting at a meeting or of drawing a dividend in respect of any accounting period, shall be deemed to have been resubmitted for the purpose of obtaining an adjudication as to his entitlement both to vote at any subsequent meeting and (so far as funds are available) to a dividend in respect of an accounting period or, as the case may be, any subsequent accounting period.

4.15(4)   A creditor, who has submitted a claim, may at any time submit a further claim specifying a different amount for his claim:

Provided that a secured creditor shall not be entitled to produce a further claim specifying a different value for the security at any time after the liquidator has required the creditor to discharge, or convey or assign, the security under paragraph 5(2) of Schedule 1 to the Bankruptcy Act, as applied by the following Rule.

4.15(5)   Votes are calculated according to the amount of–

(a)   a creditor's debt as at the date of the commencement of the winding up within the meaning of section 129, deducting any amount paid in respect of that debt after that date; or

(b)   in relation to a member State liquidator, the debt claimed to be due to creditors in proceedings in relation to which he holds office.

History

Rule 4.15(5) substituted by the Insolvency (Scotland) Regulations 2003 (SI 2003/2109 (S 8)) reg.27 as from September 8, 2003.

4.15(5A)   No vote shall be cast by virtue of a debt more than once on any resolution put to the meeting.

4.15(5B)   Where a creditor–

(a)   is entitled to vote under this Rule (as read with Rule 7.9);

(b)   has lodged his claim in one or more sets of other proceedings; and

(c)   votes (either in person or by proxy) on a resolution put to the meeting, only the creditor's vote shall be counted.

4.15(5C)   Where–

(a)   a creditor has lodged his claim in more than one set of other proceedings; and

(b)   more than one member State liquidator seeks to vote by virtue of that claim,

the entitlement to vote by virtue of that claim is exercisable by the member State liquidator in main proceedings, whether or not the creditor has lodged his claim in the main proceedings.

4.15(5D)   For the purposes of paragraphs (5B) and (5C), "other proceedings" means main proceedings, secondary proceedings or territorial proceedings in another member State.

History

Subparagraphs (5A)–(5D) inserted by the Insolvency (Scotland) Regulations 2003 (SI 2003/2109 (S 8)) reg.27 as from September 8, 2003.

4.15(6)   In this Rule and in Rule 4.16, including the provisions of the Bankruptcy Act applied by that Rule, any reference to the liquidator includes a reference to the chairman of the meeting.

4.16   Application of the Bankruptcy Act

4.16(1)   Subject to the provisions in this Chapter, the following provisions of the Bankruptcy Act shall apply in relation to a liquidation of a company in like manner as they apply in a sequestration of a debtor's estate, subject to the modifications specified in paragraphs (2) and (3) and to any other necessary modifications–

(a)   section 22(5) and (10) (criminal offence in relation to producing false claims or evidence);

(b)   section 48(5), (6) and (8), together with sections 44(2) and (3) and 47(1) as applied by those sections (further evidence in relation to claims);

(c)   section 49 (adjudication of claim);

(d)   section 50 (entitlement to vote and draw dividend);

(e)   section 60 (liabilities and rights of co-obligants); and

(f)   Schedule 1 except paragraphs 2, 4 and 6 (determination of amount of creditor's claim).

4.16(2)   Subject to paragraph (3) below, for any reference in the provisions of the Bankruptcy Act, as applied by these Rules, to any expression in column 1 below, there shall be substituted a reference to the expression in column 2 opposite thereto–

Column 1	Column 2
Interim trustee	Liquidator
Permanent trustee	Liquidator

Sequestration	Liquidation
Date of sequestration	Date of commencement of winding up within the meaning of section 129
Debtor	The company or, in the application of section 49(6) of the Bankruptcy Act, any member or contributory of the company
Debtor's estate	Company's assets
Accountant in Bankruptcy	The court
Commissioners	Liquidation committee
Sheriff	The court
Preferred debts	Preferential debts within the meaning of section 386

4.16(3)   Where the winding up was immediately preceded by an administration, the references to the date of sequestration in paragraph 1(1) of Schedule 1 to the Bankruptcy Act and the second reference to that date in paragraph 1(2) shall be construed as references to the date on which the company entered administration.

Note
See also r.4.68.
   Rule 4.16(1), (2) amended and r.4.16(3) inserted by the Insolvency (Scotland) Rules 1986 Amendment Rules 2008 (SSI 2008/393) r.3 as from December 20, 2008.
   Rule 4.16 modified by the Financial Collateral Arrangements (No.2) Regulations 2003 (SI 2003/3226) reg.15 as from December 26, 2003 in certain circumstances where a collateral-provider or a collateral-taker under a financial collateral arrangement goes into liquidation or, in the case of a partnership, sequestration.

4.17   Claims in foreign currency

4.17(1)   A creditor may state the amount of his claim in a currency other than sterling where–

(a)   his claim is constituted by decree or other order made by a court ordering the company to pay to the creditor a sum expressed in a currency other than sterling, or

(b)   where it is not so constituted, his claim arises from a contract or bill of exchange in terms of which payment is or may be required to be made by the company to the creditor in a currency other than sterling.

4.17(2)   Where a claim is stated in currency other than sterling for the purpose of the preceding paragraph, it shall be converted into sterling at the rate of exchange for that other currency at the mean of the buying and selling spot rates prevailing in the London market at the close of business on the date of commencement of winding up or, if the liquidation was immediately preceded by an administration, on the date on which the company entered administration.

Note
Rule 4.17(2) amended by the Insolvency (Scotland) Rules 1986 Amendment Rules 2008 (SSI 2008/393) r.4 as from December 20, 2008.
   Rule 4.17 modified by the Financial Collateral Arrangements (No.2) Regulations 2003 (SI 2003/3226) reg.15 as from December 26, 2003 in certain circumstances where a collateral-provider or a collateral-taker under a financial collateral arrangement goes into liquidation or, in the case of a partnership, sequestration.

CHAPTER 6

THE LIQUIDATOR

Section A: Appointment and functions of liquidator

4.18   Appointment of liquidator by the court

4.18(1)   This Rule applies where a liquidator is appointed by the court under section 138(1) (appointment of interim liquidator), 138(5) (no person appointed or nominated by the meetings of creditors and contributories), 139(4) (different persons nominated by creditors and contributories) or 140(1) or (2) (liquidation following administration or voluntary arrangement).

4.18(2)   The court shall not make the appointment unless and until there is lodged in court a statement to the effect that the person to be appointed is an insolvency practitioner, duly qualified under the Act to be the liquidator, and that he consents so to act.

4.18(3)   Thereafter, the court shall send a copy of the order to the liquidator, whose appointment takes effect from the date of the order.

4.18(4)   The liquidator shall–

(a)   within 7 days of his appointment, give notice of it to the Accountant in Bankruptcy; and

(b)   within 28 days of his appointment, give notice of it to the creditors and contributories or, if the court so permits, he shall advertise his appointment in accordance with the directions of the court.

4.18(5)   In any notice or advertisement to be given by him under this Rule, the liquidator shall state whether a liquidation committee has been established by a meeting of creditors or contributories, and, if this is not the case, he shall–

(a)   state whether he intends to summon meetings of creditors and contributories for the purpose of establishing a liquidation committee or whether he proposes to summon only a meeting of creditors for that purpose; and

(b)   if he does not propose to summon any meeting, set out the powers of the creditors under section 142(3) to require him to summon such a meeting.

4.19   Appointment by creditors or contributories

4.19(1)   This Rule applies where a person is nominated for appointment as liquidator under section 139(2) either by a meeting of creditors or by a meeting of contributories.

4.19(2)   Subject to section 139(4) the interim liquidator, as chairman of the meeting, or, where the interim liquidator is nominated as liquidator, the chairman of the meeting, shall certify the appointment of a person as liquidator by the meeting but not until and unless the person to be appointed has provided him with a written statement to the effect that he is an insolvency practitioner, duly qualified under the Act to be the liquidator and that he consents so to act.

4.19(3)   The appointment of the liquidator takes effect upon the passing of the resolution for his appointment and the date of his appointment shall be stated in the certificate.

4.19(4)   The liquidator shall–

(a)   within 7 days of his appointment, give notice of his appointment to the court and to the Accountant in Bankruptcy; and

(b)   within 28 days of his appointment, give notice of it in a newspaper circulating in the area where the company has its principal place of business, or in such newspaper as he thinks most appropriate for ensuring that it comes to the notice of the company's creditors and contributories.

4.19(5)   The provisions of Rule 4.18(5) shall apply to any notice given by the liquidator under this Rule.

4.19(6)   Paragraphs (4) and (5) need not be complied with in the case of a liquidator appointed by a meeting of contributories and replaced by another liquidator appointed on the same day by a creditors' meeting.

4.20   Authentication of liquidator's appointment

4.20   A copy certified by the clerk of court of any order of court appointing the liquidator or, as the case may be, a copy, certified by the chairman of the meeting which appointed the liquidator, of the certificate of the liquidator's appointment under Rule 4.19(2), shall be sufficient evidence for all purposes and in any proceedings that he has been appointed to exercise the powers and perform the duties of liquidator in the winding up of the company.

4.21 Hand-over of assets to liquidator

4.21(1) This Rule applies where a person appointed as liquidator (**"the succeeding liquidator"**) succeeds a previous liquidator (**"the former liquidator"**) as the liquidator.

4.21(2) When the succeeding liquidator's appointment takes effect, the former liquidator shall forthwith do all that is required for putting the succeeding liquidator into possession of the assets.

4.21(3) The former liquidator shall give to the succeeding liquidator all such information, relating to the affairs of the company and the course of the winding up, as the succeeding liquidator considers to be reasonably required for the effective discharge by him of his duties as such and shall hand over all books, accounts, statements of affairs, statements of claim and other records and documents in his possession relating to the affairs of the company and its winding up.

4.22 Taking possession and realisation of the company's assets

4.22(1) The liquidator shall–

    (a) as soon as may be after his appointment take possession of the whole assets of the company and any property, books, papers or records in the possession or control of the company or to which the company appears to be entitled; and

    (b) make up and maintain an inventory and valuation of the assets which he shall retain in the sederunt book.

4.22(2) The liquidator shall be entitled to have access to all documents or records relating to the assets or the property or the business or financial affairs of the company sent by or on behalf of the company to a third party and in that third party's hands and to make copies of any such documents or records.

4.22(3) If any person obstructs a liquidator who is exercising, or attempting to exercise, a power conferred by sub-section (2) above, the court, on the application of the liquidator, may order that person to cease so to obstruct the liquidator.

4.22(4) The liquidator may require delivery to him of any title deed or other document or record of the company, notwithstanding that a right of lien is claimed over the title deed or document or record, but this paragraph is without prejudice to any preference of the holder of the lien.

4.22(5) Section 39(4) and (7) of the Bankruptcy Act shall apply in relation to a liquidation of a company as it applies in relation to a sequestration of a debtor's estate, subject to the modifications specified in Rule 4.16(2) and to any other necessary modifications.

Section B: Removal and resignation; vacation of office

4.23 Summoning of meeting for removal of liquidator

4.23(1) Subject to section 172(3) and without prejudice to any other method of summoning the meeting, a meeting of creditors for the removal of the liquidator in accordance with section 172(2) shall be summoned by the liquidator if requested to do so by not less than one quarter in value of the creditors.

4.23(2) Where a meeting of creditors is summoned especially for the purpose of removing the liquidator in accordance with section 172(2), the notice summoning it shall draw attention to section 174(4)(a) or (b) with respect to the liquidator's release.

4.23(3) At the meeting, a person other than the liquidator or his nominee may be elected to act as chairman; but if the liquidator or his nominee is chairman and a resolution has been proposed for the liquidator's removal, the chairman shall not adjourn the meeting without the consent of at least one-half (in value) of the creditors present (in person or by proxy) and entitled to vote.

4.23(4) Where a meeting is to be held or is proposed to be summoned under this Rule, the court may, on the application of any creditor, give directions as to the mode of summoning it, the sending out and return of forms of proxy, the conduct of the meeting, and any other matter which appears to the court to require regulation or control under this Rule.

4.24 Procedure on liquidator's removal

4.24(1) Where the creditors have resolved that the liquidator be removed, the chairman of the creditors' meeting shall forthwith–

(a) if, at the meeting, another liquidator was not appointed, send a certificate of the liquidator's removal to the court and a copy of the certificate to the Accountant in Bankruptcy, and

(b) otherwise, deliver the certificate to the new liquidator, who shall forthwith send a copy of the certificate to the court and to the Accountant in Bankruptcy.

4.24(2) The liquidator's removal is effective as from such date as the meeting of the creditors shall determine, and this shall be stated in the certificate of removal.

4.25 Release of liquidator on removal

4.25(1) Where the liquidator has been removed by a creditors' meeting which has not resolved against his release, the date on which he has his release in terms of section 174(4)(a) shall be stated in the certificate of removal before a copy of it is sent to the court and to the Accountant in Bankruptcy under Rule 4.24(1).

4.25(2) Where the liquidator is removed by a creditors' meeting which has resolved against his release, or is removed by the court, he must apply to the Accountant of Court for his release.

4.25(3) When the Accountant of Court releases the former liquidator, he shall–

(a) issue a certificate of release to the new liquidator who shall send a copy of it to the court and to the Accountant in Bankruptcy, and

(b) send a copy of the certificate to the former liquidator,

and in this case release of the former liquidator is effective from the date of the certificate.

4.26 Removal of liquidator by the court

4.26(1) This Rule applies where application is made to the court for the removal of the liquidator, or for an order directing the liquidator to summon a meeting of creditors for the purpose of removing him.

4.26(2) The court may require the applicant to make a deposit or give caution for the expenses to be incurred by the liquidator on the application.

4.26(3) The applicant shall, at least 14 days before the hearing, send to the liquidator a notice stating its date, time and place and accompanied by a copy of the application, and of any evidence which he intends to adduce in support of it.

4.26(4) Subject to any contrary order of the court, the expenses of the application are not payable as an expense of the liquidation.

4.26(5) Where the court removes the liquidator–

(a) it shall send two copies of the order of removal to him;

(b) the order may include such provision as the court thinks fit with respect to matters arising in connection with the removal; and

(c)   if the court appoints a new liquidator, Rule 4.18 applies,

and the liquidator, on receipt of the two court orders under sub-paragraph (a), shall send one copy of the order to the Accountant in Bankruptcy, together with a notice of his ceasing to act as a liquidator.

4.27   Advertisement of removal

4.27   Where a new liquidator is appointed in place of the one removed, Rules 4.19 to 4.21 shall apply to the appointment of the new liquidator except that the notice to be given by the new liquidator under Rule 4.19(4) shall also state–

(a)   that his predecessor as liquidator has been removed; and

(b)   whether his predecessor has been released.

4.28   Resignation of liquidator

4.28(1)   Before resigning his office under section 172(6) the liquidator shall call a meeting of creditors for the purpose of receiving his resignation.

4.28(2)   The notice summoning the meeting shall draw attention to section 174(4)(c) and Rule 4.29(4) with respect of the liquidator's release and shall also be accompanied by an account of the liquidator's administration of the winding up, including a summary of his receipts and payments and a statement as to the amount paid to unsecured creditors by virtue of the application of section 176A (prescribed part).

History
In r.4.28(2) the words "and a statement as to the amount paid to unsecured creditors by virtue of the application of section 176A (prescribed part)" inserted by the Enterprise Act 2002 (Consequential Amendments) (Prescribed Part) (Scotland) Order 2003 (SI 2003/2108 (S 7)) art.6 as from September 15, 2003.

4.28(3)   Subject to paragraph (4), the liquidator may only proceed under this Rule on the grounds of ill health or because–

(a)   he intends ceasing to be in practice as an insolvency practitioner; or

(b)   there has been some conflict of interest or change of personal circumstances which precludes or makes impracticable the further discharge by him of the duties of the liquidator.

4.28(4)   Where two or more persons are acting as liquidator jointly, any one of them may resign (without prejudice to the continuation in office of the other or others) on the ground that, in his opinion and that of the other or others, it is no longer expedient that there should continue to be the present number of joint liquidators.

4.29   Action following acceptance of liquidator's resignation

4.29(1)   This Rule applies where a meeting is summoned to receive the liquidator's resignation.

4.29(2)   If the liquidator's resignation is accepted, it is effective as from such date as the meeting of the creditors may determine and that date shall be stated in the notice given by the liquidator under paragraph (3).

4.29(3)   The liquidator, whose resignation is accepted, shall forthwith after the meeting give notice of his resignation to the court as required by section 172(6) and shall send a copy of it to the Accountant in Bankruptcy.

4.29(4)   The meeting of the creditors may grant the liquidator his release from such date as they may determine. If the meeting resolves against the liquidator having his release, Rule 4.25(2) and (3) shall apply.

4.29(5)   Where the creditors have resolved to appoint a new liquidator in place of the one who has resigned, Rules 4.19 to 4.21 shall apply to the appointment of the new liquidator, except that the notice to be given by the new liquidator under Rule 4.19(4) shall also state that his predecessor as liquidator has resigned and whether he has been released.

4.29(6)   If there is no quorum present at the meeting summoned to receive the liquidator's resignation, the meeting is deemed to have been held, a resolution is deemed to have been passed that the liquidator's resignation be accepted, and the creditors are deemed not to have resolved against the liquidator having his release.

4.29(7)   Where paragraph (6) applies–

   (a)   the liquidator's resignation is effective as from the date for which the meeting was summoned and that date shall be stated in the notice given by the liquidator under paragraph (3), and

   (b)   the liquidator is deemed to have been released as from that date.

4.30   Leave to resign granted by the court

4.30(1)   If, at a creditors' meeting summoned to receive the liquidator's resignation, it is resolved that it be not accepted, the court may, on the liquidator's application, make an order giving him leave to resign.

4.30(2)   The court's order under this Rule may include such provision as it thinks fit with respect to matters arising in connection with the resignation including the notices to be given to the creditors and the Accountant in Bankruptcy and shall determine the date from which the liquidator's release is effective.

Section C: Release on completion of winding up

4.31   Final meeting

4.31(1)   The liquidator shall give at least 28 days' notice of the final meeting of creditors to be held under section 146. The notice shall be sent to all creditors whose claims in the liquidation have been accepted.

4.31(2)   The liquidator's report laid before the meeting shall contain an account of his administration of the winding up, including a summary of his receipts and payments and a statement as to the amount paid to unsecured creditors by virtue of the application of section 176A (prescribed part).

History
In r.4.31(2) the words "and a statement as to the amount paid to unsecured creditors by virtue of the application of section 176A (prescribed part)" inserted by the Enterprise Act 2002 (Consequential Amendments) (Prescribed Part) (Scotland) Order 2003 (SI 2003/2108 (S 7)) art.6(3) as from September 15, 2003.

4.31(3)   At the final meeting, the creditors may question the liquidator with respect to any matter contained in his report, and may resolve against the liquidator having his release.

4.31(4)   The liquidator shall within 7 days of the meeting give notice to the court and to the registrar of companies and the Accountant in Bankruptcy under section 172(8) that the final meeting has been held and the notice shall state whether or not he has been released, and be accompanied by a copy of the report laid before the meeting.

4.31(5)   If there is no quorum present at the final meeting, the liquidator shall report to the court that a final meeting was summoned in accordance with the Rules, but that there was no quorum present; and the final meeting is then deemed to have been held and the creditors not to have resolved against the liquidator being released.

4.31(6)   If the creditors at the final meeting have not resolved against the liquidator having his release, he is released in terms of section 174(4)(d)(ii) when he vacates office under section 172(8). If they have so resolved he shall apply for his release to the Accountant of Court, and Rules 4.25(2) and (3) shall apply accordingly subject to the modifications that in Rule 4.25(3) sub-paragraph (a) shall apply with the word "new" replaced by the word "former" and sub-paragraph (b) shall not apply.

Section D: Outlays and remuneration

4.32   Determination of amount of outlays and remuneration

4.32(1)   Subject to the provisions of Rules 4.33 to 4.35, claims by the liquidator for the outlays reasonably incurred by him and for his remuneration shall be made in accordance with section 53 of the Bankruptcy Act as applied by Rule 4.68 and as further modified by paragraphs (2) and (3) below.

4.32(2)   After section 53(1) of the Bankruptcy Act, there shall be inserted the following subsection–

> "**(1A)** The liquidator may, at any time before the end of an accounting period, submit to the liquidation committee (if any) an interim claim in respect of that period for the outlays reasonably incurred by him and for his remuneration and the liquidation committee may make an interim determination in relation to the amount of the outlays and remuneration payable to the liquidator and, where they do so, they shall take into account that interim determination when making their determination under subsection (3)(a)(ii).".

4.32(3)   In section 53(6) of the Bankruptcy Act, for the reference to "subsection (3)(a)(ii)" there shall be substituted a reference to "subsection (1A) or (3)(a)(ii)".

Note
Section 58 of the Bankruptcy (Scotland) Act 1985 is made to apply in company liquidations by r.4.68, subject to the modifications set out in subss.(2) and (3) above. The subsections should not be read as general amendments to the 1985 Act.

4.33   Recourse of liquidator to meeting of creditors

4.33   If the liquidator's remuneration has been fixed by the liquidation committee and he considers the amount to be insufficient, he may request that it be increased by resolution of the creditors.

4.34   Recourse to the court

4.34(1)   If the liquidator considers that the remuneration fixed for him by the liquidation committee, or by resolution of the creditors, is insufficient, he may apply to the court for an order increasing its amount or rate.

4.34(2)   The liquidator shall give at least 14 days' notice of his application to the members of the liquidation committee; and the committee may nominate one or more members to appear or be represented, and to be heard, on the application.

4.34(3)   If there is no liquidation committee, the liquidator's notice of his application shall be sent to such one or more of the company's creditors as the court may direct, which creditors may nominate one or more of their number to appear or be represented.

4.34(4)   The court may, if it appears to be a proper case, order the expenses of the liquidator's application, including the expenses of any member of the liquidation committee appearing or being represented on it, or any creditor so appearing or being represented, to be paid as an expense of the liquidation.

4.35   Creditors' claim that remuneration is excessive

4.35(1)   If the liquidator's remuneration has been fixed by the liquidation committee or by the creditors, any creditor or creditors of the company representing in value at least 25 per cent of the creditors may apply to the court for an order that the liquidator's remuneration be reduced, on the grounds that it is, in all the circumstances, excessive.

4.35(2)   If the court considers the application to be well-founded, it shall make an order fixing the remuneration at a reduced amount or rate.

4.35(3)   Unless the court orders otherwise, the expenses of the application shall be paid by the applicant, and are not payable as an expense of the liquidation.

Section E: Supplementary provisions

4.36   Liquidator deceased

4.36(1)   Subject to the following paragraph, where the liquidator has died, it is the duty of his executors or, where the deceased liquidator was a partner in a firm, of a partner in that firm to give notice of that fact to the court the Bank of England and liquidation committee and to the Accountant in Bankruptcy, specifying the date of death. This does not apply if notice has been given under the following paragraph.

4.36(2)   Notice of the death may also be given by any person producing to the court and to the Accountant in Bankruptcy a copy of the death certificate.

History
Rule 4.36(1) amended by the Bank Insolvency (Scotland) Rules 2009 (SI 2009/351) r.51(2) as from February 25, 2009.

4.37   Loss of qualification as insolvency practitioner

4.37(1)   This Rule applies where the liquidator vacates office on ceasing to be qualified to act as an insolvency practitioner in relation to the company.

4.37(2)   He shall forthwith give notice of his doing so to the court and to the Accountant in Bankruptcy.

4.37(3)   Rule 4.25(2) and (3) apply as regards the liquidator obtaining his release, as if he had been removed by the court.

4.38   Power of court to set aside certain transactions

4.38(1)   If in the course of the liquidation the liquidator enters into any transaction with a person who is an associate of his, the court may, on the application of any person interested, set the transaction aside and order the liquidator to compensate the company for any loss suffered in consequence of it.

4.38(2)   This does not apply if either–

    (a)   the transaction was entered into with the prior consent of the court, or

    (b)   it is shown to the court's satisfaction that the transaction was for value, and that it was entered into by the liquidator without knowing, or having any reason to suppose, that the person concerned was an associate.

4.38(3)   Nothing in this Rule is to be taken as prejudicing the operation of any rule of law with respect to a trustee's dealings with trust property, or the fiduciary obligations of any person.

4.39   Rule against solicitation

4.39(1)   Where the court is satisfied that any improper solicitation has been used by or on behalf of the liquidator in obtaining proxies or procuring his appointment, it may order that no remuneration be allowed as an expense of the liquidation to any person by whom, or on whose behalf, the solicitation was exercised.

4.39(2)   An order of the court under this Rule overrides any resolution of the liquidation committee or the creditors, or any other provision of the Rules relating to the liquidator's remuneration.

CHAPTER 7

THE LIQUIDATION COMMITTEE

4.40 Preliminary

4.40 For the purposes of this Chapter–

(a) an **"insolvent winding up"** takes place where a company is being wound up on grounds which include its inability to pay its debts, and

(b) a **"solvent winding up"** takes place where a company is being wound up on grounds which do not include that one.

4.41 Membership of committee

4.41(1) Subject to Rule 4.43 below, the liquidation committee shall consist as follows:–

(a) in the case of any winding up, of at least 3 and not more than 5 creditors of the company, elected by the meeting of creditors held under section 138 or 142 of the Act, and also

(b) in the case of a solvent winding up where the contributories' meeting held under either of those sections so decides, of up to 3 contributories, elected by that meeting.

4.41(2) Any creditor of the company (other than one whose debt is fully secured and who has not agreed to surrender his security to the liquidator) is eligible to be a member of the committee, so long as–

(a) he has lodged a claim of his debt in the liquidation, and

(b) his claim has neither been wholly rejected for voting purposes, nor wholly rejected for the purposes of his entitlement so far as funds are available to a dividend.

4.41(3) No person can be a member as both a creditor and a contributory.

4.41(4) A body corporate or a partnership may be a member of the committee, but it cannot act as such otherwise than by a member's representative appointed under Rule 4.48 below.

4.41(5) In this Chapter, members of the committee elected or appointed by a creditors' meeting are called **"creditor members"**, and those elected or appointed by a contributories' meeting are called **"contributory members"**.

4.41(6) Where the Deposit Protection Board exercises the right (under section 58 of the Banking Act) to be a member of the committee, the Board is to be regarded as an additional creditor member.

4.42 Formalities of establishment

4.42(1) The liquidation committee shall not come into being, and accordingly cannot act, until the liquidator has issued a certificate of its due constitution.

4.42(2) If the chairman of the meeting which resolves to establish the committee is not the liquidator, he shall forthwith give notice of the resolution to the liquidator (or, as the case may be, the person appointed as liquidator by the same meeting), and inform him of the names and addresses of the persons elected to be members of the committee.

4.42(3) No person may act as a member of the committee unless and until he has agreed to do so and, unless the relevant proxy or authorisation contains a statement to the contrary, such agreement may be given on behalf of the member by his proxy-holder or any representative under section 375 of the Companies Act who is present at the meeting at which the committee is established; and the liquidator's certificate of the committee's due constitution shall not be issued until at least the minimum number of persons in accordance with Rule 4.41 who are to be members of it have agreed to act, but shall be issued forthwith thereafter.

4.42(4) As and when the others (if any) agree to act, the liquidator shall issue an amended certificate.

4.42(5) The certificate (and any amended certificate) shall be sent by the liquidator to the Accountant in Bankruptcy.

4.42(6) If after the first establishment of the committee there is any change in its membership, the liquidator shall report the change to the Accountant in Bankruptcy.

4.43 Committee established by contributories

4.43(1) The following applies where the creditors' meeting under section 138 or 142 of the Act does not decide that a liquidation committee should be established or decides that a liquidation committee should not be established.

4.43(2) A meeting of contributories under section 138 or 142 may appoint one of their number to make application to the court for an order to the liquidator that a further creditors' meeting be summoned for the purpose of establishing a liquidation committee; and–

    (a) the court may, if it thinks that there are special circumstances to justify it, make that order, and

    (b) the creditors' meeting summoned by the liquidator in compliance with the order is deemed to have been summoned under section 142.

4.43(3) If the creditors' meeting so summoned does not establish a liquidation committee, a meeting of contributories may do so.

4.43(4) The committee shall then consist of at least 3, and not more than 5, contributories elected by that meeting; and Rule 4.42 shall apply to such a committee with the substitution of the reference to Rule 4.41 in paragraph (3) of that Rule by a reference to this paragraph.

4.44 Obligations of liquidator to committee

4.44(1) Subject as follows, it is the duty of the liquidator to report to the members of the liquidation committee all such matters as appear to him to be, or as they have indicated to him as being, of concern to them with respect to the winding up.

4.44(2) In the case of matters so indicated to him by the committee, the liquidator need not comply with any request for information where it appears to him that–

    (a) the request is frivolous or unreasonable, or

    (b) the cost of complying would be excessive, having regard to the relative importance of the information, or

    (c) there are not sufficient assets to enable him to comply.

4.44(3) Where the committee has come into being more than 28 days after the appointment of the liquidator, he shall report to them, in summary form, what actions he has taken since his appointment, and shall answer all such questions as they may put to him regarding his conduct of the winding up hitherto.

4.44(4) A person who becomes a member of the committee at any time after its first establishment is not entitled to require a report to him by the liquidator, otherwise than in summary form, of any matters previously arising.

4.44(5) Nothing in this Rule disentitles the committee, or any member of it, from having access to the liquidator's cash book and sederunt book, or from seeking an explanation of any matter within the committee's responsibility.

4.45 Meetings of the committee

4.45(1) Subject as follows, meetings of the liquidation committee shall be held when and where determined by the liquidator.

4.45(2) The liquidator shall call a first meeting of the committee to take place within 3 months of his appointment or of the committee's establishment (whichever is the later); and thereafter he shall call a meeting–

(a) if so requested by a creditor member of the committee or his representative (the meeting then to be held within 21 days of the request being received by the liquidator), and

(b) for a specified date, if the committee has previously resolved that a meeting be held on that date.

4.45(3) The liquidator shall give 7 days' written notice of the time and place of any meeting to every member of the committee (or his representative, if designated for that purpose), unless in any case the requirement of the notice has been waived by or on behalf of any member. Waiver may be signified either at or before the meeting.

4.46 The chairman at meetings

4.46(1) The chairman at any meeting of the liquidation committee shall be the liquidator, or a person nominated by him to act.

4.46(2) A person so nominated must be either–

(a) a person who is qualified to act as an insolvency practitioner in relation to the company, or

(b) an employee of the liquidator or his firm who is experienced in insolvency matters.

4.47 Quorum

4.47 A meeting of the committee is duly constituted if due notice of it has been given to all the members, and at least 2 creditor members or, in the case of a committee of contributories, 2 contributory members are present or represented.

4.48 Committee members' representatives

4.48(1) A member of the liquidation committee may, in relation to the business of the committee, be represented by another person duly authorised by him for that purpose.

4.48(2) A person acting as a committee-member's representative must hold a mandate entitling him so to act (either generally or specially) and signed by or on behalf of the committee-member, and for this purpose any proxy or authorisation under section 375 of the Companies Act in relation to any meeting of creditors (or, as the case may be, members or contributories) of the company shall, unless it contains a statement to the contrary, be treated as such a mandate to act generally signed by or on behalf of the committee-member.

4.48(3) The chairman at any meeting of the committee may call on a person claiming to act as a committee-member's representative to produce his mandate and may exclude him if it appears that his mandate is deficient.

4.48(4) No member may be represented by a body corporate or by a partnership, or by an undischarged bankrupt.

4.48(5) No person shall–

(a) on the same committee, act at one and the same time as representative of more than one committee-member, or

(b) act both as a member of the committee and as representative of another member.

4.48(6) Where a member's representative signs any document on the member's behalf, the fact that he so signs must be stated below his signature.

4.49   Resignation

4.49   A member of the liquidation committee may resign by notice in writing delivered to the liquidator.

4.50   Termination of membership

4.50   Membership of the liquidation committee of any person is automatically terminated if–

(a)   his estate is sequestrated or he becomes bankrupt or grants a trust deed for the benefit of or makes a composition with his creditors, or

(b)   at 3 consecutive meetings of the committee he is neither present nor represented (unless at the third of those meetings it is resolved that this Rule is not to apply in his case), or

(c)   that creditor being a creditor member, he ceases to be, or is found never to have been a creditor.

4.51   Removal

4.51   A creditor member of the committee may be removed by resolution at a meeting of creditors; and a contributory member may be removed by a resolution of a meeting of contributories.

4.52   Vacancy (creditor members)

4.52(1)   The following applies if there is a vacancy among the creditor members of the committee.

4.52(2)   The vacancy need not be filled if the liquidator and a majority of the remaining creditor members so agree, provided that the total number of members does not fall below the minimum required by Rule 4.41(1).

4.52(3)   The liquidator may appoint any creditor, who is qualified under the Rules to be a member of the committee, to fill the vacancy, if a majority of the other creditor members agrees to the appointment, and the creditor concerned consents to act.

4.52(4)   Alternatively, a meeting of creditors may resolve that a creditor be appointed (with his consent) to fill the vacancy. In this case, at least 14 days' notice must have been given of the resolution to make such an appointment (whether or not of a person named in the notice).

4.52(5)   Where the vacancy is filled by an appointment made by a creditors' meeting at which the liquidator is not present, the chairman of the meeting shall report to the liquidator the appointment which has been made.

4.53   Vacancy (contributory members)

4.53(1)   The following applies if there is a vacancy among the contributory members of the committee.

4.53(2)   The vacancy need not be filled if the liquidator and a majority of the remaining contributory members so agree, provided that, in the case of a committee of contributory members only, the total number of members does not fall below the minimum required by Rule 4.43(4) or, as the case may be, 4.59(4).

4.53(3)   The liquidator may appoint any contributory member (being qualified under the Rules to be a member of the committee) to fill the vacancy, if a majority of the other contributory members agree to the appointment, and the contributory concerned consents to act.

4.53(4)   Alternatively, a meeting of contributories may resolve that a contributory be appointed (with his consent) to fill the vacancy. In this case, at least 14 days' notice must have been given of the resolution to make such an appointment (whether or not of a person named in the notice).

4.53(5)   Where the vacancy is filled by an appointment made by a contributories' meeting at which the liquidator is not present, the chairman of the meeting shall report to the liquidator the appointment which has been made.

4.54 Voting rights and resolutions

4.54(1) At any meeting of the committee, each member of it (whether present himself, or by his representative) has one vote; and a resolution is passed when a majority of the creditor members present or represented have voted in favour of it.

4.54(2) Subject to the next paragraph, the votes of contributory members do not count towards the number required for passing a resolution, but the way in which they vote on any resolution shall be recorded.

4.54(3) Paragraph (2) does not apply where, by virtue of Rule 4.43(4) or 4.59, the only members of the committee are contributories. In that case the committee is to be treated for voting purposes as if all its members were creditors.

4.54(4) Every resolution passed shall be recorded in writing, either separately or as part of the minutes of the meeting. The record shall be signed by the chairman and kept as part of the sederunt book.

4.55 Resolutions by post

4.55(1) In accordance with this Rule, the liquidator may seek to obtain the agreement of members of the liquidation committee to a resolution by sending to every member (or his representative designated for the purpose) a copy of the proposed resolution.

4.55(2) Where the liquidator makes use of the procedure allowed by this Rule, he shall send out to members of the committee or their representatives (as the case may be) a copy of any proposed resolution on which a decision is sought, which shall be set out in such a way that agreement with or dissent from each separate resolution may be indicated by the recipient on the copy so sent.

4.55(3) Any creditor member of the committee may, within 7 business days from the date of the liquidator sending out a resolution, require him to summon a meeting of the committee to consider the matters raised by the resolution.

4.55(4) In the absence of such a request, the resolution is deemed to have been passed by the committee if and when the liquidator is notified in writing by a majority of the creditor members that they concur with it.

4.55(5) A copy of every resolution passed under this Rule, and a note that the committee's concurrence was obtained, shall be kept in the sederunt book.

4.56 Liquidator's reports

4.56(1) The liquidator shall, as and when directed by the liquidation committee (but not more often than once in any period of 2 months), send a written report to every member of the committee setting out the position generally as regards the progress of the winding up and matters arising in connection with it, to which the liquidator considers the committee's attention should be drawn.

4.56(2) In the absence of such directions by the committee, the liquidator shall send such a report not less often than once in every period of 6 months.

4.56(3) The obligations of the liquidator under this Rule are without prejudice to those imposed by Rule 4.44.

4.57 Expenses of members, etc.

4.57(1) The liquidator shall defray any reasonable travelling expenses directly incurred by members of the liquidation committee or their representatives in respect of their attendance at the committee's meetings, or otherwise on the committee's business, as an expense of the liquidation.

4.57(2) Paragraph (1) does not apply to any meeting of the committee held within 3 months of a previous meeting.

4.58   Dealings by committee members and others

4.58(1)   This Rule applies to–

   (a)   any member of the liquidation committee:

   (b)   any committee-member's representative;

   (c)   any person who is an associate of a member of the committee or of a committee-member's representative; and

   (d)   any person who has been a member of the committee at any time in the last 12 months.

4.58(2)   Subject as follows, a person to whom this Rule applies shall not enter into any transaction whereby he–

   (a)   receives out of the company's assets any payment for services given or goods supplied in connection with the liquidation, or

   (b)   obtains any profit from the liquidation, or

   (c)   acquires any part of the company's assets.

4.58(3)   Such a transaction may be entered into by a person to whom this Rule applies–

   (a)   with the prior leave of the court, or

   (b)   if he does so as a matter of urgency, or by way of performance of a contract in force before the date on which the company went into liquidation, and obtains the court's leave for the transaction, having applied for it without undue delay, or

   (c)   with the prior sanction of the liquidation committee, where it is satisfied (after full disclosure of the circumstances) that the transaction will be on normal commercial terms.

4.58(4)   Where in the committee a resolution is proposed that sanction be accorded for a transaction to be entered into which, without that sanction or the leave of the court, would be in contravention of this Rule, no member of the committee, and no representative of a member, shall vote if he is to participate directly or indirectly in the transaction.

4.58(5)   The court may, on the application of any person interested–

   (a)   set aside a transaction on the ground that it has been entered into in contravention of this Rule, and

   (b)   make with respect to it such other order as it thinks fit, including (subject to the following paragraph) an order requiring a person to whom this Rule applies to account for any profit obtained from the transaction and compensate the company's assets for any resultant loss.

4.58(6)   In the case of a person to whom this Rule applies as an associate of a member of the committee or of a committee-member's representative, the court shall not make any order under paragraph (5), if satisfied that he entered into the relevant transaction without having any reason to suppose that in doing so he would contravene this Rule.

4.58(7)   The expenses of an application to the court for leave under this Rule are not payable as an expense of the liquidation, unless the court so orders.

4.59   Composition of committee when creditors paid in full

4.59(1)   This Rule applies if the liquidator issues a certificate that the creditors have been paid in full, with interest in accordance with section 189.

4.59(2)   The liquidator shall forthwith send a copy of the certificate to the Accountant in Bankruptcy.

4.59(3)   The creditor members of the liquidation committee shall cease to be members of the committee.

4.59(4)　The committee continues in being unless and until abolished by decision of a meeting of contributories, and (subject to the next paragraph) so long as it consists of at least 2 contributory members.

4.59(5)　The committee does not cease to exist on account of the number of contributory members falling below 2, unless and until 28 days have elapsed since the issue of the liquidator's certificate under paragraph (1), but at any time when the committee consists of less than 2 contributory members, it is suspended and cannot act.

4.59(6)　Contributories may be co-opted by the liquidator, or appointed by a contributories' meeting, to be members of the committee; but the maximum number of members is 5.

4.59(7)　The foregoing Rules in this Chapter continue to apply to the liquidation committee (with any necessary modifications) as if all the members of the committee were creditor members.

4.59A　Formal defects

4.59A　The acts of the liquidation committee established for any winding up are valid notwithstanding any defect in the appointment, election or qualifications of any member of the committee or any committee-member's representative or in the formalities of its establishment.

CHAPTER 8

THE LIQUIDATION COMMITTEE WHERE WINDING UP FOLLOWS IMMEDIATELY ON ADMINISTRATION

4.60　Preliminary

4.60(1)　The Rules in this Chapter apply where–

(a) the winding up order has been made immediately upon the ending of administration under Part II of the Act, and

(b) the court makes an order under section 140(1) appointing as liquidator the person who was previously the administrator.

4.60(2)　In this Chapter the expressions **"insolvent winding up"**, **"solvent winding up"**, **"creditor member"**, and **"contributory member"** each have the same meaning as in Chapter 7.

4.61　Continuation of creditors' committee

4.61(1)　If under Schedule B1 to the Act a creditors' committee has been established for the purposes of the administration, then (subject as follows in this Chapter) that committee continues in being as the liquidation committee for the purposes of the winding up, and–

(a) it is deemed to be a committee established as such under section 142, and

(b) no action shall be taken under subsections (1) to (4) of that section to establish any other.

4.61(2)　This Rule does not apply if, at the time when the court's order under section 140(1) is made, the committee under Schedule B1 to the Act consists of less than 3 members; and a creditor who was, immediately before the date of that order, a member of such a committee ceases to be a member on the making of the order if his debt is fully secured (and he has not agreed to surrender his security to the liquidator).

4.62　Membership of committee

4.62(1)　Subject as follows, the liquidation committee shall consist of at least 3, and not more than 5, creditors of the company, elected by the creditors' meeting held under Schedule B1 to the Act or (in order to make up numbers or fill vacancies) by a creditors' meeting summoned by the liquidator after the company goes into liquidation.

4.62(2) In the case of a solvent winding up, the liquidator shall, on not less than 21 days' notice, summon a meeting of contributories, in order to elect (if it so wishes) contributory members of the liquidation committee, up to 3 in number.

4.63 Liquidator's certificate

4.63(1) The liquidator shall issue a certificate of the liquidation committee's continuance specifying the persons who are, or are to be, members of it.

4.63(2) It shall be stated in the certificate whether or not the liquidator has summoned a meeting of contributories under Rule 4.62(2), and whether (if so) the meeting has elected contributories to be members of the committee.

4.63(3) Pending the issue of the liquidator's certificate, the committee is suspended and cannot act.

4.63(4) No person may act, or continue to act, as a member of the committee unless and until he has agreed to do so; and the liquidator's certificate shall not be issued until at least the minimum number of persons required under Rule 4.62 to form a committee elected, whether under Rule 4.62 above or under Schedule B1 to the Act, have signified their agreement.

4.63(5) As and when the others signify their agreement, the liquidator shall issue an amended certificate.

4.63(6) The liquidator's certificate (or, as the case may be, the amended certificate) shall be sent by him to the Accountant in Bankruptcy.

4.63(7) If subsequently there is any change in the committee's membership, the liquidator shall report the change to the Accountant in Bankruptcy.

4.64 Obligations of liquidator to committee

4.64(1) As soon as may be after the issue of the liquidator's certificate under Rule 4.63, the liquidator shall report to the liquidation committee what actions he has taken since the date on which the company went into liquidation.

4.64(2) A person who becomes a member of the committee after that date is not entitled to require a report to him by the liquidator, otherwise than in a summary form, of any matters previously arising.

4.64(3) Nothing in this Rule disentitles the committee, or any member of it, from having access to the sederunt book (whether relating to the period when he was administrator, or to any subsequent period), or from seeking an explanation of any matter within the committee's responsibility.

4.65 Application of Chapter 7

4.65 Except as provided elsewhere in this Chapter, Rules 4.44 to 4.59A of Chapter 7 shall apply to a liquidation committee established under this Chapter from the date of issue of the certificate under Rule 4.63 as if it had been established under section 142.

CHAPTER 9

DISTRIBUTION OF COMPANY'S ASSETS BY LIQUIDATOR

4.66 Order of priority in distribution

4.66(1) The funds of the company's assets shall be distributed by the liquidator to meet the following expenses and debts in the order in which they are mentioned–

(a) the expenses of the liquidation;

(aa) where the court makes a winding up order in relation to a company and, at the time when the petition for winding up was first presented to the court, there was in force in relation to the company a voluntary arrangement under Part 1 of the Act, any expenses properly incurred as expenses of the administration of that arrangement;

(b) any preferential debts within the meaning of section 386 (excluding any interest which has been accrued thereon to the date of commencement of the winding up within the meaning of section 129);

(c) ordinary debts, that is to say a debt which is neither a secured debt nor a debt mentioned in any other sub-paragraph of this paragraph;

(d) interest at the official rate on–

    (i) the preferential debts, and

    (ii) the ordinary debts,

between the said date of commencement of the winding up and the date of payment of the debt; and

(e) any postponed debt.

4.66(2) In the above paragraph–

(a) **"postponed debt"** means a creditor's right to any alienation which has been reduced or restored to the company's assets under section 242 or to the proceeds of sale of such an alienation; and

(b) **"official rate"** shall be construed in accordance with subsection (4) of section 189 and, for the purposes of paragraph (a) of that subsection, as applied to Scotland by subsection (5), the rate specified in the Rules shall be 15 per centum per annum.

4.66(3) The expenses of the liquidation mentioned in sub-paragraph (a) of paragraph (1) are payable in the order of priority mentioned in Rule 4.67.

4.66(4) Subject to the provisions of section 175, any debt falling within any of sub-paragraphs (b) to (e) of paragraph (1) shall have the same priority as any other debt falling within the same sub-paragraph and, where the funds of the company's assets are inadequate to enable the debts mentioned in this sub-paragraph to be paid in full, they shall abate in equal proportions.

4.66(5) Any surplus remaining, after all expenses and debts mentioned in paragraph (1) have been paid in full, shall (unless the articles of the company otherwise provide) be distributed among the members according to their rights and interests in the company.

4.66(6) Nothing in this Rule shall affect–

(a) the right of a secured creditor which is preferable to the rights of the liquidator; or

(b) any preference of the holder of a lien over a title deed or other document which has been delivered to the liquidator in accordance with a requirement under Rule 4.22(4).

4.67 Order of priority of expenses of liquidation

4.67(1) Subject to section 156 and paragraph (2), the expenses of the liquidation are payable out of the assets in the following order of priority–

(a) any outlays properly chargeable or incurred by the provisional liquidator or liquidator in carrying out his functions in the liquidation, except those outlays specifically mentioned in the following sub-paragraphs;

(b) the cost, or proportionate cost, of any caution provided by a provisional liquidator, liquidator or special manager in accordance with the Act or the Rules;

(c) the remuneration of the provisional liquidator (if any);

(d) the expenses of the petitioner in the liquidation, and of any person appearing in the petition whose expenses are allowed by the court;

(e) the remuneration of the special manager (if any);

(f) any allowance made by the liquidator under Rule 4.9(1) (expenses of statement of affairs);

(g) the remuneration or emoluments of any person who has been employed by the liquidator to perform any services for the company, as required or authorised by or under the Act or the Rules;

(h) the remuneration of the liquidator determined in accordance with Rule 4.32;

(i) the amount of any corporation tax on chargeable gains accruing on the realisation of any asset of the company (without regard to whether the realisation is effected by the liquidator, a secured creditor or otherwise).

4.67(2) In any winding up by the court which follows immediately on a voluntary winding up (whether members' voluntary or creditors' voluntary), such outlays and remuneration of the voluntary liquidator as the court may allow, shall have the same priority as the outlays mentioned in sub-paragraph (a) of paragraph (1).

4.67(3) Nothing in this Rule applies to or affects the power of any court, in proceedings by or against the company, to order expenses to be paid by the company, or the liquidator; nor does it affect the rights of any person to whom such expenses are ordered to be paid.

4.68 Application of the Bankruptcy Act

4.68(1) Sections 52, 53 and 58 of the Bankruptcy Act shall apply in relation to the liquidation of a company as they apply in relation to a sequestration of a debtor's estate, subject to the modifications specified in Rules 4.16(2) and 4.32(2) and (3) and the following paragraph and to any other necessary modifications.

4.68(2) In section 52, the following modifications shall be made–

(a) in subsection (4)(a) for the reference to "the debts mentioned in subsection (1)(a) to (d)", there shall be substituted a reference to the expenses of the winding up mentioned in Rule 4.67(1)(a);

(b) in subsection (5), the words "with the consent of the commissioners or if there are no commissioners of the Accountant in Bankruptcy" should be deleted;

(c) in subsection (7) and (8) for the references to section 48(5) and 49(6)(b) there should be substituted a reference to those sections as applied by Rule 4.16(1); and

(d) for subsection (11) substitute–

> "**(11)** Subject to any notification by the person entitled to a dividend given to the liquidator that he wishes the dividend to be paid to another person, or that he has assigned his entitlement to another person, where both a creditor and a member State liquidator have had a claim accepted in relation to the same debt, payment shall only be made to the creditor."

History
Rule 4.68 para.(2)(d) inserted by the Insolvency (Scotland) Regulations 2003 (SI 2003/2109 (S 8)) reg.27 as from September 8, 2003.

Note
See also r.4.18 and IA 1986 s.193(3).

CHAPTER 10

SPECIAL MANAGER

4.69 Appointment and remuneration

4.69(1) This Chapter applies to an application under section 177 by the liquidator or, where one has been appointed, by the provisional liquidator for the appointment of a person to be special manager (references in this Chapter to the liquidator shall be read as including the provisional liquidator).

4.69(2) An application shall be supported by a report setting out the reasons for the appointment. The report shall include the applicant's estimate of the value of the assets in respect of which the special manager is to be appointed.

4.69(3) The order of the court appointing the special manager shall specify the duration of his appointment, which may be for a period of time or until the occurrence of a specified event. Alternatively the order may specify that the duration of the appointment is to be subject to a further order of the court.

4.69(4) The appointment of a special manager may be renewed by order of the court.

4.69(5) The special manager's remuneration shall be fixed from time to time by the court.

4.69(6) The acts of the special manager are valid notwithstanding any defect in his appointment or qualifications.

4.70 Caution

4.70(1) The appointment of the special manager does not take effect until the person appointed has found (or, being allowed by the court to do so, has undertaken to find) caution to the person who applies for him to be appointed.

4.70(2) It is not necessary that caution be found for each separate company liquidation; but it may be found either specially for a particular liquidation, or generally for any liquidation in relation to which the special manager may be employed as such.

4.70(3) The amount of the caution shall be not less than the value of the assets in respect of which he is appointed, as estimated by the applicant in his report under Rule 4.69.

4.70(4) When the special manager has found caution to the person applying for his appointment, that person shall certify the adequacy of the security and notify the court accordingly.

4.70(5) The cost of finding caution shall be paid in the first instance by the special manager; but–

   (a) where a winding up order is not made, he is entitled to be reimbursed out of the property of the company, and the court may make an order on the company accordingly, and

   (b) where a winding up order has been or is subsequently made, he is entitled to be reimbursed as an expense of the liquidation.

4.71 Failure to find or to maintain caution

4.71(1) If the special manager fails to find the required caution within the time stated for that purpose by the order appointing him, or any extension of that time that may be allowed, the liquidator shall report the failure to the court, which may thereupon discharge the order appointing the special manager.

4.71(2) If the special manager fails to maintain his caution the liquidator shall report his failure to the court, which may thereupon remove the special manager and make such order as it thinks fit as to expenses.

4.71(3) If an order is made under this Rule removing the special manager, or recalling the order appointing him, the court shall give directions as to whether any, and if so what, steps should be taken to appoint another special manager in his place.

4.72 Accounting

4.72(1) The special manager shall produce accounts containing details of his receipts and payments for the approval of the liquidator.

4.72(2) The accounts shall be in respect of 3-month periods for the duration of the special manager's appointment (or for a lesser period if his appointment terminates less than 3 months from its date, or from the date to which the last accounts were made up).

4.72(3) When the accounts have been approved, the special manager's receipts and payments shall be added to those of the liquidator.

4.73 Termination of appointment

4.73(1) The special manager's appointment terminates if the winding up petition is dismissed or, if a provisional liquidator having been appointed, he is discharged without a winding up order having been made.

4.73(2) If the liquidator is of opinion that the employment of the special manager is no longer necessary or profitable for the company, he shall apply to the court for directions, and the court may order the special manager's appointment to be terminated.

4.73(3) The liquidator shall make the same application if a resolution of the creditors is passed, requesting that the appointment be terminated.

CHAPTER 11

PUBLIC EXAMINATION OF COMPANY OFFICERS AND OTHERS

4.74 Notice of order for public examination

4.74 Where the court orders the public examination of any person under section 133(1), then, unless the court otherwise directs, the liquidator shall give at least 14 days' notice of the time and place of the examination to the persons specified in paragraphs (c) to (e) of section 133(4) and the liquidator may, if he thinks fit, cause notice of the order to be given, by public advertisement in one or more newspapers circulating in the area of the principal place of business of the company, at least 14 days before the date fixed for the examination but there shall be no such advertisement before at least 7 days have elapsed from the date when the person to be examined was served with the order.

4.75 Order on request by creditors or contributories

4.75(1) A request to the liquidator by a creditor or creditors or contributory or contributories under section 133(2) shall be made in writing and be accompanied by–

   (a) a list of the creditors (if any) concurring with the request and the amounts of their respective claims in the liquidation, or (as the case may be) of the contributories (if any) so concurring, with their respective values, and

   (b) from each creditor or contributory concurring, written confirmation of his concurrence.

4.75(2) The request must specify the name of the proposed examinee, the relationship which he has, or has had, to the company and the reasons why his examination is requested.

4.75(3)   Before an application to the court is made on the request, the requisitionists shall deposit with the liquidator such sum as the latter may determine to be appropriate by way of caution for the expenses of the hearing of a public examination, if ordered.

4.75(4)   Subject as follows, the liquidator shall, within 28 days of receiving the request, make the application to the court required by section 133(2).

4.75(5)   If the liquidator is of opinion that the request is an unreasonable one in the circumstances, he may apply to the court for an order relieving him from the obligation to make the application otherwise required by that subsection.

4.75(6)   If the court so orders, and the application for the order was made *ex parte*, notice of the order shall be given forthwith by the liquidator to the requisitionists. If the application for an order is dismissed, the liquidator's application under section 133(2) shall be made forthwith on conclusion of the hearing of the application first mentioned.

4.75(7)   Where a public examination of the examinee has been ordered by the court on a creditors' or contributories' requisition under this Rule the court may order that the expenses of the examination are to be paid, as to a specified proportion, out of the caution under paragraph (3), instead of out of the assets.

CHAPTER 12

MISCELLANEOUS

4.76   Limitation

4.76   The provisions of section 8(5) and 22(8), as read with section 73(5), of the Bankruptcy (Scotland) Act 1985 (presentation of petition or submission of claim to bar effect of limitation of actions) shall apply in relation to the liquidation as they apply in relation to a sequestration, subject to the modifications specified in Rule 4.16(2) and to any other necessary modifications.

4.77   Dissolution after winding up

4.77   Where the court makes an order under section 204(5) or 205(5), the person on whose application the order was made shall deliver to the registrar of companies a copy of the order.

CHAPTER 13

COMPANY WITH PROHIBITED NAME

4.78   Preliminary

4.78   The Rules in this Chapter–

  (a)   relate to the leave required under section 216 (restriction on re-use of name of company in insolvent liquidation) for a person to act as mentioned in section 216(3) in relation to a company with a prohibited name,

  (b)   prescribe the cases excepted from that provision, that is to say, those in which a person to whom the section applies may so act without that leave, and

  (c)   apply to all windings up to which section 216 applies, whether or not the winding up commenced before or after the coming into force of the Insolvency (Scotland) Amendment Rules 1987.

4.79   Application for leave under section 216(3)

4.79   When considering an application for leave under section 216, the court may call on the liquidator, or any former liquidator, of the liquidating company for a report of the circumstances in which that company became insolvent, and the extent (if any) of the applicant's apparent responsibility for its doing so.

4.80 First excepted case

4.80(1) This Rule applies where–

(a) a person ("**the person**") was within the period mentioned in section 216(1) a director, or shadow director, of an insolvent company that has gone into insolvent liquidation;

(b) the person acts in all or any of the ways specified in section 216(3) in connection with, or for the purposes of, the carrying on (or proposed carrying on) of the whole or substantially the whole of the business of the insolvent company where that business (or substantially the whole of it) is (or is to be) acquired from the insolvent company under arrangements–

    (i) made by its liquidator; or

    (ii) made before the insolvent company entered into insolvent liquidation by an office-holder acting in relation to it as administrator, receiver or supervisor of a voluntary arrangement under Part 1 of the Act.

4.80(2) The person will not be taken to have contravened section 216 if prior to his acting in the circumstances set out in paragraph (1) a notice is, in accordance with the requirements of paragraph (3)–

(a) given by the person to every creditor of the insolvent company whose name and address–

    (i) is known by him; or

    (ii) is ascertainable by him on the making of such enquiries as are reasonable in the circumstances; and

(b) published in the Edinburgh Gazette.

4.80(3) The notice referred to in paragraph (2)–

(a) may be given and published before the completion of the arrangements referred to in paragraph (1)(b) but must be given and published no later than 28 days after that completion;

(b) must state–

    (i) the name and registered number of the insolvent company;

    (ii) the name of the person;

    (iii) that it is his intention to act (or, where the insolvent company has not entered insolvent liquidation, to act or continue to act) in all or any of the ways specified in section 216(3) in connection with, or for the purposes of, the carrying on of the whole, or substantially the whole, of the business of the insolvent company; and

    (iv) the prohibited name or, where the company has not entered insolvent liquidation, the name under which the business is being, or is to be, carried on which would be a prohibited name in respect of the person in the event of the insolvent company entering insolvent liquidation; and

(c) must in the case of notice given to each creditor of the company be given using Form 4.32(Scot).

4.80(4) Notice may in particular be given under this Rule–

(a) prior to the insolvent company entering insolvent liquidation where the business (or substantially the whole of the business) is, or is to be, acquired by another company under arrangements made by an office-holder acting in relation to the insolvent company as administrator, receiver or supervisor of a voluntary arrangement (whether or not at the time of the giving of the notice the director is a director of that other company); or

(b) at a time where the person is a director of another company where–

    (i) the other company has acquired, or is to acquire, the whole, or substantially the whole, of the business of the insolvent company under arrangements made by its liquidator; and

    (ii) it is proposed that after the giving of the notice a prohibited name should be adopted by the other company.

History
Rule 4.80 substituted by the Insolvency (Scotland) Amendment Rules 2007 (SI 2007/2537 (S 5)) r.3, as from October 1, 2007, subject to transitional provisions in r.2.

4.81 Second excepted case

4.81(1) Where a person to whom section 216 applies as having been a director or shadow director of the liquidating company applies for leave of the court under that section not later than 7 days from the date on which the company went into liquidation, he may, during the period specified in paragraph (2) below, act in any of the ways mentioned in section 216(3), notwithstanding that he has not the leave of the court under that section.

4.81(2) The period referred to in paragraph (1) begins with the day in which the company goes into liquidation and ends either on the day falling 6 weeks after that date or on the day on which the court disposes of the application for leave under section 216, whichever of those days occurs first.

4.82 Third excepted case

4.82 The court's leave under section 216(3) is not required where the company there referred to, though known by a prohibited name within the meaning of the section,–

(a) has been known by that name for the whole of the period of 12 months ending with the day before the liquidating company went into liquidation, and

(b) has not at any time in those 12 months been dormant within the meaning of section 252(5) of the Companies Act.

CHAPTER 14

EC REGULATION—MEMBER STATE LIQUIDATOR

4.83 Interpretation of creditor and notice to member State liquidator

4.83(1) This Rule applies where a member State liquidator has been appointed in relation to the company.

4.83(2) For the purposes of the provisions referred to in paragraph (3) the member State liquidator is deemed to be a creditor.

4.83(3) The provisions referred to in paragraph (2) are–

(a) Rules 4.10(1) (report to creditors and contributories), 4.10(3) (summary of statement of affairs), 4.13 (other meetings of creditors), 4.15 (submission of claims), 4.17 (claims in foreign currency), 4.18(4) (appointment of liquidator by court), 4.23(2) and (4) (summoning of meeting for removal of liquidator), 4.31 (final meeting), 4.35 (creditors' claim that remuneration is excessive), 4.41(1), (2) and (3) (membership of liquidation committee), 4.52(3) (vacancy (creditor members)), 4.62(1) (membership of committee), 4.74 (notice of order for public examination), 7.3 (notice of meeting) (insofar as it applies to a notice of meeting of creditors under section 138(3) or (4) for the purposes of rule 4.12 and to a meeting requisitioned under rule 7.6 insofar as it applies in a winding up by the court), 7.6(2) (meetings requisitioned) (insofar as it applies in a winding up by

646

the court) and 7.9 (entitlement to vote (creditors)) (insofar as it applies in a winding up by the court); and

(b) sections 48(5), (6) and (8) and 49 of the Bankruptcy Act as applied by Rule 4.16 and section 52(3) of that Act as applied by rule 4.68(1).

4.83(4) Paragraphs (2) and (3) are without prejudice to the generality of the right to participate referred to in paragraph 3 of Article 32 of the EC Regulation (exercise of creditors' rights).

4.83(5) Where the liquidator is obliged to give notice to, or provide a copy of a document (including an order of court) to, the court or the registrar of companies, the liquidator shall give notice or provide copies, as the case may be, to the member State liquidator.

4.83(6) Paragraph (5) is without prejudice to the generality of the obligations imposed by Article 31 of the EC Regulation (duty to co operate and communicate information).

History
See history note after r.4.85.

CHAPTER 15

EC REGULATION—CREDITORS' VOLUNTARY WINDING UP—CONFIRMATION BY THE COURT

4.84 Application for confirmation

4.84(1) Where a company has passed a resolution for voluntary winding up, and no declaration under section 89 has been made, the liquidator may apply to the court for an order confirming the creditors' voluntary winding up for the purposes of the EC Regulation.

4.84(2) The application shall be in writing in the form required by Rule 7.30 and Schedule 5 and verified by affidavit by the liquidator (using the same form) and shall state–

(a) the name of the applicant;

(b) the name of the company and its registered number;

(c) the date on which the resolution for voluntary winding up was passed;

(d) that the application is accompanied by all of the documents required under paragraph (3) which are true copies of the documents required; and

(e) that the EC Regulation will apply to the company and whether the proceedings will be main proceedings, territorial proceedings or secondary proceedings.

4.84(3) The liquidator shall lodge in court two copies of the application, together with one copy of the following:–

(a) the resolution for voluntary winding up referred to by section 84(3);

(b) evidence of his appointment as liquidator of the company; and

(c) the statement of affairs required under section 99.

4.84(4) It shall not be necessary to serve the application on, or give notice of it to, any person.

4.84(5) On an application under this Rule the court may confirm the creditors' voluntary winding up.

4.84(6) If the court confirms the creditor's voluntary winding up it may do so without a hearing.

4.84(7) This Rule applies in relation to a UK insurer (within the meaning of the Insurers (Reorganisation and Winding Up) Regulations 2003) with the modification specified in paragraph (8) below.

4.84(8) For the purposes of paragraph (7), this Rule has effect as if there were substituted for paragraph (1) above–

"**(1)** Where a UK Insurer (within the meaning of the Insurers (Reorganisation and Winding Up) Regulations 2003) has passed a resolution for voluntary winding up, and no declaration under section 89 has been made, the liquidator may apply to court for an order confirming the creditors' voluntary winding up for the purposes of Articles 9 and 27 of Directive 2001/17/EC of the European Parliament and of the Council of 19th March 2001 on the reorganisation and winding up of insurance undertakings."

History
See history note after r.4.85.

4.85 Notice to member State liquidator and creditors in member States

4.85 Where the court has confirmed the creditors' voluntary winding up, the liquidator shall forthwith give notice–

(a)   if there is a member State liquidator in relation to the company, to the member State liquidator;

(b)   in accordance with Article 40 of the EC Regulation (duty to inform creditors).

History
Rules 4.83–4.85 inserted by the Insolvency (Scotland) Regulations 2003 (SI 2003/2109 (S 8)) reg.27 as from September 8, 2003.

PART 5

CREDITORS' VOLUNTARY WINDING UP

5   Application of Part 4

5   The provisions of Part 4 shall apply in a creditors' voluntary winding up of a company as they apply in a winding up by the court subject to the modifications specified in Schedule 1 and to any other necessary modifications.

PART 6

MEMBERS' VOLUNTARY WINDING UP

6   Application of Part 4

6   The provisions of Part 4, which are specified in Schedule 2, shall apply in relation to a members' voluntary winding up of a company as they apply in a winding up by the court, subject to the modifications specified in Schedule 2 and to any other necessary modifications.

PART 7

PROVISIONS OF GENERAL APPLICATION

CHAPTER 1

MEETINGS

7.1   Scope of Chapter 1

7.1(1)   This Chapter applies to any meetings held in insolvency proceedings other than meetings of a creditors' committee in administration or receivership, or of a liquidation committee.

7.1(2)   The Rules in this Chapter shall apply to any such meeting subject to any contrary provision in the Act or in the Rules, or to any direction of the court.

7.2   Summoning of meetings

7.2(1)   In fixing the date, time and place for a meeting, the person summoning the meeting (**"the convenor"**) shall have regard to the convenience of the persons who are to attend.

7.2(2)   Meetings shall in all cases be summoned for commencement between 10.00 and 16.00 hours on a business day, unless the court otherwise directs.

7.3   Notice of meeting

7.3(1)   The convenor shall give not less than 21 days' notice of the date, time and place of the meeting to every person known to him as being entitled to attend the meeting.

7.3(2)   In paragraph (1), for the reference to 21 days, there shall be substituted a reference to 14 days in the following cases:–

(a)   any meeting of the company or of its creditors under paragraph 52, 56 or 62 of Schedule B1 to the Act;

(b)   a meeting of the creditors under paragraph 51 or 54(2) (to consider administrator's proposals or proposed revisions);

(c)   a meeting of creditors under section 67(2) (meeting of unsecured creditors in receivership); and

(d)   a meeting of creditors or contributories under section 138(3) or (4).

History
Rule 7.3(2)(a) substituted by the Insolvency (Scotland) Amendment Rules 2010 (SI 2010/688 (S 2)) art.3 and Sch.1 para.105 as from April 6, 2010, subject to transitional provisions in art.4.
    In r.7.3(2)(b) the words "paragraph 51 or 54(2)" substituted for the former words "section 23(1)(b) or 25(2)(b)" by the Insolvency (Scotland) Amendment Rules 2003 (SI 2003/2111 (S 9)) r.6, Sch.2 para.7 subject to transitional and savings provisions in r.7 as from September 15, 2003.

7.3(3)   The convenor may also publish notice of the date, time and place of the meeting in a newspaper circulating in the area of the principal place of business of the company or in such other newspaper as he thinks most appropriate for ensuring that it comes to the notice of the persons who are entitled to attend the meeting.

History
In r.7.3(3) the words "paragraph 51" substituted for the former words "section 23(1)(b)" by the Insolvency (Scotland) Amendment Rules 2003 (SI 2003/2111 (S 9)) r.6 Sch.2 para.7 subject to transitional and savings provisions in r.7 as from September 15, 2003. Rule 7.3(3) amended by the Insolvency (Scotland) (Amendment) Rules 2009 (SI 2009/662 (S 1)) r.2 and Sch. para.12 as from April 6, 2009.

7.3(3A)   Any notice under this Rule or Rule 2.26A(1) or (2) shall be published not less than 21 days or, in cases to which paragraph (2) above applies, 14 days before the meeting.

History
Rule 7.3(3A) amended by the Insolvency (Scotland) (Amendment) Rules 2009 (SI 2009/662 (S 1)) r.2 and Sch. para.13 as from April 6, 2009.

7.3(4)   Any notice under this Rule shall state–

(a)   the purpose of the meeting;

(b)   the persons who are entitled to attend and vote at the meeting;

(c)   the effects of Rule 7.9 or, as the case may be, 7.10 (Entitlement to Vote) and of the relevant provisions of Rule 7.12 (Resolutions);

(d)   in the case of a meeting of creditors or contributories, that proxies may be lodged at or before the meeting and the place where they may be lodged; and

(e)   in the case of a meeting of creditors, that claims may be lodged by those who have not already done so at or before the meeting and the place where they may be lodged.

Where a meeting of creditors is summoned specially for the purpose of removing the liquidator in accordance with section 171(2) or 172(2), or of receiving his resignation under Rule 4.28, the notice summoning it shall also include the information required by Rule 4.23(2) or, as the case may be, 4.28(2).

7.3(5)   With the notice given under paragraph (1), the convenor shall also send out a proxy form.

7.3(6)   In the case of any meeting of creditors or contributories, the court may order that notice of the meeting be given by public advertisement in such form as may be specified in the order and not by individual notice to the persons concerned. In considering whether to make such an order, the court shall have regard to the cost of the public advertisement, to the amount of the assets available and to the extent of the interest of creditors or contributories or any particular class of either.

7.3(7)   The provisions of this Rule shall not apply to a meeting of creditors summoned under section 95 or 98 but any notice advertised in accordance with section 95(2)(c) or 98(1)(c) shall give not less than 7 days' notice of the meeting.

7.4   Additional notices in certain cases

7.4(1)   This Rule applies where a company goes, or proposes to go, into liquidation and it is an authorised institution or a former authorised institution within the meaning of the Banking Act.

7.4(2)   Notice of any meeting of the company at which it is intended to propose a resolution for its voluntary winding up shall be given by the directors to the Bank of England (**"the Bank"**) and to the Deposit Protection Board (**"the Board"**) as such notice is given to members of the company.

7.4(3)   Where a creditors' meeting is summoned by the liquidator under section 95 or 98, the same notice of meeting must be given to the Bank and Board as is given to the creditors under this Chapter.

7.4(4)   Where the company is being wound up by the court, notice of the first meetings of creditors and contributories within the meaning of Rule 4.12 shall be given to the Bank and the Board by the liquidator.

7.4(5)   Where in any winding up a meeting of creditors or contributories is summoned for the purpose of–

(a)   receiving the liquidator's resignation, or

(b)   removing the liquidator, or

(c)   appointing a new liquidator,

the person summoning the meeting and giving notice of it shall also give notice to the Bank and the Board.

7.4(6)   The Board is entitled to be represented at any meeting of which it is required by this Rule to be given notice; and Schedule 3 has effect with respect to the voting rights of the Board at such a meeting.

7.5   Chairman of meetings

7.5(1)   The chairman at any meeting of creditors in insolvency proceedings, other than at a meeting of creditors summoned under section 98, shall be the responsible insolvency practitioner, or except at a meeting of creditors summoned under section 95 a person nominated by him in writing.

7.5(2)   A person nominated under this Rule must be either–

(a)   a person who is qualified to act as an insolvency practitioner in relation to the company, or

(b)   an employee of the administrator, receiver or liquidator, as the case may be, or his firm who is experienced in insolvency matters.

7.5(3) This Rule also applies to meetings of contributories in a liquidation.

7.5(4) At the first meeting of creditors or contributories in a winding up by the court, the interim liquidator shall be the chairman except that, where a resolution is proposed to appoint the interim liquidator to be the liquidator, another person may be elected to act as chairman for the purpose of choosing the liquidator.

7.5(5) This Rule is subject to Rule 4.23(3) (meeting for removal of liquidator).

7.6 Meetings requisitioned

7.6(1) Subject to paragraph (8), this Rule applies to any request by a creditor or creditors–

(a) to–

(i) an administrator under paragraph 52(2) or 56(1), or

(ii) a liquidator under section 171(3) or 172(3),

for a meeting of creditors; or

(b) to a liquidator under section 142(3) for separate meetings of creditors and contributories, or for any other meeting under any other provision of the Act or the Rules.

History
In r.7.6(1)(a)(i) the words "paragraph 52(2) or 56(1)" substituted for the former words "section 17(3)" by the Insolvency (Scotland) Amendment Rules 2003 (SI 2003/2111 (S 9)) r.6, Sch.2 para.7 subject to transitional and savings provisions in r.7 as from September 15, 2003.

7.6(2) Any such request shall be accompanied by–

(a) a list of any creditors concurring with the request, showing the amounts of the respective claims against the company of the creditor making the request and the concurring creditors;

(b) from each creditor concurring, written confirmation of his concurrence; and

(c) a statement of the purpose of the proposed meeting.

7.6(3) If the administrator or, as the case may be, the liquidator considers the request to be properly made in accordance with the Act or the Rules, he shall summon a meeting of the creditors to be held on a date not more than 35 days from the date of his receipt of the request.

7.6(4) Expenses of summoning and holding a meeting under this Rule shall be paid by the creditor or creditors making the request, who shall deposit with the administrator or, as the case may be, the liquidator caution for their payment.

7.6(5) The sum to be deposited shall be such as the administrator or, as the case may be, the liquidator may determine and he shall not act without the deposit having been made.

7.6(6) The meeting may resolve that the expenses of summoning and holding it are to be payable out of the assets of the company as an expense of the administration or, as the case may be, the liquidation.

7.6(7) To the extent that any caution deposited under this Rule is not required for the payment of expenses of summoning and holding the meeting, it shall be repaid to the person or persons who made it.

7.6(8) This Rule applies to requests by a contributory or contributories for a meeting of contributories, with the modification that, for the reference in paragraph (2) to the creditors' respective claims, there shall be substituted a reference to the contributories' respective values (being the amounts for which they may vote at any meeting).

7.6(9) This Rule is without prejudice to the powers of the court under Rule 4.67(2) (voluntary winding up succeeded by winding up by the court).

7.7   Quorum

7.7(1)   Subject to the next paragraph, a quorum is–

    (a)   in the case of a creditors' meeting, at least one creditor entitled to vote;

    (b)   in the case of a meeting of contributories, at least 2 contributories so entitled, or all the contributories, if their number does not exceed 2.

7.7(2)   For the purposes of this Rule, the reference to the creditor or contributories necessary to constitute a quorum is not confined to those persons present or duly represented under section 375 of the Companies Act but includes those represented by proxy by any person (including the chairman).

7.7(3)   Where at any meeting of creditors or contributories–

    (a)   the provisions of this Rule as to a quorum being present are satisfied by the attendance of–

        (i)   the chairman alone, or

        (ii)   one other person in addition to the chairman, and

    (b)   the chairman is aware, by virtue of claims and proxies received or otherwise, that one or more additional persons would, if attending, be entitled to vote,

the meeting shall not commence until at least the expiry of 15 minutes after the time appointed for its commencement.

7.8   Adjournment

7.8(1)   This Rule applies to meetings of creditors and to meetings of contributories.

7.8(2)   If, within a period of 30 minutes from the time appointed for the commencement of a meeting, a quorum is not present, then, unless the chairman otherwise decides, the meeting shall be adjourned to the same time and place in the following week or, if that is not a business day, to the business day immediately following.

7.8(3)   In the course of any meeting, the chairman may, in his discretion, and shall, if the meeting so resolves, adjourn it to such date, time and place as seems to him to be appropriate in the circumstances.

7.8(4)   Paragraph (3) is subject to Rule 4.23(3) where the liquidator or his nominee is chairman and a resolution has been proposed for the liquidator's removal.

7.8(5)   An adjournment under paragraph (2) or (3) shall not be for a period of more than 21 days and notice of the adjourned meeting may be given by the chairman.

7.8(6)   Where a meeting is adjourned, any proxies given for the original meeting may be used at the adjourned meeting.

7.8(7)   Where a company meeting at which a resolution for voluntary winding up is to be proposed is adjourned without that resolution having been passed, any resolution passed at a meeting under section 98 held before the holding of the adjourned company meeting only has effect on and from the passing by the company of a resolution for winding up.

7.9   Entitlement to vote (creditors)

7.9(1)   This Rule applies to a creditors' meeting in any insolvency proceedings.

7.9(2)   A creditor is entitled to vote at any meeting if he has submitted his claim to the responsible insolvency practitioner and his claim has been accepted in whole or in part.

7.9(3)   Chapter 5 of Part 4 (claims in liquidation) shall apply for the purpose of determining a creditor's entitlement to vote at any creditors' meeting in any insolvency proceedings as it applies for the purpose of determining a creditor's entitlement to vote at a meeting of creditors in a liquidation, subject to the modifications specified in the following paragraphs and to any other necessary modification.

7.9(4) For any reference in the said Chapter 5, or in any provision of the Bankruptcy Act as applied by Rule 4.16(1), to–

(a) the liquidator, there shall be substituted a reference to the administrator or receiver, as the case may be;

(b) the liquidation, there shall be substituted a reference to the administration or receivership as the case may be;

(c) the date of commencement of winding up, there shall be substituted a reference–

    (ii) in the case of a meeting in the administration or receivership, to the date upon which the company entered administration or, as the case may be, the date of appointment of the receiver.

History
In r.7.9(4)(a) "supervisor" formerly appearing after "reference to the", and in r.7.9(4)(b) "voluntary arrangement" formerly appearing after "reference to the", and r.7.9(4)(c)(i) omitted by the Insolvency (Scotland) Amendment Rules 2010 (SI 2010/688 (S 2)) art.3 and Sch.1 paras106, 107 and 108 as from April 6, 2010, subject to transitional provisions in art.4.

7.9(5) In the application to meetings of creditors other than in liquidation proceedings of Schedule 1 to the Bankruptcy Act, paragraph 5(2) and (3) (secured creditors) shall not apply.

7.9(6) This Rule is subject to Rule 7.4(6) and Schedule 3.

7.10 Entitlement to vote (members and contributories)

7.10(1) Members of a company or contributories at their meetings shall vote according to their rights attaching to their shares respectively in accordance with the articles of association.

7.10(2) [Omitted by the Insolvency (Scotland) Amendment Rules 2002 (SI 2002/2709 (S 10)) r.1, 4(1) and Sch. Pt 2 para.17 as from January 1, 2003 subject to transitional provisions contained in r.4(2).]

7.10(3) Reference in this Rule to a person's share include any other interests which he may have as a member of the company.

7.11 Chairman of meeting as proxy holder

7.11(1) Where the chairman at a meeting of creditors or contributories holds a proxy which requires him to vote for a particular resolution and no other person proposes that resolution–

(a) he shall propose it himself, unless he considers that there is good reason for not doing so, and

(b) if he does not propose it, he shall forthwith after the meeting notify the person who granted him the proxy of the reason why he did not do so.

7.11(2) [Omitted by the Insolvency (Scotland) Amendment Rules 2010 (SI 2010/688 (S 2)) art.3 and Sch.1 para.109 as from April 6, 2010, subject to transitional provisions in art.4.]

7.12 Resolutions

7.12(1) Subject to any contrary provision in the Act or the Rules, at any meeting of creditors, contributories or members of a company, a resolution is passed when a majority in value of those voting, in person or by proxy, have voted in favour of it.

7.12(2) [Omitted by the Insolvency (Scotland) Amendment Rules 2010 (SI 2010/688 (S 2)) art.3 and Sch.1 para.110 as from April 6, 2010, subject to transitional provisions in art.4.]

7.12(3)   In a liquidation, in the case of a resolution for the appointment of a liquidator–

    (a)   if, on any vote, there are two nominees for appointment, the person for whom a majority in value has voted shall be appointed;

    (b)   if there are three or more nominees, and one of them has a clear majority over both or all the others together, that one is appointed; and

    (c)   in any other case, the chairman of the meeting shall continue to take votes (disregarding at each vote any nominee who has withdrawn and, if no nominee has withdrawn, the nominee who obtained the least support last time), until a clear majority is obtained for any one nominee.

The chairman may, at any time, put to the meeting a resolution for the joint appointment of any two or more nominees.

7.12(4)   Where a resolution is proposed which affects a person in respect of his remuneration or conduct as a responsible insolvency practitioner, the vote of that person, or of his firm or of any partner or employee of his shall not be reckoned in the majority required for passing the resolution. This paragraph applies with respect to a vote given by a person (whether personally or on his behalf by a proxy-holder) either as creditor or contributory or member or as proxy-holder for a creditor, contributory, or member.

7.13   Report of meeting

7.13(1)   The chairman at any meeting shall cause a report to be made of the proceedings at the meeting which shall be signed by him.

7.13(2)   The report of the meeting shall include–

    (a)   a list of all the creditors or, as the case may be, contributories who attended the meeting, either in person or by proxy;

    (b)   a copy of every resolution passed; and

    (c)   if the meeting established a creditors' committee or a liquidation committee, as the case may be, a list of the names and addresses of those elected to be members of the committee.

7.13(3)   The chairman shall keep a copy of the report of the meeting as part of the sederunt book in the insolvency proceedings.

CHAPTER 1A

PRESCRIBED PART

7.13A   Application under section 176A(5) to disapply section 176A

7.13A   An application under section 176A(5) shall include averments as to–

    (a)   the type of insolvency proceedings in which the application arises,

    (b)   the financial position of the company,

    (c)   the basis of the applicant's view that the cost of making a distribution to unsecured creditors would be disproportionate to the benefits, and

    (d)   whether any other insolvency practitioner is acting in relation to the company and, if so, his address.

History
See history note after r.7.13B.

7.13B Notice of order under section 176A(5)

7.13B(1) Where the court makes an order under section 176A(5) the applicant shall, as soon as reasonably practicable after the making of the order–

   (a) send to the company a copy of the order certified by the clerk of court,

   (b) send to the registrar of companies and, where a receiver or liquidator has been appointed, to the Accountant in Bankruptcy a copy of the order together with the form required by Rule 7.30 and Schedule 5, and

   (c) give notice of the order to each creditor of whose claim and address he is aware.

7.13B(2) The court may direct that the requirement of paragraph (1)(c) of this Rule be met by the publication of a notice in a newspaper calculated to come to the attention of the unsecured creditors stating that the court has made an order disapplying the requirement to set aside the prescribed part.

History
See history note after r.7.13B(4).

7.13B(3) In an administration, paragraph (2) does not apply and the court may direct that the requirement of paragraph (1)(c) of this Rule be met by the publication of a notice containing the standard content and stating that the Court has made an order disapplying the requirement to set aside the prescribed part.

History
See history note after r.7.13B(4).

7.13B(4) The notice referred to in paragraph (3) must be published as soon as reasonably practicable in the Edinburgh Gazette and may be advertised in such other manner as the administrator thinks fit.

History
Rule 7.13B(3) and (4) inserted by the Insolvency (Scotland) Amendment Rules 2010 (SI 2010/688 (S 2)) art.3 and Sch.1 para.111 as from April 6, 2010, subject to transitional provisions in art.4.
   Rules 7.13A and 7.13B(1) and (2) inserted by the Enterprise Act 2002 (Consequential Amendments) (Prescribed Part) (Scotland) Order 2003 (SI 2003/2108 (S 7)) art.7 as from September 15, 2003.

CHAPTER 2

PROXIES AND COMPANY REPRESENTATION

7.14 Definition of "proxy"

7.14(1) For the purposes of the Rules, a person (**"the principal"**) may authorise another person (**"the proxy-holder"**) to attend, speak and vote as his representative at meetings of creditors or contributories or of the company in insolvency proceedings, and any such authority is referred to as a proxy.

7.14(2) A proxy may be given either generally for all meetings in insolvency proceedings or specifically for any meeting or class of meetings.

7.14(3) Only one proxy may be given by the principal for any one meeting; and it may only be given to one person, being an individual aged 18 or over. The principal may nevertheless nominate one or more other such persons to be proxy-holder in the alternative in the order in which they are named in the proxy.

7.14(4) Without prejudice to the generality of paragraph (3), a proxy for a particular meeting may be given to whoever is to be the chairman of the meeting and any person to whom such a proxy is given cannot decline to be the proxy-holder in relation to that proxy.

7.14(5) A proxy may require the holder to vote on behalf of the principal on matters arising for determination at any meeting, or to abstain, either as directed or in accordance with the holder's own discretion; and it may authorise or require the holder to propose, in the principal's name, a resolution to be voted on by the meeting.

7.15 Form of proxy

7.15(1) With every notice summoning a meeting of creditors or contributories or of the company in insolvency proceedings there shall be sent out forms of proxy.

7.15(2) A form of proxy shall not be sent out with the name or description of any person inserted in it.

7.15(3) A proxy shall be in the form sent out with the notice summoning the meeting or in a form substantially to the same effect.

7.15(4) A form of proxy shall be filled out and signed by the principal, or by some person acting under his authority and, where it is signed by someone other than the principal, the nature of his authority shall be stated on the form.

7.16 Use of proxy at meeting

7.16(1) A proxy given for a particular meeting may be used at any adjournment of that meeting.

7.16(2) A proxy may be lodged at or before the meeting at which it is to be used.

7.16(3) Where the responsible insolvency practitioner holds proxies to be used by him as chairman of the meeting, and some other person acts as chairman, the other person may use the insolvency practitioner's proxies as if he were himself proxy-holder.

7.16(4) Where a proxy directs a proxy-holder to vote for or against a resolution for the nomination or appointment of a person to be the responsible insolvency practitioner, the proxy-holder may, unless the proxy states otherwise, vote for or against (as he thinks fit) any resolution for the nomination or appointment of that person jointly with another or others.

7.16(5) A proxy-holder may propose any resolution which, if proposed by another, would be a resolution in favour of which he would be entitled to vote by virtue of the proxy.

7.16(6) Where a proxy gives specific directions as to voting, this does not, unless the proxy states otherwise, preclude the proxy-holder from voting at his discretion on resolutions put to the meeting which are not dealt with in the proxy.

7.17 Retention of proxies

7.17(1) Proxies used for voting at any meeting shall be retained by the chairman of the meeting.

7.17(2) The chairman shall deliver the proxies forthwith after the meeting to the responsible insolvency practitioner (where he was not the chairman).

7.17(3) The responsible insolvency practitioner shall retain all proxies in the sederunt book.

7.18 Right of inspection

7.18(1) The responsible insolvency practitioner shall, so long as proxies lodged with him are in his hands, allow them to be inspected at all reasonable times on any business day, by–

(a) the creditors, in the case of proxies used at a meeting of creditors,

(b) a company's members or contributories, in the case of proxies used at a meeting of the company or of its contributories.

7.18(2) The reference in paragraph (1) to creditors is–

(a) in the case of a company in liquidation, those creditors whose claims have been accepted in whole or in part, and

(b) in any other case, persons who have submitted in writing a claim to be creditors of the company concerned,

but in neither case does it include a person whose claim has been wholly rejected for purposes of voting, dividend or otherwise.

7.18(3) The right of inspection given by this Rule is also exercisable, in the case of an insolvent company, by its directors.

7.18(4) Any person attending a meeting in insolvency proceedings is entitled, immediately before or in the course of the meeting, to inspect proxies and associated documents (including claims)–

(a) to be used in connection with that meeting, or

(b) sent or given to the chairman of that meeting or to any other person by a creditor, member or contributory for the purpose of that meeting, whether or not they are to be used at it.

7.19 Proxy-holder with financial interest

7.19(1) A proxy-holder shall not vote in favour of any resolution which would directly or indirectly place him, or any associate of his, in a position to receive any remuneration out of the insolvent estate, unless the proxy specifically directs him to vote in that way.

7.19(1A) Where a proxy-holder has signed the proxy as being authorised to do so by his principal and the proxy specifically directs him to vote in the way mentioned in paragraph (1), he shall nevertheless not vote in that way unless he produces to the chairman of the meeting written authorisation from his principal sufficient to show that the proxy-holder was entitled so to sign the proxy.

7.19(2) This Rule applies also to any person acting as chairman of a meeting and using proxies in that capacity in accordance with Rule 7.16(3); and in the application of this Rule to any such person, the proxy-holder is deemed an associate of his.

7.20 Representation of corporations

7.20(1) Where a person is authorised under section 375 of the Companies Act to represent a corporation at a meeting of creditors or contributories, he shall produce to the chairman of the meeting a copy of the resolution from which he derives his authority.

7.20(2) The copy resolution must be executed in accordance with the provisions of section 36(3) of the Companies Act, or certified by the secretary or a director of the corporation to be a true copy.

7.20(3) Nothing in this Rule requires the authority of a person to sign a proxy on behalf of a principal which is a corporation to be in the form of a resolution of that corporation.

7.20A Interpretation of creditor

7.20A(1) This Rule applies where a member State liquidator has been appointed in relation to a person subject to insolvency proceedings.

7.20A(2) For the purposes of the Rule 7.18(1) (right of inspection of proxies) a member State liquidator appointed in main proceedings is deemed to be a creditor.

7.20A(3) Paragraph (2) is without prejudice to the generality of the right to participate referred to in paragraph 3 of Article 32 of the EC Regulation (exercise of creditors' rights).

History
Rule 7.20A inserted by the Insolvency (Scotland) Regulations 2003 (SI 2003/2109 (S 8)) reg.28 as from September 8, 2003.

CHAPTER 3

MISCELLANEOUS

7.21 Giving of notices, etc.

7.21(1) All notices required or authorised by or under the Act or the Rules to be given, sent or delivered must be in writing, unless it is otherwise provided, or the court allows the notice to be sent or given in some other way.

7.21(1A) In Parts 1 and 2 where electronic delivery is permitted a notice or other document in electronic form is treated as being in writing if a copy of it is capable of being produced in a legible form.

History
Rule 7.21(1A) inserted by the Insolvency (Scotland) Amendment Rules 2010 (SI 2010/688 (S 2)) art.3 and Sch.1 para.112 as from April 6, 2010, subject to transitional provisions in art.4.

7.21(2) Any reference in the Act or the Rules to giving, sending or delivering a notice or any such document means, without prejudice to any other way and unless it is otherwise provided, that the notice or document may be sent by post, and that, subject to Rule 7.22, any form of post may be used. Personal service of the notice or document is permissible in all cases.

7.21(3) Where under the Act or the Rules a notice or other document is required or authorised to be given, sent or delivered by a person (**"the sender"**) to another (**"the recipient"**), it may be given, sent or delivered by any person duly authorised by the sender to do so to any person duly authorised by the recipient to receive or accept it.

7.21(4) Where two or more persons are acting jointly as the responsible insolvency practitioner in any proceedings, the giving, sending or delivering of a notice or document to one of them is to be treated as the giving, sending or delivering of a notice or document to each or all.

7.21A Contents of notices in Parts 1 and 2 to be published in the Edinburgh Gazette under the Act or Rules

7.21A(1) Where under Parts I and II of the Act or Parts 1 and 2 of the Rules a notice must be published or advertised in the Edinburgh Gazette, in addition to any content specifically required by the Act or any other provision of the Rules, the content of such a notice must be as set out in this Rule.

7.21A(2) All notices published must specify insofar as it is applicable in relation to the particular notice–

(a) the name and postal address of the office-holder acting in the proceedings to which the notice relates;

(b) the capacity in which the office holder is acting and the date of appointment;

(c) either an e-mail address, or a telephone number, through which the office holder may be contacted;

(d) the name of any person other than the office-holder (if any) who may be contacted regarding the proceedings;

(e) the number assigned to the office-holder by the Secretary of State; and

(f) the court name and any number assigned to the proceedings by the court.

7.21A(3) All notices published must specify as regards the company to which the notice relates–

(a) the registered name of the company;

(b) its registered number;

    (c)   its registered office, or if an unregistered company, the postal address of its principal place of business;

    (d)   any principal trading address if this is different from its registered office;

    (e)   any name under which it was registered in the 12 months prior to the date of the commencement of the proceedings which are the subject of the notice in the Edinburgh Gazette; and

    (f)   any name or style (other than its registered name) under which–

        (i)   the company carried on business; and

        (ii)   any debt owed to a creditor was incurred.

History
See history note after r.7.21D.

7.21B   Notices otherwise advertised under the Act or Rules

7.21B(1)   Where under Parts I and II of the Act or Parts 1 and 2 of the Rules a notice may be advertised otherwise than in the Edinburgh Gazette, in addition to any content specifically required by the Act or any other provision of the Rules, the content of such a notice must be as set out in this Rule.

7.21B(2)   All notices published must specify insofar as it is applicable in relation to the particular notice–

    (a)   the name and postal address of the office-holder acting in the proceedings to which the notice relates; and

    (b)   either an e-mail address, or a telephone number, through which the office holder may be contacted.

7.21B(3)   All notices published must specify as regards the company to which the notice relates–

    (a)   the registered name of the company;

    (b)   its registered number;

    (c)   any name under which it was registered in the 12 months prior to the date of the commencement of the proceedings which are the subject of the Edinburgh Gazette notice; and

    (d)   any name or style (other than its registered name) under which–

        (i)   the company carried on business; and

        (ii)   any debt owed to a creditor was incurred.

History
See history note after r.7.21D.

7.21C   Notices otherwise advertised—other additional provision

7.21C   The information required to be contained in a notice to which Rule 7.21B applies must be included in the advertisement of that notice in a manner that is reasonably likely to ensure, in relation to the form of the advertising used, that a person reading, hearing or seeing the advertisement, will be able to read, hear or see that information.

History
See history note after r.7.21D.

7.21D   Omission of unobtainable information

7.21D   Information required by Rules 7.21A and 7.21B to be included in a notice may be omitted if it is not reasonably practicable to obtain it.

History
Rules 7.21A–7.21D inserted by the Insolvency (Scotland) Amendment Rules 2010 (SI 2010/688 (S 2)) art.3 and Sch.1 para.113 as from April 6, 2010, subject to transitional provisions in art.4.

7.22   Sending by post

7.22(1)   For a document to be properly sent by post, it must be contained in an envelope addressed to the person to whom it is to be sent, and pre-paid for either first or second class post.

7.22(1A)   Any document to be sent by post may be sent to the last known address of the person to whom the document is to be sent.

7.22(2)   Where first class post is used, the document is to be deemed to be received on the second business day after the date of posting, unless the contrary is shown.

7.22(3)   Where second class post is used, the document is to be deemed to be received on the fourth business day after the date of posting, unless the contrary is shown.

7.23   Certificate of giving notice, etc.

7.23(1)   Where in any proceedings a notice or document is required to be given, sent or delivered by the responsible insolvency practitioner, the date of giving, sending or delivery of it may be proved by means of a certificate signed by him or on his behalf by his solicitor, or a partner or an employee of either of them, that the notice or document was duly given, posted or otherwise sent, or delivered on the date stated in the certificate.

7.23(2)   In the case of a notice or document to be given, sent or delivered by a person other than the responsible insolvency practitioner, the date of giving, sending or delivery of it may be proved by means of a certificate by that person that he gave, posted or otherwise sent or delivered the notice or document on the date stated in the certificate, or that he instructed another person (naming him) to do so.

7.23(3)   A certificate under this Rule may be endorsed on a copy of the notice to which it relates.

7.23(4)   A certificate purporting to be signed by or on behalf of the responsible insolvency practitioner, or by the person mentioned in paragraph (2), shall be deemed, unless the contrary is shown, to be sufficient evidence of the matters stated therein.

7.24   Validity of proceedings

7.24   Where in accordance with the Act or the Rules a meeting of creditors or other persons is summoned by notice, the meeting is presumed to have been duly summoned and held, notwithstanding that not all those to whom the notice is to be given have received it.

7.25   Evidence of proceedings at meetings

7.25   A report of proceedings at a meeting of the company or of the company's creditors or contributories in any insolvency proceedings, which is signed by a person describing himself as the chairman of that meeting, shall be deemed, unless the contrary is shown, to be sufficient evidence of the matters contained in that report.

7.26   Right to list of creditors and copy documents

7.26(1)   Paragraph (2) applies to–

    (a)   proceedings under Part II of the Act (company administration), and

(b)   proceedings in a creditors' voluntary winding up, or a winding up by the court.

7.26(2)   Subject to Rule 7.27, in any such proceedings, a creditor who has the right to inspect documents also has the right to require the responsible insolvency practitioner to furnish him with a list of the company's creditors and the amounts of their respective debts.

7.26(2A)   Where the responsible insolvency practitioner is requested by a creditor, member, contributory or by a member of a liquidation committee or of a creditors' committee to supply a copy of any document, he is entitled to require payment of the appropriate fee in respect of the supply of that copy.

7.26(2A)   For the purpose of this Rule a member State liquidator appointed in main proceedings in relation to a person is deemed to be a creditor.

History
Rule 7.26(2A) inserted by the Insolvency (Scotland) Regulations 2003 (SI 2003/2109 (S 8)) reg.28 as from September 8, 2003. There would appear to be a drafting error in the numbering of this insertion and the Department of Trade and Industry advise that it may be corrected in due course.

7.26(3)   Subject to Rule 7.27, where a person has the right to inspect documents, the right includes that of taking copies of those documents, on payment of the appropriate fee.

7.26(4)   In this Rule, the appropriate fee means 15 pence per A4 or A5 page and 30 pence per A3 page.

7.27   Confidentiality of documents

7.27(1)   Where, in any insolvency proceedings, the responsible insolvency practitioner considers, in the case of a document forming part of the records of those proceedings,–

(a)   that it should be treated as confidential, or

(b)   that it is of such a nature that its disclosure would be calculated to be injurious to the interests of the company's creditors or, in the case of the winding up of a company, its members or the contributories in its winding up,

he may decline to allow it to be inspected by a person who would otherwise be entitled to inspect it.

7.27(2)   The persons who may be refused the right to inspect documents under this Rule by the responsible insolvency practitioner include the members of a creditors' committee in administration or in receivership, or of a liquidation committee.

7.27(3)   Where under this Rule the responsible insolvency practitioner refuses inspection of a document, the person who made that request may apply to the court for an order to overrule the refusal and the court may either overrule it altogether, or sustain it, either unconditionally or subject to such conditions, if any, as it thinks fit to impose.

7.27(4)   Nothing in this Rule entitles the responsible insolvency practitioner to decline to allow inspection of any claim or proxy.

7.28   Insolvency practitioner's caution

7.28(1)   Wherever under the Rules any person has to appoint, or certify the appointment of, an insolvency practitioner to any office, he is under a duty to satisfy himself that the person appointed or to be appointed has caution for the proper performance of his functions.

7.28(2)   It is the duty–

(a)   of the creditors' committee in administration or in receivership,

(b)   of the liquidation committee in companies winding up, and

(c)   of any committee of creditors established for the purposes of a voluntary arrangement under Part I of the Act, to review from time to time the adequacy of the responsible insolvency practitioner's caution.

7.28(3)   In any insolvency proceedings the cost of the responsible insolvency practitioner's caution shall be paid as an expense of the proceedings.

7.29   Punishment of offences

7.29(1)   Schedule 4 has effect with respect to the way in which contraventions of the Rules are punishable on conviction.

7.29(2)   In that Schedule–

  (a)   the first column specifies the provision of the Rules which creates an offence;

  (b)   in relation to each such offence, the second column describes the general nature of the offence;

  (c)   the third column indicates its mode of trial, that is to say whether the offence is punishable on conviction on indictment, or on summary conviction, or either in the one way or the other;

  (d)   the fourth column shows the maximum punishment by way of fine or imprisonment which may be imposed on a person convicted of the offence in the mode of trial specified in relation to it in the third column (that is to say, on indictment or summarily), a reference to a period of years or months being to a maximum term of imprisonment of that duration; and

  (e)   the fifth column shows (in relation to an offence for which there is an entry in that column) that a person convicted of the offence after continued contravention is liable to a daily default fine; that is to say, he is liable on a second or subsequent conviction of the offence to the fine specified in that column for each day on which the contravention is continued (instead of the penalty specified for the offence in the fourth column of that Schedule).

7.29(3)   Section 431 (summary proceedings), as it applies to Scotland, has effect in relation to offences under the Rules as to offences under the Act.

7.30   Forms for use in insolvency proceedings

7.30   The forms contained in Schedule 5, with such variations as circumstances require, are the forms to be used for the purposes of the provisions of the Act or the Rules which are referred to in those forms.

7.30A   Electronic submission of information instead of submission of forms to the Secretary of State, office-holders, and of copies to the registrar of companies

7.30A(1)   This Rule applies in any case where information in a prescribed form is required by Part 1 or 2 of these Rules to be sent by any person to the Secretary of State, or an office-holder, or a copy of a prescribed form is to be sent to the registrar of companies.

7.30A(2)   A requirement of the kind mentioned in paragraph (1) is treated as having been satisfied where–

  (a)   the information is submitted electronically with the agreement of the person to whom the information is sent;

  (b)   the form in which the electronic submission is made satisfies the requirements of the person to whom the information is sent (which may include a requirement that the information supplied can be reproduced in the format of the prescribed form);

  (c)   that all the information required to be given in the prescribed form is provided in the electronic submission; and

  (d)   the person to whom the information is sent can produce in legible form the information so submitted.

7.30A(3)   Where information in a prescribed form is permitted to be sent electronically under paragraph (2), any requirement in the prescribed form that the prescribed form be accompanied by a signature is taken to be satisfied–

(a)   if the identity of the person who is supplying the information in the prescribed form and whose signature is required is confirmed in a manner specified by the recipient; or

(b)   where no such manner has been specified by the recipient, if the communication contains or is accompanied by a statement of the identity of the person who is providing the information in the prescribed form, and the recipient has no reason to doubt the truth of that statement.

7.30A(4)   Where information required in prescribed form has been supplied to a person, whether or not it has been supplied electronically in accordance with paragraph (2), and a copy of that information is required to be supplied to another person falling within paragraph (1), the requirements contained in paragraph (2) apply in respect of the supply of the copy to that other person as they apply in respect of the original.

History
See history note after r.7.30B.

7.30B   Electronic submission of information instead of submission of forms in all other cases

7.30B(1)   This Rule applies in any case where Rule 7.30A does not apply, where information in a prescribed form is required by Part 1 or 2 of these Rules to be sent by any person.

7.30B(2)   A requirement of the kind mentioned in paragraph (1) is treated as having been satisfied where–

(a)   the person to whom the information is sent has agreed–

(i)   to receiving the information electronically and to the form in which it is to be sent; and

(ii)   to the specified manner in which paragraph (3) is to be satisfied.

(b)   all the information required to be given in the prescribed form is provided in the electronic submission; and

(c)   the person to whom the information is sent can produce in legible form the information so sent.

7.30B(3)   Any requirement in a prescribed form that it be accompanied by a signature is taken to be satisfied if the identity of the person who is supplying the information and whose signature is required, is confirmed in the specified manner.

7.30B(4)   Where information required in prescribed form has been supplied to a person, whether or not it has been supplied electronically in accordance with paragraph (2), and a copy of that information is required to be supplied to another person falling within paragraph (1), the requirements contained in paragraph (2) apply in respect of the supply of the copy to that other person, as they apply in respect of the original.

History
Rules 7.30A and 7.30B inserted by the Insolvency (Scotland) Amendment Rules 2010 (SI 2010/688 (S 2)) art.3 and Sch.1 para.114 as from April 6, 2010, in all cases (see art.5).

7.31   Fees, expenses, etc.

7.31   All fees, costs, charges and other expenses incurred in the course of insolvency proceedings are to be regarded as expenses of those proceedings, with the exception of the fees, costs, charges and other expenses associated with the prescribed part, which shall be met out of the prescribed part.

History

In r.7.31 the words "with the exception of the fees, costs charges and other expenses associated with the prescribed part, which shall be met out of the prescribed part." inserted by the Enterprise Act 2002 (Consequential Amendments) (Prescribed Part) (Scotland) Order 2003 (SI 2003/2108 (S 7)) art.7 as from September 15, 2003.

7.32 Power of court to cure defects in procedure

7.32(1) Section 63 of the Bankruptcy Act (power of court to cure defects in procedure) shall apply in relation to any insolvency proceedings as it applies in relation to sequestration, subject to the modifications specified in paragraph (2) and to any other necessary modifications.

7.32(2) For any reference in the said section 63 to any expression in column 1 below, there shall be substituted a reference to the expression in column 2 opposite thereto–

Column 1	*Column 2*
This Act or any regulations made under it	The Act or the Rules
Permanent trustee	Responsible insolvency practitioner
Sequestration process	Insolvency proceedings
Debtor	Company
Sheriff	The court
Person who would be eligible to be elected under section 24 of this Act	Person who would be eligible to act as a responsible insolvency practitioner

7.33 Sederunt book

7.33(1) The responsible insolvency practitioner shall maintain a sederunt book during his term of office for the purpose of providing an accurate record of the administration of each insolvency proceedings.

7.33(2) Without prejudice to the generality of the above paragraph, there shall be inserted in the sederunt book a copy of anything required to be recorded in it by any provision of the Act or of the Rules.

7.33(3) The responsible insolvency practitioner shall make the sederunt book available for inspection at all reasonable hours by any interested person.

7.33(4) Any entry in the sederunt book shall be sufficient evidence of the facts stated therein, except where it is founded on by the responsible insolvency practitioner in his own interest.

7.33(5) Without prejudice to paragraph (3), the responsible insolvency practitioner shall retain, or shall make arrangements for retention of, the sederunt book for a period of ten years from the relevant date.

7.33(6) Where the sederunt book is maintained in non-documentary form it shall be capable of reproduction in legible form.

7.33(7) In this Rule **"the relevant date"** has the following meanings:–

(a) in the case of a company voluntary arrangement under Part I of the Act, the date of final completion of the voluntary arrangement;

(b) in the case of an administration under Part II of the Act, the date on which the administration ends in accordance with that Part;

(c) in the case of a receivership under Part III of the Act, the date on which the receiver resigns and the receivership terminates without a further receiver being appointed; and

(d) in the case of a winding-up, the date of dissolution of the company.

7.34 Disposal of company's books, papers and other records

7.34(1) Where a company has been the subject of insolvency proceedings (**"the original proceedings"**) which have terminated and other insolvency proceedings (**"the subsequent proceedings"**) have commenced in relation to that company, the responsible insolvency practitioner appointed in relation to the original proceedings, shall, before the expiry of the later of–

(a)   the period of 30 days following a request to him to do so by the responsible insolvency practitioner appointed in relation to the subsequent proceedings, or

(b)   the period of 6 months after the relevant date (within the meaning of Rule 7.33),

deliver to the responsible insolvency practitioner appointed in relation to the subsequent proceedings the books, papers and other records of the company.

7.34(2)   In the case of insolvency proceedings, other than winding up or administration, where–

(a)   the original proceedings have terminated, and

(b)   no subsequent proceedings have commenced within the period of 6 months after the relevant date in relation to the original proceedings,

the responsible insolvency practitioner appointed in relation to the original proceedings may dispose of the books, papers and records of the company after the expiry of the period of 6 months referred to in sub-paragraph (b), but only in accordance with directions given by–

(i)   [Deleted.]

(ii)   the members of the company by extraordinary resolution, or

(iii) the court.

7.34(3)   Where a company is being wound up the liquidator shall dispose of the books, papers and records of the company either in accordance with–

(a)   in the case of a winding up by the court, directions of the liquidation committee, or, if there is no such committee, directions of the court;

(b)   in the case of a members' voluntary winding up, directions of the members by extraordinary resolution; and

(c)   in the case of a creditors' voluntary winding up, directions of the liquidation committee, or, if there is no such committee, of the creditors given at or before the final meeting under section 106,

or, if, by the date which is 12 months after the dissolution of the company, no such directions have been given, he may do so after that date in such a way as he deems appropriate.

7.34(4)   In the case of administration proceedings, the administrator shall dispose of the books, papers and records of the company either in accordance with–

(a)   the directions of the creditors' committee (if any); or

(b)   where there is no such committee, the court,

or, if by the date which is 12 months after dissolution of the company, no such directions have been given, he may do so after that date in such a way as he deems appropriate.

7.34(5)   An administrator or former administrator shall within 14 days of a request by the Secretary of State give the Secretary of State particulars of any money in his hands or under his control representing unclaimed or undistributed assets of the company or dividends or other sums due to any person as a member or former member of the company.

History
Rule 7.34(2) amended, r.7.34(2)(i) deleted, and r.7.34(4), (5) inserted, by the Insolvency (Scotland) Amendment Rules 2006 (SI 2006/734 (S 6)) r.14, as from April 6, 2006.

7.35 Information about time spent on a case—administration and company voluntary arrangements

7.35(1) Subject as set out in this Rule, a person ("the relevant person") who has acted or is acting as–

(a) a nominee in respect of a proposed voluntary arrangements;

(b) a supervisor in respect of a voluntary arrangement; or

(c) an administrator,

must, on request in writing by any person mentioned in paragraph (2), supply free of charge to that person a statement of the kind described in paragraph (3).

7.35(2) The persons referred to in paragraph (1) are–

(a) any director of the company, or

(b) where the proposed voluntary arrangement has been approved, or where the company is in administration, any creditor or member of the company.

7.35(3) The statement referred to in paragraph (1)–

(a) must comprise the following details–

(i) the total number of hours spent on all or any of the proposal, the voluntary arrangement and administration by the relevant person, and any staff assigned to the case during that period;

(ii) for each grade of individual so engaged, the average hourly rate at which any work carried out by individuals in that grade is charged; and

(iii) the number of hours spent by each grade of staff during the period covered by the statement; and

(b) must cover the period beginning with the date of the appointment of the relevant person as nominee, supervisor or administrator (whichever is the earlier), as the case may be, and ending–

(i) with the date next before the date of making the request on which the relevant person has completed any period as nominee, supervisor or administrator, which is a multiple of 6 months, or

(ii) where the relevant person has ceased to act in any capacity in relation to the proposal, the voluntary arrangement or administration, the date upon which the person so ceased.

7.35(4) No request pursuant to this Rule may be made where more than 2 years has elapsed since the relevant person ceased to act in any capacity in relation to the proposal, any voluntary arrangement arising out of the approval of the proposal or administration.

7.35(5) Any statement required to be provided to any person under this Rule must be supplied within 28 days of the date of the receipt of the request by the person required to supply it.

History
Rules 7.35 substituted by the Insolvency (Scotland) Amendment Rules 2010 (SI 2010/688 (S 2)) art.3 and Sch.1 para.115 as from April 6, 2010 in all cases (see art.5).

Previously, r.7.35 inserted by the Insolvency (Scotland) Amendment Rules 2006 (SI 2006/734 (S 6)) r.15, as from April 6, 2006.

7.36 Information about time spent on a case

7.36(1) Subject as set out in this Rule, in respect of any liquidation or receivership in which an insolvency practitioner acts, the insolvency practitioner shall on request in writing made by any person mentioned in paragraph (2), supply free of charge to that person a statement of the kind described in paragraph (3).

7.36(2)   The persons referred to in paragraph (1) are–

(a)   any creditor in the case; and

(b)   where the case relates to a company, any director or contributory of that company.

7.36(3)   The statement referred to in paragraph (1) shall comprise in relation to the period beginning with the date of the insolvency practitioner's appointment and ending with the relevant date the following details–

(a)   the total number of hours spent on the case by the insolvency practitioner and any staff assigned to the case during that period;

(b)   for each grade of individual so engaged, the average hourly rate at which any work carried out by individuals in that grade is charged; and

(c)   the number of hours spent by each grade of staff during that period.

7.36(4)   In relation to paragraph (3) the "relevant date" means the date next before the date of the making of the request on which the insolvency practitioner has completed any period in office which is a multiple of six months or, where the insolvency practitioner has vacated office, the date that the insolvency practitioner vacated office.

7.36(5)   Where an insolvency practitioner has vacated office, an obligation to provide information under this Rule shall only arise in relation to a request that is made within 2 years of the date the insolvency practitioner vacates office.

7.36(6)   Any statement required to be provided to any person under this Rule shall be supplied within 28 days of the date of the receipt of the request by the insolvency practitioner.

History
Rule 7.36 inserted by the Insolvency (Scotland) Rules 1986 Amendment Rules 2008 (SSI 2008/393) r.5 as from December 20, 2008.

SCHEDULE 1

MODIFICATIONS OF PART 4 IN RELATION TO CREDITORS' VOLUNTARY WINDING UP

Rule 5

1   The following paragraphs describe the modifications to be made to the provisions of Part 4 in their application by Rule 5 to a creditors' voluntary winding up of a company.

General

2   Any reference, in any provision in Part 4, which is applied to a creditors' voluntary winding up, to any other Rule is reference to that Rule as so applied.

Chapter 1 (Provisional liquidator)

3   This Chapter shall not apply.

Chapter 2 (Statement of affairs)

4   Rules 4.7 and 4.8

4   For these rules, there shall be substituted the following–

"**4.7(1)**   This Rule applies with respect to the statement of affairs made out by the liquidator under section 95(3) (or as the case may be) by the directors under section 99(1).

4.7(2)   The statement of affairs shall be in the form required by Rule 7.30 and Schedule 5.

4.7(3)   Where the statement of affairs is made out by the directors under section 99(1), it shall be sent by them to the liquidator, when appointed.

4.7(3A)   Where a liquidator is nominated by the company at a general meeting held on a day prior to that on which the creditors' meeting summoned under section 98 is held, the directors shall forthwith after his nomination or the making of the statement of affairs, whichever is the later, deliver to him a copy of the statement of affairs.

4.7(4)   The liquidator shall insert a copy of the statement of affairs made out under this Rule in the sederunt book.

4.7(5)   The statement of affairs under section 99(1) shall be made up to the nearest practicable date before the date of the meeting of creditors under section 98 or to a date not more than 14 days before that on which the resolution for voluntary winding up is passed by the company, whichever is the later.

4.7(6)   At any meeting held under section 98 where the statement of affairs laid before the meeting does not state the company's affairs as at the date of the meeting, the directors of the company shall cause to be made to the meeting, either by the director presiding at the meeting or by another person with knowledge of the relevant matters, a report (written or oral) on any material transactions relating to the company occurring between the date of the making of the statement of affairs and that of the meeting and any such report shall be recorded in the report of the meeting kept under Rule 7.13."

5   Rule 4.9

5   For this Rule, there shall be substituted

"Expenses of statement of affairs

4.9(1)   Payment may be made as an expense of the liquidation, either before or after the commencement of the winding up, of any reasonable and necessary expenses of preparing the statement of affairs under section 99.

4.9(2)   Where such a payment is made before the commencement of the winding up, the director presiding at the creditors' meeting held under section 98 shall inform the meeting of the amount of the payment and the identity of the person to whom it was made.

4.9(3)   The liquidator appointed under section 100 may make such a payment (subject to the next paragraph); but if there is a liquidation committee, he must give the committee at least 7 days' notice of his intention to make it.

4.9(4)   Such a payment shall not be made by the liquidator to himself, or to any associate of his, otherwise than with the approval of the liquidation committee, the creditors, or the court.

4.9(5)   This Rule is without prejudice to the powers of the court under Rule 4.67(2) (voluntary winding up succeeded by winding up by the court)."

Chapter 3 (Information)

6   Rule 4.10

6   For this Rule, there shall be substituted the following:–

"Information to creditors and contributories

4.10(1)   The liquidator shall, within 28 days of a meeting held under section 95 or 98, send to creditors and contributories of the company–

    (a)   a copy or summary of the statement of affairs, and

    (b)   a report of the proceedings at the meeting.

4.10(2)   The report under paragraph 1(b) shall include–

    (a)   to the best of the liquidator's knowledge and belief–

(i) an estimate of the value of the prescribed part (whether or not he proposes to make an application to the court under section 176A(5) or section 176A(3) applies), and

(ii) an estimate of the value of the company's net property,

provided that such estimates shall not be required to include any information the disclosure of which could seriously prejudice the commercial interests of the company, but if such information is excluded the estimates shall be accompanied by a statement to that effect; and

(b) whether, and, if so, why, the liquidator proposes to make an application to the court under section 176A(5)."

History

Rule 4.10 as substituted by para.6 of Sch.1 to the Rules is renumbered as r.4.10(1) and para.(2) inserted by the Enterprise Act 2002 (Consequential Amendments) (Prescribed Part) (Scotland) Order 2003 (SI 2003/2108 (S 7)) art.9 as from September 15, 2003.

Chapter 4 (Meetings of creditors and contributories)

7   Rule 4.12

7 This Rule shall not apply.

8   Rule 4.14

8 After this Rule, there shall be inserted the following:–

"*Expenses of meeting under section 98*

4.14A(1) Payment may be made out of the company's assets as an expense of the liquidation, either before or after the commencement of the winding up, of any reasonable and necessary expenses incurred in connection with the summoning, advertisement and holding of a creditors' meeting under section 98.

4.14A(2) Where any such payments are made before the commencement of the winding up, the director presiding at the creditors' meeting shall inform the meeting of their amount and the identity of the persons to whom they were made.

4.14A(3) The liquidator appointed under section 100 may make such a payment (subject to the next paragraph); but if there is a liquidation committee, he must give the committee at least 7 days' notice of his intention to make the payment.

4.14A(4) Such a payment shall not be made by the liquidator to himself, or to any associate of his, otherwise than with the approval of the liquidation committee, the creditors, or the court.

4.14A(5) This Rule is without prejudice to the powers of the court under Rule 4.67(2) (voluntary winding up succeeded by winding up by the court)."

9   Rule 4.15

9(1) In paragraph (5), for the reference to section 129, there shall be substituted a reference to section 86.

9(2) In paragraph (6) there shall be inserted at the end the following:–

"and to the director who presides over any meeting of creditors as provided by section 99(1)."

10   Rule 4.16

10 In paragraph (2), for the reference to section 129, there shall be substituted a reference to section 86.

11   Rule 4.18

11(1)   For paragraph (1), there shall be substituted the following:–

"**4.18(1)**   This Rule applies where the liquidator is appointed by the court under section 100(3) or 108.".

11(2)   Paragraphs 4(a) and 5 shall be deleted.

12   Rule 4.19

12(1)   For paragraphs (1) to (3) there shall be substituted the following:–

"**4.19(1)**   This Rule applies where a person is nominated for appointment as liquidator under section 100(1) either by a meeting of the creditors or by a meeting of the company.

4.19(2)   Subject as follows, the chairman of the meeting shall certify the appointment, but not unless and until the person to be appointed has provided him with a written statement to the effect that he is an insolvency practitioner, duly qualified under the Act to be the liquidator and that he consents so to act. The liquidator's appointment takes effect on the passing of the resolution for his appointment.

4.19(3)   The chairman shall forthwith send the certificate to the liquidator, who shall keep it in the sederunt book.".

12(2)   Paragraphs (4)(a) and (5) shall not apply.

12(3)   In paragraph (6), for the reference to paragraphs (4) and (5), there shall be substituted a reference to paragraphs (3) and (4).

12(4)   After paragraph 6 there shall be inserted the following paragraph:–

"**4.19(7)**   Where a vacancy in the office of liquidator occurs in the manner mentioned in section 104, a meeting of creditors to fill the vacancy may be convened by any creditor or, if there were more liquidators than one, by any continuing liquidator."

13   Rule 4.23

13(1)   In paragraph (1), for the references to section 172(2) and (3), there shall be substituted a reference to section 171(2) and (3).

13(2)   In paragraph (2), for the references to section 172(2) and 174(4)(a) or (b), there shall be substituted a reference to section 171(2) and 173(2)(a) or (b).

14   Rule 4.24

14   In this Rule the references to the court shall be deleted.

15   Rule 4.25

15   In paragraph (1), for the reference to section 174(4)(a), there shall be substituted a reference to section 173(2)(a), and the reference to the court shall be deleted.

16   Rule 4.28

16(1)   In paragraph (1), for the reference to section 172(6), there shall be substituted a reference to section 171(5).

16(2)   In paragraph (2), for the reference to section 174(4)(c), there shall be substituted a reference to section 173(2)(c).

17   Rule 4.29

17(1)   In this Rule for paragraph (3) there shall be substituted the following:–

"**4.29(3)**   The liquidator, whose resignation is accepted, shall forthwith after the meeting give notice of his resignation to the Accountant in Bankruptcy as required by section 171(5).".

18   Rule 4.31

18   For this Rule, substitute the following:–

"*Final meeting*

4.31(1)   The liquidator shall give at least 28 days' notice of the final meeting of creditors to be held under section 106. The notice shall be sent to all creditors whose claims in the liquidation have been accepted.

4.31(2)   At the final meeting, the creditors may question the liquidator with respect to any matter contained in the account required under that section and may resolve against the liquidator having his release.

4.31(3)   The liquidator shall, within 7 days of the meeting, give notice to the Accountant in Bankruptcy under section 171(6) that the final meeting has been held. The notice shall state whether or not he has been released.

4.31(4)   If the creditors at the final meeting have not resolved against the liquidator having his release, he is released in terms of section 173(2)(e)(ii) when he vacates office under section 171(6). If they have so resolved, he must obtain his release from the Accountant of Court and Rule 4.25(2) and (3) shall apply accordingly subject to the modifications that in Rule 4.25(3) sub-paragraph (a) shall apply with the word "new" replaced by the word "former" and sub-paragraph (b) shall not apply."

History
Purported amendment in para.18 to substituted r.4.31(2) by the Enterprise Act 2002 (Consequential Amendments) (Prescribed Part) (Scotland) Order 2003 (SI 2003/2108 (S 7)) art.9(2) as from September 15, 2003 does not appear to work as it purports to insert the words "and a statement as to the amount paid to unsecured creditors by virtue of the application of section 176A (prescribed part)" after the non-existent word "payment". The problem arises because r.4.31(2) has no counterpart in this substituted rule.

19   Rule 4.36

19   For the reference to the court there shall be substituted a reference to the liquidation committee (if any) or a member of that committee.

20   Rule 4.37

20(1)   In paragraph (2), the reference to the court shall be omitted.

20(2)   At the end of this Rule, there shall be inserted the following:–

"*Vacation of office on making of winding up order*

4.37A   Where the liquidator vacates office in consequence of the court making a winding up order against the company, Rule 4.25(2) and (3) apply as regards the liquidator obtaining his release, as if he had been removed by the court.".

Chapter 7 (The liquidation committee)

21   Rule 4.40

21   This Rule shall not apply.

22   Rule 4.41

22   For paragraph (1) there shall be substituted the following:–

"**4.41(1)**   The committee must have at least 3 members before it can be established.".

23   Rule 4.43

23   This Rule shall not apply.

24   Rule 4.47

24   For this Rule, there shall be substituted the following:–

"Quorum

4.47   A meeting of the committee is duly constituted if due notice of it has been given to all the members and at least 2 members are present or represented.".

25   Rule 4.53

25   After paragraph (4) there shall be inserted the following:–

"**4.53(4A)**   Where the contributories make an appointment under paragraph (4), the creditor members of the committee may, if they think fit, resolve that the person appointed ought not to be a member of the committee; and–

   (a)   that person is not then, unless the court otherwise directs, qualified to act as a member of the committee, and

   (b)   on any application to the court for a direction under this paragraph the court may, if it thinks fit, appoint another person (being a contributory) to fill the vacancy on the committee.".

26   Rule 4.54

26   Paragraphs (2) and (3) shall not apply.

27   Rule 4.55

27   In paragraphs (3) and (4), the word "creditor" shall be omitted.

Chapter 8 (The liquidation committee where winding up follows immediately on administration)

28   This Chapter shall not apply.

Chapter 9 (Distribution of company's assets by liquidator)

29   Rule 4.66

29(1)   At the beginning of paragraph (1), insert the following:–

"Subject to the provision of section 107,".

29(2)   In paragraph (1)(b), for the reference to section 129, there shall be substituted a reference to section 86.

Chapter 10 (Special manager)

30   Rule 4.70

30   For paragraph (5), there shall be substituted the following:–

"**4.70(5)**   The cost of finding caution shall be paid in the first instance by the special manager; but he is entitled to be reimbursed out of the assets as an expense of the liquidation.".

31   Rule 4.71

31   Paragraph (1) shall not apply.

Chapter 11 (Public examination of company officers and others)

32   This Chapter shall not apply.

Chapter 12 (Miscellaneous)

33 **Rule 4.77**

33   This Rule shall not apply.

SCHEDULE 2

APPLICATION OF PART 4 IN RELATION TO MEMBERS' VOLUNTARY WINDING UP

Rule 6

1   The following paragraphs describe the provisions of Part 4 which, subject to the modifications set out in those paragraphs and any other necessary modifications, apply to a members' voluntary winding up.

General

2   Any reference in any provision of Part 4, which is applied to a members' voluntary winding up, to any other Rule is a reference to that Rule as so applied.

Chapter 3 (Information)

3 **Rule 4.11**

3   This rule shall apply subject to the modifications that for the words "accounting period" where they occur, there shall be substituted the words "period of twenty six weeks".

Chapter 6 (The liquidator)

4 **Rule 4.18**

4(1)   This Rule shall apply subject to the following modifications.

4(2)   For paragraph (1), there shall be substituted the following:–

"**4.18(1)**   This Rule applies where the liquidator is appointed by the court under section 108.".

4(3)   Paragraphs 4 and 5 shall be deleted.

5 **Rule 4.19**

5(1)   This Rule shall apply subject to the following modifications.

5(2)   For paragraphs (1) to (3) there shall be substituted the following:–

"**4.19(1)**   This Rule applies where the liquidator is appointed by a meeting of the company.

4.19(2)   Subject as follows, the chairman of the meeting shall certify the appointment, but not unless and until the person to be appointed has provided him with a written statement to the effect that he is an insolvency practitioner, duly qualified under the Act to be the liquidator and that he consents so to act. The liquidator's appointment takes effect on the passing of the resolution for his appointment.

4.19(3)   The chairman shall forthwith send the certificate to the liquidator, who shall keep it in the sederunt book.".

5(3)   Paragraphs 4(a), (5) and (6) shall be deleted.

6   Rules 4.20 to 4.22

6   These Rules shall apply.

7   Rule 4.26

7   This Rule shall apply except that in paragraph (1) for the reference to "creditors" there shall be substituted the words "the company".

8   Rule 4.27

8   This Rule shall apply.

9   Rule 4.28

9(1)   This Rule shall apply subject to the following modifications.

9(2)   In paragraph (1)–

  (a)   for the reference to section 172(6), there shall be substituted a reference to section 171(5), and

  (b)   for the reference to a meeting of creditors, there shall be substituted a reference to a meeting of the company.

9(3)   In paragraph (2)–

  (a)   for reference to section 174(4)(c) there shall be substituted a reference to section 173(2)(c), and

  (b)   for the reference to Rule 4.29(4), there shall be substituted a reference to Rule 4.28A.

9(4)   After paragraph (4) there shall be inserted the following paragraphs:–

"**4.28(5)**   The notice of the liquidator's resignation required by section 171(5) shall be given by him to the Accountant in Bankruptcy forthwith after the meeting.

4.28(6)   Where a new liquidator is appointed in place of the one who has resigned, the former shall, in giving notice of his appointment, state that his predecessor has resigned and whether he has been released.

4.28(7)   If there is no quorum present at the meeting summoned to receive the liquidator's resignation the meeting is deemed to have been held."

9(5)   After this Rule, there shall be inserted the following Rule:–

"Release of resigning or removed liquidator

4.28A(1)   Where the liquidator resigns, he has his release from the date on which he gives notice of his resignation to the Accountant in Bankruptcy.

4.28A(2)   Where the liquidator is removed by a meeting of the company, he shall forthwith give notice to the Accountant in Bankruptcy of his ceasing to act.

4.28A(3)   Where the liquidator is removed by the court, he must apply to the Accountant of Court for his release.

4.28A(4)   Where the Accountant of Court gives the release, he shall certify it accordingly, and send the certificate to the Accountant in Bankruptcy.

4.28A(5)   A copy of the certificate shall be sent by the Accountant of Court to the former liquidator, whose release is effective from the date of the certificate.".

10   Rule 4.36

10   This Rule shall apply, except that for any reference to the court, there shall be substituted a reference to the directors of the company or any one of them.

11 Rule 4.37

11(1) This Rule shall apply subject to the following modifications.

11(2) In paragraph (2), the reference to the court shall be omitted.

11(3) For paragraph (3), there shall be substituted the following:

"**(3)** Rule 4.28A applies as regards the liquidator obtaining his release, as if he had been removed by the court.".

11(4) At the end of this Rule, there shall be inserted the following:–

"*Vacation of office on making of winding up order*

4.37A Where the liquidator vacates office in consequence of the court making a winding up order against the company, Rule 4.28A applies as regards the liquidator obtaining his release, as if he had been removed by the court.".

12 Rule 4.38

12 This Rule shall apply.

13 Rule 4.39

13 This Rule shall apply.

Chapter 10 (Special manager)

14(1) This Chapter shall apply subject to the following modifications.

14(2) In Rule 4.70 for paragraph (5), there shall be substituted the following:–

"**(5)** The cost of finding caution shall be paid in the first instance by the special manager; but he is entitled to be reimbursed out of the assets as an expense of the liquidation.".

14(3) In Rule 4.71, paragraph (1) shall not apply.

SCHEDULE 3

DEPOSIT PROTECTION BOARD'S VOTING RIGHTS

Rule 7.4(6)

1 This Schedule applies where Rule 7.4 does.

2 In relation to any meeting at which the Deposit Protection Board is under Rule 7.4 entitled to be represented, the Board may submit in the liquidation, instead of a claim, a written statement of voting rights (**"the statement"**).

3 The statement shall contain details of:–

(a) the names of creditors of the company in respect of whom an obligation of the Board has arisen or may reasonably be expected to arise as a result of the liquidation or proposed liquidation;

(b) the amount of the obligation so arising; and

(c) the total amount of all such obligations specified in the statement.

4 The Board's statement shall, for the purpose of voting at a meeting (but for no other purpose), be treated in all respects as if it were a claim.

5 Any voting rights which a creditor might otherwise exercise at a meeting in respect of a claim against the company are reduced by a sum equal to the amount of that claim in relation to which the Board, by virtue of its having submitted a statement, is entitled to exercise voting rights at that meeting.

6 The Board may from time to time submit a further statement, and, if it does so, that statement supersedes any statement previously submitted.

SCHEDULE 4

PUNISHMENT OF OFFENCES UNDER THE RULES

Rule 7.29

[**Note:** In the fourth and fifth columns of this Schedule, **"the statutory maximum"** means the prescribed sum under s.289B(6) of the Criminal Procedure (Scotland) Act 1975 (C. 21).]

Rule creating offence	General nature of offence	Mode of prosecution	Punishment	Daily default fine (where applicable)
In Part 2, Rule 2.38(6)	Administrator failing to send notification as to progress of administration	Summary	One-fifth of the statutory maximum	One-fiftieth of the statutory maximum
In Part 2, Rule 2.43(3)	Administrator failing to lodge notice of automatic end of administration	Summary	One-fifth of the statutory maximum	One-fiftieth of the statutory maximum
In Part 3, Rule 3.9(5)	Receiver failing to send notification as to progress of receivership	Summary	One-fifth of the statutory maximum	One-fiftieth of the statutory maximum

History

In Sch.4 the words "Rule 2.38(6)" substituted for the former words "Rule 2.17(4)" by the Insolvency (Scotland) Amendment Rules 2003/2111 (S 9)) r.6, Sch.2 para.11 subject to transitional and savings provisions in r.7 as from September 15, 2003. In Sch.4 the entry relating to r.2.43(3) inserted by the Insolvency (Scotland) Amendment Rules 2003 (SI 2003/2111 (S 9)) r.4 subject to transitional and savings provisions in r.7 as from September 15, 2003.

SCHEDULE 5

FORMS

Rule 7.30

[Forms: not reproduced.]

Receivers (Scotland) Regulations 1986

(SI 1986/1917 (S 141))

Made on 10 November 1986 by the Secretary of State for Trade and Industry under ss.53(1), (6), 54(3), 62(1), (5), 65(1)(a), 66(1), 67(2), (6), 70(1) and 71 of the Insolvency Act 1986. Operative from 29 December 1986.

[**Note:** Changes made by the Enterprise Act 2002 (Consequential Amendments) (Prescribed Part) (Scotland) Order 2003 (SI 2003/2108 (S 7)) have been incorporated into the text. References to the registrar of companies have been substituted by references to the Accountant in Bankruptcy, pursuant to the Scotland Act 1998 (Consequential Modifications) (No.2) Order 1999 (1999/1820) arts 1(2), 4 and Sch.2 para.141 and the Scotland Act 1998 (Commencement) Order 1998 (SI 1998/3178) art.3.]

1 Citation and commencement

1 These regulations may be cited as the Receivers (Scotland) Regulations 1986 and shall come into operation on 29th December 1986.

2 Interpretation

2 In these regulations, **"the Act"** means the Insolvency Act 1986.

3 Forms

3 The forms set out in the Schedule to these regulations, with such variations as circumstances require, are the forms prescribed for the purposes of the provisions of the Act which are referred to in those forms.

4 Instrument of appointment

4 The certified copy instrument of appointment of a receiver which is required to be submitted to the registrar of companies and the Accountant in Bankruptcy by or on behalf of the person making the appointment under section 53(1) of the Act shall be certified to be a correct copy by or on behalf of that person.

5 Joint receivers

5 Where two or more persons are appointed joint receivers by the holder of a floating charge under section 53 of the Act, subsection (6) of that section shall apply subject to the following modifications:–

(a) the appointment of any of the joint receivers shall be of no effect unless the appointment is accepted by all of them in accordance with paragraph (a) of that subsection and Rule 3.1 of the Insolvency (Scotland) Rules 1986; and

(b) their appointment as joint receivers shall be deemed to be made on the day on and at the time at which the instrument of appointment is received by the last of them, as evidenced by the written docquet required by paragraph (b) of that subsection.

6 Resignation

6 For the purposes of section 62(1) of the Act, a receiver, who wishes to resign his office, shall give at least 7 days' notice of his resignation to–

(a) the holder of the floating charge by virtue of which he was appointed;

(b) the holder of any other floating charge and any receiver appointed by him;

(c) the members of any committee of creditors established under section 68 of the Act; and

   (d)   the company, or if it is then in liquidation, its liquidator,

and the notice shall specify the date on which the resignation takes effect.

7   Report to creditors

7(1)   Where the receiver determines to publish a notice under paragraph (b) of section 67(2) of the Act, the notice shall be published in a newspaper circulating in the area where the company has its principal place of business or in such other newspaper as he thinks most appropriate for ensuring that it comes to the notice of the unsecured creditors of the company.

7(2)   The receiver's report under section 67(1) shall state, to the best of his knowledge and belief–

   (a)   an estimate of the value of the prescribed part (whether or not he proposes to make an application under section 176A(5) or whether section 176A(3) applies), and

   (b)   an estimate of the value of the company's net property,

provided that such estimates shall not be required to include any information the disclosure of which could seriously prejudice the commercial interests of the company, but if such information is excluded the estimates shall be accompanied by a statement to that effect.

7(3)   The report shall also state whether, and, if so, why, the receiver proposes to make an application to the court under section 176A(5).

History
Regulation 7 renumbered as reg.7(1) and paras (2) and (3) inserted by the Enterprise Act 2002 (Consequential Amendments) (Prescribed Part) (Scotland) Order 2003 (SI 2003/2108 (S 7)) art.11 as from September 15, 2003.

SCHEDULE

FORMS

Regulation 3

[Not reproduced.]

Insolvency Proceedings (Monetary Limits) Order 1986

(SI 1986/1996)

Made on 20 November 1986 by the Secretary of State, by ss.416 and 418 of, and paras 9 and 12 of Sch.6 to, the Insolvency Act 1986. Operative from 29 December 1986.

[**Note:** Changes made by the Insolvency Proceedings (Monetary Limits) (Amendment) Order 2004 (SI 2004/547) and the Insolvency Proceedings (Monetary Limits) (Amendment) Order 2009 (SI 2009/465) have been incorporated into the text.]

1(1)   This Order may be cited as the Insolvency Proceedings (Monetary Limits) Order 1986 and shall come into force on 29th December 1986.

1(2)   In this Order **"the Act"** means the Insolvency Act 1986.

2(1)   The provisions in the first Group of Parts of the Act (companies winding up) set out in column 1 of Part 1 of the Schedule to this Order (shortly described in column 2) are hereby amended by substituting for the amounts specified in column 3 in relation to those provisions the amounts specified in column 4.

2(2)   The sum specified in column 4 of Part I of the Schedule in relation to section 184(3) of the Act is not to affect any case where the goods are sold or payment to avoid sale is made, before the coming into force of the increase.

3   The amounts prescribed for the purposes of the provisions in the second Group of Parts of the Act (bankruptcy and debt relief orders) set out in column 1 of Part II of the Schedule to this Order (shortly described in column 2) are the amounts specified in column 3 in relation to those provisions.

4   The amount prescribed for the purposes of paragraphs 9 and 12 of Schedule 6 to the Act (maximum amount for preferential status of employees' claims for remuneration and under the Reserve Forces (Safeguard of Employment) Act 1985 is £800.

5   The court shall, in determining the value of the bankrupt's interest for the purposes of section 313A(2), disregard that part of the value of the property in which the bankrupt's interest subsists which is equal to the value of:

(a)   any loans secured by mortgage or other charge against the property;

(b)   any other third party interest; and

(c)   the reasonable costs of sale.

History

Article 3 amended by the Insolvency Proceedings (Monetary Limits) (Amendment) Order 2009 (SI 2009/465) art.2 as from April 6, 2009. Article 5 inserted as from April 1, 2004 by the Insolvency Proceedings (Monetary Limits) (Amendment) Order (SI 2004/547) art.3.

SCHEDULE

PART I

INCREASES OF MONETARY AMOUNTS IN FIRST GROUP OF PARTS OF INSOLVENCY ACT 1986

Section of the Act (1)	Short Description (2)	Present Amount (3)	New Amount (4)
184(3)	Minimum value of judgment, affecting sheriff's duties on levying execution	£250	£500
206(1)(a) and (b)	Minimum value of company property concealed or fraudulently removed, affecting criminal liability of officer of company in liquidation	£120	£500

PART II

MONETARY AMOUNTS FOR PURPOSES OF SECOND GROUP OF PARTS OF INSOLVENCY ACT 1986

Section of the Act (1)	Short Description (2)	Monetary Amount (3)
251S(4)	Maximum amount of credit which a person in respect of whom a debt relief order is made may obtain without disclosure of his status	£500
273(1)(a)	Maximum level of unsecured bankruptcy debts on debtor's petition for case to be referred to insolvency practitioner to assess possibility of voluntary arrangement with creditors.	£40,000
273(1)(b)	Minimum potential value of bankrupt's estate for case to be referred as described above.	£4,000
313A(2)	Minimum value of interests in a dwelling-house for application by trustee for order for sale, possession or an order under section 313.	£1,000
346(3)	Minimum amount of judgment, determining whether amount recovered on sale of debtor's goods is to be treated as part of his estate in bankruptcy.	£1,000
354(1) and (2)	Minimum amount of concealed debt, or value of property concealed or removed, determining criminal liability under the section.	£1,000
358	Minimum value of property taken by a bankrupt out of England and Wales, determining his criminal liability.	£1,000
360(1)	Maximum amount of credit which bankrupt may obtain without disclosure of his status.	£500
364(2)(d)	Minimum value of goods removed by the bankrupt, determining his liability to arrest.	£1,000

Section of the Act (1)	Short Description (2)	Monetary Amount (3)
Schedule 4ZA–	Monetary conditions which must be satisfied for a debt relief order to be made–	
(a) paragraph 6(1)	(a) maximum amount of a person's debts:	£15,000
(b) paragraph 7(1)	(b) maximum amount of monthly surplus income:	£50
(c) paragraph 8(1)	(c) maximum total value of property:	£300

History

Part II substituted as from April 1, 2004 by the Insolvency Proceedings (Monetary Limits) (Amendment) Order (SI 2004/547) art.3, Sch. Pt 2 amended by the Insolvency Proceedings (Monetary Limits) (Amendment) Order 2009 (SI 2009/465) art.3 as from April 6, 2009.

Administration of Insolvent Estates of Deceased Persons Order 1986

(SI 1986/1999)

Made on 21 November 1986 by the Lord Chancellor under s.421 of the Insolvency Act 1986. Operative from 29 December 1986.

1   This Order may be cited as the Administration of Insolvent Estates of Deceased Persons Order 1986 and shall come into force on 29th December 1986.

2   In this Order–

"the Act" means the Insolvency Act 1986;

"insolvency administration order" means an order for the administration in bankruptcy of the insolvent estate of a deceased debtor (being an individual at the date of his death);

"insolvency administration petition" means a petition for an insolvency administration order; and

"the Rules" means the Insolvency Rules 1986.

3(1)   The provisions of the Act specified in Parts II and III of Schedule 1 to this Order shall apply to the administration in bankruptcy of the insolvent estates of deceased persons dying before presentation of a bankruptcy petition with the modifications specified in those Parts and with any further such modifications as may be necessary to render them applicable to the estate of a deceased person and in particular with the modifications specified in Part I of that Schedule, and the provisions of the Rules, the Insolvency Regulations 1986 and any order made under section 415 of the Act (fees and deposits) shall apply accordingly.

3(2)   In the case of any conflict between any provision of the Rules and any provision of this Order, the latter provision shall prevail.

4(1)   Where the estate of a deceased person is insolvent and is being administered otherwise than in bankruptcy, subject to paragraphs (2) and (3) below, the same provisions as may be in force for the time being under the law of bankruptcy with respect to the assets of individuals adjudged bankrupt shall apply to the administration of the estate with respect to the respective rights of secured and unsecured creditors, to debts and liabilities provable, to the valuation of future and contingent liabilities and to the priorities of debts and other payments.

4(2)   The reasonable funeral, testamentary and administration expenses have priority over the preferential debts listed in Schedule 6 to the Act.

4(3)   Section 292(2) of the Act shall not apply.

5(1)   If a debtor by or against whom a bankruptcy petition has been presented dies, the proceedings in the matter shall, unless the court otherwise orders, be continued as if he were alive, with the modifications specified in Schedule 2 to this Order.

5(2)   The reasonable funeral and testamentary expenses have priority over the preferential debts listed in Schedule 6 to the Act.

5(3)   If a debtor dies after presentation of a bankruptcy petition but before service, the court may order service to be effected on his personal representative or such other person as it thinks fit.

6   The definitions in Article 2 of this Order other than the first definition shall be added to those in section 385 of the Act.

SCHEDULE 1

PROVISIONS OF THE ACT APPLYING WITH RELEVANT MODIFICATIONS TO THE ADMINISTRATION IN BANKRUPTCY OF INSOLVENT ESTATES OF DECEASED PERSONS DYING BEFORE PRESENTATION OF A BANKRUPTCY PETITION

Article 3

PART I

GENERAL MODIFICATIONS OF PROVISIONS OF THE ACT

Except in so far as the context otherwise requires, for any such reference as is specified in column 1 of the Table set out below there shall be substituted the reference specified in column 2.

Table

Reference in provision of the Act specified in Part II of this Schedule (1)	*Substituted references* (2)
the bankrupt; the debtor.	the deceased debtor or his personal representative (or if there is no personal representative such person as the court may order) as the case may require.
the bankrupt's estate.	the deceased debtor's estate.
the commencement of the bankruptcy.	the date of the insolvency administration order.
a bankruptcy order.	an insolvency administration order.
an individual being adjudged bankrupt.	an insolvency administration order being made.
a debtor's petition.	a petition by the personal representative of a deceased debtor for an insolvency administration order.

PART II

PROVISIONS OF THE ACT NOT INCLUDED IN PART III OF THIS SCHEDULE

The following provisions of the Act shall apply:–

1   Section 264 with the following modifications:–

(a)   the words "against an individual" shall be omitted;

(b)   at the end of paragraph 1(a) there shall be added the words "in Form 1 set out in Schedule 3 to the Administration of Insolvent Estates of Deceased Persons Order 1986";

(c)   paragraph 1(b) shall be omitted;

(ca) at the end of paragraph 1(ba) there shall be added the words "in Form 1, with such variations as the case requires (if any), set out in Schedule 3 to the Administration of Insolvent Estates of Deceased Persons Order 1986";

(cb) at the end of paragraph 1(bb) there shall be added the words "in Form 1, with such variations as the case requires (if any), set out in Schedule 3 to the Administration of Insolvent Estates of Deceased Persons Order 1986";

(d) in paragraph 1(c) after the words "Part VIII" there shall be added the words "in Form 2 set out in the said Schedule 3";

(e) at the end of paragraph 1(d) there shall be added the words "in Form 3 set out in the said Schedule 3 in any case where a creditor could present such a petition under paragraph (a) above"; and

(f) at the end of subsection (2) there shall be added the words "in Form 4 set out in the said Schedule 3".

2   Section 266 with the following modifications:–

(a) for subsection (1) there shall be substituted the following:–

"**(1)** An insolvency administration petition shall–

    (a) if a liquidator (within the meaning of Article 2(b) of the EC Regulation) has been appointed in proceedings by virtue of Article 3(1) of the EC Regulation in relation to the deceased debtor, be served on him;

    (b) unless the court directs otherwise, be served on the personal representative; and

    (c) be served on such other persons as the court may direct."; and".

(b) in subsection (3) for the words "bankruptcy petition" there shall be substituted the words "petition to the court for an insolvency administration order with or without costs".

3   Section 267 with the following modifications to subsection (2):–

(a) before the words "at the time" there shall be inserted the words "had the debtor been alive"; and

(b) for paragraphs (a) to (d) there shall be substituted the following:–

    "(a) the amount of the debt, or the aggregate amount of the debts, owed by the debtor would have been equal to or exceeded the bankruptcy level, or

    (b) the debt, or each of the debts, owed by the debtor would have been for a liquidated sum payable to the petitioning creditor, or one or more of the petitioning creditors, either immediately or at some certain future time, and would have been unsecured.".

4   Section 269 with the modification that in subsection (2) for the words "sections 267 to 270" there shall be substituted the words "section 267 and this section".

5   Section 271 as if for that section there were substituted the following:–

"**271(1)** The court may make an insolvency administration order on a petition for such an order under section 264(1) if it is satisfied–

(a) that the debt, or one of the debts, in respect of which the petition was presented is a debt which,

    (i) having been payable at the date of the petition or having since become payable, has neither been paid nor secured or compounded for; or

    (ii) has no reasonable prospect of being able to be paid when it falls due; and

(b) that there is a reasonable probability that the estate will be insolvent.

271(2) A petition for an insolvency administration order shall not be presented to the court after proceedings have been commenced in any court of justice for the administration of the deceased debtor's estate.

271(3) Where proceedings have been commenced in any such court for the administration of the deceased debtor's estate, that court may, if satisfied that the estate is insolvent, transfer the proceedings to the court exercising jurisdiction for the purposes of the Parts in the second Group of Parts.

271(4) Where proceedings have been transferred to the court exercising jurisdiction for the purposes of the Parts in the second Group of Parts, that court may make an insolvency administration order in Form 5 set out in Schedule 3 to the Administration of Insolvent Estates of Deceased Persons Order 1986 as if a petition for such an order had been presented under section 264.

271(5)   Nothing in sections 264, 266, 267, 269 or 271 to 273 shall invalidate any payment made or any act or thing done in good faith by the personal representative before the date of the insolvency administration order.".

6   Section 272(1) with the following modifications:–

  (a)   after the word "petition" there shall be inserted the words "in Form 6 set out in Schedule 3 to the Administration of Insolvent Estates of Deceased Persons Order 1986"; and

  (b)   for the words "debtor is unable to pay his debts" there shall be substituted the words "estate of a deceased debtor is insolvent".

7   Section 273 as if for that section there were substituted the following:–

   "**273** The court shall make an insolvency administration order in Form 4 set out in Schedule 3 to the Administration of Insolvent Estates of Deceased Persons Order 1986 on the hearing of a petition presented under section 272 if it is satisfied that the deceased debtor's estate is insolvent.".

8   Section 276(2).

9   Section 277.

10   Section 278 except paragraph (b) as if for paragraph (a) there were substituted the following:–

   "(a)   commences with the day on which the insolvency administration order is made;".

11   Section 282(1) and (4).

12   Sections 283 to 285 with the modification that they shall have effect as if the petition had been presented and the insolvency administration order had been made on the date of death of the deceased debtor, and with the following modifications to section 283:–

  (a)   in subsection (2)(b), for the words "bankrupt and his family" there shall be substituted the words "family of the deceased debtor"; and

  (b)   after subsection (4) there shall be added the following subsection:–

   "(**4A**)   References in any of this Group of Parts to property, in relation to a deceased debtor, include the capacity to exercise and take proceedings for exercising all such powers over or in respect of property as might have been exercised by his personal representative for the benefit of the estate on the date of the insolvency administration order and as are specified in subsection (4) above.".

13   Section 286(1) and (3) to (8).

14   Section 287.

15   Section 288 with the modification that for subsections (1) and (2) there shall be substituted the following:–

   "(**1**) Where an insolvency administration order has been made, the personal representative, or if there is no personal representative such person as the court may on the application of the official receiver direct, shall submit to the official receiver a statement of the deceased debtor's affairs containing particulars of the assets and liabilities of the estate as at the date of the insolvency administration order together with other particulars of the affairs of the deceased debtor in Form 7 set out in Schedule 3 to the Administration of Insolvent Estates of Deceased Persons Order 1986 or as the official receiver may require.

   (**2**) The statement shall be submitted before the end of the period of fifty-six days beginning with the date of a request by the official receiver for the statement or such longer period as he or the court may allow.".

16   Section 289 as if for that section there were substituted the following:–

   "**289** The official receiver is not under any duty to investigate the conduct and affairs of the deceased debtor unless he thinks fit but may make such report (if any) to the court as he thinks fit.".

17   Section 291.

18   Sections 292 to 302, except section 297(4), with the modification that, where a meeting of creditors is summoned for the purposes of any provision in those sections, the rules regarding the trustee in bankruptcy and the creditors' committee shall apply accordingly.

19   Sections 303 and 304.

20   Section 305 with the modification that after subsection (4) there shall be added the following subsection:–

> "**(5)** In the exercise of his functions under this section where an insolvency administration order has been made, the trustee shall have regard to any claim by the personal representative to payment of reasonable funeral, testamentary and administration expenses incurred by him in respect of the deceased debtor's estate or, if there is no such personal representative, to any claim by any other person to payment of any such expenses incurred by him in respect of the estate provided that the trustee has sufficient funds in hand for the purpose, and such claims shall have priority over the preferential debts listed in Schedule 6 to this Act.".

21   Section 306.

22   Section 307 with the modification that in subsection (1) for the words "commencement of the bankruptcy" there shall be substituted the words "date of death of the deceased debtor".

23   Sections 308 to 327.

24   Sections 328 and 329 with the modification that for the words "commencement of the bankruptcy", wherever they occur, there shall be substituted the words "date of death of the deceased debtor".

25   Section 330 with the following modifications–

   (a)   in subsection (5) for the words "the bankrupt is entitled to the surplus" there shall be substituted the words "the surplus shall be paid to the personal representative unless the court otherwise orders", and

   (b)   after subsection (5) there shall be added:–

> "**(6)** Subsection (5) is subject to Article 35 of the EC Regulation (surplus in secondary proceedings to be transferred to main proceedings)."

26   Sections 331 to 340.

27   Section 341 with the modification that in subsection (1)(a) for the words "day of the presentation of the bankruptcy petition" onwards there shall be substituted the words "date of death of the deceased debtor".

28   Sections 342 to 349, 350(1), (2), (4) to (6) and 351 except paragraphs (a) and (b).

29   Section 359 with the following modifications:–

   (a)   subsection (1), and the reference to that subsection in subsection (3), shall be omitted; and

   (b)   in subsection (2), for the words "petition or in the initial period" there shall be substituted the words "the date of death of the deceased debtor".

30   Sections 363 and 365 to 381.

31   Section 382 with the modification that in the definition of "bankruptcy debt" for the words "commencement of the bankruptcy", wherever they occur, there shall be substituted the words "date of death of the deceased debtor".

32   Sections 383 and 384.

33   Section 385 with the modification that at the end of the definition of "the court" there shall be added the words "and subject thereto "the court" means the court within the jurisdiction of which the debtor resided or carried on business for the greater part of the six months immediately prior to his death".

34   Section 386.

35   Section 387(1), (5) and (6) with the modification that in subsection (6)(a) and (b) for the reference to the making of the bankruptcy order there shall be substituted a reference to the date of death of the deceased debtor.

36   Sections 388 to 410, 412, 413, 415, 418 to 420, 423 to 426, 428, 430 to 436 and 437 so far as it relates to Parts II, except paragraphs 13, IV and V of Schedule 11 to the Act.

PART III

PROVISIONS OF PART VIII OF THE ACT RELATING TO INDIVIDUAL VOLUNTARY ARRANGEMENTS

The following provisions of the Act shall apply where the court has made an interim order under section 252 of the Act in respect of an individual who subsequently dies:–

1   Section 256 with the modification that where the individual dies before he has submitted the document and statement referred to in subsection (2), after subsection (1) there shall be added the following subsections:–

> **"(1A)** The nominee shall after the death of the individual comes to his knowledge give notice to the court that the individual has died.
>
> **(1B)** After receiving such a notice the court shall discharge the order mentioned in subsection (1) above.".

2   Section 257 with the modification that where the individual dies before a creditors' meeting has been held then no such meeting shall be held and, if the individual was at the date of his death an undischarged bankrupt, the personal representative shall give notice of the death to the trustee of his estate and the official receiver.

3   Sections 258 and 259.

4   Sections 260 to 262 with the modification that they shall cease to apply on or after the death of the individual.

5   Section 263 with the modification that where the individual dies after a voluntary arrangement has been approved, then–

(a)   in subsection (3), for the words "debtor, any of his" there shall be substituted the words "personal representative of the deceased debtor, any of the deceased debtor's"; and

(b)   the supervisor shall give notice to the court that the individual has died.

SCHEDULE 2

DEATH OF DEBTOR AFTER PRESENTATION OF A BANKRUPTCY PETITION

Article 5

1   Modifications

1   For subsections (1) and (2) of section 288 of the Act there shall be substituted the following:–

> **"(1)** Where a bankruptcy order has been made otherwise than on a debtor's petition and the debtor has subsequently died without submitting a statement of his affairs to the official receiver, the personal representative or such other person as the court, on the application of the official receiver, may direct shall submit to the official receiver a statement of the deceased debtor's affairs containing particulars of the assets and liabilities of the estate as at the date of the order together with other particulars of the affairs of the deceased debtor in Form 7 set out in Schedule 3 to the Administration of Insolvent Estates of Deceased Persons

Order 1986 or as the official receiver may require, and the Rules shall apply to such a statement as they apply to an ordinary statement of affairs of a debtor.

(2) The statement shall be submitted before the end of the period of fifty-six days beginning with the date of a request by the official receiver for the statement or such longer period as he or the court may allow.".

2   At the end of section 330(4)(b) of the Act there shall be added the words "and of the personal representative of a debtor dying after the presentation of a bankruptcy petition in respect of reasonable funeral and testamentary expenses of which notice has not already been given to the trustee".

SCHEDULE 3

FORMS RELATING TO ADMINISTRATION IN BANKRUPTCY OF INSOLVENT ESTATES OF DECEASED DEBTORS

Part II of Schedule 1, paragraphs 1, 5 to 7 and 15, Schedule 2, paragraph 1

[Not reproduced.]

Act of Sederunt (Company Directors Disqualification) 1986

(SI 1986/2296 (S 168))

Made on 19 December 1986 by the Lords of Council and Session under s.32 of the Sheriff Courts (Scotland) Act 1971. Operative from 29 December 1986.

1 Citation, commencement and interpretation

1(1) This Act of Sederunt may be cited as the Act of Sederunt (Company Directors Disqualification) 1986 and shall come into operation on 29th December 1986.

1(2) This Act of Sederunt shall be inserted in the Books of Sederunt.

1(3) In this Act of Sederunt–

"disqualification order" shall have the meaning assigned to it by section 1(1) of the Company Directors Disqualification Act 1986.

2 Revocation

2 The Act of Sederunt (Disqualification of Directors etc.) 1986 is hereby revoked.

3 Applications for disqualification orders

3(1) An application to the sheriff for a disqualification order or for leave of the court under the Company Directors Disqualification Act 1986 shall be made by summary application.

3(2) In an application under sub-paragraph (1) which proceeds as unopposed, evidence submitted by way of affidavit shall be admissible in place of parole evidence.

3(3) For the purposes of this paragraph–

(a) **"affidavit"** includes affirmation and statutory declaration; and

(b) an affidavit shall be treated as admissible if it is duly emitted before a notary public or any other competent authority.

4 Orders to furnish information or for inspection

4(1) Subject to sub-paragraph (2), an application for an order of the court under rule 4(2) of the Insolvent Companies (Reports on Conduct of Directors) (No.2) (Scotland) Rules 1986 (order to furnish information, etc.) shall be made by summary application.

4(2) Where an application has been made under the Company Directors Disqualification Act 1986 for a disqualification order, an application under this paragraph may be made by minute in the proceedings in which the disqualification order is sought.

Act of Sederunt (Sheriff Court Company Insolvency Rules) 1986

(SI 1986/2297 (S 169))

Made on 19 December 1986 by the Lords of Council and Session under s.32 of the Sheriff Courts (Scotland) Act 1971. Operative from 29 December 1986.

[**Note:** Changes made by the Act of Sederunt (Sheriff Court Company Insolvency Rules 1986) Amendment 2003 (SI 2003/388), the Act of Sederunt (Sheriff Court Company Insolvency Rules 1986) Amendment (UNCITRAL Model Law on Cross-Border Insolvency) 2006 (SI 2006/200), the Act of Sederunt (Sheriff Court Company Insolvency Rules 1986) Amendment (Vulnerable Witnesses (Scotland) Act 2004) 2007 (SSI 2007/464) and the Act of Sederunt (Sheriff Court Rules) (Miscellaneous Amendments) 2008 (SSI 2008/223) have been incorporated into the text. References to administration petitions, orders, etc. have been adapted throughout, following the introduction of the new administration regime, pursuant to r.4 and Sch. paras 1 et seq. of the 2003 rules, as from September 15, 2003. Any references to a "messenger-at-arms", a "sheriff officer" and an "officer of court" are to be construed as references to a judicial officer: see the Bankruptcy and Diligence etc. (Scotland) Act 2007 s.60.]

1 Citation and commencement

1(1) This Act of Sederunt may be cited as the Act of Sederunt (Sheriff Court Company Insolvency Rules) 1986 and shall come into operation on 29th December 1986.

1(2) This Act of Sederunt shall be inserted in the Books of Sederunt.

2 Revocation and transitional provision

2(1) The Act of Sederunt (Sheriff Court Liquidations) 1930 is hereby revoked.

2(2) Notwithstanding paragraph (1), the Act of Sederunt (Sheriff Court Liquidations) 1930 shall continue to have effect in relation to proceedings commenced before the coming into operation of this Act of Sederunt.

3 Interpretation

3(1) In these rules–

"**the Act of 1986**" means the Insolvency Act 1986;

"**the Council Regulation**" means Council Regulation (E.C.) 1346/2000 of 29th May 2000 on insolvency proceedings as it may be amended from time to time;

"**the Insolvency Rules**" means the Insolvency (Scotland) Rules 1986;

"**the Model Law**" means the Model Law on Cross-Border Insolvency as set out in Schedule 1 the Cross-Border Insolvency Regulations 2006;

"**registered office**" means–

    (a) the place specified, in the statement of the company delivered to the registrar of companies under section 10 of the Companies Act 1985, as the intended place of its registered office on incorporation; or

    (b) where notice has been given by the company to the registrar of companies under section 287 of the Companies Act 1985 of a change of registered office, the place specified in the last such notice;

"**sheriff-clerk**" has the meaning assigned to it in section 3(f) of the Sheriff Courts (Scotland) Act 1907.

3(2) Unless the context otherwise requires, words and expressions used in these rules which are also used in the Act of 1986 or the Insolvency Rules have the same meaning as in that Act or those Rules.

History

See note after r.31B.

Rule 3 amended by the Act of Sederunt (Sheriff Court Rules) (Miscellaneous Amendments) 2008 (SSI 2008/223) r.10(2) as from July 1, 2008.

3A   Representation

3A(1) A party may be represented by any person authorised under any enactment to conduct proceedings in the sheriff court in accordance with the terms of that enactment.

3A(2) The person referred to in paragraph (1) may do everything for the preparation and conduct of the proceedings as may have been done by an individual conducting his own action.

3A(3) For the purposes of this rule, "enactment" includes an enactment comprised in, or in an instrument made under, an Act of the Scottish the Scottish Parliament.

3B   Expenses

3B A party who—

(a) is or has been represented by a person authorised under any enactment to conduct proceedings in the sheriff court; and

(b) would have been found entitled to expenses if he had been represented by a solicitor or an advocate,

may be awarded expenses or outlays to which a party litigant may be found entitled under the Litigants in Person (Cost and Expenses) Act 1975 or under any enactment under that Act.

History

Rules 3A, 3B inserted by the Act of Sederunt (Sheriff Court Rules) (Miscellaneous Amendments) 2008 (SSI 2008/223) r.12, as from July 1, 2008.

PART I

COMPANY VOLUNTARY ARRANGEMENTS

4   Lodging of nominee's report (Part 1, Chapter 2 of the Insolvency Rules)

4(1) This rule applies where the company is not being wound up, is not in liquidation and is not in administration.

4(2) A report of a nominee, sent to the court under section 2(2) of the Act of 1986, shall be accompanied by a covering letter, lodged in the offices of the court and marked by the sheriff-clerk with the date on which it is received.

4(3) The report shall be placed before the sheriff for consideration of any direction which he may make under section 3(1) of the Act of 1986.

4(4) An application by a nominee to extend the time within which he may lodge his report under section 2(2) of the Act of 1986 shall be made by letter addressed to the sheriff-clerk, who shall place the matter before the sheriff for determination.

4(5) The letter of application under paragraph (4) and a copy of the reply by the court shall be placed by the sheriff-clerk with the nominee's report when it is subsequently lodged.

4(6) A person who states in writing that he is a creditor, member or director of the company may, by himself or his agent, on payment of the appropriate fee, inspect the nominee's report lodged under paragraph (2).

5 Lodging of nominee's report (Part 1, Chapter 4 of The Insolvency Rules)

5(1) This rule applies where the company is being wound up, is in liquidation or is in administration.

5(2) Where a report of a nominee is sent to the court under section 2(2) of the Act of 1986, it shall be lodged in the process of the petition to wind up the company or any petition in respect of an administration which is in force in respect of it, as the case may be.

5(3) Where the nominee is not the liquidator or administrator, the report shall be placed before the sheriff for consideration of any direction which he may make under section 3(1) of the Act of 1986.

5(4) An application by a nominee to extend the time within which he may lodge his report under section 2(2) of the Act of 1986 shall be made by letter addressed to the sheriff-clerk, who shall place the matter before the sheriff for determination.

5(5) The letter of application under paragraph (4) and a copy of the reply by the court shall be placed by the sheriff-clerk in the process of the petition to wind up the company or any petition in respect of an administration which is in force in respect of it, as the case may be.

5(6) A person who states in writing that he is a creditor, member or director of the company may, by himself or his agent, on payment of the appropriate fee, inspect the nominee's report lodged under paragraph (2).

6 Applications to replace nominee

6 An application under section 2(4) of the Act of 1986 to replace a nominee who has failed to lodge a report under section 2(2) of the Act of 1986, shall be made–

(a) by petition where the company is not being wound up, is not in liquidation and there is no order in respect of an administration; or

(b) by note in the process of the petition to wind up the company or the petition in respect of an administration which is in force in respect of it, as the case may be,

and shall be intimated and served as the court shall direct.

7 Report of meetings to approve arrangement

7 The report of the result of a meeting to be sent to the court under section 4(6) of the Act of 1986 shall be sent to the sheriff-clerk who shall cause it to be lodged–

(a) in a case to which rule 4 applies, with the nominee's report lodged under that rule; or

(b) in a case to which rule 5 applies, in the process of the petition to wind up the company or the petition for an order in respect of an administration which is in force in respect of it, as the case may be.

8 Abstracts of supervisor's receipts and payments and notices of completion of arrangement

8 An abstract of receipts and payments prepared by a supervisor to be sent to the court under rule 1.21(2) of the Insolvency Rules or a notice of completion of the arrangement (together with a copy of the supervisor's report) to be sent to the court under rule 1.23(3) of those Rules shall be sent to the sheriff-clerk, who shall cause it to be lodged–

(a) in a case to which rule 4 applies, with the nominee's report lodged under that rule; or

(b) in a case to which rule 5 applies, in the process of the petition to wind up the company or the petition for an order in respect of an administration which is in force in respect of it, as the case may be.

9   Form of certain applications

9(1)   This rule applies to applications under any of the following provisions of the Act of 1986 and the Insolvency Rules:–

(a) section 6 (to challenge a decision in relation to an arrangement);

(b) section 7(3) (to challenge actings of a supervisor);

(c) section 7(4)(a) (by supervisor for directions);

(d) section 7(5) (to appoint a supervisor);

(e) rule 1.21(5) (to dispense with sending abstracts or reports or to vary dates on which obligation to send abstracts or reports arises);

(f) rule 1.23(4) (by supervisor to extend period for sending notice of implementation of arrangement); and

(g) any other provision relating to company voluntary arrangements not specifically mentioned in this Part.

9(2)   An application shall be made–

(a) in a case to which rule 4 applies, by petition; or

(b) in a case to which rule 5 applies, by note in the process of the petition to wind up the company or the petition for an order in respect of an administration which is in force in respect of it, as the case may be.

PART II

ADMINISTRATION PROCEDURE

10   Petitions for administration orders

10(1)   A petition for an administration order or any other order in an administration shall include averments in relation to–

(a) the petitioner and the capacity in which he presents the petition, if other than the company;

(b) whether it is believed that the company is, or is likely to become, unable to pay its debts and the grounds of that belief;

(c) how the making of that order will achieve–

(i) any of the purposes specified in section 8(3) of the Act of 1986; or

(ii) an objective specified in paragraph 3 of Schedule B1 to the Act of 1986;

(d) the company's financial position, specifying (so far as known) assets and liabilities, including contingent and prospective liabilities;

(e) any security known or believed to be held by creditors of the company, whether in any case the security confers power on the holder to appoint a receiver, and whether a receiver has been appointed;

(f) so far as known to the petitioner, whether any steps have been taken for the winding up of the company, giving details of them;

(g)   other matters which, in the opinion of the petitioner, will assist the court in deciding whether to grant that order;

(h)   jurisdiction under the Council Regulation, in particular stating, so far as known to the petitioner–

     (i)   where the centre of main interests of the company is and whether the company has any other establishments in another member State;

     (ii)   whether there are insolvency proceedings elsewhere in respect of the company and whether those proceedings are main or territorial proceedings; and

(i)   the person proposed to be appointed as administrator, giving his name and address and that he is qualified to act as an insolvency practitioner in relation to the company.

History

In Pt II in the heading the words "PROCEDURE" substituted for the former words "ORDERS" and in r.10(1) the words "or any other order in an administration" inserted by the Act of Sederunt (Sheriff Court Company Insolvency Rules 1986) Amendment 2003 (SI 2003/388) r.2 as from September 15, 2003.

    Paragraph 1(h) substituted by the Act of Sederunt (Sheriff Court Rules) (Miscellaneous Amendments) 2008 (SSI 2008/223) r.10(3) as from July 1, 2008.

10(2)   There shall be produced with the petition–

(a)   any document instructing the facts relied on, or otherwise founded on, by the petitioner; and

(b)   [Omitted by the Act of Sederunt (Sheriff Court Company Insolvency Rules 1986) Amendment (SI 2003/388) r.2 as from September 15, 2003.]

11   Notice of petition

11   Notice of the petition on the persons to whom notice is to be given under rule 2.3 of the Insolvency Rules shall be made in such manner as the court shall direct.

History

In r.11 "2.3" substituted for the former "2.2" by Act of Sederunt (Sheriff Court Company Insolvency Rules 1986) Amendment 2003 (SI 2003/388) r.2 as from September 15, 2003.

12   Applications during an administration

12   An application or appeal under any provision of the Act of 1986, the Insolvency Rules or an application to participate under article 12 of the Model Law in an administration during an administration shall be–

(a)   where no previous application or appeal has been made, by petition; or

(b)   where a petition for an order in respect of an administration has been made, by note in the process of that petition.

History

Rule 12 substituted by the Act of Sederunt (Sheriff Court Company Insolvency Rules 1986) Amendment 2003 (SI 2003/388) r.2 as from September 15, 2003. See also note after r.31B.

13   Report of administrator's proposals

13(1)   A report of the meeting to approve the administrator's proposals to be sent to the court under section 24(4) of the Act of 1986 shall be sent to the sheriff-clerk, who shall cause it to be lodged in the process of the petition.

13(2)   Where the report lodged under paragraph (1) discloses that the meeting has declined to approve the administrator's proposals, the court shall appoint a special diet for determination by the sheriff of any order he may make under section 24(5) of the Act of 1986.

14   Report of administrator's proposals: Schedule B1 to the Act of 1986

14(1)   Paragraph (2) shall apply where a report under paragraphs 53(2) or 54(6) of Schedule B1 to the Act of 1986 discloses a failure to approve, or to approve a revision of, an administrator's proposals.

14(2)   The sheriff clerk shall appoint a hearing for determination by the sheriff of any order that may be made under paragraph 55(2) of Schedule B1 to the Act of 1986.

14A   Time and date of lodging in an administration

14A(1)   The time and date of lodging of a notice or document relating to an administration under the Act of 1986 or the Insolvency Rules shall be noted by the sheriff clerk upon the notice or document.

14A(2)   Subject to any provision of the Insolvency Rules–

(a)   where the time of lodging of a notice or document cannot be ascertained by the sheriff clerk, the notice or document shall be deemed to be lodged at 10 a.m. on the date of lodging; and

(b)   where a notice or document under paragraph (1) is delivered on any day other than a business day, the date of lodging shall be the first business day after such delivery.

History
Rule 14 substituted and r.14A inserted by the Act of Sederunt (Sheriff Court Company Insolvency Rules 1986) Amendment 2003 (SI 2003/388) r.2 as from September 15, 2003.

Part III

Receivers

15   Petitions to appoint receivers

15(1)   A petition to appoint a receiver for a company shall include averments in relation to–

(a)   any floating charge and the property over which it is secured;

(b)   so far as known to the petitioner whether any petition for an order in respect of an administration has been made, or an administrator has been appointed, in respect of the company, giving details of it;

(c)   other matters which, in the opinion of the petitioner, will assist the court in deciding whether to appoint a receiver; and

(d)   the person proposed to be appointed as receiver, giving his name and address and that he is qualified to act as a receiver.

15(2)   There shall be produced with the petition any document instructing the facts relied on, or otherwise founded on, by the petitioner.

16   Intimation, service and advertisement

16(1)   Intimation, service and advertisement of the petition shall be made in accordance with the following provisions of this rule unless the court otherwise directs.

16(2)   There shall be included in the order for service, a requirement to serve–

(a)   upon the company;

(b)   where a petition for an order in respect of an administration has been presented, on that petitioner and any respondent to that petition; and

(c)   upon an administrator.

16(3)   Subject to paragraph (5), service of a petition on the company shall be effected at its registered office–

(a)   by registered or recorded delivery post addressed to the company; or

(b)   by sheriff officer–

    (i)   leaving the citation in the hands of a person who, after due inquiry, he has reasonable grounds for believing to be a director, other officer or responsible employee of the company or authorised to accept service on behalf of the company; or

    (ii)   if there is no such person as is mentioned in head (i) present, depositing it in the registered office in such a way that it is likely to come to the attention of such a person attending at that office.

16(4)   Where service is effected in accordance with paragraph (3)(b)(ii), the sheriff officer thereafter shall send a copy of the petition and citation by ordinary first class post to the registered office of the company.

16(5)   Where service cannot be effected at the registered office of the company or the company has no registered office–

(a)   service may be effected at the last known principal place of business of the company in Scotland or at some place in Scotland at which the company carries on business, by leaving the citation in the hands of such a person as is mentioned in paragraph (3)(b)(i) or by depositing it as specified in paragraph (3)(b)(ii); and

(b)   where the citation is deposited as is specified in paragraph (3)(b)(ii), the sheriff officer thereafter shall send a copy of the petition and citation by ordinary first class post to such place mentioned in sub-paragraph (a) of this paragraph in which the citation was deposited.

16(6)   The petition shall be advertised forthwith–

(a)   once in the Edinburgh Gazette; and

(b)   once in one or more newspapers as the court shall direct for ensuring that it comes to the notice of the creditors of the company.

16(7)   The advertisement under paragraph (6) shall state–

(a)   the name and address of the petitioner;

(b)   the name and address of the solicitor for the petitioner;

(c)   the date on which the petition was presented;

(d)   the precise order sought;

(e)   the period of notice; and

(f)   that any person who intends to appear in the petition must lodge answers to the petition within the period of notice.

16(8)   The period of notice within which answers to the petition may be lodged and after which further consideration of the petition may proceed shall be 8 days after such intimation, service and advertisement as the court may have ordered.

17   Form of certain applications where receiver appointed

17(1)   An application under any of the following sections of the Act of 1986 shall be made by petition or, where the receiver was appointed by the court, by note in the process of the petition for appointment of a receiver:–

(a)   section 61(1) (by receiver for authority to dispose of interest in property);

(b)   section 62 (for removal or resignation of receiver);

(c)   section 63(1) (by receiver for directions);

(d)   section 69(1) (to enforce receiver to make returns, etc.); and

(e)   any other section relating to receivers not specifically mentioned in this Part.

17(2)   An application under any of the following provisions of the Act of 1986 or the Insolvency Rules shall be made by motion in the process of the petition–

(a)   section 67(1) or (2) (by receiver to extend time for sending report); and

(b)   rule 3.9(2) (by receiver to extend time for sending abstract of receipts and payments).

PART IV

WINDING UP BY THE COURT OF COMPANIES REGISTERED UNDER THE COMPANIES ACTS AND OF
UNREGISTERED COMPANIES

18   Petitions to wind up a company

18(1)   A petition to wind up a company under the Act of 1986 shall include–

(a)   particulars of the petitioner, if other than the company;

(aa)   averments in relation to jurisdiction under the Council Regulation, in particular stating, so far as known to the petitioner:–

  (i)   where the centre of main interests of the company is and whether the company has any other establishments in another member State;

  (ii)   whether there are insolvency proceedings elsewhere in respect of the company and whether those proceedings are main or territorial proceedings;

(b)   in respect of the company–

  (i)   the registered name;

  (ii)   the address of the registered office and any change of that address within the last 6 months so far as known to the petitioner;

  (iii)   a statement of the nature and objects, the amount of its capital (nominal and issued) and indicating what part is called up, paid up or credited as paid, and the amount of the assets of the company so far as known to the petitioner;

(c)   a narrative of the facts on which the petitioner relies and any particulars required to instruct the title of the petitioner to present the petition;

(d)   the name and address of the person to be appointed as interim liquidator and a statement that he is qualified to act as an insolvency practitioner in relation to the company; and

(e)   a crave setting out the orders applied for, including any intimation, service and advertisement and any appointment of an interim liquidator.

18(2)   There shall be lodged with the petition any document–

(a)   instructing the title of the petitioner; and

(b)   instructing the facts relied on, or otherwise founded on, by the petitioner.

History
Rule 18(1)(aa) inserted by the Act of Sederunt (Sheriff Court Rules) (Miscellaneous Amendments) 2008 (SSI 2008/223) r.10(4) as from July 1, 2008.

19 Intimation, service and advertisement

19(1) Intimation, service and advertisement shall be in accordance with the following provisions of this rule unless the court–

(a) summarily dismisses the petition; or

(b) otherwise directs.

19(2) There shall be included in the order for intimation and service, a requirement–

(a) to intimate on the walls of the court;

(b) where the petitioner is other than the company, to serve upon the company;

(c) where the company is being wound up voluntarily and a liquidator has been appointed, to serve upon the liquidator;

(d) where a receiver has been appointed for the company, to serve upon the receiver;

(dd) where a company is in administration, to serve upon the administrator;

(e) where the company is–

    (i) a recognised bank or licensed institution within the meaning of the Banking Act 1979; or

    (ii) an institution to which sections 16 and 18 of that Act apply as if it were licensed,

and the petitioner is not the Bank of England, to serve upon the Bank of England.

History
In r.19(2) para.(dd) inserted by the Act of Sederunt (Sheriff Court Company Insolvency Rules 1986) Amendment 2003 (SI 2003/388) r.4, Sch. paras 1, 10 as from September 15, 2003.

19(3) Subject to paragraph (5), service of a petition on the company shall be executed at its registered office–

(a) by registered or recorded delivery post addressed to the company; or

(b) by sheriff officer–

    (i) leaving the citation in the hands of a person who, after due inquiry, he has reasonable grounds for believing to be a director, other officer or responsible employee of the company or authorised to accept service on behalf of the company; or

    (ii) if there is no such person as is mentioned in head (i) present, depositing it in the registered office in such a way that it is likely to come to the attention of such a person attending at that office.

19(4) Where service is effected in accordance with paragraph (3)(b)(ii), the sheriff officer thereafter shall send a copy of the petition and citation by ordinary first class post to the registered office of the company.

19(5) Where service cannot be effected at the registered office or the company has no registered office–

(a) service may be effected at the last known principal place of business of the company in Scotland or at some place in Scotland at which the company carries on business, by leaving the citation in the hands of such a person as is mentioned in paragraph (3)(b)(i) or by depositing it as specified in paragraph (3)(b)(ii); and

(b) where the citation is deposited as is specified in paragraph (3)(b)(ii), the sheriff officer thereafter shall send a copy of the petition and the citation by ordinary first class post to such place mentioned in sub-paragraph (a) of this paragraph in which the citation was deposited.

19(6)   The petition shall be advertised forthwith–

(a) once in the Edinburgh Gazette; and

(b) once in one or more newspapers as the court shall direct for ensuring that it comes to the notice of the creditors of the company.

19(7)   The advertisement under paragraph (6) shall state–

(a) the name and address of the petitioner and, where the petitioner is the company, the registered office;

(b) the name and address of the solicitor for the petitioner;

(c) the date on which the petition was presented;

(d) the precise order sought;

(e) where a provisional liquidator has been appointed, his name, address and the date of his appointment;

(f) the period of notice; and

(g) that any person who intends to appear in the petition must lodge answers to the petition within the period of notice.

19(8)   The period of notice within which answers to the petition may be lodged and after which further consideration of the petition may proceed shall be 8 days after such intimation, service and advertisement as the court may have ordered.

20   [Omitted by the Act of Sederunt (Sheriff Court Caveat Rules) 2006 (SI 2006/198) as from April 28, 2006.]

21   Substitution of creditor or contributory for petitioner

21(1)   This rule applies where a petitioner–

(a) is subsequently found not entitled to present the petition;

(b) fails to make intimation, service and advertisement as directed by the court;

(c) consents to withdraw the petition or to allow it to be dismissed or refused;

(d) fails to appear when the petition is called for hearing; or

(e) appears, but does not move for an order in terms of the prayer of the petition.

21(2)   The court may, on such terms as it considers just, sist as petitioner in room of the original petitioner any creditor or contributory who, in the opinion of the court, is entitled to present a petition.

21(3)   An application by a creditor or contributory to be sisted under paragraph (2)–

(a) may be made at any time before the petition is dismissed or refused; and

(b) shall be made by note in the process of the petition, and if necessary the court may continue the cause for a specified period to allow a note to be presented.

22 Advertisement of appointment of liquidator

22 Where a liquidator is appointed by the court, the court may order that the liquidator shall advertise his appointment once in one or more newspapers as the court shall direct for ensuring that it comes to the notice of creditors of the company.

23 Provisional liquidators

23(1) An application to appoint a provisional liquidator under section 135 of the Act of 1986 may be made–

   (a) by the petitioner, in the crave of the petition or subsequently by note in the process of the petition; or

   (b) by a creditor or contributory of the company, the company, Secretary of State or a person entitled under any enactment to present a petition to wind up the company, in a note in the process of the petition.

23(2) The petition or note, as the case may be, shall include averments in relation to–

   (a) the grounds on which it is proposed that a provisional liquidator should be appointed;

   (b) the name and address of the person to be appointed as provisional liquidator and that he is qualified to act as an insolvency practitioner in relation to the company; and

   (c) whether, to the knowledge of the applicant, there is a receiver or administrator for the company or a liquidator has been appointed for the voluntary winding up of the company.

History
In r.23(2)(c) the words "or administrator" inserted by the Act of Sederunt (Sheriff Court Company Insolvency Rules 1986) Amendment 2003 (SI 2003/388) r.4, Sch. paras 1, 11 as from September 15, 2003.

23(3) Where the court is satisfied that sufficient grounds exist for the appointment of a provisional liquidator, it shall, on making the appointment, specify the functions to be carried out by him in relation to the affairs of the company.

23(4) The applicant shall send a certified copy of the interlocutor appointing a provisional liquidator forthwith to the person appointed.

23(5) On receiving a certified copy of his appointment on an application by note, the provisional liquidator shall intimate his appointment forthwith–

   (a) once in the Edinburgh Gazette; and

   (b) once in one or more newspapers as the court shall direct for ensuring that it comes to the notice of creditors of the company.

23(6) An application for discharge of a provisional liquidator shall be by note in the process of the petition.

24 Applications and appeals in relation to a statement of affairs

24(1) An application under section 131(5) of the Act of 1986 for–

   (a) release from an obligation imposed under section 131(1) or (2) of the Act of 1986; or

   (b) an extension of time for the submission of a statement of affairs,

shall be made by note in the process of the petition.

24(2) A note under paragraph (1) shall be served on the liquidator or provisional liquidator, as the case may be.

24(3)   The liquidator or provisional liquidator may lodge answers to the note or lodge a report of any matters which he considers should be drawn to the attention of the court.

24(4)   Where the liquidator or provisional liquidator lodges a report under paragraph (3), he shall send a copy of it to the noter forthwith.

24(5)   Where the liquidator or provisional liquidator does not appear, a certified copy of the interlocutor pronounced by the court disposing of the note shall be sent by the noter forthwith to him.

24(6)   An appeal under rule 4.9(6) of the Insolvency Rules against a refusal by the liquidator of an allowance towards the expense of preparing a statement of affairs shall be made by note in the process of the petition.

25   Appeals against adjudication of claims

25(1)   An appeal under section 49(6) of the Bankruptcy (Scotland) Act 1985, as applied by rule 4.16 of the Insolvency Rules, by a creditor or contributory of the company against a decision of the liquidator shall be made by note in the process of the petition.

25(2)   A note under paragraph (1) shall be served on the liquidator.

25(3)   On receipt of the note served on him under this rule, the liquidator forthwith shall send to the court the claim in question and a copy of his adjudication for lodging in process.

25(4)   After the note has been disposed of, the court shall return the claim and the adjudication to the liquidator together with a copy of the interlocutor.

26   Appointment of liquidator by the court

26(1)   An application to appoint a liquidator under section 139(4) of the Act of 1986 shall be made by note in the process of the petition.

26(2)   Where the court appoints a liquidator under section 138(5) of the Act of 1986, the sheriff-clerk shall send a certified copy of the interlocutor pronounced by the court to the liquidator forthwith.

27   Removal of liquidator

27   An application by a creditor of the company for removal of a liquidator or provisional liquidator from office under section 172 of the Act of 1986 or for an order under section 171(3) of the Act of 1986 directing a liquidator to summon a meeting of creditors for the purpose of removing him shall be made by note in the process of the petition.

28   Applications in relation to remuneration of liquidator

28(1)   An application by a liquidator under rule 4.34 of the Insolvency Rules shall be made by note in the process of the petition.

28(2)   An application by a creditor of the company under rule 4.35 of the Insolvency Rules shall be made by note in the process of the petition.

28(3)   A note under paragraph (2) shall be served on the liquidator.

29   Application to appoint a special manager

29(1)   An application under section 177 of the Act of 1986 by a liquidator or provisional liquidator for the appointment of a special manager shall be made by note in the process of the petition.

29(2)   The cautioner, for the caution to be found by the special manager within such time as the court shall direct, may be–

(a)   a private person, if approved by the court; or

(b) a guarantee company, chosen from a list of such companies prepared for this purpose annually by the Accountant of Court and approved by the Lord President of the Court of Session.

29(3) A bond of caution certified by the noter under rule 4.70(4) of the Insolvency Rules shall be delivered to the sheriff-clerk by the noter, marked as received by him and transmitted forthwith by him to the Accountant of Court.

29(4) On receipt of the bond of caution, the sheriff-clerk shall issue forthwith to the person appointed to be special manager a certified copy of the interlocutor appointing him.

29(5) An application by a special manager to extend the time within which to find caution shall be made by motion.

30 Other applications

30 An application under the Act of 1986 or rules made under that Act in relation to a winding up by the court not specifically mentioned in this Part or an application to participate under article 12 of the Model Law in a winding up by the Court shall be made by note in the process of the petition.

History
See note after r.31B.

PART V

GENERAL PROVISIONS

31 Application

31 This Part applies to Parts I to IV of these rules.

31A Applications under section 176A of the Act of 1986

31A(1) An application by a liquidator, administrator or receiver under section 176A of the Act of 1986 shall be–

(a) where there is no existing process in relation to any liquidation, administration or receivership, by petition; or

(b) where a process exists in relation to any liquidation, administration or receivership, by note in that process.

31A(2) The sheriff clerk shall–

(a) after lodging of any petition or note fix a hearing for the sheriff to consider an application under paragraph (1); and

(b) give notice of the hearing fixed under paragraph (2)(a) to the petitioner or noter.

31A(3) The petitioner or noter shall not be required to give notice to any person of the hearing fixed under paragraph (2)(a), unless the sheriff directs otherwise.

History
Rule 31A inserted by the Act of Sederunt (Sheriff Court Company Insolvency Rules 1986) Amendment 2003 (SI 2003/388) r.3 as from September 15, 2003.

31B UNCITRAL Model Law on Cross-Border Insolvency

31B On receipt of a certified copy interlocutor of a Lord Ordinary ordering proceedings under these rules to be transferred to the Court of Session under paragraph 11 of Schedule 3 to the Cross-Border Insolvency Regulations 2006, the sheriff clerk shall within four days transmit the process to the deputy principal clerk of session.

History
Rules 3, 12 and 30 were amended and r.31B inserted by the Act of Sederunt (Sheriff Court Company Insolvency Rules 1986) Amendment (UNCITRAL Model Law on Cross-Border Insolvency) 2006 (SI 2006/200, effective April 6, 2006), to take account of the adoption by the UK of the UNCITRAL Model Law.

32   Intimation, service and advertisement of notes and appeals

32   An application by note, or an appeal, to the court under these rules shall be intimated, served and, if necessary, advertised as the court shall direct.

33   Affidavits

33   The court may accept as evidence an affidavit lodged in support of a petition or note.

34   Notices, reports and other documents sent to the court

34   Where, under the Act of 1986 or rules made under that Act–

   (a) notice of a fact is to be given to the court;

   (b) a report is to be made, or sent, to the court; or

   (c) some other document is to be sent to the court;

it shall be sent or delivered to the sheriff-clerk of the court, who shall cause it to be lodged in the appropriate process.

35   Failure to comply with rules

35(1)   The court may, in its discretion, relieve a party from the consequences of any failure to comply with the provisions of a rule shown to be due to mistake, oversight or other cause, which is not wilful non-observance of the rule, on such terms and conditions as the court considers just.

35(2)   Where the court relieves a party from the consequences of failure to comply with a rule under paragraph 1, the court may pronounce such interlocutor as may be just so as to enable the cause to proceed as if the failure to comply with the rule had not occurred.

35A   Vulnerable witnesses

35A(1)   At any hearing on an application under these rules the sheriff shall ascertain whether there is or is likely to be a vulnerable witness who is to give evidence at or for the purposes of any proof or hearing, consider any child witness notice or vulnerable witness application that has been lodged where no order has been made under section 12(1) or (6) of the Vulnerable Witnesses (Scotland) Act 2004 and consider whether any order under section 12(1) of that Act requires to be made.

35A(2)   Except where the sheriff otherwise directs, where a vulnerable witness is to give evidence at or for the purposes of any proof or hearing in an application under these rules, any application in relation to the vulnerable witness or special measure that may be ordered shall be dealt with in accordance with the rules within Chapter 45 of the Ordinary Cause Rules in the First Schedule to the Sheriff Courts (Scotland) Act 1907.

35A(3)   In this rule, "vulnerable witness" means a witness within the meaning of section 11(1) of the Vulnerable Witnesses (Scotland) Act 2004.

History
Rule 35A inserted by the Act of Sederunt (Sheriff Court Company Insolvency Rules 1986) Amendment (Vulnerable Witnesses (Scotland) Act 2004) 2007 (SSI 2007/464) r.2, as from November 1, 2007.

PART VI

APPEALS

36 Appeals to the Sheriff Principal or Court of Session

36(1)   Where an appeal to the Sheriff Principal or the Court of Session is competent, it shall be taken by note of appeal which shall–

(a)   be written by the appellant or his solicitor on–

   (i)   the interlocutor sheet or other written record containing the interlocutor appealed against; or

   (ii)   a separate document lodged with the sheriff-clerk;

(b)   be as nearly as may be in the following terms:– "The (*petitioner, noter, respondent or other party*) appeals to the Sheriff Principal [*or* Court of Session]"; and

(c)   be signed by the appellant or his solicitor and bear the date on which it is signed.

36(2)   Such an appeal shall be marked within 14 days of the date of the interlocutor appealed against.

36(3)   Where the appeal is to the Court of Session, the note of appeal shall specify the name and address of the solicitor in Edinburgh who will be acting for the appellant.

36(4)   On an appeal being taken, the sheriff-clerk shall within 4 days–

(a)   transmit the process–

   (i)   where the appeal is to Sheriff Principal, to him; or

   (ii)   where the appeal is to the Court of Session, to the Deputy Principal Clerk of Session; and

(b)   send written notice of the appeal to any other party to the cause and certify in the interlocutor sheet, or other written record containing the interlocutor appealed against, that he has done so.

36(5)   Failure of the sheriff-clerk to give notice under paragraph 4(b) shall not invalidate the appeal.

Insolvent Companies (Disqualification of Unfit Directors) Proceedings Rules 1987

(SI 1987/2023)

Made on 25 November 1987 by the Lord Chancellor, under ss.411 and 413 of the Insolvency Act 1986 and s.21 of the Company Directors Disqualification Act 1986. Operative from 11 January 1988.

[**Note:** These Regulations apply (with modifications) to limited liability partnerships by virtue of the Limited Liability Partnerships Regulations 2001 (SI 2001/1090) regs 1, 10(1) and Sch.6 Pt III para.3 as from April 6, 2001. Amendments to these Rules by the Insolvent Companies (Disqualification of Unfit Directors) Proceedings (Amendment) Rules 1999 (SI 1999/1023), the Insolvent Companies (Disqualification of Unfit Directors) Proceedings (Amendment) Rules 2003 (SI 2003/1367) and the Insolvent Companies (Disqualification of Unfit Directors) Proceedings (Amendment) Rules 2007 (SI 2007/1906) have been incorporated into the text (in the case of pre-2003 legislation without annotation).]

1 Citation, commencement and interpretation

1(1) These Rules may be cited as the Insolvent Companies (Disqualification of Unfit Directors) Proceedings Rules 1987 and shall come into force on 11th January 1988.

1(2) In these Rules–

(a) **"the Companies Act"** means the Companies Act 1985,

(b) **"the Company Directors Disqualification Act"** means the Company Directors Disqualification Act 1986,

(c) **"CPR"** followed by a Part or rule by number means that Part or rule with that number in the Civil Procedure Rules 1998.

(d) **"practice direction"** means a direction as to the practice and procedure of any court within the scope of the Civil Procedure Rules,

(e) **"registrar"** has the same meaning as in paragraphs (4) and (5) of rule 13.2 of the Insolvency Rules 1986, and

(f) **"file in court"** means deliver to the court for filing.

1(3) These Rules apply to an application made under the Company Directors Disqualification Act on or after 6th August 2007–

(a) for leave to commence proceedings for a disqualification order after the end of the period mentioned in section 7(2) of that Act;

(b) to enforce any duty arising under section 7(4) of that Act;

(c) for a disqualification order where made–

  (i) by the Secretary of State or the official receiver under section 7(1) of that Act (disqualification of unfit directors of insolvent companies);

  (ii) by the Secretary of State under section 8 of that Act (disqualification after investigation of company); or

  (iii) by the Office of Fair Trading or a specified regulator under section 9A of that Act (competition disqualification order);

(d) under section 8A of that Act (variation etc. of disqualification undertaking); or–

    (e)   for leave to act under–

        (i)   section 1A(1) or 9B(4) of that Act (and section 17 of that Act as it applies for the purposes of either of those sections); or

        (ii)   sections 1 and 17 as they apply for the purposes of section 6, 7(1), 8, 9A or 10 of that Act.

History
Rule 1(3) replaced by the Insolvent Companies (Disqualification of Unfit Directors) Proceedings (Amendment) Rules 2007 (SI 2007/1906) r.2 as from August 6, 2007.

2   Form and conduct of applications

2(1)   The Civil Procedure Rules 1998, and any relevant practice direction, apply in respect of any application to which these Rules apply, except where these Rules make provision to inconsistent effect.

2(2)   Subject to paragraph (5), an application shall be made either–

    (a) by claim form as provided by the relevant practice direction and the claimant must use the CPR Part 8 (alternative procedure for claims) procedure, or

    (b) by application notice as provided for by the relevant practice direction.

2(3)   CPR rule 8.1(3) (power of the court to order the claim to continue as if the claimant had not used the Part 8 procedure), CPR rule 8.2 (contents of the claim form) and CPR rule 8.7 (Part 20 claims) do not apply.

2(4)   Rule 7.47 (appeals and reviews of court orders) and rule 7.49 (procedure on appeal) of the Insolvency Rules 1986 apply.

2(5)   The Insolvency Rules 1986 shall apply to an application to enforce any duty arising under section 7(4) of the Company Directors Disqualification Act made against a person who at the date of the application is acting as liquidator, administrator or administrative receiver.

History
Rule 2(2) replaced, and r.2(5) inserted, by the Insolvent Companies (Disqualification of Unfit Directors) Proceedings (Amendment) Rules 2007 (SI 2007/1906) r.3 as from August 6, 2007.

2A   Application of Rules 3 to 8

2A   Rules 3 to 8 only apply to the types of application referred to in Rule 1(3)(c).

History
Rule 2A inserted by the Insolvent Companies (Disqualification of Unfit Directors) Proceedings (Amendment) Rules 2007 (SI 2007/1906) r.4 as from August 6, 2007.

3   The case against the defendant

3(1)   There shall, at the time when the claim form is issued, be filed in court evidence in support of the application for a disqualification order; and copies of the evidence shall be served with the claim form on the defendant.

3(2)   The evidence shall be by one or more affidavits, except where the claimant is the official receiver, in which case it may be in the form of a written report (with or without affidavits by other persons) which shall be treated as if it had been verified by affidavit by him and shall be prima facie evidence of any matter contained in it.

3(3)   There shall in the affidavit or affidavits or (as the case may be) the official receiver's report be included a statement of the matters by reference to which the defendant is alleged to be unfit to be concerned in the management of a company.

4   Endorsement on claim form

4   There shall on the claim form be endorsed information to the defendant as follows–

(a)   that the application is made in accordance with these Rules;

(b)   that, in accordance with the relevant enactments, the court has power to impose disqualifications as follows–

(i)   where the application is under section 7 of the Company Directors Disqualification Act, for a period of not less than 2, and up to 15, years; and

(ii)   where the application is under section 8 or 9A of that Act, for a period of up to 15 years;

(c)   that the application for a disqualification order may, in accordance with these Rules, be heard and determined summarily, without further or other notice to the defendant, and that, if it is so heard and determined, the court may impose disqualification for a period of up to 5 years;

(d)   that if at the hearing of the application the court, on the evidence then before it, is minded to impose, in the defendant's case, disqualification for any period longer than 5 years, it will not make a disqualification order on that occasion but will adjourn the application to be heard (with further evidence, if any) at a later date to be notified; and

(e)   that any evidence which the defendant wishes to be taken into consideration by the court must be filed in court in accordance with the time limits imposed under Rule 6 (the provisions of which shall be set out on the claim form).

History

In r.4(b)(ii) the words "under section 8 or 9A of that Act" substituted for the former words "under section 8 of that Act" by the Insolvent Companies (Disqualification of Unfit Directors) Proceedings (Amendment) Rules 2003 (SI 2003/1367) rr.1, 3, Sch. para.2(1), (2) as from June 20, 2003.

5   Service and acknowledgement

5(1)   The claim form shall be served on the defendant by sending it by first class post to his last known address; and the date of service shall, unless the contrary is shown, be deemed to be the 7th day next following that on which the claim form was posted.

5(2)   Where any process or order of the court or other document is required under proceedings subject to these Rules to be served on any person who is not in England and Wales, the court may order service on him of that process or order or other document to be effected within such time and in such manner as it thinks fit, and may also require such proof of service as it thinks fit.

5(3)   The claim form served on the defendant shall be accompanied by an acknowledgment of service as provided for by practice direction and CPR rule 8.3(2) (dealing with the contents of an acknowledgment of service) does not apply.

5(4)   The acknowledgement of service shall state that the defendant should indicate–

(a)   whether he contests the application on the grounds that, in the case of any particular company–

(i)   he was not a director or shadow director of the company at a time when conduct of his, or of other persons, in relation to that company is in question, or

(ii)   his conduct as director or shadow director of that company was not as alleged in support of the application for a disqualification order,

(b)   whether, in the case of any conduct of his, he disputes the allegation that such conduct makes him unfit to be concerned in the management of a company, and

(c)   whether he, while not resisting the application for a disqualification order, intends to adduce mitigating factors with a view to justifying only a short period of disqualification.

6 Evidence

6(1)   The defendant shall, within 28 days from the date of service of the claim form, file in court any affidavit evidence in opposition to the application he wishes the court to take into consideration and shall forthwith serve upon the claimant a copy of such evidence.

6(2)   The claimant shall, within 14 days from receiving the copy of the defendant's evidence, file in court any further evidence in reply he wishes the court to take into consideration and shall forthwith serve a copy of that evidence upon the defendant.

6(3)   CPR rules 8.5 (filing and serving written evidence) and 8.6(1) (requirements where written evidence is to be relied on) do not apply.

7 The hearing of the application

7(1)   When the claim form is issued, the court will fix a date for the first hearing of the claim which shall not be less than 8 weeks from the date of issue of the claim form.

7(2)   The hearing shall in the first instance be before the registrar in open court.

7(3)   The registrar shall either determine the case on the date fixed or adjourn it.

7(4)   The registrar shall adjourn the case for further consideration if–

(a)   he forms the provisional opinion that a disqualification order ought to be made, and that a period of disqualification longer than 5 years is appropriate, or

(b)   he is of opinion that questions of law or fact arise which are not suitable for summary determination.

7(5)   If the registrar adjourns the case for further consideration he shall–

(a)   direct whether the case is to be heard by a registrar or, if he thinks it appropriate, by the judge, for determination by him;

(b)   state the reasons for the adjournment; and

(c)   give directions as to the following matters–

    (i)   the manner in which and the time within which notice of the adjournment and the reasons for it are to be given to the defendant,

    (ii)   the filing in court and the service of further evidence (if any) by the parties,

    (iii)   such other matters as the registrar thinks necessary or expedient with a view to an expeditious disposal of the application, and

    (iv)   the time and place of the adjourned hearing.

7(6)   Where a case is adjourned other than to the judge, it may be heard by the registrar who originally dealt with the case or by another registrar.

8 Making and setting aside of disqualification order

8(1)   The court may make a disqualification order against the defendant, whether or not the latter appears, and whether or not he has completed and returned the acknowledgement of service of the claim form, or filed evidence in accordance with Rule 6.

8(2)   Any disqualification order made in the absence of the defendant may be set aside or varied by the court on such terms as it thinks just.

9   Commencement of disqualification order

9   [Revoked by Insolvent Companies (Disqualification of Unfit Directors) Proceedings (Amendment) Rules 2001 (SI 2001/765) rr.1, 2 as from April 2, 2001.]

10   Right of audience

10   Official receivers and deputy official receivers have right of audience in any proceedings to which these Rules apply, whether the application is made by the Secretary of State or by the official receiver at his direction, and whether made in the High Court or a county court.

11   Revocation and saving

11(1)   The Insolvent Companies (Disqualification of Unfit Directors) Proceedings Rules 1986 (**"the former Rules"**) are hereby revoked.

11(2)   Notwithstanding paragraph (1) the former Rules shall continue to apply and have effect in relation to any application described in paragraph 3(a) or (b) of Rule 1 of these Rules made before the date on which these Rules come into force.

Insolvency (ECSC Levy Debts) Regulations 1987

(SI 1987/2093)

Made on 1 December 1987 by the Secretary of State for Trade and Industry, for the purposes of s.2(2) of the European Communities Act 1972. Operative from 1 January 1988.

1 Citation and commencement

These Regulations, which extend to Great Britain, may be cited as the Insolvency (ECSC Levy Debts) Regulations 1987 and shall come into force on 1st January 1988.

2 Amendment of Insolvency Act 1986

2(1) Schedule 6 to the Insolvency Act 1986 is hereby amended by the insertion after paragraph 15 of the following paragraph–

[Insertion of para.15A—not reproduced here.]

2(2) Accordingly in section 386(1) of that Act (construction of references to preferential debts) after "remuneration etc. of employees" there shall be inserted ": levies on coal and steel production".

2(3) The amendment made by paragraph (1) above shall have effect in relation to a debtor whether the relevant date referred to in that amendment is a date falling before or after the commencement of these Regulations, but shall not affect any declaration or payment of a dividend made before that commencement.

3 Amendment of Bankruptcy (Scotland) Act 1985

3(1) Part I of Schedule 3 to the Bankruptcy (Scotland) Act 1985 is hereby amended by the insertion after paragraph 6 of the following paragraph–

[Insertion of para.6A—not reproduced here.]

3(2) The amendment made by paragraph (1) above shall have effect in relation to a debtor whether the relevant date referred to in that amendment is a date falling before or after the commencement of these Regulations, but shall not affect any declaration or payment of a dividend made before that commencement.

4 Preferential treatment under former law

4(1) Where the payment of preferential or preferred debts falls to be regulated by the law in force at any time before 29th December 1986, there shall be treated as included among those debts any sums due from the debtor at the relevant date in respect of–

(a) the levies on the production of coal and steel referred to in Articles 49 and 50 of the E.C.S.C. Treaty, or

(b) any surcharge for delay provided for in Article 50(3) of that Treaty and Article 6 of Decision 3/52 of the High Authority of the Coal and Steel Community.

4(2) In paragraph (1) above **"the relevant date"** means the date by reference to which the debtor's preferential or preferred debts fall to be ascertained in accordance with the law referred to in that paragraph.

Department of Trade and Industry (Fees) Order 1988

(SI 1988/93)

Made on 21 January 1988 by the Secretary of State for Trade and Industry under s.102(5) of the Finance (No.2) Act 1987. Operative from 22 January 1988.

[**Note:** Only those parts of this Order relevant to companies and insolvency have been reproduced—also relevant amendment by the Financial Services and Markets Act 2000 (Consequential Amendments and Repeals) Order 2001 (SI 2001/3649) (operative from December 1, 2001) included, without annotation.]

1 Citation and commencement

1(1) This Order may be cited as the Department of Trade and Industry (Fees) Order 1988, and shall come into force on the day after the day on which it is made.

2 Interpretation

2 In this Order–

(a) **"the Act"** means the Finance (No. 2) Act 1987;

    "the 1938 Act" means the Trade Marks Act 1938;

    "the 1949 Act" means the Registered Designs Act 1949;

    "the 1977 Act" means the Patents Act 1977;

    "the 1985 Act" means the Companies Act 1985;

    "the 1986 Act" means the Insolvency Act 1986;

    "wireless telegraphy", **"wireless telegraphy apparatus"** and **"interference"** have the meanings given to them in section 19 of the Wireless Telegraphy Act 1949;

(b) any reference to any provision of the 1985 Act includes any corresponding provision of any enactment repealed and re-enacted, with or without modification, by the 1985 Act.

3(1) In relation to the power of the Secretary of State under section 708 of the 1985 Act by regulations made by statutory instrument to require the payment to the registrar of companies of such fees as may be specified in the regulations in respect of–

(a) the performance by the registrar of such functions under 1985 Act or the 1986 Act as may be so specified, including the receipt by him of any notice or other document which under either of those Acts is required to be given, delivered, sent or forwarded to him,

(b) the inspection of documents or other material kept by him under either of those Acts,

the functions specified for the purpose of section 102(3) of the Act shall be those specified in Part I of Schedule 1 hereto.

3(2) In relation to the power of the Secretary of State specified in paragraph (1) above, the matters specified for the purposes of section 102(4) of the Act shall be those specified in Part I of Schedule 2 hereto.

4(1) In relation to the power of the Secretary of State to fix fees under sections 53(5), 54(4) and 71(2) of the 1986 Act, the functions specified for the purposes of section 102(3) of the Act shall be those specified in Part I of Schedule 1 hereto.

4(2) In relation to the power of the Secretary of State specified in paragraph (1) above, the matters specified for the purposes of section 102(4) of the Act shall be those specified in Part I of Schedule 2 hereto.

9(1) In relation to the power of the Lord Chancellor to fix fees under section 133(1) of the Bankruptcy Act 1914, section 663(4) of the 1985 Act and sections 414 and 415 of the 1986 Act and in relation to the power of the Secretary of State to fix fees under sections 4 and 10 of the Insolvency Act 1985 and sections 392, 414 and 419 of the 1986 Act, the functions specified for the purposes of section 102(3) of the Act shall be those specified in Part VI of Schedule 1 hereto.

SCHEDULE 1

PART I

1 Functions of the Secretary of State and the registrar of companies by virtue of the 1985 Act.

2 Functions of the registrar of companies by virtue of the 1986 Act.

3 Functions of inspectors appointed under Part XIV of the 1985 Act and of officers authorised under section 447 of that Act.

4 Functions of the Secretary of State in relation to anything done by the European Communities or any of their institutions with respect to company law, and the maintenance of relations with authorities and other persons both within the United Kingdom and abroad in respect of matters relating to company law.

5 Any other functions of the Secretary of State and the registrar of companies in relation to companies, including, without prejudice to the generality of the foregoing:–

    (a) prosecution of offences under the 1985 Act and the taking of action with a view to ensuring compliance with any obligation arising under the 1985 Act;

    (b) investigation of complaints relating to the conduct of the affairs of companies and consideration of requests for advice on questions of company law;

    (c) review of the functioning of company law and consideration and development of proposals for legislation relating to companies;

    (d) consideration, including in international fora, of accounting standards and auditing practices in relation to accounts of companies;

    (e) the conduct of civil proceedings in relation to any of the functions specified in this part of this Schedule.

PART VI

16 Functions of official receivers as provisional liquidators, interim receivers of a debtor's property, receivers and managers of a bankrupt's estate, liquidators, trustees in bankruptcy and in their capacity as official receivers, under the Companies Act 1948, the 1985 Act, the Bankruptcy Acts 1914 and 1926, the Powers of Criminal Courts Act 1973, the Insolvency Act 1976, the Insolvency Act 1985, the 1986 Act and the Company Directors Disqualification Act 1986 and subordinate legislation made under those enactments.

17 Functions of the Secretary of State, the Board of Trade and the Insolvency Practitioners Tribunal under Part V of the Companies Act 1948, Parts IX and XX of the 1985 Act, the Deeds of Arrangement Act 1914, the Bankruptcy Acts 1914 and 1926, the Insolvency Services (Accounting and Investment) Act 1970, the Insolvency Act 1976, the Insolvency Act 1985, the 1986 Act and the Company Directors Disqualification Act 1986 and subordinate legislation made under those enactments.

18 Functions of official receivers, the Secretary of State and the Board of Trade in relation to the investigation and prosecution of fraud or other malpractice in respect of the affairs of bankrupts and bodies in liquidation.

19 Functions of the Secretary of State in relation to the supervision of the operation of all the insolvency and related procedures set out in the Insolvency Act 1986, the Bankruptcy (Scotland) Act 1985, the other enactments set out in paragraphs 16 and 17 above and the Bankruptcy (Scotland) Act 1913, including the development and implementation of proposals for the modification or improvement of those procedures by primary or subordinate legislation and the consideration of and contribution to proposals for other United Kingdom legislation having an impact on those procedures.

20 Functions of the Secretary of State in relation to anything done by the European Communities or any of their institutions, or any international instruments, in relation to insolvency and the maintenance of relations with authorities and other persons both within the United Kingdom and abroad in respect of insolvency matters.

European Economic Interest Grouping Regulations 1989

(SI 1989/638)

Made on 10 April 1989 by the Secretary of State for Trade and Industry under s.2(2) of the European Communities Act 1972. Operative from 1 July 1989.

[**Note:** Changes made by the Companies Act 2006 (Consequential Amendments etc.) Order 2008 (SI 2008/948) and the European Economic Interest Grouping (Amendment) Regulations 2009 (SI 2009/2399) have been incorporated into the text.]

PART I

GENERAL

1 Citation, commencement and extent

1 These Regulations, which extend to the whole of the United Kingdom, may be cited as the European Economic Interest Grouping Regulations 1989 and shall come into force on 1st July 1989.

2 Interpretation

2(1) In these Regulations–

"**the 1985 Act**" means the Companies Act 1985;

"**the 2006 Act**" means the Companies Act 2006;

"**the Companies Acts**" has the meaning given by section 2 of the 2006 Act;

"**the contract**" means the contract for the formation of an EEIG;

"**the EC Regulation**" means Council Regulation (EEC) No. 2137/85 set out in Schedule 1 to these Regulations;

"**EEIG**" means a European Economic Interest Grouping being a grouping formed in pursuance of article 1 of the EC Regulation;

"**officer**", in relation to an EEIG, includes a manager, or any other person provided for in the contract as an organ of the EEIG; and

"**the registrar**" has the same meaning as in the Companies Acts (see section 1060 of the 2006 Act);

and other expressions used in these Regulations and defined for the purposes of the Companies Acts or in relation to insolvency and winding up by the Insolvency Act 1986 or, as regards Northern Ireland, by the Insolvency (Northern Ireland) Order 1989 have the meanings assigned to them by those provisions as if any reference to a company in any such definition were a reference to an EEIG.

2(2) In these Regulations a reference to any Form is a reference to that Form as set out in Schedule 2 to these Regulations.

2(3) In these Regulations, "**certified translation**" means a translation certified to be a correct translation–

(a) if the translation was made in the United Kingdom, by

(i) a notary public in any part of the United Kingdom;

(ii) a solicitor (if the translation was made in Scotland), a solicitor of the Supreme Court of Judicature of England and Wales (if it was made in England or Wales), or a solicitor of the Supreme Court of Judicature of Northern Ireland (if it was made in Northern Ireland); or

(iii) a person certified by a person mentioned above to be known to him to be competent to translate the document into English; or

(b) if the translation was made outside the United Kingdom, by–

(i) a notary public;

(ii) a person authorised in the place where the translation was made to administer an oath;

(iii) any of the British officials mentioned in section 6 of the Commissioners for Oaths Act 1889;

(iv) a person certified by a person mentioned in sub-paragraph (i), (ii) or (iii) of this paragraph to be known to him to be competent to translate the document into English.

History
Regulation 2(1) amended by the Companies Act 2006 (Consequential Amendments etc.) Order 2008 (SI 2008/948) art.161 as from April 6, 2008. Regulation 2(1), (2) amended by the European Economic Interest Grouping (Amendment) Regulations 2009 (SI 2009/2399) reg.5 as from October 1, 2009.

PART II

PROVISIONS RELATING TO ARTICLES 1–38 OF THE EC REGULATION

[Regulations 3–5 not reproduced.]

6 Cessation of membership (article 28(1) of the EC Regulation)

6 For the purposes of national law on liquidation, winding up, insolvency or cessation of payments, a member of an EEIG registered under these Regulations shall cease to be a member if–

(a) in the case of an individual–

(i) a bankruptcy order has been made against him in England and Wales or Northern Ireland; or

(ii) sequestration of his estate has been awarded by the court in Scotland under the Bankruptcy (Scotland) Act 1985;

(b) in the case of a partnership–

(i) a winding up order has been made against the partnership in England and Wales or Northern Ireland;

(ii) a bankruptcy order has been made against each of the partnership's members in England and Wales on a bankruptcy petition presented under Article 11(1) of the Insolvent Partnerships Order 1994;

(iia) a bankruptcy order has been made against each of the partnership's members in Northern Ireland on a bankruptcy petition presented under Article 11(1) of the Insolvent Partnerships Order (Northern Ireland) 1995; or

(iii) sequestration of the estate of the partnership has been awarded by the court in Scotland under the Bankruptcy (Scotland) Act 1985;

   (c)   in the case of a company, the company goes into liquidation in the United Kingdom; or

   (d)   in the case of any legal person or partnership, it is otherwise wound up or otherwise ceases to exist after the conclusion of winding up or insolvency.

History
Regulation 6(b)(ii) substituted and reg.6(b)(iia) inserted by the European Economic Interest Grouping (Amendment) Regulations 2009 (SI 2009/2399) reg.9 as from October 1, 2009.

7 Competent authority (articles 32(1) and (3) and 38 of the EC Regulation)

7(1) The competent authority for the purposes of making an application to the court under Article 32(1) of the EC Regulation (winding up of EEIG in certain circumstances) shall be–

   (a)   in the case of an EEIG whose official address is in Northern Ireland, the Department of Enterprise, Trade and Investment in Northern Ireland;

   (b)   in any other case, the Secretary of State.

7(2) The court may, on an application by the appropriate authority, order the winding up of an EEIG which has its official address in the United Kingdom, if the EEIG acts contrary to the public interest and it is expedient in the public interest that the EEIG should be wound up and the court is of the opinion that it is just and equitable for it to be so.

7(2A) In paragraph (2) above **"the appropriate authority"** means–

   (a)   in the case of an EEIG whose official address is in Great Britain, the Secretary of State;

   (b)   in the case of an EEIG whose official address is in Northern Ireland, the Department of Enterprise, Trade and Investment in Northern Ireland.

7(3) The court, on an application by the appropriate authority, shall be the competent authority for the purposes of prohibiting under article 38 of the EC Regulation any activity carried on in the United Kingdom by an EEIG where such an activity is in contravention of the public interest there.

7(4) In paragraph (3) above **"the appropriate authority"** means–

   (a)   in the case of any activity carried on in Great Britain, the Secretary of State;

   (b)   in the case of any activity carried on in Northern Ireland, the Department of Enterprise, Trade and Investment in Northern Ireland.

History
Regulation 7(1)–(3) amended and reg.7(4) inserted by the European Economic Interest Grouping (Amendment) Regulations 2009 (SI 2009/2399) reg.10 as from October 1, 2009.

8 Winding up and conclusion of liquidation (articles 35 and 36 of the EC Regulation)

8(1) Where an EEIG is wound up as an unregistered company under Part V of the Insolvency Act 1986, the provisions of Part V shall apply in relation to the EEIG as if any reference in that Act to a director or past director of a company included a reference to a manager of the EEIG and any other person who has or has had control or management of the EEIG's business and with the modification that in section 221(1) after the words "all the provisions" there shall be added the words "of Council Regulation (EEC) No. 2137/85 and".

8(1A) Where an EEIG is wound up as an unregistered company under Part 6 of the Insolvency (Northern Ireland) Order 1989, the provisions of Part 6 shall apply in relation to the EEIG as if–

(a) any reference in that Order to a director or past director of a company included a reference to a manager of the EEIG and any other person who has or has had control or management of the EEIG's business; and

(b) in Article 185(1) after "all the provisions" there were inserted "of Council Regulation (EEC) No 2137/85 and".

8(2)   At the end of the period of three months beginning with the day of receipt by the registrar of a notice of the conclusion of the liquidation of an EEIG, the EEIG shall be dissolved.

History

Regulation 8 amended by the Companies Act 2006 (Consequential Amendments etc.) Order 2008 (SI 2008/948) art.162 as from April 6, 2008. Regulation 8(1A) inserted by the European Economic Interest Grouping (Amendment) Regulations 2009 (SI 2009/2399) reg.11 as from October 1, 2009.

PART III

REGISTRATION ETC. (ARTICLE 39 OF THE EC REGULATION)

[Regulations 9–16 not reproduced.]

PART IV

SUPPLEMENTAL PROVISIONS

17   Application of the Business Names Act 1985

17   [Omitted by the European Economic Interest Grouping (Amendment) Regulations 2009 (SI 2009/2399) reg.18 as from October 1, 2009.]

18   Application of provisions of the Companies Acts

18(1)   The provisions of the Companies Acts specified in Schedule 4 to these Regulations apply to EEIGs, and their establishments, registered or in the process of being registered under these Regulations, as if they were companies formed and registered or in the process of being registered under the 2006 Act.

18(2)   The provisions applied have effect with the following adaptations–

(a) any reference to the 1985 Act, the 2006 Act or the Companies Acts includes a reference to these Regulations;

(b) any reference to a registered office includes a reference to an official address;

(ba) any reference to the register is to be read as a reference to the EEIG register;

(bb) any reference to an officer of a company is to be read as a reference to an officer of an EEIG, within the meaning of these Regulations;

(c) any reference to a daily default fine shall be omitted.

18(3)   The provisions applied also have effect subject to any limitations mentioned in relation to those provisions in that Schedule.

18(4)   In this regulation "the EEIG register" means–

(a) the documents and particulars required to be kept by the registrar under these Regulations; and

(b) the records falling within section 1080(1) of the 2006 Act which relate to EEIGs or their establishments.

18(5) This regulation does not affect the application of provisions of the Companies Acts to EEIGs or their establishments otherwise than by virtue of this regulation.

History
Regulation 18 substituted by the Companies Act 2006 (Consequential Amendments etc.) Order 2008 (SI 2008/948) art.163 as from April 6, 2008. Regulation 18(1), (2) amended and reg.18(4), (5) inserted by the European Economic Interest Grouping (Amendment) Regulations 2009 (SI 2009/2399) reg.19 as from October 1, 2009.

19 Application of insolvency legislation

19(1) Part III of the Insolvency Act 1986 shall apply to EEIGs, and their establishments, registered under these Regulations in England and Wales or Scotland, as if they were companies registered under the 2006 Act.

19(1A) Part 4 of the Insolvency (Northern Ireland) Order 1989 shall apply to EEIGs, and their establishments, registered under these Regulations in Northern Ireland, as if they were companies registered under the 2006 Act.

19(2) Section 120 of the Insolvency Act 1986 shall apply to an EEIG, and its establishments, registered under these Regulations in Scotland, as if it were a company registered in Scotland the paid-up or credited as paid-up share capital of which did not exceed £120,000 and as if in that section any reference to the Company's registered office were a reference to the official address of the EEIG.

History
Regulation 19(1) and the heading amended and reg.19(1A) inserted by the European Economic Interest Grouping (Amendment) Regulations 2009 (SI 2009/2399) reg.20 as from October 1, 2009.

20 Application of legislation relating to disqualification of directors

20(1) Where an EEIG is wound up as an unregistered company under Part V of the Insolvency Act 1986, the provisions of sections 1, 2, 4 to 7, 8, 9, 10, 11, 12(2), 15 to 17, 20 and 22 of, and Schedule 1 to, the Company Directors Disqualification Act 1986 shall apply in relation to the EEIG as if any reference to a director or past director of a company included a reference to a manager of the EEIG and any other person who has or has had control or management of the EEIG's business and the EEIG were a company as defined by section 22(2)(b) of that Act.

20(2) Where an EEIG is wound up as an unregistered company under Part 6 of the Insolvency (Northern Ireland) Order 1989 the provisions of Articles 2(2) to (6), 3, 5, 7 to 11, 13, 14, 15, 16(2), 19 to 21 and 23 of, and Schedule 1 to, the Company Directors Disqualification (Northern Ireland) Order 2002 shall apply in relation to the EEIG as if–

(a) any reference to a director or past director of a company included a reference to a manager of the EEIG and any other person who has or has had control or management of the EEIG's business; and

(b) the EEIG were a company as defined by Article 2(2) of that Order.

History
Regulation 20(1) and the heading amended and reg.20(2) inserted by the European Economic Interest Grouping (Amendment) Regulations 2009 (SI 2009/2399) reg.21 as from October 1, 2009.

21 Penalties

21 Nothing in these Regulations shall create any new criminal offence punishable to a greater extent than is permitted under paragraph 1(1)(d) of Schedule 2 to the European Communities Act 1972.

SCHEDULE 1

COUNCIL REGULATION (EEC) NO. 2137/85 OF 25TH JULY 1985 ON THE EUROPEAN ECONOMIC INTEREST GROUPING (EEIG)

Regulation 2(1)

THE COUNCIL OF THE EUROPEAN COMMUNITIES

Having regard to the Treaty establishing the European Economic Community, and in particular Article 235 thereof,

Having regard to the proposal from the Commission,

Having regard to the opinion of the European Parliament,

Having regard to the opinion of the Economic and Social Committee,

Whereas a harmonious development of economic activities and a continuous and balanced expansion throughout the Community depend on the establishment and smooth functioning of a common market offering conditions analogous to those of a national market; whereas to bring about this single market and to increase its unity a legal framework which facilitates the adaptation of their activities to the economic conditions of the Community should be created for natural persons, companies, firms and other legal bodies in particular; whereas to that end it is necessary that those natural persons, companies, firms and other legal bodies should be able to co-operate effectively across frontiers;

Whereas co-operation of this nature can encounter legal, fiscal or psychological difficulties; whereas the creation of an appropriate Community legal instrument in the form of a European Economic Interest Grouping would contribute to the achievement of the abovementioned objectives and therefore proves necessary;

Whereas the Treaty does not provide the necessary powers for the creation of such a legal instrument;

Whereas a grouping's ability to adapt to economic conditions must be guaranteed by the considerable freedom for its members in their contractual relations and the internal organisation of the grouping;

Whereas a grouping differs from a firm or company principally in its purpose, which is only to facilitate or develop the economic activities of its members to enable them to improve their own results, whereas, by reason of that ancillary nature, a grouping's activities must be related to the economic activities of its members but not replace them so that, to that extent, for example, a grouping may not itself, with regard to third parties, practise a profession, the concept of economic activities being interpreted in the widest sense;

Whereas access to grouping form must be made as widely available as possible to natural persons, companies, firms and other legal bodies, in keeping with the aims of this Regulation; whereas this Regulation shall not, however, prejudice the application at national level of legal rules and/or ethical codes concerning the conditions for the pursuit of business and professional activities;

Whereas this Regulation does not itself confer on any person the right to participate in a grouping, even where the conditions it lays down are fulfilled;

Whereas the power provided by this Regulation to prohibit or restrict participation in a grouping on grounds of public interest is without prejudice to the laws of Member States which govern the pursuit of activities and which may provide further prohibitions or restrictions or otherwise control or supervise participation in a grouping by any natural person, company, firm or other legal body or any class of them;

Whereas, to enable a grouping to achieve its purpose, it should be endowed with legal capacity and provision should be made for it to be represented *vis-à-vis* third parties by an organ legally separate from its membership;

Whereas the protection of third parties requires widespread publicity; whereas the members of a grouping have unlimited joint and several liability for the grouping's debts and other liabilities including those relating to tax or social security, without, however, that principle's affecting the freedom to exclude or restrict the liability of one or more of its members in respect of a particular debt or other liability by means of a specific contract between the grouping and a third party;

Whereas matters relating to the status or capacity of natural persons and to the capacity of legal persons are governed by national law;

Whereas the grounds for winding up which are peculiar to the grouping should be specific while referring to national law for its liquidation and the conclusion thereof;

Whereas groupings are subject to national laws relating to insolvency and cessation of payments; whereas such laws may provide other grounds for the winding up of groupings;

Whereas this Regulation provides that the profits or losses resulting from the activities of a grouping shall be taxable only in the hands of its members; whereas it is understood that otherwise national tax laws apply, particularly as regards the apportionment of profits, tax procedures and any obligations imposed by national tax law;

Whereas in matters not covered by this Regulation the laws of the Member States and Community law are applicable, for example with regard to:

(a) social and labour laws,

(b) competition law,

(c) intellectual property law;

Whereas the activities of groupings are subject to the provisions of Member States' laws on the pursuit and supervision of activities; whereas in the event of abuse or circumvention of the laws of a Member State by a grouping or its members that Member State may impose appropriate sanctions;

Whereas the Member States are free to apply or to adopt any laws, regulations or administrative measures which do not conflict with the scope or objectives of this Regulation;

Whereas this Regulation must enter into force immediately in its entirety; whereas the implementation of some provisions must nevertheless be deferred in order to allow the Member States first to set up the necessary machinery for the registration of groupings in their territories and the disclosure of certain matters relating to groupings; whereas, with effect from the date of implementation of this Regulation, groupings set up may operate without territorial restrictions,

HAS ADOPTED THIS REGULATION:

[Articles 1–14 not reproduced.]

Article 15

15(1) Where the law applicable to a grouping by virtue of Article 2 provides for the nullity of that grouping, such nullity must be established or declared by judicial decision. However, the court to which the matter is referred must, where it is possible for the affairs of the grouping to be put in order, allow time to permit that to be done.

15(2) The nullity of a grouping shall entail its liquidation in accordance with the conditions laid down in Article 35.

15(3) A decision establishing or declaring the nullity of a grouping may be relied on as against third parties in accordance with the conditions laid down in Article 9(1).

Such a decision shall not of itself affect the validity of liabilities, owed by or to a grouping, which originated before it could be relied on as against third parties in accordance with the conditions laid down in the previous subparagraph.

[Articles 16–23 not reproduced.]

Article 24

24(1) The members of a grouping shall have unlimited joint and several liability for its debts and other liabilities of whatever nature. National law shall determine the consequences of such liability.

24(2) Creditors may not proceed against a member for payment in respect of debts and other liabilities, in accordance with the conditions laid down in paragraph 1, before the liquidation of a grouping is concluded, unless they have first requested the grouping to pay and payment has not been made within an appropriate period.

[Articles 25–27 not reproduced.]

Article 28

28(1)   A member of a grouping shall cease to belong to it on death or when he no longer complies with the conditions laid down in Article 4(1).

In addition, a Member State may provide, for the purposes of its liquidation, winding up, insolvency or cessation of payments laws, that a member shall cease to be a member of any grouping at the moment determined by those laws.

28(2)   In the event of the death of a natural person who is a member of a grouping, no person may become a member in his place except under the conditions laid down in the contract for the formation of the grouping or, failing that, with the unanimous agreement of the remaining members.

[Article 29 not reproduced.]

Article 30

30   Except where the contract for the formation of a grouping provides otherwise and without prejudice to the rights acquired by a person under Articles 22(1) or 28(2), a grouping shall continue to exist for the remaining members after a member has ceased to belong to it, in accordance with the conditions laid down in the contract for the formation of the grouping or determined by unanimous decision of the members in question.

Article 31

31(1)   A grouping may be wound up by a decision of its members ordering its winding up. Such a decision shall be taken unanimously, unless otherwise laid down in the contract for the formation of the grouping.

31(2)   A grouping must be wound up by a decision of its members:

(a)   noting the expiry of the period fixed in the contract for the formation of the grouping or the existence of any other cause for winding up provided for in the contract, or

(b)   noting the accomplishment of the grouping's purpose or the impossibility of pursuing it further.

Where, three months after one of the situations referred to in the first subparagraph has occurred, a members' decision establishing the winding up of the grouping has not been taken, any member may petition the court to order winding up.

31(3)   A grouping must also be wound up by a decision of its members or of the remaining member when the conditions laid down in Article 4(2) are no longer fulfilled.

31(4)   After a grouping has been wound up by decision of its members, the manager or managers must take the steps required as listed in Articles 7 and 8. In addition, any person concerned may take those steps.

Article 32

32(1)   On application by any person concerned or by a competent authority, in the event of the infringement of Articles 3, 12 or 31(3), the court must order a grouping to be wound up, unless its affairs can be and are put in order before the court has delivered a substantive ruling.

32(2)   On application by a member, the court may order a grouping to be wound up on just and proper grounds.

32(3)   A Member State may provide that the court may, on application by a competent authority, order the winding up of a grouping which has its official address in the State to which that authority belongs, wherever the grouping acts in contravention of that State's public interest, if the law of that State provides for such a possibility in respect of registered companies or other legal bodies subject to it.

Article 33

33   When a member ceases to belong to a grouping for any reason other than the assignment of his rights in accordance with the conditions laid down in Article 22(1), the value of his rights and obligations shall be determined taking into account the assets and liabilities of the grouping as they stand when he ceases to belong to it.

   The value of the rights and obligations of a departing member may not be fixed in advance.

Article 34

34   Without prejudice to Article 37(1), any member who ceases to belong to a grouping shall remain answerable, in accordance with the conditions laid down in Article 24, for the debts and other liabilities arising out of the grouping's activities before he ceased to be a member.

Article 35

35(1)   The winding up of a grouping shall entail its liquidation.

35(2)   The liquidation of a grouping and the conclusion of its liquidation shall be governed by national law.

35(3)   A grouping shall retain its capacity, within the meaning of Article 1(2), until its liquidation is concluded.

35(4)   The liquidator or liquidators shall take the steps required as listed in Articles 7 and 8.

Article 36

36   Groupings shall be subject to national laws governing insolvency and cessation of payments. The commencement of proceedings against a grouping on grounds of its insolvency or cessation of payments shall not by itself cause the commencement of such proceedings against its members.

Article 37

37(1)   A period of limitation of five years after the publication, pursuant to Article 8, of notice of a member's ceasing to belong to a grouping shall be substituted for any longer period which may be laid down by the relevant national law for actions against that member in connection with debts and other liabilities arising out of the grouping's activities before he ceased to be a member.

37(2)   A period of limitation of five years after the publication, pursuant to Article 8, of notice of the conclusion of the liquidation of a grouping shall be substituted for any longer period which may be laid down by the relevant national law for actions against a member of the grouping in connection with debts and other liabilities arising out of the grouping's activities.

[Articles 38 and 39 not reproduced.]

Article 40

40   The profits or losses resulting from the activities of a grouping shall be taxable only in the hands of its members.

[Articles 41 and 42 not reproduced.]

Article 43

43   This Regulation shall enter into force on the third day following its publication in the *Official Journal of the European Communities*.

   It shall apply from 1 July 1989, with the exception of Articles 39, 41 and 42 which shall apply as from the entry into force of the Regulation.

   This Regulation shall be binding in its entirety and directly applicable in all Member States.

SCHEDULE 2

FORMS RELATING TO EEIGs

[Not reproduced.]

SCHEDULE 3

AUTHORISED EQUIVALENTS IN OTHER COMMUNITY OFFICIAL LANGUAGES OF "EUROPEAN ECONOMIC INTEREST GROUPING" AND "EEIG"

[Not reproduced.]

SCHEDULE 4

PROVISIONS OF COMPANIES ACTS APPLYING TO EEIGs AND THEIR ESTABLISHMENTS

Regulation 18

PART I

PROVISIONS OF COMPANIES ACT 1985

13   Part XVIII relating to floating charges and receivers (Scotland).

PART 2

PROVISIONS OF COMPANIES ACT 2006

...

26   Part 25 (company charges).

27   Section 993 (offence of fraudulent trading).

...

31   Section 1084 (records relating to companies that have been dissolved etc), as if subsection (4) were omitted.

...

37 Section 1112 (general false statement offence).

History

Schedule 4 amended by the Companies Act 2006 (Consequential Amendments etc.) Order 2008 (SI 2008/948) art.164 as from April 6, 2008. Schedule 4 amended by the European Economic Interest Grouping (Amendment) Regulations 2009 (SI 2009/2399) reg.23 as from October 1, 2009.

Insolvency Act 1986 (Guernsey) Order 1989

(SI 1989/2409)

Made on 19 December 1989 under s.442 of the Insolvency Act 1986. Operative from 1 February 1990.

1 This Order may be cited as the Insolvency Act 1986 (Guernsey) Order 1989 and shall come into force on 1st February 1990.

2 Subsections (4), (5), (10) and (11) of section 426 of the Insolvency Act 1986 shall extend to the Bailiwick of Guernsey with the modifications specified in the Schedule to this Order.

SCHEDULE

MODIFICATIONS IN THE EXTENSION OF PROVISIONS OF THE INSOLVENCY ACT 1986 TO THE BAILIWICK OF GUERNSEY

Article 2

1 Any reference to any provision of section 426 of the Insolvency Act 1986 shall be construed as a reference to that provision as it has effect in the Bailiwick of Guernsey.

2 In subsections (4) and (5), for "United Kingdom" there shall be substituted "Bailiwick of Guernsey."

3 For paragraphs (a), (b) and (c) of subsection (10) there shall be substituted the following paragraphs:

"(a) in relation to Guernsey:

    (i) Titres II to V of the Law entitled "Loi ayant rapport aux Débiteurs et à la Renonciation" of 1929;

    (ii) the Ordinance entitled "Ordonnance relative à la Renonciation" of 1929;

    (iii) articles LXXI to LXXXI of the Law entitled "Loi relative aux Sociétés Anonymes ou à Responsabilité Limitée" of 1908;

    (iv) sections 1, 3(3) and 4(2) of the Law of Property (Miscellaneous Provisions) (Guernsey) Law 1979;

    (v) the Preferred Debts (Guernsey) Law 1983;

    (vi) sections 12 and 32 to 39 of the Insurance Business (Guernsey) Law 1986;

    (vii) the rules of the customary law of Guernsey concerning persons who are unable to pay their judgment debts;

    (viii) any enactment for the time being in force in Guernsey which amends, modifies, supplements or replaces any of those rules or provisions;

(b) in relation to Alderney:

    (i) Part I of the Companies (Amendment) (Alderney) Law 1962;

    (ii) the Preferred Debts (Guernsey) Law 1983;

    (iii) sections 12, 32 to 39, 68(2) and 68(5) of the Insurance Business (Guernsey) Law 1986;

    (iv) the rules of the customary law of Alderney concerning persons who are unable to pay their judgment debts;

    (v) any enactment for the time being in force in Alderney which amends, modifies, supplements or replaces any of those rules or provisions;

(c) in relation to Sark:

    (i) the rules of the customary law of Sark concerning persons who are unable to pay their judgment debts;

(ii)   any enactment for the time being in force in Sark which amends, modifies, supplements or replaces any of those rules;"

4   For paragraphs (a) and (b) of subsection (11) there shall be substituted "the United Kingdom, the Bailiwick of Jersey or the Isle of Man".

Act of Sederunt (Applications Under Part VII of the Companies Act 1989) 1991

(SI 1991/145 (S 10))

Made on 30 January 1991 by the Lords of Council and Session under ss.32 and 34 of the Sheriff Courts (Scotland) Act 1971. Operative from 25 February 1991.

1 Citation and commencement

1(1)   This Act of Sederunt may be cited as the Act of Sederunt (Applications under Part VII of the Companies Act 1989) 1991 and shall come into force on 25th February 1991.

1(2)   This Act of Sederunt shall be inserted in the Books of Sederunt.

1(3)   In this Act of Sederunt, **"insolvency proceedings"** means proceedings commenced by a petition in accordance with rules 10 (administration orders), 15 (appointment of receiver) or 18 (winding up of a company) of the Act of Sederunt (Sheriff Court Company Insolvency Rules) 1986, a petition for sequestration under sections 5 or 6 of the Bankruptcy (Scotland) Act 1985 or a summary petition under section 11A of the Judicial Factors (Scotland) Act 1889.

2 Applications under Part VII of the Companies Act 1989

2(1)   An application for an order or direction under the provisions of the Companies Act 1989 (**"the Act"**) specified in sub-paragraph (2) below shall be made:

(a)   where there are before the sheriff insolvency proceedings to which the application relates, by note in the process of those proceedings; or

(b)   where there are no such proceedings before the sheriff, by summary application.

2(2)   The provisions of the Act referred to in sub-paragraph (1) above are–

(a)   section 161(1) (interim order in relation to party to market contract dissipating or applying assets to prevent recovery by relevant office-holder);

(b)   section 161(3) (order altering or dispensing from compliance with duties of relevant office-holder);

(c)   section 163(4) (direction that profit arising from a sum is not recoverable by relevant office-holder);

(d)   section 164(4) (direction that profit from a market contract or the amount or value of a margin is not recoverable by relevant office-holder);

(e)   section 175(2) (order to ensure that charge under a prior or *pari passu* ranked charge is not prejudiced by enforcement of market charge);

(f)   section 175(5) (direction that profit from a property disposition is not recoverable by relevant office-holder); and

(g)   section 182(4) (order to achieve same result as if provisions of Schedule 22 to the Act had been in force).

3 Intimation

3   Without prejudice to any other order in respect of intimation which the sheriff may make, he shall not make an order under section 175(2) of the Act unless intimation has been made to such persons having an interest as he considers necessary and any such person has had an opportunity to be heard.

Financial Markets and Insolvency Regulations 1991

(SI 1991/880)

Made on 27 March 1991 by the Secretary of State under ss.155(4), (5); 158(4), (5); 160(5); 173(4), (5); 174(2)–(4); 185; 186 and 187(3) of the Companies Act 1989. Operative from 25 April 1991.

[**Note:** Changes made by the Financial Markets and Insolvency (Amendment) Regulations 1992 (SI 1992/716), the Financial Services and Markets Act 2000 (Consequential Amendments and Repeals) Order 2001 (SI 2001/3649), the Enterprise Act 2002 (Insolvency) Order 2003 (SI 2003/2096) and the Financial Markets and Insolvency Regulations 2009 (SI 2009/853) have been incorporated into the text (in the case of pre-2003 legislation without annotation). References to administration petitions, orders, etc. have been adapted throughout, following the introduction of the new administration regime, pursuant to the Enterprise Act 2002 (Insolvency) Order 2003 (SI 2003/2096), as from September 15, 2003.]

ARRANGEMENT OF REGULATIONS

PART I

GENERAL

1 Citation and commencement

1 These Regulations may be cited as the Financial Markets and Insolvency Regulations 1991 and shall come into force on 25th April 1991.

2 Interpretation: general

2(1) In these Regulations **"the Act"** means the Companies Act 1989.

2(1A) In these Regulations "the Recognition Requirements Regulations" means the Financial Services and Markets Act 2000 (Recognition Requirements for Investment Exchanges and Clearing Houses) Regulations 2001.

2(2) A reference in any of these Regulations to a numbered regulation shall be construed as a reference to the regulation bearing that number in these Regulations.

2(3) A reference in any of these Regulations to a numbered paragraph shall, unless the reference is to a paragraph of a specified regulation, be construed as a reference to the paragraph bearing that number in the regulation in which the reference is made.

History
Regulation 2(1A) inserted by the Financial Markets and Insolvency Regulations 2009 (SI 2009/853) reg.3(1), (2) as from June 15, 2009.

PART II

FURTHER PROVISION AS TO MARKET CONTRACTS

3 Further provision as to market contracts

3 [Substitution of s.155(2) of the Act not reproduced here.]

PART III

INSOLVENCY PROCEEDINGS

4 Voting at meetings of creditors

4 [Insertion of s.159(4A) and amendment of s.159(5) of the Act not reproduced here.]

5 Ranking of expenses of relevant office-holder

5 [Amendment of s.160(4) of the Act not reproduced here.]

PART IV

REPORTS BY RECOGNISED OVERSEAS INVESTMENT EXCHANGE OR CLEARING HOUSE

6 Duty of recognised overseas investment exchange or clearing house to report on completion of default proceedings

6 [Amendment of s.162(1) and insertion of s.162(1A) of the Act not reproduced here.]

PART V

MARKET CHARGES

7 Interpretation of Part V

7 In this Part of these Regulations, unless the context otherwise requires–

"the Bank" means the Bank of England;

"business day" has the same meaning as in section 167(3) of the Act;

"CGO Service" means the computer-based system established by the Bank and The Stock Exchange to facilitate the transfer of specified securities;

"CGO Service charge" means a charge of the kind described in section 173(1)(c) of the Act;

"CGO Service member" means a person who is entitled by contract with CRESTCo Limited (which is now responsible for operating the CGO Service) to use the CGO Service;

"default fund contribution" has the same meaning as in section 188(3A) of the Act;

"former CGO Service member" means a person whose entitlement to use the CGO Service has been terminated or suspended;

"market charge" means a charge which is a market charge for the purposes of Part VII of the Act;

"settlement bank" means a person who has agreed under a contract with CRESTCo Limited (which is now responsible for operating the CGO Service) to make payments of the kind mentioned in section 173(1)(c) of the Act;

"specified securities" has the meaning given in section 173(3) of the Act;

"Talisman" means The Stock Exchange settlement system known as Talisman;

"Talisman charge" means a charge granted in favour of The Stock Exchange over property credited to an account within Talisman maintained in the name of the chargor in respect of certain property beneficially owned by the chargor; and

"transfer" when used in relation to specified securities has the meaning given in section 173(3) of the Act.

History
The entry for "default fund contribution" inserted by the Financial Markets and Insolvency Regulations 2009 (SI 2009/853) reg.3(1), (3) as from June 15, 2009.

8 Charges on land or any interest in land not to be treated as market charges

8(1) No charge, whether fixed or floating, shall be treated as a market charge to the extent that it is a charge on land or any interest in land.

8(2) For the purposes of paragraph (1), a charge on a debenture forming part of an issue or series shall not be treated as a charge on land or any interest in land by reason of the fact that the debenture is secured by a charge on land or any interest in land.

9 Amendments to section 173 of Act concerning certain charges granted in favour of The Stock Exchange and certain charges securing debts and liabilities arising in connection with allotment of specified securities

9 [Amendments of s.173(1)–(3) of the Act not reproduced here.]

10   Extent to which charge granted in favour of recognised investment exchange to be treated as market charge

10(1)   A charge granted in favour of a recognised investment exchange other than The Stock Exchange shall be treated as a market charge only to the extent that–

(a)   it is a charge over property provided as margin in respect of market contracts entered into by the exchange for the purposes of or in connection with the provision of clearing services or over property provided as a default fund contribution to the exchange;

(b)   in the case of a recognised UK investment exchange, it secures the obligation to pay to the exchange any sum due to the exchange from a member or designated non-member of the exchange or from a recognised clearing house or from another recognised investment exchange in respect of unsettled market contracts to which the member, designated non-member, clearing house or investment exchange is a party under the rules referred to in paragraph 12 of the Schedule to the Recognition Requirements Regulations in paragraph 9(2)(a) of Schedule 21 of the Act as it applies by virtue of paragraph 1(4) of that Schedule; and

(c)   in the case of a recognised overseas investment exchange, it secures the obligation to reimburse the cost (other than fees and other incidental expenses) incurred by the exchange in settling unsettled market contracts in respect of which the charged property is provided as margin.

10(2)   A charge granted in favour of The Stock Exchange shall be treated as a market charge only to the extent that–

(a)   it is a charge of the kind described in paragraph (1); or

(b)   it is a Talisman charge and secures an obligation of either or both of the kinds mentioned in paragraph (3).

10(3)   The obligations mentioned in this paragraph are–

(a)   the obligation of the chargor to reimburse The Stock Exchange for payments (including stamp duty and taxes but excluding Stock Exchange fees and incidental expenses arising from the operation by The Stock Exchange of settlement arrangements) made by The Stock Exchange in settling, through Talisman, market contracts entered into by the chargor; and

(b)   the obligation of the chargor to reimburse The Stock Exchange the amount of any payment it has made pursuant to a short term certificate.

10(4)   In paragraph (3) **"short term certificate"** means an instrument issued by The Stock Exchange undertaking to procure the transfer of property of a value and description specified in the instrument to or to the order of the person to whom the instrument is issued or his endorsee or to a person acting on behalf of either of them and also undertaking to make appropriate payments in cash, in the event that the obligation to procure the transfer of property cannot be discharged in whole or in part.

History
Regulation 10(1)(a), (b) amended by the Financial Markets and Insolvency Regulations 2009 (SI 2009/853) reg.3(1), (4) as from June 15, 2009.

11   Extent to which charge granted in favour of recognised clearing house to be treated as market charge

11   A charge granted in favour of a recognised clearing house shall be treated as a market charge only to the extent that–

(a)   it is a charge over property provided as margin in respect of market contracts entered into by the clearing house or over property provided as a default fund contribution to the clearing house;

(b)   in the case of a recognised UK clearing house, it secures the obligation to pay to the clearing house any sum due to the clearing house from a member of the clearing house or from a recognised investment exchange or from another recognised clearing house in respect of unsettled market contracts to which the member, clearing house or investment exchange is a party under the rules referred to in paragraph 25 of the Schedule to the Recognition Requirements Regulations; and

(c)   in the case of a recognised overseas clearing house, it secures the obligation to reimburse the cost (other than fees or other incidental expenses) incurred by the clearing house in settling unsettled market contracts in respect of which the charged property is provided as margin.

History
Regulation 11 amended by the Financial Markets and Insolvency Regulations 2009 (SI 2009/853) reg.3(1), (5) as from June 15, 2009.

12   Circumstances in which CGO Service charge to be treated as market charge

12   A CGO Service charge shall be treated as a market charge only if–

(a)   it is granted to a settlement bank by a person for the purpose of securing debts or liabilities of the kind mentioned in section 173(1)(c) of the Act incurred by that person through his use of the CGO Service as a CGO Service member; and

(b)   it contains provisions which refer expressly to the CGO Service.

13   Extent to which CGO Service charge to be treated as market charge

13   A CGO Service charge shall be treated as a market charge only to the extent that–

(a)   it is a charge over any one or more of the following–

   (i)   specified securities held within the CGO Service to the account of a CGO Service member or a former CGO Service member;

   (ii)   specified securities which were held as mentioned in sub-paragraph (i) above immediately prior to their being removed from the CGO Service consequent upon the person in question becoming a former CGO Service member;

   (iii)   sums receivable by a CGO Service member or former CGO Service member representing interest accrued on specified securities held within the CGO Service to his account or which were so held immediately prior to their being removed from the CGO Service consequent upon his becoming a former CGO Service member;

   (iv)   sums receivable by a CGO Service member or former CGO Service member in respect of the redemption or conversion of specified securities which were held within the CGO Service to his account at the time that the relevant securities were redeemed or converted or which were so held immediately prior to their being removed from the CGO Service consequent upon his becoming a former CGO Service member; and

   (v)   sums receivable by a CGO Service member or former CGO Service member in respect of the transfer by him of specified securities through the medium of the CGO Service; and

(b)   it secures the obligation of a CGO Service member or former CGO Service member to reimburse a settlement bank for the amount due from him to the settlement bank as a result of the settlement bank having discharged or become obliged to discharge payment obligations in respect of transfers or allotments of specified securities made to him through the medium of the CGO Service.

14 Limitation on disapplication of moratorium on certain legal processes under Schedule B1 to the Insolvency Act 1986 (administration) in relation to CGO Service charges

History
Heading to reg.14 substituted by the Enterprise Act 2002 (Insolvency) Order 2003 (SI 2003/2096) art.5, Sch. Pt 2 paras 47, 48(a) as from September 15, 2003 subject to transitional provision in art.6.

14(1) In this regulation **"qualifying period"** means the period beginning with the fifth business day before the day on which an application for the making of an administration order in relation to the relevant CGO Service member or former CGO Service member is presented and ending with the second business day after the day on which an administration order is made in relation to the relevant CGO Service member or former CGO service member pursuant to the petition.

14(1A) A reference in paragraph (1) to an application for an administration order shall be treated as including a reference to–

   (a) appointing an administrator under paragraph 14 or 22 of Schedule B1 to the Insolvency Act 1986, or

   (b) filing with the court a notice of intention to appoint an administrator under either of those paragraphs,

and a reference to **"an administration order"** shall include the appointment of an administrator under paragraph 14 or 22 of Schedule B1 to the Insolvency Act 1986.

14(2) The disapplication of paragraph 43(2) of Schedule B1 to the Insolvency Act 1986 (including that provisions as applied by paragraph 44 of that Schedule) by section 175(1)(a) of the Act shall be limited in respect of a CGO Service charge so that it has effect only to the extent necessary to enable there to be realised, whether through the sale of specified securities or otherwise, a sum equal to whichever is less of the following–

   (a) the total amount of payment obligations discharged by the settlement bank in respect of transfers and allotments of specified securities made during the qualifying period to the relevant CGO Service member or former CGO Service member through the medium of the CGO Service less the total amount of payment obligations discharged to the settlement bank in respect of transfers of specified securities made during the qualifying period by the relevant CGO Service member or former CGO Service member through the medium of the CGO Service; and

   (b) the amount (if any) described in regulation 13(b) due to the settlement bank from the relevant CGO Service member or former CGO Service member.

History
Regulation 14(2) amended by the Enterprise Act 2002 (Insolvency) Order 2003 (SI 2003/2096) art.5, Sch. Pt 2 paras 47, 48(d) as from September 15, 2003 subject to transitional provision in art.6.

15 Ability of administrator or receiver to recover assets in case of property subject to CGO Service charge or Talisman charge

15(1) The disapplication–

   (a) by section 175(1)(b) of the Act, of paragraphs 70, 71 and 72 of Schedule B1 to the Insolvency Act 1986, and

   (b) by section 175(3) of the Act, of sections 43 and 61 of the 1986 Act,

shall cease to have effect in respect of a charge which is either a CGO Service charge or a Talisman charge after the end of the second business day after the day on which an administration order is made or, as the case may be, an administrative receiver or a receiver is appointed, in relation to the grantor of the charge, in relation to property subject to it which–

(a) in the case of a CGO Service charge, is not, on the basis of a valuation in accordance with paragraph (2), required for the realisation of whichever is the less of the sum referred to in regulation 14(2)(a) and the amount referred to in regulation 14(2)(b) due to the settlement bank at the close of business on the second business day referred to above; and

(b) in the case of a Talisman charge is not, on the basis of a valuation in accordance with paragraph (2), required to enable The Stock Exchange to reimburse itself for any payment it has made of the kind referred to in regulation 10(3).

History
Regulation 15(1) amended by the Enterprise Act 2002 (Insolvency) Order 2003 (SI 2003/2096) art.5, Sch. Pt 2 paras 47, 49(a) as from September 15, 2003 subject to transitional provision in art.6.

15(1A) A reference in paragraph (1) to "an administration order" shall include the appointment of an administrator under paragraph 14 or 22 of Schedule B1 to the Insolvency Act 1986.

15(2) For the purposes of paragraph (1) the value of property shall, except in a case falling within paragraph (3), be such as may be agreed between whichever is relevant of the administrator, administrative receiver or receiver on the one hand and the settlement bank or The Stock Exchange on the other.

15(3) For the purposes of paragraph (1), the value of any investment for which a price for the second business day referred to above is quoted in the Daily Official List of The Stock Exchange shall–

(a) in a case in which two prices are so quoted, be an amount equal to the average of those two prices, adjusted where appropriate to take account of any accrued interest; and

(b) in a case in which one price is so quoted, be an amount equal to that price, adjusted where appropriate to take account of any accrued interest.

PART VI

CONSTRUCTION OF REFERENCES TO PARTIES TO MARKET CONTRACTS

16 Circumstances in which member or designated non-member dealing as principal to be treated as acting in different capacities

16(1) In this regulation **"relevant transaction"** means–

(a) a market contract, effected as principal by a member or designated non-member of a recognised investment exchange or a member of a recognised clearing house, in relation to which money received by the member or designated non-member is–

(i) clients' money for the purposes of rules relating to clients' money, or

(ii) would be clients' money for the purposes of those rules were it not money which, in accordance with those rules, may be regarded as immediately due and payable to the member or designated non-member for its own account; and

(b) a market contract which would be regarded as a relevant transaction by virtue of sub-paragraph (a) above were it not for the fact that no money is received by the member or designated non-member in relation to the contract.

16(1A) In addition "relevant transaction" means a market contract entered into by a recognised clearing house effected as principal in relation to which money is received by the recognised clearing house from a recognised investment exchange or from another recognised clearing house.

16(1B) In addition "relevant transaction" means a market contract entered into by a recognised investment exchange effected as principal in relation to which money is received by the recognised investment exchange from a recognised clearing house or from another recognised investment exchange.

16(1C) Where paragraph (1A) or (1B) apply paragraph (1) applies to the recognised clearing house or recognised investment exchange as it does to a member of the clearing house or investment exchange, and as if the clearing house or investment exchange were subject to the rules referred to in paragraph (1)(a)(i).

16(1D) In paragraph (1), "rules relating to clients' money" are rules made by the Financial Services Authority, in particular, under section 138 or 139 of the Financial Services and Markets Act 2000.

History
Regulation 16(1)(a) substituted, and reg.16(1A)–(1D) inserted, by the Financial Markets and Insolvency Regulations 2009 (SI 2009/853) reg.3(1), (6)(a)–(b) as from June 15, 2009.

16(2) For the purposes of section 187(1) of the Act (construction of references to parties to market contracts)–

(a) a recognised investment exchange or a member or designated non-member of a recognised investment exchange, or

(b) a recognised clearing house or a member of a recognised clearing house, shall be treated as effecting relevant transactions in a different capacity from other market contracts it has effected as principal.

History
Regulation 16(2) substituted, and former reg.16(3), (4) omitted, by the Financial Markets and Insolvency Regulations 2009 (SI 2009/853) reg.3(1), (6)(c)–(d) as from June 15, 2009.

PART VII

ADDITIONAL REQUIREMENTS FOR RECOGNITION

17 Restriction of paragraph 2 of Schedule 21 to Act

17 [Addition of Sch.21 para.2(4) to the Act not reproduced here.]

PART VIII

LEGAL PROCEEDINGS

18 Applications for order under section 175(2) of Act

18 [Amendment of s.175(2) of the Act not reproduced here.]

19 Court having jurisdiction in respect of proceedings under Part VII of Act

19(1) For the purposes of sections 161, 163, 164, 175(5) and 182 of the Act (various legal proceedings under Part VII of Act) **"the court"** shall be the court which has last heard an application in the proceedings under the Insolvency Act 1986 or the Bankruptcy (Scotland) Act 1985 in which the relevant office-holder is acting or, as the case may be, any court having jurisdiction to hear applications in those proceedings.

19(2) For the purposes of subsection (2) and (2A) of section 175 of the Act (administration orders etc.), **"the court"** shall be the court which has made the administration order or, as the case may be, to which the application for an administration order has been presented or the notice of intention to appoint has been filed.

19(3) The rules regulating the practice and procedure of the court in relation to applications to the court in England and Wales under sections 161, 163, 164, 175 and 182 of the Act shall be the rules applying in relation to applications to that court under the Insolvency Act 1986.

Act of Sederunt (Rules of the Court of Session 1994) 1994

(SI 1994/1443)

Made on 31 May 1994 by the Lords of Council and Session under s.5 of the Court of Session Act 1988 and other provisions specified in Sch.1 to this Act of Sederunt. Operative from 5 September 1994.

[**Note**: Changes made by the Act of Sederunt (Rules of the Court of Session Amendment No.5) (Insolvency Proceedings) 2003 (Scottish SI 2003/385), the Act of Sederunt (Rules of the Court of Session Amendment No.6) (Miscellaneous) 2004 (Scottish SI 2004/514), the Act of Sederunt (Rules of the Court of Session Amendment No.7) (Miscellaneous) 2005 (Scottish SI 2005/268), the Act of Sederunt (Rules of the Court of Session Amendment) (Miscellaneous) 2006 (Scottish SI 2006/83), the Act of Sederunt (Rules of the Court of Session Amendment No.2) (UNCITRAL Model Law on Cross-Border Insolvency) 2006 (Scottish SI 2006/199), the Act of Sederunt (Rules of the Court of Session Amendment No.8) (Miscellaneous) 2007 (SSI 2007/449) and the Act of Sederunt (Rules of the Court of Session Amendment No.9) (Miscellaneous) 2009 (SSI 2009/450) have been incorporated into the text. References to administration petitions, orders, etc. have been adapted throughout, following the introduction of the new administration regime, pursuant to the Enterprise Act 2002 (Insolvency) Order 2003 (SI 2003/2096), as from September 15, 2003. Amendments dealing with the special administration regime for insolvent banks and building societies have been omitted.]

SCHEDULE 2

THE RULES OF THE COURT OF SESSION 1994

Paragraph 2

PRELIMINARY

CHAPTER 1

CITATION, APPLICATION, ETC.

1.1 Citation

1.1 These Rules may be cited as the Rules of the Court of Session 1994.

1.2 Application

1.2 These Rules apply to any cause whether initiated before or after the coming into force of these Rules.

1.3 Interpretation etc.

1.3(1) In these Rules, unless the context otherwise requires–

"**the Act of 1988**" means the Court of Session Act 1988;

"**act**" means an order of the court which is extractable, other than a decree;

"**agent**", except in rule 16.2(2)(e) (service furth of United Kingdom by party's authorised agent) and rule 16.14(1) (arrestment of cargo), means a solicitor or person having a right to conduct the litigation:

"**the Auditor**" means the Auditor of the Court of Session;

"**cause**" means any proceedings;

"**clerk of court**" means the clerk of session acting as such;

"**clerk of session**" means a depute clerk of session or an assistant clerk of session, as the case may be;

"counsel" means a practising member of the Faculty of Advocates;

"depute clerk of session" means a depute clerk of session and justiciary;

"Deputy Principal Clerk" means the Deputy Principal Clerk of Session;

"document" has the meaning assigned to it in section 9 of the Civil Evidence (Scotland) Act 1988;

"the Extractor" means the Extractor of the Court of Session or the Extractor of the acts and decrees of the Teind Court, as the case may be;

"Keeper of the Records" means the Keeper of the Records of Scotland;

"Keeper of the Registers" means the Keeper of the Registers of Scotland;

"other person having a right of audience" means a person having a right of audience before the court by virtue of Part II of the Law Reform (Miscellaneous Provisions) (Scotland) Act 1990 (legal services) in respect of the category and nature of the cause in question;

"party" means a person who has entered appearance in an action or lodged a writ in the process of a cause (other than a minuter seeking leave to be sisted to a cause); and

"parties" shall be construed accordingly;

"period of notice" means–

(a) in relation to service, or intimation on a warrant for intimation before calling, of a summons, the period determined in accordance with rule 13.4 (period of notice in summonses); and

(b) in relation to service of any other writ, intimation of a writ other than intimation referred to in sub-paragraph (a), or the period for lodging answers to a writ, the period determined in accordance with rule 14.6 (period of notice for lodging answers);

"person having a right to conduct the litigation" means a person having a right to conduct litigation by virtue of Part II of the Law Reform (Miscellaneous Provisions) (Scotland) Act 1990 in respect of the category and nature of the cause in question;

"Principal Clerk" means the Principal Clerk of Session and Justiciary;

"principal writ" means the writ by which a cause is initiated before the court;

"proof" includes proof before answer;

"rolls" means the lists of the business of the court issued from time to time by the Keeper of the Rolls;

"send" includes deliver; and **"sent"** shall be construed accordingly;

"step of process" means a document lodged in process other than a production;

"summons" includes the condescendence and pleas-in-law annexed to it;

"vacation judge" means a judge of the court sitting as such in vacation;

"writ" means summons, petition, note, application, appeal, minute, defences, answers, counterclaim, issue or counter-issue, as the case may be.

1.3(2)   for the purpose of these Rules–

(a) **"affidavit"** includes an affirmation and a statutory or other declaration; and

(b) an affidavit shall be sworn or affirmed before a notary public or any other competent authority.

1.3(3)   Where a power is conferred in these Rules on the Lord President to make directions, the power may be exercised in his absence by the Lord Justice-Clerk.

1.3(4)   Where a provision in these Rules imposes an obligation on a principal officer, the obligation may be performed by a clerk of session authorised by him or by another principal officer; and in this paragraph

"principal officer" means the Principal Clerk, Deputy Principal Clerk, Deputy Principal Clerk (Administration), Keeper of the Rolls or Principal Extractor.

1.3(5) Unless the context otherwise requires, where a provision in these Rules requires a party to intimate, give written intimation, or send a document, to another party, it shall be sufficient compliance with that provision if intimation is given or the document is sent, as the case may be, to the agent acting in the cause for that party.

1.3(6) Unless the context otherwise requires, anything done or required to be done by a party under a provision in these Rules may be done by the agent for that party acting on his behalf.

1.3(7) Where a provision in these Rules requires a document to be lodged in an office or department of the Office of Court within or not later than a specified period and the last day of that period is a day on which that office or department is closed, the period shall be extended to include the next day on which that office or department, as the case may be, is open or on such other day as may be specified in a notice published in the rolls.

1.3(8) Unless the context otherwise requires, a reference to a specified Chapter, Part, rule or form is a reference to the Chapter, Part, rule, or the form in the appendix, so specified in these Rules; and a reference to a specified paragraph, sub-paragraph or head is a reference to that paragraph of the rule or form, that sub-paragraph of the paragraph or that head of the sub-paragraph, in which the reference occurs.

1.4 Forms

1.4 Where there is a reference to the use of a form in these Rules, that form in the appendix to these Rules, or a form substantially to the same effect, shall be used with such variation as circumstances may require.

1.5 Direction relating to Advocate General

1.5 The Lord President may, by direction, specify such arrangements as he considers necessary for, or in connection with, the appearance in court of the Advocate General for Scotland.

SPECIAL PROVISIONS IN RELATION TO PARTICULAR PROCEEDINGS

PART XIII

UNCITRAL MODEL LAW ON CROSS-BORDER INSOLVENCY

62.90 Application and interpretation of this Part

62.90(1) This Part applies to applications under the Model Law and applications under the Scottish Provisions.

62.90(2) In this Part—

"application for an interim remedy" means an application under article 19 of the Model Law for an interim remedy by a foreign representative;

"former representative" means a foreign representative who has died or who for any other reason has ceased to be the foreign representative in the foreign proceeding in relation to the debtor;

"main proceeding" means proceedings opened in accordance with Article 3(1) of the EC Insolvency Regulation and falling within the definition of insolvency proceedings in Article 2(a) of the EC Insolvency Regulation;

"the Model Law" means the UNCITRAL Model Law on Cross-Border Insolvency as set out in Schedule 1 to the Cross-Border Insolvency Regulations 2006;

"modification or termination order" means an order by the court pursuant to its powers under the Model Law modifying or terminating recognition of a foreign proceeding, the restraint, sist and suspension referred to in article 20(1) of the Model Law or any part of it or any remedy granted under article 19 or 21 of the Model Law;

"recognition application" means an application by a foreign representative in accordance with article 15 of the Model Law for an order recognising the foreign proceeding in which he has been appointed;

"recognition order" means an order by the court recognising a proceeding as a foreign main proceeding or a foreign non-main proceeding, as appropriate;

"review application" means an application to the court for a modification or termination order;

"the Scottish Provisions" are the provisions of Schedule 3 to the Cross-Border Insolvency Regulations 2006; and

words and phrases defined in the Model Law have the same meaning when used in this Part.

62.90(3)   References in this Part to a debtor who is of interest to the Financial Services Authority are references to a debtor who–

(a)   is, or has been, an authorised person within the meaning of section 31 of the Financial Services and Markets Act 2000 (authorised persons);

(b)   is, or has been, an appointed representative within the meaning of section 39 (exemption of appointed representatives) of that Act; or

(c)   is carrying on, or has carried on, a regulated activity in contravention of the general prohibition.

62.90(4)   In paragraph (3) **"the general prohibition"** has the meaning given by section 19 of the Financial Services and Markets Act 2000 and the reference to **"regulated activity"** shall be construed in accordance with–

(a)   section 22 of that Act (classes of regulated activity and categories of investment);

(b)   any relevant order under that section; and

(c)   Schedule 2 to that Act (regulated activities).

History
See note after r.62.96.

62.91   General

62.91(1)   Rule 62.1 (disapplication of certain rules to Chapter 62) shall not apply to an application to which this Part relates.

62.91(2)   Unless otherwise specified in this Part, an application under the Model Law or the Scottish Provisions shall be made by petition.

62.91(3)   For the purposes of the application of rule 14.5(1) (first order for intimation, service and advertisement) to a petition under this Part, where necessary, the petitioner shall seek an order for service of the petition on:–

(a)   the foreign representative;

(b)   the debtor;

(c)   any British insolvency officeholder acting in relation to the debtor;

(d)   any person appointed an administrative receiver of the debtor or as a receiver or manager of the property of the debtor in Scotland;

(e)   any member State liquidator who has been appointed in main proceedings in relation to the debtor;

(f)   any foreign representative who has been appointed in any other foreign proceeding regarding the debtor;

(g)   if there is pending in Scotland a petition for the winding up or sequestration of the debtor, the petitioner in those proceedings;

(h)   any person who is or may be entitled to appoint an administrator of the debtor under paragraph 14 of Schedule B1 to the Insolvency Act 1986 (appointment of administrator by holder of qualifying floating charge); and

(i)   the Financial Services Authority if the debtor is a debtor who is of interest to that Authority.

62.91(4)   On the making of–

(a)   a recognition order;

(b)   an order granting an interim remedy under article 19 of the Model Law;

(c)   an order granting a remedy under article 21 of the Model Law;

(d)   an order confirming the status of a replacement foreign representative; or

(e)   a modification or termination order,

the Deputy Principal Clerk shall send a certified copy of the interlocutor to the foreign representative.

History
See note after r.62.96.

62.92   Recognition application

62.92(1)   A petition containing a recognition application shall include averments as to–

(a)   the name of the applicant and his address for service in Scotland;

(b)   the name of the debtor in respect of which the foreign proceeding is taking place;

(c)   the name or names in which the debtor carries on business in the country where the foreign proceeding is taking place and in this country, if other than the name given under sub-paragraph (b);

(d)   the principal or last known place of business of the debtor in Great Britain (if any) and, in the case of an individual, his last known place of residence in Great Britain, (if any);

(e)   any registered number allocated to the debtor under the Companies Act 2006;

(f)   the foreign proceeding in respect of which recognition is applied for, including the country in which it is taking place and the nature of the proceeding;

(g)   whether the foreign proceeding is a proceeding within the meaning of article 2(i) of the Model Law;

(h)   whether the applicant is a foreign representative within the meaning of article 2(j) of the Model Law;

(i)   the address of the debtor's centre of main interests and, if different, the address of its registered office or habitual residence as appropriate;

(j)   if the debtor does not have its centre of main interests in the country where the foreign proceeding is taking place, whether the debtor has an establishment within the meaning of article 2(e) of the Model Law in that country, and if so, its address.

62.92(3)   There shall be lodged with the petition–

(a)   an affidavit sworn by the foreign representative as to the matters averred under paragraph (2);

(b) the evidence and statement required under article 15(2) and (3) respectively of the Model Law;

(c) any other evidence which in the opinion of the applicant will assist the court in deciding whether the proceeding in respect of which the application is made is a foreign proceeding within the meaning of article 2(i) of the Model Law and whether the applicant is a foreign representative within the meaning of article 2(j) of the Model Law; and

(d) evidence that the debtor has its centre of main interests or an establishment, as the case may be, within the country where the foreign proceeding is taking place.

62.92(4) The affidavit to be lodged under paragraph (3)(a) shall state whether, in the opinion of the applicant, the EC Insolvency Regulation applies to any of the proceedings identified in accordance with article 15(3) of the Model Law and, if so, whether those proceedings are main proceedings, secondary proceedings or territorial proceedings.

62.92(5) Any subsequent information required to be given to the court by the foreign representative under article 18 of the Model Law shall be given by amendment of the petition.

History
See note after r.62.96. There appears to be no para.2. The reference to para.(2) in para.(3) should obviously to para.(1).

62.93 Application for interim remedy

62.93(1) An application for an interim remedy shall be made by note in process.

62.93(2) There shall be lodged with the note an affidavit sworn by the foreign representative stating–

(a) the grounds on which it is proposed that the interim remedy applied for should be granted;

(b) the details of any proceeding under British insolvency law taking place in relation to the debtor;

(c) whether to the foreign representative's knowledge, an administrative receiver or receiver or manager of the debtor's property is acting in relation to the debtor;

(d) an estimate of the assets of the debtor in Scotland in respect of which the remedy is applied for;

(e) all other matters that would in the opinion of the foreign representative assist the court in deciding whether or not to grant the remedy applied for, including whether, to the best of the knowledge and belief of the foreign representative, the interests of the debtor's creditors (including any secured creditors or parties to hire-purchase agreements) and any other interested parties, including if appropriate the debtor, are adequately protected; and

(f) whether to the best of the foreign representative's knowledge and belief, the grant of any of the remedy applied for would interfere with the administration of the foreign main proceeding.

History
See note after r.62.96.

62.94 Application for remedy

62.94(1) An application under article 21 of the Model Law for a remedy shall be made by note in process.

62.94(2) There shall be lodged with the note an affidavit sworn by the foreign representative stating–

(a) the grounds on which it is proposed that the remedy applied for should be granted;

(b) an estimate of the value of the assets of the debtor in Scotland in respect of which the remedy is requested;

(c) in the case of an application by a foreign representative who is or believes that he is a representative of a foreign non-main proceeding, the reasons why the applicant believes that the remedy relates to assets that, under the law of Great Britain, should be administered in the foreign non-main proceeding or concerns information required in that proceeding; and

(d) all other matters that would in the opinion of the foreign representative assist the court in deciding whether or not it is appropriate to grant the remedy requested, including whether, to the best of the knowledge and belief of the foreign representative, the interests of the debtor's creditors (including any secured creditors or parties to hire-purchase agreements) and any other interested parties, including if appropriate the debtor, are adequately protected.

History
See note after r.62.96.

62.95   Application for confirmation of status of replacement foreign representative

62.95(1)   An application under paragraph 2(3) of the Scottish Provisions for an order confirming the status of a replacement foreign representative shall be made by note in process.

62.95(2)   The note shall include averments as to–

(a) the name of the replacement foreign representative and his address for service within Scotland;

(b) the circumstances in which the former foreign representative ceased to be foreign representative in the foreign proceeding in relation to the debtor (including the date on which he ceased to be the foreign representative);

(c) his own appointment as replacement foreign representative in the foreign proceeding (including the date of that appointment).

62.95(3)   There shall be lodged with the note–

(a) an affidavit sworn by the foreign representative as to the matters averred under paragraph (2);

(b) a certificate from the foreign court affirming–

     (i) the cessation of the appointment of the former foreign representative as foreign representative, and

     (ii) the appointment of the applicant as the foreign representative in the foreign proceeding, or

(c) in the absence of such a certificate, any other evidence acceptable to the court of the matters referred to in sub-paragraph (a).

History
See note after r.62.96.

62.96   Review application

62.96(1)   A review application shall be made by note in process.

62.96(2)   There shall be lodged with the note an affidavit sworn by the applicant as to–

(a) the grounds on which it is proposed that the remedy applied for should be granted; and

(b) all other matters that would in the opinion of the applicant assist the court in deciding whether or not it is appropriate to grant the remedy requested, including whether, to the best of the knowledge and belief of the applicant, the interests of the debtor's creditors (including any secured creditors or parties to hire-purchase agreements) and any other interested parties, including if appropriate the debtor, are adequately protected.

History
Rules 62.90 to 62.96 inserted by the Act of Sederunt ((Rules of the Court of Session Amendment No.2) (UNCITRAL Model Law on Cross-Border Insolvency) 2006 (Scottish SI 2006/199, effective April 6, 2006), to take account of the adoption by the UK of the UNCITRAL Model Law.

CHAPTER 74

COMPANIES

PART I

GENERAL PROVISIONS

74.1 Application and interpretation of this Chapter

74.1(1) This Chapter applies to causes under–

(a) the Insolvency Act 1986; and

(b) the Company Directors Disqualification Act 1986; and

(c) Chapter 3 of Part 3 of the Energy Act 2004.

74.1(2) In this Chapter–

"the Act of 1986" means the Insolvency Act 1986;

"the Act of 2004" means the Energy Act 2004;

"the Insolvency Rules" means the Insolvency (Scotland) Rules 1986;

"the Energy Administration Rules" means the Energy Administration (Scotland) Rules 2006;

"the Council Regulation" means Council Regulation (E.C.) No. 1346/2000 of 29th May 2000 on insolvency proceedings as it may be amended from time to time;

"centre of main interests" has the same meaning as in the Council Regulation;

"establishment" has the same meaning as in Article 2(h) of the Council Regulation;

"main proceedings" means proceedings opened in accordance with Article 3(1) of the Council Regulation and falling within the definition of insolvency proceedings in Article 2(a) of the Council Regulation and—

(a) in relation to England and Wales and Scotland, set out in Annex A to the Council Regulation under the heading "United Kingdom"; and

(b) in relation to another Member State, set out in Annex A to the Council Regulation under the heading relating to that Member State;

"Member State" means a Member State of the European Community that has adopted the Council Regulation;

"non GB Company" shall have the meaning assigned in section 171 of the Act of 2004;

"registered office" means–

(i) the place specified in the statement of the company delivered to the register of companies under section 9 of the Companies Act 2006 as the intended place of its registered office on incorporation, or

(ii) where notice has been given by the company to the registrar of companies under section 87 of the Companies Act 2006 of a change of registered office, the place specified in the last such notice;

"territorial proceedings" means proceedings opened in accordance with Article 3(2) and 3(4) of the Council Regulation and falling within the definition of insolvency proceedings in Article 2(a) of the Council Regulation and–

(a)   in relation to England and Wales and Scotland, set out in Annex A to the Council Regulation under the heading "United Kingdom"; and

(b)   in relation to another Member State, set out in Annex A to the Council Regulation under the heading relating to that Member State.

74.1(3)   Unless the context otherwise requires, words and expressions used in this Chapter which are also used in the Act of 1986, Chapter 3 of Part 3 of the Act of 2004, the Insolvency Rules or the Energy Administration Rules have the same meaning as in that Act or those Rules, as the case may be.

History
Rule 74.1(1)(c) and the definitions of "the Act of 2004", "the Energy Administration Rules" and "non GB company" inserted, and r.74.1(3) substituted, by the Act of Sederunt (Rules of the Court of Session Amendment) (Miscellaneous) 2006 (Scottish SI 2006/83) r.2(9), as from March 17, 2006.
   The definitions from "the Council Regulation" to "Member State" and of "territorial proceedings" inserted by the Act of Sederunt (Rules of the Court of Session Amendment No.8) (Miscellaneous) 2007 (SSI 2007/449) r.8 as from October 25, 2007.

74.2   Proceedings before insolvency judge

74.2   All proceedings in the Outer House in a cause under or by virtue of the Act of 1986, the Company Directors Disqualification Act 1986 or Chapter 3 of Part 3 of the Act of 2004, shall be brought before a judge of the court nominated by the Lord President as the insolvency judge or, where the insolvency judge is not available, any other judge of the court (including the vacation judge): and **"insolvency judge"** shall be construed accordingly.

74.3   Notices and reports, etc., sent to the court

74.3   Where, under the Act of 1986, the Act of 2004, the Insolvency Rules or the Energy Administration Rules–

(a)   notice of a fact is to be given to the court,

(b)   a report is to be made, or sent, to the court, or

(c)   any other document is to be sent to the court,

it shall be sent to the Deputy Principal Clerk who shall cause it to be lodged in the process to which it relates.

History
Rules 74.2, 74.3 substituted by the Act of Sederunt (Rules of the Court of Session Amendment) (Miscellaneous) 2006 (Scottish SI 2006/83) r.2(9), as from March 17, 2006.

PART II

COMPANY VOLUNTARY ARRANGEMENTS

74.4   Lodging of nominee's report (company not in liquidation etc.)

74.4(1)   This rule applies where the company is not being wound up by the court and is not in administration.

74.4(2)   A report of a nominee submitted to the court under section 2(2) of the Act of 1986 (procedure where nominee is not the liquidator or administrator) shall be–

(a)   lodged, with a covering letter, in the Petition Department;

(b)   marked by the clerk of session receiving it with the date on which it is received; and

(c)   placed before the insolvency judge for consideration of any direction which he may make under section 3(1) of that Act (which relates to the summoning of meetings).

74.4(3)   An application by a nominee to extend the time within which he may submit his report under section 2(2) of the Act of 1986 shall be made by letter addressed to the Deputy Principal Clerk who shall–

(a)   place the letter before the insolvency judge for determination:

(b)   intimate that determination by a written reply; and

(c)   attach the letter, and a copy of the reply, to the nominee's report when it is subsequently lodged.

74.5   Lodging of nominee's report (company in liquidation etc.)

74.5(1)   This rule applies where the company is being wound up by the court or is in administration.

74.5(2)   In this rule, **"process"** means the process of the petition under section 9 (petition for administration order), or section 124 (petition to wind up a company), of the Act of 1986, as the case may be.

74.5(3)   A report of a nominee submitted to the court under section 2(2) of the Act of 1986 (procedure where nominee is not the liquidator or administrator) shall be–

(a)   lodged in process; and

(b)   placed before the insolvency judge for consideration of any direction which he may make under section 3(1) of that Act.

74.5(4)   An application by a nominee to extend the time within which he may submit his report under section 2(2) of the Act of 1986 shall be made by letter addressed to the Deputy Principal Clerk who shall–

(a)   place the letter before the insolvency judge for determination;

(b)   intimate that determination by a written reply; and

(c)   lodge the letter, and a copy of the reply, in the process of the petition to which it relates.

74.6   Inspection of nominee's report

74.6   A person who states in a letter addressed to the Deputy Principal Clerk that he is a creditor, member or director of the company or his agent, may, on payment of the appropriate fee, inspect the nominee's report lodged under rule 74.4(2) (company not in liquidation etc.) 74.5(3) (company in liquidation etc.), as the case may be.

74.7   Report of meetings to approve arrangement

74.7   The report of the result of a meeting to be sent to the court under section 4(6) of the Act of 1986 shall be sent to the Deputy Principal Clerk who shall lodge it–

(a)   in a case to which rule 74.4 (lodging of nominee's report (company not in liquidation etc.)) applies, with the nominee's report lodged under that rule; or

(b)   in a case to which rule 74.5 (lodging of nominee's report (company in liquidation etc.)) applies, in process as defined by paragraph (2) of that rule.

74.8   Abstracts of supervisor's receipts and payments and notices of completion of arrangement

74.8   An abstract of receipts and payments prepared by a supervisor and sent to the court under rule 1.21(2) of the Insolvency Rules or a notice of completion of the arrangement (and a copy of the supervisor's report) to be sent to the court under rule 1.23(3) of those Rules shall be sent to the Deputy Principal Clerk who shall cause it to be lodged–

(a)   in a case to which rule 74.4 (lodging of nominee's report (company not in liquidation etc.)) applies, with the nominee's report lodged under that rule; or

(b)   in a case to which rule 74.5 (lodging of nominee's report (company in liquidation etc.)) applies, in process as defined by paragraph (2) of that rule.

74.9   Form of other applications

74.9(1)   An application to which this rule applies shall be made–

(a)   where the company is not being wound up by the court and is not in administration, by petition; or

(b)   where the company is being wound up by the court or is in administration, by note in the process to which it relates.

74.9(2)   This rule applies to an application under–

(a)   section 2(4) of the Act of 1986 (for the replacement of a nominee);

(b)   section 6 of that Act (to challenge a decision made in relation to an arrangement);

(c)   section 7(3) of that Act (to challenge the actings of a supervisor);

(d)   section 7(4)(a) of that Act (by a supervisor for directions);

(e)   section 7(5) of that Act (for the appointment of a supervisor);

(f)   rule 1.21(5) of the Insolvency Rules (to dispense with sending abstracts or reports or to vary the dates on which the obligation to send abstracts or reports arises);

(g)   rule 1.23(4) of those Rules (to extend the period for sending a notice of implementation of arrangement or report); or

(h)   any other provision in the Act of 1986 or the Insolvency Rules relating to company voluntary arrangements not mentioned in this Part.

PART III

ADMINISTRATION PROCEDURE

74.10   Form of petition in administration procedure

74.10(1)   In this Part, **"the petition"** means a petition under section 9 of, or section 8 of and Schedule B1 to, the Act of 1986 (petition for administration order), or section 156 of the Act of 2004 (petition for energy administration order).

74.10(2)   The petition shall include averments in relation to–

(a)   the petitioner and the capacity in which he presents the petition, if other than the company;

(b)   whether it is believed that the company is, or is likely to become, unable to pay its debts and the grounds of that belief;

(c)   in the case of a petition under the Act of 1986, how the making of that order will achieve–

(i)   any of the purposes specified in section 8(3) of the Act of 1986; or

(ii)   an objective specified in paragraph 3 of Schedule B1 to the Act of 1986;

(d)   the company's financial position specifying, so far as known, assets and liabilities, including contingent and prospective liabilities;

746

(e)   any security known or believed to be held by creditors of the company, whether in any case the security confers power on the holder to appoint a receiver or an administrator, and whether a receiver or an administrator, as the case may be, has been appointed;

(f)   so far as known to the petitioner, whether any steps have been taken for the winding up of the company;

(g)   other matters which, in the opinion of the petitioner, will assist the court in deciding whether to grant an order in respect of an administration or an energy administration, as the case may be;

(h)   [Omitted.]

(i)   the name and address of the person proposed to be appointed, and his qualification to act, as administrator or an energy administrator, as the case may be; and

(j)   in the case of a petition under the Act of 1986, jurisdiction under the Council Regulation, in particular stating, so far as known to the petitioner–

   (i)   where the centre of main interests of the company is and whether the company has any other establishments in another Member State; and

   (ii)   whether there are insolvency proceedings elsewhere in respect of the company and whether those proceedings are main or territorial proceedings;

(k)   whether the Secretary of State has certified the case as one in which he considers it would be appropriate for him to petition under section 124A of the Act of 1986 (petition for winding up on grounds of public interest);

(l)   so far as known to the petitioner in a petition for an energy administration order, whether any steps have been taken for an administration order under Schedule B1 to the Act of 1986;

(m)   whether a protected energy company in a petition for an energy administration order is a non GB company.

74.10(3)   [Omitted.]

History
Rule 74.10(1)(c) substituted by the Act of Sederunt (Rules of the Court of Session Amendment No.5) (Insolvency Proceedings) 2003 (Scottish SI 2003/385) rr.2(1), (7)(b)(i) as from September 15, 2003.
   Rule 74.10(1) substituted r.74.10(2)(c), (e), (g), (i), (j) amended, r.74.10(2)(h) and 74.10(3) omitted, and r.74.10(2)k)–(m) inserted, by the Act of Sederunt (Rules of the Court of Session Amendment) (Miscellaneous) 2006 (Scottish SI 2006/83) r.2(9), as from March 17, 2006.
   Rule 74.10(2)(j) substituted by the Act of Sederunt (Rules of the Court of Session Amendment No.8) (Miscellaneous) 2007 (SSI 2007/449) r.9 as from October 25, 2007.

74.10A   Interim orders

74.10A(1)   On making an interim order under paragraph 13(1)(d) of Schedule B1 to the Act of 1986 or section 157(1)(d) of the Act of 2004, the Lord Ordinary shall fix a hearing on the By Order Roll for a date after the expiry of the period of notice mentioned in rule 14.6 (period of notice for lodging answers).

74.10A(2)   At the hearing under paragraph (1) the Lord Ordinary shall make such order as to further procedure as he thinks fit.

History
Rule 74.10A inserted by the Act of Sederunt (Rules of the Court of Session Amendment No.7) (Miscellaneous) 2005 (Scottish SI 2005/268) r.2(1), (9) as from June 7, 2005.
   Rule 74.10A(1) amended by the Act of Sederunt (Rules of the Court of Session Amendment) (Miscellaneous) 2006 (Scottish SI 2006/83) r.2(9), as from March 17, 2006.

74.11   Notice of petition

74.11   Where–

(a)   the petition is to be served on a person mentioned in rule 2.3 of the Insolvency Rules, and

(b)   by virtue of paragraph (2) of that rule, notice requires to be given to that person, or,

(c)   the petition and a notice are to be served on a person mentioned in section 156(2)(a) to (c) of the Act of 2004 (notice of application for energy administration order) or rule 5(1) of the Energy Administration Rules,

it shall be sufficient for the petitioner, where such notice and service is to be executed by post, to enclose the statutory notice and a copy of the petition in one envelope and to certify the giving of such notice and the execution of such service by one certificate.

History
In r.74.11(a) the words "rule 2.3" substituted for the former words "rule 2.2" by the Act of Sederunt (Rules of the Court of Session Amendment No.5) (Insolvency Proceedings) 2003 (Scottish SI 2003/385) r.2(1), (8) as from September 15, 2003.
   Rule 74.11(c) inserted by the Act of Sederunt (Rules of the Court of Session Amendment) (Miscellaneous) 2006 (Scottish SI 2006/83) r.2(9), as from March 17, 2006.

74.12   Report of proposals of administrator

74.12(1)   A report of the meeting to approve the proposals of the administrator to be sent to the court under section 24(4) of the Act of 1986 shall be sent to the Deputy Principal Clerk of Session, who shall–

(a)   cause it to be lodged in the process of the petition to which it relates; and

(b)   give written intimation to the parties of the receipt and lodging of the report.

74.12(2)   Where a report under section 24(4) of the Act of 1986 discloses that the meeting has declined to approve the proposals of the administrator, the Keeper of the Rolls shall put the cause out on the By Order Roll for determination by the insolvency judge for any order he may make under section 24(5) of that Act.

74.13   Report of administrator's proposals: Schedule B1 to the Act of 1986

74.13(1)   Paragraph (2) shall apply where a report under paragraphs 53(2) or 54(6) of Schedule B1 to the Act of 1986 discloses a failure to approve, or to approve a revision of, an administrator's proposals.

74.13(2)   The Deputy Principal Clerk shall fix a hearing for determination by the insolvency judge of any order that may be made under paragraph 55(2) of Schedule B1 to the Act of 1986.

History
Rule 74.13 substituted by the Act of Sederunt (Rules of the Court of Session Amendment No.5) (Insolvency Proceedings) 2003 (Scottish SI 2003/385) r.2(1), (9) as from September 15, 2003.

74.14   Time and date of lodging in an administration or energy administration

74.14(1)   The time and date of lodging of a notice or document relating to an administration under the Act of 1986 or the Insolvency Rules, or an energy administration under the Act of 2004 or the Energy Administration Rules, shall be noted by the Deputy Principal Clerk upon the notice or document.

74.14(2)   Subject to any provision in the Insolvency Rules or the Energy Administration Rules, as the case may be–

(a)   where the time of lodging of a notice or document cannot be ascertained by the Deputy Principal Clerk, the notice or document shall be deemed to be lodged at 10 a.m. on the date of lodging; and

(b) where a notice or document under paragraph (1) is delivered on any day other than a business day, the date of lodging shall be the first business day after such delivery.

History
Rule 74.14 substituted by the Act of Sederunt (Rules of the Court of Session Amendment) (Miscellaneous) 2006 (Scottish SI 2006/83) r.2(9), as from March 17, 2006.

74.15 Applications during an administration or energy administration

74.15 An application or appeal under any provision of the Act of 1986, the Insolvency Rules, the Act of 2004 or the Energy Administration Rules during an administration or energy administration, as the case may be, shall be–

(a) where no previous application or appeal has been made, by petition; or

(b) where a petition for an order in respect of an administration, or energy administration, as the case may be, has been lodged, by note in the process of that petition.

History
Rule 74.15 substituted by the Act of Sederunt (Rules of the Court of Session Amendment) (Miscellaneous) 2006 (Scottish SI 2006/83) r.2(9), as from March 17, 2006.

PART IV

RECEIVERS

74.16 Interpretation of this Part

74.16 In this Part, **"the petition"** means a petition under section 54(1) of the Act of 1986 (petition to appoint a receiver).

74.17 Petition to appoint a receiver

74.17 The petition shall include averments in relation to–

(a) any floating charge and the property over which it is secured;

(b) so far as known to the petitioner, whether any application for an order in respect of an administration has been made, or an administrator has been appointed, in respect of the company;

(c) other matters which, in the opinion of the petitioner, will assist the court in deciding whether to appoint a receiver; and

(d) the name and address of the person proposed to be appointed, and his qualification to act, as receiver.

74.18 Intimation, service and advertisement under this Part

74.18(1) Unless the court otherwise directs, the order under rule 14.5 (first order in petitions) for intimation, service and advertisement of the petition shall include a requirement–

(a) to serve the petition–

    (i) on the company; and

    (ii) where an application for an administration order has been presented, on that applicant and any respondent to that application; and

(b) to advertise the petition forthwith–

    (i) once in the Edinburgh Gazette; and

   (ii)   once in one or more of such newspapers as the court shall direct.

74.18(2)   Subject to rule 14.6(2) (application to shorten or extend the period of notice), the period of notice for lodging answers to the petition shall be 8 days.

74.18(3)   An advertisement under paragraph (1) shall include–

   (a)   the name and address of the petitioner;

   (b)   the name and address of the agent for the petitioner;

   (c)   the date on which the petition was presented;

   (d)   the nature of the order sought;

   (e)   the period of notice for lodging answers; and

   (f)   a statement that any person who intends to appear in the petition must lodge answers within the period of notice.

74.19   Form of other applications and appeals

74.19(1)   An application under–

   (a)   section 61(1) of the Act of 1986 (by a receiver for authority to dispose of property or an interest in property),

   (b)   section 62 of that Act (for removal of a receiver),

   (c)   section 63(1) of that Act (by a receiver for directions),

   (d)   section 69(1) of that Act (to enforce the receiver's duty to make returns etc.), or

   (e)   any other provision of the Act of 1986 or the Insolvency Rules relating to receivers not mentioned in this Part,

shall, where the court has appointed the receiver, be made by note or, in any other case, by petition.

74.19(2)   An appeal against a decision of a receiver as to expenses of submitting a statement of affairs under rule 3.3(2) of the Insolvency Rules shall, where the receiver was appointed by the court, be made by note or, in any other case, by petition.

74.19(3)   An application by a receiver–

   (a)   under section 67(1) or (2) of the Act of 1986 (to extend the time for sending a report),

   (b)   under rule 3.9(2) of the Insolvency Rules (to extend the time for sending an abstract of his receipts and payments),

shall, where the court has appointed the receiver, be made by motion or, in any other case, by petition.

PART V

WINDING UP OF COMPANIES

74.20   Interpretation of this Part

74.20   In this Part, **"the petition"** means a petition under section 124 of the Act of 1986 (petition to wind up a company).

74.21   Petition to wind up a company

74.21(1)   The petition shall include averments in relation to–

   (a)   the petitioner, if other than the company, and his title to present the petition;

750

(b)   in respect of the company–

    (i)   its current and any previous registered name;

    (ii)   the address of its registered office, and any previous such address within 6 months immediately before the presentation of the petition so far as known to the petitioner;

    (iii) a statement of the nature of its business and objects, the amount of its capital (nominal and issued) indicating what part is called up, paid up or credited as paid up, and the amount of the assets of the company so far as known to the petitioner;

    (iv)   where the centre of main interests of the company is and whether the company has any other establishments in another Member State;

(c)   whether, to the knowledge of the petitioner, a receiver has been appointed in respect of any part of the property of the company or a liquidator has been appointed for the voluntary winding up of the company;

(d)   the grounds on which the petition proceeds;

(e)   the name and address of the person proposed to be appointed, and his qualification to act, as interim liquidator; and

(f)   whether there are insolvency proceedings elsewhere in respect of the company and whether those proceedings are main or territorial proceedings.

History
Rule 74.21(b)(iv) and (f) inserted by the Act of Sederunt (Rules of the Court of Session Amendment No.8) (Miscellaneous) 2007 (SSI 2007/449) r.10 as from October 25, 2007.

74.22   Intimation, service and advertisement under this Part

74.22(1)   Unless the court otherwise directs, the order under rule 14.5 (first order in petitions) for intimation, service and advertisement of the petition shall include a requirement–

(a)   to serve the petition–

    (i)   where the petitioner is not the company, on the company;

    (ii)   where the company is being wound up voluntarily and a liquidator has been appointed, on the liquidator; and

    (iii) where a receiver or administrator has been appointed, on the receiver or administrator, as the case may be;

(b)   where the company is an authorised institution or former authorised institution within the meaning assigned in section 106(1) of the Banking Act 1987 and the petitioner is not the Bank of England, to serve the petition on the Bank of England; and

(c)   to advertise the petition forthwith–

    (i)   once in the Edinburgh Gazette; and

    (ii)   once in one or more of such newspapers as the court shall direct.

74.22(2)   Subject to rule 14.6(2) (application to shorten or extend the period of notice), the period of notice for lodging answers to the petition shall be 8 days.

74.22(3)   An advertisement under paragraph (1) shall include–

(a)   the name and address of the petitioner and, where the petitioner is the company, its registered office;

(b)   the name and address of the agent for the petitioner;

   (c)   the date on which the petition was presented;

   (d)   the nature of the order sought;

   (e)   where a provisional liquidator has been appointed by the court, his name, address and the date of his appointment;

   (f)   the period of notice for lodging answers; and

   (g)   a statement that any person who intends to appear in the petition must lodge answers within the period of notice.

74.23 Remits from one court to another

74.23(1)   An application under section 120(3)(a)(i) of the Act of 1986 (application for remit of petition to a sheriff court) shall be made by motion.

74.23(2)   An application under–

   (a)   section 120(3)(a)(ii) of the Act of 1986 (application for remit of petition from a sheriff court to the court), or

   (b)   section 120(3)(b) of that Act (application for remit of petition from one sheriff court to another),

shall be made by petition.

74.24 Substitution of creditor or contributory for petitioner

74.24(1)   Where a petitioner in the petition–

   (a)   is subsequently found not entitled to present the petition,

   (b)   fails to make intimation, service and advertisement as directed by the court,

   (c)   moves or consents to withdraw the petition or to allow it to be dismissed or refused,

   (d)   fails to appear when the petition is called for hearing, or

   (e)   appears, but does not move for an order in terms of the prayer of the petition,

the court may, on such terms as it thinks fit, sist as petitioner in place of the original petitioner any creditor or contributory who, in the opinion of the court, is entitled to present the petition.

74.24(1A)   Where a member State liquidator has been appointed in main proceedings in relation to the company, without prejudice to paragraph (1) the court may, on such terms as it thinks fit, substitute the member State liquidator as petitioner, where he is desirous of prosecuting the petition.

History
Rule 74.24(1A) inserted by the Act of Sederunt (Rules of the Court of Session Amendment No.5) (Insolvency Proceedings) 2003 (Scottish SI 2003/385) r.2(1), (11) as from September 15, 2003.

74.24(2)   An application by a creditor or a contributory to be sisted under paragraph (1)–

   (a)   may be made at any time before the petition is dismissed or refused, and

   (b)   shall be made by note;

and, if necessary, the court may continue the petition for a specified period to allow a note to be presented.

74.25 Provisional liquidator

74.25(1)   An application to appoint a provisional liquidator under section 135 of the Act of 1986 may be made–

(a)   by the petitioner, in the prayer of the petition or, if made after the petition has been presented, by note; or

(b)   by a creditor or contributory of the company, the company, the Secretary of State, a member State liquidator appointed in main proceedings or a person entitled under any enactment to present a petition, by note.

History
In r.74.25(1)(b) the words ", a member State liquidator appointed in main proceedings" inserted by the Act of Sederunt (Rules of the Court of Session Amendment No.5) (Insolvency Proceedings) 2003 (Scottish SI 2003/385) r.2(1), (12) as from September 15, 2003.

74.25(2)   The application mentioned in paragraph (1) shall include averments in relation to–

(a)   the grounds for the appointment of the provisional liquidator;

(b)   the name and address of the person proposed to be appointed, and his qualification to act, as provisional liquidator; and

(c)   whether, to the knowledge of the applicant, an administrator has been appointed to the company or a receiver has been appointed in respect of any part of its property or a liquidator has been appointed voluntarily to wind it up.

74.25(3)   Where the court decides to appoint a provisional liquidator–

(a)   it shall pronounce an interlocutor making the appointment and specifying the functions to be carried out by him in relation to the affairs of the company; and

(b)   the applicant shall forthwith send a certified copy of such interlocutor to the person appointed.

74.25(4)   On receiving a certified copy of an interlocutor pronounced under paragraph (3), the provisional liquidator shall intimate his appointment forthwith–

(a)   once in the Edinburgh Gazette; and

(b)   once in one or more of such newspapers as the court has directed.

74.25(5)   An application for the discharge of a provisional liquidator shall be made by note.

74.26   Appointment of a liquidator

74.26(1)   Where the court pronounces an interlocutor appointing a liquidator–

(a)   the Deputy Principal Clerk shall send a certified copy of that interlocutor to the liquidator;

(b)   the court may, for the purposes of rule 4.18(4) of the Insolvency Rules (liquidator to give notice of appointment), give such direction as it thinks fit as to advertisement of such appointment.

74.26(2)   An application to appoint a liquidator under section 139(4) of the Act of 1986 shall be made by note.

74.27   Applications and appeals in relation to a statement of affairs

74.27(1)   An application under section 131(5) of the Act of 1986 for–

(a)   release from an obligation imposed under section 131(1) or (2) of that Act, or

(b)   an extension of time for the submission of a statement of affairs, shall be made by note.

74.27(2)   A note under paragraph (1) shall be served on the liquidator or provisional liquidator, as the case may be, who may lodge–

(a)   answers to the note; or

(b)   a report on any matters which he considers should be drawn to the attention of the court.

74.27(3)   Where the liquidator or provisional liquidator lodges a report under paragraph (2), he shall forthwith send a copy of it to the noter.

74.27(4)   Where the liquidator or the provisional liquidator does not appear at any hearing on the note, a certified copy of the interlocutor disposing of the note shall be sent to him forthwith by the noter.

74.27(5)   An appeal under rule 4.9(6) of the Insolvency Rules (appeal against refusal by liquidator of allowance towards expenses of preparing statement of affairs) shall be made by note.

74.28   Appeals against adjudication of claims

74.28(1)   An appeal under section 49(6) of the Bankruptcy (Scotland) Act 1985 as applied by rule 4.16 of the Insolvency Rules (appeal by a creditor or contributory of the company against a decision of the liquidator), shall be made by note.

74.28(2)   A note under paragraph (1) shall be served on the liquidator.

74.28(3)   On such a note being served on him, the liquidator shall send the claim in question, and a copy of his adjudication, forthwith to the Deputy Principal Clerk who shall cause them to be lodged in process.

74.28(4)   After the note has been disposed of, the Deputy Principal Clerk shall return the claim and the adjudication to the liquidator with a copy of the interlocutor disposing of the note.

74.29   Removal of liquidator

74.29   An application by a creditor of the company for an order–

   (a)   under section 171(3) of the Act of 1986 (order directing a liquidator to summon a meeting of creditors for the purpose of removing him), or

   (b)   under section 172 of that Act (order for removal of a liquidator),

shall be made by note.

74.30   Application in relation to remuneration of liquidator

74.30(1)   An application–

   (a)   by a liquidator under rule 4.34 of the Insolvency Rules (application to increase remuneration), or

   (b)   by a creditor of the company under rule 4.35 of those Rules (application to reduce liquidator's remuneration),

shall be made by note.

74.30(2)   A note under paragraph (1)(b) shall be served on the liquidator.

74.30A   Applications under section 176A of the Act of 1986

74.30A(1)   An application by a liquidator, administrator or receiver under section 176A of the Act of 1986 shall be–

   (a)   where there is no existing process in relation to any liquidation, administration or receivership, by petition; or

   (b)   where a process exists in relation to any liquidation, administration or receivership, by note in that process.

74.30A(2)   The Deputy Principal Clerk shall–

   (a)   after the lodging of any petition or note fix a hearing for the insolvency judge to consider an application under paragraph (1); and

   (b)   give notice of the hearing fixed under paragraph (2)(a) to the petitioner or noter.

74.30A(3)   The petitioner or noter shall not be required to give notice to any person of the hearing fixed under paragraph (2)(a), unless the insolvency judge directs otherwise.

History
Rule 74.30A inserted by the Act of Sederunt (Rules of the Court of Session Amendment No.5) (Insolvency Proceedings) 2003 (Scottish SI 2003/385) r.2(1), (13) as from September 15, 2003.

74.31   Application to appoint a special manager

74.31(1)   An application under section 177 of the Act of 1986 (application for the appointment of a special manager) shall be made by note.

74.31(2)   A bond of caution certified by the noter under rule 4.70(4) of the Insolvency Rules shall be sent to the Petition Department by the noter.

74.31(3)   After the Deputy Principal Clerk has satisfied himself as to the sufficiency of caution under rule 33.7(1) of these Rules, the clerk of session shall issue to the person appointed to be special manager a certified copy of the interlocutor appointing him.

74.31(4)   A special manager may, before the expiry of the period for finding caution, apply to the insolvency judge for an extension of that period.

74.32   Other applications

74.32(1)   An application under the Act of 1986 or any subordinate legislation made under that Act, or Part VII of the Companies Act 1989, in relation to a winding up by the court not mentioned in this Part shall–

(a)   if made by a party to the petition, be made by motion; or

(b)   in any other case, be made by note.

74.32(2)   At the hearing of a motion under paragraph (1)(a), the court may order that the application be made by note; and, in such a case, shall make an order for the lodging of answers to the note in process within such period as it thinks fit.

74.32A   Replacement liquidators

74.32A(1)   This rule applies where–

(a)   a person has been appointed by the court as a liquidator in respect of a petition; and

(b)   that person dies or otherwise ceases to be able to act as liquidator; and

(c)   an application is made to the court for the appointment of a replacement liquidator.

74.32A(2)   An application mentioned in paragraph (1)(c) may include a list of other petitions in which the liquidator has been appointed by the court and in respect of which the appointment of the same replacement liquidator is sought.

74.32A(3)   In an interlocutor appointing a replacement liquidator in respect of an application under paragraph (2), the court may–

(a)   order the replacement liquidator to be appointed in any or all of the petitions listed;

(b)   direct that a copy of the interlocutor be put in the process or processes of that petition or those petitions, as the case may be; and

(c)   make such orders as it thinks fit for the intimation and advertisement of such appointment.

History
Rule 74.32A inserted by the Act of Sederunt (Rules of the Court of Session Amendment) (Miscellaneous) 2006 (Scottish SI 2006/83) r.2(10), as from March 17, 2006.

PART VI

DISQUALIFICATION OF COMPANY DIRECTORS

74.33   Applications in relation to disqualification orders or undertakings

74.33   An application–

(a)   under section 3(2) of the Company Directors Disqualification Act 1986 (for disqualification for persistent breaches of companies legislation);

(b)   under section 6(1) of that Act (to disqualify unfit directors of insolvent companies);

(c)   under section 8 of that Act (for disqualification of unfit director after investigation of a company);

(ca)   under section 8A of that Act (variation or cessation of disqualification undertaking),

(d)   under section 11(1) of that Act (for leave by an undischarged bankrupt to be concerned in a company),

(e)   for leave under that Act; or

(f)   by the Secretary of State under rule 4(2) of the Insolvent Companies (Reports on Conduct of Directors (No.2) (Scotland) Rules 1986 (application for direction to comply with requirements to furnish information etc.),

shall be made by petition.

History
See history note after r.74.34.

74.34   Intimation, service and advertisement under this Part

74.34(1)   Rule 74.22, except paragraphs (1)(c) and (2) of that rule, shall apply to the intimation, service and advertisement of a petition referred to in rule 74.33 (applications in relation to disqualification orders) as it applies to a petition under that rule.

74.34(2)   A petition presented under rule 74.33 shall be intimated–

(a)   to the Secretary of State for Business, Enterprise and Regulatory Reform; or

(b)   where a petition is presented under rule 74.33(ca) and the disqualification undertaking was given under section 9B of the Company Directors Disqualification Act 1986 (competition undertaking), to the Office of Fair Trading or any specified regulator which has accepted the undertaking, as the case may be;

unless the petition is presented by that person or body.

History
Rule 7.33(ca) inserted, and r.7.34(2) substituted, by the Act of Sederunt (Rules of the Court of Session Amendment No.8) (Miscellaneous) 2005 (Scottish SI 2005/521) r.2(2), as from October 21, 2005.

APPENDIX

Rule 1.4

[Forms: not reproduced.]

Insolvent Partnerships Order 1994

(SI 1994/2421)

Made on 13 September 1994 by the Secretary of State for Trade and Industry under s.420(1), (2) of the Insolvency Act 1986 and s.21(2) of the Company Directors Disqualification Act 1986. Operative from 1 December 1994.

[**Note:** Changes made by the Financial Services and Markets Act 2000 (Consequential Amendments and Repeals) Order 2001 (SI 2001/3649), the Insolvent Partnerships (Amendment) Order 2001 (SI 2001/767), the Insolvent Partnerships (Amendment) Order 2002 (SI 2002/1308), the Insolvent Partnerships (Amendment) (No.2) Order 2002 (SI 2002/2708), the Civil Partnership Act 2004 (Amendments to Subordinate Legislation) Order 2005 (SI 2005/2114), the Insolvent Partnerships (Amendment) Order 2005 (SI 2005/1516), the Insolvent Partnerships (Amendment) Order 2006 (SI 2006/622) and the Lord Chancellor (Transfer of Functions and Supplementary Provisions) Order 2006 (SI 2006/680) have been incorporated into the text (in the case of pre-2003 legislation without annotation). References to administration petitions, orders, etc. have been adapted throughout, following the introduction of the new administration regime, pursuant to the 2005 Order.]

ARRANGEMENT OF ARTICLES

PART I

GENERAL

1 Citation, commencement and extent

1(1) This Order may be cited as the Insolvent Partnerships Order 1994 and shall come into force on 1st December 1994.

1(2) This Order–

(a) in the case of insolvency proceedings in relation to companies and partnerships, relates to companies and partnerships which the courts in England and Wales have jurisdiction to wind up; and

(b) in the case of insolvency proceedings in relation to individuals, extends to England and Wales only.

1(3) In paragraph (2) the term **"insolvency proceedings"** has the meaning ascribed to it by article 2 below.

2 Interpretation: definitions

2(1) In this Order, except in so far as the context otherwise requires–

"the Act" means the Insolvency Act 1986;

"agricultural charge" has the same meaning as in the Agricultural Credits Act 1928;

"agricultural receiver" means a receiver appointed under an agricultural charge;

"corporate member" means an insolvent member which is a company;

"the court", in relation to an insolvent partnership, means the court which has jurisdiction to wind up the partnership;

"individual member" means an insolvent member who is an individual;

"insolvency order" means–

(a)   in the case of an insolvent partnership or a corporate member, a winding-up order; and

(b)   in the case of an individual member, a bankruptcy order;

"insolvency petition" means, in the case of a petition presented to the court–

(a)   against a corporate member, a petition for its winding up by the court;

(b)   against an individual member, a petition for a bankruptcy order to be made against that individual,

where the petition is presented in conjunction with a petition for the winding up of the partnership by the court as an unregistered company under the Act;

"insolvency proceedings" means any proceedings under the Act, this Order or the Insolvency Rules 1986;

"insolvent member" means a member of an insolvent partnership, against whom an insolvency petition is being or has been presented;

"joint bankruptcy petition" means a petition by virtue of article 11 of this Order;

"joint debt" means a debt of an insolvent partnership in respect of which an order is made by virtue of Part IV or V of this Order;

"joint estate" means the partnership property of an insolvent partnership in respect of which an order is made by virtue of Part IV or V of this Order;

"joint expenses" means expenses incurred in the winding up of an insolvent partnership or in the winding up of the business of an insolvent partnership and the administration of its property;

"limited partner" has the same meaning as in the Limited Partnerships Act 1907;

"member" means a member of a partnership and any person who is liable as a partner within the meaning of section 14 of the Partnership Act 1890;

"officer", in relation to an insolvent partnership, means–

(a)   a member; or

(b)   a person who has management or control of the partnership business;

"partnership property" has the same meaning as in the Partnership Act 1890;

"postponed debt" means a debt the payment of which is postponed by or under any provision of the Act or of any other enactment;

"responsible insolvency practitioner" means–

(a)   in winding up, the liquidator of an insolvent partnership or corporate member; and

(b)   in bankruptcy, the trustee of the estate of an individual member,

and in either case includes the official receiver when so acting;

"separate debt" means a debt for which a member of a partnership is liable, other than a joint debt;

"separate estate" means the property of an insolvent member against whom an insolvency order has been made;

"separate expenses" means expenses incurred in the winding up of a corporate member, or in the bankruptcy of an individual member; and

"trustee of the partnership" means a person authorised by order made by virtue of article 11 of this Order to wind up the business of an insolvent partnership and to administer its property.

2(2) The definitions in paragraph (1), other than the first definition, shall be added to those in section 436 of the Act.

2(3) References in provisions of the Act applied by this Order to any provision of the Act so applied shall, unless the context otherwise requires, be construed as references to the provision as so applied.

2(4) Where, in any Schedule to this Order, all or any of the provisions of two or more sections of the Act are expressed to be modified by a single paragraph of the Schedule, the modification includes the combination of the provisions of those sections into the one or more sections set out in that paragraph.

3 Interpretation: expressions appropriate to companies

3(1) This article applies for the interpretation in relation to insolvent partnerships of expressions appropriate to companies in provisions of the Act and of the Company Directors Disqualification Act 1986 applied by this Order, unless the contrary intention appears.

3(2) References to companies shall be construed as references to insolvent partnerships and all references to the registrar of companies shall be omitted.

3(3) References to shares of a company shall be construed–

(a) in relation to an insolvent partnership with capital, as references to rights to share in that capital; and

(b) in relation to an insolvent partnership without capital, as references to interests–

    (i) conferring any right to share in the profits or liability to contribute to the losses of the partnership, or

    (ii) giving rise to an obligation to contribute to the debts or expenses of the partnership in the event of a winding up.

3(4) Other expressions appropriate to companies shall be construed, in relation to an insolvent partnership, as references to the corresponding persons, officers, documents or organs (as the case may be) appropriate to a partnership.

PART II

VOLUNTARY ARRANGEMENTS

4 Voluntary arrangement of insolvent partnership

4(1) The provisions of Part I of, and Schedule A1 to, the Act shall apply in relation to an insolvent partnership, certain of those provisions being modified in such manner that, after modification, they are as set out in Schedule 1 to this Order.

History
Article 4(1) substituted by the Insolvent Partnerships (Amendment) (No.2) Order 2002 (SI 2002/2708) arts 1, 4 as from January 1, 2003 subject to transitional provisions contained in art.11(1), (3).

4(2) For the purposes of the provisions of the Act applied by paragraph (1), the provisions of the Act specified in paragraph (3) below, insofar as they relate to company voluntary arrangements, shall also apply in relation to insolvent partnerships.

4(3) The provisions referred to in paragraph (2) are–

(a) section 233 in Part VI,

(b) Part VII, with the exception of section 250,

(c)   Part XII,

(d)   Part XIII,

(e)   sections 411, 413, 414 and 419 in Part XV, and

(f)   Parts XVI to XIX.

5   Voluntary arrangements of members of insolvent partnership

5(1)   Where insolvency orders are made against an insolvent partnership and an insolvent member of that partnership in his capacity as such, Part I of the Act shall apply to corporate members and Part VIII to individual members of that partnership, with the modification that any reference to the creditors of the company or of the debtor, as the case may be, includes a reference to the creditors of the partnership.

5(2)   Paragraph (1) is not to be construed as preventing the application of Part I or (as the case may be) Part VIII of the Act to any person who is a member of an insolvent partnership (whether or not a winding-up order has been made against that partnership) and against whom an insolvency order has not been made under this Order or under the Act.

PART III

ADMINISTRATION ORDERS

6   Administration in relation to insolvent partnership

6(1)   The provisions of Part II of, and Schedule B1 to, the Act shall apply in relation to an insolvent partnership, certain of those provisions being modified in such manner that, after modification, they are as set out in Schedule 2 to this Order.

6(2)   In its application to insolvent partnerships, Part II of, and Schedule B1 to, the Act (as modified as set out in Schedule 2 to this Order) shall be read subject to paragraph (3).

6(3)   For every reference to–

(a)   "administrative receiver" there shall be substituted "agricultural receiver"; and

(b)   "floating charge" there shall be substituted "agricultural floating charge".

6(4)   For the purposes of the provisions of the Act applied by paragraph (1), the provisions of the Act specified in paragraph (5) below, insofar as they relate to the appointment of an administrator, shall also apply in relation to insolvent partnerships.

6(5)   The provisions referred to in paragraph (4) are–

(a)   Part VI,

(b)   Part VII (with the exception of section 250),

(c)   Part XII,

(d)   Part XIII,

(e)   sections 411, 413, 414 and 419 in Part XV, and

(f)   Parts XVI to XIX.

6(6)   For the purposes of this Article and the provisions of the Act applied by paragraph (1), **"agricultural floating charge"** shall be construed as a reference to a floating charge created under section 5 of the Agricultural Credits Act 1928.

History
Part III (art.6) substituted by the Insolvent Partnerships (Amendment) Order 2005 (SI 2005/1516) art.3 as from July 1, 2005 subject to transitional provisions contained in art.2 of that Order.

PART IV

CREDITORS' ETC. WINDING-UP PETITIONS

7   Winding up of insolvent partnership as unregistered company on petition of creditor etc. where no concurrent petition presented against member

7(1)   Subject to paragraph (2) below, the provisions of Part V of the Act shall apply in relation to the winding up of an insolvent partnership as an unregistered company on the petition of a creditor, of a liquidator (within the meaning of Article 2(b) of the EC Regulation) appointed in proceedings by virtue of Article 3(1) of the EC Regulation, or of a temporary administrator (within the meaning of Article 38 of the EC Regulation), of a responsible insolvency practitioner, of the Secretary of State or of any other person other than a member, where no insolvency petition is presented by the petitioner against a member or former member of that partnership in his capacity as such.

7(2)   Certain of the provisions referred to in paragraph (1) are modified in their application in relation to insolvent partnerships which are being wound up by virtue of that paragraph in such manner that, after modification, they are as set out in Part I of Schedule 3 to this Order.

7(3)   The provisions of the Act specified in Part II of Schedule 3 to this Order shall apply as set out in that Part for the purposes of section 221(5) of the Act, as modified by Part I of that Schedule.

8   Winding up of insolvent partnership as unregistered company on the petition of creditor etc. where concurrent petitions presented against one or more members

8(1)   Subject to paragraph (2) below, the provisions of Part V of the Act (other than sections 223 and 224), shall apply in relation to the winding up of an insolvent partnership as an unregistered company on the petition of a creditor, of a liquidator (within the meaning of Article 2(b) of the EC Regulation) appointed in proceedings by virtue of Article 3(1) of the EC Regulation, or of a temporary administrator (within the meaning of Article 38 of the EC Regulation) where insolvency petitions are presented by the petitioner against the partnership and against one or more members or former members of the partnership in their capacity as such.

8(2)   Certain of the provisions referred to in paragraph (1) are modified in their application in relation to insolvent partnerships which are being wound up by virtue of that paragraph in such manner that, after modification, they are as set out in Part I of Schedule 4 to this Order.

8(3)   The provisions of the Act specified in Part II of Schedule 4 to this Order shall apply as set out in that Part for the purposes of section 221(5) of the Act, as modified by Part I of that Schedule.

8(4)   The provisions of the Act specified in paragraph (5) below, insofar as they relate to winding up of companies by the court in England and Wales on a creditor's petition, shall apply in relation to the winding up of a corporate member or former corporate member (in its capacity as such) of an insolvent partnership which is being wound up by virtue of paragraph (1).

8(5)   The provisions referred to in paragraph (4) are–

    (a)   Part IV,

    (b)   Part VI,

    (c)   Part VII, and

    (d)   Parts XII to XIX.

History

In art.8(5)(a) the words "(other than section 176A)" inserted by the Insolvent Partnerships (Amendment) Order 2005 (SI 2005/1516) art.4 as from July 1, 2005, and subsequently deleted by SI 2006/622 art.3.

8(6)   The provisions of the Act specified in paragraph (7) below, insofar as they relate to the bankruptcy of individuals in England and Wales on a petition presented by a creditor, shall apply in relation to the bankruptcy of an individual member or former individual member (in his capacity as such) of an insolvent partnership which is being wound up by virtue of paragraph (1).

8(7)   The provisions referred to in paragraph (6) are–

(a)   Part IX (other than sections 269, 270, 287 and 297), and

(b)   Parts X to XIX.

8(8)   Certain of the provisions referred to in paragraphs (4) and (6) are modified in their application in relation to the corporate or individual members or former corporate or individual members of insolvent partnerships in such manner that, after modification, they are as set out in Part II of Schedule 4 to this Order.

8(9)   The provisions of the Act applied by this Article shall further be modified so that references to a corporate or individual member include any former such member against whom an insolvency petition is being or has been presented by virtue of this Article.

PART V

MEMBERS' PETITIONS

9   Winding up of insolvent partnership as unregistered company on member's petition where no concurrent petition presented against member

9   The following provisions of the Act shall apply in relation to the winding up of an insolvent partnership as an unregistered company on the petition of a member where no insolvency petition is presented by the petitioner against a member of that partnership in his capacity as such–

(a)   sections 117 and 221, modified in such manner that, after modification, they are as set out in Schedule 5 to this Order; and

(b)   the other provisions of Part V of the Act, certain of those provisions being modified in such manner that, after modification, they are as set out in Part I of Schedule 3 to this Order.

10   Winding up of insolvent partnership as unregistered company on member's petition where concurrent petitions presented against all members

10(1)   The following provisions of the Act shall apply in relation to the winding up of an insolvent partnership as an unregistered company on a member's petition where insolvency petitions are presented by the petitioner against the partnership and against all its members in their capacity as such–

(a)   sections 117, 124, 125, 221, 264, 265, 271 and 272 of the Act, modified in such manner that, after modification, they are as set out in Schedule 6 to this Order; and

(b)   sections 220, 225 and 227 to 229 in Part V of the Act, section 220 being modified in such manner that, after modification, it is as set out in Part I of Schedule 4 to this Order.

10(2)   The provisions of the Act specified in paragraph (3) below, insofar as they relate to winding up of companies by the court in England and Wales on a member's petition, shall apply in relation to the winding up of a corporate member (in its capacity as such) of an insolvent partnership which is wound up by virtue of paragraph (1).

10(3)   The provisions referred to in paragraph (2) are–

(a)   Part IV,

(b)   Part VI,

(c)   Part VII, and

(d)   Parts XII to XIX.

History

In art.10(3)(a) the words "(other than section 176A)" inserted by the Insolvent Partnerships (Amendment) Order 2005 (SI 2005/1516) art.5(a) as from July 1, 2005, and subsequently deleted by SI 2006/622 art.4.

10(4) The provisions of the Act specified in paragraph (5) below, insofar as they relate to the bankruptcy of individuals in England and Wales where a bankruptcy petition is presented by a debtor, shall apply in relation to the bankruptcy of an individual member (in his capacity as such) of an insolvent partnership which is being wound up by virtue of paragraph (1).

10(5) The provisions referred to in paragraph (4) are–

    (a) Part IX (other than sections 273, 274, 287 and 297), and

    (b) Parts X to XIX.

10(6) Certain of the provisions referred to in paragraphs (2) and (4) are modified in their application in relation to the corporate or individual members of insolvent partnerships in such manner that, after modification, they are as set out in Part II of Schedule 4 to this Order.

History

Article 10(6) substituted by the Insolvent Partnerships (Amendment) Order 2005 (SI 2005/1516) art.5(b) as from July 1, 2005.

11 Insolvency proceedings not involving winding up of insolvent partnership as unregistered company where individual members present joint bankruptcy petition

11(1) The provisions of the Act specified in paragraph (2) below shall apply in relation to the bankruptcy of the individual members of an insolvent partnership where those members jointly present a petition to the court for orders to be made for the bankruptcy of each of them in his capacity as a member of the partnership, and the winding up of the partnership business and administration of its property, without the partnership being wound up as an unregistered company under Part V of the Act.

11(2) The provisions referred to in paragraph (1) are–

    (a) Part IX (other than sections 273, 274 and 287), and

    (b) Parts X to XIX,

insofar as they relate to the insolvency of individuals in England and Wales where a bankruptcy petition is presented by a debtor.

11(3) Certain of the provisions referred to in paragraph (1) are modified in their application in relation to the individual members of insolvent partnerships in such manner that, after modification, they are as set out in Schedule 7 to this Order.

PART VI

PROVISIONS APPLYING IN INSOLVENCY PROCEEDINGS IN RELATION TO INSOLVENT PARTNERSHIPS

12 Winding up of unregistered company which is a member of insolvent partnership being wound up by virtue of this Order

12 Where an insolvent partnership or other body which may be wound up under Part V of the Act as an unregistered company is itself a member of an insolvent partnership being so wound up, articles 8 and 10 above shall apply in relation to the latter insolvent partnership as though the former body were a corporate member of that partnership.

13 Deposit on petitions

13(1) Where an order under section 414(4) or 415(3) of the Act (security for fees) provides for any sum to be deposited on presentation of a winding-up or bankruptcy petition, that sum shall, in the case of petitions presented by virtue of articles 8 and 10 above, only be required to be deposited in respect of the petition for winding up the partnership, but shall be treated as a deposit in respect of all those petitions.

13(2) Production of evidence as to the sum deposited on presentation of the petition for winding up the partnership shall suffice for the filing in court of an insolvency petition against an insolvent member.

14 Supplemental powers of court

14(1) [Amends IA 1986 s.168.]

14(2) [Amends IA 1986 s.303.]

15 Meaning of "act as insolvency practitioner"

15(1) [Amends IA 1986 s.388.]

PART VII

DISQUALIFICATION

16 Application of Company Directors Disqualification Act 1986

16 Where an insolvent partnership is wound up as an unregistered company under Part V of the Act, the provisions of sections 1, 1A, 6 to 10, 13 to 15, 17, 19(c) and 20 of, and Schedule 1 to, the Company Directors Disqualification Act 1986 shall apply, certain of those provisions being modified in such manner that, after modification, they are as set out in Schedule 8 to this Order.

PART VIII

MISCELLANEOUS

17 Forms

17(1) The forms contained in Schedule 9 to this Order shall be used in and in connection with proceedings by virtue of this Order, whether in the High Court or a county court.

17(2) The forms shall be used with such variations, if any, as the circumstances may require.

18 Application of subordinate legislation

18(1) The subordinate legislation specified in Schedule 10 to this Order shall apply as from time to time in force and with such modifications as the context requires for the purpose of giving effect to the provisions of the Act and of the Company Directors Disqualification Act 1986 which are applied by this Order.

18(2) In the case of any conflict between any provision of the subordinate legislation applied by paragraph (1) and any provision of this Order, the latter provision shall prevail.

19 Supplemental and transitional provisions

19(1) This Order does not apply in relation to any case in which a winding-up or a bankruptcy order was made under the Insolvent Partnerships Order 1986 in relation to a partnership or an insolvent member of a partnership, and where this Order does not apply the law in force immediately before this Order came into force continues to have effect.

19(2) Where winding-up or bankruptcy proceedings commenced under the provisions of the Insolvent Partnerships Order 1986 were pending in relation to a partnership or an insolvent member of a partnership immediately before this Order came into force, either–

(a)   those proceedings shall be continued, after the coming into force of this Order, in accordance with the provisions of this Order, or

(b)   if the court so directs, they shall be continued under the provisions of the 1986 Order, in which case the law in force immediately before this Order came into force continues to have effect.

19(3)   For the purpose of paragraph (2) above, winding-up or bankruptcy proceedings are pending if a statutory or written demand has been served or a winding-up or bankruptcy petition has been presented.

19(4)   Nothing in this Order is to be taken as preventing a petition being presented against an insolvent partnership under section 367 of the Financial Services and Markets Act 2000, or any other enactment except where paragraph 12 of Schedule A1 to the Act, as applied by this Order, has the effect of preventing a petition being so presented.

History
In art.19(4) the words "except where paragraph 12 of Schedule A1 to the Act, as applied by this Order, has the effect of preventing a petition being so presented" inserted by the Insolvent Partnerships (Amendment) (No.2) Order 2002 (SI 2002/2708) arts 1, 5 as from January 1, 2003 subject to transitional provisions contained in arts 11(1), (3).

19(5)   Nothing in this Order is to be taken as preventing any creditor or creditors owed one or more debts by an insolvent partnership from presenting a petition under the Act against one or more members of the partnership liable for that debt or those debts (as the case may be) without including the others and without presenting a petition for the winding up of the partnership as an unregistered company.

19(6)   Bankruptcy proceedings may be consolidated by virtue of article 14(2) above irrespective of whether they were commenced under the Bankruptcy Act 1914 or the Insolvency Act 1986 or by virtue of the Insolvent Partnerships Order 1986 or this Order, and the court shall, in the case of proceedings commenced under or by virtue of different enactments, make provision for the manner in which the consolidated proceedings are to be conducted.

20   Revocation

20   The Insolvent Partnerships Order 1986 is hereby revoked.

SCHEDULE 1

MODIFIED PROVISIONS OF PART I OF, AND SCHEDULE A1 TO, THE ACT (COMPANY VOLUNTARY
ARRANGEMENTS) AS APPLIED BY ARTICLE 4

Article 4

PART I

MODIFIED PROVISIONS OF SECTIONS 1 TO 7B OF THE ACT

For sections 1 to 7B of the Act there shall be substituted:–

"PART I

PARTNERSHIP VOLUNTARY ARRANGEMENTS

The proposal

1   Those who may propose an arrangement

1(1)   The members of an insolvent partnership (other than one which is in administration, or which is being wound up as an unregistered company, or in respect of which an order has been made by virtue of article 11 of the Insolvent Partnerships Order 1994) may make a proposal under this Part to the partnership's creditors for a composition in satisfaction of the debts of the partnership or a scheme of arrangement of its affairs (from here on referred to, in either case, as a **"voluntary arrangement"**).

1(2)   A proposal under this Part is one which provides for some person (**"the nominee"**) to act in relation to the voluntary arrangement either as trustee or otherwise for the purpose of supervising its implementation; and the nominee must be a person who is qualified to act as an insolvency practitioner or authorised to act as nominee, in relation to the voluntary arrangement.

1(3)   Such a proposal may also be made–

(a)   where the partnership is in administration, by the administrator,

(b)   where the partnership is being wound up as an unregistered company, by the liquidator, and

(c)   where an order has been made by virtue of article 11 of the Insolvent Partnerships Order 1994, by the trustee of the partnership.

1(4)   (Omitted by the Insolvent Partnerships (Amendment) Order 2005 (SI 2005/1516) art.6(1), (2)(c) as from July 1, 2005.)

1A   Moratorium

1A(1)   Where the members of an eligible insolvent partnership intend to make a proposal for a voluntary arrangement, they may take steps to obtain a moratorium for the insolvent partnership.

1A(2)   Subject to subsections (3), (4), (5), (6) and (7), the provisions of Schedule A1 to this Act have effect with respect to–

(a)   insolvent partnerships eligible for a moratorium under this section,

(b)   the procedure for obtaining such a moratorium,

(c)   the effects of such a moratorium, and

(d)   the procedure applicable (in place of sections 2 to 6 and 7) in relation to the approval and implementation of a voluntary arrangement where such a moratorium is or has been in force.

1A(3)   Certain of the provisions applied in relation to insolvent partnerships by virtue of subsection (2) are modified in their application in relation to insolvent partnerships in such manner that, after modification, they are as set out in Part II of Schedule 1 to the Insolvent Partnerships Order 1994.

1A(4)   Paragraphs 4A, 4B, 4C, 4D, 4E, 4F, 4G, 4H, 4I, 4J, 4K, 5, 7(4), 8(8), 32(7), 34(2), 41(5) and 45 of Schedule A1 to this Act shall not apply.

1A(5)   An insolvent partnership is not liable to a fine under paragraphs 16(2), 17(3), 18(3), 19(3), 22 or 23(1) of Schedule A1 to the Act.

1A(6)   Notwithstanding subsection (5) an officer of an insolvent partnership may be liable to imprisonment or a fine under the paragraphs referred to in that subsection in the same manner as an officer of a company.

1A(7)   In the application of Schedule A1, and the application of the entries in Schedule 10 relating to offences under Schedule A1, to insolvent partnerships–

(a)   references to the directors or members of a company shall be construed as references to the members of an insolvent partnership,

(b)   references to officers of a company shall be construed as references to the officers of an insolvent partnership,

(c)   references to a meeting of a company shall be construed as references to a meeting of the members of an insolvent partnership, and

(d)   references to a floating charge shall be construed as references to a floating charge created under section 5 of the Agricultural Credits Act 1928.

2   Procedure where nominee is not the liquidator, administrator or trustee

2(1)   This section applies where the nominee under section 1 is not the liquidator, administrator or trustee of the insolvent partnership and the members of the partnership do not propose to take steps to obtain a moratorium under section 1A for the insolvent partnership.

2(2)   The nominee shall, within 28 days (or such longer period as the court may allow) after he is given notice of the proposal for a voluntary arrangement, submit a report to the court stating–

  (a)   whether, in his opinion, the proposed voluntary arrangement has a reasonable prospect of being approved and implemented,

  (b)   whether, in his opinion, meetings of the members of the partnership and of the partnership's creditors should be summoned to consider the proposal, and

  (c)   if in his opinion such meetings should be summoned, the date on which, and time and place at which, he proposes the meetings should be held.

2(3)   The nominee shall also state in his report whether there are in existence any insolvency proceedings in respect of the insolvent partnership or any of its members.

2(4)   For the purposes of enabling the nominee to prepare his report, the person intending to make the proposal shall submit to the nominee–

  (a)   a document setting out the terms of the proposed voluntary arrangement, and

  (b)   a statement of the partnership's affairs containing–

     (i)   such particulars of the partnership's creditors and of the partnership's debts and other liabilities and of the partnership property as may be prescribed, and

     (ii)   such other information as may be prescribed.

2(5)   The court may–

  (a)   on an application made by the person intending to make the proposal, in a case where the nominee has failed to submit the report required by this section or has died, or

  (b)   on an application made by that person or the nominee, in a case where it is impracticable or inappropriate for the nominee to continue to act as such,

direct that the nominee be replaced as such by another person qualified to act as an insolvency practitioner, or authorised to act as nominee, in relation to the voluntary arrangement.

3   Summoning of meetings

3(1)   Where the nominee under section 1 is not the liquidator, administrator or trustee of the insolvent partnership, and it has been reported to the court that such meetings as are mentioned in section 2(2) should be summoned, the person making the report shall (unless the court otherwise directs) summon those meetings for the time, date and place proposed in the report.

3(2)   Where the nominee is the liquidator, administrator or trustee of the insolvent partnership, he shall summon meetings of the members of the partnership and of the partnership's creditors to consider the proposal for such a time, date and place as he thinks fit.

3(3)   The persons to be summoned to a creditors' meeting under this section are every creditor of the partnership of whose claim and address the person summoning the meeting is aware.

Consideration and implementation of proposal

4   Decisions of meetings

4(1)   The meetings under section 3 shall decide whether to approve the proposed voluntary arrangement (with or without modifications).

4(2) The modifications may include one conferring the functions proposed to be conferred on the nominee on another person qualified to act as an insolvency practitioner, or authorised to act as nominee, in relation to the voluntary arrangement.

But they shall not include any modification by virtue of which the proposal ceases to be a proposal such as is mentioned in section 1.

4(3) A meeting so summoned shall not approve any proposal or modification which affects the right of a secured creditor of the partnership to enforce his security, except with the concurrence of the creditor concerned.

4(4) Subject as follows, a meeting so summoned shall not approve any proposal or modification under which–

    (a) any preferential debt of the partnership is to be paid otherwise than in priority to such of its debts as are not preferential debts, or

    (b) a preferential creditor of the partnership is to be paid an amount in respect of a preferential debt that bears to that debt a smaller proportion than is borne to another preferential debt by the amount that is to be paid in respect of that other debt.

However, the meeting may approve such a proposal or modification with the concurrence of the preferential creditor concerned.

4(5) Subject as above, each of the meetings shall be conducted in accordance with the rules.

4(6) After the conclusion of either meeting in accordance with the rules, the chairman of the meeting shall report the result of the meeting to the court, and, immediately after reporting to the court, shall give notice of the result of the meeting to all those who were sent notice of the meeting in accordance with the rules.

4(7) References in this section to preferential debts and preferential creditors are to be read in accordance with section 386 in Part XII of this Act.

Approval of arrangement

4A(1) This section applies to a decision, under section 4, with respect to the approval of a proposed voluntary arrangement.

4A(2) The decision has effect if, in accordance with the rules–

    (a) it has been taken by both meetings summoned under section 3, or

    (b) (subject to any order made under subsection (6)) it has been taken by the creditors' meeting summoned under that section.

4A(3) If the decision taken by the creditors' meeting differs from that taken by the meeting of the members of the partnership, a member of the partnership may apply to court.

4A(4) An application under subsection (3) shall not be made after the end of the period of 28 days beginning with–

    (a) the day on which the decision was taken by the creditors' meeting, or

    (b) where the decision of the meeting of the members of the partnership was taken on a later day, that day.

4A(5) Where a member of an insolvent partnership which is regulated applies to the court under subsection (3), the Financial Services Authority is entitled to be heard on the application.

4A(6) On an application under subsection (3), the court may–

    (a) order the decision of the meeting of the members of the partnership to have effect instead of the decision of the creditors' meeting, or

    (b) make such other order as it thinks fit.

4A(7) In this section **"regulated"** in relation to an insolvent partnership means a person who–

    (a) is, or has been, an authorised person within the meaning given by section 31 of the Financial Services and Markets Act 2000,

    (b)   is, or has been, an appointed representative within the meaning given by section 39 of that Act, or

    (c)   is carrying on, or has carried on, a regulated activity, within the meaning given by section 22 of that Act, in contravention of the general prohibition within the meaning given by section 19 of that Act.

5   Effect of approval

5(1)   This section applies where a decision approving a voluntary arrangement has effect under section 4A.

5(2)   The voluntary arrangement–

    (a)   takes effect as if made by the members of the partnership at the creditors' meeting, and

    (b)   binds every person who in accordance with the rules–

        (i)   was entitled to vote at that meeting (whether or not he was present or represented at it), or

        (ii)   would have been so entitled if he had had notice of it,

as if he were a party to the voluntary arrangement.

5(2A)   If–

    (a)   when the arrangement ceases to have effect any amount payable under the arrangement to a person bound by virtue of subsection 2(b)(ii) has not been paid, and

    (b)   the arrangement did not come to an end prematurely,

the insolvent partnership shall at that time become liable to pay to that person the amount payable under the arrangement.

5(3)   Subject as follows, if the partnership is being wound up as an unregistered company, or is in administration or an order by virtue of article 11 of the Insolvent Partnerships Order 1994 is in force, the court may do one or both of the following, namely–

    (a)   by order–

        (i)   stay all proceedings in the winding up or in the proceedings under the order made by virtue of the said article 11 (as the case may be), including any related insolvency proceedings of a member of the partnership in his capacity as such, or

        (ii)   provide for the appointment of the administrator to cease to have effect;

    (b)   give such directions as it thinks appropriate for facilitating the implementation of the voluntary arrangement with respect to–

        (i)   the conduct of the winding up, the proceedings by virtue of the said article 11 or the administration (as the case may be), and

        (ii)   the conduct of any related insolvency proceedings as referred to in paragraph (a)(i) above.

5(4)   The court shall not make an order under subsection (3)(a)–

    (a)   at any time before the end of the period of 28 days beginning with the first day on which each of the reports required by section 4(6) has been made to the court, or

    (b)   at any time when an application under the next section or an appeal in respect of such an application is pending, or at any time in the period within which such an appeal may be brought.

6   Challenge of decisions

6(1)   Subject to this section, an application to the court may be made, by any of the persons specified below, on one or both of the following grounds, namely–

    (a)   that a voluntary arrangement which has effect under section 4A unfairly prejudices the interests of a creditor, member or contributory of the partnership;

    (b)   that there has been some material irregularity at or in relation to either of the meetings.

6(2)   The persons who may apply under this section are–

(a)   a person entitled, in accordance with the rules, to vote at either of the meetings;

(b)   a person who would have been entitled, in accordance with the rules, to vote at the creditors' meeting if he had had notice of it;

(c)   the nominee or any person who has replaced him under section 2(5) or 4(2); and

(d)   if the partnership is being wound up as an unregistered company or is in administration or an order by virtue of article 11 of the Insolvent Partnerships Order 1994 is in force, the liquidator, administrator or trustee of the partnership.

6(3)   An application under this section shall not be made–

(a)   after the end of the period of 28 days beginning with the first day on which each of the reports required by section 4(6) has been made to the court, or

(b)   in the case of a person who was not given notice of the creditors' meeting, after the end of the period of 28 days beginning with the day on which he became aware that the meeting had taken place,

but (subject to that) an application made by a person within subsection (2)(b) on the ground that the voluntary arrangement prejudices his interests may be made after the voluntary arrangement has ceased to have effect, unless it came to an end prematurely.

6(4)   Where on such an application the court is satisfied as to either of the grounds mentioned in subsection (1), it may do one or both of the following, namely–

(a)   revoke or suspend any decision approving the voluntary arrangement which has effect under section 4A or, in a case falling within subsection (1)(b), any decision taken by the meeting in question which has effect under that section;

(b)   give a direction to any person for the summoning of further meetings to consider any revised proposal the person who made the original proposal may make or, in a case falling within subsection (1)(b), a further meeting of the members of the partnership or (as the case may be) of the partnership's creditors to reconsider the original proposal.

6(5)   Where at any time after giving a direction under subsection (4)(b) for the summoning of meetings to consider a revised proposal the court is satisfied that the person who made the original proposal does not intend to submit a revised proposal, the court shall revoke the direction and revoke or suspend any decision approving the voluntary arrangement which has effect under section 4A.

6(6)   In a case where the court, on an application under this section with respect to any meeting–

(a)   gives a direction under subsection (4)(b), or

(b)   revokes or suspends an approval under subsection (4)(a) or (5),

the court may give such supplemental directions as it thinks fit, and, in particular, directions with respect to things done under the voluntary arrangement since it took effect.

6(7)   Except in pursuance of the preceding provisions of this section, a decision taken at a meeting summoned under section 3 is not invalidated by any irregularity at or in relation to the meeting.

6A   False representations, etc.

6A(1)   If, for the purpose of obtaining the approval of the members or creditors of an insolvent partnership or of the members or creditors of any of its members to a proposal for a voluntary arrangement in relation to the partnership or any of its members, a person who is an officer of the partnership or an officer (which for this purpose includes a shadow director) of a corporate member in relation to which a voluntary arrangement is proposed–

(a)   makes a false representation, or

(b)   fraudulently does, or omits to do, anything,

he commits an offence.

771

6A(2)   Subsection (1) applies even if the proposal is not approved.

6A(3)   A person guilty of an offence under this section is liable to imprisonment or a fine, or both.

7   Implementation of proposal

7(1)   This section applies where a voluntary arrangement has effect under section 4A.

7(2)   The person who is for the time being carrying out in relation to the voluntary arrangement the functions conferred–

     (a)   on the nominee by virtue of the approval given at one or both of the meetings summoned under section 3, or

     (b)   by virtue of section 2(5) or 4(2) on a person other than the nominee,

shall be known as the supervisor of the voluntary arrangement.

7(3)   If any of the partnership's creditors or any other person is dissatisfied by any act, omission or decision of the supervisor, he may apply to the court; and on the application the court may–

     (a)   confirm, reverse or modify any act or decision of the supervisor,

     (b)   give him directions, or

     (c)   make such other order as it thinks fit.

7(4)   The supervisor–

     (a)   may apply to the court for directions in relation to any particular matter arising under the voluntary arrangement, and

     (b)   is included among the persons who may apply to the court for the winding up of the partnership as an unregistered company or for an administration order to be made in relation to it.

7(5)   The court may, whenever–

     (a)   it is expedient to appoint a person to carry out the functions of the supervisor, and

     (b)   it is inexpedient, difficult or impracticable for an appointment to be made without the assistance of the court,

make an order appointing a person who is qualified to act as an insolvency practitioner or authorised to act as supervisor, in relation to the voluntary arrangement, either in substitution for the existing supervisor or to fill a vacancy.

7(6)   The power conferred by subsection (5) is exercisable so as to increase the number of persons exercising the functions of supervisor or, where there is more than one person exercising those functions, so as to replace one or more of those persons.

7A   Prosecution of delinquent officers of partnership

7A(1)   This section applies where a moratorium under section 1A has been obtained for an insolvent partnership or the approval of a voluntary arrangement in relation to an insolvent partnership has taken effect under section 4A or paragraph 36 of Schedule A1.

7A(2)   If it appears to the nominee or supervisor that any past or present officer of the insolvent partnership has been guilty of any offence in connection with the moratorium or, as the case may be, voluntary arrangement for which such officer is criminally liable, the nominee or supervisor shall forthwith–

     (a)   report the matter to the Secretary of State, and

     (b)   provide the Secretary of State with such information and give him such access to and facilities for inspecting and taking copies of documents (being information or documents in the possession or under the control of the nominee or supervisor and relating to the matter in question) as the Secretary of State requires.

7A(3)   Where a prosecuting authority institutes criminal proceedings following any report under subsection (2), the nominee or supervisor, and every officer and agent of the insolvent partnership past or present (other than the defendant), shall give the authority all assistance in connection with the prosecution which he is reasonably able to give.

For this purpose–

"agent" includes any banker or solicitor of the insolvent partnership and any person employed by the insolvent partnership as auditor, whether that person is or is not an officer of the insolvent partnership,

"prosecuting authority" means the Director of Public Prosecutions or the Secretary of State.

7A(4)   The court may, on the application of the prosecuting authority, direct any person referred to in subsection (3) to comply with that subsection if he has failed to do so.

7B   Arrangements coming to an end prematurely

7B   For the purposes of this Part, a voluntary arrangement the approval of which has taken effect under section 4A or paragraph 36 of Schedule A1 comes to an end prematurely if, when it ceases to have effect, it has not been fully implemented in respect of all persons bound by the arrangement by virtue of section 5(2)(b)(i) or, as the case may be, paragraph 37(2)(b)(i) of Schedule A1."

PART II

MODIFIED PROVISIONS OF SCHEDULE A1 TO THE ACT

The following provisions of Schedule A1 to the Act are modified so as to read as follows:

"**3(1)**   An insolvent partnership meets the requirements of this paragraph if the qualifying conditions are met–

(a)   in the year ending with the date of filing, or

(b)   in the tax year of the insolvent partnership which ended last before that date.

3(2)   For the purposes of sub-paragraph (1) the qualifying conditions are met by an insolvent partnership in a period if, in that period, it satisfies two or more of the requirements set out in sub-paragraph (3).

3(3)   The qualifying conditions referred to in this paragraph are–

(a)   turnover of not more than £5.6 million,

(b)   assets of not more than £2.8 million, and

(c)   no more than 50 employees.

3(4)   For the purposes of sub-paragraph (3)–

(a)   the total of turnover is the amount which is or would be, as the case may be, entered as turnover in the partnership's tax return,

(b)   the total of assets is the amount which–

(i)   in the case of the period referred to in paragraph 3(1)(a), is entered in the partnership's statement of affairs which must be filed with the court under paragraph 7(1)(b), or

(ii)   in the case of the period referred to in paragraph 3(1)(b), would be entered in the partnership's statement of affairs had it prepared such a statement on the last day of the period to which the amount for turnover is calculated for the purposes of paragraph 3(4)(a),

(c)   the number of employees is the average number of persons employed by the insolvent partnership–

(i)   in the case of the period referred to in paragraph 3(1)(a), in the period ending with the date of filing,

(ii)   in the case of the period referred to in paragraph 3(1)(b), in the period to which the amount for turnover is calculated for the purposes of paragraph 3(4)(a).

3(5)   Where the period covered by the qualifying conditions in respect of the insolvent partnership is not a year the total of turnover referred to in paragraph 3(3)(a) shall be proportionately adjusted.

3(6)   The average number of persons employed by the insolvent partnership shall be calculated as follows–

(a)   by ascertaining the number of persons employed by it under contracts of service for each month of the year (whether throughout the month or not),

(b)   by adding those figures together, and

(c)   by dividing the resulting figure by the number of months during which persons were so employed by it during the year.

3(7)   In this paragraph–

"tax return" means a return under section 12AA of the Taxes Management Act 1970,

"tax year" means the 12 months beginning with 6th April in any year.

4(1)   An insolvent partnership is excluded from being eligible for a moratorium if, on the date of filing–

(a)   the partnership is in administration,

(b)   the insolvent partnership is being wound up as an unregistered company,

(c)   there is an agricultural receiver of the insolvent partnership,

(d)   a voluntary arrangement has effect in relation to the insolvent partnership,

(e)   there is a provisional liquidator of the insolvent partnership,

(f)   a moratorium has been in force for the insolvent partnership at any time during the period of 12 months ending with the date of filing and–

  (i)   no voluntary arrangement had effect at the time at which the moratorium came to an end, or

  (ii)   a voluntary arrangement which had effect at any time in that period has come to an end prematurely,

(g)   a voluntary arrangement in relation to the insolvent partnership which had effect in pursuance of a proposal under section 1(3) has come to an end prematurely and, during the period of 12 months ending with the date of filing, an order under section 5(3)(a) has been made, or

(h)   an order has been made by virtue of article 11 of the Insolvent Partnerships Order 1994.

4(2)   Sub-paragraph (1)(b) does not apply to an insolvent partnership which, by reason of a winding-up order made after the date of filing, is treated as being wound up on that date.

12   Effect on creditors, etc.

12(1)   During the period for which a moratorium is in force for an insolvent partnership—

(a)   no petition may be presented for the winding-up of the insolvent partnership as an unregistered company,

(b)   no meeting of the members of the partnership may be called or requisitioned except with the consent of the nominee or the leave of the court and subject (where the court gives leave) to such terms as the court may impose,

(c)   no order may be made for the winding-up of the insolvent partnership as an unregistered company,

(d)   no administration application may be made in respect of the partnership,

(da)   no administrator of the partnership may be appointed under paragraph 14 or 22 of Schedule B1,

(e)   no agricultural receiver of the partnership may be appointed except with the leave of the court and subject to such terms as the court may impose,

(f)   no landlord or other person to whom rent is payable may exercise any rights of forfeiture by peaceable re-entry in relation to premises forming part of the partnership property or let to one or more officers of the partnership in their capacity as such in respect of a failure by the partnership or one or more officers of the partnership to comply with any term or condition of the tenancy of such premises, except with the leave of the court and subject to such terms as the court may impose,

(g)   no other steps may be taken to enforce any security over the partnership property, or to repossess goods in the possession, under any hire-purchase agreement, of one or more officers of the partnership in their capacity as such, except with the leave of the court and subject to such terms as the court may impose,

(h)   no other proceedings and no execution or other legal process may be commenced or continued, and no distress may be levied, against the insolvent partnership or the partnership property except with the leave of the court and subject to such terms as the court may impose,

(i)   no petition may be presented, and no order may be made, by virtue of article 11 of the Insolvent Partnerships Order 1994, and

(j)   no application or order may be made under section 35 of the Partnership Act 1890 in respect of the insolvent partnership.

12(2)   Where a petition, other than an excepted petition, for the winding-up of the insolvent partnership has been presented before the beginning of the moratorium, section 127 shall not apply in relation to any disposition of partnership property, any transfer of an interest in the insolvent partnership or alteration in status of a member of the partnership made during the moratorium or at a time mentioned in paragraph 37(5)(a).

12(3)   Paragraph (a) of sub-paragraph (1) does not apply to an excepted petition and, where such a petition has been presented before the beginning of the moratorium or is presented during the moratorium, paragraphs (b) and (c) of that sub-paragraph do not apply in relation to proceedings on the petition.

12(4)   For the purposes of this paragraph, **"excepted petition"** means a petition under–

(a)   article 7(1) of the Insolvent Partnerships Order 1994 presented by the Secretary of State on the grounds mentioned in subsections (b), (c) and (d) of section 124A of this Act,

(b)   section 72 of the Financial Services Act 1986 on the ground mentioned in subsection (1)(b) of that section,

(c)   section 92 of the Banking Act 1987 on the ground mentioned in subsection (1)(b) of that section, or

(d)   section 367 of the Financial Services and Markets Act 2000 on the ground mentioned in subsection (3)(b) of that section.

20   Disposal of charged property, etc

20(1)   This paragraph applies where–

(a)   any partnership property of the insolvent partnership is subject to a security, or

(b)   any goods are in possession of one or more officers of the partnership in their capacity as such under a hire-purchase agreement.

20(2)   If the holder of the security consents, or the court gives leave, the insolvent partnership may dispose of the property as if it were not subject to the security.

20(3)   If the owner of the goods consents, or the court gives leave, the insolvent partnership may dispose of the goods as if all rights of the owner under the hire-purchase agreement were vested in the members of the partnership.

20(4)   Where property subject to a security which, as created, was a floating charge is disposed of under sub-paragraph (2), the holder of the security has the same priority in respect of any partnership property directly or indirectly representing the property disposed of as he would have had in respect of the property subject to the security.

20(5)   Sub-paragraph (6) applies to the disposal under sub-paragraph (2) or (as the case may be) sub-paragraph (3) of–

(a)   any property subject to a security other than a security which, as created, was a floating charge, or

(b)   any goods in the possession of one or more officers of the partnership in their capacity as such under a hire-purchase agreement.

20(6)   It shall be a condition of any consent or leave under sub-paragraph (2) or (as the case may be) sub-paragraph (3) that–

(a)   the net proceeds of the disposal, and

(b)   where those proceeds are less than such amount as may be agreed, or determined by the court, to be the net amount which would be realised on a sale of the property or goods in the open market by a willing vendor, such sums as may be required to make good the deficiency,

shall be applied towards discharging the sums secured by the security or payable under the hire-purchase agreement.

20(7)   Where a condition imposed in pursuance of sub-paragraph (6) relates to two or more securities, that condition requires–

(a)   the net proceeds of the disposal, and

(b)   where paragraph (b) of sub-paragraph (6) applies, the sums mentioned in that paragraph,

to be applied towards discharging the sums secured by those securities in the order of their priorities.

20(8)   In this paragraph **"floating charge"** means a floating charge created under section 5 of the Agricultural Credits Act 1928.

37   Effect of approval of voluntary arrangement

37(1)   This paragraph applies where a decision approving a voluntary arrangement has effect under paragraph 36.

37(2)   The approved voluntary arrangement–

(a)   takes effect as if made by the members of the partnership at the creditors' meeting, and

(b)   binds every person who in accordance with the rules–

  (i)   was entitled to vote at that meeting (whether or not he was present or represented at it), or

  (ii)   would have been so entitled if he had had notice of it,

as if he were a party to the voluntary arrangement.

37(3)   If–

(a)   when the arrangement ceases to have effect any amount payable under the arrangement to a person bound by virtue of sub-paragraph (2)(b)(ii) has not been paid, and

(b)   the arrangement did not come to an end prematurely,

the insolvent partnership shall at that time become liable to pay to that person the amount payable under the arrangement.

37(4)   Where a petition for the winding-up of the insolvent partnership as an unregistered company or a petition by virtue of article 11 of the Insolvent Partnerships Order 1994, other than an excepted petition within the meaning of paragraph 12, was presented before the beginning of the moratorium, the court shall dismiss the petition.

37(5)   The court shall not dismiss a petition under sub-paragraph (4)–

(a)   at any time before the end of the period of 28 days beginning with the first day on which each of the reports of the meetings required by paragraph 30(3) has been made to the court, or

(b)   at any time when an application under paragraph 38 or an appeal in respect of such an application is pending, or at any time in the period within which such an appeal may be brought.

40   Challenge of actions of officers of insolvent partnership

40(1)   This paragraph applies in relation to acts or omissions of the officers of a partnership during a moratorium.

40(2)   A creditor or member of the insolvent partnership may apply to the court for an order under this paragraph on the ground–

(a)   that the partnership's affairs and business and partnership property are being or have been managed by the officers of the partnership in a manner which is unfairly prejudicial to the interests of its creditors or members generally, or of some part of its creditors or members (including at least the petitioner), or

(b)   that any actual or proposed act or omission of the officers of the partnership is or would be so prejudicial.

40(3)   An application for an order under this paragraph may be made during or after the moratorium.

40(4)   On an application for an order under this paragraph the court may–

(a)   make such order as it thinks fit for giving relief in respect of the matters complained of,

(b)   adjourn the hearing conditionally or unconditionally, or

(c)   make an interim order or any other order that it thinks fit.

40(5)   An order under this paragraph may in particular–

(a)   regulate the management by the officers of the partnership of the partnership's affairs and business and partnership property during the remainder of the moratorium,

(b)   require the officers of the partnership to refrain from doing or continuing an act complained of by the petitioner, or to do an act which the petitioner has complained they have omitted to do,

(c)   require the summoning of a meeting of creditors or members of the partnership for the purpose of considering such matters as the court may direct,

(d)   bring the moratorium to an end and make such consequential provision as the court thinks fit.

40(6)   In making an order under this paragraph the court shall have regard to the need to safeguard the interests of persons who have dealt with the insolvent partnership in good faith and for value.

40(7)   Sub-paragraph (8) applies where—

(a)   the appointment of an administrator has effect in relation to the insolvent partnership and the appointment took effect before the moratorium came into force, or

(b)   the insolvent partnership is being wound up as an unregistered company or an order by virtue of article 11 of the Insolvent Partnerships Order 1994 has been made, in pursuance of a petition presented before the moratorium came into force.

40(8)   No application for an order under this paragraph may be made by a creditor or member of the insolvent partnership; but such an application may be made instead by the administrator (or as the case may be) the liquidator.

42(1)   If, for the purpose of obtaining a moratorium, or an extension of a moratorium, for an insolvent partnership or any of its members (a moratorium meaning in the case of an individual the effect of an application for, or the making of, an interim order under Part VIII of the Act), a person who is an officer of an insolvent partnership or an officer (which for this purpose includes a shadow director) of a corporate member in relation to which a voluntary arrangement is proposed–

(a)   makes any false representation, or

(b)   fraudulently does, or omits to do, anything,

he commits an offence.

42(2)   Sub-paragraph (1) applies even if no moratorium or extension is obtained.

42(3)   A person guilty of an offence under this paragraph is liable to imprisonment or a fine, or both."

History
Schedule 1 amended by the Insolvent Partnerships (Amendment) Order 2005 (SI 2005/1516) art.6 as from July 1, 2005 in keeping with the new administration regime, and also as follows:

(1)   Modified s.1(4) omitted.

(2)   In modified para.3(3)(a) of Sch.A1 "£5.6" substituted for "£2.8" and in para.3(3)(b) "£2.8" substituted for "£1.4".

(3)   Modified para.12(1)(d) and (da) of Sch.A1 substituted for the former para.12(1)(d).

(4)   Modified para.40(7) and (8) of Sch.A1 substituted for the former para.40(7).

Previously Sch.1 substituted by the Insolvent Partnerships (Amendment) (No.2) Order 2002 (SI 2002/2708) arts 1, 6 Sch.1 as from January 1, 2003 subject to transitional provisions contained in art.11(1), (3).

SCHEDULE 2

MODIFIED PROVISIONS OF PART II OF, AND SCHEDULE B1 TO, THE ACT (ADMINISTRATION) AS APPLIED BY ARTICLE 6

1   The following provisions of Schedule B1 and Schedule 1 to the Act are modified as follows.

2   Paragraph 2 is modified so as to read as follows–

"**2.**   A person may be appointed as administrator of a partnership–

(a)   by administration order of the court under paragraph 10,

(b)   by the holder of an agricultural floating charge under paragraph 14, or

(c)   by the members of the insolvent partnership in their capacity as such under paragraph 22."

3   Paragraph 7 is modified so as to read as follows–

"**7.**   A person may not be appointed as administrator of a partnership which is in administration (subject to the provisions of paragraphs 90 to 93, 95 to 97, and 100 to 103 about replacement and additional administrators)."

4   Paragraph 8 is modified so as to read as follows–

"**8(1)**   A person may not be appointed as administrator of a partnership after–

(a)   an order has been made in relation to it by virtue of Article 11 of the Insolvent Partnerships Order 1994; or

(b)   an order has been made for it to be wound up by the court as an unregistered company.

8(2)   Sub-paragraph (1)(a) is subject to paragraph 38.

8(3)   Sub-paragraph (1)(b) is subject to paragraphs 37 and 38."

5   Paragraph 11 is modified so as to read as follows–

"**11.**   The court may make an administration order in relation to a partnership only if satisfied–

(a)   that the partnership is unable to pay its debts, and

(b)   that the administration order is reasonably likely to achieve the purpose of administration."

6   Paragraph 12 is modified so as to read as follows–

"**12(1)**   An application to the court for an administration order in respect of a partnership ("an administration application") shall be by application in Form 1 in Schedule 9 to the Insolvent Partnerships Order 1994 and may be made only by–

(a)   the members of the insolvent partnership in their capacity as such;

(b)   one or more creditors of the partnership; or

(c)   a combination of persons listed in paragraphs (a) and (b).

12(2)   As soon as is reasonably practicable after the making of an administration application the applicant shall notify–

(a)   any person who has appointed an agricultural receiver of the partnership;

(b)   any person who is or may be entitled to appoint an agricultural receiver of the partnership;

    (c)   any person who is or may be entitled to appoint an administrator of the partnership under paragraph 14; and

    (d)   such other persons as may be prescribed.

12(3)   An administration application may not be withdrawn without the permission of the court.

12(4)   In sub-paragraph (1) **"creditor"** includes a contingent creditor and a prospective creditor.

12(5)   Sub-paragraph (1) is without prejudice to section 7(4)(b)."

7   Paragraph 14 is modified so as to read as follows–

"**14(1)**   The holder of a qualifying agricultural floating charge in respect of partnership property may appoint an administrator of the partnership.

14(2)   For the purposes of sub-paragraph (1) an agricultural floating charge qualifies if created by an instrument which–

    (a)   states that this paragraph applies to the agricultural floating charge,

    (b)   purports to empower the holder of the agricultural floating charge to appoint an administrator of the partnership, or

    (c)   purports to empower the holder of the agricultural floating charge to make an appointment which would be the appointment of an agricultural receiver.

14(3)   For the purposes of sub-paragraph (1) a person is the holder of a qualifying agricultural floating charge in respect of partnership property if he holds one or more charges of the partnership secured–

    (a)   by a qualifying agricultural floating charge which relates to the whole or substantially the whole of the partnership property,

    (b)   by a number of qualifying agricultural floating charges which together relate to the whole or substantially the whole of the partnership property, or

    (c)   by charges and other forms of security which together relate to the whole or substantially the whole of the partnership property and at least one of which is a qualifying agricultural floating charge."

History
Paragraph 7 amended by the Insolvent Partnerships (Amendment) Order 2006 (SI 2006/622) art.5(2)(a), as from April 6, 2006.

8   Paragraph 15 is modified so as to read as follows–

"**15(1)**   A person may not appoint an administrator under paragraph 14 unless–

    (a)   he has given at least two business days' written notice to the holder of any prior agricultural floating charge which satisfies paragraph 14(2); or

    (b)   the holder of any prior agricultural floating charge which satisfies paragraph 14(2) has consented in writing to the making of the appointment.

15(2)   For the purposes of this paragraph, one agricultural floating charge is prior to another in accordance with the provisions of section 8(2) of the Agricultural Credits Act 1928."

History
Paragraph 8 amended by the Insolvent Partnerships (Amendment) Order 2006 (SI 2006/622) art.5(2)(b), as from April 6, 2006.

9   Paragraph 22 is modified so as to read as follows–

"**22.**   The members of the insolvent partnership may appoint an administrator."

10   Paragraph 23 is modified so as to read as follows–

"**23(1)**   This paragraph applies where an administrator of a partnership is appointed–

    (a)   under paragraph 22, or

    (b)   on an administration application made by the members of the partnership.

23(2)   An administrator of the partnership may not be appointed under paragraph 22 during the period of 12 months beginning with the date on which the appointment referred to in sub-paragraph (1) ceases to have effect."

11   Paragraph 26 is modified so as to read as follows–

"**26(1)**   A person who proposes to make an appointment under paragraph 22 shall give at least five business days' written notice to–

    (a)   any person who is or may be entitled to appoint an agricultural receiver of the partnership, and

    (b)   any person who is or may be entitled to appoint an administrator of the partnership under paragraph 14.

26(2)   A person who proposes to make an appointment under paragraph 22 shall also give such notice as may be prescribed to such other persons as may be prescribed.

26(3)   A notice under this paragraph must–

    (a)   identify the proposed administrator, and

    (b)   be in Form 1A in Schedule 9 to the Insolvent Partnerships Order 1994."

12   Paragraph 27 is modified so as to read as follows–

"**27(1)**   A person who gives notice of intention to appoint under paragraph 26 shall file with the court as soon as is reasonably practicable a copy of–

    (a)   the notice, and

    (b)   any document accompanying it.

27(2)   The copy filed under sub-paragraph (1) must be accompanied by a statutory declaration made by or on behalf of the person who proposes to make the appointment–

    (a)   that the partnership is unable to pay its debts,

    (b)   that the partnership is not in liquidation, and

    (c)   that, so far as the person making the statement is able to ascertain, the appointment is not prevented by paragraphs 23 to 25, and

    (d)   to such additional effect, and giving such information, as may be prescribed.

27(3)   A statutory declaration under sub-paragraph (2) must–

    (a)   be in the prescribed form, and

    (b)   be made during the prescribed period.

27(4)   A person commits an offence if in a statutory declaration under sub-paragraph (2) he makes a statement–

    (a)   which is false, and

    (b)   which he does not reasonably believe to be true."

13   Paragraph 29 is modified so as to read as follows–

"**29(1)**   A person who appoints an administrator of a partnership under paragraph 22 shall file with the court–

    (a)   a notice of appointment, and

    (b)   such other documents as may be prescribed

29(2)   The notice of appointment must include a statutory declaration by or on behalf of the person who makes the appointment–

    (a)   that the person is entitled to make an appointment under paragraph 22,

    (b)   that the appointment is in accordance with this Schedule, and

(c)   that, so far as the person making the statement is able to ascertain, the statements made, and information given in the statutory declaration filed with the notice of intention to appoint remain accurate.

29(3)   The notice of appointment must identify the administrator and must be accompanied by a statement by the administrator–

(a)   that he consents to the appointment,

(b)   that in his opinion the purpose of administration is reasonably likely to be achieved, and giving such other information and opinions as may be prescribed.

29(4)   For the purpose of a statement under sub-paragraph (3) an administrator may rely on information supplied by members of the partnership (unless he has reason to doubt its accuracy).

29(5)   The notice of appointment must be in Form 1B in Schedule 9 to the Insolvent Partnerships Order 1994 and any document accompanying it must be in the prescribed form.

29(6)   A statutory declaration under sub-paragraph (2) must be made during the prescribed period.

29(7)   A person commits an offence if in a statutory declaration under sub-paragraph (2) he makes a statement–

(a)   which is false, and

(b)   which he does not reasonably believe to be true."

14   Paragraph 35 is modified so as to read as follows–

"**35(1)**   This paragraph applies where an administration application in respect of a partnership–

(a)   is made by the holder of a qualifying agricultural floating charge in respect of the partnership property, and

(b)   includes a statement that the application is made in reliance on this paragraph.

35(2)   The court may make an administration order–

(a)   whether or not satisfied that the partnership is unable to pay its debts; but

(b)   only if satisfied that the applicant could appoint an administrator under paragraph 14."

15   Paragraph 39 is modified so as to read as follows–

"**39(1)**   Where there is an agricultural receiver of a partnership the court must dismiss an administration application in respect of the partnership unless–

(a)   the person by or on behalf of whom the agricultural receiver was appointed consents to the making of the administration order,

(b)   the court thinks that the security by virtue of which the agricultural receiver was appointed would be liable to be released or discharged under sections 238 to 240 (transaction at undervalue and preference) if an administration order were made, or

(c)   the court thinks that the security by virtue of which the agricultural receiver was appointed would be avoided under section 245 (avoidance of floating charge) if an administration order were made.

39(2)   Sub-paragraph (1) applies whether the agricultural receiver is appointed before or after the making of the administration application."

16   Paragraph 41 is modified so as to read as follows–

"**41(1)**   When an administration order takes effect in respect of a partnership any agricultural receiver of the partnership shall vacate office.

41(2)   Where a partnership is in administration, any receiver of part of the partnership property shall vacate office if the administrator requires him to.

41(3)   Where an agricultural receiver vacates office under sub-paragraph (1) or (2), his remuneration shall be charged on and paid out of any partnership property which was in his custody or under his control immediately before he vacated office.

41(4)   In the application of sub-paragraph (3)–

(a)   'remuneration' includes expenses properly incurred and any indemnity to which the agricultural receiver is entitled out of the partnership property,

(b)   the charge imposed takes priority over security held by the person by whom or on whose behalf the agricultural receiver was appointed, and

(c)   the provision for payment is subject to paragraph 43."

17   Paragraph 42 is modified so as to read as follows–

"**42(1)**   This paragraph applies to a partnership in administration.

42(2)   No order may be made for the winding up of the partnership.

42(3)   No order may be made by virtue of Article 11 of the Insolvent Partnerships Order 1994 in respect of the partnership.

42(4)   No order may be made under section 35 of the Partnership Act 1890 in respect of the partnership.

42(5)   Sub-paragraph (2) does not apply to an order made on a petition presented under–

(a)   section 124A (public interest); or

(b)   section 367 of the Financial Services and Markets Act 2000 (c.8) (petition by Financial Services Authority).

42(6)   If a petition presented under a provision referred to in sub-paragraph (5) comes to the attention of the administrator, he shall apply to the court for directions under paragraph 63."

18   Paragraph 43 is modified so as to read as follows–

"**43(1)**   This paragraph applies to a partnership in administration.

43(2)   No step may be taken to enforce security over the partnership property except–

(a)   with the consent of the administrator, or

(b)   with the permission of the court.

43(3)   No step may be taken to repossess goods in the partnership's possession under a hire-purchase agreement except–

(a)   with the consent of the administrator, or

(b)   with the permission of the court.

43(4)   A landlord may not exercise a right of forfeiture by peaceable re-entry in relation to premises forming part of the partnership property or let to one or more officers of the partnership in their capacity as such except–

(a)   with the consent of the administrator, or

(b)   with the permission of the court.

43(5)   No legal process (including legal proceedings, execution, distress and diligence) may be instituted or continued against the partnership or partnership property except–

(a)   with the consent of the administrator, or

(b)   with the permission of the court.

43(6)   An agricultural receiver of the partnership may not be appointed.

43(7)   Where the court gives permission for a transaction under this paragraph it may impose a condition on or a requirement in connection with the transaction.

43(8)   In this paragraph **"landlord"** includes a person to whom rent is payable."

19   Paragraph 47 is modified so as to read as follows–

"**47(1)**   As soon as is reasonably practicable after appointment the administrator of a partnership shall by notice in the prescribed form require one or more relevant persons to provide the administrator with a statement of the affairs of the partnership.

47(2)   The statement must–

(a)   be verified by a statement of truth in accordance with Civil Procedure Rules,

(b)   be in the prescribed form,

(c)   give particulars of the partnership property, debts and liabilities,

(d)   give the names and addresses of the creditors of the partnership,

(e)   specify the security held by each creditor,

(f)   give the date on which each security was granted, and (g) contain such other information as may be prescribed.

47(3)   In sub-paragraph (1) **"relevant person"** means–

(a)   a person who is or has been an officer of the partnership,

(b)   a person who took part in the formation of the partnership during the period of one year ending with the date on which the partnership enters administration,

(c)   a person employed by the partnership during that period, and

(d)   a person who is or has been during that period an officer or employee of a partnership which is or has been during that year an officer of the partnership.

47(4)   For the purpose of sub-paragraph (3) a reference to employment is a reference to employment through a contract of employment or a contract for services."

20   Paragraph 49 is modified so as to read as follows–

"**49(1)**   The administrator of a partnership shall make a statement setting out proposals for achieving the purpose of administration.

49(2)   A statement under sub-paragraph (1) must, in particular–

(a)   deal with such matters as may be prescribed, and

(b)   where applicable, explain why the administrator thinks that the objective mentioned in paragraph 3(1)(a) or (b) cannot be achieved.

49(3)   Proposals under this paragraph may include a proposal for a voluntary arrangement under Part I of this Act (although this paragraph is without prejudice to section 4(3)).

49(4)   The administrator shall send a copy of the statement of his proposals–

(a)   to the court,

(b)   to every creditor of the partnership of whose claim and address he is aware, and

(c)   to every member of the partnership of whose address he is aware.

49(5)   The administrator shall comply with sub-paragraph (4)–

(a)   as soon as is reasonably practicable after the partnership enters administration, and

(b)   in any event, before the end of the period of eight weeks beginning with the day on which the partnership enters administration.

49(6)   The administrator shall be taken to comply with sub-paragraph (4)(c) if he publishes in the prescribed manner a notice undertaking to provide a copy of the statement of proposals free of charge to any member of the partnership who applies in writing to a specified address.

49(7)   An administrator commits an offence if he fails without reasonable excuse to comply with sub-paragraph (5).

49(8)   A period specified in this paragraph may be varied in accordance with paragraph 107."

21   Paragraph 52 is modified so as to read as follows–

"**52(1)**   Paragraph 51(1) shall not apply where the statement of proposals states that the administrator thinks–

(a)   that the partnership has sufficient property to enable each creditor of the partnership to be paid in full,

(b)   that the partnership has insufficient property to enable a distribution to be made to unsecured creditors, or

(c)   that neither of the objectives specified in paragraph 3(1)(a) and (b) can be achieved.

52(2)   But the administrator shall summon an initial creditors' meeting if it is requested–

(a)   by creditors of the partnership whose debts amount to at least 10 per cent of the total debts of the partnership,

(b)   in the prescribed manner, and

(c)   in the prescribed period.

52(3)   A meeting requested under sub-paragraph (2) must be summoned for a date in the prescribed period.

52(4)   The period prescribed under sub-paragraph (3) may be varied in accordance with paragraph 107."

22   Paragraph 61 is modified so as to read as follows–

"**61**   The administrator of a partnership–

(a)   may prevent any person from taking part in the management of the partnership business, and

(b)   may appoint any person to be a manager of that business."

23   Paragraph 65 is modified so as to read as follows–

"**65(1)**   The administrator of a partnership may make a distribution to a creditor of the partnership.

65(2)   Section 175(1) and (2)(a) shall apply in relation to a distribution under this paragraph as it applies in relation to a winding up.

65(3)   A payment may not be made by way of distribution under this paragraph to a creditor of the partnership who is neither secured nor preferential unless the court gives permission."

24   Paragraph 69 is modified so as to read as follows–

"**69(1)**   Subject to sub-paragraph (2) below, in exercising his function under this Schedule the administrator of a partnership acts as the agent of the members of the partnership in their capacity as such.

69(2)   An officer of the partnership shall not, unless he otherwise consents, be personally liable for the debts and obligations of the partnership incurred during the period when the partnership is in administration."

25   Paragraph 73 is modified so as to read as follows–

"**73(1)**   An administrator's statement of proposals under paragraph 49 may not include any action which–

(a)   affects the right of a secured creditor of the partnership to enforce his security,

(b)   would result in a preferential debt of the partnership being paid otherwise than in priority to its non-preferential debts, or

(c)   would result in one preferential creditor of the partnership being paid a smaller proportion of his debt than another.

73(2)   Sub-paragraph (1) does not apply to–

(a)   action to which the relevant creditor consents, or

(b)   a proposal for a voluntary arrangement under Part I of this Act (although this sub-paragraph is without prejudice to section 4(3)).

73(3)   The reference to a statement of proposals in sub-paragraph (1) includes a reference to a statement as revised or modified."

26   Paragraph 74 is modified so as to read as follows–

"**74(1)**   A creditor or member of a partnership in administration may apply to the court claiming that–

(a)   the administrator is acting or has acted so as unfairly to harm the interests of the applicant (whether alone or in common with some or all other members or creditors), or

(b)   the administrator proposes to act in a way which would unfairly harm the interests of the applicant (whether alone or in common with some or all other members or creditors).

74(2)   A creditor or member of a partnership in administration may apply to the court claiming that the administrator is not performing his functions as quickly or as efficiently as is reasonably practicable.

74(3)   The court may–

(a)   grant relief;

(b)   dismiss the application;

(c)   adjourn the hearing conditionally or unconditionally;

(d)   make an interim order;

(e)   make any other order it thinks appropriate.

74(4)   In particular, an order under this paragraph may–

(a)   regulate the administrator's exercise of his functions;

(b)   require the administrator to do or not do a specified thing;

(c)   require a creditors' meeting to be held for a specified purpose;

(d)   provide for the appointment of an administrator to cease to have effect;

(e)   make consequential provision.

74(5)   An order may be made on a claim under sub-paragraph (1) whether or not the action complained of–

(a)   is within the administrator's powers under that Schedule;

(b)   was taken in reliance on an order under paragraph 71 or 72.

74(6)   An order may not be made under this paragraph if it would impede or prevent the implementation of–

(a)   a voluntary arrangement approved under Part I, or

(b)   proposals or a revision approved under paragraph 53 or 54 more than 28 days before the day on which the application for the order under this paragraph is made."

27   Omit paragraph 83.

28   Paragraph 84 is modified so as to read as follows–

"**84(1)**   If the administrator of a partnership thinks that the partnership has no property which might permit a distribution to its creditors, he shall file a notice to that effect with the court.

84(2)   The court may on the application of the administrator of a partnership disapply sub-paragraph (1) in respect of the partnership.

84(3)   On the filing of a notice in respect of a partnership under sub-paragraph (1) the appointment of an administrator of the partnership shall cease to have effect.

84(4)   If an administrator files a notice under sub-paragraph (1) he shall as soon as is reasonably practicable send a copy of the notice to each creditor of whose claim and address he is aware.

84(5) At the end of the period of three months beginning with the date of filing of a notice in respect of a partnership under sub-paragraph (1) the partnership is deemed to be dissolved.

84(6) On an application in respect of a partnership by the administrator or another interested person the court may–

    (a)   extend the period specified in sub-paragraph (5);

    (b)   suspend that period; or

    (c)   disapply sub-paragraph (5).

84(7) An administrator commits an offence if he fails without reasonable excuse to comply with sub-paragraph (4)."

29   Paragraph 87 is modified to read as follows–

"**87(1)**   An administrator may resign only in prescribed circumstances.

87(2)   Where an administrator may resign he may do so only–

    (a)   in the case of an administrator appointed by administration order, by notice in writing to the court,

    (b)   in the case of an administrator appointed under paragraph 14, by notice in writing to the holder of the agricultural floating charge by virtue of which the appointment was made, or

    (c)   in the case of an administrator appointed under paragraph 22, by notice in writing to the members of the insolvent partnership."

30   Paragraph 89 is modified so as to read as follows–

"**89(1)**   The administrator of a partnership shall vacate office if he ceases to be qualified to act as an insolvency practitioner in relation to the partnership.

89(2)   Where an administrator vacates office by virtue of sub-paragraph (1) he shall give notice in writing–

    (a)   in the case of an administrator appointed by administration order, to the court,

    (b)   in the case of an administrator appointed under paragraph 14, to the holder of the agricultural floating charge by virtue of which the appointment was made, or

    (c)   in the case of an administrator appointed under paragraph 22, to the members of the insolvent partnership.

89(3)   An administrator who fails without reasonable excuse to comply with sub-paragraph (2) commits an offence."

31   Paragraph 90 is modified so as to read as follows–

"**90.**   Paragraphs 91 to 93 and 95 apply where an administrator–

    (a)   dies

    (b)   resigns

    (c)   is removed from office under paragraph 88, or

    (d)   vacates office under paragraph 89."

32   Paragraph 91 is modified so as to read as follows–

"**91(1)**   Where the administrator was appointed by administration order, the court may replace the administrator on an application under this sub-paragraph made by–

    (a)   a creditors' committee of the partnership,

    (b)   the members of the partnership,

    (c)   one or more creditors of the partnership, or

(d)   where more than one person was appointed to act jointly or concurrently as the administrator, any of those persons who remains in office.

91(2)   But an application may be made in reliance on sub-paragraph (1)(b) and (c) only where–

(a)   there is no creditors' committee of the partnership,

(b)   the court is satisfied that the creditors' committee or a remaining administrator is not taking reasonable steps to make a replacement, or

(c)   the court is satisfied that for another reason it is right for the application to be made."

33   Paragraph 93 is modified so as to read as follows–

"**93(1)**   Where the administrator was appointed under paragraph 22 by the members of the partnership they may replace the administrator.

93(2)   A replacement under this paragraph may be made only–

(a)   with the consent of each person who is the holder of a qualifying agricultural floating charge in respect of the partnership property, or

(b)   where consent is withheld, with the permission of the court."

34   Omit paragraph 94.

35   Paragraph 95 is modified so as to read as follows–

"**95.**   The court may replace an administrator on the application of a person listed in paragraph 91(1) if the court–

(a)   is satisfied that a person who is entitled to replace the administrator under any of paragraphs 92 and 93 is not taking reasonable steps to make a replacement, or

(b)   that for another reason it is right for the court to make the replacement."

36   Paragraph 96 is modified so as to read as follows–

"**96(1)**   This paragraph applies where an administrator of a partnership is appointed under paragraph 14 by the holder of a qualifying agricultural floating charge in respect of the partnership property.

96(2)   The holder of a prior qualifying agricultural floating charge in respect of the partnership property may apply to the court for the administrator to be replaced by an administrator nominated by the holder of the prior agricultural floating charge.

96(3)   One agricultural floating charge is prior to another for the purposes of this paragraph if–

(a)   it was created first, or

(b)   it is to be treated as having priority in accordance with an agreement to which the holder of each agricultural floating charge was party."

37   Paragraph 97 is modified so as to read as follows–

"**97(1)**   This paragraph applies where–

(a)   an administrator of a partnership is appointed by the members of the partnership under paragraph 22, and

(b)   there is no holder of a qualifying agricultural floating charge in respect of the partnership property.

97(2)   A creditor's meeting may replace the administrator.

97(3)   A creditors' meeting may act under sub-paragraph (2) only if the new administrator's written consent to act is presented to the meeting before the replacement is made."

38   Paragraph 103 is modified so as to read as follows–

"**103(1)**   Where a partnership is in administration, a person may be appointed to act as administrator jointly or concurrently with the person or persons acting as the administrator of the partnership.

103(2) Where a partnership entered administration by administration order, an appointment under sub-paragraph (1) must be made by the court on the application of–

(a)   a person or group listed in paragraph 12(1)(a) to (c), or

(b)   the person or persons acting as the administrator of the partnership.

103(3) Where a partnership entered administration by virtue of an appointment under paragraph 14, an appointment under sub-paragraph (1) must be made by–

(a)   the holder of the agricultural floating charge by virtue of which the appointment was made, or

(b)   the court on the application of the person or persons acting as the administrator of the partnership.

103(4) Where a partnership entered administration by virtue of an appointment under paragraph 22, an appointment under sub-paragraph (1) above must be made either by the court on the application of the person or persons acting as the administrator of the partnership or–

(a)   by the members of the partnership, and

(b)   with the consent of each person who is the holder of a qualifying agricultural floating charge in respect of the partnership property or, where consent is withheld, with the permission of the court.

103(5) An appointment under sub-paragraph (1) may be made only with the consent of the person or persons acting as the administrator of the partnership."

39   Omit paragraph 105.

40   Paragraph 106 is modified so as to read as follows–

"**106(1)** A person who is guilty of an offence under this Schedule is liable to a fine (in accordance with section 430 and Schedule 10).

106(2) A person who is guilty of an offence under any of the following paragraphs of this Schedule is liable to a daily default fine (in accordance with section 430 and Schedule 10)–

(a)   paragraph 20,

(b)   paragraph 32,

(c)   paragraph 46,

(d)   paragraph 48,

(e)   paragraph 49,

(f)   paragraph 51,

(g)   paragraph 53,

(h)   paragraph 54,

(i)   paragraph 56,

(j)   paragraph 78,

(k)   paragraph 80,

(l)   paragraph 84, and

(m)   paragraph 89."

41   Paragraph 111 is modified so as to read as follows–

"**111(1)** In this Schedule–

"administrator" has the meaning given by paragraph 1 and, where the context requires, includes a reference to a former administrator

"agricultural floating charge" means a charge which is an agricultural floating charge on its creation, "**correspondence**" includes correspondence by telephonic or other electronic means,

"**creditors' meeting**" has the meaning given by paragraph 50,

"**enters administration**" has the meaning given by paragraph 1,

"**in administration**" has the meaning given by paragraph 1,

"**hire-purchase agreement**" includes a conditional sale agreement, a chattel leasing agreement and a retention of title agreement,

"**holder of a qualifying agricultural floating charge**" in respect of partnership property has the meaning given by paragraph 14,

"**market value**" means the amount which would be realised on a sale of property in the open market by a willing vendor,

"**the purpose of administration**" means an objective specified in paragraph 3, and

"**unable to pay its debts**" has the meaning given by sections 222, 223, and 224.

111(2) A reference in this Schedule to a thing in writing includes a reference to a thing in electronic form.

111(3) In this Schedule a reference to action includes a reference to inaction."

42 Omit paragraphs 112–116.

43 Schedule 1 is modified to read as follows:–

"SCHEDULE 1

POWERS OF ADMINISTRATOR

Paragraph 60 of Schedule B1

1. Power to take possession of, collect and get in the partnership property and, for that purpose, to take such proceedings as may seem to him expedient.

2. Power to sell or otherwise dispose of the partnership property by public auction or private auction or private contract or, in Scotland, to sell, feu, hire out or otherwise dispose of the partnership property by public roup or private bargain.

3. Power to raise or borrow money and grant security therefor over the partnership property.

4. Power to appoint a solicitor or accountant or other professionally qualified person to assist him in the performance of his functions.

5. Power to bring or defend any action or other legal proceedings in the name and on behalf of any member of the partnership in his capacity as such or of the partnership.

6. Power to refer to arbitration any question affecting the partnership.

7. Power to effect and maintain insurances in respect of the partnership business and property.

8. Power to do all acts and execute, in the name and on behalf of the partnership or of any member of the partnership in his capacity as such, any deed, receipt or other document.

9. Power to draw, accept, make and endorse any bill of exchange or promissory note in the name and on behalf of any member of the partnership in his capacity as such or of the partnership.

10. Power to appoint any agent to do any business which he is unable to do himself or which can more conveniently be done by an agent and power to employ and dismiss employees.

11. Power to do all such things (including the carrying out of works) as may be necessary for the realisation of the partnership property.

12. Power to make any payment which is necessary or incidental to the performance of his functions.

13. Power to carry on the business of the partnership.

14.   Power to establish subsidiary undertakings of the partnership.

15.   Power to transfer to subsidiary undertakings of the partnership the whole or any part of the business of the partnership or of the partnership property.

16.   Power to grant or accept a surrender of a lease or tenancy of any of the partnership property, and to take a lease or tenancy of any property required or convenient for the business of the partnership.

17.   Power to make any arrangement or compromise on behalf of the partnership or of its members in their capacity as such.

18.   Power to rank and claim in the bankruptcy, insolvency, sequestration or liquidation of any person indebted to the partnership and to receive dividends, and to accede to trust deeds for the creditors of any such person.

19.   Power to present or defend a petition for the winding up of the partnership under the Insolvent Partnerships Order 1994.

20.   Power to do all other things incidental to the exercise of the foregoing powers."

History
Schedule 2 substituted by the Insolvent Partnerships (Amendment) Order 2005 (SI 2005/1516) art.7 and Sch.1 as from July 1, 2005 subject to the transitional provisions set out in art.2 of that Order.

SCHEDULE 3

PROVISIONS OF THE ACT WHICH APPLY WITH MODIFICATIONS FOR THE PURPOSES OF ARTICLE 7 TO WINDING UP OF INSOLVENT PARTNERSHIP ON PETITION OF CREDITOR ETC. WHERE NO CONCURRENT PETITION PRESENTED AGAINST MEMBER

Article 7

PART I

MODIFIED PROVISIONS OF PART V OF THE ACT

1   Sections 220 to 223 of the Act are set out as modified in Part I of this Schedule, and sections 117, 131, 133, 234 and Schedule 4 are set out as modified in Part II.

2   Section 220: meaning of "unregistered company"

2   Section 220 is modified so as to read as follows:–

"**220**   For the purposes of this Part, the expression '**unregistered company**' includes any insolvent partnership."

3   Section 221: winding up of unregistered companies

3   Section 221 is modified so as to read as follows:–

"**221(1)**   Subject to subsections (2) and (3) below and to the provisions of this Part, any insolvent partnership may be wound up under this Act if it has, or at any time had, in England and Wales either–

(a)   a principal place of business, or

(b)   a place of business at which business is or has been carried on in the course of which the debt (or part of the debt) arose which forms the basis of the petition for winding up the partnership.

221(2)   Subject to subsection (3) below, an insolvent partnership shall not be wound up under this Act if the business of the partnership has not been carried on in England and Wales at any time in the period of 3 years ending with the day on which the winding-up petition is presented.

221(3)   If an insolvent partnership has a principal place of business situated in Scotland or in Northern Ireland, the court shall not have jurisdiction to wind up the partnership unless it had a principal place of business in England and Wales–

(a)   in the case of a partnership with a principal place of business in Scotland, at any time in the period of 1 year, or

(b)   in the case of a partnership with a principal place of business in Northern Ireland, at any time in the period of 3 years, ending with the day on which the winding-up petition is presented.

221(3A)   The preceding subsections are subject to Article 3 of the EC Regulation (jurisdiction under the EC Regulation).

221(4)   No insolvent partnership shall be wound up under this Act voluntarily.

221(5)   To the extent that they are applicable to the winding up of a company by the court in England and Wales on the petition of a creditor or of the Secretary of State, all the provisions of this Act and the Companies Act about winding up apply to the winding up of an insolvent partnership as an unregistered company–

(a)   with the exceptions and additions mentioned in the following subsections of this section and in section 221A, and

(b)   with the modifications specified in Part II of Schedule 3 to the Insolvent Partnerships Order 1994.

221(6)   Sections 73(1), 74(2)(a) to (d) and (3), 75 to 78, 83, 122, 123, 176A, 202, 203, 205 and 250 shall not apply.

History
Modified s.221(6) amended by the Insolvent Partnerships (Amendment) Order 2006 (SI 2006/622) art.6, as from April 6, 2006.

221(7)   The circumstances in which an insolvent partnership may be wound up as an unregistered company are as follows–

(a)   if the partnership is dissolved, or has ceased to carry on business, or is carrying on business only for the purpose of winding up its affairs;

(b)   if the partnership is unable to pay its debts;

(c)   if the court is of the opinion that it is just and equitable that the partnership should be wound up;

(d)   at the time at which a moratorium for the insolvent partnership under section 1A comes to an end, no voluntary arrangement approved under Part I of this Act has effect in relation to the insolvent partnership.

221(7A)   A winding-up petition on the ground set out in section 221(7)(d) may only be presented by one or more creditors.

History
Modified ss.221(7)(d) and (7A) inserted by the Insolvent Partnerships (Amendment) (No.2) Order 2002 (SI 2002/2708) arts 1, 8 as from January 1, 2003 subject to transitional provisions contained in art.11(1), (3).

221(8)   Every petition for the winding up of an insolvent partnership under Part V of this Act shall be verified by affidavit in Form 2 in Schedule 9 to the Insolvent Partnerships Order 1994.

221A   Petition by liquidator, administrator, trustee or supervisor to wind up insolvent partnership as unregistered company

221A(1)   A petition in Form 3 in Schedule 9 to the Insolvent Partnerships Order 1994 for winding up an insolvent partnership may be presented by–

(a)   the liquidator or administrator of a corporate member or of a former corporate member, or

(b)   the administrator of the partnership, or

(c)   the trustee of an individual member's, or of a former individual member's, estate, or

(d)   the supervisor of a voluntary arrangement approved under Part I of this Act in relation to a corporate member or the partnership, or under Part VIII of this Act in relation to an individual member,

if the ground of the petition is one of the circumstances set out in section 221(7).

221A(2)   In this section **"petitioning insolvency practitioner"** means a person who has presented a petition under subsection (1).

221A(3)   If the ground of the petition presented under subsection (1) is that the partnership is unable to pay its debts and the petitioning insolvency practitioner is able to satisfy the court that an insolvency order has been made against the member whose liquidator or trustee he is because of that member's inability to pay a joint debt, that order shall, unless it is proved otherwise to the satisfaction of the court, be proof for the purposes of section 221(7) that the partnership is unable to pay its debts.

221A(4)   Where a winding-up petition is presented under subsection (1), the court may appoint the petitioning insolvency practitioner as provisional liquidator of the partnership under section 135 (appointment and powers of provisional liquidator).

221A(5)   Where a winding-up order is made against an insolvent partnership after the presentation of a petition under subsection (1), the court may appoint the petitioning insolvency practitioner as liquidator of the partnership; and where the court makes an appointment under this subsection, section 140(3) (official receiver not to become liquidator) applies as if an appointment had been made under that section.

221A(6)   Where a winding-up petition is presented under subsection (1), in the event of the partnership property being insufficient to satisfy the costs of the petitioning insolvency practitioner the costs may be paid out of the assets of the corporate or individual member, as the case may be, as part of the expenses of the liquidation, administration, bankruptcy or voluntary arrangement of that member, in the same order of priority as expenses properly chargeable or incurred by the practitioner in getting in any of the assets of the member."

4   Section 222: inability to pay debts: unpaid creditor for £750 or more

4   Section 222 is modified so as to read as follows:–

"**222(1)**   An insolvent partnership is deemed (for the purposes of section 221) unable to pay its debts if there is a creditor, by assignment or otherwise, to whom the partnership is indebted in a sum exceeding £750 then due and–

    (a)   the creditor has served on the partnership, in the manner specified in subsection (2) below, a written demand in the prescribed form requiring the partnership to pay the sum so due, and

    (b)   the partnership has for 3 weeks after the service of the demand neglected to pay the sum or to secure or compound for it to the creditor's satisfaction.

222(2)   Service of the demand referred to in subsection (1)(a) shall be effected–

    (a)   by leaving it at a principal place of business of the partnership in England and Wales, or

    (b)   by leaving it at a place of business of the partnership in England and Wales at which business is carried on in the course of which the debt (or part of the debt) referred to in subsection (1) arose, or

    (c)   by delivering it to an officer of the partnership, or

    (d)   by otherwise serving it in such manner as the court may approve or direct.

222(3)   The money sum for the time being specified in subsection (1) is subject to increase or reduction by regulations under section 417 in Part XV; but no increase in the sum so specified affects any case in which the winding-up petition was presented before the coming into force of the increase."

5   Section 223: inability to pay debts: debt remaining unsatisfied after action brought

5   Section 223 is modified so as to read as follows:–

"**223(1)**   An insolvent partnership is deemed (for the purposes of section 221) unable to pay its debts if an action or other proceeding has been instituted against any member for any debt or demand due, or claimed to be due, from the partnership, or from him in his character of member, and–

    (a)   notice in writing of the institution of the action or proceeding has been served on the partnership in the manner specified in subsection (2) below, and

    (b)   the partnership has not within 3 weeks after service of the notice paid, secured or compounded for the debt or demand, or procured the action or proceeding to be stayed or sisted, or indemnified the defendant or defender to his reasonable satisfaction against the action or proceeding, and against all costs, damages and expenses to be incurred by him because of it.

223(2)　Service of the notice referred to in subsection (1)(a) shall be effected–

(a)　by leaving it at a principal place of business of the partnership in England and Wales, or

(b)　by leaving it at a place of business of the partnership in England and Wales at which business is carried on in the course of which the debt or demand (or part of the debt or demand) referred to in subsection (1) arose, or

(c)　by delivering it to an officer of the partnership, or

(d)　by otherwise serving it in such manner as the court may approve or direct."

PART II

OTHER MODIFIED PROVISIONS OF THE ACT ABOUT WINDING UP BY THE COURT

6　Section 117: High Court and county court jurisdiction

6　Section 117 is modified so as to read as follows:–

"**117(1)**　Subject to subsections (3) and (4) below, the High Court has jurisdiction to wind up any insolvent partnership as an unregistered company by virtue of article 7 of the Insolvent Partnerships Order 1994 if the partnership has, or at any time had, in England and Wales either–

(a)　a principal place of business, or

(b)　a place of business at which business is or has been carried on in the course of which the debt (or part of the debt) arose which forms the basis of the petition for winding up the partnership.

117(2)　Subject to subsections (3) and (4) below, a petition for the winding up of an insolvent partnership by virtue of the said article 7 may be presented to a county court in England and Wales if the partnership has, or at any time had, within the insolvency district of that court either–

(a)　a principal place of business, or

(b)　a place of business at which business is or has been carried on in the course of which the debt (or part of the debt) arose which forms the basis of the winding-up petition.

117(3)　Subject to subsection (4) below, the court only has jurisdiction to wind up an insolvent partnership if the business of the partnership has been carried on in England and Wales at any time in the period of 3 years ending with the day on which the petition for winding it up is presented.

117(4)　If an insolvent partnership has a principal place of business situated in Scotland or in Northern Ireland, the court shall not have jurisdiction to wind up the partnership unless it had a principal place of business in England and Wales–

(a)　in the case of a partnership with a principal place of business in Scotland, at any time in the period of 1 year, or

(b)　in the case of a partnership with a principal place of business in Northern Ireland, at any time in the period of 3 years,

ending with the day on which the petition for winding it up is presented.

117(5)　The Lord Chancellor may, with the concurrence of the Lord Chief Justice, by order in a statutory instrument exclude a county court from having winding-up jurisdiction, and for the purposes of that jurisdiction may attach its district, or any part thereof, to any other county court, and may by statutory instrument revoke or vary any such order.

In exercising the powers of this section, the Lord Chancellor shall provide that a county court is not to have winding-up jurisdiction unless it has for the time being jurisdiction for the purposes of Parts VIII to XI of this Act (individual insolvency).

117(6)   Every court in England and Wales having winding-up jurisdiction has for the purposes of that jurisdiction all the powers of the High Court; and every prescribed officer of the court shall perform any duties which an officer of the High Court may discharge by order of a judge of that court or otherwise in relation to winding up.

117(7)   This section is subject to Article 3 of the EC Regulation (jurisdiction under the EC Regulation).

117(8)   The Lord Chief Justice may nominate a judicial office holder (as defined in section 109(4) of the Constitutional Reform Act 2005) to exercise his functions under this section."

History
Modified s.117(5) amended, and s.117(8) inserted by the Lord Chancellor (Transfer of Functions and Supplementary Provisions) Order 2006 (SI 2006/680) Sch.2 paras 5, 6 as from April 3, 2006.

7   Section 131: statement of affairs of insolvent partnership

7   Section 131 is modified so as to read as follows:–

"**131(1)**   Where the court has, by virtue of article 7 of the Insolvent Partnerships Order 1994, made a winding-up order or appointed a provisional liquidator in respect of an insolvent partnership, the official receiver may require some or all of the persons mentioned in subsection (3) below to make out and submit to him a statement in the prescribed form as to the affairs of the partnership.

131(2)   The statement shall be verified by affidavit by the persons required to submit it and shall show–

(a)   particulars of the debts and liabilities of the partnership and of the partnership property;

(b)   the names and addresses of the partnership's creditors;

(c)   the securities held by them respectively;

(d)   the dates when the securities were respectively given; and

(e)   such further or other information as may be prescribed or as the official receiver may require.

131(3)   The persons referred to in subsection (1) are–

(a)   those who are or have been officers of the partnership;

(b)   those who have taken part in the formation of the partnership at any time within one year before the relevant date;

(c)   those who are in the employment of the partnership, or have been in its employment within that year, and are in the official receiver's opinion capable of giving the information required;

(d)   those who are or have been within that year officers of, or in the employment of, a company which is, or within that year was, an officer of the partnership.

131(4)   Where any persons are required under this section to submit a statement of affairs to the official receiver, they shall do so (subject to the next subsection) before the end of the period of 21 days beginning with the day after that on which the prescribed notice of the requirement is given to them by the official receiver.

131(5)   The official receiver, if he thinks fit, may–

(a)   at any time release a person from an obligation imposed on him under subsection (1) or (2) above; or

(b)   either when giving the notice mentioned in subsection (4) or subsequently, extend the period so mentioned;

and where the official receiver has refused to exercise a power conferred by this subsection, the court, if it thinks fit, may exercise it.

131(6)   In this section–

"**employment**" includes employment under a contract for services; and

"**the relevant date**" means–

(a)   in a case where a provisional liquidator is appointed, the date of his appointment; and

(b)   in a case where no such appointment is made, the date of the winding-up order.

131(7)   If a person without reasonable excuse fails to comply with any obligation imposed under this section, he is liable to a fine and, for continued contravention, to a daily default fine."

8   Section 133: public examination of officers of insolvent partnerships

8   Section 133 is modified so as to read as follows:–

"**133(1)**   Where an insolvent partnership is being wound up by virtue of article 7 of the Insolvent Partnerships Order 1994, the official receiver may at any time before the winding up is complete apply to the court for the public examination of any person who–

(a)   is or has been an officer of the partnership; or

(b)   has acted as liquidator or administrator of the partnership or as receiver or manager or, in Scotland, receiver of its property; or

(c)   not being a person falling within paragraph (a) or (b), is or has been concerned, or has taken part, in the formation of the partnership.

133(2)   Unless the court otherwise orders, the official receiver shall make an application under subsection (1) if he is requested in accordance with the rules to do so by one-half, in value, of the creditors of the partnership.

133(3)   On an application under subsection (1), the court shall direct that a public examination of the person to whom the application relates shall be held on a day appointed by the court; and that person shall attend on that day and be publicly examined as to the formation or management of the partnership or as to the conduct of its business and affairs, or his conduct or dealings in relation to the partnership.

133(4)   The following may take part in the public examination of a person under this section and may question that person concerning the matters mentioned in subsection (3), namely–

(a)   the official receiver;

(b)   the liquidator of the partnership;

(c)   any person who has been appointed as special manager of the partnership's property or business;

(d)   any creditor of the partnership who has tendered a proof in the winding up."

9   Section 234: getting in the partnership property

9   Section 234 is modified so as to read as follows:–

"**234(1)**   This section applies where, by virtue of article 7 of the Insolvent Partnerships Order 1994–

(a)   an insolvent partnership is being wound up, or

(b)   a provisional liquidator of an insolvent partnership is appointed;

and **"the office-holder"** means the liquidator or the provisional liquidator, as the case may be.

234(2)   Any person who is or has been an officer of the partnership, or who is an executor or administrator of the estate of a deceased officer of the partnership, shall deliver up to the office-holder, for the purposes of the exercise of the office-holder's functions under this Act and (where applicable) the Company Directors Disqualification Act 1986, possession of any partnership property which he holds for the purposes of the partnership.

234(3)   Where any person has in his possession or control any property, books, papers or records to which the partnership appears to be entitled, the court may require that person forthwith (or within such period as the court may direct) to pay, deliver, convey, surrender or transfer the property, books, papers or records to the office-holder or as the court may direct.

234(4)   Where the office-holder–

(a)   seizes or disposes of any property which is not partnership property, and

(b)   at the time of seizure or disposal believes, and has reasonable grounds for believing, that he is entitled (whether in pursuance of an order of the court or otherwise) to seize or dispose of that property,

the next subsection has effect.

234(5)   In that case the office-holder–

(a)   is not liable to any person in respect of any loss or damage resulting from the seizure or disposal except in so far as that loss or damage is caused by the office-holder's own negligence, and

(b)   has a lien on the property, or the proceeds of its sale, for such expenses as were incurred in connection with the seizure or disposal."

10   Schedule 4 is modified so as to read as follows:–

"SCHEDULE 4

POWERS OF LIQUIDATOR IN A WINDING UP

Section 167

PART I

POWERS EXERCISABLE WITH SANCTION

1   Power to pay any class of creditors in full.

2   Power to make any compromise or arrangement with creditors or persons claiming to be creditors, or having or alleging themselves to have any claim (present or future, certain or contingent, ascertained or sounding only in damages) against the partnership, or whereby the partnership may be rendered liable.

3   Power to compromise, on such terms as may be agreed–

(a)   all debts and liabilities capable of resulting in debts, and all claims (present or future, certain or contingent, ascertained or sounding only in damages) subsisting or supposed to subsist between the partnership and a contributory or alleged contributory or other debtor or person apprehending liability to the partnership, and

(b)   all questions in any way relating to or affecting the partnership property or the winding up of the partnership,

and take any security for the discharge of any such debt, liability or claim and give a complete discharge in respect of it.

3A   Power to bring legal proceedings under section 213, 214, 238, 239 or 423.

4   Power to bring or defend any action or other legal proceeding in the name and on behalf of any member of the partnership in his capacity as such or of the partnership.

5   Power to carry on the business of the partnership so far as may be necessary for its beneficial winding up.

PART II

POWERS EXERCISABLE WITHOUT SANCTION

6   Power to sell any of the partnership property by public auction or private contract, with power to transfer the whole of it to any person or to sell the same in parcels.

7   Power to do all acts and execute, in the name and on behalf of the partnership or of any member of the partnership in his capacity as such, all deeds, receipts and other documents.

8   Power to prove, rank and claim in the bankruptcy, insolvency or sequestration of any contributory for any balance against his estate, and to receive dividends in the bankruptcy, insolvency or sequestration in respect of that balance, as a separate debt due from the bankrupt or insolvent, and rateably with the other separate creditors.

9 Power to draw, accept, make and endorse any bill of exchange or promissory note in the name and on behalf of any member of the partnership in his capacity as such or of the partnership, with the same effect with respect to the liability of the partnership or of any member of the partnership in his capacity as such as if the bill or note had been drawn, accepted, made or endorsed in the course of the partnership's business.

10 Power to raise on the security of the partnership property any money requisite.

11 Power to take out in his official name letters of administration to any deceased contributory, and to do in his official name any other act necessary for obtaining payment of any money due from a contributory or his estate which cannot conveniently be done in the name of the partnership.

In all such cases the money due is deemed, for the purpose of enabling the liquidator to take out the letters of administration or recover the money, to be due to the liquidator himself.

12 Power to appoint an agent to do any business which the liquidator is unable to do himself.

13 Power to do all such other things as may be necessary for winding up the partnership's affairs and distributing its property."

History
In para.10 (modified Sch.4) para.3A inserted by the Insolvent Partnerships (Amendment) Order 2005 (SI 2005/1516) art.8 as from July 1, 2005.

SCHEDULE 4

PROVISIONS OF THE ACT WHICH APPLY WITH MODIFICATIONS FOR THE PURPOSES OF ARTICLE 8 TO WINDING UP OF INSOLVENT PARTNERSHIP ON CREDITOR'S PETITION WHERE CONCURRENT PETITIONS ARE PRESENTED AGAINST ONE OR MORE MEMBERS

Article 8

PART I

MODIFIED PROVISIONS OF PART V OF THE ACT

1(1) Sections 220 to 222 of the Act are set out as modified in Part I of this Schedule, and the provisions of the Act specified in sub-paragraph (2) below are set out as modified in Part II.

1(2) The provisions referred to in sub-paragraph (1) are sections 117, 122 to 125, 131, 133, 136, 137, 139 to 141, 143, 146, 147, 168, 172, 174, 175, 189, 211, 230, 231, 234, 264, 265, 267, 268, 271, 283, 283A, 284, 288, 292 to 296, 298 to 303, 305, 313A, 314, 328, 331 and 356, and Schedule 4.

History
In para.1(2) "283A" and "313A" inserted by the Insolvent Partnerships (Amendment) Order 2005 (SI 2005/1516) art.9(1), (2) as from July 1, 2005.

2 Section 220: meaning of "unregistered company"

2 Section 220 is modified so as to read as follows:–

"**220** For the purposes of this Part, the expression **"unregistered company"** includes any insolvent partnership."

3 Section 221: winding up of unregistered companies

3 Section 221 is modified so as to read as follows:–

"**221(1)** Subject to subsections (2) and (3) below and to the provisions of this Part, any insolvent partnership may be wound up under this Act if it has, or at any time had, in England and Wales either–

(a) a principal place of business, or

(b)   a place of business at which business is or has been carried on in the course of which the debt (or part of the debt) arose which forms the basis of the petition for winding up the partnership.

221(2)   Subject to subsection (3) below, an insolvent partnership shall not be wound up under this Act if the business of the partnership has not been carried on in England and Wales at any time in the period of 3 years ending with the day on which the winding-up petition is presented.

221(3)   If an insolvent partnership has a principal place of business situated in Scotland or in Northern Ireland, the court shall not have jurisdiction to wind up the partnership unless it had a principal place of business in England and Wales–

(a)   in the case of a partnership with a principal place of business in Scotland, at any time in the period of 1 year, or

(b)   in the case of a partnership with a principal place of business in Northern Ireland, at any time in the period of 3 years,

ending with the day on which the winding-up petition is presented.

221(3A)   The preceding subsections are subject to Article 3 of the EC Regulation (jurisdiction under the EC Regulation).

221(4)   No insolvent partnership shall be wound up under this Act voluntarily.

221(5)   To the extent that they are applicable to the winding up of a company by the court in England and Wales on a creditor's petition, all the provisions of this Act and the Companies Act about winding up apply to the winding up of an insolvent partnership as an unregistered company–

(a)   with the exceptions and additions mentioned in the following subsections of this section, and

(b)   with the modifications specified in Part II of Schedule 4 to the Insolvent Partnerships Order 1994.

221(6)   Sections 73(1), 74(2)(a) to (d) and (3), 75 to 78, 83, 154, 176A, 202, 203, 205 and 250 shall not apply.

History
Modified s.221(6) amended by the Insolvent Partnerships (Amendment) Order 2006 (SI 2006/622) art.7, as from April 6, 2006.

221(7)   Unless the contrary intention appears, a member of a partnership against whom an insolvency order has been made by virtue of article 8 of the Insolvent Partnerships Order 1994 shall not be treated as a contributory for the purposes of this Act.

221(8)   The circumstances in which an insolvent partnership may be wound up as an unregistered company are as follows–

(a)   the partnership is unable to pay its debts,

(b)   at the time at which a moratorium for the insolvent partnership under section 1A comes to an end, no voluntary arrangement approved under Part I of this Act has effect in relation to the insolvent partnership.

History
Modified s.221(8) substituted by the Insolvent Partnerships (Amendment) (No.2) Order 2002 (SI 2002/2708) arts 1, 9(1), (2) as from January 1, 2003 subject to transitional provisions contained in arts 11(1), (3).

221(9)   Every petition for the winding up of an insolvent partnership under Part V of this Act shall be verified by affidavit in Form 2 in Schedule 9 to the Insolvent Partnerships Order 1994."

4   Section 222: inability to pay debts: unpaid creditor for £750 or more

4   Section 222 is modified so as to read as follows:–

"**222(1)**   An insolvent partnership is deemed (for the purposes of section 221) unable to pay its debts if there is a creditor, by assignment or otherwise, to whom the partnership is indebted in a sum exceeding £750 then due and–

(a)   the creditor has served on the partnership, in the manner specified in subsection (2) below, a written demand in Form 4 in Schedule 9 to the Insolvent Partnerships Order 1994 requiring the partnership to pay the sum so due,

(b) the creditor has also served on any one or more members or former members of the partnership liable to pay the sum due (in the case of a corporate member by leaving it at its registered office and in the case of an individual member by serving it in accordance with the rules) a demand in Form 4 in Schedule 9 to that Order, requiring that member or those members to pay the sum so due, and

(c) the partnership and its members have for 3 weeks after the service of the demands, or the service of the last of them if served at different times, neglected to pay the sum or to secure or compound for it to the creditor's satisfaction.

222(2) Service of the demand referred to in subsection (1)(a) shall be effected–

(a) by leaving it at a principal place of business of the partnership in England and Wales, or

(b) by leaving it at a place of business of the partnership in England and Wales at which business is carried on in the course of which the debt (or part of the debt) referred to in subsection (1) arose, or

(c) by delivering it to an officer of the partnership, or

(d) by otherwise serving it in such manner as the court may approve or direct.

222(3) The money sum for the time being specified in subsection (1) is subject to increase or reduction by regulations under section 417 in Part XV; but no increase in the sum so specified affects any case in which the winding-up petition was presented before the coming into force of the increase."

PART II

OTHER MODIFIED PROVISIONS OF THE ACT ABOUT WINDING UP BY THE COURT AND BANKRUPTCY OF INDIVIDUALS

5 Sections 117 and 265: High Court and county court jurisdiction

5 Sections 117 and 265 are modified so as to read as follows:–

"**117(1)** Subject to the provisions of this section, the High Court has jurisdiction to wind up any insolvent partnership as an unregistered company by virtue of article 8 of the Insolvent Partnerships Order 1994 if the partnership has, or at any time had, in England and Wales either–

(a) a principal place of business, or

(b) a place of business at which business is or has been carried on in the course of which the debt (or part of the debt) arose which forms the basis of the petition for winding up the partnership.

117(2) Subject to subsections (3) and (4) below, a petition for the winding up of an insolvent partnership by virtue of the said article 8 may be presented to a county court in England and Wales if the partnership has, or at any time had, within the insolvency district of that court either–

(a) a principal place of business, or

(b) a place of business at which business is or has been carried on in the course of which the debt (or part of the debt) arose which forms the basis of the winding-up petition.

117(3) Subject to subsection (4) below, the court only has jurisdiction to wind up an insolvent partnership if the business of the partnership has been carried on in England and Wales at any time in the period of 3 years ending with the day on which the petition for winding it up is presented.

117(4) If an insolvent partnership has a principal place of business situated in Scotland or in Northern Ireland, the court shall not have jurisdiction to wind up the partnership unless it had a principal place of business in England and Wales–

(a) in the case of a partnership with a principal place of business in Scotland, at any time in the period of 1 year, or

(b) in the case of a partnership with a principal place of business in Northern Ireland, at any time in the period of 3 years, ending with the day on which the petition for winding it up is presented.

117(5)   Subject to subsection (6) below, the court has jurisdiction to wind up a corporate member or former corporate member, or make a bankruptcy order against an individual member or former individual member, of a partnership against which a petition has been presented by virtue of article 8 of the Insolvent Partnerships Order 1994 if it has jurisdiction in respect of the partnership.

117(6)   Petitions by virtue of the said article 8 for the winding up of an insolvent partnership and the bankruptcy of one or more members or former members of that partnership may not be presented to a district registry of the High Court.

117(7)   The Lord Chancellor may, with the concurrence of the Lord Chief Justice, by order in a statutory instrument exclude a county court from having winding-up jurisdiction, and for the purposes of that jurisdiction may attach its district, or any part thereof, to any other county court, and may by statutory instrument revoke or vary any such order.

In exercising the powers of this section, the Lord Chancellor shall provide that a county court is not to have winding-up jurisdiction unless it has for the time being jurisdiction for the purposes of Parts VIII to XI of this Act (individual insolvency).

117(8)   Every court in England and Wales having winding-up jurisdiction has for the purposes of that jurisdiction all the powers of the High Court; and every prescribed officer of the court shall perform any duties which an officer of the High Court may discharge by order of a judge of that court or otherwise in relation to winding up.

117(9)   This section is subject to Article 3 of the EC Regulation (jurisdiction under the EC Regulation).

117(10)   The Lord Chief Justice may nominate a judicial office holder (as defined in section 109(4) of the Constitutional Reform Act 2005) to exercise his functions under this section."

History
Modified s.117(7) amended, and s.117(10) inserted, by the Lord Chancellor (Transfer of Functions and Supplementary Provisions) Order 2006 (SI 2006/680) Sch.2 paras 5, 7, as from April 3, 2006.

6   Circumstances in which members of insolvent partnerships may be wound up or made bankrupt by the court: Section 122—corporate member; Section 267—individual member

6(a)   Section 122 is modified so as to read as follows:–

"**122**   A corporate member or former corporate member of an insolvent partnership may be wound up by the court if–

  (a)   it is unable to pay its debts,

  (b)   there is a creditor, by assignment or otherwise, to whom the insolvent partnership is indebted and the corporate member or former corporate member is liable in relation to that debt and at the time at which a moratorium for the insolvent partnership under section 1A comes to an end, no voluntary arrangement approved under Part I of this Act has effect in relation to the insolvent partnership."

History
Modified s.122 substituted by the Insolvent Partnerships (Amendment) (No.2) Order 2002 (SI 2002/2708) arts 1, 9(1), (3) as from January 1, 2003 subject to transitional provisions contained in arts 11(1), (3).

6(b)   Section 267 is modified so as to read as follows:–

"**267(1)**   Where a petition for the winding up of an insolvent partnership has been presented to the court by virtue of article 8 of the Insolvent Partnerships Order 1994, a creditor's petition against any individual member or former individual member of that partnership by virtue of that article must be in respect of one or more joint debts owed by the insolvent partnership, and the petitioning creditor or each of the petitioning creditors must be a person to whom the debt or (as the case may be) at least one of the debts is owed.

267(2)   Subject to subsection (2A) below and section 268, a creditor's petition may be presented to the court in respect of a joint debt or debts only if, at the time the petition is presented–

  (a)   the amount of the debt, or the aggregate amount of the debts, is equal to or exceeds the bankruptcy level,

   (b) the debt, or each of the debts, is for a liquidated sum payable to the petitioning creditor, or one or more of the petitioning creditors, immediately, and is unsecured,

   (c) the debt, or each of the debts, is a debt for which the individual member or former member is liable and which he appears to be unable to pay, and

   (d) there is no outstanding application to set aside a statutory demand served (under section 268 below) in respect of the debt or any of the debts.

History

In modified s.267(2) the words "subsection (2A) below and" inserted by the Insolvent Partnerships (Amendment) (No.2) Order 2002 (SI 2002/2708) arts 1, 9(1), (4)(a) as from January 1, 2003 subject to transitional provisions contained in art.11(1), (3).

267(2A) A creditor's petition may be presented to the court in respect of a joint debt or debts if at the time at which a moratorium for the insolvent partnership under section 1A comes to an end, no voluntary arrangement approved under Part I of this Act has effect in relation to the insolvent partnership.

History

Modified s.267(2A) inserted by the Insolvent Partnerships (Amendment) (No.2) Order 2002 (SI 2002/2708) arts 1, 9(1), (4)(b) as from January 1, 2003 subject to transitional provisions contained in art.11(1), (3).

267(3) "The bankruptcy level" is £750; but the Secretary of State may by order in a statutory instrument substitute any amount specified in the order for that amount or (as the case may be) for the amount which by virtue of such an order is for the time being the amount of the bankruptcy level.

267(4) An order shall not be made under subsection (3) unless a draft of it has been laid before, and approved by a resolution of, each House of Parliament."

7 Definition of inability to pay debts: Section 123—corporate member; Section 268—individual member

7(a) Section 123 is modified so as to read as follows:–

"**123(1)** A corporate member or former member is deemed unable to pay its debts if there is a creditor, by assignment or otherwise, to whom the partnership is indebted in a sum exceeding £750 then due for which the member or former member is liable and–

   (a) the creditor has served on that member or former member and the partnership, in the manner specified in subsection (2) below, a written demand in Form 4 in Schedule 9 to the Insolvent Partnerships Order 1994 requiring that member or former member and the partnership to pay the sum so due, and

   (b) the corporate member or former member and the partnership have for 3 weeks after the service of the demands, or the service of the last of them if served at different times, neglected to pay the sum or to secure or compound for it to the creditor's satisfaction.

123(2) Service of the demand referred to in subsection (1)(a) shall be effected, in the case of the corporate member or former corporate member, by leaving it at its registered office, and, in the case of the partnership–

   (a) by leaving it at a principal place of business of the partnership in England and Wales, or

   (b) by leaving it at a place of business of the partnership in England and Wales at which business is carried on in the course of which the debt (or part of the debt) referred to in subsection (1) arose, or

   (c) by delivering it to an officer of the partnership, or

   (d) by otherwise serving it in such manner as the court may approve or direct.

123(3) The money sum for the time being specified in subsection (1) is subject to increase or reduction by order under section 416 in Part XV."

7(b) Section 268 is modified so as to read as follows:–

"**268(1)** For the purposes of section 267(2)(c), an individual member or former individual member appears to be unable to pay a joint debt for which he is liable if the debt is payable immediately and the petitioning creditor to whom the insolvent partnership owes the joint debt has served–

(a) on the individual member or former individual member in accordance with the rules a demand (known as **"the statutory demand"**), in Form 4 in Schedule 9 to the Insolvent Partnerships Order 1994, and

(b) on the partnership in the manner specified in subsection (2) below a demand (known as **"the written demand"**) in the same form,

requiring the member or former member and the partnership to pay the debt or to secure or compound for it to the creditor's satisfaction, and at least 3 weeks have elapsed since the service of the demands, or the service of the last of them if served at different times, and neither demand has been complied with nor the demand against the member set aside in accordance with the rules.

268(2) Service of the demand referred to in subsection (1)(b) shall be effected–

(a) by leaving it at a principal place of business of the partnership in England and Wales, or

(b) by leaving it at a place of business of the partnership in England and Wales at which business is carried on in the course of which the debt (or part of the debt) referred to in subsection (1) arose, or

(c) by delivering it to an officer of the partnership, or

(d) by otherwise serving it in such manner as the court may approve or direct."

8 Sections 124 and 264: applications to wind up insolvent partnership and to wind up or bankrupt insolvent member

8 Sections 124 and 264 are modified so as to read as follows:–

"**124(1)** An application to the court by virtue of article 8 of the Insolvent Partnerships Order 1994 for the winding up of an insolvent partnership as an unregistered company and the winding up or bankruptcy (as the case may be) of at least one of its members or former members shall–

(a) in the case of the partnership, be by petition in Form 5 in Schedule 9 to that Order,

(b) in the case of a corporate member or former corporate member, be by petition in Form 6 in that Schedule, and

(c) in the case of an individual member or former individual member, be by petition in Form 7 in that Schedule.

124(2) Each of the petitions mentioned in subsection (1) may be presented by a liquidator (within the meaning of Article 2(b) of the EC Regulation) appointed in proceedings by virtue of Article 3(1) of the EC Regulation, a temporary administrator (within the meaning of Article 38 of the EC Regulation) or any creditor or creditors to whom the partnership and the member or former member in question is indebted in respect of a liquidated sum payable immediately.

124(3) The petitions mentioned in subsection (1)–

(a) shall all be presented to the same court and, except as the court otherwise permits or directs, on the same day, and

(b) except in the case of the petition mentioned in subsection (1)

(c) shall be advertised in Form 8 in the said Schedule 9.

124(4) At any time after presentation of a petition under this section the petitioner may, with the leave of the court obtained on application and on such terms as it thinks just, add other members or former members of the partnership as parties to the proceedings in relation to the insolvent partnership.

124(5) Each petition presented under this section shall contain particulars of other petitions being presented in relation to the partnership, identifying the partnership and members concerned.

124(6) The hearing of the petition against the partnership fixed by the court shall be in advance of the hearing of any petition against an insolvent member.

124(7) On the day appointed for the hearing of the petition against the partnership, the petitioner shall, before the commencement of the hearing, hand to the court Form 9 in Schedule 9 to the Insolvent Partnerships Order 1994, duly completed.

124(8)   Any member of the partnership or any person against whom a winding-up or bankruptcy petition has been presented in relation to the insolvent partnership is entitled to appear and to be heard on any petition for the winding up of the partnership.

124(9)   A petitioner under this section may at the hearing withdraw a petition if–

(a)   subject to subsection (10) below, he withdraws at the same time every other petition which he has presented under this section; and

(b)   he gives notice to the court at least 3 days before the date appointed for the hearing of the relevant petition of his intention to withdraw the petition.

124(10)   A petitioner need not comply with the provisions of subsection (9)(a) in the case of a petition against an insolvent member if the court is satisfied on application made to it by the petitioner that, because of difficulties in serving the petition or for any other reason, the continuance of that petition would be likely to prejudice or delay the proceedings on the petition which he has presented against the partnership or on any petition which he has presented against any other insolvent member.

124(11)   Where notice is given under subsection (9)(b), the court may, on such terms as it thinks just, substitute as petitioner, both in respect of the partnership and in respect of each insolvent member against whom a petition has been presented, any creditor of the partnership who in its opinion would have a right to present the petitions, and if the court makes such a substitution the petitions in question will not be withdrawn.

124(12)   Reference in subsection (11) to substitution of a petitioner includes reference to change of carriage of the petition in accordance with the rules."

9   Sections 125 and 271: powers of court on hearing of petitions against insolvent partnership and members

9   Sections 125 and 271 are modified so as to read as follows:–

"**125(1)**   Subject to the provisions of section 125A, on hearing a petition under section 124 against an insolvent partnership or any of its insolvent members, the court may dismiss it, or adjourn the hearing conditionally or unconditionally or make any other order that it thinks fit; but the court shall not refuse to make a winding-up order against the partnership or a corporate member on the ground only that the partnership property or (as the case may be) the member's assets have been mortgaged to an amount equal to or in excess of that property or those assets, or that the partnership has no property or the member no assets.

125(2)   An order under subsection (1) in respect of an insolvent partnership may contain directions as to the future conduct of any insolvency proceedings in existence against any insolvent member in respect of whom an insolvency order has been made.

125A   Hearing of petitions against members

125A(1)   On the hearing of a petition against an insolvent member the petitioner shall draw the court's attention to the result of the hearing of the winding-up petition against the partnership and the following subsections of this section shall apply.

125A(2)   If the court has neither made a winding-up order, nor dismissed the winding-up petition, against the partnership the court may adjourn the hearing of the petition against the member until either event has occurred.

125A(3)   Subject to subsection (4) below, if a winding-up order has been made against the partnership, the court may make a winding-up order against the corporate member in respect of which, or (as the case may be) a bankruptcy order against the individual member in respect of whom, the insolvency petition was presented.

125A(4)   If no insolvency order is made under subsection (3) against any member within 28 days of the making of the winding-up order against the partnership, the proceedings against the partnership shall be conducted as if the winding-up petition against the partnership had been presented by virtue of article 7 of the Insolvent Partnerships Order 1994 and the proceedings against any member shall be conducted under this Act without the modifications made by that Order (other than the modifications made to sections 168 and 303 by article 14).

125A(5)   If the court has dismissed the winding-up petition against the partnership, the court may dismiss the winding-up petition against the corporate member or (as the case may be) the bankruptcy petition against the individual member. However, if an insolvency order is made against a member, the proceedings against that member shall be conducted under this Act without the modifications made by the Insolvent Partnerships Order 1994 (other than the modifications made to sections 168 and 303 of this Act by article 14 of that Order).

125A(6)   The court may dismiss a petition against an insolvent member if it considers it just to do so because of a change in circumstances since the making of the winding-up order against the partnership.

125A(7)   The court may dismiss a petition against an insolvent member who is a limited partner, if–

(a)   the member lodges in court for the benefit of the creditors of the partnership sufficient money or security to the court's satisfaction to meet his liability for the debts and obligations of the partnership; or

(b)   the member satisfies the court that he is no longer under any liability in respect of the debts and obligations of the partnership.

125A(8)   Nothing in sections 125 and 125A or in sections 267 and 268 prejudices the power of the court, in accordance with the rules, to authorise a creditor's petition to be amended by the omission of any creditor or debt and to be proceeded with as if things done for the purposes of those sections had been done only by or in relation to the remaining creditors or debts."

10   Sections 131 and 288: statements of affairs--insolvent partnerships; corporate members; individual members

10   Sections 131 and 288 are modified so as to read as follows:–

"**131(1)**   This section applies where the court has, by virtue of article 8 of the Insolvent Partnerships Order 1994–

(a)   made a winding-up order or appointed a provisional liquidator in respect of an insolvent partnership, or

(b)   made a winding-up order or appointed a provisional liquidator in respect of any corporate member of that partnership, or

(c)   made a bankruptcy order in respect of any individual member of that partnership.

131(2)   The official receiver may require some or all of the persons mentioned in subsection (4) below to make out and submit to him a statement as to the affairs of the partnership or member in the prescribed form.

131(3)   The statement shall be verified by affidavit by the persons required to submit it and shall show–

(a)   particulars of the debts and liabilities of the partnership or of the member (as the case may be), and of the partnership property and member's assets;

(b)   the names and addresses of the creditors of the partnership or of the member (as the case may be);

(c)   the securities held by them respectively;

(d)   the dates when the securities were respectively given; and

(e)   such further or other information as may be prescribed or as the official receiver may require.

131(4)   The persons referred to in subsection (2) are–

(a)   those who are or have been officers of the partnership;

(b)   those who are or have been officers of the corporate member;

(c)   those who have taken part in the formation of the partnership or of the corporate member at any time within one year before the relevant date;

(d)   those who are in the employment of the partnership or of the corporate member, or have been in such employment within that year, and are in the official receiver's opinion capable of giving the information required;

(e)   those who are or have been within that year officers of, or in the employment of, a company which is, or within that year was, an officer of the partnership or an officer of the corporate member.

131(5)   Where any persons are required under this section to submit a statement of affairs to the official receiver, they shall do so (subject to the next subsection) before the end of the period of 21 days beginning with the day after that on which the prescribed notice of the requirement is given to them by the official receiver.

131(6)   The official receiver, if he thinks fit, may–

(a)   at any time release a person from an obligation imposed on him under subsection (2) or (3) above; or

(b)   either when giving the notice mentioned in subsection (5) or subsequently, extend the period so mentioned;

and where the official receiver has refused to exercise a power conferred by this subsection, the court, if it thinks fit, may exercise it.

131(7)   In this section–

"employment" includes employment under a contract for services; and

"the relevant date" means–

(a)   in a case where a provisional liquidator is appointed, the date of his appointment; and

(b)   in a case where no such appointment is made, the date of the winding-up order.

131(8)   Any person who without reasonable excuse fails to comply with any obligation imposed under this section (other than, in the case of an individual member, an obligation in respect of his own statement of affairs), is liable to a fine and, for continued contravention, to a daily default fine.

131(9)   An individual member who without reasonable excuse fails to comply with any obligation imposed under this section in respect of his own statement of affairs, is guilty of a contempt of court and liable to be punished accordingly (in addition to any other punishment to which he may be subject)."

11   Section 133: public examination of officers of insolvent partnerships

11   Section 133 is modified so far as insolvent partnerships are concerned so as to read as follows:–

"**133(1)**   Where an insolvent partnership is being wound up by virtue of article 8 of the Insolvent Partnerships Order 1994, the official receiver may at any time before the winding up is complete apply to the court for the public examination of any person who–

(a)   is or has been an officer of the partnership; or

(b)   has acted as liquidator or administrator of the partnership or as receiver or manager or, in Scotland, receiver of its property;

(c)   not being a person falling within paragraph (a) or (b), is or has been concerned, or has taken part, in the formation of the partnership.

133(2)   Unless the court otherwise orders, the official receiver shall make an application under subsection (1) if he is requested in accordance with the rules to do so by one-half, in value, of the creditors of the partnership.

133(3)   On an application under subsection (1), the court shall direct that a public examination of the person to whom the application relates shall be held on a day appointed by the court; and that person shall attend on that day and be publicly examined as to the formation or management of the partnership or as to the conduct of its business and affairs, or his conduct or dealings in relation to the partnership.

133(4)   The following may take part in the public examination of a person under this section and may question that person concerning the matters mentioned in subsection (3), namely–

(a)   the official receiver;

(b)   the liquidator of the partnership;

(c)   any person who has been appointed as special manager of the partnership's property or business;

(d)   any creditor of the partnership who has tendered a proof in the winding up.

133(5)   On an application under subsection (1), the court may direct that the public examination of any person under this section in relation to the affairs of an insolvent partnership be combined with the public examination of any person under this Act in relation to the affairs of a corporate member of that partnership against which, or an individual member of the partnership against whom, an insolvency order has been made."

12 Sections 136, 293 and 294: functions of official receiver in relation to office of responsible insolvency practitioner

12 Sections 136, 293 and 294 are modified so as to read as follows:–

"**136(1)** The following provisions of this section and of section 136A have effect, subject to section 140 below, where insolvency orders are made in respect of an insolvent partnership and one or more of its insolvent members by virtue of article 8 of the Insolvent Partnerships Order 1994.

136(2) The official receiver, by virtue of his office, becomes the responsible insolvency practitioner of the partnership and of any insolvent member and continues in office until another person becomes responsible insolvency practitioner under the provisions of this Part.

136(3) The official receiver is, by virtue of his office, the responsible insolvency practitioner of the partnership and of any insolvent member during any vacancy.

136(4) At any time when he is the responsible insolvency practitioner of the insolvent partnership and of any insolvent member, the official receiver may summon a combined meeting of the creditors of the partnership and the creditors of such member, for the purpose of choosing a person to be responsible insolvency practitioner in place of the official receiver.

136A Duty of official receiver to summon meetings

136A(1) It is the duty of the official receiver–

(a) as soon as practicable in the period of 12 weeks beginning with the day on which the insolvency order was made against the partnership, to decide whether to exercise his power under section 136(4) to summon a meeting, and

(b) if in pursuance of paragraph (a) he decides not to exercise that power, to give notice of his decision, before the end of that period, to the court and to the creditors of the partnership and the creditors of any insolvent member against whom an insolvency order has been made, and

(c) (whether or not he has decided to exercise that power) to exercise his power to summon a meeting under section 136(4) if he is at any time requested to do so in accordance with the rules by one-quarter, in value, of either–

(i) the partnership's creditors, or

(ii) the creditors of any insolvent member against whom an insolvency order has been made,

and accordingly, where the duty imposed by paragraph (c) arises before the official receiver has performed a duty imposed by paragraph (a) or (b), he is not required to perform the latter duty.

136A(2) A notice given under subsection (1)(b) to the creditors shall contain an explanation of the creditors' power under subsection (1)(c) to require the official receiver to summon a combined meeting of the creditors of the partnership and of any insolvent member.

136A(3) If the official receiver, in pursuance of subsection (1)(a), has decided to exercise his power under section 136(4) to summon a meeting, he shall hold that meeting in the period of 4 months beginning with the day on which the insolvency order was made against the partnership.

136A(4) If (whether or not he has decided to exercise that power) the official receiver is requested, in accordance with the provisions of subsection (1)(c), to exercise his power under section 136(4) to summon a meeting, he shall hold that meeting in accordance with the rules.

136A(5) Where a meeting of creditors of the partnership and of any insolvent member has been held under section 136(4), and an insolvency order is subsequently made against a further insolvent member by virtue of article 8 of the Insolvent Partnerships Order 1994–

(a) any person chosen at that meeting to be responsible insolvency practitioner in place of the official receiver shall also be the responsible insolvency practitioner of the member against whom the subsequent order is made, and

806

(b)   subsection (1) of this section shall not apply."

13   Sections 137, 295, 296 and 300: appointment of responsible insolvency practitioner by Secretary of State

13   Sections 137, 295, 296 and 300 are modified so as to read as follows:–

"**137(1)**   This section and the next apply where the court has made insolvency orders in respect of an insolvent partnership and one or more of its insolvent members by virtue of article 8 of the Insolvent Partnerships Order 1994.

137(2)   The official receiver may, at any time when he is the responsible insolvency practitioner of the partnership and of any insolvent member, apply to the Secretary of State for the appointment of a person as responsible insolvency practitioner of both the partnership and of such member in his place.

137(3)   If a meeting is held in pursuance of a decision under section 136A(1)(a), but no person is chosen to be responsible insolvency practitioner as a result of that meeting, it is the duty of the official receiver to decide whether to refer the need for an appointment to the Secretary of State.

137A   Consequences of section 137 application

137A(1)   On an application under section 137(2), or a reference made in pursuance of a decision under section 137(3), the Secretary of State shall either make an appointment or decline to make one.

137A(2)   If on an application under section 137(2), or a reference made in pursuance of a decision under section 137(3), no appointment is made, the official receiver shall continue to be responsible insolvency practitioner of the partnership and its insolvent member or members, but without prejudice to his power to make a further application or reference.

137A(3)   Where a responsible insolvency practitioner has been appointed by the Secretary of State under subsection (1) of this section, and an insolvency order is subsequently made against a further insolvent member by virtue of article 8 of the Insolvent Partnerships Order 1994, then the practitioner so appointed shall also be the responsible insolvency practitioner of the member against whom the subsequent order is made.

137A(4)   Where a responsible insolvency practitioner has been appointed by the Secretary of State under subsection (1), or has become responsible insolvency practitioner of a further insolvent member under subsection (3), that practitioner shall give notice of his appointment or further appointment (as the case may be) to the creditors of the insolvent partnership and the creditors of the insolvent member or members against whom insolvency orders have been made or, if the court so allows, shall advertise his appointment in accordance with the directions of the court.

137A(5)   Subject to subsection (6) below, in that notice or advertisement the responsible insolvency practitioner shall–

(a)   state whether he proposes to summon, under section 141 below, a combined meeting of the creditors of the insolvent partnership and of the insolvent member or members against whom insolvency orders have been made, for the purpose of determining whether a creditors' committee should be established under that section, and

(b)   if he does not propose to summon such a meeting, set out the power under that section of the creditors of the partnership and of the insolvent member or members to require him to summon one.

137A(6)   Where in a case where subsection (3) applies a meeting has already been held under section 141 below, the responsible insolvency practitioner shall state in the notice or advertisement whether a creditors' committee was established at that meeting and–

(a)   if such a committee was established, shall state whether he proposes to appoint additional members of the committee under section 141A(3), and

(b)   if such a committee was not established, shall set out the power under section 141 of the creditors of the partnership and of the insolvent member or members to require him to summon a meeting for the purpose of determining whether a creditors' committee should be established under that section."

14   Section 139: Rules applicable to meetings of creditors

14   Section 139 is modified so as to read as follows:–

"**139(1)**   This section applies where the court has made insolvency orders against an insolvent partnership and one or more of its insolvent members by virtue of article 8 of the Insolvent Partnerships Order 1994.

139(2)   Subject to subsection (4) below, the rules relating to the requisitioning, summoning, holding and conducting of meetings on the winding up of a company are to apply (with the necessary modifications) to the requisitioning, summoning, holding and conducting of–

(a)   separate meetings of the creditors of the partnership or of any corporate member against which an insolvency order has been made, and

(b)   combined meetings of the creditors of the partnership and the creditors of the insolvent member or members.

139(3)   Subject to subsection (4) below, the rules relating to the requisitioning, summoning, holding and conducting of meetings on the bankruptcy of an individual are to apply (with the necessary modifications) to the requisitioning, summoning, holding and conducting of separate meetings of the creditors of any individual member against whom an insolvency order has been made.

139(4)   Any combined meeting of creditors shall be conducted as if the creditors of the partnership and of the insolvent member or members were a single set of creditors."

15   Section 140: appointment by the court following administration or voluntary arrangement

15   Section 140 is modified so as to read as follows:–

"**140(1)**   This section applies where insolvency orders are made in respect of an insolvent partnership and one or more of its insolvent members by virtue of article 8 of the Insolvent Partnerships Order 1994.

140(2)   Where the orders referred to in subsection (1) are made immediately upon the appointment of an administrator in respect of the partnership ceasing to have effect, the court may appoint as responsible insolvency practitioner the person whose appointment as administrator has ceased to have effect.

140(3)   Where the orders referred to in subsection (1) are made at a time when there is a supervisor of a voluntary arrangement approved in relation to the partnership under Part I, the court may appoint as responsible insolvency practitioner the person who is the supervisor at the time when the winding-up order against the partnership is made.

140(4)   Where the court makes an appointment under this section, the official receiver does not become the responsible insolvency practitioner as otherwise provided by section 136(2), and he has no duty under section 136A(1)(a) or (b) in respect of the summoning of creditors' meetings."

16   Sections 141, 301 and 302: creditors' committee: insolvent partnership and members

16   Sections 141, 301 and 302 are modified so as to read as follows:–

"**141(1)**   This section applies where–

(a)   insolvency orders are made in respect of an insolvent partnership and one or more of its insolvent members by virtue of article 8 of the Insolvent Partnerships Order 1994, and

(b)   a combined meeting of creditors has been summoned for the purpose of choosing a person to be responsible insolvency practitioner of the partnership and of any such insolvent member or members.

141(2)   The meeting of creditors may establish a committee (**"the creditors' committee"**) which shall consist of creditors of the partnership or creditors of any insolvent member against whom an insolvency order has been made, or both.

141(3)   The responsible insolvency practitioner of the partnership and of its insolvent member or members (not being the official receiver) may at any time, if he thinks fit, summon a combined general meeting of the creditors of the partnership and of such member or members for the purpose of determining whether a creditors' committee should be established and, if it is so determined, of establishing it.

The responsible insolvency practitioner (not being the official receiver) shall summon such a meeting if he is requested, in accordance with the rules, to do so by one-tenth, in value, of either–

(a)   the partnership's creditors, or

(b)   the creditors of any insolvent member against whom an insolvency order has been made.

141A   Functions and membership of creditors' committee

141A(1)   The committee established under section 141 shall act as liquidation committee for the partnership and for any corporate member against which an insolvency order has been made, and as creditors' committee for any individual member against whom an insolvency order has been made, and shall as appropriate exercise the functions conferred on liquidation and creditors' committees in a winding up or bankruptcy by or under this Act.

141A(2)   The rules relating to liquidation committees are to apply (with the necessary modifications and with the exclusion of all references to contributories) to a committee established under section 141.

141A(3)   Where the appointment of the responsible insolvency practitioner also takes effect in relation to a further insolvent member under section 136A(5) or 137A(3), the practitioner may appoint any creditor of that member (being qualified under the rules to be a member of the committee) to be an additional member of any creditors' committee already established under section 141, provided that the creditor concerned consents to act.

141A(4)   The court may at any time, on application by a creditor of the partnership or of any insolvent member against whom an insolvency order has been made, appoint additional members of the creditors' committee.

141A(5)   If additional members of the creditors' committee are appointed under subsection (3) or (4), the limit on the maximum number of members of the committee specified in the rules shall be increased by the number of additional members so appointed.

141A(6)   The creditors' committee is not to be able or required to carry out its functions at any time when the official receiver is responsible insolvency practitioner of the partnership and of its insolvent member or members; but at any such time its functions are vested in the Secretary of State except to the extent that the rules otherwise provide.

141A(7)   Where there is for the time being no creditors' committee, and the responsible insolvency practitioner is a person other than the official receiver, the functions of such a committee are vested in the Secretary of State except to the extent that the rules otherwise provide."

17   Sections 143, 168(4) and 305: general functions of responsible insolvency practitioner

17   Sections 143, 168(4) and 305 are modified so as to read as follows:–

"**143(1)**   The functions of the responsible insolvency practitioner of an insolvent partnership and of its insolvent member or members against whom insolvency orders have been made by virtue of article 8 of the Insolvent Partnerships Order 1994, are to secure that the partnership property and the assets of any such corporate member, and the estate of any such individual member, are got in, realised and distributed to their respective creditors and, if there is a surplus of such property or assets or in such estate, to the persons entitled to it.

143(2)   In the carrying out of those functions, and in the management of the partnership property and of the assets of any corporate member and of the estate of any individual member, the responsible insolvency practitioner is entitled, subject to the provisions of this Act, to use his own discretion.

143(3)   It is the duty of the responsible insolvency practitioner, if he is not the official receiver–

(a)   to furnish the official receiver with such information,

(b)   to produce to the official receiver, and permit inspection by the official receiver of, such books, papers and other records, and

(c)   to give the official receiver such other assistance,

as the official receiver may reasonably require for the purposes of carrying out his functions in relation to the winding up of the partnership and any corporate member or the bankruptcy of any individual member.

143(4)   The official name of the responsible insolvency practitioner in his capacity as trustee of an individual member shall be "the trustee of the estate of.........., a bankrupt" (inserting the name of the individual member); but he may be referred to as "the trustee in bankruptcy" of the particular member."

18   Sections 146 and 331: duty to summon final meeting of creditors

18   Sections 146 and 331 are modified so as to read as follows:–

"**146(1)**   This section applies, subject to subsection (3) of this section and section 332 below, if it appears to the responsible insolvency practitioner of an insolvent partnership which is being wound up by virtue of article 8 of the Insolvent Partnerships Order 1994 and of its insolvent member or members that the winding up of the partnership or of any corporate member, or the administration of any individual member's estate, is for practical purposes complete and the practitioner is not the official receiver.

146(2)   The responsible insolvency practitioner shall summon a final general meeting of the creditors of the partnership or of the insolvent member or members (as the case may be) or a combined final general meeting of the creditors of the partnership and of the insolvent member or members which–

(a)   shall as appropriate receive the practitioner's report of the winding up of the insolvent partnership or of any corporate member or of the administration of the estate of any individual member, and

(b)   shall determine whether the practitioner should have his release under section 174 in Chapter VII of this Part in respect of the winding up of the partnership or of the corporate member, or the administration of the individual member's estate (as the case may be).

146(3)   The responsible insolvency practitioner may, if he thinks fit, give the notice summoning the final general meeting at the same time as giving notice of any final distribution of the partnership property or the property of the insolvent member or members; but, if summoned for an earlier date, that meeting shall be adjourned (and, if necessary, further adjourned) until a date on which the practitioner is able to report to the meeting that the winding up of the partnership or of any corporate member, or the administration of any individual member's estate, is for practical purposes complete.

146(4)   In the carrying out of his functions in the winding up of the partnership and of any corporate member and the administration of any individual member's estate, it is the duty of the responsible insolvency practitioner to retain sufficient sums from the partnership property and the property of any such insolvent member to cover the expenses of summoning and holding any meeting required by this section."

19   Section 147: power of court to stay proceedings

19   Section 147 is modified, so far as insolvent partnerships are concerned, so as to read as follows:–

"**147(1)**   The court may, at any time after an order has been made by virtue of article 8 of the Insolvent Partnerships Order 1994 for winding up an insolvent partnership, on the application either of the responsible insolvency practitioner or the official receiver or any creditor or contributory, and on proof to the satisfaction of the court that all proceedings in the winding up of the partnership ought to be stayed, make an order staying the proceedings, either altogether or for a limited time, on such terms and conditions as the court thinks fit.

147(2)   If, in the course of hearing an insolvency petition presented against a member of an insolvent partnership, the court is satisfied that an application has been or will be made under subsection (1) in respect of a winding-up order made against the partnership, the court may adjourn the petition against the insolvent member, either conditionally or unconditionally.

147(3)   Where the court makes an order under subsection (1) staying all proceedings on the order for winding up an insolvent partnership–

(a)   the court may, on hearing any insolvency petition presented against an insolvent member of the partnership, dismiss that petition; and

(b)   if any insolvency order has already been made by virtue of article 8 of the Insolvent Partnerships Order 1994 in relation to an insolvent member of the partnership, the court may make an order annulling or rescinding that insolvency order, or may make any other order that it thinks fit.

147(4)   The court may, before making any order under this section, require the official receiver to furnish to it a report with respect to any facts or matters which are in his opinion relevant to the application."

20   Sections 168, 303 and 314(7): supplementary powers of responsible insolvency practitioner

20   Sections 168(1) to (3) and (5), 303 and 314(7) are modified so as to read as follows:–

"**168(1)**   This section applies where the court has made insolvency orders in respect of an insolvent partnership and one or more of its insolvent members by virtue of article 8 of the Insolvent Partnerships Order 1994.

168(2)   The responsible insolvency practitioner of the partnership and of such member or members may at any time summon either separate or combined general meetings of–

(a)   the creditors or contributories of the partnership, and

(b)   the creditors or contributories of the member or members, for the purpose of ascertaining their wishes.

168(3)   It is the duty of the responsible insolvency practitioner–

(a)   to summon separate meetings at such times as the creditors of the partnership or of the member (as the case may be), or the contributories of any corporate member, by resolution (either at the meeting appointing the responsible insolvency practitioner or otherwise) may direct, or whenever requested in writing to do so by one-tenth in value of such creditors or contributories (as the case may be); and

(b)   to summon combined meetings at such times as the creditors of the partnership and of the member or members by resolution (either at the meeting appointing the responsible insolvency practitioner or otherwise) may direct, or whenever requested in writing to do so by one-tenth in value of such creditors.

168(4)   The responsible insolvency practitioner may apply to the court (in the prescribed manner) for directions in relation to any particular matter arising in the winding up of the insolvent partnership or in the winding up or bankruptcy of an insolvent member.

168(5)   If any person is aggrieved by an act or decision of the responsible insolvency practitioner, that person may apply to the court; and the court may confirm, reverse or modify the act or decision complained of, and make such order in the case as it thinks just."

21   Sections 172 and 298: removal etc. of responsible insolvency practitioner or of provisional liquidator

21   Sections 172 and 298 are modified so as to read as follows:–

"**172(1)**   This section applies with respect to the removal from office and vacation of office of–

(a)   the responsible insolvency practitioner of an insolvent partnership which is being wound up by virtue of article 8 of the Insolvent Partnerships Order 1994 and of its insolvent member or members against whom insolvency orders have been made, or

(b)   a provisional liquidator of an insolvent partnership, and of any corporate member of that partnership, against which a winding-up petition is presented by virtue of that article,

and, subject to subsections (6) and (7) below, any removal from or vacation of office under this section relates to all offices held in the proceedings relating to the partnership.

172(2)   Subject as follows, the responsible insolvency practitioner or provisional liquidator may be removed from office only by an order of the court.

172(3)   If appointed by the Secretary of State, the responsible insolvency practitioner may be removed from office by a direction of the Secretary of State.

172(4)   A responsible insolvency practitioner or provisional liquidator, not being the official receiver, shall vacate office if he ceases to be a person who is qualified to act as an insolvency practitioner in relation to the insolvent partnership or any insolvent member of it against whom an insolvency order has been made.

172(5)   The responsible insolvency practitioner may, with the leave of the court (or, if appointed by the Secretary of State, with the leave of the court or the Secretary of State), resign his office by giving notice of his resignation to the court.

172(6)   Where a final meeting has been held under section 146 (final meeting of creditors of insolvent partnership or of insolvent members), the responsible insolvency practitioner whose report was considered at the meeting shall vacate office as liquidator of the insolvent partnership or of any corporate member or as trustee of the estate of any individual member (as the case may be) as soon as he has given notice to the court (and, in the case of a corporate member, to the registrar of companies) that the meeting has been held and of the decisions (if any) of the meeting.

172(7)   The responsible insolvency practitioner shall vacate office as trustee of the estate of an individual member if the insolvency order against that member is annulled."

22   Sections 174 and 299: release of responsible insolvency practitioner or of provisional liquidator

22   Sections 174 and 299 are modified so as to read as follows:–

"**174(1)**   This section applies with respect to the release of–

(a)   the responsible insolvency practitioner of an insolvent partnership which is being wound up by virtue of article 8 of the Insolvent Partnerships Order 1994 and of its insolvent member or members against whom insolvency orders have been made, or

(b)   a provisional liquidator of an insolvent partnership, and of any corporate member of that partnership, against which a winding-up petition is presented by virtue of that article.

174(2)   Where the official receiver has ceased to be the responsible insolvency practitioner and a person is appointed in his stead, the official receiver has his release with effect from the following time, that is to say–

(a)   in a case where that person was nominated by a combined general meeting of creditors of the partnership and of any insolvent member or members, or was appointed by the Secretary of State, the time at which the official receiver gives notice to the court that he has been replaced;

(b)   in a case where that person is appointed by the court, such time as the court may determine.

174(3)   If the official receiver while he is a responsible insolvency practitioner gives notice to the Secretary of State that the winding up of the partnership or of any corporate member or the administration of the estate of any individual member is for practical purposes complete, he has his release as liquidator or trustee (as the case may be) with effect from such time as the Secretary of State may determine.

174(4)   A person other than the official receiver who has ceased to be a responsible insolvency practitioner has his release with effect from the following time, that is to say–

(a)   in the case of a person who has died, the time at which notice is given to the court in accordance with the rules that person has ceased to hold office;

(b)   in the case of a person who has been removed from office by the court or by the Secretary of State, or who has vacated office under section 172(4), such time as the Secretary of State may, on an application by that person, determine;

(c)   in the case of a person who has resigned, such time as may be directed by the court (or, if he was appointed by the Secretary of State, such time as may be directed by the court or as the Secretary of State may, on an application by that person, determine);

(d)   in the case of a person who has vacated office under section 172(6)–

(i)   if the final meeting referred to in that subsection has resolved against that person's release, such time as the Secretary of State may, on an application by that person, determine, and

(ii)   if that meeting has not so resolved, the time at which that person vacated office.

174(5)   A person who has ceased to hold office as a provisional liquidator has his release with effect from such time as the court may, on an application by him, determine.

174(6)   Where a bankruptcy order in respect of an individual member is annulled, the responsible insolvency practitioner at the time of the annulment has his release with effect from such time as the court may determine.

174(7)   Where the responsible insolvency practitioner or provisional liquidator (including in both cases the official receiver when so acting) has his release under this section, he is, with effect from the time specified in the preceding provisions of this section, discharged from all liability both in respect of acts or omissions of his in the winding up of the insolvent partnership or any corporate member or the administration of the estate of any individual member (as the case may be) and otherwise in relation to his conduct as responsible insolvency practitioner or provisional liquidator.

But nothing in this section prevents the exercise, in relation to a person who has had his release under this section, of the court's powers under section 212 (summary remedy against delinquent directors, liquidators, etc.) or section 304 (liability of trustee)."

23   Sections 175 and 328: priority of expenses and debts

23   Sections 175 and 328(1) to (3) and (6) are modified so as to read as follows:–

"175   Priority of expenses

175(1)   The provisions of this section shall apply in a case where article 8 of the Insolvent Partnerships Order 1994 applies, as regards priority of expenses incurred by a responsible insolvency practitioner of an insolvent partnership, and of any insolvent member of that partnership against whom an insolvency order has been made.

175(2)   The joint estate of the partnership shall be applicable in the first instance in payment of the joint expenses and the separate estate of each insolvent member shall be applicable in the first instance in payment of the separate expenses relating to that member.

175(3)   Where the joint estate is insufficient for the payment in full of the joint expenses, the unpaid balance shall be apportioned equally between the separate estates of the insolvent members against whom insolvency orders have been made and shall form part of the expenses to be paid out of those estates.

175(4)   Where any separate estate of an insolvent member is insufficient for the payment in full of the separate expenses to be paid out of that estate, the unpaid balance shall form part of the expenses to be paid out of the joint estate.

175(5)   Where after the transfer of any unpaid balance in accordance with subsection (3) or (4) any estate is insufficient for the payment in full of the expenses to be paid out of that estate, the balance then remaining unpaid shall be apportioned equally between the other estates.

175(6)   Where after an apportionment under subsection (5) one or more estates are insufficient for the payment in full of the expenses to be paid out of those estates, the total of the unpaid balances of the expenses to be paid out of those estates shall continue to be apportioned equally between the other estates until provision is made for the payment in full of the expenses or there is no estate available for the payment of the balance finally remaining unpaid, in which case it abates in equal proportions between all the estates.

175(7)   Without prejudice to subsections (3) to (6) above, the responsible insolvency practitioner may, with the sanction of any creditors' committee established under section 141 or with the leave of the court obtained on application–

(a)   pay out of the joint estate as part of the expenses to be paid out of that estate any expenses incurred for any separate estate of an insolvent member; or

(b)   pay out of any separate estate of an insolvent member any part of the expenses incurred for the joint estate which affects that separate estate.

175A   Priority of debts in joint estate

175A(1)   The provisions of this section and the next (which are subject to the provisions section 9 of the Partnership Act 1890 as respects the liability of the estate of a deceased member) shall apply as regards priority of debts in a case where article 8 of the Insolvent Partnerships Order 1994 applies.

175A(2)   After payment of expenses in accordance with section 175 and subject to section 175C(2), the joint debts of the partnership shall be paid out of its joint estate in the following order of priority–

(a)   the preferential debts;

(b)   the debts which are neither preferential debts nor postponed debts;

(c)   interest under section 189 on the joint debts (other than postponed debts);

(d)   the postponed debts;

(e)   interest under section 189 on the postponed debts.

175A(3)   The responsible insolvency practitioner shall adjust the rights among themselves of the members of the partnership as contributories and shall distribute any surplus to the members or, where applicable, to the separate estates of the members, according to their respective rights and interests in it.

175A(4)   The debts referred to in each of paragraphs (a) and (b) of subsection (2) rank equally between themselves, and in each case if the joint estate is insufficient for meeting them, they abate in equal proportions between themselves.

175A(5)   Where the joint estate is not sufficient for the payment of the joint debts in accordance with paragraphs (a) and (b) of subsection (2), the responsible insolvency practitioner shall aggregate the value of those debts to the extent that they have not been satisfied or are not capable of being satisfied, and that aggregate amount shall be a claim against the separate estate of each member of the partnership against whom an insolvency order has been made which–

(a)   shall be a debt provable by the responsible insolvency practitioner in each such estate, and

(b)   shall rank equally with the debts of the member referred to in section 175B(1)(b) below.

175A(6)   Where the joint estate is sufficient for the payment of the joint debts in accordance with paragraphs (a) and (b) of subsection (2) but not for the payment of interest under paragraph (c) of that subsection, the responsible insolvency practitioner shall aggregate the value of that interest to the extent that it has not been satisfied or is not capable of being satisfied, and that aggregate amount shall be a claim against the separate estate of each member of the partnership against whom an insolvency order has been made which–

(a)   shall be a debt provable by the responsible insolvency practitioner in each such estate, and

(b)   shall rank equally with the interest on the separate debts referred to in section 175B(1)(c) below.

175A(7)   Where the joint estate is not sufficient for the payment of the postponed joint debts in accordance with paragraph (d) of subsection (2), the responsible insolvency practitioner shall aggregate the value of those debts to the extent that they have not been satisfied or are not capable of being satisfied, and that aggregate amount shall be a claim against the separate estate of each member of the partnership against whom an insolvency order has been made which–

(a)   shall be a debt provable by the responsible insolvency practitioner in each such estate, and

(b)   shall rank equally with the postponed debts of the member referred to in section 175B(1)(d) below.

175A(8)   Where the joint estate is sufficient for the payment of the postponed joint debts in accordance with paragraph (d) of subsection (2) but not for the payment of interest under paragraph (e) of that subsection, the responsible insolvency practitioner shall aggregate the value of that interest to the extent that it has not been satisfied or is not capable of being satisfied, and that aggregate amount shall be a claim against the separate estate of each member of the partnership against whom an insolvency order has been made which–

(a)   shall be a debt provable by the responsible insolvency practitioner in each such estate, and

(b)   shall rank equally with the interest on the postponed debts referred to in section 175B(1)(e) below.

175A(9)   Where the responsible insolvency practitioner receives any distribution from the separate estate of a member in respect of a debt referred to in paragraph (a) of subsection (5), (6), (7) or (8) above, that distribution shall become part of the joint estate and shall be distributed in accordance with the order of priority set out in subsection (2) above.

175B   Priority of debts in separate estate

175B(1)   The separate estate of each member of the partnership against whom an insolvency order has been made shall be applicable, after payment of expenses in accordance with section 175 and subject to section 175C(2) below, in payment of the separate debts of that member in the following order of priority–

(a)   the preferential debts;

(b)   the debts which are neither preferential debts nor postponed debts (including any debt referred to in section 175A(5)(a));

(c)   interest under section 189 on the separate debts and under section 175A(6);

(d)   the postponed debts of the member (including any debt referred to in section 175A(7)(a));

(e)   interest under section 189 on the postponed debts of the member and under section 175A(8).

175B(2)   The debts referred to in each of paragraphs (a) and (b) of subsection (1) rank equally between themselves, and in each case if the separate estate is insufficient for meeting them, they abate in equal proportions between themselves.

175B(3)   Where the responsible insolvency practitioner receives any distribution from the joint estate or from the separate estate of another member of the partnership against whom an insolvency order has been made, that distribution shall become part of the separate estate and shall be distributed in accordance with the order of priority set out in subsection (1) of this section.

175C   Provisions generally applicable in distribution of joint and separate estates

175C(1)   Distinct accounts shall be kept of the joint estate of the partnership and of the separate estate of each member of that partnership against whom an insolvency order is made.

175C(2)   No member of the partnership shall prove for a joint or separate debt in competition with the joint creditors, unless the debt has arisen–

(a)   as a result of fraud, or

(b)   in the ordinary course of a business carried on separately from the partnership business.

175C(3)   For the purpose of establishing the value of any debt referred to in section 175A(5)(a) or (7)(a), that value may be estimated by the responsible insolvency practitioner in accordance with section 322 or (as the case may be) in accordance with the rules.

175C(4)   Interest under section 189 on preferential debts ranks equally with interest on debts which are neither preferential debts nor postponed debts.

175C(5)   Sections 175A and 175B are without prejudice to any provision of this Act or of any other enactment concerning the ranking between themselves of postponed debts and interest thereon, but in the absence of any such provision postponed debts and interest thereon rank equally between themselves.

175C(6)   If any two or more members of an insolvent partnership constitute a separate partnership, the creditors of such separate partnership shall be deemed to be a separate set of creditors and subject to the same statutory provisions as the separate creditors of any member of the insolvent partnership.

175C(7)   Where any surplus remains after the administration of the estate of a separate partnership, the surplus shall be distributed to the members or, where applicable, to the separate estates of the members of that partnership according to their respective rights and interests in it.

175C(8)   Neither the official receiver, the Secretary of State nor a responsible insolvency practitioner shall be entitled to remuneration or fees under the Insolvency Rules 1986, the Insolvency Regulations 1986 or the Insolvency Fees Order 1986 for his services in connection with–

(a)   the transfer of a surplus from the joint estate to a separate estate under section 175A(3),

(b)   a distribution from a separate estate to the joint estate in respect of a claim referred to in section 175A(5), (6), (7) or (8), or

(c)   a distribution from the estate of a separate partnership to the separate estates of the members of that partnership under subsection (7) above."

24   Sections 189 and 328: interest on debts

24   Sections 189 and 328(4) and (5) are modified so as to read as follows:–

"**189(1)**   In the winding up of an insolvent partnership or the winding up or bankruptcy (as the case may be) of any of its insolvent members interest is payable in accordance with this section, in the order of priority laid down by sections 175A and 175B, on any debt proved in the winding up or bankruptcy, including so much of any such debt as represents interest on the remainder.

189(2)   Interest under this section is payable on the debts in question in respect of the periods during which they have been outstanding since the winding-up order was made against the partnership or any corporate member (as the case may be) or the bankruptcy order was made against any individual member.

189(3)   The rate of interest payable under this section in respect of any debt (**"the official rate"** for the purposes of any provision of this Act in which that expression is used) is whichever is the greater of–

(a)   the rate specified in section 17 of the Judgments Act 1838 on the day on which the winding-up or bankruptcy order (as the case may be) was made, and

(b)   the rate applicable to that debt apart from the winding up or bankruptcy."

25   Sections 211 and 356: false representations to creditors

25   Sections 211 and 356(2)(d) are modified so as to read as follows:–

"**211(1)**   This section applies where insolvency orders are made against an insolvent partnership and any insolvent member or members of it by virtue of article 8 of the Insolvent Partnerships Order 1994.

211(2)   Any person, being a past or present officer of the partnership or a past or present officer (which for these purposes includes a shadow director) of a corporate member against which an insolvency order has been made–

(a)   commits an offence if he makes any false representation or commits any other fraud for the purpose of obtaining the consent of the creditors of the partnership (or any of them) or of the creditors of any of its members (or any of such creditors) to an agreement with reference to the affairs of the partnership or of any of its members or to the winding up of the partnership or of a corporate member, or the bankruptcy of an individual member, and

(b)   is deemed to have committed that offence if, prior to the winding up or bankruptcy (as the case may be), he has made any false representation, or committed any other fraud, for that purpose.

211(3)   A person guilty of an offence under this section is liable to imprisonment or a fine, or both."

26   Sections 230, 231 and 292: appointment to office of responsible insolvency practitioner or provisional liquidator

26   Sections 230, 231 and 292 are modified so as to read as follows:–

"**230(1)**   This section applies with respect to the appointment of–

(a)   the responsible insolvency practitioner of an insolvent partnership which is being wound up by virtue of article 8 of the Insolvent Partnerships Order 1994 and of one or more of its insolvent members, or

(b)   a provisional liquidator of an insolvent partnership, or of any of its corporate members, against which a winding-up petition is presented by virtue of that article,

but is without prejudice to any enactment under which the official receiver is to be, or may be, responsible insolvency practitioner or provisional liquidator.

230(2)   No person may be appointed as responsible insolvency practitioner unless he is, at the time of the appointment, qualified to act as an insolvency practitioner both in relation to the insolvent partnership and to the insolvent member or members.

230(3)   No person may be appointed as provisional liquidator unless he is, at the time of the appointment, qualified to act as an insolvency practitioner both in relation to the insolvent partnership and to any corporate member in respect of which he is appointed.

230(4)   If the appointment or nomination of any person to the office of responsible insolvency practitioner or provisional liquidator relates to more than one person, or has the effect that the office is to be held by more than one person, then subsection (5) below applies.

230(5)   The appointment or nomination shall declare whether any act required or authorised under any enactment to be done by the responsible insolvency practitioner or by the provisional liquidator is to be done by all or any one or more of the persons for the time being holding the office in question.

230(6)   The appointment of any person as responsible insolvency practitioner takes effect only if that person accepts the appointment in accordance with the rules. Subject to this, the appointment of any person as responsible insolvency practitioner takes effect at the time specified in his certificate of appointment.

230A   Conflicts of interest

230A(1)   If the responsible insolvency practitioner of an insolvent partnership being wound up by virtue of article 8 of the Insolvent Partnerships Order 1994 and of one or more of its insolvent members is of the opinion at any time that there is a conflict of interest between his functions as liquidator of the partnership and his functions as responsible insolvency practitioner of any insolvent member, or between his functions as responsible insolvency practitioner of two or more insolvent members, he may apply to the court for directions.

230A(2)   On an application under subsection (1), the court may, without prejudice to the generality of its power to give directions, appoint one or more insolvency practitioners either in place of the applicant to act as responsible insolvency practitioner of both the partnership and its insolvent member or members or to act as joint responsible insolvency practitioner with the applicant."

27   Section 234: getting in the partnership property

27   Section 234 is modified, so far as insolvent partnerships are concerned, so as to read as follows:–

"**234(1)**   This section applies where–

(a)   insolvency orders are made by virtue of article 8 of the Insolvent Partnerships Order 1994 in respect of an insolvent partnership and its insolvent member or members, or

(b)   a provisional liquidator of an insolvent partnership and any of its corporate members is appointed by virtue of that article;

and **"the office-holder"** means the liquidator or the provisional liquidator, as the case may be.

234(2)   Any person who is or has been an officer of the partnership, or who is an executor or administrator of the estate of a deceased officer of the partnership, shall deliver up to the office-holder, for the purposes of the exercise of the office-holder's functions under this Act and (where applicable) the Company Directors Disqualification Act 1986, possession of any partnership property which he holds for the purposes of the partnership.

234(3)   Where any person has in his possession or control any property, books, papers or records to which the partnership appears to be entitled, the court may require that person forthwith (or within such period as the court may direct) to pay, deliver, convey, surrender or transfer the property, books, papers or records to the office-holder or as the court may direct.

234(4)   Where the office-holder–

(a)   seizes or disposes of any property which is not partnership property, and

(b)   at the time of seizure or disposal believes, and has reasonable grounds for believing, that he is entitled (whether in pursuance of an order of the court or otherwise) to seize or dispose of that property,

the next subsection has effect.

234(5)   In that case the office-holder–

(a)   is not liable to any person in respect of any loss or damage resulting from the seizure or disposal except in so far as that loss or damage is caused by the office-holder's own negligence, and

(b)   has a lien on the property, or the proceeds of its sale, for such expenses as were incurred in connection with the seizure or disposal."

28   Section 283: definition of individual member's estate

28   Section 283 is modified so as to read as follows:–

"**283(1)**   Subject as follows, the estate of an individual member for the purposes of this Act comprises–

(a)   all property belonging to or vested in the individual member at the commencement of the bankruptcy, and

(b)   any property which by virtue of any of the provisions of this Act is comprised in that estate or is treated as falling within the preceding paragraph.

283(2)   Subsection (1) does not apply to–

(a)   such tools, books, vehicles and other items of equipment as are not partnership property and as are necessary to the individual member for use personally by him in his employment, business or vocation;

(b)   such clothing, bedding, furniture, household equipment and provisions as are not partnership property and as are necessary for satisfying the basic domestic needs of the individual member and his family.

This subsection is subject to section 308 in Chapter IV (certain excluded property reclaimable by trustee).

283(3)   Subsection (1) does not apply to–

(a)   property held by the individual member on trust for any other person, or

(b)   the right of nomination to a vacant ecclesiastical benefice.

283(4)   References in any provision of this Act to property, in relation to an individual member, include references to any power exercisable by him over or in respect of property except in so far as the power is exercisable over or in respect of property not for the time being comprised in the estate of the individual member and–

(a)   is so exercisable at a time after either the official receiver has had his release in respect of that estate under section 174(3) or a meeting summoned by the trustee of that estate under section 146 has been held, or

(b)   cannot be so exercised for the benefit of the individual member;

and a power exercisable over or in respect of property is deemed for the purposes of any provision of this Act to vest in the person entitled to exercise it at the time of the transaction or event by virtue of which it is exercisable by that person (whether or not it becomes so exercisable at that time).

283(5)   For the purposes of any such provision of this Act, property comprised in an individual member's estate is so comprised subject to the rights of any person other than the individual member (whether as a secured creditor of the individual member or otherwise) in relation thereto, but disregarding any rights which have been given up in accordance with the rules.

283(6)   This section has effect subject to the provisions of any enactment not contained in this Act under which any property is to be excluded from a bankrupt's estate."

28A   Section 283A: individual member's home ceasing to form part of estate

28A   Section 283A is modified so as to read as follows:–

"**283A(1)**   This section applies where property comprised in the estate of an individual member consists of an interest in a dwelling-house which at the date of the bankruptcy was the sole or principal residence of–

(a)   the individual member;

(b)   the individual member's spouse or civil partner, or

(c)   a former spouse or former civil partner of the individual member.

283A(2)   At the end of the period of three years beginning with the date of the bankruptcy the interest mentioned in subsection (1) shall–

(a)   cease to be comprised in the individual member's estate, and

(b)   vest in the individual member (without conveyance, assignment or transfer).

283A(3)   Subsection (2) shall not apply if during the period mentioned in that subsection–

(a)   the trustee realises the interest mentioned in subsection (1),

(b)   the trustee applies for an order for sale in respect of the dwelling-house,

(c)   the trustee applies for an order for possession of the dwelling-house,

(d)   the trustee applies for an order under section 313 in Chapter IV in respect of that interest, or

(e)   the trustee and the individual member agree that the individual member shall incur a specified liability to his estate (with or without the addition of interest from the date of the agreement) in consideration of which the interest mentioned in subsection (1) shall cease to form part of the estate.

283A(4)   Where an application of a kind described in subsection (3)(b) to (d) is made during the period mentioned in subsection (2) and is dismissed, unless the court orders otherwise the interest to which the application relates shall on the dismissal of the application–

(a)   cease to be comprised in the individual member's estate, and

(b)   vest in the individual member (without conveyance, assignment or transfer).

283A(5)   If the individual member does not inform the trustee or the official receiver of his interest in a property before the end of the period of three months beginning with the date of the bankruptcy, the period of three years mentioned in subsection (2)–

(a)   shall not begin with the date of the bankruptcy, but

(b)   shall begin with the date on which the trustee or official receiver becomes aware of the individual member's interest.

283A(6)   The court may substitute for the period of three years mentioned in subsection (2) a longer period–

(a)   in prescribed circumstances, and

(b)   in such other circumstances as the court thinks appropriate.

283A(7)   The rules may make provision for this section to have effect with the substitution of a shorter period for the period of three years mentioned in subsection (2) in specified circumstances (which may be described by reference to action to be taken by a trustee in bankruptcy).

283A(8)   The rules may also, in particular, make provision–

(a)   requiring or enabling the trustee of an individual member's estate to give notice that this section applies or does not apply;

(b)   about the effect of a notice under paragraph (a);

(c)   requiring the trustee of an individual member's estate to make an application to the Chief Land Registrar.

283A(9)   Rules under subsection (8)(b) may, in particular–

(a)   disapply this section;

(b)   enable a court to disapply this section;

(c)   make provision in consequence of a disapplication of this section;

(d)   enable a court to make provision in consequence of a disapplication of this section;

(e)   make provision (which may include provision conferring jurisdiction on a court or tribunal) about compensation."

History
Paragraph 28A inserted by the Insolvent Partnerships (Amendment) Order 2005 (SI 2005/1516) art.9(1), (4) as from July 1, 2005.

29   Section 284: individual member: restrictions on dispositions of property

29   Section 284 is modified so as to read as follows:–

"**284(1)**   Where an individual member is adjudged bankrupt by virtue of article 8 of the Insolvent Partnerships Order 1994, any disposition of property made by that member in the period to which this section applies is void except to the extent that it is or was made with the consent of the court, or is or was subsequently ratified by the court.

284(2)   Subsection (1) applies to a payment (whether in cash or otherwise) as it applies to a disposition of property and, accordingly, where any payment is void by virtue of that subsection, the person paid shall hold the sum paid for the individual member as part of his estate.

284(3)   This section applies to the period beginning with the day of the presentation of the petition for the bankruptcy order and ending with the vesting, under Chapter IV of this Part, of the individual member's estate in a trustee.

284(4)   The preceding provisions of this section do not give a remedy against any person–

 (a)   in respect of any property or payment which he received before the commencement of the bankruptcy in good faith, for value and without notice that the petition had been presented, or

 (b)   in respect of any interest in property which derives from an interest in respect of which there is, by virtue of this subsection, no remedy.

284(5)   Where after the commencement of his bankruptcy the individual member has incurred a debt to a banker or other person by reason of the making of a payment which is void under this section, that debt is deemed for the purposes of any provision of this Act to have been incurred before the commencement of the bankruptcy unless–

 (a)   that banker or person had notice of the bankruptcy before the debt was incurred, or

 (b)   it is not reasonably practicable for the amount of the payment to be recovered from the person to whom it was made.

284(6)   A disposition of property is void under this section notwithstanding that the property is not or, as the case may be, would not be comprised in the individual member's estate; but nothing in this section affects any disposition made by a person of property held by him on trust for any other person other than a disposition made by an individual member of property held by him on trust for the partnership."

29A   Section 313A: low value home: application for sale, possession or charge

29A   Section 313A is modified so as to read as follows:–

"**313A(1)**   This section applies where-

 (a)   property comprised in the individual member's estate consists of an interest in a dwelling-house which at the date of the bankruptcy was the sole or principal residence of–

  (i)   the individual member,

  (ii)   the individual member's spouse or civil partner, or

  (iii)   a former spouse or former civil partner of the individual member, and

 (b)   the trustee applies for an order for the sale of the property, for an order for possession of the property or for an order under section 313 in respect of the property.

313A(2)   The court shall dismiss the application if the value of the interest is below the amount prescribed for the purposes of this subsection.

313A(3)   In determining the value of an interest for the purposes of this section the court shall disregard any matter which it is required to disregard by the order which prescribes the amount for the purposes of subsection (2)."

History

Paragraph 29A inserted by the Insolvent Partnerships (Amendment) Order 2005 (SI 2005/1516) art.9(1), (5) as from July 1, 2005, and modified by the Civil Partnership Act 2004 (Amendments to Subordinate Legislation) Order 2005 (SI 2005/2114) Sch.18 Pt I para.2(1), (3), as from December 5, 2005.

30   Schedule 4 is modified so as to read as follows:–

"Schedule 4

Powers of Liquidator in a Winding up

Part I

Powers Exercisable With Sanction

1 Power to pay any class of creditors in full.

2 Power to make any compromise or arrangement with creditors or persons claiming to be creditors, or having or alleging themselves to have any claim (present or future, certain or contingent, ascertained or sounding only in damages) against the partnership, or whereby the partnership may be rendered liable.

3 Power to compromise, on such terms as may be agreed–

(a) all debts and liabilities capable of resulting in debts, and all claims (present or future, certain or contingent, ascertained or sounding only in damages) subsisting or supposed to subsist between the partnership and a contributory or alleged contributory or other debtor or person apprehending liability to the partnership, and

(b) all questions in any way relating to or affecting the partnership property or the winding up of the partnership,

and take any security for the discharge of any such debt, liability or claim and give a complete discharge in respect of it.

3A Power to bring legal proceedings under section 213, 214, 238, 239 or 423.

4 Power to bring or defend any action or other legal proceeding in the name and on behalf of any member of the partnership in his capacity as such or of the partnership.

5 Power to carry on the business of the partnership so far as may be necessary for its beneficial winding up.

Part II

Powers Exercisable Without Sanction

6 Power to sell any of the partnership property by public auction or private contract, with power to transfer the whole of it to any person or to sell the same in parcels.

7 Power to do all acts and execute, in the name and on behalf of the partnership or of any member of the partnership in his capacity as such, all deeds, receipts and other documents.

8 Power to prove, rank and claim in the bankruptcy, insolvency or sequestration of any contributory for any balance against his estate, and to receive dividends in the bankruptcy, insolvency or sequestration in respect of that balance, as a separate debt due from the bankrupt or insolvent, and rateably with the other separate creditors.

9 Power to draw, accept, make and endorse any bill of exchange or promissory note in the name and on behalf of any member of the partnership in his capacity as such or of the partnership, with the same effect with respect to the liability of the partnership or of any member of the partnership in his capacity as such as if the bill or note had been drawn, accepted, made or endorsed in the course of the partnership's business.

10 Power to raise on the security of the partnership property any money requisite.

11 Power to take out in his official name letters of administration to any deceased contributory, and to do in his official name any other act necessary for obtaining payment of any money due from a contributory or his estate which cannot conveniently be done in the name of the partnership.

In all such cases the money due is deemed, for the purpose of enabling the liquidator to take out the letters of administration or recover the money, to be due to the liquidator himself.

12 Power to appoint an agent to do any business which the liquidator is unable to do himself.

13 Power to do all such other things as may be necessary for winding up the partnership's affairs and distributing its property."

History
In para.30 (modified Sch.4) para.3A inserted by the Insolvent Partnerships (Amendment) Order 2005 (SI 2005/1516) art.9(1), (6) as from July 1, 2005.

SCHEDULE 5

PROVISIONS OF THE ACT WHICH APPLY WITH MODIFICATIONS FOR THE PURPOSES OF ARTICLE 9 TO WINDING UP OF INSOLVENT PARTNERSHIP ON MEMBER'S PETITION WHERE NO CONCURRENT PETITION PRESENTED AGAINST MEMBER

Article 9

1   Section 117: High Court and county court jurisdiction

1   Section 117 is modified so as to read as follows:–

"**117(1)**   Subject to subsections (3) and (4) below, the High Court has jurisdiction to wind up any insolvent partnership as an unregistered company by virtue of article 9 of the Insolvent Partnerships Order 1994 if the partnership has, or at any time had, a principal place of business in England and Wales.

117(2)   Subject to subsections (3) and (4) below, a petition for the winding up of an insolvent partnership by virtue of the said article 9 may be presented to a county court in England and Wales if the partnership has, or at any time had, a principal place of business within the insolvency district of that court.

117(3)   Subject to subsection (4) below, the court only has jurisdiction to wind up an insolvent partnership if the business of the partnership has been carried on in England and Wales at any time in the period of 3 years ending with the day on which the petition for winding it up is presented.

117(4)   If an insolvent partnership has a principal place of business situated in Scotland or in Northern Ireland, the court shall not have jurisdiction to wind up the partnership unless it had a principal place of business in England and Wales–

   (a)   in the case of a partnership with a principal place of business in Scotland, at any time in the period of 1 year, or

   (b)   in the case of a partnership with a principal place of business in Northern Ireland, at any time in the period of 3 years,

ending with the day on which the petition for winding it up is presented.

117(5)   The Lord Chancellor may, with the concurrence of the Lord Chief Justice, by order in a statutory instrument exclude a county court from having winding-up jurisdiction, and for the purposes of that jurisdiction may attach its district, or any part thereof, to any other county court, and may by statutory instrument revoke or vary any such order.

In exercising the powers of this section, the Lord Chancellor shall provide that a county court is not to have winding-up jurisdiction unless it has for the time being jurisdiction for the purposes of Parts VIII to XI of this Act (individual insolvency).

117(6)   Every court in England and Wales having winding-up jurisdiction has for the purposes of that jurisdiction all the powers of the High Court; and every prescribed officer of the court shall perform any duties which an officer of the High Court may discharge by order of a judge of that court or otherwise in relation to winding up.

117(7)   This section is subject to Article 3 of the EC Regulation (jurisdiction under the EC Regulation).

117(8)   The Lord Chief Justice may nominate a judicial office holder (as defined in section 109(4) of the Constitutional Reform Act 2005) to exercise his functions under this section."

History
Modified s.117(5) amended, and s.117(8) inserted, by the Lord Chancellor (Transfer of Functions and Supplementary Provisions) Order 2006 (SI 2006/680) Sch.2 paras 5, 6, as from April 3, 2006.

2 Section 221: winding up of unregistered companies

2   Section 221 is modified so as to read as follows:–

"**221(1)**   Subject to subsections (2) and (3) below and to the provisions of this Part, any insolvent partnership which has, or at any time had, a principal place of business in England and Wales may be wound up under this Act.

221(2)   Subject to subsection (3) below an insolvent partnership shall not be wound up under this Act if the business of the partnership has not been carried on in England and Wales at any time in the period of 3 years ending with the day on which the winding-up petition is presented.

221(3)   If an insolvent partnership has a principal place of business situated in Scotland or in Northern Ireland, the court shall not have jurisdiction to wind up the partnership unless it had a principal place of business in England and Wales–

(a)   in the case of a partnership with a principal place of business in Scotland, at any time in the period of 1 year, or

(b)   in the case of a partnership with a principal place of business in Northern Ireland, at any time in the period of 3 years,

ending with the day on which the winding-up petition is presented.

221(3A)   The preceding subsections are subject to Article 3 of the EC Regulation (jurisdiction under the EC Regulation).

221(4)   No insolvent partnership shall be wound up under this Act voluntarily.

221(5)   To the extent that they are applicable to the winding up of a company by the court in England and Wales on a member's petition or on a petition by the company, all the provisions of this Act and the Companies Act about winding up apply to the winding up of an insolvent partnership as an unregistered company–

(a)   with the exceptions and additions mentioned in the following subsections of this section and in section 221A, and

(b)   with the modifications specified in Part II of Schedule 3 to the Insolvent Partnerships Order 1994.

221(6)   Sections 73(1), 74(2)(a) to (d) and (3), 75 to 78, 83, 122, 123, 124(2) and (3), 176A, 202, 203, 205 and 250 shall not apply.

History
Modified s.221(6) amended by the Insolvent Partnerships (Amendment) Order 2006 (SI 2006/622) art.8 as from April 6, 2006.

221(7)   The circumstances in which an insolvent partnership may be wound up as an unregistered company are as follows–

(a)   if the partnership is dissolved, or has ceased to carry on business, or is carrying on business only for the purpose of winding up its affairs;

(b)   if the partnership is unable to pay its debts;

(c)   if the court is of the opinion that it is just and equitable that the partnership should be wound up.

221(8)   Every petition for the winding up of an insolvent partnership under Part V of this Act shall be verified by affidavit in Form 2 in Schedule 9 to the Insolvent Partnerships Order 1994.

221A   Who may present petition

221A(1)   A petition for winding up an insolvent partnership may be presented by any member of the partnership if the partnership consists of not less than 8 members.

221A(2)   A petition for winding up an insolvent partnership may also be presented by any member of it with the leave of the court (obtained on his application) if the court is satisfied that–

(a)   the member has served on the partnership, by leaving at a principal place of business of the partnership in England and Wales, or by delivering to an officer of the partnership, or by otherwise serving in such manner as the court may approve or direct, a written demand in Form 10 in Schedule 9 to the Insolvent Partnerships Order 1994 in respect of a joint debt or debts exceeding £750 then due from the partnership but paid by the member, other than out of partnership property;

    (b)   the partnership has for 3 weeks after the service of the demand neglected to pay the sum or to secure or compound for it to the member's satisfaction; and

    (c)   the member has obtained a judgment, decree or order of any court against the partnership for reimbursement to him of the amount of the joint debt or debts so paid and all reasonable steps (other than insolvency proceedings) have been taken by the member to enforce that judgment, decree or order.

221A(3)   Subsection (2)(a) above is deemed included in the list of provisions specified in subsection (1) of section 416 of this Act for the purposes of the Secretary of State's order-making power under that section."

SCHEDULE 6

PROVISIONS OF THE ACT WHICH APPLY WITH MODIFICATIONS FOR THE PURPOSES OF ARTICLE 10 TO WINDING UP OF INSOLVENT PARTNERSHIP ON MEMBER'S PETITION WHERE CONCURRENT PETITIONS ARE PRESENTED AGAINST ALL THE MEMBERS

Article 10

1   Sections 117 and 265: High Court and county court jurisdiction

1   Sections 117 and 265 are modified so as to read as follows:–

"**117(1)**   Subject to the provisions of this section, the High Court has jurisdiction to wind up any insolvent partnership as an unregistered company by virtue of article 10 of the Insolvent Partnerships Order 1994 if the partnership has, or at any time had, a principal place of business in England and Wales.

117(2)   Subject to the provisions of this section, a petition for the winding up of an insolvent partnership by virtue of the said article 10 may be presented to a county court in England and Wales if the partnership has, or at any time had, a principal place of business within the insolvency district of that court.

117(3)   Subject to subsection (4) below, the court only has jurisdiction to wind up an insolvent partnership if the business of the partnership has been carried on in England and Wales at any time in the period of 3 years ending with the day on which the petition for winding it up is presented.

117(4)   If an insolvent partnership has a principal place of business situated in Scotland or in Northern Ireland, the court shall not have jurisdiction to wind up the partnership unless it had a principal place of business in England and Wales–

    (a)   in the case of a partnership with a principal place of business in Scotland, at any time in the period of 1 year, or

    (b)   in the case of a partnership with a principal place of business in Northern Ireland, at any time in the period of 3 years,

ending with the day on which the petition for winding it up is presented.

117(5)   Subject to subsection (6) below, the court has jurisdiction to wind up a corporate member, or make a bankruptcy order against an individual member, of a partnership against which a petition has been presented by virtue of article 10 of the Insolvent Partnerships Order 1994 if it has jurisdiction in respect of the partnership.

117(6)   Petitions by virtue of the said article 10 for the winding up of an insolvent partnership and the bankruptcy of one or more members of that partnership may not be presented to a district registry of the High Court.

117(7)   The Lord Chancellor may, with the concurrence of the Lord Chief Justice, by order in a statutory instrument exclude a county court from having winding-up jurisdiction, and for the purposes of that jurisdiction

824

may attach its district, or any part thereof, to any other county court, and may by statutory instrument revoke or vary any such order.

In exercising the powers of this section, the Lord Chancellor shall provide that a county court is not to have winding-up jurisdiction unless it has for the time being jurisdiction for the purposes of Parts VIII to XI of this Act (individual insolvency).

117(8)　Every court in England and Wales having winding-up jurisdiction has for the purposes of that jurisdiction all the powers of the High Court; and every prescribed officer of the court shall perform any duties which an officer of the High Court may discharge by order of a judge of that court or otherwise in relation to winding up.

117(9)　This section is subject to Article 3 of the EC Regulation (jurisdiction under the EC Regulation).

117(10)　The Lord Chief Justice may nominate a judicial office holder (as defined in section 109(4) of the Constitutional Reform Act 2005) to exercise his functions under this section."

History
Modified s.117(7) amended, and s.117(10) inserted, by the Lord Chancellor (Transfer of Functions and Supplementary Provisions) Order 2006 (SI 2006/680) Sch.2 paras 5, 7, as from April 3, 2006.

2　Sections 124, 264 and 272: applications to wind up insolvent partnership and to wind up or bankrupt insolvent members

2　Sections 124, 264 and 272 are modified so as to read as follows:–

"**124(1)**　An application to the court by a member of an insolvent partnership by virtue of article 10 of the Insolvent Partnerships Order 1994 for the winding up of the partnership as an unregistered company and the winding up or bankruptcy (as the case may be) of all its members shall–

(a)　in the case of the partnership, be by petition in Form 11 in Schedule 9 to that Order,

(b)　in the case of a corporate member, be by petition in Form 12 in that Schedule, and

(c)　in the case of an individual member, be by petition in Form 13 in that Schedule.

124(2)　Subject to subsection (3) below, a petition under subsection (1)(a) may only be presented by a member of the partnership on the grounds that the partnership is unable to pay its debts and if–

(a)　petitions are at the same time presented by that member for insolvency orders against every member of the partnership (including himself or itself); and

(b)　each member is willing for an insolvency order to be made against him or it and the petition against him or it contains a statement to this effect.

124(3)　If the court is satisfied, on application by any member of an insolvent partnership, that presentation of petitions under subsection (1) against the partnership and every member of it would be impracticable, the court may direct that petitions be presented against the partnership and such member or members of it as are specified by the court.

124(4)　The petitions mentioned in subsection (1)–

(a)　shall all be presented to the same court and, except as the court otherwise permits or directs, on the same day, and

(b)　except in the case of the petition mentioned in subsection (1)(c) shall be advertised in Form 8 in the said Schedule 9.

124(5)　Each petition presented under this section shall contain particulars of the other petitions being presented in relation to the partnership, identifying the partnership and members concerned.

124(6)　The hearing of the petition against the partnership fixed by the court shall be in advance of the hearing of the petitions against the insolvent members.

124(7)   On the day appointed for the hearing of the petition against the partnership, the petitioner shall, before the commencement of the hearing, hand to the court Form 9 in Schedule 9 to the Insolvent Partnerships Order 1994, duly completed.

124(8)   Any person against whom a winding-up or bankruptcy petition has been presented in relation to the insolvent partnership is entitled to appear and to be heard on any petition for the winding up of the partnership.

124(9)   A petitioner under this section may at the hearing withdraw the petition if–

(a)   subject to subsection (10) below, he withdraws at the same time every other petition which he has presented under this section; and

(b)   he gives notice to the court at least 3 days before the date appointed for the hearing of the relevant petition of his intention to withdraw the petition.

124(10)   A petitioner need not comply with the provisions of subsection (9)(a) in the case of a petition against a member, if the court is satisfied on application made to it by the petitioner that, because of difficulties in serving the petition or for any other reason, the continuance of that petition would be likely to prejudice or delay the proceedings on the petition which he has presented against the partnership or on any petition which he has presented against any other insolvent member."

3   Sections 125 and 271: powers of court on hearing of petitions against insolvent partnership and members

3   Sections 125 and 271 are modified so as to read as follows:–

"**125(1)**   Subject to the provisions of section 125A, on hearing a petition under section 124 against an insolvent partnership or any of its insolvent members, the court may dismiss it, or adjourn the hearing conditionally or unconditionally or make any other order that it thinks fit; but the court shall not refuse to make a winding-up order against the partnership or a corporate member on the ground only that the partnership property or (as the case may be) the member's assets have been mortgaged to an amount equal to or in excess of that property or those assets, or that the partnership has no property or the member no assets.

125(2)   An order under subsection (1) in respect of an insolvent partnership may contain directions as to the future conduct of any insolvency proceedings in existence against any insolvent member in respect of whom an insolvency order has been made.

125A   Hearing of petitions against members

125A(1)   On the hearing of a petition against an insolvent member the petitioner shall draw the court's attention to the result of the hearing of the winding-up petition against the partnership and the following subsections of this section shall apply.

125A(2)   If the court has neither made a winding-up order, nor dismissed the winding-up petition, against the partnership the court may adjourn the hearing of the petition against the member until either event has occurred.

125A(3)   Subject to subsection (4) below, if a winding-up order has been made against the partnership, the court may make a winding-up order against the corporate member in respect of which, or (as the case may be) a bankruptcy order against the individual member in respect of whom, the insolvency petition was presented.

125A(4)   If no insolvency order is made under subsection (3) against any member within 28 days of the making of the winding-up order against the partnership, the proceedings against the partnership shall be conducted as if the winding-up petition against the partnership had been presented by virtue of article 7 of the Insolvent Partnerships Order 1994, and the proceedings against any member shall be conducted under this Act without the modifications made by that Order (other than the modifications made to sections 168 and 303 by article 14).

125A(5)   If the court has dismissed the winding-up petition against the partnership, the court may dismiss the winding-up petition against the corporate member or (as the case may be) the bankruptcy petition against the individual member. However, if an insolvency order is made against a member, the proceedings against that member shall be conducted under this Act without the modifications made by the Insolvent Partnerships Order 1994 (other than the modifications made to sections 168 and 303 of this Act by article 14 of that Order).

125A(6)   The court may dismiss a petition against an insolvent member if it considers it just to do so because of a change in circumstances since the making of the winding-up order against the partnership.

125A(7)   The court may dismiss a petition against an insolvent member who is a limited partner, if–

(a)   the member lodges in court for the benefit of the creditors of the partnership sufficient money or security to the court's satisfaction to meet his liability for the debts and obligations of the partnership; or

(b)   the member satisfies the court that he is no longer under any liability in respect of the debts and obligations of the partnership."

4   Section 221: Winding up of unregistered companies

4   Section 221 is modified so as to read as follows:–

"**221(1)**   Subject to subsections (2) and (3) below and to the provisions of this Part, any insolvent partnership which has, or at any time had, a principal place of business in England and Wales may be wound up under this Act.

221(2)   Subject to subsection (3) below, an insolvent partnership shall not be wound up under this Act if the business of the partnership has not been carried on in England and Wales at any time in the period of 3 years ending with the day on which the winding-up petition is presented.

221(3)   If an insolvent partnership has a principal place of business situated in Scotland or in Northern Ireland, the court shall not have jurisdiction to wind up the partnership unless it had a principal place of business in England and Wales–

(a)   in the case of a partnership with a principal place of business in Scotland, at any time in the period of 1 year, or

(b)   in the case of a partnership with a principal place of business in Northern Ireland, at any time in the period of 3 years,

ending with the day on which the winding-up petition is presented.

221(3A)   The preceding subsections are subject to Article 3 of the EC Regulation (jurisdiction under the EC Regulation).

221(4)   No insolvent partnership shall be wound up under this Act voluntarily.

221(5)   To the extent that they are applicable to the winding up of a company by the court in England and Wales on a member's petition, all the provisions of this Act and the Companies Act about winding up apply to the winding up of an insolvent partnership as an unregistered company–

(a)   with the exceptions and additions mentioned in the following subsections of this section, and

(b)   with the modifications specified in Part II of Schedule 4 to the Insolvent Partnerships Order 1994.

221(6)   Sections 73(1), 74(2)(a) to (d) and (3), 75 to 78, 83, 124(2) and (3), 154, 176A, 202, 203, 205 and 250 shall not apply.

221(7)   Unless the contrary intention appears, the members of the partnership against whom insolvency orders are made by virtue of article 10 of the Insolvent Partnerships Order 1994 shall not be treated as contributories for the purposes of this Act.

221(8)   The circumstances in which an insolvent partnership may be wound up as an unregistered company are that the partnership is unable to pay its debts.

221(9)   Every petition for the winding up of an insolvent partnership under Part V of this Act shall be verified by affidavit in Form 2 in Schedule 9 to the Insolvent Partnerships Order 1994."

History
Modified s.221(6) amended by the Insolvent Partnerships (Amendment) Order 2006 (SI 2006/622) art.9, as from April 6, 2006.

SCHEDULE 7

PROVISIONS OF THE ACT WHICH APPLY WITH MODIFICATIONS FOR THE PURPOSES OF ARTICLE 11 WHERE JOINT BANKRUPTCY PETITION PRESENTED BY INDIVIDUAL MEMBERS WITHOUT WINDING UP PARTNERSHIP AS UNREGISTERED COMPANY

Article 11

1(1)   The provisions of the Act specified in sub-paragraph (2) below, are set out as modified in this Schedule.

1(2)   The provisions referred to in sub-paragraph (1) above are sections 264 to 266, 272, 283, 284, 290, 292 to 301, 305, 312, 328, 331 and 387.

History
In para.1(2) the reference to s.275 omitted by the Insolvent Partnerships (Amendment) Order 2005 (SI 2005/1516) art.10(1), (2) as from July 1, 2005.

2   Section 264: Presentation of joint bankruptcy petition

2   Section 264 is modified so as to read as follows:–

"**264(1)**   Subject to section 266(1) below, a joint bankruptcy petition may be presented to the court by virtue of article 11 of the Insolvent Partnerships Order 1994 by all the members of an insolvent partnership in their capacity as such provided that all the members are individuals and none of them is a limited partner.

264(2)   A petition may not be presented under paragraph (1) by the members of an insolvent partnership if the partnership–

(a)   has permission under Part 4 of the Financial Services and Markets Act 2000 to accept deposits, other than such a permission only for the purpose of carrying on another regulated activity in accordance with that permission, or

(b)   continues to have a liability in respect of a deposit which was held by it in accordance with the Banking Act 1979 or the Banking Act 1987.

264(2A)   Subsection (2)(a) must be read with–

(a)   section 22 of the Financial Services and Markets Act 2000;

(b)   any relevant order under that section; and

(c)   Schedule 2 to that Act.

264(3)   The petition–

(a)   shall be in Form 14 in Schedule 9 to the Insolvent Partnerships Order 1994; and

(b)   shall contain a request that the trustee shall wind up the partnership business and administer the partnership property without the partnership being wound up as an unregistered company under Part V of this Act.

264(4)   The petition shall either–

(a)   be accompanied by an affidavit in Form 15 in Schedule 9 to the Insolvent Partnerships Order 1994 made by the member who signs the petition, showing that all the members are individual members (and that none of them is a limited partner) and concur in the presentation of the petition, or

(b)   contain a statement that all the members are individual members and be signed by all the members.

264(5)   On presentation of a petition under this section, the court may make orders in Form 16 in Schedule 9 to the Insolvent Partnerships Order 1994 for the bankruptcy of the members and the winding up of the partnership business and administration of its property."

3 Section 265: conditions to be satisfied in respect of members

3 Section 265 is modified so as to read as follows:–

"**265(1)** Subject to the provisions of this section, a joint bankruptcy petition by virtue of article 11 of the Insolvent Partnerships Order 1994 may be presented–

(a) to the High Court (other than to a district registry of that Court) if the partnership has, or at any time had, a principal place of business in England and Wales, or

(b) to a county court in England and Wales if the partnership has, or at any time had, a principal place of business within the insolvency district of that court.

265(2) A joint bankruptcy petition shall not be presented to the court by virtue of article 11 unless the business of the partnership has been carried on in England and Wales at any time in the period of 3 years ending with the day on which the joint bankruptcy petition is presented."

4 Section 266: other preliminary conditions

4 Section 266 is modified so as to read as follows:–

"**266(1)** If the court is satisfied, on application by any member of an insolvent partnership, that the presentation of the petition under section 264(1) by all the members of the partnership would be impracticable, the court may direct that the petition be presented by such member or members as are specified by the court.

266(2) A joint bankruptcy petition shall not be withdrawn without the leave of the court.

266(3) The court has a general power, if it appears to it appropriate to do so on the grounds that there has been a contravention of the rules or for any other reason, to dismiss a joint bankruptcy petition or to stay proceedings on such a petition; and, where it stays proceedings on a petition, it may do so on such terms and conditions as it thinks fit."

5 Section 272: grounds of joint bankruptcy petition

5 Section 272 is modified so as to read as follows:–

"**272(1)** A joint bankruptcy petition may be presented to the court by the members of a partnership only on the grounds that the partnership is unable to pay its debts.

272(2) The petition shall be accompanied by–

(a) a statement of each member's affairs in Form 17 in Schedule 9 to the Insolvent Partnerships Order 1994, and

(b) a statement of the affairs of the partnership in Form 18 in that Schedule, sworn by one or more members of the partnership.

272(3) The statements of affairs required by subsection (2) shall contain–

(a) particulars of the member's or (as the case may be) partnership's creditors, debts and other liabilities and of their assets, and

(b) such other information as is required by the relevant form."

6 Section 275: summary administration

6 [Omitted by the Insolvent Partnerships (Amendment) Order 2005 (SI 2005/1516) art.10(1), (3) as from July 1, 2005.]

7 Section 283: definition of member's estate

7 Section 283 is modified so as to read as follows:–

"**283(1)** Subject as follows, a member's estate for the purposes of this Act comprises–

(a) all property belonging to or vested in the member at the commencement of the bankruptcy, and

(b) any property which by virtue of any of the provisions of this Act is comprised in that estate or is treated as falling within the preceding paragraph.

283(2) Subsection (1) does not apply to–

(a) such tools, books, vehicles and other items of equipment as are not partnership property and as are necessary to the member for use personally by him in his employment, business or vocation;

(b) such clothing, bedding, furniture, household equipment and provisions as are not partnership property and as are necessary for satisfying the basic domestic needs of the member and his family.

This subsection is subject to section 308 in Chapter IV (certain excluded property reclaimable by trustee).

283(3) Subsection (1) does not apply to–

(a) property held by the member on trust for any other person, or

(b) the right of nomination to a vacant ecclesiastical benefice.

283(4) References in any provision of this Act to property, in relation to a member, include references to any power exercisable by him over or in respect of property except insofar as the power is exercisable over or in respect of property not for the time being comprised in the member's estate and–

(a) is so exercisable at a time after either the official receiver has had his release in respect of that estate under section 299(2) in Chapter III or a meeting summoned by the trustee of that estate under section 331 in Chapter IV has been held, or

(b) cannot be so exercised for the benefit of the member;

and a power exercisable over or in respect of property is deemed for the purposes of any provision of this Act to vest in the person entitled to exercise it at the time of the transaction or event by virtue of which it is exercisable by that person (whether or not it becomes so exercisable at that time).

283(5) For the purposes of any such provision of this Act, property comprised in a member's estate is so comprised subject to the rights of any person other than the member (whether as a secured creditor of the member or otherwise) in relation thereto, but disregarding any rights which have been given up in accordance with the rules.

283(6) This section has effect subject to the provisions of any enactment not contained in this Act under which any property is to be excluded from a bankrupt's estate."

7A   Section 283A: bankrupt's home ceasing to form part of estate

7A Section 283A is modified so as to read as follows:–

"**283A(1)** This section applies where property comprised in the estate of an individual member consists of an interest in a dwelling-house which at the date of the bankruptcy was the sole or principal residence of–

(a) the individual member;

(b) the individual member's spouse or civil partner, or

(c) a former spouse or former civil partner of the individual member.

283A(2) At the end of the period of three years beginning with the date of the bankruptcy the interest mentioned in subsection (1) shall–

(a) cease to be comprised in the individual member's estate, and

(b) vest in the individual member (without conveyance, assignment or transfer).

283A(3) Subsection (2) shall not apply if during the period mentioned in that subsection–

(a) the trustee realises the interest mentioned in subsection (1),

(b) the trustee applies for an order for sale in respect of the dwelling-house,

(c) the trustee applies for an order for possession of the dwelling-house,

(d) the trustee applies for an order under section 313 in Chapter IV in respect of that interest, or

(e) the trustee and the individual member agree that the individual member shall incur a specified liability to his estate (with or without the addition of interest from the date of the agreement) in consideration of which the interest mentioned in subsection (1) shall cease to form part of the estate.

283A(4) Where an application of a kind described in subsection (3)(b) to (d) is made during the period mentioned in subsection (2) and is dismissed, unless the court orders otherwise the interest to which the application relates shall on the dismissal of the application–

(a) cease to be comprised in the individual member's estate, and

(b) vest in the individual member (without conveyance, assignment or transfer).

283A(5) If the individual member does not inform the trustee or the official receiver of his interest in a property before the end of the period of three months beginning with the date of the bankruptcy, the period of three years mentioned in subsection (2)–

(a) shall not begin with the date of the bankruptcy, but

(b) shall begin with the date on which the trustee or official receiver becomes aware of the individual member's interest.

283A(6) The court may substitute for the period of three years mentioned in subsection (2) a longer period–

(a) in prescribed circumstances, and

(b) in such other circumstances as the court thinks appropriate.

283A(7) The rules may make provision for this section to have effect with the substitution of a shorter period for the period of three years mentioned in subsection (2) in specified circumstances (which may be described by reference to action to be taken by a trustee in bankruptcy).

283A(8) The rules may also, in particular, make provision–

(a) requiring or enabling the trustee of an individual member's estate to give notice that this section applies or does not apply;

(b) about the effect of a notice under paragraph (a);

(c) requiring the trustee of an individual member's estate to make an application to the Chief Land Registrar.

283A(9) Rules under subsection (8)(b) may, in particular–

(a) disapply this section;

(b) enable a court to disapply this section;

(c) make provision in consequence of a disapplication of this section;

(d) enable a court to make provision in consequence of a disapplication of this section;

(e) make provision (which may include provision conferring jurisdiction on a court or tribunal) about compensation."

History
Paragraph 7A inserted by the Insolvent Partnerships (Amendment) Order 2005 (SI 2005/1516) art.10(1), (4) as from July 1, 2005.

8 Section 284: restrictions on dispositions of property

8 Section 284 is modified so as to read as follows:–

"**284(1)** Where a member is adjudged bankrupt on a joint bankruptcy petition, any disposition of property made by that member in the period to which this section applies is void except to the extent that it is or was made with the consent of the court, or is or was subsequently ratified by the court.

284(2) Subsection (1) applies to a payment (whether in cash or otherwise) as it applies to a disposition of property and, accordingly, where any payment is void by virtue of that subsection, the person paid shall hold the sum paid for the member as part of his estate.

284(3) This section applies to the period beginning with the day of the presentation of the joint bankruptcy petition and ending with the vesting, under Chapter IV of this Part, of the member's estate in a trustee.

284(4) The preceding provisions of this section do not give a remedy against any person–

    (a)   in respect of any property or payment which he received before the commencement of the bankruptcy in good faith, for value, and without notice that the petition had been presented, or

    (b)   in respect of any interest in property which derives from an interest in respect of which there is, by virtue of this subsection, no remedy.

284(5) Where after the commencement of his bankruptcy the member has incurred a debt to a banker or other person by reason of the making of a payment which is void under this section, that debt is deemed for the purposes of any provision of this Act to have been incurred before the commencement of the bankruptcy unless–

    (a)   that banker or person had notice of the bankruptcy before the debt was incurred, or

    (b)   it is not reasonably practicable for the amount of the payment to be recovered from the person to whom it was made.

284(6) A disposition of property is void under this section notwithstanding that the property is not or, as the case may be, would not be comprised in the member's estate; but nothing in this section affects any disposition made by a person of property held by him on trust for any other person other than a disposition made by a member of property held by him on trust for the partnership."

9   Section 290: public examination of member

9   Section 290 is modified so as to read as follows:–

"**290(1)** Where orders have been made against the members of an insolvent partnership on a joint bankruptcy petition, the official receiver may at any time before the discharge of any such member apply to the court for the public examination of that member.

290(2) Unless the court otherwise orders, the official receiver shall make an application under subsection (1) if notice requiring him to do so is given to him, in accordance with the rules, by one of the creditors of the member concerned with the concurrence of not less than one-half, in value, of those creditors (including the creditor giving notice).

290(3) On an application under subsection (1), the court shall direct that a public examination of the member shall be held on a day appointed by the court; and the member shall attend on that day and be publicly examined as to his affairs, dealings and property and as to those of the partnership.

290(4) The following may take part in the public examination of the member and may question him concerning the matters mentioned in subsection (3), namely–

    (a)   the official receiver,

    (b)   the trustee of the member's estate, if his appointment has taken effect,

    (c)   any person who has been appointed as special manager of the member's estate or business or of the partnership property or business,

    (d)   any creditor of the member who has tendered a proof in the bankruptcy.

290(5) On an application under subsection (1), the court may direct that the public examination of a member under this section be combined with the public examination of any other person.

290(6) If a member without reasonable excuse fails at any time to attend his public examination under this section he is guilty of a contempt of court and liable to be punished accordingly (in addition to any other punishment to which he may be subject)."

10   Section 292: power to appoint trustee

10   Section 292 is modified so as to read as follows:–

"**292(1)** The power to appoint a person as both trustee of the estates of the members of an insolvent partnership against whom orders are made on a joint bankruptcy petition and as trustee of the partnership is exercisable–

(a)   by a combined general meeting of the creditors of the members and of the partnership;

(b)   under section 295(2), 296(2) or 300(3) below in this Chapter, by the Secretary of State.

292(2)   No person may be appointed as trustee of the members' estates and as trustee of the partnership unless he is, at the time of the appointment, qualified to act as an insolvency practitioner both in relation to the insolvent partnership and to each of the members.

292(3)   Any power to appoint a person as trustee of the members' estates and of the partnership includes power to appoint two or more persons as joint trustees; but such an appointment must make provision as to the circumstances in which the trustees must act together and the circumstances in which one or more of them may act for the others.

292(4)   The appointment of any person as trustee of the members' estates and of the partnership takes effect only if that person accepts the appointment in accordance with the rules. Subject to this, the appointment of any person as trustee takes effect at the time specified in his certificate of appointment.

292(5)   This section is without prejudice to the provisions of this Chapter under which the official receiver is, in certain circumstances, to be trustee of the members' estates and of the partnership.

292A   Conflicts of interest

292A(1)   If the trustee of the members' estates and of the partnership is of the opinion at any time that there is a conflict of interest between his functions as trustee of the members' estates and his functions as trustee of the partnership, or between his functions as trustee of the estates of two or more members, he may apply to the court for directions.

292A(2)   On an application under subsection (1), the court may, without prejudice to the generality of its power to give directions, appoint one or more insolvency practitioners either in place of the applicant to act both as trustee of the members' estates and as trustee of the partnership, or to act as joint trustee with the applicant."

11   Sections 293 and 294: summoning of meeting to appoint trustee

11   Sections 293 and 294 are modified so as to read as follows:–

"**293(1)**   Where orders are made by virtue of article 11 of the Insolvent Partnerships Order 1994, the official receiver, by virtue of his office, becomes the trustee of the estates of the members and the trustee of the partnership and continues in office until another person becomes trustee under the provisions of this Part.

293(2)   The official receiver is, by virtue of his office, the trustee of the estates of the members and the trustee of the partnership during any vacancy.

293(3)   At any time when he is trustee, the official receiver may summon a combined meeting of the creditors of the members and the creditors of the partnership, for the purpose of appointing a trustee in place of the official receiver.

293(4)   It is the duty of the official receiver–

(a)   as soon as practicable in the period of 12 weeks beginning with the day on which the first order was made by virtue of article 11 of the Insolvent Partnerships Order 1994, to decide whether to exercise his power under subsection (3) to summon a meeting, and

(b)   if in pursuance of paragraph (a) he decides not to exercise that power, to give notice of his decision, before the end of that period, to the court and to those creditors of the members and those of the partnership who are known to the official receiver or identified in a statement of affairs submitted under section 272, and

(c)   (whether or not he has decided to exercise that power) to exercise his power to summon a meeting under subsection (3) if he is at any time requested to do so by one-quarter, in value, of either–

(i)   the creditors of any member against whom an insolvency order has been made, or

(ii)   the partnership's creditors,

and accordingly, where the duty imposed by paragraph (c) arises before the official receiver has performed a duty imposed by paragraph (a) or (b), he is not required to perform the latter duty.

293(5)   A notice given under subsection (4)(b) to the creditors shall contain an explanation of the creditors' power under subsection (4)(c) to require the official receiver to summon a combined meeting of the creditors of the partnership and of the members against whom insolvency orders have been made.

293(6)   If the official receiver, in pursuance of subsection (4)(a), has decided to exercise his power under subsection (3) to summon a meeting, he shall hold that meeting in the period of 4 months beginning with the day on which the first order was made by virtue of article 11 of the Insolvent Partnerships Order 1994.

293(7)   If (whether or not he has decided to exercise that power) the official receiver is requested, in accordance with the provisions of subsection (4)(c), to exercise his power under subsection (3) to summon a meeting, he shall hold that meeting in accordance with the rules.

293(8)   Where a meeting of creditors of the partnership and of the members has been held, and an insolvency order is subsequently made against a further insolvent member by virtue of article 11 of the Insolvent Partnerships Order 1994–

(a)   any person chosen at the meeting to be responsible insolvency practitioner in place of the official receiver shall also be the responsible insolvency practitioner of the member against whom the subsequent order is made, and

(b)   subsection (4) of this section shall not apply."

12   Section 295: failure of meeting to appoint trustee

12   Section 295 is modified so as to read as follows:–

"**295(1)**   If a meeting of creditors summoned under section 293 is held but no appointment of a person as trustee is made, it is the duty of the official receiver to decide whether to refer the need for an appointment to the Secretary of State.

295(2)   On a reference made in pursuance of that decision, the Secretary of State shall either make an appointment or decline to make one.

295(3)   If–

(a)   the official receiver decides not to refer the need for an appointment to the Secretary of State, or

(b)   on such a reference the Secretary of State declines to make an appointment,

the official receiver shall give notice of his decision or, as the case may be, of the Secretary of State's decision to the court."

13   Section 296: appointment of trustee by Secretary of State

13   Section 296 is modified so as to read as follows:–

"**296(1)**   At any time when the official receiver is the trustee of the members' estates and of the partnership by virtue of any provision of this Chapter he may apply to the Secretary of State for the appointment of a person as trustee instead of the official receiver.

296(2)   On an application under subsection (1) the Secretary of State shall either make an appointment or decline to make one.

296(3)   Such an application may be made notwithstanding that the Secretary of State has declined to make an appointment either on a previous application under subsection (1) or on a reference under section 295 or under section 300(2) below.

296(4)   Where a trustee has been appointed by the Secretary of State under subsection (2) of this section, and an insolvency order is subsequently made against a further insolvent member by virtue of article 11 of the Insolvent Partnerships Order 1994, then the trustee so appointed shall also be the trustee of the member against whom the subsequent order is made.

296(5)   Where the trustee of the members' estates and of the partnership has been appointed by the Secretary of State (whether under this section or otherwise) or has become trustee of a further insolvent member under subsection (4), the trustee shall give notice of his appointment or further appointment (as the case may be) to the creditors of the members and the creditors of the partnership or, if the court so allows, shall advertise his appointment in accordance with the court's directions.

296(6)   Subject to subsection (7) below, in that notice or advertisement the trustee shall–

(a)   state whether he proposes to summon a combined general meeting of the creditors of the members and of the creditors of the partnership for the purpose of establishing a creditors' committee under section 301, and

(b)   if he does not propose to summon such a meeting, set out the power of the creditors under this Part to require him to summon one.

296(7)   Where in a case where subsection (4) applies a meeting referred to in subsection (6)(a) has already been held, the trustee shall state in the notice or advertisement whether a creditors' committee was established at that meeting and

(a)   if such a committee was established, shall state whether he proposes to appoint additional members of the committee under section 301A(3), and

(b)   if such a committee was not established, shall set out the power of the creditors to require him to summon a meeting for the purpose of determining whether a creditors' committee should be established."

14   Section 297: rules applicable to meetings of creditors

14   Section 297 is modified so as to read as follows:–

"**297(1)**   This section applies where the court has made orders by virtue of article 11 of the Insolvent Partnerships Order 1994.

297(2)   Subject to subsection (3) below, the rules relating to the requisitioning, summoning, holding and conducting of meetings on the bankruptcy of an individual are to apply (with the necessary modifications) to the requisitioning, summoning, holding and conducting of separate meetings of the creditors of each member and of combined meetings of the creditors of the partnership and the creditors of the members.

297(3)   Any combined meeting of creditors shall be conducted as if the creditors of the members and of the partnership were a single set of creditors."

15   Section 298: removal of trustee; vacation of office

15   Section 298 is modified so as to read as follows:–

"**298(1)**   Subject as follows, the trustee of the estates of the members and of the partnership may be removed from office only by an order of the court.

298(2)   If the trustee was appointed by the Secretary of State, he may be removed by a direction of the Secretary of State.

298(3)   The trustee (not being the official receiver) shall vacate office if he ceases to be a person who is for the time being qualified to act as an insolvency practitioner in relation to any member or to the partnership.

298(4)   The trustee may, with the leave of the court (or, if appointed by the Secretary of State, with the leave of the court or the Secretary of State), resign his office by giving notice of his resignation to the court.

298(5)   Subject to subsections (6) and (7) below, any removal from or vacation of office under this section relates to all offices held in the proceedings by virtue of article 11 of the Insolvent Partnerships Order 1994.

298(6)   The trustee shall vacate office on giving notice to the court that a final meeting has been held under section 331 in Chapter IV (final meeting of creditors of insolvent partnership or of members) and of the decision (if any) of that meeting.

298(7)   The trustee shall vacate office as trustee of a member if the order made by virtue of article 11 of the Insolvent Partnerships Order 1994 in relation to that member is annulled."

16   Section 299: release of trustee

16   Section 299 is modified so as to read as follows:–

"**299(1)**   Where the official receiver has ceased to be the trustee of the members' estates and of the partnership and a person is appointed in his stead, the official receiver shall have his release with effect from the following time, that is to say–

(a)   where that person is appointed by a combined general meeting of creditors of the members and of the partnership or by the Secretary of State, the time at which the official receiver gives notice to the court that he has been replaced, and

(b)   where that person is appointed by the court, such time as the court may determine.

299(2)   If the official receiver while he is the trustee gives notice to the Secretary of State that the administration of the estate of any member, or the winding up of the partnership business and administration of its affairs, is for practical purposes complete, he shall have his release as trustee of any member or as trustee of the partnership (as the case may be) with effect from such time as the Secretary of State may determine.

299(3)   A person other than the official receiver who has ceased to be the trustee of the estate of any member or of the partnership shall have his release with effect from the following time, that is to say–

(a)   in the case of a person who has died, the time at which notice is given to the court in accordance with the rules that that person has ceased to hold office;

(b)   in the case of a person who has been removed from office by the court or by the Secretary of State, or who has vacated office under section 298(3), such time as the Secretary of State may, on an application by that person, determine;

(c)   in the case of a person who has resigned, such time as may be directed by the court (or, if he was appointed by the Secretary of State, such time as may be directed by the court or as the Secretary of State may, on an application by that person, determine);

(d)   in the case of a person who has vacated office under section 298(6)–

(i)   if the final meeting referred to in that subsection has resolved against that person's release, such time as the Secretary of State may, on an application by that person, determine; and

(ii)   if that meeting has not so resolved, the time at which the person vacated office.

299(4)   Where an order by virtue of article 11 of the Insolvent Partnerships Order 1994 is annulled in so far as it relates to any member, the trustee at the time of the annulment has his release in respect of that member with effect from such time as the court may determine.

299(5)   Where the trustee (including the official receiver when so acting) has his release under this section, he shall, with effect from the time specified in the preceding provisions of this section, be discharged from all liability both in respect of acts or omissions of his in the administration of the estates of the members and in the winding up of the partnership business and administration of its affairs and otherwise in relation to his conduct as trustee.

But nothing in this section prevents the exercise, in relation to a person who has had his release under this section, of the court's powers under section 304 (liability of trustee)."

17   Section 300: vacancy in office of trustee

17   Section 300 is modified so as to read as follows:–

"**300(1)**   This section applies where the appointment of any person as trustee of the members' estates and of the partnership fails to take effect or, such an appointment having taken effect, there is otherwise a vacancy in the office of trustee.

300(2)   The official receiver may refer the need for an appointment to the Secretary of State and shall be trustee until the vacancy is filled.

300(3)   On a reference to the Secretary of State under subsection (2) the Secretary of State shall either make an appointment or decline to make one.

300(4)   If on a reference under subsection (2) no appointment is made, the official receiver shall continue to be trustee, but without prejudice to his power to make a further reference.

300(5)   References in this section to a vacancy include a case where it is necessary, in relation to any property which is or may be comprised in a member's estate, to revive the trusteeship of that estate after the holding of a final meeting summoned under section 331 or the giving by the official receiver of notice under section 299(2)."

18   Section 301: creditors' committee

18   Section 301 is modified so as to read as follows:–

"**301(1)**   Subject as follows, a combined general meeting of the creditors of the members and of the partnership (whether summoned under the preceding provisions of this Chapter or otherwise) may establish a committee (known as **"the creditors' committee"**) to exercise the functions conferred on it by or under this Act.

301(2)   A combined general meeting of the creditors of the members and of the partnership shall not establish such a committee, or confer any functions on such a committee, at any time when the official receiver is the trustee, except in connection with an appointment made by that meeting of a person to be trustee instead of the official receiver.

301A   Functions and membership of creditors' committee

301A(1)   The committee established under section 301 shall act as creditors' committee for each member and as liquidation committee for the partnership, and shall as appropriate exercise the functions conferred on creditors' and liquidation committees in a bankruptcy or winding up by or under this Act.

301A(2)   The rules relating to liquidation committees are to apply (with the necessary modifications and with the exclusion of all references to contributories) to a committee established under section 301.

301A(3)   Where the appointment of the trustee also takes effect in relation to a further insolvent member under section 293(8) or 296(4), the trustee may appoint any creditor of that member (being qualified under the rules to be a member of the committee) to be an additional member of any creditors' committee already established under section 301, provided that the creditor concerned consents to act.

301A(4)   The court may at any time, on application by a creditor of any member or of the partnership, appoint additional members of the creditors' committee.

301A(5)   If additional members of the creditors' committee are appointed under subsection (3) or (4), the limit on the maximum number of members of the committee specified in the rules shall be increased by the number of additional members so appointed."

19   Section 305: general functions and powers of trustee

19   Section 305 is modified so as to read as follows:

"**305(1)**   The function of the trustee of the estates of the members and of the partnership is to get in, realise and distribute the estates of the members and the partnership property in accordance with the following provisions of this Chapter.

305(2)   The trustee shall have all the functions and powers in relation to the partnership and the partnership property that he has in relation to the members and their estates.

305(3)   In the carrying out of his functions and in the management of the members' estates and the partnership property the trustee is entitled, subject to the following provisions of this Chapter, to use his own discretion.

305(4)   It is the duty of the trustee, if he is not the official receiver–

(a)   to furnish the official receiver with such information,

(b)   to produce to the official receiver, and permit inspection by the official receiver of, such books, papers and other records, and

(c)   to give the official receiver such other assistance,

as the official receiver may reasonably require for the purpose of enabling him to carry out his functions in relation to the bankruptcy of the members and the winding up of the partnership business and administration of its property."

305(5) The official name of the trustee in his capacity as trustee of a member shall be "the trustee of the estate of…………, a bankrupt" (inserting the name of the member concerned); but he may be referred to as "the trustee in bankruptcy" of the particular member.

305(6) The official name of the trustee in his capacity as trustee of the partnership shall be "the trustee of…………, a partnership" (inserting the name of the partnership concerned)."

20   Section 312: obligation to surrender control to trustee

20   Section 312 is modified so as to read as follows:–

"**312(1)** This section applies where orders are made by virtue of article 11 of the Insolvent Partnerships Order 1994 and a trustee is appointed.

312(2) Any person who is or has been an officer of the partnership in question, or who is an executor or administrator of the estate of a deceased officer of the partnership, shall deliver up to the trustee of the partnership, for the purposes of the exercise of the trustee's functions under this Act, possession of any partnership property which he holds for the purposes of the partnership.

312(3) Each member shall deliver up to the trustee possession of any property, books, papers or other records of which he has possession or control and of which the trustee is required to take possession.
This is without prejudice to the general duties of the members as bankrupts under section 333 in this Chapter.

312(4) If any of the following is in possession of any property, books, papers or other records of which the trustee is required to take possession, namely–

    (a)   the official receiver,

    (b)   a person who has ceased to be trustee of a member's estate,

    (c)   a person who has been the administrator of the partnership or supervisor of a voluntary arrangement approved in relation to the partnership under Part I,

    (d)   a person who has been the supervisor of a voluntary arrangement approved in relation to a member under Part VIII,

the official receiver or, as the case may be, that person shall deliver up possession of the property, books, papers or records to the trustee.

312(5) Any banker or agent of a member or of the partnership, or any other person who holds any property to the account of, or for, a member or the partnership shall pay or deliver to the trustee all property in his possession or under his control which forms part of the member's estate or which is partnership property and which he is not by law entitled to retain as against the member, the partnership or the trustee.

312(6) If any person without reasonable excuse fails to comply with any obligation imposed by this section, he is guilty of a contempt of court and liable to be punished accordingly (in addition to any other punishment to which he may be subject)."

20A   Section 313A: low value home: application for sale, possession or charge

20A   Section 313A is modified so as to read as follows:–

"**313A(1)** This section applies where–

    (a)   property comprised in the individual member's estate consists of an interest in a dwelling-house which at the date of the bankruptcy was the sole or principal residence of–

        (i)   the individual member,

        (ii)   the individual member's spouse or civil partner, or

        (iii)   a former spouse or former civil partner of the individual member, and

    (b)   the trustee applies for an order for the sale of the property, for an order for possession of the property or for an order under section 313 in respect of the property.

313A(2)   The court shall dismiss the application if the value of the interest is below the amount prescribed for the purposes of this subsection.

313A(3)   In determining the value of an interest for the purposes of this section the court shall disregard any matter which it is required to disregard by the order which prescribes the amount for the purposes of subsection (2)."

History
Paragraph 20A inserted by the Insolvent Partnerships (Amendment) Order 2005 (SI 2005/1516) art.10(1), (5) as from July 1, 2005.

21   Section 328: priority of expenses and debts

21   Section 328 is modified so as to read as follows:–

"328   Priority of expenses

328(1)   The provisions of this section shall apply in a case where article 11 of the Insolvent Partnerships Order 1994 applies, as regards priority of expenses incurred by a person acting as trustee of the estates of the members of an insolvent partnership and as trustee of that partnership.

328(2)   The joint estate of the partnership shall be applicable in the first instance in payment of the joint expenses and the separate estate of each insolvent member shall be applicable in the first instance in payment of the separate expenses relating to that member.

328(3)   Where the joint estate is insufficient for the payment in full of the joint expenses, the unpaid balance shall be apportioned equally between the separate estates of the insolvent members against whom insolvency orders have been made and shall form part of the expenses to be paid out of those estates.

328(4)   Where any separate estate of an insolvent member is insufficient for the payment in full of the separate expenses to be paid out of that estate, the unpaid balance shall form part of the expenses to be paid out of the joint estate.

328(5)   Where after the transfer of any unpaid balance in accordance with subsection (3) or (4) any estate is insufficient for the payment in full of the expenses to be paid out of that estate, the balance then remaining unpaid shall be apportioned equally between the other estates.

328(6)   Where after an apportionment under subsection (5) one or more estates are insufficient for the payment in full of the expenses to be paid out of those estates, the total of the unpaid balances of the expenses to be paid out of those estates shall continue to be apportioned equally between the other estates until provision is made for the payment in full of the expenses or there is no estate available for the payment of the balance finally remaining unpaid, in which case it abates in equal proportions between all the estates.

328(7)   Without prejudice to subsections (3) to (6) above, the trustee may, with the sanction of any creditors' committee established under section 301 or with the leave of the court obtained on application–

    (a)   pay out of the joint estate as part of the expenses to be paid out of that estate any expenses incurred for any separate estate of an insolvent member; or

    (b)   pay out of any separate estate of an insolvent member any part of the expenses incurred for the joint estate which affects that separate estate.

328A   Priority of debts in joint estate

328A(1)   The provisions of this section and the next (which are subject to the provisions of section 9 of the Partnership Act 1890 as respects the liability of the estate of a deceased member) shall apply as regards priority of debts in a case where article 11 of the Insolvent Partnerships Order 1994 applies.

328A(2)   After payment of expenses in accordance with section 328 and subject to section 328C(2), the joint debts of the partnership shall be paid out of its joint estate in the following order of priority–

    (a)   the preferential debts;

(b)   the debts which are neither preferential debts nor postponed debts;

(c)   interest under section 328D on the joint debts (other than postponed debts);

(d)   the postponed debts;

(e)   interest under section 328D on the postponed debts.

328A(3)   The responsible insolvency practitioner shall adjust the rights among themselves of the members of the partnership as contributories and shall distribute any surplus to the members or, where applicable, to the separate estates of the members, according to their respective rights and interests in it.

328A(4)   The debts referred to in each of paragraphs (a) and (b) of subsection (2) rank equally between themselves, and in each case if the joint estate is insufficient for meeting them, they abate in equal proportions between themselves.

328A(5)   Where the joint estate is not sufficient for the payment of the joint debts in accordance with paragraphs (a) and (b) of subsection (2), the responsible insolvency practitioner shall aggregate the value of those debts to the extent that they have not been satisfied or are not capable of being satisfied, and that aggregate amount shall be a claim against the separate estate of each member of the partnership against whom an insolvency order has been made which–

(a)   shall be a debt provable by the responsible insolvency practitioner in each such estate, and

(b)   shall rank equally with the debts of the member referred to in section 328B(1)(b) below.

328A(6)   Where the joint estate is sufficient for the payment of the joint debts in accordance with paragraphs (a) and (b) of subsection (2) but not for the payment of interest under paragraph (c) of that subsection, the responsible insolvency practitioner shall aggregate the value of that interest to the extent that it has not been satisfied or is not capable of being satisfied, and that aggregate amount shall be a claim against the separate estate of each member of the partnership against whom an insolvency order has been made which–

(a)   shall be a debt provable by the responsible insolvency practitioner in each such estate, and

(b)   shall rank equally with the interest on the separate debts referred to in section 328B(1)(c) below.

328A(7)   Where the joint estate is not sufficient for the payment of the postponed joint debts in accordance with paragraph (d) of subsection (2), the responsible insolvency practitioner shall aggregate the value of those debts to the extent that they have not been satisfied or are not capable of being satisfied, and that aggregate amount shall be a claim against the separate estate of each member of the partnership against whom an insolvency order has been made which–

(a)   shall be a debt provable by the responsible insolvency practitioner in each such estate, and

(b)   shall rank equally with the postponed debts of the member referred to in section 328B(1)(d) below.

328A(8)   Where the joint estate is sufficient for the payment of the postponed joint debts in accordance with paragraph (d) of subsection (2) but not for the payment of interest under paragraph (e) of that subsection, the responsible insolvency practitioner shall aggregate the value of that interest to the extent that it has not been satisfied or is not capable of being satisfied, and that aggregate amount shall be a claim against the separate estate of each member of the partnership against whom an insolvency order has been made which–

(a)   shall be a debt provable by the responsible insolvency practitioner in each such estate, and

(b)   shall rank equally with the interest on the postponed debts referred to in section 328B(1)(e) below.

328A(9)   Where the responsible insolvency practitioner receives any distribution from the separate estate of a member in respect of a debt referred to in paragraph (a) of subsection (5), (6), (7) or (8) above, that distribution shall become part of the joint estate and shall be distributed in accordance with the order of priority set out in subsection (2) above.

328B   Priority of debts in separate estate

328B(1)   The separate estate of each member of the partnership against whom an insolvency order has been made shall be applicable, after payment of expenses in accordance with section 328 and subject to section 328C(2) below, in payment of the separate debts of that member in the following order of priority–

(a)   the preferential debts;

(b)   the debts which are neither preferential debts nor postponed debts (including any debt referred to in section 328A(5)(a));

(c)   interest under section 328D on the separate debts and under section 328A(6);

(d)   the postponed debts of the member (including any debt referred to in section 328A(7)(a));

(e)   interest under section 328D on the postponed debts of the member and under section 328A(8).

328B(2)   The debts referred to in each of paragraphs (a) and (b) of subsection (1) rank equally between themselves, and in each case if the separate estate is insufficient for meeting them, they abate in equal proportions between themselves.

328B(3)   Where the responsible insolvency practitioner receives any distribution from the joint estate or from the separate estate of another member of the partnership against whom an insolvency order has been made, that distribution shall become part of the separate estate and shall be distributed in accordance with the order of priority set out in subsection (1) of this section.

328C   Provisions generally applicable in distribution of joint and separate estates

328C(1)   Distinct accounts shall be kept of the joint estate of the partnership and of the separate estate of each member of that partnership against whom an insolvency order is made.

328C(2)   No member of the partnership shall prove for a joint or separate debt in competition with the joint creditors, unless the debt has arisen–

(a)   as a result of fraud, or

(b)   in the ordinary course of a business carried on separately from the partnership business.

328C(3)   For the purpose of establishing the value of any debt referred to in section 328A(5)(a) or (7)(a), that value may be estimated by the responsible insolvency practitioner in accordance with section 322.

328C(4)   Interest under section 328D on preferential debts ranks equally with interest on debts which are neither preferential debts nor postponed debts.

328C(5)   Sections 328A and 328B are without prejudice to any provision of this Act or of any other enactment concerning the ranking between themselves of postponed debts and interest thereon, but in the absence of any such provision postponed debts and interest thereon rank equally between themselves.

328C(6)   If any two or more members of an insolvent partnership constitute a separate partnership, the creditors of such separate partnership shall be deemed to be a separate set of creditors and subject to the same statutory provisions as the separate creditors of any member of the insolvent partnership.

328C(7)   Where any surplus remains after the administration of the estate of a separate partnership, the surplus shall be distributed to the members or, where applicable, to the separate estates of the members of that partnership according to their respective rights and interests in it.

328C(8)   Neither the official receiver, the Secretary of State nor a responsible insolvency practitioner shall be entitled to remuneration or fees under the Insolvency Rules 1986, the Insolvency Regulations 1986 or the Insolvency Fees Order 1986 for his services in connection with–

(a)   the transfer of a surplus from the joint estate to a separate estate under section 328A(3),

(b)   a distribution from a separate estate to the joint estate in respect of a claim referred to in section 328A (5), (6), (7) or (8), or

(c)   a distribution from the estate of a separate partnership to the separate estates of the members of that partnership under subsection (7) above.

328D   Interest on debts

328D(1)   In the bankruptcy of each of the members of an insolvent partnership and in the winding up of that partnership's business and administration of its property, interest is payable in accordance with this section, in the order of priority laid down by sections 328A and 328B, on any debt proved in the bankruptcy including so much of any such debt as represents interest on the remainder.

328D(2)   Interest under this section is payable on the debts in question in respect of the periods during which they have been outstanding since the relevant order was made by virtue of article 11 of the Insolvent Partnerships Order 1994.

328D(3)   The rate of interest payable under this section in respect of any debt (**"the official rate"** for the purposes of any provision of this Act in which that expression is used) is whichever is the greater of–

(a)   the rate specified in section 17 of the Judgments Act 1838 on the day on which the relevant order was made, and

(b)   the rate applicable to that debt apart from the bankruptcy or winding up."

22   Section 331: final meeting

22   Section 331 is modified so as to read as follows:–

"**331(1)**   Subject as follows in this section and the next, this section applies where–

(a)   it appears to the trustee of the estates of the members and of the partnership that the administration of any member's estate or the winding up of the partnership business and administration of the partnership property is for practical purposes complete, and

(b)   the trustee is not the official receiver.

331(2)   The trustee shall summon a final general meeting of the creditors of any such member or of the partnership (as the case may be) or a combined final general meeting of the creditors of any such members or (as the case may be) the creditors of any such members and of the partnership which–

(a)   shall as appropriate receive the trustee's report of the administration of the estate of the member or members or of the winding up of the partnership business and administration of the partnership property, and

(b)   shall determine whether the trustee should have his release under section 299 in Chapter III in respect (as the case may be) of the administration of the estate of the member or members, or of the winding up of the partnership business and administration of the partnership property.

331(3)   The trustee may, if he thinks fit, give the notice summoning the final general meeting at the same time as giving notice under section 330(1); but, if summoned for an earlier date, that meeting shall be adjourned (and, if necessary, further adjourned) until a date on which the trustee is able to report that the administration of the estate of the member or members or the winding up of the partnership business and administration of the partnership property is for practical purposes complete.

331(4)   In the administration of the members' estates and the winding up of the partnership business and administration of the partnership property it is the trustee's duty to retain sufficient sums from the property of the members and of the partnership to cover the expenses of summoning and holding any meeting required by this section."

23   Section 387: the "relevant date"

23   Section 387 is modified so as to read as follows:–

"**387**   Where an order has been made in respect of an insolvent partnership by virtue of article 11 of the Insolvent Partnerships Order 1994, references in Schedule 6 to this Act to the relevant date (being the date which determines the existence and amount of a preferential debt) are to the date on which the said order was made."

SCHEDULE 8

MODIFIED PROVISIONS OF COMPANY DIRECTORS DISQUALIFICATION ACT 1986
FOR THE PURPOSES OF ARTICLE 16

Article 16

The following provisions of the Company Directors Disqualification Act 1986 are modified so as to read as follows:–

"Section 6: Duty of court to disqualify unfit officers of insolvent partnerships

6(1)   The court shall make a disqualification order against a person in any case where, on an application under this section, it is satisfied–

(a)   that he is or has been an officer of a partnership which has at any time become insolvent (whether while he was an officer or subsequently), and

(b)   that his conduct as an officer of that partnership (either taken alone or taken together with his conduct as an officer of any other partnership or partnerships, or as a director of any company or companies) makes him unfit to be concerned in the management of a company.

6(2)   For the purposes of this section and the next–

(a)   a partnership becomes insolvent if–

     (i)   the court makes an order for it to be wound up as an unregistered company at a time when its assets are insufficient for the payment of its debts and other liabilities and the expenses of the winding up; or

     (ii)   the partnership enters administration; and

(b)   a company becomes insolvent if–

     (i)   the company goes into liquidation at a time when its assets are insufficient for the payment of its debts and other liabilities and the expenses of the winding up,

     (ii)   the company enters administration, or

     (iii)   an administrative receiver of the company is appointed.

6(3)   For the purposes of this section and the next, references to a person's conduct as an officer of any partnership or partnerships, or as a director of any company or companies, include, where the partnership or company concerned or any of the partnerships or companies concerned has become insolvent, that person's conduct in relation to any matter connected with or arising out of the insolvency of that partnership or company.

6(4)   In this section and section 7(2), **"the court"** means–

(a)   where the partnership in question is being or has been wound up as an unregistered company by the court, that court,

(b)   where the preceding paragraph does not apply but an administrator has at any time been appointed in relation to the partnership in question, any court which has jurisdiction to wind it up.

6(4A)   Section 117 of the Insolvency Act 1986 (High Court and county court jurisdiction), as modified and set out in Schedule 5 to the 1994 Order, shall apply for the purposes of subsection (4) as if in a case within paragraph (b) of that subsection the references to the presentation of the petition for winding up in sections 117(3) and 117(4) of the Insolvency Act 1986, as modified and set out in that Schedule, were references to the making of the administration order.

6(4B)   Nothing in subsection (4) invalidates any proceedings by reason of their being taken in the wrong court; and proceedings–

(a)   for or in connection with a disqualification order under this section, or

(b)   in connection with a disqualification undertaking accepted under section 7, may be retained in the court in which the proceedings were commenced, although it may not be the court in which they ought to have been commenced.

6(4C)   In this section and section 7, **"director"** includes a shadow director.

6(5)   Under this section the minimum period of disqualification is 2 years, and the maximum period is 15 years.

Section 7: Disqualification order or undertaking; and reporting provisions

7(1)   If it appears to the Secretary of State that it is expedient in the public interest that a disqualification order under section 6 should be made against any person, an application for the making of such an order against that person may be made–

   (a)   by the Secretary of State, or

   (b)   if the Secretary of State so directs in the case of a person who is or has been an officer of a partnership which is being or has been wound up by the court as an unregistered company, by the official receiver.

7(2)   Except with the leave of the court, an application for the making under that section of a disqualification order against any person shall not be made after the end of the period of 2 years beginning with the day on which the partnership of which that person is or has been an officer became insolvent.

7(2A)   If it appears to the Secretary of State that the conditions mentioned in section 6(1) are satisfied as respects any person who has offered to give him a disqualification undertaking, he may accept the undertaking if it appears to him that it is expedient in the public interest that he should do so (instead of applying, or proceeding with an application, for a disqualification order).

7(3)   If it appears to the office-holder responsible under this section, that is to say–

   (a)   in the case of a partnership which is being wound up by the court as an unregistered company, the official receiver, or

   (b)   in the case of a partnership which is in administration, the administrator, that the conditions mentioned in section 6(1) are satisfied as respects a person who is or has been an officer of that partnership, the office-holder shall forthwith report the matter to the Secretary of State.

7(4)   The Secretary of State or the official receiver may require any of the persons mentioned in subsection (5) below–

   (a)   to furnish him with such information with respect to any person's conduct as an officer of a partnership or as a director of a company, and

   (b)   to produce and permit inspection of such books, papers and other records relevant to that person's conduct as such an officer or director, as the Secretary of State or the official receiver may reasonably require for the purpose of determining whether to exercise, or of exercising, any function of his under this section.

7(5)   The persons referred to in subsection (4) are–

   (a)   the liquidator or administrator, or former liquidator or administrator of the partnership,

   (b)   the liquidator, administrator or administrative receiver, or former liquidator, administrator or administrative receiver, of the company.

Section 8: disqualification after investigation

8(1)   If it appears to the Secretary of State from–

   (a)   a report made by an inspector or person appointed to conduct an investigation under a provision mentioned in subsection (1A), or

   (b)   information or documents obtained under a provision mentioned in subsection (1B),

that it is expedient in the public interest that a disqualification order should be made against any person who is or has been an officer of an insolvent partnership, he may apply to the court for such an order to be made against that person.

8(1A)   The provisions are–

(a)   section 437 of the Companies Act,

(b)   section 167, 168, 169(1)(b) or 284 of the Financial Services and Markets Act 2000, or

(c)   regulations made as a result of section 262(2)(k) of that Act.

8(1B)   The provisions are–

(a)   section 447 or 448 of the Companies Act,

(b)   section 2 of the Criminal Justice Act 1987,

(c)   section 52 of the Criminal Justice (Scotland) Act 1987,

(d)   section 83 of the Companies Act 1989, or

(e)   section 171 or 173 of the Financial Services and Markets Act 2000.

8(2)   The court may make a disqualification order against a person where, on an application under this section, it is satisfied that his conduct in relation to the partnership makes him unfit to be concerned in the management of a company.

8(2A)   Where it appears to the Secretary of State from such report, information or documents that, in the case of a person who has offered to give him a disqualification undertaking–

(a)   the conduct of the person in relation to an insolvent partnership of which the person is or has been an officer makes him unfit to be concerned in the management of a company, and

(b)   it is expedient in the public interest that he should accept the undertaking (instead of applying, or proceeding with an application, for a disqualification order),

he may accept the undertaking.

8(3)   In this section **"the court"** means the High Court.

8(4)   The maximum period of disqualification under this section is 15 years.

Section 9: matters for determining unfitness of officers of partnerships

9(1)   This section applies where it falls to a court to determine whether a person's conduct as an officer of a partnership (either taken alone or taken together with his conduct as an officer of any other partnership or partnerships or as a director of any company or companies) makes him unfit to be concerned in the management of a company.

9(1A)   In determining whether he may accept a disqualification undertaking from any person the Secretary of State shall, as respects the person's conduct as an officer of any partnership or a director of any company concerned, have regard in particular–

(a)   to the matters mentioned in Part I of Schedule 1 to this Act, and

(b)   where the partnership or the company (as the case may be) has become insolvent, to the matters mentioned in Part II of that Schedule;

and references in that Schedule to the officer and the partnership or, as the case may be, to the director and the company are to be read accordingly.

9(2)   The court shall, as respects that person's conduct as an officer of that partnership or each of those partnerships or as a director of that company or each of those companies, have regard in particular–

(a)   to the matters mentioned in Part I of Schedule 1 to this Act, and

(b)   where the partnership or company (as the case may be) has become insolvent, to the matters mentioned in Part II of that Schedule;

and references in that Schedule to the officer and the partnership or, as the case may be, to the director and the company, are to be read accordingly and in this section and that Schedule **"director"** includes a shadow director.

9(3)   Subsections (2) and (3) of section 6 apply for the purposes of this section and Schedule 1 as they apply for the purposes of sections 6 and 7.

9(4)   Subject to the next subsection, any reference in Schedule 1 to an enactment contained in the Companies Act or the Insolvency Act includes, in relation to any time before the coming into force of that enactment, the corresponding enactment in force at that time.

9(5)   The Secretary of State may by order modify any of the provisions of Schedule 1; and such an order may contain such transitional provisions as may appear to the Secretary of State necessary or expedient.

9(6)   The power to make orders under this section is exercisable by statutory instrument subject to annulment in pursuance of a resolution of either House of Parliament.

Section 13: Criminal penalties

13   If a person acts in contravention of a disqualification order or disqualification undertaking he is liable–

     (a)   on conviction on indictment, to imprisonment for not more than 2 years or a fine or both; and

     (b)   on summary conviction, to imprisonment for not more than 6 months or a fine not exceeding the statutory maximum, or both.

Section 14: Offences by body corporate

14(1)   Where a body corporate is guilty of an offence of acting in contravention of a disqualification order or disqualification undertaking and it is proved that the offence occurred with the consent or connivance of, or was attributable to any neglect on the part of any director, manager, secretary or other similar officer of the body corporate, or any person who was purporting to act in any such capacity he, as well as the body corporate, is guilty of the offence and liable to be proceeded against and punished accordingly.

14(2)   Where the affairs of a body corporate are managed by its members, subsection (1) applies in relation to the acts and defaults of a member in connection with his functions of management as if he were a director of the body corporate.

Section 15: Personal liability for company's debts where person acts while disqualified

15(1)   A person is personally responsible for all the relevant debts of a company if at any time–

     (a)   in contravention of a disqualification order or disqualification undertaking he is involved in the management of the company, or

     (b)   as a person who is involved in the management of the company, he acts or is willing to act on instructions given without the leave of the court by a person whom he knows at that time to be the subject of a disqualification order or disqualification undertaking or a disqualification order under Part II of the Companies (Northern Ireland) Order 1989 or to be an undischarged bankrupt.

15(2)   Where a person is personally responsible under this section for the relevant debts of a company, he is jointly and severally liable in respect of those debts with the company and any other person who, whether under this section or otherwise, is so liable.

15(3)   For the purposes of this section the relevant debts of a company are–

     (a)   in relation to a person who is personally responsible under paragraph (a) of subsection (1), such debts and other liabilities of the company as are incurred at a time when that person was involved in the management of the company, and

     (b)   in relation to a person who is personally responsible under paragraph (b) of that subsection, such debts and other liabilities of the company as are incurred at a time when that person was acting or was willing to act on instructions given as mentioned in that paragraph.

15(4)   For the purposes of this section, a person is involved in the management of a company if he is a director of the company or if he is concerned, whether directly or indirectly, or takes part, in the management of the company.

15(5)   For the purposes of this section a person who, as a person involved in the management of a company, has at any time acted on instructions given without the leave of the court by a person whom he knew at that time to be the subject of a disqualification order or disqualification undertaking or a disqualification order under Part II of the

Companies (Northern Ireland) Order 1989 or to be an undischarged bankrupt is presumed, unless the contrary is shown, to have been willing at any time thereafter to act on any instructions given by that person.

Section 17: Application for leave under an order or undertaking

17(1)   Where a person is subject to a disqualification order made by a court having jurisdiction to wind up partnerships, any application for leave for the purposes of section 1(1)(a) shall be made to that court.

17(2)   Where a person is subject to a disqualification undertaking accepted at any time under section 7 or 8, any application for leave for the purposes of section 1A(1)(a) shall be made to any court to which, if the Secretary of State had applied for a disqualification order under the section in question at that time, his application could have been made.

17(3)   But where a person is subject to two or more disqualification orders or undertakings (or to one or more disqualification orders and to one or more disqualification undertakings), any application for leave for the purposes of section 1(1)(a) or 1A(1)(a) shall be made to any court to which any such application relating to the latest order to be made, or undertaking to be accepted, could be made.

17(4)   On the hearing of an application for leave for the purposes of section 1(1)(a) or 1A(1)(a), the Secretary of State shall appear and call the attention of the court to any matters which seem to him to be relevant, and may himself give evidence or call witnesses.

SCHEDULE 1

MATTERS FOR DETERMINING UNFITNESS OF OFFICERS OF PARTNERSHIPS

Section 9

PART I

MATTERS APPLICABLE IN ALL CASES

1   Any misfeasance or breach of any fiduciary or other duty by the officer in relation to the partnership or, as the case may be, by the director in relation to the company.

2   Any misapplication or retention by the officer or the director of, or any conduct by the officer or the director giving rise to an obligation to account for, any money or other property of the partnership or, as the case may be, of the company.

3   The extent of the officer's or the director's responsibility for the partnership or, as the case may be, the company entering into any transaction liable to be set aside under Part XVI of the Insolvency Act (provisions against debt avoidance).

4   The extent of the director's responsibility for any failure by the company to comply with any of the following provisions of the Companies Act, namely–

(a)   section 221 (companies to keep accounting records);

(b)   section 222 (where and for how long records to be kept);

(c)   section 288 (register of directors and secretaries);

(d)   section 352 (obligation to keep and enter up register of members);

(e)   section 353 (location of register of members);

(f)   section 363 (duty of company to make annual returns); and

(g)   sections 399 and 415 (company's duty to register charges it creates).

5   The extent of the director's responsibility for any failure by the directors of the company to comply with–

(a)   section 226 or 227 of the Companies Act (duty to prepare annual accounts), or

(b)   section 233 of that Act (approval and signature of accounts).

6   Any failure by the officer to comply with any obligation imposed on him by or under any of the following provisions of the Limited Partnerships Act 1907–

(a)   section 8 (registration of particulars of limited partnership);

(b)   section 9 (registration of changes in particulars);

(c)   section 10 (advertisement of general partner becoming limited partner and of assignment of share of limited partner).

PART II

MATTERS APPLICABLE WHERE PARTNERSHIP OR COMPANY HAS BECOME INSOLVENT

7   The extent of the officer's or the director's responsibility for the causes of the partnership or (as the case may be) the company becoming insolvent.

8   The extent of the officer's or the director's responsibility for any failure by the partnership or (as the case may be) the company to supply any goods or services which have been paid for (in whole or in part).

9   The extent of the officer's or the director's responsibility for the partnership or (as the case may be) the company entering into any transaction or giving any preference, being a transaction or preference–

(a)   liable to be set aside under section 127 or sections 238 to 240 of the Insolvency Act, or

(b)   challengeable under section 242 or 243 of that Act or under any rule of law in Scotland.

10   The extent of the director's responsibility for any failure by the directors of the company to comply with section 98 of the Insolvency Act (duty to call creditors' meeting in creditors' voluntary winding up).

11   Any failure by the director to comply with any obligation imposed on him by or under any of the following provisions of the Insolvency Act–

(a)   section 47 (statement of affairs to administrative receiver);

(b)   section 66 (statement of affairs in Scottish receivership);

(c)   section 99 (directors' duty to attend meeting; statement of affairs in creditors' voluntary winding up).

12   Any failure by the officer or the director to comply with any obligation imposed on him by or under any of the following provisions of the Insolvency Act (both as they apply in relation to companies and as they apply in relation to insolvent partnerships by virtue of the provisions of the Insolvent Partnerships Order 1994)–

(a)   paragraph 48 of Schedule B1 (statement of affairs in administration);

(b)   section 131 (statement of affairs in winding up by the court);

(c)   section 234 (duty of any one with property to deliver it up);

(d)   section 235 (duty to co-operate with liquidator, etc.)."

History
Modified Sch.1 para.12(a) amended by the Insolvent Partnerships (Amendment) Order 2005 (SI 2005/1516) art.11(1), (4), as from July 1, 2005.

SCHEDULE 9

FORMS

Article 17

[Not reproduced.]

Schedule 10

Subordinate Legislation Applied

Article 18

The Insolvency Practitioners Tribunal (Conduct of Investigations) Rules 1986

The Insolvency Practitioners (Recognised Professional Bodies) Order 1986

The Insolvency Rules 1986

The Insolvency Proceedings (Monetary Limits) Order 1986

The Administration of Insolvent Estates of Deceased Persons Order 1986

The Insolvency (Amendment of Subordinate Legislation) Order 1986

The Co-operation of Insolvency Courts (Designation of Relevant Countries and Territories) Order 1986

The Insolvent Companies (Disqualification of Unfit Directors) Proceedings Rules 1987

The Insolvency Regulations 1994

The Insolvent Companies (Reports on Conduct of Directors) Rules 1996

The Companies (Disqualification Orders) Regulations 2001

The Insolvency Practitioners and Insolvency Services Accounts (Fees) Order 2003

The Insolvency Proceedings (Fees) Order 2004

The Insolvency Practitioners Regulations 2005

Insolvency Regulations 1994

(SI 1994/2507)

Made on 26 September 1994 by the Secretary of State for Trade and Industry under r.12.1 of the Insolvency Rules 1986 and ss.411, 412 of and para.27 of Sch.8 and para.30 of Sch.9 to the Insolvency Act 1986. Operative from 24 October 1994.

[**Note:** These Regulations apply (with modifications) to limited liability partnerships by virtue of the Limited Liability Partnerships Regulations 2001 (SI 2001/1090) regs 1, 10(1) and Sch.6 Pt II para.10 as from April 6, 2001. Changes made by the Insolvency (Amendment) Regulations 2000 (SI 2000/485), the Insolvency (Amendment) Regulations 2001 (SI 2001/762), the Financial Services and Markets Act 2000 (Consequential Amendments and Repeals) Order 2001 (SI 2001/3649), the Insolvency (Amendment) Regulations 2004 (SI 2004/472), the Insolvency (Amendment) Regulations 2005 (SI 2005/512), the Insolvency (Amendment) Regulations 2008 (SI 2008/670), the Insolvency (Amendment) Regulations 2009 (SI 2009/482) and the Insolvency (Amendment) Regulations 2011 (SI 2011/2203) have been incorporated into the text (in the case of pre-2003 legislation without annotation).]

PART 1

GENERAL

1 Citation and commencement

1 These Regulations may be cited as the Insolvency Regulations 1994 and shall come into force on 24th October 1994.

2 Revocations

2 Subject to regulation 37 below, the Regulations listed in Schedule 1 to these Regulations are hereby revoked.

3 Interpretation and application

3(1) In these Regulations, except where the context otherwise requires–

"bank" means–

(a) a person who has permission under Part 4 of the Financial Services and Markets Act 2000 to accept deposits, or

(b) an EEA firm of the kind mentioned in paragraph 5(b) of Schedule 3 to that Act, which has permission under paragraph 15 of that Schedule (as a result of qualifying for authorisation under paragraph 12(1) of that Schedule) to accept deposits;

"bankrupt" means the bankrupt or his estate;

"company" means the company which is being wound up;

"creditors' committee" means any committee established under section 301;

"electronic transfer" means transmission by any electronic means;

"liquidation committee" means, in the case of a winding up by the court, any committee established under section 141 and, in the case of a creditors' voluntary winding up, any committee established under section 101;

"liquidator" includes, in the case of a company being wound up by the court, the official receiver when so acting;

"local bank" means any bank in, or in the neighbourhood of, the insolvency district, or the district in respect of which the court has winding-up jurisdiction, in which the proceedings are taken, or in the locality in which any business of the company or, as the case may be, the bankrupt is carried on;

"local bank account" means, in the case of a winding up by the court, a current account opened with a local bank under regulation 6(2) below and, in the case of a bankruptcy, a current account opened with a local bank under regulation 21(1) below;

"payment instrument" means a cheque or payable order;

"the Rules" means the Insolvency Rules 1986; and

"trustee", subject to regulation 19(2) below, means trustee of a bankrupt's estate including the official receiver when so acting;

and other expressions used in these Regulations and defined by the Rules have the meanings which they bear in the Rules.

3(2)   A Rule referred to in these Regulations by number means the Rule so numbered in the Rules.

3(3)   Any application to be made to the Secretary of State or to the Department or anything required to be sent to the Secretary of State or to the Department under these Regulations shall be addressed to the Department for Business, Innovation and Skills, The Insolvency Service, PO Box 3690, Birmingham B2 4UY.

3(4)   Where a regulation makes provision for the use of a form obtainable from the Department, the Department may provide different forms for different cases arising under that regulation.

3(5)   Subject to regulation 37 below, these Regulations (except for regulations 3A and 36A) apply–

(a)   to winding-up proceedings commenced on or after 29th December 1986; and

(b)   to bankruptcy proceedings where the bankruptcy petition is or was presented on or after that day.

History
In reg.3(5) the words in round brackets inserted by the Insolvency (Amendment) Regulations 2005 (SI 2005/512) reg.5(1), (2) as from April 1, 2005.

3(6)   Regulation 3A applies in any case where a company entered into administration on or after 15th September 2003 other than a case where the company entered into administration by virtue of a petition presented before that date.

History
Regulation 3(6) inserted by the Insolvency (Amendment) Regulations 2005 (SI 2005/512) reg.5(1), (3) as from April 1, 2005.

3(7)   Regulation 36A applies in any case where an insolvency practitioner is appointed on or after 1st April 2005.

History
Regulation 3(7) inserted by the Insolvency (Amendment) Regulations 2005 (SI 2005/512) reg.5(1), (3) as from April 1, 2005.

PART 1A

ADMINISTRATION

3A   Disposal of company's records and provision of information to the Secretary of State

3A(1)   The person who was the last administrator of a company which has been dissolved may, at any time after the expiration of a period of one year from the date of dissolution, destroy or otherwise dispose of the books, papers and other records of the company.

3A(2)   An administrator or former administrator shall within 14 days of a request by the Secretary of State give the Secretary of State particulars of any money in his hands or under his control representing unclaimed or undistributed assets of the company or dividends or other sums due to any person as a member or former member of the company.

History

Regulation 3A inserted by the Insolvency (Amendment) Regulations 2005 (SI 2005/512) reg.6 as from April 1, 2005.

3B   Payment of unclaimed dividends or other money

3B(1)   This regulation applies to monies which–

   (a)   are held by the former administrator of a dissolved company, and

   (b)   represent either or both of the following–

      (i)   unclaimed dividends due to creditors, or

      (ii)   sums held by the company in trust in respect of dividends or other sums due to any person as a member or former member of the company.

3B(2)   Any monies to which this regulation applies may be paid into the Insolvency Services Account.

3B(3)   Where under this regulation the former administrator pays any sums into the Insolvency Services Account, he shall at the same time give notice to the Secretary of State of–

   (a)   the name of the company,

   (b)   the name and address of the person to whom the dividend or other sum is payable,

   (c)   the amount of the dividend or other sum, and

   (d)   the date on which it was paid.

3B(4)   Where a dividend or other sum is paid to a person by way of a payment instrument, any payment into the Insolvency Services Account in respect of that dividend or sum pursuant to paragraph (2) may not be made earlier than on or after the expiry of 6 months from the date of the payment instrument.

PART 1B

ADMINISTRATIVE RECEIVERSHIP

3C   Payment of unclaimed dividends or other money

3C(1) This regulation applies to monies which–

   (a)   are held by the former administrative receiver of a dissolved company, and

   (b)   represent either or both of the following–

      (i)   unclaimed dividends due to creditors, or

      (ii)   sums held by the company in trust in respect of dividends or other sums due to any person as a member or former member of the company.

3C(2)   Any monies to which this regulation applies may be paid into the Insolvency Services Account.

3C(3)   Where under this regulation the former administrative receiver pays any sums into the Insolvency Services Account, he shall at the same time give notice to the Secretary of State of–

   (a)   the name of the company,

   (b)   the name and address of the person to whom the dividend or other sum is payable,

(c)   the amount of the dividend or other sum, and

(d)   the date on which it was paid.

3C(3)   Where a dividend or other sum is paid to a person by way of a payment instrument, any payment in respect of that dividend or sum into the Insolvency Services Account pursuant to paragraph (2) may not be made earlier than on or after the expiry of 6 months from the date of the payment instrument.

History
Regulations 3B, 3C inserted by the Insolvency (Amendment) Regulations 2008 (SI 2008/670) reg.3(1), (2) as from April 6, 2008.

PART 2

WINDING UP

4   Introductory

4   This Part of these Regulations relates to–

(a)   voluntary winding up and

(b)   winding up by the court

of companies which the courts in England and Wales have jurisdiction to wind up.

Payments into and out of the Insolvency Services Account

5   Payments into the Insolvency Services Account

5(1)   In the case of a winding up by the court, subject to regulation 6 below, the liquidator shall pay all money received by him in the course of carrying out his functions as such without any deduction into the Insolvency Services Account kept by the Secretary of State with the Bank of England to the credit of the company once every 14 days or forthwith if £5,000 or more has been received.

5(2)   [Omitted by the Insolvency (Amendment) Regulations 2011 (SI 2011/2203) Sch. para.1 as from October 1, 2011.]

5(3)   Every payment of money into the Insolvency Services Account under this regulation shall be–

(a)   made through the Bank Giro system; or

(b)   sent direct to the Bank of England, Threadneedle Street, London EC2R 8AH by cheque drawn in favour of the "Insolvency Services Account" and crossed "A/c payee only" "Bank of England"; or

(c)   made by electronic transfer,

and the liquidator shall on request be given by the Department a receipt for the money so paid.

5(4)   Every payment of money made under sub-paragraph (a) or (b) of paragraph (3) above shall be accompanied by a form obtainable from the Department for that purpose or by a form that is substantially similar. Every payment of money made under sub-paragraph (c) of paragraph (3) above shall specify the name of the liquidator making the payment and the name of the company to whose credit such payment is made.

5(5)   Where in a voluntary winding up a liquidator pays any unclaimed dividend into the Insolvency Services Account, he shall at the same time give notice to the Secretary of State, on a form obtainable from the Department or on one that is substantially similar, of the name and address of the person to whom the dividend is payable and the amount of the dividend.

6 Local bank account and handling of funds not belonging to the company

6(1)   This regulation does not apply in the case of a voluntary winding up.

6(2)   Where the liquidator intends to exercise his power to carry on the business of the company, he may apply to the Secretary of State for authorisation to open a local bank account, and the Secretary of State may authorise him to make his payments into and out of a specified bank, subject to a limit, instead of into and out of the Insolvency Services Account if satisfied that an administrative advantage will be derived from having such an account.

6(3)   Money received by the liquidator relating to the purpose for which the account was opened may be paid into the local bank account to the credit of the company to which the account relates.

6(4)   Where the liquidator opens a local bank account pursuant to an authorisation granted under paragraph (2) above, he shall open and maintain the account in the name of the company.

6(5)   Where money which is not an asset of the company is provided to the liquidator for a specific purpose, it shall be clearly identifiable in a separate account.

6(6)   The liquidator shall keep proper records, including documentary evidence of all money paid into and out of every local bank account opened and maintained under this regulation.

6(7)   The liquidator shall pay without deduction any surplus over any limit imposed by an authorisation granted under paragraph (2) above into the Insolvency Services Account in accordance with regulation 5 above as that regulation applies in the case of a winding up by the court.

6(8)   As soon as the liquidator ceases to carry on the business of the company or vacates office or an authorisation given in pursuance of an application under paragraph (2) above is withdrawn, he shall close the account and pay any balance into the Insolvency Services Account in accordance with regulation 5 above as that regulation applies in the case of a winding up by the court.

7 Payment of disbursements etc. out of the insolvency services account

7(A1)   Paragraphs (1) and (2) of this regulation are subject to paragraph (3A).

7(1)   In the case of a winding up by the court, on application to the Department, the liquidator shall be repaid all necessary disbursements made by him, and expenses properly incurred by him, in the course of his administration to the date of his vacation of office out of any money standing to the credit of the company in the Insolvency Services Account.

7(2)   In the case of a winding up by the court, the liquidator shall on application to the Department obtain payment instruments to the order of the payee for sums which become payable on account of the company for delivery by the liquidator to the persons to whom the payments are to be made.

7(3)   [Omitted.]

7(3A)   In respect of an application made by the liquidator under paragraph (1) or (2) above, the Secretary of State, if requested to do so by the liquidator, may, at his discretion,

    (a)   make the payment which is the subject of the application to the liquidator by electronic transfer; or

    (b)   as an alternative to the issue of payment instruments, make payment by electronic transfer to the persons to whom the liquidator would otherwise deliver payment instruments.

7(4)   Any application under this regulation shall be made by the liquidator on a form obtainable from the Department for the purpose or on a form that is substantially similar.

7(5)   In the case of a winding up by the court, on the liquidator vacating office, he shall be repaid by any succeeding liquidator out of any funds available for the purpose any necessary disbursements made by him and any expenses properly incurred by him but not repaid before he vacates office.

History
Regulation 7(A1), 7(3A) amended and reg.7(3) omitted by the Insolvency (Amendment) Regulations 2011 (SI 2011/2203) regs 2–4 as from October 1, 2011.

Dividends to creditors and returns of capital to contributories of a company

8 Payment

8(A1) Paragraphs (1) and (2) of this regulation are subject to paragraph (3A).

8(1) In the case of a winding up by the court, the liquidator shall pay every dividend by payment instruments which shall be prepared by the Department on the application of the liquidator and transmitted to him for distribution amongst the creditors.

8(2) In the case of a winding up by the court, the liquidator shall pay every return of capital to contributories by payment instruments which shall be prepared by the Department on application.

8(3) [Omitted.]

8(3A) In respect of an application made by the liquidator under paragraph (1) or (2) above, the Secretary of State, if requested to do so by the liquidator, may, at his discretion,

(a) as an alternative to the issue of payment instruments, make payment by electronic transfer to the persons to whom the liquidator would otherwise deliver payment instruments; or

(b) make the payment which is the subject of the application to the liquidator by electronic transfer.

8(4) Any application under this regulation for a payment instrument or payment by electronic transfer shall be made by the liquidator on a form obtainable from the Department for the purpose or on a form which is substantially similar.

8(5) In the case of a winding up by the court, the liquidator shall enter the total amount of every dividend and of every return to contributories that he desires to pay under this regulation in the records to be kept under regulation 10 below in one sum.

8(6) On the liquidator vacating office, he shall send to the Department any valid unclaimed or undelivered payment instruments for dividends or returns to contributories after endorsing them with the word "cancelled".

History
Regulation 8(A1) inserted by the Insolvency (Amendment) Regulations 2000 (SI 2000/485), regs 1, 3 and Sch. para.6 as from March 31, 2000. Regulation 8(A1), 8(3A) amended and reg.8(3) omitted by the Insolvency (Amendment) Regulations 2011 (SI 2011/2203) regs 5–7 as from October 1, 2011.

9 Investment or otherwise handling of funds in winding up of companies and payment of interest

9(1) When the cash balance standing to the credit of the company in the account in respect of that company kept by the Secretary of State is in excess of the amount which, in the opinion of the liquidator, is required for the immediate purposes of the winding up and should be invested, he may request the Secretary of State to invest the amount not so required in Government securities, to be placed to the credit of that account for the company's benefit.

9(2) When any of the money so invested is, in the opinion of the liquidator, required for the immediate purposes of the winding up, he may request the Secretary of State to raise such sum as may be required by the sale of such of those securities as may be necessary.

9(3) In cases where investments have been made at the request of the liquidator in pursuance of paragraph (1) above and additional sums to the amounts so invested, including money received under paragraph (7) below, are paid into the Insolvency Services Account to the credit of the company, a request shall be made to the Secretary of State by the liquidator if it is desired that these additional sums should be invested.

9(4)   Any request relating to the investment in, or sale of, as the case may be, Treasury Bills made under paragraphs (1), (2) or (3) above shall be made on a form obtainable from the Department or on one that is substantially similar and any request relating to the purchase or sale, as the case may be, of any other type of Government security made under the provisions of those paragraphs shall be made in writing.

9(5)   Any request made under paragraphs (1), (2) or (3) above shall be sufficient authority to the Secretary of State for the investment or sale as the case may be.

9(6)   Subject to paragraphs (6A) and (6B), at any time after 1st April 2004 whenever there are any monies standing to the credit of the company in the Insolvency Services Account the company shall be entitled to interest on those monies at the rate of 4.25 per cent per annum.

9(6A)   Interest shall cease to accrue pursuant to paragraph (6) from the date of receipt by the Secretary of State of a notice in writing from the liquidator that in the opinion of the liquidator it is necessary or expedient in order to facilitate the conclusion of the winding up that interest should cease to accrue but interest shall start to accrue again pursuant to paragraph (6) where the liquidator gives a further notice in writing to the Secretary of State requesting that interest should start to accrue again.

9(6B)   The Secretary of State may by notice published in the London Gazette vary the rate of interest prescribed by paragraph (6) and such variation shall have effect from the day after the date of publication of the notice in the London Gazette or such later date as may be specified in the notice.

9(7)   All money received in respect of investments and interest earned under this regulation shall be paid into the Insolvency Services Account to the credit of the company.

9(8)   [Omitted.]

History
Regulation 9(6) substituted and reg.9(6A), (6B) inserted by the Insolvency (Amendment) Regulations 2004 (SI 2004/472) reg.2 and Sch. para.2 as from April 1, 2004. Regulation 9(8) omitted by the Insolvency (Amendment) Regulations 2011 (SI 2011/2203) reg.9 as from October 1, 2011.

Records to be maintained by liquidators and the provision of information

10   Financial records

10(1)   This regulation does not apply in the case of a members' voluntary winding up.

10(2)   The liquidator shall prepare and keep–

(a)   separate financial records in respect of each company; and

(b)   such other financial records as are required to explain the receipts and payments entered in the records described in sub-paragraph (a) above or regulation 12(2) below, including an explanation of the source of any receipts and the destination of any payments;

and shall, subject to regulation 12(2) below as to trading accounts, from day to day enter in those records all the receipts and payments made by him.

10(3)   In the case of a winding up by the court, the liquidator shall obtain and keep bank statements relating to any local bank account in the name of the company.

10(4)   The liquidator shall submit financial records to the liquidation committee when required for inspection.

10(5)   In the case of a winding up by the court, if the liquidation committee is not satisfied with the contents of the financial records submitted under paragraph (4) above it may so inform the Secretary of

State, giving the reasons for its dissatisfaction, and the Secretary of State may take such action as he thinks fit.

History
Regulation 10(2) amended by the Insolvency (Amendment) Regulations 2011 (SI 2011/2203) reg.9 as from October 1, 2011.

11   Provision of information by liquidator

11(1)   In the case of a winding up by the court, the liquidator shall, within 14 days of the receipt of a request for a statement of his receipts and payments as liquidator from any creditor, contributory or director of the company, supply free of charge to the person making the request, a statement of his receipts and payments as liquidator during the period of one year ending on the most recent anniversary of his becoming liquidator which preceded the request.

11(2)   In the case of a voluntary winding up, the liquidator shall, on request from any creditor, contributory or director of the company for a copy of a statement for any period, including future periods, sent to the registrar of companies under section 192, send such copy free of charge to the person making the request and the copy of the statement shall be sent within 14 days of the liquidator sending the statement to the registrar or the receipt of the request whichever is the later.

12   Liquidator carrying on business

12(1)   This regulation does not apply in the case of a members' voluntary winding up.

12(2)   Where the liquidator carries on any business of the company, he shall–

(a)   keep a separate and distinct account of the trading, including, where appropriate, in the case of a winding up by the court, particulars of all local bank account transactions; and

(b)   incorporate in the financial records required to be kept under regulation 10 above the total weekly amounts of the receipts and payments made by him in relation to the account kept under sub-paragraph (a) above.

13   Retention and delivery of records

13(1)   All records kept by the liquidator under regulations 10 and 12(2) and any such records received by him from a predecessor in that office shall be retained by him for a period of 6 years following–

(a)   his vacation of office, or

(b)   in the case of the official receiver, his release as liquidator under section 174,

unless he delivers them to another liquidator who succeeds him in office.

13(2)   Where the liquidator is succeeded in office by another liquidator, the records referred to in paragraph (1) above shall be delivered to that successor forthwith, unless, in the case of a winding up by the court, the winding up is for practical purposes complete and the successor is the official receiver, in which case the records are only to be delivered to the official receiver if the latter so requests.

14   Provision of accounts by liquidator and audit of accounts

14(1)   The liquidator shall, if required by the Secretary of State at any time, send to the Secretary of State an account in relation to the company of the liquidator's receipts and payments covering such period as the Secretary of State may direct and such account shall, if so required by the Secretary of State, be certified by the liquidator.

14(2)   Where the liquidator in a winding up by the court vacates office prior to the holding of the final general meeting of creditors under section 146, he shall within 14 days of vacating office send to the Secretary of State an account of his receipts and payments as liquidator for any period not covered by an account previously so sent by him or if no such account has been sent, an account of his receipts and payments in respect of the whole period of his office.

14(3)   In the case of a winding up by the court, where:

  (a)   a final general meeting of creditors has been held pursuant to section 146, or

  (b)   a final general meeting is deemed to have been held by virtue of Rule 4.125(5),

the liquidator shall send to the Secretary of State, in case (a), within 14 days of the holding of the final general meeting of creditors and, in case (b), within 14 days of his report to the court pursuant to Rule 4.125(5), an account of his receipts and payments as liquidator which are not covered by any previous account so sent by him, or if no such account has been sent an account of his receipts and payments in respect of the whole period of his office.

14(4)   In the case of a winding up by the court, where a statement of affairs has been submitted under the Act, any account sent under this regulation shall be accompanied by a summary of that statement of affairs and shall show the amount of any assets realised and explain the reasons for any non-realisation of any assets not realised.

14(5)   In the case of a winding up by the court, where a statement of affairs has not been submitted under the Act, any account sent under this regulation shall be accompanied by a summary of all known assets and their estimated values and shall show the amounts actually realised and explain the reasons for any non-realisation of any assets not realised.

14(6)   Any account sent to the Secretary of State shall, if he so requires, be audited, but whether or not the Secretary of State requires the account to be audited, the liquidator shall send to the Secretary of State on demand any documents (including vouchers and bank statements) and any information relating to the account.

15   Production and inspection of records

15(1)   The liquidator shall produce on demand to the Secretary of State, and allow him to inspect, any accounts, books and other records kept by him (including any passed to him by a predecessor in office), and this duty to produce and allow inspection shall extend–

  (a)   to producing and allowing inspection at the premises of the liquidator; and

  (b)   to producing and allowing inspection of any financial records of the kind described in regulation 10(2)(b) above prepared by the liquidator (or any predecessor in office of his) before 24th October 1994 and kept by the liquidator;

and any such demand may–

  (i)   require the liquidator to produce any such accounts, books or other records to the Secretary of State, and allow him to inspect them–

    (A) at the same time as any account is sent to the Secretary of State under regulation 14 above; or

    (B) at any time after such account is sent to the Secretary of State;

    whether or not the Secretary of State requires the account to be audited; or

  (ii) where it is made for the purpose of ascertaining whether the provisions of these Regulations relating to the handling of money received by the liquidator in the course of carrying out his functions have been or are likely to be complied with, be made at any time, whether or not an account has been sent or should have been sent to the Secretary of State under regulation 14 above and whether or not the Secretary of State has required any account to be audited.

15(2)   The liquidator shall allow the Secretary of State on demand to remove and take copies of any accounts, books and other records kept by the liquidator (including any passed to him by a predecessor in office), whether or not they are kept at the premises of the liquidator.

16   Disposal of company's books, papers and other records

16(1)   The liquidator in a winding up by the court, on the authorisation of the official receiver, during his tenure of office or on vacating office, or the official receiver while acting as liquidator, may at any time sell, destroy or otherwise dispose of the books, papers and other records of the company.

16(2)   In the case of a voluntary winding up, the person who was the last liquidator of a company which has been dissolved may, at any time after the expiration of a period of one year from the date of dissolution, destroy or otherwise dispose of the books, papers and other records of the company.

17   Voluntary liquidator to provide information to Secretary of State

17(1)   In the case of a voluntary winding up, a liquidator or former liquidator, whether the winding up has been concluded under Rule 4.223 or not, shall, within 14 days of a request by the Secretary of State, give the Secretary of State particulars of any money in his hands or under his control representing unclaimed or undistributed assets of the company or dividends or other sums due to any person as a member or former member of the company.

17(2)   [Omitted.]

History
Regulation 17(1) amended and reg.17(2) omitted by the Insolvency (Amendment) Regulations 2011 (SI 2011/2203) regs 10–11 as from October 1, 2011.

18   Payment of unclaimed dividends or other money

18(1)   This regulation applies to monies which–

    (a)   are held by the former liquidator of a dissolved company, and

    (b)   represent either or both of the following–

        (i)   unclaimed dividends due to creditors, or

        (ii)   sums held by the company in trust in respect of dividends or other sums due to any person as a member or former member of the company.

18(2)   Monies to which this regulation applies–

    (a)   may in the case of a voluntary winding up,

    (b)   must in the case of a winding up by the court,

be paid into the Insolvency Services Account.

18(3)   Where the former liquidator pays any sums into the Insolvency Services Account pursuant to paragraph (2), he shall at the same time give notice to the Secretary of State of–

    (a)   the name of the company,

    (b)   the name and address of the person to whom the dividend or other sum is payable,

    (c)   the amount of the dividend, and

    (d)   the date on which it was paid.

18(4) Where a dividend or other sum is paid to a person by way of a payment instrument, any payment into the Insolvency Services Account in respect of that dividend or sum pursuant to paragraph (2) may not be made earlier than on or after the expiry of 6 months from the date of the payment instrument.

History
Regulation 18 substituted by the Insolvency (Amendment) Regulations 2008 (SI 2008/670) reg.3(1), (3) as from April 6, 2008.

PART 3

BANKRUPTCY

19 Introductory

19(1) This Part of these Regulations relates to bankruptcy and extends to England and Wales only.

19(2) In addition to the application of the provisions of this Part to the official receiver when acting as trustee, the provisions of this Part (other than regulations 30 and 31) shall also apply to him when acting as receiver or manager under section 287 and the term **"trustee"** shall be construed accordingly.

Payments into and out of the Insolvency Services Account

20 Payments into the Insolvency Services Account

20(1) Subject to regulation 21 below, the trustee shall pay all money received by him in the course of carrying out his functions as such without any deduction into the Insolvency Services Account kept by the Secretary of State with the Bank of England to the credit of the bankrupt once every 14 days or forthwith if £5,000 or more has been received.

20(2) Every payment of money into the Insolvency Services Account under this regulation shall be–

  (a) made through the Bank Giro system; or

  (b) sent direct to the Bank of England, Threadneedle Street, London EC2R 8AH by cheque drawn in favour of the "Insolvency Services Account" and crossed "A/c payee only" "Bank of England"; or

  (c) made by electronic transfer,

and the trustee shall on request be given by the Department a receipt for the money so paid.

20(3) Every payment of money made under sub-paragraph (a) or (b) of paragraph (2) above shall be accompanied by a form obtainable from the Department for that purpose or by a form that is substantially similar. Every payment of money made under sub-paragraph (c) of paragraph (2) above shall specify the name of the trustee making the payment and the name of the bankrupt to whose credit such payment is made.

21 Local bank account and handling of funds not forming part of the bankrupt's estate

21(1) Where the trustee intends to exercise his power to carry on the business of the bankrupt, he may apply to the Secretary of State for authorisation to open a local bank account, and the Secretary of State may authorise him to make his payments into and out of a specified bank, subject to a limit, instead of into and out of the Insolvency Services Account if satisfied that an administrative advantage will be derived from having such an account.

21(2) Money received by the trustee relating to the purpose for which the account was opened may be paid into the local bank account to the credit of the bankrupt to whom the account relates.

21(3)   Where the trustee opens a local bank account pursuant to an authorisation granted under paragraph (1) above he shall open and maintain the account in the name of the bankrupt.

21(4)   Where money which does not form part of the bankrupt's estate is provided to the trustee for a specific purpose it shall be clearly identifiable in a separate account.

21(5)   The trustee shall keep proper records, including documentary evidence of all money paid into and out of every local bank account opened and maintained under this regulation.

21(6)   The trustee shall pay without deduction any surplus over any limit imposed by an authorisation granted under paragraph (1) above into the Insolvency Services Account in accordance with regulation 20(1) above.

21(7)   As soon as the trustee ceases to carry on the business of the bankrupt or vacates office or an authorisation given in pursuance of an application under paragraph (1) above is withdrawn, he shall close the account and pay any balance into the Insolvency Services Account in accordance with regulation 20(1) above.

22   Payment of disbursements etc. out of the Insolvency Services Account

22(A1)   Paragraphs (1) and (2) of this regulation are subject to paragraph (2A).

History
Regulation 22(A1) inserted by the Insolvency (Amendment) Regulations 2000 (SI 2000/485) regs 1, 3 and Sch. para.11 as from March 31, 2000.

22(1)   On application to the Department, the trustee shall be repaid all necessary disbursements made by him, and expenses properly incurred by him, in the course of his administration to the date of his vacation of office out of any money standing to the credit of the bankrupt in the Insolvency Services Account.

22(2)   The trustee shall on application to the Department obtain payment instruments to the order of the payee for sums which become payable on account of the bankrupt for delivery by the trustee to the persons to whom the payments are to be made.

22(2A)   In respect of an application made by the trustee under paragraph (1) or (2) above, the Secretary of State, if requested to do so by the trustee, may, at his discretion,

   (a)   make the payment which is the subject of the application to the trustee by electronic transfer; or

   (b)   as an alternative to the issue of payment instruments, make payment by electronic transfer to the persons to whom the trustee would otherwise deliver payment instruments.

22(3)   Any application under this regulation shall be made on a form obtainable from the Department or on one that is substantially similar.

22(4)   On the trustee vacating office, he shall be repaid by any succeeding trustee out of any funds available for the purpose any necessary disbursements made by him and any expenses properly incurred by him but not repaid before he vacates office.

Dividends to creditors

23   Payment

23(1)   Subject to paragraph (1A), the trustee shall pay every dividend by payment instruments which shall be prepared by the Department on the application of the trustee and transmitted to him for distribution amongst the creditors.

23(1A)   In respect of an application made by the trustee under paragraph (1) above, the Secretary of State, if requested to do so by the trustee, may, at his discretion, as an alternative to the issue of payment instruments, make payment by electronic transfer to the persons to whom the trustee would otherwise deliver payment instruments.

23(2) Any application under this regulation for a payment instrument or payment by electronic transfer shall be made by the trustee on a form obtainable from the Department for the purpose or on a form which is substantially similar.

23(3) The trustee shall enter the total amount of every dividend that he desires to pay under this regulation in the records to be kept under regulation 24 below in one sum.

23(4) On the trustee vacating office, he shall send to the Department any valid unclaimed or undelivered payment instruments for dividends after endorsing them with the word "cancelled."

Investment or otherwise handling of funds in bankruptcy and payment of interest

23A(1) When the cash balance standing to the credit of the bankrupt in the account in respect of that bankrupt kept by the Secretary of State is in excess of the amount which, in the opinion of the trustee, is required for the immediate purposes of the bankruptcy and should be invested, he may request the Secretary of State to invest the amount not so required in Government securities, to be placed to the credit of that account for the benefit of the bankrupt.

23A(2) When any of the money so invested is, in the opinion of the trustee, required for the immediate purposes of the bankruptcy, he may request the Secretary of State to raise such sum as may be required by the sale of such of those securities as may be necessary.

23A(3) In cases where investments have been made at the request of the trustee in pursuance of paragraph (1) above and additional sums to the amounts so invested, including money received under paragraph (7) below, are paid into the Insolvency Services Account to the credit of the bankrupt, a request shall be made to the Secretary of State by the trustee if it is desired that these additional funds should be invested.

23A(4) Any request relating to the investment in, or sale of, as the case may be, Treasury Bills under paragraphs (1), (2) or (3) above shall be made on a form obtainable from the Department or on one that is substantially similar and any request relating to the purchase or sale, as the case may be, of any other type of Government security made under the provisions of those paragraphs shall be made in writing.

23A(5) Any request made under paragraphs (1), (2) or (3) above shall be sufficient authority to the Secretary of State for the investment or sale as the case may be.

23A(6) Subject to paragraphs (6A) and (6B), at any time after 1st April 2004 whenever there are any monies standing to the credit of the estate of the bankrupt in the Insolvency Services Account the estate shall be entitled to interest on those monies at the rate of 4.25 per cent per annum.

23A(6A) Interest shall cease to accrue pursuant to paragraph (6) from the date of receipt by the Secretary of State of a notice in writing from the trustee that in the opinion of the trustee it is necessary or expedient in order to facilitate the conclusion of the bankruptcy that interest should cease to accrue but interest shall start to accrue again pursuant to paragraph (6) where the trustee gives a further notice in writing to the Secretary of State requesting that interest should start to accrue again.

23A(6B) The Secretary of State may by notice published in the London Gazette vary the rate of interest prescribed by paragraph (6) and such variation shall have effect from the day after the date of publication of the notice in the London Gazette or such later date as may be specified in the notice.

23A(7) All money received in respect of investments and interest earned under this regulation shall be paid into the Insolvency Services Account to the credit of the bankrupt.

History
Regulation 23A(6) substituted and reg.23A(6A) and (6B) added by the Insolvency (Amendment) Regulations 2004 (SI 2004/472) reg.2, Sch. para.3 as from April 1, 2004.

Records to be maintained by trustees and the provision of information

24   Financial records

24(1)   The trustee shall prepare and keep–

(a)   separate financial records in respect of each bankrupt; and

(b)   such other financial records as are required to explain the receipts and payments entered in the records described in sub-paragraph (a) above or regulation 26 below, including an explanation of the source of any receipts and the destination of any payments;

and shall, subject to regulation 26 below as to trading accounts, from day to day enter in those records all the receipts and payments made by him.

24(2)   The trustee shall obtain and keep bank statements relating to any local bank account in the name of the bankrupt.

24(3)   The trustee shall submit financial records to the creditors' committee when required for inspection.

24(4)   If the creditors' committee is not satisfied with the contents of the financial records submitted under paragraph (3) above it may so inform the Secretary of State, giving the reasons for its dissatisfaction and the Secretary of State may take such action as he thinks fit.

25   Provision of information by trustee

25   The trustee shall, within 14 days of the receipt of a request from any creditor or the bankrupt for a statement of his receipts and payments as trustee, supply free of charge to the person making the request, a statement of his receipts and payments as trustee during the period of one year ending on the most recent anniversary of his becoming trustee which preceded the request.

26   Trustee carrying on business

26   Subject to paragraph (2) below, where the trustee carries on any business of the bankrupt, he shall–

(a)   keep a separate and distinct account of the trading, including, where appropriate, particulars of all local bank account transactions; and

(b)   incorporate in the financial records required to be kept under regulation 24 above the total weekly amounts of the receipts and payments made by him in relation to the account kept under paragraph (a) above.

27   Retention and delivery of records

27(1)   All records kept by the trustee under regulations 24 and 26 and any such records received by him from a predecessor in that office shall be retained by him for a period of 6 years following–

(a)   his vacation of office, or

(b)   in the case of the official receiver, his release as trustee under section 299,

unless he delivers them to another trustee who succeeds him in office.

27(2)   Where the trustee is succeeded in office by another trustee, the records referred to in paragraph (1) above shall be delivered to that successor forthwith, unless the bankruptcy is for practical purposes complete and the successor is the official receiver, in which case the records are only to be delivered to the official receiver if the latter so requests.

28   Provision of accounts by trustee and audit of accounts

28(1)   The trustee shall, if required by the Secretary of State at any time, send to the Secretary of State an account of his receipts and payments as trustee of the bankrupt covering such period as the Secretary of State may direct and such account shall, if so required by the Secretary of State, be certified by the trustee.

28(2)   Where the trustee vacates office prior to the holding of the final general meeting of creditors under section 331, he shall within 14 days of vacating office send to the Secretary of State an account of his receipts and payments as trustee for any period not covered by an account previously so sent by him, or if no such account has been sent, an account of his receipts and payments in respect of the whole period of his office.

28(3)   Where:

(a)   a final general meeting of creditors has been held pursuant to section 331, or

(b)   a final general meeting is deemed to have been held by virtue of Rule 6.137(5),

the trustee shall send to the Secretary of State, in case (a), within 14 days of the holding of the final general meeting of creditors and, in case (b), within 14 days of his report to the court pursuant to Rule 6.137(5), an account of his receipts and payments as trustee which are not covered by any previous account so sent by him, or if no such account has been sent, an account of his receipts and payments in respect of the whole period of his office.

28(4)   Where a statement of affairs has been submitted under the Act, any account sent under this regulation shall be accompanied by a summary of that statement of affairs and shall show the amount of any assets realised and explain the reasons for any non-realisation of any assets not realised.

28(5)   Where a statement of affairs has not been submitted under the Act, any account sent under this regulation shall be accompanied by a summary of all known assets and their estimated values and shall show the amounts actually realised and explain the reasons for any non-realisation of any assets not realised.

28(6)   Any account sent to the Secretary of State shall, if he so requires, be audited, but whether or not the Secretary of State requires the account to be audited, the trustee shall send to the Secretary of State on demand any documents (including vouchers and bank statements) and any information relating to the account.

29   Production and inspection of records

29(1)   The trustee shall produce on demand to the Secretary of State, and allow him to inspect, any accounts, books and other records kept by him (including any passed to him by a predecessor in office), and this duty to produce and allow inspection shall extend–

(a)   to producing and allowing inspection at the premises of the trustee; and

(b)   to producing and allowing inspection of any financial records of the kind described in regulation 24(1)(b) above prepared by the trustee before 24th October 1994 and kept by him;

and any such demand may–

(i) require the trustee to produce any such accounts, books or other records to the Secretary of State, and allow him to inspect them–

    (A) at the same time as any account is sent to the Secretary of State under regulation 28 above; or

    (B) at any time after such account is sent to the Secretary of State;

    whether or not the Secretary of State requires the account to be audited; or

(ii) where it is made for the purpose of ascertaining whether the provisions of these Regulations relating to the handling of money received by the trustee in the course of carrying out his functions have been or are likely to be complied with, be made at any time, whether or not an account has been sent or should have been sent to the Secretary of State under regulation 28 above and whether or not the Secretary of State has required any account to be audited.

29(2) The trustee shall allow the Secretary of State on demand to remove and take copies of any accounts, books and other records kept by the trustee (including any passed to him by a predecessor in office), whether or not they are kept at the premises of the trustee.

30 Disposal of bankrupt's books, papers and other records

30 The trustee, on the authorisation of the official receiver, during his tenure of office or on vacating office, or the official receiver while acting as trustee, may at any time sell, destroy or otherwise dispose of the books, papers and other records of the bankrupt.

31 Payment of unclaimed or undistributed assets, dividends or other money

31 Notwithstanding anything in these Regulations, any money–

(a) in the hands of the trustee at the date of his vacation of office, or

(b) which comes into the hands of any former trustee at any time after his vacation of office,

representing, in either case, unclaimed or undistributed assets of the bankrupt or dividends, shall forthwith be paid by him into the Insolvency Services Account.

PART 4

CLAIMING MONEY PAID INTO THE INSOLVENCY SERVICES ACCOUNT

32(1) Any person claiming to be entitled to any money paid into the Insolvency Services Account may apply to the Secretary of State for payment and shall provide such evidence of his claim as the Secretary of State may require.

32(2) Any person dissatisfied with the decision of the Secretary of State in respect of his claim made under this regulation may appeal to the court.

PART 5

REMUNERATION OF OFFICIAL RECEIVER

33 Official receiver's remuneration while acting as liquidator or trustee calculated as a percentage of the value of assets realised or distributed

33 [Revoked by the Insolvency (Amendment) Regulations 2004 (SI 2004/472) reg.2, Sch. para.4 as from April 1, 2004.]

34 Limits on official receiver's remuneration as trustee

34 [Revoked by the Insolvency (Amendment) Regulations 2004 (SI 2004/472) reg.2, Sch. para.4 as from April 1, 2004.]

35 Official receiver's general remuneration while acting as interim receiver, provisional liquidator, liquidator or trustee

35(1) The official receiver shall be entitled to remuneration calculated in accordance with the applicable hourly rates set out in paragraph (2) for services provided by him (or any of his officers) in relation to–

  (a) a distribution made by him when acting as liquidator or trustee to creditors (including preferential or secured creditors or both such classes of creditor);

  (b) the realisation of assets on behalf of the holder of a fixed or floating charge or both types of those charges;

  (c) the supervision of a special manager;

  (d) the performance by him of any functions where he acts as provisional liquidator; or

  (e) the performance by him of any functions where he acts as an interim receiver.

35(2) The applicable hourly rates referred to in paragraph (1) are–

  (a) in relation to the official receiver of the London insolvency district, those set out in Table 2 in Schedule 2; and

  (b) in relation to any other official receiver, those set out in Table 3 in Schedule 2.

History
Regulation 35 substituted by the Insolvency (Amendment) Regulations 2005 (SI 2005/512) reg.7 as from April 1, 2005 subject to transitional provisions contained in reg.3 of those Regulations.

36 Official receiver's remuneration while acting as liquidator or provisional liquidator in respect of the realisation of property charged

36 [Revoked by the Insolvency (Amendment) Regulations 2004 (SI 2004/472) reg.2, Sch. para.4 as from April 1, 2004.]

PART 5A

INFORMATION ABOUT TIME SPENT ON A CASE TO BE PROVIDED BY INSOLVENCY PRACTITIONER TO CREDITORS ETC.

36A(1) Subject as set out in this regulation, in respect of any case in which he acts, an insolvency practitioner shall on request in writing made by any person mentioned in paragraph (2), supply free of charge to that person a statement of the kind described in paragraph (3).

36A(2) The persons referred to in paragraph (1) are–

  (a) any creditor in the case;

  (b) where the case relates to a company, any director or contributory of that company; and

  (c) where the case relates to an individual, that individual.

36A(3) The statement referred to in paragraph (1) shall comprise in relation to the period beginning with the date of the insolvency practitioner's appointment and ending with the relevant date the following details–

866

(a)   the total number of hours spent on the case by the insolvency practitioner and any staff assigned to the case during that period;

(b)   for each grade of individual so engaged, the average hourly rate at which any work carried out by individuals in that grade is charged; and

(c)   the number of hours spent by each grade of staff during that period.

36A(4)   In relation to paragraph (3) the **"relevant date"** means the date next before the date of the making of the request on which the insolvency practitioner has completed any period in office which is a multiple of six months or, where the insolvency practitioner has vacated office, the date that he vacated office.

36A(5)   Where an insolvency practitioner has vacated office, an obligation to provide information under this regulation shall only arise in relation to a request that is made within 2 years of the date he vacates office.

36A(6)   Any statement required to be provided to any person under this regulation shall be supplied within 28 days of the date of the receipt of the request by the insolvency practitioner.

36A(7)   In this regulation the expression **"insolvency practitioner"** shall be construed in accordance with section 388 of the Insolvency Act 1986.

History
Regulation 36A inserted by the Insolvency (Amendment) Regulations 2005 (SI 2005/512) reg.8 as from April 1, 2005.

PART 6

TRANSITIONAL AND SAVING PROVISIONS

37   The Regulations shall have effect subject to the transitional and saving provisions set out in Schedule 3 to these Regulations.

SCHEDULE 1

Regulation 2

The Insolvency Regulations 1986

The Insolvency (Amendment) Regulations 1987

The Insolvency (Amendment) Regulations 1988

The Insolvency (Amendment) Regulations 1991

SCHEDULE 2

Regulations 33 to 36

Table 1

[Omitted by the Insolvency (Amendment) Regulations 2004 (SI 2004/472) reg.2, Sch. para.6 as from April 1, 2004.]

Table 2—London Rates

Grade according to the Insolvency Service grading structure/Status of Official	Total hourly rate £
D2/Official Receiver	75
C2/Deputy or Assistant Official Receiver	63
C1/Senior Examiner	58
L3/Examiner	46
L2/Examiner	42
B2/Administrator	46
L1/Examiner	40
B1/Administrator	46
A2/Administrator	40
A1/Administrator	35

Table 3—Provincial Rates

Grade according to the Insolvency Service grading structure/Status of Official	Total hourly rate £
D2/Official Receiver	69
C2/Deputy or Assistant Official Receiver	58
C1/Senior Examiner	52
L3/Examiner	46
L2/Examiner	40
B2/Administrator	43
L1/Examiner	38
B1/Administrator	42
A2/Administrator	36
A1/Administrator	31

History
Table 2 and Table 3 substituted by the Insolvency (Amendment) Regulations 2004 (SI 2004/472) reg.2, Sch. para.7 as from April 1, 2004, and further substituted by the Insolvency (Amendment) Regulations 2009 (SI 2009/482) reg.2 as from April 6, 2009.

SCHEDULE 3

Regulation 37

1 Interpretation

1 In this Schedule the expression **"the former Regulations"** means the Insolvency Regulations 1986 as amended by the Insolvency (Amendment) Regulations 1987, the Insolvency (Amendment) Regulations 1988 and the Insolvency (Amendment) Regulations 1991.

2 Requests pursuant to regulation 13(1) of the former Regulations

2 Any request made pursuant to regulation 13(1) of the former Regulations which has not been complied with prior to 24th October 1994 shall be treated, in the case of a company that is being wound up by the court, as a request made pursuant to regulation 11(1) of these Regulations and, in the case of a bankruptcy, as a request made pursuant to regulation 25 of these Regulations and in each case the request shall be treated as if it had been made on 24th October 1994.

3 Things done under the provisions of the former Regulations

3 So far as anything done under, or for the purposes of, any provision of the former Regulations could have been done under, or for the purposes of, the corresponding provision of these Regulations, it is not invalidated by the revocation of that provision but has effect as if done under, or for the purposes of, the corresponding provision.

4 Time periods

4 Where any period of time specified in a provision of the former Regulations is current immediately before 24th October 1994, these Regulations have effect as if the corresponding provision of these Regulations had been in force when the period began to run; and (without prejudice to the foregoing) any period of time so specified and current is deemed for the purposes of these Regulations–

(a) to run from the date or event from which it was running immediately before 24th October 1994, and

(b) to expire whenever it would have expired if these Regulations had not been made;

and any rights, obligations, requirements, powers or duties dependent on the beginning, duration or end of such period as above-mentioned shall be under these Regulations as they were or would have been under the former Regulations.

5 References to other provisions

5 Where in any provision of these Regulations there is reference to another provision of these Regulations, and the first-mentioned provision operates, or is capable of operating, in relation to things done or omitted, or events occurring or not occurring, in the past (including in particular past acts of compliance with the former Regulations), the reference to that other provision is to be read as including a reference to the corresponding provision of the former Regulations.

6 Provisions of Schedule to be without prejudice to the operation of sections 16 and 17 of the Interpretation Act 1978

6 The provisions of this Schedule are to be without prejudice to the operation of sections 16 and 17 of the Interpretation Act 1978 (saving from, and effect of, repeals) as they are applied by section 23 of that Act.

7 Meaning of "corresponding provision"

7(1) A provision in the former Regulations, except regulation 13(1) of those Regulations, is to be regarded as the corresponding provision of a provision in these Regulations notwithstanding any modifications made to the provision as it appears in these Regulations.

7(2) Without prejudice to the generality of the term **"corresponding provision"** the following table shall, subject to sub-paragraph (3) below, have effect in the interpretation of that expression with a provision of these Regulations listed in the left hand column being regarded as the corresponding provision of a provision of the former Regulations listed opposite it in the right hand column and that latter provision being regarded as the corresponding provision of the first-mentioned provision:

TABLE

Provision in these Regulations	Provision in the former Regulations
5(1), 5(3), 5(4)	4
5(2), 5(3), 5(4)	24
6	6
7(1), 7(2), 7(4), 7(5)	5
7(3), 7(4)	25
8(1), 8(2), 8(4), 8(5), 8(6)	15
8(3), 8(4)	25
9	18, 34
10	9, 27
11(2)	31
12	10, 28
13	10A, 28A
15	12A, 30A
16(1)	14
16(2)	32
17	35
18	16, 33
20	4
21	6
22	5
23	15
24	9
26	10
27	10A
29	12A
30	14
31	16A
32	17, 33
33, Table 1 in Schedule 2	19
35, Tables 2 and 3 in Schedule 2	20
36, Table 1 in Schedule 2	22

7(3) Where a provision of the former Regulations is expressed in the Table in sub-paragraph (2) above to be the corresponding provision of a provision in these Regulations and the provision in the former Regulations was capable of applying to other proceedings in addition to those to which the provision in these Regulations is capable of applying, the provision in the former Regulations shall be construed as the corresponding provision of the provision in these Regulations only to the extent that they are both capable of applying to the same type of proceedings.

Financial Markets and Insolvency Regulations 1996

(SI 1996/1469)

Made on 5 June 1996 by the Treasury and the Secretary of State for Trade and Industry under ss.185 and 186 of the Companies Act 1989. Operative from 15 July 1996.

[**Note:** Changes made by the Uncertificated Securities Regulations 2001 (SI 2001/3755) and the Enterprise Act 2002 (Insolvency) Order 2003 (SI 2003/2096) have been incorporated into the text (in the case of pre-2003 legislation without annotation). Where references to administration petitions, orders, etc. and to the original IA 1986 Pt II have been altered by the Enterprise Act 2002 (Insolvency) Order 2003 (SI 2003/2096) art.5 and Sch. Pt 2 as from September 15, 2003 (subject to transitional provision in art.6), following the introduction of the new administration regime, history notes have been omitted.]

PART I

GENERAL

1 Citation and commencement

1 These Regulations may be cited as the Financial Markets and Insolvency Regulations 1996 and shall come into force on 15th July 1996.

2 Interpretation

2(1) In these Regulations–

"the Act" means the Companies Act 1989;

"business day" means any day which is not a Saturday or Sunday, Christmas Day, Good Friday or a bank holiday in any part of the United Kingdom under the Banking and Financial Dealings Act 1971;

"issue", in relation to an uncertificated unit of a security, means to confer on a person title to a new unit;

"register of securities"–

(a) in relation to shares, means a register of members; and

(b) in relation to units of a security other than shares, means a register, whether maintained by virtue of the Uncertificated Securities Regulations 2001 or otherwise, of persons holding the units;

"relevant nominee" means a system-member who is a subsidiary undertaking of the Operator designated by him as such in accordance with such rules and practices as are mentioned in paragraph 25(f) of Schedule 1 to the Uncertificated Securities Regulations 2001;

"settlement bank" means a person who has contracted with an Operator to make payments in connection with transfers, by means of a relevant system, of title to uncertificated units of a security and of interests of system-beneficiaries in relation to such units;

"system-beneficiary" means a person on whose behalf a system-member or former system-member holds or held uncertificated units of a security;

"system-charge" means a charge of a kind to which regulation 3(2) applies;

"system-member" means a person who is permitted by an Operator to transfer by means of a relevant system title to uncertificated units of a security held by him; and **"former system-member"** means a person whose participation in the relevant system is terminated or suspended;

"transfer", in relation to title to uncertificated units of a security, means the registration of a transfer of title to those units in the relevant Operator register of securities; and in relation to an interest of a system-beneficiary in relation to uncertificated units of a security, means the transfer of the interest to another system-beneficiary by means of a relevant system; and

other expressions used in these Regulations which are also used in the Uncertificated Securities Regulations 2001 have the same meanings as in those Regulations.

2(2)　For the purposes of these Regulations, a person holds a unit of a security if–

　(a)　in the case of an uncertificated unit, he is entered on a register of securities in relation to the unit in accordance with regulation 20, 21 or 22 of the Uncertificated Securities Regulations 2001; and

　(b)　in the case of a certificated unit, he has title to the unit.

2(3)　A reference in any of these Regulations to a numbered regulation shall be construed as a reference to the regulation bearing that number in these Regulations.

2(4)　A reference in any of these Regulations to a numbered paragraph shall, unless the reference is to a paragraph of a specified regulation, be construed as a reference to the paragraph bearing that number in the regulation in which the reference is made.

PART II

SYSTEM-CHARGES

3　Application of Part VII of the Act in relation to system-charges

3(1)　Subject to the provisions of these Regulations, Part VII of the Act shall apply in relation to–

　(a)　a charge to which paragraph (2) applies (**"a system-charge"**) and any action taken to enforce such a charge; and

　(b)　any property subject to a system-charge,

in the same way as it applies in relation to a market charge, any action taken to enforce a market charge and any property subject to a market charge.

3(2)　This paragraph applies in relation to a charge granted in favour of a settlement bank for the purpose of securing debts or liabilities arising in connection with any of the following–

　(a)　a transfer of uncertificated units of a security to a system-member by means of a relevant system whether the system-member is acting for himself or on behalf of a system-beneficiary;

　(b)　a transfer, by one system-beneficiary to another and by means of a relevant system, of his interests in relation to uncertificated units of a security held by a relevant nominee where the relevant nominee will continue to hold the units;

　(c)　an agreement to make a transfer of the kind specified in paragraph (a);

　(d)　an agreement to make a transfer of the kind specified in paragraph (b): and

　(e)　an issue of uncertificated units of a security to a system-member by means of a relevant system whether the system-member is acting for himself or on behalf of a system-beneficiary.

3(3)　In its application, by virtue of these Regulations, in relation to a system-charge, section 173(2) of the Act shall have effect as if the references to "purposes specified" and "specified purposes" were references to any one or more of the purposes specified in paragraph (2).

4　Circumstances in which Part VII applies in relation to system-charge

4(1)　Part VII of the Act shall apply in relation to a system-charge granted by a system-member and in relation to property subject to such a charge only if–

872

(a) it is granted to a settlement bank by a system-member for the purpose of securing debts or liabilities arising in connection with any of the transactions specified in regulation 3(2), being debts or liabilities incurred by that system-member or by a system-beneficiary on whose behalf he holds uncertificated units of a security; and

(b) it contains provisions which refer expressly to the relevant system in relation to which the grantor is a system-member.

4(2) Part VII of the Act shall apply in relation to a system-charge granted by a system-beneficiary and in relation to property subject to such a charge only if–

(a) it is granted to a settlement bank by a system-beneficiary for the purpose of securing debts or liabilities arising in connection with any of the transactions specified in regulation 3(2), incurred by that system-beneficiary or by a system-member who holds uncertificated units of a security on his behalf; and

(b) it contains provisions which refer expressly to the relevant system in relation to which the system-member who holds the uncertificated units of a security in relation to which the system-beneficiary has the interest is a system-member.

5   Extent to which Part VII applies to a system-charge

5   Part VII of the Act shall apply in relation to a system-charge only to the extent that–

(a) it is a charge over any one or more of the following–

    (i) uncertificated units of a security held by a system-member or a former system-member;

    (ii) interests of a kind specified in regulation 31(2)(b) or 31(4)(b) of the Uncertificated Securities Regulations 2001 in uncertificated units of a security in favour of a system-member or a former system-member;

    (iii) interests of a system-beneficiary in relation to uncertificated units of a security;

    (iv) units of a security which are no longer in uncertificated form because the person holding the units has become a former system-member;

    (v) sums or other benefits receivable by a system-member or former system-member by reason of his holding uncertificated units of a security, or units which are no longer in uncertificated form because the person holding the units has become a former system-member;

    (vi) sums or other benefits receivable by a system-beneficiary by reason of his having an interest in relation to uncertificated units of a security or in relation to units which are no longer in uncertificated form because the person holding the units has become a former system-member;

    (vii) sums or other benefits receivable by a system-member or former system-member by way of repayment, bonus, preference, redemption, conversion or accruing or offered in respect of uncertificated units of a security, or units which are no longer in uncertificated form because the person holding the units has become a former system-member;

    (viii) sums or other benefits receivable by a system-beneficiary by way of repayment, bonus, preference, redemption, conversion or accruing or offered in respect of uncertificated units of a security in relation to which he has an interest or in respect of units in relation to which the system-beneficiary has an interest and which are no longer in uncertificated form because the person holding the units has become a former system-member;

(ix) sums or other benefits receivable by a system-member or former system-member in respect of the transfer of uncertificated units of a security by or to him by means of a relevant system;

(x) sums or other benefits receivable by a system-member or former system-member in respect of an agreement to transfer uncertificated units of a security by or to him by means of a relevant system;

(xi) sums or other benefits receivable by a system-beneficiary in respect of the transfer of the interest of a system-beneficiary in relation to uncertificated units of a security by or to him by means of a relevant system or in respect of the transfer of uncertificated units of a security by or to a system-member acting on his behalf by means of a relevant system;

(xii) sums or other benefits receivable by a system-beneficiary in respect of an agreement to transfer the interest of a system-beneficiary in relation to uncertificated units of a security by or to him by means of a relevant system, or in respect of an agreement to transfer uncertificated units of a security by or to a system-member acting on his behalf by means of a relevant system; and

(b) it secures–

(i) the obligation of a system-member or former system-member to reimburse a settlement bank, being an obligation which arises in connection with any of the transactions specified in regulation 3(2) and whether the obligation was incurred by the system-member when acting for himself or when acting on behalf of a system-beneficiary; or

(ii) the obligation of a system-beneficiary to reimburse a settlement bank, being an obligation which arises in connection with any of the transactions specified in regulation 3(2) and whether the obligation was incurred by the system-beneficiary when acting for himself or by reason of a system-member acting on his behalf.

6 Limitation on disapplication of moratorium on certain legal processes under Schedule B1 to the Insolvency Act 1986 (administration) in relation to system-charges

History
Heading to reg.6 substituted by the Enterprise Act 2002 (Insolvency) Order 2003 art.5, Sch. Pt 2 paras 61, 62(a) as from September 15, 2003 subject to transitional provision in art.6.

6(1) This regulation applies where an administration order is made in relation to a system-member or former system-member.

6(1A) A reference in paragraph (1) to "an administration order" shall include the appointment of an administrator under paragraph 14 or 22 of Schedule B1 to the Insolvency Act 1986.

History
Regulation 6(1A) inserted by the Enterprise Act 2002 (Insolvency) Order 2003 art.5, Sch. Pt 2 paras 61, 62(b) as from September 15, 2003 subject to transitional provision in art.6.

6(2) The disapplication of paragraph 43(2) of Schedule B1 to the Insolvency Act 1986 (including that provision as applied by paragraph 44 of that Schedule) by section 175(1)(a) of the Act shall have effect, in relation to a system-charge granted by a system-member or former system-member, only to the extent necessary to enable there to be realised, whether through the sale of uncertificated units of a security or otherwise, the lesser of the two sums specified in paragraphs (3) and (4).

6(3) The first sum of the two sums referred to in paragraph (2) is the net sum of–

(a) all payment obligations discharged by the settlement bank in connection with–

(i)   transfers of uncertificated units of a security by means of a relevant system made during the qualifying period to or by the relevant system-member or former system-member, whether acting for himself or on behalf of a system-beneficiary;

(ii) agreements made during the qualifying period to transfer uncertificated units of a security by means of a relevant system to or from the relevant system-member or former system-member, whether acting for himself or on behalf of a system-beneficiary; and

(iii) issues of uncertificated units of a security by means of a relevant system made during the qualifying period to the relevant system-member or former system-member, whether acting for himself or on behalf of a system-beneficiary; less

(b)   all payment obligations discharged to the settlement bank in connection with transactions of any kind described in paragraph (3)(a)(i) and (ii).

6(4)   The second of the two sums referred to in paragraph (2) is the sum (if any) due to the settlement bank from the relevant system-member or former system-member by reason of an obligation of the kind described in regulation 5(b)(i).

6(5)   In this regulation and regulation 7, **"qualifying period"** means the period–

(a)   beginning with the fifth business day before the day on which the application for the making of the administration order was presented; and

(b)   ending with the second business day after the day on which the administration order is made.

6(5A)   A reference in paragraph (5) to an application for an administration order shall be treated as including a reference to–

(a)   appointing an administrator under paragraph 14 or 22 of Schedule B1 to the Insolvency Act 1986, or

(b)   filing with the court a notice of intention to appoint an administrator under either of those paragraphs,

and a reference to "an administration order" shall include the appointment of an administrator under paragraph 14 or 22 of Schedule B1 to the Insolvency Act 1986.

7   Limitation on disapplication of moratorium on certain legal processes under Schedule B1 to the Insolvency Act 1986 (administration) in relation to system-charges granted by a system-beneficiary

7(1)   This regulation applies where an administration order is made in relation to a system-beneficiary.
   A reference in paragraph (1) to "an administration order" shall include the appointment of an administrator under paragraph 14 or 22 of Schedule B1 to the Insolvency Act 1986.

7(2)   The disapplication of paragraph 43(2) of Schedule B1 to the Insolvency Act 1986 (including that provision as applied by paragraph 44 of that Schedule) by section 175(1)(a) of the Act shall have effect, in relation to a system-charge granted by a system-beneficiary, only to the extent necessary to enable there to be realised, whether through the sale of interests of a system-beneficiary in relation to uncertificated units of a security or otherwise, the lesser of the two sums specified in paragraphs (3) and (4).

7(3)   The first of the two sums referred to in paragraph (2) is the net sum of–

(a)   all payment obligations discharged by the settlement bank in connection with–

(i)   transfers, to or by the relevant system-beneficiary by means of a relevant system made during the qualifying period, of interests of the system-beneficiary in relation to uncertificated units of a security held by a relevant nominee, where the relevant nominee has continued to hold the units;

(ii) agreements made during the qualifying period to transfer, to or from the relevant system-beneficiary by means of a relevant system, interests of the system-beneficiary in relation to uncertificated units of a security held by a relevant nominee, where the relevant nominee will continue to hold the units;

(iii) transfers, during the qualifying period and by means of a relevant system, of uncertificated units of a security, being transfers made to or by a system-member acting on behalf of the relevant system-beneficiary;

(iv) agreements made during the qualifying period to transfer uncertificated units of a security by means of a relevant system to or from a system-member acting on behalf of the relevant system-beneficiary; and

(v) issues of uncertificated units of a security made during the qualifying period and by means of a relevant system, being issues to a system-member acting on behalf of the relevant system-beneficiary; less

(b) all payment obligations discharged to the settlement bank in connection with transactions of any kind described in paragraph (3)(a)(i) to (iv).

7(4)   The second of the two sums referred to in paragraph (2) is the sum (if any) due to the settlement bank from the relevant system-beneficiary by reason of an obligation of the kind described in regulation 5(b)(ii).

8   Ability of administrator or receiver to recover assets in case of property subject to system-charge

8(1)   This regulation applies where an administration order is made or an administrator or an administrative receiver or a receiver is appointed, in relation to a system-member, former system-member or system-beneficiary.

8(1A)   A reference in paragraph (1) to "an administration order" shall include the appointment of an administrator under paragraph 14 or 22 of Schedule B1 to the Insolvency Act 1986.

8(2)   The disapplication–

(a) by section 175(1)(b) of the Act, of paragraphs 70, 71 and 72 of Schedule B1 to the Insolvency Act 1986, and

(b) by section 175(3) of the Act, of sections 43 and 61 of the 1986 Act,

shall cease to have effect after the end of the relevant day in respect of any property which is subject to a system-charge granted by the system-member, former system-member or system-beneficiary if on the basis of a valuation in accordance with paragraph (3), the charge is not required for the realisation of the sum specified in paragraph (4) or (5).

8(3)   For the purposes of paragraph (2), the value of property shall, except in a case falling within paragraph (6), be such as may be agreed between the administrator, administrative receiver or receiver on the one hand and the settlement bank on the other.

8(4)   Where the system-charge has been granted by a system-member or former system-member, the sum referred to in paragraph (2) is whichever is the lesser of–

(a) the sum referred to in regulation 6(3);

(b) the sum referred to in regulation 6(4) due to the settlement bank at the close of business on the relevant day.

8(5)   Where the system-charge has been granted by a system-beneficiary, the sum referred to in paragraph (2) is whichever is the lesser of–

    (a)   the sum referred to in regulation 7(3);

    (b)   the sum referred to in regulation 7(4) due to the settlement bank at the close of business on the relevant day.

8(6)   For the purposes of paragraph (2), the value of any property for which a price for the relevant day is quoted in the Daily Official List of The London Stock Exchange Limited shall–

    (a)   in a case in which two prices are so quoted, be an amount equal to the average of those two prices, adjusted where appropriate to take account of any accrued dividend or interest; and

    (b)   in a case in which one price is so quoted, be an amount equal to that price, adjusted where appropriate to take account of any accrued dividend or interest.

8(7)   In this regulation **"the relevant day"** means the second business day after the day on which the company enters administration, or the administrative receiver or receiver is appointed.

PART III

MARKET CONTRACTS

9   Amendments to section 156 of the Act

9   [Insertion of s.156(3A) into the Act.]

Insolvent Companies (Reports on Conduct of Directors) Rules 1996

(SI 1996/1909)

Made on 22 July 1996 by the Lord Chancellor and the Secretary of State for Trade and Industry, under ss.411 and 413 of the Insolvency Act 1986 and s.21(2) of the Company Directors Disqualification Act 1986. Operative from 30 September 1996.

[**Note:** These Rules apply (with modifications) to limited liability partnerships by virtue of the Limited Liability Partnerships Regulations 2001 (SI 2001/1090) regs 1, 10(1) and Sch.6 Pt III para.6 as from April 6, 2001. Changes made by the Insolvent Companies (Reports on Conduct of Directors) (Amendment) Rules 2001 (SI 2001/764) and the Enterprise Act 2002 (Insolvency) Order 2003 (SI 2003/2096) have been incorporated into the text (in the case of pre-2003 legislation without annotation). References to administration petitions, orders, etc. have been adapted throughout, following the introduction of the new administration regime, pursuant to the Enterprise Act 2002 (Insolvency) Order 2003 (SI 2003/2096), as from September 15, 2003.]

1 Citation, commencement and interpretation

1(1) These Rules may be cited as the Insolvent Companies (Reports on Conduct of Directors) Rules 1996.

1(2) These Rules shall come into force on 30th September 1996.

1(3) In these Rules–

"**the Act**" means the Company Directors Disqualification Act 1986;

"**the former Rules**" means the Insolvent Companies (Reports on Conduct of Directors) No. 2 Rules 1986; and

"**the commencement date**" means 30th September 1996.

2 Revocation

2 Subject to rule 7, below the former Rules are hereby revoked.

3 Reports required under section 7(3) of the Act

3(1) This rule applies to any report made to the Secretary of State under section 7(3) of the Act by:–

(a) the liquidator of a company which the courts in England and Wales have jurisdiction to wind up which passes a resolution for voluntary winding up on or after the commencement date;

(b) an administrative receiver of a company appointed otherwise than under section 51 of the Insolvency Act 1986 (power to appoint receiver under the law of Scotland) on or after the commencement date; or

(c) the administrator of a company which the courts in England and Wales have jurisdiction to wind up which enters administration on or after the commencement date.

3(2) Such a report shall be made in the Form D1 set out in the Schedule hereto, or in a form which is substantially similar, and in the manner and to the extent required by the Form D1.

4 Return by office-holder

4(1) This rule applies where it appears to a liquidator of a company as mentioned in rule 3(1)(a), to an administrative receiver as mentioned in rule 3(l)(b), or to an administrator as mentioned in rule 3(1)(c) (each of whom is referred to hereinafter as **"an office-holder"**) that the company has at any time become insolvent within the meaning of section 6(2) of the Act.

4(2)   Subject as follows there may be furnished to the Secretary of State by an office-holder at any time during the period of 6 months from the relevant date (defined in paragraph (4) below) a return with respect to every person who:–

(a)   was, on the relevant date, a director or shadow director of the company, or

(b)   had been a director or shadow director of the company at any time in the 3 years immediately preceding that date.

4(3)   The return shall be made in the Form D2 set out in the Schedule hereto, or in a form which is substantially similar, and in the manner and to the extent required by the Form D2.

4(4)   For the purposes of this rule, **"the relevant date"** means:–

(a)   in the case of a company in creditors' voluntary winding up (there having been no declaration of solvency by the directors under section 89 of the Insolvency Act 1986), the date of the passing of the resolution for voluntary winding up,

(b)   in the case of a company in members' voluntary winding up, the date on which the liquidator forms the opinion that, at the time when the company went into liquidation, its assets were insufficient for the payment of its debts and other liabilities and the expenses of winding up,

(c)   in the case of the administrative receiver, the date of his appointment,

(d)   in the case of the administrator, the date that the company enters administration,

and for the purposes of sub-paragraph (c) above the only appointment of an administrative receiver to be taken into account in determining the relevant date shall be that appointment which is not that of a successor in office to an administrative receiver who has vacated office either by death or pursuant to section 45 of the Insolvency Act 1986.

4(5)   Subject to paragraph (6) below, it shall be the duty of an office-holder to furnish a return complying with the provisions of paragraphs (3) and (4) of this rule to the Secretary of State:–

(a)   where he is in office in relation to the company on the day one week before the expiry of the period of 6 months from the relevant date, not later than the expiry of such period;

(b)   where he vacates office (otherwise than by death) before the day one week before the expiry of the period of 6 months from the relevant date, within 14 days after his vacation of office except where he has furnished such a return on or prior to the day one week before the expiry of such period.

4(6)   A return need not be provided under this rule by an office-holder if he has, whilst holding that office in relation to the company, since the relevant date, made a report under rule 3 with respect to all persons falling within paragraph (2) of this rule and (apart from this paragraph) required to be the subject of a return.

4(7)   If an office-holder without reasonable excuse fails to comply with the duty imposed by paragraph (5) of this rule, he is guilty of an offence and–

(a)   on summary conviction of the offence, is liable to a fine not exceeding level 3 on the standard scale, and

(b)   after continued contravention, is liable to a daily default fine; that is to say, he is liable on a second or subsequent summary conviction of the offence to a fine of one-tenth of level 3 on the standard scale for each day on which the contravention is continued (instead of the penalty specified in sub-paragraph (a)).

4(8)   Section 431 of the Insolvency Act 1986 (summary proceedings), as it applies to England and Wales, has effect in relation to an offence under this rule as to offences under Parts I to VII of that Act.

5   Forms

5   The forms referred to in rule 3(2) and rule 4(3) shall be used with such variations, if any, as the circumstances may require.

6   Enforcement of section 7(4)

6(1)   This rule applies where under section 7(4) of the Act (power to call on liquidators, former liquidators and others to provide information) the Secretary of State or the official receiver requires or has required a person:–

   (a)   to furnish him with information with respect to a person's conduct as director or shadow director of a company, and

   (b)   to produce and permit inspection of relevant books, papers and other records.

6(2)   On the application of the Secretary of State or (as the case may be) the official receiver, the court may make an order directing compliance within such period as may be specified.

6(3)   The court's order may provide that all costs of and incidental to the application shall be borne by the person to whom the order is directed.

7   Transitional and saving provisions

7(1)   Subject to paragraph (2) below, rules 3 and 4 of the former Rules shall continue to apply as if the former Rules had not been revoked when any of the events mentioned in sub-paragraphs (a), (b) or (c) of rule 3(1) of the former Rules (passing of resolution for voluntary winding up, appointment of administrative receiver, making of administration order) occurred on or after 29th December 1986 but before the commencement date.

7(2)   Until 31st December 1996–

   (a)   the forms contained in the Schedule to the former Rules which were required to be used for the purpose of complying with those Rules, or

   (b)   the Form D1 or D2 as set out in the Schedule to these Rules, as appropriate, or a form which is substantially similar thereto, with such variations, if any, as the circumstances may require,

may be used for the purpose of complying with rules 3 and 4 of the former Rules as applied by paragraph (1) above; but after that date the forms mentioned in sub-paragraph (b) of this paragraph shall be used for that purpose.

7(3)   When a period referred to in rule 5(2) of the former Rules is current immediately before the commencement date, these Rules have effect as if rule 6(2) of these Rules had been in force when the period began and the period is deemed to expire whenever it would have expired if these Rules had not been made and any right, obligation or power dependent on the beginning, duration or end of such period shall be under rule 6(2) of these Rules as it was or would have been under the said rule 5(2).

7(4)   The provisions of this rule are to be without prejudice to the operation of section 16 of the Interpretation Act 1978 (saving from repeals) as it is applied by section 23 of that Act.

SCHEDULE

Rules 3(2), 4(3) and 7(2)

[Forms: not reproduced.]

Insolvent Companies (Reports on Conduct of Directors) (Scotland) Rules 1996

(SI 1996/1910 (S 154))

Made on 22 July 1996 by the Secretary of State for Trade and Industry under s.411 of the Insolvency Act 1986 and s.21(2) of the Company Directors Disqualification Act 1986. Operative from 30 September 1996.

[**Note:** Changes made by the Insolvent Companies (Reports on Conduct of Directors) (Scotland) (Amendment) Rules 2001 (SI 2001/768) have been incorporated into the text (without annotation). The Rules do not appear to have been updated to take account of the introduction of the new administration regime by the Enterprise Act 2002.]

1 Citation, commencement and interpretation

1(1) These Rules may be cited as the Insolvent Companies (Reports on Conduct of Directors) (Scotland) Rules 1996.

1(2) These Rules shall come into force on 30th September 1996.

1(3) In these Rules–

"the Act" means the Company Directors Disqualification Act 1986;

"the former Rules" means the Insolvent Companies (Reports on Conduct of Directors) (No. 2) (Scotland) Rules 1986;

"the commencement date" means 30th September 1996; and

"a company" means a company which the courts in Scotland have jurisdiction to wind up.

2 Revocation

2 Subject to rule 7 below the former Rules are hereby revoked.

3 Reports required under section 7(3) of the Act

3(1) This rule applies to any report made to the Secretary of State under section 7(3) of the Act by:–

   (a) the liquidator of a company which is being wound up by an order of the court made on or after the commencement date;

   (b) the liquidator of a company which passes a resolution for voluntary winding up on or after that date;

   (c) a receiver of a company appointed under section 51 of the Insolvency Act 1986 (power to appoint receiver under the law of Scotland) on or after that date, who is an administrative receiver; or

   (d) the administrator of a company in relation to which the court makes an administration order on or after that date.

3(2) Such a report shall be made in the Form D1 (Scot) set out in the Schedule hereto, or in a form which is substantially similar, and in the manner and to the extent required by the Form D1 (Scot).

4 Return by office-holder

4(1) This rule applies where it appears to a liquidator of a company as mentioned in rule 3(1)(a) or (b), to an administrative receiver as mentioned in rule 3(1)(c), or to an administrator as mentioned in rule 3(1)(d) (each of whom is referred to hereinafter as **"an office-holder"**) that the company has at any time become insolvent within the meaning of section 6(2) of the Act.

4(2)   Subject as follows there may be furnished to the Secretary of State by an office-holder at any time during the period of 6 months from the relevant date (defined in paragraph (4) below) a return with respect to every person who:–

(a)   was, on the relevant date, a director or shadow director of the company, or

(b)   had been a director or shadow director of the company at any time in the 3 years immediately preceding that date.

4(3)   The return shall be made in the Form D2 (Scot) set out in the Schedule hereto, or in a form which is substantially similar, and in the manner and to the extent required by the Form D2 (Scot).

4(4)   For the purposes of this rule, **"the relevant date"** means:–

(a)   in the case of a company in liquidation (except in the case mentioned in paragraph (4)(b) below), the date on which the company goes into liquidation within the meaning of section 247(2) of the Insolvency Act 1986,

(b)   in the case of a company in members' voluntary winding up, the date on which the liquidator forms the opinion that, at the time when the company went into liquidation, its assets were insufficient for the payment of its debts and other liabilities and the expenses of winding up,

(c)   in the case of the administrative receiver, the date of his appointment,

(d)   in the case of the administrator, the date of the administration order made in relation to the company,

and for the purposes of sub-paragraph (c) above the only appointment of an administrative receiver to be taken into account in determining the relevant date shall be that appointment which is not that of a successor in office to an administrative receiver who has vacated office either by death or pursuant to section 62 of the Insolvency Act 1986.

4(5)   Subject to paragraph (6) below, it shall be the duty of an office-holder to furnish a return complying with the provisions of paragraphs (3) and (4) of this rule to the Secretary of State:–

(a)   where he is in office in relation to the company on the day one week before the expiry of the period of 6 months from the relevant date, not later than the expiry of such period;

(b)   where he vacates office (otherwise than by death) before the day one week before the expiry of the period of 6 months from the relevant date, within 14 days after his vacation of office except where he has furnished such a return on or prior to the day one week before the expiry of such period.

4(6)   A return need not be provided under this rule by an office-holder if he has, whilst holding that office in relation to the company, since the relevant date, made a report under rule 3 with respect to all persons falling within paragraph (2) of this rule and (apart from this paragraph) required to be the subject of a return.

4(7)   If an office-holder without reasonable excuse fails to comply with the duty imposed by paragraph (5) of this rule, he is guilty of an offence and–

(a)   on summary conviction of the offence, is liable to a fine not exceeding level 3 on the standard scale, and

(b)   after continued contravention, is liable to a daily default fine; that is to say, he is liable on a second or subsequent summary conviction of the offence to a fine of one-tenth of level 3 on the standard scale for each day on which the contravention is continued (instead of the penalty specified in sub-paragraph (a)).

4(8)   Section 431 of the Insolvency Act 1986 (summary proceedings), as it applies to Scotland, has effect in relation to an offence under this rule as to offences under Parts I to VII of that Act.

5   Forms

5   The forms referred to in rule 3(2) and rule 4(3) shall be used with such variations, if any as the circumstances may require.

6   Enforcement of section 7(4)

6(1)   This rule applies where under section 7(4) of the Act (power to call on liquidators, former liquidators and others to provide information) the Secretary of State requires or has required a person:–

    (a)   to furnish him with information with respect to a person's conduct as director or shadow director of a company, and

    (b)   to produce and permit inspection of relevant books, papers and other records.

6(2)   On the application of the Secretary of State, the court may make an order directing compliance within such period as may be specified.

6(3)   The court's order may provide that all expenses of and incidental to the application shall be borne by the person to whom the order is directed.

SCHEDULE

Rules 3(2) and 4(3) and 7(2)

[Forms: not reproduced.]

Civil Procedure Rules 1998

(SI 1998/3132)

Made on 10 December 1998. Operative from 26 April 1999.

[**Note**: The text which follows includes all updates to February 29, 2012, without detailed annotation.]

PART 2

APPLICATION AND INTERPRETATION OF THE RULES

2.1 Application of the Rules

2.1(1) Subject to paragraph (2), these Rules apply to all proceedings in–

  (a) county courts;

  (b) the High Court; and

  (c) the Civil Division of the Court of Appeal.

2.1(2) These Rules do not apply to proceedings of the kinds specified in the first column of the following table (proceedings for which rules may be made under the enactments specified in the second column) except to the extent that they are applied to those proceedings by another enactment–

PROCEEDINGS	ENACTMENTS
1. Insolvency proceedings	Insolvency Act 1986, ss. 411 and 412

Note

IA 1986 ss.411 and 412 are, of course, the provisions under which the Insolvency Rules 1986 were made; and IR 1986 r.7.51 (as amended) provides for the application generally of the CPR to insolvency proceedings in the High Court and county court.

PART 6

SERVICE OF DOCUMENTS

I Scope of this part and interpretation

6.1 Part 6 rules about service apply generally

6.1 This Part applies to the service of documents, except where–

  (a) another Part, any other enactment or a practice direction makes different provision; or

  (b) the court orders otherwise.

(Other Parts, for example, Part 54 (Judicial Review) and Part 55 (Possession Claims) contain specific provisions about service.)

6.2 Interpretation

6.2 In this Part–

  (a) "bank holiday" means a bank holiday under the Banking and Financial Dealings Act 1971 in the part of the United Kingdom where service is to take place;

  (b) "business day" means any day except Saturday, Sunday, a bank holiday, Good Friday or Christmas Day;

(c) "claim" includes petition and any application made before action or to commence proceedings and "claim form", "claimant" and "defendant" are to be construed accordingly; and

(d) "solicitor" includes any other person who, for the purposes of the Legal Services Act 2007, is an authorised person in relation to an activity which constitutes the conduct of litigation (within the meaning of that Act); and

(e) "European Lawyer" has the meaning set out in article 2 of the European Communities (Services of Lawyers) Order 1978 (S. I. 1978/1910).

(The European Communities (Services of Lawyers) Order 1978 is annexed to Practice Direction 6A.)

III   Service of documents other than the claim form in the United Kingdom or in specified circumstances within the EEA

6.20   Methods of service

6.20(1)   Subject to Section IV of this Part and the rules in this Section relating to service out of the jurisdiction on solicitors, European Lawyers and parties, a document may be served by any of the following methods–

(a) personal service, in accordance with rule 6.22;

(b) first class post, document exchange or other service which provides for delivery on the next business day, in accordance with Practice Direction 6A;

(c) leaving it at a place specified in rule 6.23;

(d) fax or other means of electronic communication in accordance with Practice Direction 6A; or

(e) any method authorised by the court under rule 6.27.

6.20(2)   A company may be served–

(a) by any method permitted under this Part; or

(b) by any of the methods of service permitted under the Companies Act 2006.

6.20(3)   A limited liability partnership may be served–

(a) by any method permitted under this Part; or

(b) by any of the methods of service permitted under the Companies Act 2006 as applied with modification by regulations made under the Limited Liability Partnerships Act 2000.

6.21   Who is to serve

6.21(1)   Subject to Section IV of this Part and the rules in this Section relating to service out of the jurisdiction on solicitors, European Lawyers and parties, a party to proceedings will serve a document which that party has prepared except where–

(a) a rule or practice direction provides that the court will serve the document; or

(b) the court orders otherwise.

6.21(2)   The court will serve a document which it has prepared except where–

(a) a rule or practice direction provides that a party must serve the document;

(b) the party on whose behalf the document is to be served notifies the court that the party wishes to serve it; or

(c)   the court orders otherwise.

6.21(3)   Where the court is to serve a document, it is for the court to decide which method of service is to be used.

6.21(4)   Where the court is to serve a document prepared by a party, that party must provide a copy for the court and for each party to be served.

6.22   Personal service

6.22(1)   Where required by another Part, any other enactment, a practice direction or a court order, a document must be served personally.

6.22(2)   In other cases, a document may be served personally except–

(a)   where the party to be served has given an address for service under rule 6.23; or

(b)   in any proceedings by or against the Crown.

6.22(3)   A document may be served personally as if the document were a claim form in accordance with rule 6.5(3).

(For service out of the jurisdiction see rules 6.40 to 6.47.)

6.23   Address for service to be given after proceedings are started

6.23(1)   A party to proceedings must give an address at which that party may be served with documents relating to those proceedings. The address must include a full postcode or its equivalent in any EEA state (if applicable) unless the court orders otherwise.

(Paragraph 2.4 of Practice Direction 16 contains provisions about postcodes.)

6.23(2)   Except where any other rule or practice direction makes different provision, a party's address for service must be–

(a)   the business address either within the United Kingdom or any other EEA state of a solicitor acting for the party to be served; or

(b)   the business address in any EEA state of a European Lawyer nominated to accept service of documents; or

(c)   where there is no solicitor acting for the party or no European Lawyer nominated to accept service of documents–

(i)   an address within the United Kingdom at which the party resides or carries on business; or

(ii)   an address within any other EEA state at which the party resides or carries on business.

(For Production Centre Claims see paragraph 2.3(7) of Practice Direction 7C; for Money Claims Online see paragraph 4(6) of Practice Direction 7E; and for Possession Claims Online see paragraph 5.1(4) of Practice Direction 55B.)

6.23(3)   Where none of sub-paragraphs (2)(a), (b) or (c) applies, the party must give an address for service within the United Kingdom. (Part 42 contains provisions about change of solicitor. Rule 42.1 provides that where a party gives the business address of a solicitor as that party's address for service, that solicitor will be considered to be acting for the party until the provisions of Part 42 are complied with.)

6.23(4)   Subject to the provisions of Section IV of this Part (where applicable), any document to be served in proceedings must be sent or transmitted to, or left at, the party's address for service under paragraph (2) or (3) unless it is to be served personally or the court orders otherwise.

6.23(5) Where, in accordance with Practice Direction 6A, a party indicates or is deemed to have indicated that they will accept service by fax, the fax number given by that party must be at the address for service.

6.23(6) Where a party indicates in accordance with Practice Direction 6A that they will accept service by electronic means other than fax, the e-mail address or electronic identification given by that party will be deemed to be at the address for service.

6.23(7) In proceedings by or against the Crown, service of any document in the proceedings on the Crown must be effected in the same manner prescribed in rule 6.10 as if the document were a claim form.

6.23(8) This rule does not apply where an order made by the court under rule 6.27 (service by an alternative method or at an alternative place) specifies where a document may be served.

(For service out of the jurisdiction see rules 6.40 to 6.47.)

6.24 Change of address for service

6.24 Where the address for service of a party changes, that party must give notice in writing of the change as soon as it has taken place to the court and every other party.

6.25 Service on children and protected parties

6.25(1) An application for an order appointing a litigation friend where a child or protected party has no litigation friend must be served in accordance with rule 21.8(1) and (2).

6.25(2) Any other document which would otherwise be served on a child or a protected party must be served on the litigation friend conducting the proceedings on behalf of the child or protected party.

6.25(3) The court may make an order permitting a document to be served on the child or protected party or on some person other than the person specified in rule 21.8 or paragraph (2).

6.25(4) An application for an order under paragraph (3) may be made without notice.

6.25(5) The court may order that, although a document has been sent or given to someone other than the person specified in rule 21.8 or paragraph (2), the document is to be treated as if it had been properly served.

6.25(6) This rule does not apply where the court has made an order under rule 21.2(3) allowing a child to conduct proceedings without a litigation friend.

6.26 Deemed Service

6.26 A document, other than a claim form, served within the United Kingdom in accordance with these Rules or any relevant practice direction is deemed to be served on the day shown in the following table–

Method of service	*Deemed date of service*
1. First class post (or other service which provides for delivery on the next business day)	The second day after it was posted, left with, delivered to or collected by the relevant service provider provided that day is a business day; or if not, the next business day after that day.
2. Document exchange	The second day after it was left with, delivered to or collected by the relevant service provider provided that day is a business day; or if not, the next business day after that day.
3. Delivering the document to or leaving it at a permitted address	If it is delivered to or left at the permitted address on a business day before 4.30p.m., on that day; or in any other case, on the next business day after that day.

4. Fax	If the transmission of the fax is completed on a business day before 4.30p.m., on that day; or in any other case, on the next business day after the day on which it was transmitted.
5. Other electronic method	If the e-mail or other electronic transmission is sent on a business day before 4.30p.m., on that day; or in any other case, on the next business day after the day on which it was sent.
6. Personal service	If the document is served personally before 4.30p.m. on a business day, on that day; or in any other case, on the next business day after that day.

(Paragraphs 10.1 to 10.7 of Practice Direction 6A contain examples of how the date of deemed service is calculated.)

6.27   Service by an alternative method or at an alternative place

6.27   Rule 6.15 applies to any document in the proceedings as it applies to a claim form and reference to the defendant in that rule is modified accordingly.

6.28   Power to dispense with service

6.28(1)   The court may dispense with service of any document which is to be served in the proceedings.

6.28(2)   An application for an order to dispense with service must be supported by evidence and may be made without notice.

6.29   Certificate of service

6.29   Where a rule, practice direction or court order requires a certificate of service, the certificate must state the details required by the following table–

Method of Service	*Details to be certified*
1. Personal service	Date and time of personal service.
2. First class post, document exchange or other service which provides for delivery on the next business day	Date of posting, or leaving with, delivering to or collection by the relevant service provider.
3. Delivery of document to or leaving it at a permitted place	Date and time of when the document was delivered to or left at the permitted place.
4. Fax	Date and time of completion of the transmission.
5. Other electronic method	Date and time of sending the e-mail or other electronic transmission.
6. Alternative method or place permitted by the court	As required by the court.

IV   Service of the claim form and other documents out of the jurisdiction

[Not reproduced.]

PART 49

SPECIALIST PROCEEDINGS

49   These Rules apply to proceedings under–

(a)   the Companies Act 1985;

(b)   the Companies Act 2006; and

(c)   other legislation relating to companies and limited liability partnerships,

subject to the provision of the relevant practice direction which applies to those proceedings.

[**Note**: Part 49 is supplemented by *Practice Direction 49A—Applications under the Companies Acts and Related Legislation*. The *Practice Direction* applies (para.2) to proceedings under:

(a)   CA 1985;

(b)   CA 2006 (except proceedings under Chapter 1 of Pt 11 or Pt 30);

(c)   Criminal Justice and Police Act 2001 s.59;

(d)   Articles 22, 25 and 26 of the EC Regulation;

(e)   FSMA 2000 Pt VII;

(f)   the Companies (Cross-Border Mergers) Regulations 2007 (SI 2007/2974).

Part 49 is further supplemented by *Practice Direction 49B—Order under section 127 of the Insolvency Act 1986* (reproduced in App.V, below).]

Financial Markets and Insolvency (Settlement Finality) Regulations 1999

(SI 1999/2979)

Made on 2 November 1999 by the Treasury under s.2(2) of the European Communities Act 1972.
Operative from 11 December 1999.

[**Note**: Changes made by the Financial Services and Markets Act 2000 (Consequential Amendments) Order 2000 (SI 2000/1555), the Banking Consolidation Directive (Consequential Amendments) Regulations 2000 (SI 2000/2952), the Civil Jurisdiction and Judgments Regulations 2001 (SI 2001/3929), the Electronic Money (Miscellaneous Amendments) Regulations 2002 (SI 2002/765), the Enterprise Act (Insolvency) Order 2003 (SI 2003/2096), the Financial Markets and Insolvency (Settlement Finality) (Amendment) Regulations 2006 (SI 2006/50), the Capital Requirements Regulations 2006 (SI 2006/3221), the Financial Services and Insolvency (Settlement Finality) (Amendment) Regulations 2007 (SI 2007/832), the Financial Services (EEA State) Regulations 2007 (SI 2007/108), the Civil Jurisdiction and Judgments Regulations 2007 (SI 2007/1655), the Financial Markets and Insolvency (Settlement Finality) Regulations 2009 (SI 2009/902), the Financial Markets and Insolvency (Settlement Finality and Financial Collateral Arrangements) (Amendment) Regulations 2010 (SI 2010/2993) and the Electronic Money Regulations 2011 (SI 2011/99) have been incorporated into the text (in the case of pre-2003 legislation without annotation). Where references to administration petitions, orders, etc. and to the original IA 1986 Pt II have been altered by the Enterprise Act 2002 (Insolvency) Order 2003 (SI 2003/2096) art.5 and Sch. Pt 2 as from September 15, 2003 (subject to transitional provision in art.6), following the introduction of the new administration regime, history notes have been omitted. The text has been amended throughout (without detailed annotation) to reflect the extension of the Regulations to Northern Ireland, pursuant to the Financial Markets and Insolvency (Settlement Finality) (Amendment) Regulations 2006 (SI 2006/50), effective February 2, 2006.]

PART I

GENERAL

1 Citation, commencement and extent

1(1) These Regulations may be cited as the Financial Markets and Insolvency (Settlement Finality) Regulations 1999 and shall come into force on 11th December 1999.

1(2) [Deleted: the Regulations now extend to Northern Ireland.]

2 Interpretation

2(1) In these Regulations

"the 2000 Act" means the Financial Services and Markets Act 2000;

"business day" shall cover both day and night-time settlements and shall encompass all events happening during the business cycle of a system;

"central bank" means a central bank of an EEA State or the European Central Bank;

"central counterparty" means a body corporate or unincorporated association interposed between the institutions in a system and which acts as the exclusive counterparty of those institutions with regard to transfer orders;

"charge" means any form of security, including a mortgage and, in Scotland, a heritable security;

"clearing house" means a body corporate or unincorporated association which is responsible for the calculation of the net positions of institutions and any central counterparty or settlement agent in a system;

"collateral security" means any realisable assets provided under a charge or a repurchase or similar agreement, or otherwise (including credit claims and money provided under a charge)–

(a) for the purpose of securing rights and obligations potentially arising in connection with a system ("collateral security in connection with participation in a system"); or

(b) to a central bank for the purpose of securing rights and obligations in connection with its operations in carrying out its functions as a central bank ("collateral security in connection with the functions of a central bank");

"collateral security charge" means, where collateral security consists of realisable assets (including money) provided under a charge, that charge;

"credit claims" means pecuniary claims arising out of an agreement whereby a credit institution grants credit in the form of a loan;

"credit institution" means a credit institution as defined in Article 4(1) of Directive 2006/48/EC of the European Parliament and of the Council of 14 June 2006 relating to the taking up and pursuit of the business of credit institutions (as last amended by Directive 2009/111/EC), including the bodies set out in the list in Article 2;

History
Definition of "credit institution" amended by the Capital Requirements Regulations 2006 (SI 2006/3221) reg.29(4) and Sch.6 para.3 as from January 1, 2007 and by the Electronic Money Regulations 2011 (SI 2011/99) reg.79 and Sch.4 para.8 as from April 30, 2011.

"creditors' voluntary winding-up resolution" means a resolution for voluntary winding up (within the meaning of the Insolvency Act 1986 or the Insolvency (Northern Ireland) Order 1989) where the winding up is a creditors' winding up (within the meaning of that Act or that Order);

"default arrangements" means the arrangements put in place by a designated system or by a system which is an interoperable system in relation to that system to limit systemic and other types of risk which arise in the event of a participant or a system operator of an interoperable system appearing to be unable, or likely to become unable, to meet its obligations in respect of a transfer order, including, for example, any default rules within the meaning of Part VII or Part V or any other arrangements for–

(a) netting,

(b) the closing out of open positions, or

(c) the application or transfer of collateral security;

"defaulter" means a person in respect of whom action has been taken by a designated system under its default arrangements;

"designated system" means a system which is declared by a designation order for the time being in force to be a designated system for the purposes of these Regulations;

"designating authority" means–

(a) in the case of a system–

  (i) which is, or the operator of which is, a recognised investment exchange or a recognised clearing house for the purposes of the 2000 Act,

  (ii) which is, or the operator of which is, a listed person within the meaning of the Financial Markets and Insolvency (Money Market) Regulations 1995, or

  (iii) through which securities transfer orders are effected (whether or not payment transfer orders are also effected through that system),

  the Financial Services Authority;

(b) in any other case, the Bank of England;

"designation order" has the meaning given by regulation 4;

"EEA State" has the meaning given by Schedule 1 to the Interpretation Act 1978;

History

Definition of "EEA State" substituted by the Financial Services (EEA State) Regulations 2007 (SI 2007/108) reg.5 as from February 13, 2007. The definition was inserted into the 1978 Act by the Legislative and Regulatory Reform Act 2006.

"guidance", in relation to a designated system, means guidance issued or any recommendation made by it which is intended to have continuing effect and is issued in writing or other legible form to all or any class of its participants or users or persons seeking to participate in the system or to use its facilities and which would, if it were a rule, come within the definition of a rule;

"indirect participant" means an institution, central counterparty, settlement agent, clearing house or system operator–

(a) which has a contractual relationship with a participant in a designated system that enables the indirect participant to effect transfer orders through that system, and

(b) the identity of which is known to the system operator;

"institution" means–

(a) a credit institution;

(aa) an electronic money institution within the meaning of Article 2.1 of Directive 2009/110/EC of the European Parliament and of the Council of 16 September 2009 on the taking up, pursuit and prudential supervision of the business of electronic money institutions amending Directives 2005/60/EC and 2006/48/EC and repealing Directive 2000/46/EC;

(b) an investment firm as defined in Article 4.1.1 of Directive 2004/39/EC of the European Parliament and of the Council of 21 April 2004 on markets in financial instruments, other than a person to whom Article 2 applies;

(c) a public authority or publicly guaranteed undertaking;

(d) any undertaking whose head office is outside the European Community and whose functions correspond to those of a credit institution or investment firm as defined in (a) and (b) above; or

(e) any undertaking which is treated by the designating authority as an institution in accordance with regulation 8(1),

which participates in a system and which is responsible for discharging the financial obligations arising from transfer orders which are effected through the system;

"interoperable system" in relation to a system (**"the first system"**), means a second system whose system operator has entered into an arrangement with the system operator of the first system that involves cross-system execution of transfer orders;

"netting" means the conversion into one net claim or obligation of different claims or obligations between participants resulting from the issue and receipt of transfer orders between them, whether on a bilateral or multilateral basis and whether through the interposition of a clearing house, central counterparty or settlement agent or otherwise;

"Part V" means Part V of the Companies (No. 2) (Northern Ireland) Order 1990;

"Part VII" means Part VII of the Companies Act 1989;

"participant" means–

(a) an institution,

(aa) a system operator;

(b) a body corporate or unincorporated association which carries out any combination of the functions of a central counterparty, a settlement agent or a clearing house, with respect to a system, or

(c) an indirect participant which is treated as a participant, or is a member of a class of indirect participants which are treated as participants, in accordance with regulation 9;

"protected trust deed" and

"trust deed" shall be construed in accordance with section 73(1) of the Bankruptcy (Scotland) Act 1985 (interpretation);

"relevant office-holder" means–

(a) the official receiver;

(b) any person acting in relation to a company as its liquidator, provisional liquidator, or administrator;

(c) any person acting in relation to an individual (or, in Scotland, any debtor within the meaning of the Bankruptcy (Scotland) Act 1985) as his trustee in bankruptcy or interim receiver of his property or as permanent or interim trustee in the sequestration of his estate or as his trustee under a protected trust deed;

(d) any person acting as administrator of an insolvent estate of a deceased person; or

(e) any person appointed pursuant to insolvency proceedings of a country or territory outside the United Kingdom;

and in sub-paragraph (b), **"company"** means any company, society, association, partnership or other body which may be wound up under the Insolvency Act 1986 or the Insolvency (Northern Ireland) Order 1989;

"rules", in relation to a designated system, means rules or conditions governing the system with respect to the matters dealt with in these Regulations;

"securities" means (except for the purposes of the definition of "charge") any instruments referred to in C of Annex I to Directive 2004/39/EC of the European Parliament and of the Council of 21 April 2004 on markets in financial instruments;

"settlement account" means an account at a central bank, a settlement agent or a central counterparty used to hold funds or securities (or both) and to settle transactions between participants in a system;

"settlement agent" means a body corporate or unincorporated association providing settlement accounts to the institutions and any central counterparty in a system for the settlement of transfer orders within the system and, as the case may be, for extending credit to such institutions and any such central counterparty for settlement purposes;

"the Settlement Finality Directive" means Directive 98/26/EC of the European Parliament and of the Council of 19th May 1998 on settlement finality in payment and securities settlement systems as amended by Directive 2009/44/EC of the European Parliament and of the Council of 6 May 2009 amending Directive 98/26/EC on settlement finality in payment and securities settlement systems and Directive 2002/47/EC on financial collateral arrangements as regards linked systems and credit claims;

"system operator" means the entity or entities legally responsible for the operation of a system. A system operator may also act as a settlement agent, central counterparty or clearing house;

"transfer order" means–

(a) an instruction by a participant to place at the disposal of a recipient an amount of money by means of a book entry on the accounts of a credit institution, a central bank, a central counterparty or a settlement agent, or an instruction which results in the assumption or discharge of a payment obligation as defined by the rules of a designated system (**"a payment transfer order"**); or

(b)   an instruction by a participant to transfer the title to, or interest in, securities by means of a book entry on a register, or otherwise (**"a securities transfer order"**);

"winding-up" means–

(a)   winding up by the court or creditors' voluntary winding up within the meaning of the Insolvency Act 1986 or the Insolvency (Northern Ireland) Order 1989 (but does not include members' voluntary winding up within the meaning of that Act or that Order);

(b)   sequestration of a Scottish partnership under the Bankruptcy (Scotland) Act 1985;

(c)   bank insolvency within the meaning of the Banking Act 2009.

2(2)   In these Regulations–

(a)   references to the law of insolvency include references to every provision made by or under the Insolvency Act 1986, the Insolvency (Northern Ireland) Order 1989 or the Bankruptcy (Scotland) Act 1985; and in relation to a building society references to insolvency law or to any provision of the Insolvency Act 1986 or the Insolvency (Northern Ireland) Order 1989 are to that law or provision as modified by the Building Societies Act 1986;

(b)   in relation to Scotland, references to–

(i)   sequestration include references to the administration by a judicial factor of the insolvent estate of a deceased person,

(ii)   an interim or permanent trustee include references to a judicial factor on the insolvent estate of a deceased person, and

(iii) "set off" include compensation.

2(3)   Subject to paragraph (1), expressions used in these Regulations which are also used in the Settlement Finality Directive have the same meaning in these Regulations as they have in the Settlement Finality Directive.

2(4)   References in these Regulations to things done, or required to be done, by or in relation to a designated system shall, in the case of a designated system which is neither a body corporate nor an unincorporated association, be treated as references to things done, or required to be done, by or in relation to the operator of that system.

History
Definitions of "business day", "credit claims", "interoperable system" and "system operator" inserted and reg.2(1)–(3) extensively amended by the Financial Markets and Insolvency (Settlement Finality and Financial Collateral Arrangements) (Amendment) Regulations 2010 (SI 2010/2993) reg.2(1), (2) as from April 6, 2011.

PART II

DESIGNATED SYSTEMS

3   Application for designation

3(1)   Any body corporate or unincorporated association may apply to the designating authority for an order declaring it, or any system of which it is the operator, to be a designated system for the purposes of these Regulations.

3(2)   Any such application–

(a)   shall be made in such manner as the designating authority may direct; and

(b)   shall be accompanied by such information as the designating authority may reasonably require for the purpose of determining the application.

3(3) At any time after receiving an application and before determining it, the designating authority may require the applicant to furnish additional information.

3(4) The directions and requirements given or imposed under paragraphs (2) and (3) may differ as between different applications.

3(5) Any information to be furnished to the designating authority under this regulation shall be in such form or verified in such manner as it may specify.

3(6) Every application shall be accompanied by copies of the rules of the system to which the application relates and any guidance relating to that system.

4 Grant and refusal of designation

4(1) Where–

    (a) an application has been duly made under regulation 3;

    (b) the applicant has paid any fee charged by virtue of regulation 5(1); and

    (c) the designating authority is satisfied that the requirements of the Schedule are satisfied with respect to the system to which the application relates;

the designating authority may make an order (a **"designation order"**) declaring the system to be a designated system and identifying the system operator of that system for the purposes of these Regulations.

4(2) In determining whether to make a designation order, the designating authority shall have regard to systemic risks.

4(3) Where an application has been made to the Financial Services Authority under regulation 3 in relation to a system through which both securities transfer orders and payment transfer orders are effected, the Authority shall consult the Bank of England before deciding whether to make a designation order.

4(4) A designation order shall state the date on which it takes effect.

4(5) Where the designating authority refuses an application for a designation order it shall give the applicant a written notice to that effect stating the reasons for the refusal.

History
Regulation 4 amended by the Financial Markets and Insolvency (Settlement Finality and Financial Collateral Arrangements) (Amendment) Regulations 2010 (SI 2010/2993) reg.2(3) as from April 6, 2011.

5 Fees

5(1) The designating authority may charge a fee to an applicant for a designation order.

5(2) The designating authority may charge the system operator of a designated system a periodical fee.

5(3) Fees chargeable by the designating authority under this regulation shall not exceed an amount which reasonably represents the amount of costs incurred or likely to be incurred–

    (a) in the case of a fee charged to an applicant for a designation order, in determining whether the designation order should be made; and

    (b) in the case of a periodical fee, in satisfying itself that the designated system and its system operator continue to meet the requirements of the Schedule and are complying with any obligations to which they are subject by virtue of these Regulations.

History
Regulation 5 amended by the Financial Markets and Insolvency (Settlement Finality and Financial Collateral Arrangements) (Amendment) Regulations 2010 (SI 2010/2993) reg.2(4) as from April 6, 2011.

6 Certain bodies deemed to satisfy requirements for designation

6(1) Subject to paragraph (2), an investment exchange or clearing house declared by an order for the time being in force to be a recognised investment exchange or recognised clearing house for the purposes of the 2000 Act, whether that order was made before or is made after the coming into force of these Regulations, shall be deemed to satisfy the requirements in paragraphs 2 and 3 of the Schedule.

6(2) Paragraph (1) does not apply to overseas investment exchanges or overseas clearing houses within the meaning of the 2000 Act.

7 Revocation of designation

7(1) A designation order may be revoked by a further order made by the designating authority if at any time it appears to the designating authority–

(a) that any requirement of the Schedule is not satisfied in the case of the system to which the designation order relates; or

(b) that the system or the system operator of that system has failed to comply with any obligation to which they are subject by virtue of these Regulations.

7(2) Subsections (1) to (7) of section 298 of the 2000 Act shall apply in relation to the revocation of a designation order under paragraph (1) as they apply in relation to the revocation of a recognition order section 297(2) of that Act; and in those subsections as they so apply–

(a) any reference to a recognised body shall be taken to be a reference to a designated system;

(b) any reference to members of a recognised body shall be taken to be a reference to participants in a designated system;

(c) references to the Authority shall, in cases where the Bank of England is the designating authority, be taken to be a reference to the Bank of England; and

(d) subsection (4)(a) shall have effect as if for "two months" there were substituted "three months".

7(3) An order revoking a designation order–

(a) shall state the date on which it takes effect, being no earlier than three months after the day on which the revocation order is made; and

(b) may contain such transitional provisions as the designating authority thinks necessary or expedient.

7(4) A designation order may be revoked at the request or with the consent of the system operator of the designated system, and any such revocation shall not be subject to the restriction imposed by paragraph (3)(a), or to the requirements imposed by subsections (1) to (6) of section 298 of the 2000 Act.

History
Regulation 7 amended by the Financial Markets and Insolvency (Settlement Finality and Financial Collateral Arrangements) (Amendment) Regulations 2010 (SI 2010/2993) reg.2(5) as from April 6, 2011.

8 Undertakings treated as institutions

8(1) A designating authority may treat as an institution any undertaking which participates in a designated system and which is responsible for discharging financial obligations arising from transfer orders effected through that system, provided that–

(a) the designating authority considers such treatment to be required on grounds of systemic risk, and

(b) the designated system is one in which at least three institutions (other than any undertaking treated as an institution by virtue of this paragraph) participate and through which securities transfer orders are effected.

8(2)   Where a designating authority decides to treat an undertaking as an institution in accordance with paragraph (1), it shall give written notice of that decision to the designated system in which the undertaking is to be treated as a participant and to the system operator of that system.

History
Regulation 8 amended by the Financial Markets and Insolvency (Settlement Finality and Financial Collateral Arrangements) (Amendment) Regulations 2010 (SI 2010/2993) reg.2(7) as from April 6, 2011.

9   Indirect participants treated as participants

9(1)   A designating authority may treat–

   (a)   an indirect participant as a participant in a designated system, or

   (b)   a class of indirect participants as participants in a designated system, where it considers this to be required on grounds of systemic risk, and shall give written notice of any decision to that effect to the designated system and to the system operator of that system.

9(2)   Where a designating authority, in accordance with paragraph (1), treats an indirect participant as a participant in a designated system, the liability of the participant through which that indirect participant passes transfer orders to the designated system is not affected.

History
Regulation 9 amended by the Financial Markets and Insolvency (Settlement Finality and Financial Collateral Arrangements) (Amendment) Regulations 2010 (SI 2010/2993) reg.2(8) as from April 6, 2011.

10   Provision of information by designated systems

10(1)   The system operator of a designated system shall, when that system is declared to be a designated system, provide to the designating authority in writing a list of the participants (including the indirect participants) in the designated system and shall give written notice to the designating authority of any amendment to the list within seven days of such amendment.

10(2)   The designating authority may, in writing, require the system operator of a designated system to furnish to it such other information relating to that designated system as it reasonably requires for the exercise of its functions under these Regulations, within such time, in such form, at such intervals and verified in such manner as the designating authority may specify.

10(3)   When the system operator of a designated system amends, revokes or adds to its rules or its guidance, it shall within fourteen days give written notice to the designating authority of the amendment, revocation or addition.

10(4)   The system operator of a designated system shall give the designating authority at least fourteen days' written notice of any proposal to amend, revoke or add to its default arrangements.

10(5)   Nothing in this regulation shall require the system operator of a designated system to give any notice or furnish any information to the Financial Services Authority which it has given or furnished to the Authority pursuant to any requirement imposed by or under section 293 of the 2000 Act (notification requirements) or any other enactment.

History
Regulation 10 amended by the Financial Markets and Insolvency (Settlement Finality and Financial Collateral Arrangements) (Amendment) Regulations 2010 (SI 2010/2993) reg.2(9) as from April 6, 2011.

11   Exemption from liability in damages

11(1)   Neither the designating authority nor any person who is, or is acting as, a member, officer or member of staff of the designating authority shall be liable in damages for anything done or omitted in the discharge, or purported discharge, of the designating authority's functions under these Regulations.

11(2) Paragraph (1) does not apply–

(a) if the act or omission is shown to have been in bad faith; or

(b) so as to prevent an award of damages made in respect of an act or omission on the ground that the act or omission was unlawful as a result of section 6(1) of the Human Rights Act 1998 (acts of public authorities).

12 Publication of information and advice

12 A designating authority may publish information or give advice, or arrange for the publication of information or the giving of advice, in such form and manner as it considers appropriate with respect to any matter dealt with in these Regulations.

PART III

TRANSFER ORDERS EFFECTED THROUGH A DESIGNATED SYSTEM AND COLLATERAL SECURITY

13 Modifications of the law of insolvency

13(1) The general law of insolvency has effect in relation to–

(a) transfer orders effected through a designated system and action taken under the rules of a designated system with respect to such orders; and

(b) collateral security,

subject to the provisions of this Part.

13(2) Those provisions apply in relation to–

(a) insolvency proceedings in respect of a participant in a designated system, or of a participant in a system which is an interoperable system in relation to that designated system;

(b) insolvency proceedings in respect of a provider of collateral security in connection with the functions of a central bank, in so far as the proceedings affect the rights of the central bank to the collateral security; and

(c) insolvency proceedings in respect of a system operator of a designated system or of a system which is an interoperable system in relation to that designated system;

but not in relation to any other insolvency proceedings, notwithstanding that rights or liabilities arising from transfer orders or collateral security fall to be dealt with in the proceedings.

13(3) Subject to regulation 21, nothing in this Part shall have the effect of disapplying Part VII or Part V.

13(4) References in this Part to "insolvency proceedings" shall include–

(a) bank insolvency under Part 2 of the Banking Act 2009; and

(b) bank administration under Part 3 of the Banking Act 2009.

History

Regulation 13(3) amended by the Financial Markets and Insolvency (Settlement Finality) (Amendment) Regulations 2006 (SI 2006/50) reg.2(1), (5) as from February 2, 2006 and by the Financial Markets and Insolvency (Settlement Finality and Financial Collateral Arrangements) (Amendment) Regulations 2010 (SI 2010/2993) reg.2(10) as from April 6, 2011.

14 Proceedings of designated system take precedence over insolvency proceedings

14(1) None of the following shall be regarded as to any extent invalid at law on the ground of inconsistency with the law relating to the distribution of the assets of a person on bankruptcy, winding up, administration, sequestration or under a protected trust deed, or in the administration of an insolvent estate or with the law relating to other insolvency proceedings of a country or territory outside the United Kingdom–

  (a) a transfer order;

  (b) the default arrangements of a designated system;

  (c) the rules of a designated system as to the settlement of transfer orders not dealt with under its default arrangements;

  (d) a contract for the purpose of realising collateral security in connection with participation in a designated system or in a system which is an interoperable system in relation to that designated system otherwise than pursuant to its default arrangements; or

  (e) a contract for the purpose of realising collateral security in connection with the functions of a central bank.

14(2) The powers of a relevant office-holder in his capacity as such, and the powers of the court under the Insolvency Act 1986, the Insolvency (Northern Ireland) Order 1989 or the Bankruptcy (Scotland) Act 1985, shall not be exercised in such a way as to prevent or interfere with–

  (a) the settlement in accordance with the rules of a designated system of a transfer order not dealt with under its default arrangements;

  (b) any action taken under the default arrangements of a designated system;

  (c) any action taken to realise collateral security in connection with participation in a designated system or in a system which is an interoperable system in relation to that designated system otherwise than pursuant to its default arrangements; or

  (d) any action taken to realise collateral security in connection with the functions of a central bank.

14(3) Nothing in the following provisions of this Part shall be construed as affecting the generality of the above provisions.

14(4) A debt or other liability arising out of a transfer order which is the subject of action taken under default arrangements may not be proved in a winding up, bankruptcy, or administration, or in Scotland claimed in a winding up, sequestration or under a protected trust deed, until the completion of the action taken under default arrangements.

A debt or other liability which by virtue of this paragraph may not be proved or claimed shall not be taken into account for the purposes of any set-off until the completion of the action taken under default arrangements.

14(5) Paragraph (1) has the effect that the following provisions (which relate to preferential debts and the payment of expenses etc) apply subject to paragraph (6), namely–

  (a) in the case of collateral security provided by a company (within the meaning of section 1 of the Companies Act 2006) or by a building society (within the meaning of section 119 of the Building Societies Act 1986)–

    (i) sections 175, 176ZA and 176A of, and paragraph 65(2) of Schedule B1 to, the Insolvency Act 1986 or Articles 149, 150ZA, and 150A of, and paragraph 66(2) of Schedule B1 to, the Insolvency (Northern Ireland) Order 1989;

   (ii)   Rules 4.30(3) and 4.218(2)(b) of the Insolvency Rules 1986, Rules 4.033(3) and 4.228(2)(b) of the Insolvency Rules (Northern Ireland) 1991 and rule 4.5(3) of the Insolvency (Scotland) Rules 1986;

   (iii)   section 40 (or in Scotland, section 59 and 60(1)(e)) of the Insolvency Act 1986, paragraph 99(3) of Schedule B1 to that Act and section 19(4) of that Act as that section has effect by virtue of section 249(1) of the Enterprise Act 2002;

   (iv)   paragraph 100(3) of Schedule B1 to the Insolvency (Northern Ireland) Order 1989, Article 31(4) of that Order, as it has effect by virtue of Article 4(1) of the Insolvency (Northern Ireland) Order 2005, and Article 50 of the Insolvency (Northern Ireland) Order 1989; and

   (v)   section 754 of the Companies Act 2006 (including that section as applied or modified by any enactment made under the Banking Act 2009); and

(b)   in the case of collateral security provided by an individual, section 328(1) and (2) of the Insolvency Act 1986 or, in Northern Ireland, Article 300(1) and (2) of the Insolvency (Northern Ireland) Order 1989 or, in Scotland, in the case of collateral security provided by an individual or a partnership, section 51 of the Bankruptcy (Scotland) Act 1985 and any like provision or rule of law affecting a protected trust deed.

14(6)   The claim of a participant, system operator or central bank to collateral security shall be paid in priority to–

(a)   the expenses of the winding up mentioned in sections 115 and 156 of the Insolvency Act 1986 or Articles 100 and 134 of the Insolvency (Northern Ireland) Order 1989, the expenses of the bankruptcy within the meaning of that Act or that Order or, as the case may be, the remuneration and expenses of the administrator mentioned in paragraph 99(3) of Schedule B1 to that Act and in section 19(4) of that Act as that section has effect by virtue of section 249(1) of the Enterprise Act 2002 or in paragraph 100(3) to Schedule B1 to that Order and Article 31(4) of that Order, as that Article has effect by virtue of Article 4(1) of the Insolvency (Northern Ireland) Order 2005, and

(b)   the preferential debts of the company or the individual (as the case may be) within the meaning given by section 386 of that Act or Article 346 of that Order, and

(c)   the debts or liabilities arising or incurred under contracts mentioned in–

   (i)   paragraph 99(4) of Schedule B1 to the Insolvency Act 1986 and section 19(5) of that Act, as that section has effect by virtue of section 249(1) of the Enterprise Act 2002, or

   (ii)   paragraph 100(4) of Schedule B1 to, the Insolvency (Northern Ireland) Order 1989 and Article 31(5) of that Order as that article has effect by virtue of Article 4(1) of the Insolvency (Northern Ireland) Order 2005,

unless the terms on which the collateral security was provided expressly provide that such expenses, remuneration or preferential debts are to have priority.

14(7)   As respects Scotland–

(a)   the reference in paragraph (6)(a) to the expenses of bankruptcy shall be taken to be a reference to the matters mentioned in paragraphs (a) to (d) of section 51(1) of the Bankruptcy (Scotland) Act 1985, or any like provision or rule of law affecting a protected trust deed; and

(b)   the reference in paragraph (6)(b) to the preferential debts of the individual shall be taken to be a reference to the preferred debts of the debtor within the meaning of the Bankruptcy (Scotland) Act 1985, or any like definition applying with respect to a protected trust deed by virtue of any provision or rule of law affecting it.

History
Regulation 14(5)(a)(ii) and 14(6)(a) amended by the Financial Markets and Insolvency (Settlement Finality) (Amendment) Regulations 2007 (SI 2007/832) reg.2(1)–(3), as from April 6, 2007. Regulation 14(1), (2), (4)–(7) amended by the Financial Markets and Insolvency (Settlement Finality) (Amendment) Regulations 2009 (SI 2009/1972) reg.4 as from October 1, 2009. Regulation 14 further amended by the Financial Markets and Insolvency (Settlement Finality and Financial Collateral Arrangements) (Amendment) Regulations 2010 (SI 2010/2993) reg.2(11) as from April 6, 2011.
    Regulation 14 modified in relation to building societies which receive financial assistance from the Bank of England by the Building Societies (Financial Assistance) Order 2008 (SI 2008/1427) art.12 from June 5, 2008.

15   Net sum payable on completion of action taken under default arrangements

15(1)   The following provisions apply with respect to any sum which is owed on completion of action taken under default arrangements of a designated system by or to a defaulter but do not apply to any sum which (or to the extent that it) arises from a transfer order which is also a market contract within the meaning of Part VII or Part V, in which case sections 162 and 163 of the Companies Act 1989 or Articles 85 and 86 of the Companies (No. 2) (Northern Ireland) Order 1990 apply subject to the modification made by regulation 21.

15(2)   If, in England and Wales or Northern Ireland, a bankruptcy, winding-up or administration order has been made or a creditors' voluntary winding-up resolution has been passed, the debt–

   (a)   is provable in the bankruptcy, winding-up or administration or, as the case may be, is payable to the relevant office-holder; and

   (b)   shall be taken into account, where appropriate, under section 323 of the Insolvency Act 1986 or Article 296 of the Insolvency (Northern Ireland) Order 1989 or Rule 2.85 of the Insolvency Rules 1986 or Rule 2.086 of the Insolvency Rules (Northern Ireland) 1991 (mutual dealings and set-off) or the corresponding provision applicable in the case of winding-up or administration;

in the same way as a debt due before the commencement of bankruptcy, the date on which the body corporate goes into liquidation (within the meaning of section 247 of the Insolvency Act 1986 or Article 6 of the Insolvency (Northern Ireland) Order 1989) or enters into administration (within the meaning of paragraph 1 of Schedule B1 to the Insolvency Act 1986 or paragraph 2 of Schedule B1 to the Insolvency (Northern Ireland) Order 1989) or, in the case of a partnership, the date of the winding-up order.

15(3)   If, in Scotland, an award of sequestration or a winding-up order has been made, or a creditors' voluntary winding-up resolution has been passed, or a trust deed has been granted and it has become a protected trust deed, the debt–

   (a)   may be claimed in the sequestration or winding up or under the protected trust deed or, as the case may be, is payable to the relevant office-holder; and

   (b)   shall be taken into account for the purposes of any rule of law relating to set-off applicable in sequestration, winding up or in respect of a protected trust deed;

in the same way as a debt due before the date of sequestration (within the meaning of section 73(1) of the Bankruptcy (Scotland) Act 1985) or the commencement of the winding up (within the meaning of section 129 of the Insolvency Act 1986) or the grant of the trust deed.

15(4)   A reference in this regulation to **"administration order"** shall include–

   (a)   the appointment of an administrator under paragraph 14 or 22 of Schedule B1 to the Insolvency Act 1986 or under paragraph 15 or 23 of Schedule B1 to the Insolvency (Northern Ireland) Order 1989;

   (b)   the making of an order under section 8 of that Act as it has effect by virtue of section 249(1) of the Enterprise Act 2002; and

(c) the making of an order under Article 21 of that Order as it has effect by virtue of Article 4(1) of the Insolvency (Northern Ireland) Order 2005;

and "administration" shall be construed accordingly.

History
Regulation 15(2) amended and reg.15(4) inserted by the Financial Markets and Insolvency (Settlement Finality) (Amendment) Regulations 2009 (SI 2009/1972) reg.5 as from October 1, 2009. Regulation 15(1) amended by the Financial Markets and Insolvency (Settlement Finality and Financial Collateral Arrangements) (Amendment) Regulations 2010 (SI 2010/2993) reg.2(12) as from April 6, 2011.

16 Disclaimer of property, rescission of contracts, &c

16(1) Sections 178, 186, 315 and 345 of the Insolvency Act 1986 or Articles 152, 157, 288 and 318 of the Insolvency (Northern Ireland) Order 1989 (power to disclaim onerous property and court's power to order rescission of contracts, &c) do not apply in relation to–

(a) a transfer order; or

(b) a contract for the purpose of realising collateral security.

In the application of this paragraph in Scotland, the reference to sections 178, 315 and 345 shall be construed as a reference to any rule of law having the like effect as those sections.

16(2) In Scotland, a permanent trustee on the sequestrated estate of a defaulter or a liquidator or a trustee under a protected trust deed granted by a defaulter is bound by any transfer order given by that defaulter and by any such contract as is mentioned in paragraph (1)(b) notwithstanding section 42 of the Bankruptcy (Scotland) Act 1985 or any rule of law having the like effect applying in liquidations or any like provision or rule of law affecting the protected trust deed.

16(3) Sections 88, 127, 245 and 284 of the Insolvency Act 1986 or Articles 74, 107, 207 and 257 of the Insolvency (Northern Ireland) Order 1989 (avoidance of property dispositions effected after commencement of winding up or presentation of bankruptcy petition), section 32(8) of the Bankruptcy (Scotland) Act 1985 (effect of dealing with debtor relating to estate vested in permanent trustee) and any like provision or rule of law affecting a protected trust deed, do not apply to–

(a) a transfer order, or any disposition of property in pursuance of such an order;

(b) the provision of collateral security;

(c) a contract for the purpose of realising collateral security or any disposition of property in pursuance of such a contract; or

(d) any disposition of property in accordance with the rules of a designated system as to the application of collateral security.

History
Regulation 16(3) amended by the Financial Markets and Insolvency (Settlement Finality) (Amendment) Regulations 2009 (SI 2009/1972) reg.6 as from October 1, 2009.

17 Adjustment of prior transactions

17(1) No order shall be made in relation to a transaction to which this regulation applies under–

(a) section 238 or 339 of the Insolvency Act 1986 or Article 202 or 312 of the Insolvency (Northern Ireland) Order 1989 (transactions at an undervalue);

(b) section 239 or 340 of that Act or Article 203 or 313 of that Order (preferences); or

(c) section 423 of that Act or Article 367 of that Order (transactions defrauding creditors).

17(2)   As respects Scotland, no decree shall be granted in relation to any such transaction–

(a)   under section 34 or 36 of the Bankruptcy (Scotland) Act 1985 or section 242 or 243 of the Insolvency Act 1986 (gratuitous alienations and unfair preferences); or

(b)   at common law on grounds of gratuitous alienations or fraudulent preferences.

17(3)   This regulation applies to–

(a)   a transfer order, or any disposition of property in pursuance of such an order;

(b)   the provision of collateral security;

(c)   a contract for the purpose of realising collateral security or any disposition of property in pursuance of such a contract; or

(d)   any disposition of property in accordance with the rules of a designated system as to the application of collateral security.

Collateral security charges

18   Modifications of the law of insolvency

18   The general law of insolvency has effect in relation to a collateral security charge and the action taken to enforce such a charge, subject to the provisions of regulation 19.

19   Administration orders, &c

19(1)   The following provisions of Schedule B1 to the Insolvency Act 1986 (which relate to administration orders and administrators) do not apply in relation to a collateral security charge–

(a)   paragraph 43(2) including that provision as applied by paragraph 44; and

(b)   paragraphs 70, 71 and 72 of that Schedule;

and paragraph 41(2) of that Schedule (receiver to vacate office when so required by administrator) does not apply to a receiver appointed under such a charge.

19(1ZA)   The following provisions of the Insolvency Act 1986 (which relate to administration orders and administrators), as they have effect by virtue of section 249(1) of the Enterprise Act 2002, do not apply in relation to a collateral security charge–

(a)   sections 10(1)(b) and 11(3)(c) (restriction on enforcement of security while petition for administration order pending or order in force); and

(b)   sections 15(1) and (2) (power of administrator to deal with charged property);

and section 11(2) (receiver to vacate office when so required by administrator) does not apply to a receiver appointed under such a charge.

19(1A)   The following provisions of Schedule B1 to the Insolvency (Northern Ireland) Order 1989 (which relate to administration orders and administrators) do not apply in relation to a collateral security charge–

(a)   paragraph 44(2), including that provision as applied by paragraph 45 (restrictions on enforcement of security where company in administration or where administration application has been made); and

(b)   paragraphs 71, 72 and 73 (charged and hire purchase property);

and paragraph 42(2) (receiver to vacate office when so required by administrator) does not apply to a receiver appointed under such a charge.

19(1B)   The following provisions of the Insolvency (Northern Ireland) Order 1989 (administration), as they have effect by virtue of Article 4(1) of the Insolvency (Northern Ireland) Order 2005, do not apply in relation to a collateral security charge–

(a)   Article 23(1)(b) and Article 24(3)(c) (restriction on enforcement of security while petition for administration order pending or order in force); and

(b)   Article 28(1) and (2) (power of administrator to deal with charged property);

and Article 24(2) of that Order (receiver to vacate office at request of administrator) shall not apply to a receiver appointed under such a charge.

19(2)   However, where a collateral security charge falls to be enforced after an administration order has been made or a petition for an administration order has been presented, and there exists another charge over some or all of the same property ranking in priority to or *pari passu* with the collateral security charge, on the application of any person interested, the court may order that there shall be taken after enforcement of the collateral security charge such steps as the court may direct for the purpose of ensuring that the chargee under the other charge is not prejudiced by the enforcement of the collateral security charge.

19(2A)   A reference in paragraph (2) to **"an administration order"** shall include the appointment of an administrator under paragraph 14 or 22 of Schedule B1 to the Insolvency Act 1986 or under paragraph 15 or 23 of Schedule B1 to the Insolvency (Northern Ireland) Order 1989.

19(3)   Sections 127 and 284 of the Insolvency Act 1986 or Articles 107 and 257 of the Insolvency (Northern Ireland) Order 1989 (avoidance of property dispositions effected after commencement of winding up or presentation of bankruptcy petition), section 32(8) of the Bankruptcy (Scotland) Act 1985 (effect of dealing with debtor relating to estate vested in permanent trustee) and any like provision or rule of law affecting a protected trust deed, do not apply to a disposition of property as a result of which the property becomes subject to a collateral security charge or any transactions pursuant to which that disposition is made.

19(4)   Paragraph 20 and paragraph 12(1)(g) of Schedule A1 to the Insolvency Act 1986, and paragraph 31 and paragraph 23(1)(g) of Schedule A1 to the Insolvency (Northern Ireland) Order 1989 (effect of moratorium on creditors) shall not apply (if they would otherwise do so) to any collateral security charge.

History
Regulation 19(1A), (2A) amended by the Financial Markets and Insolvency (Settlement Finality) (Amendment) Regulations 2007 (SI 2007/832) reg.2(1), (4), (5), as from April 6, 2007. Regulation 19(1ZA), (1B), (4) inserted by the Financial Markets and Insolvency (Settlement Finality) (Amendment) Regulations 2009 (SI 2009/1972) reg.7 as from October 1, 2009.

General

20   Transfer order entered into designated system following insolvency

20(1)   This Part does not apply in relation to any transfer order given by a participant which is entered into a designated system after–

(a)   a court has made an order of a type referred to in regulation 22 in respect of–

(i)   that participant;

(ii)   a participant in a system which is an interoperable system in relation to the designated system; or

(iii)   a system operator which is not a participant in the designated system, or

(b)   that participant, a participant in a system which is an interoperable system in relation to the designated system or a system operator of that designated system has passed a creditors' voluntary winding-up resolution, or

(c)   a trust deed granted by that participant, a participant in a system which is an interoperable system in relation to the designated system or a system operator of that designated system has become a protected trust deed,

unless the conditions mentioned in paragraph (2) are satisfied.

20(2)   The conditions referred to in paragraph (1) are that–

(a)   the transfer order is carried out on the same business day of the designated system that the event specified in paragraph (1)(a), (b) or (c) occurs, and

(b)   the system operator can show that it did not have notice of that event at the time the transfer order became irrevocable.

20(3)   For the purposes of paragraph (2)(b), the relevant system operator shall be taken to have notice of an event specified in paragraph (1)(a), (b) or (c) if it deliberately failed to make enquiries as to that matter in circumstances in which a reasonable and honest person would have done so.

History
Regulation 20 amended by the Financial Markets and Insolvency (Settlement Finality and Financial Collateral Arrangements) (Amendment) Regulations 2010 (SI 2010/2993) reg.2(13) as from April 6, 2011.

21   Disapplication of certain provisions of Part VII and Part V

21(1)   The provisions of the Companies Act 1989 or the Companies (No. 2) (Northern Ireland) Order 1990 mentioned in paragraph (2) do not apply in relation to–

(a)   a market contract which is also a transfer order effected through a designated system; or

(b)   a market charge which is also a collateral security charge.

21(2)   The provisions referred to in paragraph (1) are as follows–

(a)   section 163(4) to (6) and Article 86(3) to (5) (net sum payable on completion of default proceedings);

(b)   section 164(4) to (6) and Article 87(3) to (5) (disclaimer of property, rescission of contracts, &c); and

(c)   section 175(5) and (6) and Article 97(5) and (6) (administration orders, &c).

22   Notification of insolvency order or passing of resolution for creditors' voluntary winding up

22(1)   Upon the making of an order for bankruptcy, sequestration, administration or winding up in respect of a participant in a designated system, the court shall forthwith notify both the system operator of that designated system and the designating authority that such an order has been made.

22(2)   Following receipt of–

(a)   such notification from the court, or

(b)   notification from a participant of the passing of a creditors' voluntary winding-up resolution or of a trust deed becoming a protected trust deed, pursuant to paragraph 5(4) of the Schedule,

the designating authority shall forthwith inform the Treasury of the notification.

History
Regulation 22(1) amended by the Financial Markets and Insolvency (Settlement Finality and Financial Collateral Arrangements) (Amendment) Regulations 2010 (SI 2010/2993) reg.2(14) as from April 6, 2011.

23   Applicable law relating to securities held as collateral security

23   Where–

(a)   securities (including rights in securities) are provided as collateral security to a participant, a system operator or a central bank (including any nominee, agent or third party acting on behalf of the participant, the system operator or the central bank), and

(b)   a register, account or centralised deposit system located in an EEA State legally records the entitlement of that person to the collateral security,

the rights of that person as a holder of collateral security in relation to those securities shall be governed by the law of the EEA State or, where appropriate, the law of the part of the EEA State, where the register, account, or centralised deposit system is located.

History
Regulation 23 amended by the Financial Markets and Insolvency (Settlement Finality and Financial Collateral Arrangements) (Amendment) Regulations 2010 (SI 2010/2993) reg.2(15) as from April 6, 2011.

24   Applicable law where insolvency proceedings are brought

24   Where insolvency proceedings are brought in any jurisdiction against a person who participates, or has participated, in a system designated for the purposes of the Settlement Finality Directive, any question relating to the rights and obligations arising from, or in connection with, that participation and falling to be determined by a court in England and Wales, the High Court in Northern Ireland or in Scotland shall (subject to regulation 23) be determined in accordance with the law governing that system.

25   Insolvency proceedings in other jurisdictions

25(1)   The references to insolvency law in section 426 of the Insolvency Act 1986 (co-operation between courts exercising jurisdiction in relation to insolvency) include, in relation to a part of the United Kingdom, this Part and, in relation to a relevant country or territory within the meaning of that section, so much of the law of that country or territory as corresponds to this Part.

25(2)   A court shall not, in pursuance of that section or any other enactment or rule of law, recognise or give effect to–

(a)   any order of a court exercising jurisdiction in relation to insolvency law in a country or territory outside the United Kingdom, or

(b)   any act of a person appointed in such a country or territory to discharge any functions under insolvency law,

in so far as the making of the order or the doing of the act would be prohibited in the case of a court in England and Wales or Scotland, the High Court in Northern Ireland or a relevant office-holder by this Part.

25(3)   Paragraph (2) does not affect the recognition or enforcement of a judgment required to be recognised or enforced under or by virtue of the Civil Jurisdiction and Judgments Act 1982 or Council Regulation(EC) No.44/2001 of 22nd December 2000 on jurisdiction and the recognition and enforcement of judgments in civil and commercial matters, as amended from time to time and as applied by the Agreement made on 19th October 2005 between the European Community and the Kingdom of Denmark on jurisdiction and the recognition and enforcement of judgments in civil and commercial matters.

History
Paragraph (3) amended by the Civil Jurisdiction and Judgments Regulations 2007 (SI 2007/1655) reg.5 and Sch. para.32 as from July 1, 2007.

26   Systems designated in other EEA States and Gibraltar

26(1)   Where an equivalent overseas order or equivalent overseas security is subject to the insolvency law of England and Wales or Scotland or Northern Ireland, this Part shall apply–

(a)   in relation to the equivalent overseas order as it applies in relation to a transfer order; and

(b)   in relation to the equivalent overseas security as it applies in relation to collateral security.

26(2)   In paragraph (1)–

(a)   **"equivalent overseas order"** means an order having the like effect as a transfer order which is effected through a system designated for the purposes of the Settlement Finality Directive in another EEA State or Gibraltar; and

(b)   **"equivalent overseas security"** means any realisable assets provided under a charge or a repurchase or similar agreement, or otherwise (including credit claims and money provided under a charge)–

(i)   for the purpose of securing rights and obligations potentially arising in connection with such a system, or

(ii)   to a central bank for the purpose of securing rights and obligations in connection with its operations in carrying out its functions as a central bank.

History
Regulation 26 amended by the Financial Markets and Insolvency (Settlement Finality and Financial Collateral Arrangements) (Amendment) Regulations 2010 (SI 2010/2993) reg.2(16) as from April 6, 2011.

SCHEDULE

REQUIREMENTS FOR DESIGNATION OF SYSTEM

Regulation 4(1)

1   Establishment, participation and governing law

1(1)   The head office of at least one of the participants in the system must be in the United Kingdom and the law of England and Wales, Northern Ireland or Scotland must be the governing law of the system.

1(2)   There must be not less than three institutions participating in the system, unless otherwise determined by the designating authority in any case where–

(a)   there are two institutions participating in a system; and

(b)   the designating authority considers that designation is required on the grounds of systemic risk.

1(3)   The system must be a system through which transfer orders are effected.

1(4)   Where orders relating to financial instruments other than securities are effected through the system–

(a)   the system must primarily be a system through which securities transfer orders are effected; and

(b)   the designating authority must consider that designation is required on grounds of systemic risk.

1(5)   An arrangement entered into between interoperable systems shall not constitute a system.

2   Arrangements and resources

2   The system must have adequate arrangements and resources for the effective monitoring and enforcement of compliance with its rules or, as respects monitoring, arrangements providing for that function to be performed on its behalf (and without affecting its responsibility) by another body or person who is able and willing to perform it.

3   Financial resources

3   The system operator must have financial resources sufficient for the proper performance of its functions as a system operator.

4   Co-operation with other authorities

4   The system operator must be able and willing to co-operate, by the sharing of information and otherwise, with–

(a)   the Financial Services Authority,

(b)   the Bank of England,

(c)   any relevant office-holder, and

(d)   any authority, body or person having responsibility for any matter arising out of, or connected with, the default of a participant.

5   Specific provision in the rules

5(1)   The rules of the system must–

(a)   specify the point at which a transfer order takes effect as having been entered into the system,

(b)   specify the point after which a transfer order may not be revoked by a participant or any other party, and

(c)   prohibit the revocation by a participant or any other party of a transfer order from the point specified in accordance with paragraph (b).

5(1A)   Where the system has one or more interoperable systems, the rules required under paragraph (1)(a) and (b) shall, as far as possible, be co-ordinated with the rules of those interoperable systems.

5(1B)   The rules of the system which are referred to in paragraph (1)(a) and (b) shall not be affected by any rules of that system's interoperable systems in the absence of express provision in the rules of the system and all of those interoperable systems.

5(2)   The rules of the system must require each institution which participates in the system to provide upon payment of a reasonable charge the information mentioned in sub-paragraph (3) to any person who requests it, save where the request is frivolous or vexatious. The rules must require the information to be provided within fourteen days of the request being made.

5(3)   The information referred to in sub-paragraph (2) is as follows–

(a)   details of the systems which are designated for the purposes of the Settlement Finality Directive in which the institution participates, and

(b)   information about the main rules governing the functioning of those systems.

5(4)   The rules of the system must require each participant upon–

(a)   the passing of a creditors' voluntary winding up resolution, or

(b)   a trust deed granted by him becoming a protected trust deed,

to notify forthwith both the system and the designating authority that such a resolution has been passed, or, as the case may be, that such a trust deed has become a protected trust deed.

6   Default arrangements

6   The system must have default arrangements which are appropriate for that system in all the circumstances.

History

Paragraphs 1, 3–5 amended by the Financial Markets and Insolvency (Settlement Finality and Financial Collateral Arrangements) (Amendment) Regulations 2010 (SI 2010/2993) reg.2(17) as from April 6, 2011.

Limited Liability Partnerships (Scotland) Regulations 2001

(Scottish SI 2001/128)

Made on 28 March 2001 by the Scottish Ministers under ss.14(1) and (2), 15, 16 and 17(1) and (3) of the Limited Liability Partnerships Act 2000. Operative from 6 April 2001.

[**Note**: Changes made by the Limited Liability Partnerships (Scotland) Amendment Regulations 2009 (SSI 2009/310) have been incorporated into the text.]

PART I

CITATION, COMMENCEMENT, EXTENT AND INTERPRETATION

1 Citation, commencement and extent

1(1) These Regulations may be cited as the Limited Liability Partnerships (Scotland) Regulations 2001 and shall come into force on 6th April 2001.

1(2) These Regulations extend to Scotland only.

2 Interpretation

2 In these Regulations–

"the 1985 Act" means the Companies Act 1985;

"the 1986 Act" means the Insolvency Act 1986;

"limited liability partnership agreement", in relation to a limited liability partnership, means any agreement, express or implied, made between the members of the limited liability partnership or between the limited liability partnership and the members of the limited liability partnership which determines the mutual rights and duties of the members, and their rights and duties in relation to the limited liability partnership;

"the principal Act" means the Limited Liability Partnerships Act 2000; and

"shadow member", in relation to a limited liability partnership, means a person in accordance with whose directions or instructions the members of the limited liability partnership are accustomed to act (but so that a person is not deemed a shadow member by reason only that the members of the limited liability partnership act on advice given by that person in a professional capacity).

PART II

COMPANIES ACT

3 Application of the 1985 Act to limited liability partnerships

3 The provisions of the 1985 Act specified in the first column of Schedule 1 to these Regulations shall apply to limited liability partnerships, with the following modifications–

(a) references to a company shall include references to a limited liability partnership;

(b) references to the Companies Acts shall include references to the principal Act and any regulations made thereunder;

(c) references to the 1986 Act shall include references to that Act as it applies to limited liability partnerships by virtue of Part III of these Regulations;

910

(d) references in a provision of the 1985 Act to other provisions of that Act shall include references to those other provisions as they apply to limited liability partnerships by virtue of these Regulations; and

(e) the modifications, if any, specified in the second column of Schedule 1 of the provision specified opposite them in the first column.

Part III

Winding Up and Insolvency

4 Application of the 1986 Act to limited liability partnerships

4(1) Subject to paragraph (2), the provisions of the 1986 Act listed in Schedule 2 shall apply in relation to limited liability partnerships as they apply in relation to companies.

4(2) The provisions of the 1986 Act referred to in paragraph (1) shall so apply, with the following modifications–

(a) references to a company shall include references to a limited liability partnership;

(b) references to a director or to an officer of a company shall include references to a member of a limited liability partnership;

(c) references to a shadow director shall include references to a shadow member;

(d) references to the 1985 Act, the Company Directors Disqualification Act 1986, the Companies Act 1989 or to any provisions of those Acts or to any provisions of the 1986 Act shall include references to those Acts or provisions as they apply to limited liability partnerships by virtue of the principal Act or these Regulations; and

(e) the modifications set out in Schedule 3 to these Regulations.

Part IV

Miscellaneous

5 General and consequential amendments

5 The enactments referred to in Schedule 4 shall have effect subject to the amendments specified in that Schedule.

6 Application of subordinate legislation

6(1) The Insolvency (Scotland) Rules 1986 shall apply to limited liability partnerships with such modifications as the context requires for the purpose of giving effect to the provisions of the Insolvency Act 1986 which are applied by these Regulations.

6(2) In the case of any conflict between any provision of the subordinate legislation applied by paragraph (1) and any provision of these Regulations, the latter shall prevail.

SCHEDULE 1

MODIFICATIONS TO PROVISIONS OF THE 1985 ACT

Regulation 3

Formalities of Carrying on Business	
36B (execution of documents by companies)	
Floating Charges and Receivers (Scotland)	
462 (power of incorporated company to create floating charge)	In subsection (1), for the words "an incorporated company (whether a company within the meaning of this Act or not)," substitute "a limited liability partnership", and the words "(including uncalled capital)" are omitted.
463 (effect of floating charge on winding up)	
466 (alteration of floating charges) Subsections (1), (2), (3) and (6)	
486 (interpretation for Part XVIII generally)	For the definition of "company" substitute ""company" means a limited liability partnership;"
487 (extent of Part XVIII)	

SCHEDULE 2

PROVISIONS OF THE 1986 ACT

Regulation 4(1)

The relevant provisions of the 1986 Act are as follows:

Sections 50 to 52;

Section 53(1) and (2), to the extent that those subsections do not relate to the requirement for a copy of the instrument and notice being delivered to the registrar of companies;

Section 53(4), (6) and (7);

Section 54(1), (2), (3) (to the extent that that subsection does not relate to the requirement for a copy of the interlocutor to be delivered to the registrar of companies), and subsections (5), (6) and (7);

Sections 55 to 58;

Section 60, other than subsection (1);

Section 61, including subsections (6) and (7) to the extent that those subsections do not relate to anything to be done or which may be sent to the registrar of companies;

Section 62, including subsection (5) to the extent that that subsection does not relate to anything to be done or which may be sent to the registrar of companies;

Sections 63 to 66;

Section 67, including subsections (1) and (8) to the extent that those subsections do not relate to anything to be sent to the registrar of companies;

Section 68;

Section 69, including subsections (1) and (2) to the extent that those subsections do not relate to anything to be done or which may be done by the registrar of companies;

Sections 70 and 71;

Subsection 84(3) to the extent that it does not concern the copy of the resolution being forwarded to the registrar of companies within 15 days;

Sections 91 to 93;

Section 94, including subsections (3) and (4) to the extent that those subsections do not relate to the liquidator being required to send to the registrar of companies a copy of the account and a return of the final meeting;

Section 95;

Section 97;

Sections 100 to 102;

Sections 104 to 105;

Section 106, including subsections (3), (4) and (5) to the extent that those subsections do not relate to the liquidator being required to send to the registrar of companies a copy of the account of winding up and a return of the final meeting/quorum;

Sections 109 to 111;

Section 112, including subsection (3) to the extent that that subsection does not relate to the liquidator being required to send to the registrar of companies a copy of the order made by the court;

Sections 113 to 115;

Sections 126 to 128;

Section 130(1) to the extent that that subsection does not relate to a copy of the order being forwarded by the court to the registrar of companies;

Section 131;

Sections 133 to 135;

Sections 138 to 140;

Sections 142 to 146;

Section 147, including subsection (3) to the extent that that subsection does not relate to a copy of the order being forwarded by the company to the registrar of companies;

Section 162 to the extent that the section concerns the matters set out in Section C.2 of Schedule 5 to the Scotland Act 1998 as being exceptions to the reservation of insolvency;

Sections 163 to 167;

Section 169;

Section 170, including subsection (2) to the extent that that subsection does not relate to an application being made by the registrar to make good the default;

Section 171;

Section 172, including subsection (8) to the extent that that subsection does not relate to the liquidator being required to give notice to the registrar of companies;

Sections 173 and 174;

Section 177;

Sections 185 to 189;

Sections 191 to 194;

Section 196;

Section 199;

Section 200;

Sections 206 to 215;

Section 218 subsections (1), (2), (4) and (6);

Sections 231 to 232 to the extent that the sections apply to administrative receivers, liquidators and provisional liquidators;

Section 233 to the extent that that section applies in the case of the appointment of an administrative receiver, of a voluntary arrangement taking effect, of a company going into liquidation or where a provisional liquidator is appointed;

Section 234 to the extent that that section applies to situations other than those where an administration has been entered into;

Section 235 to the extent that that section applies to situations other than those where an administration has been entered into;

Sections 236 to 237 to the extent that those sections apply to situations other than administrations entered into and winding up;

Sections 242 to 243;

Section 244 to the extent that that section applies in circumstances other than a company which has entered into administration;

Section 245;

Section 251;

Section 416(1) and (4) to the extent that those subsections apply to section 206(1)(a) and (b) in connection with the offence provision relating to the winding up of a limited liability partnership;

Section 430;

Section 436;

Schedule 2;

Schedule 3;

Schedule 4;

Schedule 8 to the extent that that Schedule does not apply to voluntary arrangements or administrations within the meaning of Parts I and II of the 1986 Act;

Schedule 10 to the extent that it refers to any of the sections referred to above.

SCHEDULE 3

MODIFICATIONS TO PROVISIONS OF THE 1986 ACT

Regulation 4(2)

Provisions	Modifications
Section 84 (circumstances in which company may be wound up voluntarily)	
Subsection (3)	For subsection (3) substitute the following— "(3) Within 15 days after a limited liability partnership has determined that it be wound up there shall be forwarded to the registrar of companies either a printed copy or a copy in some other form approved by the registrar of the determination." After subsection (3) insert a new subsection—
Subsection (3A)	"(3A) If a limited liability partnership fails to comply with this regulation the limited liability partnership and every designated member of it who is in default is liable on summary conviction to a fine not exceeding level 3 on the standard scale."
Section 91 (appointment of liquidator)	
Subsection (1)	Delete "in general meeting".
Subsection (2)	For subsection (2) substitute the following— "(2) On the appointment of a liquidator the powers of the members of the limited liability partnership shall cease except to the extent that a meeting of the members of the limited liability partnership summoned for the purpose or the liquidator sanctions their continuance." After subsection (2) insert— "(3) Subsections (3) and (4) of section 92 shall apply for the purposes of this section as they apply for the purposes of that section."
Section 92 (power to fill vacancy in office of liquidator)	
Subsection (1)	For "the company in general meeting" substitute "a meeting of the members of the limited liability partnership summoned for the purpose".
Subsection (2)	For "a general meeting" substitute "a meeting of the members of the limited liability partnership".
Subsection (3)	In subsection (3), for "articles" substitute "limited liability partnership agreement".
new subsection (4)	Add a new subsection (4) as follows— "(4) The quorum required for a meeting of the members of the limited liability partnership shall be any quorum required by the limited liability partnership agreement for meetings of the members of the limited liability partnership and if no requirement for a quorum has been agreed upon the quorum shall be 2 members."
Section 93 (general company meeting at each year's end)	
subsection (1)	For "a general meeting of the company" substitute "a meeting of the members of the limited liability partnership".

Provisions	Modifications
new subsection (4)	Add a new subsection (4) as follows— "(4) Subsections (3) and (4) of section 92 shall apply for the purposes of this section as they apply for the purposes of that section."
Section 94 (final meeting prior to dissolution)	
subsection (1)	For "a general meeting of the company" substitute "a meeting of the members of the limited liability partnership".
new subsection 5(A)	Add a new subsection (5A) as follows— "(5A) Subsections (3) and (4) of section 92 shall apply for the purposes of this section as they apply for the purposes of that section."
subsection (6)	For "a general meeting of the company" substitute "a meeting of the members of the limited liability partnership".
Section 95 (effect of company's insolvency)	
subsection (1)	For "directors" substitute "designated members".
subsection (7)	For subsection (7) substitute the following— "(7) In this section 'the relevant period' means the period of 6 months immediately preceding the date on which the limited liability partnership determined that it be wound up voluntarily."
Section 100 (appointment of liquidator)	
subsection (1)	For "The creditors and the company at their respective meetings mentioned in section 98" substitute "The creditors at their meeting mentioned in section 98 and the limited liability partnership".
subsection (3)	Delete "director,".
Section 101 (appointment of liquidation committee)	
subsection (2)	For subsection (2) substitute the following— "(2) If such a committee is appointed, the limited liability partnership may, when it determines that it be wound up voluntarily or at any time thereafter, appoint such number of persons as they think fit to act as members of the committee, not exceeding 5."
Section 105 (meetings of company and creditors at each year's end)	
subsection (1)	For "a general meeting of the company" substitute "a meeting of the members of the limited liability partnership".
new subsection (5)	Add a new subsection (5) as follows— "(5) Subsections (3) and (4) of section 92 shall apply for the purposes of this section as they apply for the purposes of that section."
Section 106 (final meeting prior to dissolution)	
subsection (1)	For "a general meeting of the company" substitute "a meeting of the members of the limited liability partnership".
new subsection (5A)	After subsection (5) insert a new subsection (5A) as follows— "(5A) Subsections (3) and (4) of section 92 shall apply for the purposes of this section as they apply for the purposes of that section."

Provisions	Modifications
subsection (6)	For "a general meeting of the company" substitute "a meeting of the members of the limited liability partnership".
Section 110 (acceptance of shares, etc, as consideration for sale of company property)	
	For the existing section substitute the following:
	"(1) This section applies, in the case of a limited liability partnership proposed to be, or being, wound up voluntarily, where the whole or part of the limited liability partnership's business or property is proposed to be transferred or sold to another company whether or not it is a company within the meaning of the Companies Act ("the transferee company") or to a limited liability partnership ("the transferee limited liability partnership").
	(2) With the requisite sanction, the liquidator of the limited liability partnership being, or proposed to be, wound up ("the transferor limited liability partnership") may receive, in compensation or part compensation for the transfer or sale, shares, policies or other like interests in the transferee company or the transferee limited liability partnership for distribution among the members of the transferor limited liability partnership.
	(3) The sanction required under subsection (2) is—
	(a) in the case of a members' voluntary winding up, that of a determination of the limited liability partnership at a meeting of the members of the limited liability partnership conferring either a general authority on the liquidator or an authority in respect of any particular arrangement, (subsections (3) and (4) of section 92 to apply for this purpose as they apply for the purposes of that section), and
	(b) in the case of a creditor's voluntary winding up, that of either court or the liquidation committee.
	(4) Alternatively to subsection (2), the liquidator may (with the sanction) enter into any other arrangement whereby the members of the transferor limited liability partnership may, in lieu of receiving cash, shares, policies or other like interests (or in addition thereto), participate in the profits, or receive any other benefit from the transferee company or the transferee limited liability partnership.
	(5) A sale or arrangement in pursuance of this section is binding on members of the transferor limited liability partnership.
	(6) A determination by the limited liability partnership is not invalid for the purposes of this section by reason that it is made before or concurrently with a determination by the limited liability partnership that it be wound up voluntarily or for appointing liquidators; but, if an order is made within a year for winding up the limited liability partnership by the court, the determination by the limited liability partnership is not valid unless sanctioned by the court."
Section 111 (dissent from arrangement under section 110)	
subsections (1)–(3)	For subsections (1)–(3) substitute the following—
	"(1) This section applies in the case of a voluntary winding up where, for the purposes of section 110(2) or (4), a determination of the limited liability partnership has provided the sanction requisite for the liquidator under that section.

Provisions	Modifications
	(2) If a member of the transferor limited liability partnership who did not vote in a favour of providing the sanction required for the liquidator under section 110 expresses his dissent from it in writing addressed to the liquidator and left at the registered office of the limited liability partnership within 7 days after the date on which that sanction was given, he may require the liquidator either to abstain from carrying the arrangement so sanctioned into effect or to purchase his interest at a price to be determined by agreement or arbitration under this section. (3) If the liquidator elects to purchase the member's interest, the purchase money must be paid before the limited liability partnership is dissolved and be raised by the liquidator in such manner as may be determined by the limited liability partnership."
subsection (4)	Omit subsection (4).
Section 126 (power to stay or restrain proceedings against company)	
subsection (2)	Delete subsection (2).
Section 127 (avoidance of property dispositions, etc)	
	For "any transfer of shares" substitute "any transfer by a member of the limited liability partnership of his interest in the property of the limited liability partnership".
Section 165 (voluntary winding up)	
subsection (2)	In paragraph (a) for "an extraordinary resolution of the company" substitute "a determination by a meeting of the members of the limited liability partnership".
subsection (4)	For paragraph (c) substitute the following— "(c) summon meetings of the members of the limited liability partnership for the purpose of obtaining their sanction or for any other purpose he may think fit."
new subsection (4A)	Insert a new subsection (4A) as follows— "(4A) Subsections (3) and (4) of section 92 shall apply for the purposes of this section as they apply for the purposes of that section."
Section 166 (creditors' voluntary winding up)	
subsection (5)	In paragraph (b) for "directors" substitute "designated members".
Section 171 (removal, etc (voluntary winding up))	
subsection (2)	For paragraph (a) substitute the following— "(a) in the case of a members' voluntary winding up, by a meeting of the members of the limited liability partnership summoned specially for that purpose, or".
subsection (6)	In paragraph (a) for "final meeting of the company" substitute "final meeting of the members of the limited liability partnership" and in paragraph (b) for "final meetings of the company" substitute "final meetings of the members of the limited liability partnership".
new subsection (7)	Insert a new subsection (7) as follows— "(7) Subsections (3) and (4) of section 92 apply for the purposes of this section as they apply for the purposes of that section."

Provisions	Modifications
Section 173 (release (voluntary winding up))	
subsection (2)	In paragraph (a) for "a general meeting of the company" substitute "a meeting of the members of the limited liability partnership".
Section 187 (power to make over assets to employees)	
	Delete section 187
Section 194 (resolutions passed at adjourned meetings)	
	After "contributories" insert "or of the members of a limited liability partnership".
Section 206 (fraud, etc in anticipation of winding up)	
subsection (1)	For "passes a resolution for voluntary winding up" substitute "makes a determination that it be wound up voluntarily".
Section 207 (transactions in fraud of creditors)	
subsection (1)	For "passes a resolution for voluntary winding up" substitute "makes a determination that it be wound up voluntarily".
Section 210 (material omissions from statement relating to company's affairs)	
subsection (2)	For "passed a resolution for voluntary winding up" substitute "made a determination that it be wound up voluntarily".
Section 214 (wrongful trading)	
subsection (2)	Delete from "but the court shall not" to the end of the subsection.
After section 214	Insert the following new section 214A
"Adjustment of withdrawals
214A(1) This section has effect in relation to a person who is or has been a member of a limited liability partnership where, in the course of the winding up of that limited liability partnership, it appears that subsection (2) of this section applies in relation to that person.
(2) This subsection applies in relation to a person if—
(a) within the period of two years ending with the commencement of the winding up, he was a member of the limited liability partnership who withdrew property of the limited liability partnership, whether in the form of a share of profits, salary, repayment of or payment of interest on a loan to the limited liability partnership or any other withdrawal of property, and
(b) it is proved by the liquidator to the satisfaction of the court that at the time of the withdrawal he knew or had reasonable grounds for believing that the limited liability partnership—
(i) was at the time of the withdrawal unable to pay its debts within the meaning of section 123 of the Act, or
(ii) would become so unable to pay its debts after the assets of the limited liability partnership had been depleted by that withdrawal taken together with all other withdrawals (if any) made by any members contemporaneously with that withdrawal or in contemplation when that withdrawal was made.

Provisions	Modifications
	(3) Where this section has effect in relation to any person the court, on the application of the liquidator, may declare that that person is to be liable to make such contribution (if any) to the limited liability partnership's assets as the court thinks proper.

(4) The court shall not make a declaration in relation to any person the amount of which exceeds the aggregate of the amounts or values of all the withdrawals referred to in subsection (2) made by that person within the period of 2 years referred to in that subsection.

(5) The court shall not make a declaration under this section with respect to any person unless that person knew or ought to have concluded that after each withdrawal referred to in subsection (2) there was no reasonable prospect that the limited liability partnership would avoid going into insolvent liquidation.

(6) For the purposes of subsection (5) the facts which a member ought to know or ascertain, the conclusions which he ought to reach and the steps which he ought to have taken are those which would be known or ascertained, or reached or taken, by a reasonably diligent person having both:

    (a) the general knowledge, skill and experience that may reasonably be expected of a person carrying out the same functions as are carried out by that member in relation to the limited liability partnership, and

    (b) the general knowledge, skill and experience that that member has.

(7) For the purposes of this section a limited liability partnership goes into insolvent liquidation if it goes into liquidation at a time when its assets are insufficient for the payment of its debts and other liabilities and the expenses of the winding up.

(8) In this section "member" includes a shadow member.

(9) This section is without prejudice to section 214." |
Section 215 (proceedings under ss 213, 214)	
subsection (1)	Omit the word "or" between the words "213" and "214" and insert after "214" "or 214A".
subsection (2)	For "either section" substitute "any of those sections".
subsection (4)	For "either section" substitute "any of those sections".
subsection (5)	For "Sections 213 and 214" substitute "Sections 213, 214 or 214A".
Section 218 (prosecution of delinquent officers and members of company)	
subsection (1)	For "officer, or any member, of the company" substitute "member of the limited liability partnership"
subsections (4) and (6)	For "officer of the company, or any member of it," substitute "officer or member of the limited liability partnership".
subsection (4)	For paragraph (c) substitute the following—

    "(c) the date on which the voluntary arrangement took effect in accordance with section 5". |
| Section 251 (expressions used generally) | |
| | Delete the word "and" appearing after the definition of "the rules" and insert the word "and" after the definition of "shadow director". |

Provisions	Modifications
	After the definition of "shadow director" insert the following—
	" "shadow member", in relation to a limited liability partnership, means a person in accordance with whose directions or instructions the members of the limited liability partnership are accustomed to act (but so that a person is not deemed a shadow member by reason only that the members of the limited liability partnership act on advice given by him in a professional capacity);"
Section 416 (monetary limits (companies winding up))	
subsection (1)	In subsection (1), omit the words "section 117(2) (amount of company's share capital determining whether county court has jurisdiction to wind it up);" and the words "section 120(3) (the equivalent as respects sheriff court jurisdiction in Scotland);".
Section 436 (expressions used generally)	
	The following expressions and definitions shall be added to the section—
	"designated member" has the same meaning as it has in the Limited Liability Partnerships Act 2000;
	"limited liability partnership" means a limited liability partnership formed and registered under the Limited Liability Partnership Act 2000;
	"limited liability partnership agreement", in relation to a limited liability partnership, means any agreement, express or implied, made between the members of the limited liability partnership or between the limited liability partnership and the members of the limited liability partnership which determines the mutual rights and duties of the members, and their rights and duties in relation to the limited liability partnership.
Schedule 2	
Paragraph 17	For paragraph 17 substitute the following— "**17.** Power to enforce any rights the limited liability partnership has against the members under the terms of the limited liability partnership agreement"
Schedule 10	
Section 93(3)	In the entry relating to section 93(3) for "general meeting of the company" substitute "meeting of members of the limited liability partnership".
Section 105(3)	In the entry relating to section 105(3) for "company general meeting" substitute "meeting of the members of the limited liability partnership".
Section 106(6)	In the entry relating to section 106(6) for "company" substitute "the members of the limited liability partnership"

History
The entry relating to s.84 amended and that to s.233 omitted by the Limited Liability Partnerships (Scotland) Amendment Regulations 2009 (SSI 2009/310) reg.4 and Sch.2 as from October 1, 2009.

SCHEDULE 4

GENERAL AND CONSEQUENTIAL AMENDMENTS IN OTHER LEGISLATION

Regulation 5

[Not reproduced.]

Limited Liability Partnerships Regulations 2001

(SI 2001/1090)

Made on 19 March 2001 by the Secretary of State under ss.14, 15, 16 and 17 of the Limited Liability Partnerships Act 2000. Operative from 6 April 2001.

[**Note:** Changes made by the Financial Services and Markets Act 2000 (Consequential Amendments) Order 2004 (SI 2004/355), the Limited Liability Partnerships (Amendment) Regulations 2005 (SI 2005/1989) (in this latter case, minor amendments to Sch.3 have been made without annotation), the Limited Liability Partnerships (Amendment) Regulations 2007 (SI 2007/2073), the Limited Liability Partnerships (Accounts and Audit) (Application of Companies Act 2006) Regulations 2008 (SI 2008/1911), the Limited Liability Partnerships (Application of Companies Act 2006) Regulations 2009 (SI 2009/1804) and the Companies Act 2006 (Consequential Amendments, Transitional Provisions and Savings) Order 2009 (SI 2009/1941) have been incorporated into the text (in the case of pre-2003 legislation without annotation). Note also that the Companies Act 2006 (Commencement No.3, Consequential Amendments, Transitional Provisions and Savings) Order 2007 (SI 2007/2194 (C. 84)) art.12(2) provides that "nothing in this order affects any provision of the 1985 Act [CA 1985]…as applied by the Limited Liability Partnership Regulations 2001…to limited liability partnerships"—i.e. the old law is kept alive for LLPs.]

PART I

CITATION, COMMENCEMENT AND INTERPRETATION

1 Citation and commencement

1 These Regulations may be cited as the Limited Liability Partnerships Regulations 2001 and shall come into force on 6th April 2001.

2 Interpretation

2 In these Regulations–

"**the 1985 Act**" means the Companies Act 1985;

"**the 1986 Act**" means the Insolvency Act 1986;

"**the 2000 Act**" means the Financial Services and Markets Act 2000;

"**devolved**", in relation to the provisions of the 1986 Act, means the provisions of the 1986 Act which are listed in Schedule 4 and, in their application to Scotland, concern wholly or partly, matters which are set out in Section C.2 of Schedule 5 to the Scotland Act 1998 as being exceptions to the reservations made in that Act in the field of insolvency;

"**limited liability partnership agreement**", in relation to a limited liability partnership, means any agreement express or implied between the members of the limited liability partnership or between the limited liability partnership and the members of the limited liability partnership which determines the mutual rights and duties of the members, and their rights and duties in relation to the limited liability partnership;

"**the principal Act**" means the Limited Liability Partnerships Act 2000; and

"**shadow member**", in relation to limited liability partnerships, means a person in accordance with whose directions or instructions the members of the limited liability partnership are accustomed to act (but so that a person is not deemed a shadow member by reason only that the members of the limited partnership act on advice given by him in a professional capacity).

2A   Application of provisions

2A(1)   The provisions of these Regulations applying–

(a) the Company Directors Disqualification Act 1986, or

(b) provisions of the Insolvency Act 1986, have effect only in relation to limited liability partnerships registered in Great Britain.

2A(2)   The other provisions of these Regulations have effect in relation to limited liability partnerships registered in any part of the United Kingdom.

History

Regulation 2A inserted by the Limited Liability Partnerships (Application of Companies Act 2006) Regulations 2009 (SI 2009/1804) Sch.3 Pt 2 para.13(1), (2) as from October 1, 2009.

PART II

ACCOUNTS AND AUDIT

3   Application of the accounts and audit provisions of the 1985 Act to limited liability partnerships

3   [Revoked by the Limited Liability Partnerships (Accounts and Audit) (Application of Companies Act 2006) Regulations 2008 (SI 2008/1911) reg.58 as from October 1, 2008.]

PART III

COMPANIES ACT 1985 AND COMPANY DIRECTORS DISQUALIFICATION ACT 1986

4   Application of certain provisions of the 1985 Act and of the provisions of the Company Directors Disqualification Act 1986 to limited liability partnerships

4(1)   The provisions of the 1985 Act specified in the first column of Part I of Schedule 2 to these Regulations shall apply to limited liability partnerships, except where the context otherwise requires, with the following modifications–

(a) references to a company shall include references to a limited liability partnership;

(b) [Omitted.]

(c) references to the Insolvency Act 1986 shall include references to that Act as it applies to limited liability partnerships by virtue of Part IV of these Regulations;

(d) references in a provision of the 1985 Act to–

(i) other provisions of that Act, or

(ii) provisions of the Companies Act 2006,

shall include references to those provisions as they apply to limited liability partnerships;

(e), (f) [Omitted.]

(g) references to a director of a company or to an officer of a company shall include references to a member of a limited liability partnership;

(h) the modifications, if any, specified in the second column of Part I of Schedule 2 opposite the provision specified in the first column; and

(i) such further modifications as the context requires for the purpose of giving effect to that legislation as applied by these Regulations.

4(2)   The provisions of the Company Directors Disqualification Act 1986 shall apply to limited liability partnerships, except where the context otherwise requires, with the following modifications–

   (a)   references to a company shall include references to a limited liability partnership;

   (b)   references to the Companies Acts shall include references to the principal Act and regulations made thereunder and references to the companies legislation shall include references to the principal Act, regulations made thereunder and to any enactment applied by regulations to limited liability partnerships;

   (d)   references to the Insolvency Act 1986 shall include references to that Act as it applies to limited liability partnerships by virtue of Part IV of these Regulations;

   (e)   [Omitted by the Companies Act 2006 (Consequential Amendments, Transitional Provisions and Savings) Order 2009 (SI 2009/1941) art.2(1) and Sch.1 para.192(2), as from October 1, 2009.]

   (f)   references to a shadow director shall include references to a shadow member;

   (g)   references to a director of a company or to an officer of a company shall include references to a member of a limited liability partnership;

   (h)   the modifications, if any, specified in the second column of Part II of Schedule 2 opposite the provision specified in the first column; and

   (i)   such further modifications as the context requires for the purpose of giving effect to that legislation as applied by these Regulations.

History

Regulation 4 (heading) amended, reg.4(1)(b), (e), (f) omitted and reg.4(1)(d) substituted by the Limited Liability Partnerships (Application of Companies Act 2006) Regulations 2009 (SI 2009/1804) Sch.3 Pt 2 para.13(3) and the Companies Act 2006 (Consequential Amendments, Transitional Provisions and Savings) Order 2009 (SI 2009/1941) Sch.1 para.192(2) as from October 1, 2009.

PART IV

WINDING UP AND INSOLVENCY

5   Application of the 1986 Act to limited liability partnerships

5(1)   Subject to paragraphs (2) and (3), the following provisions of the 1986 Act, shall apply to limited liability partnerships–

   (a)   Parts I, II, III, IV, VI and VII of the First Group of Parts (company insolvency; companies winding up),

   (b)   the Third Group of Parts (miscellaneous matters bearing on both company and individual insolvency; general interpretation; final provisions).

5(2)   The provisions of the 1986 Act referred to in paragraph (1) shall apply to limited liability partnerships, except where the context otherwise requires, with the following modifications–

   (a)   references to a company shall include references to a limited liability partnership;

   (b)   references to a director or to an officer of a company shall include references to a member of a limited liability partnership;

   (c)   references to a shadow director shall include references to a shadow member;

   (d)   references to the Companies Acts, the Company Directors Disqualification Act 1986, the Companies Act 1989 or to any provisions of those Acts or to any provisions of the 1986 Act shall include references to those Acts or provisions as they apply to limited liability partnerships by virtue of the principal Act;

   (e)   references to the articles of association of a company shall include references to the limited liability partnership agreement of a limited liability partnership;

(f)   the modifications set out in Schedule 3 to these Regulations; and

(g)   such further modifications as the context requires for the purpose of giving effect to that legislation as applied by these Regulations.

5(3)   In the application of this regulation to Scotland, the provisions of the 1986 Act referred to in paragraph (1) shall not include the provisions listed in Schedule 4 to the extent specified in that Schedule.

PART V

FINANCIAL SERVICES AND MARKETS

6   Application of provisions contained in Parts XV and XXIV of the 2000 Act to limited liability partnerships

6(1)   Subject to paragraph (2), sections 215(3),(4) and (6), 356, 359(1) to (4), 361 to 365, 367, 370 and 371 of the 2000 Act shall apply to limited liability partnerships.

6(2)   The provisions of the 2000 Act referred to in paragraph (1) shall apply to limited liability partnerships, except where the context otherwise requires, with the following modifications–

(a)   references to a company shall include references to a limited liability partnership;

(b)   references to body shall include references to a limited liability partnership; and

(c)   references to the 1985 Act, the 1986 Act or to any of the provisions of those Acts shall include references to those Acts or provisions as they apply to limited liability partnerships by virtue of the principal Act.

PART VI

DEFAULT PROVISION

7   Default provision for limited liability partnerships

7   The mutual rights and duties of the members and the mutual rights and duties of the limited liability partnership and the members shall be determined, subject to the provisions of the general law and to the terms of any limited liability partnership agreement, by the following rules:

7(1)   All the members of a limited liability partnership are entitled to share equally in the capital and profits of the limited liability partnership.

7(2)   The limited liability partnership must indemnify each member in respect of payments made and personal liabilities incurred by him–

(a)   in the ordinary and proper conduct of the business of the limited liability partnership; or

(b)   in or about anything necessarily done for the preservation of the business or property of the limited liability partnership.

7(3)   Every member may take part in the management of the limited liability partnership.

7(4)   No member shall be entitled to remuneration for acting in the business or management of the limited liability partnership.

7(5)   No person may be introduced as a member or voluntarily assign an interest in a limited liability partnership without the consent of all existing members.

7(6)   Any difference arising as to ordinary matters connected with the business of the limited liability partnership may be decided by a majority of the members, but no change may be made in the nature of the business of the limited liability partnership without the consent of all the members.

7(7)   The books and records of the limited liability partnership are to be made available for inspection at the registered office of the limited liability partnership or at such other place as the members think fit and every member of the limited liability partnership may when he thinks fit have access to and inspect and copy any of them.

7(8)   Each member shall render true accounts and full information of all things affecting the limited liability partnership to any member or his legal representatives.

7(9)   If a member, without the consent of the limited liability partnership, carries on any business of the same nature as and competing with the limited liability partnership, he must account for and pay over to the limited liability partnership all profits made by him in that business.

7(10)   Every member must account to the limited liability partnership for any benefit derived by him without the consent of the limited liability partnership from any transaction concerning the limited liability partnership, or from any use by him of the property of the limited liability partnership, name or business connection.

8 Expulsion

8   No majority of the members can expel any member unless a power to do so has been conferred by express agreement between the members.

PART VII

MISCELLANEOUS

9 General and consequential amendments

9(1)   Subject to paragraph (2), the enactments mentioned in Schedule 5 shall have effect subject to the amendments specified in that Schedule.

9(2)   In the application of this regulation to Scotland–

(a) paragraph 15 of Schedule 5 which amends section 110 of the 1986 Act shall not extend to Scotland; and

(b) paragraph 22 of Schedule 5 which applies to limited liability partnerships the culpable officer provisions in existing primary legislation shall not extend to Scotland insofar as it relates to matters which have not been reserved by Schedule 5 to the Scotland Act 1998.

10 Application of subordinate legislation

10(1)   The subordinate legislation specified in Schedule 6 shall apply as from time to time in force to limited liability partnerships and–

(a) in the case of the subordinate legislation listed in Part I of that Schedule with such modifications as the context requires for the purpose of giving effect to the provisions of the Companies Act 1985 which are applied by these Regulations;

(b) in the case of the subordinate legislation listed in Part II of that Schedule with such modifications as the context requires for the purpose of giving effect to the provisions of the Insolvency Act 1986 which are applied by these Regulations; and

(c) in the case of the subordinate legislation listed in Part III of that Schedule with such modifications as the context requires for the purpose of giving effect to the provisions of the Company Directors Disqualification Act 1986 which are applied by these Regulations.

10(2)   In the case of any conflict between any provision of the subordinate legislation applied by paragraph (1) and any provision of these Regulations, the latter shall prevail.

History
Regulation 10(1)(c) amended by the Limited Liability Partnerships (Application of Companies Act 2006) Regulations 2009 (SI 2009/1804) as from October 1, 2009.

SCHEDULE 1

MODIFICATIONS TO PROVISIONS OF PART VII OF THE 1985 ACT APPLIED BY THESE REGULATIONS

[Revoked by the Limited Liability Partnerships (Accounts and Audit) (Application of Companies Act 2006) Regulations 2008 (SI 2008/1911) reg.58 as from October 1, 2008.]

SCHEDULE 2

Regulation 4

PART I

MODIFICATIONS TO PROVISIONS OF THE 1985 ACT APPLIED TO LIMITED LIABILITY PARTNERSHIPS

Provisions	*Modifications*
Investigation of companies and their affairs: Requisition of documents	
431 (investigation of a company on its own application or that of its members)	For subsection (2) substitute the following: "(2)—The appointment may be made on the application of the limited liability partnership or on the application of not less than one-fifth in number of those who appear from notifications made to the registrar of companies to be currently members of the limited liability partnership."
432 (other company investigations)	
subsection (4)	For the words "but to whom shares in the company have been transferred or transmitted by operation of law" substitute "but to whom a member's share in the limited liability partnership has been transferred or transmitted by operation of law."
433 (inspectors' powers during investigation)	
434 (production of documents and evidence to inspectors)	
436 (obstruction of inspectors treated as contempt of court)	
437 (inspectors' reports)	
439 (expenses of investigating a company's affairs)	
subsection (5)	Omit paragraph (b) together with the word "or" at the end of paragraph (a).

Provisions	Modifications
441 (inspectors' report to be evidence)	
section 446A (general powers to give directions)	
section 446B (direction to terminate investigation)	
section 446C (resignation and revocation of appointment)	
section 446D (appointment of replacement inspectors)	
section 446E (obtaining information from former inspectors etc)	
447 (Secretary of State's power to require production of documents)	
447A (information provided: evidence)	
448 (entry and search of premises)	
448A (protection in relation to certain disclosures: information provided to Secretary of State)	
449 (provision for security of information obtained)	
450 (punishment for destroying, mutilating etc. company documents)	Omit subsection (1A).
451 (punishment for furnishing false information)	
451A (disclosure of information by Secretary of State or inspector)	In subsection (1), for the words "sections 434 to 446" substitute "sections 434 to 441 and 446E". Omit subsection (5).
452 (privileged information)	In subsection (1), for the words "sections 431 to 446" substitute "sections 431 to 441 and 446E". In subsection (1A), for the words "sections 434, 443 or 446" substitute "section 434".

Provisions	Modifications
453A (power to enter and remain on premises)	In subsection (7), for the words "section 431, 432 or 442" substitute "section 431 or 432.
453B (power to enter and remain on premises: procedural)	
453C (failure to comply with certain requirements)	
Fraudulent Trading	
458 (punishment for fraudulent trading)	
Floating Charges and Receivers (Scotland)	
464 (ranking of floating charges)	In subsection (1), for the words " section 462 " substitute "the law of Scotland".
466 (alteration of floating charges)	Omit subsections (1), (2), (3) and (6).
486 (interpretation for Part XVIII generally)	For the current definition of "company" substitute " "company" means a limited liability partnership;" Omit the definition of "Register of Sasines"
487 (extent of Part XVIII)	

History
Entries for ss.447A, 448A and 453A–453C inserted by the Limited Liability Partnerships (Amendment) Regulations 2007 (SI 2007/2073) reg.2 as from October 1, 2007. The modification to s.450 substituted as from March 4, 2004 by the Financial Services and Markets Act 2000 (Consequential Amendments) Order 2004 (SI 2004/355). Schedule 2 Pt 1 extensively amended by the Limited Liability Partnerships (Application of Companies Act 2006) Regulations 2009 (SI 2009/1804) Sch.3 Pt 2 para.13(5) as from October 1, 2009.

PART II

MODIFICATIONS TO THE COMPANY DIRECTORS DISQUALIFICATION ACT 1986

Provisions	Modifications
Part II of Schedule I	After paragraph 8 insert— "**8A** The extent of the member's and shadow members' responsibility for events leading to a member or shadow member, whether himself or some other member or shadow member, being declared by the court to be liable to make a contribution to the assets of the limited liability partnership under section 214A of the Insolvency Act 1986."

SCHEDULE 3

MODIFICATIONS TO THE 1986 ACT

Regulation 5

Provisions	Modifications
Section 1 (those who may propose an arrangement)	
subsection (1)	For "The directors of a company" substitute "A limited liability partnership" and delete "to the company and".
subsection (3)	At the end add "but where a proposal is so made it must also be made to the limited liability partnership".
Section 1A (moratorium)	
Subsection (1)	For "the directors of an eligible company intend" substitute "an eligible limited liability partnership intends". For "they" substitute "it".
The following modifications to sections 2 to 7 apply where a proposal under section 1 has been made by the limited liability partnership.	
Section 2 (procedure where the nominee is not the liquidator or administrator)	
subsection (1)	For "the directors do" substitute "the limited liability partnership does".
subsection (2)	In paragraph (aa) for "meetings of the company and of it creditors" substitute "a meeting of the creditors of the limited liability partnership"; In paragraph (b) for the first "meetings" substitute "a meeting" and for the second "meetings" substitute "meeting".
subsection (3)	For "the person intending to make the proposal" substitute "the designated members of the limited liability partnership".
subsection (4)	In paragraph (a) for "the person intending to make the proposal" substitute "the designated members of the limited liability partnership".

Provisions	Modifications
	In paragraph (b) for "that person" substitute "those designated members".
Section 3 (summoning of meetings)	
subsection (1)	For "such meetings as are mentioned in section 2(2)" substitute "a meeting of creditors" and for "those meetings" substitute "that meeting".
subsection (2)	Delete subsection (2).
Section 4 (decisions of meetings)	
subsection (1)	For "meetings" substitute "meeting".
subsection (5)	For "each of the meetings" substitute "the meeting".
new subsection (5A)	Insert a new subsection (5A) as follows— "(5A) If modifications to the proposal are proposed at the meeting the chairman of the meeting shall, before the conclusion of the meeting, ascertain from the limited liability partnership whether or not it accepts the proposed modifications; and if at that conclusion the limited liability partnership has failed to respond to a proposed modification it shall be presumed not to have agreed to it."
subsection (6)	For "either" substitute "the"; after "the result of the meeting", in the first place where it occurs, insert "(including, where modifications to the proposal were proposed at the meeting, the response to those proposed modifications made by the limited liability partnership)"; and at the end add "and to the limited liability partnership".
Section 4A (approval of arrangement)	
subsection (2)	Omit "—(a)". For "both meetings" substitute "the meeting". Omit the words from ", or" to "that section".
subsection (3)	Omit.
subsection (4)	Omit.
subsection (5)	Omit.

Provisions	Modifications
subsection (6)	Omit.
Section 5 (effect of approval)	
subsection (4)	For "each of the reports" substitute "the report".
Section 6 (challenge of decisions)	
subsection (1)	For "either of the meetings" substitute "the meeting".
subsection (2)	For "either of the meetings" substitute "the meeting" and after paragraph (aa) add a new paragraph (ab) as follows— (ab) any member of the limited liability partnership; and". Omit the word "and" at the end of paragraph (b) and omit paragraph (c).
subsection (3)	For "each of the reports" substitute "the report".
subsection (4)	For subsection (4) substitute the following— "(4) Where on such an application the court is satisfied as to either of the, grounds mentioned in subsection (1) it may do one or both of the following, namely— (a) revoke or suspend any decision approving the voluntary arrangement which has effect under section 4A; (b) give a direction to any person for the summoning of a further meeting to consider any revised proposal the limited liability partnership may make or, in a case falling within subsection (1)(b), a further meeting to consider the original proposal."
subsection (5)	For "meetings" substitute "a meeting", and for "person who made the original proposal" substitute "limited liability partnership".
Section 6A (false representations, etc)	
subsection (1)	Omit "members or".
Section 7 (implementation of proposal)	
subsection (2)	In paragraph (a) omit "one or both of" and for "meetings" substitute "meeting".

Provisions	Modifications
The following modifications to sections 2 and 3 apply where a proposal under section 1 has been made, where the limited liability partnership is in administration, by the administrator or, where the limited liability partnership is being wound up, by the liquidator.	
Section 2 (procedure where the nominee is not the liquidator or administrator)	
subsection (2)	In paragraph (a) for "meetings of the company" substitute "meetings of the members of the limited liability partnership".
Section 3 (summoning of meetings)	
subsection (2)	For "meetings of the company" substitute "a meeting of the members of the limited liability partnership".
Section 73 (alternative modes of winding up)	
subsection (1)	Delete ", within the meaning given to that expression by section 735 of the Companies Act,".
Section 74 (liability as contributories of present and past members)	
For section 74 there shall be substituted the following—	"**74** When a limited liability partnership is wound up every present and past member of the limited liability partnership who has agreed with the other members or with the limited liability partnership that he will, in circumstances which have arisen, be liable to contribute to the assets of the limited liability partnership in the event that the limited liability partnership goes into liquidation is liable, to the extent that he has so agreed, to contribute to its assets to any amount sufficient for payment of its debts and liabilities, and the expenses of the winding up, and for the adjustment of the rights of the contributories among themselves. However, a past member shall only be liable if the obligation arising from such agreement survived his ceasing to be a member of the limited liability partnership."
Section 75 to 78	Delete sections 75 to 78.
Section 79 (meaning of "contributory")	

Provisions	Modifications
subsection (1)	In subsection (1) for "every person" substitute "(a) every present member of the limited liability partnership and (b) every past member of the limited liability partnership".
subsection (2)	After "section 214 (wrongful trading)" insert "or 214A (adjustment of withdrawals)".
subsection (3)	Delete subsection (3).
Section 83 (companies registered under Companies Act, Part XXII, Chapter II)	Delete Section 83.
Section 84 (circumstances in which company may be wound up voluntarily)	
subsection (1)	For subsection (1) substitute the following— "(1) A limited liability partnership may be wound up voluntarily when it determines that it is to be wound up voluntarily."
subsection (2)	Omit subsection (2).
subsection (2A)	For "company passes a resolution for voluntary winding up" substitute "limited liability partnership determines that it is to be wound up voluntarily" and for "resolution" where it appears for the second time substitute "determination".
subsection (2B)	For "resolution for voluntary winding up may be passed only" substitute "determination to wind up voluntarily may only be made" and in sub-paragraph (b), for "passing of the resolution" substitute "making of the determination".
subsection (3)	For subsection (3) substitute the following— "(3) Within 15 days after a limited liability partnership has determined that it be wound up there shall be forwarded to the registrar of companies either a printed copy or else a copy in some other form approved by the registrar of the determination."
subsection (4)	After subsection (4) insert a new subsection (5)— "(5) If a limited liability partnership fails to comply with this regulation the limited liability partnership and every designated member of it who is in default

Provisions	Modifications
	is liable on summary conviction to a fine not exceeding level 3 on the standard scale."
Section 85 (notice of resolution to wind up)	
subsection (1)	For subsection (1) substitute the following— "(1) When a limited liability partnership has determined that it shall be would up voluntarily, it shall within 14 days after the making of the determination give notice of the determination by advertisement in the Gazette."
Section 86 (commencement of winding up)	
	Substitute the following new section— "**86.** A voluntary winding up is deemed to commence at the time when the limited liability partnership determines that it be wound up voluntarily.".
Section 87 (effect on business and status of company)	
subsection (2)	In subsection (2), for "articles" substitute "limited liability partnership agreement".
Section 88 (avoidance of share transfers, etc. after winding-up resolution)	
	For "shares" substitute "the interest of any member in the property of the limited liability partnership".
Section 89 (statutory declaration of solvency)	
	For "director(s)" wherever it appears in section 89 substitute "designated member(s)";
subsection (2)	For paragraph (a) substitute the following—"(a) it is made within the 5 weeks immediately preceding the date when the limited liability partnership determined that it be wound up voluntarily or on that date but before the making of the determination, and".
subsection (3)	For "the resolution for winding up is passed" substitute "the limited liability partnership determined that it be wound up voluntarily".

Provisions	Modifications
subsection (5)	For "in pursuance of a resolution passed" substitute "voluntarily".
Section 90 (distinction between "members" and "creditors" voluntary winding up)	
	For "directors" substitute "designated members".
Section 91 (appointment of liquidator)	
subsection (1)	Delete "in general meeting".
subsection (2)	For the existing wording substitute "(2) On the appointment of a liquidator the powers of the members of the limited liability partnership shall cease except to the extent that a meeting of the members of the limited liability partnership summoned for the purpose or the liquidator sanctions their continuance."
	After subsection (2) insert— "(3) Subsections (3) and (4) of section 92 shall apply for the purposes of this section as they apply for the purposes of that section."
Section 92 (power to fill vacancy in office of liquidator)	
subsection (1)	For "the company in general meeting" substitute "a meeting of the members of the limited liability partnership summoned for the purpose".
subsection (2)	For "a general meeting" substitute "a meeting of the members of the limited liability partnership".
subsection (3)	In subsection (3), for "articles" substitute "limited liability partnership agreement".
new subsection (4)	Add a new subsection (4) as follows— "(4) The quorum required for a meeting of the members of the limited liability partnership shall be any quorum required by the limited liability partnership agreement for meetings of the members of the limited liability partnership and if no requirement for a quorum has been agreed upon the quorum shall be 2 members."

Provisions	Modifications
Section 93 (general company meeting at each year's end)	
subsection (1)	For "a general meeting of the company" substitute "a meeting of the members of the limited liability partnership".
new subsection (4)	Add a new subsection (4) as follows— "(4) Subsections (3) and (4) of section 92 shall apply for the purposes of this section as they apply for the purposes of that section."
Section 94 (final meeting prior to dissolution)	
subsection (1)	For "a general meeting of the company" substitute "a meeting of the members of the limited liability partnership".
new subsection (5A)	Add a new subsection (5A) as follows— "(5A) Subsections (3) and (4) of section 92 shall apply for the purposes of this section as they apply for the purposes of that section."
subsection (6)	For "a general meeting of the company" substitute "a meeting of the members of the limited liability partnership".
Section 95 (effect of company's insolvency)	
subsection (1)	For "directors"' substitute "designated members".
subsection (7)	For subsection (7) substitute the following— "(7) In this section 'the relevant period' means the period of 6 months immediately preceding the date on which the limited liability partnership determined that it be would up voluntarily."
Section 96 (conversion to creditors' voluntary winding up)	
paragraph (a)	For "directors"' substitute "designated members"'.
paragraph (b)	Substitute a new paragraph (b) as follows— "(b) the creditors' meeting was the meeting mentioned in section 98 in the next Chapter;".
Section 98 (meeting of creditors)	

Provisions	*Modifications*
subsection (1)	For paragraph (a) substitute the following— "(a) cause a meeting of its creditors to be summoned for a day not later than the 14th day after the day on which the limited liability partnership determines that it be wound up voluntarily;".
subsection (5)	For "were sent the notices summoning the company meeting at which it was resolved that the company be wound up voluntarily" substitute "the limited liability partnership determined that it be wound up voluntarily".
Section 99 (directors to lay statement of affairs before creditors)	
subsection (1)	For "the directors of the company" substitute "the designated members" and for "the director so appointed" substitute "the designated member so appointed".
subsection (2)	For "directors" substitute "designated members".
subsection (3)	For "directors" substitute "designated members" and for "director" substitute "designated member".
Section 100 (appointment of liquidator)	
subsection (1)	For "The creditors and the company at their respective meetings mentioned in section 98" substitute "The creditors at their meeting mentioned in section 98 and the limited liability partnership".
subsection (3)	Delete "director,".
Section 101 (appointment of liquidation committee)	
subsection (2)	For subsection (2) substitute the following— "(2) If such a committee is appointed, the limited liability partnership may, when it determines that it be wound up voluntarily or at any time thereafter, appoint such number of persons as they think fit to act as members of the committee, not exceeding 5."
Section 105 (meetings of company and creditors at each year's end)	

Provisions	Modifications
subsection (1)	For "a general meeting of the company" substitute "a meeting of the members of the limited liability partnership".
new subsection (5)	Add a new subsection (5) as follows— "(5) Subsections (3) and (4) of section 92 shall apply for the purposes of this section as they apply for the purposes of that section."
Section 106 (final meeting prior to dissolution)	
subsection (1)	For "a general meeting of the company" substitute "a meeting of the members of the limited liability partnership".
new subsection (5A)	After subsection (5) insert a new subsection (5A) as follows— "(5A) Subsections (3) and (4) of section 92 shall apply for the purposes of this section as they apply for the purposes of that section."
subsection (6)	For "a general meeting of the company" substitute "a meeting of the members of the limited liability partnership".
Section 110 (acceptance of shares, etc., as consideration for sale of company property)	
	For the existing section substitute the following: "(1) This section applies, in the case of a limited liability partnership proposed to be, or being, wound up voluntarily, where the whole or part of the limited liability partnership's business or property is proposed to be transferred or sold to another company whether or not it is a company within the meaning of the Companies Act ("the transferee company") or to a limited liability partnership ("the transferee limited liability partnership"). (2) With the requisite sanction, the liquidator of the limited liability partnership being, or proposed to be, wound up ("the transferor limited liability partnership") may receive, in compensation or part compensation for the transfer or sale, shares, policies or other like interests in the transferee company or the transferee limited liability partnership for distribution among the members of the transferor limited liability partnership.

Provisions	Modifications
	(3) The sanction required under subsection (2) is— (a) in the case of a members' voluntary winding up, that of a determination of the limited liability partnership at a meeting of the members of the limited liability partnership conferring either a general authority on the liquidator or an authority in respect of any particular arrangement, (subsections (3) and (4) of section 92 to apply for this purpose as they apply for the purposes of that section), and (b) in the case of a creditor's voluntary winding up, that of either court or the liquidation committee. (4) Alternatively to subsection (2), the liquidator may (with the sanction) enter into any other arrangement whereby the members of the transferor limited liability partnership may, in lieu of receiving cash, shares, policies or other like interests (or in addition thereto), participate in the profits, or receive any other benefit from the transferee company or the transferee limited liability partnership. (5) A sale or arrangement in pursuance of this section is binding on members of the transferor limited liability partnership. (6) A determination by the limited liability partnership is not invalid for the purposes of this section by reason that it is made before or concurrently with a determination by the limited liability partnership that it be wound up voluntarily or for appointing liquidators; but, if an order is made within a year for winding up the limited liability partnership by the court, the determination by the limited liability partnership is not valid unless sanctioned by the court."
Section 111 (dissent from arrangement under section 110)	
subsections (1)–(3)	For subsections (1)–(3) substitute the following— "(1) This section applies in the case of a voluntary winding up where, for the purposes of section 110(2) or (4), a determination of the limited liability partnership has provided the sanction requisite for the liquidator under that section. (2) If a member of the transferor limited liability partnership who did not vote in favour of providing the sanction required for the liquidator under section 110 expresses his dissent from it in writing addressed to the liquidator and left at the registered

Provisions	Modifications
	office of the limited liability partnership within 7 days after the date on which that sanction was given, he may require the liquidator either to abstain from carrying the arrangement so sanctioned into effect or to purchase his interest at a price to be determined by agreement or arbitration under this section.
	(3) If the liquidator elects to purchase the member's interest, the purchase money must be paid before the limited liability partnership is dissolved and be raised by the liquidator in such manner as may be determined by the limited liability partnership."
subsection (4)	Omit subsection (4).
Section 117 (high court and county court jurisdiction)	
subsection (2)	Delete "Where the amount of a company's share capital paid up or credited as paid up does not exceed £120,000, then (subject to this section)".
subsection (3)	Delete subsection (3).
Section 120 (court of session and sheriff court jurisdiction)	
subsection (3)	Delete "Where the amount of a company's share capital paid up or credited as paid up does not exceed £120,000,".
subsection (5)	Delete subsection (5).
Section 122 (circumstances in which company may be wound up by the court)	
subsection (1)	For subsection (1) substitute the following— "(1) A limited liability partnership may be wound up by the court if— (a) the limited liability partnership has determined that the limited liability partnership be wound up by the court, (b) the limited liability partnership does not commence its business within a year from its incorporation or suspends its business for a whole year, (c) the number of members is reduced below two,

Provisions	*Modifications*
	(d) the limited liability partnership is unable to pay its debts,
	(da) at the time at which a moratorium for the limited liability partnership under section 1A comes to an end, no voluntary arrangement approved under Part I has effect in relation to the limited liability partnership,
	(e) the court is of the opinion that it is just and equitable that the limited liability partnership should be wound up."
Section 124 (application for winding up)	
subsections (2), (3) and (4)(a)	Delete these subsections.
subsection (3A)	For "122(1)(fa)" substitute "122(1)(da)".
Section 124A (petition for winding-up on grounds of public interest)	
subsection (1)	Omit paragraphs (b) and (bb).
Section 126 (power to stay or restrain proceedings against company)	
subsection (2)	Delete subsection (2).
Section 127 (avoidance of property dispositions, etc.)	
subsection (1)	For "any transfer of shares" substitute "any transfer by a member of the limited liability partnership of his interest in the property of the limited liability partnership".
Section 129 (commencement of winding up by the court)	
subsection (1)	For "a resolution has been passed by the company" substitute "a determination has been made" and for "at the time of the passing of the resolution" substitute "at the time of that determination".
Section 130 (consequences of winding-up order)	
subsection (3)	Delete subsection (3).

Provisions	Modifications
Section 148 (settlement of list of contributories and application of assets)	
subsection (1)	Delete ", with power to rectify the register of members in all cases where rectification is required in pursuance of the Companies Act or this Act,".
Section 149 (debts due from contributory to company)	
subsection (1)	Delete "the Companies Act or".
subsection (2)	Delete subsection (2).
subsection (3)	Delete ", whether limited or unlimited,".
Section 160 (delegation of powers to liquidator (England and Wales))	
subsection (1)	In subsection (1)(b) delete "and the rectifying of the register of members".
subsection (2)	For subsection (2) substitute the following— "(2) But the liquidator shall not make any call without the special leave of the court or the sanction of the liquidation committee."
Section 165 (voluntary winding up)	
subsection (2)	In paragraph (a) for "an extraordinary resolution of the company" substitute "a determination by a meeting of the members of the limited liability partnership".
subsection (4)	For paragraph (c) substitute the following— "(c) summon meetings of the members of the limited liability partnership for the purpose of obtaining their sanction or for any other purpose he may think fit."
new subsection (4A)	Insert a new subsection (4A) as follows— "(4A) Subsections (3) and (4) of section 92 shall apply for the purposes of this section as they apply for the purposes of that section."
Section 166 (creditors' voluntary winding up)	

Provisions	Modifications
subsection (5)	In paragraph (b) for "directors" substitute "designated members".
Section 171 (removal, etc. (voluntary winding up))	
subsection (2)	For paragraph (a) substitute the following— "(a) in the case of a members' voluntary winding up, by a meeting of the members of the limited liability partnership summoned specially for that purpose, or"
subsection (6)	In paragraph (a) for "final meeting of the company" substitute "final meeting of the members of the limited liability partnership" and in paragraph (b) for "final meetings of the company" substitute "final meetings of the members of the limited liability partnership".
new subsection (7)	Insert a new subsection (7) as follows— "(7) Subsections (3) and (4) of section 92 are to apply for the purposes of this section as they apply for the purposes of that section."
Section 173 (release (voluntary winding up))	
subsection (2)	In paragraph (a) for "a general meeting of the company" substitute "a meeting of the members of the limited liability partnership".
Section 183 (effect of execution or attachment (England and Wales))	
subsection (2)	Delete paragraph (a).
Section 184 (duties of sheriff (England and Wales))	
subsection (1)	For "a resolution for voluntary winding up has been passed" substitute "the limited liability partnership has determined that it be wound up voluntarily".
subsection (4)	Delete "or of a meeting having been called at which there is to be proposed a resolution for voluntary winding up," and "or a resolution is passed (as the case may be)".

Provisions	Modifications
Section 187 (power to make over assets to employees)	
	Delete section 187.
Section 194 (resolutions passed at adjourned meetings)	
	After "contributories" insert "or of the members of a limited liability partnership".
Section 195 (meetings to ascertain wishes of creditors or contributories)	
subsection (3)	Delete "the Companies Act or".
Section 206 (fraud, etc. in anticipation of winding up)	
subsection (1)	For "passes a resolution for voluntary winding up" substitute "makes a determination that it be wound up voluntarily".
Section 207 (transactions in fraud of creditors)	
subsection (1)	For "passes a resolution for voluntary winding up" substitute "makes a determination that it be wound up voluntarily".
Section 210 (material omissions from statement relating to company's affairs)	
subsection (2)	For "passes a resolution for voluntary winding up" substitute "made a determination that it be wound up voluntarily".
Section 214 (wrongful trading)	
subsection (2)	Delete from "but the court shall not" to the end of the subsection.
After section 214	
	Insert the following new section 214A **"214A Adjustment of withdrawals** (1) This section has effect in relation to a person who is or has been a member of a limited liability

Provisions	Modifications
	partnership where, in the course of the winding up of that limited liability partnership, it appears that subsection (2) of this section applies in relation to that person.
	(2) This subsection applies in relation to a person if—
	(a) within the period of two years ending with the commencement of the winding up, he was a member of the limited liability partnership who withdrew property of the limited liability partnership, whether in the form of a share of profits, salary, repayment of or payment of interest on a loan to the limited liability partnership or any other withdrawal of property, and
	(b) it is proved by the liquidator to the satisfaction of the court that at the time of the withdrawal he knew or had reasonable ground for believing that the limited liability partnership—
	(i) was at the time of the withdrawal unable to pay its debts within the meaning of section 123, or
	(ii) would become so unable to pay its debts after the assets of the limited liability partnership had been depleted by that withdrawal taken together with all other withdrawals (if any) made by any members contemporaneously with that withdrawal or in contemplation when that withdrawal was made.
	(3) Where this section has effect in relation to any person the court, on the application of the liquidator, may declare that that person is to be liable to make such contribution (if any) to the limited liability partnership's assets as the court thinks proper.
	(4) The court shall not make a declaration in relation to any person the amount of which exceeds the aggregate of the amounts or values of all the withdrawals referred to in subsection (2) made by that person within the period of two years referred to in that subsection.
	(5) The court shall not make a declaration under this section with respect to any person unless that person knew or ought to have concluded that after each withdrawal referred to in subsection (2) there was no reasonable prospect that the limited liability partnership would avoid going into insolvent liquidation.
	(6) For the purposes of subsection (5) the facts which a member ought to know or ascertain and the conclusions which he ought to reach are those which

Provisions	Modifications
	would be known, ascertained, or reached by a reasonably diligent person having both: (a) the general knowledge, skill and experience that may reasonably be expected of a person carrying out the same functions as are carried out by that member in relation to the limited liability partnership, and (b) the general knowledge, skill and experience that that member has. (7) For the purposes of this section a limited liability partnership goes into insolvent liquidation if it goes into liquidation at a time when its assets are insufficient for the payment of its debts and other liabilities and the expenses of the winding up. (8) In this section "member" includes a shadow member. (9) This section is without prejudice to section 214."
Section 215 (proceedings under ss 213, 214)	
subsection (1)	Omit the word "or" between the words "213" and "214" and insert after "214" or "214A".
subsection (2)	For "either section" substitute "any of those sections".
subsection (4)	For "either section" substitute "any of those sections".
subsection (5)	For "Sections 213 and 214" substitute "Sections 213, 214 or 214A".
Section 218 (prosecution of delinquent officers and members of company)	
subsection (1)	For "officer, or any member, of the company" substitute "member of the limited liability partnership".
subsections (3), (4) and (6)	For "officer of the company, or any member of it," substitute "officer or member of the limited liability partnership".
Section 247 ("insolvency" and "go into liquidation")	
subsection (2)	For "passes a resolution for voluntary winding up" substitute "makes a determination that it be wound

Provisions	Modifications
	up voluntarily" and for "passing such a resolution" substitute "making such a determination".
subsection (3)	For "resolution for voluntary winding up" substitute "determination to wind up voluntarily".
Section 249 ("connected with a company")	For the existing words substitute— "For the purposes of any provision in this Group of Parts, a person is connected with a company (including a limited liability partnership) if— (a) he is a director or shadow director of a company or an associate of such a director or shadow director (including a member or a shadow member of a limited liability partnership or an associate of such a member or shadow member); or (b) he is an associate of the company or of the limited liability partnership."
Section 250 ("member" of a company)	
	Delete section 250.
Section 251 (expressions used generally)	
	Delete the word "and" appearing after the definition of "the rules" and insert the word "and" after the definition of "shadow director". After the definition of "shadow director" insert the following— " 'shadow member', in relation to a limited liability partnership, means a person in accordance with whose directions or instructions the members of the limited liability partnership are accustomed to act (but so that a person is not deemed a shadow member by reason only that the members of the limited liability partnership act on advice given by him in a professional capacity);".
Section 386 (categories of preferential debts)	
subsection (1)	In subsection (1), omit the words "or an individual".
subsection (2)	In subsection (2), omit the words "or the individual".
Section 387 ("the relevant date")	

Provisions	Modifications
subsection (3)	In paragraph (ab) for "passed a resolution for voluntary winding up" substitute "made a determination that it be wound up voluntarily". In paragraph (c) for "passing of the resolution for the winding up of the company" substitute "making of the determination by the limited liability partnership that it be wound up voluntarily".
subsection (5)	Omit subsection (5).
subsection (6)	Omit subsection (6).
Section 388 (meaning of "act as insolvency practitioner")	
subsection (2)	Omit subsection (2).
subsection (3)	Omit subsection (3).
subsection (4)	Delete " "company" means a company within the meaning given by section 735(1) of the Companies Act or a company which may be wound up under Part V of this Act (unregistered companies);" and delete " "interim trustee" and "permanent trustee" mean the same as the Bankruptcy (Scotland) Act 1985".
Section 389 (acting without qualification an offence)	
subsection (1)	Omit the words "or an individual".
Section 389A (authorisation of nominees and supervisors)	
subsection (1)	Omit "or Part VIII".
Section 402 (official petitioner)	Delete section 402.
Section 412 (individual insolvency rules (England and Wales))	Delete section 412.
Section 415 (Fees orders (individual insolvency proceedings in England and Wales))	Delete section 415.
Section 416 (monetary limits (companies winding up))	

Provisions	Modifications
subsection (1)	In subsection (1), omit the words "section 117(2) (amount of company's share capital determining whether county court has jurisdiction to wind it up);" and the words "section 120(3) (the equivalent as respects sheriff court jurisdiction in Scotland),".
subsection (3)	In subsection (3), omit the words "117(2), 120(3) or".
Section 418 (monetary limits (bankruptcy))	Delete section 418.
Section 420 (insolvent partnerships)	
	Delete section 420.
Section 421 (insolvent estates of deceased persons)	
	Delete section 421.
Section 422 (recognised banks, etc.)	
	Delete section 422.
Section 426A (disqualification from Parliament (England and Wales))	Omit.
Section 426B (devolution)	Omit.
Section 426C (irrelevance of privilege)	Omit.
Section 427 (parliamentary disqualification)	Delete section 427.
Section 429 (disabilities on revocation or administration order against an individual)	
	Delete section 429.
Section 432 (offences by bodies corporate)	
subsection (2)	Delete "secretary or".
Section 435 (meaning of "associate")	
new subsection (3A)	Insert a new subsection (3A) as follows— "(3A) A member of a limited liability partnership is an associate of that limited liability partnership and

Provisions	Modifications
	of every other member of that limited liability partnership and of the husband or wife or civil partner or relative of every other member of that limited liability partnership.".
subsection (11)	For subsection (11) there shall be substituted "(11) In this section "company" includes any body corporate (whether incorporated in Great Britain or elsewhere); and references to directors and other officers of a company and to voting power at any general meeting of a company have effect with any necessary modifications."
Section 436 (expressions used generally)	
	The following expressions and definitions shall be added to the section— "designated member" has the same meaning as it has in the Limited Liability Partnerships Act 2000; "limited liability partnership" means a limited liability partnership formed and registered under the Limited Liability Partnerships Act 2000; "limited liability partnership agreement", in relation to a limited liability partnership, means any agreement, express or implied, made between the members of the limited liability partnership or between the limited liability partnership and the members of the limited liability partnership which determines the mutual rights and duties of the members, and their rights and duties in relation to the limited liability partnership.
Section 437 (transitional provisions, and savings)	Delete section 437.
Section 440 (extent (Scotland))	
subsection (2)	In subsection (2), omit paragraph (b).
Section 441 (extent (Northern Ireland))	
	Delete section 441.
Section 442 (extent (other territories))	
	Delete section 442.
Schedule A1	

Provisions	Modifications
Paragraph 6	
sub-paragraph (1)	For "directors of a company wish" substitute "limited liability partnership wishes". For "they" substitute "the designated members of the limited liability partnership".
sub-paragraph (2)	For "directors" substitute "the designated members of the limited liability partnership". In sub-paragraph (c), for "meetings of the company and" substitute "a meeting of".
Paragraph 7	
sub-paragraph (1)	For "directors of a company" substitute "designated members of the limited liability partnership". In sub-paragraph (e)(iii), for "meetings of the company and" substitute "a meeting of".
Paragraph 8	
sub-paragraph (2)	For "meetings" substitute "meeting". For "are" substitute "is". Omit the words in parenthesis.
sub-paragraph (3)	For "either of those meetings" substitute "the meeting". For "those meetings were" substitute "that meeting was". Omit the words in parenthesis.
sub-paragraph (4)	For "either" substitute "the".
sub-paragraph (6)(c)	For "one or both of the meetings" substitute "the meeting".
Paragraph 9	
sub-paragraph (1)	For "directors" substitute "designated members of the limited liability partnership".
sub-paragraph (2)	For "directors" substitute "designated members of the limited liability partnership".
Paragraph 12	
sub-paragraph (1)(b)	Omit.

Provisions	Modifications
sub-paragraph (1)(c)	For "resolution may be passed" substitute "determination that it may be wound up may be made".
sub-paragraph (2)	For "transfer of shares" substitute "any transfer by a member of the limited liability partnership of his interest in the property of the limited liability partnership".
Paragraph 20	
sub-paragraph (8)	For "directors" substitute "designated members of the limited liability partnership".
sub-paragraph (9)	For "directors" substitute "designated members of the limited liability partnership".
Paragraph 24	
sub-paragraph (2)	For "directors" substitute "designated members of the limited liability partnership".
Paragraph 25	
sub-paragraph (2)(c)	For "directors" substitute "designated members of the limited liability partnership".
Paragraph 26	
sub-paragraph (1)	Omit ", director".
Paragraph 29	
sub-paragraph (1)	For "meetings of the company and its creditors" substitute "a meeting of the creditors of the limited liability partnership".
Paragraph 30	
sub-paragraph (1)	For "meetings" substitute "meeting".
new sub-paragraph (2A)	Insert new sub-paragraph (2A) as follows— "(2A) If modifications to the proposal are proposed at the meeting the chairman of the meeting shall, before the conclusion of the meeting, ascertain from the limited liability partnership whether or not it accepts the proposed modifications; and if at that

Provisions	Modifications
	conclusion the limited liability partnership has failed to respond to a proposed modification it shall be presumed not to have agreed to it.".
sub-paragraph (3)	For "either" substitute "the". After "the result of the meeting" in the first place where it occurs insert "(including, where modifications to the proposal were proposed at the meeting, the response to those proposed modifications made by the limited liability partnership)". At the end add "and to the limited liability partnership".
Paragraph 31	
sub-paragraph (1)	For "meetings" substitute "meeting".
sub-paragraph (7)	For "directors of the company" substitute "designated members of the limited liability partnership". For "meetings (or either of them)" substitute "meeting". For " directors" substitute "limited liability partnership". For "those meetings" substitute "that meeting".
Paragraph 32	
sub-paragraph (2)	For sub-paragraphs (a) and (b) substitute "with the day on which the meeting summoned under paragraph 29 is first held.".
Paragraph 36	
sub-paragraph (2)	For sub-paragraph (2) substitute— "(2) The decision has effect if, in accordance with the rules, it has been taken by the creditors' meeting summoned under paragraph 29.".
sub-paragraph (3)	Omit.
sub-paragraph (4)	Omit.
sub-paragraph (5)	Omit.
Paragraph 37	

Provisions	Modifications
sub-paragraph (5)	For "each of the reports of the meetings" substitute "the report of the meeting".
Paragraph 38	
sub-paragraph (1)(a)	For "one or both of the meetings" substitute "the meeting".
sub-paragraph (1)(b)	For "either of those meetings" substitute "the meeting".
sub-paragraph (2)(a)	For "either of the meetings" substitute "the meeting". After sub-paragraph (2)(a) insert new (aa) as follows— "(aa) any member of the limited liability partnership;".
sub-paragraph (2)(b)	Omit "creditors'".
sub-paragraph (3)(a)	For "each of the reports" substitute "the report".
sub-paragraph (3)(b)	Omit "creditors'".
sub-paragraph (4)(a)(ii)	Omit "in question".
sub-paragraph (4)(b)(i)	For "further meetings" substitute "a further meeting" and for "directors" substitute "limited liability partnership".
sub-paragraph (4)(b)(ii)	Omit "company or (as the case may be) creditors'".
sub-paragraph (5)	For "directors do" substitute "limited liability partnerships does".
Paragraph 39	
sub-paragraph (1)	For "one or both of the meetings" substitute "the meeting".
Schedule B1	
Paragraph 2	
sub-paragraph (c)	For "company or its directors" substitute "limited liability partnership".

Provisions	Modifications
Paragraph 8	
sub-paragraph (1)(a)	For "resolution for voluntary winding up" substitute "determination to wind up voluntarily".
Paragraph 9	Omit.
Paragraph 12	
sub-paragraph (1)(b)	Omit.
Paragraph 22	For sub-paragraph (1) substitute— "(1) A limited liability partnership may appoint an administrator.". Omit sub-paragraph (2).
Paragraph 23	
sub-paragraph (1)(b)	Omit "or its directors".
Paragraph 42	
sub-paragraph (2)	For "resolution may be passed for the winding up of" substitute "determination to wind up voluntarily may be made by".
Paragraph 61	For paragraph 61 substitute— "**61.** The administrator has power to prevent any person from taking part in the management of the business of the limited liability partnership and to appoint any person to be a manager of that business.".
Paragraph 62	At the end add the following— Subsections (3) and (4) of section 92 shall apply for the purposes of this paragraph as they apply for the purposes of that section.
Paragraph 83	
sub-paragraph (6)(b)	For "resolution for voluntary winding up" substitute "determination to wind up voluntarily".
sub-paragraph (8)(b)	For "passing of the resolution for voluntary winding up" substitute "determination to wind up voluntarily".

Provisions	Modifications
sub-paragraph (8)(e)	For "passing of the resolution for voluntary winding up" substitute "determination to wind up voluntarily".
Paragraph 87	
sub-paragraph (2)(b)	Insert at the end "or".
sub-paragraph (2)(c)	Omit ", or".
sub-paragraph (2)(d)	Omit the words from "(d)" to "company".
Paragraph 89	
sub-paragraph (2)(b)	Insert at the end "or".
sub-paragraph (2)(c)	Omit ", or".
sub-paragraph (2)(d)	Omit the words from "(d)" to "company".
Paragraph 91	
sub-paragraph (1)(c)	Omit.
Paragraph 94	Omit.
Paragraph 95	For "to 94" substitute "and 93".
Paragraph 97	
sub-paragraph (1)(a)	Omit "or directors".
Paragraph 103	
sub-paragraph (5)	Omit.
Paragraph 105	Omit.
Schedule 1	
Paragraph 19	For paragraph 19 substitute the following— "**19.** Power to enforce any rights the limited liability partnership has against the members under the terms of the limited liability partnership agreement."
Schedule 10	

Provisions	Modifications
Section 6A(1)	In the entry relating to section 6A omit "members' or".
Section 85(2)	In the entry relating to section 85(2) for "resolution for voluntary winding up" substitute "making of determination for voluntary winding up".
Section 89(4)	In the entry relating to section 89(4) for "Director" substitute "Designated member".
Section 93(3)	In the entry relating to section 93(3) for "general meeting of the company" substitute "meeting of members of the limited liability partnership".
Section 99(3)	In the entries relating to section 99(3) for "director" and "directors" where they appear substitute "designated member" or "designated members" as appropriate.
Section 105(3)	In the entry relating to section 105(3) for "company general meeting" substitute "meeting of the members of the limited liability partnership".
Section 106(6)	In the entry relating to section 106(6) for "final meeting of the company" substitute "final meeting of the members of the limited liability partnership".
Sections 353(1) to 362	Delete the entries relating to sections 353(1) to 362 inclusive.
Section 429(5)	Delete the entry relating to section 429(5).
Schedule A1, paragraph 9(2)	For "Directors" substitute "Designated Members".
Schedule A1, paragraph 20(9)	For "Directors" substitute "Designated Members".
Schedule B1, paragraph 27(4)	Omit "or directors".
Schedule B1, paragraph 29(7)	Omit "or directors".
Schedule B1, paragraph 32	Omit "or directors".

History

The modification to s.8(1A) was revoked and the modification to s.8(5), (6) inserted as from March 4, 2004 by the Financial Services and Markets Act 2000 (Consequential Amendments) Order 2004 (SI 2004/355) art.10(2).

The modification to s.124A(1) substituted as from March 4, 2004 by the Financial Services and Markets Act 2000 (Consequential Amendments) Order 2004 (SI 2004/355) art.10(3).

Numerous minor amendments made to Sch.3 by the Limited Liability Partnerships (Amendment) Regulations 2005 (SI 2005/1989), as from October 1, 2005.

APPLICATION OF PROVISIONS TO SCOTLAND

Regulation 5(3)

The provisions listed in this Schedule are not applied to Scotland to the extent specified below:

Sections 50 to 52;

Section 53(1) and (2), to the extent that those subsections do not relate to the requirement for a copy of the instrument and notice being forwarded to the registrar of companies;

Section 53(4) (6) and (7);

Section 54(1), (2), (3) (to the extent that that subsection does not relate to the requirement for a copy of the interlocutor to be sent to the registrar of companies), and subsections (5), (6) and (7);

Sections 55 to 58;

Section 60, other than subsection (1);

Section 61, including subsections (6) and (7) to the extent that those subsections do not relate to anything to be done or which may be done to or by the registrar of companies;

Section 62, including subsection (5) to the extent that that subsection does not relate to anything to be done or which may be done to or by the registrar of companies;

Sections 63 to 66;

Section 67, including subsections (1) and (8) to the extent that those subsections do not relate to anything to be done or which may be done to the registrar of companies;

Section 68;

Section 69, including subsections (1) and (2) to the extent that those subsections do not relate to anything to be done or which may be done by the registrar of companies;

Sections 70 and 71;

Subsection 84(3), to the extent that it does not concern the copy of the resolution being forwarded to the registrar of companies within 15 days;

Sections 91 to 93;

Section 94, including subsections (3) and (4) to the extent that those subsections do not relate to the liquidator being required to send to the registrar of companies a copy of the account and a return of the final meeting;

Section 95;

Section 97;

Sections 100 to 102;

Sections 104 to 105;

Section 106, including subsections (3), (4) and (5) to the extent that those subsections do not relate to the liquidator being required to send to the registrar of companies a copy of the account of winding up and a return of the final meeting/quorum;

Sections 109 to 111;

Section 112, including subsection (3) to the extent that that subsection does not relate to the liquidator being required to send to the registrar a copy of the order made by the court;

Sections 113 to 115;

Sections 126 to 128;

Section 130(1) to the extent that that subsection does not relate to a copy of the order being forwarded by the court to the registrar;

Section 131;

Sections 133 to 135;

Sections 138 to 140;

Sections 142 to 146;

Section 147, including subsection (3) to the extent that that subsection does not relate to a copy of the order being forwarded by the company to the registrar;

Section 162 to the extent that that section concerns the matters set out in Section C.2 of Schedule 5 to the Scotland Act 1998 as being exceptions to the insolvency reservation;

Sections 163 to 167;

Section 169;

Section 170, including subsection (2) to the extent that that subsection does not relate to an application being made by the registrar to make good the default;

Section 171;

Section 172, including subsection (8) to the extent that that subsection does not relate to the liquidator being required to give notice to the registrar;

Sections 173 and 174;

Section 177;

Sections 185 to 189;

Sections 191 to 194;

Section 196 to the extent that that section applies to the specified devolved functions of Part IV of the Insolvency Act 1986;

Section 199;

Section 200 to the extent that it applies to the specified devolved functions of Part IV of the First Group of Parts of the 1986 Act;

Sections 206 to 215;

Section 218 subsections (1), (2), (4) and (6);

Section 231 to 232 to the extent that the sections apply to administrative receivers, liquidators and provisional liquidators;

Section 233, to the extent that that section applies in the case of the appointment of an administrative receiver, of a voluntary arrangement taking effect, of a company going into liquidation or where a provisional liquidator is appointed;

Section 234 to the extent that that section applies to situations other than those where an administration order applies;

Section 235 to the extent that that section applies to situations other than those where an administration order applies;

Sections 236 to 237 to the extent that those sections apply to situations other than administration orders and winding up;

Sections 242 to 243;

Section 244 to the extent that that section applies in circumstances other than a company which is subject to an administration order;

Section 245;

Section 251, to the extent that that section contains definitions which apply only to devolved matters;

Section 416(1) and (4), to the extent that those subsections apply to section 206(1)(a) and (b) in connection with the offence provision relating to the winding up of a limited liability partnership;

Schedule 2;

Schedule 3;

Schedule 4;

Schedule 8, to the extent that that Schedule does not apply to voluntary arrangements or administrations within the meaning of Parts I and II of the 1986 Act.

In addition, Schedule 10, which concerns punishment of offences under the Insolvency Act 1986, lists various sections of the Insolvency Act 1986 which create an offence. The following sections, which are listed in Schedule 10, are devolved in their application to Scotland:

Section 51(4);

Section 51(5);

Sections 53(2) to 62(5) to the extent that those subsections relate to matters other than delivery to the registrar of companies;

Section 64(2);

Section 65(4);

Section 66(6);

Section 67(8) to the extent that that subsection relates to matters other than delivery to the registrar of companies;

Section 93(3);

Section 94(4) to the extent that that subsection relates to matters other than delivery to the registrar of companies;

Section 94(6);

Section 95(8);

Section 105(3);

Section 106(4) to the extent that that subsection relates to matters other than delivery to the registrar of companies;

Section 106(6);

Section 109(2);

Section 114(4);

Section 131(7);

Section 164;

Section 166(7);

Section 188(2);

Section 192(2);

Sections 206 to 211; and

Section 235(5) to the extent that it relates to matters other than administration orders.

SCHEDULE 5

GENERAL AND CONSEQUENTIAL AMENDMENTS IN OTHER LEGISLATION

Regulation 9

[Not reproduced but noted where relevant elsewhere in this *Guide*.]

SCHEDULE 6

APPLICATION OF SUBORDINATE LEGISLATION

Regulation 10

PART I

REGULATIONS MADE UNDER THE 1985 ACT

1–3   [Revoked.]

4   [Omitted.]

5   [Omitted.]

6   [Revoked.]

7   The Companies Act 1985 (Power to Enter and Remain on Premises: Procedural) Regulations 2005

History
Paragraph 7 inserted by the Limited Liability Partnerships (Amendment) Regulations 2007 (SI 2007/2073) reg.3 as from October 1, 2007.
    Paragraphs 1–3 and 6 revoked by the Limited Liability Partnerships (Accounts and Audit) (Application of Companies Act 2006) Regulations 2008 (SI 2008/1911) reg.58 as from October 1, 2008.
    Paragraphs 4 and 5 omitted by the Limited Liability Partnerships (Application of Companies Act 2006) Regulations 2009 (SI 2009/1804) Sch.3 Pt 2 para.13(7) as from October 1, 2009.

PART II

REGULATIONS MADE UNDER THE 1986 ACT

1   Insolvency Practitioners Regulations 1990

2   The Insolvency Practitioners (Recognised Professional Bodies) Order 1986

3   The Insolvency Rules 1986 and the Insolvency (Scotland) Rules 1986 (except in so far as they relate to the exceptions to the reserved matters specified in section C.2 of Part II of Schedule 5 to the Scotland Act 1998)

4   The Insolvency Fees Order 1986

5 The Co-operation of Insolvency Courts (Designation of Relevant Countries and Territories) Order 1986

6 The Co-operation of Insolvency Courts (Designation of Relevant Countries and Territories) Order 1996

7 The Co-operation of Insolvency Courts (Designation of Relevant Country) Order 1998

8 Insolvency Proceedings (Monetary Limits) Order 1986

9 Insolvency Practitioners Tribunal (Conduct of Investigations) Rules 1986

10 Insolvency Regulations 1994

11 Insolvency (Amendment) Regulations 2000

PART III

REGULATIONS MADE UNDER OTHER LEGISLATION

1 [Omitted by the Limited Liability Partnerships (Application of Companies Act 2006) Regulations 2009 (SI 2009/1804) Sch.3 Pt 2 para.13(7)(b) as from October 1, 2009.]

2 The Companies (Disqualification Orders) Regulations 1986

3 The Insolvent Companies (Disqualification of Unfit Directors) Proceedings Rules 1987

4 The Contracting Out (Functions of the Official Receiver) Order 1995

5 The Uncertificated Securities Regulations 1995

6 The Insolvent Companies (Reports on Conduct of Directors) Rules 1996

7 The Insolvent Companies (Reports on Conduct of Directors) (Scotland) Rules 1996

Financial Services and Markets Act 2000 (Insolvency) (Definition of Insurer) Order 2001

(SI 2001/2634)

Made on 20 July 2001 by the Treasury under ss.355(2) and 428(3) of the Financial Services and Markets Act 2000. Operative from 1 December 2001.

1(1)　This Order may be cited as the Financial Services and Markets Act 2000 (Insolvency) (Definition of "Insurer") Order 2001 and comes into force on the day on which section 19 of the Act comes into force.

1(2)　In this Order, the **"Regulated Activities Order"** means the Financial Services and Markets Act 2000 (Regulated Activities) Order 2001.

2　In Part XXIV of the Act (insolvency), **"insurer"** means any person who is carrying on a regulated activity of the kind specified by article 10(1) or (2) of the Regulated Activities Order (effecting and carrying out contracts of insurance) but who is not–

    (a)　exempt from the general prohibition in respect of that regulated activity;

    (b)　a friendly society; or

    (c)　a person who effects or carries out contracts of insurance all of which fall within paragraphs 14 to 18 of Part I of Schedule 1 to the Regulated Activities Order in the course of, or for the purposes of, a banking business.

History
In art.2 the words "except section 360 (administration orders in relation to insurers)," omitted by the Financial Services and Markets Act 2000 (Administration Orders Relating to Insurers) Order 2002 (SI 2002/1242) arts 1, 2 as from May 31, 2002.

Bankruptcy (Financial Services and Markets Act 2000) Rules 2001

(SI 2001/3634)

Made on 9 November 2001 by the Lord Chancellor, in the exercise of his powers under s.412 of the Insolvency Act 1986 with the concurrence of the Secretary of State, and after consulting the committee existing for that purpose under s.413 of that Act. Operative from 1 December 2001.

1 Citation and commencement

1 These Rules may be cited as the Bankruptcy (Financial Services and Markets Act 2000) Rules 2001 and come into force on 1st December 2001.

2 Interpretation

2 In these Rules–

"the Act" means the Financial Services and Markets Act 2000;

"the Authority" means the Financial Services Authority;

"debt" means the sum referred to in section 372(4)(a) of the Act;

"demand" means a demand made under section 372(4)(a) of the Act;

"individual" has the meaning given by section 372(7) of the Act;

"person" excludes a body of persons corporate or unincorporate;

"the 1986 Rules" means the Insolvency Rules 1986.

3 Modification of the 1986 Rules

3 The 1986 Rules apply in relation to a demand with the following modifications.

4 Rule 6.1

4(1) Rule 6.1 (form and content of statutory demand) is disapplied.

4(2) A demand must be dated and signed by a member of the Authority's staff authorised by it for that purpose.

4(3) A demand must specify that it is made under section 372(4)(a) of the Act.

4(4) A demand must state the amount of the debt, to whom it is owed and the consideration for it or, if there is no consideration, the way in which it arises; but if the person to whom the debt is owed holds any security in respect of the debt of which the Authority is aware–

(a) the demand must specify the nature of the security and the value which the Authority puts upon it as at the date of the demand; and

(b) the amount of which payment is claimed by the demand must be the full amount of the debt less the amount specified as the value of the security.

4(5) A demand must state the grounds on which it is alleged that the individual appears to have no reasonable prospect of paying the debt.

5   Rule 6.2

5(1)   Rule 6.2 (information to be given in statutory demand) is disapplied–

5(2)   The demand must include an explanation to the individual of the following matters–

   (a)   the purpose of the demand and the fact that, if the individual does not comply with the demand, bankruptcy proceedings may be commenced against him;

   (b)   the time within which the demand must be complied with, if that consequence is to be avoided;

   (c)   the methods of compliance which are open to the individual; and

   (d)   the individual's right to apply to the court for the demand to be set aside.

5(3)   The demand must specify the name and address (and telephone number, if any) of one or more persons with whom the individual may, if he wishes, enter into communication with a view to establishing to the Authority's satisfaction that there is a reasonable prospect that the debt will be paid when it falls due or (as the case may be) that the debt will be scoured or compounded.

6   Rules 6.3, 6.5, 6.11 and 6.25

6(1)   Rules 6.3 (requirements as to service), 6.5 (hearing of application to set aside), 6.11, (proof of service of statutory demand) and 6.25 (decision on the hearing) apply as if–

   (a)   references to the debtor were references to an individual;

   (b)   references (other than in rule 6.5(2) and (4)(c)) to the creditor were references to the Authority; and

   (c)   references to the creditor in rule 6.5(2) and (4)(c) were references to the person to whom the debt is owed.

6(2)   Rule 6.5(2) applies as if the reference to the creditor also included a reference to the Authority.

6(3)   Rule 6.5(5) is disapplied and there is substituted the following–

"Where the person to whom the debt is owed holds some security in respect of his debt, and rule 4(4) of the Bankruptcy (Financial Services and Markets Act 2000) Rules 2001 is complied with in respect of it but the court is satisfied that the security is undervalued in the demand, the Authority may be required to amend the demand accordingly (but without prejudice to its right to present a bankruptcy by reference to the original demand)."

7   Rule 6.4

7   Rule 6.4 (application to set aside statutory demand) applies as if–

   (a)   references to the debtor were references to an individual;

   (b)   the words in paragraph (2), "the creditor issuing the statutory demand is a Minister of the Crown or a Government Department, and" were omitted; and

   (c)   the reference to the creditor in paragraph (2)(b) was a reference to the Authority.

8   Rule 6.9

8   Rule 6.9 (court in which petition to be presented) applies as if, for paragraph (1)(a), there were substituted–

"(a) if in any demand on which the petition is based the Authority has indicated the intention to present a bankruptcy petition to that Court,".

Insurers (Winding Up) Rules 2001

(SI 2001/3635)

Made on 9 November 2001 by the Lord Chancellor, in exercise of the powers conferred on him by s.411 of the Insolvency Act 1986 and s.379 of the Financial Services and Markets Act 2000, with the concurrence of the Secretary of State, and after consulting the committee existing for that purpose under s.413 of the 1986 Act. Operative from 1 December 2001.

[**Note**: Changes made by the Insurers (Reorganisation and Winding Up) Regulations 2003 (SI 2003/1102), the Insurers (Reorganisation and Winding Up) Regulations 2004 (SI 2004/353) and the Insurers (Reorganisation and Winding Up) (Amendment) Regulations 2004 (SI 2004/546) have been incorporated into the text.]

1 Citation, commencement and revocation

1(1) These Rules may be cited as the Insurers (Winding Up) Rules 2001 and come into force on 1st December 2001.

1(2) The Insurance Companies (Winding Up) Rules 1985 are revoked.

2 Interpretation

2(1) In these Rules, unless the context otherwise requires–

"the 1923 Act" means the Industrial Assurance Act 1923;

"the 1985 Act" means the Companies Act 1985;

"the 1986 Act" means the Insolvency Act 1986;

"the 2000 Act" means the Financial Services and Markets Act 2000;

"the Authority" means the Financial Services Authority;

"company" means an insurer which is being wound up;

"contract of general insurance" and **"contract of long-term insurance"** have the meaning given by article 3(1) of the Financial Services and Markets Act 2000 (Regulated Activities) Order 2001;

"excess of the long-term business assets" means the amount, if any, by which the value of the assets representing the fund or funds maintained by the company in respect of its long-term business as at the liquidation date exceeds the value as at that date of the liabilities of the company attributable to that business;

"excess of the other business assets" means the amount, if any, by which the value of the assets of the company which do not represent the fund or funds maintained by the company in respect of its long-term business as at the liquidation date exceeds the value as at that date of the liabilities of the company (other than liabilities in respect of share capital) which are not attributable to that business;

"Financial Services Compensation Scheme" means the scheme established under section 213 of the 2000 Act;

"general business" means the business of effecting or carrying out a contract of general insurance;

"the general regulations" means the Insolvency Regulations 1994;

"the Industrial Assurance Acts" means the 1923 Act and the Industrial Assurance and Friendly Societies Act 1948;

"insurer" has the meaning given by article 2 of the Financial Services and Markets Act 2000 (Insolvency) (Definition of "Insurer") Order 2001;

967

"linked liability" means any liability under a policy the effecting of which constitutes the carrying on of long-term business the amount of which is determined by reference to–

(a)   the value of property of any description (whether or not specified in the policy),

(b)   fluctuations in the value of such property,

(c)   income from any such property, or

(d)   fluctuations in an index of the value of such property

"linked policy" means a policy which provides for linked liabilities and a policy which when made provided for linked liabilities is deemed to be a linked policy even if the policy holder has elected to convert his rights under the policy so that at the liquidation date there are no longer linked liabilities under the policy;

"liquidation date" means the date of the winding-up order or the date on which a resolution for the winding up of the company is passed by the members of the company (or the policyholders in the case of a mutual insurance company) and, if both a winding-up order and winding-up resolution have been made, the earlier date;

"long-term business" means the business of effecting or carrying out any contract of long-term insurance;

"non-linked policy" means a policy which is not a linked policy;

"other business," in relation to a company carrying on long-term business, means such of the business of the company as is not long-term business;

"the principal rules" means the Insolvency Rules 1986;

"stop order," in relation to a company, means an order of the court, made under section 376(2) of the 2000 Act, ordering the liquidator to stop carrying on the long-term business of the company;

"unit" in relation to a policy means any unit (whether or not described as a unit in the policy) by reference to the numbers and value of which the amount of the liabilities under the policy at any time is measured.

2(2)   Unless the context otherwise requires, words or expressions contained in these Rules bear the same meaning as in the principal rules, the general regulations, the 1986 Act, the 2000 Act or any statutory modification thereof respectively.

3   Application

3(1)   These Rules apply to proceedings for the winding up of an insurer which commence on or after the date on which these Rules come into force.

3(2)   These Rules supplement the principal rules and the general regulations which continue to apply to the proceedings in the winding up of an insurer under the 1986 Act as they apply to proceedings in the winding up of any company under that Act; but in the event of a conflict between these Rules and the principal rules or the general regulations these Rules prevail.

4   Appointment of liquidator

4   Where the court is considering whether to appoint a liquidator under–

(a)   section 139(4) of the 1986 Act (appointment of liquidator where conflict between creditors and contributories), or

(b)   section 140 of the 1986 Act (appointment of liquidator following administration or voluntary arrangement), the manager of the Financial Services Compensation Scheme may appear and make representations to the court as to the person to be appointed.

5 Maintenance of separate financial records for long-term and other business in winding up

5(1) This rule applies in the case of a company carrying on long-term business in whose case no stop order has been made.

5(2) The liquidator shall prepare and keep separate financial records in respect of the long-term business and the other business of the company.

5(3) Paragraphs (4) and (5) apply in the case of a company to which this rule applies which also carries on permitted general business (**"a hybrid insurer"**).

5(4) Where, before the liquidation date, a hybrid insurer has, or should properly have, apportioned the assets and liabilities attributable to its permitted general business to its long term business for the purposes of any accounts, those assets and liabilities must be apportioned to its long term business for the purposes of complying with paragraph (2) of this rule.

5(5) Where, before the liquidation date, a hybrid insurer has, or should properly have, apportioned the assets and liabilities attributable to its permitted general business other than to its long term business for the purposes of any accounts, those assets and liabilities must be apportioned to its other business for the purposes of complying with paragraph (2) of this rule.

5(6) Regulation 10 of the general regulations (financial records) applies only in relation to the company's other business.

5(7) In relation to the long-term business, the liquidator shall, with a view to the long-term business of the company being transferred to another insurer, maintain such accounting, valuation and other records as will enable such other insurer upon the transfer being effected to comply with the requirements of any rules made by the Authority under Part X of the 2000 Act relating to accounts and statements of insurers.

5(8) In paragraphs (4) and (5)–

    (a) **"accounts"** means any accounts or statements maintained by the company in compliance with a requirement under the Companies Act 1985 or any rules made by the Authority under Part X of the 2000 Act;

    (b) **"permitted general business"** means the business of effecting or carrying out a contract of general insurance where the risk insured against relates to either accident or sickness.

History
Rule 5 revoked and replaced by the Insurers (Reorganisation and Winding Up) Regulations 2003 (SI 2003/1102) regs 1, 52, 53(1) as from April 20, 2003.

6 Valuation of general business policies

6 Except in relation to amounts which have fallen due for payment before the liquidation date and liabilities referred to in paragraph 2(1)(b) of Schedule 1, the holder of a general business policy shall be admitted as a creditor in relation to his policy without proof for an amount equal to the value of the policy and for this purpose the value of a policy shall be determined in accordance with Schedule 1.

7 Valuation of long-term policies

7(1) This rule applies in relation to a company's long-term business where no stop order has been made.

7(2) In relation to a claim under a policy which has fallen due for payment before the liquidation date, a policy holder shall be admitted as a creditor without proof for such amount as appears from the records of the company to be due in respect of that claim.

7(3) In all other respects a policy holder shall be admitted as a creditor in relation to his policy without proof for an amount equal to the value of the policy and for this purpose the value of a policy of any class shall be determined in the manner applicable to policies of that class provided by Schedules 2, 3 and 4.

7(4) This rule applies in relation to a person entitled to apply for a free paid-up policy under section 24 of the 1923 Act (provisions as to forfeited policies) and to whom no such policy has been issued before the liquidation date (whether or not it was applied for) as if such a policy had been issued immediately before the liquidation date–

(a) for the minimum amount determined in accordance with section 24(2) of the 1923 Act, or

(b) if the liquidator is satisfied that it was the practice of the company during the five years immediately before the liquidation date to issue policies under that section in excess of the minimum amounts so determined, for the amount determined in accordance with that practice.

8(1) This rule applies in relation to a company's long-term business where a stop order has been made.

8(2) In relation to a claim under a policy which has fallen due for payment on or after the liquidation date and before the date of the stop order, a policy holder shall be admitted as a creditor without proof for such amount as appears from the records of the company and of the liquidator to be due in respect of that claim.

8(3) In all other respects a policy holder shall be admitted as a creditor in relation to his policy without proof for an amount equal to the value of the policy and for this purpose the value of a policy of any class shall be determined in the manner applicable to policies of that class provided by Schedule 5.

8(4) Paragraph (4) of rule 7 applies for the purposes of this rule as if references to the liquidation date (other than that in sub-paragraph (b) of that paragraph) were references to the date of the stop order.

9 Attribution of liabilities to company's long-term business

9(1) This rule applies in the case of a company carrying on long-term business if at the liquidation date there are liabilities of the company in respect of which it is not clear from the accounting and other records of the company whether they are or are not attributable to the company's long-term business.

9(2) The liquidator shall, in such manner and according to such accounting principles as he shall determine, identify the liabilities referred to in paragraph (1) as attributable or not attributable to a company's long-term business and those liabilities shall for the purposes of the winding-up be deemed as at the liquidation date to be attributable or not as the case may be.

9(3) For the purposes of paragraph (2) the liquidator may–

(a) determine that some liabilities are attributable to the company's long-term business and that others are not (the first method); or

(b) determine that a part of a liability shall be attributable to the company's long-term business and that the remainder of the liability is not (the second method),

and he may use the first method for some of the liabilities and the second method for the remainder of them.

9(4) Notwithstanding anything in the preceding paragraphs of this rule, the court may order that the determination of which (if any) of the liabilities referred to in paragraph (1) are attributable to the company's long-term business and which (if any) are not shall be made in such manner and by such methods as the court may direct or the court may itself make the determination.

10   Attribution of assets to company's long-term business

10(1)   This rule applies in the case of a company carrying on long-term business if at the liquidation date there are assets of the company in respect of which–

(a)   it is not clear from the accounting and other records of the company whether they do or do not represent the fund or funds maintained by the company in respect of its long-term business, and

(b)   it cannot be inferred from the source of the income out of which those assets were provided whether they do or do not represent those funds.

10(2)   Subject to paragraph (6) the liquidator shall determine which (if any) of the assets referred to in paragraph (1) are attributable to those funds and which (if any) are not and those assets shall, for the purposes of the winding up, be deemed as at the liquidation date to represent those funds or not in accordance with the liquidator's determination.

10(3)   For the purposes of paragraph (2) the liquidator may–

(a)   determine that some of those assets shall be attributable to those funds and that others of them shall not (the first method); or

(b)   determine that a part of the value of one of those assets shall be attributable to those funds and that the remainder of that value shall not (the second method),

and he may use the first method for some of those assets and the second method for others of them.

10(4)

(a)   In making the attribution the liquidator's objective shall in the first instance be so far as possible to reduce any deficit that may exist, at the liquidation date and before any attribution is made, either in the company's long-term business or in its other business.

(b)   If there is a deficit in both the company's long-term business and its other business the attribution shall be in the ratio that the amount of the one deficit bears to the amount of the other until the deficits are eliminated.

(c)   Thereafter the attribution shall be in the ratio which the aggregate amount of the liabilities attributable to the company's long-term business bears to the aggregate amount of the liabilities not so attributable.

10(5)   For the purposes of paragraph (4) the value of a liability of the company shall, if it falls to be valued under rule 6 or 7, have the same value as it has under that rule but otherwise it shall have such value as would have been included in relation to it in a balance sheet of the company prepared in accordance with the 1985 Act as at the liquidation date; and, for the purpose of determining the ratio referred to in paragraph (4) but not for the purpose of determining the amount of any deficit therein referred to, the net balance of shareholders' funds shall be included in the liabilities not attributable to the company's long-term business.

10(6)   Notwithstanding anything in the preceding paragraphs of this rule, the court may order that the determination of which (if any) of the assets referred to in paragraph (1) are attributable to the fund or funds maintained by the company in respect of its long-term business and which (if any) are not shall be made in such manner and by such methods as the court may direct or the court may itself make the determination.

11   Excess of long-term business assets

11(1)   Where the company is one carrying on long-term business and in whose case no stop order has been made, for the purpose of determining the amount, if any, of the excess of the long-term business assets, there shall be included amongst the liabilities of the company attributable to its long-term business an amount determined by the liquidator in respect of liabilities and expenses likely to be incurred in connection with the transfer of the company's long-term business as a going concern to another insurance company being liabilities not included in the valuation of the long-term policies made in pursuance of rule 7.

History
In r.11(1) the words "and in whose case no stop order has been made" inserted by the Insurers (Reorganisation and Winding Up) Regulations 2003 (SI 2003/1102) regs 1, 52, 54 as from April 20, 2003.

11(2)   Where the liquidator is carrying on the long-term business of an insurer with a view to that business being transferred as a going concern to a person or persons ("transferee") who may lawfully carry out those contracts (or substitute policies being issued by another insurer), the liquidator may, in addition to any amounts paid by the Financial Services Compensation Scheme for the benefit of the transferee to secure such a transfer or to procure substitute policies being issued, pay to the transferee or other insurer all or part of such funds or assets as are attributable to the long-term business being transferred or substituted.

12   Actuarial advice

12(1)   Before doing any of the following, that is to say–

(a)   determining the value of a policy in accordance with Schedules 1 to 5 (other than paragraph 3 of Schedule 1);

(b)   identifying long-term liabilities and assets in accordance with rules 9 and 10;

(c)   determining the amount (if any) of the excess of the long-term business assets in accordance with rule 11;

(d)   determining the terms on which he will accept payment of overdue premiums under rule 21(1) or the amount and nature of any compensation under rule 21(2);

the liquidator shall obtain and consider advice thereon (including an estimate of any value or amount required to be determined) from an actuary.

12(2)   Before seeking, for the purpose of valuing a policy, the direction of the court as to the assumption of a particular rate of interest or the employment of any rates of mortality or disability, the liquidator shall obtain and consider advice thereon from an actuary.

13   Utilisation of excess of assets

13(1)   Except at the direction of the court, no distribution may be made out of and no transfer to another insurer may be made of–

(a)   any part of the excess of the long-term business assets which has been transferred to the other business; or

(b)   any part of the excess of the other business assets, which has been transferred to the long-term business.

13(2)   Before giving a direction under paragraph (1) the court may require the liquidator to advertise the proposal to make a distribution or a transfer in such manner as the court shall direct.

14   In the case of a company carrying on long-term business in whose case no stop order has been made, regulation 5 of the general regulations (payments into the Insolvency Services Account) applies only in relation to the company's other business.

15 Custody of assets

15(1) The Secretary of State may, in the case of a company carrying on long-term business in whose case no stop order has been made, require that the whole or a specified proportion of the assets representing the fund or funds maintained by the company in respect of its long-term business shall be held by a person approved by him for the purpose as trustee for the company.

15(2) No assets held by a person as trustee for a company in compliance with a requirement imposed under this rule shall, so long as the requirement is in force, be released except with the consent of the Secretary of State but they may be transposed by the trustee into other assets by any transaction or series of transactions on the written instructions of the liquidator.

15(3) The liquidator may not grant any mortgage or charge of assets which are held by a person as trustee for the company in compliance with a requirement imposed under this rule except with the consent of the Secretary of State.

16 Maintenance of accounting, valuation and other records

16(1) In the case of a company carrying on long-term business in whose case no stop order has been made, regulation 10 of the general regulations (financial records) applies only in relation to the company's other business.

16(2) The liquidator of such company shall, with a view to the long-term business of the company being transferred to another insurer, maintain such accounting, valuation and other records as will enable such other insurer upon the transfer being effected to comply with the requirements of any rules made by the Authority under Part X of the 2000 Act relating to accounts and statements of insurers.

17 Additional powers in relation to long-term business

17(1) In the case of a company carrying on long-term business in whose case no stop order has been made, regulation 9 of the general regulations (investment or otherwise handling of funds in winding up of companies and payment of interest) applies only in relation to the company's other business.

17(2) The liquidator of a company carrying on long-term business shall, so long as no stop order has been made, have power to do all such things as may be necessary to the performance of his duties under section 376(2) of the 2000 Act (continuation of contracts of long-term insurance where insurer in liquidation) but the Secretary of State may require him–

  (a) not to make investments of a specified class or description,

  (b) to realise, before the expiration of a specified period, the whole or a specified proportion of investments of a specified class or description held by the liquidator.

18 Accounts and audit

18(1) In the case of a company carrying on long-term business in whose case no stop order has been made, regulation 12 of the general regulations (liquidator carrying on business) applies only in relation to the company's other business.

18(2) The liquidator of such a company shall supply the Secretary of State, at such times or intervals as he may specify, with such accounts as he may specify and audited in such manner as he may require and with such information about specified matters and verified in such specified manner as he may require.

18(3) The liquidator of such a company shall, if required to do so by the Secretary of State, instruct at actuary to investigate the financial condition of the company's long-term business and to report thereon in such manner as the Secretary of State may specify.

19   Security by the liquidator and special manager

19   In the case of a company carrying on long-term business in whose case no stop order has been made, rule 4.207 of the principal rules (security) applies separately to the company's long-term business and to its other business.

20   Proof of debts

20(1)   This rule applies in the case of a company carrying on long-term business in whose case no stop order has been made.

History
In r.20(1) the words "and in whose case no stop order has been made" inserted by the Insurers (Reorganisation and Winding Up) Regulations 2003 (SI 2003/1102) regs 1, 52, 55 as from April 20, 2003.

20(2)   The liquidator may in relation to the company's long-term business and to its other business fix different days on or before which the creditors of the company who are required to prove their debts or claims are to prove their debts or claims and he may fix one of those days without at the same time fixing the other.

20(3)   In submitting a proof of any debt a creditor may claim the whole or any part of such debt as attributable to the company's long-term business or to its other business or he may make no such attribution.

20(4)   When he admits any debt, in whole or in part, the liquidator shall state in writing how much of what he admits is attributable to the company's long-term business and how much to the company's other business.

21   Failure to pay premiums

21(1)   The liquidator may in the course of carrying on the company's long-term business and on such terms as he thinks fit accept payment of a premium even though the payment is tendered after the date on which under the terms of the policy it was finally due to be paid.

21(2)   The liquidator may in the course of carrying on the company's long-term business, and having regard to the general practice of insurers, compensate a policy holder whose policy has lapsed in consequence of a failure to pay any premium by issuing a free paid-up policy for reduced benefits or otherwise as the liquidator thinks fit.

22   Notice of valuation of policy

22(1)   Before paying a dividend respect of claims other than under contracts of long-term insurance, the liquidator shall give notice of the value of each general business policy, as determined by him in accordance with rule 6, to the persons appearing from the records of the company or otherwise to be entitled to an interest in that policy and he shall do so in such manner as the court may direct.

22(2)   Before paying a dividend in respect of claims under contracts of long-term insurance and where a stop order has not been made in relation to the company, the liquidator shall give notice to the persons appearing from the records of the company or otherwise to be entitled to a payment under or to an interest in a long-term policy of the amount of that payment or the value of that policy as determined by him in accordance with rule 7(2) or (3), as the case may be.

22(3)   If a stop order is made in relation to the company, the liquidator shall give notice to all the persons appearing from the records of the company or otherwise to be entitled to a payment under or to an interest in a long-term policy of the amount of that payment or the value of that policy as determined by him in accordance with rule 8(2) or (3), as the case may be, and he shall give that notice in such manner as the court may direct.

22(4) Any person to whom notice is so given shall be bound by the value so determined unless and until the court otherwise orders.

22(5) Paragraphs (2) and (3) of this rule have effect as though references therein to persons appearing to be entitled to an interest in a long-term policy and to the value of that policy included, respectively, references to persons appearing to be entitled to apply for a free paid-up policy under section 24 of the 1923 Act and to the value of that entitlement under rule 7 (in the case of paragraph (2) of this rule) or under rule 8 (in the case of paragraph (3) of this rule).

22(6) Where the liquidator summons a meeting of creditors in respect of liabilities of the company attributable to either or both its long-term business or other business, he may adopt any valuation carried out in accordance with rules 6, 7 or 8 as the case may be or, if no such valuation has been carried out by the time of the meeting, he may conduct the meeting using such estimates of the value of policies as he thinks fit.

History
In r.22(6) the words "attributable to either or both" substituted for the former words "attributable either to" by the Insurers (Reorganisation and Winding Up) Regulations 2003 (SI 2003/1102) regs 1, 52, 56 as from April 20, 2003.

23 Dividends to creditors

23(1) This rule applies in the case of a company carrying on long-term business.

23(2) Part II of the principal rules applies separately in relation to the two separate companies assumed for the purposes of rule 5 above.

23(3) The court may, at any time before the making of a stop order, permit a dividend to be declared and paid on such terms as thinks fit in respect only of debts which fell due to payment before the liquidation date or, in the case of claims under long-term policies, which have fallen due for payment on or after the liquidation date.

24 Meetings of creditors

24(1) In the case of a company carrying on long-term business in whose case no stop order has been made, the creditors entitled to participate in creditors' meetings may be–

   (a)   in relation to the long-term business assets of the company, only those who are creditors in respect of liabilities attributable to the long-term business of the company; and

   (b)   in relation to the other business assets of the company, only those who are creditors in respect of liabilities attributable to the other business of the company.

24(1A) In a case where separate general meetings of the creditors are summoned by the liquidator pursuant to–

   (a)   paragraph (1) above; or

   (b)   regulation 29 of the Insurers (Reorganisation and Winding Up) Regulations 2004 (composite insurers: general meetings of creditors),

chapter 8 of Part 4 and Part 8 of the principal rules apply to each such separate meeting.

History
In r.24(1A), the words "regulation 29 Insurers (Reorganisation and Winding Up) (No.2) Regulations 2004" substituted for the former words "regulation 29 Insurers (Reorganisation and Winding Up) Regulations 2003" as from February 18, 2004 by the Insurers (Reorganisation and Winding Up) (No.2) Regulations 2004 (SI 2004/353) regs 51(1), (2). The amendment was later corrected by deleting the erroneous words "(No. 2)" by the Insurers (Reorganisation and Winding Up) (Amendment) Regulations 2004 (SI 2004/546) reg.2(6), as from March 3, 2004.
  Previously r.24(1), (1A) substituted for the former r.24(1) by the Insurers (Reorganisation and Winding Up) Regulations 2003 (SI 2003/1102) regs 1, 52, 57(1), (2) as from April 20, 2003.

24(2) In relation to any such separate meeting–

(a) rule 4.61(3) of the principal rules (expenses of summoning meetings) has effect as if the reference therein to assets were a reference to the assets available under the above-mentioned Regulations for meeting the liabilities of the company owed to the creditors summoned to the meeting, and

(b) rule 4.63 of the principal rules (resolutions) applies as if the reference therein to value in relation to a creditor who is not, by virtue of rule 6, 7 or 8 above, required to prove his debt, were a reference to the value most recently notified to him under rule 22 above or, if the court has determined a different value in accordance with rule 22(4), as if it were a reference to that different value.

24(3) In paragraph (1)–

"long-term business assets" means the assets representing the fund or funds maintained by the company in respect of its long-term business;

"other business assets" means any assets of the company which are not long-term business assets.

History
Rule 24(3) inserted by the Insurers (Reorganisation and Winding Up) Regulations 2003 (SI 2003/1102) regs 1, 52, 57(1), (3) as from April 20, 2003.

25 Remuneration of liquidator carrying on long-term business

25(1) So long as no stop order has been made in relation to a company carrying on long-term business, the liquidator is entitled to receive remuneration for his services as such in relation to the carrying on of that business provided for in this rule.

25(2) The remuneration shall be fixed by the liquidation committee by reference to the time properly given by the liquidator and his staff in attending to matters arising in the winding up.

25(3) If there is no liquidation committee or the committee does not make the requisite determination, the liquidator's remuneration may be fixed (in accordance with paragraph (2)) by a resolution of a meeting of creditors.

25(4) If not fixed as above, the liquidator's remuneration shall be in accordance with the scale laid down for the Official Receiver by the general regulations.

25(5) If the liquidator's remuneration has been fixed by the liquidation committee, and the liquidator considers the amount to be insufficient, he may request that it be increased by resolution of the creditors.

26 Apportionment of costs payable out of the assets

26(1) Where no stop order has been made in relation to a company, rule 4.218 of the principal rules (general rule as to priority) applies separately to the assets of the company's long-term business and to the assets of the company's other business.

History
In r.26(1) the words "Where no stop order has been made in relation to a company, rule 4.218" substituted for the former words "Rule 4.218" by the Insurers (Reorganisation and Winding Up) Regulations 2003 (SI 2003/1102) regs 1, 52, 58(1) as from April 20, 2003.

26(2) But where any fee, expense, cost, charge, disbursement or remuneration does not relate exclusively to the assets of the company's long-term business or to the assets of the company's other business, the liquidator shall apportion it amongst those assets in such manner as he shall determine.

27 Notice of stop order

27(1) When a stop order has been made in relation to the company, the court shall, on the same day send to the Official Receiver a notice informing him that the stop order has been made.

27(2)   The notice shall be in Form No 1 set out in Schedule 6 with such variation as circumstances may require.

27(3)   Three copies of the stop order sealed with the seal of the court shall forthwith be sent by the court to the Official Receiver.

27(4)   The Official Receiver shall cause a sealed copy of the order to be served upon the liquidator by prepaid letter or upon such other person or persons, or in such other manner as the court may direct, and shall forward a copy of the order to the registrar of companies.

27(5)   The liquidator shall forthwith on receipt of a sealed copy of the order–

(a)   cause notice of the order in Form 2 set out in Schedule 6 to be gazetted, and

(b)   advertise the making of the order in the newspaper in which the liquidation date was advertised, by notice in Form No 3 set out in Schedule 6.

SCHEDULE 1

RULES FOR VALUING GENERAL BUSINESS POLICIES

Rule 6

1(1)   This paragraph applies in relation to periodic payments under a general business policy which fall due for payment after the liquidation date where the event giving rise to the liability to make the payments occurred before the liquidation date.

1(2)   The value to be attributed to such periodic payments shall be determined on such actuarial principles and assumptions in regard to all relevant factors as the court shall direct.

2(1)   This paragraph applies in relation to liabilities under a general business policy which arise from events which occurred before the liquidation date but which have not–

(a)   fallen due for payment before the liquidation date; or

(b)   been notified to the company before the liquidation date.

2(2)   The value to be attributed to such liabilities shall be determined on such actuarial principles and assumptions in regard to all relevant factors as the court shall direct.

3(1)   This paragraph applies in relation to liabilities under a general business policy not dealt with by paragraphs 1 or 2.

3(2)   The value to be attributed to those liabilities shall–

(a)   if the terms of the policy provide for a repayment of premium upon the early termination of the policy or the policy is expressed to run from one definite date to another or the policy may be terminated by any of the parties with effect from a definite date, be the greater of the following two amounts:

(i)   the amount (if any) which under the terms of the policy would have been repayable on early termination of the policy had the policy terminated on the liquidation date, and

(ii)   where the policy is expressed to run from one definite date to another or may be terminated by any of the parties with effect from a definite date, such proportion of the last premium paid as is proportionate to the unexpired portion of the period in respect of which that premium was paid; and

(b)   in any other case, be a just estimate of that value.

SCHEDULE 2

RULES FOR VALUING NON-LINKED LIFE POLICIES, NON-LINKED DEFERRED ANNUITY POLICIES, NON-LINKED ANNUITIES IN PAYMENT, UNITISED NON-LINKED POLICIES AND CAPITAL REDEMPTION POLICIES

Rule 7

1 General

1 In valuing a policy–

(a) where it is necessary to calculate the present value of future payments by or to the company, interest shall be assumed at such fair and reasonable rate or rates as the court may direct;

(b) where relevant, the rates of mortality and the rates of disability to be employed shall be such rates as the court considers appropriate after taking into account:

(i) relevant published tables of rates of mortality and rates of disability, and

(ii) the rates of mortality and the rates of disability experienced in connection with similar policies issued by the company;

(c) there shall be determined:

(i) the present value of the ordinary benefits,

(ii) the present value of additional benefits;

(iii) the present value of options, and

(iv) if further premiums fall to be paid under the policy on or after the liquidation date, the present value of the premiums;

and for the purposes of this Schedule if the ordinary benefits only take into account premiums paid to date, the present value of future premiums shall be taken as nil.

2 Present value of the ordinary benefits

2(1) Ordinary benefits are the benefits which will become payable to the policy holder on or after the liquidation date without his having to exercise any option under the policy (including any bonus or addition to the sum assured or the amount of annuity declared before the liquidation date) and for this purpose "option" includes a right to surrender the policy.

2(2) Subject to sub-paragraph (3), the present value of the ordinary benefits shall be the value at the liquidation date of the reversion in the ordinary benefits according to the contingency upon which those benefits are payable calculated on the basis of the rates of interest, mortality and disability referred to in paragraph 1.

2(3) For accumulating with profits policies–

(a) where the benefits are not expressed in the form of units in a with-profits fund, the value of the ordinary benefits is the amount that would have been payable, excluding any discretionary additions, if the policyholder had been able to exercise a right to terminate the policy at the liquidation date; and

(b) where the benefits are expressed in the form of units in a with-profits fund, the value of the ordinary benefits is the number of units held by the policy holder at the liquidation date valued at the unit price in force at that time or, if that price is not calculated on a daily basis, such price as the court may determine having regard to the last published unit price and any change in the value of assets attributable to the fund since the date of the last published unit price.

2(4) Where–

(a) sub-paragraph (3) applies, and

(b) paragraph 3(1) of Schedule 3 applies to the calculation of the unit price (or as the case may be) the fund value,

the value shall be adjusted on the basis set out in paragraph 3(3) to (5) of Schedule 3.

2(5) Where sub-paragraph (3) applies, the value may be further adjusted by reference to the value of the assets underlying the unit price (or as the case may be) the value of the fund, if the liquidator considers such an adjustment to be necessary.

3 Present value of additional benefits

3(1) Where under the terms of the policy or on the basis of the company's established practice the policy holder has a right to receive or an expectation of receiving benefits additional to the minimum benefits guaranteed under those terms, the court shall determine rates of interest, bonus (whether reversionary, terminal or any other type of bonus used by the company), mortality and disability to provide for the present value (if any) of that right or expectation.

3(2) In determining what (if any) value to attribute to any such expectations the court shall have regard to the premium payable in relation to the minimum guaranteed benefits and the amount (if any) an insurer is required to provide in respect of those expectations in any rules made by the Authority under Part X of the 2000 Act.

4 Present value of options

4 The amount of the present value of options shall be the amount which, in the opinion of the liquidator, is necessary to be provided at the liquidation date (in addition to the amount of the present value of the ordinary benefits) to cover the additional liabilities likely to arise upon the exercise on or after that date by the policy holder of any option conferred upon him by the terms of the policy or, in the case of an industrial assurance policy, by the Industrial Assurance Acts other than an option whereby the policy holder can secure a guaranteed cash payment within the period of 12 months beginning with that date.

5 Present value of premiums

5 The present value of the premiums shall be the value at the liquidation date of the premiums which fall due to be paid by the policy holder after the liquidation date calculated on the basis of the rates of interest, mortality and disability referred to in paragraph 1.

6 Value of the policy

6(1) Subject to sub-paragraph (2)–

(a) if no further premiums fall due to be paid under the policy on or after the liquidation date, the value of the policy shall be the aggregate of:

(i) the present value of the ordinary benefits;

(ii) the present value of options; and

(iii) the present value of additional benefits;

(b) if further premiums fall due to be so paid and the aggregate value referred to in sub-paragraph (a) exceeds the present value of the premiums, the value of the policy shall be the amount of that excess; and

(c) if further premiums fall due to be so paid and that aggregate does not exceed the present value of the premiums, the policy shall have no value.

6(2)   Where the policy holder has a right conferred upon him by the terms of the policy or by the Industrial Assurance Acts whereby the policy holder can secure a guaranteed cash payment within the period of 12 months beginning with the liquidation date, the liquidator shall determine the amount which in his opinion it is necessary to provide at that date to cover the liabilities which will accrue when that option is exercised (on the assumption that it will be exercised) and the value of the policy shall be that amount if it exceeds the value of the policy (if any) determined in accordance with sub-paragraph (1).

SCHEDULE 3

RULES FOR VALUING LIFE POLICIES AND DEFERRED ANNUITY POLICIES WHICH ARE LINKED POLICIES

Rule 7

1(1)   Subject to sub-paragraph (2) the value of the policy shall be the aggregate of the value of the linked liabilities (calculated in accordance with paragraphs 2 or 4) and the value of other than linked liabilities (calculated in accordance with paragraph 5) except where that aggregate is a negative amount it which case the policy shall have no value.

1(2)   Where the terms of the policy include a right whereby the policy holder can secure a guaranteed cash payment within the period of 12 months beginning with the liquidation date then, if the amount which in the opinion of the liquidator is necessary to be provided at that date to cover any liabilities which will accrue when that option is exercised (on the assumption that it will be exercised) is greater than the value determined under sub-paragraph (1) of this paragraph, the value of the policy shall be that greater amount.

2(1)   Where the linked liabilities are expressed in terms of units the value of those liabilities shall, subject to paragraph 3, be the amount arrived at by taking the product of the number of units of each class of units allocated to the policy on the liquidation date and the value of each such unit on that date and then adding those products.

2(2)   For the purposes of sub-paragraph (1)–

   (a)   where under the terms of the policy the value of a unit at any time falls to be determined by reference to the value at that time of the assets of a particular fund maintained by the company in relation to that and other policies, the value of a unit on the liquidation date shall be determined by reference to the net realisable value of the assets credited to that fund on that date (after taking account of disposal costs, any tax liabilities resulting from the disposal of assets insofar as they have not already been provided for by the company and any other amounts which under the terms of those policies are chargeable to the fund), and

   (b)   in any other case, the value of a unit on the liquidation date shall be the value which would have been ascribed to each unit credited to the policy holder, after any deductions which may be made under the terms of the policy, for the purpose of determining the benefits payable under the policy on the liquidation date had the policy matured on that date.

3(1)   This paragraph applies where–

   (a)   paragraph 2(2)(a) applies and the company has a right under the terms of the policy either to make periodic withdrawals from the fund referred to in that paragraph or to retain any part of the income accruing in respect of the assets of that fund,

   (b)   paragraph 2(2)(b) applies and the company has a right under the terms of the policy to receive the whole or any part of any distributions made in respect of the units referred to in that paragraph, or

   (c)   paragraph 2(2)(a) or paragraph 2(2)(b) applies and the company has a right under the terms of the policy to make periodic cancellations of a proportion of the number of units credited to the policy.

980

3(2) Where this paragraph applies, the value of the linked liabilities calculated in accordance with paragraph 2(1) shall be reduced by an amount calculated in accordance with sub-paragraph (3) of this paragraph.

3(3) The said amount is–

(a) where this paragraph applies by virtue of head (a) or (b) of sub-paragraph (1), the value as at the liquidation date, calculated on actuarial principles, of the future income of the company in respect of the units in question arising from the rights referred to in head (a) or (b) of sub-paragraph (1) as the case may be, or

(b) where this paragraph applies by virtue of head (c) of sub-paragraph (1), the value as at the liquidation date, calculated on actuarial principles, of the liabilities of the company in respect of the units which fall to be cancelled in the future under the right referred to in head (c) of sub-paragraph (1).

3(4) In calculating any amount in accordance with sub-paragraph (3) there shall be disregarded–

(a) such part of the rights referred to in the relevant head of sub-paragraph (1) which in the opinion of the liquidator constitutes appropriate provision for future expenses and mortality risks, and

(b) such part of those rights (if any) which the court considers to constitute appropriate provision for any right or expectation of the policy holder to receive benefits additional to the benefits guaranteed under the terms of the policy.

3(5) In determining the said amount–

(a) interest shall be assumed at such rate or rates as the court may direct, and

(b) where relevant, the rates of mortality and the rates of disability to be employed shall be such rates as the court considers appropriate after taking into account:

(i) relevant published tables of rates of mortality and rates of disability, and

(ii) the rates of mortality and the rates of disability experienced in connection with similar policies issued by the company.

4 Where the linked liabilities are not expressed in terms of units the value of those liabilities shall be the value (subject to adjustment for any amounts which would have been deducted for taxation) which would have been ascribed to those liabilities had the policy matured on the liquidation date.

5(1) The value of any liabilities other than linked liabilities including reserves for future expenses, options and guarantees shall be determined on actuarial principles and appropriate assumptions in regard to all relevant factors including the assumption of such rate or rates of interest, mortality and disability as the court may direct.

5(2) In valuing liabilities under this paragraph credit shall be taken for those parts of future premiums which do not fall to be applied in the allocation of further units to the policy and for any rights of the company which have been disregarded under paragraph 3(4)(a) in valuing the linked liabilities.

Schedule 4

Rules for Valuing Long-Term Policies which are not Dealt with in Schedules 2 or 3

Rule 7

The value of a long-term policy not covered by Schedule 2 or 3 shall be the value of the benefits due to the policy holder determined on such actuarial principles and assumptions in regard to all relevant factors as the court shall determine.

SCHEDULE 5

RULES FOR VALUING LONG-TERM POLICIES WHERE A STOP ORDER HAS BEEN MADE

Rule 8

1   Subject to paragraphs 2 and 3, in valuing a policy Schedules 2, 3 or 4 shall apply according to the class of that policy as if those Schedules were herein repeated but with a view to a fresh valuation of each policy on appropriate assumptions in regard to all relevant factors and subject to the following modifications–

    (a)   references to the stop order shall be substituted for references to the liquidation date,

    (b)   in paragraph 4 of Schedule 2 for the words "whereby the policy holder can secure a guaranteed cash payment within the period of 12 months beginning with that date" there shall be substituted the words "to surrender the policy which can be exercised on that date",

    (c)   paragraph 6(2) of Schedule 2 shall be deleted, and

    (d)   paragraph 1(2) of Schedule 3 shall be deleted.

2(1)   This paragraph applies where the policy holder has a right conferred upon him under the terms of the policy or by the Industrial Assurance Acts to surrender the policy and that right is exercisable on the date of the stop order.

2(2)   Where this paragraph applies and the amount required at the date of the stop order to provide for the benefits payable upon surrender of the policy (on the assumption that the policy is surrendered on the date of the stop order) is greater than the value of the policy determined in accordance with paragraph 1, the value of the policy shall, subject to paragraph 3, be the said amount so required.

2(3)   Where any part of the surrender value is payable after the date of the stop order, sub-paragraph (2) shall apply but the value therein referred to shall be discounted at such a rate of interest as the court may direct.

3(1)   This paragraph applies in the case of a linked policy where–

    (a)   the terms of the policy include a guarantee that the amount assured will on maturity of the policy be worth a minimum amount calculable in money terms, or

    (b)   the terms of the policy include a right on the part of the policy holder to surrender the policy and a guarantee that the payment on surrender will be worth a minimum amount calculable in money terms and that right is exercisable on or after the date of the stop order.

3(2)   Where this paragraph applies the value of the policy shall be the greater of the following two amounts–

    (a)   the value the policy would have had at the date of the stop order had the policy been a non-linked policy, that is to say, had the linked liabilities provided by the policy not been so provided but the policy had otherwise been on the same terms, and

    (b)   the value the policy would have had at the date of the stop order had the policy not included any guarantees of payments on maturity or surrender worth a minimum amount calculable in money terms.

SCHEDULE 6

FORMS

Rule 27

[Not reproduced.]

Insurers (Winding Up) (Scotland) Rules 2001

(2001/4040 (S 21))

Made on 20 December 2001 by the Secretary of State for Trade and Industry under s.411 of the Insolvency Act 1986 and s.379 of the Financial Services and Markets Act 2000. Operative from 18 January 2002.

[**Note**: Changes made by the Insurers (Reorganisation and Winding Up) Regulations 2003 (SI 2003/1102), the Insurers (Reorganisation and Winding Up) Regulations 2004 (SI 2004/353) and the Insurers (Reorganisation and Winding Up) (Amendment) Regulations 2004 (SI 2004/546) have been incorporated into the text.]

1 Citation, commencement and revocation

1(1) These Rules may be cited as the Insurers (Winding Up) (Scotland) Rules 2001 and shall come into force on 18th January 2002.

1(2) The Insurance Companies (Winding Up) (Scotland) Rules 1986 are revoked.

2 Interpretation

2(1) In these Rules, unless the context otherwise requires–

"**the 1923 Act**" means the Industrial Assurance Act 1923;

"**the 1985 Act**" means the Companies Act 1985;

"**the 1986 Act**" means the Insolvency Act 1986;

"**the 2000 Act**" means the Financial Services and Markets Act 2000;

"**the Authority**" means the Financial Services Authority;

"**company**" means an insurer which is being wound up;

"**contract of general insurance**" and "**contract of long-term insurance**" have the meaning given by article 3(1) of the Financial Services and Markets Act 2000 (Regulated Activities) Order 2001;

"**excess of the long-term business assets**" means the amount, if any, by which the value of the assets representing the fund or funds maintained by the company in respect of its long-term business as at the liquidation date exceeds the value as at that date of the liabilities of the company attributable to that business;

"**excess of the other business assets**" means the amount, if any, by which the value of the assets of the company which do not represent the fund or funds maintained by the company in respect of its long-term business as at the liquidation date exceeds the value as at that date of the liabilities of the company (other than liabilities in respect of share capital) which are not attributable to that business;

"**Financial Services Compensation Scheme**" means the scheme established under section 213 of the 2000 Act;

"**general business**" means the business of effecting or carrying out a contract of general insurance;

"**the Industrial Assurance Acts**" means the 1923 Act and the Industrial Assurance and Friendly Societies Act 1948;

"**insurer**" has the meaning given by article 2 of the Financial Services and Markets Act 2000 (Insolvency) (Definition of "Insurer") Order 2001;

"**linked liability**" means any liability under a policy the effecting of which constitutes the carrying on of long-term business the amount of which is determined by reference to–

983

(a)   the value of property of any description (whether or not specified in the policy),

(b)   fluctuations in the value of such property,

(c)   income from any such property, or

(d)   fluctuations in an index of the value of such property;

"linked policy" means a policy which provides for linked liabilities, and a policy which when made provided for linked liabilities is deemed to be a linked policy even if the policy holder has elected to convert his rights under the policy so that at the liquidation date there are no longer linked liabilities under the policy;

"liquidation date" means the date of the winding-up order or the date on which a resolution for the winding up of the company is passed by the members of the company (or the policyholders in the case of a mutual insurance company) and, if both a winding-up order and a winding-up resolution have been made, the earlier date;

"long-term business" means the business of effecting or carrying out any contract of long-term insurance;

"non-linked policy" means a policy which is not a linked policy;

"other business", in relation to a company carrying on long-term business, means such of the business of the company as is not long-term business;

"the principal rules" means the Insolvency (Scotland) Rules 1986;

"stop order", in relation to a company, means an order of the court, made under section 376(2) of the 2000 Act, ordering the liquidator to stop carrying on the long-term business of the company;

"unit" in relation to a policy means any unit (whether or not described as a unit in the policy) by reference to the numbers and the value of which the amount of the liabilities under the policy at any time is measured.

2(2)   Unless the context otherwise requires, words or expressions contained in these Rules bear the same meaning as in the principal rules, the 1986 Act, the 2000 Act or any statutory modification thereof respectively.

3   Application

3(1)   These Rules apply in relation to an insurer which the courts in Scotland have jurisdiction to wind up.

3(2)   These Rules apply to proceedings for the winding up of such an insurer which commence on or after the date on which these Rules come into force.

3(3)   These Rules supplement the principal rules which also apply to the proceedings in the winding up of such an insurer under the 1986 Act as they apply to proceedings in the winding up of any company under that Act; but in the event of a conflict between these Rules and the principal rules these Rules prevail.

4   Financial Services Compensation Scheme

4   In any proceedings for the appointment of a liquidator by the court under–

(a)   section 139(4) of the 1986 Act (appointment of liquidator where conflict between creditors and contributories), or

(b)   section 140 of that Act (appointment of liquidator following administration or voluntary arrangement), the manager of the Financial Services Compensation Scheme shall be entitled to appear and make representations as to the person to be appointed.

5 Maintenance of separate financial records for long-term and other business in winding up

5(1) This rule applies in the case of a company carrying on long-term business in whose case no stop order has been made.

5(2) The liquidator shall prepare and keep separate financial records in respect of the long-term business and the other business of the company.

5(3) Paragraphs (4) and (5) apply in the case of a company to which this rule applies which also carries on permitted general business ("a hybrid insurer").

5(4) Where, before the liquidation date, a hybrid insurer has, or should properly have, apportioned the assets and liabilities attributable to its permitted general business to its long term business for the purposes of any accounts, those assets and liabilities must be apportioned to its long term business for the purposes of complying with paragraph (2) of this rule.

5(5) Where, before the liquidation date, a hybrid insurer has, or should properly have, apportioned the assets and liabilities attributable to its permitted general business other than to its long term business for the purposes of any accounts, those assets and liabilities must be apportioned to its other business for the purposes of complying with paragraph (2) of this rule.

5(6) Regulation 10 of the general regulations (financial records) applies only in relation to the company's other business.

5(7) In relation to the long-term business, the liquidator shall, with a view to the long-term business of the company being transferred to another insurer, maintain such accounting, valuation and other records as will enable such other insurer upon the transfer being effected to comply with the requirements of any rules made by the Authority under Part X of the 2000 Act relating to accounts and statements of insurers.

5(8) In paragraphs (4) and (5)–

    (a) **"accounts"** means any accounts or statements maintained by the company in compliance with a requirement under the Companies Act 1985 or any rules made by the Authority under Part X of the 2000 Act;

    (b) **"permitted general business"** means the business of effecting or carrying out a contract of general insurance where the risk insured against relates to either accident or sickness.

History
Rule 5 revoked and replaced by the Insurers (Reorganisation and Winding Up) Regulations 2003 (SI 2003/1102) regs 1, 52, 53(2) as from April 20, 2003.

6 Valuation of general business policies

6 Except in relation to amounts which have fallen due for payment before the liquidation date and liabilities referred to in paragraph 2(1)(b) of Schedule 1, the holder of a general business policy shall be accepted as a creditor in relation to his policy, without submitting or lodging a claim, for an amount equal to the value of the policy and for this purpose the value of a policy shall be determined in accordance with Schedule 1.

7 Valuation of long-term policies

7(1) This rule applies in relation to a company's long-term business where no stop order has been made.

7(2) In relation to a claim under a policy which has fallen due for payment before the liquidation date, a policy holder shall be accepted as a creditor, without submitting or lodging a claim, for such amount as appears from the records of the company to be due in respect of that claim.

7(3) In all other respects a policy holder shall be accepted as a creditor in relation to his policy, without submitting or lodging a claim, for an amount equal to the value of the policy and for this purpose the value of a policy of any class shall be determined in the manner applicable to policies of that class provided by Schedules 2, 3 and 4.

7(4) This rule applies in relation to a person entitled to apply for a free paid-up policy under section 24 of the 1923 Act (provisions as to forfeited policies) and to whom no such policy has been issued before the liquidation date (whether or not it was applied for) as if such a policy had been issued immediately before the liquidation date–

    (a) for the minimum amount determined in accordance with section 24(2) of the 1923 Act, or

    (b) if the liquidator is satisfied that it was the practice of the company during the five years immediately before the liquidation date to issue policies under that section in excess of the minimum amounts so determined, for the amount determined in accordance with that practice.

8 Valuation of long-term policies: stop order made

8(1) This rule applies in relation to a company's long-term business where a stop order has been made.

8(2) In relation to a claim under a policy which has fallen due for payment on or after the liquidation date and before the date of the stop order, a policy holder shall be accepted as a creditor, without submitting or lodging a claim, for such amount as appears from the records of the company and of the liquidator to be due in respect of that claim.

8(3) In all other respects a policy holder shall be accepted as a creditor in relation to his policy, without submitting or lodging a claim, for an amount equal to the value of the policy and for this purpose the value of a policy of any class shall be determined in the manner applicable to the policies of that class provided by Schedule 5.

8(4) Paragraph (4) of rule 7 applies for the purposes of this rule as if references to the liquidation date (other than that in sub-paragraph (b) of that paragraph) were references to the date of the stop order.

9 Attribution of liabilities to company's long-term business

9(1) This rule applies in the case of a company carrying on long-term business if at the liquidation date there are liabilities of the company in respect of which it is not clear from the accounting and other records of the company whether they are or are not attributable to the company's long-term business.

9(2) The liquidator shall, in such manner and according to such accounting principles as he shall determine, identify the liabilities referred to in paragraph (1) as attributable or not attributable to a company's long-term business and those liabilities shall for the purposes of the winding up be deemed as at the liquidation date to be so attributable or not as the case may be.

9(3) For the purposes of paragraph (2) the liquidator may–

    (a) determine that some liabilities are attributable to the company's long-term business and that others are not (the first method); or

    (b) determine that a part of a liability shall be attributable to the company's long-term business and that the remainder of the liability is not (the second method),

and he may use the first method for some of the liabilities and the second method for the remainder of them.

9(4)   Notwithstanding anything in the preceding paragraphs of this rule, the court may order that the determination of which (if any) of the liabilities referred to in paragraph (1) are attributable to the company's long-term business and which (if any) are not shall be made in such manner and by such methods as the court may direct or the court may itself make the determination.

10   Attribution of assets to company's long-term business

10(1)   This rule applies in the case of a company carrying on long-term business if at the liquidation date there are assets of the company in respect of which–

  (a)   it is not clear from the accounting and other records of the company whether they do or do not represent the fund or funds maintained by the company in respect of its long-term business, and

  (b)   it cannot be inferred from the source of the income out of which those assets were provided whether they do or do not represent those funds.

10(2)   Subject to paragraph (6) the liquidator shall determine which (if any) of the assets referred to in paragraph (1) are attributable to those funds and which (if any) are not and those assets shall, for the purposes of the winding up, be deemed as at the liquidation date to represent those funds or not in accordance with the liquidator's determination.

10(3)   For the purposes of paragraph (2) the liquidator may–

  (a)   determine that some of those assets shall be attributable to those funds and that others of them shall not (the first method); or

  (b)   determine that a part of the value of one of those assets shall be attributable to those funds and that the remainder of that value shall not (the second method),

and he may use the first method for some of those assets and the second method for others of them.

10(4)

  (a)   In making the attribution the liquidator's objective shall in the first instance be so far as possible to reduce any deficit that may exist, at the liquidation date and before any attribution is made, either in the company's long-term business or in its other business.

  (b)   If there is a deficit in both the company's long-term business and its other business the attribution shall be in the ratio that the amount of the one deficit bears to the amount of the other until the deficits are eliminated.

  (c)   Thereafter the attribution shall be in the ratio which the aggregate amount of the liabilities attributable to the company's long-term business bears to the aggregate amount of the liabilities not so attributable.

10(5)   For the purposes of paragraph (4) the value of a liability of the company shall, if it falls to be valued under rule 6 or 7, have the same value as it has under that rule but otherwise it shall have such value as would have been included in relation to it in a balance sheet of the company prepared in accordance with the 1985 Act as at the liquidation date; and, for the purpose of determining the ratio referred to in paragraph (4) but not for the purpose of determining the amount of any deficit therein referred to, the net balance of the shareholders' funds shall be included in the liabilities not attributable to the company's long-term business.

10(6)   Notwithstanding anything in the preceding paragraphs of this rule, the court may order that the determination of which (if any) of the assets referred to in paragraph (1) are attributable to the fund or funds maintained by the company in respect of its long-term business and which (if any) are not shall be made in such manner and by such methods as the court may direct or the court may itself make the determination.

11 Excess of long-term business assets

11(1) Where the company is one carrying on long-term business and in whose case no stop order has been made, for the purpose of determining the amount, if any, of the excess of the long-term business assets, there shall be included amongst the liabilities of the company attributable to its long-term business an amount determined by the liquidator in respect of liabilities and expenses likely to be incurred in connection with the transfer of the company's long-term business as a going concern to another insurance company being liabilities not included in the valuation of the long-term policies made in pursuance of rule 7.

History
In r.11(1) the words "and in whose case no stop order has been made" inserted by the Insurers (Reorganisation and Winding Up) Regulations 2003 (SI 2003/1102) regs 1, 52, 54 as from April 20, 2003.

11(2) Where the liquidator is carrying on the long-term business of an insurer with a view to that business being transferred as a going concern to a person or persons ("the transferee") who may lawfully carry out those contracts (or substitute policies being issued by another insurer), the liquidator may, in addition to any amounts paid by the Financial Services Compensation Scheme for the benefit of the transferee to secure such a transfer or to procure substitute policies being issued, pay to the transferee or other insurer all or part of such funds or assets as are attributable to the long-term business being transferred or substituted.

12 Actuarial advice

12(1) Before–

    (a) determining the value of a policy in accordance with Schedules 1 to 5 (other than paragraph 3 of Schedule 1);

    (b) identifying long-term liabilities and assets in accordance with rules 9 and 10;

    (c) determining the amount (if any) of the excess of the long-term business assets in accordance with rule 11;

    (d) determining the terms on which he will accept payment of overdue premiums under rule 20(1) or the amount and nature of any recompense under rule 20(2);

the liquidator shall obtain and consider advice thereon (including an estimate of any value or amount required to be determined) from an actuary.

12(2) Before seeking, for the purpose of valuing a policy, the direction of the court as to the assumption of a particular rate of interest or the employment of any rates of mortality or disability, the liquidator shall obtain and consider advice thereon from an actuary.

13 Utilisation of excess of assets

13(1) Except at the direction of the court, no distribution may be made out of and no transfer to another insurer may be made of–

    (a) any part of the excess of the long-term business assets which has been transferred to the other business; or

    (b) any part of the excess of the other business assets, which has been transferred to the long-term business.

13(2) Before giving a direction under paragraph (1) the court may require the liquidator to advertise the proposal to make a distribution or a transfer in such manner as the court shall direct.

14   Custody of assets

14(1)   The Secretary of State may, in the case of a company carrying on long-term business in whose case no stop order has been made, require that the whole or a specified proportion of the assets representing the fund or funds maintained by the company in respect of its long-term business shall be held by a person approved by him for the purpose as trustee for the company.

14(2)   No assets held by a person as trustee for a company in compliance with a requirement imposed under this rule shall, so long as the requirement is in force, be released except with the consent of the Secretary of State but they may be transposed by the trustee into other assets by any transaction or series of transactions on the written instructions of the liquidator.

14(3)   The liquidator may not, except with the consent of the Secretary of State, grant any security over assets which are held by a person as trustee for the company in compliance with a requirement imposed under this rule.

15   Maintenance of accounting, valuation and other records

15   The liquidator of a company carrying on long-term business in whose case no stop order has been made shall, with a view to the long-term business of the company being transferred to another insurance company, maintain such accounting, valuation and other records as will enable such other insurer upon the transfer being effected to comply with the requirements of any rules made by the Authority under Part X of the 2000 Act relating to accounts and statements of insurers.

16   Additional powers in relation to long-term business

16   The liquidator of a company carrying on long-term business shall, so long as no stop order has been made, have power to do all such things as may be necessary to the performance of his duties under section 376(2) of the 2000 Act (continuation of contracts of long-term insurance where insurer in liquidation) but the Secretary of State may require him–

(a)   not to make investments of a specified class or description,

(b)   to realise, before the expiration of a specified period, the whole or a specified proportion of investments of a specified class or description held by the liquidator.

17   Accounts and audit

17(1)   The liquidator of a company carrying on long-term business in whose case no stop order has been made shall supply the Secretary of State, at such times or intervals as he may specify, with such accounts as he may specify and audited in such manner as he may require and with such information about specified matters and verified in such specified manner as he may require.

17(2)   The liquidator of such a company shall, if required to do so by the Secretary of State, instruct an actuary to investigate the financial condition of the company's long-term business and to report thereon in such manner as the Secretary of State may specify.

18   Caution for long-term and other business

18   Where a company carries on long-term business and–

(a)   no stop order has been made; and

(b)   a special manager has been appointed,

rule 4.70 of the principal rules (caution) applies separately to the company's long-term business and to its other business.

19   Claims

19(1)   This rule applies to a company carrying on long-term business in whose case no stop order has been made.

History

In r.19(1) the words "and in whose case no stop order has been made" inserted by the Insurers (Reorganisation and Winding Up) Regulations 2003 (SI 2003/1102) regs 1, 52, 55 as from April 20, 2003.

19(2)   The liquidator may, in relation to the long-term business of the company and to its other business, fix different days on or before which the creditors of the company, who are required to submit or lodge claims, are to do so and he may fix one of those days without at the same time fixing the other.

19(3)   In submitting or lodging a claim, a creditor may claim the whole or part of such claim as attributable to the long-term business of the company or to its other business or he may make no such attribution.

19(4)   When he accepts any claim, in whole or in part, the liquidator shall state in writing how much of what he accepts is attributable to the long-term business of the company and how much to the other business of the company.

20   Failure to pay premiums

20(1)   The liquidator may in the course of carrying on the company's long-term business and on such terms as he thinks fit accept payment of a premium even though the payment is tendered after the date on which under the terms of the policy it was finally due to be paid.

20(2)   The liquidator may in the course of carrying on the company's long-term business, and having regard to the general practice of insurers, compensate a policy holder whose policy has lapsed in consequence of a failure to pay any premium by issuing a free paid-up policy for reduced benefits or otherwise as the liquidator thinks fit.

21   Notice of valuation of policy

21(1)   Before paying a dividend in respect of claims other than under contracts of long-term insurance, the liquidator shall give notice of the value of each general business policy, as determined by him in accordance with rule 6, to the persons appearing from the records of the company or otherwise to be entitled to an interest in that policy and he shall do so in such manner as the court may direct.

21(2)   Before paying a dividend in respect of claims under contracts of long-term insurance and where a stop order has not been made in relation to the company, the liquidator shall give notice to the persons appearing from the records of the company or otherwise to be entitled to a payment under or to an interest in a long-term policy of the amount of that payment or the value of that policy as determined by him in accordance with rule 7(2) or (3), as the case may be.

21(3)   If a stop order is made in relation to the company, the liquidator shall give notice to all the persons appearing from the records of the company or otherwise to be entitled to a payment under or to an interest in a long-term policy of the amount of that payment or the value of that policy as determined by him in accordance with rule 8(2) or (3), as the case may be, and he shall give that notice in such manner as the court may direct.

21(4)   Any person to whom notice is so given shall be bound by the value so determined unless and until the court otherwise orders.

21(5)   Paragraphs (2) and (3) of this rule have effect as though references therein to persons appearing to be entitled to an interest in a long-term policy and to the value of that policy included, respectively, references to persons appearing to be entitled to apply for a free paid-up policy under section 24 of the 1923 Act and to the value of that entitlement under rule 7 (in the case of paragraph (2) of this rule) or under rule 8 (in the case of paragraph (3) of this rule).

21(6) Where the liquidator summons a meeting of creditors in respect of liabilities of the company attributable to either or both its long-term business or other business, he may adopt any valuation carried out in accordance with rules 6, 7 or 8 as the case may be or, if no such valuation has been carried out by the time of the meeting, he may conduct the meeting using such estimates of the value of policies as he thinks fit.

History
In r.21(6) the words "attributable to either or both" substituted for the former words "attributable either to" by the Insurers (Reorganisation and Winding Up) Regulations 2003 (SI 2003/1102) regs 1, 52, 56 as from April 20, 2003.

22 Dividends to creditors

22(1) This rule applies in the case of a company carrying on long-term business.

22(2) The procedure for payment of dividends to creditors under Chapter 9 of Part 4 of the principal rules (distribution of company's assets by liquidator) applies separately in relation to the two separate companies assumed for the purposes of rule 5 above.

22(3) The court may, at any time before the making of a stop order, permit a dividend to be declared and paid on such terms as it thinks fit in respect only of debts which fell due for payment before the liquidation date or, in the case of claims under long-term policies, which have fallen due for payment on or after the liquidation date.

23 Meetings of creditors

23(1) In the case of a company carrying on long-term business in whose case no stop order has been made, the creditors entitled to participate in creditors' meetings may be–

(a) in relation to the long-term business assets of the company, only those who are creditors in respect of liabilities attributable to the long-term business of the company; and

(b) in relation to the other business assets of the company, only those who are creditors in respect of liabilities attributable to the other business of the company.

23(1A) In a case where separate general meetings of the creditors are summoned by the liquidator pursuant to–

(a) paragraph (1) above; or

(b) regulation [29] of the Insurers (Reorganisation and Winding Up) Regulations 2004 (composite insurers: general meetings of creditors),

chapter 4 (meetings of creditors) and rule 4.31 (final meeting) of Part 4 and Chapters 1 and 2 of Part 7 (meetings and proxies and company representation) of the principal rules apply to each such separate meeting.

History
Purported substitution in "r.24(1A)(b)" of "regulation 28 of the Insurers (Reorganisation and Winding Up) Regulations 2004" for "regulation 28 of the Insurers (Reorganisation and Winding Up) Regulations 2003" by the Insurers (Regulation and Winding Up) Regulations 2004 (SI 2004/353) regs 5(1), (3) as from February 18, 2004: however, the rule in question should plainly be r.23(1A)(b) and the reference in each case to reg.29.
    Previously r.23(1), (1A) substituted for the former r.23(1) by the Insurers (Reorganisation and Winding Up) Regulations 2003 (SI 2003/1102) regs 1, 52, 57(4), (5) as from April 20, 2003.

23(2)   In relation to any such separate meeting–

(a)   rule 7.6(6) of the principal rules (meetings requisitioned) has effect as if the reference therein to assets of the company was a reference to the assets available under the above-mentioned Regulations for meeting the liabilities of the company owed to the creditors summoned to the meeting, and

(b)   rule 7.12 of the principal rules (resolutions) applies as if the reference therein to value in relation to a creditor who is not, by virtue of rule 6, 7 or 8, required to submit or lodge a claim, was a reference to the value most recently notified to him under rule 21 above or, if the court has determined a different value in accordance with rule 21(4), as if it were a reference to that different value.

23(3)   In paragraph (1)–

"long-term business assets" means the assets representing the fund or funds maintained by the company in respect of its long-term business;

"other business assets" means any assets of the company which are not long-term business assets.

History
Rule 23(3) inserted by the Insurers (Reorganisation and Winding Up) Regulations 2003 (SI 2003/1102) regs 1, 52, 57(4), (6) as from April 20, 2003.

24   Apportionment of expenses of liquidation

24(1)   Where no stop order has been made in relation to a company, rule 4.67 of the principal rules (appointment and remuneration) applies separately to the assets of the long-term business of the company and to the assets of the other business of the company.

History
In r.24(1) the words "Where no stop order has been made in relation to a company, rule 4.67" substituted for the former words "Rule 4.67" by the Insurers (Reorganisation and Winding Up) Regulations 2003 (SI 2003/1102) regs 1, 52, 58(2) as from April 20, 2003.

24(2)   Where any fee, expense, cost, charge, outlay or remuneration does not relate exclusively to the assets of the company's long-term business or to the assets of the company's other business, the liquidator shall apportion it amongst those assets in such manner as he shall determine.

25   Notice of stop order

25(1)   When a stop order has been made in relation to the company, the clerk of court shall, on the same day, send–

(a)   to the liquidator,

(b)   to the registrar of companies for Scotland, and

(c)   to such other person as the court may direct,

a certified copy of the stop order.

25(2)   The liquidator shall forthwith after receiving a certified copy give notice of the order in the Form in Schedule 6–

(a)   in the Edinburgh Gazette, and

(b)   in the newspaper in which the winding-up order was advertised.

SCHEDULES

SCHEDULE 1

RULES FOR VALUING GENERAL BUSINESS POLICIES

Rule 6

1(1) This paragraph applies in relation to periodic payments under a general business policy which fall due for payment after the liquidation date where the event giving rise to the liability to make the payments occurred before the liquidation date.

1(2) The value to be attributed to such periodic payments shall be determined on such actuarial principles and assumptions in regard to all relevant factors as the court shall direct.

2(1) This paragraph applies in relation to liabilities under a general business policy which arise from events which occurred before the liquidation date but which have not–

   (a)   fallen due for payment before the liquidation date; or

   (b)   been notified to the company before the liquidation date.

2(2) The value to be attributed to such liabilities shall be determined on such actuarial principles and assumptions in regard to all relevant factors as the court shall direct.

3(1) This paragraph applies in relation to liabilities under a general business policy not dealt with by paragraphs 1 or 2.

3(2) The value to be attributed to those liabilities shall–

   (a)   if the terms of the policy provide for a repayment of premium upon the early termination of the policy or the policy is expressed to run from one definite date to another or the policy may be terminated by any of the parties with effect from a definite date, be the greater of the following two amounts:

      (i)   the amount (if any) which under the terms of the policy would have been repayable on early termination of the policy had the policy terminated on the liquidation date, and

      (ii)   where the policy is expressed to run from one definite date to another or may be terminated by any of the parties with effect from a definite date, such proportion of the last premium paid as is proportionate to the unexpired portion of the period in respect of which that premium was paid; and

   (b)   in any other case, be a just estimate of that value.

SCHEDULE 2

RULES FOR VALUING NON-LINKED LIFE POLICIES, NON-LINKED DEFERRED ANNUITY POLICIES, NON-LINKED ANNUITIES IN PAYMENT, UNITISED NON-LINKED POLICIES AND CAPITAL REDEMPTION POLICIES

Rule 7

1   General

1   In valuing a policy–

   (a)   where it is necessary to calculate the present value of future payments by or to the company, interest shall be assumed at such fair and reasonable rate or rates as the court may direct;

   (b)   where relevant, the rates of mortality and the rates of disability to be employed shall be such rates as the court considers appropriate after taking into account:

     (i)   relevant published tables of rates of mortality and rates of disability, and

     (ii) the rates of mortality and the rates of disability experienced in connection with similar policies issued by the company;

(c) there shall be determined:

     (i)   the present value of the ordinary benefits,

     (ii) the present value of additional benefits;

     (iii) the present value of options, and

     (iv) if further premiums fall due to be paid under the policy on or after the liquidation date, the present value of the premiums;

and for the purposes of this Schedule if the ordinary benefits only take into account premiums paid to date, the present value of future premiums shall be taken as nil.

2   Present value of the ordinary benefits

2(1)   Ordinary benefits are the benefits which will become payable to the policy holder on or after the liquidation date without his having to exercise any option under the policy (including any bonus or addition to the sum assured or the amount of annuity declared before the liquidation date) and for this purpose **"option"** includes a right to surrender the policy.

2(2)   Subject to sub-paragraph (3), the present value of the ordinary benefits shall be the value at the liquidation date of the reversion in the ordinary benefits according to the contingency upon which those benefits are payable calculated on the basis of the rates of interest, mortality and disability referred to in paragraph 1.

2(3)   For accumulating with profits policies–

(a) where the benefits are not expressed in the form of units in a with-profits fund, the value of the ordinary benefits is the amount that would have been payable, excluding any discretionary additions, if the policyholder had been able to exercise a right to terminate the policy at the liquidation date; and

(b) where the benefits are expressed in the form of units in a with-profits fund, the value of the ordinary benefits is the number of units held by the policy holder at the liquidation date valued at the unit price in force at that time or, if that price is not calculated on a daily basis, such price as the court may determine having regard to the last published unit price and any change in the value of assets attributable to the fund since the date of the last published unit price.

2(4)   Where–

(a) sub-paragraph (3) applies, and

(b) paragraph 3(1) of Schedule 3 applies to the calculation of the unit price (or as the case may be) the fund value,

the value shall be adjusted on the basis set out in paragraph 3(3) to (5) of Schedule 3.

2(5)   Where sub-paragraph (3) applies, the value may be further adjusted by reference to the value of the assets underlying the unit price (or as the case may be) the value of the fund, if the liquidator considers such an adjustment to be necessary.

3   Present value of additional benefits

3(1)   Where under the terms of the policy or on the basis of the company's established practice the policy holder has a right to receive or an expectation of receiving benefits additional to the minimum benefits guaranteed under those terms, the court shall determine rates of interest, bonus (whether reversionary, terminal or any other type of bonus used by the company), mortality and disability to provide for the present value (if any) of that right or expectation.

3(2) In determining what (if any) value to attribute to any such expectations the court shall have regard to the premium payable in relation to the minimum guaranteed benefits and the amount (if any) an insurer is required to provide in respect of those expectations in any rules made by the Authority under Part X of the 2000 Act.

4 Present value of options

4 The amount of the present value of options shall be the amount which, in the opinion of the liquidator, is necessary to be provided at the liquidation date (in addition to the amount of the present value of the ordinary benefits) to cover the additional liabilities likely to arise upon the exercise on or after that date by the policy holder of any option conferred upon him by the terms of the policy or, in the case of an industrial assurance policy, by the Industrial Assurance Acts other than an option whereby the policy holder can secure a guaranteed cash payment within the period of 12 months beginning with that date.

5 Present value of premiums

5 The present value of the premiums shall be the value at the liquidation date of the premiums which fall due to be paid by the policy holder after the liquidation date calculated on the basis of the rates of interest, mortality and disability referred to in paragraph 1.

6 Value of the policy

6(1) Subject to sub-paragraph (2)–

  (a) if no further premiums fall due to be paid under the policy on or after the liquidation date, the value of the policy shall be the aggregate of:

    (i)   the present value of the ordinary benefits;

    (ii) the present value of options; and

    (iii) the present value of additional benefits;

  (b) if further premiums fall due to be so paid and the aggregate value referred to in sub-paragraph (a) exceeds the present value of the premiums, the value of the policy shall be the amount of that excess; and

  (c) if further premiums fall due to be so paid and that aggregate does not exceed the present value of the premiums, the policy shall have no value.

6(2) Where the policy holder has a right conferred upon him by the terms of the policy or by the Industrial Assurance Acts whereby the policy holder can secure a guaranteed cash payment within the period of 12 months beginning with the liquidation date, the liquidator shall determine the amount which in his opinion it is necessary to provide at that date to cover the liabilities which will accrue when that option is exercised (on the assumption that it will be exercised) and the value of the policy shall be that amount if it exceeds the value of the policy (if any) determined in accordance with sub-paragraph (1).

SCHEDULE 3

RULES FOR VALUING LIFE POLICIES AND DEFERRED ANNUITY POLICIES WHICH ARE LINKED POLICIES

Rule 7

1(1) Subject to sub-paragraph (2) the value of the policy shall be the aggregate of the value of the linked liabilities (calculated in accordance with paragraphs 2 or 4) and the value of other than linked liabilities (calculated in accordance with paragraph 5) except where that aggregate is a negative amount in which case the policy shall have no value.

1(2)   Where the terms of the policy include a right whereby the policy holder can secure a guaranteed cash payment within the period of 12 months beginning with the liquidation date then, if the amount which in the opinion of the liquidator is necessary to be provided at that date to cover any liabilities which will accrue when that option is exercised (on the assumption that it will be exercised) is greater than the value determined under sub-paragraph (1) of this paragraph, the value of the policy shall be that greater amount.

2(1)   Where the linked liabilities are expressed in terms of units the value of those liabilities shall, subject to paragraph 3, be the amount arrived at by taking the product of the number of units of each class of units allocated to the policy on the liquidation date and the value of each such unit on that date and then adding those products.

2(2)   For the purposes of sub-paragraph (1)–

(a)   where under the terms of the policy the value of a unit at any time falls to be determined by reference to the value at that time of the assets of a particular fund maintained by the company in relation to that and other policies, the value of a unit on the liquidation date shall be determined by reference to the net realisable value of the assets credited to that fund on that date (after taking account of disposal costs, any tax liabilities resulting from the disposal of assets insofar as they have not already been provided for by the company and any other amounts which under the terms of those polices are chargeable to the fund), and

(b)   in any other case, the value of a unit on the liquidation date shall be the value which would have been ascribed to each unit credited to the policy holder, after any deductions which may be made under the terms of the policy, for the purpose of determining the benefits payable under the policy on the liquidation date had the policy matured on that date.

3(1)   This paragraph applies where–

(a)   paragraph 2(2)(a) applies and the company has a right under the terms of the policy either to make periodic withdrawals from the fund referred to in that paragraph or to retain any part of the income accruing in respect of the assets of that fund,

(b)   paragraph 2(2)(b) applies and the company has a right under the terms of the policy to receive the whole or any part of any distributions made in respect of the units referred to in that paragraph, or

(c)   paragraph 2(2)(a) or paragraph 2(2)(b) applies and the company has a right under the terms of the policy to make periodic cancellations of a proportion of the number of units credited to the policy.

3(2)   Where this paragraph applies, the value of the linked liabilities calculated in accordance with paragraph 2(1) shall be reduced by an amount calculated in accordance with sub-paragraph (3) of this paragraph.

3(3)   The said amount is–

(a)   where this paragraph applies by virtue of head (a) or (b) of sub-paragraph (1), the value as at the liquidation date, calculated on actuarial principles, of the future income of the company in respect of the units in question arising from the rights referred to in head (a) or (b) of sub-paragraph (1) as the case may be, or

(b)   where this paragraph applies by virtue of head (c) of sub-paragraph (1), the value as at the liquidation date, calculated on actuarial principles, of the liabilities of the company in respect of the units which fall to be cancelled in the future under the right referred to in head (c) of sub-paragraph (1).

3(4)   In calculating any amount in accordance with sub-paragraph (3) there shall be disregarded–

   (a)   such part of the rights referred to in the relevant head of sub-paragraph (1) which in the opinion of the liquidator constitutes appropriate provision for future expenses and mortality risks, and

   (b)   such part of those rights (if any) which the court considers to constitute appropriate provision for any right or expectation of the policy holder to receive benefits additional to the benefits guaranteed under the terms of the policy.

3(5)   In determining the said amount–

   (a)   interest shall be assumed at such rate or rates as the court may direct, and

   (b)   where relevant, the rates of mortality and the rates of disability to be employed shall be such rates as the court considers appropriate after taking into account:

      (i)   relevant published tables of rates of mortality and rates of disability, and

      (ii)   the rates of mortality and the rates of disability experienced in connection with similar policies issued by the company.

4   Where the linked liabilities are not expressed in terms of units the value of those liabilities shall be the value (subject to adjustment for any amounts which would have been deducted for taxation) which would have been ascribed to those liabilities had the policy matured on the liquidation date.

5(1)   The value of any liabilities other than linked liabilities including reserves for future expenses, options and guarantees shall he determined on actuarial principles and appropriate assumptions in regard to all relevant factors including the assumption of such rate or rates of interest, mortality and disability as the court may direct.

5(2)   In valuing liabilities under this paragraph credit shall be taken for those parts of future premiums which do not fall to be applied in the allocation of further units to the policy and for any rights of the company which have been disregarded under paragraph 3(4)(a) in valuing the linked liabilities.

SCHEDULE 4

RULES FOR VALUING LONG-TERM POLICIES WHICH ARE NOT DEALT WITH IN SCHEDULES 2 OR 3

Rule 7

The value of a long-term policy not covered by Schedule 2 or 3 shall be the value of the benefits due to the policy holder determined on such actuarial principles and assumptions in regard to all relevant factors as the court shall determine.

SCHEDULE 5

RULES FOR VALUING LONG-TERM POLICIES WHERE A STOP ORDER HAS BEEN MADE

Rule 8

1   Subject to paragraphs 2 and 3, in valuing a policy Schedules 2, 3 or 4 shall apply according to the class of that policy as if those Schedules were herein repeated but with a view to a fresh valuation of each policy on appropriate assumptions in regard to all relevant factors and subject to the following modifications–

   (a)   references to the stop order shall be substituted for references to the liquidation date,

   (b)   in paragraph 4 of Schedule 2 for the words "whereby the policy holder can secure a guaranteed cash payment within the period of 12 months beginning with that date" there shall be substituted the words "to surrender the policy which can be exercised on that date",

997

    (c)   paragraph 6(2) of Schedule 2 shall be deleted, and

    (d)   paragraph 1(2) of Schedule 3 shall be deleted.

2(1)   This paragraph applies where the policy holder has a right conferred upon him under the terms of the policy or by the Industrial Assurance Acts to surrender the policy and that right is exercisable on the date of the stop order.

2(2)   Where this paragraph applies and the amount required at the date of the stop order to provide for the benefits payable upon surrender of the policy (on the assumption that the policy is surrendered on the date of the stop order) is greater than the value of the policy determined in accordance with paragraph 1, the value of the policy shall, subject to paragraph 3, be the said amount so required.

2(3)   Where any part of the surrender value is payable after the date of the stop order, sub-paragraph (2) shall apply but the value therein referred to shall be discounted at such rate of interest as the court may direct.

3(1)   This paragraph applies in the case of a linked policy where–

    (a)   the terms of the policy include a guarantee that the amount assured will on maturity of the policy be worth a minimum amount calculable in money terms, or

    (b)   the terms of the policy include a right on the part of the policy holder to surrender the policy and a guarantee that the payment on surrender will be worth a minimum calculable in money terms and that right is exercisable on or after the date of the stop order.

3(2)   Where this paragraph applies the value of the policy shall be the greater of the following two amounts–

    (a)   the value the policy would have had at the date of the stop order had the policy been a non-linked policy, that is to say, had the linked liabilities provided by the policy not been so provided but the policy had otherwise been on the same terms, and

    (b)   the value the policy would have had at the date of the stop order had the policy not included any guarantees of payments on maturity or surrender worth a minimum amount calculable in money terms.

SCHEDULE 6

FORM

Rule 25

[Not reproduced.]

Insolvency Act 1986 (Prescribed Part) Order 2003

(SI 2003/2097)

Made on 8 August 2002 by the Secretary of State for Trade and Industry under s.176A of the Insolvency Act 1986. Operative from 15 September 2003.

1 Citation, Commencement And Interpretation

1(1) This Order may be cited as the Insolvency Act 1986 (Prescribed Part) Order 2003 and shall come into force on 15th September 2003.

1(2) In this Order **"the 1986 Act"** means the Insolvency Act 1986.

2 Minimum value of the company's net property

2 For the purposes of section 176A(3)(a) of the 1986 Act the minimum value of the company's net property is £10,000.

3 Calculation of prescribed part

3(1) The prescribed part of the company's net property to be made available for the satisfaction of unsecured debts of the company pursuant to section 176A of the 1986 Act shall be calculated as follows–

    (a) where the company's net property does not exceed £10,000 in value, 50% of that property;

    (b) subject to paragraph (2), where the company's net property exceeds £10,000 in value the sum of–

        (i) 50% of the first £10,000 in value; and

        (ii) 20% of that part of the company's net property which exceeds £10,000 in value.

3(2) The value of the prescribed part of the company's net property to be made available for the satisfaction of unsecured debts of the company pursuant to section 176A shall not exceed £600,000.

Financial Collateral Arrangements (No.2) Regulations 2003

(SI 2003/3226)

Made on December 10, 2003 by the Treasury, being a government department designated for the purposes of s.2(2) of the European Communities Act 1972 in relation to collateral security, in exercise of the powers conferred on them by that section. Operative from December 26, 2003.

[**Note**: Changes made by the Financial Collateral Arrangements (No.2) Regulations 2003 (Amendment) Regulations 2009 (SI 2009/2462) and the Financial Markets and Insolvency (Settlement Finality and Financial Collateral Arrangements) (Amendment) Regulations 2010 (SI 2010/2993) have been incorporated into the text.]

PART 1

GENERAL

1 Citation and commencement

1(1) These Regulations may be cited as the Financial Collateral Arrangements (No. 2) Regulations 2003.

1(2) Regulation 2 shall come into force on 11th December 2003 and all other Regulations thereof shall come into force on 26th December 2003.

2 Revocation

2 The Financial Collateral Arrangements Regulations 2003 are hereby revoked.

[**Note:** These Regulations were never brought into force.]

3 Interpretation

3(1) In these Regulations–

"**book entry securities collateral**" means financial collateral subject to a financial collateral arrangement which consists of financial instruments, title to which is evidenced by entries in a register or account maintained by or on behalf of an intermediary;

"**cash**" means money in any currency, credited to an account, or a similar claim for repayment of money and includes money market deposits and sums due or payable to, or received between the parties in connection with the operation of a financial collateral arrangement or a close-out netting provision;

"**close-out netting provision**" means a term of a financial collateral arrangement, or of an arrangement of which a financial collateral arrangement forms part, or any legislative provision under which on the occurrence of an enforcement event, whether through the operation of netting or set-off or otherwise–

(a) the obligations of the parties are accelerated to become immediately due and expressed as an obligation to pay an amount representing the original obligation's estimated current value or replacement cost, or are terminated and replaced by an obligation to pay such an amount; or

(b) an account is taken of what is due from each party to the other in respect of such obligations and a net sum equal to the balance of the account is payable by the party from whom the larger amount is due to the other party;

"**credit claims**" means pecuniary claims which arise out of an agreement whereby a credit institution, as defined in Article 4(1) of Directive 2006/48/EC of the European Parliament and of the Council relating to the taking up and pursuit of the business of credit institutions (recast), including the institutions listed in Article 2 of that Directive, grants credit in the form of a loan;

"enforcement event" means an event of default, or any similar event as agreed between the parties, on the occurrence of which, under the terms of a financial collateral arrangement or by operation of law, the collateral-taker is entitled to realise or appropriate financial collateral or a close-out netting provision comes into effect;

"equivalent financial collateral" means–

(a)   in relation to cash, a payment of the same amount and in the same currency;

(b)   in relation to financial instruments, financial instruments of the same issuer or debtor, forming part of the same issue or class and of the same nominal amount, currency and description or, where the financial collateral arrangement provides for the transfer of other assets following the occurrence of any event relating to or affecting any financial instruments provided as financial collateral, those other assets;

and includes the original financial collateral provided under the arrangement;

"financial collateral arrangement" means a title transfer financial collateral arrangement or a security financial collateral arrangement, whether or not these are covered by a master agreement or general terms and conditions;

"financial collateral" means either cash, financial instruments or credit claims;

"financial instruments" means–

(a)   shares in companies and other securities equivalent to shares in companies;

(b)   bonds and other forms of instruments giving rise to or acknowledging indebtedness if these are tradeable on the capital market; and

(c)   any other securities which are normally dealt in and which give the right to acquire any such shares, bonds, instruments or other securities by subscription, purchase or exchange or which give rise to a cash settlement (excluding instruments of payment);

and includes units of a collective investment scheme within the meaning of the Financial Services and Markets Act 2000, eligible debt securities within the meaning of the Uncertificated Securities Regulations 2001, money market instruments, claims relating to or rights in or in respect of any of the financial instruments included in this definition and any rights, privileges or benefits attached to or arising from any such financial instruments;

"intermediary" means a person that maintains registers or accounts to which financial instruments may be credited or debited, for others or both for others and for its own account but does not include–

(a)   a person who acts as a registrar or transfer agent for the issuer of financial instruments; or

(b)   a person who maintains registers or accounts in the capacity of operator of a system for the holding and transfer of financial instruments on records of the issuer or other records which constitute the primary record of entitlement to financial instruments as against the issuer;

"non-natural person" means any corporate body, unincorporated firm, partnership or body with legal personality except an individual, including any such entity constituted under the law of a country or territory outside the United Kingdom or any such entity constituted under international law;

"relevant account" means, in relation to book entry securities collateral which is subject to a financial collateral arrangement, the register or account, which may be maintained by the collateral-taker, in which entries are made, by which that book entry securities collateral is transferred or designated so as to be in the possession or under the control of the collateral-taker or a person acting on its behalf;

"relevant financial obligations" means the obligations which are secured or otherwise covered by a financial collateral arrangement, and such obligations may consist of or include–

(a) present or future, actual or contingent or prospective obligations (including such obligations arising under a master agreement or similar arrangement);

(b) obligations owed to the collateral-taker by a person other than the collateral-provider;

(c) obligations of a specified class or kind arising from time to time;

"reorganisation measures" means–

(a) administration within the meaning of the Insolvency Act 1986 or the Insolvency (Northern Ireland) Order 1989;

(b) a company voluntary arrangement within the meaning of that Act or that Order;

(c) administration of a partnership within the meaning of that Act or that Order or, in the case of a Scottish partnership, a protected trust deed within the meaning of the Bankruptcy (Scotland) Act 1985;

(d) a partnership voluntary arrangement within the meaning of the Insolvency Act 1986 or the Insolvency (Northern Ireland) Order 1989 or, in the case of a Scottish partnership, a protected trust deed within the meaning of the Bankruptcy (Scotland) Act 1985; and

(e) the making of an interim order on an administration application;

"security financial collateral arrangement" means an agreement or arrangement, evidenced in writing, where–

(a) the purpose of the agreement or arrangement is to secure the relevant financial obligations owed to the collateral-taker;

(b) the collateral-provider creates or there arises a security interest in financial collateral to secure those obligations;

(c) the financial collateral is delivered, transferred, held, registered or otherwise designated so as to be in the possession or under the control of the collateral-taker or a person acting on its behalf; any right of the collateral-provider to substitute financial collateral of the same or greater value or withdraw excess financial collateral or to collect the proceeds of credit claims until further notice shall not prevent the financial collateral being in the possession or under the control of the collateral-taker; and

(d) the collateral-provider and the collateral-taker are both non-natural persons;

"security interest" means any legal or equitable interest or any right in security, other than a title transfer financial collateral arrangement, created or otherwise arising by way of security including–

(a) a pledge;

(b) a mortgage;

(c) a fixed charge;

(d) a charge created as a floating charge where the financial collateral charged is delivered, transferred, held, registered or otherwise designated so as to be in the possession or under the control of the collateral-taker or a person acting on its behalf; any right of the collateral-provider to substitute financial collateral of the same or greater value or withdraw excess financial collateral or to collect the proceeds of credit claims until further notice shall not prevent the financial collateral being in the possession or under the control of the collateral-taker; or

(e) a lien;

"title transfer financial collateral arrangement" means an agreement or arrangement, including a repurchase agreement, evidenced in writing, where–

(a) the purpose of the agreement or arrangement is to secure or otherwise cover the relevant financial obligations owed to the collateral-taker;

(b) the collateral-provider transfers legal and beneficial ownership in financial collateral to a collateral-taker on terms that when the relevant financial obligations are discharged the collateral-taker must transfer legal and beneficial ownership of equivalent financial collateral to the collateral-provider; and

(c) the collateral-provider and the collateral-taker are both non-natural persons;

"winding-up proceedings" means–

(a) winding up by the court or voluntary winding up within the meaning of the Insolvency Act 1986 or the Insolvency (Northern Ireland) Order 1989;

(b) sequestration of a Scottish partnership under the Bankruptcy (Scotland) Act 1985;

(c) bank insolvency within the meaning of the Banking Act 2009.

3(2) For the purposes of these Regulations **"possession"** of financial collateral in the form of cash or financial instruments includes the case where financial collateral has been credited to an account in the name of the collateral-taker or a person acting on his behalf (whether or not the collateral-taker, or person acting on his behalf, has credited the financial collateral to an account in the name of the collateral-provider on his, or that person's, books) provided that any rights the collateral-provider may have in relation to that financial collateral are limited to the right to substitute financial collateral of the same or greater value or to withdraw excess financial collateral.

History
Definitions of "financial collateral", "reorganisation measures", "security financial collateral arrangement", "security interest" and "winding up proceedings" amended and definition of "credit claims" and reg.3(1) inserted by the Financial Markets and Insolvency (Settlement Finality and Financial Collateral Arrangements) (Amendment) Regulations 2010 (SI 2010/2993) reg.4(2) as from April 6, 2011.

PART 2

MODIFICATION OF LAW REQUIRING FORMALITIES

4   Certain legislation requiring formalities not to apply to financial collateral arrangements

4(1) Section 4 of the Statute of Frauds 1677 (no action on a third party's promise unless in writing and signed) shall not apply (if it would otherwise do so) in relation to a financial collateral arrangement.

4(2) Section 53(1)(c) of the Law of Property Act 1925 (disposition of equitable interest to be in writing and signed) shall not apply (if it would otherwise do so) in relation to a financial collateral arrangement.

4(3) Section 136 of the Law of Property Act 1925 (legal assignments of things in action) shall not apply (if it would otherwise do so) in relation to a financial collateral arrangement, to the extent that the section requires an assignment to be signed by the assignor or a person authorised on its behalf, in order to be effectual in law.

4(4) Sections 860 (charges created by a company) and 874 (consequence of failure to register charges created by a company) of the Companies Act 2006 shall not apply (if they would otherwise do so) in relation to a security financial collateral arrangement or any charge created or otherwise arising under a security financial collateral arrangement or, in Scotland, to relation to any charge created or arising under a financial collateral arrangement.

4(5) Section 4 of the Industrial and Provident Societies Act 1967 (filing of information relating to charges) shall not apply (if it would otherwise do so) in relation to a financial collateral arrangement or any charge created or otherwise arising under a financial collateral arrangement.

(See history note after reg.7.)

5   Certain legislation affecting Scottish companies not to apply to financial collateral arrangements

5 Sections 878 (charges created by a company) and 889 (charges void unless registered) of the Companies Act 2006 shall not apply (if they would otherwise do so) in relation to a financial collateral arrangement or any charge created or otherwise arising under a financial collateral arrangement.

(See history note after reg.7.)

6   No additional formalities required for creation of a right in security over book entry securities collateral in Scotland

6(1) Where under the law of Scotland an act is required as a condition for transferring, creating or enforcing a right in security over any book entry securities collateral, that requirement shall not apply (if it would otherwise do so).

6(2) For the purposes of paragraph (1) an **"act"**–

(a) is any act other than an entry on a register or account maintained by or on behalf of an intermediary which evidences title to the book entry securities collateral;

(b) includes the entering of the collateral-taker's name in a company's register of members.

(See history note after reg.7.)

6A   Certain legislation affecting overseas companies not to apply to financial collateral arrangements

6A Any provision about registration of charges made by regulations under section 1052 of the Companies Act 2006 (overseas companies) does not apply (if it would otherwise do so) in relation to a security financial collateral arrangement or any charge created or otherwise arising under a security financial collateral arrangement or, in Scotland, to any charge created or arising under a financial collateral arrangement.

(See history note after reg.7.)

7   Certain legislation affecting Northern Ireland companies and requiring formalities not to apply to financial collateral arrangements [Omitted.]

History
Regulations 4, 5 amended, reg.6A inserted and reg.7 omitted by the Financial Collateral Arrangements (No.2) Regulations 2003 (Amendment) Regulations 2009 (SI 2009/2462) reg.2(1)–(5) as from October 1, 2009. Regulations

4, 5, 6A amended by the Financial Markets and Insolvency (Settlement Finality and Financial Collateral Arrangements) (Amendment) Regulations 2010 (SI 2010/2993) reg.4(3)–(5) as from April 6, 2011.

PART 3

MODIFICATION OF INSOLVENCY LAW

8   Certain legislation restricting enforcement of security not to apply to financial collateral arrangements

8(1)   The following provisions of Schedule B1 to the Insolvency Act 1986 (administration) shall not apply to any security interest created or otherwise arising under a financial collateral arrangement–

(a)   paragraph 43(2) (restriction on enforcement of security or repossession of goods) including that provision as applied by paragraph 44 (interim moratorium);

(aa)   paragraph 65(2) (distribution);

(b)   paragraphs 70 and 71 (power of administrator to deal with charged property); and

(c)   paragraph 99(3) and (4) (administrator's remuneration, expenses and liabilities).

8(2)   Paragraph 41(2) of Schedule B1 to the Insolvency Act 1986 (receiver to vacate office when so required by administrator) shall not apply to a receiver appointed under a charge created or otherwise arising under a financial collateral arrangement.

8(3)   The following provisions of the Insolvency Act 1986 (administration) shall not apply in relation to any security interest created or otherwise arising under a financial collateral arrangement–

(a)   sections 10(1)(b) and 11(3)(c) (restriction on enforcement of security while petition for administration order pending or order in force); and

(b)   section 15(1) and 15(2) (power of administrator to deal with charged property); and

(c)   section 19(4) and 19(5) (administrator's remuneration, expenses and liabilities).

8(4)   Section 11(2) of the Insolvency Act 1986 (receiver to vacate office when so required by administrator) shall not apply to a receiver appointed under a charge created or otherwise arising under a financial collateral arrangement.

8(5)   Paragraph 20 and sub-paragraph 12(1)(g) of Schedule A1 to the Insolvency Act 1986 (Effect of moratorium on creditors) shall not apply (if it would otherwise do so) to any security interest created or otherwise arising under a financial collateral arrangement.

History
Regulation 8 amended by the Financial Markets and Insolvency (Settlement Finality and Financial Collateral Arrangements) (Amendment) Regulations 2010 (SI 2010/2993) reg.4(6) as from April 6, 2011.

9   Certain Northern Ireland legislation restricting enforcement of security not to apply to financial collateral arrangements

9(1)   The following provisions of the Insolvency (Northern Ireland) Order 1989 (administration) shall not apply to any security interest created or otherwise arising under a financial collateral arrangement–

(a)   Article 23(1)(b) and Article 24(3)(c) (restriction on enforcement of security while petition for administration order pending or order in force);

(b)   Article 28(1) and (2) (power of administrator to deal with charged property);

(c)   Article 31(4) and (5) (administrator's remuneration, expenses and liabilities); and

(d)   Paragraphs 44(2), 45 (restriction on enforcement of security), 66(2) (distribution), 71, 72 (power of administrator to deal with charged property), 100(3) and (4) (administrator's remuneration, expenses and liabilities) of Schedule B1 to the Order.

9(2)   Article 24(2) of that Order (receiver to vacate office at request of administrator) shall not apply to a receiver appointed under a charge created or otherwise arising under a financial collateral arrangement.

(See history note after reg.11.)

10   Certain insolvency legislation on avoidance of contracts and floating charges not to apply to financial collateral arrangements

10(1)   In relation to winding-up proceedings of a collateral-taker or collateral-provider, section 127 of the Insolvency Act 1986 (avoidance of property dispositions, etc) shall not apply (if it would otherwise do so)–

(a)   to any property or security interest subject to a disposition or created or otherwise arising under a financial collateral arrangement; or

(b)   to prevent a close-out netting provision taking effect in accordance with its terms.

10(2)   Section 88 of the Insolvency Act 1986 (avoidance of share transfers, etc after winding-up resolution) shall not apply (if it would otherwise do so) to any transfer of shares under a financial collateral arrangement.

10(2A)   Sections 40 (or in Scotland, sections 59, 60(1)(e)) and 175 of the Insolvency Act 1986 (preferential debts) shall not apply to any debt which is secured by a charge created or otherwise arising under a financial collateral arrangement.

10(2B)   Section 176ZA of the Insolvency Act 1986 (expenses of winding up) 4 shall not apply in relation to any claim to any property which is subject to a disposition or created or otherwise arising under a financial collateral arrangement.

10(3)   Section 176A of the Insolvency Act 1986 (share of assets for unsecured creditors) shall not apply (if it would otherwise do so) to any charge created or otherwise arising under a financial collateral arrangement.

10(4)   Section 178 of the Insolvency Act 1986 (power to disclaim onerous property) or, in Scotland, any rule of law having the same effect as that section, shall not apply where the collateral-provider or collateral-taker under the arrangement is subject to winding-up proceedings, to any financial collateral arrangement.

10(5)   Section 245 of the Insolvency Act 1986 (avoidance of certain floating charges) shall not apply (if it would otherwise do so) to any charge created or otherwise arising under a security financial collateral arrangement.

10(6)   Section 754 of the Companies Act 2006 (priorities where debentures secured by floating charge) (including that section as applied or modified by any enactment made under the Banking Act 2009) shall not apply (if it would otherwise do so) to any charge created or otherwise arising under a financial collateral arrangement.

(See history note after reg.11.)

11 Certain Northern Ireland insolvency legislation on avoidance of contracts and floating charges not to apply to financial collateral arrangements

11(1)   In relation to winding-up proceedings of a collateral-provider or collateral-taker, Article 107 of the Insolvency (Northern Ireland) Order 1989 (avoidance of property dispositions effected after commencement of winding up) shall not apply (if it would otherwise do so)–

(a)   to any property or security interest subject to a disposition or created or otherwise arising under a financial collateral arrangement; or

(b)   to prevent a close-out netting provision taking effect in accordance with its terms.

11(1A)   Article 50 of that Order (payment of debts out of assets subject to floating charge) shall not apply (if it would otherwise do so), to any charge created or otherwise arising under a financial collateral arrangement.

11(2)   Article 74 of that Order (avoidance of share transfers, etc after winding-up resolution) shall not apply (if it would otherwise do so) to any transfer of shares under a financial collateral arrangement.

11(2A)   Articles 149 of that Order (preferential debts) and 150ZA (expenses of winding up) shall not apply (if they would otherwise do so) to any charge created or otherwise arising under a financial collateral arrangement.

11(3)   Article 152 of that Order (power to disclaim onerous property) shall not apply where the collateral-provider or collateral-taker under the arrangement is being wound-up, to any financial collateral arrangement.

11(4)   Article 207 of that Order (avoidance of certain floating charges) shall not apply (if it would otherwise do so) to any charge created or otherwise arising under a security financial collateral arrangement.

11(5)   [Omitted.]

History
Regulation 10(6) amended and reg.11(5) omitted by the Financial Collateral Arrangements (No.2) Regulations 2003 (Amendment) Regulations 2009 (SI 2009/2462) reg.2(6), (7) as from October 1, 2009. Regulations 9–11 amended by the Financial Markets and Insolvency (Settlement Finality and Financial Collateral Arrangements) (Amendment) Regulations 2010 (SI 2010/2993) reg.4(7)–(9) as from April 6, 2011.

12 Close-out netting provisions to take effect in accordance with their terms

12(1)   A close-out netting provision shall, subject to paragraph (2), take effect in accordance with its terms notwithstanding that the collateral-provider or collateral-taker under the arrangement is subject to winding-up proceedings or reorganisation measures.

12(2)   Paragraph (1) shall not apply if at the time that a party to a financial collateral arrangement entered into such an arrangement or that the relevant financial obligations came into existence–

(a)   that party was aware or should have been aware that winding up proceedings or re-organisation measures had commenced in relation to the other party;

(b)   that party had notice that a meeting of creditors of the other party had been summoned under section 98 of the Insolvency Act 1986, or Article 84 of the Companies (Northern Ireland) Order 1989 or that a petition for the winding-up of or, in Scotland, a petition for winding-up proceedings in relation to the other party was pending;

(c)   that party had notice that an application for an administration order was pending or that any person had given notice of an intention to appoint an administrator; or

(d)   that party had notice that an application for an administration order was pending or that any person had given notice of an intention to appoint an administrator and liquidation of the other party to the financial collateral arrangement was immediately preceded by an administration of that party.

12(3)   For the purposes of paragraph (2)–

 (a) winding-up proceedings commence on the making of a winding-up order or, in the case of a Scottish partnership, the award of sequestration by the court; and

 (b) reorganisation measures commence on the appointment of an administrator, whether by a court or otherwise or, in the case of a Scottish partnership, when a protected trust deed is entered into.

12(4)   Rules 2.85(4)(a) and (c) and 4.90(3)(b) of the Insolvency Rules 1986 (mutual credit and set-off), or in Scotland, any rule of law with the same or similar effect to the effect of these Rules shall not apply to a close-out netting provision unless sub-paragraph (2)(a) applies.

[**Note**: the references in reg.12(4) are to provisions which were in force when these Regulations were made. They correspond approximately to the present r.2.85(2)(a) and (d) and r.4.90(2)(c).]

History
Regulation 12 amended by the Financial Markets and Insolvency (Settlement Finality and Financial Collateral Arrangements) (Amendment) Regulations 2010 (SI 2010/2993) reg.4(10) as from April 6, 2011.

13   Financial collateral arrangements to be enforceable where collateral-taker not aware of commencement of winding-up proceedings or reorganisation measures

13(1)   Where any of the events specified in paragraph (2) occur on the day of, but after the moment of commencement of, winding-up proceedings or reorganisation measures those events, arrangements and obligations shall be legally enforceable and binding on third parties if the collateral-taker can show that he was not aware, nor should have been aware, of the commencement of such proceedings or measures.

13(2)   The events referred to in paragraph (1) are–

 (a) a financial collateral arrangement coming into existence;

 (b) a relevant financial obligation secured by a financial collateral arrangement coming into existence; or

 (c) the delivery, transfer, holding, registering or other designation of financial collateral so as to be in the possession or under the control of the collateral-taker.

13(3)   For the purposes of paragraph (1)–

 (a) the commencement of winding-up proceedings means the making of a winding-up order or, in the case of a Scottish partnership, the award of sequestration by the court; and

 (b) commencement of reorganisation measures means the appointment of an administrator, whether by a court or otherwise or, in the case of a Scottish partnership, the date of registration of a protected trust deed.

History
Regulation 13 amended by the Financial Markets and Insolvency (Settlement Finality and Financial Collateral Arrangements) (Amendment) Regulations 2010 (SI 2010/2993) reg.4(11) as from April 6, 2011.

14   Modification of the Insolvency Rules 1986 and the Insolvency Rules (Northern Ireland) 1991

14   Where the collateral-provider or the collateral-taker under a financial collateral arrangement goes into liquidation or administration and the arrangement or a close out netting provision provides for, or the mechanism provided under the arrangement permits, either–

 (a) the debt owed by the party in liquidation or administration under the arrangement, to be assessed or paid in a currency other than sterling; or

(b) the debt to be converted into sterling at a rate other than the official exchange rate prevailing on the date when that party went into liquidation or administration;

then rule 4.91 (liquidation), or rule 2.86 (administration) of the Insolvency Rules 1986 (debt in foreign currency), or rule 4.097 of the Insolvency Rules (Northern Ireland) 1991 (liquidation, debt in foreign currency), as appropriate, shall not apply unless the arrangement provides for an unreasonable exchange rate or the collateral-taker uses the mechanism provided under the arrangement to impose an unreasonable exchange rate in which case the appropriate rule shall apply.

15   Modification of the Insolvency (Scotland) Rules 1986

15   Where the collateral-provider or the collateral-taker under a financial collateral arrangement goes into liquidation or administration or, in the case of a partnership, sequestration and the arrangement provides for, or the mechanism provided under the arrangement permits, either–

(a) the debt owed by the party in liquidation or sequestration under the arrangement, to be assessed or paid in a currency other than sterling; or

(b) the debt to be converted into sterling at a rate other than the official exchange rate prevailing on the date when that party went into liquidation or sequestration;

then rules 4.16 and 4.17 of the Insolvency (Scotland) Rules 1986 and the provisions of the Bankruptcy (Scotland) Act 1985 referred to in those rules and such rules and provisions as applied by rule 2.41 of the Insolvency (Scotland) Rules 1986, as appropriate, shall not apply unless the arrangement provides for an unreasonable exchange rate or the collateral-taker uses the mechanism provided under the arrangement to impose an unreasonable exchange rate in which case the appropriate rule shall apply.

History
Regulation 15 amended by the Financial Markets and Insolvency (Settlement Finality and Financial Collateral Arrangements) (Amendment) Regulations 2010 (SI 2010/2993) reg.4(12) as from April 6, 2011.

15A   Insolvency proceedings in other jurisdictions

15A(1)   The references to insolvency law in section 426 of the Insolvency Act 1986 (co-operation between courts exercising jurisdiction in relation to insolvency) include, in relation to a part of the United Kingdom, this Part of these Regulations and, in relation to a relevant country or territory within the meaning of that section, so much of the law of that country or territory as corresponds to this Part

15A(2)   A court shall not, in pursuance of that section or any other enactment or rule of law, recognise or give effect to–

(a) any order of a court exercising jurisdiction in relation to insolvency law in a country or territory outside the United Kingdom, or

(b) any act of a person appointed in such a country or territory to discharge any functions under insolvency law,

in so far as the making of the order or the doing of the act would be prohibited by this Part in the case of a court in England and Wales or Scotland, the High Court in Northern Ireland or a relevant office holder.

15A(3)   Paragraph (2) does not affect the recognition of a judgment required to be recognised or enforced under or by virtue of the Civil Jurisdiction and Judgments Act 1982 or Council Regulation (EC) No 44/2001 of 22nd December 2000 on jurisdiction and the recognition and enforcement of judgments in civil and commercial matters, as amended from time to time and as applied by the Agreement made on 19th October 2005 between the European Community and the Kingdom of Denmark on jurisdiction and the recognition and enforcement of judgments in civil and commercial matters.

History
Regulation 15A inserted by the Financial Markets and Insolvency (Settlement Finality and Financial Collateral Arrangements) (Amendment) Regulations 2010 (SI 2010/2993) reg.4(13) as from April 6, 2011.

PART 4

RIGHT OF USE AND APPROPRIATION

16   Right of use under a security financial collateral arrangement

16(1)   If a security financial collateral arrangement provides for the collateral-taker to use and dispose of any financial collateral provided under the arrangement, as if it were the owner of it, the collateral-taker may do so in accordance with the terms of the arrangement.

16(2)   If a collateral-taker exercises such a right of use, it is obliged to replace the original financial collateral by transferring equivalent financial collateral on or before the due date for the performance of the relevant financial obligations covered by the arrangement or, if the arrangement so provides, it may set off the value of the equivalent financial collateral against or apply it in discharge of the relevant financial obligations in accordance with the terms of the arrangement.

16(3)   The equivalent financial collateral which is transferred in discharge of an obligation as described in paragraph (2), shall be subject to the same terms of the security financial collateral arrangement as the original financial collateral was subject to and shall be treated as having been provided under the security financial collateral arrangement at the same time as the original financial collateral was first provided.

16(3A)   In Scotland, paragraphs (1) and (3) apply to title transfer financial collateral arrangements as they apply to security financial collateral arrangements.

16(4)   If a collateral-taker has an outstanding obligation to replace the original financial collateral with equivalent financial collateral when an enforcement event occurs, that obligation may be the subject of a close-out netting provision.

16(5)   This regulation does not apply in relation to credit claims.

History
Regulation 16 amended by the Financial Markets and Insolvency (Settlement Finality and Financial Collateral Arrangements) (Amendment) Regulations 2010 (SI 2010/2993) reg.4(14) as from April 6, 2011.

17   Appropriation of financial collateral under a security financial collateral arrangement

17(1)   Where a security interest is created or arises under a security financial collateral arrangement on terms that include a power for the collateral-taker to appropriate the financial collateral, the collateral-taker may exercise that power in accordance with the terms of the security financial collateral arrangement, without any order for foreclosure from the courts (and whether or not the remedy of foreclosure would be available).

17(2)   Upon the exercise by the collateral-taker of the power to appropriate the financial collateral, the equity of redemption of the collateral-provider shall be extinguished and all legal and beneficial interest of the collateral-provider in the financial collateral shall vest in the collateral taker.

History
Regulation 17 substituted by the Financial Markets and Insolvency (Settlement Finality and Financial Collateral Arrangements) (Amendment) Regulations 2010 (SI 2010/2993) reg.4(15) as from April 6, 2011.

18   Duty to value collateral and account for any difference in value on appropriation

18(1)   Where a collateral-taker exercises a power contained in a security financial collateral arrangement to appropriate the financial collateral the collateral-taker must value the financial collateral in accordance with the terms of the arrangement and in any event in a commercially reasonable manner.

18(2)   Where a collateral-taker exercises such a power and the value of the financial collateral appropriated differs from the amount of the relevant financial obligations, then as the case may be, either–

(a)   the collateral-taker must account to the collateral-provider for the amount by which the value of the financial collateral exceeds the relevant financial obligations; or

(b)   the collateral-provider will remain liable to the collateral-taker for any amount whereby the value of the financial collateral is less than the relevant financial obligations.

PART 5

CONFLICT OF LAWS

19   Standard test regarding the applicable law to book entry securities financial collateral arrangements

19(1)   This regulation applies to financial collateral arrangements where book entry securities collateral is used as collateral under the arrangement and are held through one or more intermediaries.

19(2)   Any question relating to the matters specified in paragraph (4) of this regulation which arises in relation to book entry securities collateral which is provided under a financial collateral arrangement shall be governed by the domestic law of the country in which the relevant account is maintained.

19(3)   For the purposes of paragraph (2) "domestic law" excludes any rule under which, in deciding the relevant question, reference should be made to the law of another country.

19(4)   The matters referred to in paragraph (2) are–

(a)   the legal nature and proprietary effects of book entry securities collateral;

(b)   the requirements for perfecting a financial collateral arrangement relating to book entry securities collateral and the transfer or passing of control or possession of book entry securities collateral under such an arrangement;

(c)   the requirements for rendering a financial collateral arrangement which relates to book entry securities collateral effective against third parties;

(d)   whether a person's title to or interest in such book entry securities collateral is overridden by or subordinated to a competing title or interest; and

(e)   the steps required for the realisation of book entry securities collateral following the occurrence of any enforcement event.

Insolvency Practitioners and Insolvency Services Account (Fees) Order 2003

(SI 2003/3363)

Made on 30 December 2003 by the Secretary of State under s.415A of the Insolvency Act 1986. Operative from 1 April 2004.

[**Note**: Changes made by the Insolvency Practitioners and Insolvency Services Account (Fees) Order 2004 (SI 2004/476), the Insolvency Practitioners and Insolvency Services Account (Fees) (Amendment) Order 2005 (SI 2005/523), the Insolvency Practitioners and Insolvency Services Account (Fees) (Amendment) (No.2) Order 2005 (SI 2005/3524), the Insolvency Practitioners and Insolvency Services Account (Fees) (Amendment) Order 2007 (SI 2007/133), the Insolvency Practitioners and Insolvency Services Account (Fees) (Amendment) Order 2008 (SI 2008/3), the Insolvency Practitioners and Insolvency Services Account (Fees) (Amendment) (No.2) Order 2008 (SI 2008/672), the Insolvency Practitioners and Insolvency Services Account (Fees) (Amendment) Order (SI 2009/487) and the Provision of Services (Insolvency Practitioners) Regulations 2009 (SI 2009/3081) have been incorporated into the text.]

1 Citation, commencement, interpretation and extent

1(1) This Order may be cited as the Insolvency Practitioners and Insolvency Services Account (Fees) Order 2003 and shall come into force on 1st April 2004 (**"the principal commencement date"**) except for Article 2(3) which shall come into force on 30th January 2004.

1(2) In this Order any reference to a numbered section is to the section so numbered in the Insolvency Act 1986.

1(3) All the provisions of this Order except Article 5 and the Schedule to this Order extend to England and Wales and Scotland and Article 5 and the Schedule to this Order extend only to England and Wales.

2 Fees payable in connection with the recognition of professional bodies pursuant to section 391

2(1) Every application by a body for recognition pursuant to section 391 shall be accompanied by a fee of £4,500.

2(2) On or before 6th April 2009 and on or before 6th April in each subsequent year, there shall be paid to the Secretary of State by each body recognised pursuant to section 391 in respect of the maintenance of that body's recognition pursuant to that section, a fee calculated by multiplying £300 by the number of persons who as at the 1st January in that year were authorised to act as insolvency practitioners by virtue of membership of that body.

2(3) Each body recognised pursuant to section 391 shall on or before 31st January in each year submit to the Secretary of State a list of its members who as at 1st January in that year were authorised to act as insolvency practitioners by virtue of membership of that body.

History

Article 2 substituted, and former art.2(2A), 2(2B) deleted, by the Insolvency Practitioners and Insolvency Services Account (Fees) (Amendment) Order 2008 (SI 2008/3) art.3 as from January 30, 2008, subject to transitional provisions in art.4. Article 2(2) further substituted by the Insolvency Practitioners and Insolvency Services Account (Fees) (Amendment) Order 2009 (SI 2009/487) arts 2, 3 as from April 6, 2009, subject to transitional provisions in art.4.

3 Fees payable in connection with authorisations by the Secretary of State under section 393

3(1) Subject to paragraph (1A), every person who on the principal commencement date is the holder of an authorisation to act as an insolvency practitioner granted by the Secretary of State pursuant to section

393 shall within 7 days of that date pay to the Secretary of State a fee in respect of the maintenance of that authorisation calculated in accordance with paragraph (2).

History
In art.3(1) the words "Subject to paragraph (1A), every person" substituted for the former words "Every person" by the Insolvency Practitioners and Insolvency Services Account (Fees) (Amendment) Order 2004 (SI 2004/476) art.2(1), (2) as from March 31, 2004.

3(1A) Paragraph (1) does not apply to–

    (a) any authorisation granted on the principal commencement date; or

    (b) any authorisation granted on the 1st April in any year prior to the year 2004.

History
Article 3(1A) inserted by the Insolvency Practitioners and Insolvency Services Account (Fees) (Amendment) Order 2004 (SI 2004/476) art.2(3) as from March 31, 2004.

3(2) The fee payable by virtue of paragraph (1) shall be calculated by multiplying £2,100 by the number of days in the period starting with the principal commencement date and ending with the date immediately before the next anniversary of the granting of the authorisation or the date of expiry of the authorisation (whichever occurs first) and dividing the result by 365.

3(3) Every application made to the Secretary of State pursuant to section 392 for authorisation to act as an insolvency practitioner shall be accompanied by a fee of £850, in connection with the grant of the application.

3(3A) Where the application is granted, the individual to whom authorisation has been granted must pay to the Secretary of State as soon as reasonably practicable a fee of £2,400 in connection with the maintenance of the authorisation for the period of 12 months commencing with the date of the grant of the authorisation.

3(4) Subject to paragraph (5), every person who holds an authorisation granted by the Secretary of State pursuant to section 393 to act as an insolvency practitioner shall, on each anniversary of the granting of that authorisation when it is in force, pay to the Secretary of State in connection with the maintenance of that authorisation a fee of £3,250.

3(5) Where on the relevant anniversary the authorisation mentioned in paragraph (4) has less than a year to run, the fee shall be calculated by multiplying £3,250 by the number of days that the authorisation has to run (starting with the day of the anniversary) and dividing the result by 365.

History
The figure "£2100" substituted for "£2000" in art.3(2) by the Insolvency Practitioners and Insolvency Services Account (Fees) (Amendment) (No.2) Order 2005 (SI 2005/3524) art.3(2), as from April 1, 2006. Article 3(3), (4), (5) amended, and art.3(3A) inserted, by the Provision of Services (Insolvency Practitioners) Regulations 2009 (SI 2009/3081) reg.3, 5 as from December 28, 2009.

4 Transitional cases early applications for authorisation

4(1) This article applies to an application made to the Secretary of State pursuant to section 392 for the granting of an authorisation to act as an insolvency practitioner–

    (a) where the applicant was as at the date of its making the holder of an authorisation granted pursuant to section 393;

    (b) where the application was made–

        (i) after the date of the making of this Order but before the principal commencement date; and

        (ii) more than three months before the expiry of the authorisation mentioned in sub-paragraph (a); and

    (c)   in respect of which as at the principal commencement date no decision as to whether to grant or refuse it has been taken.

4(2)   In respect of an application to which this article applies, there shall be paid to the Secretary of State by the applicant within 7 days of the principal commencement date a fee of £1,500.

5   Fees payable in connection with the operation of the Insolvency Services Account

5   There shall be payable in connection with the operation of the Insolvency Services Account fees as provided for in the Schedule to this Order.

6   Value added tax

6   Where Value Added Tax is chargeable in respect of the provision of a service for which a fee is prescribed by any provision of this Order, there shall be payable in addition to that fee the amount of the Value Added Tax.

SCHEDULE

FEES PAYABLE IN CONNECTION WITH THE OPERATION OF THE INSOLVENCY SERVICES ACCOUNT

Article 5

1   Interpretation for the purposes of the Schedule

1(1)   In this Schedule a reference to a numbered regulation is to the regulation so numbered in the Insolvency Regulations 1994

1(2)   In this Schedule **"payment date"** means any of the following dates in any year

    (a)   1st January;

    (b)   1st April;

    (c)   1st July; and

    (d)   1st October.

1(2A)   In this Schedule **"working day"** means any day other than a Saturday, a Sunday, Good Friday, Christmas Day or a Bank Holiday in England and Wales in accordance with the Banking and Financial Dealings Act 1971.

History
Paragraph 1(2A) inserted by the Insolvency Practitioners and Insolvency Services Account (Fees) (Amendment) Order 2005 (SI 2005/523) art.2(2) as from April 1, 2005.

1(3)   Subject to paragraphs (4) and (5), for the purposes of this Schedule an account is "maintained with the Secretary of State in respect of monies which may from time to time be paid into the Insolvency Services Account" where–

    (a)   in a winding up by the court or a bankruptcy the Secretary of State creates a record in relation to the winding up or, as the case may be, the bankruptcy for the purpose of recording payments into and out of the Insolvency Services Account relating to the winding up or, as the case may be, the bankruptcy; and

    (b)   in a voluntary winding up on the request of the liquidator the Secretary of State creates a record in relation to the winding up for the purposes of recording payments into and out of the Insolvency Services Account relating to the winding up.

1(4)   An account ceases to be maintained with the Secretary of State in the case of a winding up by the court or a bankruptcy where–

(a) the liquidator or the trustee has filed a receipts and payments account with the Secretary of State pursuant to regulation 14 or regulation 28;

(b) the account contains, or is accompanied by, a statement that it is a final receipts and payments account; and

(c) four working days have elapsed since the requirements of paragraphs (a) and (b) have been met,

but an account is revived in the circumstances mentioned in paragraph (5).

1(4A) An account ceases to be maintained with the Secretary of State in the case of a voluntary winding up where–

(a) no monies to which that account relates are held in the Insolvency Services Account (other than any unclaimed dividends or any amount that it is impracticable to distribute to creditors or is required for the payment of fees that are or will become payable while the account is maintained); and

(b) notice in writing has been given to the Secretary of State that the account is no longer required and four working days have elapsed since the receipt of that notice by the Secretary of State,

but an account is revived in the circumstances mentioned in paragraph (5).

History
Paragraph 1(4), (4A) substituted for the original para.1(4) by the Insolvency Practitioners and Insolvency Services Account (Fees) (Amendment) Order 2005 (SI 2005/523) art.2(3) as from April 1, 2005.

1(5) The circumstances referred to in paragraphs (4) and (4A) are–

(a) the receipt by the Secretary of State of notice in writing given by the trustee or liquidator for the revival of the account; or

(b) the payment into the Insolvency Services Account of any sums to the credit of the company or, as the case may be, the estate of the bankrupt,

and on the occurrence of either of the circumstances mentioned above, an account is "maintained with the Secretary of State in respect of monies which may from time to time be paid into the Insolvency Services Account".

History
In para.1(5) the words "paragraphs (4) and (4A)" substituted for the former words "paragraph (4)" by the Insolvency Practitioners and Insolvency Services Account (Fees) (Amendment) Order 2005 (SI 2005/523) art.2(4) as from April 1, 2005.

1(6) References to a bankruptcy include a bankruptcy under the Bankruptcy Act 1914 and references to a winding up include a winding up under the provisions of the Companies Act 1985.

2   Fees payable in connection with the operation of the Insolvency Services Account

2 Fees shall be payable in relation to the operation of the Insolvency Services Account (including payments into and out of that account) in the circumstances set out in the table below–

No. of fee	Description of fee and circumstances in which it is payable	Amount
1.	**Banking fee; winding up by the court and bankruptcy** Where in any bankruptcy or winding up by the court an account is maintained with the Secretary of State in respect of monies which may from time to time be paid into the Insolvency Services Account, there shall be payable out of the estate of the bankrupt or, as the case may be, the assets of the company on each payment date where the liquidator or the trustee is not the official receiver, a fee of–	£18

2.   **Banking fee; voluntary winding up** Where in a voluntary winding up an account is maintained with the Secretary of State in respect of monies which may from time to time be paid into the Insolvency Services Account there shall be payable out of the assets of the company on each payment date a fee of–   £23

2A.   **Payment of unclaimed dividends or other money—administration** Where any money is paid into the Insolvency Services Account pursuant to regulation 3B, that payment shall be accompanied by a fee in respect of each company to which it relates of–   £25

2B.   **Payment of unclaimed dividends or other money—administrative receivership** Where any money is paid into the Insolvency Services Account pursuant to regulation 3C, that payment shall be accompanied by a fee in respect of each company to which it relates of–   £25

2C.   **Payment of unclaimed dividends or other money—voluntary winding up** Where any money is paid into the Insolvency Services Account pursuant to regulation 18(2)(a), that payment shall be accompanied by a fee in respect of each company to which it relates of–   £25.00

3.   **Cheque etc. issue fee** Where a cheque, money order or payable order in respect of monies in the Insolvency Services Account is issued or reissued on the application of–

   (a) a liquidator pursuant to regulations 7 or 8;

   (b) a trustee pursuant to regulations 22 or 23; or

   (c) any person claiming any monies in that account pursuant to regulation 32,

there shall be payable out of the assets of the company, the estate of the bankrupt or, as the case may be, by the claimant–

(i) where the application is made before principal commencement date, a fee in respect of that cheque, money order or payable order of–   £0.65

(ii) where the application is made on or after the principal commencement date, a fee in respect of that cheque, money order or payable order of–   £1

4.   **Electronic funds systems (CHAPs and BACs etc.) fees** On the making or remaking of a transfer in respect of funds held in the Insolvency Services Account on an application made by–

   (a) a liquidator pursuant to regulations 7 or 8;

   (b) a trustee pursuant to regulations 22 or 23; or

   (c) any person claiming pursuant to regulation 32 any monies held in the Insolvency Services Account,

there shall be payable out of the assets of the company, the estate of the bankrupt or, as the case may be, by the claimant, a fee in respect of that transfer as follows:

(i) where it is made through the Clearing House Automated Payments System (CHAPs), a fee of–   £10

(ii) where it is made through the Banker's Clearing System (BACs) or any electronic funds transfer system other than CHAPS, a fee of–   £0.15

History
Paragraphs 2A, 2B inserted by the Insolvency Practitioners and Insolvency Services Account (Fees) (Amendment) (No.2) Order 2008 (SI 2008/672) art.4 as from April 6, 2008. Paragraph 4 substituted by the Insolvency Practitioners and Insolvency Services Account (Fees) (Amendment) Order 2007 (SI 2007/133) art.4 as from April 1, 2007. Paragraph 2C inserted and paras 1, 2A, 3(ii) amended by the Insolvency Practitioners and Insolvency Services Account (Fees) (Amendment) Order 2009 (SI 2009/487) arts 2, 6 as from April 6, 2009.

Insurers (Reorganisation and Winding Up) Regulations 2004

(SI 2004/353)

Made on 12 February 2004 by the Treasury under s.2(2) of the European Communities Act 1972.
Operative from 18 February 2004.

[**Note:** Changes made by the Insurers (Reorganisation and Winding Up) (Amendment) Regulations 2004 (SI 2004/546), the Insurers (Reorganisation and Winding Up) (Lloyd's) Regulations 2005 (SI 2005/1998), the Financial Services (EEA State) Regulations 2007 (SI 2007/108), the Financial Services and Markets Act 2000 (Markets in Financial Instruments) Regulations 2007 (SI 2007/126), the Insurers (Reorganisation and Winding Up) (Amendment) Regulations 2007 (SI 2007/851) and the Companies Act 2006 (Consequential Amendments and Transitional Provisions) Order 2011 (SI 2011/1265) have been incorporated into the text. Where the 2007 Regulations simply add references to paragraphs of Sch.B1 to the Insolvency (Northern Ireland) Order 1989 corresponding to those of Sch.B1 to IA 1986, annotations have been omitted.]

PART I

GENERAL

1   Citation and commencement

1   These Regulations may be cited as the Insurers (Reorganisation and Winding Up) Regulations 2004, and come into force on 18th February 2004.

2   Interpretation

2(1)   In these Regulations–

"**the 1986 Act**" means the Insolvency Act 1986;

"**the 2000 Act**" means the Financial Services and Markets Act 2000;

"**the 2006 Act**" means the Companies Act 2006;

"**the 1989 Order**" means the Insolvency (Northern Ireland) Order 1989;

"**administrator**" has the meaning given by paragraph 13 of Schedule B1, or by paragraph 14 of Schedule B1 to the 1989 Order;

"**the Authority**" means the Financial Services Authority;

"**branch**", in relation to an EEA or UK insurer has the meaning given by Article 1(b) of the life insurance directive or the third non-life insurance directive;

"**claim**" means a claim submitted by a creditor of a UK insurer in the course of–

(a)   a winding up,

(b)   an administration, or

(c)   a voluntary arrangement,

with a view to recovering his debt in whole or in part, and includes a proof of debt, within the meaning of Rule 4.73(4) of the Insolvency Rules, Rule 4.079(4) of the Insolvency Rules (Northern Ireland) or in Scotland a claim made in accordance with rule 4.15 of the Insolvency (Scotland) Rules;

"**creditors' voluntary winding up**" has the meaning given by section 90 of the 1986 Act or Article 76 of the 1989 Order;

"**debt**"–

(a)   in England and Wales and Northern Ireland–

   (i)   in relation to a winding up or administration of a UK insurer, has the meaning given by Rule 13.12 of the Insolvency Rules or Article 5 of the 1989 Order, and

   (ii)   in a case where a voluntary arrangement has effect, in relation to a UK insurer, means a debt which would constitute a debt in relation to the winding up of that insurer, except that references in paragraph (1) of Rule 13.12 or paragraph (1) of Article 5 of the 1989 Order to the date on which the company goes into liquidation are to be read as references to the date on which the voluntary arrangement has effect;

(b)   in Scotland–

   (i)   in relation to a winding up of a UK insurer, shall be interpreted in accordance with Schedule 1 to the Bankruptcy (Scotland) Act 1985 as applied by Chapter 5 of Part 4 of the Insolvency (Scotland) Rules, and

   (ii)   in a case where a voluntary arrangement has effect in relation to a UK insurer, means a debt which would constitute a debt in relation to the winding up of that insurer, except that references in Chapter 5 of Part 4 of the Insolvency (Scotland) Rules to the date of commencement of winding up are to be read as references to the date on which the voluntary arrangement has effect;

"directive reorganisation measure" means a reorganisation measure as defined in Article 2(c) of the reorganisation and winding-up directive which was adopted or imposed on or after 20th April 2003;

"directive winding up proceedings" means winding up proceedings as defined in Article 2(d) of the reorganisation and winding-up directive which were opened on or after 20th April 2003;

"EEA creditor" means a creditor of a UK insurer who–

(a)   in the case of an individual, is ordinarily resident in an EEA State, and

(b)   in the case of a body corporate or unincorporated association of persons, has its head office in an EEA State;

"EEA insurer" means an undertaking, other than a UK insurer, pursuing the activity of direct insurance (within the meaning of Article 1 of the first life insurance directive or the first non-life insurance directive) which has received authorisation under Article 6 from its home state regulator;

"EEA regulator" means a competent authority (within the meaning of Article 1(1) of the life insurance directive or Article 1(k) of the third non-life insurance directive, as the case may be) of an EEA State;

"EEA State" has the meaning given by Schedule 1 to the Interpretation Act 1978;

"the first non-life insurance directive" means the Council Directive (73/239/EEC) of 24 July 1973 on the co-ordination of laws, regulations and administrative provisions relating to the taking up and pursuit of the business of direct insurance other than life assurance;

"home state regulator", in relation to an EEA insurer, means the relevant EEA regulator in the EEA State where its head office is located;

"the Insolvency Rules" means the Insolvency Rules 1986;

"the Insolvency Rules (Northern Ireland)" means the Insolvency Rules (Northern Ireland) 1991;

"the Insolvency (Scotland) Rules" means the Insolvency (Scotland) Rules 1986;

"insurance claim" means any claim in relation to an insurance debt;

"insurance creditor" means a person who has an insurance claim against a UK insurer (whether or not he has claims other than insurance claims against that insurer);

"insurance debt" means a debt to which a UK insurer is, or may become liable, pursuant to a contract of insurance, to a policyholder or to any person who has a direct right of action against that insurer, and includes any premium paid in connection with a contract of insurance (whether or not that contract was concluded) which the insurer is liable to refund;

"life insurance directive" means the Directive (2002/83/EC) of the European Parliament and of the Council concerning life assurance;

"officer", in relation to a company, has the meaning given by section 1173(1) of the Companies Act 2006;

"official language" means a language specified in Article 1 of Council Regulation No 1 of 15th April 1958 determining the languages to be used by the European Economic Community (Regulation 1/58/EEC), most recently amended by paragraph (a) of Part XVIII of Annex I to the Act of Accession 1994 (194 N);

"policyholder" has the meaning given by the Financial Services and Markets Act 2000 (Meaning of "Policy" and "Policyholder") Order 2001;

"the reorganisation and winding-up directive" means the Directive (2001/17/EC) of the European Parliament and of the Council of 19 March 2001 on the reorganisation and winding-up of insurance undertakings;

"Schedule B1" means Schedule B1 to the 1986 Act as inserted by section 248 of the Enterprise Act 2002, unless specified otherwise;

"section 899 compromise or arrangement" means a compromise or arrangement sanctioned by the court in relation to a UK insurer under section 899 of the 2006 Act but does not include a compromise or arrangement falling within section 900 (powers of court to facilitate reconstruction or amalgamation) or Part 27 (mergers and divisions of public companies) of that Act;

"supervisor" has the meaning given by section 7 of the 1986 Act or Article 20 of the 1989 Order;

"the third non-life insurance directive" means the Council Directive (92/49/EEC) of 18th June 1992 on the co-ordination of laws, etc, and amending directives 73/239/EEC and 88/357/EEC);

"UK insurer" means a person who has permission under Part IV of the 2000 Act to effect or carry out contracts of insurance, but does not include a person who, in accordance with that permission, carries on that activity exclusively in relation to reinsurance contracts;

"voluntary arrangement" means a voluntary arrangement which has effect in relation to a UK insurer in accordance with section 4A of the 1986 Act or Article 17A of the 1989 Order; and

"winding up" means–

(a) winding up by the court, or

(b) a creditors' voluntary winding up.

History

Definition of "Schedule B1" amended by the Insurers (Reorganisation and Winding Up) (Amendment) Regulations 2007 (SI 2007/851) reg.2(1), (2)(b), as from April 6, 2007. Definition of "EEA State" substituted by the Financial Services (EEA State) Regulations 2007 (SI 2007/108) reg.8 as from February 13, 2007. The definition was inserted into the 1978 Act by the Legislative and Regulatory Reform Act 2006. Definition of "officer" amended, definitions of "the 2006 Act" and of "section 899 compromise or arrangement" inserted and various definitions deleted by the Companies Act 2006 (Consequential Amendments and Transitional Provisions) Order 2011 (SI 2011/1265) art.23(2) as from May 12, 2011.

2(2)   In paragraph (1)–

(a)   for the purposes of the definition of **"directive reorganisation measure"**, a reorganisation measure is adopted or imposed at the time when it is treated as adopted or imposed by the law of the relevant EEA State; and

(b)   for the purposes of the definition of **"directive winding up proceedings"**, winding up proceedings are opened at the time when they are treated as opened by the law of the relevant EEA State,

and in this paragraph **"relevant EEA State"** means the EEA State under the law of which the reorganisation is adopted or imposed, or the winding up proceedings are opened, as the case may be.

2(3)   In these Regulations, references to the general law of insolvency of the United Kingdom include references to every provision made by or under the 1986 Act or the 1989 Order; and in relation to friendly societies or to industrial and provident societies references to the law of insolvency or to any provision of the 1986 Act or the 1989 Order are to that law as modified by the Friendly Societies Act 1992 or by the Industrial and Provident Societies Act 1965 or the Industrial and Provident Societies Act (Northern Ireland) 1969 (as the case may be).

2(4)   References in these Regulations to a **"contract of insurance"** must be read with–

(a)   section 22 of the 2000 Act;

(b)   any relevant order made under that section; and

(c)   Schedule 2 to that Act,

but for the purposes of these Regulations a contract of insurance does not include a reinsurance contract.

2(5)   Functions imposed or falling on the Authority by or under these Regulations shall be deemed to be functions under the 2000 Act.

3   Scope

3   For the purposes of these Regulations, neither the Society of Lloyd's nor the persons specified in section 316(1) of the 2000 Act are UK insurers.

Note
In regard to Lloyd's, see now the Insurers (Reorganisation and Winding Up) (Lloyd's) Regulations 2005 (SI 2005/1998), effective August 10, 2005.

PART II

INSOLVENCY MEASURES AND PROCEEDINGS: JURISDICTION IN RELATION TO INSURERS

4   Prohibition against winding up etc. EEA insurers in the United Kingdom

4(1)   On or after the relevant date a court in the United Kingdom may not, in relation to an EEA insurer or any branch of an EEA insurer–

(a)   make a winding up order pursuant to section 221 of the 1986 Act or Article 185 of the 1989 Order;

(b)   appoint a provisional liquidator;

(c)   make an administration order.

4(2)   Paragraph (1)(a) does not prevent–

(a)   the court from making a winding up order after the relevant date in relation to an EEA insurer if–

      (i)   a provisional liquidator was appointed in relation to that insurer before the relevant date, and

      (ii)   that appointment continues in force until immediately before that winding up order is made;

   (b)   the winding up of an EEA insurer after the relevant date pursuant to a winding up order which was made, and has not been discharged, before that date.

4(3)   Paragraph (1)(b) does not prevent a provisional liquidator of an EEA insurer appointed before the relevant date from acting in relation to that insurer after that date.

4(4)   Paragraph (1)(c) does not prevent an administrator appointed before the relevant date from acting after that date in a case in which the administration order under which he or his predecessor was appointed remains in force after that date.

4(5)   An administrator may not, in relation to an EEA insurer, be appointed under paragraphs 14 or 22 of Schedule B1 or paragraph 15 or 23 of Schedule B1 to the 1989 Order.

4(6)   A proposed voluntary arrangement shall not have effect in relation to an EEA insurer if a decision, under section 4 of the 1986 Act or Article 17 of the 1989 Order, with respect to the approval of that arrangement was made after the relevant date.

4(7)   Section 377 of the 2000 Act (reducing the value of contracts instead of winding up) does not apply in relation to an EEA insurer.

4(8)   An order under section 254 of the Enterprise Act 2002 (application of insolvency law to a foreign company) or under Article 9 of the Insolvency (Northern Ireland) Order 2005 (application of insolvency law to company incorporated outside Northern Ireland) may not provide for any of the following provisions of the 1986 Act or of the 1989 Order to apply in relation to an EEA insurer–

   (a)   Part I of the 1986 Act or Part II of the 1989 Order (company voluntary arrangements);

   (b)   Part II of the 1986 Act or Part III of the 1989 Order (administration);

   (c)   Chapter VI of Part IV of the 1986 Act (winding up by the Court) or Chapter VI of Part V of the 1989 Order (winding up by the High Court).

4(9)   In this regulation and regulation 5, **"relevant date"** means 20th April 2003.

History

Regulation 4(8) substituted by the Insurers (Reorganisation and Winding Up) (Amendment) Regulations 2007 (SI 2007/851) reg.2(1), (4), as from April 6, 2007.

5   Schemes of arrangement: EEA insurers

5(1)   For the purposes of section 895(2)(b) of the 2006 Act, an EEA insurer or a branch of an EEA insurer is to be treated as a company liable to be wound up under the 1986 Act or the 1989 Order if it would be liable to be wound up under that Act or Order but for the prohibition in regulation 4(1)(a).

5(2)   But a court may not make a relevant order under section 899 of the 2006 Act in relation to an EEA insurer which is subject to a directive reorganisation measure or directive winding up proceedings, or a branch of an EEA insurer which is subject to such a measure or proceedings unless the conditions set out in paragraph (3) are satisfied.

5(3)   Those conditions are–

   (a)   the person proposing the section 899 compromise or arrangement (**"the proposal"**) has given–

      (i)   the administrator or liquidator, and

      (ii)   the relevant competent authority,

     reasonable notice of the details of that proposal; and

(b)   no person notified in accordance with sub-paragraph (a) has objected to the proposal.

5(4)   Nothing in this regulation invalidates a compromise or arrangement which was sanctioned by the court by an order made before the relevant date.

5(5)   For the purposes of paragraph (2), a relevant order means an order sanctioning a section 899 compromise or arrangement which–

(a)   is intended to enable the insurer, and the whole or any part of its undertaking, to survive as a going concern and which affects the rights of persons other than the insurer or its contributories; or

(b)   includes among its purposes a realisation of some or all of the assets of the EEA insurer to which the order relates and the distribution of the proceeds to creditors, with a view to terminating the whole or any part of the business of that insurer.

5(6)   For the purposes of this regulation–

(a)   **"administrator"** means an administrator, as defined by Article 2(i) of the reorganisation and winding up directive, who is appointed in relation to the EEA insurer in relation to which the proposal is made;

(b)   **"liquidator"** means a liquidator, as defined by Article 2(j) of the reorganisation and winding up directive, who is appointed in relation to the EEA insurer in relation to which the proposal is made;

(c)   **"competent authority"** means the competent authority, as defined by Article 2(g) of the reorganisation and winding up directive, which is competent for the purposes of the directive reorganisation measure or directive winding up proceedings mentioned in paragraph (2).

History
Regulation 5(1), 5(2), 5(3) and 5(5) amended by the Companies Act 2006 (Consequential Amendments and Transitional Provisions) Order 2011 (SI 2011/1265) art.23(3) as from May 12, 2011.

6   Reorganisation measures and winding up proceedings in respect of EEA insurers effective in the United Kingdom

6(1)   An EEA insolvency measure has effect in the United Kingdom in relation to–

(a)   any branch of an EEA insurer,

(b)   any property or other assets of that insurer,

(c)   any debt or liability of that insurer

as if it were part of the general law of insolvency of the United Kingdom.

6(2)   Subject to paragraph (4)–

(a)   a competent officer who satisfies the condition mentioned in paragraph (3); or

(b)   a qualifying agent appointed by a competent officer who satisfies the condition mentioned in paragraph (3),

may exercise in the United Kingdom, in relation to the EEA insurer which is subject to an EEA insolvency measure, any function which, pursuant to that measure, he is entitled to exercise in relation to that insurer in the relevant EEA State.

6(3)   The condition mentioned in paragraph (2) is that the appointment of the competent officer is evidenced–

(a) by a certified copy of the order or decision by a judicial or administrative authority in the relevant EEA State by or under which the competent officer was appointed; or

(b) by any other certificate issued by the judicial or administrative authority which has jurisdiction in relation to the EEA insolvency measure,

and accompanied by a certified translation of that order, decision or certificate (as the case may be).

6(4)   In exercising functions of the kind mentioned in paragraph (2), the competent officer or qualifying agent–

(a) may not take any action which would constitute an unlawful use of force in the part of the United Kingdom in which he is exercising those functions;

(b) may not rule on any dispute arising from a matter falling within Part V of these Regulations which is justiciable by a court in the part of the United Kingdom in which he is exercising those functions; and

(c) notwithstanding the way in which functions may be exercised in the relevant EEA State, must act in accordance with relevant laws or rules as to procedure which have effect in the part of the United Kingdom in which he is exercising those functions.

6(5)   For the purposes of paragraph (4)(c), **"relevant laws or rules as to procedure"** mean–

(a) requirements as to consultation with or notification of employees of an EEA insurer;

(b) law and procedures relevant to the realisation of assets;

(c) where the competent officer is bringing or defending legal proceedings in the name of, or on behalf of, an EEA insurer, the relevant rules of court.

6(6)   In this regulation–

"competent officer" means a person appointed under or in connection with an EEA insolvency measure for the purpose of administering that measure;

"qualifying agent" means an agent validly appointed (whether in the United Kingdom or elsewhere) by a competent officer in accordance with the relevant law in the relevant EEA State;

"EEA insolvency measure" means, as the case may be, a directive reorganisation measure or directive winding up proceedings which has effect in relation to an EEA insurer by virtue of the law of the relevant EEA State;

"relevant EEA State", in relation to an EEA insurer, means the EEA State in which that insurer has been authorised in accordance with Article 4 of the life insurance directive or Article 6 of the first non-life insurance directive.

7   Confirmation by the court of a creditors' voluntary winding up

7(1)   Rule 7.62 of the Insolvency Rules or Rule 7.56 of the Insolvency Rules (Northern Ireland) applies in relation to a UK insurer with the modification specified in paragraph (2) or (3).

7(2)   In Rule 7.62, paragraph (1), after the words "the Insurers (Reorganisation and Winding Up) Regulations 2003" insert the words "or the Insurers (Reorganisation and Winding Up) Regulations 2004".

7(3)   In Rule 7.56 of the Insolvency Rules (Northern Ireland) paragraph (1), after the words "the Insurers (Reorganisation and Winding Up) Regulations 2003" insert the words "or the Insurers (Reorganisation and Winding Up) Regulations 2004".

PART III

MODIFICATIONS OF THE LAW OF INSOLVENCY: NOTIFICATION AND PUBLICATION

8   Modifications of the law of insolvency

8   The general law of insolvency has effect in relation to UK insurers subject to the provisions of this Part.

9   Notification of relevant decision to the Authority

9(1)   Where on or after 3rd March 2004 the court makes a decision, order or appointment of any of the following kinds–

(a)   an administration order under paragraph 13 of Schedule B1 or paragraph 14 of Schedule B1 to the 1989 Order;

(b)   a winding up order under section 125 of the 1986 Act or Article 105 of the 1989 Order;

(c)   the appointment of a provisional liquidator under section 135(1) of the 1986 Act or Article 115(1) of the 1989 Order;

(d)   an interim order under paragraph 13(1)(d) of Schedule B1 or paragraph 14(1)(d) of Schedule B1 to the 1989 Order;

(e)   a decision to reduce the value of one or more of the insurer's contracts, in accordance with section 377 of the 2000 Act,

it must immediately inform the Authority, or cause the Authority to be informed of the decision, order or appointment which has been made.

History
The date "3rd March 2004" substituted for "[] February 2004" (or, in some printed versions "18th February 2004") by the Insurers (Reorganisation and Winding Up) (Amendment) Regulations 2004 (SI 2004/546) reg.2(2), as from March 3, 2004.

9(2)   Where a decision with respect to the approval of a voluntary arrangement has effect, and the arrangement which is the subject of that decision is a qualifying arrangement, the supervisor must forthwith inform the Authority of the arrangement.

9(3)   Where a liquidator is appointed as mentioned in section 100 of the 1986 Act, paragraph 83 of Schedule B1, paragraph 84 of Schedule B1 to the 1989 Order or Article 86 of the 1989 Order (appointment of liquidator in a creditors' voluntary winding up), the liquidator must inform the Authority forthwith of his appointment.

9(4)   Where in the case of a members' voluntary winding up, section 95 of the 1986 Act (effect of company's insolvency) or Article 81 of the 1989 Order applies, the liquidator must inform the Authority forthwith that he is of that opinion.

Note
There does not appear to be a reg.9(5).

9(6)   Paragraphs (1), (2) and (3) do not apply in any case where the Authority was represented at all hearings in connection with the application in relation to which the decision, order or appointment is made.

9(7)   For the purposes of paragraph (2), a **"qualifying arrangement"** means a voluntary arrangement which–

(a)   varies the rights of creditors as against the insurer and is intended to enable the insurer, and the whole or any part of its undertaking, to survive as a going concern; or

(b)   includes a realisation of some or all of the assets of the insurer and distribution of the proceeds to creditors, with a view to terminating the whole or any part of the business of that insurer.

9(8)   An administrator, supervisor or liquidator who fails without reasonable excuse to comply with paragraph (2), (3), or (4) (as the case may be) commits an offence and is liable on summary conviction to a fine not exceeding level 3 on the standard scale.

10   Notification of relevant decision to EEA regulators

10(1)   Where the Authority is informed of a decision, order or appointment in accordance with regulation 9, the Authority must as soon as is practicable inform the EEA regulators in every EEA State–

(a)   that the decision, order or appointment has been made; and

(b)   in general terms, of the possible effect of a decision, order or appointment of that kind on–

    (i)   the business of an insurer, and

    (ii)   the rights of policyholders under contracts of insurance effected and carried out by an insurer.

10(2)   Where the Authority has been represented at all hearings in connection with the application in relation to which the decision, order or appointment has been made, the Authority must inform the EEA regulators in every EEA State of the matters mentioned in paragraph (1) as soon as is practicable after that decision, order or appointment has been made.

11   Publication of voluntary arrangement, administration order, winding up order or scheme of arrangement

11(1)   This regulation applies where a qualifying decision has effect, or a qualifying order or qualifying appointment is made, in relation to a UK insurer on or after 20th April 2003.

11(2)   For the purposes of this regulation–

(a)   a qualifying decision means a decision with respect to the approval of a proposed voluntary arrangement, in accordance with section 4A of the 1986 Act or Article 17A of the 1989 Order;

(b)   a qualifying order means–

    (i)   an administration order under paragraph 13 of Schedule B1 or under paragraph 14 of Schedule B1 to the 1989 Order,

    (ii)   an order appointing a provisional liquidator in accordance with section 135 of the 1986 Act or Article 115 of the 1989 Order, or

    (iii)   a winding up order made by the court under Part IV of the 1986 Act or Part V of the 1989 Order.

(c)   a qualifying appointment means the appointment of a liquidator as mentioned in section 100 of the 1986 Act or Article 86 of the 1989 Order (appointment of liquidator in a creditors' voluntary winding up).

11(3)   Subject to paragraph (8), as soon as is reasonably practicable after a qualifying decision has effect, or a qualifying order or a qualifying appointment has been made, the relevant officer must publish, or cause to be published, in the Official Journal of the European Communities the information mentioned in paragraph (4) and (if applicable) paragraphs (5), (6) or (7).

11(4)   That information is–

(a)   a summary of the terms of the qualifying decision or qualifying appointment or the provisions of the qualifying order (as the case may be);

(b)   the identity of the relevant officer; and

(c)   the statutory provisions in accordance with which the qualifying decision has effect or the qualifying order or appointment has been made or takes effect.

11(5)   In the case of a qualifying appointment falling within paragraph (2)(c), that information includes the court to which an application under section 112 of the 1986 Act (reference of questions to the court) or Article 98 of the 1989 Order (reference of questions to the High Court) may be made.

11(6)   In the case of a qualifying decision, that information includes the court to which an application under section 6 of the 1986 Act or Article 19 of the 1989 Order (challenge of decisions) may be made.

11(7)   Paragraph (3) does not apply where a qualifying decision or qualifying order falling within paragraph (2)(b)(i) affects the interests only of the members, or any class of members, or employees of the insurer (in their capacity as members or employees).

11(8)   This regulation is without prejudice to any requirement to publish information imposed upon a relevant officer under any provision of the general law of insolvency.

11(9)   A relevant officer who fails to comply with paragraph (3) of this regulation commits an offence and is liable on summary conviction to a fine not exceeding level 3 on the standard scale.

11(10)   A qualifying decision, qualifying order or qualifying appointment is not invalid or ineffective if the relevant official fails to comply with paragraph (3) of this regulation.

11(11)   In this regulation, **"relevant officer"** means–

(a)   in the case of a voluntary arrangement, the supervisor;

(b)   in the case of an administration order or the appointment of an administrator, the administrator;

(c)   in the case of a creditors' voluntary winding up, the liquidator;

(d)   in the case of winding up order, the liquidator;

(e)   in the case of an order appointing a provisional liquidator, the provisional liquidator.

12   Notification to creditors: winding up proceedings

12(1)   When a relevant order or appointment is made, or a relevant decision is taken, in relation to a UK insurer on or after 20th April 2003, the appointed officer must as soon as is reasonably practicable–

(a)   notify all known creditors of that insurer in writing of–

(i)   the matters mentioned in paragraph (4), and

(ii)   the matters mentioned in paragraph (5); and

(b)   notify all known insurance creditors of that insurer in writing of the matters mentioned in paragraph 6, in any case.

12(2)   The appointed officer may comply with the requirement in paragraph (1)(a)(i) and the requirement in paragraph (1)(a)(ii) by separate notifications.

12(3)   For the purposes of this regulation–

(a)   **"relevant order"** means–

(i)   an administration order made under section 8 of the 1986 Act before 15th September 2003, or made on or after that date under paragraph 13 of Schedule B1 in the prescribed circumstances or under paragraph 14 of Schedule B1 to the 1989 Order in the prescribed circumstances,

    (ii) a winding up order under section 125 of the 1986 Act (powers of the court on hearing a petition) or Article 105 of the 1989 Order (powers of High Court on hearing of petition),

    (iii) the appointment of a liquidator in accordance with section 138 of the 1986 Act (appointment of a liquidator in Scotland), and

    (iv) an order appointing a provisional liquidator in accordance with section 135 of that Act or Article 115 of the 1989 Order;

  (b) **"relevant appointment"** means the appointment of a liquidator as mentioned in section 100 of the 1986 Act or Article 86 of the 1989 Order (appointment of liquidator in a creditors' voluntary winding up); and

  (c) **"relevant decision"** means a decision as a result of which a qualifying voluntary arrangement has effect.

12(4) The matters which must be notified to all known creditors in accordance with paragraph (1)(a)(i) are as follows–

  (a) that a relevant order or appointment has been made, or a relevant decision taken, in relation to the UK insurer; and

  (b) the date from which that order, appointment or decision has effect.

12(5) The matters which must be notified to all known creditors in accordance with paragraph (1)(a)(ii) are as follows–

  (a) if applicable, the date by which a creditor must submit his claim in writing;

  (b) the matters which must be stated in a creditor's claim;

  (c) details of any category of debt in relation to which a claim is not required;

  (d) the person to whom any such claim or any observations on a claim must be submitted; and

  (e) the consequences of any failure to submit a claim by any specified deadline.

12(6) The matters which must be notified to all known insurance creditors, in accordance with paragraph (1)(b), are as follows–

  (a) the effect which the relevant order, appointment or decision will, or is likely, to have on the kind of contract of insurance under, or in connection with, which that creditor's insurance claim against the insurer is founded; and

  (b) the date from which any variation (resulting from the relevant order or relevant decision) to the risks covered by, or the sums recoverable under, that contract has effect.

12(7) Subject to paragraph (8), where a creditor is notified in accordance with paragraph (1)(a)(ii), the notification must be headed with the words "Invitation to lodge a claim: time limits to be observed", and that heading must be given in–

  (a) the official language, or one of the official languages, of the EEA State in which that creditor is ordinarily resident; or

  (b) every official language.

12(8) Where a creditor notified in accordance with paragraph (1) is–

  (a) an insurance creditor; and

  (b) ordinarily resident in an EEA State,

the notification must be given in the official language, or one of the official languages, of that EEA State.

12(9)   The obligation under paragraph (1)(a)(ii) may be discharged by sending a form of proof in accordance with Rule 4.74 of the Insolvency Rules, Rule 4.080 of the Insolvency Rules (Northern Ireland) or Rule 4.15(2) of the Insolvency (Scotland) Rules as applicable in cases where any of those rules applies, provided that the form of proof complies with paragraph (7) or (8) (whichever is applicable).

12(10)   The prescribed circumstances are where the administrator includes in the statement required under Rule 2.3 of the Insolvency Rules or under Rule 2.003 of the Insolvency Rules (Northern Ireland) a statement to the effect that the objective set out in paragraph 3(1)(a) of Schedule B1 or in paragraph 4(1)(a) of Schedule B1 to the 1989 Order is not reasonably likely to be achieved.

12(11)   Where, after the appointment of an administrator, the administrator concludes that it is not reasonably practicable to achieve the objective specified in paragraph 3(1)(a) of Schedule B1 or in paragraph 4(1)(a) of Schedule B1 to the 1989 Order, he shall inform the court and the Authority in writing of that conclusion and upon so doing the order by which he was appointed shall be a relevant order for the purposes of this regulation and the obligation under paragraph (1) shall apply as from the date on which he so informs the court and the Authority.

12(12)   An appointed officer commits an offence if he fails without reasonable excuse to comply with an applicable requirement under this regulation, and is liable on summary conviction to a fine not exceeding level 3 on the standard scale.

12(13)   For the purposes of this regulation–

(a)   **"appointed officer"** means–

    (i)   in the case of a relevant order falling within paragraph (3)(a)(i) or a relevant appointment falling within paragraph (3)(b)(i), the administrator,

    (ii)   in the case of a relevant order falling within paragraph (3)(a)(ii) or (iii) or a relevant appointment falling within paragraph (3)(b)(ii), the liquidator,

    (iii)   in the case of a relevant order falling within paragraph (3)(a)(iv), the provisional liquidator, or

    (iv)   in the case of a relevant decision, the supervisor; and

(b)   a creditor is a "known" creditor if the appointed officer is aware, or should reasonably be aware of–

    (i)   his identity,

    (ii)   his claim or potential claim, and

    (iii)   a recent address where he is likely to receive a communication.

12(14)   For the purposes of paragraph (3), and of regulations 13 and 14, a voluntary arrangement is a qualifying voluntary arrangement if its purposes include a realisation of some or all of the assets of the UK insurer to which the order relates and a distribution of the proceeds to creditors, with a view to terminating the whole or any part of the business of that insurer.

History
Regulation 12(10) substituted by the Insurers (Reorganisation and Winding Up) (Amendment) Regulations 2007 (SI 2007/851) reg.2(1), (9), as from April 6, 2007.

13   Submission of claims by EEA creditors

13(1)   An EEA creditor who on or after 20th April 2003 submits a claim or observations relating to his claim in any relevant proceedings (irrespective of when those proceedings were commenced or had effect) may do so in his domestic language, provided that the requirements in paragraphs (3) and (4) are complied with.

13(2)   For the purposes of this regulation, **"relevant proceedings"** means–

   (a)   a winding up;

   (b)   a qualifying voluntary arrangement;

   (c)   administration.

13(3)   Where an EEA creditor submits a claim in his domestic language, the document must be headed with the words "Lodgement of claim" (in English).

13(4)   Where an EEA creditor submits observations on his claim (otherwise than in the document by which he submits his claim), the observations must be headed with the words "Submission of observations relating to claims" (in English).

13(5)   Paragraph (3) does not apply where an EEA creditor submits his claim using–

   (a)   in the case of a winding up, a form of proof supplied by the liquidator in accordance with Rule 4.74 of the Insolvency Rules, Rule 4.080 of the Insolvency Rules (Northern Ireland) or rule 4.15(2) of the Insolvency (Scotland) Rules as the case may be;

   (b)   in the case of a qualifying voluntary arrangement, a form approved by the court for that purpose.

13(6)   In this regulation–

   (a)   **"domestic language"**, in relation to an EEA creditor, means the official language, or one of the official languages, of the EEA State in which he is ordinarily resident or, if the creditor is not an individual, in which the creditor's head office is located; and

   (b)   **"qualifying voluntary arrangement"** has the meaning given by regulation 12(12).

14   Reports to creditors

14(1)   This regulation applies where, on or after 20th April 2003–

   (a)   a liquidator is appointed in accordance with section 100 of the 1986 Act or Article 86 of the 1989 Order (creditors' voluntary winding up: appointment of liquidator) or, on or after 15th September 2003, paragraph 83 of Schedule B1 or paragraph 84 of Schedule B1 to the 1989 Order (moving from administration to creditors' voluntary liquidation);

   (b)   a winding up order is made by the court;

   (c)   a provisional liquidator is appointed; or

   (d)   an administrator is appointed under paragraph 13 of Schedule B1 or under paragraph 14 of Schedule B1 to the 1989 Order.

History
The words "an administrator is appointed under paragraph 13 of Schedule B1" substituted for the word "administration" by the Insurers (Reorganisation and Winding Up) (Amendment) Regulations 2004 (SI 2004/546) reg.2(3), as from March 3, 2004.

14(2)   The liquidator or provisional liquidator (as the case may be) must send to every known creditor a report once in every 12 months beginning with the date when his appointment has effect.

14(3)   The requirement in paragraph (2) does not apply where a liquidator or provisional liquidator is required by order of the court to send a report to creditors at intervals which are more frequent than those required by this regulation.

14(4)   This regulation is without prejudice to any requirement to send a report to creditors, imposed by the court on the liquidator or provisional liquidator, which is supplementary to the requirements of this regulation.

14(5)   A liquidator or provisional liquidator commits an offence if he fails without reasonable excuse to comply with an applicable requirement under this regulation, and is liable on summary conviction to a fine not exceeding level 3 on the standard scale.

14(6)   For the purposes of this regulation–

(a)   **"known creditor"** means–

   (i)   a creditor who is known to the liquidator or provisional liquidator, and

   (ii)   in a case falling within paragraph (1)(b) or (c), a creditor who is specified in the insurer's statement of affairs (within the meaning of section 131 of the 1986 Act or Article 111 of the 1989 Order); and

(b)   **"report"** means a written report setting out the position generally as regards the progress of the winding up or provisional liquidation (as the case may be).

15   Service of notices and documents

15(1)   This regulation applies to any notification, report or other document which is required to be sent to a creditor of a UK insurer by a provision of this Part (**"a relevant notification"**).

15(2)   A relevant notification may be sent to a creditor by either of the following methods–

(a)   posting it to the proper address of the creditor;

(b)   transmitting it electronically, in accordance with paragraph (4).

15(3)   For the purposes of paragraph (2)(a), the proper address of a creditor is any current address provided by that creditor as an address for service of a relevant notification or, if no such address is provided–

(a)   the last known address of that creditor (whether his residence or a place where he carries on business);

(b)   in the case of a body corporate, the address of its registered or principal office; or

(c)   in the case of an unincorporated association, the address of its principal office.

15(4)   A relevant notification may be transmitted electronically only if it is sent to–

(a)   an electronic address notified to the relevant officer by the creditor for this purpose; or

(b)   if no such address has been notified, an electronic address at which the relevant officer reasonably believes the creditor will receive the notification.

15(5)   Any requirement in this part to send a relevant notification to a creditor shall also be treated as satisfied if–

(a)   the creditor has agreed with–

   (i)   the UK insurer which is liable under the creditor's claim, or

   (ii)   the relevant officer,

   that information which is required to be sent to him (whether pursuant to a statutory or contractual obligation, or otherwise) may instead be accessed by him on a web site;

(b)   the agreement applies to the relevant notification in question;

   (c)   the creditor is notified of–

        (i)   the publication of the relevant notification on a web site,

        (ii) the address of that web site,

        (iii) the place on that web site where the relevant notification may be accessed, and how it may be accessed; and

   (d)   the relevant notification is published on that web site throughout a period of at least one month beginning with the date on which the creditor is notified in accordance with sub-paragraph (c).

15(6)   Where, in a case in which paragraph (5) is relied on for compliance with a requirement of regulation 12 or 14–

   (a)   a relevant notification is published for a part, but not all, of the period mentioned in paragraph (5)(d); but

   (b)   the failure to publish it throughout that period is wholly attributable to circumstances which it would not be reasonable to have expected the relevant officer to prevent or avoid,

no offence is committed under regulation 12(10) or regulation 14(5) (as the case may be) by reason of that failure.

15(7)   In this regulation–

   (a)   **"electronic address"** includes any number or address used for the purposes of receiving electronic communications;

   (b)   **"electronic communication"** means an electronic communication within the meaning of the Electronic Communications Act 2000 the processing of which on receipt is intended to produce writing; and

   (c)   **"relevant officer"** means (as the case may be) an administrator, liquidator, provisional liquidator or supervisor who is required to send a relevant notification to a creditor by a provision of this Part.

16   Disclosure of confidential information received from an EEA regulator

16(1)   This regulation applies to information (**"insolvency information"**) which–

   (a)   relates to the business or affairs of any other person; and

   (b)   is supplied to the Authority by an EEA regulator acting in accordance with Articles 5, 8 or 30 of the reorganisation and winding up directive.

16(2)   Subject to paragraphs (3) and (4), sections 348, 349 and 352 of the 2000 Act apply in relation to insolvency information in the same way as they apply in relation to confidential information within the meaning of section 348(2) of the 2000 Act.

16(3)   Insolvency information is not subject to the restrictions on disclosure imposed by section 348(1) of the 2000 Act (as it applies by virtue of paragraph (2)) if it satisfies any of the criteria set out in section 348(4) of the 2000 Act.

16(4)   The Disclosure Regulations apply in relation to insolvency information as they apply in relation to single market directive information (within the meaning of those Regulations).

16(5)   In this regulation, **"the Disclosure Regulations"** means the Financial Services and Markets Act 2000 (Disclosure of Confidential Information) Regulations 2001.

PART IV

PRIORITY OF PAYMENT OF INSURANCE CLAIMS IN WINDING UP ETC.

17   Interpretation of this Part

17(1)   For the purposes of this Part–

"composite insurer" means a UK insurer who is authorised to carry on both general business and long term business, in accordance with article 18(2) of the life insurance directive;

"floating charge" has the meaning given by section 251 of the 1986 Act or paragraph (1) of Article 5 of the 1989 Order;

"general business" means the business of effecting or carrying out a contract of general insurance;

"general business assets" means the assets of a composite insurer which are, or should properly be, apportioned to that insurer's general business, in accordance with the requirements of Article 18(3) of the life insurance directive (separate management of long term and general business of a composite insurer);

"general business liabilities" means the debts of a composite insurer which are attributable to the general business carried on by that insurer;

"general insurer" means a UK insurer who carries on exclusively general business;

"long term business" means the business of effecting or carrying out a contract of long term insurance;

"long term business assets" means the assets of a composite insurer which are, or should properly be, apportioned to that insurer's long term business, in accordance with the requirements of Article 18(3) of the first life insurance directive (separate management of long term and general business of a composite insurer);

"long term business liabilities" means the debts of a composite insurer which are attributable to the long term business carried on by that insurer;

"long term insurer" means a UK insurer who–

(a)   carries on long term business exclusively, or

(b)   carries on long term business and permitted general business;

"non-transferring composite insurer" means a composite insurer the long term business of which has not been, and is not to be, transferred as a going concern to a person who may lawfully carry out those contracts, in accordance with section 376(2) of the 2000 Act;

"other assets" means any assets of a composite insurer which are not long term business assets or general business assets;

"other business", in relation to a composite insurer, means such of the business (if any) of the insurer as is not long term business or general business;

"permitted general business" means the business of effecting or carrying out a contract of general insurance where the risk insured against relates to either accident or sickness;

"preferential debt" means a debt falling into any of categories 4 or 5 of the debts listed in Schedule 6 to the 1986 Act or Schedule 4 to the 1989 Order, that is–

(a)   contributions to occupational pension schemes, etc., and

(b)   remuneration etc. of employees;

"society" means–

(a) a friendly society incorporated under the Friendly Societies Act 1992;

(b) a society which is a friendly society within the meaning of section 7(1)(a) of the Friendly Societies Act 1974, and registered within the meaning of that Act, or

(c) an industrial and provident society registered or deemed to be registered under the Industrial and Provident Societies Act 1965 or the Industrial and Provident Societies Act (Northern Ireland) 1969.

17(2)   In this Part, references to assets include a reference to proceeds where an asset has been realised, and any other sums representing assets.

17(3)   References in paragraph (1) to a contract of long term or of general insurance must be read with–

(a) section 22 of the 2000 Act;

(b) any relevant order made under that section; and

(c) Schedule 2 to that Act.

18   Application of regulations 19 to 27

18(1)   Subject to paragraph (2), regulations 19 to 27 apply in the winding up of a UK insurer where–

(a) in the case of a winding up by the court, the winding up order is made on or after 20th April 2003; or

(b) in the case of a creditors' voluntary winding up, the liquidator is appointed, as mentioned in section 100 of the 1986 Act, paragraph 83 of Schedule B1, paragraph 84 of Schedule B1 to the 1989 Order or Article 86 of the 1989 Order, on or after 20th April 2003.

18(2)   Where a relevant compromise or arrangement is in place,

(a) no winding up proceedings may be opened without the permission of the court, and

(b) the permission of the court is to be granted only if required by the exceptional circumstances of the case.

18(3)   For the purposes of paragraph (2), winding up proceedings include proceedings for a winding up order or for a creditors' voluntary liquidation with confirmation by the court.

18(4)   Regulations 20 to 27 do not apply to a winding up falling within paragraph (1) where, in relation to a UK insurer–

(a) an administration order was made before 20th April 2003, and that order is not discharged until the commencement date; or

(b) a provisional liquidator was appointed before 20th April 2003, and that appointment is not discharged until the commencement date.

18(5)   For purposes of this regulation, **"the commencement date"** means the date when a UK insurer goes into liquidation within the meaning given by section 247(2) of the 1986 Act or Article 6(2) of the 1989 Order.

18(6)   In paragraph (2) **"relevant compromise or arrangement"** means–

(a) a section 899 compromise or arrangement, or

(b) a compromise or arrangement sanctioned by the court in relation to a UK insurer before 6th April 2008 under–

(i) section 425 of the Companies Act 1985 (excluding a compromise or arrangement falling within section 427 or 427A of that Act), or

    (ii)   Article 418 of the Companies (Northern Ireland) Order 1986 (excluding a compromise or arrangement falling within Article 420 or 420A of that Order).

History
Regulation 18(2) amended and reg.18(6) inserted by the Companies Act 2006 (Consequential Amendments and Transitional Provisions) Order 2011 (SI 2011/1265) art.23(4) as from May 12, 2011.

19 Application of this Part: certain assets excluded from insolvent estate of UK insurer

19(1)   For the purposes of this Part, the insolvent estate of a UK insurer shall not include any assets which at the commencement date are subject to a relevant compromise or arrangement.

19(2)   In this regulation–

    (a)   **"assets"** has the same meaning as **"property"** in section 436 of the 1986 Act or Article 2(2) of the 1989 Order;

    (b)   **"commencement date"** has the meaning given in regulation 18(5);

    (c)   **"insolvent estate"**–

        (i)   in England, Wales and Northern Ireland has the meaning given by Rule 13.8 of the Insolvency Rules or Rule 0.2 of the Insolvency Rules (Northern Ireland), and

        (ii)   in Scotland means the company's assets;

    (d)   **"relevant compromise or arrangement"** means–

        (i)   a compromise or arrangement sanctioned by the court in relation to a UK insurer before 20th April 2003 under–

            (aa)   section 425 of the Companies Act 1985 (excluding a compromise or arrangement falling within section 427 or 427A of that Act), or

            (bb)   Article 418 of the Companies (Northern Ireland) Order 1986 (excluding a compromise or arrangement falling within Article 420 or 420A of that Order); or

        (ii)   any subsequent compromise or arrangement sanctioned by the court to amend or replace a compromise or arrangement of a kind mentioned in paragraph (i) which is–

            (aa)   itself of a kind mentioned in sub-paragraph (aa) or (bb) of paragraph (i) (whether sanctioned before, on or after 20th April 2003), or

            (bb)   a section 899 compromise or arrangement.

History
In reg.19(2)(b), "18(5)" substituted for "18(4)" by the Insurers (Reorganisation and Winding Up) (Lloyd's) Regulations 2005 (SI 2005/1998) art.49, as from August 10, 2005. Heading and reg.19(1) amended and reg.19(2)(d) substituted by the Companies Act 2006 (Consequential Amendments and Transitional Provisions) Order 2011 (SI 2011/1265) art.23(5), (6) as from May 12, 2011.

20 Preferential debts: disapplication of section 175 of the 1986 Act or article 149 of the 1989 Order

20   Except to the extent that they are applied by regulation 27, section 175 of the 1986 Act or Article 149 of the 1989 Order (preferential debts (general provision)) does not apply in the case of a winding up of a UK insurer, and instead the provisions of regulations 21 to 26 have effect.

21   Preferential debts: long term insurers and general insurers

21(1)   This regulation applies in the case of a winding up of–

(a)   a long term insurer;

(b)   a general insurer;

(c)   a composite insurer, where the long term business of that insurer has been or is to be transferred as a going concern to a person who may lawfully carry out the contracts in that long term business in accordance with section 376(2) of the 2000 Act.

21(2)   Subject to paragraph (3), the debts of the insurer must be paid in the following order of priority–

(a)   preferential debts;

(b)   insurance debts;

(c)   all other debts.

21(3)   Preferential debts rank equally among themselves after the expenses of the winding up and must be paid in full, unless the assets are insufficient to meet them, in which case they abate in equal proportions.

History

The words "after the expenses of the winding up" inserted by the Insurers (Reorganisation and Winding Up) (Amendment) Regulations 2004 (SI 2004/546) reg.2(4), as from March 3, 2004.

21(4)   Insurance debts rank equally among themselves and must be paid in full, unless the assets available after the payment of preferential debts are insufficient to meet them, in which case they abate in equal proportions.

21(5)   Subject to paragraph (6), so far as the assets of the insurer available for the payment of unsecured creditors are insufficient to meet the preferential debts, those debts (and only those debts) have priority over the claims of holders of debentures secured by, or holders of, any floating charge created by the insurer, and must be paid accordingly out of any property comprised in or subject to that charge.

21(6)   The order of priority specified in paragraph (2)(a) and (b) applies for the purposes of any payment made in accordance with paragraph (5).

21(7)   Section 176A of the 1986 Act and Article 150A of the 1989 Order have effect with regard to an insurer so that insurance debts must be paid out of the prescribed part in priority to all other unsecured debts.

22   Composite insurers: preferential debts attributable to long term and general business

22(1)   This regulation applies in the case of the winding up of a non-transferring composite insurer.

22(2)   Subject to the payment of costs in accordance with regulation 30, the long term business assets and the general business assets must be applied separately in accordance with paragraphs (3) and (4).

22(3)   Subject to paragraph (6), the long term business assets must be applied in discharge of the long term business preferential debts in the order of priority specified in regulation 23(1).

22(4)   Subject to paragraph (8), the general business assets must be applied in discharge of the general business preferential debts in the order of priority specified in regulation 24(1).

22(5)   Paragraph (6) applies where the value of the long term business assets exceeds the long term business preferential debts and the general business assets are insufficient to meet the general business preferential debts.

22(6)   Those long term business assets which represent the excess must be applied in discharge of the outstanding general business preferential debts of the insurer, in accordance with the order of priority specified in regulation 24(1).

22(7)   Paragraph (8) applies where the value of the general business assets exceeds the general business preferential debts, and the long term business assets are insufficient to meet the long term business preferential debts.

22(8)   Those general business assets which represent the excess must be applied in discharge of the outstanding long term business preferential debts of the insurer, in accordance with the order of priority specified in regulation 23(1).

22(9)   For the purposes of this regulation and regulations 23 and 24–

"long term business preferential debts" means those debts mentioned in regulation 23(1) and, unless the court orders otherwise, any expenses of the winding up which are apportioned to the long term business assets in accordance with regulation 30;

"general business preferential debts" means those debts mentioned in regulation 24(1) and, unless the court orders otherwise, any expenses of the winding up which are apportioned to the general business assets in accordance with regulation 30.

22(10)   For the purposes of paragraphs (6) and (8)–

"outstanding long term business preferential debts" means those long term business preferential debts, if any, which remain unpaid, either in whole or in part, after the application of the long term business assets, in accordance with paragraph (3);

"outstanding general business preferential debts" means those general business preferential debts, if any, which remain unpaid, either in whole or in part, after the application of the general business assets, in accordance with paragraph (3).

23   Preferential debts: long term business of a non-transferring composite insurer

23(1)   For the purpose of compliance with the requirement in regulation 22(3), the long term business assets of a non-transferring composite insurer must be applied in discharge of the following debts and in the following order of priority–

(a)   relevant preferential debts;

(b)   long term insurance debts.

23(2)   Relevant preferential debts rank equally among themselves, unless the long term business assets, any available general business assets and other assets (if any) applied in accordance with regulation 24 are insufficient to meet them, in which case they abate in equal proportions.

23(3)   Long term insurance debts rank equally among themselves, unless the long term business assets available after the payment of relevant preferential debts and any available general business assets and other assets (if any) applied in accordance with regulation 25 are insufficient to meet them, in which case they abate in equal proportions.

23(4)   So far as the long term business assets, and any available general business assets, which are available for the payment of unsecured creditors are insufficient to meet the relevant preferential debts, those debts (and only those debts) have priority over the claims of holders of debentures secured by, or holders of, any floating charge created by the insurer over any of its long term business assets, and must be paid accordingly out of any property comprised in or subject to that charge.

23(5)   The order of priority specified in paragraph (1) applies for the purposes of any payment made in accordance with paragraph (4).

23(6) For the purposes of this regulation–

"**available general business assets**" means those general business assets which must be applied in discharge of the insurer's outstanding long term business preferential debts, in accordance with regulation 22(8);

"**long term insurance debt**" means an insurance debt which is attributable to the long term business of the insurer;

"**relevant preferential debt**" means a preferential debt which is attributable to the long term business of the insurer.

24 Preferential debts: general business of a composite insurer

24(1) For the purpose of compliance with the requirement in regulation 22(4), the long term business assets of a non-transferring composite insurer must be applied in discharge of the following debts and in the following order of priority–

   (a)   relevant preferential debts;

   (b)   general insurance debts.

24(2) Relevant preferential debts rank equally among themselves, unless the general business assets, any available long term business assets, and other assets (if any) applied in accordance with regulation 25 are insufficient to meet them, in which case they abate in equal proportions.

24(3) General insurance debts rank equally among themselves, unless the general business assets available after the payment of relevant preferential debts, any available long term business assets, and other assets (if any) applied in accordance with regulation 26 are insufficient to meet them, in which case they abate in equal proportions.

24(4) So far as the other business assets and available long term assets of the insurer which are available for the payment of unsecured creditors are insufficient to meet relevant preferential debts, those debts (and only those debts) have priority over the claims of holders of debentures secured by, or holders of, any floating charge created by the insurer, and must be paid accordingly out of any property comprised in or subject to that charge.

24(5) The order of priority specified in paragraph (1) applies for the purposes of any payment made in accordance with paragraph (4).

24(6) For the purposes of this regulation–

"**available long term business assets**" means those long term business assets which must be applied in discharge of the insurer's outstanding general business preferential debts, in accordance with regulation 22(6);

"**general insurance debt**" means an insurance debt which is attributable to the general business of the insurer;

"**relevant preferential debt**" means a preferential debt which is attributable to the general business of the insurer.

25 Insufficiency of long term business assets and general business assets

25(1) This regulation applies in the case of the winding up of a non-transferring composite insurer where the long term business assets and the general business assets, applied in accordance with regulation 22, are insufficient to meet in full the preferential debts and insurance debts.

25(2) In a case in which this regulation applies, the other assets (if any) of the insurer must be applied in the following order of priority–

(a)   outstanding preferential debts;

(b)   unattributed preferential debts;

(c)   outstanding insurance debts;

(d)   all other debts.

25(3)   So far as the long term business assets, and any available general business assets, which are available for the payment of unsecured creditors are insufficient to meet the outstanding preferential debts and the unattributed preferential debts, those debts (and only those debts) have priority over the claims of holders of debentures secured by, or holders of, any floating charge created by the insurer over any of its other assets, and must be paid accordingly out of any property comprised in or subject to that charge.

25(4)   For the purposes of this regulation–

"outstanding insurance debt" means any insurance debt, or any part of an insurance debt, which was not discharged by the application of the long term business assets and the general business assets in accordance with regulation 22;

"outstanding preferential debt" means any preferential debt attributable either to the long term business or the general business of the insurer which was not discharged by the application of the long term business assets and the general business assets in accordance with regulation 23;

"unattributed preferential debt" means a preferential debt which is not attributable to either the long term business or the general business of the insurer.

26   Composite insurers: excess of long term business assets and general business assets

26(1)   This regulation applies in the case of the winding up of a non-transferring composite insurer where the value of the long term business assets and the general business assets, applied in accordance with regulation 22, exceeds the value of the sum of the long term business preferential debts and the general business preferential debts.

26(2)   In a case to which this regulation applies, long term business assets or general business assets which have not been applied in discharge of long term business preferential debts or general business preferential debts must be applied in accordance with regulation 27.

26(3)   In this regulation, **"long term business preferential debts"** and **"general business preferential debts"** have the same meaning as in regulation 22.

27   Composite insurers: application of other assets

27(1)   This regulation applies in the case of the winding up of a non-transferring composite insurer where regulation 25 does not apply.

27(2)   The other assets of the insurer, together with any outstanding business assets, must be paid in discharge of the following debts in accordance with section 175 of the 1986 Act or Article 149 of the 1989 Order–

(a)   unattributed preferential debts;

(b)   all other debts.

27(3)   In this regulation–

"unattributed preferential debt" has the same meaning as in regulation 25;

"outstanding business assets" means assets of the kind mentioned in regulation 26(2).

28   Composite insurers: proof of debts

28(1)   This regulation applies in the case of the winding up of a non-transferring composite insurer in compliance with the requirement in regulation 23(2).

28(2)   The liquidator may in relation to the insurer's long term business assets and its general business assets fix different days on or before which the creditors of the company who are required to prove their debts or claims are to prove their debts or claims, and he may fix one of those days without at the same time fixing the other.

28(3)   In submitting a proof of any debt a creditor may claim the whole or any part of such debt as is attributable to the company's long term business or to its general business, or he may make no such attribution.

28(4)   When he admits any debt, in whole or in part, the liquidator must state in writing how much of what he admits is attributable to the company's long term business, how much is attributable to the company's general business, and how much is attributable to its other business (if any).

28(5)   Paragraph (2) does not apply in Scotland.

29   Composite insurers: general meetings of creditors

29(1)   This regulation applies in the same circumstances as regulation 28.

29(2)   The creditors mentioned in section 168(2) of the 1986 Act, Article 143(2) of the 1989 Order or rule 4.13 of the Insolvency (Scotland) Rules (power of liquidator to summon general meetings of creditors) are to be–

(a)   in relation to the long term business assets of that insurer, only those who are creditors in respect of long term business liabilities; and

(b)   in relation to the general business assets of that insurer, only those who are creditors in respect of general business liabilities,

and, accordingly, any general meetings of creditors summoned for the purposes of that section, Article or rule are to be separate general meetings of creditors in respect of long term business liabilities and general business liabilities.

30   Composite insurers: apportionment of costs payable out of the assets

30(1)   In the case of the winding up of a non-transferring composite insurer, Rule 4.218 of the Insolvency Rules or Rule 4.228 of the Insolvency Rules (Northern Ireland) (general rules as to priority) or rule 4.67 (order of priority of expenses of liquidation) of the Insolvency (Scotland) Rules applies separately to long-term business assets and to the general business assets of that insurer.

30(2)   But where any fee, expense, cost, charge, or remuneration does not relate exclusively to the long-term business assets or to the general business assets of that insurer, the liquidator must apportion it amongst those assets in such manner as he shall determine.

31   Summary remedy against liquidators

31   Section 212 of the 1986 Act or Article 176 of the 1989 Order (summary remedy against delinquent directors, liquidators etc.) applies in relation to a liquidator who is required to comply with regulations 21 to 27, as it applies in relation to a liquidator who is required to comply with section 175 of the 1986 Act or Article 149 of the 1989 Order.

32   Priority of subrogated claims by the Financial Services Compensation Scheme

32(1)   This regulation applies where an insurance creditor has assigned a relevant right to the scheme manager (**"a relevant assignment"**).

32(2)   For the purposes of regulations 21, 23 and 24, where the scheme manager proves for an insurance debt in the winding up of a UK insurer pursuant to a relevant assignment, that debt must be paid to the scheme manager in the same order of priority as any other insurance debt.

32(3)   In this regulation–

"relevant right" means any direct right of action against a UK insurer under a contract of insurance, including the right to prove for a debt under that contract in a winding up of that insurer;

"scheme manager" has the meaning given by section 212(1) of the 2000 Act.

33   Voluntary arrangements: treatment of insurance debts

33(1)   The modifications made by paragraph (2) apply where a voluntary arrangement is proposed under section 1 of the 1986 Act or Article 14 of the 1989 Order in relation to a UK insurer, and that arrangement includes–

(a)   a composition in satisfaction of any insurance debts; and

(b)   a distribution to creditors of some or all of the assets of that insurer in the course of, or with a view to, terminating the whole or any part of the business of that insurer.

33(2)   Section 4 of the 1986 Act (decisions of meetings) has effect as if–

(a)   after subsection (4) there were inserted

"**(4A)** A meeting so summoned and taking place on or after 20th April 2003 shall not approve any proposal or modification under which any insurance debt of the company is to be paid otherwise than in priority to such of its debts as are not insurance debts or preferential debts.

(4B) Paragraph (4A) does not apply where–

(a)   a winding up order made before 20th April 2003 is in force; or

(b)   a relevant insolvency appointment made before 20th April 2003 has effect, in relation to the company.";

(b)   for subsection (7) there were substituted

"**(7)** References in this section to preferential debts mean debts falling into any of categories 4 and 5 of the debts listed in Schedule 6 to this Act; and references to preferential creditors are to be construed accordingly."; and

(c)   after subsection (7) as so substituted there were inserted–

"**(8)** For the purposes of this section–

(a)   'insurance debt' has the meaning it has in the Insurers (Reorganisation and Winding up) Regulations 2004; and

(b)   'relevant insolvency measure' means–

(i)   the appointment of a provisional liquidator, or

(ii)   the appointment of an administrator,

where an effect of the appointment will be, or is intended to be, a realisation of some or all of the assets of the insurer and the distribution of the proceeds to creditors, with a view to terminating the whole or any part of the business of that insurer.".

33(3)   Article 17 of the 1989 Order (decisions of meetings) has effect as if–

(a)   after paragraph (4) there were inserted–

"**(4A)** A meeting so summoned and taking place on or after 20th April 2003 shall not approve any proposal or modification under which any insurance debt of the company is to be paid otherwise than in priority to such of its debts as are not insurance debts or preferential debts.

(4B) Paragraph (4A) does not apply where–

(a)   a winding up order made before 20th April 2003 is in force; or

(b)   a relevant insolvency appointment made before 20th April 2003 has effect, in relation to the company.";

(b)   for paragraph (7) there were substituted–

"**(7)** References in this Article to preferential debts mean debts falling into any of categories 4 and 5 of the debts listed in Schedule 4 to this Order, and references to preferential creditors are to be construed accordingly."; and

(c)   after paragraph (7) as so substituted there were inserted–

"**(8)** For the purposes of this section–

(a)   'insurance debt' has the meaning it has in the Insurers (Reorganisation and Winding Up) Regulations 2004 and

(b)   'relevant insolvency measure' means–

(i)   the appointment of a provisional liquidator, or

(ii)   the appointment of an administrator,

where an effect of the appointment will be, or is intended to be, a realisation of some or all of the assets of the insurer and the distribution of the proceeds to creditors, with a view to terminating the whole or any part of the business of that insurer.".

History
The date "2003", originally omitted in two places after "20th April" in reg.32(2), (3) inserted by the Insurers (Reorganisation and Winding Up) (Amendment) Regulations 2004 (SI 2004/546) reg.2(5), as from March 3, 2004.

PART V

REORGANISATION OR WINDING UP OF UK INSURERS: RECOGNITION OF EEA RIGHTS

34   Application of this Part

34(1)   This Part applies–

(a)   where a decision with respect to the approval of a proposed voluntary arrangement having a qualifying purpose is made under section 4A of the 1986 Act or Article 17A of the 1989 Order on or after 20th April 2003 in relation to a UK insurer;

(b)   where an administration order made under section 8 of the 1986 Act on or after 20th April 2003 or, on or after 15th September 2003, made under paragraph 13 of Schedule B1 or under paragraph 14 of Schedule B1 to the 1989 Order is in force in relation to a UK insurer;

(c)   where on or after 20th April 2003 the court reduces the value of one or more of the contracts of a UK insurer under section 377 of the 2000 Act or section 24(5) of the Friendly Societies Act 1992;

(d)   where a UK insurer is subject to a relevant winding up;

(e)   where a provisional liquidator is appointed in relation to a UK insurer on or after 20th April 2003.

34(2)   For the purposes of paragraph (1)(a), a voluntary arrangement has a qualifying purpose if it–

(a)   varies the rights of the creditors as against the insurer and is intended to enable the insurer, and the whole or any part of its undertaking, to survive as a going concern; or

(b)   includes a realisation of some or all of the assets of the insurer to which it relates and the distribution of the proceeds to creditors, with a view to terminating the whole or any part of the business of that insurer.

34(3)   For the purposes of paragraph (1)(d), a winding up is a relevant winding up if–

    (a)   in the case of a winding up by the court, the winding up order is made on or after 20th April 2003; or

    (b)   in the case of a creditors' voluntary winding up, the liquidator is appointed in accordance with section 100 of the 1986 Act, paragraph 83 of Schedule B1, paragraph 84 of Schedule B1 to the 1989 Order or Article 86 of the 1989 Order on or after 20th April 2003.

35   Application of this Part: certain assets excluded from insolvent estate of UK insurer

35(1)   For the purposes of this Part, the insolvent estate of a UK insurer shall not include any assets which at the commencement date are subject to a relevant compromise or arrangement.

35(2)   In this regulation–

    (a)   **"assets"** has the same meaning as **"property"** in section 436 of the 1986 Act or Article 2(2) of the 1989 Order;

    (b)   **"commencement date"** has the meaning given in regulation 18(4);

    (c)   **"insolvent estate"** in England and Wales and Northern Ireland has the meaning given by Rule 13.8 of the Insolvency Rules or Rule 0.2 of the Insolvency Rules (Northern Ireland) and in Scotland means the company's assets;

    (d)   **"relevant compromise or arrangement"** means–

        (i)   a compromise or arrangement sanctioned by the court in relation to a UK insurer before 20th April 2003 under–

            (aa) section 425 of the Companies Act 1985 (excluding a compromise or arrangement falling within section 427 or 427A of that Act), or

            (bb) Article 418 of the Companies (Northern Ireland) Order 1986 (excluding a compromise or arrangement falling within Article 420 or 420A of that Order); or

        (ii) any subsequent compromise or arrangement sanctioned by the court to amend or replace a compromise or arrangement of a kind mentioned in paragraph (i) which is–

            (aa) itself of a kind mentioned in sub-paragraph (aa) or (bb) of paragraph (i) (whether sanctioned before, on or after 20th April 2003), or

            (bb) a section 899 compromise or arrangement.)

History
Heading and reg.35(1) amended and reg.35(2)(d) substituted by the Companies Act 2006 (Consequential Amendments and Transitional Provisions) Order 2011 (SI 2011/1265) art.23(7), (8) as from May 12, 2011.

36   Interpretation of this Part

36(1)   For the purposes of this Part–

    (a)   **"affected insurer"** means a UK insurer which is the subject of a relevant reorganisation or a relevant winding up;

    (b)   **"relevant reorganisation or a relevant winding up"** means any voluntary arrangement, administration order, winding up, or order referred to in regulation 34(1)(d) to which this Part applies; and

    (c)   **"relevant time"** means the date of the opening of a relevant reorganisation or a relevant winding up.

36(2)   In this Part, references to the opening of a relevant reorganisation or a relevant winding up mean–

(a)   in the case of winding up proceedings–

    (i)   in the case of a winding up by the court, the date on which the winding up order is made, or

    (ii)   in the case of a creditors' voluntary winding up, the date on which the liquidator is appointed in accordance with section 100 of the 1986 Act, paragraph 83 of Schedule B1 or Article 86 of the 1989 Order or paragraph 84 of Schedule B1 to the 1989 Order;

(b)   in the case of a voluntary arrangement, the date when a decision with respect to that voluntary arrangement has effect in accordance with section 4A(2) of the 1986 Act or Article 17A(2) of the 1989 Order;

(c)   in a case where an administration order under paragraph 13 of Schedule B1 or under paragraph 14 of Schedule B1 to the 1989 Order is in force, the date of the making of that order;

(d)   in a case where an administrator is appointed under paragraphs 14 or 22 of Schedule B1 or under paragraph 15 or 23 of Schedule B1 to the 1989 Order the date on which that appointment takes effect;

(e)   in a case where the court reduces the value of one or more of the contracts of a UK insurer under section 377 of the 2000 Act or section 24(5) of the Friendly Societies Act 1992, the date the court exercises that power; and

(f)   in a case where a provisional liquidator has been appointed, the date of that appointment, and references to the time of an opening must be construed accordingly.

37   EEA rights: applicable law in the winding up of a UK insurer

37(1)   This regulation is subject to the provisions of regulations 38 to 47.

37(2)   In a relevant winding up, the matters mentioned in paragraph (3) in particular are to be determined in accordance with the general law of insolvency of the United Kingdom.

37(3)   Those matters are–

(a)   the assets which form part of the estate of the affected insurer;

(b)   the treatment of assets acquired by, or devolving on, the affected insurer after the opening of the relevant winding up;

(c)   the respective powers of the affected insurer and the liquidator or provisional liquidator;

(d)   the conditions under which set-off may be revoked;

(e)   the effects of the relevant winding up on current contracts to which the affected insurer is a party;

(f)   the effects of the relevant winding up on proceedings brought by creditors;

(g)   the claims which are to be lodged against the estate of the affected insurer;

(h)   the treatment of claims against the affected insurer arising after the opening of the relevant winding up;

(i)   the rules governing–

    (i)   the lodging, verification and admission of claims,

    (ii)   the distribution of proceeds from the realisation of assets,

    (iii)   the ranking of claims,

    (iv)   the rights of creditors who have obtained partial satisfaction after the opening of the relevant winding up by virtue of a right in rem or through set-off;

(j)   the conditions for and the effects of the closure of the relevant winding up, in particular by composition;

(k)   the rights of creditors after the closure of the relevant winding up;

(l)   who is to bear the cost and expenses incurred in the relevant winding up;

(m)   the rules relating to the voidness, voidability or unenforceability of legal acts detrimental to all the creditors.

37(4)   In this regulation, **"relevant winding up"** has the meaning given by regulation 34(3).

38   Employment contracts and relationships

38(1)   The effects of a relevant reorganisation or a relevant winding up on any EEA employment contract and any EEA employment relationship are to be determined in accordance with the law of the EEA State to which that contract or that relationship is subject.

38(2)   In this regulation, an employment contract is an EEA employment contract, and an employment relationship is an EEA employment relationship, if it is subject to the law of an EEA State.

39   Contracts in connection with immovable property

39   The effects of a relevant reorganisation or a relevant winding up on a contract conferring the right to make use of or acquire immovable property situated within the territory of an EEA State are to be determined in accordance with the law of that State.

40   Registrable rights

40   The effects of a relevant reorganisation or a relevant winding up on rights of the affected insurer with respect to–

(a)   immovable property,

(b)   a ship, or

(c)   an aircraft

which is subject to registration in a public register kept under the authority of an EEA State are to be determined in accordance with the law of that State.

41   Third parties' rights in rem

41(1)   A relevant reorganisation or a relevant winding up shall not affect the rights in rem of creditors or third parties in respect of tangible or intangible, movable or immovable assets (including both specific assets and collections of indefinite assets as a whole which change from time to time) belonging to the affected insurer which are situated within the territory of an EEA State at the relevant time.

41(2)   The rights in rem referred to in paragraph (1) shall in particular include–

(a)   the right to dispose of the assets in question or have them disposed of and to obtain satisfaction from the proceeds of or the income from those assets, in particular by virtue of a lien or a mortgage;

(b)   the exclusive right to have a claim met out of the assets in question, in particular a right guaranteed by a lien in respect of the claim or by assignment of the claim by way of guarantee;

(c)   the right to demand the assets in question from, or to require restitution by, any person having possession or use of them contrary to the wishes of the party otherwise entitled to the assets;

(d) a right in rem to the beneficial use of assets.

41(3) A right, recorded in a public register and enforceable against third parties, under which a right in rem within the meaning of paragraph (1) may be obtained, is also to be treated as a right in rem for the purposes of this regulation.

41(4) Paragraph (1) does not preclude actions for voidness, voidability or unenforceability of legal acts detrimental to creditors under the general law of insolvency of the United Kingdom, as referred to in regulation 37(3)(m).

42   Reservation of title agreements etc.

42(1) The opening of a relevant reorganisation or a relevant winding up in relation to an insurer purchasing an asset shall not affect the seller's rights based on a reservation of title where at the time of that opening the asset is situated within the territory of an EEA State.

42(2) The opening of a relevant reorganisation or a relevant winding up in relation to an insurer selling an asset, after delivery of the asset, shall not constitute grounds for rescinding or terminating the sale and shall not prevent the purchaser from acquiring title where at the time of that opening the asset sold is situated within the territory of an EEA State.

42(3) Paragraphs (1) and (2) do not preclude actions for voidness, voidability or unenforceability of legal acts detrimental to creditors under the general law of insolvency of the United Kingdom, as referred to in regulation 37(3)(m).

43   Creditors' rights to set off

43(1) A relevant reorganisation or a relevant winding up shall not affect the right of creditors to demand the set-off of their claims against the claims of the affected insurer, where such a set-off is permitted by the applicable EEA law.

43(2) In paragraph (1), **"applicable EEA law"** means the law of the EEA State which is applicable to the claim of the affected insurer.

43(3) Paragraph (1) does not preclude actions for voidness, voidability or unenforceability of legal acts detrimental to creditors under the general law of insolvency of the United Kingdom, as referred to in regulation 37(3)(m).

44   Regulated markets

44(1) Without prejudice to regulation 40, the effects of a relevant reorganisation measure or winding up on the rights and obligations of the parties to a regulated market operating in an EEA State must be determined in accordance with the law applicable to that market.

44(2) Paragraph (1) does not preclude actions for voidness, voidability or unenforceability of legal acts detrimental to creditors under the general law of insolvency of the United Kingdom, as referred to in regulation 37(3)(m).

44(3) For the purposes of this regulation, **"regulated market"** has the meaning given by Article 4.1.14 of Directive 2004/39/EC of the European Parliament and of the Council of 21 April 2004 on markets in financial instruments.

History
Regulation 44 amended by the Financial Services and Markets Act 2000 (Markets in Financial Instruments) Regulations 2007 (SI 2007/126) reg.6 and Sch.6 para.17, as from April 1, 2007 for the purposes specified in reg.1(2) and from November 1, 2007 for all other purposes.

45   Detrimental acts pursuant to the law of an EEA State

45(1)   In a relevant reorganisation or a relevant winding up, the rules relating to detrimental transactions shall not apply where a person who has benefited from a legal act detrimental to all the creditors provides proof that–

(a)   the said act is subject to the law of an EEA State; and

(b)   that law does not allow any means of challenging that act in the relevant case.

45(2)   For the purposes of paragraph (1), **"the rules relating to detrimental transactions"** means any provisions of the general law of insolvency relating to the voidness, voidability or unenforceability of legal acts detrimental to all the creditors, as referred to in regulation 37(3)(m).

46   Protection of third party purchasers

46(1)   This regulation applies where, by an act concluded after the opening of a relevant reorganisation or a relevant winding up, an affected insurer disposes for a consideration of–

(a)   an immovable asset situated within the territory of an EEA State;

(b)   a ship or an aircraft subject to registration in a public register kept under the authority of an EEA State; or

(c)   securities whose existence or transfer presupposes entry into a register or account laid down by the law of an EEA State or which are placed in a central deposit system governed by the law of an EEA State.

46(2)   The validity of that act is to be determined in accordance with the law of the EEA State within whose territory the immovable asset is situated or under whose authority the register, account or system is kept, as the case may be.

47   Lawsuits pending

47(1)   The effects of a relevant reorganisation or a relevant winding up on a relevant lawsuit pending in an EEA State shall be determined solely in accordance with the law of that EEA State.

47(2)   In paragraph (1), **"relevant lawsuit"** means a lawsuit concerning an asset or right of which the affected insurer has been divested.

PART VI

THIRD COUNTRY INSURERS

48   Interpretation of this Part

48(1)   In this Part–

(a)   **"relevant measure"**, in relation to a third country insurer, means

(i)   a winding up;

(ii)   an administration order made under paragraph 13 of Schedule B1 or under paragraph 14 of Schedule B1 to the 1989 Order; or

(iii)   a decision of the court to reduce the value of one or more of the insurer's contracts, in accordance with section 377 of the 2000 Act;

(b)   **"third country insurer"** means a person–

(i)   who has permission under the 2000 Act to effect or carry out contracts of insurance; and

(ii)   whose head office is not in the United Kingdom or an EEA State.

48(2)   In paragraph (1), the definition of **"third country insurer"** must be read with–

(a)   section 22 of the 2000 Act;

(b)   any relevant order made under that section; and

(c)   Schedule 2 to that Act.

49   Application of these Regulations to a third country insurer

49   Parts III, IV and V of these Regulations apply where a third country insurer is subject to a relevant measure, as if references in those Parts to a UK insurer included a reference to a third country insurer.

50   Disclosure of confidential information: third country insurers

50(1)   This regulation applies to information (**"insolvency practitioner information"**) which–

(a)   relates to the business or other affairs of any person; and

(b)   is information of a kind mentioned in paragraph (2).

50(2)   Information falls within paragraph (1)(b) if it is supplied to–

(a)   the Authority by an EEA regulator; or

(b)   an insolvency practitioner by an EEA administrator or liquidator,

in accordance with or pursuant to Article 30 of the reorganisation and winding up directive.

50(3)   Subject to paragraphs (4), (5) and (6), sections 348, 349 and 352 of the 2000 Act apply in relation to insolvency practitioner information in the same way as they apply in relation to confidential information within the meaning of section 348(2) of that Act.

50(4)   For the purposes of this regulation, sections 348, 349 and 352 of the 2000 Act and the Disclosure Regulations have effect as if the primary recipients specified in subsection (5) of section 348 of the 2000 Act included an insolvency practitioner.

50(5)   Insolvency practitioner information is not subject to the restrictions on disclosure imposed by section 348(1) of the 2000 Act (as it applies by virtue of paragraph (3)) if it satisfies any of the criteria set out in section 348(4) of the 2000 Act.

50(6)   The Disclosure Regulations apply in relation to insolvency practitioner information as they apply in relation to single market directive information (within the meaning of those Regulations).

50(7)   In this regulation–

"the Disclosure Regulations" means the Financial Services and Markets Act 2000 (Disclosure of Confidential Information) Regulations 2001;

"EEA administrator" and **"EEA liquidator"** mean respectively an administrator or liquidator within the meaning of the reorganisation and winding up directive;

"insolvency practitioner" means an insolvency practitioner, within the meaning of section 388 of the 1986 Act or Article 3 of the 1989 Order, who is appointed or acts in relation to a third country insurer.

PART VII

REVOCATION AND AMENDMENTS

51   Amendment of the Insurers (Winding Up) Rules 2001 and the Insurers (Winding Up) (Scotland) Rules 2001

51   [Amends reg.29 of each of the above.]

52   Financial Services and Markets Act 2000 (Administration Orders Relating to Insurers) Order 2002

52   [Revoked by the Financial Services and Markets Act 2000 (Administration Orders Relating to Insurers) Order 2010 (SI 2010/3023) art.5(c) as from February 1, 2011.]

53   Revocation and transitional

53(1)   Except as provided in this regulation, the Insurers (Reorganisation and Winding Up) Regulations 2003 are revoked.

53(2)   Subject to (3), the provisions of Parts III and IV shall continue in force in respect of decisions orders or appointments referred to therein and made before the coming into force of these Regulations.

53(3)   Where an administrator has been appointed in respect of a UK insurer on or after 15th September 2003, he shall be treated as being so appointed on the date these regulations come into force.

Insolvency Proceedings (Fees) Order 2004

(SI 2004/593)

Made on 4 March 2004 by the Lord Chancellor, under ss.414 and 415 of the Insolvency Act 1986 s.133 of the Bankruptcy Act 1914 and s.663(4) of the Companies Act 1985 and with the sanction of the Treasury. Operative from 1 April 2004.

[**Note:** Changes made by the Insolvency Proceedings (Fees) (Amendment) Order 2005 (SI 2005/544), the Insolvency Proceedings (Fees) (Amendment) Order 2006 (SI 2006/561), the Insolvency Proceedings (Fees) (Amendment) Order 2007 (SI 2007/521), the Insolvency Proceedings (Fees) (Amendment) Order 2008 (SI 2008/714), the Insolvency Proceedings (Fees) (Amendment) Order 2009 (SI 2009/645), the Insolvency Proceedings (Fees) (Amendment) Order 2010 (SI 2010/732) and the Insolvency Proceedings (Fees) (Amendment) Order 2011 (SI 2011/1167) have been incorporated into the text.]

1 Citation and commencement

1 This Order may be cited as the Insolvency Proceedings (Fees) Order 2004 and shall come into force on 1st April 2004.

2 Interpretation

2(1) In this Order–

"**the Act**" means the Insolvency Act 1986 (any reference to a numbered section being to the section so numbered in that Act);

"**the commencement date**" is the date referred to in Article 1;

"**individual voluntary arrangement**" means a voluntary arrangement pursuant to Part VIII of the Act; and

"**the Rules**" means the Insolvency Rules 1986 (any reference to a numbered Rule being to the Rule so numbered in the Rules).

2(2) A reference to a fee by a means of letters and a number is a reference to the fee so designated in the table in Schedule 2.

3 Revocations and transitional provisions

3 The instruments listed in the Schedule 1 to this Order are revoked to the extent set out in that Schedule.

4 Fees payable in connection with bankruptcies, debt relief orders, individual voluntary arrangements and winding up

4(1) Subject to paragraphs (2) and (3) and article 8, the fees payable to the Secretary of State in respect of the costs of persons acting as approved intermediaries under Part 7A of the Act, proceedings under Parts I to XI of the Act and the performance by the official receiver or Secretary of State of functions under those Parts shall be determined in accordance with the provisions of Schedule 2 to this Order.

History
The heading to art.4 and art.4(1) amended by the Insolvency Proceedings Fees (Amendment) Order 2009 (SI 2009/645) art.4(1)(a), (b) as from April 6, 2009.

4(2) Paragraph (1) and the provisions of Schedule 2 shall not apply to a bankruptcy where the bankruptcy order was made before the commencement date except insofar as is necessary to enable the charging of–

  (a)   fee INV1; or

  (b)   as regards an individual voluntary arrangement proposed by, or entered into by, the bankrupt, fees IVA1, IVA2 or IVA3.

4(3) Paragraph (1) and the provisions of Schedule 2 shall not apply to a winding up by the court where the winding-up order was made before the commencement date except insofar as is necessary to enable the charging of fee INV1.

4(4) Each request for the purchase of any government securities made by a trustee in bankruptcy under the Bankruptcy Act 1914 or a liquidator in a winding up under the provisions of the Companies Act 1985 shall be accompanied by the appropriate amount of fee INV1.

History
Article 4(4) amended by the Insolvency Proceedings Fees (Amendment) Order 2009 (SI 2009/645) art.4(1)(c) as from April 6, 2009.

5   Fees payable to an insolvency practitioner appointed under section 273

5   Where a court appoints an insolvency practitioner under section 273(2) to prepare and submit a report under section 274 the court shall, on submission of the report, pay to the practitioner a fee of £450 (that sum being inclusive of Value Added Tax).

History
The specified sum increased by the Insolvency Proceedings Fees (Amendment) Order 2009 (SI 2009/645) art.4(2) as from April 6, 2009 and further by the Insolvency Proceedings (Fees) (Amendment) Order 2010 (SI 2010/732) art.4 as from April 6, 2010.

6   Deposits—winding up by the court and bankruptcy

6(1)   In this Article–

  "appropriate deposit" means–

   (a)   in relation to a winding-up petition to be presented under the Act the sum of £1,165;

   (b)   in relation to a bankruptcy petition to be presented under section 264(1)(b) the sum of £525; or

   (c)   in relation to a bankruptcy petition to be presented under sections 264(1)(a), (ba), (bb), (c) or (d) the sum of £700;

  "order" means a winding-up, or as the case may be, bankruptcy order;

  "petition" means a winding-up, or as the case may be, bankruptcy petition;

  "relevant assets" means the assets of the company or, as the case may be the assets comprised in the estate of the bankrupt; and

  "relevant fees" means in relation to winding-up proceedings fee W1 and in relation to bankruptcy proceedings fee B1 together with any fees payable under section 273.

History
In the definition of "appropriate deposit" the words "(ba), (bb)," inserted by the Insolvency Proceedings (Fees) (Amendment) Order 2005 (SI 2005/544) regs 4, 5(a) as from April 1, 2005 and the specified sums increased by the

Insolvency Proceedings (Fees) (Amendment) Order 2006 (SI 2006/561) art.2(2), as from April 1, 2006. The specified sums further increased by the Insolvency Proceedings (Fees) (Amendment) Order 2008 (SI 2008/714) reg.2(1)–(3) as from April 6, 2008, by the Insolvency Proceedings Fees (Amendment) Order 2009 (SI 2009/645) art.4(3) as from April 6, 2009, by the Insolvency Proceedings (Fees) (Amendment) Order 2010 (SI 2010/732) art.5 as from April 6, 2010 and by the Insolvency Proceedings (Fees) (Amendment) Order 2011 (SI 2011/1167) art.2 as from June 1, 2011.

6(2) Where a bankruptcy or winding-up petition is presented the appropriate deposit is payable by the petitioner and the deposit shall be security for the payment of the relevant fees and shall be used to discharge those fees to the extent that the relevant assets are insufficient for that purpose.

History
In art.6(2) the words "Where a bankruptcy or winding-up petition is presented the appropriate deposit is payable by the petitioner and the deposit" substituted for the former words "The deposit" by the Insolvency Proceedings (Fees) (Amendment) Order 2005 (SI 2005/544) arts 4, 5(b) as from April 1, 2005.

6(3) Where a deposit is paid to the court, the court shall (except to the extent that a fee is payable by virtue of Article 5) transmit the deposit paid to the official receiver attached to the court.

6(4) A deposit shall be repaid to the person who made it in a case where a petition is dismissed or withdrawn except in the case of a bankruptcy petition where it is required to pay any fees arising under Article 5.

6(5) In any case where an order is made (including any case where the order is subsequently annulled, rescinded or recalled), any deposit made shall be returned to the person who made it save to the extent that the relevant assets are insufficient to discharge the fees for which the deposit is security.

7 Deposits—official receiver acting as nominee in individual voluntary arrangement

7(1) Where a proposal for an individual voluntary arrangement with the official receiver acting as nominee is notified to the official receiver, the notification shall be accompanied by a deposit of £315 as security for fee IVA1 and fee IVA2.

7(2) The deposit shall be used to discharge fee IVA1 and fee IVA2.

7(3) Where the official receiver declines to act in relation to a proposal of the kind mentioned in paragraph (1) the deposit mentioned in that paragraph shall be refunded to the person entitled to it.

7(4) Where the official receiver agrees to act as nominee in relation to a proposal of the kind mentioned in paragraph (1) but the proposal is rejected by the bankrupt's creditors, any balance of the deposit after deducting fee IVA2 shall be returned to the person who is entitled to it.

History
The sum specified in art.7(1) increased by the Insolvency Proceedings Fees (Amendment) Order 2009 (SI 2009/645) art.4(4) as from April 6, 2009.

8 Reduction and refund of fees—individual voluntary arrangement following bankruptcy

8 Where proposals made by a bankrupt for an individual voluntary arrangement with the official receiver acting as supervisor are approved by the bankrupt's creditors, fee B1 shall be reduced to £857.50 and any payments made in respect of fee B1 which exceed that amount shall be refunded to the credit of the estate of the bankrupt.

9 Value Added Tax

9 Where Valued Added Tax is chargeable in respect of the provision of a service for which a fee is prescribed by virtue of any provision of this Order (other than Article 5), there shall be payable in addition to that fee the amount of the Value Added Tax.

SCHEDULE 1

REVOCATIONS

[Not reproduced.]

SCHEDULE 2

FEES PAYABLE IN INSOLVENCY PROCEEDINGS

1(1)   In this Schedule–

"the bankruptcy ceiling" means in relation to a bankruptcy, the sum which is arrived at by adding together–

(a)   the bankruptcy debts required to be paid under the Rules;

(b)   any interest payable by virtue of sections 328(4) and 329(2)(b); and

(c)   the expenses of the bankruptcy as set out in Rule 6.224 other than–

    (i)   any sums spent out of money received in carrying on the business of the bankrupt; and

    (ii)   fee B2 in the Table set out in paragraph 2;

"chargeable receipts" means those sums which are paid into the Insolvency Services Account after first deducting any amounts paid into the Insolvency Services Account which are subsequently paid out to secured creditors in respect of their securities or in carrying on the business of the company or the bankrupt; and

"the insolvency legislation" means the Insolvency Act 1986, the Insolvency Rules 1986 and the Insolvency Regulations 1994.

1(2)   In this Schedule, references to the performance of the "general duties" of the official receiver on the making of a winding-up or bankruptcy order–

(a)   include the payment by the official receiver of any fees, costs or disbursements except for those associated with the realisation of assets or the distribution of funds to creditors; but

(b)   does not include anything done by the official receiver in connection with or for the purposes of–

    (i)   the appointment of agents for the purposes of, or in connection with, the realisation of assets;

    (ii)   the making of a distribution to creditors (including preferential or secured creditors or both such classes of creditor);

    (iii)   the realisation of assets on behalf of the holder of a fixed or floating charge or both types of those charges; or

    (iv)   the supervision of a special manager.

History
Entries for "excepted bankruptcy" and "excepted winding-up" in para.1(1) inserted by the Insolvency Proceedings Fees (Amendment) Order 2009 (SI 2009/645) art.5 as from April 6, 2009 and revoked by the Insolvency Proceedings (Fees) (Amendment) Order 2010 (SI 2010/732) art.7(1) as from April 6, 2010.

2   Fees payable to the Secretary of State in respect of proceedings under Parts I to XI of the Act and the performance by the official receiver and the Secretary of State of functions under those Parts shall be determined in accordance with the provisions of the Table of Fees set out below–

Table of Fees

Fees payable in respect of individual voluntary arrangements only

Designation of Fee	Description of fee and circumstances in which it is charged	Amount of fee or applicable %
IVA1	**Individual voluntary arrangement registration fee** On the registration of an individual voluntary arrangement by the Secretary of State there is payable a fee of–	£15
IVA2	**Individual voluntary arrangement— official receiver's nominee fee** For the performance by the official receiver in relation to an individual voluntary arrangement of the functions of nominee there shall be payable on the agreement of the official receiver so to act a fee of–	£300
IVA3	**Individual voluntary arrangement— official receiver's supervisor fee** For the performance by the official receiver in relation to an individual voluntary arrangement of the functions of supervisor, there shall be payable, a fee calculated as a percentage of any monies realised whilst he acts as supervisor at the rate of–	15%

Fees payable in bankruptcies only

Designation of Fee	Description of fee and circumstances in which it is charged	Amount of fee or applicable %
B1	**Bankruptcy—Official receiver's administration fee** For the performance by the official receiver of his general duties as official receiver on the making of a bankruptcy order, including his duty to investigate and report upon the affairs of bankrupts, there shall be payable a fee of–	£1,715

Designation of Fee	*Description of fee and circumstances in which it is charged*	*Amount of fee or applicable %*
B2	**Bankruptcy—Secretary of State's administration fee applicable to bankruptcy orders made on or after 6 April 2010**	
	For the performance of the Secretary of State's general duties under the insolvency legislation in relation to the administration of the estate of each bankrupt, there shall be payable a fee calculated in accordance with the following scale as a percentage of chargeable receipts relating to the bankruptcy (but ignoring that part of the chargeable receipts which exceeds the bankruptcy ceiling) at the rate of–	0% of the first £2,000
		100% of the next £1,700
		75% of the next £1,500
		15% of the next £396,000
		1% of the remainder, subject to a maximum of £80,000.

Fees payable in relation to debt relief orders

Designation of Fee	*Description of fee and circumstances in which it is charged*	*Amount of fee or applicable %*
DRO1	**Application for a debt relief order—official receiver's administration fee and costs of persons acting as approved intermediaries**	
	For the performance by the official receiver of his functions, and for the payment of an amount not exceeding £10 in respect of the costs of persons acting as approved intermediaries, under Part 7A of the Act, there shall be payable in connection with an application for a debt relief order, a fee of–	£90

Fees payable in relation to winding up by the court only

Designation of Fee	*Description of fee and circumstances in which it is charged*	*Amount of fee or applicable %*
W1	**Winding up by the court—official receiver's administration fee**	
	For the performance by the official receiver of his general duties as official receiver on the making of a winding-up order, including his duty to investigate and report upon the affairs of bodies in liquidation, there shall be payable a fee of–	£2,235

Designation of Fee	Description of fee and circumstances in which it is charged	Amount of fee or applicable %
W2	**Winding up by the court—Secretary of State's administration fee applicable to winding up orders made on or after 6 April 2010**	
	For the performance of the Secretary of State's general duties under the insolvency legislation in relation to the administration of the affairs of each company which is being wound up by the court, there shall be payable a fee calculated in accordance with the following scale as a percentage of chargeable receipts relating to the company at the rate of–	0% of the first £2,500
		100% of the next £1,700
		75% of the next £1,500
		15% of the next £396,000
		1% of the remainder, subject to a maximum of £80,000.

Fees payable in bankruptcies and both types of winding up

Designation of Fee	Description of fee and circumstances in which it is charged	Amount of fee or applicable %
INV1	**Investment fee on purchase or sale of government securities—**	
	For each purchase or sale of any government securities made at the request of a trustee in bankruptcy or a liquidator in a compulsory or voluntary winding up–	
	(a) in respect of a purchase, where the cost of the securities (including accrued interest, if any)–	
	(i) does not exceed £5,000, a fee of–	£50
	(ii) exceeds £5,000, a fee of–	£50 plus 0.3% of the cost in excess of £5,000
	(b) in respect of a sale, where the proceeds of sale of the securities (including accrued interest, if any) exceed £5,000, a fee of–	£50 plus 0.3% of the proceeds in excess of £5,000

History

Fees B2, W1 and W2 amended by the Insolvency Proceedings (Fees) (Amendment) Order 2008 (SI 2008/714) reg.2(4) as from April 6, 2008. The entries for fees IVA1, B2, W2 and INV1 amended, and that for DRO inserted, by the Insolvency Proceedings Fees (Amendment) Order 2009 (SI 2009/645) art.6 as from April 6, 2009. The entries for fees B2, W1 and W2 further amended by the Insolvency Proceedings (Fees) (Amendment) Order 2010 (SI 2010/732) art.6 as from April 6, 2010.

Credit Institutions (Reorganisation and Winding Up) Regulations 2004

(SI 2004/1045)

Made on 1 April 2004 by the Treasury under s.2(2) of the European Communities Act 1972. Operative from 5 May 2004.

Part 1

GENERAL

[**Note:** Changes made by the Capital Requirement Regulations 2006 (SI 2006/3221), the Financial Services (EEA State) Regulations 2007 (SI 2007/108), the Financial Services and Markets Act 2000 (Markets in Financial Instruments) Regulations 2007 (SI 2007/126), the Credit Institutions (Reorganisation and Winding Up) (Amendment) Regulations 2007 (SI 2007/830), the Electronic Money Regulations 2011 (SI 2011/99) and the Companies Act 2006 (Consequential Amendments and Transitional Provisions) Order 2011 (SI 2011/1265) have been incorporated into the text. Where the 2007 Regulations simply add references to articles and paragraphs of Sch.B1 to the Insolvency (Northern Ireland) Order 1989 corresponding to sections and paragraphs of Sch.B1 to IA 1986, annotations have been omitted.]

1 Citation and commencement

1 These Regulations may be cited as the Credit Institutions (Reorganisation and Winding up) Regulations 2004, and come into force on 5th May 2004.

2 Interpretation

2(1) In these Regulations–

"**the 1986 Act**" means the Insolvency Act 1986;

"**the 2000 Act**" means the Financial Services and Markets Act 2000;

"**the 2006 Act**" means the Companies Act 2006;

"**the 1989 Order**" means the Insolvency (Northern Ireland) Order 1989;

"**administrator**" has the meaning given by paragraph 13 of Schedule B1 to the 1986 Act, paragraph 14 of Schedule B1 to the 1989 Order, section 8(2) of the 1986 Act, or Article 21(2) of the 1989 Order as the case may be;

"**the Authority**" means the Financial Services Authority;

"**banking consolidation directive**" means Directive 2006/48/EC of the European Parliament and of the Council of 14 June 2006 relating to the taking up and pursuit of the business of credit institutions as last amended by Directive 2009/111/EC;

"**branch**", in relation to an EEA or UK credit institution has the meaning given by Article 4(3) of the banking consolidation directive;

"**claim**" means a claim submitted by a creditor of a UK credit institution in the course of–

(a) a winding up,

(b) an administration, or

(c) a voluntary arrangement,

with a view to recovering his debt in whole or in part, and includes a proof, within the meaning of rule 2.72 of the Insolvency Rules, or a proof of debt within the meaning of rule 4.73(4) of the Insolvency Rules or Rule 4.079(4) of the Insolvency Rules (Northern Ireland), as the case may be, or in Scotland a claim made in accordance with rule 4.15 of the Insolvency (Scotland) Rules;

"creditors' voluntary winding up" has the meaning given by section 90 of the 1986 Act or Article 76 of the 1989 Order as the case may be;

"debt"–

(a) in relation to a winding up or administration of a UK credit institution, has the meaning given by rule 13.12 of the Insolvency Rules or Article 5(1) of the 1989 Order except that where the credit institution is not a company, references in rule 13.12 or Article 5(1) to a company are to be read as references to the credit institution, and

(b) in a case where a voluntary arrangement has effect, in relation to a UK credit institution, means a debt which would constitute a debt in relation to the winding up of that credit institution, except that references in paragraph (1) of rule 13.12 or paragraph (1) of Article 5 of the 1989 Order to the date on which the company goes into liquidation are to be read as references to the date on which the voluntary arrangement has effect;

(c) in Scotland–

  (i) in relation to the winding up of a UK credit institution, shall be interpreted in accordance with Schedule 1 of the Bankruptcy (Scotland) Act 1985 as applied by Chapter 5 of Part 4 of the Insolvency (Scotland) Rules; and

  (ii) in a case where a voluntary arrangement has effect in relation to a UK credit institution, means a debt which would constitute a debt in relation to the winding up of that credit institution, except that references in Chapter 5 of Part 4 of the Insolvency (Scotland) Rules to the date of commencement of winding up are to be read as references to the date on which the voluntary arrangement has effect;

"directive reorganisation measure" means a reorganisation measure as defined in Article 2 of the reorganisation and winding up directive which was adopted or imposed on or after the 5th May 2004;

"directive winding-up proceedings" means winding-up proceedings as defined in Article 2 of the reorganisation and winding up directive which were opened on or after the 5th May 2004;

"Disclosure Regulations" means the Financial Services and Markets Act 2000 (Disclosure of Confidential Information) Regulations 2001;

"EEA credit institution" means an EEA undertaking, other than a UK credit institution, of the kind mentioned in Article 4(1) and (3) and subject to the exclusion of the undertakings referred to in Article 2 of the banking consolidation directive;

"EEA creditor" means a creditor of a UK credit institution who–

(a) in the case of an individual, is ordinarily resident in an EEA State; and

(b) in the case of a body corporate or unincorporated association of persons, has its head office in an EEA State;

"EEA regulator" means a competent authority (within the meaning of Article 4(4) of the banking consolidation directive) of an EEA State;

"EEA State" has the meaning given by Schedule 1 to the Interpretation Act 1978;

"home state regulator", in relation to an EEA credit institution, means the relevant EEA regulator in the EEA State where its head office is located;

"the Insolvency Rules" means the Insolvency Rules 1986;

"the Insolvency Rules (Northern Ireland)" means the Insolvency Rules (Northern Ireland) 1991;

"the Insolvency (Scotland) Rules" means the Insolvency (Scotland) Rules 1986;

"liquidator", except for the purposes of regulation 4, includes any person or body appointed by the administrative or judicial authorities whose task is to administer winding-up proceedings in respect of a UK credit institution which is not a body corporate;

"officer", in relation to a company, has the meaning given by section 1173(1) of the Companies Act 2006;

"official language" means a language specified in Article 1 of Council Regulation No 1 of 15 April 1958 determining the languages to be used by the European Economic Community (Regulation 1/58/EEC), most recently amended by paragraph (a) of Part XVIII of Annex I to the Act of Accession 1994 (194 N);

"the reorganisation and winding up directive" means the directive of the European Parliament and of the Council of 4 April 2001 on the reorganisation and winding up of credit institutions (2001/24/EC);

"section 899 compromise or arrangement" means a compromise or arrangement sanctioned by the court in relation to a UK credit institution under section 899 of the 2006 Act but does not include a compromise or arrangement falling within section 900 (powers of court to facilitate reconstruction or amalgamation) or Part 27 (mergers and divisions of public companies) of that Act;

"supervisor" has the meaning given by section 7 of the 1986 Act or Article 20 of the 1989 Order as the case may be;

"UK credit institution" means an undertaking whose head office is in the United Kingdom with permission under Part 4 of the 2000 Act to accept deposits or to issue electronic money as the case may be but does not include–

(a) an undertaking which also has permission under Part 4 of the 2000 Act to effect or carry out contracts of insurance; or

(b) a credit union within the meaning of section 1 of the Credit Unions Act 1979;

"voluntary arrangement" means a voluntary arrangement which has effect in relation to a UK credit institution in accordance with section 4A of the 1986 Act or Article 17A of the 1989 Order as the case may be; and

"winding up" means–

(a) winding up by the court, or

(b) a creditors' voluntary winding up.

History
Definition of "banking consolidation directive" substituted, and definitions of "branch", "EEA credit institution" and "EEA regulator" amended, by the Capital Requirements Regulations 2006 (SI 2006/3221) reg.29(4) and Sch.6 para.17(1), (2) as from January 1, 2007. Definition of "banking consolidation directive" further amended by the Electronic Money Regulations 2011 (SI 2011/99) reg.79 and Sch.4 para.16 as from April 30, 2011. Definition of "EEA State" substituted by the Financial Services (EEA State) Regulations 2007 (SI 2007/108) reg.9 as from February 13, 2007. This definition was inserted into the 1978 Act by the Legislative and Regulatory Reform Act 2006. Definitions of "the 2006 Act" and "officer" amended, definitions of "the 2006 Act" and "section 899 compromise or arrangement" inserted and various other definitions deleted by the Companies Act 2006 (Consequential Amendments and Transitional Provisions) Order 2011 (SI 2011/1265) art.24(2) as from May 12, 2011.

2(2)   In paragraph (1)–

(a)   for the purposes of the definition of **"directive reorganisation measure"**, a reorganisation measure is adopted at the time when it is treated as adopted or imposed by the law of the relevant EEA State; and

(b)   for the purposes of the definition of **"directive winding-up proceedings"**, winding-up proceedings are opened at the time when they are treated as opened by the law of the relevant EEA State,

and in this paragraph **"relevant EEA State"** means the EEA State under the law of which the reorganisation is adopted or imposed, or the winding-up proceedings are opened, as the case may be.

2(3)   In these Regulations, references to the law of insolvency of the United Kingdom include references to every provision made by or under the 1986 Act or the 1989 Order as the case may be; and in relation to partnerships, limited liability partnerships or building societies, references to the law of insolvency or to any provision of the 1986 Act or the 1989 Order are to that law as modified by the Insolvent Partnerships Order 1994, the Insolvent Partnerships Order (Northern Ireland) 1995, the Limited Liability Partnerships Regulations 2001, the Limited Liability Partnerships Regulations (Northern Ireland) 2004 or the Building Societies Act 1986 (as the case may be).

2(4)   References in these Regulations to "accepting deposits" and a "contract of insurance" must be read with–

(a)   section 22 of the 2000 Act;

(b)   any relevant order made under that section; and

(c)   Schedule 2 to that Act.

2(5)   For the purposes of the 2000 Act, functions imposed or falling on the Authority under these Regulations shall be deemed to be functions under the 2000 Act.

History
Regulation 2(3) amended by the Credit Institutions (Reorganisation and Winding Up) (Amendment) Regulations 2007 (SI 2007/830) reg.2(1), (3) as from April 6, 2007.

Part 2

Insolvency Measures and Proceedings: Jurisdiction in Relation to Credit Institutions

3   Prohibition against winding up etc. EEA credit institutions in the United Kingdom

3(1)   On or after the relevant date a court in the United Kingdom may not, in relation to an EEA credit institution or any branch of an EEA credit institution–

(a)   make a winding-up order pursuant to section 221 of the 1986 Act or Article 185 of the 1989 Order;

(b)   appoint a provisional liquidator;

(c)   make an administration order.

3(2)   Paragraph (1)(a) does not prevent–

(a)   the court from making a winding-up order on or after the relevant date in relation to an EEA credit institution if–

(i)   a provisional liquidator was appointed in relation to that credit institution before the relevant date, and

(ii)   that appointment continues in force until immediately before that winding-up order is made;

1060

(b) the winding up of an EEA credit institution on or after the relevant date pursuant to a winding-up order which was made, and has not been discharged, before that date.

3(3) Paragraph (1)(b) does not prevent a provisional liquidator of an EEA credit institution appointed before the relevant date from acting in relation to that credit institution on or after that date.

3(4) Paragraph (1)(c) does not prevent an administrator appointed before the relevant date from acting on or after that date in a case in which the administration order under which he or his predecessor was appointed remains in force after that date.

3(5) On or after the relevant date, an administrator may not, in relation to an EEA credit institution, be appointed under paragraphs 14 or 22 of Schedule B1 to the 1986 Act or paragraphs 15 or 23 of Schedule B1 to the 1989 Order.

3(6) A proposed voluntary arrangement shall not have effect in relation to an EEA credit institution if a decision under section 4 of the 1986 Act or Article 17 of the 1989 Order with respect to the approval of that arrangement was taken on or after the relevant date.

3(7) An order under section 254 of the Enterprise Act 2002 (application of insolvency law to a foreign company) or under Article 9 of the Insolvency (Northern Ireland) Order 2005 (application of insolvency law to company incorporated outside Northern Ireland) may not provide for any of the following provisions of the 1986 Act or of the 1989 Order to apply in relation to an incorporated EEA credit institution–

(a) Part 1 of the 1986 Act or Part 2 of the 1989 Order (company voluntary arrangements);

(b) Part 2 of the 1986 Act or Part 3 of the 1989 Order (administration);

(c) Chapter 4 of Part 4 of the 1986 Act or chapter 4 of Part 5 of the 1989 Order (creditors' voluntary winding up);

(d) Chapter 6 of Part 4 of the 1986 Act (winding up by the Court).

3(8) In this regulation and regulation 4, **"relevant date"** means the 5th May 2004.

History
Regulation 3(7) substituted by the Credit Institutions (Reorganisation and Winding Up) (Amendment) Regulations 2007 (SI 2007/830) reg.2(1), (5) as from April 6, 2007.

4 Schemes of arrangement

4(1) For the purposes of section 895(2)(b) of the 2006 Act, an EEA credit institution or a branch of an EEA credit institution is to be treated as a company liable to be wound up under the 1986 Act or the 1989 Order if it would be liable to be wound up under that Act or Order but for the prohibition in regulation 3(1)(a).

4(2) But a court may not make a relevant order under section 899 of the 2006 Act in relation to an EEA credit institution which is subject to a directive reorganisation measure or directive winding-up proceedings, or a branch of an EEA credit institution which is subject to such a measure or proceedings, unless the conditions set out in paragraph (3) are satisfied.

4(3) Those conditions are–

(a) the person proposing the section 899 compromise or arrangement (**"the proposal"**) has given–

(i) the administrator or liquidator, and

(ii) the relevant administrative or judicial authority,

reasonable notice of the details of that proposal; and

(b) no person notified in accordance with sub-paragraph (a) has objected to the proposal.

4(4)   Nothing in this regulation invalidates a compromise or arrangement which was sanctioned by the court by an order made before the relevant date.

4(5)   For the purposes of paragraph (2), a relevant order means an order sanctioning a section 899 compromise or arrangement which–

(a)   is intended to enable the credit institution, and the whole or any part of its undertaking, to survive as a going concern and which affects the rights of persons other than the credit institution or its contributories; or

(b)   includes among its purposes a realisation of some or all of the assets of the EEA credit institution to which the order relates and the distribution of the proceeds to creditors, with a view to terminating the whole or any part of the business of that credit institution.

4(6)   For the purposes of this regulation–

(a)   **"administrator"** means an administrator, as defined by Article 2 of the reorganisation and winding up directive, who is appointed in relation to the EEA credit institution in relation to which the proposal is made;

(b)   **"liquidator"** means a liquidator, as defined by Article 2 of the reorganisation and winding up directive, who is appointed in relation to the EEA credit institution in relation to which the proposal is made;

(c)   **"administrative or judicial authority"** means the administrative or judicial authority, as defined by Article 2 of the reorganisation and winding up directive, which is competent for the purposes of the directive reorganisation measure or directive winding-up proceedings mentioned in paragraph (2).

History
Regulation 4(1)–(3) and 4(5) amended by the Companies Act 2006 (Consequential Amendments and Transitional Provisions) Order 2011 (SI 2011/1265) art.24(3) as from May 12, 2011.

5   Reorganisation measures and winding-up proceedings in respect of EEA credit institutions effective in the United Kingdom

5(1)   An EEA insolvency measure has effect in the United Kingdom in relation to–

(a)   any branch of an EEA credit institution,

(b)   any property or other assets of that credit institution,

(c)   any debt or liability of that credit institution,

as if it were part of the general law of insolvency of the United Kingdom.

5(2)   Subject to paragraph (4)–

(a)   a competent officer who satisfies the condition mentioned in paragraph (3); or

(b)   a qualifying agent appointed by a competent officer who satisfies the condition mentioned in paragraph (3),

may exercise in the United Kingdom, in relation to the EEA credit institution which is subject to an EEA insolvency measure, any function which, pursuant to that measure, he is entitled to exercise in relation to that credit institution in the relevant EEA State.

5(3)   The condition mentioned in paragraph (2) is that the appointment of the competent officer is evidenced–

(a)   by a certified copy of the order or decision by a judicial or administrative authority in the relevant EEA State by or under which the competent officer was appointed; or

(b) by any other certificate issued by the judicial or administrative authority which has jurisdiction in relation to the EEA insolvency measure,

and accompanied by a certified translation of that order, decision or certificate (as the case may be).

5(4) In exercising the functions of the kind mentioned in paragraph (2), the competent officer or qualifying agent–

(a) may not take any action which would constitute an unlawful use of force in the part of the United Kingdom in which he is exercising those functions;

(b) may not rule on any dispute arising from a matter falling within Part 4 of these Regulations which is justiciable by a court in the part of the United Kingdom in which he is exercising those functions; and

(c) notwithstanding the way in which functions may be exercised in the relevant EEA State, must act in accordance with relevant laws or rules as to procedure which have effect in the part of the United Kingdom in which he is exercising those functions.

5(5) For the purposes of paragraph (4)(c), **"relevant laws or rules as to procedure"** means–

(a) requirements as to consultation with or notification of employees of an EEA credit institution;

(b) law and procedures relevant to the realisation of assets;

(c) where the competent officer is bringing or defending legal proceedings in the name of, or on behalf of an EEA credit institution, the relevant rules of court.

5(6) In this regulation–

"competent officer" means a person appointed under or in connection with an EEA insolvency measure for the purpose of administering that measure;

"qualifying agent" means an agent validly appointed (whether in the United Kingdom or elsewhere) by a competent officer in accordance with the relevant law in the relevant EEA State;

"EEA insolvency measure" means, as the case may be, a directive reorganisation measure or directive winding-up proceedings which have effect in relation to an EEA credit institution by virtue of the law of the relevant EEA State;

"relevant EEA State", in relation to an EEA credit institution, means the EEA State in which that credit institution has been authorised in accordance with Article 6 of the banking consolidation directive.

History
Definition of "relevant EEA State" amended by the Capital Requirements Regulations 2006 (SI 2006/3221) reg.29(4) and Sch.6 para.17(1), (3) as from January 1, 2007.

6 Confirmation by the court of a creditors' voluntary winding up

6(1) Rule 7.62 of the Insolvency Rules or Rule 7.56 of the Insolvency Rules (Northern Ireland) applies in relation to a UK credit institution with the modification specified in paragraph (2) or (3).

6(2) For the purposes of this regulation, rule 7.62 has effect as if there were substituted for paragraph (1)–

"**(1)** Where a UK credit institution (within the meaning of the Credit Institutions (Reorganisation and Winding up) Regulations 2004) has passed a resolution for voluntary winding up, and no declaration under section 89 has been made, the liquidator may apply to court for an order confirming the creditors' voluntary winding up for the purposes of Articles 10 and 28 of directive 2001/24/EC of the European Parliament and of the Council of 4 April 2001 on the reorganisation and winding up of credit institutions.".

6(3)   For the purposes of this regulation, Rule 7.56 of the Insolvency Rules (Northern Ireland) has effect as if there were substituted for paragraph (1)–

> "**(1)** Where a UK credit institution (within the meaning of the Credit Institutions (Reorganisation and Winding up) Regulations 2004) has passed a resolution for voluntary winding up, and no declaration under Article 75 has been made, the liquidator may apply to court for an order confirming the creditors' voluntary winding up for the purposes of Articles 10 and 28 of directive 2001/24/EC of the European Parliament and of the Council of 4 April 2001 on the reorganisation and winding up of credit institutions.".

PART 3

MODIFICATIONS OF THE LAW OF INSOLVENCY: NOTIFICATION AND PUBLICATION

7   Modifications of the law of insolvency

7   The general law of insolvency has effect in relation to UK credit institutions subject to the provisions of this Part.

8   Consultation of the Authority prior to a voluntary winding up

8(1)   Where, on or after 5th May 2004, a UK credit institution (**"the institution"**) intends to pass a resolution to wind up the institution under paragraph (b) or (c) of section 84(1) of the 1986 Act or sub-paragraph (b) or (c) of Article 70(1) of the 1989 Order, the institution must give written notice of the resolution to the Authority before it passes the resolution.

8(2)   Where notice is given under paragraph (1), the resolution may be passed only after the end of the period of five business days beginning with the day on which the notice was given.

9   Notification of relevant decision to the Authority

9(1)   Where on or after 5th May 2004 the court makes a decision, order or appointment of any of the following kinds–

(a)   an administration order under paragraph 13 of Schedule B1 to the 1986 Act, paragraph 14 of Schedule B1 to the 1989 Order, section 8(1) of the 1986 Act or Article 21(1) of the 1989 Order;

(b)   a winding-up order under section 125 of the 1986 Act or Article 105 of the 1989 Order;

(c)   the appointment of a provisional liquidator under section 135(1) of the 1986 Act or Article 115(1) of the 1989 Order;

(d)   the appointment of an administrator in an interim order under paragraph 13(1)(d) of Schedule B1 to the 1986 Act, paragraph 14(1)(d) of Schedule B1 to the 1989 Order, section 9(4) of the 1986 Act or Article 22(4) of the 1989 Order,

it must immediately inform the Authority, or cause the Authority to be informed, of the order or appointment which has been made.

9(2)   Where a decision with respect to the approval of a voluntary arrangement has effect, and the arrangement which is the subject of that decision is a qualifying arrangement, the supervisor must forthwith inform the Authority of the arrangement which has been approved.

9(3)   Where a liquidator is appointed as mentioned in section 100 of the 1986 Act, paragraph 83 of Schedule B1 to the 1986 Act, paragraph 84 of Schedule B1 to the 1989 Order or Article 86 of the 1989 Order (appointment of liquidator in a creditors' voluntary winding up), the liquidator must inform the Authority forthwith of his appointment.

9(4)   Where in the case of a members' voluntary winding up, section 95 of the 1986 Act (effect of company's insolvency) or Article 81 of the 1989 Order applies, the liquidator must inform the Authority forthwith that he is of that opinion.

9(5) Paragraphs (1), (2) and (3) do not apply in any case where the Authority was represented at all hearings in connection with the application in relation to which the order or appointment is made.

9(6) For the purposes of paragraph (2), a **"qualifying arrangement"** means a voluntary arrangement which–

(a) varies the rights of creditors as against the credit institution and is intended to enable the credit institution, and the whole or any part of its undertaking, to survive as a going concern; or

(b) includes a realisation of some or all of the assets of the credit institution, with a view to terminating the whole or any part of the business of that credit institution.

9(7) A supervisor, administrator or liquidator who fails without reasonable excuse to comply with paragraph (2), (3), or (4) (as the case may be) commits an offence and is liable on summary conviction to a fine not exceeding level 3 on the standard scale.

10 Notification to EEA regulators

10(1) Where the Authority is informed of a decision, order or appointment in accordance with regulation 9, the Authority must as soon as is practicable inform the relevant person–

(a) that the decision, order or appointment has been made; and

(b) in general terms, of the possible effect of a decision, order or appointment of that kind on the business of a credit institution.

10(2) Where the Authority has been represented at all hearings in connection with the application in relation to which the decision, order or appointment has been made, the Authority must inform the relevant person of the matters mentioned in paragraph (1) as soon as is practicable after that decision, order or appointment has been made.

10(3) Where, on or after 5th May 2004, it appears to the Authority that a directive reorganisation measure should be adopted in relation to or imposed on an EEA credit institution which has a branch in the United Kingdom, it will inform the home state regulator as soon as is practicable.

10(4) In this regulation, the **"relevant person"** means the EEA regulator of any EEA State in which the UK credit institution has a branch.

11 Withdrawal of authorisation

11(1) For the purposes of this regulation–

(a) a qualifying decision means a decision with respect to the approval of a voluntary arrangement where the voluntary arrangement includes a realisation of some or all of the assets of the credit institution with a view to terminating the whole or any part of the business of that credit institution;

(b) a qualifying order means–

    (i) a winding-up order under section 125 of the 1986 Act or Article 105 of the 1989 Order; or

    (ii) an administration order under paragraph 13 of Schedule B1 to the 1986 Act or paragraph 14 of Schedule B1 to the 1989 Order in the prescribed circumstances;

(c) a qualifying appointment means–

    (i) the appointment of a provisional liquidator under section 135(1) of the 1986 Act or Article 115(1) of the 1989 Order; or

    (ii) the appointment of a liquidator as mentioned in section 100 of the 1986 Act, Article 86 of the 1989 Order (appointment of liquidator in a creditors' voluntary winding up) or paragraph 83 of Schedule B1 to the 1986 Act or paragraph 84 of Schedule B1 to the 1989 Order (moving from administration to creditors' voluntary liquidation).

11(2)   The prescribed circumstances are where, after the appointment of an administrator, the administrator concludes that it is not reasonably practicable to achieve the objective specified in paragraph 3(1)(a) of Schedule B1 to the 1986 Act or paragraph 4(1)(a) of Schedule B1 to the 1989 Order.

11(3)   When the Authority is informed of a qualifying decision, qualifying order or qualifying appointment, the Authority will as soon as reasonably practicable exercise its power under section 45 of the 2000 Act to vary or to cancel the UK credit institution's permission under Part 4 of that Act to accept deposits or to issue electronic money as the case may be.

12   Publication of voluntary arrangement, administration order, winding-up order or scheme of arrangement

12(1)   This regulation applies where a qualifying decision is approved, or a qualifying order or qualifying appointment is made, in relation to a UK credit institution on or after 5th May 2004.

12(2)   For the purposes of this regulation–

(a)   a qualifying decision means a decision with respect to the approval of a proposed voluntary arrangement, in accordance with section 4A of the 1986 Act or Article 17A of the 1989 Order;

(b)   a qualifying order means–

   (i)   an administration order under paragraph 13 of Schedule B1 to the 1986 Act, paragraph 14 of Schedule B1 to the 1989 Order, section 8(1) of the 1986 Act or Article 21(1) of the 1989 Order,

   (ii)   an order appointing a provisional liquidator in accordance with section 135 of that Act or Article 115 of that Order, or

   (iii)   a winding-up order made by the court under Part 4 of that Act or Part V of the 1989 Order;

(c)   a qualifying appointment means the appointment of a liquidator as mentioned in section 100 of the 1986 Act or Article 86 of the 1989 Order (appointment of liquidator in a creditors' voluntary winding up).

12(3)   Subject to paragraph (7), as soon as is reasonably practicable after a qualifying decision has effect or a qualifying order or a qualifying appointment has been made, the relevant officer must publish, or cause to be published, in the Official Journal of the European Communities and in 2 national newspapers in each EEA State in which the UK credit institution has a branch the information mentioned in paragraph (4) and (if applicable) paragraphs (5) or (6).

12(4)   That information is–

(a)   a summary of the terms of the qualifying decision, qualifying appointment or the provisions of the qualifying order (as the case may be);

(b)   the identity of the relevant officer;

(c)   the statutory provisions in accordance with which the qualifying decision has effect or the qualifying order or appointment has been made or takes effect.

12(5)   In the case of a qualifying appointment, that information includes the court to which an application under section 112 of the 1986 Act (reference of questions to the court) or Article 98 of the 1989 Order (reference of questions to the High Court) may be made.

12(6)   In the case of a qualifying decision, that information includes the court to which an application under section 6 of the 1986 Act or Article 19 of the 1989 Order (challenge of decisions) may be made.

12(7)   Paragraph (3) does not apply where a qualifying decision or qualifying order falling within paragraph (2)(b)(i) affects the interests only of the members, or any class of members, or employees of the credit institution (in their capacity as members or employees).

12(8)   This regulation is without prejudice to any requirement to publish information imposed upon a relevant officer under any provision of the general law of insolvency.

12(9)   A relevant officer who fails to comply with paragraph (3) of this regulation commits an offence and is liable on summary conviction to a fine not exceeding level 3 on the standard scale.

12(10)   A qualifying decision, qualifying order or qualifying appointment is not invalid or ineffective if the relevant official fails to comply with paragraph (3) of this regulation.

12(11)   In this regulation, **"relevant officer"** means–

(a)   in the case of a voluntary arrangement, the supervisor;

(b)   in the case of an administration order, the administrator;

(c)   in the case of a creditors' voluntary winding up, the liquidator;

(d)   in the case of winding-up order, the liquidator; or

(e)   in the case of an order appointing a provisional liquidator, the provisional liquidator.

12(12)   The information to be published in accordance with paragraph (3) of this regulation shall be–

(a)   in the case of the Official Journal of the European Communities, in the official language or languages of each EEA State in which the UK credit institution has a branch;

(b)   in the case of the national newspapers of each EEA State in which the UK credit institution has a branch, in the official language or languages of that EEA State.

History
Regulation 12(5) amended by the Credit Institutions (Reorganisation and Winding Up) (Amendment) Regulations 2007 (SI 2007/830) reg.2(1), (11) as from April 6, 2007.

13   Honouring of certain obligations

13(1)   This regulation applies where, on or after 5th May 2004, a relevant obligation has been honoured for the benefit of a relevant credit institution by a relevant person.

13(2)   Where a person has honoured a relevant obligation for the benefit of a relevant credit institution, he shall be deemed to have discharged that obligation if he was unaware of the winding up of that credit institution.

13(3)   For the purposes of this regulation–

(a)   a relevant obligation is an obligation which, after the commencement of the winding up of a relevant credit institution, should have been honoured for the benefit of the liquidator of that credit institution;

(b)   a relevant credit institution is a UK credit institution which–

(i)   is not a body corporate; and

(ii)   is the subject of a winding up;

(c)   a relevant person is a person who at the time the obligation is honoured–

(i)   is in the territory of an EEA State; and

(ii)   is unaware of the winding up of the relevant credit institution.

13(4)   For the purposes of paragraph (3)(c)(ii) of this regulation–

    (a)   a relevant person shall be presumed, in the absence of evidence to the contrary, to have been unaware of the winding up of a relevant credit institution where the relevant obligation was honoured before date of the publication provided for in regulation 12 in relation to that winding up;

    (b)   a relevant person shall be presumed, in the absence of evidence to the contrary, to have been aware of the winding up of the relevant credit institution where the relevant obligation was honoured on or after the date of the publication provided for in regulation 12 in relation to that winding up.

14   Notification to creditors: winding-up proceedings

14(1)   When a relevant order or appointment is made, or a relevant decision is taken, in relation to a UK credit institution on or after 5th May 2004, the appointed officer must, as soon as is reasonably practicable, notify in writing all known creditors of that credit institution–

    (a)   of the matters mentioned in paragraph (4); and

    (b)   of the matters mentioned in paragraph (5).

14(2)   The appointed officer may comply with the requirement in paragraphs (1)(a) and the requirement in paragraph (1)(b) by separate notifications.

14(3)   For the purposes of this regulation–

    (a)   **"relevant order"** means–

        (i)   an administration order under paragraph 13 of Schedule B1 to the 1986 Act or paragraph 14 of Schedule B1 to the 1989 Order in the prescribed circumstances or an administration order made for the purposes set out in section 8(3)(b) or (d) of the 1986 Act or Article 21(3)(b) or (d) of the 1989 Order, as the case may be,

        (ii)   a winding-up order under section 125 of the 1986 Act (powers of the court on hearing a petition) or Article 105 of the 1989 Order (powers of High Court on hearing of petition),

        (iii)   the appointment of a liquidator in accordance with section 138 of the 1986 Act (appointment of a liquidator in Scotland), or

        (iv)   an order appointing a provisional liquidator in accordance with section 135 of that Act or Article 115 of the 1989 Order;

    (b)   a **"relevant appointment"** means the appointment of a liquidator as mentioned in section 100 of the 1986 Act or Article 86 of the 1989 Order (appointment of liquidator in a creditors' voluntary winding up); and

    (c)   a **"relevant decision"** means a decision as a result of which a qualifying voluntary arrangement has effect.

14(4)   The matters which must be notified to all known creditors in accordance with paragraph (1)(a) are as follows–

    (a)   that a relevant order or appointment has been made, or a relevant decision taken, in relation to the UK credit institution; and

    (b)   the date from which that order, appointment or decision has effect.

14(5)   The matters which must be notified to all known creditors in accordance with paragraph (1)(b) are as follows–

    (a)   if applicable, the date by which a creditor must submit his claim in writing;

(b)   the matters which must be stated in a creditor's claim;

(c)   details of any category of debt in relation to which a claim is not required;

(d)   the person to whom any such claim or any observations on a claim must be submitted; and

(e)   the consequences of any failure to submit a claim by any specified deadline.

14(6)   Where a creditor is notified in accordance with paragraph (1)(b), the notification must be headed with the words "Invitation to lodge a claim. Time limits to be observed", and that heading must be given in every official language.

14(7)   The obligation under paragraph (1)(b) may be discharged by sending a form of proof in accordance with rule 4.74 of the Insolvency Rules, Rule 4.080 of the Insolvency Rules (Northern Ireland) or Rule 4.15(2) of the (Insolvency) Scotland Rules as applicable in cases where any of those rules applies, provided that the form of proof complies with paragraph (6).

14(8)   The prescribed circumstances are where the administrator includes in the statement required under Rule 2.3 of the Insolvency Rules or under Rule 2.003 of the Insolvency Rules (Northern Ireland) a statement to the effect that the objective set out in paragraph 3(1)(a) of Schedule B1 to the 1986 Act or in paragraph 4(1)(a) of Schedule B1 to the 1989 Order is not reasonably likely to be achieved.

14(9)   Where, after the appointment of an administrator, the administrator concludes that it is not reasonably practicable to achieve the objective specified in paragraph 3(1)(a) of Schedule B1 to the 1986 Act or paragraph 4(1)(a) of Schedule B1 to the 1989 Order, he shall inform the court and the Authority in writing of that conclusion and upon so doing the order by which he was appointed shall be a relevant order for the purposes of this regulation and the obligation under paragraph (1) shall apply as from the date on which he so informs the court and the Authority.

14(10)   An appointed officer commits an offence if he fails without reasonable excuse to comply with a requirement under paragraph (1) of this regulation, and is liable on summary conviction to a fine not exceeding level 3 on the standard scale.

14(11)   For the purposes of this regulation–

(a)   **"appointed officer"** means–

   (i)   in the case of a relevant order falling within paragraph (3)(a)(i), the administrator,

   (ii)   in the case of a relevant order falling within paragraph (3)(a)(ii) or (iii) or a relevant appointment falling within paragraph (3)(b), the liquidator,

   (iii)   in the case of a relevant order falling within paragraph (3)(a)(iv), the provisional liquidator, or

   (iv)   in the case of a relevant decision, the supervisor; and

(b)   a creditor is a "known" creditor if the appointed officer is aware of–

   (i)   his identity,

   (ii)   his claim or potential claim, and

   (iii)   a recent address where he is likely to receive a communication.

14(12)   For the purposes of paragraph (3), a voluntary arrangement is a qualifying voluntary arrangement if its purposes include a realisation of some or all of the assets of the UK credit institution to which the order relates with a view to terminating the whole or any part of the business of that credit institution.

History
Regulation 14(8) substituted by the Credit Institutions (Reorganisation and Winding Up) (Amendment) Regulations 2007 (SI 2007/830) reg.2(1), (12) as from April 6, 2007.

15   Submission of claims by EEA creditors

15(1)   An EEA creditor who, on or after 5th May 2004, submits a claim or observations relating to his claim in any relevant proceedings (irrespective of when those proceedings were commenced or had effect) may do so in his domestic language, provided that the requirements in paragraphs (3) and (4) are complied with.

15(2)   For the purposes of this regulation, **"relevant proceedings"** means–

    (a)   a winding up;

    (b)   a qualifying voluntary arrangement; or

    (c)   administration.

15(3)   Where an EEA creditor submits a claim in his domestic language, the document must be headed with the words "Lodgement of claim" (in English).

15(4)   Where an EEA creditor submits observations on his claim (otherwise than in the document by which he submits his claim), the observations must be headed with the words "Submission of observations relating to claims" (in English).

15(5)   Paragraph (3) does not apply where an EEA creditor submits his claim using–

    (a)   in the case of a winding up, a form of proof supplied by the liquidator in accordance with rule 4.74 of the Insolvency Rules, Rule 4.080 of the Insolvency Rules (Northern Ireland) or rule 4.15(2) of the Insolvency (Scotland) Rules;

    (b)   in the case of a qualifying voluntary arrangement, a form approved by the court for that purpose.

15(6)   In this regulation–

    (a)   **"domestic language"**, in relation to an EEA creditor, means the official language, or one of the official languages, of the EEA State in which he is ordinarily resident or, if the creditor is not an individual, in which the creditor's head office is located; and

    (b)   **"qualifying voluntary arrangement"** means a voluntary arrangement whose purposes include a realisation of some or all of the assets of the UK credit institution to which the order relates with a view to terminating the whole or any part of the business of that credit institution.

16   Reports to creditors

16(1)   This regulation applies where, on or after 5th May 2004–

    (a)   a liquidator is appointed in accordance with section 100 of the 1986 Act, Article 86 of the 1989 Order (creditors' voluntary winding up: appointment of liquidator) or paragraph 83 of Schedule B1 to the 1986 Act or paragraph 84 of Schedule B1 to the 1989 Order (moving from administration to creditors' voluntary liquidation);

    (b)   a winding-up order is made by the court;

    (c)   a provisional liquidator is appointed; or

    (d)   an administrator is appointed under paragraph 13 of Schedule B1 to the 1986 Act or paragraph 14 of Schedule B1 to the 1989 Order.

16(2)   The liquidator, provisional liquidator or administrator (as the case may be) must send a report to every known creditor once in every 12 months beginning with the date when his appointment has effect.

16(3)   The requirement in paragraph (2) does not apply where a liquidator, provisional liquidator or administrator is required by order of the court to send a report to creditors at intervals which are more frequent than those required by this regulation.

16(4)   This regulation is without prejudice to any requirement to send a report to creditors, imposed by the court on the liquidator, provisional liquidator or administrator, which is supplementary to the requirements of this regulation.

16(5)   A liquidator, provisional liquidator or administrator commits an offence if he fails without reasonable excuse to comply with an applicable requirement under this regulation, and is liable on summary conviction to a fine not exceeding level 3 on the standard scale.

16(6)   For the purposes of this regulation–

(a)   **"known creditor"** means–

(i)   a creditor who is known to the liquidator, provisional liquidator or administrator, and

(ii)   in a case falling within paragraph (1)(b) or (c), a creditor who is specified in the credit institution's statement of affairs (within the meaning of section 131 of the 1986 Act or Article 111 of the 1989 Order);

(b)   **"report"** means a written report setting out the position generally as regards the progress of the winding up, provisional liquidation or administration (as the case may be).

History
Regulation 16(1)(d) substituted by the Credit Institutions (Reorganisation and Winding Up) (Amendment) Regulations 2007 (SI 2007/830) reg.2(1), (13) as from April 6, 2007.

17   Service of notices and documents

17(1)   This regulation applies to any notification, report or other document which is required to be sent to a creditor of a UK credit institution by a provision of this Part ("a relevant notification").

17(2)   A relevant notification may be sent to a creditor by one of the following methods–

(a)   by posting it to the proper address of the creditor;

(b)   by transmitting it electronically, in accordance with paragraph (4).

17(3)   For the purposes of paragraph (2)(a), the proper address of a creditor is any current address provided by that person as an address for service of a relevant notification and, if no such address is provided–

(a)   the last known address of that creditor (whether his residence or a place where he carries on business);

(b)   in the case of a body corporate, the address of its registered or principal office; or

(c)   in the case of an unincorporated association, the address of its principal office.

17(4)   A relevant notification may be transmitted electronically only if it is sent to–

(a)   an electronic address notified to the relevant officer by the creditor for this purpose; or

(b)   if no such address has been notified, to an electronic address at which the relevant officer reasonably believes the creditor will receive the notification.

17(5)   Any requirement in this Part to send a relevant notification to a creditor shall also be treated as satisfied if the conditions set out in paragraph (6) are satisfied.

17(6)   The conditions of this paragraph are satisfied in the case of a relevant notification if–

(a)   the creditor has agreed with–

(i)   the UK credit institution which is liable under the creditor's claim, or

(ii)   the relevant officer,

that information which is required to be sent to him (whether pursuant to a statutory or contractual obligation, or otherwise) may instead be accessed by him on a web site;

(b)   the agreement applies to the relevant notification in question;

(c)   the creditor is notified of–

(i)   the publication of the relevant notification on a web site,

(ii)   the address of that web site,

(iii)   the place on that web site where the relevant notification may be accessed, and how it may be accessed; and

(d)   the relevant notification is published on that web site throughout a period of at least one month beginning with the date on which the creditor is notified in accordance with sub-paragraph (c).

17(7)   Where, in a case in which paragraph (5) is relied on for compliance with a requirement of regulation 14 or 16–

(a)   a relevant notification is published for a part, but not all, of the period mentioned in paragraph (6)(d) but

(b)   the failure to publish it throughout that period is wholly attributable to circumstances which it would not be reasonable to have expected the relevant officer to prevent or avoid,

no offence is committed under regulation 14(10) or regulation 16(5) (as the case may be) by reason of that failure.

17(8)   In this regulation–

(a)   **"electronic address"** includes any number or address used for the purposes of receiving electronic communications which are sent electronically;

(b)   **"electronic communication"** means an electronic communication within the meaning of the Electronic Communications Act 2000 the processing of which on receipt is intended to produce writing; and

(c)   **"relevant officer"** means (as the case may be) an administrator, liquidator, provisional liquidator or supervisor who is required to send a relevant notification to a creditor by a provision of this Part.

18   Disclosure of confidential information received from an EEA regulator

18(1)   This regulation applies to information ("insolvency information") which–

(a)   relates to the business or affairs of any other person; and

(b)   is supplied to the Authority by an EEA regulator acting in accordance with Articles 4, 5, 9, or 11 of the reorganisation and winding up directive.

18(2)   Subject to paragraphs (3) and (4), sections 348, 349 and 352 of the 2000 Act apply in relation to insolvency information as they apply in relation to confidential information within the meaning of section 348(2) of the 2000 Act.

18(3)   Insolvency information is not subject to the restrictions on disclosure imposed by section 348(1) of the 2000 Act (as it applies by virtue of paragraph (2)) if it satisfies any of the criteria set out in section 348(4) of the 2000 Act.

18(4)   The Disclosure Regulations apply in relation to insolvency information as they apply in relation to single market directive information (within the meaning of those Regulations).

PART 4

REORGANISATION OR WINDING UP OF UK CREDIT INSTITUTIONS: RECOGNITION OF EEA RIGHTS

19   Application of this Part

19(1)   This Part applies as follows–

(a)   where a decision with respect to the approval of a proposed voluntary arrangement having a qualifying purpose is made under section 4A of the 1986 Act or Article 17A of the 1989 Order on or after 5th May 2004 in relation to a UK credit institution;

(b)   where an administration order made under paragraph 13 of Schedule B1 to the 1986 Act, paragraph 14 of Schedule B1 to the 1989 Order, section 8(1) of the 1986 Act or Article 21(1) of the 1989 Order on or after 5th May 2004 is in force in relation to a UK credit institution;

(c)   where a UK credit institution is subject to a relevant winding up; or

(d)   where a provisional liquidator is appointed in relation to a UK credit institution on or after 5th May 2004.

19(2)   For the purposes of paragraph (1)(a), a voluntary arrangement has a qualifying purpose if it–

(a)   varies the rights of the creditors as against the credit institution and is intended to enable the credit institution, and the whole or any part of its undertaking, to survive as a going concern; or

(b)   includes a realisation of some or all of the assets of the credit institution to which the compromise or arrangement relates, with a view to terminating the whole or any part of the business of that credit institution.

19(3)   For the purposes of paragraph (1)(c), a winding up is a relevant winding up if–

(a)   in the case of a winding up by the court, the winding-up order is made on or after 5th May 2004; or

(b)   in the case of a creditors' voluntary winding up, the liquidator is appointed in accordance with section 100 of the 1986 Act, Article 86 of the 1989 Order or paragraph 83 of Schedule B1 to the 1986 Act or paragraph 84 of Schedule B1 to the 1989 Order on or after 5th May 2004.

20   Application of this Part: certain assets excluded from insolvent estate of UK credit institution

20(1)   For the purposes of this Part, the insolvent estate of a UK credit institution shall not include any assets which at the commencement date are subject to a relevant compromise or arrangement.

20(2)   In this regulation–

(a)   **"assets"** has the same meaning as **"property"** in section 436 of the 1986 Act or Article 2(2) of the 1989 Order;

(b)   **"commencement date"** means the date when a UK credit institution goes into liquidation within the meaning given by section 247(2) of the 1986 Act or Article 6(2) of the 1989 Order;

(c)   **"insolvent estate"** has the meaning given by rule 13.8 of the Insolvency Rules or Rule 0.2 of the Insolvency Rules (Northern Ireland) and in Scotland means the company's assets;

(d)   **"relevant compromise or arrangement"** means–

(i)   a compromise or arrangement sanctioned by the court before 5th May 2004 under–

(aa) section 425 of the Companies Act 1985 (excluding a compromise or arrangement falling within section 427 or 427A of that Act), or

(bb) Article 418 of the Companies (Northern Ireland) Order 1986 (excluding a compromise or arrangement falling within Article 420 or 420A of that Order); or

    (ii)   any subsequent compromise or arrangement sanctioned by the court to amend or replace a compromise or arrangement of a kind mentioned in paragraph (i) which is–

        (aa) itself of a kind mentioned in sub-paragraph (aa) or (bb) of paragraph (i) (whether sanctioned before, on or after 5th May 2004), or

        (bb) a section 899 compromise or arrangement.

History
Heading of reg.20 and reg.20(1) amended and reg.20(2)(d) substituted by the Companies Act 2006 (Consequential Amendments and Transitional Provisions) Order 2011 (SI 2011/1265) art.24(4), (5) as from May 12, 2011.

21   Interpretation of this Part

21(1)   For the purposes of this Part–

   (a)   **"affected credit institution"** means a UK credit institution which is the subject of a relevant reorganisation or winding up;

   (b)   **"relevant reorganisation"** or **"relevant winding up"** means any voluntary arrangement, administration, winding up, or order referred to in regulation 19(1) to which this Part applies; and

   (c)   **"relevant time"** means the date of the opening of a relevant reorganisation or a relevant winding up.

21(2)   In this Part, references to the opening of a relevant reorganisation or a relevant winding up mean–

   (a)   in the case of winding-up proceedings–

      (i)   in the case of a winding up by the court, the date on which the winding-up order is made, or

      (ii)   in the case of a creditors' voluntary winding up, the date on which the liquidator is appointed in accordance with section 100 of the 1986 Act, Article 86 of the 1989 Order or paragraph 83 of Schedule B1 to the 1986 Act or paragraph 84 of Schedule B1 to the 1989 Order;

   (b)   in the case of a voluntary arrangement, the date when a decision with respect to the approval of that voluntary arrangement has effect in accordance with section 4A(2) of the 1986 Act or Article 17A(2) of the 1989 Order;

   (c)   in a case where an administration order under paragraph 13 of Schedule B1 to the 1986 Act, paragraph 14 of Schedule B1 to the 1989 Order, section 8(1) of the 1986 Act or Article 21(1) of the 1989 Order is in force, the date of the making of that order; and

   (d)   in a case where a provisional liquidator has been appointed, the date of that appointment,

and references to the time of an opening must be construed accordingly.

22   EEA rights: applicable law in the winding up of a UK credit institution

22(1)   This regulation is subject to the provisions of regulations 23 to 35.

22(2)   In a relevant winding up, the matters mentioned in paragraph (3) are to be determined in accordance with the general law of insolvency of the United Kingdom.

22(3)   Those matters are–

   (a)   the assets which form part of the estate of the affected credit institution;

   (b)   the treatment of assets acquired by the affected credit institution after the opening of the relevant winding up;

   (c)   the respective powers of the affected credit institution and the liquidator or provisional liquidator;

   (d)   the conditions under which set-off may be invoked;

(e)   the effects of the relevant winding up on current contracts to which the affected credit institution is a party;

(f)   the effects of the relevant winding up on proceedings brought by creditors;

(g)   the claims which are to be lodged against the estate of the affected credit institution;

(h)   the treatment of claims against the affected credit institution arising after the opening of the relevant winding up;

(i)   the rules governing–

    (i)   the lodging, verification and admission of claims,

    (ii)   the distribution of proceeds from the realisation of assets,

    (iii)   the ranking of claims,

    (iv)   the rights of creditors who have obtained partial satisfaction after the opening of the relevant winding up by virtue of a right in rem or through set-off;

(j)   the conditions for and the effects of the closure of the relevant winding up, in particular by composition;

(k)   the rights of creditors after the closure of the relevant winding up;

(l)   who is to bear the cost and expenses incurred in the relevant winding up;

(m)   the rules relating to the voidness, voidability or unenforceability of legal acts detrimental to all the creditors.

23   Employment contracts and relationships

23(1)   The effects of a relevant reorganisation or a relevant winding up on EEA employment contracts and EEA employment relationships are to be determined in accordance with the law of the EEA State to which that contract or that relationship is subject.

23(2)   In this regulation, an employment contract is an EEA employment contract, and an employment relationship is an EEA employment relationship if it is subject to the law of an EEA State.

24   Contracts in connection with immovable property

24(1)   The effects of a relevant reorganisation or a relevant winding up on a contract conferring the right to make use of or acquire immovable property situated within the territory of an EEA State shall be determined in accordance with the law of that State.

24(2)   The law of the EEA State in whose territory the property is situated shall determine whether the property is movable or immovable.

25   Registrable rights

25   The effects of a relevant reorganisation or a relevant winding up on rights of the affected UK credit institution with respect to–

(a)   immovable property,

(b)   a ship, or

(c)   an aircraft

which is subject to registration in a public register kept under the authority of an EEA State are to be determined in accordance with the law of that State.

26   Third parties' rights in rem

26(1)   A relevant reorganisation or a relevant winding up shall not affect the rights in rem of creditors or third parties in respect of tangible or intangible, movable or immovable assets (including both specific assets and collections of indefinite assets as a whole which change from time to time) belonging to the affected credit institution which are situated within the territory of an EEA State at the relevant time.

26(2)   The rights in rem referred to in paragraph (1) shall mean–

(a)   the right to dispose of assets or have them disposed of and to obtain satisfaction from the proceeds of or the income from those assets, in particular by virtue of a lien or a mortgage;

(b)   the exclusive right to have a claim met, in particular a right guaranteed by a lien in respect of the claim or by assignment of the claim by way of guarantee;

(c)   the right to demand the assets from, or to require restitution by, any person having possession or use of them contrary to the wishes of the party so entitled;

(d)   a right in rem to the beneficial use of assets.

26(3)   A right, recorded in a public register and enforceable against third parties, under which a right in rem within the meaning of paragraph (1) may be obtained, is also to be treated as a right in rem for the purposes of this regulation.

26(4)   Paragraph (1) does not preclude actions for voidness, voidability or unenforceability of legal acts detrimental to creditors under the general law of insolvency of the United Kingdom.

27   Reservation of title agreements etc.

27(1)   The adoption of a relevant reorganisation or opening of a relevant winding up in relation to a credit institution purchasing an asset shall not affect the seller's rights based on a reservation of title where at the time of that adoption or opening the asset is situated within the territory of an EEA State.

27(2)   The adoption of a relevant reorganisation or opening of a relevant winding up in relation to a credit institution selling an asset, after delivery of the asset, shall not constitute grounds for rescinding or terminating the sale and shall not prevent the purchaser from acquiring title where at the time of that adoption or opening the asset sold is situated within the territory of an EEA State.

27(3)   Paragraphs (1) and (2) do not preclude actions for voidness, voidability or unenforceability of legal acts detrimental to creditors under the general law of insolvency of the United Kingdom.

28   Creditors' rights to set off

28(1)   A relevant reorganisation or a relevant winding up shall not affect the right of creditors to demand the set-off of their claims against the claims of the affected credit institution, where such a set-off is permitted by the law applicable to the affected credit institution's claim.

28(2)   Paragraph (1) does not preclude actions for voidness, voidability or unenforceability of legal acts detrimental to creditors under the general law of insolvency of the United Kingdom.

29   Regulated markets

29(1)   Subject to regulation 33, the effects of a relevant reorganisation or winding up on transactions carried out in the context of a regulated market operating in an EEA State must be determined in accordance with the law applicable to those transactions.

29(2)   For the purposes of this regulation, **"regulated market"** has the meaning given by the Article 4.1.14 of Directive 2004/39/EC of the European Parliament and of the Council of 21 April 2004 on markets in financial instruments.

History
See note after reg.31.

30   Detrimental acts pursuant to the law of an EEA State

30(1)   In a relevant reorganisation or a relevant winding up, the rules relating to detrimental transactions shall not apply where a person who has benefited from a legal act detrimental to all the creditors provides proof that–

    (a)   the said act is subject to the law of an EEA State; and

    (b)   that law does not allow any means of challenging that act in the relevant case.

30(2)   For the purposes of paragraph (1), **"the rules relating to detrimental transactions"** means any provision of the general law of insolvency relating to the voidness, voidability or unenforceability of legal acts detrimental to all the creditors.

31   Protection of third party purchasers

31(1)   This regulation applies where, by an act concluded after the adoption of a relevant reorganisation or opening of a relevant winding up, an affected credit institution disposes for a consideration of–

    (a)   an immovable asset situated within the territory of an EEA State;

    (b)   a ship or an aircraft subject to registration in a public register kept under the authority of an EEA State;

    (c)   relevant instruments or rights in relevant instruments whose existence or transfer presupposes entry into a register or account laid down by the law of an EEA State or which are placed in a central deposit system governed by the law of an EEA State.

31(2)   The validity of that act is to be determined in accordance with the law of the EEA State within whose territory the immoveable asset is situated or under whose authority the register, account or system is kept, as the case may be.

31(3)   In this regulation, **"relevant instruments"** means the instruments referred to in Section C of Annex I to Directive 2004/39/EC of the European Parliament and of the Council of 21 April 2004 on markets in financial instruments.

History
Regulations 29(2) and 31(3) amended by the Financial Services and Markets Act 2000 (Markets in Financial Instruments) Regulations 2007 (SI 2007/126) reg.6 and Sch.6 paras 17, 18 as from April 1, 2007 for the purposes specified in reg.1(2) and from November 1, 2007 for all other purposes.

32   Lawsuits pending

32(1)   The effects of a relevant reorganisation or a relevant winding up on a relevant lawsuit pending in an EEA State shall be determined solely in accordance with the law of that EEA State.

32(2)   In paragraph (1), **"relevant lawsuit"** means a lawsuit concerning an asset or right of which the affected credit institution has been divested.

33   Lex rei sitae

33(1)   The effects of a relevant reorganisation or a relevant winding up on the enforcement of a relevant proprietary right shall be determined by the law of the relevant EEA State.

33(2)   In this regulation–

"relevant proprietary right" means proprietary rights in relevant instruments or other rights in relevant instruments the existence or transfer of which is recorded in a register, an account or a centralised deposit system held or located in an EEA state;

"relevant EEA State" means the Member State where the register, account or centralised deposit system in which the relevant proprietary right is recorded is held or located;

"relevant instrument" has the meaning given by regulation 31(3).

34   Netting agreements

34   The effects of a relevant reorganisation or a relevant winding up on a netting agreement shall be determined in accordance with the law applicable to that agreement.

35   Repurchase agreements

35   Subject to regulation 33, the effects of a relevant reorganisation or a relevant winding up on a repurchase agreement shall be determined in accordance with the law applicable to that agreement.

PART 5

THIRD COUNTRY CREDIT INSTITUTIONS

36   Interpretation of this Part

36(1)   In this Part–

(a)   **"relevant measure"**, in relation to a third country credit institution, means–

   (i)   a winding up;

   (ii)   a provisional liquidation; or

   (iii)   an administration order made under paragraph 13 of Schedule B1 to the 1986 Act, paragraph 14 of Schedule B1 to the 1989 Order, section 8(1) of the 1986 Act or Article 21(1) of the 1989 Order as the case may be.

(b)   **"third country credit institution"** means a person–

   (i)   who has permission under the 2000 Act to accept deposits or to issue electronic money as the case may be; and

   (ii)   whose head office is not in the United Kingdom or an EEA State.

36(2)   In paragraph (1), the definition of "third country credit institution" must be read with–

(a)   section 22 of the 2000 Act;

(b)   any relevant order made under that section; and

(c)   Schedule 2 to that Act.

37   Application of these Regulations to a third country credit institution

37   Regulations 9 and 10 apply where a third country credit institution is subject to a relevant measure, as if references in those regulations to a UK credit institution included a reference to a third country credit institution.

38   Disclosure of confidential information: third country credit institution

38(1)   This regulation applies to information (**"insolvency practitioner information"**) which–

(a)   relates to the business or other affairs of any person; and

(b)   is information of a kind mentioned in paragraph (2).

1078

38(2)   Information falls within paragraph (1)(b) if it is supplied to–

(a)   the Authority by an EEA regulator; or

(b)   an insolvency practitioner by an EEA administrator or liquidator,

in accordance with or pursuant to Articles 8 or 19 of the reorganisation and winding up directive.

38(3)   Subject to paragraphs (4), (5) and (6), sections 348, 349 and 352 of the 2000 Act apply in relation to insolvency practitioner information in the same way as they apply in relation to confidential information within the meaning of section 348(2) of that Act.

38(4)   For the purposes of this regulation, sections 348, 349 and 352 of the 2000 Act and the Disclosure Regulations have effect as if the primary recipients specified in subsection (5) of section 348 of the 2000 Act included an insolvency practitioner.

38(5)   Insolvency practitioner information is not subject to the restrictions on disclosure imposed by section 348(1) of the 2000 Act (as it applies by virtue of paragraph (2)) if it satisfies any of the criteria set out in section 348(4) of the 2000 Act.

38(6)   The Disclosure Regulations apply in relation to insolvency practitioner information as they apply in relation to single market directive information (within the meaning of those Regulations).

38(7)   In this regulation–

"EEA administrator" "and EEA liquidator" mean an administrator or liquidator of a third country credit institution as the case may be within the meaning of the reorganisation and winding up directive;

"insolvency practitioner" means an insolvency practitioner, within the meaning of section 388 of the 1986 Act or Article 3 of the 1989 Order, who is appointed or acts in relation to a third country credit institution.

Insolvency Practitioners Regulations 2005

(SI 2005/524)

Made on March 8, 2005 by the Secretary of State under ss.390, 392, 393 and 419 of the Insolvency Act 1986. Operative from April 1, 2005.

[**Note**: Changes made by the Provision of Services (Insolvency Practitioners) Regulations 2009 (SI 2009/3081) have been incorporated into the text.]

PART 1

INTRODUCTORY

1 Citation and commencement

1 These Regulations may be cited as the Insolvency Practitioners Regulations 2005 and shall come into force on 1st April 2005.

2 Interpretation: General

2(1) In these Regulations–

"**the Act**" means the Insolvency Act 1986;

"**commencement date**" means the date on which these Regulations come into force;

"**initial capacity**" shall be construed in accordance with regulation 3;

"**insolvency practitioner**" means a person who is authorised to act as an insolvency practitioner by virtue of–

(a) membership of a body recognised pursuant to section 391 of the Act; or

(b) an authorisation granted pursuant to section 393 of the Act;

"**insolvent**" means a person in respect of whom an insolvency practitioner is acting;

"**interim trustee**"

"**permanent trustee**"

and

"**trust deed for creditors**" have the same meanings as in the Bankruptcy (Scotland) Act 1985;

"**subsequent capacity**" shall be construed in accordance with regulation 3.

2(2) In these Regulations a reference to the date of release or discharge of an insolvency practitioner includes–

(a) where the insolvency practitioner acts as nominee in relation to proposals for a voluntary arrangement under Part I or VIII of the Act, whichever is the earlier of the date on which–

(i) the proposals are rejected by creditors;

(ii) he is replaced as nominee by another insolvency practitioner; or

(iii) the arrangement takes effect without his becoming supervisor in relation to it; and

(b) where an insolvency practitioner acts as supervisor of a voluntary arrangement, whichever is the earlier of the date on which–

(i) the arrangement is completed or terminated; or

(ii) the insolvency practitioner otherwise ceases to act as supervisor in relation to the arrangement.

3   Interpretation—meaning of initial and subsequent capacity

3(1)   In these Regulations an insolvency practitioner holds office in relation to an insolvent in a **"subsequent capacity"** where he holds office in relation to that insolvent in one of the capacities referred to in paragraph (3) and immediately prior to his holding office in that capacity, he held office in relation to that insolvent in another of the capacities referred to in that paragraph.

3(2)   The first office held by the insolvency practitioner in the circumstances referred to in paragraph (1) is referred to in these Regulations as the **"initial capacity"**.

3(3)   The capacities referred to in paragraph (1) are, nominee in relation to proposals for a voluntary arrangement under Part I of the Act, supervisor of a voluntary arrangement under Part I of the Act, administrator, provisional liquidator, liquidator, nominee in relation to proposals for a voluntary arrangement under Part VIII of the Act, supervisor of a voluntary arrangement under Part VIII of the Act, trustee, interim trustee and permanent trustee.

4   Revocations and transitional and saving provisions

4(1)   Subject to paragraphs (2), (3) and (4), the Regulations listed in Schedule 1 are revoked.

4(2)   Parts I and II of the Insolvency Practitioners Regulations 1990 shall continue to apply in relation to an application for authorisation under section 393 of the Act to act as an insolvency practitioner made to the Secretary of State before the commencement date and accordingly nothing in these Regulations shall apply to such an application.

4(3)   Parts I, III and IV of the Insolvency Practitioners Regulations 1990 shall continue to apply in relation to any case in respect of which an insolvency practitioner is appointed–

(a) before the commencement date; or

(b) in a subsequent capacity and he was appointed in an initial capacity in that case before the commencement date.

4(4)   Only regulations 16 and 17 of these Regulations shall apply in relation to the cases mentioned in paragraph (3).

Part 2

Authorisation of Insolvency Practitioners by Competent Authorities

5   Interpretation of Part

5   In this Part–

"advisory work experience" means experience obtained in providing advice to the office-holder in insolvency proceedings or anyone who is a party to, or whose interests are affected by, those proceedings;

"application" means an application made by an individual to the competent authority for authorisation under section 393 of the Act to act as an insolvency practitioner and "applicant" shall be construed accordingly;

"authorisation" means an authorisation to act as an insolvency practitioner granted under section 393 of the Act;

"continuing professional development" has the meaning given to it by regulation 8(3);

"higher insolvency work experience" means engagement in work in relation to insolvency proceedings where the work involves the management or supervision of the conduct of those proceedings on behalf of the office-holder acting in relation to them;

"insolvency legislation" means the provisions of, or any provision made under, the Act, the Bankruptcy (Scotland) Act 1985 or the Deeds of Arrangement Act 1914 and any other enactment past or present applying to Great Britain (or any part of it) that relates to the insolvency of any person;

"insolvency practice" means the carrying on of the business of acting as an insolvency practitioner or in a corresponding capacity under the law of any country or territory outside Great Britain, and for this purpose acting as an insolvency practitioner shall include acting as a judicial factor on the bankrupt estate of a deceased person;

"insolvency proceedings" means any proceedings in which an office-holder acts under any provision of insolvency legislation or the corresponding provision of the law of any country or territory outside Great Britain;

"insolvency work experience" means engagement in work related to the administration of insolvency proceedings–

(a)   as the office-holder in those proceedings;

(b)   in the employment of a firm or body whose members or employees act as insolvency practitioners; or

(c)   in the course of employment in the Insolvency Service of the Department of Trade and Industry, of the Department for Business, Enterprise and Regulatory Reform or of the Department for Business, Innovation and Skills.

"office-holder" means a person who acts as an insolvency practitioner or a judicial factor on the bankrupt estate of a deceased person or in a corresponding capacity under the law of any country or territory outside Great Britain and includes the official receiver acting as liquidator, provisional liquidator, trustee, interim receiver or nominee or supervisor of a voluntary arrangement; and

"regulatory work experience" means experience of work relating to the regulation of insolvency practitioners for or on behalf of a competent authority or a body recognised pursuant to section 391 of the Act or experience of work in connection with any function of the Secretary of State under that section.

6   Matters for determining whether an applicant for an authorisation is a fit and proper person

6   The matters to be taken into account by a competent authority in deciding whether an individual is a fit and proper person to act as an insolvency practitioner for the purpose of section 393(2)(a) or 393(4)(a) shall include:–

(a)   whether the applicant has been convicted of any offence involving fraud or other dishonesty or violence;

(b)   whether the applicant has contravened any provision in any enactment contained in insolvency legislation;

(c)   whether the applicant has engaged in any practices in the course of carrying on any trade, profession or vocation or in the course of the discharge of any functions relating to any office or employment appearing to be deceitful or oppressive or otherwise unfair or improper, whether unlawful or not, or which otherwise cast doubt upon his probity or competence for discharging the duties of an insolvency practitioner;

(d)   whether in respect of any insolvency practice carried on by the applicant at the date of or at any time prior to the making of the application, there were established adequate systems of control of the practice and adequate records relating to the practice, including accounting records, and whether such systems of control and records have been or were maintained on an adequate basis;

(e) whether the insolvency practice of the applicant is, has been or, where the applicant is not yet carrying on such a practice, will be, carried on with the independence, integrity and the professional skills appropriate to the range and scale of the practice and the proper performance of the duties of an insolvency practitioner and in accordance with generally accepted professional standards, practices and principles;

(f) whether the applicant, in any case where he has acted as an insolvency practitioner, has failed to disclose fully to such persons as might reasonably be expected to be affected thereby circumstances where there is or appears to be a conflict of interest between his so acting and any interest of his own, whether personal, financial or otherwise, without having received such consent as might be appropriate to his acting or continuing to act despite the existence of such circumstances.

7   Requirements as to education and training—applicants who have never previously been authorised to act as insolvency practitioners

7(1)   The requirements as to education, training and practical experience prescribed for the purposes of section 393(2)(b) of the Act in relation to an applicant who has never previously been authorised to act as an insolvency practitioner (whether by virtue of membership of a body recognised under section 391 of the Act or by virtue of an authorisation granted by a competent authority under section 393 of the Act) shall be as set out in this regulation.

7(2)   An applicant must at the date of the making of his application have passed the Joint Insolvency Examination set by the Joint Insolvency Examination Board or have acquired in, or been awarded in, a country or territory outside Great Britain professional or vocational qualifications which indicate that the applicant has the knowledge and competence that is attested by a pass in that examination.

7(3)   An applicant must either–

(a) have held office as an office-holder in not less than 30 cases during the period of 10 years immediately preceding the date on which he made his application for authorisation; or

(b) have acquired not less than 2000 hours of insolvency work experience of which no less than 1400 hours must have been acquired within the period of two years immediately prior to the date of the making of his application and show that he satisfies one of the three requirements set out in paragraph (4).

History
Regulation 7(3)(b) amended by the Provision of Services (Insolvency Practitioners) Regulations 2009 (SI 2009/3081) reg.4 and Sch. para.3 as from December 28, 2009.

7(4)   The three requirements referred to in paragraph (3)(b) are–

(a) the applicant has become an office-holder in at least 5 cases within the period of 5 years immediately prior to the date of the making of his application;

(b) the applicant has acquired 1,000 hours or more of higher insolvency work experience or experience as an office-holder within the period referred to in sub-paragraph (a); and

(c) the applicant can show that within the period referred to in sub-paragraph (a) he has achieved one of the following combinations of positions as an office-holder and hours acquired of higher insolvency work experience–

(i) 4 cases and 200 hours;

(ii) 3 cases and 400 hours;

    (iii) 2 cases and 600 hours; or

    (iv) 1 case and 800 hours.

7(5)   Where in order to satisfy all or any of the requirements set out in paragraphs (3) and (4) an applicant relies on appointment as an office-holder or the acquisition of insolvency work experience or higher insolvency work experience in relation to cases under the laws of a country or territory outside the United Kingdom, he shall demonstrate that he has no less than 1,400 hours of insolvency work experience in cases under the law of any part of the United Kingdom acquired within the period of two years immediately prior to the date of the making of his application.

7(6)   In ascertaining whether an applicant meets all or any of the requirements of paragraphs (3) and (4)–

    (a) no account shall be taken of any case where–

        (i) he was appointed to the office of receiver (or to a corresponding office under the law of a country or territory outside Great Britain) by or on behalf of a creditor who at the time of the appointment was an associate of the applicant; or

        (ii) in a members' voluntary winding up or in a corresponding procedure under the laws of a country or territory outside Great Britain he was appointed liquidator at a general meeting where his associates were entitled to exercise or control the exercise of one third or more of the voting power at that general meeting;

    (b) where the applicant has been an office-holder in relation to–

        (i) two or more companies which were associates at the time of appointment; or

        (ii) two or more individuals who were carrying on business in partnership with each other at the time of appointment,

he shall be treated as having held office in only one case in respect of all offices held in relation to the companies which were associates or in respect of all offices held in relation to the individuals who were in partnership, as the case may be.

7(7)   An applicant must have a good command of the English language.

8 Requirements relating to education and training etc—applicants previously authorised to act as insolvency practitioners

8(1)   The requirements prescribed for the purposes of section 393(2)(b) of the Act in relation to an applicant who has at any time been authorised to act as an insolvency practitioner (whether by virtue of membership of a body recognised under section 391 of the Act or an authorisation granted by a competent authority under section 393 of the Act) shall be as set out in this regulation.

8(2)   The applicant must–

    (a) satisfy the requirements set out in regulation 7(3) to (5) or have acquired within the period of three years preceding the date of the making of his application 450 hours of any combination of the following types of experience–

        (i) experience as an office-holder;

        (ii) higher insolvency work experience;

        (iii) regulatory work experience; or

        (iv) advisory work experience; and

(b) subject to paragraph (4), have completed at least 108 hours of continuing professional development in the period of three years ending on the day before the date of the making of his application of which–

    (i) a minimum of 12 hours must be completed in each of those years; and

    (ii) 54 hours must fall into the categories in paragraphs (3)(b)(i) to (v).

8(3) **"Continuing professional development"** means any activities which–

(a) relate to insolvency law or practice or the management of the practice of an insolvency practitioner; and

(b) fall into any of the following categories–

    (i) the production of written material for publication;

    (ii) attendance at courses, seminars or conferences;

    (iii) the viewing of any recording of a course, seminar or conference;

    (iv) the giving of lectures or the presentation of papers at courses, seminars or conferences;

    (v) the completion of on-line tests; and

    (vi) the reading of books or periodical publications (including any on-line publication).

8(4) The requirement in paragraph (2)(b) shall only apply in relation to any application made on or after the third anniversary of the commencement date.

8(5) For the purposes of paragraph (3)(b)(i), **"publication"** includes making material available to a body recognised in pursuance of section 391 of the Act or any association or body representing the interests of those who act as insolvency practitioners.

History
Regulation 8(2)(a) amended by the Provision of Services (Insolvency Practitioners) Regulations 2009 (SI 2009/3081) reg.4 and Sch. para.4(1), (2) as from December 28, 2009.

8A   Requirements relating to education and training etc.—further authorisation to act as insolvency practitioners

8A(1) The requirements prescribed under section 393(2)(b) of the Act in relation to further authorisation under section 393(3A) of the Act are as set out in this regulation.

8A(2) The individual must–

(a) have acquired within the period in regulation 11(1A) 150 hours of any combination of the following types of experience–

    (i) experience as an office-holder;

    (ii) higher insolvency work experience;

    (iii) regulatory work experience; or

    (iv) advisory work experience; and

(b) have completed within the period in regulation 11(1A) at least 36 hours of continuing professional development of which 18 hours must fall into the categories in regulation 8(3)(b)(i) to (v).

8A(3) In the first period after the grant of an authorisation an individual must comply with–

(a) paragraph (2)(a) where the number of hours is 125; and

(b)   paragraph (2)(b) where the number of hours are 30 and 15 respectively.

History
Regulation 8A inserted by the Provision of Services (Insolvency Practitioners) Regulations 2009 (SI 2009/3081) reg.4 and Sch. para.4(1, (3) as from December 28, 2009.

9   Records of continuing professional development activities

9(1)   Every holder of an authorisation granted by the Secretary of State shall maintain a record of each continuing professional development activity undertaken by him for a period of six years from the date on which the activity was completed.

9(2)   The record shall contain details of–

(a)   which of the categories in regulation 8(3)(b) the activity comes within;

(b)   the date that the activity was undertaken;

(c)   the duration of the activity; and

(d)   the topics covered by the activity.

9(3)   Where the continuing professional development comprises–

(a)   attendance at a course, seminar or conference; or

(b)   the giving of a lecture or presentation of a paper at a course, seminar or conference,

the holder of the authorisation shall keep with the record evidence from the organiser of the course, seminar or conference of the attendance of the holder at the course, seminar or conference.

9(4)   The Secretary of State may, on the giving of reasonable notice, inspect and take copies of any records or evidence maintained pursuant to this regulation.

10   Maximum period of authorisation

10   [Revoked by the Provision of Services (Insolvency Practitioners) Regulations 2009 (SI 2009/3081) reg.4 and Sch. para.5 as from December 28, 2009.]

11   Returns by insolvency practitioners authorised by the Secretary of State

11(1)   Every holder of an authorisation granted by the Secretary of State shall make a return to the Secretary of State in respect of each period in paragraph (1A) during the whole or any part of which he held an authorisation granted by the Secretary of State containing the following information–

(a)   the number of cases in respect of whom the holder of the authorisation has acted as an insolvency practitioner during the period;

(b)   in respect of each case where the holder of the authorisation has acted as an insolvency practitioner–

(i)   the name of the person in respect of whom the insolvency practitioner is acting,

(ii)   the date of the appointment of the holder of the authorisation,

(iii)   the type of proceedings involved, and

(iv)   the number of hours worked in relation to the case by the holder of the authorisation and any person assigned to assist him in the case;

(c)   the following details of any continuing professional development undertaken activity during the period by the holder of the authorisation–

(i)   the nature of the activity;

(ii)   the date that the activity was undertaken;

(iii) the duration of the activity; and

(iv) the topics covered by the activity; and

(d)   the number of hours of any experience of the types in regulation 8A(2)(a)(i) to (iv).

11(1A)   The period is the period of 12 months ending two months before the anniversary of the grant of the authorisation or the last further authorisation.

11(2)   Every return required to be submitted pursuant to this regulation shall be submitted no later than 6 weeks before the end of the period to which it relates.

11(3)   The Secretary of State may at any time request the holder of an authorisation to provide any information relating to any matters of the kind referred to in paragraph (1) and any such request shall be complied with by the holder of the authorisation within one month of its receipt or such longer period as the Secretary of State may allow.

History
Regulation 11(1), (2) amended and reg.11(1A) inserted by the Provision of Services (Insolvency Practitioners) Regulations 2009 (SI 2009/3081) reg.4 and Sch. para.6 as from December 28, 2009.

PART 3

THE REQUIREMENTS FOR SECURITY AND CAUTION FOR THE PROPER PERFORMANCE OF THE FUNCTIONS OF AN INSOLVENCY PRACTITIONER ETC.

12(1)   Schedule 2 shall have effect in respect of the requirements prescribed for the purposes of section 390(3)(b) in relation to security or caution for the proper performance of the functions of an insolvency practitioner and for related matters.

12(2)   Where two or more persons are appointed jointly to act as insolvency practitioners in relation to any person, the provisions of this regulation shall apply to each of them individually.

12(3)   Where, in accordance with section 390(2)(c) of the Act a person is qualified to act as an insolvency practitioner by virtue of an authorisation granted by the Department of Enterprise, Trade and Investment for Northern Ireland under Article 352 of the Insolvency (Northern Ireland) Order 1989, this Part applies in relation to that person as if that authorisation had been granted pursuant to section 393 of the Act.

History
Regulation 12(3) inserted by the Provision of Services (Insolvency Practitioners) Regulations 2009 (SI 2009/3081) reg.4 and Sch. para.7 as from December 28, 2009.

PART 4

RECORDS TO BE MAINTAINED BY INSOLVENCY PRACTITIONERS—INSPECTION OF RECORDS

13   Records to be maintained by insolvency practitioners

13(1)   In respect of each case in which he acts, an insolvency practitioner shall maintain records containing at least the information specified in Schedule 3 to these Regulations as is applicable to the case.

13(2)   Where at any time the records referred to in paragraph (1) do not contain all the information referred to in Schedule 3 as is applicable to the case, the insolvency practitioner shall forthwith make such changes to the records as are necessary to ensure that the records contains all such information.

13(3) References in Schedule 3 to "the Accountant in Bankruptcy" shall be construed in accordance with section 1 of the Bankruptcy (Scotland) Act 1985.

13(4) Each record maintained pursuant to paragraph (1) shall be capable of being produced by the insolvency practitioner separately from any other record.

13(5) Any records created in relation to a case pursuant to this regulation shall be preserved by the insolvency practitioner until whichever is the later of–

(a) the sixth anniversary of the date of the grant to the insolvency practitioner of his release or discharge in that case; or

(b) the sixth anniversary of the date on which any security or caution maintained in that case expires or otherwise ceases to have effect.

14 Notification of whereabouts of records

14 The insolvency practitioner shall notify the persons referred to in regulation 15(1)(a) and 15(1)(b) of the place where the records required to be maintained under this Part are so maintained and the place (if different) where they may be inspected pursuant to regulation 15.

15 Inspection of records

15(1) Any records maintained by an insolvency practitioner pursuant to this Part shall on the giving of reasonable notice be made available by him for inspection by–

(a) any professional body recognised under section 391 of the Act of which he is a member and the rules of membership of which entitle him to act as an insolvency practitioner;

(b) any competent authority by whom the insolvency practitioner is authorised to act pursuant to section 393 of the Act; and

(c) the Secretary of State.

15(2) Any person who is entitled to inspect any record pursuant to paragraph (1) shall also be entitled to take a copy of those records.

16 Inspection of practice records

16(1) This regulation applies to any relevant records which are held by–

(a) the holder of an authorisation to act as an insolvency practitioner granted by the Secretary of State pursuant to section 393 of the Act;

(b) his employer or former employer; or

(c) any firm or other body of which he is or was a member or partner.

16(2) In this regulation **"relevant records"** mean any records which relate to any case where the holder of the authorisation mentioned in paragraph (1) has acted as an insolvency practitioner and which–

(a) record receipts and payments made in relation to, or in connection with, that case;

(b) record time spent on that case by the holder of the authorisation or any person assigned to assist the holder;

(c) relate to any business carried on in the case by or at the direction of the holder of the authorisation; or

(d) otherwise relate to the management of that case.

16(3) The Secretary of State may, on the giving of reasonable notice to their holder, inspect and take copies of any records to which this regulation applies.

17   Inspection of records in administration and administrative receiverships

17   On the giving of reasonable notice to the insolvency practitioner, the Secretary of State shall be entitled to inspect and take copies of any records in the possession or control of that insolvency practitioner which–

(a)   were required to be created by or under any provision of the Act (or any provision made under the Act); and

(b)   relate to an administration or an administrative receivership.

Schedule 1

Regulations Revoked

Regulation 4

The Insolvency Practitioners Regulations 1990

The Insolvency Practitioners (Amendment) Regulations 1993

The Insolvency Practitioners (Amendment) Regulations 2002

The Insolvency Practitioners (Amendment) (No 2) Regulations 2002

The Insolvency Practitioners (Amendment) Regulations 2004

Schedule 2

Requirements for Security or Caution and Related Matters

Regulation 12

Part 1

Interpretation

1   Interpretation

1   In this Schedule–

"cover schedule" means the schedule referred to in paragraph 3(2)(c);

"the insolvent" means the individual or company in relation to which an insolvency practitioner is acting;

"general penalty sum" shall be construed in accordance with paragraph 3(2)(b);

"insolvent's assets" means all assets comprised in the insolvent's estate together with any monies provided by a third party for the payment of the insolvent's debts or the costs and expenses of administering the insolvent's estate;

"professional liability insurance" means insurance taken out by the insolvency practitioner in respect of potential liabilities to the insolvent and third parties arising out of acting as an insolvency practitioner;

"specific penalty sum" shall be construed in accordance with paragraph 3(2)(a).

History

Definition of "professional liability insurance" amended by the Provision of Services (Insolvency Practitioners) Regulations 2009 (SI 2009/3081) reg.4 and Sch. para.8(1), (2) as from December 28, 2009.

PART 2

REQUIREMENTS RELATING TO SECURITY AND CAUTION

2   Requirements in respect of security or caution

2   The requirements in respect of security or caution for the proper performance of the duties of insolvency practitioners prescribed for the purposes of section 390(3)(b) shall be as set out in this Part.

2A   Requirement for bond or professional liability insurance

2A   Where an insolvency practitioner is appointed to act in respect of an insolvent there must be in force–

(a)   a bond in a form approved by the Secretary of State which complies with paragraph 3; or

(b)   where the insolvency practitioner is already established in another EEA state and is already covered in that state by professional liability insurance or a guarantee, professional liability insurance or a guarantee which complies with paragraph 8A.

History
Paragraph 2A inserted by the Provision of Services (Insolvency Practitioners) Regulations 2009 (SI 2009/3081) reg.4 and Sch. para.8(1), (3) as from December 28, 2009.

3   Terms of the bond

3(1)   The bond must–

(a)   be in writing or in electronic form;

(b)   contain provision whereby a surety or cautioner undertakes to be jointly and severally liable for losses in relation to the insolvent caused by–

(i)   the fraud or dishonesty of the insolvency practitioner whether acting alone or in collusion with one or more persons; or

(ii)   the fraud or dishonesty of any person committed with the connivance of the insolvency practitioner; and

(c)   otherwise conform to the requirements of this paragraph and paragraphs 4 to 8.

3(2)   The terms of the bond shall provide–

(a)   for the payment, in respect of each case where the insolvency practitioner acts, of claims in respect of liabilities for losses of the kind mentioned in sub-paragraph (1) up to an aggregate maximum sum in respect of that case (**"the specific penalty sum"**) calculated in accordance with the provisions of this Schedule;

(b)   in the event that any amounts payable under (a) are insufficient to meet all claims arising out of any case, for a further sum of £250,000 (**"the general penalty sum"**) out of which any such claims are to be met;

(c)   for a schedule containing the name of the insolvent and the value of the insolvent's assets to be submitted to the surety or cautioner within such period as may be specified in the bond;

(d)   that where at any time before the insolvency practitioner obtains his release or discharge in respect of his acting in relation to an insolvent, he forms the opinion that the value of that insolvent's assets is greater than the current specific penalty sum, a revised specific penalty sum shall be applicable on the submission within such time as may be specified in the bond of a cover schedule containing a revised value of the insolvent's assets;

(e) for the payment of losses of the kind mentioned in sub-paragraph (1), whether they arise during the period in which the insolvency practitioner holds office in the capacity in which he was initially appointed or a subsequent period where he holds office in a subsequent capacity;

3(3) The terms of the bond may provide–

(a) that total claims in respect of the acts of the insolvency practitioner under all bonds relating to him are to be limited to a maximum aggregate sum (which shall not be less than £25,000,000); and

(b) for a time limit within which claims must be made.

History
Title of para.3 amended and para.(1) substituted by the Provision of Services (Insolvency Practitioners) Regulations 2009 (SI 2009/3081) reg.4 and Sch. para.8(4) as from December 28, 2009.

4 Subject to paragraphs 5, 6 and 7, the amount of the specific penalty in respect of a case in which the insolvency practitioner acts, shall equal at least the value of the insolvent's assets as estimated by the insolvency practitioner as at the date of his appointment but ignoring the value of any assets–

(a) charged to a third party to the extent of any amount which would be payable to that third party; or

(b) held on trust by the insolvent to the extent that any beneficial interest in those assets does not belong to the insolvent.

5 In a case where an insolvency practitioner acts as a nominee or supervisor of a voluntary arrangement under Part I or Part VIII of the Act, the amount of the specific penalty shall be equal to at least the value of those assets subject to the terms of the arrangement (whether or not those assets are in his possession) including, where under the terms of the arrangement the debtor or a third party is to make payments, the aggregate of any payments to be made.

6 Where the value of the insolvent's assets is less than £5,000, the specific penalty sum shall be £5,000.

7 Where the value of the insolvent's assets is more than £5,000,000 the specific penalty sum shall be £5,000,000.

8 In estimating the value of an insolvent's assets, unless he has reason to doubt their accuracy, the insolvency practitioner may rely upon–

(a) any statement of affairs produced in relation to that insolvent pursuant to any provision of the Act; and

(b) in the case of a sequestration–

(i) the debtor's list of assets and liabilities under section 19 of the Bankruptcy (Scotland) Act 1985;

(ii) the preliminary statement under that Act; or

(iii) the final statement of the debtor's affairs by the interim trustee under section 23 of the Bankruptcy (Scotland) Act 1985.

8A Compliance of professional liability insurance cover in another EEA state

8A Where paragraph 2A(b) applies to an insolvency practitioner, the professional liability insurance or guarantee complies with this paragraph if the Secretary of State determines that it is equivalent or essentially comparable to the bond referred to in paragraph 3 as regards–

(a) its purpose, and

(b) the cover it provides in terms of–

(i) the risk covered,

(ii)   the amount covered, and

(iii)   exclusions from the cover.

8B   Procedure for determining compliance of professional liability insurance or guarantee

8B(1)   Where an insolvency practitioner seeks a determination under paragraph 8A, the insolvency practitioner must send to the Secretary of State–

(a)   a copy of the document providing the professional liability insurance or guarantee cover in the EEA state in which the insolvency practitioner is established;

(b)   where the document in sub-paragraph (a) is not in English, a translation of it into English; and

(c)   a notice–

(i)   where the insolvency practitioner intends to act in respect of an insolvent, specifying–

(aa)   the name of the insolvent; and

(bb)   the time and date when the insolvency practitioner intends to consent to be appointed to act; or

(ii)   that the insolvency practitioner seeks a determination without reference to a specific appointment.

8B(2)   Where there is a notice sent under sub-paragraph (1)(c)(i), the documents sent under sub-paragraph (1) must be sent to the Secretary of State such that the Secretary of State receives them no later than 5 business days before the date in the notice.

8B(3)   Where the Secretary of State receives the documents sent under sub-paragraph (1), the Secretary of State must–

(a)   as soon as is reasonably practicable, notify the insolvency practitioner whether they were received in accordance with sub-paragraph (2);

(b)   consider them; and

(c)   determine whether the document sent under sub-paragraph (1)(a) complies with paragraph 8A.

8B(4)   Where the Secretary of State determines that the document sent under sub-paragraph (1)(a) complies with paragraph 8A, the Secretary of State must–

(a)   notify the insolvency practitioner that it complies with paragraph 8A; and

(b)   determine whether it contains a term equivalent or essentially comparable to a requirement to provide–

(i)   a specific penalty sum; or

(ii)   a cover schedule.

8B(5)   Where the Secretary of State determines under sub-paragraph (4)(b) that the document sent under sub-paragraph (1)(a)–

(a)   contains a term equivalent or essentially comparable to a requirement to provide a specific penalty sum or a cover schedule, the notice sent under paragraph (4)(a) must specify–

(i)   the term equivalent or essentially comparable to a requirement to provide a specific penalty sum or a cover schedule; and

(ii) the thing in the term in sub-paragraph (i) which is equivalent or essentially comparable to a specific penalty sum or a cover schedule; or

(b) does not contain a term equivalent or essentially comparable to a requirement to provide a specific penalty sum or a cover schedule, the notice sent under paragraph (4)(a) must state that determination.

8B(6) Where the Secretary of State determines that the document sent under sub-paragraph (1)(a) does not comply with paragraph 8A, the Secretary of State must notify the insolvency practitioner and–

(a) give reasons for the determination; and

(b) specify any terms which, if included in a supplementary guarantee, will cause the Secretary of State to make a determination in accordance with paragraph 8A.

8B(7) In this paragraph a "business day" means any day other than a Saturday, a Sunday, Christmas Day, Good Friday or a day which is a bank holiday in England and Wales under or by virtue of the Banking and Financial Dealings Act 1971.

8B(8) Any documents in this paragraph or paragraph 8C or 8D may be sent electronically.

8C Procedure for determining compliance of supplementary guarantee

8C(1) Where the Secretary of State has made a determination under paragraph 8B(6), the insolvency practitioner may send to the Secretary of State–

(a) a supplementary guarantee purporting to provide for the matters specified in paragraph 8B(6)(b); and

(b) where the supplementary guarantee is not in English, a translation of it into English.

8C(2) Where the Secretary of State receives the documents sent under sub-paragraph (1), the Secretary of State must–

(a) as soon as is reasonably practicable, notify the insolvency practitioner of the date and time of their receipt;

(b) consider them; and

(c) determine whether the document sent under sub-paragraph (1)(a) provides for the matters specified in paragraph 8B(6)(b).

8C(3) Where the Secretary of State determines that the document sent under sub-paragraph (1)(a)–

(a) provides for the matters in specified in paragraph 8B(6)(b); and

(b) together with the document in paragraph 8B(1)(a) complies with paragraph 8A, the Secretary of State must notify the insolvency practitioner that the documents sent under sub-paragraph (1)(a) and paragraph 8B(1)(a) together comply with paragraph 8A.

8C(4) Where the Secretary of State determines in accordance with sub-paragraph (3), the Secretary of State must also determine whether the document sent under sub-paragraph (1)(a) or paragraph 8B(1)(a) contains a term equivalent or essentially comparable to a requirement to provide–

(a) a specific penalty sum; or

(b) a cover schedule.

8C(5) Where the Secretary of State determines under sub-paragraph (4) that the document sent under sub-paragraph (1)(a) or paragraph 8B(1)(a)–

(a) contains a term equivalent or essentially comparable to a requirement to provide a specific penalty sum or a cover schedule, the notice sent under sub-paragraph (3) must specify–

  (i) the term equivalent or essentially comparable to a requirement to provide a specific penalty sum or a cover schedule;

  (ii) the thing in the term in sub-paragraph (i) which is equivalent or essentially comparable to a requirement to a specific penalty sum or a cover schedule; and

  (iii) the document in which the term in sub-paragraph (i) and the thing in sub-paragraph (ii) are to be found; or

(b) does not contain a term equivalent or essentially comparable to a requirement to provide a specific penalty sum or a cover schedule, the notice sent under sub-paragraph (3) must state that determination.

8C(6) Where the Secretary of State determines that the document sent under sub-paragraph (1)(a)–

(a) does not provide for the matters specified in paragraph 8B(6)(b), or

(b) together with the document sent under paragraph 8B(1)(a) does not comply with paragraph 8A, the Secretary of State must notify the insolvency practitioner that the documents sent under sub-paragraphs (1)(a) and paragraph 8B(1)(a) together do not comply with paragraph 8A.

8D Time for notification of determinations

8D(1) The Secretary of State must notify the insolvency practitioner of the determinations under paragraph 8B or 8C in the periods set out in this paragraph.

8D(2) The Secretary of State must notify the insolvency practitioner–

(a) where a notice under paragraph 8B(1)(c)(i) is received by the Secretary of State in accordance with paragraph 8B(2) and the determination is under–

  (i) paragraph 8B(4), (5) or (6), such that the insolvency practitioner receives the notice sent under paragraph 8B(4) or (6) or before the time and date in the notice sent under paragraph 8B(1)(c)(i); or

  (ii) paragraph 8C(4), (5) or (6), as soon as is reasonably practicable after receipt of the documents sent under paragraph 8C(1);

(b) where a notice sent under paragraph 8B(1)(c)(i) is received by the Secretary of State but not in accordance with paragraph 8B(2), and the determination is under–

  (i) paragraph 8B(4), (5) or (6), as soon as is reasonably practicable after receipt of the documents sent under paragraph 8B(1); or

  (ii) paragraph 8C(3), (5) or (6), as soon as is reasonably practicable after receipt of the documents sent under paragraph 8C(1); or

(c) where the notice is sent under paragraph 8B(1)(c)(ii), and the determination is under–

  (i) paragraph 8B(4), (5) or (6), within 28 days of receipt of the documents sent under paragraph 8B(1); or

  (ii) paragraph 8C(3), (5) or (6), within 14 days of receipt of the documents sent under paragraph 8C(1).

8E   Notification of determination out of time

8E(1)   This paragraph applies where the insolvency practitioner–

(a)   sends a notice under paragraph 8B(1)(c)(i);

(b)   receives notification sent under paragraph 8B(3)(a) that the Secretary of State received the documents in paragraph 8B(1) in accordance with paragraph 8B(2); and

(c)   does not receive the notifications in the time in paragraph 8D(2)(a)(i).

8E(2)   The insolvency practitioner is qualified to act as an insolvency practitioner in respect of the insolvent specified in the notice under paragraph 8B(1)(c)(i) until the Secretary of State notifies the insolvency practitioner of the determination under paragraph 8B or 8C.

8E(3)   Subject to sub-paragraph (4), where the Secretary of State notifies the insolvency practitioner of the determination under paragraph 8B or 8C–

(a)   the determination applies; and

(b)   the insolvency practitioner ceases to be qualified to act as an insolvency practitioner under sub-paragraph (2).

8E(4)   Where–

(a)   the Secretary of State gives notice under paragraph 8B(6); and

(b)   the insolvency practitioner sends the documents in paragraph 8C(1), the insolvency practitioner is qualified to act as an insolvency practitioner under sub-paragraph (2) until the Secretary of State determines in accordance with paragraph 8C(4) or (6).

History
Paragraphs 8A–8E inserted by the Provision of Services (Insolvency Practitioners) Regulations 2009 (SI 2009/3081) reg.4 and Sch. para.8(5) as from December 28, 2009.

PART 3

RECORDS RELATING TO BONDING AND CONNECTED MATTERS

9   Record of specific penalty sums to be maintained by insolvency practitioner

9(1)   An insolvency practitioner shall maintain a record of all specific penalty sums that are applicable in relation to any case where he is acting and such record shall contain the name of each person to whom the specific penalty sum relates and the amount of each penalty sum that is in force.

9(2)   Any record maintained by an insolvency practitioner pursuant to this paragraph shall, on the giving of reasonable notice, be made available for inspection by–

(a)   any professional body recognised under section 391 of the Act of which he is or was a member and the rules of membership of which entitle or entitled him to act as an insolvency practitioner;

(b)   any competent authority by whom the insolvency practitioner is or was authorised to act pursuant to section 393 of the Act; and

(c)   the Secretary of State.

9(3)   Subject to sub-paragraph (4), where the Secretary of State has notified the insolvency practitioner in accordance with paragraph 8B(5)(a) or 8C(5)(a) in relation to a specific penalty sum, the thing notified under paragraph 8B(5)(a)(ii) or 8C(5)(a)(ii) is construed as a specific penalty sum for the purposes of this paragraph and Schedule 3.

9(4) Where the Secretary of State has notified the insolvency practitioner in accordance with paragraph 8B(5)(b) or 8C(5)(b) in relation to a specific penalty sum, this paragraph does not apply.

History
Paragraphs 9(3), (4) inserted by the Provision of Services (Insolvency Practitioners) Regulations 2009 (SI 2009/3081) reg.4 and Sch. para.8(6) as from December 28, 2009.

10 Retention of bond by recognised professional body or competent authority

10(1) The documents in sub-paragraph (2) or a copy must be sent by the insolvency practitioner to–

(a) any professional body recognised under section 391 of the Act of which he is a member and the rules of membership of which entitle him to act as an insolvency practitioner; or

(b) any competent authority by whom the insolvency practitioner is authorised to act pursuant to section 393 of the Act.

10(2) The documents in this sub-paragraph are–

(a) the bond referred to in paragraph 3;

(b) where the Secretary of State has determined under paragraph 8B(4)–

(i) the document in paragraph 8B(1)(a) and (b); and

(ii) the notice under paragraph 8B(4);

(c) where the Secretary of State has determined under paragraph 8C(4)–

(i) the documents in paragraphs 8B(1)(a) and (b) and 8C(1)(a) and (b); and

(ii) the notice under paragraph 8C(3).

10(3) The document in sub-paragraph (2) or a copy of it may be sent electronically.

History
Paragraph 10 amended and renumbered as para.10(1) and paras 10(2), (3) inserted by the Provision of Services (Insolvency Practitioners) Regulations 2009 (SI 2009/3081) reg.4 and Sch. para.8(7) as from December 28, 2009.

11 Inspection and retention requirements relating to cover schedule—England and Wales

11(1) This regulation applies to an insolvency practitioner appointed in insolvency proceedings under the Act to act–

(a) in relation to a company which the courts in England and Wales have jurisdiction to wind up; or

(b) in respect of an individual.

11(2) The insolvency practitioner shall retain a copy of the cover schedule submitted by him in respect of his acting in relation to the company or, as the case may be, individual until the second anniversary of the date on which he is granted his release or discharge in relation to that company or, as the case may be, that individual.

11(3) The copy of a schedule kept by an insolvency practitioner in pursuance of sub-paragraph (2) shall be produced by him on demand for inspection by–

(a) any creditor of the person to whom the schedule relates;

(b) where the schedule relates to an insolvent who is an individual, that individual;

(c) where the schedule relates to an insolvent which is a company, any contributory or director or other officer of the company; and

(d) the Secretary of State.

11(4) Subject to sub-paragraph (5), where the Secretary of State has notified the insolvency practitioner in accordance with paragraph 8B(5)(a) or 8C(5)(a) in relation to a cover schedule, the thing notified under paragraph 8B(5)(a)(ii) or 8C(5)(a)(ii) is construed as a cover schedule for the purposes of this paragraph, paragraph 12, paragraph 13 and Schedule 3.

11(5) Where the Secretary of State has notified the insolvency practitioner in accordance with paragraph 8B(5)(b) or 8C(5)(b) in relation to a cover schedule, this paragraph, paragraph 12 and paragraph 13 do not apply.

History
Paragraph 11(4), (5) inserted by the Provision of Services (Insolvency Practitioners) Regulations 2009 (SI 2009/3081) reg.4 and Sch. para.8(8) as from December 28, 2009.

12 Inspection and retention requirements relating to the cover schedule—Scotland

12(1) Where an insolvency practitioner is appointed to act in relation to a company which the courts in Scotland have jurisdiction to wind up, he shall retain in the sederunt book kept under rule 7.33 of the Insolvency (Scotland) Rules 1986, the principal copy of any cover schedule containing entries in relation to his so acting.

12(2) Where an insolvency practitioner is appointed to act as interim trustee or permanent trustee or as a trustee under a trust deed for creditors, he shall retain in the sederunt book kept for those proceedings, the principal copy of any cover schedule containing entries in relation to his so acting.

13 Requirements to submit cover schedule to authorising body

13(1) Every insolvency practitioner shall submit to his authorising body not later than 20 days after the end of each month during which he holds office in a case–

(a) the information submitted to a surety or cautioner in any cover schedule related to that month;

(b) where no cover schedule is submitted in relation to the month, a statement either that there are no relevant particulars to be supplied or, as the case may be, that it is not practicable to supply particulars in relation to any appointments taken in that month; and

(c) a statement identifying any case in respect of which he has been granted his release or discharge.

13(2) In this regulation **"authorising body"** means in relation to an insolvency practitioner–

(a) any professional body recognised under section 391 of the Act of which he is a member and the rules of membership of which entitle him to act as an insolvency practitioner; or

(b) any competent authority by whom he is authorised to act as an insolvency practitioner pursuant to section 393 of the Act.

SCHEDULE 3

RECORDS TO BE MAINTAINED—MINIMUM REQUIREMENTS

Regulation 13

1 Details of the insolvency practitioner acting in the case

1 The name of the insolvency practitioner acting in the case.

2 The identifying number or reference issued to the insolvency practitioner by–

(a) a competent authority;

(b) the Department of Enterprise, Trade and Investment for Northern Ireland; or

(c) any body recognised under section 391 of the Act".

History
Paragraph 2 amended by the Provision of Services (Insolvency Practitioners) Regulations 2009 (SI 2009/3081) reg.4 and Sch. para.9(1), (2) as from December 28, 2009.

3 The principal business address of the insolvency practitioner.

4 Either–

(a) the name of–

(i) any body by virtue of whose rules the insolvency practitioner is entitled to practise; or

(ii) any competent authority by whom the insolvency practitioner is authorised; or

(b) where the insolvency practitioner is authorised by the Department of Enterprise, Trade and Investment for Northern Ireland under Article 352 of the Insolvency (Northern Ireland) Order 1989, that such an authorisation has been granted.

History
Paragraph 4 substituted by the Provision of Services (Insolvency Practitioners) Regulations 2009 (SI 2009/3081) reg.4 and Sch. para.9(3) as from December 28, 2009.

5 **Details of the insolvent**

5 The name of the person in respect of whom the insolvency practitioner is acting.

6 The type of the insolvency proceedings.

7 **Progress of administration**

7 As regards the progress of the administration of the case the following details if applicable–

(a) the date of commencement of the proceedings;

(b) the date of appointment of the insolvency practitioner;

(c) the date on which the appointment was notified to–

(i) the Registrar of Companies; or

(ii) the Accountant in Bankruptcy.

8 **Bonding arrangements in the case**

8 As regards the arrangements for security or caution in the case–

(a) the date of submission of the cover schedule which has the details of the specific penalty sum applicable in the case;

(b) the amount of the specific penalty sum;

(c) the name of the surety or cautioner;

(d) the date of submission to surety or cautioner of a cover schedule with any increase in the amount of the specific penalty sum;

(e) the amount of any revised specific penalty sum; and

(f) the date of submission to the surety or cautioner of details of termination of the office held by the insolvency practitioner.

9   Matters relating to remuneration

9   As regards the remuneration of the insolvency practitioner–

   (a)   the basis on which the remuneration of the insolvency practitioner is to be calculated; and

   (b)   the date and content of any resolution of creditors in relation to the remuneration of the insolvency practitioner.

10   Meetings (other than any final meeting of creditors)

10   The dates of–

   (a)   the meeting of members;

   (b)   the date of first meeting of creditors–

      (i)   to consider an administrator's proposals;

      (ii)   to consider an administrative receiver's report;

      (iii) in liquidation or bankruptcy;

      (iv)   to consider a voluntary arrangement proposal; or

      (v)   according to a trust deed for creditors;

   (c)   the date of the statutory meeting in sequestration; and

   (d)   the dates and purposes of any subsequent meetings.

11   Disqualification of directors

11   As regards the insolvency practitioner's duties under section 7 of the Company Directors Disqualification Act 1986 to report the conduct of directors–

   (a)   the date a return under section 7 is due;

   (b)   the date a return is submitted to the Secretary of State;

   (c)   the date a conduct report is submitted to the Secretary of State; and

   (d)   the date on which any further reports are submitted to the Secretary of State.

12   Vacation of office etc.

12   The following details regarding the completion of the case–

   (a)   the date of the final notice to, or meeting of, creditors;

   (b)   the date that the insolvency practitioner vacates office; and

   (c)   the date of release or discharge of the insolvency practitioner (or if there is no final meeting of creditors, the date of the final return of receipts and payments to the Secretary of State).

13   Distributions to creditors etc.

13   As regards distributions–

   (a)   in relation to each payment to preferential or preferred creditors–

      (i)   the name of the person to whom the payment was made;

      (ii)   the date of the payment;

      (iii) the amount of the payment;

    (b) in relation to each payment to unsecured creditors–

        (i) the name of the person to whom the payment was made;

        (ii) the date of the payment;

        (iii) the amount of the payment; and

    (c) in relation to each return of capital–

        (i) the name of the person to whom the return of capital was made;

        (ii) the date of the payment; and

        (iii) the amount of capital returned or the value of any assets returned.

14 Statutory returns

14 As regards any returns or accounts to be made to the Secretary of State, the Registrar of Companies or the Accountant in Bankruptcy–

    (a) as regards each interim return or abstract of receipts and payments;

        (i) the date the return or abstract is due;

        (ii) the date on which the return is filed; and

    (b) as regards any final return or abstract of receipts and payments–

        (i) the date that the return or abstract is due; and

        (ii) the date on which the return is filed.

15 Time recording

15 Records of the amount of time spent on the case by the insolvency practitioner and any persons assigned to assist in the administration of the case.

Community Interest Company Regulations 2005

(SI 2005/1788)

Made on June 30, 2005 by the Secretary of State for Trade and Industry under ss.30(1) to (4), 30(7), 31, 32(3), (4) and (6), 34(3), 35(4) to (6), 36(2), 37(7), 47(12) and (13), 57(1) and (2), 58, 59(1) and 62(2) and (3) of and para.4 of Sch.4 to the Companies (Audit, Investigations and Community Enterprise) Act 2004. Operative from July 1, 2005.

[**Note**: Changes made by the Companies Act 2006 (Commencement No.2, Consequential Amendments, Transitional Provisions and Savings) Order 2007 and the Housing and Regeneration Act 2008 (Consequential Provisions) (No.2) Order 2010 (SI 2010/671) have been incorporated into the text.]

PART 6

RESTRICTIONS ON DISTRIBUTIONS AND INTEREST

23   Distribution of assets on a winding up

23(1)   This regulation applies where–

(a)   a community interest company is wound up under the Insolvency Act 1986 or the Insolvency (Northern Ireland) Order 1989; and

(b)   some property of the company (the **"residual assets"**) remains after satisfaction of the company's liabilities.

23(2)   Subject to paragraph (3), the residual assets shall be distributed to those members of the community interest company (if any) who are entitled to share in any distribution of assets on the winding up of the company according to their rights and interests in the company.

23(3)   No member shall receive under paragraph (2) an amount which exceeds the paid up value of the shares which he holds in the company.

23(4)   If any residual assets remain after any distribution to members under paragraph (2) (the **"remaining residual assets"**), they shall be distributed in accordance with paragraphs (5) and (6).

23(5)   If the articles of the company specify an asset-locked body to which any remaining residual assets of the company should be distributed, then, unless either of the conditions specified in sub-paragraphs (b) and (c) of paragraph (6) is satisfied, the remaining residual assets shall be distributed to that asset-locked body in such proportions or amounts as the Regulator shall direct.

23(6)   If–

(a)   the articles of the company do not specify an asset-locked body to which any remaining residual assets of the company should be distributed;

(b)   the Regulator is aware that the asset-locked body to which the articles of the company specify that the remaining residual assets of the company should be distributed is itself in the process of being wound up; or

(c)   the Regulator–

(i)   has received representations from a member or director of the company stating, with reasons, that the asset-locked body to which the articles of the company specify that the remaining residual assets of the company should be distributed is not an appropriate recipient of the company's remaining residual assets; and

(ii)   has agreed with those representations,

then the remaining residual assets shall be distributed to such asset-locked bodies, and in such proportions or amounts, as the Regulator shall direct.

23(7)   In considering any direction to be made under this regulation, the Regulator must–

(a)   consult the directors and members of the company, to the extent that he considers it practicable and appropriate to do so; and

(b)   have regard to the desirability of distributing assets in accordance with any relevant provisions of the company's articles.

23(8)   The Regulator must give notice of any direction under this regulation to the company and the liquidator.

23(9)   This regulation has effect notwithstanding anything in the Insolvency Act 1986 or the Insolvency (Northern Ireland) Order 1989.

23(10)   This regulation has effect subject to the provisions of the Housing Act 1996, Part 2 of the Housing and Regeneration Act 2008 and the Housing (Scotland) Act 2001.

23(11)   Any member or director of the company may appeal to the Appeal Officer against a direction of the Regulator made under this regulation.

Note
"Asset-locked body" is defined in reg.2 as follows:

"'**asset-locked body**' means–

(a)   a community interest company, charity or Scottish charity; or

(b)   a body established outside Great Britain that is equivalent to any of those persons."

History
Paragraph 23(1)(a), (9) amended by the Companies Act 2006 (Commencement No.2, Consequential Amendments, Transitional Provisions and Savings) Order 2007 (SI 2007/1093 (C. 49) art.6(2) and Sch.4 para.36, as from April 6, 2007. Paragraph 23(10) amended by the Housing and Regeneration Act 2008 (Consequential Provisions) (No.2) Order 2010 (SI 2010/671) art.4 and Sch.1 para.42 as from April 1, 2010.

Transfer of Undertakings (Protection of Employment) Regulations 2006

(SI 2006/246)

Made on February 6, 2006 by the Secretary of State under the European Communities Act 1972 s.2(2) and the Employment Relations Act 1999 s.38. Operative from April 6, 2006

[**Note:** Changes made by the Transfer of Undertakings (Protection of Employment) (Amendment) Regulations 2009 (SI 2009/592) and by the Agency Workers Regulations 2010 (SI 2010/93) have been incorporated into the text.]

1 Citation, commencement and extent

1(1) These Regulations may be cited as the Transfer of Undertakings (Protection of Employment) Regulations 2006.

1(2) These Regulations shall come into force on 6 April 2006.

1(3) These Regulations shall extend to Northern Ireland, except where otherwise provided.

2 Interpretation

2(1) In these Regulations–

"assigned" means assigned other than on a temporary basis;

"collective agreement", **"collective bargaining"** and **"trade union"** have the same meanings respectively as in the 1992 Act;

"contract of employment" means any agreement between an employee and his employer determining the terms and conditions of his employment;

references to **"contractor"** in regulation 3 shall include a sub-contractor;

"employee" means any individual who works for another person whether under a contract of service or apprenticeship or otherwise but does not include anyone who provides services under a contract for services and references to a person's employer shall be construed accordingly;

"insolvency practitioner" has the meaning given to the expression by Part XIII of the Insolvency Act 1986;

references to **"organised grouping of employees"** shall include a single employee;

"recognised" has the meaning given to the expression by section 178(3) of the 1992 Act;

"relevant transfer" means a transfer or a service provision change to which these Regulations apply in accordance with regulation 3 and **"transferor"** and **"transferee"** shall be construed accordingly and in the case of a service provision change falling within regulation 3(1)(b), **"the transferor"** means the person who carried out the activities prior to the service provision change and **"the transferee"** means the person who carries out the activities as a result of the service provision change;

"the 1992 Act" means the Trade Union and Labour Relations (Consolidation) Act 1992;

"the 1996 Act" means the Employment Rights Act 1996;

"the 1996 Tribunals Act" means the Employment Tribunals Act 1996;

"the 1981 Regulations" means the Transfer of Undertakings (Protection of Employment) Regulations 1981.

2(2)   For the purposes of these Regulations the representative of a trade union recognised by an employer is an official or other person authorised to carry on collective bargaining with that employer by that trade union.

2(3)   In the application of these Regulations to Northern Ireland the Regulations shall have effect as set out in Schedule 1.

3   A relevant transfer

3(1)   These Regulations apply to–

(a)   a transfer of an undertaking, business or part of an undertaking or business situated immediately before the transfer in the United Kingdom to another person where there is a transfer of an economic entity which retains its identity;

(b)   a service provision change, that is a situation in which–

(i)   activities cease to be carried out by a person (**"a client"**) on his own behalf and are carried out instead by another person on the client's behalf (**"a contractor"**);

(ii)   activities cease to be carried out by a contractor on a client's behalf (whether or not those activities had previously been carried out by the client on his own behalf) and are carried out instead by another person (**"a subsequent contractor"**) on the client's behalf; or

(iii)   activities cease to be carried out by a contractor or a subsequent contractor on a client's behalf (whether or not those activities had previously been carried out by the client on his own behalf) and are carried out instead by the client on his own behalf,

and in which the conditions set out in paragraph (3) are satisfied.

3(2)   In this regulation **"economic entity"** means an organised grouping of resources which has the objective of pursuing an economic activity, whether or not that activity is central or ancillary.

3(3)   The conditions referred to in paragraph (1)(b) are that–

(a)   immediately before the service provision change–

(i)   there is an organised grouping of employees situated in Great Britain which has as its principal purpose the carrying out of the activities concerned on behalf of the client;

(ii)   the client intends that the activities will, following the service provision change, be carried out by the transferee other than in connection with a single specific event or task of short-term duration; and

(b)   the activities concerned do not consist wholly or mainly of the supply of goods for the client's use.

3(4)   Subject to paragraph (1), these Regulations apply to–

(a)   public and private undertakings engaged in economic activities whether or not they are operating for gain;

(b)   a transfer or service provision change howsoever effected notwithstanding–

(i)   that the transfer of an undertaking, business or part of an undertaking or business is governed or effected by the law of a country or territory outside the United Kingdom or that the service provision change is governed or effected by the law of a country or territory outside Great Britain;

(ii)   that the employment of persons employed in the undertaking, business or part transferred or, in the case of a service provision change, persons employed in the organised grouping of employees, is governed by any such law;

(c)   a transfer of an undertaking, business or part of an undertaking or business (which may also be a service provision change) where persons employed in the undertaking, business or part transferred ordinarily work outside the United Kingdom.

3(5)   An administrative reorganisation of public administrative authorities or the transfer of administrative functions between public administrative authorities is not a relevant transfer.

3(6)   A relevant transfer–

(a)   may be effected by a series of two or more transactions; and

(b)   may take place whether or not any property is transferred to the transferee by the transferor.

3(7)   Where, in consequence (whether directly or indirectly) of the transfer of an undertaking, business or part of an undertaking or business which was situated immediately before the transfer in the United Kingdom, a ship within the meaning of the Merchant Shipping Act 1995 registered in the United Kingdom ceases to be so registered, these Regulations shall not affect the right conferred by section 29 of that Act (right of seamen to be discharged when ship ceases to be registered in the United Kingdom) on a seaman employed in the ship.

4   Effect of relevant transfer on contracts of employment

4(1)   Except where objection is made under paragraph (7), a relevant transfer shall not operate so as to terminate the contract of employment of any person employed by the transferor and assigned to the organised grouping of resources or employees that is subject to the relevant transfer, which would otherwise be terminated by the transfer, but any such contract shall have effect after the transfer as if originally made between the person so employed and the transferee.

4(2)   Without prejudice to paragraph (1), but subject to paragraph (6), and regulations 8 and 15(9), on the completion of a relevant transfer–

(a)   all the transferor's rights, powers, duties and liabilities under or in connection with any such contract shall be transferred by virtue of this regulation to the transferee; and

(b)   any act or omission before the transfer is completed, of or in relation to the transferor in respect of that contract or a person assigned to that organised grouping of resources or employees, shall be deemed to have been an act or omission of or in relation to the transferee.

4(3)   Any reference in paragraph (1) to a person employed by the transferor and assigned to the organised grouping of resources or employees that is subject to a relevant transfer, is a reference to a person so employed immediately before the transfer, or who would have been so employed if he had not been dismissed in the circumstances described in regulation 7(1), including, where the transfer is effected by a series of two or more transactions, a person so employed and assigned or who would have been so employed and assigned immediately before any of those transactions.

4(4)   Subject to regulation 9, in respect of a contract of employment that is, or will be, transferred by paragraph (1), any purported variation of the contract shall be void if the sole or principal reason for the variation is–

(a)   the transfer itself; or

(b)   a reason connected with the transfer that is not an economic, technical or organisational reason entailing changes in the workforce.

4(5)   Paragraph (4) shall not prevent the employer and his employee, whose contract of employment is, or will be, transferred by paragraph (1), from agreeing a variation of that contract if the sole or principal reason for the variation is–

    (a)   a reason connected with the transfer that is an economic, technical or organisational reason entailing changes in the workforce; or

    (b)   a reason unconnected with the transfer.

4(6)   Paragraph (2) shall not transfer or otherwise affect the liability of any person to be prosecuted for, convicted of and sentenced for any offence.

4(7)   Paragraphs (1) and (2) shall not operate to transfer the contract of employment and the rights, powers, duties and liabilities under or in connection with it of an employee who informs the transferor or the transferee that he objects to becoming employed by the transferee.

4(8)   Subject to paragraphs (9) and (11), where an employee so objects, the relevant transfer shall operate so as to terminate his contract of employment with the transferor but he shall not be treated, for any purpose, as having been dismissed by the transferor.

4(9)   Subject to regulation 9, where a relevant transfer involves or would involve a substantial change in working conditions to the material detriment of a person whose contract of employment is or would be transferred under paragraph (1), such an employee may treat the contract of employment as having been terminated, and the employee shall be treated for any purpose as having been dismissed by the employer.

4(10)   No damages shall be payable by an employer as a result of a dismissal falling within paragraph (9) in respect of any failure by the employer to pay wages to an employee in respect of a notice period which the employee has failed to work.

4(11)   Paragraphs (1), (7), (8) and (9) are without prejudice to any right of an employee arising apart from these Regulations to terminate his contract of employment without notice in acceptance of a repudiatory breach of contract by his employer.

5   Effect of relevant transfer on collective agreements

5   Where at the time of a relevant transfer there exists a collective agreement made by or on behalf of the transferor with a trade union recognised by the transferor in respect of any employee whose contract of employment is preserved by regulation 4(1) above, then–

    (a)   without prejudice to sections 179 and 180 of the 1992 Act (collective agreements presumed to be unenforceable in specified circumstances) that agreement, in its application in relation to the employee, shall, after the transfer, have effect as if made by or on behalf of the transferee with that trade union, and accordingly anything done under or in connection with it, in its application in relation to the employee, by or in relation to the transferor before the transfer, shall, after the transfer, be deemed to have been done by or in relation to the transferee; and

    (b)   any order made in respect of that agreement, in its application in relation to the employee, shall, after the transfer, have effect as if the transferee were a party to the agreement.

6   Effect of relevant transfer on trade union recognition

6(1)   This regulation applies where after a relevant transfer the transferred organised grouping of resources or employees maintains an identity distinct from the remainder of the transferee's undertaking.

6(2)   Where before such a transfer an independent trade union is recognised to any extent by the transferor in respect of employees of any description who in consequence of the transfer become employees of the transferee, then, after the transfer–

    (a)   the trade union shall be deemed to have been recognised by the transferee to the same extent in respect of employees of that description so employed; and

    (b)   any agreement for recognition may be varied or rescinded accordingly.

7 Dismissal of employee because of relevant transfer

7(1) Where either before or after a relevant transfer, any employee of the transferor or transferee is dismissed, that employee shall be treated for the purposes of Part X of the 1996 Act (unfair dismissal) as unfairly dismissed if the sole or principal reason for his dismissal is–

   (a) the transfer itself; or

   (b) a reason connected with the transfer that is not an economic, technical or organisational reason entailing changes in the workforce.

7(2) This paragraph applies where the sole or principal reason for the dismissal is a reason connected with the transfer that is an economic, technical or organisational reason entailing changes in the workforce of either the transferor or the transferee before or after a relevant transfer.

7(3) Where paragraph (2) applies–

   (a) paragraph (1) shall not apply;

   (b) without prejudice to the application of section 98(4) of the 1996 Act (test of fair dismissal), the dismissal shall, for the purposes of sections 98(1) and 135 of that Act (reason for dismissal), be regarded as having been for redundancy where section 98(2)(c) of that Act applies, or otherwise for a substantial reason of a kind such as to justify the dismissal of an employee holding the position which that employee held.

7(4) The provisions of this regulation apply irrespective of whether the employee in question is assigned to the organised grouping of resources or employees that is, or will be, transferred.

7(5) Paragraph (1) shall not apply in relation to the dismissal of any employee which was required by reason of the application of section 5 of the Aliens Restriction (Amendment) Act 1919 to his employment.

7(6) Paragraph (1) shall not apply in relation to a dismissal of an employee if the application of section 94 of the 1996 Act to the dismissal of the employee is excluded by or under any provision of the 1996 Act, the 1996 Tribunals Act or the 1992 Act.

8 Insolvency

8(1) If at the time of a relevant transfer the transferor is subject to relevant insolvency proceedings paragraphs (2) to (6) apply.

8(2) In this regulation **"relevant employee"** means an employee of the transferor–

   (a) whose contract of employment transfers to the transferee by virtue of the operation of these Regulations; or

   (b) whose employment with the transferor is terminated before the time of the relevant transfer in the circumstances described in regulation 7(1).

8(3) The relevant statutory scheme specified in paragraph (4)(b) (including that sub-paragraph as applied by paragraph 5 of Schedule 1) shall apply in the case of a relevant employee irrespective of the fact that the qualifying requirement that the employee's employment has been terminated is not met and for those purposes the date of the transfer shall be treated as the date of the termination and the transferor shall be treated as the employer.

8(4) In this regulation the **"relevant statutory schemes"** are–

   (a) Chapter VI of Part XI of the 1996 Act;

   (b) Part XII of the 1996 Act.

8(5) Regulation 4 shall not operate to transfer liability for the sums payable to the relevant employee under the relevant statutory schemes.

8(6) In this regulation **"relevant insolvency proceedings"** means insolvency proceedings which have been opened in relation to the transferor not with a view to the liquidation of the assets of the transferor and which are under the supervision of an insolvency practitioner.

8(7) Regulations 4 and 7 do not apply to any relevant transfer where the transferor is the subject of bankruptcy proceedings or any analogous insolvency proceedings which have been instituted with a view to the liquidation of the assets of the transferor and are under the supervision of an insolvency practitioner.

9 Variations of contract where transferors are subject to relevant insolvency proceedings

9(1) If at the time of a relevant transfer the transferor is subject to relevant insolvency proceedings these Regulations shall not prevent the transferor or transferee (or an insolvency practitioner) and appropriate representatives of assigned employees agreeing to permitted variations.

9(2) For the purposes of this regulation **"appropriate representatives"** are–

- (a) if the employees are of a description in respect of which an independent trade union is recognised by their employer, representatives of the trade union; or

- (b) in any other case, whichever of the following employee representatives the employer chooses–

  - (i) employee representatives appointed or elected by the assigned employees (whether they make the appointment or election alone or with others) otherwise than for the purposes of this regulation, who (having regard to the purposes for, and the method by which they were appointed or elected) have authority from those employees to agree permitted variations to contracts of employment on their behalf;

  - (ii) employee representatives elected by assigned employees (whether they make the appointment or election alone or with others) for these particular purposes, in an election satisfying requirements identical to those contained in regulation 14 except those in regulation 14(1)(d).

9(3) An individual may be an appropriate representative for the purposes of both this regulation and regulation 13 provided that where the representative is not a trade union representative he is either elected by or has authority from assigned employees (within the meaning of this regulation) and affected employees (as described in regulation 13(1)).

9(4) In section 168 of the 1992 Act (time off for carrying out trade union duties) in subsection (1), after paragraph (c) there is inserted–

" , or

- (d) negotiations with a view to entering into an agreement under regulation 9 of the Transfer of Undertakings (Protection of Employment) Regulations 2006 that applies to employees of the employer, or

- (e) the performance on behalf of employees of the employer of functions related to or connected with the making of an agreement under that regulation.".

9(5) Where assigned employees are represented by non-trade union representatives–

- (a) the agreement recording a permitted variation must be in writing and signed by each of the representatives who have made it or, where that is not reasonably practicable, by a duly authorised agent of that representative; and

- (b) the employer must, before the agreement is made available for signature, provide all employees to whom it is intended to apply on the date on which it is to come into effect with copies of the text of the agreement and such guidance as those employees might reasonably require in order to understand it fully.

9(6)   A permitted variation shall take effect as a term or condition of the assigned employee's contract of employment in place, where relevant, of any term or condition which it varies.

9(7)   In this regulation–

"assigned employees" means those employees assigned to the organised grouping of resources or employees that is the subject of a relevant transfer;

"permitted variation" is a variation to the contract of employment of an assigned employee where–

(a)   the sole or principal reason for it is the transfer itself or a reason connected with the transfer that is not an economic, technical or organisational reason entailing changes in the workforce; and

(b)   it is designed to safeguard employment opportunities by ensuring the survival of the undertaking, business or part of the undertaking or business that is the subject of the relevant transfer;

"relevant insolvency proceedings" has the meaning given to the expression by regulation 8(6).

10   Pensions

10(1)   Regulations 4 and 5 shall not apply–

(a)   to so much of a contract of employment or collective agreement as relates to an occupational pension scheme within the meaning of the Pension Schemes Act 1993; or

(b)   to any rights, powers, duties or liabilities under or in connection with any such contract or subsisting by virtue of any such agreement and relating to such a scheme or otherwise arising in connection with that person's employment and relating to such a scheme.

10(2)   For the purposes of paragraphs (1) and (3), any provisions of an occupational pension scheme which do not relate to benefits for old age, invalidity or survivors shall not be treated as being part of the scheme.

10(3)   An employee whose contract of employment is transferred in the circumstances described in regulation 4(1) shall not be entitled to bring a claim against the transferor for–

(a)   breach of contract; or

(b)   constructive unfair dismissal under section 95(1)(c) of the 1996 Act,

arising out of a loss or reduction in his rights under an occupational pension scheme in consequence of the transfer, save insofar as the alleged breach of contract or dismissal (as the case may be) occurred prior to the date on which these Regulations took effect.

11   Notification of employee liability information

11(1)   The transferor shall notify to the transferee the employee liability information of any person employed by him who is assigned to the organised grouping of resources or employees that is the subject of a relevant transfer–

(a)   in writing; or

(b)   by making it available to him in a readily accessible form.

11(2)   In this regulation and in regulation 12 **"employee liability information"** means–

(a)   the identity and age of the employee;

(b)   those particulars of employment that an employer is obliged to give to an employee pursuant to section 1 of the 1996 Act;

(c)   information of any–

(i)   disciplinary procedure taken against an employee;

(ii)   grievance procedure taken by an employee,

within the previous two years, in circumstances where a Code of Practice issued under Part IV of the Trade Union and Labour Relations Act 1992 which relates exclusively or primarily to the resolution of disputes applies;

(d)   information of any court or tribunal case, claim or action–

(i)   brought by an employee against the transferor, within the previous two years;

(ii)   that the transferor has reasonable grounds to believe that an employee may bring against the transferee, arising out of the employee's employment with the transferor; and

(e)   information of any collective agreement which will have effect after the transfer, in its application in relation to the employee, pursuant to regulation 5(a).

History
Regulation 11(2)(c) amended by the Transfer of Undertakings (Protection of Employment) (Amendment) Regulations 2009 (SI 2009/592) reg.2(1), (2) as from April 6, 2009.

11(3)   Employee liability information shall contain information as at a specified date not more than fourteen days before the date on which the information is notified to the transferee.

11(4)   The duty to provide employee liability information in paragraph (1) shall include a duty to provide employee liability information of any person who would have been employed by the transferor and assigned to the organised grouping of resources or employees that is the subject of a relevant transfer immediately before the transfer if he had not been dismissed in the circumstances described in regulation 7(1), including, where the transfer is effected by a series of two or more transactions, a person so employed and assigned or who would have been so employed and assigned immediately before any of those transactions.

11(5)   Following notification of the employee liability information in accordance with this regulation, the transferor shall notify the transferee in writing of any change in the employee liability information.

11(6)   A notification under this regulation shall be given not less than fourteen days before the relevant transfer or, if special circumstances make this not reasonably practicable, as soon as reasonably practicable thereafter.

11(7)   A notification under this regulation may be given–

(a)   in more than one instalment;

(b)   indirectly, through a third party.

12   Remedy for failure to notify employee liability information

12(1)   On or after a relevant transfer, the transferee may present a complaint to an employment tribunal that the transferor has failed to comply with any provision of regulation 11.

12(2)   An employment tribunal shall not consider a complaint under this regulation unless it is presented–

(a)   before the end of the period of three months beginning with the date of the relevant transfer;

(b) within such further period as the tribunal considers reasonable in a case where it is satisfied that it was not reasonably practicable for the complaint to be presented before the end of that period of three months.

12(3)   Where an employment tribunal finds a complaint under paragraph (1) well-founded, the tribunal–

(a) shall make a declaration to that effect; and

(b) may make an award of compensation to be paid by the transferor to the transferee.

12(4)   The amount of the compensation shall be such as the tribunal considers just and equitable in all the circumstances, subject to paragraph (5), having particular regard to–

(a) any loss sustained by the transferee which is attributable to the matters complained of; and

(b) the terms of any contract between the transferor and the transferee relating to the transfer under which the transferor may be liable to pay any sum to the transferee in respect of a failure to notify the transferee of employee liability information.

12(5)   Subject to paragraph (6), the amount of compensation awarded under paragraph (3) shall be not less than £500 per employee in respect of whom the transferor has failed to comply with a provision of regulation 11, unless the tribunal considers it just and equitable, in all the circumstances, to award a lesser sum.

12(6)   In ascertaining the loss referred to in paragraph (4)(a) the tribunal shall apply the same rule concerning the duty of a person to mitigate his loss as applies to any damages recoverable under the common law of England and Wales, Northern Ireland or Scotland, as applicable.

12(7)   Section 18 of the 1996 Tribunals Act (conciliation) shall apply to the right conferred by this regulation and to proceedings under this regulation as it applies to the rights conferred by that Act and the employment tribunal proceedings mentioned in that Act.

13   Duty to inform and consult representatives

13(1)   In this regulation and regulations 14 and 15 references to affected employees, in relation to a relevant transfer, are to any employees of the transferor or the transferee (whether or not assigned to the organised grouping of resources or employees that is the subject of a relevant transfer) who may be affected by the transfer or may be affected by measures taken in connection with it; and references to the employer shall be construed accordingly.

13(2)   Long enough before a relevant transfer to enable the employer of any affected employees to consult the appropriate representatives of any affected employees, the employer shall inform those representatives of–

(a) the fact that the transfer is to take place, the date or proposed date of the transfer and the reasons for it;

(b) the legal, economic and social implications of the transfer for any affected employees;

(c) the measures which he envisages he will, in connection with the transfer, take in relation to any affected employees or, if he envisages that no measures will be so taken, that fact; and

(d) if the employer is the transferor, the measures, in connection with the transfer, which he envisages the transferee will take in relation to any affected employees who will become employees of the transferee after the transfer by virtue of regulation 4 or, if he envisages that no measures will be so taken, that fact.

13(2A)   Where information is to be supplied under paragraph (2) by an employer–

(a) this must include suitable information relating to the use of agency workers (if any) by that employer; and

(b) "suitable information relating to the use of agency workers" means–

(i) the number of agency workers working temporarily for and under the supervision and direction of the employer;

(ii) the parts of the employer's undertaking in which those agency workers are working; and

(iii) the type of work those agency workers are carrying out.

13(3)   For the purposes of this regulation the appropriate representatives of any affected employees are–

(a) if the employees are of a description in respect of which an independent trade union is recognised by their employer, representatives of the trade union; or

(b) in any other case, whichever of the following employee representatives the employer chooses–

(i) employee representatives appointed or elected by the affected employees otherwise than for the purposes of this regulation, who (having regard to the purposes for, and the method by which they were appointed or elected) have authority from those employees to receive information and to be consulted about the transfer on their behalf;

(ii) employee representatives elected by any affected employees, for the purposes of this regulation, in an election satisfying the requirements of regulation 14(1).

13(4)   The transferee shall give the transferor such information at such a time as will enable the transferor to perform the duty imposed on him by virtue of paragraph (2)(d).

13(5)   The information which is to be given to the appropriate representatives shall be given to each of them by being delivered to them, or sent by post to an address notified by them to the employer, or (in the case of representatives of a trade union) sent by post to the trade union at the address of its head or main office.

13(6)   An employer of an affected employee who envisages that he will take measures in relation to an affected employee, in connection with the relevant transfer, shall consult the appropriate representatives of that employee with a view to seeking their agreement to the intended measures.

13(7)   In the course of those consultations the employer shall–

(a) consider any representations made by the appropriate representatives; and

(b) reply to those representations and, if he rejects any of those representations, state his reasons.

13(8)   The employer shall allow the appropriate representatives access to any affected employees and shall afford to those representatives such accommodation and other facilities as may be appropriate.

13(9)   If in any case there are special circumstances which render it not reasonably practicable for an employer to perform a duty imposed on him by any of paragraphs (2) to (7), he shall take all such steps towards performing that duty as are reasonably practicable in the circumstances.

13(10)   Where–

(a) the employer has invited any of the affected employee to elect employee representatives; and

(b) the invitation was issued long enough before the time when the employer is required to give information under paragraph (2) to allow them to elect representatives by that time,

the employer shall be treated as complying with the requirements of this regulation in relation to those employees if he complies with those requirements as soon as is reasonably practicable after the election of the representatives.

13(11)   If, after the employer has invited any affected employees to elect representatives, they fail to do so within a reasonable time, he shall give to any affected employees the information set out in paragraph (2).

13(12) The duties imposed on an employer by this regulation shall apply irrespective of whether the decision resulting in the relevant transfer is taken by the employer or a person controlling the employer.

History

Regulation 13(2A) inserted by the Agency Workers Regulations 2010 (SI 2010/93) reg.2 and Sch.2(2) para.29 as from October 1, 2011.

14   Election of employee representatives

14(1) The requirements for the election of employee representatives under regulation 13(3) are that—

  (a) the employer shall make such arrangements as are reasonably practicable to ensure that the election is fair;

  (b) the employer shall determine the number of representatives to be elected so that there are sufficient representatives to represent the interests of all affected employees having regard to the number and classes of those employees;

  (c) the employer shall determine whether the affected employees should be represented either by representatives of all the affected employees or by representatives of particular classes of those employees;

  (d) before the election the employer shall determine the term of office as employee representatives so that it is of sufficient length to enable information to be given and consultations under regulation 13 to be completed;

  (e) the candidates for election as employee representatives are affected employees on the date of the election;

  (f) no affected employee is unreasonably excluded from standing for election;

  (g) all affected employees on the date of the election are entitled to vote for employee representatives;

  (h) the employees entitled to vote may vote for as many candidates as there are representatives to be elected to represent them or, if there are to be representatives for particular classes of employees, may vote for as many candidates as there are representatives to be elected to represent their particular class of employee;

  (i) the election is conducted so as to secure that—

    (i) so far as is reasonably practicable, those voting do so in secret; and

    (ii) the votes given at the election are accurately counted.

14(2) Where, after an election of employee representatives satisfying the requirements of paragraph (1) has been held, one of those elected ceases to act as an employee representative and as a result any affected employees are no longer represented, those employees shall elect another representative by an election satisfying the requirements of paragraph (1)(a), (e), (f) and (i).

15   Failure to inform or consult

15(1) Where an employer has failed to comply with a requirement of regulation 13 or regulation 14, a complaint may be presented to an employment tribunal on that ground—

  (a) in the case of a failure relating to the election of employee representatives, by any of his employees who are affected employees;

  (b) in the case of any other failure relating to employee representatives, by any of the employee representatives to whom the failure related;

  (c) in the case of failure relating to representatives of a trade union, by the trade union; and

(d)   in any other case, by any of his employees who are affected employees.

15(2)   If on a complaint under paragraph (1) a question arises whether or not it was reasonably practicable for an employer to perform a particular duty or as to what steps he took towards performing it, it shall be for him to show–

(a)   that there were special circumstances which rendered it not reasonably practicable for him to perform the duty; and

(b)   that he took all such steps towards its performance as were reasonably practicable in those circumstances.

15(3)   If on a complaint under paragraph (1) a question arises as to whether or not an employee representative was an appropriate representative for the purposes of regulation 13, it shall be for the employer to show that the employee representative had the necessary authority to represent the affected employees.

15(4)   On a complaint under paragraph (1)(a) it shall be for the employer to show that the requirements in regulation 14 have been satisfied.

15(5)   On a complaint against a transferor that he had failed to perform the duty imposed upon him by virtue of regulation 13(2)(d) or, so far as relating thereto, regulation 13(9), he may not show that it was not reasonably practicable for him to perform the duty in question for the reason that the transferee had failed to give him the requisite information at the requisite time in accordance with regulation 13(4) unless he gives the transferee notice of his intention to show that fact; and the giving of the notice shall make the transferee a party to the proceedings.

15(6)   In relation to any complaint under paragraph (1), a failure on the part of a person controlling (directly or indirectly) the employer to provide information to the employer shall not constitute special circumstances rendering it not reasonably practicable for the employer to comply with such a requirement.

15(7)   Where the tribunal finds a complaint against a transferee under paragraph (1) well-founded it shall make a declaration to that effect and may order the transferee to pay appropriate compensation to such descriptions of affected employees as may be specified in the award.

15(8)   Where the tribunal finds a complaint against a transferor under paragraph (1) well-founded it shall make a declaration to that effect and may–

(a)   order the transferor, subject to paragraph (9), to pay appropriate compensation to such descriptions of affected employees as may be specified in the award; or

(b)   if the complaint is that the transferor did not perform the duty mentioned in paragraph (5) and the transferor (after giving due notice) shows the facts so mentioned, order the transferee to pay appropriate compensation to such descriptions of affected employees as may be specified in the award.

15(9)   The transferee shall be jointly and severally liable with the transferor in respect of compensation payable under sub-paragraph (8)(a) or paragraph (11).

15(10)   An employee may present a complaint to an employment tribunal on the ground that he is an employee of a description to which an order under paragraph (7) or (8) relates and that–

(a)   in respect of an order under paragraph (7), the transferee has failed, wholly or in part, to pay him compensation in pursuance of the order;

(b)   in respect of an order under paragraph (8), the transferor or transferee, as applicable, has failed, wholly or in part, to pay him compensation in pursuance of the order.

15(11)   Where the tribunal finds a complaint under paragraph (10) well-founded it shall order the transferor or transferee as applicable to pay the complainant the amount of compensation which it finds is due to him.

15(12)   An employment tribunal shall not consider a complaint under paragraph (1) or (10) unless it is presented to the tribunal before the end of the period of three months beginning with–

    (a) in respect of a complaint under paragraph (1), the date on which the relevant transfer is completed; or

    (b) in respect of a complaint under paragraph (10), the date of the tribunal's order under paragraph (7) or (8),

or within such further period as the tribunal considers reasonable in a case where it is satisfied that it was not reasonably practicable for the complaint to be presented before the end of the period of three months.

16   Failure to inform or consult: supplemental

16(1)   Section 205(1) of the 1996 Act (complaint to be sole remedy for breach of relevant rights) and section 18 of the 1996 Tribunals Act (conciliation) shall apply to the rights conferred by regulation 15 and to proceedings under this regulation as they apply to the rights conferred by those Acts and the employment tribunal proceedings mentioned in those Acts.

16(2)   An appeal shall lie and shall lie only to the Employment Appeal Tribunal on a question of law arising from any decision of, or arising in any proceedings before, an employment tribunal under or by virtue of these Regulations; and section 11(1) of the Tribunals and Inquiries Act 1992 (appeals from certain tribunals to the High Court) shall not apply in relation to any such proceedings.

16(3)   **"Appropriate compensation"** in regulation 15 means such sum not exceeding thirteen weeks' pay for the employee in question as the tribunal considers just and equitable having regard to the seriousness of the failure of the employer to comply with his duty.

16(4)   Sections 220 to 228 of the 1996 Act shall apply for calculating the amount of a week's pay for any employee for the purposes of paragraph (3) and, for the purposes of that calculation, the calculation date shall be–

    (a) in the case of an employee who is dismissed by reason of redundancy (within the meaning of sections 139 and 155 of the 1996 Act) the date which is the calculation date for the purposes of any entitlement of his to a redundancy payment (within the meaning of those sections) or which would be that calculation date if he were so entitled;

    (b) in the case of an employee who is dismissed for any other reason, the effective date of termination (within the meaning of sections 95(1) and (2) and 97 of the 1996 Act) of his contract of employment;

    (c) in any other case, the date of the relevant transfer.

17   Employers' Liability Compulsory Insurance

17(1)   Paragraph (2) applies where–

    (a) by virtue of section 3(1)(a) or (b) of the Employers' Liability (Compulsory Insurance) Act 1969 (**"the 1969 Act"**), the transferor is not required by that Act to effect any insurance; or

    (b) by virtue of section 3(1)(c) of the 1969 Act, the transferor is exempted from the requirement of that Act to effect insurance.

17(2)   Where this paragraph applies, on completion of a relevant transfer the transferor and the transferee shall be jointly and severally liable in respect of any liability referred to in section 1(1) of the 1969 Act, in so far as such liability relates to the employee's employment with the transferor.

18   Restriction on contracting out

18   Section 203 of the 1996 Act (restrictions on contracting out) shall apply in relation to these Regulations as if they were contained in that Act, save for that section shall not apply in so far as these Regulations provide for an agreement (whether a contract of employment or not) to exclude or limit the operation of these Regulations.

19   Amendment to the 1996 Act

19   In section 104 of the 1996 Act (assertion of statutory right) in subsection (4)–

(a)   the word "and" at the end of paragraph (c) is omitted; and

(b)   after paragraph (d), there is inserted–

", and

(e)   the rights conferred by the Transfer of Undertakings (Protection of Employment) Regulations 2006.".

20   Repeals, revocations and amendments

20(1)   Subject to regulation 21, the 1981 Regulations are revoked.

20(2)   Section 33 of, and paragraph 4 of Schedule 9 to, the Trade Union Reform and Employment Rights Act 1993 are repealed.

20(3)   Schedule 2 (consequential amendments) shall have effect.

21   Transitional provisions and savings

21(1)   These Regulations shall apply in relation to–

(a)   a relevant transfer that takes place on or after 6 April 2006;

(b)   a transfer or service provision change, not falling within sub-paragraph (a), that takes place on or after 6 April 2006 and is regarded by virtue of any enactment as a relevant transfer.

21(2)   The 1981 Regulations shall continue to apply in relation to–

(a)   a relevant transfer (within the meaning of the 1981 Regulations) that took place before 6 April 2006;

(b)   a transfer, not falling within sub-paragraph (a), that took place before 6 April 2006 and is regarded by virtue of any enactment as a relevant transfer (within the meaning of the 1981 Regulations).

21(3)   In respect of a relevant transfer that takes place on or after 6 April 2006, any action taken by a transferor or transferee to discharge a duty that applied to them under regulation 10 or 10A of the 1981 Regulations shall be deemed to satisfy the corresponding obligation imposed by regulations 13 and 14 of these Regulations, insofar as that action would have discharged those obligations had the action taken place on or after 6 April 2006.

21(4)   The duty on a transferor to provide a transferee with employee liability information shall not apply in the case of a relevant transfer that takes place on or before 19 April 2006.

21(5)   Regulations 13, 14, 15 and 16 shall not apply in the case of a service provision change that is not also a transfer of an undertaking, business or part of an undertaking or business that takes place on or before 4 May 2006.

21(6)   The repeal of paragraph 4 of Schedule 9 to the Trade Union Reform and Employment Rights Act 1993 does not affect the continued operation of that paragraph so far as it remains capable of having effect.

SCHEDULE 1

APPLICATION OF THE REGULATION TO NORTHERN IRELAND

[Not reproduced.]

SCHEDULE 2

CONSEQUENTIAL AMENDMENTS

[Not reproduced.]

Banks (Former Authorised Institutions) (Insolvency) Order 2006

(SI 2006/3107)

Made on November 20, 2006 by the Secretary of State under the Insolvency Act 1986 s.422, having consulted the Financial Services Authority in accordance with s.422(1). Operative from December 15, 2006.

1 Citation and commencement

1(1) This Order may be cited as the Banks (Former Authorised Institutions) (Insolvency) Order 2006 and shall come into force on 15th December 2006 (**"the commencement date"**).

1(2) In this Order, **"the 1986 Act"** means the Insolvency Act 1986.

2 Revocation of the Banks (Administration Proceedings) Order 1989

2(1) Subject to paragraph (2), the Banks (Administration Proceedings) Order 1989 (**"the 1989 Order"**) is revoked.

2(2) The 1989 Order shall continue in effect for the purposes of any proceedings begun before the commencement date under the first Group of Parts of the 1986 Act in relation to a former authorised institution within the meaning of Article 1A of that Order.

3 Modification of first Group of Parts of the Insolvency Act 1986 in their application to companies that are former authorised institutions

3(1) This article applies to a person of the kind mentioned in section 422(1) of the 1986 Act that is a company within the meaning of section 735(1) of the Companies Act 1985.

3(2) The first Group of Parts of the 1986 Act shall apply in relation to a person to which this article applies with the modifications set out in the Schedule to this Order.

SCHEDULE

MODIFICATIONS OF PART 2 OF THE INSOLVENCY ACT IN ITS APPLICATION TO COMPANIES THAT ARE FORMER AUTHORISED INSTITUTIONS

Article 3

1 References to a numbered paragraph in this Schedule are references to the paragraph so numbered in Schedule B1 to the Insolvency Act 1984.

2 In their application to a person falling within article 3(1), section 8 of, and Schedule B1 to, the 1986 Act shall apply subject to the modifications set out below.

3 Paragraph 9 shall apply with the omission of sub-paragraph (1).

4 For paragraph 12(1) there is substituted–

"**12.**—(1) An application to the court for an administration order in respect of a company ("an administration application") may be made only by—

　　(a)　the company,

　　(b)　the directors of the company,

　　(c)　one or more creditors of the company,

    (d)   the Financial Services Authority,

    (e)   the designated officer for a magistrates' court in exercise of the power conferred by section 87A of the Magistrates' Courts Act 1980 (c.43) (fine imposed on company), or,

    (f)   a combination of persons listed in paragraphs (a) to (e).

(1A) Where an administration application is made to which the Financial Services Authority is not a party, the applicant shall, as soon as is reasonably practicable after the making of the application give notice of the making of the application to the Financial Services Authority.".

5   For paragraph 22 there is substituted–

"**22.**—(1) Subject as set out in this paragraph–

    (a)   a company may appoint an administrator; and

    (b)   the directors of a company may appoint an administrator.

(2) An administrator may not be appointed under this paragraph without the consent in writing of the Financial Services Authority.

(3) The written consent under paragraph (2) must be filed in court–

    (a)   at the same time that any notice of intention to appoint under paragraph 26 is filed in court pursuant to paragraph 27; or,

    (b)   where no such notice of intention to appoint is required to be given, at the same time that notice of appointment is filed under paragraph 29.".

6   After paragraph 91 there is inserted–

"**91A.** Where the administrator was appointed by administration order, the court may replace the administrator on an application under this paragraph made by the Financial Services Authority.

91B. Where the administrator was appointed otherwise than by administration order any replacement administrator may only be appointed with the consent of the Financial Services Authority.".

7   After paragraph 116 there is inserted—

"Miscellaneous—Powers of the Financial Services Authority

"**117.**—(1) in this paragraph "the Authority" means the Financial Services Authority.

(2) The Authority is entitled to be heard at the hearing of an administration application or at any other court hearing in relation to the company pursuant to any provision of Schedule B1.

(3) Any notice or other document required to be sent to a creditor of the company must also be sent to the Authority.

(4) The Authority may apply to the court under paragraph 74 and in such a case paragraphs 74(1)(a) and 74(1)(b) shall have effect as if the words "harm the interests of the applicant (whether alone or in common with some or all other members or creditors)" there were substituted the words "harm the interests of some or all members or creditors".

(5) A person appointed for the purpose by the Authority is entitled–

    (a)   to attend any meeting of creditors of the company summoned under this Act;

    (b)   to attend any meeting of a committee established under paragraph 57; and

    (c)   to make representations as to any matter for decision at such a meeting."

European Grouping of Territorial Cooperation Regulations 2007

(SI 2007/1949)

Made on July 9, 2007 by the Secretary of State under the European Communities Act 1972. Operative from August 1, 2007.

PART 1

GENERAL

2 Interpretation

2(1) In these Regulations–

"the 1986 Act" means the Insolvency Act 1986;

"the 1989 Order" means the Insolvency (Northern Ireland) Order 1989;

"the EC Regulation" means Regulation (EC) No.1082/2006 of the European Parliament and of the Council on a European grouping of territorial cooperation;

"EGTC" means a European grouping of territorial cooperation formed under the EC Regulation;

"The Insolvency Rules" means in the case of a UK EGTC with its registered office in England and Wales the Insolvency Rules 1986, in the case of a UK EGTC with its registered office in Scotland the Insolvency (Scotland) Rules 1986, or in the case of a UK EGTC with its registered office in Northern Ireland the Insolvency Rules (Northern Ireland) 1991;

"UK EGTC" means an EGTC which has its registered office in the United Kingdom.

PART 2

PROVISIONS RELATING TO ARTICLES 4, 5, 11, 12, 13 AND 14 OF THE EC REGULATION

7 Insolvency and winding up (Article 12(1) of the EC Regulation)

7 A UK EGTC shall be wound up as an unregistered company under Part 5 of the 1986 Act, or in the case of a UK EGTC with a registered office in Northern Ireland, under Part 6 of the 1989 Order, and the provisions of–

(a) that Act (or in the case of Northern Ireland, that Order), and

(b) the Insolvency Rules,

shall apply to that UK EGTC with the modifications set out in Parts 2 and 3 of the Schedule to these Regulations.

SCHEDULE

Regulations 6 and 7

PART 2

MODIFICATIONS TO THE INSOLVENCY ACT 1986 AND THE INSOLVENCY (NORTHERN IRELAND) ORDER 1989

6 Sections 117(2) to (5) (county court jurisdiction), 118 (proceedings taken in the wrong court), 119 (proceedings in county court) and 120(3) and (5) (sheriff court jurisdiction) of the 1986 Act do not apply.

7 In section 221(1) of the 1986 Act and article 185(1) of the 1989 Order (winding up of unregistered companies) after the words "all the provisions" there shall be added the words "of Regulation (EC) No 1082/2006 of the European Parliament and of the Council and".

Part 3

Modifications To The Insolvency Rules

8 Any requirement in the Insolvency Rules to provide the registrar of companies with information in relation to the winding up of an unregistered company, shall not apply where such a company is a UK EGTC.

9 In rule 4.21 of the Insolvency Rules 1986 and rule 4.021 of the Insolvency Rules (Northern Ireland) 1991 (transmission and advertisement of order) the court is required to serve two copies of the winding-up order on the official receiver.

Regulated Covered Bonds Regulations 2008

(SI 2008/346)

Made on February 13, 2008 by the Treasury under the European Communities Act 1972 s.2(2). Operative from March 6, 2008.

[**Note:** Changes made by the Regulated Covered Bonds (Amendment) Regulations 2008 (SI 2008/1714) and the Housing and Regeneration Act 2008 (Consequential Provisions) (No.2) Order 2010 (SI 2010/671) have been incorporated into the text. Note prospective amendments (from January 1, 2013) to be made by SI 2011/2859.]

PART 1

INTRODUCTION

1 Citation, commencement and interpretation

1(1) These Regulations may be cited as the Regulated Covered Bonds Regulations 2008 and come into force on 6th March 2008.

1(2) In these Regulations–

"**the 1986 Act**" means the Insolvency Act 1986;

"**the 2006 Act**" means the Companies Act 2006;

"**the 1989 Order**" means the Insolvency (Northern Ireland) Order 1989;

"**the Act**" means the Financial Services and Markets Act 2000;

"**asset**" means any property, right, entitlement or interest;

"**asset pool**" has the meaning given by regulation 3;

"**covered bond**" means a bond in relation to which the claims attaching to that bond are guaranteed to be paid by an owner from an asset pool it owns;

"**eligible property**" has the meaning given by regulation 2;

"**issuer**" means a person which issues a covered bond;

"**owner**" has the meaning given by regulation 4;

"**programme**" means issues, or series of issues, of covered bonds which have substantially similar terms and are subject to a framework contract or contracts;

"**regulated covered bond**" means a covered bond or a programme of covered bonds, as the case may be, which is admitted to the register of regulated covered bonds;

"**relevant asset pool**" in relation to a regulated covered bond means the asset pool from which the claims attaching to that bond are guaranteed to be paid by the owner of that pool in the event of the failure of the issuer;

"**relevant persons**" has the meaning given by regulation 27(2).

1(3) Unless otherwise defined, any expression used in these Regulations and in Article 22(4) of directive 85/611/EEC of the Council of 20 December 1985 relating to undertakings for collective investment in transferable securities has the same meaning as in that Article of that Directive.

2 Eligible property

2(1) In these Regulations "eligible property" means any interest in–

(a) eligible assets specified in and compliant with the requirements contained in paragraph 68 of Annex VI of the banking consolidation directive, provided that–

    (i) exposures to a body qualifying for credit quality step 2 on the credit quality assessment scale set out in that Annex shall not be eligible property; and

    (ii) senior units, issued by French Fonds Communs de Creances or by equivalent securitisation entities governed by the laws of the United Kingdom or an EEA state, securitising residential real estate or commercial real estate exposures may only be assessed as eligible assets if–

        (aa) the residential real estate or commercial real estate exposures secured were originated or acquired by the issuer or a connected person; and

        (bb) the senior units have a credit assessment by a nominated external credit assessment institution which is the most favourable category of credit assessment made by that external credit assessment institution;

(b) loans to a registered social landlord or, in Northern Ireland, to a registered housing association where the loans are secured–

    (i) over housing accommodation; or

    (ii) by rental income from housing accommodation;

(c) loans to a person ("A") which provides loans directly to a registered social landlord or, in Northern Ireland, to a registered housing association, where the loans to A are secured directly or indirectly–

    (i) over housing accommodation; or

    (ii) by rental income from housing accommodation;

(d) loans to a project company of a project which is a public-private partnership project where the loans are secured by payments made by a public body with step-in rights;

(e) loans to a person ("B") which provides loans directly to a project company of a project which is a public-private partnership project where the loans to B are secured directly or indirectly by payments made by a public body with step-in rights.

2(2) Eligible property (and any relevant security) must be situated in an EEA state, Switzerland, the United States of America, Japan, Canada, Australia, New Zealand, the Channel Islands or the Isle of Man.

2(3) In this regulation–

"the 1996 Act" means the Housing Act 1996;

"the 2001 Act" means the Housing (Scotland) Act 2001;

"housing accommodation"–

(a) in England and Wales, has the meaning given by section 63 of the 1996 Act (minor modifications: Part 1);

(b) in Scotland, has the meaning given by section 111 of the 2001 Act (interpretation); and

(c) in Northern Ireland, has the meaning given by Article 2 of the Housing (Northern Ireland) Order 1981;

"project company" has the meaning given by paragraph 4H of Schedule A1 to the 1986 Act or, in Northern Ireland, paragraph 12 of Schedule A1 to the 1989 Order;

"public body" means a body which exercises public functions;

"public-private partnership project" has the meaning given by paragraph 4I of Schedule A1 to the 1986 Act or, in Northern Ireland, paragraph 13 of Schedule A1 to the 1989 Order;

"registered housing association" means a body registered as a housing association under Chapter II of Part II of the Housing (Northern Ireland) Order 1992;

"registered social landlord"–

(a) in England and Wales, means a private registered provider of social housing or a body registered as a social landlord under Part 1 of the 1996 Act; and

(b) in Scotland, means a body registered as a social landlord under Part 3 of the 2001 Act;

"step-in rights" has the meaning given by paragraph 4J of Schedule A1 to the 1986 Act or, in Northern Ireland, paragraph 14 of Schedule A1 to the 1989 Order.

History
Definition of "registered social landlord" amended by the Housing and Regeneration Act 2008 (Consequential Provisions) (No.2) Order 2010 (SI 2010/671) Sch.1 para.68 as from April 1, 2010.

2(4) Unless otherwise defined, any expression used in this regulation and the banking consolidation directive has the same meaning as in that directive.

3 Asset Pool

3(1) Subject to paragraph (2), in these Regulations an "asset pool" comprises the following assets–

(a) sums derived from the issue of regulated covered bonds and lent to the owner in accordance with regulation 16;

(b) eligible property which is acquired by the owner using sums lent to it in accordance with regulation 22;

(c) eligible property transferred to the asset pool by the issuer or a connected person to enable the issuer or owner, as the case may be, to comply with–

    (i) the requirements specified in regulation 17(2);

    (ii) a direction of the Authority under regulation 30; or

    (iii) an order of the court under regulation 33;

(d) eligible property transferred to the asset pool by the issuer or a connected person for the purpose of over collateralisation;

(e) contracts relating to the asset pool or to a regulated covered bond;

(f) eligible property acquired by the owner using sums derived from any of the assets referred to in sub-paragraph (b), (c), (d) or (e);

(g) sums derived from any of the assets referred to in sub-paragraph (b), (c), (d), (e) or (f); and

(h) sums lent by persons (other than the issuer) to the owner to enable it to comply with the requirements specified in regulation 24(1)(a).

3(2) Any of the assets referred to in sub-paragraphs (a) to (f) and (h) of paragraph (1) may only form part of an asset pool at any time if they are recorded at that time, pursuant to arrangements made in accordance with regulation 17, 23 or 24, as being in that pool.

3(3) In paragraph (1), "over collateralisation" means the provision of additional assets that assist the payment from the relevant asset pool of claims attaching to a regulated covered bond in the event of the failure of the issuer.

4 Owner

4 In these Regulations "owner" means a person which–

(a) owns an asset pool; and

(b) issues a guarantee to pay from that asset pool claims attaching to a regulated covered bond in the event of a failure of the issuer of that bond.

PART 6

PRIORITY OF PAYMENT

27 Priority in a winding up

27(1) Subject to–

(a) section 115 of the 1986 Act (expenses of voluntary winding up) or, in Northern Ireland, article 100 of the 1989 Order (expenses of voluntary winding up); and

(b) the priority of the expenses of the winding up in a compulsory liquidation; where an owner is wound up, the claims of relevant persons shall be paid from the relevant asset pool in priority to all other creditors.

27(2) "Relevant persons" are–

(a) regulated covered bond holders;

(b) persons providing services for the benefit of those bond holders;

(c) the counter-parties to hedging instruments which are incidental to the maintenance and administration of the asset pool or to the terms of the regulated covered bond; and

(d) persons (other than the issuer) providing a loan to the owner to enable it to satisfy the claims of the persons mentioned in sub-paragraph (a), (b) or (c).

27(3) The claims of the persons mentioned in paragraph (2)(b), (c) and (d) may rank equally with, but not in priority to, the claims of the persons mentioned in paragraph (2)(a).

28 Realisation of a charge

28(1) Subject to regulation 29, if–

(a) any asset comprised in the asset pool is charged as security for claims in priority to any charge over that asset granted to secure the claims of relevant persons; and

(b) the charge which has priority is realised at any time when the owner is not in the course of being wound up;

the proceeds of the realisation of that charge must, after payment of the expenses referred to in regulation 29 and any other expenses relating to that charge, be first applied to satisfy the claims of relevant persons at such time as those claims fall due for payment.

28(2) Subject to regulation 29, if–

(a) any asset comprised in the asset pool is charged as security for several claims;

(b) any agreement between the creditors of that charge gives priority to the claims of any person above the claims of the relevant persons; and

(c) that charge is realised at any time when the owner is not in the course of being wound up;

the proceeds of the realisation of that charge must, after payment of the expenses referred to in regulation 29 and any other expenses relating to that charge, be first applied to satisfy the claims of the relevant persons at such time as those claims fall due for payment.

28(3) For the purposes of paragraphs (1) and (2) the claims of the persons mentioned in regulation 27(2)(b), (c) and (d) may rank equally with, but not in priority to, the claims of the persons mentioned in regulation 27(2)(a).

History
Regulation 28(3) inserted by the Regulated Covered Bonds (Amendment) Regulations 2008 (SI 2008/1714) reg.2(1), (5) as from July 22, 2008.

29 Expenses

29(1) Disbursements made by a liquidator, provisional liquidator, administrator, administrative receiver, receiver or manager of the owner in respect of costs which–

(a) are incurred after the commencement of any winding up, administration, administrative receivership or receivership; and

(b) relate to any of the persons mentioned in paragraph (2);

shall be expenses of the winding up, administration, administrative receivership or receivership, as the case may be, and shall rank equally among themselves in priority to all other expenses.

29(2) The persons referred to in paragraph (1)(b) are–

(a) persons providing services for the benefit of regulated covered bond holders;

(b) the counter-parties to hedging instruments which are incidental to the maintenance and administration of the asset pool or to the terms of the regulated covered bonds; and

(c) persons (other than the issuer) providing a loan to the owner to enable it to meet the claims of regulated covered bond holders or pay costs which relate to persons falling within sub-paragraph (a) or (b).

History
Regulation 29 substituted by the Regulated Covered Bonds (Amendment) Regulations 2008 (SI 2008/1714) reg.2(1), (6) as from July 22, 2008.

PART 9

MISCELLANEOUS

46 Modifications of primary and secondary legislation

46 The Schedule (which modifies primary and secondary legislation) has effect.

Regulation 46

MODIFICATIONS TO PRIMARY AND SECONDARY LEGISLATION

PART 1

PRIMARY LEGISLATION

1   Modification of the Companies Act 1985

1   Section 196 (payment of debts out of assets subject to floating charge (England and Wales)) of the Companies Act 1985 shall not apply to an owner.

2   Modifications of the 1986 Act

2(1)   Sections 40 (payment of debts out of assets subject to floating charge) and 43 (power to dispose of charged property) of the 1986 Act shall not apply to an owner.

2(2)   Section 107 of the 1986 Act (distribution of company's property) shall apply only after payment has been made of the claims of relevant persons.

2(3)   Section 156 of the 1986 Act (payment of expenses of winding up) shall apply only after payment has been made of the expenses referred to in regulation 29.

2(4)   Section 175 (preferential debts (general provision)) and 176A (share of assets for unsecured creditors) of the 1986 Act shall not apply to an owner.

2(5)   Paragraphs 65(1) and 66 of Schedule B1 (distributions) to the 1986 Act shall apply only after payment has been made of the claims of relevant persons.

6   Modification of the 2006 Act

6   Where an owner is wound up, section 754 of the 2006 Act (priorities where debentures secured by floating charge) shall apply only after payment has been made of the claims of relevant persons.

PART 2

SECONDARY LEGISLATION

7   Modifications of the Insolvency Rules 1986

7(1)   Rule 4.181(1) of the Insolvency Rules 1986 (debts of insolvent company to rank equally) shall apply only after payment has been made of the claims of relevant persons.

7(2)   Rules 2.67, 4.218 and 4.219 of the Insolvency Rules 1986 (priority of expenses) shall apply to an owner subject to the provisions of regulation 29.

8   Modification to the Insolvency (Scotland) Rules 1986

8   Rules 2.39B (expenses of the administration) and 4.67 (order of priority of expenses of liquidation) of the Insolvency (Scotland) Rules 19862 shall apply to an owner subject to the provisions of regulation 29.

History
Paragraph 8 substituted by the Regulated Covered Bonds (Amendment) Regulations 2008 (SI 2008/1714) reg.2(1), (7) as from July 22, 2008.

11   Modification of the Cross-Border Insolvency Regulations 2006

11   The Cross-Border Insolvency Regulations 2006 shall not apply to an owner.

Non-Domestic Rating (Unoccupied Property) (England) Regulations 2008

(SI 2008/386)

Made on February 18, 2008 by the Secretary of State under the Local Government Finance Act 1988 ss.45(1)(d), (9) and (10), 143(2) and 146(6). Effective April 1, 2008.

[**Note**: Changes made by the Non-Domestic Rating (Unoccupied Property) (England) (Amendment) Regulations 2010 (SI 2010/408) have been incorporated into the text.]

1 Citation, application and commencement

1 These Regulations, which apply in relation to England only, may be cited as the Non-Domestic Rating (Unoccupied Property) (England) Regulations 2008 and shall come into force on 1st April 2008.

2 Interpretation

2 In these Regulations–

"qualifying industrial hereditament" means any hereditament other than a retail hereditament in relation to which all buildings comprised in the hereditament are–

(a) constructed or adapted for use in the course of a trade or business; and

(b) constructed or adapted for use for one or more of the following purposes, or one or more such purposes and one or more purposes ancillary thereto–

    (i) the manufacture, repair or adaptation of goods or materials, or the subjection of goods or materials to any process;

    (ii) storage (including the storage or handling of goods in the course of their distribution);

    (iii) the working or processing of minerals; and

    (iv) the generation of electricity;

"relevant non-domestic hereditament" means any non-domestic hereditament consisting of, or of part of, any building, together with any land ordinarily used or intended for use for the purposes of the building or part;

"retail hereditament" means any hereditament where any building or part of a building comprised in the hereditament is constructed or adapted for the purpose of the retail provision of–

(a) goods, or

(b) services, other than storage for distribution services, where the services are to be provided on or from the hereditament; and

"the Act" means the Local Government Finance Act 1988.

3 Hereditaments prescribed for the purposes of section 45(1)(d) of the Act

3 The class of non-domestic hereditaments prescribed for the purposes of section 45(1)(d) of the Act consists of all relevant non-domestic hereditaments other than those described in regulation 4.

4   Hereditaments not prescribed for the purposes of section 45(1)(d) of the Act

4   The relevant non-domestic hereditaments described in this regulation are any hereditament–

(a)   which, subject to regulation 5, has been unoccupied for a continuous period not exceeding three months;

(b)   which is a qualifying industrial hereditament that, subject to regulation 5, has been unoccupied for a continuous period not exceeding six months;

(c)   whose owner is prohibited by law from occupying it or allowing it to be occupied;

(d)   which is kept vacant by reason of action taken by or on behalf of the Crown or any local or public authority with a view to prohibiting the occupation of the hereditament or to acquiring it;

(e)   which is the subject of a building preservation notice within the meaning of the Planning (Listed Buildings and Conservation Areas) Act 1990 or is included in a list compiled under section 1 of that Act;

(f)   which is included in the Schedule of monuments compiled under section 1 of the Ancient Monuments and Archaeological Areas Act 1979;

(g)   whose rateable value is less than £2,600 [but see note below];

(h)   whose owner is entitled to possession only in his capacity as the personal representative of a deceased person;

(i)   where, in respect of the owner's estate, there subsists a bankruptcy order within the meaning of section 381(2) of the Insolvency Act 1986;

(j)   whose owner is entitled to possession of the hereditament in his capacity as trustee under a deed of arrangement to which the Deeds of Arrangement Act 1914 applies;

(k)   whose owner is a company which is subject to a winding-up order made under the Insolvency Act 1986 or which is being wound up voluntarily under that Act;

(l)   whose owner is a company in administration within the meaning of paragraph 1 of Schedule B1 to the Insolvency Act 1986 or is subject to an administration order made under the former administration provisions within the meaning of article 3 of the Enterprise Act 2002 (Commencement No. 4 and Transitional Provisions and Savings) Order 2003;

(m)   whose owner is entitled to possession of the hereditament in his capacity as liquidator by virtue of an order made under section 112 or section 145 of the Insolvency Act 1986.

History
Regulation 4(g) amended by the Non-Domestic Rating (Unoccupied Property) (England) (Amendment) Regulations 2010 (SI 2010/408) reg.2(2)(a) as from April 1, 2010. Note however that in relation to the financial year beginning on April 1, 2010 the figure "£18,000" is substituted for "£2,600" (reg.2(2)(b)).

5   Continuous occupation

5   A hereditament which has been unoccupied and becomes occupied on any day shall be treated as having been continuously unoccupied for the purposes of regulation 4(a) and (b) if it becomes unoccupied again on the expiration of a period of less than six weeks beginning with that day.

6   Hereditaments not previously occupied

6   For the purposes of regulation 4(a) and (b), a hereditament which has not previously been occupied shall be treated as becoming unoccupied–

(a)   on the day determined under paragraph 8 of Schedule 1 to the General Rate Act 1967, or on the day determined under Schedule 4A to the Act, whichever day first occurs; or

    (b)   where paragraph (a) does not apply, on the day for which the hereditament is first shown in a local rating list.

7   Revocation and saving

7(1)   Subject to paragraph (2), the Non-Domestic Rating (Unoccupied Property) Regulations 1989 are revoked in their application to England.

7(2)   Those Regulations shall continue to apply for the purposes of calculating liability for rates in respect of financial years beginning before 1st April 2008.

Non-Domestic Rating (Unoccupied Property) (Scotland) (Amendment) Regulations 2008

(SSI 2008/83)

Made on March 4, 2008 by the Scottish Ministers under the Local Government (Scotland) Act 1966, ss.24(2) and 24A(4). Effective April 1, 2008.

1 Citation and commencement

1 These Regulations may be cited as the Non-Domestic Rating (Unoccupied Property) (Scotland) Amendment Regulations 2008 and come into force on 1st April 2008.

2 Amendment of Regulations

2 In Part 1 of the Schedule to the Non-Domestic Rating (Unoccupied Property) (Scotland) Regulations 1994, insert–

(a) in paragraph (e) after "company", "or limited liability partnership"; and

(b) after paragraph (e)–

"(f) the owner of the lands and heritages is a company or limited liability partnership, which on or after 1st April 2008–

(i) remains subject to an administration order made under Part II of the Insolvency Act 1986; or

(ii) is in administration (within the meaning of paragraph 1 of Schedule B1 to that Act)."

Companies (Trading Disclosures) Regulations 2008

(SI 2008/495)

Made on February 23, 2008 by the Secretary of State in exercise of the powers conferred by ss.82, 84, 1292(1)(a) and 1294 of the Companies Act 2006. Operative from October 1, 2008

[**Note**: Changes made by the Companies (Trading Disclosures) (Amendment) Regulations 2009 (SI 2009/218) have been incorporated into the text.]

3 Requirement to display registered name at registered office and inspection place

3(1) A company shall display its registered name at–

(a) its registered office; and

(b) any inspection place.

3(2) But paragraph (1) does not apply to any company which has at all times since its incorporation been dormant.

3(3) Paragraph (1) shall also not apply to the registered office or an inspection place of a company where–

(a) in respect of that company, a liquidator, administrator or administrative receiver has been appointed; and

(b) the registered office or inspection place is also a place of business of that liquidator, administrator or administrative receiver.

History
Regulation 3(3) inserted by the Companies (Trading Disclosures) (Amendment) Regulations 2009 (SI 2009/218) reg.2 as from October 1, 2009.

4 Requirement to display registered name at other business locations

4(1) This regulation applies to a location other than a company's registered office or any inspection place.

4(2) A company shall display its registered name at any such location at which it carries on business.

4(3) But paragraph (2) shall not apply to a location which is primarily used for living accommodation.

4(4) Paragraph (2) shall also not apply to any location at which business is carried on by a company where–

(a) in respect of that company, a liquidator, administrator or administrative receiver has been appointed; and

(b) the location is also a place of business of that liquidator, administrator or administrative receiver.

4(5) Paragraph (2) shall also not apply to any location at which business is carried on by a company of which every director who is an individual is a relevant director.

4(6)   In this regulation–

   (a)   "administrative receiver" has the meaning given—

      (i)   in England and Wales or Scotland, by section 251 of the Insolvency Act 1986, and

      (ii)   in Northern Ireland, by Article 5 of the Insolvency (Northern Ireland) Order 1989;

   (b)   "credit reference agency" has the meaning given in section 243(7) of the Act;

   (c)   "protected information" has the meaning given in section 240 of the Act; and

   (d)   "relevant director" means an individual in respect of whom the registrar is required by regulations made pursuant to section 243(4) of the Act to refrain from disclosing protected information to a credit reference agency.

History
Regulation 4(4)–(6) inserted by the Companies (Trading Disclosures) (Amendment) Regulations 2009 (SI 2009/218) reg.3 as from October 1, 2009.

Civil Proceedings Fees Order 2008

(SI 2008/1053 (L. 5))

Made on 7 April 2008 by the Lord Chancellor, with the consent and sanction of the Treasury under the Courts Act 2003 s.92 and the Insolvency Act 1986 ss.414 and 415. Operative from 1 May 2008.

[**Note**: Changes made by the Civil Proceedings Fees (Amendment) Order 2008 (SI 2008/2853 (L.19)), the Civil Proceedings Fees (Amendment) Order 2009 (SI 2009/1498 (L. 15)) and by Civil Proceedings Fees (Amendment) Order 2011 (SI 2011/586 (L. 2)) have been incorporated into the text.]

1 Citation and commencement

1(1) This Order may be cited as the Civil Proceedings Fees Order 2008 and shall come into force on 1st May 2008.

1(2) In this Order–

(a) "**CCBC**" means County Court Bulk Centre;

(b) "**the CPR**" means the Civil Procedure Rules 1998;

(c) "**LSC**" means the Legal Services Commission established under section 1 of the Access to Justice Act 1999;

(d) expressions also used in the CPR have the same meaning as in those Rules.

2 Fees payable

2 The fees set out in column 2 of Schedule 1 are payable in the Supreme Court and in county courts in respect of the items described in column 1 in accordance with and subject to the directions specified in that column.

SCHEDULE 1

Article 2

FEES TO BE TAKEN

Column 1	Column 2
Number and description of fee	Amount of fee
3 Companies Act 1985, Companies Act 2006 and Insolvency Act 1986 (High Court and county court)	
3.1 On entering a bankruptcy petition–	
(a) if presented by a debtor or the personal representative of a deceased debtor;	£175
(b) if presented by a creditor or other person.	£220
3.2 On entering a petition for an administration order.	£175

Column 1	Column 2
Number and description of fee	Amount of fee
3.3 On entering any other petition.	£220
One fee only is payable where more than one petition is presented in relation to a partnership.	
3.4(a) On a request for a certificate of discharge from bankruptcy;	£70
3.4(b) after the first certificate, for each copy.	£5
3.5 On an application under the Companies Act 1985, the Companies Act 2006 or the Insolvency Act 1986 other than one brought by petition and where no other fee is specified.	£155
Fee 3.5 is not payable where the application is made in existing proceedings.	
3.6 On an application for the conversion of a voluntary arrangement into a winding up or bankruptcy under Article 37 of Council Regulation (EC) No 1346/2000.	£155
3.7 On an application, for the purposes of Council Regulation (EC) No 1346/2000, for an order confirming creditors' voluntary winding up (where the company has passed a resolution for voluntary winding up, and no declaration under section 89 of the Insolvency Act 1986 has been made).	£35
3.8 On filing–	
• a notice of intention to appoint an administrator under paragraph 14 of Schedule B1 to the Insolvency Act 1986 or in accordance with paragraph 27 of that Schedule; or	£35
• a notice of appointment of an administrator in accordance with paragraphs 18 or 29 of that Schedule.	
Where a person pays fee 3.8 on filing a notice of intention to appoint an administrator, no fee is payable on that same person filing a notice of appointment of that administrator.	
3.9 On submitting a nominee's report under section 2(2) of the Insolvency Act 1986.	£35
3.10 On filing documents in accordance with paragraph 7(1) of Schedule A1 to the Insolvency Act 1986.	£35

Column 1	Column 2
Number and description of fee	Amount of fee
3.11 On an application by consent or without notice within existing proceedings where no other fee is specified.	£35
3.12 On an application with notice within existing proceedings where no other fee is specified.	£70
3.13 On a search in person of the bankruptcy and companies records, in a county court.	£45
Requests and applications with no fee	
No fee is payable on a request or on an application to the Court by the Official Receiver when applying only in the capacity of Official Receiver to the case (and not as trustee or liquidator), or on an application to set aside a statutory demand.	
7 Enforcement in the High Court	
7.1. On sealing a writ of execution/possession/ delivery.	£60
Where the recovery of a sum of money is sought in addition to a writ of possession and delivery, no further fee is payable.	
7.2 On an application for an order requiring a judgment debtor or other person to attend court to provide information in connection with enforcement of a judgment or order.	£50
7.3(a) On an application for a third party debt order or the appointment of a receiver by way of equitable execution.	£100
7.3(b) On an application for a charging order.	£100
Fee 7.3(a) is payable in respect of each third party against whom the order is sought.	
Fee 7.3(b) is payable in respect of each charging order applied for.	
7.4 On an application for a judgment summons.	£100
7.5 On a request or application to register a judgment or order or for permission to enforce an arbitration award, or for a certificate or a certified copy of a judgment or order for use abroad.	£60

Column 1	Column 2
Number and description of fee	Amount of fee
8 Enforcement in the county court	
8.1 On an application for or in relation to enforcement of a judgment or order of a county court or through a county court, by the issue of a warrant of execution against goods except a warrant to enforce payment of a fine:	
(a) in cases other than CCBC cases;	£100
(b) in CCBC cases.	£70
8.2 On a request for a further attempt at execution of a warrant at a new address following a notice of the reason for non-execution (except a further attempt following suspension and CCBC cases brought by Centre users).	£30
8.3 On an application for an order requiring a judgment debtor or other person to attend court to provide information in connection with enforcement of a judgment or order.	£50
8.4(a) On an application for a third party debt order or the appointment of a receiver by way of equitable execution.	£100
(b) On an application for a charging order.	£100
Fee 8.4(a) is payable in respect of each third party against whom the order is sought.	
Fee 8.4(b) is payable in respect of each charging order applied for.	
8.5 On an application for a judgment summons.	£100
8.6 On the issue of a warrant of possession or a warrant of delivery.	£110
Where the recovery of a sum of money is sought in addition, no further fee is payable.	
8.7 On an application for an attachment of earnings order (other than a consolidated attachment of earnings order) to secure payment of a judgment debt.	£100
Fee 8.7 is payable for each defendant against whom an order is sought.	
Fee 8.7 is not payable where the attachment of earnings order is made on the hearing of a judgment summons.	

Column 1	*Column 2*
Number and description of fee	Amount of fee
8.8 On a consolidated attachment of earnings order or on an administration order.	For every £1 or part of a £1 of the money paid into court in respect of debts due to creditors—10p
Fee 8.8 is calculated on any money paid into court under any order at the rate in force at the time when the order was made (or, where the order has been amended, at the time of the last amendment before the date of payment).	
FEES PAYABLE IN HIGH COURT ONLY	
10 Miscellaneous proceedings or matters	
Searches	
10.3 On a search in person of the bankruptcy and companies records, including inspection, for each 15 minutes or part of 15 minutes.	£7

History

Amendments made in respect of fees 7.3(b), 8.1 and 8.4(b) by the Civil Proceedings Fees (Amendment) Order 2008 (SI 2008/2853 (L. 19)) arts 2–5, as from November 26, 2008. Amendments made in respect of fees 8.1, 8.3–8.5, 8.7 by the Civil Proceedings Fees (Amendment) Order 2009 (SI 2009/1498 (L. 15)) art.11–16 as from July 13, 2009. Amendments made in respect of fees 3.1–3.13, 7.1, 7.5, 8.2, 8.6, 10.3 by the Civil Proceedings Fees (Amendment) Order 2011 (SI 2011/586 (L. 2)) Sch. as from April 4, 2011.

Non-Domestic Rating (Unoccupied Property) (Wales) Regulations 2008

SI 2008/2499 (W 217)

Made on September 20, 2008 by the Welsh Ministers in exercise of the powers conferred on the Secretary of State by the Local Government Finance Act 1988 and now vested in them. Effective November 1, 2008.

[**Note**: changes made by the Non-Domestic Rating (Unoccupied Property) (Wales) (Amendment) Regulations 2009 (SI 2009/272) and Non-Domestic Rating (Unoccupied Property) (Wales) (Amendment) Regulations 2011 (SI 2011/197) have been incorporated into the text.]

1 Title, application and commencement

1(1) The title of these Regulations is The Non-Domestic Rating (Unoccupied Property) (Wales) Regulations 2008 and they come into force on 1 November 2008.

1(2) These Regulations apply in relation to Wales.

2 Interpretation

2 In these Regulations–

"the Act" ("*y Ddeddf*") means the Local Government Finance Act 1988;

"qualifying industrial hereditament" ("*hereditament diwydiannol cymwys*") means any hereditament, other than a retail hereditament, in relation to which all buildings comprised in the hereditament are–

(a) constructed or adapted for use in the course of a trade or business; and

(b) constructed or adapted for use for one or more of the following purposes, or one or more such purposes and one or more purposes ancillary thereto–

    (i) the manufacture, repair or adaptation of goods or materials, or the subjection of goods or materials to any process;

    (ii) storage (including the storage or handling of goods in the course of their distribution);

    (iii) the working or processing of minerals; and

    (iv) the generation of electricity;

"relevant non-domestic hereditament" ("*hereditament annomestig perthnasol*") means any non-domestic hereditament consisting of, or of part of, any building, together with any land ordinarily used or intended for use for the purposes of the building or part; and

"retail hereditament" ("*hereditament masnachol*") means any hereditament where any building or part of a building comprised in the hereditament is constructed or adapted for the purpose of the retail provision of–

(a) goods, or

(b) services, other than storage for distribution services, where the services are to be provided on or from the hereditament.

3 Hereditaments prescribed for the purposes of section 45(1)(d) of the Act

3 The class of non-domestic hereditaments prescribed for the purposes of section 45(1)(d) of the Act consists of all relevant non-domestic hereditaments other than those described in regulation 4.

4   Hereditaments not prescribed for the purposes of section 45(1)(d) of the Act

4   The relevant non-domestic hereditaments described in this regulation are any hereditament–

(a)   the whole of which, subject to regulation 5, has been unoccupied for a continuous period not exceeding three months;

(b)   which is a qualifying industrial hereditament and the whole of which, subject to regulation 5, has been unoccupied for a continuous period not exceeding six months;

(c)   whose owner is prohibited by law from occupying it or allowing it to be occupied;

(d)   which is kept vacant by reason of action taken by or on behalf of the Crown or any local or public authority with a view to prohibiting the occupation of the hereditament or to acquiring it;

(e)   which is the subject of a building preservation notice within the meaning of the Planning (Listed Buildings and Conservation Areas) Act 1990 or is included in a list compiled under section 1 of that Act;

(f)   which is included in the Schedule of monuments compiled under section 1 of the Ancient Monuments and Archaeological Areas Act 1979;

(g)   whose rateable value is less than £2,600;

(h)   whose owner is entitled to possession only in his or her capacity as the personal representative of a deceased person;

(i)   where, in respect of the owner's estate, there subsists a bankruptcy order within the meaning of section 381(2) of the Insolvency Act 1986;

(j)   whose owner is entitled to possession in his or her capacity as trustee under a deed of arrangement to which the Deeds of Arrangement Act 1914 applies;

(k)   whose owner is a company which is subject to a winding-up order made under the Insolvency Act 1986 or which is being wound up voluntarily under that Act;

(l)   whose owner is a company in administration within the meaning of paragraph 1 of Schedule B1 to the Insolvency Act 1986 or is subject to an administration order made under the former administration provisions within the meaning of article 3 of the Enterprise Act 2002 (Commencement No. 4 and Transitional Provisions and Savings) Order 2003;

(m)   whose owner is entitled to possession in his or her capacity as liquidator by virtue of an order made under section 112 or section 145 of the Insolvency Act 1986.

History
Regulation 4(g) amended (in relation to the financial year beginning with April 1, 2010) by the Non-Domestic Rating (Unoccupied Property) (Wales) (Amendment) Regulations 2009 (SI 2009/272 (W 27)) reg.2 as from March 7, 2009. The figure "£2,600" substituted for £18,000" by the Non-Domestic Rating (Unoccupied Property) (Wales) (Amendment) Regulations 2011 (SI 2011/197) reg.2 as from April 1, 2011.

5   Continuous occupation

5   A hereditament which has been unoccupied and becomes occupied on any day is to be treated as having been continuously unoccupied for the purposes of regulation 4(a) and (b) if it becomes unoccupied again on the expiration of a period of less than six weeks beginning with that day.

6   Hereditaments not previously occupied

6   For the purposes of regulation 4(a) and (b), a hereditament which has not previously been occupied is to be treated as becoming unoccupied–

(a) on the day determined under paragraph 8 of Schedule 1 to the General Rate Act 1967, or on the day determined under Schedule 4A to the Act, whichever day first occurs; or

(b) where paragraph (a) does not apply, on the day for which the hereditament is first shown in a local rating list.

7 Revocation and saving

7(1) Subject to paragraph (2), the Non-Domestic Rating (Unoccupied Property) Regulations 1989 are revoked in their application to Wales.

7(2) Those Regulations continue to apply for the purposes of calculating liability for rates in respect of any day before 1 November 2008.

Overseas Companies Regulations 2009

(SI 2009/1801)

Made on July 8, 2009 by the Secretary of State in exercise of the powers conferred by various sections of the Companies Act 2006. Operative from October 1, 2009.

PART 8

RETURNS IN CASE OF WINDING UP ETC

68 Application of Part

68   This Part applies to an overseas company that has one or more UK establishments.

69 Return in case of winding up

69(1)   Where a company to which this Part applies is being wound up, it must deliver to the registrar a return containing the following particulars–

(a)   the company's name;

(b)   whether the company is being wound up by an order of a court and if so, the name and address of the court and the date of the order;

(c)   if the company is not being so wound up, as a result of what action the winding up has commenced;

(d)   whether the winding up has been instigated by–

    (i)   the company's members,

    (ii)   the company's creditors, or

    (iii)   some other person (stating the person's identity); and

(e)   the date on which the winding up became or will become effective.

69(2)   The return must be delivered not later than–

(a)   if the winding up began before the company had a UK establishment, one month after the company first opens a UK establishment;

(b)   if the winding up begins when the company has a UK establishment, 14 days after the date on which the winding up begins.

69(3)   Where the company has more than one UK establishment the obligation to deliver a return under this regulation applies in respect of each of them, but a return giving the registered numbers of more than one UK establishment is regarded as a return in respect of each establishment whose number is given.

69(4)   No return is required under this regulation in respect of winding up under the Insolvency Act 1986 or the Insolvency (Northern Ireland) Order 1989.

70 Returns to be made by liquidator

70(1)   A person appointed to be the liquidator of a company to which this Part applies must deliver to the registrar a return containing the following particulars–

(a)   their name and address,

(b)   date of the appointment, and

(c)   a description of such of the person's powers, if any, as are derived otherwise than from the general law or the company's constitution.

70(2)   The period allowed for delivery of the return required by paragraph (1) is–

(a)   if the liquidator was appointed before the company had a UK establishment (and continues in office at the date of the opening), one month after the company first opens a UK establishment;

(b)   if the liquidator is appointed when the company has a UK establishment, 14 days after the date of the appointment.

70(3)   The liquidator of a company to which this Part applies must–

(a)   on the termination of the winding up of the company, deliver a return to the registrar stating the name of the company and the date on which the winding up terminated;

(b)   on the company ceasing to be registered in circumstances where ceasing to be registered is an event of legal significance, deliver a return to the registrar stating the name of the company and the date on which it ceased to be registered.

70(4)   The period allowed for delivery of the return required by paragraph (3)(a) or (b) is 14 days from the date of the event.

70(5)   Where the company has more than one UK establishment the obligation to deliver a return under this regulation applies in respect of each of them, but a return giving the registered numbers of more than one UK establishment is regarded as a return in respect of each establishment whose number is given.

70(6)   No return is required under this regulation in respect of a liquidator appointed under the Insolvency Act 1986 or the Insolvency (Northern Ireland) Order 1989.

71   Return in case of insolvency proceedings etc (other than winding up)

71(1)   Where a company to which this Part applies becomes subject to insolvency proceedings or an arrangement or composition or any analogous proceedings (other than proceedings for winding up of the company), it must deliver to the registrar a return containing the following particulars–

(a)   the company's name;

(b)   whether the proceedings are by an order of a court and if so, the name and address of the court and the date of the order;

(c)   if the proceedings are not by an order of a court, as a result of what action the proceedings have been commenced;

(d)   whether the proceedings have been commenced by–

(i)   the company's members,

(ii)   the company's creditors, or

(iii) some other person (giving the person's identity);

(e)   the date on which the proceedings became or will become effective.

71(2) The period allowed for delivery of the return required by paragraph (1) is–

(a) if the company became subject to the proceedings before it had a UK establishment, one month after the company first opens a UK establishment;

(b) if the company becomes subject to the proceedings when it has a UK establishment,

14 days from the date on which it becomes subject to the proceedings.

71(3) Where a company to which this Part applies ceases to be subject to any of the proceedings referred to in paragraph (1) it must deliver to the registrar a return stating–

(a) the company's name, and

(b) the date on which it ceased to be subject to the proceedings.

71(4) The period allowed for delivery of the return required by paragraph (3) is 14 days from the date on which it ceases to be subject to the proceedings.

71(5) Where the company has more than one UK establishment the obligation to deliver a return under this regulation applies in respect of each of them, but a return giving the registered numbers of more than one UK establishment is regarded as a return in respect of each establishment whose number is given.

71(6) No return is required under this regulation in respect of–

(a) a company's becoming or ceasing to be subject to a voluntary arrangement under Part 1 of the Insolvency Act 1986 or Part 2 of the Insolvency (Northern Ireland) Order 1989, or

(b) a company's entering administration under Part 2 and Schedule B1 of that Act or becoming or ceasing to be subject to an administration order under Part 3 of that Order.

72 Penalties for non-compliance

72(1) If a company fails to comply with regulation 69(1) or 71(1) or (3) within the period allowed for compliance, an offence is committed by–

(a) the company, and

(b) every person who immediately before the end of that period was a director of the company.

72(2) A liquidator who fails to comply with regulation 70(1) or (3)(a) or (b) within the period allowed for compliance commits an offence.

72(3) A person who takes all reasonable steps to secure compliance with the requirements concerned does not commit an offence under this regulation.

72(4) A person guilty of an offence under this regulation is liable–

(a) on conviction on indictment, to a fine;

(b) on summary conviction to a fine not exceeding the statutory maximum and, for continued contravention, a daily default fine not exceeding one-fiftieth of the statutory maximum.

73 Notice of appointment of judicial factor

73(1) Notice must be given to the registrar of the appointment in relation to a company to which this Part applies of a judicial factor (in Scotland).

73(2) The notice must be given by the judicial factor.

73(3)   The notice must specify an address at which service of documents (including legal process) may be effected on the judicial factor.

73(4)   Notice of a change in the address for service may be given to the registrar by the judicial factor.

73(5)   A judicial factor who has notified the registrar of the appointment must also notify the registrar of the termination of the appointment.

74   Offence of failure to give notice

74(1)   A judicial factor who fails to give notice of the appointment in accordance with regulation 73 within the period of 14 days after the appointment commits an offence.

74(2)   A person guilty of an offence under this regulation is liable on summary conviction to–

(a)   a fine not exceeding level 5 on the standard scale, and

(b)   for continued contravention, a daily default fine not exceeding one-tenth of level 5 on the standard scale.

Debt Relief Orders (Designation of Competent Authorities) Regulations 2009

(SI 2009/457)

Made on March 2, 2009 by the Secretary of State in exercise of the powers conferred by the Insolvency Act 1986 s.251U(4). Effective April 6, 2009.

[**Note:** Changes made by the Debt Relief Orders (Designation of Competent Authorities) (Amendment) Regulations 2009 (SI 2009/1553) have been incorporated into the text.]

1   Citation, commencement and interpretation

These Regulations may be cited as the Debt Relief Orders (Designation of Competent Authorities) Regulations and come into force on 6th April 2009.

2   "The Act" means the Insolvency Act 1986.

PART I

COMPETENT AUTHORITIES

3   Designated competent authorities

3(1)   The Secretary of State may designate a body which appears to him to fall within paragraph (2) to be a competent authority for the purposes of granting approvals under section 251U of the Act.

3(2)   A body may be designated by the Secretary of State if–

(a)   it makes an application to the Secretary of State to be designated as a competent authority in accordance with the Act and these Regulations;

(b)   it provides or ensures–

    (i)   the provision of debt management or debt counselling services through intermediaries, and

    (ii)   the provision to those intermediaries of education, training and development (including continuing education, training and development) in debt management or debt counselling services, and

(c)   it appears to the Secretary of State that it is a fit and proper body to approve individuals to act as intermediaries between a person wishing to make an application for a debt relief order and the official receiver.

4   Application for designation as a competent authority

4(1)   An application by a body ("the applicant body") for designation as a competent authority for the purposes of granting approvals under section 251U of the Act ("the application") shall be made to the Secretary of State in writing and contain–

(a)   the applicant body's full name;

(b)   the address of its registered office or, if it has no registered office, the address of its centre of administration or principal place of business;

(c)   its registered number (if any);

(d) if registered outside the United Kingdom, the state in which it is registered and the place where the register is maintained;

(e) if not registered, the nature of the applicant body;

(f) a copy of its constitution;

(g) if a charitable body, the objects or purposes of the charity (if not set out in the constitution) and–

   (i) if registered as a charity, its registered number as such and (if registered outside the United Kingdom) the state in which it is registered and the place where the register is maintained, or,

   (ii) if not registered as a charity, reasons why it is not so registered;

(h) a description of the applicant body's current occupation or activities;

(i) reasons why the applicant body should be considered for designation;

(j) a copy of its most recent–

   (i) audited accounts and balance sheet, and

   (ii) other statutorily required report, if any;

(k) a statement of the sources of the applicant body's income over the past 24 months and of its assets and liabilities not earlier than 12 months before the day on which the application is made;

(l) details of the nature of the applicant body's connection with the provision of debt management or debt counselling services to the public;

(m) details of existing or proposed education, training and development programmes which are, or which are to be, made available to individuals who are to be approved as, or who are acting as, approved intermediaries;

(n) a description and explanation of–

   (i) the procedure which the applicant body proposes to adopt for the approval of individuals to act as intermediaries;

   (ii) the manner in which the applicant body will ensure that individuals meet the conditions set out in these Regulations subject to compliance with which an intermediary may be approved;

   (iii) any additional criteria which the applicant body proposes to adopt against which it will assess the competence of individuals to act as intermediaries;

(o) an undertaking on the part of the applicant body that–

   (i) it will not grant approval to individuals to act as intermediaries except as provided in these Regulations;

   (ii) it will withdraw approvals of individuals to act as intermediaries as provided in these Regulations; and

   (iii) it will adopt an accessible, effective, fair and transparent procedure for dealing with complaints about its functions as a competent authority, including complaints about–

      (aa) any intermediary approved by it, or

      (bb) the activities of any such intermediary;

(p) details of the procedures referred to in subparagraph (o)(iii) and how and to what extent they are or will be published;

(q) a statement that such procedures will include the giving of notice to any complainant to the applicant body under subparagraph (o)(iii) that, if dissatisfied with the applicant body's response to the complaint, the complainant may refer the complaint and the response to the Secretary of State;

(r) details of any consumer credit licence and public liability or indemnity insurance which the applicant body holds;

(s) if the applicant body holds a consumer credit licence, whether it provides cover for persons approved by it to act as, and in the course of acting as such intermediaries.

4(2)   The application may be accompanied by further information in support of the application;

and the Secretary of State may request the applicant body to supply further information or evidence.

5   Fit and proper body

5(1)   A body may not be designated a competent authority unless it is a fit and proper body to act as such.

5(2)   Without prejudice to the generality of paragraph (1), a body is not a fit and proper body qualified to act as a competent authority if it–

(a) has committed any offence under any enactment contained in insolvency legislation;

(b) has engaged in any deceitful or oppressive or otherwise unfair or improper practices, whether unlawful or not, or any practices which otherwise cast doubt upon the probity of the body; or

(c) has not carried on its activities with integrity and the skills appropriate to the proper performance of the duties of–

(i) a body which purports to ensure the provision of, or to provide, debt management or debt counselling services to the public, or

(ii) a competent authority; or

(d) has entered into a company voluntary arrangement under Part 1 of the Act.

6   Extent of designation

6   The Secretary of State shall designate a competent authority by sending to the applicant body a letter of designation which shall contain–

(a) a statement that the applicant body as competent authority is designated to approve persons of any description ("unlimited designation"), or

(b) a statement that the applicant body as competent authority is designated to approve persons only of a particular description ("limited designation") and the description of person to which the designation is limited.

7   Withdrawal of designation as competent authority

7(1)   The Secretary of State may at any time–

(a) modify or withdraw an existing designation where a competent authority so requests or with its consent, or

(b) withdraw an existing designation where it appears to the Secretary of State that a body–

   (i) is not or is no longer a fit and proper body to act as a competent authority;

   (ii) has failed to comply with any provision of Part 7A of the Act or any rules, regulations or order made under it, including any failure to approve an intermediary, or failure to withdraw approval of an intermediary, in accordance with these regulations;

   (iii) has furnished the Secretary of State with any false, inaccurate or misleading information.

7(2)   The Secretary of State may from time to time request a competent authority to supply such information or evidence about–

(a) itself and its activities as a competent authority, or

(b) any intermediary appointed by it or the activities of any such intermediary,

as may be required by him or her for the purpose of ensuring that the requirements of these regulations are being met.

PART II

APPROVAL OF INTERMEDIARIES

8   Approval by competent authority

8(1)   A competent authority may approve an individual to act as an intermediary between a person wishing to make an application for a debt relief order and the official receiver subject as follows.

8(2)   An individual may be approved–

(a) if the individual makes an application to a competent authority to be approved as an intermediary in accordance with the Act and these regulations; and

(b) it appears to the competent authority that the individual is a fit and proper person to act as intermediary between a person wishing to make an application for a debt relief order and the official receiver.

9   Ineligibility

9   Individuals of any of the following descriptions are ineligible to be approved by a competent authority to act as intermediaries–

(a) individuals convicted of any offence involving fraud or other dishonesty or violence whose convictions are not spent;

(b) individuals who have committed any offence in any enactment contained in insolvency legislation;

(c) individuals who, in the course of carrying on any trade, profession or vocation or in the course of the discharge of any functions relating to any office or employment have engaged in any deceitful or oppressive or otherwise unfair or improper practices, whether unlawful or not, or which otherwise cast doubt upon their probity;

(d) individuals who have no experience, education or other training in the provision of debt management or debt counselling services;

(e) individuals who have not acted with the independence, integrity and the skills appropriate to the proper performance of the duties of a provider of debt management or debt counselling services or of an approved intermediary;

1149

(f) undischarged bankrupts;

(g) individuals in respect of whom there is or has been in force a bankruptcy restrictions order or undertaking or an interim bankruptcy restrictions order or undertaking or any bankruptcy restrictions order or undertaking made under the Insolvency (Northern Ireland) Order 1989 or the Bankruptcy (Scotland) Act 1985

(h) individuals to whom a moratorium period applies or in respect of whom a debt relief order or application for a debt relief order, has been made;

(i) individuals in respect of whom there is or has been in force a debt relief restrictions order or undertaking or an interim debt relief restrictions order or undertaking;

(j) individuals who are or have been subject to a disqualification order or undertaking accepted under the Company Directors Disqualification Act 1986 or to a disqualification order made under Part 11 of the Companies (Northern Ireland) Order 1989 or to a disqualification undertaking accepted under the Company Directors Disqualification (Northern Ireland) Order 2002;

(k) individuals who are patients within meaning of section 329(1) of the Mental Health (Care and Treatment) (Scotland) Act 2003 or have had a guardian appointed to them under the Adults with Incapacity (Scotland) Act 2000;

(l) individuals who lack capacity within the meaning of the Mental Health Capacity Act 2005 to act as intermediaries between a person wishing to make an application for a debt relief order and the official receiver;

(m) individuals who, subject to any exemption from the requirement to possess or be covered by a relevant consumer credit licence which would otherwise apply to or in relation to them, neither possess nor are validly covered by such a licence; and

(n) individuals who are not covered, either individually or by way of a group policy, by public liability or personal indemnity insurance.

10 Applications to a competent authority for approval to act as intermediary

10(1) Applications to a competent authority by an individual for approval to act as an intermediary shall be in writing and contain–

(a) the individual's full name and address, date of birth and gender;

(b) any name or names used by the applicant for any purpose, if different from the above;

(c) a description of the individual's current occupation or activities;

(d) a description giving reasons why the individual should be considered suitable for approval;

(e) whether the individual is a member of a relevant body and if so which;

(f) the individual's educational and professional qualifications;

(g) the source of the individual's income and the individual's current financial status;

(h) details of the individual's expertise in the provision of debt management or debt counselling services including details of any education, training and development which the individual has undergone and any qualifications the individual has acquired in connection with the provision of debt management or debt counselling services;

(i) details of any consumer credit licence which the individual has in place or of any exemption claimed by him or her from the requirement to possess or be covered by such a licence (as the case may be), or, if none, how the individual proposes to secure that he or she has in place, or is validly covered by, a consumer credit licence;

(j)   details of any public liability or personal indemnity insurance which the individual has in place, or, if none, how the individual proposes to secure that he or she has in place, or is validly covered by, appropriate public liability or personal indemnity insurance;

(k)   copies of–

    (i)   documents confirming the individual's name, address and date of birth;

    (ii)   material relating to the educational, training and development experience referred to in sub-paragraph (h);

    (iii)   material relating to the individual's professional or other qualifications.

10(2)   In this regulation, **"relevant body"** means a body concerned with the regulation of persons who provide or ensure the provision of debt management or debt counselling services.

10(3)   The application may be accompanied by further information in support of the application; and the competent authority may request the individual to supply further information or evidence.

History
Regulation 10(3) amended by the Debt Relief Orders (Designation of Competent Authorities) (Amendment) Regulations 2009 (SI 2009/1553) reg.2 as from July 20, 2009.

11   Procedure for withdrawal of approval to act as intermediary

11   A competent authority shall withdraw an approval to act as intermediary from any individual–

(a)   where the individual so requests or with the individual's consent;

(b)   where it becomes clear to the competent authority after approval that the individual–

    (i)   was ineligible at the time of approval, or

    (ii)   has become ineligible for approval;

    (iii)   is at any time not or no longer a fit and proper person to act as intermediary;

    (iv)   has failed to comply with any provision of Part 7A of the Act or any rule, regulations or orders made under it, including these regulations;

    (v)   has furnished the competent authority with any false, inaccurate or misleading information.

11(2)   The competent authority may from time to time request an approved intermediary to supply such information or evidence about that intermediary or his or her activities as may be required by that authority for the purpose of ensuring that the requirements of these Regulations are being met.

Companies (Disqualification Orders) Regulations 2009

(SI 2009/2471)

Made on September 8, 2009 by the Secretary of State in exercise of the powers conferred by the Company Directors Disqualification Act 1986 s.18. Effective October 1, 2009.

1 Citation and commencement

1 These Regulations may be cited as the Companies (Disqualification Orders) Regulations 2009 and come into force on 1st October 2009.

2 Definitions

2(1) In these Regulations–

"the Act" means the Company Directors Disqualification Act 1986;

"disqualification order" means an order of the court under any of sections 2 to 6, 8, 9A and 10 of the Act;

"disqualification undertaking" means an undertaking accepted by the Secretary of State under section 7, 8 or 9B of the Act;

"grant of leave" means a grant by the court of leave under section 17 of the Act to any person in relation to a disqualification order or a disqualification undertaking.

2(2) For the purposes of regulations 5 and 9, "leave granted"–

(a) in relation to a disqualification order granted under Part 2 of the Companies (Northern Ireland) Order 1989 means leave granted by a court for a person subject to such an order to do anything which otherwise the order prohibits that person from doing; and

(b) in relation to a disqualification undertaking accepted under the Company Directors Disqualification (Northern Ireland) Order 2002 means leave granted by a court for a person subject to such an undertaking to do anything which otherwise the undertaking prohibits that person from doing.

3 Revocations

3 The following instruments are revoked–

(a) the Companies (Disqualification Orders) Regulations 2001;

(b) the Companies (Disqualification Orders) (Amendment No. 2) Regulations 2002; and

(c) the Companies (Disqualification Orders) (Amendment) Regulations 2004.

4 Transitional provisions

4 Other than regulation 9, these Regulations apply–

(a) in relation to a disqualification order made after the coming into force of these Regulations; and

(b) in relation to–

(i) a grant of leave made after the coming into force of these Regulations; or

(ii) any action taken by a court after the coming into force of these Regulations in consequence of which a disqualification order or a disqualification undertaking is varied or ceases to be in force,

whether the disqualification order or disqualification undertaking to which the grant of leave or the action relates was made by the court or accepted by the Secretary of State before or after the coming into force of these Regulations.

5 Regulation 9 applies to–

(a) particulars of disqualification orders made and leave granted under Part 2 of the Companies (Northern Ireland) Order 1989 received by the Secretary of State on or after 1st October 2009 other than particulars of disqualification orders made and leave granted under that Order which relate to disqualification orders made by the courts of Northern Ireland before 2nd April 2001; and

(b) particulars of undertakings accepted under the Company Directors Disqualification (Northern Ireland) Order 2002 on or after 1st October 2009, and to leave granted under that Order in relation to such undertakings.

6 Particulars to be furnished by officers of the court

6(1) The following officers of the court must furnish to the Secretary of State the particulars specified in regulation 7(a) to (c) in the form and manner there specified–

(a) where a disqualification order is made by the Crown Court, the Court Manager;

(b) where a disqualification order or grant of leave is made by the High Court, the Court Manager;

(c) where a disqualification order or grant of leave is made by a County Court, the Court Manager;

(d) where a disqualification order is made by a Magistrates' Court, the designated officer for a Magistrates' Court;

(e) where a disqualification order is made by the High Court of Justiciary, the Deputy Principal Clerk of Justiciary;

(f) where a disqualification order or grant of leave is made by a Sheriff Court, the Sheriff Clerk;

(g) where a disqualification order or grant of leave is made by the Court of Session, the Deputy Principal Clerk of Session;

(h) where a disqualification order or grant of leave is made by the Court of Appeal, the Court Manager; and

(i) where a disqualification order or grant of leave is made by the Supreme Court, the Registrar of the Supreme Court.

6(2) Where–

(a) a disqualification order has been made by any of the courts mentioned in paragraph (1), or

(b) a disqualification undertaking has been accepted by the Secretary of State,

and subsequently any action is taken by a court in consequence of which that order or that undertaking is varied or ceases to be in force, the officer specified in paragraph (1) of the court which takes such action must furnish to the Secretary of State the particulars specified in regulation 7(d) in the form and manner there specified.

7   The form in which the particulars are to be furnished is–

(a)   that set out in Schedule 1 to these Regulations with such variations as circumstances require when the person against whom the disqualification order is made is an individual, and the particulars contained therein are the particulars specified for that purpose;

(b)   that set out in Schedule 2 to these Regulations with such variations as circumstances require when the person against whom the disqualification order is made is a body corporate, and the particulars contained therein are the particulars specified for that purpose;

(c)   that set out in Schedule 3 to these Regulations with such variations as circumstances require when a grant of leave is made by the court in relation to a disqualification order or a disqualification undertaking, and the particulars contained therein are the particulars specified for that purpose;

(d)   that set out in Schedule 4 to these Regulations with such variations as circumstances require when any action is taken by a court in consequence of which a disqualification order or a disqualification undertaking is varied or ceases to be in force, and the particulars contained therein are the particulars specified for that purpose.

8   The time within which the officer specified in regulation 6(1) is to furnish the Secretary of State with the said particulars is the period of 14 days beginning with the day on which the disqualification order or grant of leave is made or on which action is taken by a court in consequence of which the disqualification order or disqualification undertaking is varied or ceases to be in force.

9   Extension of certain of the provisions of section 18 of the Act to orders made, undertakings accepted and leave granted in Northern Ireland

9(1)   Section 18(2) of the Act is extended to the particulars furnished to the Secretary of State of disqualification orders made and leave granted under Part 2 of the Companies (Northern Ireland) Order 1989.

9(2)   Section 18(2A) of the Act is extended to the particulars of disqualification undertakings accepted under and leave granted in relation to disqualification undertakings under the Company Directors Disqualification (Northern Ireland) Order 2002.

9(3)   Section 18(3) of the Act is extended to all entries in the register and particulars relating to them furnished to the Secretary of State in respect of orders made under Part 2 of the Companies (Northern Ireland) Order 1989 or disqualification undertakings accepted under the Company Directors Disqualification (Northern Ireland) Order 2002.

[Schedules 1–4 not reproduced]

Financial Services and Markets Act 2000 (Administration Orders Relating to Insurers) Order 2010

(SI 2010/3023)

Made on December 20, 2010 in exercise of the powers conferred on them by ss.360, 426(1) and 428(3) of the Financial Services and Markets Act 2000 by the Treasury with the consent of the Secretary of State for Business, Innovation and Skills. Operative from February 1, 2011.

1 Citation, commencement and interpretation

1(1) This Order may be cited as the Financial Services and Markets Act 2000 (Administration Orders Relating to Insurers) Order 2010 and comes into force on 1st February 2011.

1(2) In this Order–

"the 1986 Act" means the Insolvency Act 1986;

"Schedule B1" means Schedule B1 to the 1986 Act.

2 Application and modification of Part 2 of the 1986 Act in relation to insurers

2(1) Part 2 of the 1986 Act (administration), other than paragraph 14 of Schedule B1 (power of holder of floating charge to appoint administrator) and paragraph 22 of Schedule B1 (power of company or directors to appoint administrator), applies in relation to insurers with the modifications specified in the Schedule to this Order.

2(2) Accordingly paragraph 9(2) of Schedule B1 does not preclude the making of an administration order in relation to an insurer.

3 Application and modification of the Insolvency Rules 1986 in relation to insurers

3 The Insolvency Rules 1986, so far as they give effect to Part 2 of the 1986 Act, have effect in relation to insurers with the following modifications–

(a) in Rule 2.12(1) (the hearing) after sub-paragraph (a) insert–

"(aa) the Financial Services Authority;

(ab) the scheme manager of the Financial Services Compensation Scheme;".

4 Application and modification of the Insolvency (Scotland) Rules 1986 in relation to insurers

4 The Insolvency (Scotland) Rules 1986, so far as they give effect to Part 2 of the 1986 Act, have effect in relation to insurers with the following modifications–

(a) in Rule 2.3(1) (service of petition) after subparagraph (a) insert–

"(aa) the Financial Services Authority;"

(ab) the scheme manager of the Financial Services Compensation Scheme;".

5 Revocation

5 The following are revoked–

(a) the Financial Services and Markets Act 2000 (Administration Orders Relating to Insurers) Order 2002;

(b) articles 2 to 8 of the Financial Services and Markets Act 2000 (Administration Orders Relating to Insurers) (Amendment) Order 2003;

(c) regulation 52 of the Insurers (Reorganisation and Winding Up) Regulations 2004.

6 Saving

6 Nothing in articles 2 to 5 applies in relation to any case where the appointment of an administrator takes effect before the coming into force of this Order.

SCHEDULE

MODIFICATIONS OF PART 2 OF THE INSOLVENCY ACT 1986 IN RELATION TO INSURERS

Article 2

1(1) In paragraph 3 of Schedule B1 (purpose of administration)–

(a) at the beginning of sub-paragraph (1) insert "Subject to sub-paragraph (1A)";

(b) after sub-paragraph (1) insert–

"(1A) The administrator of an insurer which effects or carries out contracts of insurance shall, at the request of the scheme manager of the Financial Services Compensation Scheme, provide any assistance identified by the scheme manager as being necessary–

(a) to enable the scheme manager to administer the compensation scheme in relation to contracts of insurance, and

(b) to enable the scheme manager to secure continuity of insurance in relation to contracts of long-term insurance.

(1B) For the purposes of this Schedule–

(a) "compensation scheme" has the same meaning as in section 213 of the Financial Services and Markets Act 2000;

(b) "contracts of insurance" and "contracts of long-term insurance" have the same meaning as in article 3 of the Financial Services and Markets Act 2000 (Regulated Activities) Order 2001;

(c) "scheme manager" means the body corporate established by the Financial Services Authority under section 212 of the Financial Services and Markets Act 2000.".

1(2) In sub-paragraph (2), for "sub-paragraph (4)," substitute "sub-paragraphs (1A) and (4) and to paragraph 3A".

2(1) After paragraph 3 of Schedule B1, insert–

"3A.-

(1) This paragraph applies in relation to the administration of an insurer which effects or carries out contracts of long-term insurance.

(2) Unless the court orders otherwise, the administrator must carry on the insurer's business so far as that business consists of carrying out the insurer's contracts of long-term insurance ("the long-term insurance business") with a view to the business being transferred as a going concern to a person who may lawfully carry out those contracts.

(3) In carrying on the long-term insurance business, the administrator–

(a) may agree to the variation of any contracts of insurance in existence when the administration order is made; but

(b) must not effect any new contracts of insurance without the approval of the Financial Services Authority.

(4)   If the administrator is satisfied that the interests of the creditors in respect of liabilities of the insurer attributable to contracts of long-term insurance effected by it require the appointment of a special manager, the administrator may apply to the court.

(5)   On such an application, the court may appoint a special manager to act during such time, and to have such powers (including powers of a receiver or manager) as the court may direct.

(6)   Section 177(5) of this Act (duties of special manager) applies to a special manager appointed under sub-paragraph (5) as it applies to a special manager appointed under section 177.

(7)   If the court thinks fit, it may reduce the value of one or more of the contracts of long-term insurance effected by the insurer.

(8)   Any reduction is to be on such terms and subject to such conditions (if any) as the court thinks fit.

(9)   The court may, on the application of an official, appoint an independent actuary to investigate the insurer's long-term insurance business and to report to the official–

    (a)   on the desirability or otherwise of the insurer's long-term insurance business being continued; and

    (b)   on any reduction in the contracts of long-term insurance effected by the insurer that may be necessary for successful continuation of the insurer's long-term insurance business.

(10)   "Official" means–

    (a)   the administrator;

    (b)   a special manager appointed under sub-paragraph (5); or

    (c)   the Financial Services Authority.".

3   In paragraph 49(4) of Schedule B1 (administrator's proposals), omit "and" at the end of paragraph (b) and at the end of paragraph (c) add–

    "(d)   to the Financial Services Authority, and

    (e)   to the scheme manager of the Financial Services Compensation Scheme."

4   In paragraph 53(2) of Schedule B1 (business and result of initial creditors' meeting), omit "and" at the end of paragraph (b) and at the end of paragraph (c), add–

    "(d)   the Financial Services Authority, and

    (e)   to the scheme manager of the Financial Services Compensation Scheme."

5   In paragraph 54(2)(b) of Schedule B1 (revision of administrator's proposals), after "creditor" insert ", to the Financial Services Authority and to the scheme manager of the Financial Services Compensation Scheme.".

6   In paragraph 76(1) of Schedule B1 (automatic end of administration), for "one year" substitute "30 months".

7   In paragraph 76(2)(b) of Schedule B1 for "six" substitute "twelve".

8   In paragraph 79(1) of Schedule B1 (court ending administration on application of administrator), after the first reference to "company" insert "or the Financial Services Authority".

9   In paragraph 91(1) of Schedule B1 (supplying vacancy in office of administrator)–

    (a)   at the end of sub-paragraph (d), omit "or";

    (b)   at the end of sub-paragraph (e), insert "or";

    (c)   after sub-paragraph (e), insert

        "(f)   the Financial Services Authority".

10(1) The powers of the administrator specified in Schedule 1 to the 1986 Act (powers of administrator or administrative receiver) include the power to make–

(a) any payments due to a creditor; or

(b) any payments on account of any sum which may become due to a creditor.

10(2) Any payments to a creditor made pursuant to sub-paragraph (1) must not exceed, in aggregate, the amount which the administrator reasonably considers that the creditor would be entitled to receive on a distribution of the insurer's assets in a winding up.

10(3) The powers conferred by sub-paragraph (1) may be exercised until an initial creditors' meeting but may only be exercised thereafter–

(a) if the following conditions are met–

(i) the administrator has laid before that meeting or any subsequent creditors' meeting ("the relevant meeting") a statement containing the information mentioned in subparagraph (4); and

(ii) the powers are exercised with the consent of a majority in number representing three fourths in value of the creditors present and voting either in person or by proxy at the relevant meeting; or

(b) with the consent of the court.

10(4) The information referred to in sub-paragraph (3)(a)(i) is an estimate of the aggregate amount of–

(a) the insurer's assets and liabilities (whether actual, contingent or prospective); and

(b) all payments which the administrator proposes to make to creditors pursuant to subparagraph (1);

including any assumptions which the administrator has made in calculating that estimate.

10(5) In this paragraph, "initial creditors' meeting" has the meaning given by paragraph 51(1) of Schedule B1.

London Insolvency District (Central London County Court) Order 2011

(SI 2011/761)

Made on March 11, 2011 by the Lord Chancellor in exercise of the powers conferred on him by s.1 of the Courts and Legal Services Act 1990 and by s.374 of the Insolvency Act 1986. Operative from April 6, 2011.

1 Citation and commencement

1 This Order may be cited as the London Insolvency District (Central London County Court) Order 2011 and comes into force on 6th April 2011.

2 Areas within the London insolvency district

2 The London insolvency district shall comprise the areas situated within the districts of the following county courts–

(a) Barnet;

(b) Bow;

(c) Brentford;

(d) Central London;

(e) Clerkenwell and Shoreditch;

(f) Edmonton;

(g) Lambeth;

(h) Mayor's and City of London;

(i) Wandsworth;

(j) West London; and

(k) Willesden.

3 Jurisdiction under the Insolvency Act 1986

3 Jurisdiction in relation to proceedings under Parts 7A to 11 of the Insolvency Act 1986 that are allocated to the London insolvency district in accordance with the Insolvency Rules shall be conferred on the Central London County Court.

4 For the purposes of section 374 of the Insolvency Act 1986 the districts of the county courts falling within the London insolvency district are attached to the Central London County Court.

5 Amendment to the Insolvency Act 1986

5 In section 373(3)(a) of the Insolvency Act 1986, after "the High Court" insert "or the Central London County Court".

6 Amendments to the Civil Courts Order 1983

6–7 [Not reproduced.]

8 Amendments to the Civil Courts (Amendment No. 3) Order 1992

8 [Not reproduced.]

9 Transitional provisions

9 Proceedings under the Insolvency Act 1986 that–

(a) were, immediately before this Order came into force, being dealt with in the High Court; and

(b) would have been allocated to the Central London County Court if this Order had been in force when proceedings were commenced,

may either be continued in the High Court or transferred to the Central London County Court.

Appendix IV

Practice Direction: Insolvency Proceedings [2012] B.C.C. 265

This *Practice Direction* ("PD") is the latest in a succession of PDs relating to insolvency proceedings going back to 1999. It was issued on February 23, 2012 and came into effect immediately on that date. A PD may be amended from time to time and the current version at any time is to be found at *http://www.justice.gov.uk/civil/procrules_fin/ contents/practice_directions/insolvency_pd.htm*.

It should be noted that the statement in para.1.2 that this PD "shall replace all previous Practice Notes and Practice Directions relating to insolvency proceedings" is probably misleading. For example, there is no overlap between the present PD and the *Practice Note* reported in [1994] 1 W.L.R. 160; [1994] B.C.C. 35 discussed above in the note to the original r.2.2; but it would be surprising if there had been any intention to repeal that Note and leave a void. Again, the *Practice Direction: Applications under the Companies Acts and Related Legislation* [2007] B.C.C. 833, which deals with petitions in which relief is sought under both CA 2006 s.994 and IA 1986 s.122(1)(g), covers matters which are not addressed by the new PD (and continues to be included in the CPR as PD 49B), and so we have reproduced it below as App.V. See further the note to IA 1986 s.127.

CONTENTS OF THIS PRACTICE DIRECTION

PART ONE: GENERAL PROVISIONS

1. Definitions

1.1 In this Practice Direction:

(1) 'The Act' means the Insolvency Act 1986 and includes the Act as applied to limited liability partnerships by the Limited Liability Partnerships Regulations 2001 or to any other person or body by virtue of the Act or any other legislation;

(2) 'The Insolvency Rules' means the rules for the time being in force and made under s.411 and s.412 of the Act in relation to insolvency proceedings, and, save where otherwise provided, any reference to a rule is to a rule in the Insolvency Rules;

(3) 'CPR' means the Civil Procedure Rules and 'CPR' followed by a Part or rule identified by number means the Part or rule with that number in those Rules;

(4) 'EC Regulation on Insolvency Proceedings' means Council Regulation (EC) No 1346/2000 of 29 May 2000 on Insolvency Proceedings;

(5) 'Service Regulation' means Council Regulation (EC) No. 1393/2007 of 13 November 2007 on the service in the Member States of judicial and extrajudicial documents in civil and commercial matters (service of documents);

(6) 'Insolvency proceedings' means:

    (a) any proceedings under the Act, the Insolvency Rules, the Administration of Insolvent Estates of Deceased Persons Order 1986 (S.I. 1986 No.1999), the Insolvent Partnerships Order 1994 (S.I. 1994 No. 2421) or the Limited Liability Partnerships Regulations 2001;

    (b) any proceedings under the EC Regulation on Insolvency Proceedings or the Cross-Border Insolvency Regulations 2006 (S.I. 2006/1030);

(7) References to a 'company' include a limited liability partnership and references to a 'contributory' include a member of a limited liability partnership;

(8) References to a 'Registrar' are to a Registrar in Bankruptcy of the High Court and (save in cases where it is clear from the context that a particular provision applies only to the Royal Courts of Justice) include a District Judge in a District Registry of the High Court and in any county court having insolvency jurisdiction;

(9) 'Court' means any court having insolvency jurisdiction;

(10) 'Royal Courts of Justice' means the Royal Courts of Justice, Strand, London WC2A 2LL or such other place in London where the Registrars sit;

(11) In Part Five of this Practice Direction:

    (a) "appointee" means:

        (i) a provisional liquidator appointed under section 135 of the Act;

        (ii) a special manager appointed under section 177 or section 370 of the Act;

        (iii) a liquidator appointed by the members of a company or partnership or by the creditors of a company or partnership or by the Secretary of State pursuant to section 137 of the Act, or by the court pursuant to section 140 of the Act;

        (iv) an administrator of a company appointed to manage the property, business and affairs of that company under the Act or other enactment and to which the provisions of the Act are applicable;

        (v) a trustee in bankruptcy (other than the Official Receiver) appointed under the Act;

    (vi)   a nominee or supervisor of a voluntary arrangement under Part I or Part VIII of the Act;

    (vii) a licensed insolvency practitioner appointed by the court pursuant to section 273 of the Act;

    (viii) an interim receiver appointed by the court pursuant to section 286 of the Act;

(b)   "assessor" means a person appointed in accordance with CPR 35.15;

(c)   "remuneration application" means any application to fix, approve or challenge the remuneration or expenses of an appointee or the basis of remuneration;

(d)   "remuneration" includes expenses (where the Act or the Insolvency Rules give the court jurisdiction in relation thereto) and, in the case of an administrator, any pre-appointment administration costs or remuneration.

2.   Coming into force

2.1   This Practice Direction shall come into force on 23 February 2012 and shall replace all previous Practice Directions, Practice Statements and Practice Notes relating to insolvency proceedings.

3.   Distribution of business

3.1   As a general rule all petitions and applications (except those listed in paragraphs 3.2 and 3.3 below) should be listed for initial hearing before a Registrar in accordance with rule 7.6A(2) and (3).

3.2   The following applications relating to insolvent companies should always be listed before a Judge:

(1)   applications for committal for contempt;

(2)   applications for an administration order;

(3)   applications for an injunction;

(4)   applications for the appointment of a provisional liquidator;

(5)   interim applications and applications for directions or case management after any proceedings have been referred or adjourned to the Judge (except where liberty to apply to the Registrar has been given).

3.3   The following applications relating to insolvent individuals should always be listed before a Judge:

(1)   applications for committal for contempt;

(2)   applications for an injunction;

(3)   interim applications and applications for directions or case management after any proceedings have been referred or adjourned to the Judge (except where liberty to apply to the Registrar has been given).

3.4   When deciding whether to hear proceedings or to refer or adjourn them to the Judge, the Registrar should have regard to the following factors:

(1)   the complexity of the proceedings;

(2)   whether the proceedings raise new or controversial points of law;

(3)   the likely date and length of the hearing;

(4)   public interest in the proceedings.

4.   Court documents

4.1   All insolvency proceedings should be commenced and applications in proceedings should be made using the forms prescribed by the Act, the Insolvency Rules or other legislation under which the same is or are brought or made and/or should contain the information prescribed by the Act, the Insolvency Rules or other legislation.

4.2   Every court document in insolvency proceedings under Parts I to VII of the Act shall be headed:

IN THE HIGH COURT OF JUSTICE

CHANCERY DIVISION

[DISTRICT REGISTRY] or in the Royal Courts of Justice [COMPANIES COURT]

or

IN THE [   ] COUNTY COURT

followed by

IN THE MATTER OF [name of company]

AND IN THE MATTER OF THE INSOLVENCY ACT 1986

4.3   Every court document in insolvency proceedings under Parts IX to XI of the Act shall be headed:

IN THE [HIGH COURT OF JUSTICE] or [[   ] COUNTY COURT]

IN BANKRUPTCY

IN THE MATTER OF [name of bankrupt]

or

RE: [name of bankrupt].

Every application should also be headed:

AND IN THE MATTER OF THE INSOLVENCY ACT 1986

4.4   Every court document in proceedings to which the Act applies by virtue of other legislation should also be headed:

IN THE MATTER OF [THE FINANCIAL SERVICES AND MARKETS ACT 2000 or as the case may be]

AND IN THE MATTER OF THE INSOLVENCY ACT 1986

5.   Evidence

5.1   Subject to the provisions of rule 7.9 or any other provisions or directions as to the form in which evidence should be given, written evidence in insolvency proceedings must be given by witness statement.

6.   Service of court documents in insolvency proceedings

6.1   Except where the Insolvency Rules otherwise provide, CPR Part 6 applies to the service of court documents both within and out of the jurisdiction as modified by this Practice Direction or as the court may otherwise direct.

6.2   Except where the Insolvency Rules otherwise provide or as may be required under the Service Regulation, service of documents in insolvency proceedings will be the responsibility of the parties and will not be undertaken by the court.

6.3   A document which, pursuant to rule 12A.16(3)(b), is treated as a claim form, is deemed to have been served on the date specified in CPR Part 6.14, and any other document is deemed to have been served on the date specified in CPR Part 6.26, unless the court otherwise directs.

6.4   Except as provided below, service out of the jurisdiction of an application which is to be treated as a claim form under rule 12A.16(3) requires the permission of the court.

6.5   An application which is to be treated as a claim form under rule 12A.16(3) may be served out of the jurisdiction without the permission of the court if:

(1)   the application is by an office-holder appointed in insolvency proceedings in respect of a company with its centre of main interests within the jurisdiction exercising a statutory power under the Act, and the person to be served is to be served within the EU; or

(2)   it is a copy of an application, being served on a member State liquidator.

6.6   An application for permission to serve out of the jurisdiction must be supported by a witness statement setting out:

(1)   the nature of the claim or application and the relief sought;

(2)   that the applicant believes that the claim has a reasonable prospect of success; and

(3)   the address of the person to be served or, if not known, in what place or country that person is, or is likely, to be found.

6.7   CPR 6.36 and 6.37(1) and (2) do not apply in insolvency proceedings.

7.   Jurisdiction

7.1   Where CPR 2.4 provides for the court to perform any act, that act may be performed by a Registrar.

8.   Drawing up of orders

8.1   The court will draw up all orders except orders on the application of the Official Receiver or for which the Treasury Solicitor is responsible or where the court otherwise directs.

9.   Urgent applications

9.1   In the Royal Courts of Justice the Registrars (and in other courts exercising insolvency jurisdiction the District Judges) operate urgent applications lists for urgent and time-critical applications and may be available to hear urgent applications at other times. Parties asking for an application to be dealt with in the urgent applications lists or urgently at any other time must complete the certificate below:

<u>No:</u>

<u>Heading of action</u>

I estimate that this matter is likely to occupy the court for .... mins/hours.

I certify that it is urgent for the following reasons:

....

[name of representative]

....

[telephone number]

Counsel/Solicitor for the ....

WARNING. If, in the opinion of the Registrar/District Judge, the application is not urgent then such sanction will be applied as is thought appropriate in all the circumstances.

PART TWO: COMPANY INSOLVENCY

10. Administrations

10.1 In the absence of special circumstances, an application for the extension of an administration should be made not less than one month before the end of the administration. The evidence in support of any later application must explain why the application is being made late. The court will consider whether any part of the costs should be disallowed where an application is made less than one month before the end of the administration.

11. Winding-up petitions

11.1 Before presenting a winding-up petition the creditor must conduct a search to ensure that no petition is already pending. Save in exceptional circumstances a second winding up petition should not be presented whilst a prior petition is pending. A petitioner who presents his own petition while another petition is pending does so at risk as to costs.

11.2 Every creditor's winding-up petition must (in the case of a company) contain the following:

(1) the full name and address of the petitioner;

(2) the name and number of the company in respect of which a winding up order is sought;

(3) the date of incorporation of the company and the Companies Act or Acts under which it was incorporated;

(4) the address of the company's registered office;

(5) a statement of the nominal capital of the company, the manner in which its shares are divided up and the amount of the capital paid up or credited as paid up;

(6) brief details of the principal objects for which the company was established followed, where appropriate, by the words "and other objects stated in the memorandum of association of the company";

(7) details of the basis on which it is contended that the company is insolvent including, where a debt is relied on, sufficient particulars of the debt (the amount, nature and approximate date(s) on which it was incurred) to enable the company and the court to identify the debt;

(8) a statement that the company is insolvent and unable to pay its debts;

(9) a statement that for the reasons set out in the evidence verifying the petition the EC Regulation on Insolvency Proceedings either applies or does not and if the former whether the proceedings will be main, territorial or secondary proceedings;

(10) the statement that, "In the circumstances it is just and equitable that the company be wound up under the provisions of the Insolvency Act 1986";

(11) a prayer that the company be wound up, for such other order as the court thinks fit and any other specific relief sought.

Similar information (so far as is appropriate) should be given where the petition is presented against a partnership.

11.3 The statement of truth verifying the petition in accordance with rule 4.12 should be made no more than ten business days before the date of issue of the petition.

11.4 Where the company to be wound up has been struck off the register, the petition should state that fact and include as part of the relief sought an order that it be restored to the register. Save where the petition has been presented by a Minister of the Crown or a government department, evidence of service on the Treasury Solicitor or the Solicitor for the affairs of the Duchy of Lancaster (as appropriate) should be filed exhibiting the bona vacantia waiver letter.

11.5 *Gazetting of the petition*

11.5.1 Rule 4.11 must be complied with (unless waived by the court): it is designed to ensure that the class remedy of winding up by the court is made available to all creditors, and is not used as a means of putting improper pressure on the company to pay the petitioner's debt or costs. Failure to comply with the rule, without good reason accepted by the court, may lead to the summary dismissal of the petition on the return date (rule 4.11(6)) or to the court depriving the petitioner of the costs of the hearing. If the court, in its discretion, grants an adjournment, this will usually be on terms that notice of the petition is gazetted or otherwise given in accordance with the rule in due time for the adjourned hearing. No further adjournment for the purpose of gazetting will normally be granted.

11.5.2 Copies of every notice gazetted in connection with a winding up petition, or where this is not practicable a description of the form and content of the notice, must be lodged with the court as soon as possible after publication and in any event not later than five business days before the hearing of the petition. This direction applies even if the notice is defective in any way (e.g. is published on a date not in accordance with the Insolvency Rules, or omits or misprints some important words) or if the petitioner decides not to pursue the petition (e.g. on receiving payment).

11.6 Errors in petitions

11.6.1 Applications for permission to amend errors in petitions which are discovered after a winding up order has been made should be made to the member of court staff in charge of the winding up list in the Royal Courts of Justice or to a District Judge in any other court.

11.6.2 Where the error is an error in the name of the company, the member of court staff in charge of the winding up list in the Royal Courts of Justice or a District Judge in any other court may make any necessary amendments to ensure that the winding up order is drawn up with the correct name of the company inserted. If there is any doubt, e.g. where there might be another company in existence which could be confused with the company to be wound up, the member of court staff in charge of the winding up list will refer the application to a Registrar at the Royal Courts of Justice and a District Judge may refer it to a Judge.

11.6.3 Where it is discovered that the company has been struck off the Register of Companies prior to the winding up order being made, the matter must be restored to the list as soon as possible to enable an order for the restoration of the name to be made as well as the order to wind up.

11.7 *Rescission of a winding up order*

11.7.1 An application to rescind a winding up order must be made by application.

11.7.2 The application should normally be made within five business days after the date on which the order was made (rule 7.47(4)) failing which it should include an application to extend time. Notice of any such application must be given to the petitioning creditor, any supporting or opposing creditor and the Official Receiver.

11.7.3 Applications will only be entertained if made (a) by a creditor, or (b) by a contributory, or (c) by the company jointly with a creditor or with a contributory. The application must be supported by a witness statement which should include details of assets and liabilities and (where appropriate) reasons for any failure to apply within five business days.

11.7.4 In the case of an unsuccessful application the costs of the petitioning creditor, any supporting creditors and of the Official Receiver will normally be ordered to be paid by the creditor or the contributory making or joining in the application. The reason for this is that if the costs of an unsuccessful application are made payable by the company, they fall unfairly on the general body of creditors.

11.8 *Validation orders*

11.8.1 A company against which a winding up petition has been presented may apply to the court after presentation of the petition for relief from the effects of section 127(1) of the Act by seeking an order that a disposition or dispositions of its property, including payments out of its bank account (whether such account is in credit or overdrawn), shall not be void in the event of a winding up order being made on the hearing of the petition (a validation order).

11.8.2 An application for a validation order should generally be made to the Registrar. An application should be made to the Judge only if: (a) it is urgent and no Registrar is available to hear it; or (b) it is complex or raises new or controversial points of law; or (c) it is estimated to last longer than 30 minutes.

11.8.3 Save in exceptional circumstances, notice of the making of the application should be given to: (a) the petitioning creditor; (b) any person entitled to receive a copy of the petition pursuant to rule 4.10; (c) any creditor who has given notice to the petitioner of his intention to appear on the hearing of the petition pursuant to rule 4.16; and (d) any creditor who has been substituted as petitioner pursuant to rule 4.19.

11.8.4 The application should be supported by a witness statement which, save in exceptional circumstances, should be made by a director or officer of the company who is intimately acquainted with the company's affairs and financial circumstances. If appropriate, supporting evidence in the form of a witness statement from the company's accountant should also be produced.

11.8.5 The extent and contents of the evidence will vary according to the circumstances and the nature of the relief sought, but in the majority of cases it should include, as a minimum, the following information:

(1) when and to whom notice has been given in accordance with paragraph 11.8.3 above;

(2) the company's registered office;

(3) the company's nominal and paid up capital;

(4) brief details of the circumstances leading to presentation of the petition;

(5) how the company became aware of presentation of the petition;

(6) whether the petition debt is admitted or disputed and, if the latter, brief details of the basis on which the debt is disputed;

(7) full details of the company's financial position including details of its assets (including details of any security and the amount(s) secured) and liabilities, which should be supported, as far as possible, by documentary evidence, e.g. the latest filed accounts, any draft audited accounts, management accounts or estimated statement of affairs;

(8) a cash flow forecast and profit and loss projection for the period for which the order is sought;

(9) details of the dispositions or payments in respect of which an order is sought;

(10) the reasons relied on in support of the need for such dispositions or payments to be made;

(11) any other information relevant to the exercise of the court's discretion;

(12) details of any consents obtained from the persons mentioned in paragraph 11.8.3 above (supported by documentary evidence where appropriate);

(13) details of any relevant bank account, including its number and the address and sort code of the bank at which such account is held.

11.8.6 Where an application is made urgently to enable payments to be made which are essential to continued trading (e.g. wages) and it is not possible to assemble all the evidence listed above, the court may consider granting limited relief for a short period, but there should be sufficient evidence to satisfy the court that the interests of creditors are unlikely to be prejudiced.

11.8.7 Where the application involves a disposition of property the court will need details of the property (including its title number if the property is land) and to be satisfied that any proposed disposal will be at a proper value. Accordingly, an independent valuation should be obtained and exhibited to the evidence.

11.8.8 The court will need to be satisfied by credible evidence either that the company is solvent and able to pay its debts as they fall due or that a particular transaction or series of transactions in respect of which the order is sought will be beneficial to or will not prejudice the interests of all the unsecured creditors as a class (*Denney v John Hudson & Co Ltd* [1992] BCLC 901; *Re Fairway Graphics Ltd* [1991] BCLC 468).

11.8.9 A draft of the order sought should be attached to the application.

11.8.10 Similar considerations to those set out above are likely to apply to applications seeking ratification of a transaction or payment after the making of a winding-up order.

12. Applications

12.1 In accordance with rule 13.2(2), in the Royal Courts of Justice the member of court staff in charge of the winding up list has been authorised to deal with applications:

(1) to extend or abridge time prescribed by the Insolvency Rules in connection with winding up (rule 4.3);

(2) for permission to withdraw a winding up petition (rule 4.15);

(3) for the substitution of a petitioner (rule 4.19);

(4) by the Official Receiver for limited disclosure of a statement of affairs (rule 4.35);

(5) by the Official Receiver for relief from duties imposed upon him by the Insolvency Rules (rule 4.47);

(6) by the Official Receiver for permission to give notice of a meeting by advertisement only (rule 4.59);

(7) to transfer proceedings from the High Court (Royal Courts of Justice) to a county court after the making of a winding-up order (rule 7.11).

12.2 In District Registries or a county court such applications must be made to a District Judge.

PART THREE: PERSONAL INSOLVENCY

13. Statutory demands

13.1 *Deemed date of service*

13.1.1 A statutory demand is deemed to be served on the date applicable to the method of service set out in CPR Part 6.26 unless the statutory demand is advertised in which case it is deemed served on the date of the appearance of the advertisement pursuant to rule 6.3.

13.2 *Service abroad of statutory demands*

13.2.1 A statutory demand is not a document issued by the court. Permission to serve out of the jurisdiction is not, therefore, required.

13.2.2 Rule 6.3(2) ('Requirements as to service') applies to service of the statutory demand whether within or out of the jurisdiction.

13.2.3 A creditor wishing to serve a statutory demand out of the jurisdiction in a foreign country with which a civil procedure convention has been made (including the Hague Convention) may and, if the assistance of a British Consul is desired, must adopt the procedure prescribed by CPR Part 6.42 and 6.43. In the case of any doubt whether the country is a 'convention country', enquiries should be made of the Queen's Bench Masters' Secretary Department, Room E216, Royal Courts of Justice.

13.2.4 In all other cases, service of the demand must be effected by private arrangement in accordance with rule 6.3(2) and local foreign law.

13.2.5 When a statutory demand is to be served out of the jurisdiction, the time limits of 21 days and 18 days respectively referred to in the demand must be amended as provided in the next paragraph. For this purpose reference should be made to the table set out in the practice direction supplementing Section IV of CPR Part 6.

13.2.6 A creditor should amend the statutory demand as follows:

(1) for any reference to 18 days there must be substituted the appropriate number of days set out in the table plus 4 days;

(2) for any reference to 21 days there must be substituted the appropriate number of days in the table plus 7 days.

13.2.7 Attention is drawn to the fact that in all forms of the statutory demand the figure 18 and the figure 21 occur in more than one place.

13.3 *Substituted service of statutory demands*

13.3.1 The creditor is under an obligation to do all that is reasonable to bring the statutory demand to the debtor's attention and, if practicable, to cause personal service to be effected (rule 6.3(2)).

13.3.2 In the circumstances set out in rule 6.3(3) the demand may instead be advertised. As there is no statutory form of advertisement, the court will accept an advertisement in the following form:

STATUTORY DEMAND

(Debt for liquidated sum payable immediately following a judgment or order of the court)

To (Block letters)

of

TAKE NOTICE that a statutory demand has been issued by:

Name of Creditor:

Address:

The creditor demands payment of £   the amount now due on a judgment or order of the (High Court of Justice   Division) (................County Court) dated the [day] of [month] 20[   ].

The statutory demand is an important document and it is deemed to have been served on you on the date of the first appearance of this advertisement. You must deal with this demand within 21 days of the service upon you or you could be made bankrupt and your property and goods taken away from you. If you are in any doubt as to your position, you should seek advice immediately from a solicitor or your nearest Citizens' Advice Bureau. The statutory demand can be obtained or is available for inspection and collection from:

Name:

Address:

(Solicitor for) the creditor

Tel. No.   Reference:

You have only 21 days from the date of the first appearance of this advertisement before the creditor may present a bankruptcy petition. You have only 18 days from the date of the first appearance of this advertisement within which to apply to the court to set aside the demand.

13.3.3 Where personal service is not effected or the demand is not advertised in the limited circumstances permitted by rule 6.3(3), substituted service is permitted, but the creditor must have taken all those steps which would justify the court making an order for substituted service of a petition. The steps to be taken to obtain an order for substituted service of a petition are set out below. Failure to comply with these requirements may result in the court declining to issue the petition (rule 6.11(9)) or dismissing it.

13.3.4 In most cases, evidence of the following steps will suffice to justify acceptance for presentation of a petition where the statutory demand has been served by substituted service (or to justify making an order for substituted service of a petition):

(1) One personal call at the residence and place of business of the debtor where both are known or at either of such places as is known. Where it is known that the debtor has more than one residential or business address, personal calls should be made at all the addresses.

(2) Should the creditor fail to effect personal service, a first class prepaid letter should be written to the debtor referring to the call(s), the purpose of the same and the failure to meet the debtor, adding that a further call will be made for the same purpose on the [day] of [month] 20[ ] at [ ] hours at [place]. At least two business days' notice should be given of the appointment and copies of the letter sent to all known addresses of the debtor. The appointment letter should also state that:

(a) in the event of the time and place not being convenient, the debtor should propose some other time and place reasonably convenient for the purpose;

(b) (In the case of a statutory demand) if the debtor fails to keep the appointment the creditor proposes to serve the debtor by [advertisement] [post] [insertion through a letter box] or as the case may be, and that, in the event of a bankruptcy petition being presented, the court will be asked to treat such service as service of the demand on the debtor;

(c) (In the case of a petition) if the debtor fails to keep the appointment, application will be made to the Court for an order for substituted service either by advertisement, or in such other manner as the court may think fit.

(3) When attending any appointment made by letter, inquiry should be made as to whether the debtor has received all letters left for him. If the debtor is away, inquiry should also be made as to whether or not letters are being forwarded to an address within the jurisdiction (England and Wales) or elsewhere.

(4) If the debtor is represented by a solicitor, an attempt should be made to arrange an appointment for personal service through such solicitor. The Insolvency Rules enable a solicitor to accept service of a statutory demand on behalf of his client but there is no similar provision in respect of service of a bankruptcy petition.

(5) The certificate of service of a statutory demand filed pursuant to rule 6.11 should deal with all the above matters including all relevant facts as to the debtor's whereabouts and whether the appointment letter(s) have been returned. It should also set out the reasons for the belief that the debtor resides at the relevant address or works at the relevant place of business and whether, so far as is known, the debtor is represented by a solicitor.

13.4 *Setting aside a statutory demand*

13.4.1 The application (Form 6.4) and witness statement in support (Form 6.5) exhibiting a copy of the statutory demand must be filed in court within 18 days of service of the statutory demand on the debtor. Where service is effected by advertisement the period of 18 days is calculated from the date of the first appearance of the advertisement. Three copies of each document must be lodged with the application to enable the court to serve notice of the hearing date on the applicant, the creditor and the person named in Part B of the statutory demand.

13.4.2 Where copies of the documents are not lodged with the application, any order of the Registrar fixing a venue is conditional upon copies of the documents being lodged on the next business day after the Registrar's order otherwise the application will be deemed to have been dismissed.

13.4.3 Where the debt claimed in the statutory demand is based on a judgment, order, liability order, costs certificate, tax assessment or decision of a tribunal, the court will not at this stage inquire into the validity of the debt nor, as a general rule, will it adjourn the application to await the result of an application to set aside the judgment, order decision, costs certificate or any appeal.

13.4.4   Where the debtor (a) claims to have a counterclaim, set-off or cross demand (whether or not he could have raised it in the action in which the judgment or order was obtained) which equals or exceeds the amount of the debt or debts specified in the statutory demand or (b) disputes the debt (not being a debt subject to a judgment, order, liability order, costs certificate or tax assessment) the court will normally set aside the statutory demand if, in its opinion, on the evidence there is a genuine triable issue.

13.4.5   A debtor who wishes to apply to set aside a statutory demand after the expiration of 18 days from the date of service of the statutory demand must apply for an extension of time within which to apply. If the applicant wishes to apply for an injunction to restrain presentation of a petition the application must be made to the Judge. Paragraphs 1 and 2 of Form 6.5 (witness statement in support of application to set aside statutory demand) should be used in support of the application for an extension of time with the following additional paragraphs:

"(3) To the best of my knowledge and belief the creditor(s) named in the demand has/have not presented a petition against me.

(4) The reasons for my failure to apply to set aside the demand within 18 days after service are as follows:…"

If application is made to restrain presentation of a bankruptcy petition the following additional paragraph should be added:

"(5) Unless restrained by injunction the creditor(s) may present a bankruptcy petition against me".

14.   Bankruptcy petitions

14.1   *Listing of petitions*

14.1.1   All petitions presented will be listed under the name of the debtor unless the court directs otherwise.

14.2   *Content of petitions*

14.2.1   The attention of practitioners is drawn to the following points:

(1)   A creditor's petition does not require dating, signing or witnessing but must be verified in accordance with rule 6.12.

(2)   In the heading it is only necessary to recite the debtor's name e.g. Re John William Smith or Re J W Smith (Male). Any alias or trading name will appear in the body of the petition.

14.2.2   Where the petition is based solely on a statutory demand, only the debt claimed in the demand may be included in the petition.

14.2.3   The attention of practitioners is also drawn to rules 6.7 and 6.8, and in particular to rule 6.8(1) where the 'aggregate sum' is made up of a number of debts.

14.2.4   The date of service of the statutory demand should be recited as follows:

(1)   In the case of personal service, the date of service as set out in the certificate of service should be recited and whether service is effected before/after 1700 hours on Monday to Friday or at any time on a Saturday or a Sunday.

(2)   In the case of substituted service (other than by advertisement), the date alleged in the certificate of service should be recited.

(3) In the strictly limited case of service by advertisement under rule 6.3, the date to be alleged is the date of the advertisement's appearance or, as the case may be, its first appearance (see rules 6.3(3) and 6.11(8)).

14.3 *Searches*

14.3.1 The petitioning creditor shall, before presenting a petition, conduct a search for petitions presented against the debtor in the previous 18 months (a) in the Royal Courts of Justice, (b) in the Central London County Court and (c) in any county court which he believes is or was within that period the debtor's own county court within the meaning of rule 6.9A(3) and shall include the following certificate at the end of the petition:

"I/we certify that I/we have conducted a search for petitions presented against the debtor in the period of 18 months ending today and that [no prior petitions have been presented in the said period which are still pending] [a prior petition (No [   ]) has been presented and is pending in the [Court] and we are issuing this petition at risk as to costs].
Signed .... Dated ...."

14.4 *Deposit*

14.4.1 The deposit will be taken by the court and forwarded to the Official Receiver. In the Royal Courts of Justice the petition fee and deposit should be paid in the Fee Room, which will record the receipt and will impress two entries on the original petition, one in respect of the court fee and the other in respect of the deposit. In a District Registry or a county court, the petition fee and deposit should be handed to the duly authorised officer of the court's staff who will record its receipt.

14.4.2 In all cases cheque(s) for the whole amount should be made payable to 'HM Courts and Tribunals Service' or 'HMCTS'.

14.5 *Certificates of continuing debt and of notice of adjournment*

14.5.1 On the hearing of a petition where a bankruptcy order is sought, in order to satisfy the court that the debt on which the petition is founded has not been paid or secured or compounded for the court will normally accept as sufficient a certificate signed by the person representing the petitioning creditor in the following form:

"I certify that I have/my firm has made enquiries of the petitioning creditor(s) within the last business day prior to the hearing/adjourned hearing and to the best of my knowledge and belief the debt on which the petition is founded is still due and owing and has not been paid or secured or compounded for save as to...
Signed .... Dated ...."

14.5.2 For convenience, in the Royal Courts of Justice this certificate is incorporated in the attendance sheet for the parties to complete when they come to court and which is filed after the hearing. A fresh certificate will be required on each adjourned hearing.

14.5.3 On any adjourned hearing of a petition where a bankruptcy order is sought, in order to satisfy the court that the petitioner has complied with rule 6.29, the petitioner will be required to file evidence of the date on which, manner in which and address to which notice of the making of the order of adjournment and of the venue for the adjourned hearing has been sent to:

(1) the debtor, and

(2) any creditor who has given notice under rule 6.23 but was not present at the hearing when the order for adjournment was made or was present at the hearing but the date of the adjourned hearing was not fixed at that hearing. For convenience, in the Royal Courts of Justice this certificate is incorporated in the attendance sheet for the parties to complete when they come to court and which is filed after the hearing and is as follows:

"I certify that the petitioner has complied with rule 6.29 by sending notice of adjournment to the debtor [supporting/opposing creditor(s)] on [date] at [address]".

A fresh certificate will be required on each adjourned hearing.

14.6   *Extension of hearing date of petition*

14.6.1   Late applications for extension of hearing dates under rule 6.28, and failure to attend on the listed hearing of a petition, will be dealt with as follows:

(1)   If an application is submitted less than two clear working days before the hearing date (for example, later than Monday for Thursday, or Wednesday for Monday) the costs of the application will not be allowed under rule 6.28(3).

(2)   If the petition has not been served and no extension has been granted by the time fixed for the hearing of the petition, and if no one attends for the hearing, the petition may be dismissed or re-listed for hearing about 21 days later. The court will notify the petitioning creditor's solicitors (or the petitioning creditor in person), and any known supporting or opposing creditors or their solicitors, of the new date and times. Written evidence should then be filed on behalf of the petitioning creditor explaining fully the reasons for the failure to apply for an extension or to appear at the hearing, and (if appropriate) giving reasons why the petition should not be dismissed.

(3)   On the re-listed hearing the court may dismiss the petition if not satisfied it should be adjourned or a further extension granted.

14.6.2   All applications for an extension should include a statement of the date fixed for the hearing of the petition.

14.6.3   The petitioning creditor should contact the court (by solicitors or in person) on or before the hearing date to ascertain whether the application has reached the file and been dealt with. It should not be assumed that an extension will be granted.

14.7   *Substituted service of bankruptcy petitions*

14.7.1   In most cases evidence that the steps set out in paragraph 13.3.4 have been taken will suffice to justify an order for substituted service of a bankruptcy petition.

14.8   *Validation orders*

14.8.1   A person against whom a bankruptcy petition has been presented ('the debtor') may apply to the court after presentation of the petition for relief from the effects of section 284(1)–(3) of the Act by seeking an order that any disposition of his assets or payment made out of his funds, including any bank account (whether it is in credit or overdrawn) shall not be void in the event of a bankruptcy order being made on the petition (a 'validation order').

14.8.2   Save in exceptional circumstances, notice of the making of the application should be given to (a) the petitioning creditor(s) or other petitioner, (b) any creditor who has given notice to the petitioner of his intention to appear on the hearing of the petition pursuant to r 6.23 1986, (c) any creditor who has been substituted as petitioner pursuant to r 6.30 Insolvency Rules 1986 and (d) any creditor who has carriage of the petition pursuant to r 6.31 Insolvency Rules 1986.

14.8.3   The application should be supported by a witness statement which, save in exceptional circumstances, should be made by the debtor. If appropriate, supporting evidence in the form of a witness statement from the debtor's accountant should also be produced.

14.8.4   The extent and contents of the evidence will vary according to the circumstances and the nature of the relief sought, but in a case where the debtor is trading or carrying on business it should include, as a minimum, the following information:

(1)   when and to whom notice has been given in accordance with paragraph 14.8.2 above;

(2) brief details of the circumstances leading to presentation of the petition;

(3) how the debtor became aware of the presentation of the petition;

(4) whether the petition debt is admitted or disputed and, if the latter, brief details of the basis on which the debt is disputed;

(5) full details of the debtor's financial position including details of his assets (including details of any security and the amount(s) secured) and liabilities, which should be supported, as far as possible, by documentary evidence, e.g. accounts, draft accounts, management accounts or estimated statement of affairs;

(6) a cash flow forecast and profit and loss projection for the period for which the order is sought;

(7) details of the dispositions or payments in respect of which an order is sought;

(8) the reasons relied on in support of the need for such dispositions or payments to be made;

(9) any other information relevant to the exercise of the court's discretion;

(10) details of any consents obtained from the persons mentioned in paragraph 14.8.2 above (supported by documentary evidence where appropriate);

(11) details of any relevant bank account, including its number and the address and sort code of the bank at which such account is held.

14.8.5   Where an application is made urgently to enable payments to be made which are essential to continued trading (e.g. wages) and it is not possible to assemble all the evidence listed above, the court may consider granting limited relief for a short period, but there must be sufficient evidence to satisfy the court that the interests of creditors are unlikely to be prejudiced.

14.8.6   Where the debtor is not trading or carrying on business and the application relates only to a proposed sale, mortgage or re-mortgage of the debtor's home evidence of the following will generally suffice:

(1) when and to whom notice has been given in accordance with 14.8.2 above;

(2) whether the petition debt is admitted or disputed and, if the latter, brief details of the basis on which the debt is disputed;

(3) details of the property to be sold, mortgaged or re-mortgaged (including its title number);

(4) the value of the property and the proposed sale price, or details of the mortgage or re-mortgage;

(5) details of any existing mortgages or charges on the property and redemption figures;

(6) the costs of sale (e.g. solicitors' or agents' costs);

(7) how and by whom any net proceeds of sale (or sums coming into the debtor's hands as a result of any mortgage or re-mortgage) are to be held pending the final hearing of the petition;

(8) any other information relevant to the exercise of the court's discretion;

(9) details of any consents obtained from the persons mentioned in 14.8.2 above (supported by documentary evidence where appropriate).

14.8.7   Whether or not the debtor is trading or carrying on business, where the application involves a disposition of property the court will need to be satisfied that any proposed disposal will be at a proper value. Accordingly an independent valuation should be obtained and exhibited to the evidence.

14.8.8   The court will need to be satisfied by credible evidence that the debtor is solvent and able to pay his debts as they fall due or that a particular transaction or series of transactions in respect of which the order is sought will be beneficial to or will not prejudice the interests of all the unsecured creditors as a class (Denney v John Hudson & Co Ltd [1992] BCLC 901, [1992] BCC 503, CA; Re Fairway Graphics Ltd [1991] BCLC 468).

14.8.9   A draft of the order sought should be attached to the application.

14.8.10   Similar considerations to those set out above are likely to apply to applications seeking ratification of a transaction or payment after the making of a bankruptcy order.

15.   Applications

15.1   In accordance with rule 13.2(2), in the Royal Courts of Justice the member of court staff in charge of the winding up list has been authorised to deal with applications:

(1)   by petitioning creditors to extend the time for hearing petitions (rule 6.28);

(2)   by the Official Receiver:

    (a)   to transfer proceedings from the High Court to a county court (rule 7.13);

    (b)   to amend the title of the proceedings (rules 6.35 and 6.47).

15.2   In District Registries or a county court such applications must be made to the District Judge.

16.   Orders without attendance

16.1   In suitable cases the court will normally be prepared to make orders under Part VIII of the Act (Individual Voluntary Arrangements), without the attendance of the parties, provided there is no bankruptcy order in existence and (so far as is known) no pending petition. The orders are:

(1)   A 14 day interim order adjourning the application for 14 days for consideration of the nominee's report, where the papers are in order, and the nominee's signed consent to act includes a waiver of notice of the application or the consent by the nominee to the making of an interim order without attendance.

(2)   A standard order on consideration of the nominee's report, extending the interim order to a date seven weeks after the date of the proposed meeting, directing the meeting to be summoned and adjourning to a date about three weeks after the meeting. Such an order may be made without attendance if the nominee's report has been delivered to the court and complies with section 256(1) of the Act and rule 5.11(2) and (3) and proposes a date for the meeting not less than 14 days from that on which the nominee's report is filed in court under rule 5.11 nor more than 28 days from that on which that report is considered by the court under rule 5.13.

(3)   A 'concertina' order, combining orders as under (1) and (2) above. Such an order may be made without attendance if the initial application for an interim order is accompanied by a report of the nominee and the conditions set out in (1) and (2) above are satisfied.

(4)   A final order on consideration of the chairman's report. Such an order may be made without attendance if the chairman's report has been filed and complies with rule 5.27(1). The order will record the effect of the chairman's report and may discharge the interim order.

16.2   Provided that the conditions under sub-paragraphs (2) and (4) above are satisfied and that the appropriate report has been lodged with the court in due time the parties need not attend or be represented on the adjourned hearing for consideration of the nominee's report or of the chairman's report (as the case may be) unless they are notified by the court that attendance is required. Sealed copies of the order made (in all four cases as above) will be posted by the court to the applicant or his solicitor and to the nominee.

16.3   In suitable cases the court may also make consent orders without attendance by the parties. The written consent of the parties will be required. Examples of such orders are as follows:

(1)   on applications to set aside a statutory demand, orders:

    (a)   dismissing the application, with or without an order for costs as may be agreed (permission will be given to present a petition on or after the seventh day after the date of the order, unless a different date is agreed);

(b) setting aside the demand, with or without an order for costs as may be agreed; or

(2) On petitions where there is a negative list of supporting or opposing creditors in Form 6.21, or a statement signed by or on behalf of the petitioning creditor that no notices have been received from supporting or opposing creditors, orders:

(a) dismissing the petition, with or without an order for costs as may be agreed; or

(b) if the petition has not been served, giving permission to withdraw the petition (with no order for costs).

(3) On other applications, orders:

(a) for sale of property, possession of property, disposal of proceeds of sale;

(b) giving interim directions;

(c) dismissing the application, with or without an order for costs as may be agreed;

(d) giving permission to withdraw the application, with or without an order for costs as may be agreed.

16.4 If, as may often be the case with orders under subparagraphs 3(a) or (b) above, an adjournment is required, whether generally with liberty to restore or to a fixed date, the order by consent may include an order for the adjournment. If adjournment to a date is requested, a time estimate should be given and the court will fix the first available date and time on or after the date requested.

16.5 The above lists should not be regarded as exhaustive, nor should it be assumed that an order will be made without attendance as requested.

16.6 Applications for consent orders without attendance should be lodged at least two clear working days (and preferably longer) before any hearing date.

16.7 Whenever a document is lodged or a letter sent, the correct case number should be quoted. A note should also be given of the date and time of the next hearing (if any).

17. Bankruptcy restrictions undertakings

17.1 Where a bankrupt has given a bankruptcy restrictions undertaking, the Secretary of State or official receiver must file a copy in court and send a copy to the bankrupt as soon as reasonably practicable (rule 6.250). In addition the Secretary of State must notify the court immediately that the bankrupt has given such an undertaking in order that any hearing date can be vacated.

18. Persons at risk of violence

18.1 Where an application is made pursuant to rule 5.67, 5.68, 5A 18, or 6.235B or otherwise to limit disclosure of information as to a person's current address by reason of the possibility of violence, the relevant application should be accompanied by a witness statement which includes the following:

(1) The grounds upon which it is contended that disclosure of the current address as defined by the Insolvency Rules might reasonably be expected to lead to violence against the debtor or a person who normally resides with him or her as a member of his or her family or where appropriate any other person.

(2) Where the application is made in respect of the address of the debtor, the debtor's proposals with regard to information which may safely be given to potential creditors in order that they can recognise that the debtor is a person who may be indebted to them, in particular the address at which the debtor previously resided or carried on business and the nature of such business.

(3) The terms of the order sought by the applicant by reference to the court's particular powers as set out in the rule under which the application is made and, unless impracticable, a draft of the order sought.

(4)   Where the application is made by the debtor in respect of whom a nominee or supervisor has been appointed or against whom a bankruptcy order has been made, evidence of the consent of the nominee/supervisor, or, in the case of bankruptcy, the trustee in bankruptcy, if one has been appointed, and the official receiver if a trustee in bankruptcy has not been appointed. Where such consent is not available the statement must indicate whether such consent has been refused.

The application shall in any event make such person a respondent to the application.

18.2   The application shall be referred to the Registrar who will consider it without a hearing in the first instance but without prejudice to the right of the court to list it for hearing if:

(1)   the court is minded to refuse the application;

(2)   the consent of any respondent is not attached;

(3)   the court is of the view that there is another reason why listing is appropriate.

PART FOUR: APPEALS

19. Appeals

19.1   An appeal from a decision of a county court (whether made by a District Judge, a Recorder or a Circuit Judge) or of a Registrar in insolvency proceedings lies to a Judge of the High Court.

19.2   An appeal from a decision of a Judge of the High Court, whether at first instance or on appeal, lies to the Court of Appeal.

19.3   A first appeal, whether under 19.1 or 19.2 above, is subject to the permission requirements of CPR Part 52, rule 3.

19.4   An appeal from a decision of a Judge of the High Court which was made on a first appeal requires the permission of the Court of Appeal.

19.5 *Filing Appeals*

19.5.1   An appeal from a decision of a Registrar must be filed at the Royal Courts of Justice in London.

19.5.2   An appeal from a decision of a District Judge sitting in a district registry of the High Court may be filed:

(1)   at the Royal Courts of Justice in London; or

(2)   in that district registry.

19.6   The court centres at which appeals from decisions of county courts on any particular Circuit must be filed, managed and heard (unless the appeal court otherwise orders) are as follows:

Midland Circuit: Birmingham

North Eastern Circuit: Leeds or Newcastle upon Tyne

Northern Circuit: Manchester or Liverpool

Wales Circuit: Cardiff, Caernarfon or Mold

Western Circuit: Bristol

South Eastern Circuit: Royal Courts of Justice.

19.7   Where the lower court is a county court:

(1)   an appeal or application for permission to appeal from a decision of a District Judge will be heard or considered by a High Court Judge or by any person authorised under section 9 of the Senior Courts Act 1981 to act as a judge of the High Court in the Chancery Division;

(2) an appeal or application for permission to appeal from a decision of a Recorder or a Circuit Judge will be heard or considered by a High Court Judge or by a person authorised under paragraphs (1), (2) or (4) of the table in section 9(1) of the Senior Courts Act 1981 to act as a judge of the High Court in the Chancery Division;

(3) other applications in any appeal or application for permission to appeal may be heard or considered and directions may be given by a High Court Judge or by any person authorised under section 9 of the Senior Courts Act 1981 to act as a judge of the High Court in the Chancery Division.

19.8 In the case of appeals from decisions of Registrars or District Judges in the High Court, appeals, applications for permission to appeal and other applications may be heard or considered and directions may be given by a High Court Judge or by any person authorised under section 9 of the Senior Courts Act 1981 to act as a judge of the High Court in the Chancery Division.

19.9.1 CPR Part 52 and sections I and IV of Practice Direction 52 and its Forms shall, as appropriate, apply to appeals in insolvency proceedings, save as provided below.

19.9.2 Paragraphs 8.2 to 8.8, 8.13, 8.14 and 8A.1 of Practice Direction 52 shall not apply, and paragraph 8.9 shall apply with the exclusion of the last sentence.

PART FIVE: APPLICATIONS RELATING TO THE REMUNERATION OF APPOINTEES

20. Remuneration of Appointees

20.1 *Introduction*

20.1.1 This Part of the Practice Direction applies to any remuneration application made under the Act or the Insolvency Rules.

20.2 *The objective and guiding principles*

20.2.1 The objective of this Part of the Practice Direction is to ensure that the remuneration of an appointee which is fixed and approved by the court is fair, reasonable and commensurate with the nature and extent of the work properly undertaken by the appointee in any given case and is fixed and approved by a process which is consistent and predictable.

20.2.2 Set out below are the guiding principles by reference to which remuneration applications are to be considered both by applicants, in the preparation and presentation of their application, and by the court determining such applications.

20.2.3 The guiding principles are as follows:

(1) "Justification"

It is for the appointee who seeks to be remunerated at a particular level and / or in a particular manner to justify his claim and in order to do so the appointee should be prepared to provide full particulars of the basis for and the nature of his claim for remuneration.

(2) "The benefit of the doubt"

The corollary of guiding principle (1) is that on any remuneration application, if after considering the evidence before it and after having regard to the guiding principles (in particular guiding principle (3)), the matters contained in paragraph 20.4.2 (in particular paragraph 20.4.2 (10)) and the matters referred to in paragraph 20.4.3 (as appropriate) there remains any element of doubt as to the appropriateness, fairness or reasonableness of the remuneration sought or to be fixed (whether arising from a lack of particularity as to the basis for and the nature of the appointee's claim to remuneration or otherwise) such element of doubt should be resolved by the court against the appointee.

(3) "Professional integrity"

The court should (where this is the case) give weight to the fact that the appointee is a member of a regulated profession and as such is subject to rules and guidance as to professional conduct and the fact that (where this is the case) the appointee is an officer of the court.

(4) "The value of the service rendered"

The remuneration of an appointee should reflect the value of the service rendered by the appointee, not simply reimburse the appointee in respect of time expended and cost incurred.

(5) "Fair and reasonable"

The amount of the appointee's remuneration should represent fair and reasonable remuneration for the work properly undertaken or to be undertaken.

(6) "Proportionality"

(a) "Proportionality of information"

In considering the nature and extent of the information which should be provided by an appointee in respect of a remuneration application the court, the appointee and any other parties to the application shall have regard to what is proportionate by reference to the amount of remuneration to be fixed, the nature, complexity and extent of the work to be completed (where the application relates to future remuneration) or that has been completed by the appointee and the value and nature of the assets and liabilities with which the appointee will have to deal or has had to deal.

(b) "Proportionality of remuneration"

The amount of remuneration to be fixed by the court should be proportionate to the nature, complexity and extent of the work to be completed (where the application relates to future remuneration) or that has been completed by the appointee and the value and nature of the assets and/or potential assets and the liabilities and/or potential liabilities with which the appointee will have to deal or has had to deal, the nature and degree of the responsibility to which the appointee has been subject in any given case, the nature and extent of the risk (if any) assumed by the appointee and the efficiency (in respect of both time and cost) with which the appointee has completed the work undertaken.

(7) "Professional guidance"

In respect of an application for the fixing and approval of the remuneration of an appointee, the appointee may have regard to the relevant and current statements of practice promulgated by any relevant regulatory and professional bodies in relation to the fixing of the remuneration of an appointee. In considering a remuneration application, the court may also have regard to such statements of practice and the extent of compliance with such statements of practice by the appointee.

(8) "Timing of application"

The court will take into account whether any application should have been made earlier and if so the reasons for any delay in making it.

20.3 *Hearing of remuneration applications*

20.3.1 On the hearing of the application the court shall consider the evidence then available to it and may either summarily determine the application or adjourn it giving such directions as it thinks appropriate.

20.3.2   Whilst the application will normally be determined summarily by a Registrar sitting alone, where it is sufficiently complex, the court may direct that:

(1)   an assessor or a Costs Judge prepare a report to the court in respect of the remuneration which is sought to be fixed and approved; and/or

(2)   the application be heard by the Registrar sitting with or without an assessor or a Costs Judge or by a Judge sitting with or without an assessor or a Costs Judge.

20.4   *Relevant criteria and procedure*

20.4.1   When considering a remuneration application the court shall have regard to the objective, the guiding principles and all relevant circumstances including the matters referred to in paragraph 20.4.2 and where appropriate paragraph 20.4.3, each of which should be addressed in the evidence placed before the court.

20.4.2   On any remuneration application, the appointee should:

(1)   Provide a narrative description and explanation of:

   (a)   the background to, the relevant circumstances of and the reasons for the appointment;

   (b)   the work undertaken or to be undertaken in respect of the appointment; the description should be divided, insofar as possible, into individual tasks or categories of task (general descriptions of work, tasks, or categories of task should (insofar as possible) be avoided);

   (c)   the reasons why it is or was considered reasonable and/or necessary and/or beneficial for such work to be done, giving details of why particular tasks or categories of task were undertaken and why such tasks or categories of task are to be undertaken or have been undertaken by particular individuals and in a particular manner;

   (d)   the amount of time to be spent or that has been spent in respect of work to be completed or that has been completed and why it is considered to be fair, reasonable and proportionate;

   (e)   what is likely to be and has been achieved, the benefits that are likely to and have accrued as a consequence of the work that is to be or has been completed, the manner in which the work required in respect of the appointment is progressing and what, in the opinion of the appointee, remains to be achieved.

(2)   Provide details sufficient for the court to determine the application by reference to the criteria which are required to be taken into account by reference to the Insolvency Rules and any other applicable enactments or rules relevant to the fixing of the remuneration.

(3)   Provide a statement of the total number of hours of work undertaken or to be undertaken in respect of which the remuneration is sought, together with a breakdown of such hours by individual member of staff and individual tasks or categories of tasks to be performed or that have been performed. Where appropriate, a proportionate level of detail should also be given of:

   (a)   the tasks or categories of tasks to be undertaken as a proportion of the total amount of work to be undertaken in respect of which the remuneration is sought and the tasks or categories of tasks that have been undertaken as a proportion of the total amount of work that has been undertaken in respect of which the remuneration is sought; and

   (b)   the tasks or categories of task to be completed by individual members of staff or grade of personnel including the appointee as a proportion of the total amount of work to be completed by all members of staff including the appointee in respect of which the remuneration is sought, or the tasks or categories of task that have been completed by individual members of staff or grade of personnel as a proportion of the total amount of work that has been completed by all members of staff including the appointee in respect of which the remuneration is sought.

(4) Provide a statement of the total amount to be charged for the work to be undertaken or that has been undertaken in respect of which the remuneration is sought which should include:

(a) a breakdown of such amounts by individual member of staff and individual task or categories of task performed or to be performed;

(b) details of the time expended or to be expended and the remuneration charged or to be charged in respect of each individual task or category of task as a proportion (respectively) of the total time expended or to be expended and the total remuneration charged or to be charged.

In respect of an application pursuant to which some or all of the amount of the appointee's remuneration is to be fixed on a basis other than time properly spent, the appointee shall provide (for the purposes of comparison) the same details as are required by this paragraph (4), but on the basis of what would have been charged had he been seeking remuneration on the basis of the time properly spent by him and his staff.

(5) Provide details of each individual to be engaged or who has been engaged in work in respect of the appointment and in respect of which the remuneration is sought, including details of their relevant experience, training, qualifications and the level of their seniority.

(6) Provide an explanation of:

(a) the steps, if any, to be taken or that have been taken by the appointee to avoid duplication of effort and cost in respect of the work to be completed or that has been completed in respect of which the remuneration is sought;

(b) the steps to be taken or that have been taken to ensure that the work to be completed or that has been completed is to be or was undertaken by individuals of appropriate experience and seniority relative to the nature of the work to be or that has been undertaken.

(7) Provide details of the individual rates charged by the appointee and members of his staff in respect of the work to be completed or that has been completed and in respect of which the remuneration is sought. Such details should include:

(a) a general explanation of the policy adopted in relation to the fixing or calculation of such rates and the recording of time spent;

(b) where, exceptionally, the appointee seeks remuneration in respect of time spent by secretaries, cashiers or other administrative staff whose work would otherwise be regarded as an overhead cost forming a component part of the rates charged by the appointee and members of his staff, a detailed explanation as to why such costs should be allowed should be provided.

(8) Where the remuneration application is in respect of a period of time during which the charge-out rates of the appointee and/or members of his staff engaged in work in respect of the appointment have increased, provide an explanation of the nature, extent and reason for such increase and the date when such increase took effect. This paragraph (8) does not apply to applications to which paragraph 20.4.3 applies.

(9) Provide details of any remuneration previously fixed or approved in relation to the appointment (whether by the court or otherwise) including in particular the amounts that were previously sought to be fixed or approved and the amounts that were in fact fixed or approved and the basis upon which such amounts were fixed or approved.

(10) In order that the court may be able to consider the views of any persons who the appointee considers have an interest in the assets that are under his control, provide details of:

   (a)   what (if any) consultation has taken place between the appointee and those persons and if no such consultation has taken place an explanation as to the reason why;

   (b)   the number and value of the interests of the persons consulted including details of the proportion (by number and by value) of the interests of such persons by reference to the entirety of those persons having an interest in the assets under the control of the appointee.

(11) Provide such other relevant information as the appointee considers, in the circumstances, ought to be provided to the court.

20.4.3   This paragraph applies to applications where some or all of the remuneration of the appointee is to be fixed and approved on a basis other than time properly spent. On such applications in addition to the matters referred to in paragraph 20.4.2 (as applicable) the appointee shall:

   (1)   Provide a full description of the reasons for remuneration being sought by reference to the basis contended for.

   (2)   Where the remuneration is sought to be fixed by reference to a percentage of the value of the assets which are realised or distributed, provide a full explanation of the basis upon which any percentage rates to be applied to the values of the assets realised and/or distributed have been chosen.

   (3)   Provide a statement that to the best of the appointee's belief the percentage rates or other bases by reference to which some or all of the remuneration is to be fixed are similar to the percentage rates or other bases that are applied or have been applied in respect of other appointments of a similar nature.

   (4)   Provide a comparison of the amount to be charged by reference to the basis contended for and the amount that would otherwise have been charged by reference to the other available bases of remuneration, including the scale of fees in Schedule 6 to the Insolvency Rules.

20.4.4   If and insofar as any of the matters referred to in paragraph 20.4.2 or 20.4.3 (as appropriate) are not addressed in the evidence, an explanation for why this is the case should be included in such evidence.

20.4.5   For the avoidance of doubt and where appropriate and proportionate, paragraphs 20.4.2 to 20.4.4 (inclusive) are applicable to applications for the apportionment of remuneration as between a new appointee and a former appointee in circumstances where some or all of the former appointee's remuneration was based upon a set amount under the Insolvency Rules and the former appointee has ceased (for whatever reason) to hold office before the time has elapsed or the work has been completed in respect of which the set amount of remuneration was fixed.

20.4.6   The evidence placed before the court by the appointee in respect of any remuneration application should include the following documents:

   (1)   a copy of the most recent receipts and payments account;

   (2)   copies of any reports by the appointee to the persons having an interest in the assets under his control relevant to the period for which the remuneration sought to be fixed and approved relates;

   (3)   any schedules or such other documents providing the information referred to in paragraphs 20.4.2 and 20.4.3 where these are likely to be of assistance to the court in considering the application;

   (4)   evidence of any consultation with those persons having an interest in the assets under the control of appointee in relation to the remuneration of the appointee.

20.4.7   On any remuneration application the court may make an order allowing payments of remuneration to be made on account subject to final approval whether by the court or otherwise.

20.4.8 Unless otherwise ordered by the court (or as may otherwise be provided for in any enactment or rules of procedure) the costs of and occasioned by an application for the fixing and/or approval of the remuneration of an appointee, including those of any assessor, shall be paid out of the assets under the control of the appointee.

Appendix V

Practice Direction—Order under section 127 Insolvency Act 1986 [2007] B.C.C. 839

This Practice Direction supplements Part 49.

1. Attention is drawn to the undesirability of asking as a matter of course for a winding up order as an alternative to an order under s.994 of the Companies Act 2006. The petition should not ask for a winding up order unless that is the remedy which the petitioner prefers or it is thought that it may be the only remedy to which the petitioner is entitled.

2. Whenever a winding up order is asked for in a contributory's petition, the petition must state whether the petitioner consents or objects to an order under s.127 of the Insolvency Act 1986 ('a s.127 order') in the standard form. If he objects, the written evidence in support must contain a short statement of his reasons.

3. If the petitioner objects to a s.127 order in the standard form but consents to such an order in a modified form, the petition must set out in the form of order to which he consents, and the written evidence in support must contain a short statement of his reasons for seeking the modification.

4. If the petition contains a statement that the petitioner consents to a s.127 order, whether in the standard or a modified form, but the petitioner changes his mind before the first hearing of the petition, he must notify the respondents and may apply on notice to a Judge for an order directing that no s.127 order or a modified order only (as the case may be) shall be made by the Registrar, but validating dispositions made without notice of the order made by the Judge.

5. If the petition contains a statement that the petitioner consents to a s.127 order, whether in the standard or a modified form, the Registrar shall without further enquiry make an order in such form at the first hearing unless an order to the contrary has been made by the Judge in the meantime.

6. If the petition contains a statement that the petitioner objects to a s.127 order in the standard form, the company may apply (in the case of urgency, without notice) to the Judge for an order.

7. Section 127 Order—Standard Form:

(Title etc.)

ORDER that notwithstanding the presentation of the said petition

(1) payments made into or out of the bank accounts of the Company in the ordinary course of business of the Company and

(2) dispositions of the property of the Company made in the ordinary course of its business for proper value between the date of presentation of the Petition and the date of judgment on the Petition or further order in the meantime

shall not be void by virtue of the provisions of section 127 of the Insolvency Act 1986 in the event of an Order for the winding up of the Company being made on the said Petition provided that (the relevant bank) shall be under no obligation to verify for itself whether any transaction through the company's bank accounts is in the ordinary course of business, or that it represents full market value for the relevant transaction.

This form of Order may be departed from where the circumstances of the case require.

GENERAL NOTE

This *Practice Direction* should be read with para.11.8 of the *Practice Direction: Insolvency Proceedings* [2012] B.C.C. 265 (reproduced as App.IV to this *Guide*). See the note to IA 1986 s.127.

Appendix VI

Practice Direction: Directors Disqualification Proceedings [2007] B.C.C. 862

This *Practice Direction* (PD) was first issued in 1999 and is most recently reported in [2007] B.C.C. 862. It has since been amended from time to time and the text below shows the PD as at February 29, 2012. The current version at any time is to be found at *http://www.justice.gov.uk/civil/procrules_fin/contents/ practice_directions/disqualification_proceedings.htm*.

CONTENTS OF THIS PRACTICE DIRECTION

1. Application and interpretation

1.1 In this practice direction:

  (1) "the Act" means the Company Directors Disqualification Act 1986;

  (2) "the Disqualification Rules" means the rules for the time being in force made under section 411 of the Insolvency Act 1986 in relation to disqualification proceedings [the current rules are the Insolvent Companies (Disqualification of Unfit Directors) Proceedings Rules 1987 (SI 1987/2023)];

  (3) "the Insolvency Rules" means the rules for the time being in force made under sections 411 and 412 of the Insolvency Act 1986 in relation to insolvency proceedings;

  (4) "CPR" means the Civil Procedure Rules 1998 and "CPR" followed by "Part" or "rule" and a number means the part or rule with that number in those Rules;

  (5) "disqualification proceedings" has the meaning set out in paragraph 1.3 below;

  (6) "a disqualification application" is an application under the Act for the making of a disqualification order;

  (7) "registrar" means any judge of the High Court or the county court who is a registrar within the meaning of the Insolvency Rules;

  (8) "companies court registrar" means any judge of the High Court sitting in the Royal Courts of Justice in London who is a registrar within the meaning of the Insolvency Rules.

  (9) except where the context otherwise requires references to;

    (a) 'company' or 'companies' shall include references to 'partnership' or 'partnerships' and to 'limited liability partnership' and 'limited liability partnerships'

    (b) 'director' shall include references to an 'officer' of a partnership and to a 'member' of a limited liability partnership:

    (c) 'shadow director' shall include references to a 'shadow member' of a limited liability partnership

  and, in appropriate cases, the forms annexed to this practice direction shall be varied accordingly;

  (10) 'disqualification order' has the meaning set out in section 1 of the Act and 'disqualification undertaking' has the meaning set out in section 1A or section 9B of the Act (as the context requires);

  (11) a 'Section 8A application' is an application under section 8A of the Act to reduce the period for which a disqualification undertaking is in force or to provide for it to cease to be in force;

  (12) 'specified regulator' has the meaning set out in section 9E(2) of the Act.

1.2 This practice direction shall come into effect on 26 April 1999 and shall replace all previous practice directions relating to disqualification proceedings.

1.3 This practice direction applies to the following proceedings ("disqualification proceedings"):

  (1) disqualification applications made:

    (a) under section 2(2)(a) of the Act (after the person's conviction of an indictable offence in connection with the affairs of a company);

    (b) under section 3 of the Act (on the ground of persistent breaches of provisions of companies legislation);

    (c)   under section 4 of the Act (on the ground of fraud, etc.);

    (d)   by the Secretary of State or the official receiver under section 7(1) of the Act (on the ground that the person is or has been a director of a company which has at any time become insolvent and his conduct makes him unfit to be concerned in the management of a company);

    (e)   by the Secretary of State under section 8 of the Act (on it appearing to the Secretary of State from investigative material that it is expedient in the public interest that a disqualification order should be made); or

    (f)   by the Office of Fair Trading or a specified regulator under section 9A of the Act (on the ground of breach of competition law by an undertaking and unfitness to be concerned in the management of a company);

  (2)   any application made under section 7(2) or 7(4) of the Act; and

  (3)   any application for permission to act made under section 17 of the Act for the purposes of any of sections 1(1)(a), 1A(1)(a) or 9B(4), or made under section 12(2) of the Act;

  (4)   any application for a court order made under CPR Part 23 in the course of any of the proceedings set out in sub-paragraphs (1) to (3) above;

  (5)   any application under the Act to the extent provided for by subordinate legislation;

  (6)   any section 8A application.

2. Multi-track

2.1   All disqualification proceedings are allocated to the multi-track. The CPR relating to allocation questionnaires and track allocation shall not apply.

3. Rights of audience

3.1   Official receivers and deputy official receivers have right of audience in any proceedings to which this Practice Direction applies, including cases where a disqualification application is made by the Secretary of State or by the official receiver at his direction, and whether made in the High Court or a county court [r.10 of the *Insolvent Companies (Disqualification of Unfit Directors) Proceedings Rules 1987*].

PART TWO

DISQUALIFICATION APPLICATIONS

4. Commencement

4.1   Sections 2(2)(a), 3(4), 4(2), 6(3), 8(3) and 9E(3) of the Act identify the civil courts which have jurisdiction to deal with disqualification applications.

4.1A   A disqualification application must be commenced by a claim form issued:

  (1)   in the case of a disqualification application under section 9A of the Act, in the High Court out of the office of the companies court registrar at the Royal Courts of Justice;

  (2)   in any other case,

    (a)   in the High Court out of the office of the companies court registrar or a chancery district registry; and

    (b)   in the county court, out of a county court office.

4.2 Disqualification applications shall be made by the issue of a claim form in the form annexed hereto and the use of the procedure set out in CPR Part 8 [r.2(2) of the *Insolvent Companies (Disqualification of Unfit Directors) Proceedings Rules* 1987 as amended], as modified by this practice direction and (where the application is made under sections 7, 8 or 9A of the Act) the Disqualification Rules. [For convenience, relevant references to the *Insolvent Companies (Disqualification of Unfit Directors) Proceedings Rules* 1987, which apply to disqualification applications under sections 7 and 8 of the Act (see r.1(3)(a) and (b)) are set out in notes to this Practice Direction.] CPR rule 8.1(3) (power of the Court to order the application to continue as if the claimant had not used the Part 8 procedure) shall not apply.

4.3 When the claim form is issued, the claimant will be given a date for the first hearing of the disqualification application. This date is to be not less than eight weeks from the date of issue of the claim form [r.7(1) of the *Insolvent Companies (Disqualification of Unfit Directors) Proceedings Rules* 1987]. The first hearing will be before a registrar.

5. Headings

5.1 Every claim form by which an application under the Act is begun and all affidavits, notices and other documents in the proceedings must be entitled in the matter of the company or companies in question and in the matter of the Act. In the case of any disqualification application under section 7 or 9A of the Act it is not necessary to mention in the heading any company other than that referred to in section 6(1)(a) or 9A(2) of the Act (as the case may be).

6. The claim form

6.1 CPR r. 8.2 does not apply. The claim form must state:

(1) that CPR Part 8 (as modified by this practice direction) applies, and (if the application is made under sections 7, 8 or 9A of the Act) that the application is made in accordance with the Disqualification Rules [r.4(a) of the *Insolvent Companies (Disqualification of Unfit Directors) Proceedings Rules* 1987];

(2) that the claimant seeks a disqualification order, and the section of the Act pursuant to which the disqualification application is made;

(3) the period for which, in accordance with the Act, the court has power to impose a disqualification period. The periods are as follows:–

   (a) where the application is under section 2 of the Act, for a period of up to 15 years;

   (b) where the application is under section 3 of the Act, for a period of up to five years;

   (c) where the application is under section 4 of the Act, for a period of up to 15 years;

   (d) where the application is under section 7 of the Act, for a period of not less than two, and up to 15, years [r.4(b)(i) of the *Insolvent Companies (Disqualification of Unfit Directors) Proceedings Rules* 1987];

   (e) where the application is under section 8 or 9A of the Act, for a period of up to 15 years [r.4(b)(ii) of the *Insolvent Companies (Disqualification of Unfit Directors) Proceedings Rules* 1987].

(4) in cases where the application is made under sections 7, 8 or 9A of the Act, that on the first hearing of the application, the court may hear and determine it summarily, without further or other notice to the defendant, and that, if the application is so determined, the court may impose a period of disqualification of up to five years but that if at the hearing of the application the court, on the evidence then before it, is minded to impose, in the case of any defendant, disqualification for any period longer than five years, it will not make a disqualification order on that occasion but will adjourn the application to be heard (with further evidence, if any) at a later date that will be

notified to the defendant [r.4(c) and (d) of the *Insolvent Companies (Disqualification of Unfit Directors) Proceedings Rules* 1987];

(5) that any evidence which the defendant wishes the court to take into consideration must be filed in court in accordance with the time limits set out in paragraph 9 below (which time limits shall be set out in the notes to the Claim Form) [r.4(e) of the *Insolvent Companies (Disqualification of Unfit Directors) Proceedings Rules* 1987].

7. Service of the claim form

7.1 Service of claim forms in disqualification proceedings will be the responsibility of the claimant and will not be undertaken by the court.

7.2 The claim form shall be served by the claimant on the defendant. It may be served by sending it by first class post to his last known address; and the date of service shall, unless the contrary is shown, be deemed to be the seventh day following that on which the claim form was posted [r.5(1) of the *Insolvent Companies (Disqualification of Unfit Directors) Proceedings Rules* 1987]. CPR r. 6.7(1) shall be modified accordingly. Otherwise sections I and II of CPR Part 6 apply.

7.3 Where any claim form or order of the court or other document is required under any disqualification proceedings to be served on any person who is not in England and Wales, the court may order service on him to be effected within such time and in such manner as it thinks fit, may require such proof of service as it thinks fit [r.5(2) of the *Insolvent Companies (Disqualification of Unfit Directors) Proceedings Rules* 1987], and may give such directions as to acknowledgement of service as it thinks fit. Section III of CPR Part 6 shall not apply.

7.4 The claim form served on the defendant shall be accompanied by an acknowledgement of service.

8. Acknowledgment of service

8.1 The form of acknowledgment of service is annexed to this practice direction. CPR rules 8.3(2) and 8.3(3)(a) do not apply to disqualification applications.

8.2 In cases brought under section 7, 8 or 9A of the Act, the form of acknowledgement of service shall state that the defendant should indicate [r.5(4) of the *Insolvent Companies (Disqualification of Unfit Directors) Proceedings Rules* 1987]:

(1) whether he contests the application on the grounds that, in the case of any particular company:–

    (a) he was not a director or shadow director of that company at a time when conduct of his, or of other persons, in relation to that company is in question;

    (b) his conduct as director or shadow director of that company was not as alleged in support of the application for a disqualification order;

    (c) in the case of an application made under section 7 of the Act, the company has at no time become insolvent within the meaning of section 6; or

    (d) in the case of an application under section 9A of the Act, the undertaking which is a company did not commit a breach of competition law within the meaning of that section.

(2) whether, in the case of any conduct of his, he disputes the allegation that such conduct makes him unfit to be concerned in the management of a company; and

(3) whether he, while not resisting the application for a disqualification order, intends to adduce mitigating factors with a view to reducing the period of disqualification.

8.3 The defendant shall:

(1) (subject to any directions to the contrary given under paragraph 7.3 above) file an acknowledgement of service in the prescribed form not more than 14 days after service of the claim form; and

(2) serve the acknowledgement of service on the claimant and any other party.

8.4 Where the defendant has failed to file an acknowledgement of service and the time period for doing so has expired, the defendant may attend the hearing of the application but may not take part in the hearing unless the court gives permission.

9. Evidence

9.1 Evidence in disqualification applications shall be by affidavit, except where the official receiver is a party, in which case his evidence may be in the form of a written report (with or without affidavits by other persons) which shall be treated as if it had been verified by affidavit by him and shall be prima facie evidence of any matter contained in it [r.3(2) of the *Insolvent Companies (Disqualification of Unfit Directors) Proceedings Rules* 1987. Section 441 of the *Companies Act* 1985 makes provision for the admissibility in legal proceedings of a certified copy of a report of inspectors appointed under Part XIV of the *Companies Act* 1985 (these provisions are not affected by 2006)].

9.2 In the affidavits or (as the case may be) the official receiver's report in support of the application, there shall be included:

(1) a statement of the matters by reference to which it is alleged that a disqualification order should be made against the defendant [r.3(3) of the *Insolvent Companies (Disqualification of Unfit Directors) Proceedings Rules* 1987]; and

(2) a statement of the steps taken to comply with any requirements imposed by sections 16(1) and 9C(4) of the Act.

9.3 When the claim form is issued:

(1) the affidavit or report in support of the disqualification application must be filed in court;

(2) exhibits must be lodged with the court where they shall be retained until the conclusion of the proceedings; and

(3) copies of the affidavit/report and exhibits shall be served with the claim form on the defendant [r.3(1) of the *Insolvent Companies (Disqualification of Unfit Directors) Proceedings Rules* 1987].

9.4 The defendant shall, within 28 days from the date of service of the claim form [r.6(1) of the *Insolvent Companies (Disqualification of Unfit Directors) Proceedings Rules* 1987]:

(1) file in court any affidavit evidence in opposition to the disqualification application that he or she wishes the court to take into consideration; and

(2) lodge the exhibits with the court where they shall be retained until the conclusion of the proceedings; and

(3) at the same time, serve upon the claimant a copy of the affidavits and exhibits.

9.5 In cases where there is more than one defendant, each defendant is required to serve his evidence on the other defendants unless the court otherwise orders.

9.6 The claimant shall, within 14 days from receiving the copy of the defendant's evidence [r.6(2) of the *Insolvent Companies (Disqualification of Unfit Directors) Proceedings Rules* 1987]:

(1) file in court any further affidavit or report in reply he wishes the court to take into consideration; and

(2) lodge the exhibits with the court where they shall be retained until the conclusion of the proceedings; and

(3) at the same time serve a copy of the affidavits/reports and exhibits upon the defendant.

9.7 Prior to the first hearing of the disqualification application, the time for serving evidence may be extended by written agreement between the parties. After the first hearing, the extension of time for serving evidence is governed by CPR rules 2.11 and 29.5.

9.8 So far as is possible all evidence should be filed before the first hearing of the disqualification application.

10. The first hearing of the disqualification application

10.1 The date fixed for the hearing of the disqualification application shall be not less than eight weeks from the date of issue of the claim form [r.7(1) of the *Insolvent Companies (Disqualification of Unfit Directors) Proceedings Rules* 1987].

10.2 The hearing shall in the first instance be before the registrar [r.7(2) of the *Insolvent Companies (Disqualification of Unfit Directors) Proceedings Rules* 1987].

10.3 The registrar shall either determine the case on the date fixed or give directions and adjourn it [r.7(3) of the *Insolvent Companies (Disqualification of Unfit Directors) Proceedings Rules* 1987].

10.4 All interim directions should insofar as possible be sought at the first hearing of the disqualification application so that the disqualification application can be determined at the earliest possible date. The parties should take all such steps as they respectively can to avoid successive directions hearings.

10.5 In the case of disqualification applications made under sections 7, 8 or 9A of the Act, the registrar shall adjourn the case for further consideration if:–

 (1) he forms the provisional opinion that a disqualification order ought to be made, and that a period of disqualification longer than five years is appropriate [r.7(4)(a) of the *Insolvent Companies (Disqualification of Unfit Directors) Proceedings Rules* 1987], or

 (2) he is of opinion that questions of law or fact arise which are not suitable for summary determination [r.7(4)(b) of the *Insolvent Companies (Disqualification of Unfit Directors) Proceedings Rules* 1987].

10.6 If the registrar adjourns the application for further consideration he shall:–

 (1) direct whether the application is to be heard by a registrar or by a judge [r.7(5)(a) of the *Insolvent Companies (Disqualification of Unfit Directors) Proceedings Rules* 1987]. This direction may at any time be varied by the court either on application or of its own initiative. If the court varies the direction in the absence of any of the parties, notice will be given to the parties;

 (2) consider whether or not to adjourn the application to a judge so that the judge can give further directions;

 (3) consider whether or not to make any direction with regard to fixing the trial date or a trial window;

 (4) state the reasons for the adjournment [r.7(5)(b) of the *Insolvent Companies (Disqualification of Unfit Directors) Proceedings Rules* 1987].

11. Case management

11.1 On the first or any subsequent hearing of the disqualification application, the registrar may also give directions as to the following matters:

 (1) the filing in court and the service of further evidence (if any) by the parties [r.7(5)(c)(ii) of the *Insolvent Companies (Disqualification of Unfit Directors) Proceedings Rules* 1987];

 (2) the time-table for the steps to be taken between the giving of directions and the hearing of the application;

(3) such other matters as the registrar thinks necessary or expedient with a view to an expeditious disposal of the application or the management of it generally [r.7(5)(c)(iii) of the *Insolvent Companies (Disqualification of Unfit Directors) Proceedings Rules* 1987];

(4) the time and place of the adjourned hearing [r.7(5)(c)(iv) of the *Insolvent Companies (Disqualification of Unfit Directors) Proceedings Rules* 1987]; and

(5) the manner in which and the time within which notice of the adjournment and the reasons for it are to be given to the parties [r.7(5)(c)(i) of the *Insolvent Companies (Disqualification of Unfit Directors) Proceedings Rules* 1987].

11.2   Where a case is adjourned other than to a judge, it may be heard by the registrar who originally dealt with the case or by another registrar [r.7(6) of the *Insolvent Companies (Disqualification of Unfit Directors) Proceedings Rules* 1987].

11.3   If the companies court registrar adjourns the application to a judge, all directions having been complied with and the evidence being complete, the application will be referred to the Listing Office and any practice direction relating to listing shall apply accordingly.

11.4   In all disqualification applications, the court may direct a pre-trial review ("PTR"), a case management conference or pre-trial check lists (listing questionnaires) (in the form annexed to this practice direction) and will fix a trial date or trial period in accordance with the provisions of CPR Part 29: the Multi Track as modified by any relevant practice direction made thereunder.

11.5   At the hearing of the PTR, the registrar may give any further directions as appropriate and, where the application is to be heard in the Royal Courts of Justice in London, unless the trial date has already been fixed, may direct (by Counsel's clerks if applicable), to attend the Registrar at a specified time and place in order solely to fix a trial date. the court will give notice of the date fixed for the trial to the parties.

11.6   In all cases, the parties must inform the court immediately of any material change to the information provided in a pre-trial check list.

12.   The trial

12.1   Trial bundles containing copies of:–

(1)   the claim form;

(2)   the acknowledgement of service;

(3)   all evidence filed by or on behalf of each of the parties to the proceedings, together with the exhibits thereto;

(4)   all relevant correspondence; and

(5)   such other documents as the parties consider necessary;

shall be lodged with the court.

12.2   Skeleton arguments should be prepared by all the parties in all but the simplest cases whether the case is to be heard by a registrar or a judge. They should comply with all relevant guidelines.

12.3   The advocate for the claimant should also in all but the simplest cases provide: (a) a chronology; (b) a dramatis personae; (c) in respect of each defendant, a list of references to the relevant evidence.

12.4   The documents mentioned in paragraph 12.1–12.3 above must be delivered to the court in accordance with any order of the court and/or any relevant practice direction. [Attention is drawn to the provisions of the Chancery Guide. Chapter 7 of that Guide dated September 2000 provides guidance on the preparation of trial bundles and skeleton arguments. Unless the Court otherwise orders, paragraph 7.16 of the Chancery Guide requires that trial bundles be delivered to the Court 7 days before trial and paragraph 7.21 requires that skeleton arguments be delivered to the Court not less than 2 clear days before trial.]

(1) If the case is to be heard by a judge sitting in the Royal Courts of Justice, London, but the name of the judge is not known, or the judge is a deputy judge, these documents must be delivered to the Clerk of the Lists. If the name of the judge (other than a deputy judge) is known, these documents must be delivered to the judge's clerk;

(2) If the case is to be heard by a companies court registrar, these documents must be delivered to Room 409, Thomas More Building, Royal Courts of Justice. Copies must be provided to the other party so far as possible when they are delivered to the court;

(3) If the case is to be heard in the Chancery district registries in Birmingham, Bristol, Caernarfon, Cardiff, Leeds, Liverpool, Manchester, Mold, Newcastle upon Tyne or Preston, the addresses for delivery are set out in Annex 1;

(4) If the case is to be heard in a county court, the documents should be delivered to the relevant county court office.

12.5 Copies of documents delivered to the court must, so far as possible, be provided to each of the other parties to the claim.

12.6 The provisions in paragraphs 12.1 to 12.5 above are subject to any order of the court making different provision.

13. Summary procedure

13.1 If the parties decide to invite the court to deal with the application under the procedure adopted in *Re Carecraft Construction Co Ltd* [1993] BCC 336; [1944] 1 WLR 172, they should inform the court immediately and obtain a date for the hearing of the application.

13.2 Whenever the *Carecraft* procedure is adopted, the claimant must:

(1) except where the court otherwise directs, submit a written statement containing in respect of each defendant any material facts which (for the purposes of the application) are either agreed or not opposed (by either party); and

(2) specify in writing the period of disqualification which the parties accept that the agreed or unopposed facts justify or the band of years (e.g. four to six years) or bracket (i.e. two to five years; six to ten years; 11 to 15 years) into which they will submit the case fails.

13.3 Paragraph 12.4 of the above applies to the documents mentioned in paragraph 13.2 above unless the court otherwise directs.

13.4 Unless the court otherwise orders, a hearing under the *Carecraft* procedure will be held in private.

13.5 If the court is minded to make a disqualification order having heard the parties' representations, it will usually give judgment and make the disqualification order in public. Unless the court otherwise orders, the written statement referred to in paragraph 13.2 shall be annexed to the disqualification order.

13.6 If the court refuses to make the disqualification order under the *Carecraft* procedure, the court shall give further directions for the hearing of the application.

14. Making and setting aside of disqualification order

14.1 The court may make a disqualification order against the defendant, whether or not the latter appears, and whether or not he has completed and returned the acknowledgment of service of the claim form, or filed evidence [r.8(1) of the *Insolvent Companies (Disqualification of Unfit Directors) Proceedings Rules* 1987].

14.2   Any disqualification order made in the absence of the defendant may be set aside or varied by the court on such terms as it thinks just [r.8(2) of the *Insolvent Companies (Disqualification of Unfit Directors) Proceedings Rules* 1987].

15.   Service of disqualification orders

15.1   Service of disqualification orders will be the responsibility of the claimant.

16.   Commencement of disqualification order

16.1   Unless the court otherwise orders, the period of disqualification imposed by a disqualification order shall begin at the end of the period of 21 days beginning with the date of the order.

Part Three

Applications under sections 7(2) and 7(4) of the Act

17.   Applications for permission to make a disqualification application after the end of the period of two years specified in section 7(2) of the Act

17.1   Such applications shall be made by Practice Form N208 under CPR Part 8 save where it is sought to join a director or former director to existing proceedings, in which case such application shall be made by Application Notice under CPR Part 23, and Practice Direction 23A shall apply save as modified below.

18.   Applications for extra information made under section 7(4) of the Act

18.1   Such applications may be made:

(1)   by Practice Form N.208 under CPR Part 8;

(2)   by Application Notice in existing disqualification claim proceedings; or

(3)   by application under the Insolvency Rules in the relevant insolvency, if the insolvency practitioner against whom the application is made remains the officeholder.

19.   Provisions applicable to applications under sections 7(2) and 7(4) of the Act

19.1   Headings: Every claim form and notice by which such an application is begun and all witness statements affidavits, notices and other documents in relation thereto must be entitled in the matter of the company or companies in question and in the matter of the Act.

19.2   Service:

(1)   Service of claim forms and application notices seeking orders under section 7(2) or 7(4) of the Act will be the responsibility of the applicant and will not be undertaken by the court.

(2)   Where any claim form, application notice or order of the court or other document is required in any application under section 7(2) or section 7(4) of the Act to be served on any person who is not in England and Wales, the court may order service on him to be effected within such time and in such manner as it thinks fit, may require such proof of service as it thinks fit, and may make such directions as to acknowledgment of service as it thinks fit. Section III of CPR Part 6 does not apply.

1195

20. Commencing an application for permission to act

20.1 This practice direction governs applications for permission made under:

(1)   section 17 of the Act for the purposes of any of sections 1(1)(a), 1A(1)(a) or 9B(4); and

(2)   section 12(2) of the Act.

20.2 Sections 12 and 17 of the Act identify the courts which have jurisdiction to deal with applications for permission to act. Subject to these sections, such applications may be made:

(1)   by Practice Form N.208 under CPR Part 8; or

(2)   by application notice in an existing disqualification application.

20.3 In the case of a person subject to disqualification under section 12A or 12B (by reason of being disqualified in Northern Ireland), permission to act notwithstanding disqualification can only be granted by the High Court of Northern Ireland.

21. Headings

21.1 Every claim form by which an application for permission to act is begun, and all affidavits, notices and other documents in the application must be entitled in the matter of the company or companies in question and in the matter of the Act.

21.2 Every application notice by which an application for permission to act is made and all affidavits, notices and other documents in the application shall be entitled in the same manner as the heading of the claim form in the existing disqualification application.

22. Evidence

22.1 Evidence in support of an application for permission to act shall be by affidavit.

23. Service

23.1 Where a disqualification application has been made under section 9A of the Act or a disqualification undertaking has been accepted under section 9B of the Act, the claim form or application notice (as appropriate), together with the evidence in support thereof, must be served on the Office of Fair Trading or specified regulator which made the relevant disqualification application or accepted the disqualification undertaking (as the case may be).

23.2 In all other cases, the claim form or application notice (as appropriate), together with the evidence in support thereof, must be served on the Secretary of State.

24. Form of application

24.1 CPR Part 23 and Practice Direction 23A shall apply in relation to applications governed by this practice direction (see paragraph 1.3(4) above) save as modified below.

25. Headings

25.1 Every notice and all affidavits in relation thereto must be entitled in the same manner as the Claim Form in the proceedings in which the application is made.

26. Service

26.1 Service of application notices in disqualification proceedings will be the responsibility of the parties and will not be undertaken by the court.

26.2 Where any application notice or order of the court or other document is required in any application to be served on any person who is not in England and Wales, the court may order service on him to be effected within such time and in such manner as it thinks fit, and may also require such proof of service as it thinks fit. Section III of CPR Part 6 does not apply.

PART SIX

DISQUALIFICATION PROCEEDINGS OTHER THAN IN THE ROYAL COURTS OF JUSTICE

27.1 Where a disqualification application or a section 8A application is made by a claim form issued other than in the Royal Courts of Justice this practice direction shall apply with the following modifications:

(1) Upon the issue of the claim form the court shall endorse it with the date and time for the first hearing before a district judge. The powers exercisable by a registrar under this practice direction shall be exercised by a district judge.

(2) If the district judge (either at the first hearing or at any adjourned hearing before him) directs that the disqualification claim is to be heard by a High Court judge or by an authorised circuit judge he will direct that the case be entered forthwith in the list for hearing by that judge and the court will allocate (i) a date for the hearing of the trial by that judge and (ii) unless the district judge directs otherwise a date for the hearing of a PTR by the trial judge.

PART SEVEN

DISQUALIFICATION UNDERTAKINGS

28. Costs

28.1 The general rule is that the court will order the defendant to pay–

(1) the costs of the Secretary of State (and, in the case of a disqualification application made under section 7(1)(b) of the Act, the costs of the official receiver) if:

    (a) a disqualification application under section 7 or 8 of the Act has been commenced; and

    (b) that application is discontinued because the Secretary of State has accepted a disqualification undertaking under section 1A of the Act;

(2) the costs of the Office of Fair Trading or a specified regulator if:

    (a) a disqualification application under section 9A of the Act has been commenced; and

    (b) that application is discontinued because the Office of Fair Trading or specified regulator (as the case may be) has accepted a disqualification undertaking under section 9B of the Act.

28.2 The general rule will not apply where the court considers that the circumstances are such that it should make another order.

APPLICATIONS UNDER SECTION 8A OF THE ACT TO REDUCE THE PERIOD FOR WHICH A DISQUALIFICATION UNDERTAKING IS IN FORCE OR TO PROVIDE FOR IT TO CEASE TO BE IN FORCE

29. Headings

29.1 Every claim form by which a section 8A application is begun and all affidavits, notices and other documents in the proceedings must be entitled in the matter of a disqualification undertaking and its date and in the matter of the Act.

30. Commencement: the claim form

30.1 Section 8A(3) of the Act identifies the courts which have jurisdiction to deal with section 8A applications.

30.1A A section 8A application must be commenced by a claim form issued:

(1) in the case of a disqualification undertaking given under section 9B of the Act, in the High Court out of the office of the companies court registrar at the Royal Courts of Justice;

(2) in any other case,

     (a) in the High Court out of the office of the companies court registrar or a chancery district registry; and

     (b) in the county court, out of a county court office.

30.2 A section 8A application shall be made by the issue of a Part 8 claim form in the form annexed hereto and the use of the procedure set out in CPR Part 8, as modified by this practice direction. CPR rule 8.1(3) (power of the Court to order the application to continue as if the claimant had not used the Part 8 procedure) shall not apply.

30.3 When the claim form is issued, the claimant will be given a date for the first hearing of the section 8A application. This date is to be not less than eight weeks from the date of issue of the claim form. The first hearing will be before registrar.

30.4 CPR Rule 8.2 does not apply. The claim form must state:

(1) that CPR Part 8 (as modified by this practice direction) applies;

(2) the form of order the claimant seeks.

30.5 In the case of a disqualification undertaking given under section 9B of the Act, the defendant to the section 8A application shall be the Office of Fair Trading or specified regulator which accepted the undertaking. In all other cases, the Secretary of State shall be made the defendant to the section 8A application.

30.6 Service of claim forms in section 8A applications will be the responsibility of the claimant and will not be undertaken by the court. The claim form may be served by sending it by first class post and the date of service shall, unless the contrary is shown, be deemed to be the 7th day following that on which the claim form was posted. CPR r. 6.7(1) shall be modified accordingly. Otherwise Sections I and II of CPR Part 6 apply.

30.7 Where any order of the court or other document is required to be served on any person who is not in England and Wales, the court may order service on him to be effected within such time and in such manner as it thinks fit and may require such proof of service as it thinks fit. Section III of CPR Part 6 shall not apply. [Attention is drawn to CPR r.6.14(2) regarding a certificate of service of the claim form.]

30.8 The claim form served on the defendant shall be accompanied by an acknowledgement of service in the form annexed hereto.

31. Acknowledgement of service

31.1 The defendant shall:

(1) file an acknowledgement of service in the relevant practice form not more than 14 days after service of the claim form; and

(2) serve a copy of the acknowledgement of service on the claimant and any other party.

31.2 Where the defendant has failed to file an acknowledgement of service and the time period for doing so has expired, the defendant may nevertheless attend the hearing of the application and take part in the hearing as provided for by section 8A(2) or (2A) of the Act. However, this is without prejudice to the Court's case management powers and its powers to make costs orders.

32. Evidence

32.1 Evidence in section 8A applications shall be by affidavit. The undertaking (or a copy) shall be exhibited to the affidavit.

32.2 When the claim form is issued:

(1) the affidavit in support of the section 8A application must be filed in court;

(2) exhibits must be lodged with the court where they shall be retained until the conclusion of the proceedings; and

(3) copies of the affidavit and exhibits shall be served with the claim form on the defendant.

32.3 The defendant shall, within 28 days from the date of service of the claim form:

(1) file in court any affidavit evidence that he wishes the court to take into consideration on the application; and

(2) lodge the exhibits with the court where they shall be retained until the conclusion of the proceedings; and

(3) at the time, serve upon the claimant a copy of the affidavits and exhibits.

32.4 The claimant shall, within 14 days from receiving the copy of the defendant's evidence:

(1) file in court any further affidavit evidence in reply he wishes the court to take into consideration; and

(2) lodge the exhibits with the court where they shall be retained until the conclusion of the proceedings; and

(3) at the same time serve a copy of the affidavits and exhibits upon the defendant.

32.5 Prior to the first hearing of the section 8A application, the time for serving evidence may be extended by written agreement between the parties. After the first hearing, the extension of time for serving evidence is governed by CPR rules 2.11 and 29.5.

32.6 So far as is possible all evidence should be filed before the first hearing of the section 8A application.

33. Hearings and case management

33.1 The date fixed for the first hearing of the section 8A application shall be not less than 8 weeks from the date of issue of the claim form.

33.2 The hearing shall in the first instance be before the registrar.

33.3 The registrar shall either determine the case on the date fixed or give directions and adjourn it.

33.4   All interim directions should insofar as possible be sought at the first hearing of the section 8A application so that the section 8A application can be determined at the earliest possible date. The parties should take all such steps as they respectively can to avoid successive directions hearings.

33.5   If the registrar adjourns the application for further consideration he shall:

(1)   direct whether the application is to be heard by a registrar or by a judge. This direction may at any time be varied by the court either on application or of its own initiative. If the court varies the direction in the absence of any of the parties, notice will be given to the parties;

(2)   consider whether or not to adjourn the application to a judge so that the judge can give further directions;

(3)   consider whether or not to make any direction with regard to fixing the trial date or a trial window.

33.6   On the first or any subsequent hearing of the section 8A application, the registrar may also give directions as to the following matters:

(1)   the filing in court and the service of further evidence (if any) by the parties;

(2)   the time-table for the steps to be taken between the giving of directions and the hearing of the section 8A application;

(3)   such other matters as the registrar thinks necessary or expedient with a view to an expeditious disposal of the section 8A application or the management of it generally;

(4)   the time and place of the adjourned hearing.

33.7   Where a case is adjourned other than to a judge, it may be heard by the registrar who originally dealt with the case or by another registrar.

33.8   If the companies court registrar adjourns the application to a judge, all directions having been complied with and the evidence being complete, the application will be referred to the Listing Office and any practice direction relating to listing shall apply accordingly.

33.9   In all section 8A applications, the Court may direct a pre-trial review ('PTR'), a case management conference or pre-trial check lists (listing questionnaires) (in the form annexed to this practice direction) and will fix a trial date or trial period in accordance with the provisions of CPR Part 29: The Multi-Track, as modified by any relevant practice direction made thereunder.

33.10   At the hearing of the PTR, the registrar may give any further directions as appropriate and, where the application is to be heard in the Royal Courts of Justice in London, unless the trial date has already been fixed, may direct the parties (by Counsel's clerks, if applicable) to attend the Registrar at a specified time and place in order solely to fix a trial date. The court will give notice of the date fixed for the trial to the parties.

33.11   In all cases, the parties must inform the court immediately of any material change to the information provided in a pre-trial check list.

34. The trial

34.1   Trial bundles containing copies of–

(1)   the claim form;

(2)   the acknowledgement of service;

(3)   all evidence filed by or on behalf of each of the parties to the proceedings, together with the exhibits thereto;

(4)   all relevant correspondance; and

(5)   such other documents as the parties consider necessary.

shall be lodged with the court.

34.2 Skeleton arguments should be prepared by all the parties in all but the simplest cases whether the case is to be heard by a registrar or a judge. They should comply with all relevant guidelines.

34.3 The advocate for the claimant should also in all but the simplest cases provide: (a) a chronology; (b) a dramatis personae.

34.4 The documents mentioned in paragraph 34.1–34.3 above must be delivered to the court in accordance with any order of the court and/or and relevant practice direction.

(1) If the case is to be heard by a judge sitting in the Royal Courts of Justice, London, but the name of the judge is not known, or the judge is a deputy judge, these documents must be delivered to the Clerk of the Lists. If the name of the judge (other than a deputy judge) is known, these documents must be delivered to the judge's clerk;

(2) If the case is to be heard by a companies court registrar, these documents must be delivered to Room 409, Thomas More Building, Royal Courts of Justice. Copies must be provided to the other party so far as possible when they are delivered to the court;

(3) If the case is to be heard in the Chancery district registries in Birmingham, Bristol, Cardiff, Leeds, Liverpool, Manchester, Newcastle, or Preston, the addresses for delivery are set out in Annex 1;

(4) If the case is to be heard in a county court, the documents should be delivered to the relevant county court office.

34.5 Copies of documents delivered to the court must, so far as possible, be provided to each of the other parties to the claim.

34.6 The provisions in paragraphs 34.1 to 34.5 above are subject to any order of the court making different provision.

35. Appeals

35.1 Rules 7.47 and 7.49 of the Insolvency Rules, as supplemented by Part Four of the Insolvency Proceedings Practice Direction, apply to an appeal from, or review of, a decision made by the court in the course of:

(1) disqualification proceedings under any of sections 6 to 8A or 9A of the Act;

(2) an application made under section 17 of the Act for the purposes of any of sections 1(1)(a), 1A(1)(a) or 9B(4), for permission to act notwithstanding a disqualification order made, or a disqualification undertaking accepted, under any of sections 6 to 10.

Any such decision, and any appeal from it, constitutes 'insolvency proceedings' for the purposes of the Insolvency Proceedings Practice Direction.

35.2 An appeal from a decision made by the court in the course of disqualification proceedings under any of sections 2(2)(a), 3 or 4 of the Act or on an application for permission to act notwithstanding a disqualification order made under any of those sections is governed by CPR Part 52 and Practice Direction 52.

ANNEX 1

Birmingham: The Chancery Listing Officer, The District Registry of the Chancery Division of the High Court, 33 Bull Street, Birmingham B4 6DS.

Bristol: The Chancery Listing Officer, The District Registry of the Chancery Division of the High Court, 3rd Floor, Greyfriars, Lewins Mead, Bristol BS1 2NR.

Caernarfon: The Chancery Listing Officer, The District Registry of the Chancery Division of the High Court, 1st Floor, Llanberis Road, Caernarfon, LL55 2DF.

Cardiff: The Chancery Listing Officer, The District Registry of the Chancery Division of the High Court, 1st Floor, 2 Park Street, Cardiff CF10 1ET.

Leeds: The Chancery Listing Officer, The District Registry of the Chancery Division of the High Court, Leeds Combined Court Centre, The Court House, 1 Oxford Row, Leeds LS1 3BG.

Liverpool and Manchester: The Chancery Listing Officer, The District Registry of the Chancery Division of the High Court, Manchester Courts of Justice, Crown Square, Manchester M60 9DJ.

Mold: The Chancery Listing Officer, The District Registry of the Chancery Division of the High Court, Law Courts, Civic Centre, Mold, CH7 1AE.

Newcastle upon Tyne: The Chancery Listing Officer, The District Registry of the Chancery Division of the High Court, The Law Courts, Quayside, Newcastle upon Tyne NE1 3LA.

Preston: The Chancery Listing Officer, The District Registry of the Chancery Division of the High Court, The Combined Court Centre, Ringway, Preston PR1 2LL.

Index

This index has been prepared using Sweet & Maxwell's Legal Taxonomy. Main index entries conform to keywords provided by the Legal Taxonomy except where references to specific documents or non-standard terms (denoted by quotation marks) have been included. These keywords provide a means of identifying similar concepts in other Sweet & Maxwell publications and online services to which keywords from the Legal Taxonomy have been applied. Readers may find some minor differences between terms used in the text and those which appear in the index. Suggestions to *sweet&maxwell.taxonomy@thomson.com*.

Where the provision is shown in *italics*, this denotes the administration regime prior to the introduction of the Enterprise Act 2002.

References within square brackets are located in Volume 2.

The following abbreviations are used to denote the location of entries:

[CBIR]	Cross-Border Insolvency Regulations 2006
[CDDA]	Company Directors Disqualification Act 1986
EA	Enterprise Act 2002
[ER]	EC Regulation on Insolvency Proceedings 2000
IA	Insolvency Act 1986
IA 2000	Insolvency Act 2000
IR	Insolvency Rules 1986
[UML]	UNCITRAL Model Law on Cross-Border Insolvency

Provision

Provision

Index